P9-DHC-865

A GUIDE TO TREATMENTS THAT WORK

A GUIDE TO TREATMENTS THAT WORK

2nd EDITION

EDITED BY

PETER E. NATHAN
JACK M. GORMAN

New York Oxford
Oxford University Press
2002

Oxford University Press

Oxford New York
Athens Auckland Bangkok Bogotá Buenos Aires Cape Town
Chennai Dar es Salaam Delhi Florence Hong Kong Istanbul Karachi
Kolkata Kuala Lumpur Madrid Melbourne Mexico City Mumbai Nairobi
Paris São Paulo Shanghai Singapore Taipei Tokyo Toronto Warsaw

and associated companies in
Berlin Ibadan

Published by Oxford University Press, Inc.
198 Madison Avenue, New York, New York 10016

Library of Congress Cataloging-in-Publication Data
A guide to treatments that work / [edited by] Peter E. Nathan, Jack M. Gorman.—2nd ed.
p. cm.
Includes bibliographical references and index.
ISBN 0-19-514072-9
1. Mental illness—Treatment—Evaluation. I. Nathan, Peter E. II. Gorman, Jack M.
[DNLM: 1. Mental Disorders—therapy. 2. Psychotherapy—methods. WM 400 G946 2002]
RC480.5 .G85 2002
616.89'1—dc21 2001034636
ISBN 0-19-514072-9

4 6 8 9 7 5 3

Printed in the United States of America
on acid-free paper

Preface

In the absence of science, opinion prevails

The first edition of *A Guide to Treatments That Work* filled a need neither of us fully recognized at the time. Countless books and articles on treatment are published every year. Some focus on diverse treatments for a single disorder, others on a specific approach to treatment applied across the diagnostic range. But no single volume had succinctly presented the empirical findings on pharmacological and psychosocial treatments across a broad range of disorders in a way that encouraged comparisons across both treatments and syndromes. The first edition of *A Guide to Treatments That Work* met that need. As a result, it sold very well and was reviewed very favorably.

It is a mark of the rapidity with which new findings on treatment are now being generated that the second edition of this book follows so closely on the first. While few treatment breakthroughs have taken place during the 4 years between the first and second editions of this volume, sufficient new research has been reported to justify a thorough update of the book. Each chapter author has returned to the literature in his or her research domain, surveyed the new findings, and integrated them into the revised chapter. We estimate that 30% or more of most chapters has been rewritten or extensively modified with this new information.

One of the features of the first edition most often remarked on and approved of was our specification of the standards by which we wished our authors to judge the methodological adequacy of outcome studies. These standards were shared with chapter authors before they commenced their work, and the authors, in turn, make frequent reference to them in their chapters. We have retained these standards in this edition, in the belief that treatments with good outcomes revealed by a substantial number of methodologically sound studies are more likely to prove efficacious than those with support that derives from research of lesser quality. Those standards are reproduced here:

> The purpose of these chapters is to present the most rigorous, scientifically based evidence for the efficacy of treatments that is available. At the same time, it is clear that, for some disorders, there are treatments widely recognized by experienced clinicians to be useful that may not have been subjected to rigorous investigation for a variety of reasons. Our aim is to be clear with readers what treatments are felt by a large number of experts to be valuable but have never been properly scientifically examined and what treatments are known to be of little value.
>
> To achieve this aim, it is useful to establish some criteria for evaluating the validity of articles in the literature that are reviewed in writing the chapters. We would like you to keep in mind the following classification when you are reviewing the literature and writing your chapter:
>
> *Type 1 studies:* These are the most rigorous and involve a randomized, prospective clinical trial. Such studies also must involve comparison groups with random assignment, blinded assess-

ments, clear presentation of exclusion and inclusion criteria, state-of-the-art diagnostic methods, adequate sample size to offer statistical power, and clearly described statistical methods.

Type 2 studies: These are clinical trials in which an intervention is made, but some aspects of the Type 1 study requirement are missing, for example, a trial in which a double blind cannot be maintained; a trial in which two treatments are compared but the assignment is not randomized; and a trial in which there is a clear but not fatal flaw, such as a period of observation that is felt to be too short to make full judgments on treatment efficacy. Such studies clearly do not merit the same consideration as Type 1 studies but often make important contributions and generally should not be ignored.

Type 3 studies: These are clearly methodologically limited. Generally, Type 3 studies are open-treatment studies aiming at obtaining pilot data. They are highly subject to observer bias and can usually do little more than indicate if a treatment is worth pursuing in a more rigorous design. Also included in this category are case control studies in which patients are identified and then information about treatment is obtained from them retrospectively. Such studies can, of course, provide a great deal of naturalistic information but are prone to all of the problems of uncontrolled data collection and retrospective recall error.

Type 4 studies: Reviews with secondary data analysis can be useful, especially if the data-analytic techniques are sophisticated. Modern methods of meta-analysis attempt to account for the fact that, for example, negative studies tend to be reported at a substantially lower rate than positive outcome studies.

Type 5 studies: Reviews without secondary data analysis are helpful to give an impression of the literature but are clearly subject to the writer's opinion and sometimes are highly biased.

Type 6 studies: These encompass a variety of reports that have marginal value, such as case studies, essays, and opinion papers.

Another of the features of the first edition that has been retained in this edition is the table "Summary of Treatments that Work," which appears at the beginning of the volume. It lists the syndromes for which treatments have been examined, the results of research on outcomes of both psychosocial and pharmacological treatments, and the methodological adequacy of the research ("Standards of Proof") that yielded the outcome findings. The summary table, which begins on page xiii, makes it easy for the reader to compare and contrast syndromes and treatments by the methodological adequacy of their supporting research.

The same table also facilitates comparisons between pharmacological and psychosocial treatments for the same or related disorders. As more and more research is published suggesting that combined treatments—those combining drug treatment and psychotherapy—work best for an increasing number of disorders, it becomes even more important to provide clinicians and researchers alike the most current data on the efficacy and effectiveness of these integrated treatments. It seems clear that we can no longer permit disciplinary boundaries to interfere with the provision of the most effective treatments—pharmacological, psychosocial, or a combination of the two—for our patients.

The book concludes with a chapter by the coeditors reviewing the literature contrasting research on psychotherapy efficacy and effectiveness. This issue, of central importance to psychotherapy researchers but of relevance to everyone with responsibility for treating psychiatric patients, has been debated widely in the past few years, in large part because of the long-recognized and lamentable lack of impact the efforts of psychotherapy researchers appear to have had on the clinical work of psychotherapists. One popular explanation is that most current psychotherapy research, epitomized by the extensively controlled efficacy study, has little relevance to psychological treatment in the real world. Another is that common factors, rather than differences in techniques, play a more important role in determining therapeutic effectiveness. This chapter considers the recent literature on both matters in considerable detail in the effort to weigh the relative contributions that efficacy and effectiveness research, as well as common factors, have made to the psychotherapeutic enterprise. The goal of the chapter, like that of the volume as a whole, is to examine as carefully as possible the data in support of the view that psychosocial and pharmacological interventions with patients do make a difference, in the belief that the difference is heightened when what we do is informed as much as possible by empirically based findings.

Iowa City, Iowa P. E. N.
New York, New York J. M. G.

Contents

Contributors

Abikoff, Howard B., M.D.: Professor, Child Study Center, New York University School of Medicine

Althof, Stanley, Ph.D.: Associate Professor, Department of Psychiatry, Case Western Reserve School of Medicine

Barber, Jacques P., Ph.D.: Department of Psychiatry, University of Pennsylvania Health System

Barlow, David H., Ph.D.: Professor and Director, Center for Anxiety and Related Disorders, Boston University

Bradford, Daniel, M.D.: Department of Psychiatry, School of Medicine, University of North Carolina at Chapel Hill

Butler, Lisa D., Ph.D.: Psychosocial Research Laboratory, Department of Psychiatry and Behavioral Sciences, Stanford University School of Medicine

Buysse, Daniel J., M.D.: Associate Professor, Department of Psychiatry and Sleep and Chronobiology Center, University of Pittsburgh School of Medicine

Cohen, Elizabeth M.: Center for Anxiety and Related Disorders, Boston University

Cowley, Deborah S., M.D.: Associate Professor, Department of Psychiatry and Behavioral Sciences, University of Washington School of Medicine at Harborview Medical Center

Craighead, Linda Wilcoxon, Ph.D.: Professor, Department of Psychology, University of Colorado at Boulder

Craighead, W. Edward, Ph.D.: Professor and Director of Clinical Training, Department of Psychology, University of Colorado at Boulder

Crits-Christoph, Paul, Ph.D.: Associate Professor of Psychology in Psychiatry and Director, Center for Psychotherapy Research, Department of Psychiatry, University of Pennsylvania Health System

Dougherty, Darin D., M.D.: Department of Psychiatry, Massachusetts General Hospital and Harvard Medical School

Fairburn, Christopher G., D.M., M.Phil., FRCPsych.: Wellcome Principal Research Fellow and Professor, Department of Psychiatry, Oxford University, Warneford Hospital, Oxford, UK

Finney, John W., Ph.D.: Associate Director, Center for Health Care Evaluation and Program Evaluation and Resource Center, VA Palo Alto Health Care System and Stanford University Medical Center

Foa, Edna B., Ph.D.: Professor and Director, Center for the Treatment and Study of Anxiety, University of Pennsylvania School of Medicine

Ford, Rebecca E., M.D.: Child Psychiatry, New York State Psychiatric Institute

Frank, Ellen, Ph.D.: Professor, Department of Psychiatry, University of Pittsburgh College of Medicine

Franklin, Martin E., Ph.D.: Associate Professor, Center for the Treatment and Study of Anxiety, University of Pennsylvania School of Medicine

Gorman, Jack M., M.D.: Lieber Professor and Vice Chair for Research, Department of Psychiatry, College of Physicians and Surgeons of Columbia University

Greenhill, Laurence L., M.D.: Associate Professor of Clinical Psychiatry, College of Physicians and Surgeons of Columbia University

Hart, Alisha B.: Department of Psychology, University of Colorado at Boulder

Hinshaw, Stephen P., Ph.D.: Professor, Department of Psychology, University of California at Berkeley

Ilardi, Stephen S., Ph.D.: Assistant Professor, Department of Psychology, University of Kansas

Jenike, Michael A., M.D.: Professor, Department of Psychiatry, Massachusetts General Hospital and Harvard Medical School

Kazdin, Alan E., Ph.D.: Professor, Department of Psychology, Yale University

Keck, Paul E., Jr., M.D.: Professor and Vice Chairman for Research, Biological Psychiatry Program, Department of Psychiatry, College of Medicine, University of Cincinnati

Klein, Rachel G., Ph.D.: Professor, Child Study Center, New York University School of Medicine

Koenigsberg, Harold W., M.D.: Department of Psychiatry, Mount Sinai School of Medicine

Kopelowicz, Alex, M.D.: Department of Psychiatry, Stanford University School of Medicine

Kupfer, David J., M.D.: Thomas Detre Professor and Chairman, Department of Psychiatry, University of Pittsburgh School of Medicine

Liberman, Robert Paul, M.D.: Professor, Department of Psychiatry, Stanford University School of Medicine

Lieberman, Jeffrey, M.D.: Professor and Vice Chairman, Department of Psychiatry, School of Medicine, University of North Carolina at Chapel Hill

Maldonado, Jose R., M.D.: Assistant Professor and Chief, Medical and Forensic Psychiatry Section, Department of Psychiatry and Behavioral Sciences, Stanford University School of Medicine

Maletzky, Barry M., M.D.: Professor of Clinical Psychiatry and Director of the Sexual Abuse Clinic, Department of Psychiatry, Oregon Health Sciences University

Marshall, Randall, M.D.: Department of Psychiatry, College of Physicians and Surgeons of Columbia University

McElroy, Susan L., M.D.: Professor and Director, Biological Psychiatry Program, Department of Psychiatry, College of Medicine, University of Cincinnati

McKay, James, M.D.: Assistant Professor, Department of Psychiatry, University of Pennsylvania School of Medicine

Miklowitz, David J., Ph.D.: Associate Professor, Department of Psychology, University of Colorado at Boulder

Moos, Rudolf H., Ph.D.: Director, Center for Health Care Evaluation and Program Evaluation and Resource Center, VA Palo Alto Health Care System and Stanford University Medical Center

Morin, Charles, Ph.D.: Professor, School of Psychology, Université Laval

Nathan, Peter E., Ph.D.: University of Iowa Foundation Distinguished Professor, Department of Psychology, College of Liberal Arts and Sciences, and Department of Community and Behavioral Health, College of Public Health, University of Iowa

Nemeroff, Charles B., M.D.: Reunette W. Harris Professor and Chairman, Department of Psychiatry and Behavioral Sciences, Emory University School of Medicine

Nowell, Peter D., M.D.: Department of Psychiatry and Sleep and Chronobiology Center, University of Pittsburgh School of Medicine

O'Brien, Charles P., M.D.: Professor, Department of Psychiatry, University of Pennsylvania School of Medicine

Penkower, Ariel, M.D.: Department of Psychiatry, Mount Sinai School of Medicine

Raffa, Susan D.: Center for Anxiety and Related Disorders, Boston University

Rauch, Scott L., M.D.: Assistant Professor, Department of Psychiatry, Massachusetts General Hospital and Harvard Medical School

Reynolds, Charles F., III, M.D.: Professor, Department of Psychiatry and Sleep and Chronobiology Center, University of Pittsburgh School of Medicine

Roy-Byrne, Peter P., M.D.: Professor and Vice Chairman, Department of Psychiatry and Behavioral Sciences, University of Washington School of Medicine at Harborview Medical Center

Schatzberg, Alan F., M.D.: Kenneth T. Norris Professor and Chairman, Department of Psychiatry and Behavioral Sciences, Stanford University School of Medicine

Segraves, Taylor, M.D., Ph.D.: Professor, Department of Psychiatry, Case Western Reserve School of Medicine

Siever, Larry J., M.D.: Professor, Department of Psychiatry, Mount Sinai School of Medicine

Simon, Gregory E., M.D.: Center for Health Studies, Group Health Cooperative, and Department of Psychiatry and Behavioral Sciences, University of Washington School of Medicine

Spiegel, David, M.D.: Professor and Vice Chairman, Department of Psychiatry and Behavioral Sciences and Director, Psychosocial Treatment Laboratory, Stanford University School of Medicine

Stroup, Scott, M.D.: Department of Psychiatry, School of Medicine, University of North Carolina at Chapel Hill

Tune, Larry, M.D.: Professor, Department of Psychiatry and Behavioral Sciences, Emory University School of Medicine

Vajk, Fiona C.: Department of Psychology, University of Colorado at Boulder

Wilson, G. Terence, Ph.D.: Oscar K. Buros Professor of Psychology, Graduate School of Applied and Professional Psychology, Rutgers, State University of New Jersey

Wong, Cheryl M., M.D.: Assistant Professor, Department of Psychiatry, Mount Sinai School of Medicine

Woo-Ming, Anne Marie, M.D.: Associate Professor, Department of Psychiatry, Mount Sinai School of Medicine

Yehuda, Rachel, Ph.D.: Associate Professor, Department of Psychiatry, Mount Sinai School of Medicine

Zarate, Roberto, Ph.D.: Department of Psychiatry, Stanford University School of Medicine

Summary of Treatments That Work

Syndromes	*Treatments*	*Standards of Proof*	*References*
Alcohol use disorders	• Several *cognitive behavioral treatments* appear to help patients shape and adapt to their life circumstances. • Two recent multisite evaluations suggest that *12-step treatment* may be as effective as cognitive behavioral treatments. • Therapist characteristics may have a stronger impact on outcome than type of treatment. • Lower intensity treatment for a longer duration may be an effective treatment strategy for many patients. • There appears to be little difference in outcome between inpatient and outpatient treatment for many patients.	• Several Type 1 and, especially, Type 2 RCTs, including two substantial multisite evaluations.	Finney and Moos, Chapter 6, pp. 157–168
	• *Naltrexone* appears to be particularly effective in preventing full-blown relapses in alcoholics who have had a "slip" after achieving abstinence.	• Nine of 13 RCTs have yielded positive results over placebo.	O'Brien and McKay, Chapter 5, pp. 125–156
Avoidant personality disorder	A *group-administered behavioral intervention* (graded exposure, standard social skills training, or intimacy-focused social skills training) was more efficacious than the wait-list control.	A single Type 2 RCT, which compared three group-administered behavioral interventions with a wait-list control.	Crits-Christoph and Barber, Chapter 24, pp. 611–623

Syndromes	*Treatments*	*Standards of Proof*	*References*
Avoidant personality disorder (*cont.*)	*Antidepressants* may be helpful for this disorder.	Two Type 2 RCTs and several case reports.	Koenigsberg, Woo-Ming, and Siever, Chapter 25, pp. 625–641
Bipolar disorders	• *Lithium, divalproex, and olanzapine* are all effective in reducing the symptoms of acute bipolar manic episodes.	• A substantial number of Type 1 and Type 2 RCTs.	Keck and McElroy, Chapter 12, pp. 277–299
	• *Carbamazepine, typical antipsychotics, risperidone, and ziprasidone* have also been shown to have efficacy in the treatment of acute mania.	• A number of Type 1 and Type 2 RCTs.	
	• Although understudied, the pharmacological treatment of acute bipolar depression suggests that *lithium, most antidepressants, and lamotrigine* are effective antidepressants.	• Several Type 1 and Type 2 RCTs.	
	• *Lithium*, the most well-studied medication for the maintenance treatment of bipolar I disorder, is effective with a substantial percentage of bipolar patients (e.g., 35–50% within a year) in preventing or reducing the frequency of recurrent affective episodes; side effects have been a problem with drug compliance.	• A moderate number of Type 2 RCTs and Type 3 case reports.	
	• *Divalproex and carbamazepine* have also been shown to be efficacious as preventive treatments.	• A few Type 1 and Type 2 RCTs.	
	• While pharmacological interventions are treatments of choice, *psychosocial treatments, including psychoeducation, cognitive behavior therapy*, IPSRT, *and marital/family therapy*, have shown the potential to increase medication adherence, improve quality of life, and enhance mechanisms for coping with stress in patients with bipolar disorder.	• Several Type 2 and Type 3 studies of psychoeducation; three Type 1 studies of cognitive-behavior therapy; one Type 1 study of IPSRT; and several Type 1 studies of marital/family therapy.	Craighead, Miklowitz, Frank, and Vajk, Chapter 11, pp. 263–275
Body dysmorphic disorder	A *focused form of cognitive behavioral therapy* may be an effective treatment.	One RCT each reported superior outcomes for group and individual CBT when compared to a no-treatment control group.	Simon, Chapter 18, pp. 447–461

Syndromes	*Treatments*	*Standards of Proof*	*References*
Borderline personality disorder	• *Dialectical behavioral therapy* produced lower attrition, fewer and less severe episodes of parasuicidal behavior, and fewer days of hospitalization than the control condition. • Partial hospitalization involving *group and individual psychoanalytic psychotherapy* for 18 months decreased the number of suicidal attempts, acts of self-harm, psychiatric symptoms, and inpatient days and increased the quality of social and interpersonal functioning.	• A single Type 2 RCT, which randomized 44 women to either DBT or treatment-as-usual in the community. • A single Type 1 RCT, with standard psychiatric care as the comparison treatment.	Crits-Christoph and Barber, Chapter 24, pp. 611–623
	• *Noradrenergic agents* tend to improve mood but not irritability or dyscontrol, whereas *serotonergic agents* may act to decrease impulsivity.	• Several Type 1 and Type 2 RCTs and a large number of Type 3 studies.	Koenigsberg, Woo-Ming, and Siever, Chapter 25, pp. 625–641
Bulimia nervosa (BN)	• *Several different classes of antidepressant drugs* produce significant, short-term reductions in binge eating and purging. • *Manual-based cognitive behavioral therapy (CBT)* is currently the treatment of choice: Roughly half the patients receiving CBT cease binge eating and purging. Long-term maintenance of improvement appears to be reasonably good.	• A large number of Type 1 and Type 2 RCTs, utilizing placebo as comparison. • A very substantial number of Type 1 and Type 2 RCTs.	Wilson and Fairburn, Chapter 22, pp. 559–592
Childhood attention-deficit hyperactivity disorder (ADHD)	• *Psychostimulants (e.g., methylphenidate, the amphetamines, and magnesium pemoline)* have shown short-term efficacy in reducing overactivity, increasing concentration and prosocial behavior, and eliminating disruptive classroom behavior.	• A very large number of Type 1 RCTs, in comparison with placebo.	Greenhill and Ford, Chapter 2, pp. 25–55
	• *Contingency management* produces impressive behavioral and academic gains in specialized classrooms so long as contingencies are enforced; they may also enable a reduction in the stimulant dosage needed for optimal classroom behavior.	• Several substantial reviews of single-case experimental designs (Type 3 studies).	Hinshaw, Klein, and Abikoff, Chapter 1, pp. 3–23

Syndromes	*Treatments*	*Standards of Proof*	*References*
Childhood attention-deficit hyperactivity disorder (ADHD) (*cont.*)	• Systematic combinations of *direct contingency management plus clinical behavior therapy* have yielded significant behavioral improvements, although their effects are smaller than those from medication. • *Combining intensive behavioral intervention with well-delivered pharmacological agents* typically ranks better than either treatment component alone; this is the only modality that tends to normalize behavior patterns.	• Three large-scale Type 1 studies. • One very large-scale Type 1 clinical trial comparing behavioral intervention alone and medication alone with the two together.	
Conduct disorder in children	*Parent management training (PMT)* with the parents of a variety of troubled children and adolescents; *multisystemic therapy (MST)* with troubled families and their conduct-disordered adolescents; *problem-solving skills training (PSST)* with impulsive, aggressive, and conduct disorder (CT) children and adolescents; *functional family therapy (FFT)* with difficult-to-treat CD populations; and *brief strategic family therapy (BSFT)* with Hispanic families with maladaptive interactional styles—all have been used with success with this population.	A large number of Type 1 and Type 2 RCTs of PMT over a 30-year span; multiple Type 1 RCTs of MST; several Type 1 and Type 2 RCTs of PSST; a few Type 1 and Type 2 RCTs of FFT; a few Type 2 studies of BSFT.	Kazdin, Chapter 3, pp. 57–85
Dissociative disorders	• *Sodium pentobarbital, sodium amobarbital, and hypnosis* have proven useful in facilitating the recovery of repressed and dissociated memories. • *Psychotherapy* has been reported to help patients work through, and ultimately control access to, traumatic memories.	These treatments have been studied by case report methods; no Type 1 or Type 2 RCTs of any treatments for dissociative disorders have been reported.	Maldonado, Butler, and Spiegel, Chapter 19, pp. 463–496
Generalized anxiety disorder (GAD)	• The most successful psychosocial treatments for GAD combine *relaxation exercises and cognitive behavior therapy* in the effort to bring the worry process itself under the patient's control.	• A few recent Type 1 and Type 2 RCTs.	Barlow, Raffa, and Cohen, Chapter 13, pp. 301–335

Syndromes	*Treatments*	*Standards of Proof*	*References*
	• *Benzodiazepines, buspirone, tricyclic antidepressants (TCAs), venlafaxine, and SSRIs* have all been found to be superior to placebo in reducing anxiety, although the first two are subject to abuse/dependence.	• Benzodiazepines: numerous Type 1 and Type 2 RCTs; buspirone: several Type 1 RCTs; TCAs: several Type 1 RCTs; venlafaxine and SSRIs: several Type 1 RCTs	Roy-Byrne and Cowley, Chapter 14, pp. 337–365
Hypochondriasis	*Cognitive behavior therapy* has proven helpful in reducing attention to distressing bodily sensations, correcting misinformation and exaggerated beliefs, and addressing cognitive processes (selective perception, misattribution, etc.) that maintain disease fears.	Several recent Type 1 and Type 2 controlled trials, demonstrating the clear superiority of CBT to no treatment and its marginal superiority to nonspecific treatments (i.e., relaxation training).	Simon, Chapter 18, pp. 447–461
Major depressive disorder (MDD)	• Interventions utilizing *behavior therapy, cognitive behavior therapy, and interpersonal therapy* have all yielded substantial reductions in scores on the two major depression-rating scales and in a percentage of patients meeting MDD criteria posttreatment; all three have also produced significant maintenance of effect after discontinuation of treatment.	• At least two Type 1 or Type 2 RCTs (seven in the case of cognitive behavior therapy) for each of these psychosocial interventions, as well as four meta-analytic reports in the literature.	Craighead, Hart, Craighead, and Ilardi, Chapter 10, pp. 245–261
	• At least one major study lends strong support for the superior effectiveness of *combined psychosocial and pharmacological treatment.*	• One Type 1 RCT.	
	• *TCAs* have now largely been replaced as first-line treatments for MDD by *SSRIs*: *fluoxetine, sertraline, paroxetine, and citalopram,* along with such new compounds as *venlafaxine, mirtazapine, bupropion, and nefazodone.*	• Many, many Type 1 and Type 2 studies of the SSRIs; several Type 1 and Type 2 studies of new compounds.	Nemeroff and Schatzberg, Chapter 9, pp. 229–243
Mixed personality disorder (excluding Cluster A disorders)	An average of 40 weeks of *brief dynamic therapy* yielded substantial symptomatic improvement at both the end of treatment and after 1.5 years.	A single Type 2 RCT, which randomized 81 patients to two forms of brief dynamic therapy and a wait-list control condition.	Crits-Christoph and Barber, Chapter 24, pp. 611–623

Syndromes	*Treatments*	*Standards of Proof*	*References*
Obsessive compulsive disorder (OCD)	• *Serotonergic reuptake inhibitors (SRIs)*, which reduce or eliminate both obsessions and compulsions, represent one of two first-line treatments for OCD.	• A very large number of Type 1 RCTs, which randomized patients to SRI and non-SRI antidepressant treatments in both placebo-controlled and non placebo-controlled studies.	Dougherty, Rauch, and Jenike, Chapter 16, pp. 387–409
	• Augmentation of SRIs with *clonazepam or buspirone*, and with high-potency *neuroleptics* in cases of a comorbid tic disorder, is provisionally recommended based on marginal available data.	• A few recent Type 2 and Type 3 studies.	
	• *Cognitive behavioral therapy* involving exposure and ritual prevention methods, which reduce or eliminate the obsessions and behavioral and mental rituals of this disorder, is the other first-line treatment for OCD.	• A very substantial number of Type 1 and Type 2 RCTs.	Franklin and Foa, Chapter 15, pp. 367–386
Panic disorder with agoraphobia	*Situational in vivo exposure* substantially reduced symptoms.	A substantial number of Type 1 RCTs.	Barlow, Raffa, and Cohen, Chapter 13, pp. 301–335
Panic disorder without agoraphobia	*Cognitive behavioral treatments* that focused on education about the nature of anxiety and panic and provided some form of exposure and coping skills acquisition have proven efficacious.	A substantial number of Type 1 RCTs.	Barlow, Raffa, and Cohen, Chapter 13, pp. 301–335
Panic disorder with and without agoraphobia	• *Tricyclic antidepressants (e.g., imipramine, clomipramine)* reduced the number of panic attacks and also reduced anticipatory anxiety and phobic avoidance, although side effects caused patients to drop from clinical trials.	• A large number of Type 1 and Type 2 RCTs, with comparisons primarily to placebo.	Roy-Byrne and Cowley, Chapter 14, pp. 337–365
	• *High-potency benzodiazepines (e.g., alprazolam, clonazepam)* were subsequently found to eliminate panic attacks in 55–75% of patients.	• Twelve Type 1 and Type 2 RCTs, with comparisons to placebo.	

Syndromes	*Treatments*	*Standards of Proof*	*References*
	• *Serotonin reuptake inhibitors (SRIs) (including selective SRIs)* have more recently shown effects on panic frequency, generalized anxiety, disability, and phobic avoidance.	• Several Type 1 and Type 2 RCTs, with comparisons to placebo.	
Paraphilias	• *Cognitive, behavioral, and cognitive behavioral treatments* have been reported to lower rates of recidivism, although methodological difficulties in carrying out the research reduce confidence in these results.	• A few Type 2 RCTs, a larger number of Type 3 open trials, and several Type 4 reviews.	Maletzky, Chapter 21, pp. 525–557
	• *Somatic treatments (e.g., medroxyprogesterone and cyproterone acetate)* that lower testosterone levels have also been reported to have shown some success.	• Large-scale outcome evaluations of these treatments are lacking.	
Posttraumatic stress disorder (PTSD)	• *Antidepressants* reduced both PTSD symptoms and those of comorbid conditions; they also made it easier for patients to benefit from psychotherapy; three varieties of antidepressants have been most commonly used:	• Several Type 1 and Type 2 RCTs.	Yehuda, Marshall, Penkower, and Wong, Chapter 17, pp. 411–445
	• *Monoamine oxidase inhibitors* reduced intrusive thoughts, improved sleep, and moderated anxiety and depression.	• One Type 1 and one Type 2 RCTs; three Type 3 open trials.	
	• *Tricyclic antidepressants* reduced intrusive thoughts and obsessions and moderated depression.	• Two Type 1 and one Type 2 RCTs; three Type 3 open trials.	
	• *Selective serotonin reuptake inhibitors* markedly reduced intrusive thoughts, avoidance, and sleep problems.	• One Type 1 RCT and six Type 3 open trials.	
	• Future research must also address the interaction of *psychopharmacology* and *psychosocial* (largely *behavioral* and *cognitive-behavioral*) treatments.		

Syndromes	*Treatments*	*Standards of Proof*	*References*
Schizophrenia	• *Behavior therapy and social-learning–token-economy programs* help structure, support, and reinforce prosocial behaviors in persons with schizophrenia.	• Many Type 1 and Type 2 RCTs and a very large number of Type 3 studies of behavior therapy and social-learning–token-economy programs.	Kopelowicz, Liberman, and Zarate, Chapter 8, pp. 201–228
	• *Structured, educational family interventions* help patients with schizophrenia maintain gains achieved with medication and customary case management.	• Over 20 Type 1 and Type 2 RCTs of educational family interventions.	
	• *Social skills training* has enabled persons with schizophrenia to acquire instrumental and affiliative skills to improve functioning in their communities.	• More than 40 Type 1 and Type 2 RCTs of social skills training.	
	• *Pharmacological treatment* has had a profoundly positive impact on the course of schizophrenia. The recent introduction of *atypical antipsychotics* has been promising because of their reduced side effects and enhanced efficacy in some refractory patients.	A very large number of RCTs over 40 years.	Bradford, Stroup, and Lieberman, Chapter 7, pp. 169–199
Schizotypal personality disorder	*Antipsychotic medications* may be useful for some aspects of this disorder.	Two Type 1, three Type 2, and two Type 3 studies.	Koenigsberg, Woo-Ming, and Siever, Chapter 25, pp. 625–641
Sexual dysfunctions	The introduction of effective pharmacological therapies for both erectile disorders (*sildenafil*) and rapid ejaculation (*SSRIs: fluoxetine, sertraline, clomipramine, paroxetine*) has shifted many physicians from the psychobiological model that previously held sway to a narrower biological model. There is considerable evidence that these therapies are frequently successful in reversing sexual dysfunction; there is less evidence concerning their long-term efficacy in subjective sense of sexual satisfaction and couple interaction. As well, the evi-	• Erectile disorders: multiple double-blind, placebo-controlled, multicenter Type 1 studies. • Rapid ejaculation: a large number of placebo-controlled, double-blind Type 1 studies.	Segraves and Althof, Chapter 20, pp. 497–524

Syndromes	*Treatments*	*Standards of Proof*	*References*
	dence concerning pharmacological treatment of female sexual disorders is extremely limited.		
Sleep disorders	• *Benzodiazepines, zolpidem, and zaleplon* have been shown to be effective, typically reducing sleep onset by 15–30 minutes, decreasing the number of awakenings to an absolute level of 1–3 per night, and increasing total sleep time about 15–45 minutes; these pharmacological agents act more reliably than behavioral interventions in the short term.	• A large number of Type 1 and, especially, Type 2 RCTs, in comparison to placebo and a variety of pharmacological agents.	Nowell, Buysse, Morin, Reynolds, and Kupfer, Chapter 23, pp. 593–609
	• *Behavioral interventions, including stimulus control, sleep restriction, relaxation strategies, and cognitive behavioral therapy*, have shown effectiveness, especially over the longer term, in reducing sleep onset, decreasing awakenings, and increasing total sleep time; these behavioral interventions produce more sustained effects than pharmacological agents.	• A moderate number of Type 2 RCTs, in comparison to wait-list controls, partial behavioral interventions, and pharmacological agents.	
Social phobia	• *Exposure-based procedures and multicomponent cognitive behavioral treatments* most effectively reduced or eliminated the symptoms of social phobia.	• A large number of Type 1 and Type 2 RCTs.	Barlow, Raffa, and Cohen, Chapter 13, pp. 301–335
	• *Social skills training and relaxation techniques* have also been used with some success to treat social phobia.	• A substantial number of Type 1 and Type 2 RCTs.	
	• *Monoamine oxidase inhibitors (e.g., phenelzine)* relieved the key symptoms of social phobia.	• Three Type 1 and Type 2 RCTs.	Roy-Byrne and Cowley, Chapter 14, pp. 337–365
	• The *benzodiazepine clonazepam* has shown that it might be helpful in reducing the symptoms of this disorder.	• One Type 1 RCT.	
	• The *SSRIs fluvoxamine, sertraline, and paroxetine* have demonstrated efficacy for some aspects of this disorder.	• Several Type 1 RCTs.	

Syndromes	*Treatments*	*Standards of Proof*	*References*
Somatoform pain disorder	• *Individual and group cognitive behavior therapy* are useful in reducing pain-related distress and disability. • *Antidepressants* reduce pain intensity.	• Several Type 2 RCTs. • A large number of Type 1 and Type 2 placebo-controlled RCTs.	Simon, Chapter 18, pp. 447–461
Specific phobias	• *Exposure-based procedures, especially in vivo exposure,* reduce or eliminate most or all components of specific phobic disorders. • No pharmacological intervention has been shown to be effective for specific phobias.	• A very large number of Type 1 RCTs.	Barlow, Raffa, and Cohen, Chapter 13, pp. 301–335 Roy-Byrne and Cowley, Chapter 14, pp. 337–365
Substance use disorders	• The *nicotine patch and nicotine chewing gum* significantly increase the nicotine abstinence rate. • *Naltrexone* is particularly effective in preventing full-blown relapses in alcoholics who have had a "slip" after achieving abstinence. • Maintenance treatment using *methadone* for heroin dependence has proven to be the treatment of choice for heroin dependence; more recently, *LAAM*, a longer-acting opioid, has also been used successfully.	• A large number of Type 1 and Type 2 RCTs. • Nine of thirteen Type 1 and Type 2 RCTs have shown positive results for naltrexone over placebo. • A very large number of Type 1 and Type 2 RCTs, and a large number of reviews, have established the efficacy of methadone.	O'Brien and McKay, Chapter 5, pp. 125–156

A GUIDE TO TREATMENTS THAT WORK

1

Childhood Attention-Deficit Hyperactivity Disorder: Nonpharmacological Treatments and Their Combination with Medication

Stephen P. Hinshaw

Rachel G. Klein

Howard B. Abikoff

Attention-deficit hyperactivity disorder (ADHD) is an impairing and persistent disorder of childhood and adolescence that mandates early and effective intervention. Although neurobiological models of etiology predominate, interaction patterns at home and school are relevant to the exacerbation of symptomatology and impairments. Regarding psychosocial intervention, direct contingency management features systematic manipulation of rewards and punishments in specialized settings. It typically yields large effects on behavior and academic performance, but (a) outcomes are typically appraised through single-case experimental designs, outside the typology of clinical trials used in this volume; (b) their effects tend not to generalize or maintain beyond the settings in which they are applied; and (c) research in the past decade suggests larger effects for stimulant medications. Clinical behavior therapy involves consultation with parents and teachers regarding optimal home and school management practices. A number of Type 2 trials demonstrate the clinical value of such procedures for the behavior problems of children with ADHD as rated by parents and teachers but not as directly observed. Three Type 1 investigations of systematic combinations of direct contingency management plus clinical behavior therapy have appeared since the first edition of this book. Although such interventions have yielded significant improvements, effects are, again, smaller than those found with medication. Multimodal treatment—combining intensive behavioral intervention with well-delivered pharmacological agents—typically ranks better than either treatment component alone. Whereas it is not always significantly superior to medication only, combined treatment is the only modality that tends to normalize behavior patterns among children with ADHD. Further work is needed on tailoring psychosocial interventions to ADHD-related deficits and impairments.

The prevalence, impairment, and persistence associated with attention-deficit hyperactivity disorder (ADHD) in children provide a clarion call for the application of effective treatment strategies to youngsters with this condition (e.g., Barkley, 1998; Hinshaw, 1994). We feature nonpharmacological intervention strategies, the most effective of which for ADHD are behavioral approaches. We highlight at the outset that the documented efficacy of medication treatments for ADHD (Campbell & Cueva, 1995; Klein & Wender, 1995) provides a standard for judging other treatments (Hinshaw, 2000). Therefore, in addition to describing studies of nonpharmacological/behavioral treatments themselves, we also examine (a) comparisons of behavioral with medication treatments and (b) combinations of behavioral and pharmacological intervention strategies for ADHD (see Greenhill & Ford, this volume, regarding medication treatments per se). The frequent co-occurrence of ADHD with aggressive and antisocial behavior patterns (Abikoff & Klein, 1992; Fergusson, Horwood, & Lloyd, 1991; Hinshaw, 1987) dictates the salience of these outcome domains, and we refer readers to Kazdin (this volume) for specific discussion of the treatment of conduct disorders. In addition, we highlight at the outset that youth with ADHD have proven distressingly refractory to long-term amelioration with any treatment strategies, pharmacological or psychosocial, a point to which we return at the conclusion of the chapter (see also Hinshaw, 2000).

BACKGROUND INFORMATION REGARDING ADHD

Considerable knowledge has accumulated about ADHD, the latest title for a constellation of symptoms that has been described for well over a century and that has undergone many name changes over time (Barkley, 1998; Schachar, 1986). First, the constituent symptoms of this disorder fall into two main clusters: inattention-disorganization and hyperactivity-impulsivity (American Psychiatric Association [APA], 1994; Barkley, 1998). Because such behavior patterns are ubiquitous in young children, clear impairment in academic, family, interpersonal, and self-related domains must be demonstrated to justify the diagnosis. Indeed, the diagnostic criteria for ADHD in the fourth edition of the *Diagnostic and Statistical Manual of Mental Disorders* (DSM-IV; APA, 1994) mandate the presence, from early ages, of developmentally atypical levels of the constituent behaviors leading to impairment in multiple settings (see Table 1.1). Individuals can be classified into predominantly inattentive, predominantly hyperactive-impulsive, or combined subtypes. Distinctions between inattentive-type youth and those with inattention plus hyperactive/impulsive features have been found with respect to family history, gender distribution, neuropsychological profiles, and some aspects of treatment response (see Hinshaw, 1994).

When stringent diagnostic criteria are applied, the prevalence of childhood ADHD appears to be approximately 3 to 5% of elementary-school-aged boys and 1 to 2% of girls (APA, 1994). ADHD has been shown to exist across multiple cultures and in multiple nations, but precise cross-national comparisons of prevalence rates are hampered by disparate screening thresholds and diverse diagnostic criteria (Barkley, 1998; Schachar, 1991).

Crucially, children with ADHD are highly likely to show substantial impairment in key functional domains. They are prone to serious accidents and injuries; they are likely to be academic underachievers (even in the absence of formal learning disabilities); they are highly rejected by peers; their families are often in conflict; and, not surprisingly, they have lowered self-esteem (e.g., Hinshaw, 1992; Hinshaw & Melnick, 1995; Slomkowski, Klein, & Mannuzza, 1995; see review in Hinshaw, in press). Furthermore, prospective studies have shown that children with ADHD are likely to show persisting symptomatology and impairment into adolescence, with a substantial minority proceeding to demonstrate marked problems in young adulthood (Gittelman, Mannuzza, Shenker, & Bonagura, 1985; Klein & Mannuzza, 1991; Mannuzza & Klein, 1999; Weiss & Hechtman, 1993). In short, clear impairment and a highly negative course speak to the ongoing need for concerted prevention and treatment efforts.

The underlying nature of ADHD remains an area of active debate. For many years, in keeping with earlier labels of *hyperactivity* or *hyperkinesis*, basic research focused on motoric overactivity and implicated subcortical brain regions in neural models (Laufer & Denhoff, 1957). Two decades ago, focus shifted to underlying attentional processes and deficient self-regulation (e.g., Douglas, 1983). Current work capitalizes on more precise and differentiated views of attentional style, cognitive processing, and behavioral regulation, with increasing recognition that children with ADHD show pronounced diffi-

TABLE 1.1 Diagnostic Criteria for Attention-Deficit Hyperactivity Disorder

A. Either (1) or (2):
   (1) Six (or more) of the following symptoms of **inattention** have persisted for at least 6 months to a degree that is maladaptive and inconsistent with developmental level:
   Inattention
   (a) often fails to give close attention to details or makes careless mistakes in schoolwork, work, or other activities
   (b) often has difficulty sustaining attention in tasks or play activities
   (c) often does not seem to listen when spoken to directly
   (d) often does not follow through on instructions and fails to finish schoolwork, chores, or duties in the workplace (not due to oppositional behavior or failure to understand directions)
   (e) often has difficulty organizing tasks and activities
   (f) often avoids, dislikes, or is reluctant to engage in tasks that require sustained mental effort (such as schoolwork or homework)
   (g) often loses things necessary for tasks or activities (e.g., toys, school assignments, pencils, books, or tools)
   (h) is often easily distracted by extraneous stimuli
   (i) is often forgetful in daily activities
   (2) Six (or more) of the following symptoms of **hyperactivity-impulsivity** have persisted for at least 6 months to a degree that is maladaptive and inconsistent with developmental level:
   Hyperactivity
   (a) often fidgets with hands or feet or squirms in seat
   (b) often leaves seat in classroom or in other situations in which remaining seated is expected
   (c) often runs about or climbs excessively in situations in which it is inappropriate (in adolescents or adults, may be limited to subjective feelings of restlessness)
   (d) often has difficulty playing or engaging in leisure activities quietly
   (e) is always "on the go" or often acts as if "driven by a motor"
   (f) often talks excessively
   Impulsivity
   (g) often blurts out answers before questions have been completed
   (h) often has difficulty awaiting turn
   (i) often interrupts or intrudes on others (e.g., butts into conversations or games)
B. Some hyperactive-impulsive or inattentive symptoms that caused impairment were present before age 7 years.
C. Some impairment from the symptoms is present in two or more settings (e.g., at school [or work] and at home).
D. There must be clear evidence of clinically significant impairment in social, academic, or occupational functioning.
E. The symptoms do not occur exclusively during the course of a Pervasive Developmental Disorder, Schizophrenia, or other Psychotic Disorder and are not better accounted for by another mental disorder (e.g., Mood Disorder, Anxiety Disorder, Dissociative Disorder, or a Personality Disorder).

Attention-Deficit Hyperactivity Disorder, Combined Type: If both criteria A1 and A2 are met for the past 6 months.

Attention-Deficit Hyperactivity Disorder, Predominantly Inattentive Type: If criterion A1 is met but criterion A2 is not met for the past 6 months.

Attention-Deficit Hyperactivity Disorder, Predominantly Hyperactive-Impulsive Type: If criterion A2 is met but criterion A1 is not met for the past 6 months.

Note. From American Psychiatric Association, 1994, *Diagnostic and Statistical Manual of Mental Disorders* (4th ed.). Reprinted by permission.

culties in response inhibition and in organization of motoric output (Barkley, 1997; Schachar, Tannock, Marriott, & Logan, 1995). There is evidence that frontal and prefrontal impairment is implicated, but nonspecifically (Barkley, 1997). The lack of agreement on basic mechanisms dictates that clinical evaluation focus on systematically documenting behavioral signs, obtaining a thorough developmental history, and addressing key domains of impairment. As with nearly all other mental disorders, treatment approaches for ADHD are not yet directed toward known underlying causal mechanisms and are instead based on empirical support.

The search for causal mechanisms has uncovered a host of potentially interacting risk factors but limited evidence for unimodal, overarching etiologies (e.g., Tannock, 1998). Evidence is increasing for strong heritability of both dimensional and categorical conceptions of ADHD (Faraone et al., 1992; Levy, Hay, McStephen, Wood, & Waldman, 1997).

In addition, a host of nongenetic risk factors, such as prenatal and perinatal difficulties and maternal smoking and alcohol abuse, appear to be nonspecifically linked with attentional deficits and hyperactivity (Breslau, 1995; Sprich-Buckminster, Biederman, Milberger, Faraone, & Lehman, 1993). Some investigations of high-risk, low-income samples have implicated overly stimulating parenting during infancy and toddlerhood in the later display of ADHD (Carlson, Jacobvitz, & Sroufe, 1995; Jacobvitz & Sroufe, 1987), but child-rearing practices or attitudes are not likely candidates as "main effect" causes of ADHD. Indeed, birdirectional and transactional conceptions of parent-child influence are necessary. The clear role of coercive parenting styles in the development of aggressive and antisocial behaviors that often accompany ADHD (Anderson, Hinshaw, & Simmel, 1994; Patterson, Reid, & Dishion, 1992) implicates family intervention as a cornerstone of psychosocial treatment approaches.

It is in the classroom setting that ADHD often yields its most harmful effects. Underfocused attention, disruptive behavior, and poor rule following place youth with ADHD at high risk for underachievement, peer rejection, and consequent decrements in self-esteem (Barkley, 1998; Hinshaw, 1994). School-based intervention is therefore a key aspect of psychosocial interventions.

In summary, ADHD is a persistent and cross-situational behavior disorder that yields substantial impairment. Cormorbidity with aggressive-spectrum disorders is commonplace, and associations with learning disorders as well as anxiety and mood disorders are above chance levels (Biederman, Newcorn, & Sprich, 1991; Jensen, Martin, & Cantwell, 1997). Prevalence of ADHD is estimated to approach 3 to 7% of the school-aged population, with a male preponderance (APA, 1994). Interacting causal factors include genetic predispositions and early biological triggers, with negative familial patterns serving as potential escalating variables. Home- and school-based intervention strategies constitute the backbone of psychosocial treatments.

HISTORICAL CONCEPTIONS OF INTERVENTION

For many decades the child guidance model and its underlying psychodynamic conceptualization held court as the primary approach for nearly all clinically referred children in the United States. Thus, play therapy constituted the predominant psychosocial treatment strategy for youngsters with ADHD. Evidence for the efficacy of insight-oriented treatments for youngsters with ADHD is lacking. The application of behavioral, social learning approaches to youngsters specifically diagnosed as "hyperactive" began in the 1960s (e.g., Patterson, 1965). During the 1970s and 1980s, both behavioral and cognitive behavioral interventions—the latter promising greater durability of treatment gains through self-management training—became far more widespread. Because cognitive behavioral treatments, particularly those emphasizing the use of verbal self-instructions, have not shown clinically significant benefits for children with ADHD (Abikoff, 1991; Hinshaw, 2000), we focus on systematically applied behavioral interventions in our review.

As discussed in greater detail by Greenhill (this volume), psychopharmacological approaches to ADHD have been scientifically appraised for nearly 60 years. Stimulants were first noted to yield impressive short-term benefits for youth with behavioral and emotional disturbances in the 1930s, and hundreds of controlled intervention studies have continued to document impressive gains in core symptom areas and in domains of associated impairment when youngsters with ADHD are treated with stimulants (Campbell & Cueva, 1995; Greenhill & Osman, 2000; Klein, 1987; Swanson, McBurnett, Christian, & Wigal, 1995). However, evidence for a relative advantage of prognosis or long-term outcome in children treated with medication has eluded empirical verification. As a result, evaluation of (a) more intensive psychosocial strategies and (b) integrations of psychosocial and pharmacological interventions is a priority (Pelham & Murphy, 1986; Richters et al., 1995).

PROGRAMMATIC AND METHODOLOGICAL ISSUES IN DETERMINING TREATMENT BENEFITS

Before appraising specific evidence regarding the documented benefits of psychosocial treatments for ADHD, we discuss the different types of behavioral interventions as well as the research designs and assessment methods used to evaluate these types of nonpharmacological treatments.

Direct Contingency Management Versus Clinical Behavior Therapy

Two types of behavioral intervention approaches for youngsters with behavior disorders are salient: (a) direct contingency management, in which intensive reward and punishment procedures are established in specialized treatment facilities or demonstration classrooms, and (b) clinical behavior therapy procedures, in which consultation (via group or individual sessions) is provided to families and teachers, who in turn implement behavior management programs in the child's natural environment. With direct contingency management, a variety of systematic reward and response cost procedures are implemented with frequent and intensive schedules of administration. The heavy reinforcement schedules implemented in specialized settings, however, may not be readily applicable in the natural environment, and effects may not be generalizable to other settings. Furthermore, gains seen under conditions of direct prompting may dissipate without explicit programming for generalization. Thus, evaluation during explicitly prompted performance (e.g., in the presence of a teacher's aide who delivers strict contingencies) is likely to yield greater estimates of efficacy than appraisal during unprompted periods; in the vast majority of investigations of contingency management, treatment evaluation is made during the period of active contingencies.

Clinical behavior therapy procedures involve a structured curriculum of parent and/or teacher consultation. A prototypical sequence of activities for parent training involves (a) directing positive attention to the child; (b) targeting performance goals and collecting baseline data; (c) implementing individualized, systematic, and coordinated home- and school-based reinforcement programs; and (d) utilizing contingent, nonphysical punishment procedures such as time-out or response cost (e.g., Barkley, 1987; Wells et al., 2000). Teachers receive consultation in such areas as modifying expectations, classroom seating patterns, individualized reward programs, and coordination of home-school reinforcement systems. Clinical behavior therapy programs originated in the 1960s for children with oppositional or aggressive behavior patterns; during the 1970s, applications began to be targeted specifically to youth with hyperactivity or ADHD (O'Leary, Pelham, Rosenbaum, & Price, 1976).

A key research issue is that the two types of behavioral treatment strategies are typically evaluated in different ways, confounding easy comparison across investigations. Specifically, direct contingency management interventions, which emanate from the applied behavior analysis tradition, usually employ single-case experimental designs (e.g., reversal, multiple-baseline) to ascertain the causal effect of specific contingencies on the dependent measures of interest, such as behavior problems and academic productivity. Such interventions are appraised nearly exclusively in specialized programs containing only youth with ADHD (or other disruptive behavior disorders), with extremely short periods of intervention (measured in hours or days). As a result, such investigations do not readily fit into the standards-of-proof framework (i.e., Type 1, Type 2, Type 3) used in the current volume. Clinical behavior therapy procedures, on the other hand, are usually implemented in home and regular-education settings and are evaluated by means of randomized, parallel group clinical trials, with subjects assigned to contrasting treatments for periods of several months (or more). Note that we have designated most of the investigations of clinical behavior therapy that we review herein as Type 2. That is, although they employ random assignment to treatment condition, they have relatively short intervention periods and little or no manualization of treatment procedures. We reserve Type 1 status for the few large-scale and longer term randomized clinical trials with manualization and with at least some objective observations or other blinded outcome assessments (Barkley et al., 2000; Klein & Abikoff, 1997; MTA Cooperative Group, 1999a).

Finally, we include in the second edition of this volume a recent randomized investigation of a third type of behavioral intervention for ADHD: social skills training. Earlier work with social skills training in the field had not focused on youth specifically diagnosed with ADHD, had embedded social skills training in multicomponent treatments, or had used single-case experimental designs. As noted below, the controlled (albeit small-scale) investigation of Pfiffner and McBurnett (1997) shows that behaviorally oriented social skills training groups, incorporating copious rehearsal and reinforcement of important social skills, can yield positive outcomes for children with ADHD, at least as reported by parents.

OUTCOME STUDIES

Our review focuses on investigations of direct contingency management, clinical behavior therapy, and social skills training for children diagnosed specifically with ADHD (or with earlier diagnostic conceptions that correspond with ADHD, e.g., attention deficit disorder with or without hyperactivity). We include designs that (a) directly compare behavioral interventions with wait-list controls, placebo treatments, or contrasting psychosocial treatments; (b) contrast behavioral treatments with medication conditions; and/or (c) examine combinations of behavioral and pharmacological treatments in relation to single-treatment modalities. The comprehensive reviews of early studies in the field (see Mash & Dalby, 1979; Sprague, 1983) allow us to restrict our coverage to treatment investigations published from the year 1980 onward. Note that we exclude interventions that focus on cognitive mediational approaches, as the systematic reviews of Abikoff (1987, 1991), Hinshaw and Erhardt (1991), and Hinshaw (2000) document the lack of efficacy of these treatments for this population. Indeed, despite their initial promise, self-instructional strategies have failed to produce any significant cognitive or behavioral gains for youngsters with ADHD, even though youth rated as impulsive by teachers (who fall short of meeting diagnostic criteria for ADHD) may show some positive response (e.g., Kendall & Braswell, 1982).

Direct Contingency Management

Building on the explosion of single-case-experiment research in the 1960s and 1970s—in which it was repeatedly demonstrated that specific contingencies produced strong, acute effects on observed child behavior—more recent studies have focused on (a) comparisons of varying types of contingencies (e.g., positive vs. negative consequences) and (b) contrasts between behaviorally oriented and medication-related strategies for children with ADHD. The large number of specific investigations precludes a study-by-study analysis (for a thorough review, see Pfiffner & O'Leary, 1993). We note that investigators of contingency management programs often deemphasize formal diagnosis; thus, results pertain to a wide range of attention-disordered and behavior-disordered children.

The prototypical investigation of direct contingency management takes place in a specialized classroom, in which all of the participating children have behavioral disorders. The teacher or "behavioral engineer" is trained to implement classroomwide contingencies, typically incorporating (a) such positive incentives as praise or individualized reward programs for targeted behaviors (see Pfiffner, Rosen, & O'Leary, 1985); (b) negative consequences, such as reprimands, response cost contingencies (the subtraction of earned points; see Rapport, Murphy, & Bailey, 1982), or time-out; or (c) combinations of positive and negative contingencies (e.g., Rosen, O'Leary, Joyce, Conway, & Pfiffner, 1984). The contingencies are altered over periods of hours or, at most, days; outcome measures are usually restricted to observations of on-task or disruptive classroom behavior (see Pelham et al., 1993, for a wider range of outcome measures); and single-case or within-subject experimental methodologies are typically employed to yield causal inferences. Given their specialized and time-restricted nature, most investigations of direct contingency management programs can best be viewed as demonstrations of the acute effects of reward and punishment procedures rather than as integrative treatments per se.

The behavioral gains reported from these studies are often impressive (e.g., Robinson, Newby, & Ganzell, 1981). For instance, Rosen et al. (1984, Experiment 1) reported an average increase in on-task behavior (across 8 subjects) from 35% during no-contingency periods to 79% during intervals of active contingent reinforcement or punishment. Importantly, in some reports academic productivity has been found to parallel the behavioral improvements (e.g., Rapport et al., 1982). The systematic work of Susan O'Leary and colleagues has demonstrated that stringently implemented, individualized reward programs can yield benefit for hyperactive/disruptive youth (see Pfiffner et al., 1985), but the use of prudent, low-intensity negative consequences (e.g., brief reprimands backed up with privilege loss; response cost) is an extremely valuable component of contingency management (Rosen et al., 1984; see also Rapport et al., 1982).

Intensive and broader applications of direct contingency management for children with ADHD can be found in the summer-treatment-program model of Pelham and Hoza (1996), which has been adopted at a number of locations throughout the United States. Here, academic skills training, social skills groups, and playground and sports activities are applied in a contingency-rich environment with five counselors working with units of 12 children during 9-hour days.

Another example of direct contingency management is the systematic, special kindergarten classroom provided by Barkley et al. (2000) for young children meeting screening criteria for both inattentive/hyperactive and aggressive behavior. In this heavily supervised, 9-month program—which featured an intensive positive and negative contingency program as well as social skills training, anger-management training, and academic readiness training—significant gains were found at the end of the school year across some outcome measures, including both adult informant reports and objective classroom observations. Yet, as discussed below, there was almost no maintenance of these gains in subsequent school years.

Indeed, from another perspective, the experimental success of demonstrating stimulus control (i.e., improvements over baseline that remit when contingencies are removed) reflects a lack of sustained treatment-related clinical benefits. In other words, the lack of generalized and persisting gains when contingencies are lifted highlights the key deficiency of direct contingency management (Pelham & Hinshaw, 1992). A parallel acuteness of effects is salient for stimulant medication treatments for children and adolescents with ADHD (Greenhill & Ford, this volume). Providing lasting benefit is the key treatment issue in the field.

In some early investigations, effects of behavioral manipulations appeared stronger than those from medication-related changes (Rapport et al., 1982). Yet the more recent, systematic research of Pelham and colleagues (Carlson, Pelham, Milich, & Dixon, 1992; Pelham et al., 1993) in intensive summer-treatment-program settings demonstrates otherwise. In both reports, systematic behavioral contingencies in special classroom settings produced significant benefit (compared to nonsystematic contingencies) regarding observed classroom behavior but did not yield significant improvement in academic productivity or accuracy. Stimulant medication, on the other hand, improved both behavioral and academic outcome domains, with an effect size approximately twice that of the behavioral contingencies (Pelham et al., 1993). Furthermore, whereas stimulants added significant benefit when combined with direct contingency management, the converse was not typically the case (see, however, Kolko, Bukstein, & Barron, 1999, who did find at least some outcome measures for which combination interventions, in a day treatment program, were superior to medication alone). We do note that contingency management procedures may permit a reduction in stimulant dosage for optimal classroom behavior in specialized settings (Carlson et al., 1992; see also Horn et al., 1991; Pelham, Schnedler, Bologna, & Contreras, 1980).

In summary, direct contingency management procedures produce significant, short-term benefits regarding core symptoms of ADHD, as rated by adults and as objectively observed, as well as regarding off-task and disruptive behavior patterns and some measures of academic productivity. These benefits, however, are largely confined to specialized settings. The lack of maintenance of behavior change and the artificiality of the settings in which contingency management has been implemented constitute key limitations; in addition, even intensive, systemic behavioral contingency programs show significantly weaker effects than those from stimulant medication. Moreover, the addition of contingency procedures has not typically provided significant increments to medication-related gains (Carlson et al., 1992; Pelham et al., 1993). As noted earlier, the types of studies used to show the efficacy of direct contingency management for children with ADHD are not readily classifiable by the framework for standards of proof used in the current volume. Whereas single-case demonstrations of contingency-related effects on observed behavior are heuristic, they do not, in and of themselves, translate into comprehensive interventions for groups of youngsters in natural settings (see, for example, discussion in Kolko et al., 1999). Overall, we believe that incorporating the power of direct contingency management approaches into generalizable treatment strategies is a continuing challenge for the field, yet we contend that investigators also need to consider carefully the development of other types of psychosocial interventions for children with ADHD.

Clinical Behavior Therapy and Social Skills Training

Table 1.2 lists key experimental investigations of clinical behavior therapy investigations for children with ADHD that have been published since the early 1980s. Between-group clinical trials are included in this table. The typical treatment period spans several months, parent-training procedures and teacher consultation sessions being the key clinical activities.

TABLE 1.2 Findings from Clinical Behavior Therapy Trials for ADHD from 1980 Onward

Authors	N/M Age (yr)	Behavioral Treatment	Study Design	Outcome Domains	Key Findings
Firestone et al. (1981)[a]	43/7.3	3 months: 3 individual and 6 group parent-training sessions plus 2 teacher consultations	Type 2 1. BT + placebo 2. MPH 3. BT + MPH (pre-post)	A. Academic achievement B. Laboratory reaction time C. Behavior ratings (P, T)	A. and B. 2 = 3 > 1 C.[b]
Dubey et al. (1983)	37/8.4	9 weeks: weekly group parent-training sessions	Type 2 1. BT 2. Parent effectiveness training 3. Delayed treatment control (pre-post 9-mo. FU)	A. Behavior ratings (P) B. Videotaped PC interaction, scored for parent and child behavior	A. 1 = 2 > 3, with 1 and 2 showing significant pre-post and pre-FU change for several scales B. No effects
Horn et al. (1987)	19/9.7	8 weeks: 8 weekly group parent-training sessions	Type 2 1. BT 2. SI 3. BT + SI (pre-post 1-mo. FU)	A. Child self-report and lab measures B. Behavior ratings (P, T) C. Classroom observations	Equal improvement across groups for all but 1 of 32 outcome measures[c]
Pelham et al. (1988)	30[d]/$M = 10$	5 months: $M = 10$ individual and group parent-training sessions plus $M = 10$ teacher consultations	Type 2 1. BT + SS + MPH 2. BT + SS + placebo 3. BT + MPH 4. BT + placebo 5. SS only (not random) (pre-post)	A. Behavior ratings (P, T) B. Academic achievement C. Peer sociometrics D. Classroom observations	1 = 2 = 3 = 4; for A (parent), B, C, and D, with all 4 groups showing significant pre-post improvement (whereas 5 did not). For teacher ratings, 1 and 3 improved more than 2 and 4, during periods of active medication
Pisterman et al. (1989)	46/4.2	12 weeks: 10 group parent-training sessions plus 2 individual sessions	Type 2 1. BT 2. Delayed treatment control group (pre-post 3-mo. FU)	A. Videotaped PC interaction, scored for parent and child behavior B. Behavior ratings (P)	A. 1 > 2 re: child compliance and some parenting measures B. 1 = 2 re: Conners ratings[e]
Horn et al. (1990)	31/8.8	12 weeks: 12 group parent-training sessions plus 3 teacher consultations	Type 2 1. BT 2. SI 3. BT + SI (pre-post 8-mo. FU)	A. Child achievement, attention, and self-concept B. Behavior ratings (P, T)	No treatment differences (no group × time interactions); all groups showed gains pre-post and pre-FU[f]
Horn et al. (1991)[g]	78/7–11	12 weeks: 12 group parent-training sessions plus 12 child SI sessions plus 3 teacher consultations	Type 2 1. Placebo 2. Low-dose MPH 3. High-dose MPH 4. 1 + BT/SI 5. 2 + BT/SI 6. 3 + BT/SI (pre-post)	A. Child achievement, attention, and self-concept B. Classroom observations C. Behavior ratings (P, T)	Groups with MPH showed greater improvement than placebo; Groups 5 and 6 did not outperform 2 and 3[h]

Barkley et al. (1992)	61/13.9	10 weeks: 8–10 weekly parent sessions	Type 2 1. Behavioral parent training 2. Problem solving and communication therapy 3. Structural family therapy (pre-post 3-mo. FU)	A. Behavior ratings (P, A) B. Family ratings (P, A) C. Videotaped P-A interaction D. Rated depression (M)	1 = 2 = 3 for all outcomes; all groups yielded pre-post improvement for A, B, and D (with maintenance at FU)[i]
Pisterman et al. (1992)	45/4.0	12 weekly group parent-training sessions	Type 2 1. BT 2. Delayed treatment group (pre-post 3-mo. FU)	A. Behavior ratings (P) B. Videotaped PC interaction, scored for parent and child behavior and child attention	1 > 2, for pre-post and pre-FU comparisons regarding parent behavior and child behavior, but not child attention
Anastopoulos et al. (1993)	34/8.1	2 months: 9 sessions of parent training	Type 3 1. BT 2. Delayed treatment group (pre-post FU)	A. Behavior ratings (P) B. Parent-reported stress, parenting efficacy, marital satisfaction	1 > 2, for pre-post comparisons regarding ADHD symptoms and some aspects of parental functioning; gains maintained at FU
Klein & Abikoff (1997)[j]	86/8.25	8 weeks: weekly individual sessions with parents and with teacher augmented by child attendance when needed and by telephone contact	Type 1 1. BT + placebo 2. MPH 3. BT + MPH (pre-post)	A. Behavior ratings (M, T) B. Classroom observations C. Global improvement ratings (M, T, Psy) D. Academic/cognitive tests	A. [k] B. [l] C. [m] D. Few effects[n]
Pfiffner & McBurnett (1997)	27 (8–10)	Eight 90-minute sessions (weekly) for children in SS groups or parents in generalization training groups	Type 2 1. SS 2. SS + parent generalization 3. Wait-list control (pre-post 4-mo. FU)	A. Behavior ratings (P, T) B. Social skills knowledge (C)	A. 1 = 2 > 3 for parent ratings, but not teacher ratings, despite moderate effect sizes for the latter. Parent effects larger for social skills than disruptive behavior. B. 1 = 2 > 3[o]
MTA Cooperative Group (1999a)[p]	579/8.5	Integrated clinical behavior therapy and direct contingency management across 14 months, with parent, school, and child components (see text)	Type 1 1. Medication management 2. Behavioral treatment 3. Combined 1 + 2 4. Community-treated comparison (pre-post)	A. ADHD symptoms (P, T, Obs) B. Oppositional symptoms (P, T, Obs) C. Internalizing (P, T, C) D. Social/peer (P, T, sociometrics) E. Family (P, C, Obs) F. Achievement	A. 1 = 3 > 2 = 4 B.–F. 3 > 4 across all 5 domains, according to at least one informant; additionally, for D., 1 > 4 (teacher) and for E., 2 > 4 (parent)
Barkley et al. (2000)	158/4.8	Special day-class kindergarten program (9 mo.; see text) and 10 weekly group parent-training sessions	Type 1 1. Special class 2. Parent training 3. Combined 1 + 2 4. Regular class, no parent training (pre-post 24-mo. FU—for FU, see Shelton et al., 2000)	A. Diagnostic interviews B. Parent ratings C. Teacher ratings D. Psychoeducational testing E. Clinic behavior observations F. PC interactions G. Classroom observations	No main effects or interactions of parent training. Significant effects of special class for parent ratings of adaptive behavior, multiple teacher ratings, classroom observations of externalizing behavior. Effects not maintained at follow-up.

(continued)

TABLE 1.2 (continued)

Note. N = number of subjects completing the investigation. BT = clinical behavior therapy; SI = self-instructional training for child; SS = social skills training for child; MPH = methylphenidate; M = mother; P = parent; T = teacher; C = child; PC = parent-child; Psy = psychiatrist; A = adolescent; PA = parent-adolescent; Obs = observations.

[a]See also Firestone, Crowe, Goodman, and McGrath (1986), for presentation of 1-year ($N = 52$) and 2-year ($N = 30$) follow-up data for subsets of this sample who remained for assessment. At each follow-up period, no significant between-group differences were found for any outcome measure, in part because a noteworthy subgroup of parent-training-plus-placebo subjects had "switched" to medication treatment.

[b]Results of covariance analysis are difficult to interpret, but it appears as though the medicated groups outperformed the behavior-therapy-plus-placebo children for teacher Conners scores. MPH was individually titrated, averaging 22 mg/day. All three groups showed significant within-subject change on Metropolitan Achievement Tests and on parent- and teacher-rated behavior, but only the medicated youngsters improved on the Gates-MacGinitie Verbal Grade score.

[c]SI treatment involved weekly group sessions for the children. One-month follow-up data showed persistence of within-subject changes across treatment groups for several outcome measures.

[d]For the 20 children in Groups 1–4 who received behavior therapy, MD age was reported to be 7 years; for the 10 children in Group 5, MD = 8 years. MPH dosages were fixed at 0.3 mg/kg, with most children receiving b.i.d. dosages.

[e]Immediate posttreatment gains for treated vs. delayed-treatment control group were maintained at 3-month follow-up.

[f]Pre-FU changes were found, across groups, for parent ratings only.

[g]See also Ialongo et al. (1991) for presentation of 9-month FU data, which revealed a general deterioration of performance for all groups and extremely limited evidence for Groups 5 and 6 to outperform Groups 2 and 3 (i.e., marginally significant finding, and only for parental ratings).

[h]Low-dose MPH = 0.4 mg/kg; high dose = 0.8 mg/kg.

[i]When clinical significance of effects was ascertained via procedures of Jacobson and Truax (1991), only 5–30% improved sufficiently across treatment groups, and only 5–20% "recovered" (rates did not differ across treatment groups).

[j]This report supplants the partial sample report of Gittelman et al. (1980), which included the initial 61 participants. For Treatments 2 and 3, MPH was individually titrated, averaging 40.6 mg/day.

[k]For parent ratings, Treatment 3 was significantly better than Treatment 1 for 5/19 scales; no other group comparisons were significant. For teacher ratings, Treatment 3 was significantly better than Treatment 1 for 16/17 scales, Treatment 3 was significantly better than Treatment 2 for 3/17 scales, and Treatment 2 was significantly better than Treatment 1 for 11/17 scales.

[l]For classroom observations, Treatment 3 was significantly better than Treatment 1 for 9/14 codes; Treatment 3 was significantly better than Treatment 2 for 2/14 codes; and Treatment 2 was significantly better than Treatment 1 for 5/14 codes. Importantly, by the end of treatment, Treatment 3 did not differ significantly from normal classroom controls on any observational measure, reflecting normalization of behavior with combination treatment.

[m]For Clinical Global Improvement ratings by parents, 93% were rated as improved for Treatment 3, 76% for Treatment 2, and 64% for Treatment 1, the only significant difference being between 3 and 1. For ratings by teachers, respective percentages were 93%, 69%, and 57% (Treatment 3 significantly different from 1 and 2, which did not differ). By psychiatrists, respective percentages were 97%, 79%, and 50% (all three contrasts significant).

[n]Across 9 test scores (derived from WISC, WRAT, Matching Familiar Figures, and Paired Associate Test measures) × 3 treatment contrasts, only 2/27 comparisons were significant (both favoring Treatment 2 over Treatment 1: Matching Familiar Figures and Paired Associate Test). Note that psychologists who administered the tests rated participants' test behavior. Across 8 different behavior ratings × 3 treatment group contrasts, only 2/24 comparisons were significant, both favoring Treatment 2 over Treatment 1.

[o]There was modest evidence that Treatment 2 facilitated greater generalization of social skills gains to the classroom.

[p]MPH dosages initially titrated through 4-week trial and maintained during monthly pharmacotherapist visits (Treatment 1 $M = 37.7$ mg/day; Treatment 3 $M = 31.2$ mg/day). With composite outcome measures (Conners et al., 2001; Swanson et al., 2001), the contrast between Treatment 3 and 2 became significant, with a small effect size (see text). Note that data are not yet available for longitudinal follow-up of the MTA sample.

Several recent investigations, however, have included longer intervention periods of up to 9 to 14 months. An important feature of many such programs is the establishment of a joint, home-school reward program such as a "daily report card," through which key school targets are monitored by the teacher, with home reinforcement contingent on positive teacher report or even with response cost contingent on negative report. The sole experimental trial of social skills training utilized group therapy with children diagnosed with ADHD, supplemented by a treatment condition combining social skills child groups with parent generalization training (Pfiffner & McBurnett, 1997).

The cited investigations are diverse in treatment methods and research design parameters. For example, some studies compare behavior therapy directly to medication (e.g., Klein & Abikoff, 1997, which supersedes the initial report of Gittelman et al., 1980, cited in the Hinshaw, Klein, & Abikoff, 1998, chapter in the first edition of this volume; Firestone et al., 1981; MTA Cooperative Group, 1999a). Others evaluate combination medication-psychosocial treatments (Firestone et al., 1981; Klein & Abikoff, 1997; MTA Cooperative Group, 1999a; Pelham et al., 1988). Still others employ either delayed treatment controls (Anastopoulos et al., 1993; Dubey et al., 1983; Pfiffner & McBurnett, 1997; Pisterman et al., 1989, 1992) or alternative treatment control groups (Barkley et al., 1992, 2000; Dubey et al., 1983; Horn et al., 1987, 1990, 1991; Pelham et al., 1988). Several investigations, in fact, perform more than one type of comparison. Furthermore, some of the clinical behavior therapy interventions include school consultation (Firestone et al., 1981; Horn et al., 1990, 1991; Klein & Abikoff, 1997; Pelham et al., 1988); and two include integrative combinations of direct contingency management and clinical behavior therapy (Barkley et al., 2000; MTA Cooperative Group, 1999a).

Several potentially informative investigations are not included in Table 1.2 for reasons of sampling (e.g., Strayhorn & Weidman, 1989, who evaluated preventive parent-child interaction training for low-income preschoolers not designated as having ADHD) or design (i.e., within-subject investigations of Pelham et al., 1980, and Pollard, Ward, & Barkley, 1983). Note also that the year-long New York-Montreal study of Abikoff and Hechtman (1996) is not included because its results are not yet published (see below for description).

Despite the diversity of the reported investigations, it is apparent from Table 1.2 that clinical behavior therapy procedures often yield statistically significant benefits with regard to ADHD-related problem behavior, particularly when the source of outcome measures is the parents and teachers who deliver the treatments. In several cases, the effects reveal clinical significance as well (e.g., Anastopoulos et al., 1993; Pelham et al., 1988; Pfiffner & McBurnett, 1997), for at least some domains of outcome. Overall, clinical behavior therapy procedures have received empirical support for the treatment of childhood ADHD, in terms of both core symptoms of the disorder and associated areas of impairment (see Table 1.2; see also review of Pelham, Wheeler, & Chronis, 1998). Behaviorally oriented social skills training has also received initial, empirical support.

Limitations and Qualifications

Five key limitations and qualifications are noteworthy. First, only three recent studies (Barkley et al., 2000; Klein & Abikoff, 1997; MTA Cooperative Group, 1999a) qualify as Type 1 investigations (the New York-Montreal Study also meets criteria for this designation but is not included in Table 1.2 because the research is not published), a designation reserved for rigorous, randomized clinical trials with (a) sufficient sample sizes to yield at least moderate power and (b) evaluation of multiple outcome domains that include objective measures. These stringent standards for a Type 1 designation must be kept in mind while reviewing the contents of the table. Indeed, the lack of full manualization of treatments in Klein and Abikoff (1997) qualifies its placement as a Type 1 study.

Second, in nearly all reports significant effects are found on parent or teacher rating scales but rarely on objectively observed behavior (e.g., Dubey et al., 1983; Klein & Abikoff, 1997; MTA Cooperative Group, 1999a). Although the best established rating scales are well normed and treatment-sensitive (see Hinshaw & Nigg, 1999), the potential for bias is real with such measures, in that the adults who determine child outcomes are precisely those individuals who receive treatment services and implement the behavioral programs. A parent's or teacher's increased sense of efficacy or coping resulting from intervention—as well as consumer satisfaction with the interventions or even dissonance reduction—may underlie improved behavior ratings of the child (Klein & Abikoff, 1997). Objective assessment procedures (e.g., direct observations, sociometric appraisals from peers, tests of academic performance) are needed to supplement and validate rating-scale measures obtained from those involved in treatment delivery.

Third, the average effects of clinical behavior therapy procedures are smaller in magnitude than those from stimulant medications (Firestone et al., 1981; Horn et al., 1991; Klein & Abikoff, 1997; MTA Cooperative Group, 1999a; see also Carlson et al., 1992, and Pelham et al., 1993, from the contingency management section). This finding is particularly noteworthy with respect to the long-term, intensive, integrated behavioral program that was performed and evaluated in the multicenter Multimodal Treatment Study of Children with ADHD (MTA Study; MTA Cooperative Group, 1999a). In this, the largest clinical trial to date supported by the National Institute of Mental Health, 579 children, aged 7 to 9.9 years and carefully diagnosed with ADHD, combined type, were assigned randomly for 14 months of treatment to (a) medication management (initial titration followed by monthly maintenance medication sessions); (b) intensive behavioral treatment; (c) combined treatment (integrating these two systematic intervention strategies); or (d) community care, in which the families sought services on their own from local providers. The behavioral intervention in conditions (b) and (c) was designed to be intensive and well coordinated (see Wells et al., 2000, for details). It involved 35 group and individual parent-training sessions with a psychologist; biweekly teacher consultation from the same psychologist that focused on setting up a daily report card; an 8-week summer treatment program for the child (Pelham & Hoza, 1996); and 12 weeks of paraprofessional aide intervention in the child's classroom, supervised by the psychologist.

Treatment outcome data, obtained from parents and teachers, reveal two key findings with regard to the behavioral treatment condition (MTA Cooperative Group, 1999a):

1. For the core outcome domains of ADHD symptoms, comorbid symptoms, and school, family, and peer-related impairments, it yielded gains that were comparable to those from regular community care, which included the use of stimulant medications in two thirds of the participants.
2. Its benefits were significantly smaller than those from medication management regarding ADHD-related symptomatology.

Measures were ratings from parents and teachers, who were active participants in the behavioral intervention; objective behavior observations did not yield evidence for gains from the behavioral treatment, in contrast to medication. The long-term nature and rigor of the MTA study significantly add to the conclusions from other reports that behavioral treatments do not provide the same degree of benefit as well-delivered pharmacological interventions for ADHD, even when improvement ratings are obtained from adults involved in the child's treatment.

Fourth, full normalization of problem behavior is rarely attained with behavior therapy programs. The analysis of Abikoff and Gittelman (1984), which utilizes partial data from the Klein and Abikoff (1997) investigation, is heuristic in this regard. From direct observation procedures, the main behaviors relevant to ADHD (e.g., interference, off-task, out of chair, noncompliance) did not show normalization for the behavior therapy condition, whereas medication normalized three of these four categories. Only aggressive behavior—which showed low initial levels—was brought into normative ranges with the clinical behavior therapy procedures. In addition, peer sociometric status has not been found to be normalized with behavior therapy (see Pelham et al., 1980, 1988), a limitation shared by medication treatment (Whalen et al., 1989).

Fifth, analysis of long-term carryover of effects has rarely been undertaken. Those investigations with any follow-through data (ranging from 1 to 24 months) have yielded only tentative evidence for significant maintenance of gains following the end of treatment. Especially pertinent in this regard is the intensive, special classroom, kindergarten intervention of Barkley et al. (2000). In this Type 1 study, clinical behavior therapy (in the form of 10-session parent training) and systematic contingency management (9 months of a special treatment classroom) were compared and combined for young children meeting screening criteria for both ADHD and aggression. Results were as follows: The parent training intervention, for which attendance was low, yielded no main effects or interactions. Thus, this form of clinical behavior therapy may have limited appeal and benefit to community samples of parents of young disruptive children who have not been clinically referred. In addition, whereas the intensive 9-month classroom environment yielded posttreatment gains that were stronger than those found with a control group that received regular kindergarten education, chiefly for reports from adult informants who were aware of treatment assignment but also for some objective classroom observation codes, these benefits did not persist at 1- or 2-year follow-up (see Shelton et al., 2000). The results provide a sobering message, as it was hoped that early, intensive intervention could alter the trajectory of externalizing symptomatology. Parallel to stimulant treatment, it appears that psychosocial interventions need to be maintained if gains are to persist.

We note, in passing, that despite the lack of evidence for cognitive therapy procedures based on self-instruction for children with ADHD (see earlier discussion), self-management programs may still constitute an important extension of traditional reward systems. Specifically, as shown in the short-term study of Hinshaw, Henker, and Whalen (1984), when children with ADHD were trained to evaluate their own behavior while receiving reinforcement programs and were then rewarded for the accuracy of their self-evaluations, reductions in negative social behavior were effected. Thus, the potential for approaches based on problem-solving and self-management to extend the benefits gained from structured contingency management programs is real. Given the continuing problems regarding generalization and maintenance of gains from behavioral interventions, alternative approaches are worthy of study.

Incremental Effects of Combination Treatments

Can clinical behavior therapy procedures increment the effects of medication for youngsters with ADHD? The evidence is suggestive but not definitive. We note, for historical reasons, a Type 3 study involving tailored combinations of medication, family therapy, tutoring, marital therapy, and individual child therapy decided upon by careful clinical appraisal that was undertaken over 2 decades ago (Satterfield, Cantwell, & Satterfield, 1979). Because (a) random assignment of children and families to treatment combinations was not made, (b) a control group was not utilized, and (c) only a minority of families who began the intervention were available for follow-up assessments, attributions of decreased delinquency in adolescence (several years after the termination of treatment) to the multimodality intervention may be unwarranted (Satterfield, Satterfield, & Schell, 1987). Nonetheless, this investigation spurred the field to consider integrative combination interventions for youth with ADHD.

Negative results were found in the randomized dual-site 2-year New York–Montreal Study (Abikoff & Hechtman, 1994; Hechtman & Abikoff, 1995). In this investigation, positive responders (N = 102) to stimulant medication, aged 7 to 9 years, were assigned to one of three treatments for 12 months: (a) optimal-dose methylphenidate (MPH) alone; (b) MPH in combination with active parent, child, and teacher intervention; or (c) MPH in combination with an attention control intervention (mean dose of MPH = 34 mg/day). One year of maintenance "booster" therapy followed the year-long intensive intervention phase. The psychosocial adjuncts to medication included social skills training, remedial tutoring, organization skills training, and individual psychotherapy for the child; parent management training and counseling for the parents; and a home-based reinforcement program for targeted school behavior. Assessments from multiple sources yielded no evidence of incremental efficacy for the psychosocial intervention. That is, children and parents in each condition improved in all outcome domains, and multimodal treatment did not permit medication to be discontinued, as all children deteriorated and had to be placed back on active medication (with the majority requiring remedication within 2 weeks of placebo substitution). Note that although points were awarded during the child social skills groups and home reward programs were established, direct contingency management as defined above did not play a major role in the intervention.

Other reports provide evidence for the incremental benefits of combination treatments. In Klein and Abikoff (1997), (a) combined medication plus clinical behavior therapy ranked best across all outcome measures (adult-reported as well as blinded); (b) the combined treatment was significantly superior to methylphenidate alone for some teacher rating scales, for psychiatrist and teacher global ratings of improvement, and for some objective classroom observational codes of classroom behavior; (c) and only the combination condition yielded consistent normalization of key observational outcome measures. As stated by Klein and Abikoff (1997, p. 111): "The study provides clear support for the potential usefulness of adding behavior therapy to methylphenidate treatment," at least for partial responders to medication. They noted, however, that withdrawing medication from such a combined treatment regimen invariably led to clinical deterioration.

An interesting parallel to such results is found in the MTA Study (MTA Cooperative Group, 1999a), the investigation with the greatest statistical power of any study in the field. Initial outcome analyses showed that whereas combined treatment was typically ranked best across diverse outcome measures and that it was the only treatment that significantly outperformed the community care intervention for non-ADHD-symptom outcome domains, it was not significantly superior to medication management for the 19 individual outcome measures investigated. However, the secondary analyses of Swanson et al. (2001) reveal that, when outcome measures of ADHD-related and disruptive symptomatology were composited, combination treatment significantly outperformed medication management, with a small effect size of approximately .3 for this contrast. Furthermore, utilizing a categorical measure of excellent treatment response (scores on a composite ADHD/ODD rating-scale measure that reflect the absence of significant symptomatology), 68% of combined treatment participants, 56% of medication alone, and 34% of behavioral treatment alone reached this criterion at the conclusion of treatment (Swanson et al., 2001). Thus, although incremental effects of multimodal (medication plus psychosocial) treatments may not be large, they are significant—at least when parent and teacher reports are the outcome measures.

Along this line, the within-subject study of Pelham, Schnedler, Bologna, and Contreras (1980) complements several of the studies reported in Table 1.2. It incorporated a 5-month regimen of clinical behavior therapy (parent training plus regular-classroom teacher consultation), with 3-week-long MPH probes performed at baseline and following 3 and 13 weeks of behavioral treatment. After 3 weeks of treatment, the high medication dosage yielded stronger effects than the low dosage level, but following 13 weeks, low and high medication dosages were equivalent, both leading to normalization of behavior. The suggestion is that, over time, concerted behavioral intervention may allow a reduction in the dosage of stimulant medication that is required for optimal behavior. In the MTA Study, for example, we note that the equivalent (and—as shown by Swanson et al., 2001—better) performance of the combined treatment condition relative to medication management was effected with a lower average dosage of medication (31.2 mg of methylphenidate per day at treatment end point with combined vs. 37.7 mg per day with medication management).

Moderators and Mediators of Treatment Outcome

Do any subject characteristics predict or moderate treatment response for behavioral treatments? The MTA Cooperative Group (1999b) found that overall study outcomes were parallel for boys and girls with ADHD, for children previously treated with medications and those who had never been medicated, and for those with comorbid oppositional defiant or conduct disorder and noncomorbid youth. Yet comorbid anxiety disorder status did serve to moderate treatment response, so that children with ADHD plus anxiety receiving the intensive behavior treatment were significantly more improved than ADHD/anxious children treated in the community, in fact showing equivalent response to ADHD/anxious children who received medication management or combined treatment. Some indications, as well, pointed to the relatively stronger response to combination treatment for low-SES MTA participants (MTA Cooperative Group, 1999b).

Regarding mediators, defined as treatment-related processes that may help to explain how treatments work, Hinshaw et al. (2000) performed secondary analyses of MTA data with respect to self-reported parenting practices as potential mediators of school-based outcomes. In brief, the success of combined medication-behavioral treatment for teacher-reported disruptive behavior was related to the family's reduction of negative and ineffective parenting practices during the 14 months of active intervention. That is, the only subgroup of children in the MTA study whose teacher-reported levels of disruptive (ADHD and oppositional) behavior were normalized at the end of treatment were those (a) who were receiving combined treatment *and* (b) whose parents showed substantial reductions of negative/ineffective discipline during the trial. Children of families in the unimodal treatments or the community-treated comparison group whose families showed comparable improvements in negative/ineffective discipline did not yield such normalization of school behavior, a finding pointing to the importance of changes in parenting in predicting outcome for recipients of multimodal intervention. Considerable work remains to be done to understand additional mechanisms through which behavioral and combined treatments provide benefit for youth with ADHD.

Summary of Findings from Contingency Management and Behavior Therapy Studies

1. Direct contingency management, provided in special classroom settings over brief time periods, yields significant and large reductions in problem behavior and, in some cases, enhancement of academic performance for youngsters with ADHD. Such gains are transitory, however; and stimulants yield stronger effects than those from such classroom contingencies (Carlson et al., 1992; Pelham et al., 1993).

2. Clinical behavior therapy procedures, involving consultation with teachers and the conducting of parent management sessions, yield statistically significant improvement in child behavior as rated by parents and teachers but less consistent benefit for directly observed behavior. Benefits fall short of normalization of functioning, however, and are significantly weaker than those from medication. Behavioral treatments can significantly enhance the gains yielded from medication. Although increments are typically small, children receiving combination treatments are the most likely to show outcomes that reflect normalization of behavior. Some reports indicate that, while contingencies are in effect in specialized settings, behavioral programs combined with low-dosage medication appear to yield effects that are similar to benefits from higher doses of medication.

3. Because of the importance of defiant, aggressive, and antisocial behavior patterns for the persistence and magnification of ADHD related impairment, it is essential that treatment studies document effects for this domain. Medication effects are substantial for aggressive behavior (Hinshaw & Lee, 2000), and behavioral contingencies are also effective in reducing aggression.

4. The maintenance of gains from intensive behavioral intervention is not assured (Shelton et al., 2000). Medication treatments for ADHD clearly need to be continued if gains are to persist; the same may well be true for behavioral contingencies, which are admittedly more difficult, expensive, and time-consuming to maintain.

5. As reviewed elsewhere and noted above, cognitive approaches (particularly those emphasizing self-instructional therapies) have not yielded statistically or clinically significant benefit for youth with ADHD (Abikoff, 1987, 1991; Hinshaw, 2000; Hinshaw & Erhardt, 1991). The use of self-management procedures to extend the benefits of well-implemented behavioral intervention may be worth further investigation.

Overall, our review attests to the significant benefits of behavioral treatments for children with ADHD; at the same time, we cannot offer a carte blanche endorsement of nonpharmacological interventions for ADHD, as they are currently operationalized and delivered. Indeed, although benefits have been shown to accrue from well-delivered behavioral treatments, they are rarely long-lasting or sufficient to the child and family, and their effects are not as strong as those yielded from well-delivered medication treatment. Given the limitations of pharmacological interventions, however (see Greenhill & Ford, this volume), psychosocial/behavioral interventions may be required for families unwilling to utilize medication, for children who show an adverse response, and as an adjunct to pharmacological intervention in order to approach normalization of functioning.

How many children respond? A host of investigations of medication treatments for children with ADHD reveal that positive response to treatment occurs in 70 to 80% of children who have been studied; estimates are even higher if alternative stimulants are tried following the clinical failure of an initial trial (see Greenhill & Ford, this volume). Nonetheless, some children with ADHD do not show benefit. Furthermore, some families are philosophically opposed to medicating their children for behavior disorders. A clear impetus for developing and promoting psychosocial treatments for ADHD is that a minority of afflicted children require nonpharmacological intervention.

Ascertaining the response rate of children with ADHD to behavioral treatments is harder to determine. When systematic contingencies are employed, the vast majority of children with ADHD appear to respond. The important clinical issue, however, is whether parents and teachers are willing and motivated for the often substantial investments of time and effort required to make the environmental modifications required by clinical behavior therapy approaches. Furthermore, the strongly familial nature of ADHD means that biological parents at risk for disorganization and impulsivity are being asked to become far more regular and consistent in their parenting practices, a difficult task for any parent but particularly so for parents with problems in behavioral regulation themselves. Our objective in making this statement is not to blame families for any shortcomings of behavioral interventions but to point out the clinical realities of effecting change in the most affected cases. Certainly, nonattendance and less-than-complete adherence to treatment regimens is a critical issue for parent management approaches to ADHD (Barkley et al., 2000). We also highlight that the types of psychosocial intervention most available to concerned families still constitute play therapy and other nonvalidated strategies.

One means of estimating treatment response to behaviorally based intervention appears in the analyses of Swanson et al. (2001) regarding the MTA study. As noted above, 34% of the behavioral treatment group showed an "excellent response" at the end of treatment, defined as parent and teacher ratings of ADHD and oppositional symptomatology at or below the cutoff of "just a little" severity. In contrast, 68% of the combined group and 56% of medication management met this criterion. An interesting comparison is the rate of excellent response in the community care group, in which families were assigned randomly to care from community practitioners. Here, the rate was only 25%, even though over two thirds of these families obtained stimulant treatment. It therefore appears that intensive behavioral treatment yields rates of response that are equivalent to or somewhat stronger than routine community care, even when such treatment includes medication (delivered and monitored in nonoptimal fashion). The additional question of how many families of children with ADHD have access to behavioral treatments is a thorny one, which goes beyond the scope of this chapter.

CONCLUSION

As we have highlighted throughout this chapter, psychosocial approaches to the treatment of childhood ADHD require the application of systematic contingencies in home and school environments. Direct contingency management in specialized settings is a powerful treatment, but one that lacks applicability to most children with the diagnosis. Clinical behavior therapy approaches, in which parents and teachers are taught to implement regular contingencies, are effective with respect to parent- and teacher-rated outcomes but fall short of clinically sufficient benefits for the treatment of children with ADHD. The emphasis has therefore moved to more intensive and ambitious multimodal treatment programs, which explicitly target multiple functions over extended periods of time, in the hope of influencing posttreatment adjustment and functioning (see, for example, Kazdin, 1987, who argued for a "chronic disease" model of externalizing behavior patterns, requiring long-term treatment strategies). Indeed, combinations of intensive behavioral approaches and pharmacological treatments may be required, in many cases, for normalization. Given the clear impairment and negative course associated with ADHD in childhood, continued efforts to improve behavioral and combination interventions and to enhance the access to high-quality care are highly desired.

From another perspective, however, it is essential that clinicians and investigators seek to develop other types of psychosocial intervention for the distressingly persistent and pervasive problems and impairments related to ADHD. Although behavioral approaches are the only validated nonpharmacological treatments for this disorder (Pelham et al., 1998), we cannot be satisfied with the rates of success for behavioral treatments as typically implemented. Basic science on the underlying mechanisms of the disorder will need to be coordinated with clinical science intended to foster maximum benefit from treatment. Along this line, specific strategies for enhancing organizational skills may be promising. In addition, alternative means of measuring the effectiveness of both psychosocial and pharmacological treatments for ADHD need to be considered. For example, Abikoff (2001) advocates the utilization of outcome measures that are tailored to each individual's particular target goals, as is done via goal attainment scaling. In all, the clinical realities of ADHD mandate both promotion of treatments known to be effective and development of even more effective interventions in the future.

ACKNOWLEDGMENT Work on this chapter was supported, in part, by National Institute of Mental

Health Grants R01 MH45064 and U01 MH50461 (Stephen P. Hinshaw), R01 MH35779 (Rachel G. Klein), and U01 MH50453 (Howard B. Abikoff). Address correspondence to Stephen P. Hinshaw, Department of Psychology, Tolman Hall #1650, University of California, Berkeley, CA 94720-1650. e-mail: hinshaw@socrates.berkeley.edu

References

Abikoff, H. (1987). An evaluation of cognitive behavior therapy for hyperactive children. In B. B. Lahey & A. E. Kazdin (Eds.), *Advances in clinical child psychology* (Vol. 10, pp. 171–216). New York: Plenum Press.

Abikoff, H. (1991). Cognitive training in ADHD children: Less to it than meets the eye. *Journal of Learning Disabilities, 24*, 205–209.

Abikoff, H. (2001). Tailored psychosocial treatments for ADHD: The search for a good fit. *Journal of Clinical Child Psychology*.

Abikoff, H., & Gittelman, R. (1984). Does behavior therapy normalize the class-room behavior of hyperactive children? *Archives of General Psychiatry, 41*, 449–454.

Abikoff, H., & Hechtman, L. T. (1994, October). Methylphenidate and multimodal treatment for ADHD. In B. Geller (Chair), *Advanced topics in psychopharmacology*. Paper presented at the annual meeting of the American Academy of Child and Adolescent Psychiatry, New York.

Abikoff, H., & Hechtman, L. (1996). Multimodal therapy and stimulants in the treatment of children with ADHD. In E. D. Hibbs & P. Jensen (Eds.), *Psychosocial treatment for child and adolescent disorders: Empirically based approaches* (pp. 341–369). Washington, DC: American Psychological Association.

Abikoff, H., & Klein, R. (1992). Attention-deficit hyperactivity and conduct disorder: Comorbidity and implications for treatment. *Journal of Consulting and Clinical Psychology, 60*, 881–892.

American Psychiatric Association. (1994). *Diagnostic and statistical manual of mental disorders* (4th ed.). Washington, DC: Author.

Anastopoulos, A. D., Shelton, T., DuPaul, G. J., & Guevremont, D. C. (1993). Parent training for attention-deficit hyperactivity disorder: Its impact on parent functioning. *Journal of Abnormal Child Psychology, 21*, 581–596.

Anderson, C. A., Hinshaw, S. P., & Simmel, C. (1994). Mother-child interactions in ADHD and comparison boys: Relationships to overt and covert externalizing behavior. *Journal of Abnormal Child Psychology, 22*, 247–265.

Barkley, R. A. (1987). *Defiant children: A clinician's manual for parent training*. New York: Guilford Press.

Barkley, R. A. (1997). *ADHD and the nature of self-control*. New York: Guilford Press.

Barkley, R. A. (1998). *Attention deficit hyperactivity disorder: A handbook for diagnosis and treatment* (2nd ed.). New York: Guilford Press.

Barkley, R. A., Guevremont, D. C., Anastopoulos, A. D., & Fletcher, K. E. (1992). A comparison of three family therapy programs for treating family conflicts in adolescents with attention-deficit hyperactivity disorder. *Journal of Consulting and Clinical Psychology, 60*, 450–462.

Barkley, R. A., Shelton, T. L., Crosswait C., Moorehouse, M., Fletcher, K., Barrett, S., Jenkins, L., & Metevia, L. (2000). Multi-method psycho-educational intervention for preschool children with disruptive behavior: Preliminary results at post-treatment. *Journal of Child Psychology and Psychiatry, 41*, 319–332.

Biederman, J., Newcorn, J., & Sprich, S. (1991). Comorbidity of attention deficit hyperactivity disorder with conduct, depressive, anxiety, and other disorders. *American Journal of Psychiatry, 148*, 564–577.

Breslau, N. (1995). Psychiatric sequelae of low birth weight. *Epidemiologic Reviews, 17*, 96–104.

Campbell, M., & Cueva, J. E. (1995). Psychopharmacology in child and adolescent psychiatry: A review of the past seven years. *Journal of the American Academy of Child and Adolescent Psychiatry, 34*, 1124–1132.

Carlson, C. L., Pelham, W. E., Milich, R., & Dixon, J. (1992). Single and combined effects of methylphenidate and behavior therapy on the classroom performance of children with attention-deficit hyperactivity disorder. *Journal of Abnormal Child Psychology, 20*, 213–232.

Carlson, E. A., Jacobvitz, D., & Sroufe, L. A. (1995). A developmental investigation of inattentiveness and hyperactivity. *Child Development, 66*, 37–54.

Conners, C. K., Epstein J. N., March, J. S., Angold, A., Wells, K. C., Klaric, J., Swanson, J. M., Abikoff, H. B., Arnold, L. E., Elliott, G. R., Greenhill, L. L., Hechtman, L., Hinshaw, S. P., Hoza, B., Jensen, P. S., Kraemer, H. C., Newcorn, J., Pelham, W. E., Severe, J. B., Vitiello, B., & Wigal, T. (2001). Multimodal treatment of ADHD in the MTA: An alternative outcome analysis. *Journal of the American Academy of Child and Adolescent Psychiatry, 40*, 159–167.

Douglas, V. I. (1983). Attention and cognitive problems. In M. Rutter (Ed.), *Developmental neuropsychiatry* (pp. 280–329). New York: Guilford Press.

Dubey, D. R., O'Leary, S. G., & Kaufman, K. F. (1983). Training parents of hyperactive children in child management: A comparative outcome study. *Journal of Abnormal Child Psychology, 11,* 229–246.

Faraone, S., Biederman, J., Chen, W. J., Krifcher, B., Keenan, K., Moore, C., Sprich, S., & Tsuang, M. (1992). Segregation analysis of attention-deficit hyperactivity disorder: Evidence for single-gene transmission. *Psychiatric Genetics, 2,* 257–276.

Fergusson, D. M., Horwood, L. J., & Lloyd, M. (1991). Confirmatory factor models of attention deficit and conduct disorder. *Journal of Child Psychology and Psychiatry, 32,* 257–274.

Firestone, P., Crowe, D., Goodman, J. T., & McGrath, P. (1986). Vicissitudes of follow-up studies. Differential effects of parent training and stimulant medication with hyperactives. *American Journal of Orthopsychiatry, 56,* 184–194.

Firestone, P., Kelly, M. J., Goodman, J. T., & Davey, J. (1981). Differential treatment effects of parent training and stimulant medication with hyperactives. *Journal of the American Academy of Child Psychiatry, 20,* 135–147.

Gittelman, R., Abikoff, H., Pollack, E., Klein, D., Katz, S., & Mattes, J. (1980). A controlled trial of behavior modification and methylphenidate in hyper-active children. In C. K. Whalen & B. Henker (Eds.), *Hyperactive children: The social ecology of identification and treatment* (pp. 221–243). New York: Academic Press.

Gittelman, R., Mannuzza, S., Shenker, R., & Bonagura, N. (1985). Hyperactive boys almost grown up: 1. Psychiatric status. *Archives of General Psychiatry, 42,* 937–947.

Greenhill, L. L., & Osman, B. (2000). *Ritalin: Theory and practice* (2nd ed.). Larchmont, NY: Mary Ann Liebert.

Hechtman, L., & Abikoff, H. (1995, October). Multimodal treatment plus stimulants vs. stimulant treatment in ADHD children: Results from a two-year comparative treatment study. In R. J. Schachar (Chair), *Recent studies of the treatment of attention-deficit hyperactivity disorder.* Paper presented at the annual meeting of the American Academy of Child and Adolescent Psychiatry, New Orleans.

Hinshaw, S. P. (1987). On the distinction between attentional deficits/hyperactivity and conduct problems/aggression in child psychopathology. *Psychological Bulletin, 101,* 443–463.

Hinshaw, S. P. (1992). Externalizing behavior problems and academic underachievement in childhood and adolescence: Causal relationships and underlying mechanisms. *Psychological Bulletin, 111,* 127–155.

Hinshaw, S. P. (1994). *Attention deficits and hyperactivity in children.* Thousand Oaks, CA: Sage.

Hinshaw, S. P. (2000). Attention-deficit hyperactivity disorder: The search for viable treatments. In P. C. Kendall (Ed.), *Child and adolescent therapy: Cognitive-behavioral procedures* (2nd ed., pp. 88–128). New York: Guilford Press.

Hinshaw, S. P. (in press). Is ADHD an impairing condition in childhood and adolescence? In P. S. Jensen & J. R. Cooper (Eds.), *Diagnosis and treatment of attention-deficit hyperactivity disorder: An evidence-based approach.* Washington, DC: American Psychiatric Press.

Hinshaw, S. P., & Erhardt, D. (1991). Attention-deficit hyperactivity disorder. In P. C. Kendall (Ed.), *Child and adolescent therapy: Cognitive-behavioral perspectives* (pp. 98–128). New York: Guilford Press.

Hinshaw, S. P., Henker, B., & Whalen, C. K. (1984). Cognitive-behavioral and pharmacological interventions for hyperactive boys: Comparative and combined effects. *Journal of Consulting and Clinical Psychology, 52,* 739–749.

Hinshaw, S. P., Klein, R., & Abikoff, H. B. (1998). Childhood attention deficit hyperactivity disorder: Nonpharmacological and combination treatments. In P. E. Nathan & J. M. Gorman (Eds.), *A guide to treatments that work* (pp. 26–41). New York: Oxford University Press.

Hinshaw, S. P., & Lee, S. S. (2000). Ritalin effects on aggression and antisocial behavior. In L. L. Greenhill & B. B. Osman (Eds.), *Ritalin: Theory and practice* (2nd ed.). Larchmont, NY: Mary Ann Liebert.

Hinshaw, S. P., & Melnick, S. M. (1995). Peer relationships in boys with attention-deficit hyperactivity disorder with and without comorbid aggression. *Development and Psychopathology, 7,* 627–647.

Hinshaw, S. P., & Nigg, J. T. (1999). Behavior rating scales in the assessment of disruptive behavior disorders in childhood. In D. Shaffer, C. P. Lucas, & J. Richters (Eds.), *Diagnostic assessment in child and adolescent psychopathology* (pp. 91–126). New York: Guilford Press.

Hinshaw, S. P., Owens, E. B., Wells, K. C., Kraemer, H. C., Abikoff, H. B., Arnold, L. E., Conners, C. K., Elliott, G., Greenhill, L. L., Hechtman, L., Hoza, B., Jensen, P. S., March, J. S., Newcorn, J., Pelham, W. E., Swanson, J. M., Vitiello, B., & Wigal, T. (2000). Family processes and treatment outcome in the MTA: Negative/ineffective parenting practices in relation to multimodal treatment. *Journal of Abnormal Child Psychology, 28*, 555–568.

Horn, W. F., Ialongo, N., Greenberg, G., Packard, T., & Smith-Winberry, C. (1990). Additive effects of behavioral parent training and self-control therapy with attention deficit hyperactivity disordered children. *Journal of Clinical Child Psychology, 19*, 98–110.

Horn, W. F., Ialongo, N. S., Pascoe, J. M., Greenberg, G. A., Packard, T., Lopez, M., Wagner, A., & Puttler, L. (1991). Additive effects of psychostimulants, parent training, and self-control therapy with ADHD children. *Journal of the American Academy of Child and Adolescent Psychiatry, 30*, 233–240.

Horn, W. F., Ialongo, N., Popvich, S., & Perdatto, D. (1987). Behavioral parent training and cognitive-behavioral self-control therapy with ADD-H children: Comparative and combined effects. *Journal of Clinical Child Psychology, 16*, 57–68.

Ialongo, N. S., Horn, W. F., Pascoe, J. M., Greenberg, G., Packard, T., Lopez, M., Wagner, A., & Puttler, L. (1993). The effects of a multimodal intervention with attention-deficit hyperactivity disorder children: A 9-month follow-up. *Journal of the American Academy of Child and Adolescent Psychiatry, 32*, 182–189.

Jacobson, N. S., & Truax, P. (1991). Clinical significance: A statistical approach to defining meaningful change in psychotherapy research. *Journal of Consulting and Clinical Psychology, 59*, 12–19.

Jacobvitz, D., & Sroufe, L. A. (1987). The early caregiver-mother relationship and attention deficit disorder with hyperactivity in kindergarten: A prospective study. *Child Development, 58*, 1488–1495.

Jensen, P. S., Martin, D., & Cantwell, D. P. (1997). Comorbidity in ADHD: Implications for research, practice, and *DSM-V*. *Journal of the American Academy of Child and Adolescent Psychiatry, 36*, 1065–1079.

Kazdin, A. E. (1987). Treatment of antisocial behavior in children: Current status and future directions. *Psychological Bulletin, 102*, 187–203.

Kendall, P. C., & Braswell, L. (1982). Cognitive-behavioral self-control therapy for children: A components analysis. *Journal of Consulting and Clinical Psychology, 50*, 672–689

Klein, R. G. (1987). Pharmacotherapy of childhood hyperactivity: An update. In H. Y. Meltzer (Ed.), *Psychopharmacology: The third generation of progress* (pp. 1215–1224). New York: Raven Press.

Klein, R. G., & Abikoff, H. (1997). Behavior therapy and methylphenidate in the treatment of children with ADHD. *Journal of Attention Disorders, 2*, 89–114.

Klein, R., & Mannuzza, S. (1991). Long-term outcome of hyperactive children: A review. *Journal of the American Academy of Child and Adolescent Psychiatry, 30*, 383–387.

Klein, R. G., & Wender, P. (1995). The role of methylphenidate in psychiatry. *Archives of General Psychiatry, 52*, 429–433.

Kolko, D. J., Bukstein, O. G., & Barron, J. (1999). Methylphenidate and behavior modification in children with ADHD and comorbid ODD or CD: Main and incremental effects across settings. *Journal of the American Academy of Child and Adolescent Psychiatry, 38*, 578–586.

Laufer, M. W., & Denhoff, E. (1957). Hyperkinetic behavior syndrome in children. *Journal of Pediatrics, 50*, 463–473.

Levy, F., Hay, D. A., McStephen, M., Wood, C., & Waldman, I. (1997). Attention-deficit hyperactivity disorder: A category or a continuum? Genetic analysis of a large-scale twin study. *Journal of the American Academy of Child and Adolescent Psychiatry, 36*, 737–744.

Mannuzza, S., & Klein, R. G. (1999). Adolescent and adult outcomes of attention-deficit/hyperactivity disorder. In H. C. Quay & A. E. Hogan (Eds.), *Handbook of disruptive behavior disorders* (pp. 279–294). New York: Kluwer Academic.

Mash, E. J., & Dalby, T. (1979). Behavioral interventions for hyperactivity. In R. Trites (Ed.), *Hyperactivity in children: Etiology, measurement, and treatment implications* (pp. 161–216). Baltimore: University Park Press.

MTA Cooperative Group. (1999a). Fourteen-month randomized clinical trial of treatment strategies for attention-deficit hyperactivity disorder. *Archives of General Psychiatry, 56*, 1073–1086.

MTA Cooperative Group. (1999b). Moderators and mediators of treatment response in children with attention-deficit/hyperactivity disorder: The MTA Study. *Archives of General Psychiatry, 56*, 1088–1096.

O'Leary, K. D., Pelham, W. E., Rosenbaum, A., & Price, G. H. (1976). Behavioral treatment of hyperkinetic children. *Clinical Pediatrics, 15*, 510–515.

Patterson, G. R. (1965). An application of conditioning techniques to the control of a hyperactive child. In L. P. Ullmann & L. Krasner (Eds.), *Case studies in behavior modification* (pp. 370–375). New York: Holt, Rinehart & Winston.

Patterson, G. R., Reid, J. B., & Dishion, T. J. (1992). *Antisocial boys*. Eugene, OR: Castalia.

Pelham, W. E., Carlson, C., Sams, S. E., Dixon, M. J., & Hoza, B. (1993). Separate and combined effects of methylphenidate and behavior modification on boys with attention-deficit hyperactivity disorder in the classroom. *Journal of Consulting and Clinical Psychology, 61,* 506–515.

Pelham, W. E., & Hinshaw, S. P. (1992). Behavioral intervention for attention-deficit hyperactivity disorder. In S. M. Turner, K. S. Calhoun, & H. E. Adams (Eds.), *Handbook of clinical behavior therapy* (2nd ed., pp. 259–283). New York: Wiley.

Pelham, W. E., & Hoza, B. (1996). Comprehensive treatment for ADHD: A proposal for intensive summer treatment programs and outpatient follow-up. In E. Hibbs & P. Jensen (Eds.), *Psychosocial treatment of child and adolescent disorders: Empirically-based approaches* (pp. 311–340). Washington, DC: American Psychological Association Press.

Pelham, W. E., & Murphy, H. A. (1986). Behavioral and pharmacological treatment of attention deficit and conduct disorders. In M. Hersen (Ed.), *Pharmacological and behavioral treatment: An integrative approach* (pp. 108–148). New York: Wiley.

Pelham, W. E., Schnedler, R. W., Bender, M., Nilsson, D., Miller, J., Budrow, M., Ronnei, M., Paluchowski, C., & Marks, D. (1988). The combination of behavior therapy and methylphenidate in the treatment of attention deficit disorder: A therapy outcome study. In L. M. Bloomingdale (Ed.), *Attention deficit disorder* (Vol. 3, pp. 29–48). Oxford, UK: Pergamon.

Pelham, W. E., Schnedler, R. W., Bologna, N. C., & Contreras, J. A. (1980). Behavioral and stimulant treatment of hyperactivity children: A therapy study with methylphenidate probes in a within-subject design. *Journal of Applied Behavior Analysis, 13,* 221–236.

Pelham, W. E., Wheeler, T., & Chronis, A. (1998). Empirically supported psychosocial treatments for attention deficit hyperactivity disorder. *Journal of Clinical Child Psychology, 27,* 190–205.

Pfiffner, L., & McBurnett, K. (1997). Social skills training with parent generalization: Treatment effects for children with attention deficit disorder. *Journal of Consulting and Clinical Psychology, 65,* 749–757.

Pfiffner, L. J., & O'Leary, S. G. (1993). School-based psychological treatments. In J. L. Matson (Ed.), *Handbook of hyperactivity in children* (pp. 234–255). Boston: Allyn & Bacon.

Pfiffner, L. J., Rosen, L. A., & O'Leary, S. G. (1985). The efficacy of an all-positive approach to classroom management. *Journal of Applied Behavior Analysis, 18,* 257–261.

Pisterman, S., Firestone, P., McGrath, P., Goodman, J., Webster, I., Mallory, R., & Goffin, B. (1992). The role of parent training in treatment of preschoolers with ADDH. *American Journal of Orthopsychiatry, 62,* 397–408.

Pisterman, S., McGrath, P., Firestone, P., Goodman, J. T., Webster, I., & Mallory, R. (1989). Outcome of parent-mediated treatment of preschoolers with attention deficit disorder with hyperactivity. *Journal of Consulting and Clinical Psychology, 57,* 628–635.

Pollard, S., Ward, E., & Barkley, R. A. (1983). The effects of parent training and Ritalin on the parent-child interactions of hyperactive boys. *Child and Family Behavior Therapy, 5,* 51–69.

Rapport, M. D., Murphy, H. A., & Bailey, J. S. (1982). Ritalin vs. response cost in the control of hyperactive children: A within-subject comparison. *Journal of Applied Behavior Analysis, 15,* 205–216.

Richters, J. E., Arnold, L. E., Jensen, P. S., Abikoff, H., Conners, C. K., Greenhill, L. L., Hechtman, L. T., Hinshaw, S. P., Pelham, W. E., & Swanson, J. M. (1995). The National Institute of Mental Health Collaborative Multisite Multimodal Treatment Study of Children with Attention-Deficit Hyperactivity Disorder (MTA): 1. Background and rationale. *Journal of the American Academy of Child and Adolescent Psychiatry, 34,* 987–1000.

Robinson, P. W., Newby, T. J., & Ganzell, S. L. (1981). A token system for a class of underachieving hyperactive children. *Journal of Applied Behavior Analysis, 14,* 307–315.

Rosen, L. A., O'Leary, S. G., Joyce, S. A., Conway, G., & Pfiffner, L. J. (1984). The importance of prudent negative consequences for maintaining the appropriate behavior of hyperactive students. *Journal of Abnormal Child Psychology, 12,* 581–604.

Satterfield, J. H., Cantwell, D. P., & Satterfield, B. T. (1979). Multimodality treatment: A one-year follow-up of 84 hyperactive boys. *Archives of General Psychiatry, 36,* 965–974.

Satterfield, J. H., Satterfield, B. T., & Schell, A. M. (1987). Therapeutic interventions to prevent delinquency in hyperactive boys. *Journal of the American Academy of Child and Adolescent Psychiatry, 26,* 56–64.

Schachar, R. (1986). Hyperkinetic syndrome: Historical development of the concept. In E. A. Taylor (Ed.), *The overactive child* (pp. 19–40). London: MacKeith.

Schachar, R. (1991). Childhood hyperactivity. *Journal of Child Psychology and Psychiatry, 32,* 155–191.

Schachar, R., Tannock, R., Marriott, M., & Logan, G. (1995). Deficient inhibitory control in attention deficit hyperactivity disorder. *Journal of Abnormal Child Psychology, 23,* 411–437.

Shelton, T. L., Barkley, R. A., Crosswait, C., Moorehouse, M., Fletcher, K., Barrett, S., Jenkins, L., & Metevia, L. (2000). Multimethod psychoeducational intervention for preschool children with disruptive behavior: Two-year post-treatment follow-up. *Journal of Abnormal Child Psychology, 28,* 253–266.

Slomkowski, C., Klein, R. G., & Mannuzza, S. (1995). Is self-esteem an important outcome in hyperactive children? *Journal of Abnormal Child Psychology, 23,* 303–315.

Sprague, R. L. (1983). Behavior modification and educational techniques. In M. Rutter (Ed.), *Developmental neuropsychiatry* (pp. 404–421). New York: Guilford Press.

Sprich-Buckminster, S., Biederman, J., Milberger, S., Faraone, S. V., & Lehman, B. K. (1993). Are perinatal complications relevant to the manifestation of ADD? Issues of comorbidity and familiality. *Journal of the American Academy of Child and Adolescent Psychiatry, 32,* 1032–1037.

Strayhorn, J. M., & Weidman, C. S. (1989). Reduction of attention deficit and internalizing symptoms in preschoolers through parent-child interaction training. *Journal of the American Academy of Child and Adolescent Psychiatry, 28,* 888–896.

Swanson, J. M., Kraemer, H. C., Hinshaw, S. P., Arnold, L. E., Conners, C. K., Abikoff, H. B., Clevenger, W., Davies, M., Elliott, G., Greenhill, L. L., Hechtman, L., Hoza, B., Jensen, P. S., March, J. S., Newcorn, J. H., Owens, E. B., Pelham, W. E., Schiller, E., Severe, J., Simpson, S., Vitiello, B., Wells, K. C., Wigal, T., & Wu, M. (2001). Clinical relevance of the primary findings of the MTA: Success rates based on severity of symptoms at the end of treatment. *Journal of the American Academy of Child and Adolescent Psychiatry, 40,* 168–179.

Swanson, J. M., McBurnett, K., Christian, D. L., & Wigal, T. (1995). Stimulant medications and the treatment of children with ADHD. In T. H. Ollendick & R. J. Prinz (Eds.), *Advances in clinical child psychology* (Vol. 17, pp. 265–322). New York: Plenum Press.

Tannock, R. (1998). Attention deficit hyperactivity disorder: Advances in cognitive, neurobiological, and genetic research. *Journal of Child Psychology and Psychiatry, 39,* 65–99.

Weiss, G., & Hechtman, L. T. (1993). *Hyperactive children grown up* (2nd ed.). New York: Guilford Press.

Wells, K. C., Pelham, W. E., Kotkin, R. A., Hoza, B., Abikoff, H., Abramowitz, A., Arnold, L. E., Cantwell, D. P., Conners, C. K., Del Carmen, R., Elliott, G., Greenhill, L. L., Hechtman, L., Hibbs, E., Hinshaw, S. P., Jensen, P. S., March, J., Swanson, J., & Wigal, T. (2000). Psychosocial treatment strategies in the MTA Study: Rationale, methods, and critical issues in design and implementation. *Journal of Abnormal Child Psychology, 28,* 483–505.

Whalen, C. K., Henker, B., Buhrmester, D., Hinshaw, S. P., Huber, A., & Laski, K. (1989). Does stimulant medication improve the peer status of hyperactive children? *Journal of Consulting and Clinical Psychology, 57,* 545–549.

2

Childhood Attention-Deficit Hyperactivity Disorder: Pharmacological Treatments

Laurence L. Greenhill

Rebecca E. Ford

More than 180 placebo-controlled investigations demonstrate that psychostimulants—the methylphenidates, the amphetamines, or pemoline—are effective in reducing core symptoms of childhood attention-deficit hyperactivity disorder (ADHD). (See below for common abbreviations used in this chapter.) Approximately 70% of patients respond to stimulants compared with 13% to placebo. Short-term efficacy is more pronounced for behavioral rather than cognitive and learning abnormalities associated with ADHD. The stimulant treatment evidence base was supplemented at the end of the 1990s by large multisite randomized controlled trials—particularly the Multimodal Treatment Study of ADHD (the MTA Study)—that further support the short-term efficacy in schoolage children. This study, plus the 1998 NIH Consensus Development Conference on ADHD and the publication of the McMaster Evidence Based Review of ADHD Treatments, emphasized the strong evidence base for ADHD stimulant treatments. In contrast, there remains much less evidence for the efficacy of psychostimulants in the treatment of ADHD in preschoolers, adolescents, and adults because of the lack of large-scale randomized clinical trials for those age groups. The main side effects of psychostimulant therapy in placebo-controlled trials—insomnia, decreased appetite, stomachache, and headache—occur more frequently in patients on an active drug than on a placebo. Although psychostimulants are clearly effective in the short term up through 14 months, concern remains that long-term benefits over years have not yet been adequately assessed. Other nonstimulant agents for which there is limited evidence of efficacy include atomoxetine, the tricyclics, bupropion, buspirone, clonidine, and venlafaxine.

COMMON ABBREVIATIONS

AMP	mixed salts of amphetamine
CLON	clonidine
DA	dopamine
DEX	dextroamphetamine
DMI	desipramine
MPH	methylphenidate
NE	norepinephrine
OROS-MPH	oros methylphenidate
PEM	pemoline
RCT	randomized clinical trial
SE	side effects

Attention-deficit hyperactivity disorder (ADHD), as diagnosed in the United States, is regarded as a major public health problem, because it is responsible for 30 to 50% of referrals to mental health services for children. The prevalence of ADHD may be gleaned from comprehensive reviews (Bird et al., 1988; Bauermeister et al., 1994; Szatmari, 1992) of epidemiological studies conducted in Australia (Connell et al., 1982); Norway (Vikan, 1985); the Netherlands (Verhulst et al., 1992); Ontario, Canada (Szatmari et al., 1989); Manheim, Germany (Esser et al., 1996); New Zealand (Anderson et al., 1987); Pittsburgh, Pennsylvania (Costello, 1989); Puerto Rico (Bird et al., 1988); East London (Taylor et al., 1991); and the Great Smoky Mountain area of rural North Carolina. Rates for ADHD range between 2.0% and 6.3% (Szatmari et al., 1989), while ADD (attention deficit disorder without hyperactivity) shows a wider range, between 2.2% and 12.6% (Velez et al., 1989).

Fortunately, ADHD responds to both psychosocial and psychopharmacological treatments (Richters et al., 1995). It has been estimated that between 2% and 2.5% of all school-aged children in North America receive some pharmacological intervention for hyperactivity (Bosco & Robin, 1980), more than 90% of them being treated with the psychostimulant, methylphenidate (MPH) (Greenhill, 1995; Wilens & Biederman, 1992). Estimates (Swanson et al., 1995a) suggest that from 1990 to 1993, the number of outpatient visits for ADHD has increased from 1.6 to 4.2 million per year and the amount of MPH manufactured increased from 1,784 to 5,110 kg per year.

Experts and clinicians find psychostimulants highly effective in reducing core ADHD symptoms in as many as 80% of children treated. This unusually high rate of drug response explains, to some degree, why published drug research in the past decade has focused on these medications for study (Vitiello & Jensen, 1995). Rather than explore new compounds, researchers have used one drug, methylphenidate, to study responses in mentally retarded ADHD children, adverse events, the determination of "normalization" during drug treatment, and patient characteristics among nonresponders.

This chapter provides a review of the ADHD treatment literature in the late 1990s. As in other chapters in this volume, the study classification system listed below will be used to guide the reader. Unlike in other chapters, a thorough description of the *DSM-IV* (American Psychiatric Association [APA], 1994) syndrome of ADHD, its principal diagnostic criteria, and information on incidence, prevalence, and epidemiology will not be given, as they are well covered elsewhere (see Hinshaw, Klein, & Abikoff, this volume). Instead, the chapter will include (a) a brief historical perspective on ADHD drug treatment studies, using Type 5 reviews to highlight conceptual notions driving drug research; (b) a description of current psychopharmacological treatments of choice, supported by recently published Type 1 RCTs; and (c) a perspective on future areas of ADHD psychopharmacological investigation. New medications, current ongoing ADHD treatment studies involving drug treatments, and alternative new psychopharmacological agents are surveyed, drawing upon Type 1 clinical trials and Type 3 pilot studies.

Types of Drug Studies
Type 1—randomized clinical trials
Type 2—quasi-experimental trials
Type 3—pilot studies
Type 4—review with meta-analyses
Type 5—reviews without meta-analyses
Type 6—retrospectives, case reports

HISTORICAL PERSPECTIVE: PHARMACOLOGICAL INTERVENTIONS FOR ADHD

In 1937, Bradley (1937), looking for a new treatment for headache, serendipitously observed that disturbed children and adolescents responded to benzedrine, a racemic form of amphetamine. This treatment produced a dramatic calming effect, while simultaneously producing an increase in academic productivity and a "zest for work." Bradley published other Type 6 studies reporting the improvement of children during amphetamine treatment (Bradley, 1941; Bradley & Bowen, 1941).

More detailed investigations of these drugs were carried out between 1960 and 1970. During that period, studies showed that psychostimulants increased the seizure threshold to photometrizol (Laufer et al., 1957), decreased oppositional behavior of boys with conduct disorder in a residential school (Eisenberg et al., 1961), and reliably improved the target symptoms of ADHD as measured by standardized rating forms filled out by parents and teachers (Conners et al., 1967). These early studies lacked many refinements available today, such as the use of uniform diagnostic criteria, reliability measures, and multiple observers, so must be judged Type 2 studies.

Since then, there have been several waves of published Type 2 ADHD psychostimulant studies, first in the mid-1980s and then at the end of the 1990s. The rapid onset of these medications and clinicians' growing knowledge of ADHD in children facilitated the publication of many studies, all confirming Bradley's initial observations. The drugs DEX and MPH, in particular, can produce statistically significant and clinically meaningful improvements in controlled studies within days. Starting in 1977 (Barkley, 1977), a series of Type 5 literature reviews have summarized these studies. Wilens and Biederman's (Wilens et al., 1992) 1992 MEDLINE search retrieved over 990 psychostimulant treatment publications between 1982 and 1991. Summaries of these open-label and controlled studies (Barkley, 1977, 1982; Gittelman, 1987; Gittelman-Klein, 1980) conclude that the psychostimulants have major beneficial effects on the behavior of children with ADHD over short time periods. Verification of this agreement appeared in a Type 4 meta-analysis (Swanson, 1993) that utilized 250 reviews of psychostimulant studies of children with ADHD children. These reports showed the most marked effects can be observed on teacher measures of classroom behavior, with effect sizes ranging from 0.63 to 0.85, with lesser effects—in the range of 0.19–0.47—on measures of intelligence or academic achievement. The effect sizes observed on teacher ratings would satisfy a rigorous Phase III, premarketing, investigational new drug application to the Food and Drug Administration (FDA). A small sample of frequently cited reviews appears in Table 2.1.

These reviews summarize the evidence that the psychostimulants MPH, DEX, and PEM, in short-duration trials, effectively reduce ADHD behaviors in school-age children such as task-irrelevant activity and classroom disturbance (Barkley, 1977; Gittelman-Klein, 1980; Jacobvitz et al., 1990). One such review in 1992 (Wilens & Biederman, 1992) encompassed 4 preschool, 96 school-age, 6 adolescent, and 6 adult controlled studies of psychostimulant treatment. Of these controlled trials, 84 compared MPH to placebo, 21 compared DEX to placebo, and 6 evaluated PEM. Treatment response occurred in 65 to 75% of 4,777 ADHD children treated. More recent, large, systematic, evidence-based reviews include "A Review of Therapies for Attention Deficit Hyperactivity Disorder" by the Canadian Coordinating Office for Health Technology Assessment (Pelham et al., 2000a), "The Treatment of Attention Deficit Hyperactivity Disorder: An Evidence Report" by the McMaster University Evidence-Based Practice Center (McMaster University Evidence-Based Practice Center, 1998), and others (Campbell & Ewing, 1990; Leech et al., 1999).

These reviews discuss the reduction of core ADHD behaviors (Barkley, 1977, 1982; DuPaul & Barkley, 1990), psychostimulant mechanisms of action (Solanto, 1984), the question of diagnostic specificity for stimulant response (Gittelman, 1980), and the ability of these medications to enhance other therapies (Gittelman, 1987). In addition, dosing methods, paradoxical stimulant effects, and whether stimulants improved academic performance (DuPaul et al., 1990; Jacobvitz et al., 1990) have been addressed.

Dosing methods and dose-response issues were ushered in by the seminal paper of Sprague and Sleator (1977), which reported dissociation of cognitive and behavioral MPH responses in ADHD children. Using weight-adjusted doses, Sprague reported that children responded optimally to a memory task at a low dose (0.3 mg/kg) but needed higher doses (1.0 mg/kg) to attain behavioral control in the classroom. This paper set the customary weight-adjusted MPH dosing standard that would permeate the ADHD drug-treatment literature until the present and also raised the question of whether MPH doses optimized for behavior might not be best for learning.

Reviews of pre-1990 drug studies (Jacobvitz et al., 1990; Wilens et al., 1992) concluded that there was no diagnostically specific positive response to stimulants for ADHD children. No differences in response were found between stimulant-treated ADHD children, stimulant-treated normal children, and clinically referred non-ADHD children (Rapoport et al., 1980). Also rejected was the notion that ADHD children show a "paradoxical" slow-down response to stimulants. Rather, the literature shows a decrease in aimless activity, an increase in attention, and an increase in heart rate and blood pressure.

These reviews also grappled with the question of whether stimulants, so successful in short-term trials, lead to long-term improvements. ADHD follow up studies (Barkley et al., 1990a; Mannuzza et al., 1993; Weiss & Hechtman, 1993) have shown that ADHD core symptoms persist into late adolescence and even into adult life. Some of these studies also report no stimulant benefit persisting when children are treated over years. The early psychostimulant treatment stud-

TABLE 2.1 Selected Reviews of Psychostimulant Treatments: School-age Children

Study (Year)	*Type*	*Drugs*	*No. Studies*	*Subjects*	*Response Rate %*	*Placebo Response %*	*References*
Barkley (1977)	3	DEX	15	915	74	29	159
		MPH	14	866	77	23	
		PEM	2	105	73	27	
		PL	8	417	39	—	
Klein[a] (1980)	3	DEX	6	225	Mod	Low	398
		MPH	18	528	69	24	
		PEM	4	228	69	23	
Gittelman[a] (1987)	3	MPH	25	777	N/A	N/A	82
		PEM	1	20	N/A	N/A	
Hinshaw (1991)	3	MPH	10	187	Situation[b]	N/A	82
Jacobvitz (1991)	4	MPH	136	N/A	N/A	N/A	175
Wilens (1992)	3	MPH	37	1,113	73	222	121
Schachar (1993)	4	MPH	18	531	Resp.	26 attrition	88
Greenhill (1995)	3	MPH	15	236	70	20	229
		SR	7	181	75	20	
		DEX	2	2	High	Low	
		PEM	1	22	75	20	
Spencer (1996)	3	MPH	133	N/A	70	N/A	202
		DEX	22	N/A			
		PEM	6	N/A			
Jadad (2001) (78 studies)	3	MPH	56	N/A	N/A	N/A	116
		SR	N/A				
		DEX	18				
		PEM	5				

Resp. = Only responders included in Schachar et al.'s examination of long-term stimulant treatment. [a] = author of both reviews is Rachel Klein, Ph.D. [b] = Hinshaw's review focuses on aggression and reports different rates depending on age and setting. N/A = Information not given in the review.

Based on Wilens et al., 1992.

ies showed strong behavioral improvements and less impressive academic gains in ADHD children who were treated. Although there is evidence for short-term gains in arithmetic performance (Pelham et al., 1985), other work (Charles et al., 1979) shows no differences in long-term academic achievement when treated and untreated ADHD children were compared.

Yet these studies are hobbled by major methodological weaknesses, such as lack of uniform diagnostic criteria, no use of standardized outcome measures, no random assignment, high attrition rate, or no compliance checks. It is encouraging, then, that one careful review (Schachar & Tannock, 1993) finds evidence that drug treatment studies lasting 3 to 7 months show stimulants to be more effective than placebo, nonpharmacological therapies, or no treatment in ameliorating core ADHD symptoms.

Despite the breadth and depth of this pre-1990 treatment literature, with its attention to concerns of finding optimal dose level, tracking compliance, understanding time-action effects of the psychostimulants (Hinshaw, 1994), interpreting concurrent interventions, and studying individual differences in response, a number of weaknesses exist (Pelham, 1993). These included the use of academic measures to test treatment response in a group of ADHD children heterogeneous for learning disabilities and the use of global measures of improvement rather than objective measures of cognitive skill to adjust doses in titration. No mention is made of a tight standardization of dosing times for all subjects, so some subjects may have differed greatly in the time of dosing within the same study. Because most clinical studies treated behavioral targets, attempts were not made to synchronize the time of peak drug effectiveness with the child's daily academic tasks. The majority of drug studies covered by reviews in Table 2.1 lasted 6 weeks or less, too brief to generalize to typical medication treatments, which average 3 years. No common definition of a categorical treatment responder existed much before 1985, so it was difficult to do meta-analytic studies, looking across studies for identical response patterns in children.

LONG-TERM OUTCOME: RANDOMIZED CONTROLLED TRIALS OF STIMULANT MEDICATION

Although short-duration stimulant studies have shown robust efficacy, their effects last only as long as the patient continues medication. ADHD is a chronic disorder lasting many years, and thus maintenance treatment constitutes the main component of care. Unfortunately, most stimulant RCTs last less than 3 months, with only 22 published studies lasting longer (Schachar & Tannock, 1993). Most long-duration studies started before the 1990s were constrained by their retrospective methods, lack of nonstandard outcome measures, restrictive inclusion criteria that rejected patients with comorbid disorders, irregular prescribing patterns (Sherman, 1991), and the lack of compliance measures (Richters et al., 1995). Long-duration trials have shown maintenance of stimulant medication effects over periods ranging from 12 months (Gillberg et al., 1997) to 24 months (Abikoff & Hechtman, 1998).

The NIMH Multimodal Treatment Study of Children with Attention Deficit Hyperactivity Disorder (MTA Study) compared the relative effectiveness of four randomly assigned, 14-month treatments of children with ADHD: medication management (Medmgt), behavioral treatment (Beh), the combination (Comb), or a community comparison group (CC) getting treatment as usual (Arnold et al., 1997). The study questions included (a) Do Beh and Medmgt treatments result in comparable levels of improvement over time? (b) Do participants assigned to Comb show greater improvement over time than those assigned to either Medmgt or to Beh? (c) Do participants assigned to any of the 3 MTA intensive treatments show greater improvement over time than those assigned to treatment as usual in the community (CC)?

To have sufficient power to address these questions, 579 children with ADHD, combined subtype, aged 7 to 9 years, were recruited at seven sites and assessed across six domains at four different points in time (Hinshaw et al., 1997). They were assigned to 14 months of (a) medication management (b) intensive behavioral treatment (Beh—parent, school, and child components, with therapist involvement gradually faded over time), (c) the two combined, or (d) treatments by community providers). Outcomes were assessed in multiple domains before, during, and at treatment end point (with Comb and Medmgt subjects on medication at time of assesment).

Children randomized to medication management alone (Medmgt, N = 144) or to combined treatment (Comb, N = 145) in the MTA Study participated in a 28-day double-blind, placebo-controlled titration study that identified each child's optimal dose of MPH. Three doses of methylphenidate and placebo were used in a three-times-daily protocol (Greenhill et al., 1996, 2001). Medication conditions were switched daily to reduce error variance. Parents and teachers rated ADHD symptoms and impairment daily.

During titration, a repeated-measures ANOVA revealed a main effect of MPH/placebo dose with greater effects on teacher's ratings ($F(3) = 100.6$, $N = 223$, $p = 0.0001$; effect sizes 0.8–1.3) than on parent's ratings ($F(3) = 55.61$, $N = 253$, $p = 0.00001$; effect sizes 0.4–0.6). Dose did not interact with between-subjects factors (period, dose order, comorbid diagnosis, site or treatment group). Drug-related adverse events were reported more often by parents than by teachers, who rated irritability highest on placebo. The distribution of the best MPH starting doses determined during titration (10 to 50 mg/day), response rate (77%), and adverse event profile across six sites and multiple subgroups suggest that MPH titration in office practice should explore MPH's full dosage range in 7- to 10-year-old children over 25 kg in weight. Parent weekend symptom ratings showed daytime drug effects, but not as clearly as weekday after-school ratings. Nonresponders to MPH were older, had less severe symptoms, and were medication-naive. Thus, the MTA controlled multisite titration trial using daily dose switches replicated the published, single-site MPH trial effect sizes and adverse event rates (Spencer et al., 1996a).

Data were analyzed through intent-to-treat, random-effects regression. When analyzed, all four groups showed sizable reductions in symptoms over time, with significant differences among them in degrees of change. For most ADHD symptoms, children in the combined and medication management groups showed significantly greater improvement than those given intensive behavioral treatment or community care. Combined and medication management treatments did not differ significantly on any direct comparisons, but in several instances (internalizing symptoms, teacher-rated social skills, parent-child relations, and reading achievement), combined treatment proved significantly better at reducing symptom scores, compared to intensive behavioral treatment and/or community care, while medication management did not. MTA medication strategies were superior to treatment as usual in the community, despite the fact that two thirds of community-treated subjects received medication during the study period. The combined treatment did not yield significantly greater benefits than medication management for core ADHD symptoms, but may have provided modest additional advantages for non-ADHD-symptom and positive functioning outcomes.

The MTA is the largest and most methodologically sophisticated randomized multisite treatment study to date in ADHD children that includes monomodal and combined treatments. These therapeutic methods had been shown previously to be effective in simpler two-arm (active versus placebo) controlled studies (Pelham, 1989; Pelham & Murphy, 1986). Because of its size, the MTA was able to address certain treatment questions. First, it shows that stimulant medication efficacy can be realized across diverse settings and patient groups and can be maintained during chronic therapy lasting more than a year. The MTA's findings replicate those from smaller long duration stimulant trials—the 102-child New York/Montreal Study (Abikoff & Hechtman, 1998), the 91-child Toronto study (Schachar et al., 1997), and 62-child Gillberg (Gillberg et al., 1997) studies.

Collectively, these multisite studies show a persistence of medication effects over time. Within-subject effect sizes reported after 12 to 24 months of MPH treatment resembled those previously reported in short-duration studies (Elia et al., 1991; Thurber & Walker, 1983). Domain of greatest improvement differs among studies, with some (Gillberg et al., 1997) showing greater effects at home and another (Schachar et al., 1997) showing greater effects at school. The total mean MPH daily doses reported by three long-duration studies ranged between 33 and 37.5 mg. The one DEX study reported a mean dose half of this level, agreeing with the general ratio of DEX to MPH doses. Persistent stimulant drug side effects or assignment to placebo treatment were associated with dropout. Fortunately, attrition from placebo assignment was slow, allowing ample time for standard 8-week efficacy trials to be conducted.

USE OF PSYCHOSTIMULANTS IN CHILDREN YOUNGER THAN 6 YEARS

The signs and symptoms of ADHD may be evident before age 3, particularly pronounced motor activity, excessive climbing, aggressivity, and destructiveness. These signs may be disruptive to family life and make nursery school attendance impossible. Campbell found that hyperactive preschoolers did not "grow out of" this behavior but maintained their hyperkinesis when they went on to grade school (Campbell et al., 1977). Even though these early ADHD symptoms resemble the behaviors of older ADHD patients, the diagnostic manuals give little guidance about the validity of the ADHD diagnosis in the preschool years. School-age norms gathered on standard teacher global rating forms, such as the Conners Teacher Questionnaire (CTQ), have not included preschoolers until recently (Conners, personal communication).

Unfortunately, there are only a handful of published treatment studies on preschoolers. No pharmacokinetic studies have been done in this age group to determine if younger children, with their larger liver-to-body size ratio, might show more accelerated metabolism of psychostimulants than seen in older children. To date there are no studies that would validate or refute clinicians' concerns that preschoolers suffer more pronounced stimulant withdrawal effects.

Comprehensive reviews (Spencer et al., 1996a) have identified only five controlled studies ($N = 144$) of methylphenidate in preschoolers (Barkley, 1988; Barkley et al., 1984; Conners, 1975; Mayes et al., 1994; Musten et al., 1997; Schleifer et al., 1975). MPH produced improvements in structured situations, but not in free play (Schleifer et al., 1975). Four of these six studies showed strongly positive results. Two reported higher rates of side effects, such as tearfulness and irritability, than would be expected in school-age children (Barkley et al., 1990). However, the six studies utilized very different inclusion/

exclusion criteria, diagnostic definition, ratings forms, and study designs, so that a meta-analysis would not be appropriate. Current labeling warns against using MPH in children below age 6. Even so, there has been a 180% increase since 1996 in the prescriptions of MPH for preschoolers. Clearly, more controlled data are needed.

A single-case intensive study design noted that dextroamphetamine reduced temper outbursts in a toddler (Speltz et al., 1988). The MPH treatment studies have found that the mother-child interactions involving preschoolers are ameliorated by MPH (Barkley, 1988). MPH appeared to have a linear dose-response effect on improvements in the mother-child interaction, perhaps related to increasing child compliance and decreased symptomatic intensity in the child. No disabling side effects were noted.

USE OF PSYCHOSTIMULANTS IN THE TREATMENT OF ADULTS WITH ADHD

The prevalence of ADHD in adults, its severity, and indications for treatment are issues that are not settled among clinicians. Although it had been assumed that children with ADHD outgrow their problems, recent prospective follow-up studies have shown that ADHD signs and symptoms continue into adult life (APA, 1980). Adults with concentration problems, impulsivity, poor anger control, job instability, and marital difficulties sometimes seek help for problems they believe to be the manifestation of ADHD in adult life. Parents may decide that they themselves are impaired by the same attentional and impulse control problems found during an evaluation of their ADHD children.

Attention deficit disorder, residual state (ADD-R), was placed in the the third edition of the *Diagnostic and Statistical Manual* (*DSM-III*) (APA, 1980), to include patients over age 18, who had been diagnosed as children with ADD and were no longer motorically hyperactive but had impairment from residual impulsivity, overactivity, or inattention. The diagnosis of ADD-R was dropped from the *DSM-III-R* (APA, 1987). Since the publication of *DSM-III-R*, a small but steady stream of publications has supported the existence of the adult ADD disorder, and clinicians and parent groups find it to be a useful and realistic clinical condition. These clinicians requested that future manuals include ADHD descriptors that would cover both adults and children with ADD difficulties, not just those that applied only to children. These clinicians noted that ADHD may be overlooked in adults because it is widely viewed as a disorder of childhood.

Although the *DSM-IV* (APA, 1994) did not restore the diagnosis of ADD-R, the item lists for the ADHD syndrome were rewritten to include adult manifestations. Furthermore, the *DSM-IV* contains a category "in partial remission" that covers the adult with ADHD who retains some, but not all, of the childhood problems. Three ADHD symptoms in an adult might be more impairing than six ADHD symptoms in a child. One method to discover the extent of residual disorders in this population is to follow ADHD children prospectively. Follow-up studies carried out by Weiss and Hechtman (Weiss et al., 1985) compared adults who had had ADHD since childhood (index group) with adults who had no mental disorder as children (control group). Compared to controls, the index group reported fewer years of education completed, a higher incidence of antisocial personality disorder, lower scores on clinician-rated global assessment scores, more complaints of restlessness, sexual problems, and interpersonal problems. Manuzza and colleagues (1991) found little evidence of a residual ADHD syndrome because approximately 50% had the full syndrome by age 25 (Mannuzza et al., 1991). The *DSM-IV* agrees with the Mannuzza group's finding and does not specifically include a diagnostic category for this problem. Rather, the category "not otherwise specified" (NOS) allows adult patients whose past childhood histories are unclear, but who have ADHD symptoms as adults, to receive a diagnosis of ADHD NOS. Such patients might not recall if their ADHD symptoms had appeared before the age of 7 years (American Psychiatric Association Workgroup on *DSM-IV*, 1991).

Shaffer (1994), in an invited editorial, urged clinicians to be wary of making the diagnosis and treating ADHD in adults. First, the diagnosis of "adult" ADD is difficult to make because adults cannot easily recall their own childhood history of ADHD symptoms with sufficient accuracy. Second, the high incidence of comorbid Axis 1 (e.g., major depressive disorder) and Axis 2 (e.g., antisocial personality disorder) disorders makes it difficult to determine if the adult's current impairment is from the comorbid condition or from the ADHD.

Wilens and Biederman (1992) disagree with Shaffer's concern.They point out that the initial studies of stimulant-treated adults were inconclusive due to the low stimulant dosages used, the high rate of comorbid disorders in the patients, and/or the lack of a clear childhood history of ADHD. A number of these studies used self-report outcome measures, even though adult ADHD patients appear to be unreliable reporters of their own behaviors. A double-blind comparison of MPH (1 mg/kg/dose) and placebo was carried out in 23 adult patients with ADHD, and 78% showed improvement on MPH versus 4%, who responded on placebo (Spencer et al., 1995). The same group, in a chart review study, reported that 32 adult patients with ADHD, demonstrated a positive response to treatment with tricyclics (Wilens et al., 1994a).

Controlled stimulant treatment studies have been conducted with adults with ADHD including over 200 patients, some involving MPH (Gualtieri et al., 1981; Mattes et al., 1984; Wender et al., 1981). A recent review identified 15 studies ($N = 435$) of stimulants and 22 studies of nonstimulant medications (Swanson et al., 2000) . Although there was considerable variability in diagnostic criteria, dosing parameters and response rates among these studies, there appeared to be significant improvement in ADHD symptoms for those adults assigned randomly to stimulants and antidepressants compared to placebo.

With the caveat that sample selection criteria differ greatly from study to study, different pharmacological treatment strategies have been applied to ADHD in adults with varying success. Although Mattes and Boswell (Mattes et al., 1984) showed little benefit from MPH, others have found robust effects (Ratey et al., 1991; Wender et al., 1985). In a study by Spencer and colleagues (1995), the response to MPH was independent of gender, comorbidity, or family history of psychiatric disorders. Treatment was generally well tolerated at the target dose of 1.0 mg/kg; side effects included loss of appetite, insomnia, and anxiety. Other drugs that have been reported to be beneficial include fluoxetine (Sabelsky, 1990), nomifensine (Shekim et al., 1989), pargyline (Wender et al., 1994), bupropion (Wender & Reimherr, 1990), the MAO inhibitor selegiline (Ernst et al., 1995), and the long-acting methamphetamine compound Desoxyn Gradumets (Wender, 1994).

Novel compounds have been used with varying amounts of success. Although the nicotinic analogue (ABT 418) significantly reduced ADHD symptoms (Pelham et al., 2000b), the antinarcoleptic modafinil failed to separate from placebo in a multisite controlled trial of three doses (100, 200, and 400 mg) (Cephalon Press Release, 7/31/00).

Barkley (DuPaul & Barkley, 1990) and Wender et al. (1994) recommended a number of medications that can be used to treat the adult with ADHD. These include MPH, 5 tid to 20 tid; DEX, 5 tid to 20 bid; methamphetamine (Desoxyn Gradumets), 5 to 25 mg once in A.M.; bupropion (Wellbutrin), 100 mg bid to 100 mg tid; and selegiline (Eldepryl), 5 mg bid only. The database is limited for the efficacy of these medications, so practitioners should be cautious in their use until proof of efficacy is available. Of particular concern is the danger of prescribing psychostimulants for adults with comorbid substance abuse disorder. In these patients, it is preferable to use drugs with lower abuse potential, such as pemoline or tricyclic antidepressants, for the treatment of adults with ADHD who suffer from such comorbid problems.

CURRENT PSYCHOPHARMACOLOGICAL AGENTS: EFFICACY AND UTILITY

Three groups of stimulants are currently approved by the FDA for treatment of ADHD in children and are available in both brand and generic: the amphetamines (Adderall®, Dextrostat, Dexedrine), the methylphenidates (Concerta®, Metadate-ER®, Metadate-CD®, methylphenidate, Methylin, Ritalin®, Ritalin-SR®, Ritalin-LA®, and Ritadex®), and magnesium pemoline (Cylert®). Characteristics of these stimulants can be found in Table 2.2. While dextroamphetamine (DEX) and methylphenidate (MPH) are structurally related to the catecholamines (DA and NE), pemoline (PEM) has a different structure, although it, too, has strong DA effects on the central nervous system (CNS) (McCracken, 1991). The term *psychostimulant* used for these compounds refers to their ability to increase CNS activity in some but not all brain regions.

Compared to placebo, psychostimulants have a significantly greater ability to reduce ADHD symptoms such as overactivity (fidgetiness, off-task behavior during direct observation) and to eliminate behavior that disrupts the classroom (constant requests of the teacher during direct observation) (Jacobvitz et al., 1990). In experimental settings, stimulants

TABLE 2.2 Stimulant Drugs, Doses, and Pharmacodynamics

Medication	*Tablets/Dosages*	*Dose Range (mg/day)*	*Administration*	*Peak Effect (hours)*	*Duration of Action (hours)*
Amphetamines					
Dexedrine®	5 mg	10–40	bid or tid	1–3	5
Adderall®	5, 10, 20, 30 mg	10–40	bid or tid	1–3	5
Dextrostat® (generic)	5 mg	10–40	bid or tid	1–3	5
Long-Duration Type					
Dexedrine Spansule®	5, 10, 15 mg capsule	10–45	once-daily	1–4	6–9
Adderall XL®	10, 20, 30 mg capsules	10–40	once-daily	1–4	9
Methylphenidates					
Ritalin®	5, 10, 20 mg	10–60	tid	1–3	2–4
Methylphenidate	5, 10, 20 mg	10–60	tid	1–3	2–4
Methylin®	5, 10, 20 mg	10–60	tid	1–3	2–4
Ritadex®	2.5, 5, 10 mg	5–30	bid	1–4	2–5
Long-Duration Type					
Ritalin-SR®	20 mg	20–60	Q.D. in A.M. or bid	3	5
Metadate-ER®	10 mg, 20 mg	20–60	Q.D. in A.M. or bid	3	5
Medadate-CD®	20 mg	20–60	Q.D. in A.M.	5	8
Concerta®	18 mg, 36 mg, 54 mg	18–54	Q.D. in A.M.	8	12
Ritalin-LA®	20 mg	20–60	Q.D. in A.M.	5	8
Pemoline (Cylert®)	18.75, 37.5, 75mg; 37.5 chewable	37.5–112.5	Q.D. in A.M. or bid	2–4	7

have been shown to improve child behavior during parent-child interactions (Barkley & Cunningham, 1979) and problem-solving activities with peers (Whalen et al., 1989). The behavior of children with ADHD has a tendency to elicit negative, directive, and controlling behavior from parents and peers (Campbell, 1973). When these children are placed on stimulants, their mothers' rate of disapproval, commands, and control diminishes to the extent seen between other mothers and their non-ADHD children (Barkley & Cunningham, 1979; Barkley et al., 1984; Humphries et al., 1978). In the laboratory, stimulant-treated children with ADHD demonstrate major improvements during experimenter-paced continuous performance tests (Halperin et al., 1992), paired-associate learning, cued and free recall, auditory and reading comprehension, spelling recall, and arithmetic computation (Pelham & Bender, 1982; Stephens et al., 1984). Some studies show correlations between plasma levels of MPH and performance on a laboratory task (Greenhill, 1995), but plasma levels rarely correlate with clinical response. Likewise, hyperactive conduct-disordered children and preadolescents show reductions in aggressive behavior when treated with stimulants and observed in structured and unstructured school settings (Hinshaw, 1991). Stimulants also can reduce the display of covert antisocial behaviors such as stealing and property destruction (Hinshaw et al., 1992).

No single theory explains the psychostimulant mechanism of action on the central nervous system that ameliorates ADHD symptoms. The drug's effect based on a single neurotransmitter has been discounted (Zametkin & Rapoport, 1987) as well as its ability to correct the ADHD child's under- or over-aroused central nervous system (Solanto, 1984). More recently, a two-part theory of stimulant action has been postulated (McCracken, 1991) in which stimulants increase DA release, producing enhanced autoreceptor-mediated inhibition of ascending DA neurons, while simultaneously increasing adrenergic-mediated inhibition of the noradrenergic locus coeruleus via epinephrine activity. This theory awaits confirmation from basic research in animals and imaging studies in humans.

To date, brain imaging has reported few consistent psychostimulant effects on glucose metabolism. While some studies in ADHD adults using positron emission tomography (PET) and $[^{18}F]$fluorodeoxyglucose show that stimulants lead to increased brain glucose metabolism in the striatal and frontal regions (Ernst & Zametkin, 1995), others (Matochik et al.,

1993, 1994) are unable to find a change in glucose metabolism during acute and chronic stimulant treatment.

Psychostimulants are thought to release catecholamines and block their reuptake. Methylphenidate, like cocaine, has affinity for the dopamine transporter (DAT), and DAT blockade is now regarded as the putative mechanism for psychostimulant action in the human central nervous system. Positron emission tomography (PET) scan data show that [^{11}C]methylphenidate concentration in brain is maximal in striatum, an area rich in dopamine terminals where DAT resides (Volkow et al., 1995). These PET scans reveal a significant difference in the pharmacokinetics of [^{11}C]methylphenidate and [^{11}C]cocaine (Volkow et al., 1995). Although both drugs display rapid uptake into striatum, MPH is more slowly cleared from brain. The authors speculate that this low reversal of binding to the DA transporter means that MPH is not as reinforcing as cocaine and therefore does not lead to as much self-administration as does cocaine. More recently, the same authors (Wolraich, 2001) were able to show that therapeutic doses of oral MPH significantly increase extracellular dopamine in the human brain: "DA decreases the background firing rates and increases signal-to-noise in target neurons, we postulate that the amplification of weak DA signals in subjects with ADHD by MPH would enhance task-specific signaling, improving attention and decreasing distractibility" (p. 3).

One of the most important findings in the stimulant treatment literature is the high degree of short-term efficacy for *behavioral* targets, with weaker effects for *cognition and learning*. Conners (personal communication, 1993) noted that 0.8, 1.0, and 0.9 effect sizes are reported for behavioral improvements in Type 4 meta-analytic reviews of stimulant drug actions (Kavale, 1982; Ottenbach & Cooper, 1983; Thurber & Walker, 1983). These behavioral responses to stimulant treatment, when compared to placebo, resemble the treatment efficacy of antibiotics. Less powerful effects are found for laboratory measures for cognitive changes, in particular on the continuous performance task, for which effect sizes of these medications range between 0.6 and 0.5 for omissions and commissions, respectively, in a within-subject design (Milich et al., 1989); and 0.6 and 1.8 in a between-subject study (Schechter & Keuezer, 1985).

Psychostimulants continue to show behavioral efficacy in the Type 1 RCTs published over the last 10 years (see Table 2.2). These modern-day controlled trials have matured with the field and now utilize multiple-dose conditions with multiple stimulants (Elia et al., 1991), parallel designs (Spencer et al., 1995), and a common definition of response as normalization (Abikoff & Gittelman, 1985; Rapport et al., 1994). These studies now test psychostimulants in special ADHD populations, including adolescents (Klorman et al., 1990), adults (Spencer et al., 1995), the mentally retarded (Horn et al., 1991), ADHD subjects with anxiety disorders and internalizing disorders, and ADHD subjects with tic disorders (Gadow et al., 1995). As shown in Table 2.3, 70% of ADHD subjects respond to stimulants and less than 13% to placebo (Greenhill et al., 2001).

Studies also have attempted to study stimulant nonresponders. Some drug trials (Douglas et al., 1988) report a 100% response rate in small samples in which multiple doses of MPH are used. Others find that a trial involving two stimulants effectively lowers the nonresponse rate. Elia and colleagues (1991) reduced the 32% nonresponse rate to a single psychostimulant to less than 4% when two stimulants, DEX and MPH, were titrated sequentially in the same subject. However, if one includes children with comorbidity in the sample, the rate of medication nonresponse might be higher. Finally, few studies have used the double-blind or single-blind placebo discontinuation model to determine if the child continues to respond to stimulants after being treated for 1 year or more. One study found that 80% of ADHD children relapsed when switched single blind from MPH to a placebo after 8 months of treatment (H. Abikoff, personal communication, 1994). Even so, these observations about the "rare nonresponder" do not address the rate of placebo response. Few, if any, of the current RCTs are parallel designs, which can test to see if placebo response emerges at some point over the entire drug trial. Few treatment studies prescreen for placebo responders, so the numbers of actual medication responders in any sample of ADHD children might be closer to 55%, not the 75 to 96% often quoted. Furthermore, these estimates apply to group effects and do not inform the clinician about the individual patient.

Increasing Use of Stimulants in Clinical Practice

Outpatient visits devoted to ADHD increased from 1.6 to 4.2 million per year during the years 1990–

1993 (Swanson et al., 1995a); by 1995, these figures had climbed to 2 million visits and 6 million stimulant drug prescriptions (Jensen et al., 1999a). During those visits, 90% of the children were given prescriptions, 71% of which were for the stimulant methylphenidate (MPH). MPH production in the United States increased from 1,784 kg to 5,110 kg during the same time period, so that over 10 million prescriptions for MPH were written in 1996 (Vitiello & Jensen, 1997). It has been estimated that 2.8% of U.S. youth, ages 5 to 18 years, were prescribed stimulants in 1995 (Goldman et al., 1998). However, specific epidemiological surveys suggest that 12-month prescription rates for the school-age group—ages 6 to 12 years—may be higher, ranging from 6% urban (Safer et al., 1996) to 7% rural (Angold et al., 2000) and extending up to 10% in some communities (LeFever et al., 1999).

Psychostimulant use has increased fivefold since 1989, and this increase has raised concerns at the U.S. Drug Enforcement Administration (DEA)—which regulates their production—about the risk of abuse and diversion. Production of MPH tripled over a 10-year period, and 90% of U.S.-produced MPH is used in the United States. Increased MPH use could mean increases in ADHD prevalence, a change in the ADHD diagnosis, improved recognition of ADHD by physicians, broadened indications for use, or an increase in drug diversion and prescription for profit or abuse (Goldman et al., 1998). Analyses of managed-care datasets reveals a 2.5-fold increase in prescribing in the 1990–1995 time period, accounted for by longer durations of treatment, inclusion of girls and those with predominantly inattention, and treatment of high school students (Safer et al., 1996). An epidemiologically based survey in four different communities found only one-eighth of diagnosed ADHD children received adequate stimulant treatment (Jensen et al., 1999b), while another survey in rural North Carolina found that many school-age children on stimulants did not meet *DSM-IV* criteria for ADHD (Angold et al., 2000).

The Controversy and Politics of Stimulant Treatments for Children with ADHD

Even though the psychostimulants are the most widely researched, clinically effective, and commonly prescribed treatments for ADHD, their use in children has become the focus of a major controversy. A 1998 Consensus Development Conference (CDC) on ADHD sponsored by the National Institutes of Health concluded that stimulants were effective in reducing the defining symptoms of ADHD in children in the short term but indicated that the controversy about their use demanded serious consideration. It also noted the lack of evidence of the long-term benefit and safety; the considerable risks of treatment; the wide variation in prescribing practices among practitioners; and the absence of evidence regarding the appropriate AD/HD diagnostic threshold above which the benefits of psychostimulant therapy outweigh the risks.

The CDC's conclusions were much less sanguine than a similar report published the same year by the Council on Scientific Affairs of the American Medical Association. After reviewing hundreds of trials involving thousands of patients, the Council concluded that "the risk-benefit ratio of stimulant treatment in AD/HD must be evaluated and monitored on an ongoing basis in each case, but in general is highly favorable" (Goldman et al., 1998, p. 1106).

Stimulant Medications in Practice

Currently, over 85% of psychostimulant prescriptions in the United States are written for MPH (Safer et al., 1996; Williams & Swanson, 1996). The rate of MPH prescription writing increased fourfold from 1990 to 1995. The indications, pharmacology, adverse effects, and usage directions for MPH are frequently highlighted in reviews (Dulcan, 1990; Greenhill, 1995; Wilens & Biederman, 1992). MPH has become the "first-line" psychostimulant for ADHD, followed by DEX and PEM (Richters et al., 1995). Within the group of stimulants, practitioners order MPH first, DEX second, and PEM third. The popularity of MPH as the first choice in psychostimulants is not supported by the literature, however. DEX and PEM have identical efficacy to MPH (Arnold et al., 1978; Elia et al., 1991; Pelham et al., 1990, 1995a; Vyborova et al., 1984; Winsberg et al., 1974). Arnold noted (Greenhill et al., 1996) that of the 141 subjects in these studies, 50 responded better to DEX, and only 37 better to MPH.

Because of reports of hepatotoxicity during postmarketing surveillance, 1975–1990, by the Food and Drug Administration, PEM is now not recommended as a first-line treatment for ADHD (Burns et al., 1999). As a result of manufacturer's warning letters, sales of PEM declined between 1996 and 1999, and it has been taken off formulary in various parts of the

TABLE 2.3 Type 1 Studies Showing Efficacy in ADHD Drug Treatments (N=1702)

Study (Year)	N	*Age Range*	*Design*	*Drug (Dose)*	*Duration*	*Response*	*Comment*
Abikoff (1985)	28	6–12	ADHD Controls	MPH (PB, 41 mg)	8 weeks	80.9%	ADHD kids normalized
Abikoff (1998)	103	6–12	ADHD	MPH tid (33.7 mg)	2 years	100% 2.7 *SD*	Multisite, multimodal study; all children on MPH
Barkley (1989)	74	6–13	Xover 37 agg 37 nonagg	MPH (PB, 0.3, 0.5)	4 weeks	80%	Aggression responsive to MPH
Barkley (1991)	40	6–12	Xover 23 ADHD 17 ADHD-W	MPH bid (5, 10, 15 bid) PB bid	6 weeks	ADHD 95% ADHD-W 76%	Fewer ADHD-W respond, need low dose
Castellanos (1997)	20	6–13	Xover	MPH 45 mg bid DEX 22.5 mg bid	9 weeks	ADHD + TS	Tics dose-related at high doses
Douglas (1988)	19	7–13	Xover	MPH (PB, 0.15, 0.3, 0.6)	2 weeks	100%	Linear D/R relationships
Douglas (1995)	17	6–11	Xover	MPH (0.3, 0.6, 0.9) PB	4 weeks	behavior 70%	No cognitive toxicity at high doses, linear D/R curves
DuPaul (1993)	31	6–12	Xover 31 ADHD 25 normals	MPH (20 mg) PB bid	6 weeks	behavior 78% attention 61%	MPH can normalize classroom behavior; 25% of ADHD subjects didn't normalize academics
DuPaul (1994)	40	6–12	Xover 12 high ANX 17 mid ANX 11 low ANX	MPH (5, 10, 15 mg) PB single dose	6 weeks	high 68% nor mid 70% nor low 82% nor	25% in internalizing group deteriorated on meds ADHD; subjects with comorbid int disorders less to be normalized or to respond to MPH
Elia (1991)	48	6–12	Xover	MPH (0.5; 0.8, 1.5) PB bid DEX (0.25, (0.5, 0.75)	6 weeks	MPH 79% DEX 86%	Response rate for two stimulants = 96%
Gadow (1995)	34	6–12	Xover ADHD + tic disorder	MPH (0.1, 0.3, 0.5) PB bid	8 weeks	100% MPH	No nonresponders to behavior; MD's motor tic ratings show 2 min increases on drug; Only shows effects of 8 weeks treatment

Gillberg (1997)	62	6–12	Parallel	AMP (17 mg) PB bid	60 weeks	70% respond 27–40% impr	No dropouts but only 25% placebo groups at 15-month assessment
Greenhill (2001)	277	6–12	Parallel	Metadate-CD Placebo	3 weeks	70% respond	Mean total daily dose 40 mg. FDA registration
Klorman (1990)	48	12–18	Xover	MPH tid (0.26) PB bid	6 weeks	MPH 60%	Less med benefits for adolescents
Klein (1997)	84	6–15	Parallel	MPH bid (1.0)	5 weeks	MPH 59–78% PB 9–29%	MPH reduced ratings of antisocial behaviors
MTA (1999)	579	7–9	Parallel	MPH tid (< 0.8)	4 weeks (14 months)	MPH 77% DEX 10% None 13%	Titration Trial for multisite, multimodal study, full study data for 288 on 38.7 mg MPH
Musten (1997)	31	4–6	Xover	MPH bid (0.3, 0.5)	3 weeks	MPH > NA	MPH improves attention in preschoolers
Pelham (1990)	22	8–13	Xover	MPH 10 bid; PB bid; DEX span 10 mg PEM 56.25 daily	24 days	Stim 68%	DEX Span, PEM best for behavior 27% did best on DEX; 18% on SR; 18% on PEM; 5% on MPH bid.
Pelham (1995)	28	5–12	Xover	PEM (18.75, 37.5, 75, 112.5 mg) PB OD	7 weeks	PEM resp 89% PB resp 0%	PEM dose ≥ 37.5 mg/day lasts 2–7 hours. Efficacy and time course = MPH
Rapport (1988)	22	6–10	Xover	MPH (PB, 5, 10, 15 mg)	5 weeks	72%	MPH response same in home and school
Rapport (1994)	76	6–12	Xover	MPH (5,10, 15, 20 mg) PB bid	5 weeks	94% beh 53% att	MPH normalizes behavior > academics. Higher doses better, linear D/R curve
Schachar (1997)	91	6–12	Parallel	MPH (33.5 mg) PB bid	52 weeks	0.7 *SD* effect size	15% side effects: affective, overfocusing led to dropouts
Spencer (1995)	23	18–60	Xover	MPH (1 mg/kg/d)	7 weeks	78% PB 4%	MPH at 1 mg/kg/d produces improvement in adults equivalent to that seen in kids

(*continued*)

TABLE 2.3 (continued)

Study (Year)	N	*Age Range*	*Design*	*Drug (Dose)*	*Duration*	*Response*	*Comment*
Swanson (1998)	29	7–14	Xover	Adderall (5, 10, 15, 20, PB, MPH)	7 weeks	100%*	Adderall peaks at 3 hr, MPH at 1.5 hr
Tannock (1995)	40	6–12	Xover	MPH (0.3, 0.6) 17 ADHD-Anx	2 weeks	70%	Activity level better in both groups; working memory not improved in anxious kids
Tannock (1995)	28	6–12	Xover	MPH (0.3, 0.6, 0.9) PB	2 weeks	70% 70%	Effects on behavior D/R curve linear, but effects on resp inhibition U-shaped suggest adjust dose on obj measures
Taylor (1987)	38	6–10	Xover	MPH (PB 0.2–1.4)	6 weeks	58%	Severe ADHD symptoms, better response
Whalen (1989)	25	6.3–12	Xover	MPH (PB, 0.3, 0.5)	5 weeks	48–72%	MPH helps, not normalizes, peer status
Wolraich (2001)	277	6–12	Parallel	Concerta 36 mg Placebo MPH tid	4 weeks	62%	Concerta rated effective by teachers and parents

Doses listed as mg/kg/dose, and medication is given twice daily unless otherwise stated.

Abbreviations: PB = placebo; Xover = crossover design; Anx = anxiety; MPH = methylphenidate; DEX = dextroamphetamine; PEM = pemoline; AMP = d,l-amphetamine (Adderall); mg/kg/d = dosage in milligram/kilogram/day; Agg = aggression; ADHD-W = ADD without hyperactivity; sx = symptoms; obj = objective; resp = response.

United Kingdom. Practitioners are advised to obtain informed consent from parents before treatment using a form attached to the package insert, and to monitor liver function via biweekly blood tests. Children with ADHD, especially those with needle phobias, may refuse the tests. Also, PEM is more expensive than the other psychostimulants. For these reasons, practitioners are reluctant to prescribe the drug. However, PEM is effective. Pelham's RCT (Pelham et al., 1995b) comparing four doses of once daily PEM with a placebo showed a 72% rate of response for PEM in doses of 37.5 mg per day.

Stimulant responsiveness or rates of side effects were originally thought to be affected by the presence of comorbid anxiety symptoms. Pliszka (1989) treated 43 subjects with ADHD with MPH (0.25–0.4 mg/kg, and 0.45–0.70 mg/kg) and placebo for 4 weeks. The 22 subjects comorbid for anxiety symptoms and ADHD (the ADHD + ANX group) showed less efficacy when active stimulant treatment was compared to placebo, as judged by teachers' global ratings, with no increase in side effects. This might be explained by strong placebo response in the ADHD + ANX group. Tannock, Ickowicz, and Schachar (1995) reported that children with ADHD, some with (*N* = 18) and some without (*N* = 22) comorbid anxiety symptoms, treated in a double-blind randomized, crossover design with three MPH doses (0.3, 0.6, 0.9 mg/kg), showed equal decreases in motor activity, but the group with comorbid anxiety did poorer on a serial addition task and had a differential heart rate response to MPH. DuPaul, Barkley, and McMurray (1994) found that 40 children with ADHD and comorbid anxiety were less likely to respond to MPH and showed more side effects for three doses of MPH (5, 10, 15 mg) and placebo. However, the study did not collect ratings for anxiety symptoms, so the direct effect of MPH on such symptoms was not recorded.

More recent data do not support these early impressions. The one controlled study (Gadow et al., 1995) that tested the effects of MPH in children with comorbid symptoms found equally good response in both those with and those without the anxiety disorder. These divergent data leave open the question of whether comorbid anxiety symptoms predict poor response to stimulant treatment.

Predicting drug response in the individual ADHD child is difficult. While pretreatment patient characteristics (young age, low rates of anxiety, low severity of disorder, and high IQ) may predict a good response to methylphenidate on global rating scales (Buitelaar et al., 1995), most research shows that no neurological, physiological, or psychological measures of functioning have been identified that are reliable predictors of response to psychostimulants (Pelham & Milich, 1991; Zametkin et al., 1987). Once a child responds, there has been no universally agreed-upon criterion for how much the symptoms must change before the clinician stops increasing the dose. Furthermore, there is no standard for the outcome measure. For example, should global ratings alone be used, or should they be combined with more "objective" academic measures such as percentage correct or percentage completed lists of math problems? Some have advocated a 25% reduction of ADHD symptoms, while others suggest that the dose continue to be adjusted until the child's behavior and classroom performance is normalized.

The concept of *normalization* has helped standardize the definition of a categorical responder across domains and across studies. Studies now determine if the improvement from treatment is clinically meaningful, using normal classroom controls, instead of just being statistically significant. Treatment was noted to remove differences between ADHD children and nonreferred classmates on measures of activity and attention (Abikoff & Gittelman, 1985), but not for positive peer nominations (Whalen et al., 1989). Further advances occurred when investigators used statistically derived definitions of clinically meaningful change during psychotherapeutic treatment (Jacobsen & Truax, 1991). Rapport and colleagues (1994) used this technique to calculate reliable change and normalization on the Abbreviated Conners Teacher Rating Scale (ACTRS) using national norms. They determined that a child would be normalized when his or her ACTRS score fell closer to the mean of the normal population than to the mean of the ADHD population. Using this technique in a controlled trial of four doses of MPH in ADHD children, they found that MPH normalized behavior and, to a lesser extent, academics (94% versus 53%). Similarly, DuPaul and colleagues (DuPaul & Rapport, 1993) found that MPH normalized behavior for all ADHD children treated, but only 75% of the ADHD children normalized for academics. In another study, the same group (DuPaul et al., 1994) reported that normalization in behavior and academics occurred less often when

ADHD subjects were comorbid for high levels of internalizing disorders. Swanson applied this approach to the cumulative-distribution curves of the Swanson, Nolan, and Pelham (SNAP) parent and teacher ratings at the end of the MTA study and found that 88% of classroom controls, 65% of ADHD children treated with combined treatment, and 55% of ADHD children treated with MTA medication strategies had mean symptom scores of 1 or less, equivalent to a "normal" response on those scales.

RISKS ASSOCIATED WITH STIMULANT USE

Both the risk-benefit and cost-benefit ratios for the psychostimulants are very favorable (Klein & Wender, 1995). Two double-blind, placebo-controlled studies (Ahmann et al., 1993; Barkley et al., 1990b) identified only four active drug side effects that exceeded placebo rates associated with MPH treatment. One study (Ahmann et al., 1993) involving 234 children, ages 5–15, used the Barkley Side Effect Questionnaire and found that only five side effects during MPH treatment showed a significant increase over placebo: insomnia (58.8% vs. 36.7%); decreased appetite (55.7% vs. 25.4%); stomachache (33.8% vs. 18.4%); headache (30.4% vs. 21.4%), and dizziness (12.5% vs. 4.5%).

Motor or vocal tics have been reported to appear in as many as 1% of children taking MPH (Ickowicz et al., 1992). A controlled trial of MPH in children with ADHD and chronic tic disorder (Gadow et al., 1995) reported significant improvement in ADHD symptoms for all subjects, but no consistent worsening or increase in tic frequency. However, the total daily MPH doses used never exceeded 20 mg/day. These low doses and the short 8-week study do not resemble the higher doses or longer treatment duration found in clinical practice, where tics may appear after several months of MPH administration. The clinical literature has held that MPH lowers the seizure threshold, although treatment of patients with ADHD and seizures with MPH shows no change in seizure frequency (Klein et al., 1995).

Growth slowdown is another infrequent psychostimulant adverse reaction. Psychostimulant-induced reductions in growth velocity have been the most consistently researched long-term side effect for this type of medication (Greenhill, 1984). Even with the many studies in this area (Greenhill, 1981), myriad methodological difficulties prevent an easy interpretation. Few studies employ the optimal controls needed, which include untreated ADHD children, a psychiatric control group, and an ADHD group treated with a class of medications other than stimulants. Studies differ in quality of compliance measures, whether the children are off stimulants on weekends, and whether the stimulants are used through the summer. One large controlled study (Gittelman-Klein et al., 1988) reported growth rate reductions among a subgroup of children, but growth resumes immediately when treatment is interrupted (Safer et al., 1975).

Safer and Allen (Safer et al., 1972, 1975; Safer & Allen, 1973) first reported that treatment for 2 or more years with MPH and DEX could produce decrements in weight velocity on age-adjusted growth rate charts; stopping the medication produced a quick return to baseline growth velocities. Dextroamphetamine, with a half-life of two to three times that of MPH, produces more sustained effects than does MPH on weight velocity, as well as suppressing mean sleep-related prolactin concentrations (Greenhill, 1981). In MPH-treated ADHD children, followed for 2 to 4 years, dose-related decreases in weight velocity are seen (Gittelman-Klein et al., 1988; Satterfield et al., 1979), with some tolerance of the suppressive effect developing in the second year (Satterfield et al., 1979). Hechtman and Weiss (1984) report growth slowdown in untreated children with ADHD, suggesting that there may be differential growth in such children associated with the ADHD disorder itself. Spencer and colleagues (1996b) detected similar different growth rates for children with ADHD that could be associated with the disorder itself and not only with stimulant treatment.

The actual psychostimulant mechanism for any growth slowdown is unknown. Early theories blamed the drug's putative growth suppressant action on its effects on growth hormone or prolactin, but research studies on 13 children treated for 18 months with 0.8 mg/day of DEX (Greenhill et al., 1981) or on 9 children treated for 12 months on 1.2 mg/kg/day of MPH (Greenhill et al., 1984) failed to demonstrate a consistent change in growth hormone release. The most parsimonious explanation for this drug effect is the medication's suppression of appetite, leading to reduced caloric intake. No study, however, has collected the standardized diet diaries necessary to track calories consumed by ADHD children on psychostimulants (Greenhill, 1981).

In any case, the growth effects of MPH appear to be minimal. Satterfield et al. (1979) followed 110 children and found decreases in height velocity during the first year of psychostimulant treatment, but this reversed during the second year of treatment. An initial growth loss during MPH treatment was seen in 65 children followed to age 18, but these children "caught up" during adolescence and reached heights predicted from their parents' heights (Gittelman & Mannuzza, 1988). These results confirm the observations by Roche and colleagues (1979) that psychostimulants have mild and transitory effects on weight and only rarely interfere with height acquisition. Height and weight should be measured at 6-month intervals during stimulant treatment and recorded on age-adjusted growth forms to determine the presence of a drug-related reduction in height or weight velocity. If such a decrement is discovered during maintenance therapy with psychostimulants, a reduction in dosage or change to another class of medication can be carried out.

LIMITATIONS OF STIMULANTS FOR THE TREATMENT OF ADHD

Although 3- to 7-month treatment studies carried out on groups of children with ADHD (Schachar & Tannock, 1993) show impressive reductions in ADHD symptoms, clinicians must manage individual ADHD children over years. Although psychostimulants produce moderate to marked short-term improvement in motor restlessness, on-task behavior, compliance, and classroom academic performance (DuPaul & Barkley, 1990), these effects have been demonstrated convincingly only in short-term studies. When examined over periods greater than 6 months, these medications fail to maintain academic improvement (Cadow, 1991) or to improve the social problem-solving deficits that accompany ADHD. Many of the long-term studies reporting lack of academic improvement have been uncontrolled, with many of the children followed not taking stimulants consistently, so it is not possible to draw conclusions about whether stimulant treatment reverses academic failure over time. Although there are over 100 controlled studies of stimulant efficacy in the literature, only 18 studies lasted as long as 3 months according to a recent authoritative review (Schachar & Tannock, 1993). Because literally 4 million psychostimulant prescriptions were written in 1994 and because the duration of treatment extends from first grade through college, there is growing interest in showing that stimulant treatment is effective over the long run.

A dual-site multimodal treatment study (Abikoff, 1991) treated children over 2 years and found that medication-alone treatment is as effective as combination treatment involving medication plus psychosocial interventions. However, that study did not have a no-medication group. This concern about drawing long-term conclusions from short-term benefits in the psychostimulant literature became one of the driving forces behind the implementation of the 14-month NIMH Cooperative Multimodal Treatment Study of Children with Attention Deficit Hyperactivity Disorder (NIMH MTA Study) (Richters et al., 1995). This study attempts to address long-term stimulant use by including a no-medication psychosocial-treatment-only arm in a sample of 576 children with ADHD.

Other caveats have been expressed about the use of psychostimulants for the treatment of children with ADHD. First, the behavioral benefits from a single dose of a psychostimulant last only a few hours during its absorption phase (Perel et al., 1991) and are often gone by the afternoon if given in the morning. Second, even with the new understanding about the relatively small numbers of nonresponders (Elia et al., 1991), a small number improve but experience unmanageable side effects. Approximately 25% of children with ADHD are not helped by the first psychostimulant given or experience side effects so bothersome that meaningful dose adjustments cannot be made (DuPaul & Barkley, 1990). Third, the indications for choosing a particular psychostimulant and the best methods for adjusting the dose remain unclear and thus may prove confusing to the clinician and family. Although MPH is regarded as the drug of choice for the treatment of ADHD, controlled treatment studies show no particular advantage of this medication over dextroamphetamine. Fourth, many treatment studies are troubled by methodological problems, including failure to control for prior medication treatment and inappropriately short washout periods.

In addition to widely accepted short-term side effects of stimulants, other concerns have been more theoretical, but still controversial. A few studies have reported that there are problems with dissociation of cognitive and behavioral responses to MPH (Sprague & Sleator, 1977), or that the response to MPH treatment may be diminished by the presence of comorbid internalizing disorders (Pliszka, 1989; Tannock et al., 1993). There has also been the concern that children treated with stimulants may develop negative self-attributions, coming to believe that they are incapable of functioning without the medication. In addition, investigators have sometimes found that stimulant effects may be influenced by the patient's IQ or age (Buitelaar et al., 1995). Fifth, some have speculated that dose-response measures of academic performance in stimulant-treated ADHD children may be influenced by state-dependent learning (Swanson & Kinsbourne, 1976). Sixth, the possibility that stimulant medication response may be related to the presence of minor physical anomalies, neurological soft signs, or metabolic/nutritional status has yet to be explored.

The practitioner may find it difficult to cull specific guidelines about dosing the individual patient from these studies involving groups of children with ADHD. There is no universally agreed-upon method for dosing with these medications; some practitioners use the child's weight as a guideline (dose-by-weight method), and others titrate each child's response through the approved dose range until clinical response occurs or side effects limit further dose increases (stepwise-titration method). Rapport and colleages (1989) have shown that there is no consistent relationship between weight-adjusted MPH doses and behavioral responses, calling into question the widely accepted practice in research of standardizing MPH doses by weight adjustment. Some children with ADHD show dose-responses that can be conceptualized as a simple linear function (Gittelman & Kanner, 1986), while others show curvilinear patterns. These relationships may vary in the same child, one type for cognitive performance and another type for the behavioral domain (Sprague & Sleator, 1977).

Adverse reactions to medications show the same variability and may appear unpredictably during different phases of the drug's absorption or metabolic phases. Although long-term adverse reactions, such as inhibition of linear growth in children, have been shown to resolve by adult life, no long-term, prospective studies have been published maintaining adolescents on psychostimulants through the critical period when their long bone epiphyses fuse. Therefore, the final evidence remains to be gathered showing that continuously treated adolescents will reach the final height predicted from their parents' size (Greenhill, 1981).

NEW STIMULANT PREPARATIONS

In recent years, the pharmaceutical industry has renewed its interest in the ADHD market and has submitted many new drug applications to the Food and Drug Administration (FDA). Under the Food and Drug Administration Modernization Act (FDAMA), the agency has responded to the need for more child dosing and safety data by offering a 6-month extension of patent exclusivity to a manufacturer who gathers pharmacokinetic data on already approved active drug moieties in this age group. Under this provision, new pediatric psychopharmacology research has been conducted on fluoxetine, fluvoxamine, and gabapentin.

In parallel to the FDA's incentives, pharmaceutical companies have been launching new drug development projects. By the fall of 2001, two new psychoactive drugs, OROS-Methylphenidate (Concerta®) and beaded-methylphenidate (Metadate-CD®) had been approved for use in children. OROS-methylphenidate was evaluated in a 13-site, placebo-controlled, double-blind trial involving 277 children (Wolraich et al., 2001). The subjects were randomized in a three-arm, 4-week study to either OROS-methylphenidate (18, 36, or 54 mg QD in the A.M.), to methylphenidate (5, 10, or 15 mg tid), or placebo. Teacher's IOWA Conners ratings showed significant reductions for both active drugs over placebo at 1 and 4 weeks. Beaded-methylphenidate was evaluated in a 3-week, placebo-controlled, randomized, double-blind, multisite trial (Lord et al., 1994). A total of 312 children were randomized to either beaded-methylphenidate or placebo. Teacher's Conners rating forms were collected in the morning and afternoon during each of the 3 weeks and showed significant improvements over the entire schoolday for the beaded-methylphenidate given once in the morning at a mean dose of 40.2 mg/day.

Three more products, beaded-mixed-amphetamine salts (Adderall XL®), beaded-brand-methylphenidate (Ritalin LA®), and dextromethylphenidate (Ritadex®) were in review at the Food and Drug Administration at the time of this writing. All of these new agents have the advantage of permitting-once-daily dosing.

USING NONSTIMULANT MEDICATION TREATMENTS FOR ADHD

Because of the controversy surrounding the use of scheduled drugs in children, clinicians and parents may prefer nonstimulant medications in the treatment of ADHD. Besides the controversy, other problems face the family using stimulants for ADHD. Short-acting stimulants require cooperation from the school personnel for midday dosing, and this may not always be possible. Stimulants, which cause insomnia, cannot be given too late in the day. MPH's attention-enhancing effects, which last only 3 to 4 hours, are often needed in the late evening to help school-age children with their homework but may result in delayed sleep onset and insomnia. Adverse effects, including severe weight loss, headaches, insomnia, and tics, can occur.

March and colleagues (1994) suggested that a nonstimulant may be used when there is an unsatisfactory response to two different stimulants; this suggestion agrees with the studies of Elia et al. (1991). Other ADHD treatment parameters, as well as the Texas Children's Medication Algorithm Program (C-MAP), recommend the use of nonstimulants when stimulants cannot be used because of inadequate response, unwanted side effects, or parental preference (Pliszka et al., 2000).

Type 1 studies of alternative medications have appeared since 1996. These are listed in Table 2.4.

The tricyclic antidepressants (TCAs) have been considered as an alternative treatment for ADHD. Their efficacy in reducing ADHD symptoms is supported by well-designed, controlled-type RCTs (Biederman et al., 1989) of DMI, as shown in Table 2.1 TCAs are long-acting, allow flexible dosing, and are not drugs of abuse. Dosages can be checked with plasma levels. However, TCAs affect cardiac conduction time, so electrocardiographic monitoring is necessary and a possible inconvenience for families. A series of four deaths in 1988 of ADHD children treated with DMI has made therapists cautious about its use (Werry et al., 1995), although careful statistical analyses showed that these unfortunate occurrences probably were too rare to be causally linked to DMI administration (Biederman et al., 1995).

Bupropion, an antidepressant with noradrenergic activity, was reported to be effective for some of the symptoms of ADHD in placebo-controlled trials (Casat et al., 1989; Clay et al., 1988; Simeon et al., 1986). Barrickman and colleagues (1995) reported that bupropion was equivalent to MPH in the treatment of 15 children with ADHD, who showed equal improvements for both medications on the CGI, Conners teacher and parent ratings, the continuous performance test, and ratings of anxiety and depression. The study shows an order effect, which suggests a carryover from one drug condition to the next. Also, subjects were not placed on placebo in the crossover, so the study is not placebo-controlled. The multisite, double-blind, placebo-controlled trial of bupropion revealed that teachers could detect a reduction of ADHD symptoms at a significant level, but parents could not (Conners et al., 1996). This finding suggests that bupropion is a second-line agent for the treatment of ADHD.

Atomoxetine is a selective noradrenergic reuptake inhibitor that has shown promise in the treatment of adults with ADHD (Greenhill, 2000). Two identical randomized controlled trials to treat ADHD were conducted at 17 sites in the United States. Patients were both genders, 7 to 13 years old, who met *DSM-IV* criteria for ADHD. The atomoxetine dose was titrated based on clinical response to a maximum daily dose of 2.0 mg/kg/day (maximum allowable dose = 90 mg). Atomoxetine was superior to placebo on the primary outcome measure, the ADHD RS total score, as well as on parent and clinician global measures (Wolraich, 2000).

Buspirone is an anxiolytic compound with weak DA activity. Data to date for children with ADHD come from a small, 10-patient controlled study (McCormick et al., 1994) and case reports. One of these case reports (Quaison et al., 1991) suggests that buspirone may reduce aggressivity as well as ameliorate the symptoms of ADHD. A large multisite, placebo-controlled, randomized controlled trial of buspirone transdermal patches for treating children with ADHD failed to show a separation between active drug and placebo on ADHD symptoms.

Clonidine (CLON) is an alpha-2 presynaptic receptor agonist indicated for adult hypertension. The drug has been touted as a nonstimulant treatment for aggressive children with ADHD, although much of its popularity among practitioners and families for treatment of ADHD may be based on its sedating

TABLE 2.4 Studies (Arranged by Drug) of Alternative Medications for ADHD

Study (Year)	N	*Age Range*	*Design*	*Drug (Dose)*	*Duration*	*Response*	*Comment*
Spencer (2000)	20	18–65	Parallel	Atomoxetine	8 weeks	Atomox > PB	Atomox dosed up to 2 mg/kg/day
Simeon (1986)	17	7–13	Single-blind	Bupropion (135 mg/d)	8 weeks	70% improve	CGI, Conners Rating Scales
Casat (1987)	30	6–12	DB parallel	Bupropion (150–250 mg/d)	4 weeks	Mod improve	Teacher, CGI improved
Clay (1988)	33	6–12	DB parallel	Bupropion (5.3 mg/kg/d)	3 weeks	Mod improve	Teacher, parent, CGI improve
Spencer (1993) (Spencer et al., 1993)	4	7–12	Open-L	Bupropion (75–225 mg/d)	1 week–2 months	50% improve	Increased tics, so stopped BPR
Jacobsen (1994) (Jacobsen et al., 1994)	1	7	Open-L	Bupropion (75 mg tid)	4 weeks	Mod improve	Increased compulsions, so stopped BPR
Barrickman (1995)	15	7–17	Xover	Bupropion (3.3 mg/kg/d) MPH (0.7 mg/kg/d)	6 weeks	BPR = MPH	CGI, IOWA-Conners, CDI, CMAS, CPT. No placebo group; order effects
McCormick (1994)	10	6–12	Xover	Buspirone (10 mg/d) PB	6 weeks	BPR > PB	Teacher ratings better
Quiason (1991)	1	8	Open-L	Buspirone (15 mg tid)	10 days	Improved	Decreased aggression
Hunt (1985)	10	11.6	Open	Clonidine	12 weeks	70% improve	Observers disagree about improvement
Ernst (1995)	36	37.6	Xover	*l*-Deprenyl (20 mg, 60 mg)	6 weeks	PB = active	High-dose *l*-deprenyl decreased p-HVA
Barrickman (1991)	22	7–15	Open	Fluoxetine (20–60 mg)	6 weeks	58% improve	19 completers

Chappell (1995)	10	8–16	Open	Guanfacine (1.5 mg/d)	4–20 weeks	Improve tics 40% ADHD	ADHD + Tourette's patients 40% behavior improve
Hunt (1995)	13	8–17	Open	Guanfacine (0.5–4.0 mg)	4 weeks	Improve	Compares baseline versus end point
Conners (1995) (Conners et al., 1995)	17	N/A	Xover	Nicotine patch 11 nonsmoke 6 smokers	3 sessions (7 mg patch) (21 mg patch)	Improve	Improved CGI, reaction time
Hinton (1995) (Hinton et al., 1995)	10	N/A	Xover	Nicotine patch A-B-A	3 sessions (7 mg patch)	Improve	Improve deficits in timing accuracy
Spencer (1998) (Schnipper et al., 2000)	22	adults (76 mg/d)	Xover	Tomoxetin 10% placebo	6 weeks	52% active	Found mild appetite suppression for this NE reuptake inhibitor
Pleak (1995)	1	11	Open-L	Venlafaxine (75 mg tid)	6 weeks	Improved	Diastolic blood pressure increases on doses over 100 mg twice daily
Wilens (1995)	2	45–48	Open	Venlafaxine (18.75 tid–75 bid)	2 months	Improved	52–60% reduction of ADHD symptoms
Reimherr (1995)	20	35	Open	Venlafaxine (50–150 mg/d)	N/A	40% improved	8 patients unable to tolerate lowest dose
Adler (1995)	12	19–59	Open	Venlafaxine (110.4 mg/d)	8 weeks	49.6% improve	4 dropped: sedation
Hornig-Rohan (1995)	17	43	Open	Venlafaxine (N/A)	N/A	80% improve	Small samples, some on multiple meds
Luh (1995)	15	8–17	Open	Venlafaxine (12.5–75 mg)	5 weeks	50% improve	Well tolerated
Derivan (1995)	25	6–15	Open PK	Venlafaxine	6 weeks	Significant	AUC, clearance kids > adults
Castellanos (1996) (Review)	12	6–12	1 Xover	CMI	3 weeks	N/A	CMI > MPH for depressive symptoms
	55	3–39	5 Open	Fluoxetine	6 weeks–3 months	Improvement	All open studies
	1	24	1 Open	Sertraline	N/A	Improvement	Temper, distractibility improved

Studies arranged alphabetically by drug generic name. Most studies open or letters (see "L" added to study type column).

effects, useful for counteracting stimulant-related insomnia (Wilens et al., 1994b). However, a recent review (Swanson et al., 1995b) reveals that there was a fivefold increase in physicians writing CLON prescriptions for children with ADHD from 1990 to 1995. Safety and efficacy issues have not been addressed in this age group. Only one small controlled study of 10 ADHD children (Hunt et al., 1985) suggests that CLON may be effective in ADHD, with reductions in hyperactivity and aggression. Another review (Williams & Swanson, 1996) shows that publications mention only 124 CLON-treated children, 42 with ADHD, 74 with Tourette's, and 8 with early infantile autism. Improvements averaged 22.9% for parent ADHD ratings in the five published studies of children with ADHD (Williams & Swanson, 1996). Connor conducted a pilot study comparing methylphenidate, clonidine, or the combination in 24 ADHD children comorbid with aggression, with either oppositional-defiant or conduct-disorders children (Connor et al., 2000). While all groups showed improvement, the group on clonidine showed a decrease in fine motor speed. Connor, in reviewing this clonidine study and others in a meta-analysis, concluded that clonidine has a moderate effect size of 0.56 on symptoms of ADHD in children and adolescents with ADHD and ADHD comorbid with conduct disorder, developmental delay, and tic disorders (Connor et al., 1999).

Although Connor concluded that clonidine may be an effective second-tier treatment for the symptoms of ADHD, its clinical use is associated with many side effects. This conclusion was seconded by reports coming into the FDA's Post Marketing Surveillance MEDWATCH system, whereby 23 children treated simultaneously with CLON and MPH were reported for drug reactions, including heart rate and blood pressure abnormalities. Among that group, 4 experienced severe adverse effects, including death (Swanson et al., 1995b). Guanfacine, a similar alpha-2 presynaptic agonist, has been studied in two open trials involving 23 children (Chappell et al., 1995; Hunt et al., 1995), but no efficacy or safety data are available.

Venlafaxine is a new antidepressant that acts as a reuptake inhibitor at both the serotonin and norepinephrine neuron. Investigators have reported venlafaxine-related improvements in single patients with ADHD in open trials (Adler et al., 1995; Hornig-Roher & Amsterdam, 1995; Reimherr et al., 1995; Wilens et al., 1995), with symptom reductions in the 40 to 60% range. Other investigators have run small open trials with school-age children and adolescents (Luh et al., 1995; Pleak & Gornly, 1995) and found that venlafaxine was well tolerated and improved ADHD symptoms. Derivan and colleagues (1995) completed a pharmacokinetic study of 25 children and adolescents with ADHD and conduct disorder and showed that these youth needed a higher oral dose than adults to achieve the same blood level. He also reported improvement in CGI (Clinical Global Impression Rating Form) scores for these children and adolescents. No direct comparison has been done between venlafaxine and stimulants, although early impressions suggest that it is less effective in reducing the symptoms of ADHD.

Selective serotonin reuptake inhibitors (SSRIs) enjoy a reputation for high efficacy and low adverse event reporting in adults with major depressive disorder. Castellanos (1996) found no signs of efficacy for SSRIs in the treatment of ADHD symptoms in children in the seven studies (68 children) he reviewed.

CONCLUSIONS

Psychostimulant medications have become a mainstay in the American treatment of ADHD, primarily based on the proven efficacy of these compounds during short-term controlled studies. In fact, the majority of children with ADHD will respond to either MPH or DEX, so that nonresponders are rare (Elia et al., 1991). Although the long-term response of ADHD children to psychostimulants has not been examined in a controlled study much longer than 24 months (Jacobvitz et al., 1990), anecdotal reports suggest that children with ADHD relapse when their medication is withdrawn and respond when the medication is restarted. Optimal treatment involves initial titration to optimize dose, followed by regular appointments and a clinician who remains in regular contact with the teacher or school (Greenhill et al., 2001).

Stimulants continue to be a mainstay of the practice of child psychiatry. The effects of psychostimulants are rapid, dramatic, and normalizing. The risk of long-term side effects remains low, and no substantial impairments have emerged to lessen the remarkable therapeutic benefit-to-risk ratio of these medications. More expensive and demanding treatments, including behavior modification and cognitive behavioral therapies, have, at best, only equaled the treatment with psychostimulants. The combination of behavioral and medication therapies is only slightly more effective than the medication alone in reducing ADHD symptoms (MTA Cooperative Group, 1999). The NIMH MTA Follow-Up Study will test whether combined treatment results in better long-term functioning and decreased appearance of comorbid conditions than does monomodal treatment with psychostimulants alone.

Psychostimulant treatment research has also flourished, but there is ample opportunity for more studies. Not all patients respond to psychostimulants, in particular, patients with comorbid psychiatric disorders. It is also important to determine medication effects on the acquisition of social skills in ADHD children (Hinshaw, 1991). The aim of the new psychopharmacological studies will be to target populations with comorbid disoders (e.g., the child with ADHD and comorbid anxiety disorder) and to examine differential responses to medications in these patients versus patients without the additional psychiatric diagnoses.

ACKNOWLEDGMENT This work was supported, in part, by the grant No. 5 UO1-MH50454–07 (Dr. Greenhill) from the National Institute of Mental Health.

References

Abikoff, H. (1991), Interaction of methylphenidate and multimodal therapy in the treatment of attention deficit hyperactivity disorder. In B. Osman & L. L. Greenhill (Eds.), *Ritalin: Theory and patient management.* New York: Mary Ann Liebert.

Abikoff, H., & Gittelman, R. (1985). Hyperactive children treated with stimulants: Is cognitive training a useful adjunct? *Archives of General Psychiatry, 42,* 953–961.

Abikoff, H., & Hechtman, L. (1998). *Multimodal treatment for children with ADHD: Effects on ADHD and social behavior and diagnostic status* (unpublished)

Adler, L., Resnick, S., Kunz, M., & McDevinsky, O. (1995). Open-label trial of venlafaxine (Effexor) in attention deficit disorder. *Psychological Bulletin, 31,* 544.

Ahmann, P., Waltonen, S., Olson, K., Theye, F., Van Erem, A., & LaPlant, R. (1993). Placebo-controlled evaluation of Ritalin side effects. *Pediatrics, 91,* 1101–1106.

American Psychiatric Association. (1980). *Diagnostic and statistical manual of mental disorders (DSM-III).* Washington, DC: Author.

American Psychiatric Association. (1987). *Diagnostic and statistical manual of mental disorders (DSM-III-R).* Washington, DC: Author.

American Psychiatric Association. (1994). *Diagnostic and statistical manual of mental disorders (DSM-IV).* Washington, DC: Author.

American Psychiatric Association Workgroup on DSM-IV. (1991). *DSM-IV options book.* Washington, DC: Author.

Anderson, J., Williams, S., McGee, R., & Silva, P. (1987). *DSM-III* disorders in pre-adolescent children; Prevalence in a large sample for the general population. *Archives of General Psychiatry, 44,* 69–76.

Angold, A., Erkanli, A., Egger, H., & Costello, J. (2000). Stimulant treatment for children: A community perspective. *Journal of the Academy of Child and Adolescent Psychiatry, 39,* 975–983. (abstract)

Arnold, L., Jensen, P., Richters, J., Abikoff, H., Conners, K., Greenhill, L., Hechtman, L., Hinshaw, S., Pelham, W., & Swanson, J. (1997). The National Institute of Mental Health Collaborative Multisite Multimodal Treatment Study of Children with Attention-Deficit Hyperactivity Disorder (MTA): Design challenges and choices. *Archives of General Psychiatry, 54,* 865–870. (abstract)

Arnold, L. E., Christopher, J., Huestis, R., & Smeltzer, D. (1978). Methylphenidate vs. dextroamphetamine vs. caffeine in minimal brain dysfunction. *Archives of General Psychiatry, 35,* 463–473.

Barkley, R., Fischer, M., Edelbroch, C., & Smallish, L. (1990a). The adolescent outcome of hyperactive children diagnosed by research criteria: An 8-year prospective follow-up. *Journal of the American Academy of Child and Adolescent Psychiatry, 29,* 546–557.

Barkley, R., McMurray, M., Edelbroch, C., & Robbins, K. (1990b). Side effects of MPH in children with attention deficit hyperactivity disorder: A systematic placebo-controlled evaluation. *Pediatrics, 86,* 184–192.

Barkley, R. A. (1977). A review of stimulant drug research with hyperactive children. *Journal of Child Psychology and Psychiatry, 18,* 137–165.

Barkley, R. A. (1982). *Hyperactive children: A handbook for diagnosis and treatment.* New York: Guilford Press.

Barkley, R. A. (1988). The effects of methylphenidate on the interactions of preschool ADHD children with their mothers. *Journal of the American Academy of Child and Adolescent Psychiatry, 27,* 336–341.

Barkley, R. A., & Cunningham, C. E. (1979). The effects of methylphenidate on the mother-child interactions of hyperactive children. *Archives of General Psychiatry, 36,* 201–208.

Barkley, R. A., Karlsson, J., & Strzilecki, E. (1984). Effects of age and Ritalin dosage on mother-child interactions of hyperactive children. *Journal of Consulting and Clinical Psychology, 52,* 750–758.

Barrickman, L., Perry, P., Allen, A., Kuperman, S., Arndt, S., Herrnan, K., & Schumacher, E. (1995). A double-blind crossover trial of bupropion and methylphendiate. *Journal of the American Academy of Child and Adolescent Psychiatry, 34,* 649–657.

Bauermeister, J., Canino, G., & Bird, H. (1994). Epidemiology of disruptive behavior disorders. *Child Adolescent Psychiatric Clinics, 3,* 177–194.

Biederman, J., Baldessarini, R. J., Wright, V., Keenan, K., & Faraone, S. (1989). A double-blind placebo controlled study of desipramine in the treatment of ADD: I. Efficacy. *Journal of the American Academy of Child and Adolescent Psychiatry, 28*(5), 777–784.

Biederman, J., Thisted, R., Greenhill, L., & Ryan, N. (1995). Estimation of the association between desipramine and the risk for sudden death in 5 and 14 old children. *Journal of Clinical Psychiatry, 56,* 87–93.

Bird, H. R., Canino, G., Rubio-Stipec, M., Gould, M. S., Ribera, J., Sesman, M., Woodbury, M., Heurtas-Goldman, S., Pagan, A., Sanchez-Lacay, A., & Moscoso, M. (1988). Estimates of the prevalence of childhood maladjustment in a community sample in Puerto Rico. *Archives of General Psychiatry, 45,* 1120–1126.

Bosco, J., & Robin, S. (1980). Hyperkinesis: prevalence and treatment. In C. Whalen & B. Henker (Eds.), *Hyperkinetic children: The social ecology of identification and treatment.* New York: Academic Press.

Bradley, C. (1937). The behavior of children receiving benzedrine. *American Journal of Psychiatry, 94,* 577–585.

Bradley, C. (1941). The behavior of children receiving benzedrine. *American Journal of Orthopsychiatry, 11,* 92–103.

Bradley, C., & Bowen, M. (1941). Amphetamine (benzedrine) therapy of children's behavior disorders. *American Journal of Orthopsychiatry, 11,* 92–103.

Buitelaar, J., Gary, R., Swaab-Barneveld, H., & Kuiper, M. (1995). Prediction of clinical response to methylphenidate in children with attention deficit hyperactivity disorder. *Journal of the American Academy of Child and Adolescent Psychiatry, 34,* 1025–1032.

Burns, B. J., Hoagwood, K., & Mrazek, P. J. (1999). Effective treatment for mental disorders in children and adolescents. *Clinical Child and Family Psychology Review, 2,* 199–254. (abstract)

Campbell, S. (1973). Mother-child interaction in reflective, impulsive, and hyperactive children. *Developmental Psychology, 8,* 341–349. (abstract)

Campbell, S. B., Endman, M., & Bernfield, G. (1977). A three-year follow-up of hyperactive preschoolers into elementary school. *Journal of Child Psychology and Psychiatry, 18,* 239–249.

Campbell, S. B., & Ewing, L. J. (1990). Follow-up of hard-to-manage preschoolers: Adjustment at age 9 and predictors of continuing symptoms. *Journal of Child Psychology & Psychiatry and Allied Disciplines, 31,* 871–889. (abstract)

Casat, C. D., Pleasants, D. Z., Schroeder, D., & Parker, D. (1989). Bupropion in children with attention deficit disorder. *Psychopharmacology Bulletin, 25*(2), 198–201.

Castellanos, X. (1996). *SSRIs in ADHD.* (unpublished)

Chappell, P., Riddle, M., Scahill, L., Lynch, K., Shultz, R., Arnsten, A., Leckman, J., & Cohen, D. (1995). Guanfacine treatment of comorbid ADHD and Tourette's syndrome: Preliminary clinical experience. *Journal of the American Academy of Child and Adolescent Psychiatry, 34,* 1140–1146.

Charles, L., Schain, R. J., & Guthrie, D. (1979). Long-term use and discontinuation of methylphenidate with hyperactive children. *Developmental Medicine in Child Neurology, 21*(6), 758–764.

Clay, T., Gualtieri, C., Evans, P., & Guillian, C. (1988). Clinical and neurophysiological effects of the novel antidepressant buproprion. *Psychological Bulletin, 24,* 143–148.

Connell, H., Irvine, L., & Rodney, J. (1982). Psychiatric disorder in Queensland primary school children. *Australian Pediatrics, 18,* 177–180.

Conners, C. K., Casat, C., Gualtieri, C. T., Weller, E., Reader, M., Reiss, A., Weller, R., Khayrallah, M., & Ascher, J. (1996). Buproprion hydrochloride in attention deficit disorder with hyperactivity. *Journal of the American Academy of Child and Adolescent Psychiatry, 35,* 1314–1321. (abstract)

Conners, C., Levin, E., March, J., Sparrow, E., & Erhardt, D. (1995). Neurocognitive and behavioral effects of nicotine in adult attention-deficit hyperactivity disorder (ADHD). *Psychopharmacology Bulletin, 31,* 559.

Conners, C. K., Eisenberg, L., & Barcai, A. (1967). Effect of dextroamphetamine on children: Studies on subjects with learning disabilities and school behavior problems. *Archives of General Psychiatry, 17,* 478–485.

Conners, K. C. (1975). Controlled trial of methylphenidate in preschool children with minimal brain dysfunction. *International Journal of Mental Health, 4*, 61–74. (abstract)

Connor, D. F., Barkley, R. A., & Davis, H. T. (2000). A pilot study of methylphenidate, clonidine, or the combination in ADHD comorbid with aggressive oppositional defiant or conduct disorder. *Clinical Pediatrics, 39*, 15–25.

Connor, D. F., Fletcher, K. E., & Swanson, J. (1999). A meta-analysis of clonidine for symptoms of attention-deficit hyperactivity disorder. *Journal of the Academy of Child and Adolescent Psychiatry, 38*, 1551–1559.

Costello, E. (1989). Child psychiatric disorders and their correlates: A primary care pediatric sample. *Journal of the American Academy of Child and Adolescent Psychiatry, 28*, 851–858. (abstract)

Derivan, A., Aquir, L., Preskorn, S., D'Amico, D., & Troy, S. (1995). A study of venlafaxine in children and adolescents with conduct disorder. In *Proceedings of the Annual Meeting of the American Academy of Child and Adolescent Psychiatry, 11*, 128. (abstract)

Douglas, V. I., Barr, R. G., Amin, K., O'Neill, M. E., & Britton, B. G. (1988). Dose effects and individual responsivity to methylphenidate in attention deficit disorder. *Journal of Child Psychology and Psychiatry, 29*, 453–475.

Dulcan, M. (1990). Using psychostimulants to treat behavior disorders of children and adolescents. *Journal of Child and Adolescent Psychopharmacology, 1*, 7–20.

DuPaul, G., Barkley, R., & McMurray, M. (1994). Response of children with ADHD to methylphenidate: Interaction with internalizing symptoms. *Journal of the American Academy of Child and Adolescent Psychiatry*, 33(6), 894–903.

DuPaul, G., & Rapport, M. (1993). Does MPH normalize the classroom performance of children with attention deficit disorder? *Journal of the American Academy of Child and Adolescent Psychiatry, 32*, 190–198.

DuPaul, G. J., & Barkley, R. A. (1990). Medication therapy. In R. A. Barkley (Ed.), *Attention deficit hyperactivity disorder: A handbook for diagnosis and treatment* (2nd ed., pp. 573–612). New York: Guilford Press.

Eisenberg, L., Lachman, R., Molling, P., Lockner, A., Mizelle, J., & Conners, C. (1961). A psychopharmacologic experiment in a training school for deliquent boys: Methods, problems and findings. *American Journal of Orthopsychiatry, 33*, 431–447.

Elia, J., Borcherding, B., Rapoport, J., & Keysor, C. (1991). Methylphenidate and dextroamphetamine treatments of hyperactivity: Are there true nonresponders? *Psychiatry Research, 36*, 141–155.

Ernst, M., Liebenauer, L., Jons, P., Murphy, D., & Zametkin, A. (1995). L-Deprenyl on behavior and plasma monoamine metabolites in hyperactive adults. *Psychopharmacology Bulletin, 31*, 565.

Ernst, M., & Zametkin, A. (1995). The interface of genetics, neuroimaging, and neurochemistry in attention-deficit hyperactivity disorder. In F. Bloom & D. Kupfer (Eds.), *Psychopharmacology: The fourth generation of progress* (4th ed., pp. 1643–1652). New York: Raven Press.

Esser, G., Schmidt, M., & Woerner, W. (1996). Epidemiology and course of psychiatric disorders in school-age children—results of a longitudinal study. *Journal of Child Psychology and Psychiatry, 31*, 243–253.

Gadow, K. (1991). Effects of stimulant drugs on academic performance in hyperactive and learning disabled children. *Journal of Learning Disorders, 16*, 190–199.

Gadow, K., Sverd, J., Sprafkin, J., Nolan, E., & Ezor, S. (1995). Efficacy of methylphenidate for attention deficit hyperactivity in children with tic disorder. *Archives of General Psychiatry, 52*, 444–455.

Gillberg, C., Melander, H., von Knorring, A., Janols, L., Thernlund, G., Heggel, B., Edievall-Walin, L., Gustafsson, P., & Kopp, S. (1997). Long-term central stimulant treatment of children with attention-deficit hyperactivity disorder. A randomized double-blind placebo-controlled trial. *Archives of General Psychiatry, 54*, 857–864. (abstract)

Gittelman, K. (1987). Pharmacotherapy of childhood hyperactivity: An update. In H. Y. Meltzer (Ed.), *Psychopharmacology: The third generation of progress.* (3rd ed.). New York: Raven.

Gittelman, R. (1980). Drug treatment of child psychiatric disorders. In D. F. Klein, R. Gittelman, F. Quitkin, & A. Rifkin (Eds.), *Diagnosis and drug treatment of psychiatric disorders* (2nd ed.). Baltimore: Williams & Wilkins.

Gittelman, R., & Kanner, A. (1986). Psychopharmacotherapy. In H. Quay & J. Werry (Eds.), *Psychopathological disorders of childhood* (3rd ed.). New York: Wiley.

Gittelman, R., & Mannuzza, S. (1988). Hyperactive boys almost grown up: 3. Methylphenidate effects on ultimate height. *Archives of General Psychiatry, 45*, 1131–1134.

Gittelman-Klein, R. (1980). Diagnosis and drug treatment of childhood disorders: Attention deficit disorder with hyperactivity. In R. Klein & F. Quitkin (Eds.), *Diagnosis and drug treatment of psychiatric disorders: Adults and children.* (2nd ed.). Baltimore: Williams & Wilkins.

Gittelman-Klein, R., Landa, B., Mattes, J. A., & Klein, D. F. (1988). Methylphenidate and growth in hyperactive children. *Archives of General Psychiatry, 45,* 1127–1130.

Goldman, L., Genel, M., Bazman, R., & Slanetz, P. (1998). Diagnosis and treatment of attention-deficit/hyperactivity disorder. *Journal of the American Medical Association, 279,* 1100–1107. (abstract)

Greenhill, L. (1995). Attention-deficit hyperativity disorder: The stimulants. *Child and Adolescent Psychiatric Clinics, 4*(1), 123–168.

Greenhill, L., Abikoff, H., Conners, C. K., Elliott, G., Hechtman, L., Hinshaw, S., Hoza, B., Jensen, P., Kraemer, H., March, J., Newcorn, J., Pelham, W., Richters, J., Schiller, E., Severe, J., Swanson, J., Vereen, D., & Wells, K. (1996). Medication treatment strategies in the MTA: Relevance to clinicians and researchers. *Journal of the American Academy of Child and Adolescent Psychiatry Psychiatry, 35,* 444–454.

Greenhill, L., Swanson, J. M., Vitiello, B., Davies, M., Clevenger, W., Wu, M., Arnold, L. E., Abikoff, H. B., Conners, C. K., Elliott, G., Hechtman, L., Hinshaw, S. P., Hoza, B., Jensen, P. S., Kraemer, H. C., March, J. S., Newcorn, J. H., Pelham, W. E., Severe, J. B., Wells, K., & Wigal, T. (2001). Determining the best dose of methylphenidate under controlled conditions: Lessons from the MTA titration. *Journal of the American Academy of Child and Adolescent Psychiatry, 40,* 180–187.

Greenhill, L. L. (1981). Stimulant-relation growth inhibition in children: A review. In M. Gittelman (Ed.), *Strategic interventions for hyperactive children.* Armonk, NY: M. E. Sharpe.

Greenhill, L. L. (1984). Stimulant related growth inhibition in children: A review. In B. Shopsin (Ed.), *The psychobiology of childhood.* New York: SP Medical & Scientific Books.

Greenhill, L. L., Puig-Antich, J., Chambers, W., Rubinstein, B., Halpern, F., & Sachar, E. J. (1981). Growth hormone, prolactin, and growth responses in hyperkinetic males treated with D-amphetamine. *Journal of the American Academy of Child and Adolescent Psychiatry, 20,* 84–103.

Greenhill, L. L., Puig-Antich, J., Novacenko, H., Solomon, M., Anghern, C., Florea, J., Goetz, R., Fiscina, B., & Sachar, E. J. (1984). Prolactin, growth hormone and growth responses in boys with attention deficit disorder and hyperactivity treated with methylphenidate. *Journal of the American Academy of Child and Adolescent Psychiatry, 23*(1), 58–67.

Gualtieri, C. T., Kanoy, R., Koriath, U., Schroeder, S., Youngblood, W., Breese, G. R., & Prange, A. J. (1981). Growth hormone and prolactin secretion in adults and hyperactive children relation to methylphenidate serum levels. *Psychoneurology, 6*(4), 331–339.

Halperin, J. M., Matier, K., Bedi, G., Sharma, S., & Newcorn, J. H. (1992). Specificity of inattention, impulsivity, and hyperactivity to the diagnosis of attention-deficit disorder. *Journal of the American Academy of Child and Adolescent Psychiatry, 31*(2), 190–196. (abstract)

Hechtman, L., & Weiss, G. (1984). Hyperactives as young adults: Initial predictors of adult outcome. *Journal of the American Academy of Child and Adolescent Psychiatry, 23,* 250–260.

Hinshaw, S. (1991). Effects of methylphenidate on aggressive and antisocial behavior. *Proceedings of the American Academy of Child and Adolescent Psychiatry, 7,* 31–32. (abstract)

Hinshaw, S. (1994). *Attention deficits and hyperactivity in children.* Thousand Oaks, CA: Sage.

Hinshaw, S., Heller, T., & McHale, J. (1992). Covert antisocial behavior in boys with attention-deficit hyperactivity disorder: External validation and effects of methylphendiate. *Journal of Consulting and Clinical Psychology, 60,* 274–281.

Hinshaw, S., March, J., Abikoff, H., Arnold, L., Cantwell, D., Conners, C., Elliott, G., Halperin, J., Greenhill, L., Hechtman, L., Hoza, B., Jensen, P., Newcorn, J., McBurnett, K., Pelham, W., Richters, J., Severe, J., Schiller, E., Swanson, J., Vereen, D., Wells, K., & Wigal, T. (1997). Comprehensive assessment of childhood attention-deficit hyperactivity disorder in the context of a multisite, multimodal clinical trial. *Journal of Attention Disorders, 1,* 217–234. (abstract)

Hinton, S., Conners, C., Levin, E., & Meck, W. (1995). Nicotine and attention-deficit disorder: Effects on temporal generalization. *Psychopharmacology Bulletin, 31,* 579. (abstract)

Horn, W. F., Islongo, N. S., Pascoe, J. M., Greenberg, G., Packard, T., Lopez, M., Wagner, A., & Puttler, L. (1991). Additive effects of psychostimulants, parent training, and self-control therapy with ADHD children. *Journal of the American Academy of Child and Adolescent Psychiatry, 30*(2), 233–240.

Hornig-Roher, M., & Amsterdam, J. (1995). Venlafaxine verus stimulant therapy in patients with dual diagnosis of attention deficit disorder and depression. *Psychological Bulletin, 3,* 580. (abstract)

Humphries, T., Kinsbourne, M., & Swanson, J. (1978). Stimulant effects on cooperation and social interaction between hyperactive children and their mothers. *Journal of Child Psychology and Psychiatry, 19*, 13–22.

Hunt, R., Arnstan, A., & Asbell, M. (1995). An open trial of guanfacine in the treatment of attention-deficit hyperactivity disorder. *Journal of the American Academy of Child and Adolescent Psychiatry, 34*, 41–50.

Hunt, R., Minderaa, R., & Cohen, D. (1985). Clonidine benefits children with attention deficit disorder and hyperactivity: Report of a double-blind placebo-crossover therapeutic trial. *Journal of the American Academy of Child and Adolescent Psychiatry, 24*, 617–629.

Ickowicz, A., Tannock, R., Fulford, P., Purvis, K., & Schachar, R. (1992). Transient tics and compulsive behaviors following methylphenidate: Evidence from a placebo controlled double blind clinical trial. *American Academy of Child and Adolescent Psychiatry, Scientific Proceedings of the Annual Meeting, 8*, 70.

Jacobsen, L., Chappell, P., & Woolish, J. (1994). Buproprion and compulsive behavior. *Journal of the American Academy of Child and Adolescent Psychiatry, 33*, 140–144. (abstract)

Jacobsen, N., & Truax, P. (1991). Clinical significance: A statistical approach to defining meaningful change in psychotherapy research. *Journal of Consulting and Clinical Psychology, 50*, 12–19.

Jacobvitz, D., Srouge, L. A., Stewart, M., & Leffert, N. (1990). Treatment of attentional and hyperactivity problems in children with sympathomimetic drugs: A comprehensive review. *Journal of the American Academy of Child and Adolescent Psychiatry*, 29(5), 677–688.

Jensen, P., Bhatara, V., Vitiello, B., Hoagwood, K., Feil, M., & Burke, L. (1999a). Psychoactive medication prescribing practices for US children: Gaps between research and clinical practice. *Journal of the American Academy of Child and Adolescent Psychiatry, 38*, 557–565.

Jensen, P., Kettle, L., Roper, M., Sloan, M., Dulcan, M., Hoven, C., Bird, H., Bauermeister, J. & Payne, J. (1999b). Are stimulants overprescribed? Treatment of ADHD in 4 US communities. *Journal of the American Academy of Child and Adolescent Psychiatry, 38*, 797–804.

Kavale, K. (1982). The efficacy of stimulant drug treatment for hyperactivity: A meta-analysis. *Journal of Learning Disorders, 15*, 280–289.

Klein, R., & Wender, P. (1995). The role of methylphenidate in psychiatry. *Archives of General Psychiatry, 52*, 429–433.

Klorman, R., Brumagham, J., Fitzpatrick, P., & Burgstedt, A. (1990). Clinical effects of a controlled trial of methylphenidate on adolescents with attention deficit disorder. *Journal of the American Academy of Child and Adolescent Psychiatry, 29*, 702–709.

Laufer, M. W., Denhoff, E., & Solomon, G. (1957). Hyperkinetic impulsive disorder in children's behavior problems. *Psychosomatic Medicine, 19*, 38–49.

Leech, S. L., Richardson, G. A., Goldschmidt, L., & Day, N. L. (1999). Prenatal substance exposure: Effects on attention and impulsivity of 6-year-olds. *Neurotoxicology and Teratology, 21*, 109–118. (abstract)

LeFever, G., Sawson, K. V., & Morrow, A. L. (1999). The extent of drug therapy for attention deficit-hyperactivity disorder among children in public schools. *American Journal of Public Health, 89*, 1359–1364.

Lord, C., Rutter, M., & Le Couteur, A. (1994). Autism diagnostic interview—revised: A revised version of a diagnostic interview for caregivers of individuals with possible pervasive developmental disorders. *Journal of Autism and Developmental Disorders, 24*, 659–685. (abstract)

Luh, J., Pliszka, S. R., Olvera, R., & Taton, R. (1995). An open trial of venlafaxine in the treatment of ADHD. *Proceedings of the Annual Meeting of the American Academy of Child and Adolescent Psychiatry, 11*, 122. (abstract)

Mannuzza, S., Klein, R., Bessler, A., Malloy, P., & LaPadula, M. (1993). Adult outcome of hyperactive boys: Educational achievement, occupational rank and psychiatric status. *Archives of General Psychiatry, 50*, 565–576.

Mannuzza, S., Klein, R., Bonagura, N., Malloy, P., Giampino, T., & Addlii, K. (1991). Hyperactive boys almost grown up: 5. Replication of psychiatric status. *Archives of General Psychiatry, 48*, 77–83.

March, J., Conners, C. K., Erhardt, D., & Johnston, H. (1994). Pharmacotherapy of attention-deficit hyperactivity disorder. *Annals of Drug Therapy, 2*, 187–213.

Matochik, J., Liebenauer, L., King, A., Szymanski, H., Cohen, R., & Zametkin, A. (1994). Cerebral glucose metabolism in adults with attention deficit hyperactivity disorder after chronic stimulant treatment. *American Journal of Psychiatry, 151*, 658–664.

Matochik, J., Nordahl, T., Gross, M., Semple, M., King, A., Cohen, R., & Zametkin, A. (1993). Effects of acute stimulant medication on cerebral metabolism in adults with hyperactivity. *Neuropsychopharmacology, 8*, 377–386.

Mattes, J. A., Boswell, J., & Oliver, H. (1984). Methylphenidate effects on symptoms of attention deficit disorder in adults. *Archives of General Psychiatry, 41*, 449–456.

Mayes, S., Crites, D., Bixler, E., Humphrey, B., & Mattison, R. (1994). Methylphenidate and ADHD: Influence of age, IQ and neurodevelopmental status. *Developmental Medical Child Neurology, 36,* 1099–1107. (abstract)

McCormick, L., Rizzuo, G., & Knickes, H. (1994). A pilot study of buspirone in ADHD. *Archives of General Psychiatry, 3,* 68–70.

McCracken, J. (1991). A two-part model of stimulant action on attention-deficit hyperactivity disorder in children. *Journal of Neuropsychiatry in Clinical Neuroscience,* 3(2), 201–209.

McMaster University Evidence-Based Practice Center. (1998). The treatment of attention-deficit/hyperactivity disorder: An evidence report (contract 290–97-0017). (abstract)

Milich, R., Licht, B., & Murphy, D. (1989). Attention-deficit hyperactivity disorder in boys: Evaluations of and attributions for task performance on medication versus placebo. *Journal of Abnormal Psychology, 98,* 280–284.

MTA Cooperative Group. (1999). 14-month randomized clinical trial of treatment strategies for attention deficit hyperactivity disorder. *Archives of General Psychiatry, 56,* 1073–1086.

Musten, L., Firestone, P., Pisterman, S., Bennett, S., & Mercer, J. (1997). Effects of methylphenidate on preschool children with ADHD: Cognitive and behavioral functions. *Journal of the American Academy of Child and Adolescent Psychiatry, 36,* 1407–1415. (abstract)

Ottenbach, J., & Cooper, H. (1983). Drug treatment of hyperactivity in children. *Developmental Medicine in Child Neurology, 25,* 358–366.

Pelham, W. (1993). Pharmacotherapy for children with attention-deficit hyperactivity disorder. *School Psychology Review, 23,* 199–227.

Pelham, W., & Murphy, H. (1986). Behavioral and pharmacological treatment of hyperactivity and attention deficit disorders. In M. Hersen & J. Breuning (Eds.), *Pharmacological and behavioral treatment: An integrative approach.* New York: Wiley.

Pelham, W., Swanson, J., Forman, M., & Schwint, H. (1995a). Pemoline effects on children with ADHD: A time response by dose-reponse analysis on classroom measures. *Journal of the American Academy of Child and Adolescent Psychiatry, 34,* 1504–1514.

Pelham, W. E. (1989). Behavior therapy, behavioral assessment and psychostimulant medication in the treatment of attention deficit disorders: An interactive approach. In J. Swanson & L. Bloomingdale (Eds.), *Attention deficit disorder: 4. Emerging trends in the treatment of attention and behavioral problems in children.* London: Pergamon.

Pelham, W. E., & Bender, M. E. (1982). Peer relationships in hyperactive children: Description and treatment. In K. D. B. I. Gadow (Ed.), *Advances in learning and behavioral disabilities.* Greenwich, CT: JAI Press.

Pelham, W. E., Bender, M. E., Cadell, J., Booth, S., & Moorer, S. (1985). The dose-response effects of methylphenidate on classroom academic and social behavior in children with attention deficit disorder. *Archives of General Psychiatry, 42,* 948–952.

Pelham, W., Gnagy, E. M., Burrows-Maclean, L., Fabiano, W. A., Morrisey, S. M., Chronis, A. M., Forehand, G. L., Nguyen, C. A., Hoffman, M. T., Lock, T. M., Fiefelkon, K., Coles, E. K., Panahon, C. J., Strom, R. L., Meichenbaum, D. L. Onyango, A. W., & Morse, G. D. (2000a). Once-a-day concerta methylphenidate versus three-times-daily methylphenidate in laboratory and natural settings. *Pediatrics, 107,* E105.

Pelham, W. E., Greenslade, K. E., Vodde-Hamilton, M. A., Murphy, D. A, Greenstein, J. J., Gnagy, E. M., & Dahl, R. E. (1990). Relative efficacy of long-acting stimulants on ADHD children: A comparison of standard methylphenidate, Ritalin-SR, Dexedrine spansule, and pemoline. *Pediatrics, 86,* 226–237.

Pelham, W. E., Hoffman, M. T., Lock, T., & SUNY CONCERTA Study Group. (2000b). *Evaluation of once-a-day OROS methylphenidate HCl (MPH extended-release tablet versus MPH tid in children with ADHD in natural school settings.* Presented at the Pediatric Academic Societies and American Academy of Pediatrics Joint Meeting, Boston, MA, May 12–16, 2000. (abstract)

Pelham, W. E., & Milich, R. (1991). Individual differences in response to Ritalin in classwork and social behavior. In L. L. Greenhill & B. Osman (Eds.), *Ritalin: Theory and patient management.* New York: Mary Ann Liebert.

Pelham, W. E., Swanson, J., Furman, M., & Schwindt, H. (1995b). Pemoline effects of children with ADHD: A time-reponse by dose-response analysis on classroom measures. *Journal of the American Academy of Child and Adolescent Psychiatry, 34,* 1504–1514.

Perel, J. M., Greenhill, L. L., Curran, S., Feldman, B., & Puig-Antich, J. (1991). Correlates of pharmacokinetics and attentional measures in methylphenidate treated hyperactive children. *Clinical Pharmacology and Therapy,* 49(2), 160–161.

Pleak, R., & Gornly, L. (1995). Effects of venlafaxine treatment for ADHD in a child. *American Journal of Psychiatry, 152,* 1099.

Pliszka, S. R. (1989). Effect of anxiety on cognition, behavior, and stimulant response in ADHD. *Journal of the American Academy of Child and Adolescent Psychiatry*, 28(6), 882–887.

Pliszka, S. R., Greenhill, L., Crismon, L., Sedillo, A., Carlson, C., Conners, C. K., McCracken, J., Swanson, J., Hughes, C. W., Llana, M., Lopez, M., & Toprac, M., Texas Consensus Conference Panel on Medication Treatment of Childhood Attention Deficit Hyperactivity Disorder. (2000). The Texas Children's Medication Algorithm Project: Report of the Texas Expert Consensus Conference Panel on Medication Treatment of Childhood Attention Deficit Hyperactivity Disorder: 2. Tactics. *Journal of the Academy of Child and Adolescent Psychiatry*, 39, 920–927.

Quaison, N., Ward, D., & Kitchen, T. (1991). Buspirone for aggression. *Journal of the American Academy of Child and Adolescent Psychiatry*, 30, 1026.

Rapoport, J. L., Buchsbaum, M. S., Weingartner, H., Zahn, P., Ludlow, C., & Mikkelsen, E.J. (1980). Dextroamphetamine: Cognitive and behavioral effects in normal and hyperactive boys and normal men. *Archives of General Psychiatry*, 37, 933–943.

Rapport, M., Denney, C., DuPaul, G., & Gardner, M. (1994). Attention deficit disorder and methylphenidate: Normalization rates, clinical effectiveness and response prediction in 76 children. *Journal of the American Academy of Child and Adolescent Psychiatry*, 33(6), 882–893.

Rapport, M. D., DuPaul, G. J., & Kelly, K. L. (1989). Attention deficit hyperactivity disorder and methylphenidate: The relationship between gross body weight and drug response in children. *Psychopharmacology Bulletin*, 25(2), 285–290.

Ratey, J., Greenberg, M., & Lindem, K. (1991). Combination of treatments for attention deficit hyperactivity disorder in adults. *Journal of Nervous and Mental Disease*, 179(11), 699–701.

Reimherr, F., Hedges, D., Strong, R., & Wender, P. (1995). An open trial of venlafaxine in adult patients with ADHD. *Psychological Bulletin*, 31, 609–614.

Richters, J., Arnold, L., Abikoff, H., Conners, C., Greenhill, L., Hechtman, L., Hinshaw, S., Pelham, W., & Swanson, J. (1995). The National Institute of Mental Health Collaborative Multisite Multimodal Treatment Study of Children with Attention-Deficit Hyperactivity Disorder (MTA): 1. Background and rationale. *Journal of the American Academy of Child and Adolescent Psychiatry*, 34, 987–1000.

Roche, A. F., Lipman, R. S., Overall, J. E., & Hung, W. (1979). The effects of stimulant medication on the growth of hyperactive children. *Pediatrics*, 63(6), 847–849.

Sabelsky, D. (1990). Fluoxetine in adults with residual attention deficit disorder and hypersomnolence. *Journal of Neuropsychiatry and Clinical Neuroscience*, 2(4), 463–464.

Safer, D., & Allen, R. (1973). Factors influencing the suppressant effects of two stimulant drugs on the growth of hyperactive children. *Pediatrics*, 51, 660–667.

Safer, D., Allen, R., & Barr, E. (1972). Depression of growth in hyperactive children on stimulant drugs. *New England Journal of Medicine*, 287, 217–220.

Safer, D., Allen, R., & Barr, E. (1975). Growth rebound after termination of stimulant drugs. *Journal of Pediatrics*, 86, 113–116.

Safer, D., Zito, J., & Fine, E. (1996). Increased methylphenidate usage for attention deficit hyperactivity disorder in the 1990s. *Pediatrics*, 98, 1084–1088.

Satterfield, J. H., Cantwell, D. P., Schell, A., & Blaschke, T. (1979). Growth of hyperactive children with methylphenidate. *Archives of General Psychiatry*, 36, 212–217.

Schachar, R., & Tannock, R. (1993). Childhood hyperactivity and psychostimulants: A review of extended treatment studies. *Journal of Child and Adolescent Psychopharmacology*, 3, 81–97.

Schachar, R., Tannock, R., Cunningham, C., & Corkum, P. (1997). Behavioral, situational, and temporal effects of treatment of ADHD with methylphenidate. *Journal of the American Academy of Child and Adolescent Psychiatry*, 36, 754–763

Schechter, M., & Keuezer, E. (1985). Learning in hyperactive children: Are there stimulant-related and state-dependent effects? *Journal of Clinical Pharmacology*, 25, 276–280.

Schleifer, M., Weiss, G., Cohen, N., Elman, M., Cvejic, H., & Kruger, E. (1975). Hyperactivity in preschoolers and the effect of methylphenidate. *American Journal of Orthopsychiatry*, 45, 38–50.

Shaffer, D. (1994). Attention deficit hyperactivity disorder in adults. *American Journal of Psychiatry*, 151(5), 633–638.

Shekim, W., Masterson, A., Cantwell, D., & Hanna, G. (1989). Nomifensine maleate in adult attention deficit disorder. *Journal of Nervous and Mental Disease*, 177(5), 296–299.

Sherman, M. (1991). Prescribing practice of methylphenidate: The Suffolk County study. In B. Osman & L. L. Greenhill (Eds.), *Ritalin: Theory and patient management*. New York: Mary Ann Liebert.

Simeon, J. G., Ferguson, H. B., & Van Wyck Fleet, J. (1986). Buproprion effects in attention deficit and conduct disorders. *Canadian Journal of Psychiatry, 31,* 581–585.

Solanto, M. V. (1984). Neuropharmacological basis of stimulant drug action in attention deficit disorder with hyperactivity: A review and synthesis. *Psychological Bulletin, 95,* 387–409.

Speltz, M. L., Varley, C. K., Peterson, K., & Beilke, R. L. (1988). Effects of dextroamphetamine and contingecy management on a preschooler with ADHD and oppositional defiant disorder. *Journal of the American Academy of Child and Adolescent Psychiatry,* 27(2), 175–178.

Spencer, T., Biederman, J., Harding, M., Faraone, S., & Wilens, T. (1996b). Growth deficits in ADHD children revisited: Evidence for disorder related growth delays. *Journal of the American Academy of Child and Adolescent Psychiatry, 35,* 1460–1467. (abstract)

Spencer, T., Biederman, J., Wilens, T., Harding, M., O'Donnell, D., & Griffin, S. (1996a). Pharmacotherapy of attention-deficit hyperactivity disorder across the life cycle. *Journal of the American Academy of Child and Adolescent Psychiatry, 35,* 409–432.

Spencer, T., Biederman, J., Wilens, T., Steingard, R., & Geist, D. (1993). Buproprion exacerbates tics in children with attention-deficit hyperactivity disorder and Tourette's syndrome. *Journal of the American Academy of Child and Adolescent Psychiatry,* 32(1), 211–214.

Spencer, T., Wilens, T., Biederman, J., Farone, S., Ablen, S., & Lapey, K. (1995). A double-blind, crossover comparison of methylphenidate and placebo in adults with childhood onset ADHD. *Archives of General Psychiatry, 52,* 434–443.

Sprague, R. L., & Sleator, E. K. (1977). Methylphenidate in hyperkinetic children: Differences in dose effects on learning and social behavior. *Science, 198,* 1274–1276.

Stephens, R., Pelham, W. E., & Skinner, R. (1984). The state-dependent and main effects of pemoline and methylphenidate on paired-associates learning and spelling in hyperactive children. *Journal of Consulting and Clinical Psychology, 52,* 104–113.

Swanson, J. (1993). Effect of stimulant medication on hyperactive children: A review of reviews. *Exceptional Child, 60,* 154–162.

Swanson, J., Flockhart, D., Udrea, D., Cantwell, D., Conner, D., & Williams, L. (1995b). Clonidine in the treatment of ADHD: Questions about the safety and efficacy. *Journal of Child and Adolescent Psychopharmacology, 5,* 301–305.

Swanson, J., & Kinsbourne, M. (1976). Stimulant-related state-dependent learning in hyperactive children. *Science,* 192(4246), 1354–1357.

Swanson, J., Lerner, M., & Williams, L. (1995a). More frequent diagnosis of attention deficit-hyperactivity disorder. *New England Journal of Medicine, 333,* 944.

Swanson, J., Sale, M., & Laurenza, A. (2000). Pediatric pharmacokinetics/pharmacodynamics of GW320659 in attention-deficit/hyperactivity disorder. Unpublished manuscript.

Szatmari, P. (1992). The epidemiology of attention-deficit hyperactivity disorders. *Child and Adolescent Psychiatric Clinics, 1,* 361–371.

Szatmari, P., Offord, D., & Boyle, M. (1989). Ontario child health study: Prevalence of attention deficit disorder with hyperactivity. *Journal of Child Psychology and Psychiatry & Allied Disciplines, 30,* 219–230.

Tannock, R., Ickowicz, A., & Schachar, R. (1995). Differential effects of MPH on working memory in ADHD children with and without comorbid anxiety. *Journal of the American Academy of Child and Adolescent Psychiatry, 34,* 886–896.

Tannock, R., Schachar, R., & Logan, R. (1993). Methylphenidate and working memory: Differential effects in attention-deficit hyperactivity disorder (ADHD) with and without memory. *AACAP, Scientific Proceedings of the Annual Meeting, 9,* 42.

Taylor, E., Sandberg, S., Thorley, G., & Rutter, M. (1991). The epidemiology of childhood hyperactivity. In E. Taylor & M. Rutter (Eds.), *Child Psychiatry.* London: Oxford University Press.

Thurber, S., & Walker, C. (1983). Medication and hyperactivity: A meta-analysis. *Journal of General Psychiatry, 108,* 79–86.

Velez, C., Johnson, J., & Cohen, P. (1989). A longitudinal analysis of selected risk factors for childhood psychopathology. *Journal of the American Academy of Child and Adolescent Psychiatry, 28,* 861–871.

Verhulst, F., Eussen, M., & Berden, G. (1992). Pathways of problem behaviors from childhood to adolescence. *Journal of the American Academy of Child and Adolescent Psychiatry,* 32, 388–392.

Vikan, A. (1985). Psychiatric epidemiology in a sample of 1,510 ten-year-old children: 1. Prevalence. *Journal of Child Psychology and Psychiatry, 26,* 55–60. (abstract)

Vitiello, B., & Jensen, P. (1995). Developmental perspectives in pediatric psychopharmacology. *Psychopharmacology Bulletin, 31,* 75–81.

Vitiello, B., & Jensen, P. (1997). Medication development and testing in children and adolescents. *Archives of General Psychiatry, 54,* 871–876. (abstract)

Volkow, N., Ding, J., Fowler, G., Wang, J., Logan, J., Gatley, J., Dewey, S., Ashby, C., Lieberman, J., Hitzemann, R., & Wolf, A. (1995). Is methylphenidate like cocaine? *Archives of General Psychiatry, 52*, 456–464.

Vyborova, L., Nahunek, K., Drtilkova, I., Balastikova, B., & Misurec, J. (1984). Intraindividual comparison of 21-day application of amphetamine and methylphenidate in hyperkinetic children. *Activas Nervosa Superior, 26*, 268–269.

Weiss, G., & Hechtman, L. (1993). *Hyperactive children grown up*. New York: Guilford Press.

Weiss, G., Hechtman, L., Milroy, T., & Perlman, T. (1985). Psychiatric status of hyperactives as adults: A controlled prospective 15-year follow-up of 63 hyperactive children. *Journal of the American Academy of Child and Adolescent Psychiatry, 24*, 211–220.

Wender, P. (1994). *Attention deficit/hyperactivity disorder in adults*. Grand Rounds, New York State Psychiatric Institute, September 9, 1994, New York. (unpublished)

Wender, P., & Reimherr, F. (1990). Bupropion treatment of attention-deficit hyperactivity disorder in adults. *American Journal of Psychiatry, 147*(8), 1018–1020.

Wender, P., Reimherr, F., & Wood, D. (1985). A controlled study of methylphenidate in the treatment of attention deficit disorder. *American Journal of Psychiatry, 142*, 547–552.

Wender, P., Wood, D., Reimherr, F., & Ward, M. (1994). An open trial of pargyline in the treatment of adult attention deficit disorder, residual type. *Psychiatry Research, 9*, 329–336.

Wender, P. H., Reimherr, F., & Wood, D. (1981). Attention deficit disorder in adults. *Archives of General Psychiatry, 38*, 449–456.

Werry, J., Biederman, J., Thisted, R., Greenhill, L., & Ryan, N. (1995). Resolved: Cardiac arryhthmias make desipramine an unacceptable choice in children. *Journal of the American Academy of Child and Adolescent Psychiatry, 34*, 1239–1248.

Whalen, C., Henker, B., Buhrmester, D., Hinshaw, S., Huber, A., & Laski, K. (1989). Does stimulant medication improve the peer status of hyperactive children? *Journal of Consulting and Clinical Psychology, 57*, 545–549.

Wilens, T. E., & Biederman, J. (1992). The stimulants. *Psychiatric Clinic of North America, 15*(1), 191–222.

Wilens, T., Biederman, J., Mick, E., & Spencer, T. (1994a). Treatment of adult attention-deficit hyperactivity disorder (ADHD) with tricyclic antidepressants: Clinical experience with 23 patients. *American Academy of Child and Adolescent Psychiatry, Scientific Proceedings of the Annual Meeting, 9*, 45.

Wilens, T., Biederman, J., & Spencer, T. (1994b). Clonidine for sleep disturbances associated with attention deficit hyperactivity disorder. *Journal of the American Academy of Child and Adolescent Psychiatry, 33*, 424–427.

Wilens, T., Biederman, J., & Spencer, T. (1995). Venlafaxine for adult ADHD. *American Journal of Psychiatry, 152*, 1099–1100.

Williams, L., & Swanson, J. (1996). *Some aspects of the efficacy and safety of clonidine in children with ADHD*. (unpublished)

Winsberg, B. G., Press, M., Bialer, I., & Kupietz, S. (1974). Dextroamphetamine and methylphenidate in the treatment of hyperactive/aggressive children. *Pediatrics, 53*, 236–241.

Wolraich, M., Greenhill, L. L., Abikoff, H., Atkins, M., August, G., Biederman, J., Bukstein, O., Conners, C., Chinglin, L., Gupta, S., Hoffman, M., Lerner, M., MacBurnett, K., McDaniel, D., O'Connell, M., Polombo, D., Pelham, W. E., Quinta, D., Ryan, K., Seither, K., Stein, M., Strasser, B., Swanson, J., & Waxman, D. (2000). *Randomized controlled trial of OROS methylphenidate Q.D. in children with attention-deficit/hyperactivity disorder*. (unpublished)

Wolraich, M., Greenhill, L., Pelham, W., Swanson, J., Wilens, T., Palumbo, D., Atkins, M., McBurnett, K., Bukstein, O., & August, G. (2001). Randomized, controlled trial of OROS methylphenidate once a day in children with Attention-Deficit/Hyperactivity disorder. *Pediatrics, 108*, 833–892.

Zametkin, A. J., & Rapoport, J. L. (1987). Neurobiology of attention deficit disorder with hyperactivity: Where have we come in 50 years? *Journal of the American Academy of Child and Adolescent Psychiatry Psychiatry, 26*, 676–686.

3

Psychosocial Treatments for Conduct Disorder in Children and Adolescents

Alan E. Kazdin

Antisocial and aggressive behavior in children (conduct disorder) is extremely difficult to treat in light of the stability of the problem, the untoward long-term prognosis, and the diverse domains of dysfunction in the child, parent, and family with which the problem is associated. Significant advances have been made in treatment. Five Type 1 treatments with strong evidence in their behalf (randomized controlled clinical trials) with children and adolescents are reviewed: *Parent management training* is directed at altering parent-child interactions in the home, particularly those interactions related to child-rearing practices and coercive interchanges. *Multisystemic therapy* focuses on the individual, family, and extrafamilial systems and their interrelations as a way to reduce symptoms and promote prosocial behavior. Multiple treatments are used in combination to address domains that affect the child. *Cognitive problem-solving skills training* focuses on cognitive processes that underlie social behavior and response repertoires in interpersonal situations. *Functional family therapy* utilizes principles of systems theory and behavior modification for altering interaction, communication patterns, and problem solving among family members. *Brief strategic family therapy* focuses on the structure of the family and concrete strategies that can be used to promote improved patterns of interaction. This treatment has been developed with Hispanic children and adolescents and has integrated culturally pertinent issues to engage the families. Questions remain about the long-term impact of various treatments, the persons for whom one or more of these treatments is well suited, and ways of optimizing therapeutic change. Even so, extensive evidence suggests there are treatments of choice for conduct disorder.

Antisocial behaviors in children refer to a variety of acts that reflect social rule violations and actions against others. Such behaviors as fighting, lying, and stealing are seen in varying degrees in most children over the course of development. Conduct disorder (CD) refers to antisocial behavior that is clinically significant and clearly beyond the realm of "normal" functioning. The extent to which antisocial behaviors are sufficiently severe to constitute CD depends on several characteristics of the behaviors, including their frequency, intensity, and chronicity; whether they are isolated acts or part of a larger syndrome with other deviant behaviors, and whether they lead to significant impairment of the child, as judged by parents, teachers, or others.

The significance of CD as a clinical and social problem derives from several factors (Kazdin, 1995b; Stoff, Breiling, & Maser, 1997). Conduct disorder is one of the most frequent bases of clinical referral in child and adolescent treatment services and encompasses from one third to one half of referral cases. Moreover the disorder has a poor long-term prognosis and is transmitted across generations. Because children with CD often traverse multiple social services in childhood, adolescence, and adulthood (e.g., special education, mental health, juvenile justice), the disorder is one of the most costly mental disorders in the United States (Robins, 1981).

Until recently, there has been little in the way of effective treatments for such children and adolescents.[1] This chapter reviews significant advances in treatments including those with well-established evidence and others that show considerable promise. The treatments were selected because they have been carefully evaluated in controlled clinical trials with children and adolescents. The chapter describes and evaluates the underpinnings, techniques, and evidence in behalf of these treatments. Limitations of the current evidence and research priorities are also examined.

CHARACTERISTICS OF CONDUCT DISORDER

Descriptive Features: Diagnosis and Prevalence

The overriding feature of CD is a persistent pattern of behavior in which the rights of others and age-appropriate social norms are violated. Isolated acts of physical aggression, destruction of property, stealing, and fire setting are sufficiently severe to warrant concern and attention in their own right. Although these behaviors may occur in isolation, several of them are likely to appear together as a constellation or syndrome and form the basis of a clinical diagnosis. For example, in the fourth edition of the *Diagnostic and Statistical Manual of Mental Disorders* (*DSM-IV*; American Psychiatric Association [APA], 1994), the diagnosis of Conduct Disorder is reached if the child shows at least 3 of the 15 symptoms within the past 12 months, with at least 1 symptom evident within the past 6 months. The symptoms include bullying others, initiating fights, using a weapon, being physically cruel to others or to animals, stealing items of nontrivial value, stealing while confronting a victim, fire setting, destroying property, breaking into others' property, staying out late, running away, lying, and truancy.[2]

Based on these diagnostic criteria or criteria from prior versions of the *DSM*, the prevalence of the disorder among community samples of school-aged youth is approximately 2 to 6% (see Zoccolillo, 1993). One of the most frequent findings is that boys show approximately three to four times higher rates of CD than girls. Rates of CD tend to be higher for adolescents (approximately 7% for youths ages 12 to 16) than for children (approximately 4% for children age 4 to 11 years, Offord, Boyle, & Racine, 1991). The higher prevalence rate for boys is associated primarily with childhood-onset CD; the boy-to-girl ratio evens out in adolescence. Characteristic symptom patterns tend to differ as well. Child-onset conduct problems tend to reflect aggressive behavior, whereas adolescent-onset problems tend to reflect delinquent behavior (theft, vandalism).

The prevalence rates are only approximations of CD as a dysfunction among children and adolescents. Moreover, they are likely to reflect a gross underestimation of the extent of the problem. The criteria for delineating individual symptoms and the diagnosis are recognized to be somewhat arbitrary. Youths who approximate but fail to meet the diagnosis, sometimes referred to as *subsyndromal*, often are significantly impaired (Angold, Costello, Farmer, Burns, & Erkanli, 1999). It is likely that CD is better represented as a continuum or set of continua based on the number, severity, and duration of symptoms and degree of impairment rather than as a condition achieved by a particular cutoff (Boyle et al., 1996; Offord et al., 1992). Individuals who miss the cutoff criteria for the diagnosis are likely to show impairment and poor long-term prognoses, although to a lesser extent as a function of the degree of dysfunction.

The general pattern of conduct-disordered behavior has been studied extensively using varied populations (e.g., clinical referrals and delinquent samples) and defining criteria (Kazdin, 1995b; Stoff et al., 1997). There is widespread agreement and evidence that a constellation of antisocial behaviors can be identified and has correlates related to child, parent, and family functioning. Moreover, antisocial behaviors included in the constellation extend beyond those included in the diagnosis (e.g., substance abuse, associating with delinquent peers).

Onset and Long-Term Clinical Course

Conduct disorder is not a homogeneous disorder. Indeed, two children might meet diagnostic criteria for the disorder but not share any of the symptoms. Even for a group of children who closely resemble each other in symptoms, it is unlikely that CD results from a single cause or simple set of antecedents. Current work tends to focus on characteristics, events, and experiences that influence the likelihood (increase the risk) of CD. Numerous factors that predispose children and adolescents to CD have been identified in the context of clinically referred and adjudicated youths. Table 3.1 highlights several risk factors that have been studied.

Merely enumerating risk factors is misleading without conveying some of the complexities of how they operate. These complexities have direct implications for interpreting the findings, for understanding the disorder, and for identifying at-risk children for preventive interventions. First, risk factors tend to come in "packages." Thus, at a given point in time, several factors may be present, such as low income, large family size, overcrowding, poor housing, poor parental supervision, parent criminality, and marital discord, to mention a few (Kazdin, 1995b). Second, over time, several risk factors become interrelated, because the presence of one factor can lead to the accumulation of other risk factors. For example, early aggression can lead to poor peer relations, aca-

TABLE 3.1 Factors That Place Youths at Risk for the Onset of Conduct Disorder

Child Factors

Child Temperament. A more difficult child temperament (on a dimension of "easy-to-difficult"), as characterized by more negative mood, lower levels of approach toward new stimuli, and less adaptability to change

Neuropsychological Deficits and Difficulties. Deficits in diverse functions related to language (e.g., verbal learning, verbal fluency, verbal IQ), memory, motor coordination, integration of auditory and visual cues, and "executive" functions of the brain (e.g., abstract reasoning, concept formation, planning, control of attention)

Subclinical Levels of Conduct Disorder. Early signs (e.g., elementary school) of mild ("subclinical") levels of unmanageability and aggression, especially with early age of onset; multiple types of antisocial behaviors; and multiple situations in which they are evident (e.g., at home and school, in the community)

Poor Bonding/Attachment to Conventional Values. Little interest in or commitment to school and family life

Academic and Intellectual Performance. Academic deficiencies and lower levels of intellectual functioning

Parent and Family Factors

Psychopathology and Criminal Behavior in the Family. Criminal behavior, antisocial personality disorder, and alcoholism of the parent

Parent-Child Punishment. Harsh (e.g., severe corporal punishment) and inconsistent punishment

Monitoring of the Child. Poor supervision, lack of monitoring of whereabouts, and few rules about where youth can go and when they can return

Quality of the Family Relationships. Less parental acceptance of their children; less warmth, affection, and emotional support; and less attachment

Family Activities. Few activities with the family (e.g., recreational, religious)

Marital Discord. Unhappy marital relationships, interpersonal conflict, and aggression of the parents

Family Size. Larger family size (i.e., more children in the family)

Sibling with Antisocial Behavior. Presence of a sibling, especially an older brother, with antisocial behavior

Socioeconomic Disadvantage. Poverty, overcrowding, unemployment, receipt of social assistance ("welfare"), and poor housing

Other Factors

Prenatal and Perinatal Complications. Pregnancy- and birth-related complications, including maternal infection, prematurity and low birth weight, impaired respiration at birth, and minor birth injury

Exposure to Violence. Exposure in the home, in neighborhood, on TV, and other forms of violence

Antisocial Peers. Association of the child with peers who engage in aggressive and antisocial behavior

School-Related Factors. Attending schools where there is little emphasis on academic work, little teacher time spent on lessons, infrequent teacher use of praise and appreciation of schoolwork, little emphasis on individual responsibility of the students, poor working conditions for pupils (e.g., furniture in poor repair), unavailability of the teacher to deal with children's problems, and low teacher expectancies

Note. The list of risk factors highlights major influences. The number of factors and the relations of specific factors to risk are more complex than the summary statements noted here. For a more detailed discussion, other sources can be consulted (e.g., Kazdin, 1995b; Loeber & Farrington, 1998; Stoff et al., 1997).

demic dysfunction, and dropping out of school, which further increase risk for CD.

Third, risk factors may interact with (i.e., be moderated or influenced by) each other and with other variables such as age, sex, and ethnicity of the child. As one example, large family size has been repeatedly shown to be a risk factor for CD. However, the importance of family size as a predictor is moderated by income. If family income and living accommodations are adequate, family size is less likely to be a risk factor (West, 1982). As another example, risk factors often interact with age of the child (e.g., infancy, early or middle childhood). For example, marital discord or separation appear to serve as risk factors primarily when they occur early in the child's life (e.g., within the first 4 or 5 years; Wadsworth, 1979). How risk factors exert impact in childhood and why some periods of development are sensitive to particular influences underscore the importance of understanding "normal" developmental processes.

No single characteristic or factor seems to be necessary or sufficient for the onset of the disorder. Even though some risk factors are more important than others, the accumulation of factors (i.e., number present) itself is important. One or two risk factors may not increase risk very much. With several risk factors, however, the likelihood of the outcome may increase sharply (e.g., Rutter, Tizard, & Whitmore, 1970; Sanson et al., 1991). Even with the presence of multiple risk factors, the outcome is not determined. Some individuals at high risk may not show any dysfunction (Werner & Smith, 1992). Many factors that contribute to reducing risk, referred to as *protective factors*, have been identified, but these are less well studied than risk factors (see Kazdin, 1995b).

Risk factors are usually discussed in relation to onset of a disorder, identification of cases for preventive intervention, and long-term course. Risk factors are quite relevant to treatment as well. For example, children referred to treatment for CD vary in the extent to which the risk factors (in Table 3.1) are present. A greater number of risk factors present among clinically referred youths predict lower response to treatment (Kazdin & Wassell, 1999).

Longitudinal studies have consistently shown that CD identified in childhood predicts a continued course of social dysfunction, problematic behavior, and poor school adjustment. The classic study in this area showed that antisocial child behavior predicts multiple problems in adulthood 30 years later (Robins, 1966). Youths who are referred for their antisocial behavior, compared to youths with other clinical problems or matched "normal" controls, are likely to show psychiatric symptoms, criminal behavior, physical health problems, and social maladjustment in adulthood. Even though CD portends a number of other significant problems, not all antisocial children suffer impairment as adults. Drawing from multiple samples, Robins (1978) noted that among the most severely antisocial children, less than 50% become antisocial adults. If diverse diagnoses are considered, rather than serious antisocial behavior alone, the picture of impairment in adulthood is much worse. Among youths referred for antisocial behavior, 84% received a diagnosis of some psychiatric disorder as adults (Robins, 1966). Similar patterns have been found in other follow-up studies of conduct-disordered youths. In brief, the data suggest that the majority of children with clinically referred antisocial behavior will suffer from a significant degree of impairment over the course of their lives.

The Scope of Dysfunction

If one were to consider "only" the symptoms of CD and the persistence of impairment, the challenge of identifying effective treatments would be great enough. However, the presenting characteristics of children and their families usually raise other considerations that are central to treatment. Consider characteristics of children, families, and contexts that are associated with CD, as a backdrop for later comments on treatment.

Child Characteristics

Children who meet criteria for CD are likely to meet criteria for other disorders as well. The coexistence of two or more disorders is referred to as *comorbidity*. In general, diagnoses involving disruptive or externalizing behaviors (CD, Oppositional Defiant Disorder [ODD], and Attention Deficit Hyperactivity Disorder [ADHD]) often go together. In studies of community and clinic samples, a large percentage of youth with CD or ADHD (e.g., 45 to 70%) also meet criteria for the other disorder (e.g., Fergusson, Horwood, & Lloyd, 1991; Offord et al., 1991). The co-occurrence of CD and ODD is common as well. Among clinic-referred youths who meet criteria for CD, 84 to 96% also meet concurrent diagnostic criteria for ODD (see

Hinshaw, Lahey, & Hart, 1993).[3] CD is sometimes comorbid with anxiety disorders and depression (Hinshaw et al., 1993; Walker et al., 1991).

Several other associated features of CD are relevant to treatment. For example, children with CD are also likely to show academic deficiencies, as reflected in achievement level, grades, being left behind in school, early termination from school, and deficiencies in specific skill areas such as reading. Youths with the disorder are likely to evince poor interpersonal relations, as reflected in diminished social skills in relation to peers and adults and higher levels of peer rejection. They are likely to show deficits and distortions in cognitive problem-solving skills, attributions of hostile intent to others, and resentment and suspiciousness. Clearly, CD is pervasive in the scope of characteristics that are affected.

Parent and Family Characteristics

Several parent and family characteristics are associated with CD (see Kazdin, 1995b; Robins, 1991; Stoff et al., 1997). Criminal behavior and alcoholism are two of the stronger and more consistently demonstrated parental characteristics. Harsh, lax, erratic, and inconsistent parent disciplinary practices and attitudes often characterize the families of CD children. Dysfunctional relations are also evident, as reflected in less acceptance of their children, less warmth, less affection, less emotional support, and less attachment than in parents of nonreferred youths. Less supportive and more defensive communications among family members, less participation in activities as a family, and more clear dominance of one family member are also evident. In addition, unhappy marital relations, interpersonal conflict, and aggression characterize the parental relations of antisocial children. Poor parental supervision and monitoring of the child and lack of knowledge of the child's whereabouts also are associated with CD.

Contextual Conditions

Conduct disorder is associated with a variety of untoward living conditions such as large family size, overcrowding, poor housing, and disadvantaged school settings (see Kazdin, 1995b). Many of the untoward conditions in which families live place stress on the parents or diminish their threshold for coping with everyday stressors. The net effect can be evident in strained parent-child interactions in which parent behavior inadvertently sustains or exacerbates child antisocial and aggressive behavior (e.g., Dumas & Wahler, 1985; Patterson, Capaldi, & Bank, 1991).

Quite often the child's dysfunction is embedded in a larger context that cannot be neglected in conceptual views about the development, maintenance, and course of CD nor in the actual delivery of treatment. For example, at our outpatient clinical service (Yale Child Conduct Clinic), it is likely that a family referred for treatment will experience a subset of these characteristics: financial hardship (unemployment, significant debt, bankruptcy), untoward living conditions (dangerous neighborhood, small living quarters), transportation obstacles (no car or car in frequent repair, state-provided taxi service), psychiatric impairment of one of the parents, stress related to significant others (former spouses, boyfriends, or girlfriends), and adversarial contact with an outside agency (schools, youth services, courts). Conduct disorder is conceived of as a dysfunction of children and adolescents. The accumulated evidence regarding the symptom constellation, risk factors, and course over the life span attests to the heuristic value of focusing on characteristics of the child. At the same time, there is a child-parent-family-context Gestalt that includes multiple and reciprocal influences that affect each participant (child and parent) and the systems in which they operate (family, school). For treatment to be effective, it is likely that multiple domains will have to be addressed.

EVIDENCE-BASED TREATMENTS

Overview of Child and Adolescent Therapy Research

The context for examining psychosocial treatments for CD is the broader child and adolescent therapy literature (see Kazdin, 2000b). There has been remarkable progress in research in the quantity and quality of the evidence. Over 1,500 controlled outcome studies exist (e.g., Kazdin, 2000a). Quantitative reviews have consistently concluded that treatments for children are effective and produce rather strong effects (large effect sizes; e.g., Weisz, Weiss, Han, Granger, & Morton, 1995). Outcome studies continue to emerge, and their methodological quality continues to improve (Durlak, Wells, Cotten, & Johnson, 1995). Empirically supported treatments have been identified for several problem domains including anxiety, depression, and CD, to mention a few (Kazdin & Weisz, 1998; Lonigan & Elbert, 1998). Guidelines for clinical practice have emerged to take into account mounting empirical evidence (e.g., American Academy of Child and Adolescent Psychiatry, 1998). In short, the progress has been enormous.

There are notable limitations as well. For example, the main conclusion about the effects of psychotherapy is that those who receive treatment are better off than those who do not. Yet, effect sizes from which these conclusions are drawn are not easily translated into meaningful or clinically important reductions in symptoms or improvement of adaptive functioning for those who have been treated. Also, characteristics of the treatment studies greatly limit what can be said about the effects of treatment and their relevance to treatment in clinical practice (Kazdin, Bass, Ayers, & Rodgers, 1990). In the majority of cases, child and adolescent therapy research focuses on youths recruited, rather than referred, for treatment. This means that characteristics such as comorbid diagnoses, impairment in multiple domains of functioning, and parent and family dysfunction are likely to be appreciably less than cases seen in clinical work. Also, treatment research focuses on group treatments provided in the schools. The most commonly investigated treatments are behavioral or cognitive behavioral interventions. Treatment is relatively brief (e.g., 8 to 10 hours) and does not involve the family or address many of the child, parent, and contextual characteristics noted previously. In light of these characteristics, the question remains about the extent to which the favorable results in therapy research would characterize the likely effects if treatments were extended to clinical practice.

The connection between research and clinical practice raises its own issues. Surveys spanning decades have shown that psychodynamic, psychoanalytic, family, and eclectic treatments are the most commonly used interventions for children and adolescents (Kazdin, Siegel, & Bass, 1990; Koocher & Pedulla, 1977; Silver & Silver, 1983). Clearly, most of the treatments shown to work in research are not in use in clinical practice, and most of the treatments in use in clinical practice have never been investigated empirically. There continues to be a proliferation of treatments for use with children and adolescents, with a conservative count documenting over 550 treatments (Kazdin, 2000b). The vast majority of these have never been studied empirically. In relation to CD, there have been important exceptions in which controlled studies and indeed programs of research have developed effective treatments.

Many different treatments have been applied to conduct-disordered youths, including variations of psychotherapy, pharmacotherapy, psychosurgery, home, school, and community-based programs; residential and hospital treatment; and social services (e.g., Brandt & Zlotnick, 1988; Dumas, 1989; U.S. Congress, 1991). Only a few treatments have strong evidence in their behalf and these are highlighted here. The outcome data for these treatments derive from randomized, controlled clinical trials (Type 1 and 2 studies). In highlighting the approaches, the purpose is not to convey that these are the only promising treatments. Yet, these are clearly among the most well developed in relation to the number of controlled clinical trials and replications across investigators and samples.[4]

Parent Management Training

Background and Underlying Rationale

Parent management training (PMT) refers to procedures in which parents are trained to alter their child's behavior in the home. The parents meet with a therapist or trainer who teaches them to use specific procedures to alter interactions with their child, to promote prosocial behavior, and to decrease deviant behavior. Training reflects the general view that conduct problem behavior is inadvertently developed and sustained in the home by maladaptive parent-child interactions and that altering these interactions can reduce these behaviors.

There are multiple facets of parent-child interaction that promote aggressive and antisocial behavior. These patterns include directly reinforcing deviant behavior, frequently and ineffectively using commands and harsh punishment, and failing to attend to appropriate behavior (Patterson, 1982; Patterson, Reid, & Dishion, 1992). Among the many interaction patterns, those involving coercion have received the greatest attention. *Coercion* refers to deviant behavior on the part of one person (e.g., the child) that is rewarded by another person (e.g., the parent). Aggressive children are inadvertently rewarded for their aggressive interactions and their escalation of coercive behaviors, as part of the discipline practices that sustain aggressive behavior.

There has been an excellent set of studies and conceptual models to elaborate the role of parent-child discipline practices in the development and maintenance of aggressive child behavior (Patterson, 1982; Patterson et al., 1992). The studies have included observation of family interactions in the home and the sequences and progressions of these interactions in relation to child aggressive behavior. In addition, PMT has been used to alter parent-child interaction patterns. Overall, the results have shown that child-rearing practices directly foster and increase aggressive child behavior and that altering these practices reduces child aggressive behavior and related conduct problems (Dishion & Andrews, 1995; Dishion, Patterson, & Kavanagh, 1992; Forgatch, 1991; Forgatch & DeGarmo, 1999). These are powerful demonstrations in the sense that parenting practices have been shown to be causally related to aggressive behavior in children.

It would be misleading to imply that the parent generates and is solely responsible for the child-parent sequences of interactions. Influences are bidirectional, so that the child influences the parent as well (see Bell & Harper, 1977; Lytton, 1990). Indeed, in some cases, children engage in deviant behavior to help prompt the parent-child interaction sequences. For example, when parents behave inconsistently and unpredictably (e.g., not attending to the child in the usual ways), the child may engage in some deviant behavior (e.g., whining, throwing some object). The effect is to cause the parent to respond in more predictable ways (see Wahler & Dumas, 1986). Essentially, inconsistent and unpredictable parent behavior is an aversive condition for the child. Terminating parent unpredictability negatively reinforces the child's deviant behavior. However, the result is also to increase the parental punishment of the child.

The primary goal of PMT is to alter the pattern of interchanges between parent and child so that prosocial, rather than coercive, behavior is directly reinforced and supported within the family. This goal requires developing several different parenting behaviors, such as establishing the rules for the child to follow, providing positive reinforcement for appropriate behavior, delivering mild forms of punishment to suppress behavior, negotiating compromises, and other procedures. These parenting behaviors are systematically and progressively developed within the sessions in which the therapist shapes (develops through successive approximations) parenting skills. The programs that parents eventually implement in the home also serve as the basis for the focus of the sessions in which the procedures are modified and refined.

The methods to alter parent and child behavior are based on principles and procedures of operant conditioning. Operant conditioning, elaborated by B. F. Skinner (1938) in animal laboratory research, describes and explains how behavior can be acquired and influenced by a variety of antecedents and consequences. Beginning in the late 1950s and early 1960s, extensions of this work led to applications across a broad range of settings (psychiatric hospitals, rehabilitation facilities, nursing homes, special-education and regular classrooms, the military, business and industry; Kazdin, 2001). Experimental demonstrations have repeatedly shown that persons (e.g., parents, teachers, peers, hospital and institutional staff) can be trained to administer consequences for behavior and to achieve therapeutic changes in diverse clients (e.g., patients, students, residents, and inmates). Early applications with children focused on mental retardation, autism, and special problems in institutional or special-education settings. Many extensions in the home focused on everyday concerns of parents rather than clinical dysfunction or impairment (e.g., tantrums, thumb sucking, toileting, completing homework, complying with requests). Applications in the home, begun initially in the late 1960s and early 1970s (e.g., Hanf, 1969), stimulated a vigorous line of research that continues today.

Characteristics of Treatment

Although many variations of PMT exist, several common characteristics can be identified. First, treatment is conducted primarily with the parent(s) who implement several procedures in the home. There usually is little direct intervention of the therapist with the child. With young children, the child may be brought into the session to help train both parent and child how to interact and to show the parent precisely how to deliver antecedents (prompts) and consequences (reinforcement, time-out from reinforcement). Older youths may participate to negotiate and to develop behavior-change programs in the home. Second, parents are trained to identify, define, and observe problem behaviors in new ways. Careful specification of the problem is essential for delivering reinforcing or punishing consequences and for evaluating if the program is achieving the desired goals. Third, the treatment sessions cover social learning principles and the procedures that follow from them, including positive reinforcement (e.g., the use of social praise and tokens or points for prosocial behavior), mild punishment (e.g., use of time-out from reinforcement, loss of privileges), negotiation, and contingency contracting. Fourth, the sessions provide opportunities for parents to see how the techniques are implemented, to practice using the techniques, and to review the behavior-change programs in the home. The immediate goal of the program is to develop specific skills in the parents. As the parents become more proficient, the program can address the child's most severely problematic behaviors and encompass other problem domains (e.g., school behavior). Over the course of treatment, more complex repertoires are developed, both in the parents and in the child. Finally, child functioning at school is usually incorporated into the program. Parent-managed reinforcement programs for child deportment and performance at school, completion of homework, and activities on the playground often are integrated into the behavior-change programs. If available, teachers can play an important role in monitoring or providing consequences for behaviors at school.

Overview of the Evidence

Since the early 1970s, a large number of randomized, controlled (Type 1 and 2) studies of PMT have been completed with youths varying in age (e.g., 2 to 17 years old) and severity of oppositional and conduct problems (see Graziano & Diament, 1992; Kazdin, 1997a; Patterson, Dishion, & Chamberlain, 1993; Serketich & Dumas, 1996). Indeed, a recent review of treatments for CD identified PMT as the only intervention that is well established, that is, has been shown to be effective in independently replicated controlled clinical trials (Brestan & Eyberg, 1998).[5]

The outcome studies support several conclusions. PMT has led to marked improvements in child behavior on parent and teacher reports of deviant behavior, direct observation of behavior at home and at school, and institutional records (e.g., school truancy, police contacts, arrest rates, institutionalization). The improvements can be traced to the specific changes in parenting practices in the home and hence support directly the conceptual model on which treatment is based (Forgatch & DeGarmo, 1999). The magnitude of therapeutic change has placed conduct problem behaviors to within nonclinic levels of functioning at home and at school, based on normative data from nonreferred peers (e.g., same age, sex). The improvements extend to child behaviors that have not been focused on directly, to behaviors of siblings, to maternal psychopathology, and to family relations. Treatment gains have been maintained in several studies 1 to 3 years after treatment, although one program reported maintenance of gains 10 to 14 years later (Long, Forehand, Wierson, & Morgan, 1994).

Considerable attention has been devoted to identifying parent and family characteristics that contribute to outcome. Family socioeconomic disadvantage, marital discord, high parental stress and low social support, single-parent families, harsh punishment practices, and parent history of antisocial behavior predict (a) who remains in treatment, (b) the magnitude of change among those who complete treatment, and (c) the extent to which changes are maintained at follow-up (e.g., Dadds & McHugh, 1992; Dumas & Wahler, 1983; Kazdin, 1995a; Webster-Stratton & Hammond, 1990). Those families at greatest risk often respond to treatment, but the magnitude of effects is attenuated as a function of the extent to which these factors are present. Among child characteristics, more severe and chronic antisocial behavior and comorbidity predict reduced responsiveness to treatment (e.g., Kazdin, 1995a; Ruma, Burke, & Thompson, 1996).

Characteristics of treatment also contribute to outcome. Providing parents with in-depth knowledge of social learning principles, rather than just teaching them the techniques, improves outcomes. Also, including mild punishment (e.g., brief time-out from reinforcement) along with reinforcement programs in the home enhances treatment effects. These components are now standard in most PMT programs. Processes within treatment have also been studied to identify who responds to treatment. Measures of parent resistance (e.g., parents saying, "I can't," "I won't") correlate with parent discipline practices at home; changes in resistance during therapy predict changes in parent behavior. Moreover, specific therapist ploys during the sessions (e.g., reframing, confronting) can overcome or contribute to resistance (Patterson & Chamberlain, 1994). This work begins to identify ways to enhance the administration of PMT.

In much of the outcome research, PMT has been administered to families individually in clinic settings. PMT has been extended to community settings to bring treatment to those persons least likely to come to or remain in treatment (e.g., Cunningham, Bremner, & Boyle, 1995; Irvine, Biglan, Smolkowski, Metzler, & Ary, 1999; Thompson et al., 1996; Webster-Stratton, 1998). PMT is effective and highly cost-effective when provided in small parent groups in neighborhoods where the families reside. Occasionally, community-based PMT has been more effective than clinic-based treatment. Of course, it is not clear that one form of treatment can replace another for all children. Community applications may permit dissemination of treatment to families that otherwise might not attend the usual mental health services.

Overall Evaluation

No other technique for CD has been studied as often or as well in controlled trials as has PMT (Brestan & Eyberg, 1998). The outcome evidence makes PMT one of the most promising treatments. Related lines of work bolster the evidence. First, the study of family interaction processes that contribute to antisocial behavior in the home and evidence that changing these processes alters child behavior provide a strong empirical base for treatment. Second, the procedures and practices that are used in PMT (e.g., various forms of reinforcement and punishment practices) have been widely and effectively applied outside the context of CD. For example, the procedures have been applied with parents of children with autism, language delays, developmental disabilities, and medical disorders for which compliance with special treatment regimens is required, and with parents who physically abuse or neglect their children (see Kazdin, 2001). Third, a great deal is known about the procedures and the parameters that influence the reinforcement and punishment practices that form the core of PMT. Consequently, very concrete recommendations can be provided to change behavior and to alter programs when behavior change has not occurred.

Treatment manuals and training materials for PMT are available for parents and therapists (e.g., Forehand & Long, 1996; Forgatch, 1994; Sanders & Dadds, 1993). Also noteworthy is the development of self-administered videotapes of treatment that present themes, principles, and procedures to the parents (see Webster-Stratton, 1994). Randomized controlled trials have shown that video-based treatment, particularly in group format and when supplemented with therapist-led discussions, leads to clinically significant changes at posttreatment and that these changes are maintained at follow-up 1 and 3 years later. The potential for extension of PMT with readily available and empirically tested videotapes presents a unique feature in child treatment.

Several limitations of PMT can be identified as well. First, some families may not respond to treatment. PMT makes several demands on the parents, such as mastering educational materials that convey major principles underlying the program, systematically observing deviant child behavior and implementing specific procedures at home, attending weekly sessions, and responding to frequent telephone contacts made by the therapist. For some families, the demands may be too great to continue in treatment. Interestingly, within the approach, several procedures (e.g., shaping parent behavior through reinforcement) provide guidelines for developing parent compliance and the desired response repertoire in relation to their children.

Second, and perhaps the greatest limitation or obstacle in using PMT, there are few training opportunities for professionals to learn the approach. Training programs in child psychiatry, clinical psychology, and social work are unlikely to provide exposure to the technique, much less opportunities for formal training. PMT requires mastery of social learning principles and multiple procedures that derive from them (Cooper, Heron, & Heward, 1987; Kazdin, 2001). For example, the administration of reinforcement by the parent in the home (to alter child behavior) and by the therapist in the session (to change parent behavior) requires more than passing familiarity with the principle and the parametric variations that dictate its effectiveness (e.g., administration of reinforcement contingently, immediately, frequently; use of varied and high-quality reinforcers; use of prompts, shaping). The requisite skills in administering the procedures within the treatment sessions can be readily trained but they are not trivial.

Finally, the applicability of PMT to adolescents, compared with children, is less clear. PMT has reduced offense rates among delinquent adolescents (Bank et al., 1991) and school behavioral problems and substance use among adolescents at risk for serious conduct problems (Dishion & Andrews, 1995). Yet, some studies suggest that adolescents respond less well to PMT than preadolescents (Dishion & Patterson, 1992). This effect may be accounted for by severity of symptoms at pretreatment. Adolescents referred for treatment tend to be more severely and chronically impaired than preadolescents; once severity is controlled, age does not influence outcome (Ruma et al., 1996). In light of limited applications with adolescents, the strength of conclusions about the efficacy of PMT applies mainly to preadolescent children.

Multisystemic Therapy

Background and Underlying Rationale

Multisystemic therapy (MST) focuses on systems in which behavior is embedded and on altering these systems in concrete ways that can influence behavior (Henggeler et al., 1998). The primary focus of treatment has been with delinquent adolescents, including seriously disturbed repeat offenders. The adolescent is influenced by a number of systems, including the family (immediate and extended-family members), peers, schools, and neighborhood. Multiple influences within these systems may be involved in development, maintenance, or amelioration of the problem. For example, within the context of the family, some tacit alliance between one parent and the adolescent may contribute to disagreement and conflict over discipline in relation to the adolescent. Treatment may be required to address the alliance and sources of conflict in an effort to alter adolescent behavior. Also, adolescent functioning at school may involve limited and poor peer relations; treatment may address these areas as well. Finally, the systems approach entails a focus on the individual's own behavior insofar as it affects others. Individual treatment of the adolescent or parents may be included in treatment.

The focus of treatment is on current systems within the life of the adolescent that can be mobilized to promote adaptive and prosocial behavior and to reduce influences within the home or between peers that foster or contribute to maladaptive behavior. Thus, current areas of functioning, rather than past determinants, serve as the focus of treatment. Factors identified earlier as risk factors for CD (e.g., family discipline, parent conflict) often serve as the focus of intervention insofar as they are identified as influences on current child functioning.

Characteristics of Treatment

The goals of treatment are to help the parents develop positive, prosocial behaviors of the adolescent; to overcome difficulties (e.g., marital) that impede the parents' ability to function as parents to eliminate negative interactions between parent and adolescent; and to develop or build cohesion and emotional warmth among family members. Emphasis on systems and contexts requires mobilizing many influences and aspects of the interpersonal environment, as feasible and available. Two key systems are the family and peers. At the family level, MST makes an effort to improve family structure and cohesion and provide parents with resources and skills to monitor and discipline their children. Efforts are made to improve communication of the parents with the children, develop skills in the parent that diffuse family conflict, and encourage parents to spend more time with their children. At the peer level, treatment focuses on increasing youth's association with prosocial peers (e.g., through organized athletics, church) and helping parents disengage youths from interactions with deviant peers (e.g., gang members, school dropouts).

Treatment draws on several different techniques, including PMT, contingency management, problem-solving skills therapy, and marital therapy. Domains may be addressed in treatment (e.g., parent unemployment) because they raise issues for one or more systems (e.g., marital conflict, parent stress, alcohol consumption, child-discipline practices) and affect how the adolescent is functioning. Much of the therapy is conducted outside the treatment sessions, in which parents and significant others engage in new strategies (e.g., reinforcement techniques) that alter behavior at home, at school, and in the community.

Treatment procedures are used on an "as-needed" basis, as determined by assessment of the individual, family, and system issues that may contribute to problem behavior. The key foci of treatment are: concentrating on present behavior, directing interventions to achieve concrete observable changes in the family and adolescent, treating specific and well-defined problems, and empowering parents in relation to family interaction, the school, and peers. In some cases, treatment consists of helping the parents address a significant domain through practical advice and guidance (e.g., to involve the adolescent in prosocial peer activities at school, to restrict specific activities with a deviant peer group). In short, treatment is problem-focused and action-oriented. Parents are directly involved in treatment both as administrators of behavior change strategies for the adolescent and as direct targets of intervention so their own behaviors and interaction patterns change.

Much of therapy is based on assessment and hypothesis testing. That is, an evaluation is made about how or what the adolescent is doing in a particular context, a hypothesis is generated by the therapist regarding what factors might be influencing these behaviors, and the hypothesis is tested by intervening to alter the factor to see if there are concrete changes in adolescent behavior. Domains that are known to influence delinquent behavior, as mentioned above, alert the therapists to likely targets of treatment (e.g., parent marital discord, child-rearing practices, child-peer relations). The assessment, hypothesis generation, and hypothesis testing are sometimes said to characterize all clinical work. The approach is much more explicit in MST.

Overview of the Evidence

There is strong evidence in behalf of MST. Treatment has been evaluated in multiple randomized controlled clinical trials (Type 1 studies) with very seriously disturbed adjudicated delinquent youths and their families, including chronic juvenile offenders, juvenile sexual offenders, youths with substance use and abuse, and maltreating (abusing, neglectful) families (see Henggeler et al., 1998, for a review). MST has led to greater reductions in delinquency and emotional and behavioral problems and improvements in family functioning than other procedures, including "usual services" provided to adolescents (e.g., probation or court-ordered activities that are monitored, such as school attendance), individual counseling, and community-based eclectic treatment. For seriously disturbed youths, a recent randomized controlled trial showed that MST is more effective than hospitalization in improving symptoms and family functioning (Henggeler et al., 1999). For studies with the outpatient samples, the benefits of treatment, in comparison to other treatment and control conditions, have been evident on measures of adolescent and parent psychopathology, family relations and functioning, rearrest rates, severity of offenses, drug use, and reinstitutionalization (e.g., incarceration, hospitalization). Follow-up studies up to 2, 4, and 5 years later with separate samples have shown that MST adolescents have lower arrest rates than those who receive other services. Cost-effectiveness data have also shown that the treatment is a bargain in comparison to alternative diversion and institutional programs to which such youths are ordinarily assigned.

Treatment influences key processes proposed in the underlying conceptual model. Improvements in family relations (improved cohesion, family functioning, parent monitoring) and decreased delinquent peer affiliations are associated with reductions in delinquent adolescent behavior (Huey, Henggeler, Brondino, & Pickrel, 2000). Critical family processes are altered with treatment. For example, parents and adolescents show a reduction in coalitions (e.g., less verbal activity, conflict, and hostility) and increases in support, and parents show increases in verbal communication and decreases in conflict (Mann, Borduin, Henggeler, & Blaske, 1990). Moreover, decreases in adolescent symptoms are positively correlated with increases in supportiveness and decreases in conflict between the mother and father. This work provides an important link between theoretical underpinnings of treatment and outcome effects.

Evidence suggests that the fidelity with which MST is carried out influences treatment outcome. Therapist adherence to treatment predicts reductions in arrest, self-reported offenses, psychiatric symptoms, and delinquent peer affiliation and improved family relations (Henggeler et al., 1997; Huey et al., 2000). Few studies of child and adolescent therapy have evaluated the relation of treatment adherence and clinical outcomes.

Overall Evaluation

The evidence in behalf of MST has several strengths including the focus on very seriously disturbed adolescents, replication of treatment outcomes in several randomized controlled clinical trials, evaluation of clinically and socially important outcomes (e.g., arrest, criminal activity, reinstitutionalization), and assessment of long-term follow-up. Another strength is the conceptualization of conduct problems at multiple levels, namely, as dysfunction in relation to the individual, family, and extrafamilial systems and the transactions among these. In fact, youths with conduct problems experience dysfunction at multiple levels, including individual repertoires, family interactions, and extrafamilial systems (e.g., peers, schools, employment among later adolescents). MST begins with the view that many different domains are likely to be relevant; they need to be evaluated and then addressed in treatment.

There remain important challenges for the approach. First, treatment is guided by broad principles, and moving from the principles to specific action plans within the session is not entirely straightforward. However, several illustrations are available (Henggeler et al., 1998). Second, the administration of MST is demanding in light of the need to provide several different interventions in a high-quality fashion. Individual treatments alone are difficult to provide; multiple combinations of different treatments invite all sorts of challenges (e.g., therapist training; ensuring treatments of high quality, strength, and integrity). Third and related, MST is intensive. In some projects, therapists are available 24 hours a day, 7 days a week. Sometimes a team of therapists is involved rather than merely one therapist. It may be the case that this model of treatment delivery is precisely what is needed for clinical problems that are multiply determined, protracted, and recalcitrant to more abbreviated interventions. However, the model of how MST is delivered will very much influence its adoption as a treatment.

Fourth, further replications will be needed for this treatment. The treatment has already provided multiple replications across problems, therapists, and settings (Henggeler et al., 1998), but these have been completed largely by the same team of researchers. Replications by others not involved with the original development of the program is the next logical step. Finally, the treatment already has impressive evidence in its behalf and is undergoing further treatment trials. The central issue is understanding what treatment components to provide to whom and how the decisions are made, and to identify whether these rules can be reliably implemented across settings and investigators. These questions ought not detract from the superb evidence and consistency of the outcomes already established.

Cognitive Problem-Solving Skills Training

Background and Underlying Rationale

Cognitive processes refers to a broad class of constructs that pertain to how the individual perceives, codes, and experiences the world. Individuals who engage in conduct-disordered behaviors, particularly aggression, show distortions and deficiencies in various cognitive processes. These distortions and deficiencies are not merely reflections of intellectual functioning. Several cognitive processes have been studied. Examples include generating alternative solutions to interpersonal problems (e.g., different ways of handling social situations); identifying the means to obtain particular ends (e.g., making friends) or consequences of one's actions (e.g., what could happen after a particular behavior); making attributions to others of the motivation of their actions; perceiving how others feel; and modifying expectations of the effects of one's own actions (see Lochman, Whidby, & FitzGerald, 2000; Shirk, 1988; Spivack & Shure, 1982). Deficits and distortion among these processes relate to teacher ratings of disruptive behavior, peer evaluations, and direct assessment of overt behavior (e.g., Lochman & Dodge, 1994; Rubin, Bream, & Rose-Krasnor, 1991).

An example of cognitive processes implicated in CD can be seen in the work on attributions and aggressive behavior. Aggression is triggered not merely by environmental events, but through the way in which these events are perceived and processed. The processing refers to the child's appraisals of the situation, anticipated reactions of others, and self-statements in response to particular events. Attribution of intent to others represents a salient cognitive disposition critically important to understanding aggressive behavior. Aggressive children and adolescents tend to attribute hostile intent to others, especially in social situations where the cues of actual intent are ambiguous (see Crick & Dodge, 1994). Understandably, when situations are initially perceived as hostile, children are more likely to react aggressively. Although many studies have shown that conduct-disordered children experience various cognitive distortions and deficiencies, the specific contribution of these processes to CD, as opposed to risk factors with which they may be associated (e.g., untoward living conditions, low IQ), has not been established. Nevertheless, research on cognitive processes among aggressive children has served as a heuristic base for conceptualizing treatment and for developing specific treatment strategies (Kendall, 2000).

Characteristics of Treatment

Problem-solving skills training (PSST) consists of developing interpersonal cognitive problem-solving skills. Although many variations of PSST have been applied to conduct problem children, several characteristics usually are shared. First, the emphasis is on how children approach situations (i.e., the thought processes in which the child engages to guide responses to interpersonal situations). The children are taught to engage in a step-by-step approach to solve interpersonal problems. They make statements to themselves that direct attention to certain aspects of the problem or tasks that lead to effective solutions. Second, the behaviors (solutions to the interpersonal problems) that are selected are important as well. Prosocial behaviors are fostered through modeling and direct reinforcement as part of the problem-solving process. Third, treatment utilizes structured tasks involving games, academic activities, and stories. Over the course of treatment, the cognitive problem-solving skills are increasingly applied to real-life situations. Fourth, therapists play an active role in treatment. They model the cognitive processes by making verbal self-statements, apply the sequence of statements to particular problems, provide cues to prompt use of the skills, and deliver feedback and praise to develop correct use of the skills. Finally, treatment usually combines several different procedures, including modeling and practice, role playing, and reinforcement and mild punishment (loss of points or tokens). These are deployed in systematic ways to develop increasingly complex response repertoires of the child.

Overview of the Evidence

Several randomized clinical trials (Type 1 and 2 studies) have been completed with impulsive, aggressive, and conduct-disordered children and adolescents (see Baer & Nietzel, 1991; Durlak, Furhman, & Lampman, 1991, for reviews). Cognitively based treatments have significantly reduced aggressive and antisocial behavior at home, at school, and in the community. At follow-up, these gains have been evident up to 1 year later. Many early studies in the field (e.g., 1970s and 1980s) focused on impulsive children and nonpatient samples. Since that time, several additional (Type 1 and 2) studies have shown treatment effects with inpatient and outpatient cases (see Kazdin, 1997b, 2000; Pepler & Rubin, 1991).

The strength of the evidence in the context of treatment for referred cases stands on its own in support of PSST as a promising treatment for CD. Evidence outside the context of treatment is quite pertinent to the evaluation of this intervention. PSST has been studied for a period spanning 20 years in a very well-developed program of research (Shure, 1997, 1999). In one of the reports, PSST was provided in the classrooms of economically disadvantaged elementary-school children. Those who received the training, compared to those who did not, showed decreases in disruptive student behavior and increases in positive, prosocial behavior. Although the effects were evident when training was conducted for 1 year (kindergarten), the impact was greater when training was continued for 2 years (kindergarten and first grade). Either way, the benefits of the intervention were still evident at least up to 2 years after the program ended. The program is noteworthy because it can be implemented on a large scale in the schools and used to improve outcomes of children who are at high risk for academic, social, emotional, and behavioral problems.

In the context of treatment, there is only sparse evidence that addresses the child, parent, family, contextual, or treatment factors that influence treatment outcome. Evidence suggests that older children (>10–11 years of age) profit more from treatment than younger children, perhaps due to their cognitive development (Durlak et al., 1991). However, the basis for differential responsiveness to treatment as a function of age has not been well tested. Conduct-disordered children who show comorbid diagnoses, academic delays and dysfunction, and lower reading achievement and who come from families with high levels of impairment (parent psychopathology, stress, and family dysfunction) respond less well to treatment than do children with less dysfunction in these domains (Kazdin, 1995a; Kazdin & Crowley, 1997). These child, parent, and family characteristics may influence the effectiveness of several different treatments for CD rather than PSST in particular. Much further work is needed to evaluate factors that contribute to responsiveness to treatment.

Overall Evaluation

There are features of PSST that make it an extremely promising approach. Several controlled outcome studies with clinic samples have shown that cognitively based treatment leads to therapeutic change. Basic research in developmental psychology continues to elaborate the relation of maladaptive cognitive processes among children and adolescents and conduct problems that serve as underpinnings of treatment (Crick & Dodge, 1994; Lochman et al., 2000). An advantage of the approach is that versions of treatment are available in manual form (e.g., Feindler & Ecton, 1986; Finch, Nelson, & Ott, 1993; Shure, 1992, 1996). Consequently, the treatment can be readily evaluated in research and explored further in clinical practice.

Critical questions remain to be addressed in research. Primary among these is the role of cognitive processes in clinical dysfunction. Evidence is not entirely clear in showing that a specific pattern of cognitive processes characterizes children with conduct problems, rather than adjustment or externalizing problems more generally. Also, although evidence has shown that cognitive processes change with treatment, evidence has not established that change in these processes mediates or is responsible for improvements in treatment outcome. Thus, the basis for therapeutic change has yet to be established. Although central questions about treatment and its effects remain to be resolved, PSST is highly promising in light of its effects in several controlled outcome studies with conduct-disordered children.

Other Treatments Briefly Noted

The strongest outcome evidence for the treatment of CD serves as the basis for reviewing PMT, MST, and PSST. Two other treatments are mentioned briefly here. They, too, have randomized controlled trials in their behalf (Type 1 and 2 studies). However, the extent of the evidence and replication across investigators and settings is less than for the other treatments.

Functional Family Therapy

Functional family therapy (FFT) reflects an integrative approach to treatment that relies on systems, behavioral, and cognitive views of dysfunction (Alexander, Holtzworth-Munroe, & Jameson, 1994; Alexander & Parsons, 1982). Clinical problems are conceptualized from the standpoint of the functions they serve in the family as a system, as well as for individual family members. Problem behavior evident in the child is assumed to be the way in which some interpersonal functions (e.g., intimacy, distancing, support) are met among family members. Maladaptive processes within the family are considered to preclude a more direct means of fulfilling these functions. The goal of treatment is to alter interaction and communication patterns in such a way as to foster more adaptive functioning. Treatment is also based on learning theory and focuses on specific stimuli and responses that can be used to produce change. Social learning concepts and procedures, such as identifying specific behaviors for change, reinforcing new adaptive ways of responding, and evaluating and monitoring change, are included in this perspective. *Cognitive processes* in this context refers to the attributions, attitudes, assumptions, expectations, and emotions of the family. Family members may begin treatment with attributions that focus on blaming others or themselves. New perspectives may be needed to help serve as the basis for developing new ways of behaving.

The underlying rationale emphasizes a family systems approach, especially family communication patterns and their meaning. As an illustration of salient constructs, research underlying FFT has found that families of delinquents show higher rates of defensiveness in their communications, in both parent-child and parent-parent interactions, blaming, and negative attributions and also lower rates of mutual support than families of nondelinquents (see Alexander & Parsons, 1982). Improving these communication and support functions is a goal of treatment.

FFT requires that the family see the clinical problem from the relational functions it serves within the family. The therapist points out interdependencies and contingencies between family members in their day-to-day functioning and with specific reference to the problem that has served as the basis for seeking treatment. Once the family sees alternative ways of viewing the problem, the incentive for interacting more constructively is increased.

The main goals of treatment are to increase reciprocity and positive reinforcement among family members, to establish clear communication, to help specify behaviors that family members desire from each other, to negotiate constructively, and to help identify solutions to interpersonal problems. Specific treatment strategies draw on findings that underlie PMT in relation to maladaptive and coercive parent-child interactions, discussed previously. In therapy, family members identify behaviors they would like others to perform. Responses are incorporated into a reinforcement system in the home to promote adaptive behavior in exchange for privileges. However, the primary focus is within the treatment sessions, where family communication patterns are altered directly. During the sessions, the therapist provides social reinforcement (verbal and nonverbal praise) for communications that suggest solutions to problems, clarify problems, or offer feedback.

Relatively few outcome studies have evaluated FFT (see Alexander et al., 1994). However, the available studies (Type 1 and 2) have focused on populations that are difficult to treat (e.g., adjudicated delinquent adolescents, multiple offender delinquents) and have produced clear effects. In controlled studies, FFT has led to greater change than other treatments (e.g., client-centered family groups, psychodynamically oriented family therapy) and various control conditions (e.g., group discussion and expression of feeling, no-treatment control groups). Treatment outcome has been reflected in improved family communication and interactions and lower rates of referral to and contact of youths with the courts. Moreover, gains have been evident in separate studies up to 2 1/2 years after treatment.

Research has examined processes in therapy to identify in-session behaviors of the therapist and how these influence responsiveness among family members (Alexander, Barton, Schiavo, & Parsons, 1976; Newberry, Alexander, & Turner, 1991). For example, providing support and structure and reframing (recasting the attributions and bases of a problem) influence family member responsiveness and blaming of others. The relations among such variables are complex insofar as the impact of various type of statements (e.g., supportive) can vary as a function of gender of the therapist and family member. Evidence of changes in processes proposed to be critical to FFT (e.g., improved communication in treatment, more spontaneous discussion) supports the conceptual view of treatment.

Overall, the outcome evidence indicates that FFT alters conduct problems among delinquent youths who vary in severity and chronicity of antisocial behavior (e.g., youths with status offenses; others who have multiple offenses and who have served in maximum-security wards). The evaluation of processes that contribute to family member responsiveness within the sessions, as well as to treatment outcome, represents a significant line of work not often seen among treatment techniques for children and adolescents. Some of this process work has extended to laboratory (analogue) studies to examine more precisely how specific types of therapist statements (e.g., reframing) can reduce blaming among group members (e.g., Morris, Alexander, & Turner, 1991). A treatment manual has been provided (Alexander & Parsons, 1982) to facilitate further evaluation and extension of treatment.

Further extensions are needed to replicate the treatment beyond the original program from which it emerged. One such effort demonstrated that delinquent youths who received FFT showed lower recidivism rates up to 2 1/2 years later than a comparison group of lower risk delinquent youths (Gordon, Arbuthnot, Gustafson, & McGreen, 1988). These results suggest that FFT can be replicated. Further replication efforts in randomized controlled trials are needed.

Brief Strategic Family Therapy

Brief strategic family therapy (BSFT) has emerged from a programmatic series of studies with Hispanic youths (see Coatsworth, Szapocznik, Kurtines, & Santisteban, 1997; Szapocznik & Kurtines, 1989). The youths have included those referred for externalizing behaviors such as CD, drug abuse, and a broader range of problems as well. BSFT views child behavior within the context of the family system. Integrated into a family approach is a cultural frame of reference that draws from the study of Hispanic families. Among the key foci of this frame of reference is the importance of strong family cohesion, parental control, and communication issues that may arise from cultural and intergenerational conflicts (e.g., individualism of the adolescent vs. family ties).

Both family and individual behavior are considered interdependent and interactive. Individuals are jointly responsible for the state of the family system and for the changes that are to be made in treatment. Patterns of interaction, conceptualized as the structure of the family system, are identified as the likely bases for maladaptive functioning. Thus, a child's "problem" brought to treatment is reconceptualized as dysfunction in relation to the family. Persistent maladaptive behavior in one or more family members must in some way be maintained by the family.

Treatment focuses on strategies that can be used to alter interaction patterns. The focus is on providing concrete and direct changes in the family situation to promote improved interactions. This is distinguished from more traditional strategies that have focused on insight and understanding. The treatment sessions are problem-focused whenever possible. The therapist identifies what can be altered within the family to promote change. Formal assessment is provided by a set of family tasks (e.g., planning a menu, discussing a prior family argument) that allow the therapist to identify areas of focus. Structure of the family, alliance, conflict resolution, roles (e.g., patient, model child), and flexibility of the family are some of the dimensions that are examined in assessment and focused on in treatment. During treatment, the therapist challenges interaction patterns, reformulates (reframes) ways of considering interaction and communication patterns, and encourages new ways of interacting to break up established sequences.

There have been several studies (Type 1 and 2) to develop and evaluate the intervention with youths referred for diverse problems. The results have shown improvements in child and family functioning as a result of treatment when compared to other treatment and control (e.g., minimal contact conditions; see Coatsworth et al., 1997; Szapocznik & Kurtines, 1989). For example, in one investigation, BFST and psychodynamic therapy were equally effective in reducing symptoms of clinically referred children, but BFST was more effective in improving family functioning (Szapocznik et al., 1989).

Conceptually interesting findings have been obtained in the context of the outcome studies. For example, family therapy is usually conceptualized as an intervention in which the entire family is seen in treatment. Szapocznik and his colleagues have argued that family therapy is a way of conceptualizing problems and interventions. Seeing the entire family or most members may not necessarily be important. Indeed, a controlled comparison found that seeing the individual is as effective as seeing the entire family, when these two variants of family therapy are compared (Szapocznik et al., 1986). The research has focused as well on engaging the family so that they remain in treatment. Special attention to the family early in treatment in an effort to address family and cultural barriers to treatment participation, evaluated in randomized controlled trials, has significantly reduced dropping out of treatment (e.g., Santisteban et al., 1996; Szapocznik et al., 1988).

Overall, BFST has been studied in a well-developed program of research. As with FFT, the research has been restricted primarily to a particular research center and set of investigators. Treatment has been replicated in several studies and with children presenting diverse clinical problems. The research program is unique in directly developing a treatment sensitive to critical cultural issues and developing methods to assess these issues. Apart from the accomplishments of the studies in relation to BFST, the broader approach of assessing and studying cultural features of families and then integrating them into therapy may reflect a model for developing ethnically relevant and sensitive treatment.

LIMITATIONS OF WELL-INVESTIGATED TREATMENTS

Each treatment reviewed has randomized controlled trials in its behalf, includes replications of treatment effects, focuses on youths whose aggressive and antisocial behavior have led to impairment and referral to social services (e.g., clinics, hospitals, courts), and has assessed outcome over the course of follow-up, at least up to a year, but often longer. Even though these treatments have made remarkable gains, they also bear limitations worth highlighting.

Impact of Treatment and Magnitude of Therapeutic Change

Promising treatments have achieved change, but is the change enough to make a difference in the lives of the youths who are treated? Also, what proportion of children improves with treatment and improves in ways that materially affect their functioning at home and at school? There are no clear answers to these important questions. Since the early 1980s, outcome research has attempted to address these questions by studying the clinical significance of therapeutic change. *Clinical significance* refers to the practical value or importance of the effect of an intervention, that is, whether it makes any "real" difference to the patients or to others with whom they interact. Clinical significance is important because it is quite possible for treatment effects to be statistically significant, but not to have impact on most or any of the cases in a way that improves their functioning or adjustment in daily life.

There are several ways to evaluate clinical significance (see Kazdin, 1998). The most commonly used method is to evaluate the extent to which treated children are functioning within normative levels at the end of treatment. This evaluation is accomplished by comparing youths who received treatment on measures of problems and social functioning before and after treatment with youths of the same age and sex who are not clinically referred and who are functioning well in everyday life. Comparison in the context of normative peers may be especially important in relation to children and adolescents because base rates of emotional and behavioral problems can vary greatly as a function of age. Promising treatments occasionally have shown that treatment returns individuals to normative levels in relation to behavioral problems and prosocial functioning at home and at school (see Kazdin, 1995b).

A difficulty is interpreting the findings of studies that focus on clinically significant changes. Clinical significance has been defined by researchers on an a priori basis. Performance on commonly used measures at the end of treatment (e.g., parent and teacher checklists) may not necessarily reflect adaptive and normative functioning of the individual, as defined in performance in everyday life. Measures of clinical significance have not been systematically validated in relation to what consumers (e.g., parents, teachers, youths) would identify as an important change or in relation to everyday measures of performance (Kazdin, 1999).

The problem of validating measures can be conveyed by examining another treatment focus. Treatments of obesity use weight and pounds lost as outcome measures. The clinical significance of treatment outcome can be more easily interpreted in light of the measure. We know that if a male 5 feet 5 inches (1.65 meters) tall who weighs 350 pounds (158.8 kilograms) loses 15 pounds (6.8 kilograms) over the course of treatment, this change is not likely to be clinically significant. Current and future health benefits (e.g., risk of heart disease, diabetes) are not likely to be altered because of the low magnitude of change. In contrast, a loss of 150 pounds (68.1 kilograms) might make an important difference in the functioning of the individual (e.g., daily activities) and in the current and future health benefits.[6] In the evaluation of therapeutic change for CD, there is no measure equivalent to weight to anchor measures such as parent and teacher ratings. Consequently, when CD children and "normal" children are functioning within the same range on parent and teacher ratings, the interpretation is not at all clear. We do not yet know if this means that CD children are actually functioning just as well as their peers in everyday life and if no differences (statistically) between treated and well-functioning children really means no difference on non-rating-scale dimensions. Validity research to convey what level or what amount of change on commonly used psychological measures (e.g., parent and teacher ratings) is significant has not been completed to allow such interpretations.

In some outcome studies, behaviors are observed directly at home and at school and show that marked changes have been achieved (e.g., no more fighting episodes at school, improved compliance in the home). Such measures often are more easily interpreted in the sense that they convey referents that directly reflect the problem for which treatment was sought. However, measures of overt behavior often are restricted to artificial or restricted situations and may not reflect functioning outside these assessment situations.

Overall, evidence suggests that children receiving one of the treatments reviewed earlier make marked changes. Even so, interpretation of the impact of treatment on everyday functioning is not clear. Part of the problem stems from the focus of treatment. In some cases, complete elimination of the behavior (e.g., fire setting, cruelty to animals, brandishing a weapon) would provide clear evidence that treatment had significant impact. Yet, more commonly, changes in such behaviors as rule breaking, getting into trouble, and arguing are less readily interpretable because the changes may be a matter of degree and because changes on the usual parent and teacher ratings do not automatically translate into actual functioning in everyday situations. In some of the studies reviewed previously (e.g., for MST), the outcome measures have included rearrest and reincarceration rates among adjudicated delinquents. These measures convey significant impact of treatment on outcomes well beyond the usual rating scales.

Although the goal of treatment is to effect clinically significant change, other less dramatic goals are not trivial. For many conduct-disordered youths, symptoms may escalate, comorbid diagnoses (e.g., substance abuse, depression) may emerge, and family dysfunction may increase. Also, such youths are at risk for teen marriage, dropping out of school, and running away. If treatment were to achieve stability in symptoms and family life and prevent or delimit future dysfunction, that would be a significant achievement. In other words, conceivably, for some children, *no change* over the course of treatment could represent an important intervention effect. Control conditions in therapy studies are so central in part because they allow a comparison of the course of change of those who receive treatment with those who do not. The within-group changes over the course of treatment (e.g., no change at all) may be viewed quite differently as a function of between-group changes (e.g., if the no-treatment control group becomes worse).

Maintenance of Change

Promising treatments have included follow-up assessment, usually up to a year after treatment. Yet, CD has a poor long-term prognosis, so it is especially important to identify whether treatment has enduring effects. Also, in evaluating the relative merit of different treatments, follow-up data play a critical role. When two (or more) treatments are compared, the treatment that is more (or most) effective immediately after treatment is not always the one that proves to be the most effective treatment in the long run (see Kazdin, 2000b). Consequently, the conclusions about treatment may be very different depending on the timing of the outcome assessment. Apart from conclusions about treatment, follow-up may provide important information that permits differentiation among youths. Over time, youths who maintain the benefits of treatment may differ in important ways from those who do not. Understanding who responds and who responds poorly or well to a particular treatment can be very helpful in understanding, treating, and preventing CD.

The evidence for long-term effects of treatment is sparse. Among the treatments reviewed, the evidence for MST is the most extensive. Studies have shown that the benefits of treatment, relative to control or alternative conditions, are still evident 5 years after treatment has ended (see Henggeler et al., 1998). The evidence is particularly impressive because of the severity of the dysfunction of the samples included in treatment. In general, much more evidence is needed on the long-term effects of treatment and these effects across multiple domains of functioning.

The study of long-term effects of treatment is difficult in general, but the usual problems are exacerbated by a focus on CD. Among clinic samples, families of conduct-disordered youths have high rates of dropping out of treatment or the follow-up assessment period. Many of the child, parent, family, and contextual factors (e.g., parent stress and psychopathology, socioeconomic disadvantage) associated with the problem also predict premature termination of treatment (Kazdin, 1996b). Indeed, evaluating the short-term effects of treatment is difficult because of the high attrition rates. Following such samples long after treatment is terminated merely exacerbates the problem. As the sample size decreases over time, conclusions about the impact of treatment become increasingly difficult to draw because of reduced power and increased prospect that those families remaining do not represent the original sample that began the study. Nevertheless, evaluation of the long-term effects of treatment remains a high priority for research. Embedding treatment studies within longitudinal investigations may be especially useful because longitudinal studies often use multiple procedures to remain in contact with and to obtain cooperation from samples over extended periods.

Limited Assessment of Outcome Domains

In the majority of child therapy studies, child symptoms are the exclusive focus of outcome assessment (Kazdin, Bass, et al., 1990). Other domains such as prosocial behavior, peer relations, and academic functioning are neglected, even though they relate to concurrent and long-term adjustment. Perhaps the greatest single deficit in the evaluation of treatment is absence of attention to impairment. Impairment reflects the extent to which the individual's functioning in everyday life is impeded. School and academic functioning, peer relations, and participation in activities are some of key areas of functioning. Impairment can be distinguished from symptoms insofar as individuals with similar levels of symptoms, diagnoses, and patterns of comorbidity are likely to be distinguishable in their ability to function adaptively. Indeed, impairment is associated with significant disturbance whether or not youths meet criteria for psychiatric diagnosis (Angold et al., 1999). Understandably, referral to clinical services is more likely to be related to impairment in everyday life than to meeting criteria for a psychiatric disorder (e.g., Bird et al., 1990). Treatment may significantly reduce symptoms, but is there any change or reduction in impairment? The impact of treatment on impairment is arguably as important as the impact on the CD symptoms.

Beyond child functioning, parent and family functioning may also be relevant as outcome domains of child and adolescent therapy. Parents and family members of conduct-disordered youths often experience dysfunction (e.g., psychiatric impairment, high levels of stress in the home, marital conflict). Also, the problem behaviors of the child are often part of complex, dynamic, and reciprocal influences that affect all relations in the home. Consequently, parent and family functioning and the quality of life for family members are relevant outcomes and may be appropriate goals for treatment. There is some evidence that parent dysfunction (e.g., depression, symptoms across diverse disorders) and perceived stress and family relations improve with child treatment, even though these are not focused on directly (Kazdin & Wassell, 2000). The effects are reliable but not large (in terms of effect sizes), even when changes in the children are large.

In general, many outcomes are of interest in evaluating treatment. From existing research we already know that the conclusions reached about a given treatment can vary depending on the outcome criterion. Within a given study, one set of measures (e.g., child functioning) may show no differences between two treatments, but another measure (e.g., family functioning) may show that one treatment is clearly better than another (e.g., Kazdin et al., 1992; Szapocznik et al., 1989; Webster-Stratton & Hammond, 1997). Thus, in examining different outcomes of interest, we must be prepared for the different conclusions that these outcomes may yield.

General Comments

Even among the most well-investigated treatments, several critical questions remain. Even so, it is important to place these treatments in perspective. The most commonly used treatments in clinical practice consist of "traditional" approaches, including psychodynamic, relationship, play, and family therapies (other than those mentioned above; Kazdin, Siegel, & Bass, 1990). These treatments have rarely been tested in controlled outcome studies to show that they achieve therapeutic change in referred (or nonreferred) samples of youth with conduct problems. Many forms of behavior therapy have a rather extensive literature showing that various techniques (e.g., reinforcement programs, social skills training) can alter aggressive and other antisocial behaviors. Yet, the focus has tended to be on isolated behaviors, rather than on a constellation of symptoms evident among children referred for inpatient or outpatient treatment.

Pharmacotherapy represents a line of work that deserves comment. Stimulant medication (e.g., methylphenidate) is frequently used with children diagnosed with Attention-Deficit Hyperactivity Disorder, which is often comorbid with Conduct Disorder. Moreover, occasionally, stimulant medication has some impact on aggressive and other antisocial behaviors (see Hinshaw, 1994). Yet, no strong evidence exists that stimulant medication can alter the constellation of symptoms (e.g., fighting, stealing) central to the diagnosis. A review of various medications for aggression in children and adolescents has raised leads, but the bulk of research consists of uncontrolled studies (Campbell & Cueva, 1995; Stewart, Myers, Burket, & Lyles, 1990). Controlled studies (e.g., random assignment, placebo controls) have shown antiaggressive effects with some medications (e.g., lithium; Campbell et al., 1995) but not others (e.g., carbamazepine; Cueva et al., 1996). Reliable psychopharmacological treatments for aggression, leaving aside the constellation of CD (e.g., fire setting and stealing), remain to be developed.

There is a genre of interventions that is worth mentioning in passing. Occasionally, interventions are advocated and implemented such as sending conduct-disordered youths to a camp out in the country where they learn how to "rough it," to assume responsibility (e.g., take care of horses), or to experience military (e.g., basic training) regimens. The conceptual bases of such treatments and supportive research on the processes involved in the onset or maintenance of CD are rarely provided. On the one hand, developing treatments that emerge outside the mainstream of the mental health professions is to be encouraged precisely because traditional treatments have not resolved the problem. On the other hand, this genre of intervention tends to eschew evaluation. Evaluation is key because well-intentioned and costly interventions can have little or no effect on youths they serve (Weisz et al., 1990) and sometimes may actually increase antisocial behavior (Lundman, 1984).

DEVELOPING MORE EFFECTIVE TREATMENTS

A number of issues emerge in the treatment of conduct-disordered youths and decision making about what interventions to provide to whom. These issues reflect obstacles in delivering treatment, lacunae in our knowledge base, and limitations in the models of providing care. Addressing these issues in research is likely to increase the effectiveness of treatment.

What Treatments Do Not Work

With hundreds of treatments available for children, it would be quite helpful to know which among these do not work or do not work very well. As noted earlier, the vast majority of treatments have not been evaluated empirically. Thus, there is no accumulated body of evidence in which treatments have consistently emerged as weak or ineffective. Moreover, the nature of the dominant scientific research paradigm (inability to prove the null hypothesis) precludes firm demonstration of no effects of treatment. Even so, some comments can be made. Variations of psychodynamic therapy, relationship-based treatment, and play therapy, commonly used in clinical practice, have been shown to be less effective than one of the promising treatments noted previously (e.g., Borduin et al., 1995; Kazdin et al., 1987, 1989; Weiss, Catron, Harris, & Phung, 1999). From this limited research, it is premature to conclude that these latter treatments are ineffective. Yet, at best, their benefits for CD have yet to be demonstrated, and more promising treatments with firmer empirical bases are currently the treatments of choice.

The absence of empirical evidence is only one criterion, albeit an obviously important one. In advance of, and eventually along with, the evidence, scrutiny of the conceptual underpinnings of treatment and the treatment focus is important in relation to what we know about CD. We know, for example, that conduct-disordered youths usually show problems in multiple domains, including overt behavior, social relations (with, e.g., peers, teachers, family members), and academic performance. For a treatment to be effective, it is likely that several domains have to be addressed explicitly within the sessions, or a conceptual model (with supporting evidence) is needed to convey why a narrow or delimited focus (e.g., on psychic conflicts or a small set of overt behaviors) is likely to have broad effects on domains not explicitly addressed in treatment. Although one cannot say for certain what techniques will not work, it is much safer to say that treatments that neglect multiple domains are likely to have limited effects.

Second, some evidence has emerged that is useful for selecting what treatments to avoid or to use with great caution. Often, conduct-disordered youths are treated in group therapy. Yet, placing youths together could impede improvement. For example, in one demonstration, youths (ages 8 to 17) were randomly assigned to variations of group therapy (Feldman, Caplinger, & Wodarski, 1983). In one type of group, all members were individuals referred for CD; in another type of group, conduct-disordered youths were placed with some non-CD youths (without clinical problems). Those placed in a group of their deviant peers did not improve; those placed with nondeviant peers did improve. Interpretation is based on the likelihood that peer bonding to others can improve one's behavior, if those peers engage in more normative behavior; bonding to a deviant group can sustain deviant behavior.

Similarly, another study compared interventions for nonreferred youths (ages 10 to 14) with conduct problems (Dishion & Andrews, 1995). One of the treatment conditions included youths meeting in a group with a focus on self-regulation, monitoring, and developing behavior-change programs. This condition, whether alone or in combination with parent training, was associated with *increases* in behavioral problems and substance use (cigarette smoking). Again, placing conduct problem teens in a group situation exacerbated their problems. Other research has shown that individuals may become worse (e.g., increase in arrest rates) through association with deviant peers as part of treatment (Dishion, McCord, & Poulin, 1999; O'Donnell, 1992).

Treatments for conduct-disordered youths in such settings as hospitals, schools, and correctional facilities are often conducted in a group therapy format in which several conduct problem youths are together to talk about or work on their problems or go to the country for some fresh air experience to get better. There may be conditions under which this arrangement is beneficial. However, current research suggests that placing such youths together can impede therapeutic change and have deleterious effects.

Understanding the Basis of Therapeutic Change

A salient limitation of child and adolescent therapy research, in relation to CD and to other disorders as well, is the paucity of studies that attempt to understand the basis of therapeutic change. There appears to be little interest in developing theoretical views about the change processes and testing these views empirically. For this reason, it is not clear why treatment works (i.e., through what processes or mechanisms). Research would profit immeasurably by generating and testing theories of therapeutic change. In much of current theory research, theory is used to refer to the approach toward treatment and reflects an orientation or statement of key constructs (e.g., faulty cognitions, faulty family functioning). What is needed is research on the mechanisms of why and how people change.

Theories of therapeutic change and their empirical tests would serve several important purposes. There is a vast number of treatments, as noted previously. Perhaps a small set of common mechanisms or processes could be identified that span several techniques. Second, therapy outcome effects can be broad and affect mental and physical health and social, emotional, and behavioral functioning. In the context of adult treatment, psychotherapy improves symptoms of physical health and affects life (e.g., increases fertility among infertile couples) and death (e.g., increases survival among terminally ill patients; see Kazdin, 2000b). How are such changes possible and through what processes? Third, there are likely to be all sorts of moderators of treatment (i.e., factors on which treatment outcome depends). Theory is needed to sort through an indefinite range of factors and to explain how these factors relate to the treatment process. Finally, in both research and clinical practice, we wish to maximize therapeutic change. This requires knowing what the critical factors are in treatment and how change occurs.

Who Responds Well to Treatment

We have known for many years that the critical question of psychotherapy is not what technique is effective, but what technique works for whom, under what conditions, as administered by what type of therapists (Kiesler, 1971). The adult psychotherapy literature has focused on a range of questions to identify factors (e.g., patient, therapist, treatment process) that contribute to outcome. Child and adolescent therapy research has neglected the role of child, parent, family, and therapist factors that may moderate outcome.

In the case of CD, a few studies have looked at who responds to treatment, mostly in the context of PMT. As mentioned previously, evidence suggests that risk factors for onset of CD and poor long-term prognosis (e.g., early onset, severe aggressive behavior, family adversity) influence responsiveness to treatment. Our own work has shown that even those youths with multiple risk factors still improve with treatment, but the changes are not as great as those achieved for cases with fewer risk factors. At present and in the absence of very much research on the matter, a useful guideline to predict responsiveness to treatment is to consider loading of the child, parent, and family on risk factors that portend a poor long-term prognosis (see Kazdin, 1995b; Robins, 1991).

A goal of research is to identify whether some children respond to one type of treatment more than another. At this point, the literature cannot speak to this issue. The characteristics that have been studied in relation to treatment outcome (e.g., comorbidity) have not been examined across different treatments. Consequently, we do not know whether these factors affect responsiveness to any treatment or to particular forms of treatment.

Combining Treatments

There is keen interest, both in clinical work and in research, in using combinations of treatment (i.e., multiple psychosocial and/or pharmacological interventions; see Kazdin, 1996a). The benefits of combining treatment require showing that the combination is better than the constituent components provided alone. Little work of this ilk is available in the child and adolescent therapy literature, leaving aside the more restricted focus on CD.

Some studies have suggested that combining PMT and PSST is more effective than the individual components (e.g., Kazdin et al., 1992; Webster-Stratton & Hammond, 1997). Also, some of the promising treatments reviewed previously (MST, FFT) *are* combined treatments. For example, MST provides many different treatments for antisocial youths. Two points are worth noting. First, the constituent treatments that form a major part of treatment are those that have evidence on their behalf (e.g., PSST, PMT), so that not any combination is used. Second, we do not yet know that MST as a combined treatment package is more effective than the most effective constituent component administered for the same duration. The comparisons of MST mostly included individual psychotherapy and counseling—important comparison groups, to be sure. Although treatment has surpassed traditional therapy practices, this is not the same as showing that combinations of treatment per se are necessary to achieve therapeutic changes.

Combined treatments may be very useful and should be pursued. At the same time, the effects of combined treatment obviously depend very much on the treatments that are combined. For example, mentioned already was a study in which parent training and a teen-focused group were evaluated alone and in combination (Dishion & Andrews, 1995). Conditions that received the teen group component, whether alone or in combination with parent training, became worse. Obviously, one cannot assume that combined treatments will automatically be no different from or better than their constituent treatments. There is another more subtle and perhaps worrisome facet of combined treatments. A danger in promoting treatment combinations is that it may unwittingly continue to promote techniques with little evidence in their behalf. Poorly understood, poorly investigated, or ineffective treatments may be promoted as filled with new potential as a component of a larger package of techniques. With promising treatments available, we have a comparative base to evaluate novel treatments, treatment combinations, and unevaluated treatments in current use. If a promising treatment is not used in clinical work, we would want evidence that it has clearly failed, that other promising treatments for whatever reason cannot be used, and that the treatment that is to be applied has a reasonable basis for addressing the scope of dysfunction.

Models of Delivering Treatment

The model of treatment delivery in current research is to provide a relatively brief and time-limited intervention (e.g., typically 8 to 10 sessions). For several clinical dysfunctions or for a number of children with a particular dysfunction such as CD, the course of maladjustment may be long term. In such cases, the notion of providing a brief, time-limited treatment may very much limit outcome effects. More extended and enduring treatment in some form may be needed to achieve clinically important effects with the greatest number of youths. Two ways of delivering extended treatment illustrate the point.

The first variation can be referred to simply as *continued care*. The model of treatment delivery that may be needed can be likened to the model used in the treatment of diabetes mellitus. With diabetes, ongoing treatment (insulin) is needed to ensure that the benefits of treatment are sustained. The benefits of treatment would end with discontinuation of treatment. Analogously, in the context of CD, a variation of ongoing treatment may be needed. Perhaps after the child is referred, treatment is provided to address the current crises and to have impact on functioning at home, at school, and in the community. After improvement is achieved, treatment is modified rather than terminated. At that point, the child could enter into maintenance therapy, that is, continued treatment, perhaps in varying schedules ("doses"). Treatment would continue, but perhaps on a more intermittent basis. Continued treatment in this fashion has been effective as a model for treating recurrent depression in adults (see Kupfer et al., 1992).

The second variation is referred to as *periodic monitoring and treatment* and reflects a different way of extending treatment. After initial treatment and demonstrated improvement in functioning in everyday life, treatment is suspended. At this point, the child's functioning begins to be monitored regularly (e.g., every 3 months) and systematically (with standardized measures). Treatment could be provided *pro re nata* (PRN) based on the assessment data or emergent issues raised by the family, teachers, or others. The approach might be likened to the more familiar model of dental care in the United States in which "checkups" are recommended every 6 months; an intervention is provided if needed based on these periodic checks.

Obviously, the use of ongoing treatment is not advocated in cases where there is evidence that short-term treatment is effective. A difficulty with most of the research on treatment of CD, whether promising, poorly investigated, or combined treatments, is that the conventional treatment model of brief, time-limited therapy has been adopted. Without considering alternative models of delivery, current treatments may be quite limited in the effects they can produce. Although more effective treatments are sorely needed, the way of delivering currently available treatments ought to be reconsidered.

CONCLUSIONS

Many different types of treatment have been applied to CD. Five treatments with the strongest evidence to date were detailed. *Parent management training* is directed at altering parent-child interactions in the home, particularly those interactions related to child-rearing practices and coercive interchanges. *Multisystemic therapy* focus on the individual, family, and extrafamilial systems and their interrelations as a way to reduce symptoms and to promote prosocial behavior. Multiple treatments (e.g., PSST, PMT, family therapy) are used in combination to address domains that affect the child. *Cognitive problem-solving skills training* focuses on cognitive processes that underlie social behavior and response repertoires in interpersonal situations. *Functional family therapy* utilizes principles of systems theory and behavior modification for altering interaction, communication patterns, and problem solving among family members. *Brief strategic family therapy* focuses on the structure of the family and concrete strategies that can be used to promote improved patterns of interaction. This treatment has been developed with Hispanic children and adolescents and has integrated culturally pertinent issues to engage the families.

Evidence in behalf of these treatments was reviewed. The first three treatments (PMT, MST, PSST) were reviewed in greater detail because of the more extensive evidence (Type 1 and 2 studies) and follow-up data in their behalf. FFT and BSFT have controlled trials in their behalf, but the scope of the evidence (e.g., replications, range of tests, number of outcome studies) has not approached that for the other treatments. Nevertheless, they are quite promising, and their empirical base places them at the front of the small group of evidence-based treatments for conduct problems.

What is striking about the treatments is that there is a strong emphasis on the family; four of the five treatments explicitly focus on parents and family interaction in some way. The evidence does not establish that the family is the only or best way to intervene. At the same time, a striking feature of CD among those who treat clinically referred cases is the significant parent, family, and contextual influences in which the child's function is embedded. This, too, does not mean that the child's problem is caused by these influences, but it does mean that with any intervention, it is difficult and perhaps not even possible to ignore the parent and family. Indeed, parent functioning, stress, and perceptions about treatment strongly influence whether children come to, remain in, and profit from therapy. Consequently, engaging the family in special ways to participate in treatment and directly addressing parent and family functioning are high-priority foci. Better assessment and diagnosis of parent, family, and contextual factors are needed to provide a systematic way of identifying whether multiple foci and which foci are optimal for a particular child or type of child-parent-family-context Gestalt.

We cannot yet say that one intervention can ameliorate CD and overcome the poor long-term prognosis. On the other hand, much can be said. Much of what is practiced in clinical settings is based on psychodynamically oriented treatment, general relationship counseling, various forms of family therapy (other than those reviewed above), and group therapy (with all antisocial youths as members). These and other procedures, alone and in various combinations in which they are often used, have not been evaluated carefully in controlled trials. Of course, absence of evidence is not tantamount to ineffectiveness. At the same time, promising treatments have advanced considerably, and a very special argument might be needed to justify administration of treatments that have neither basic research on their conceptual underpinnings in relation to CD nor outcome evidence from controlled clinical trials on their behalf.

Even considering only the evidence-based treatments for CD, important questions remain unanswered. The short- and long-term impact on children and the extent to which the changes materially alter their everyday lives are not clear from current research. Further development of treatments clearly is needed. Apart from treatment studies, further progress in understanding the nature of CD is likely to have very important implications for improving treatment outcome. Improved triage of patients to treatments that are likely to work will require understanding of characteristics of children, parents, and families that will make them more-or-less amenable to current treatments. And perhaps most important, research is needed that attempts to understand the bases of therapeutic change. Understanding the change process is the best long-term investment in developing effective treatments for clinical use.

ACKNOWLEDGMENTS Completion of this chapter was facilitated by support from the Leon Lowenstein Foundation, the William T. Grant Foundation (98-1872-98), and the National Institute of Mental Health (MH59029). Address correspondence to Alan E. Kazdin, Department of Psychology, Yale University, P.O. Box 208205, New Haven, Connecticut, USA 06520-8205.

Notes

1. *Children* refers to both children and adolescents. When pertinent to the discussion, a distinction is made.

2. *Conduct Disorder*, when capitalized, refers to the diagnosis and meeting diagnostic criteria for the disorder; when not capitalized, the term refers to children and adolescents with antisocial and aggressive behavior and impaired functioning whether or not they meet diagnostic criteria.

3. In *DSM-IV*, if the child meets criteria for CD, ODD is not diagnosed, because the former is likely to include many symptoms of the latter. Yet, invoking and evaluating the criteria for these diagnoses ignoring this consideration has been useful in understanding the relation and overlap of these diagnoses.

4. The rationale, empirical underpinnings, outcome research, and treatment procedures cannot be fully elaborated for each of the techniques. References will be made to reviews of the evidence and to treatment manuals that elaborate each of the treatments.

5. Although many researchers contributed to the extensive literature on behalf of PMT, a few research programs (e.g., Eyberg, University of Florida; Forehand, University of Georgia; Patterson, Oregon Social Learning Research Center; Webster-Stratton, University of Washington) have made special inroads in developing the treatment, assessing factors that contribute to change, evaluating follow-up, and replicating treatment effects across multiple samples. Samples of this work are cited in the chapter.

6. The comments on treatment of obesity greatly oversimplify outcomes of weight control studies. For example, individuals receiving treatment wish to attain much greater weight losses from treatment than they actually do or that are recommended for health reasons (see Foster, Wadden, Vogt, & Brewer, 1997). Body image, self-esteem, and measures of related psychological constructs convey that physical and mental health outcomes of treatment may vary considerably.

References

Alexander, J. F., Barton, C., Schiavo, R. S., & Parsons, B. V. (1976). Systems-behavioral intervention with families of delinquents: Therapist characteristics, family behavior, and outcome. *Journal of Consulting and Clinical Psychology, 44*, 656–664.

Alexander, J. F., Holtzworth-Munroe, A., & Jameson, P. B. (1994). The process and outcome of marital and family therapy research: Review and evaluation. In A. E. Bergin & S. L. Garfield (Eds.), *Handbook of psychotherapy and behavior change* (4th ed., pp. 595–630). New York: Wiley.

Alexander, J. F., & Parsons, B. V. (1982). *Functional family therapy*. Monterey, CA: Brooks/Cole.

American Academy of Child and Adolescent Psychiatry. (1998). Practice parameters. *Journal of the American Academy of Child and Adolescent Psychiatry*, 37(10, 1s-89s, supplement).

American Psychiatric Association. (1994). *Diagnostic and statistical manual of mental disorders* (4th ed.). Washington, DC: Author.

Angold, A., Costello, J., Farmer, E. M. Z., Burns, B. J., & Erkanli, A. (1999). Impaired but undiagnosed. *Journal of the American Academy of Child and Adolescent Psychiatry*, 38, 129–137.

Baer, R. A., & Nietzel, M. T. (1991). Cognitive and behavioral treatment of impulsivity in children: A meta-analytic review of the outcome literature. *Journal of Clinical Child Psychology, 20*, 400–412.

Bank, L., Marlowe, J. H., Reid, J. B., Patterson, G. R., & Weinrott, M. R. (1991). A comparative evaluation of parent-training interventions for families of chronic delinquents. *Journal of Abnormal Child Psychology, 19*, 15–33.

Bell, R. Q., & Harper, L. (1977). *Child effects on adults*. New York: Wiley.

Bird, H. R., Yager, T. J., Staghezza, B., Gould, M. S., Canino, G., & Rubio-Stipec, M. (1990). Impairment in the epidemiological measurement of psychopathology in the community. *Journal of the American Academy of Child and Adolescent Psychiatry, 29*, 796–803.

Borduin, C. M., Mann, B. J., Cone, L. T., Henggeler, S. W., Fucci, B. R., Blaske, D. M., & Williams, R. A. (1995). Multisystemic treatment of serious juvenile offenders: Long-term prevention of criminality and violence. *Journal of Consulting and Clinical Psychology, 63*, 569–578.

Boyle, M. H., Offord, D., Racine, Y. A., Szatmari, P., Fleming, J. E., & Sanford, M. N. (1996). Identifying thresholds for classifying psychiatric disorder: Issues and prospects. *Journal of the American Academy of Child and Adolescent Psychiatry, 35*, 1440–1448.

Brandt, D. E., & Zlotnick, S. J. (1988). *The psychology and treatment of the youthful offender*. Springfield, IL: Charles C Thomas.

Brestan, E. V., & Eyberg, S. M. (1998). Effective psychosocial treatments of conduct-disordered children and adolescents: 29 years, 82 studies, and 5,272 kids. *Journal of Clinical Child Psychology, 27*, 180–189.

Campbell, M., Adams, P. B., Small, A. M., Kafantaris, V., Silva, R. R., Shell, J., Perry, R., & Overall, J. E. (1995). Lithium in hospitalized aggressive children with conduct disorder: A double-blind and placebo-controlled study. *Journal of the American Academy of Child and Adolescent Psychiatry, 34*, 445–453.

Campbell, M., & Cueva, J. E. (1995). Psychopharmacology in child and adolescent psychiatry: A review of the past seven years. Part 2. *Journal of the American Academy of Child and Adolescent Psychiatry, 34*, 1262–1272.

Coatsworth, J. D., Szapocznik, J., Kurtines, W., & Santisteban, D. A. (1997). Culturally competent psychosocial interventions with antisocial problem behavior in Hispanic youths. In D. M. Stoff, J. Breiling, & J. D. Maser (Eds.), *Handbook of antisocial behavior* (pp. 395–404). New York: Wiley.

Cooper, J. O., Heron, T. E., & Heward, W. L. (1987). *Applied behavior analysis*. Columbus, OH: Merrill.

Crick, N. R., & Dodge, K. A. (1994). A review and reformulation of social information processing mechanisms in children's social adjustment. *Psychological Bulletin, 115*, 74–101.

Cueva, J. E., Overall, J. E., Small, A. M., Armenteros, J. L., Perry, R., & Campbell, M. (1996). Carbamazepine in aggressive children with conduct disorder: A double-blind and placebo controlled study. *Journal of the American Academy of Child and Adolescent Psychiatry, 35*, 480–490.

Cunningham, C. E., Bremner, R., & Boyle, M. (1995). Large group community-based parenting programs for families of preschoolers at risk for disruptive behaviour disorders: Utilization, cost effectiveness, and outcome. *Journal of Child Psychology and Psychiatry, 36*, 1141–1159.

Dadds, M. R., & McHugh, T. A. (1992). Social support and treatment outcome in behavioral family therapy for child conduct problems. *Journal of Consulting and Clinical Psychology, 60*, 252–259.

Dishion, T. J., & Andrews, D. W. (1995). Preventing escalation in problem behaviors with high-risk young adolescents: Immediate and 1-year outcomes. *Journal of Consulting and Clinical Psychology, 63*, 538–548.

Dishion, T. J., McCord, J., & Poulin, F. (1999). When interventions harm: Peer groups and problem behavior. *American Psychologist, 54*, 755–764.

Dishion, T. J., & Patterson, G. R. (1992). Age effects in parent training outcomes. *Behavior Therapy, 23*, 719–729.

Dishion, T. J., Patterson, G. R., & Kavanagh, K. A. (1992). An experimental test of the coercion model: Linking theory, measurement, and intervention. In J. McCord & R. E. Tremblay (Eds.), *Preventing antisocial behavior* (pp. 253–282). New York: Guilford Press.

Dumas, J. E. (1989). Treating antisocial behavior in children: Child and family approaches. *Clinical Psychology Review, 9*, 197–222.

Dumas, J. E., & Wahler, R. G. (1983). Predictors of treatment outcome in parent training: Mother insularity and socioeconomic disadvantage. *Behavioral Assessment, 5*, 301–313.

Dumas, J. E., & Wahler, R. G. (1985). Indiscriminate mothering as a contextual factor in aggressive oppositional child behavior: "Damned if you do and damned if you don't." *Journal of Applied Behavior Analysis, 13*, 1–17.

Durlak, J. A., Fuhrman, T., & Lampman, C. (1991). Effectiveness of cognitive-behavioral therapy for maladapting children: A meta-analysis. *Psychological Bulletin, 110,* 204–214.

Durlak, J. A., Wells, A. M., Cotten, J. K., & Johnson, S. (1995). Analysis of selected methodological issues in child psychotherapy research. *Journal of Clinical Child Psychology, 24,* 141–148.

Feindler, E. L., & Ecton, R. B. (1986). *Adolescent anger control: Cognitive-behavioral techniques.* Elmsford, NY: Pergamon Press.

Feldman, R. A., Caplinger, T. E., & Wodarski, J. S. (1983). *The St. Louis conundrum: The effective treatment of antisocial youths.* Englewood Cliffs, NJ: Prentice Hall.

Fergusson, D. M., Horwood, L. J., & Lloyd, M. (1991). Confirmatory factor models of attention deficit and conduct disorder. *Journal of Child Psychology and Psychiatry, 32,* 257–274.

Finch, A. J., Jr., Nelson, W. M., & Ott, E. S. (1993). *Cognitive-behavioral procedures with children and adolescents: A practical guide.* Needham Heights, MA: Allyn & Bacon.

Forehand, R., & Long, N. (1996). *Parenting the strong-willed child.* Chicago: Contemporary Books.

Forgatch, M. S. (1991). The clinical science vortex: A developing theory of antisocial behavior. In D. J. Pepler & K. H. Rubin (Eds.), *The development and treatment of childhood aggression* (pp. 291–315). Hillsdale, NJ: Erlbaum.

Forgatch, M. S. (1994). *Parenting through change: A training manual.* Eugene: Oregon Social Learning Center.

Forgatch, M. S., & DeGarmo, D. S. (1999). Parenting through change: An effective prevention program for single mothers. *Journal of Consulting and Clinical Psychology, 67,* 711–724.

Foster, G. D., Wadden, T. A., Vogt, R. A., & Brewer, G. (1997). What is a reasonable weight loss? Patients' expectations and evaluations of obesity treatment outcomes. *Journal of Consulting and Clinical Psychology, 65,* 79–85.

Gordon, D. A., Arbuthnot, J., Gustafson, K. E., & McGreen, P. (1988). Home-based behavioral-systems family therapy with disadvantaged juvenile delinquents. *American Journal of Family Therapy, 163,* 243–255.

Graziano, A. M., & Diament, D. M. (1992). Parent behavioral training: An examination of the paradigm. *Behavior Modification, 16,* 3–38.

Hanf, C. (1969). *A two-stage program for modifying maternal controlling during mother-child interaction.* Paper presented at the meeting of the Western Psychological Association, Vancouver, British Columbia.

Henggeler, S. W., Melton, G. B., Brondino, M. J., Scherer, D. G., & Hanley, J. H. (1997). Multisystemic therapy with violent and chronic juvenile offenders and their families: The role of treatment fidelity in successful dissemination. *Journal of Consulting and Clinical Psychology, 65,* 821–833.

Henggeler, S. W., Rowland, M. D., Randall, J., Ward, D. M., Pickrel, S. G., Cunningham, P. B., Miller, S. L., Edwards, J., Zealberg, J. J., Hand, L. D., & Santos, A. B. (1999). Home-based multisystemic therapy as an alternative to hospitalization of youths in psychiatric crisis: Clinical outcomes. *Journal of the American Academy of Child and Adolescent Psychiatry, 38,* 1331–1339.

Henggeler, S. W., Schoenwald, S. K., Borduin, C. M., Rowland, M. D., & Cunningham, P. B. (1998). *Multisystemic treatment of antisocial behavior in children and adolescents.* New York: Guilford Press.

Hinshaw, S. P. (1994). *Attention deficits and hyperactivity in children.* Thousand Oaks, CA: Sage.

Hinshaw, S. P., Lahey, B. B., & Hart, E. L. (1993). Issues of taxonomy and comorbidity in the development of conduct disorder. *Development and Psychopathology, 5,* 31–49.

Huey, S. J., Jr., Henggeler, S. W., Brondino, M. J., & Pickrel, S. G. (2000). Mechanisms of change in multisystemic therapy: Reducing delinquent behavior through therapist adherence and improved family and peer functioning. *Journal of Consulting and Clinical Psychology, 68,* 451–467.

Irvine, A. B., Biglan, A., Smolkowski, K., Metzler, C. W., & Ary, D. V. (1999). The effectiveness of a parenting skills program for parents of middle school students in small communities. *Journal of Consulting and Clinical Psychology, 67,* 811–825.

Kazdin, A. E. (1995a). Child, parent, and family dysfunction as predictors of outcome in cognitive-behavioral treatment of antisocial children. *Behaviour Research and Therapy, 33,* 271–281.

Kazdin, A. E. (1995b). *Conduct disorder in childhood and adolescence* (2nd ed.). Thousand Oaks, CA: Sage.

Kazdin, A. E. (1996a). Combined and multimodal treatments in child and adolescent psychotherapy: Issues, challenges, and research directions. *Clinical Psychology: Science and Practice, 3,* 69–100.

Kazdin, A. E. (1996b). Dropping out of child psychotherapy: Issues for research and implications for practice. *Clinical Child Psychology and Psychiatry, 1,* 133–156.

Kazdin, A. E. (1997a). Parent management training: Evidence, outcomes, and issues. *Journal of the American Academy of Child and Adolescent Psychiatry, 36,* 1349–1356.

Kazdin, A. E. (1997b). Psychosocial treatments for conduct disorder in children. *Journal of Child Psychology and Psychiatry, 38,* 161–178.

Kazdin, A. E. (1998). *Research design in clinical psychology* (3rd ed.). Needham Heights, MA: Allyn & Bacon.

Kazdin, A. E. (1999). The meanings and measurement of clinical significance. *Journal of Consulting and Clinical Psychology, 67,* 332–339.

Kazdin, A. E. (2000a). Developing a research agenda for child and adolescent psychotherapy research. *Archives of General Psychiatry, 57,* 829–835.

Kazdin, A. E. (2000b). *Psychotherapy for children and adolescents: Directions for research and practice.* New York: Oxford University Press.

Kazdin, A. E. (2001). *Behavior modification in applied settings* (6th ed.). Pacific Grove, CA: Wadsworth.

Kazdin, A. E., Bass, D., Ayers, W. A., & Rodgers, A. (1990). Empirical and clinical focus of child and adolescent psychotherapy research. *Journal of Consulting and Clinical Psychology, 58,* 729–740.

Kazdin, A. E., Bass, D., Siegel, T., & Thomas, C. (1989). Cognitive-behavioral treatment and relationship therapy in the treatment of children referred for antisocial behavior. *Journal of Consulting and Clinical Psychology, 57,* 522–535.

Kazdin, A. E., & Crowley, M. (1997). Moderators of treatment outcome in cognitively based treatment of antisocial behavior. *Cognitive Therapy and Research, 21,* 185–207.

Kazdin, A. E., Esveldt-Dawson, K., French, N. H., & Unis, A. S. (1987). Problem-solving skills training and relationship therapy in the treatment of antisocial child behavior. *Journal of Consulting and Clinical Psychology, 55,* 76–85.

Kazdin, A. E., Siegel, T. C., & Bass, D. (1990). Drawing upon clinical practice to inform research on child and adolescent psychotherapy: A survey of practitioners. *Professional Psychology: Research and Practice, 21,* 189–198.

Kazdin, A. E., Siegel, T., & Bass, D. (1992). Cognitive problem-solving skills training and parent management training in the treatment of antisocial behavior in children. *Journal of Consulting and Clinical Psychology, 60,* 733–747.

Kazdin, A. E., & Wassell, G. (1999). Barriers to treatment participation and therapeutic change among children referred for conduct disorder. *Journal of Clinical Child Psychology, 28,* 160–172.

Kazdin, A. E., & Wassell, G. (2000). Therapeutic changes in children, parents, and families resulting from treatment of children with conduct problems. *Journal of the American Academy of Child and Adolescent Psychiatry, 39,* 414–420.

Kazdin, A. E., & Weisz, J. R. (1998). Identifying and developing empirically supported child and adolescent treatments. *Journal of Consulting and Clinical Psychology, 66,* 19–36.

Kendall, P. C. (Ed.). (2000). *Child and adolescent therapy: Cognitive-behavioral procedures* (2nd ed.). New York: Guilford Press.

Kiesler, D. J. (1971). Experimental designs in psychotherapy research. In A. E. Bergin & S. L. Garfield (Eds.), *Handbook of psychotherapy and behavior change: An empirical analysis* (pp. 36–74). New York: Wiley.

Koocher, G. P., & Pedulla, B. M. (1977). Current practices in child psychotherapy. *Professional Psychology, 8,* 275–287.

Kupfer, D. J., Frank, E., Perel, J. M., Cornes, C., Mallinger, A. G., Thase, M. E., McEachran, A. B., & Grochocinski, V. J. (1992). Five-year outcome for maintenance therapies in recurrent depression. *Archives of General Psychiatry, 49,* 769–773.

Lochman, J. E., & Dodge, K. A. (1994). Social-cognitive processes of severely violent, moderately aggressive, and nonaggressive boys. *Journal of Consulting and Clinical Psychology, 62,* 366–374.

Lochman, J. E., Whidby, J. M., & FitzGerald, D. P. (2000). Cognitive-behavioral assessment and treatment with aggressive children. In P. C. Kendall (Ed.), *Child and adolescent therapy: Cognitive-behavioral procedures* (2nd ed., pp. 31–87). New York: Guilford Press.

Loeber, R., & Farrington, D. P. (Eds.). (1998). *Serious and violent juvenile offenders: Risk factors and successful interventions.* Thousand Oaks, CA: Sage.

Long, P., Forehand, R., Wierson, M., & Morgan, A. (1994). Does parent training with young noncompliant children have long-term effects? *Behaviour Research and Therapy, 32,* 101–107.

Lonigan, C. J., & Elbert, J. C. (Eds.). (1998). Special issue on empirically supported psychosocial interventions for children. *Journal of Clinical Child Psychology, 27,* 138–226.

Lundman, R. J. (1984). *Prevention and control of juvenile delinquency.* New York: Oxford University Press.

Lytton, H. (1990). Child and parent effects in boys' conduct disorder: A reinterpretation. *Developmental Psychology, 26,* 683–697.

Mann, B. J., Borduin, C. M., Henggeler, S. W., & Blaske, D. M. (1990). An investigation of systemic conceptualizations of parent-child coalitions and symptom change. *Journal of Consulting and Clinical Psychology, 58,* 336–344.

Morris, S. M., Alexander, J. F., & Turner, C. W. (1991). Do reattributions reduce blame? *Journal of Family Psychology, 5,* 192–203.

Newberry, A. M., Alexander, J. F., & Turner, C. W. (1991). Gender as a process variable in family therapy. *Journal of Family Psychology, 5*, 158–175.

O'Donnell, C. R. (1992). The interplay of theory and practice in delinquency prevention: From behavior modification to activity settings. In J. McCord & R. E. Tremblay (Eds.), *Preventing antisocial behavior* (pp. 209–232). New York: Guilford Press.

Offord, D. R., Boyle, M. H., & Racine, Y. A. (1991). The epidemiology of antisocial behavior. In D. J. Pepler & K. H. Rubin (Eds.), *The development and treatment of childhood aggression* (pp. 31–54). Hillsdale, NJ: Erlbaum.

Offord, D., Boyle, M. H., Racine, Y. A., Fleming, J. E., Cadman, D. T., Blum, H. M., Byrne, C., Links, P. S., Lipman, E. L., MacMillan, H. L., Rae Grant, N. I., Sanford, M. N., Szatmari, P., Thomas, H., & Woodward, C. A. (1992). Outcome, prognosis, and risk in a longitudinal follow-up study. *Journal of the American Academy of Child and Adolescent Psychiatry, 31*, 916–923.

Patterson, G. R. (1982). *Coercive family process*. Eugene, OR: Castalia.

Patterson, G. R., Capaldi, D., & Bank, L. (1991). An early starter model for predicting delinquency. In D. J. Pepler & K. H. Rubin (Eds.), *The development and treatment of childhood aggression* (pp. 139–168). Hillsdale, NJ: Erlbaum.

Patterson, G. R., & Chamberlain, P. (1994). A functional analysis of resistance during parent training therapy. *Clinical Psychology: Science and Practice, 1*, 53–70.

Patterson, G. R., Dishion, T. J., & Chamberlain, P. (1993). Outcomes and methodological issues relating to treatment of antisocial children. In T. R. Giles (Ed.), *Handbook of effective psychotherapy* (pp. 43–87). New York: Plenum Press.

Patterson, G. R., Reid, J. B., & Dishion, T. J. (1992). *Antisocial boys*. Eugene, OR: Castalia.

Pepler, D. J., & Rubin, K. H. (Eds.). (1991). *The development and treatment of childhood aggression*. Hillsdale, NJ: Erlbaum.

Robins, L. N. (1966). *Deviant children grown up*. Baltimore: Williams & Wilkins.

Robins, L. N. (1978). Sturdy childhood predictors of adult antisocial behavior: Replications from longitudinal studies. *Psychological Medicine, 8*, 611–622.

Robins, L. N. (1981). Epidemiological approaches to natural history research: Antisocial disorders in children. *Journal of the American Academy of Child Psychiatry, 20*, 566–680.

Robins, L. N. (1991). Conduct disorder. *Journal of Child Psychology and Psychiatry, 32*, 193–212.

Rubin, K. H., Bream, L. A., & Rose-Krasnor, L. (1991). Social problem solving and aggression in childhood. In D. J. Pepler & K. H. Rubin (Eds.), *The development and treatment of childhood aggression* (pp. 219–248). Hillsdale, NJ: Erlbaum.

Ruma, P. R., Burke, R. V., & Thompson, R. W. (1996). Group parent training: Is it effective for children of all ages? *Behavior Therapy, 27*, 159–169.

Rutter, M., Tizard, J., & Whitmore, K. (Eds.). (1970). *Education, health and behaviour*. London: Longmans.

Sanders, M. R., & Dadds, M. R. (1993). *Behavioral family intervention*. Needham Heights, MA: Allyn & Bacon.

Sanson, A., Oberklaid, F., Pedlow, R., & Prior, M. (1991). Risk indicators: Assessment of infancy predictors of pre-school behavioural maladjustment. *Journal of Child Psychology and Psychiatry, 32*, 609–626.

Santisteban, D. A., Szapocznik, J., Perez-Vidal, A., Kurtines, W. H., Murray, E. J., & LaPerriere, A. (1996). Efficacy of intervention for engaging youth and families into treatment and some variables that may contribute to differential effectiveness. *Journal of Family Psychology, 10*, 35–44.

Serketich, W. J., & Dumas, J. E. (1996). The effectiveness of behavioral parent training to modify antisocial behavior in children: A meta-analysis. *Behavior Therapy, 27*, 171–186.

Shirk, S. R. (Ed.). (1988). *Cognitive development and child psychotherapy*. New York: Plenum Press.

Shure, M. B. (1992). *I can problem solve (ICPS): An interpersonal cognitive problem solving program*. Champaign, IL: Research Press.

Shure, M. B. (1996). *Raising a thinking child: Help your young child to resolve everyday conflicts and get along with others*. New York: Pocket Books.

Shure, M. B. (1997). Interpersonal cognitive problem solving: Primary prevention of early high-risk behaviors in the preschool and primary years. In G. W. Albee & T. P. Gulotta (Eds.), *Primary prevention works* (pp. 167–188). Thousand Oaks, CA: Sage.

Shure, M. B. (1999). Preventing violence the problem-solving way. *Juvenile Justice Bulletin*, April 1–11. Publication of the US Department of Justice, Office of Juvenile Justice and Delinquency Prevention, Washington, DC.

Silver, L. B., & Silver, B. J. (1983). Clinical practice of child psychiatry: A survey. *Journal of the American Academy of Child Psychiatry, 22*, 573–579.

Skinner, B. F. (1938). *The behavior of organisms: An experimental analysis*. New York: Appleton-Century.

Spivack, G., & Shure, M. B. (1982). The cognition of social adjustment: Interpersonal cognitive problem solving thinking. In B. B. Lahey & A. E. Kazdin (Eds.), *Advances in clinical child psychology* (Vol. 5, pp. 323–372). New York: Plenum Press.

Stewart, J. T., Myers, W. C., Burket, R. C., & Lyles, W. B. (1990). A review of the psychopharmacology of aggression in children and adolescents. *Journal of the American Academy of Child and Adolescent Psychiatry, 29,* 269–277.

Stoff, D. M., Breiling, J., & Maser, J. D. (Eds.). (1997). *Handbook of antisocial behavior*. New York: Wiley.

Szapocznik, J., & Kurtines, W. M. (1989). *Breakthroughs in family therapy with drug-abusing problem youth*. New York: Springer.

Szapocznik, J., Kurtines, W. H., Foote, F. H., Perez-Vidal, A., & Hervis, O. (1986). Conjoint versus one person family therapy: Further evidence for the effectiveness of conducting family therapy through one person. *Journal of Consulting and Clinical Psychology, 54,* 395–397.

Szapocznik, J., Perez-Vidal, A., Brickman, A., Foote, F. H., Santisteban, D. A., Hervis, O., & Kurtines, W. H. (1988). Engaging adolescent drug abusers and their families into treatment: A strategic structural systems approach. *Journal of Consulting and Clinical Psychology, 56,* 552–557.

Szapocznik, J., Rio, A., Murray, E., Cohen, R., Scopetta, M., Rivas-Vasquez, A., Hervis, O., Posada, V., & Kurtines, W. (1989). Structural family versus psychodynamic child therapy for problematic Hispanic boys. *Journal of Consulting and Clinical Psychology, 57,* 571–578.

Thompson, R. W., Ruma, P. R., Schuchmann, L. F., & Burke, R. V. (1996). A cost-effectiveness evaluation of parent training. *Journal of Child and Family Studies, 5,* 415–429.

U.S. Congress, Office of Technology Assessment. (1991). *Adolescent health*. (OTA-H-468). Washington, DC: U.S. Government Printing Office.

Wadsworth, M. (1979). *Roots of delinquency: Infancy, adolescence and crime*. New York: Barnes & Noble.

Wahler, R. G., & Dumas, J. E. (1986). Maintenance factors in coercive mother-child interactions: The compliance and predictability hypotheses. *Journal of Applied Behavior Analysis, 19,* 13–22.

Walker, J. L., Lahey, B. B., Russo, M. F., Christ, M. A. G., McBurnett, K., Loeber, R., Stouthamer-Loeber, M., & Green, S. M. (1991). Anxiety, inhibition, and conduct disorder in children: 1. Relation to social impairment. *Journal of the American Academy of Child and Adolescent Psychiatry, 30,* 187–191.

Webster-Stratton, C. (1994). Advancing videotape parent training: A comparison study. *Journal of Consulting and Clinical Psychology, 62,* 583–593.

Webster-Stratton, C. (1998). Preventing conduct problems in Head Start children: Strengthening parenting competencies. *Journal of Consulting and Clinical Psychology, 66,* 715–730.

Webster-Stratton, C., & Hammond, M. (1990). Predictors of treatment outcome in parent training for families with conduct problem children. *Behavior Therapy, 21,* 319–337.

Webster-Stratton, C., & Hammond, M. (1997). Treating children with early-onset conduct problems: A comparison of child and parent training interventions. *Journal of Consulting and Clinical Psychology, 65,* 93–109.

Weiss, B., Catron, T., Harris, V., & Phung, T. M. (1999). The effectiveness of traditional child therapy. *Journal of Consulting and Clinical Psychology, 67,* 82–94.

Weisz, J. R., Walter, B. R., Weiss, B., Fernandez, G. A., & Mikow, V. A. (1990). Arrests among emotionally disturbed violent and assaultive individuals following minimal versus lengthy intervention through North Carolina's Willie M. Program. *Journal of Consulting and Clinical Psychology, 58,* 720–728.

Weisz, J. R., Weiss, B., Han, S. S., Granger, D. A., & Morton, T. (1995). Effects of psychotherapy with children and adolescents revisited: A meta-analysis of treatment outcome studies. *Psychological Bulletin, 117,* 450–468.

Werner, E. E., & Smith, R. S. (1992). *Overcoming the odds: High risk children from birth to adulthood*. Ithaca: Cornell University Press.

West, D. J. (1982). *Delinquency: Its roots, careers and prospects*. Cambridge: Harvard University Press.

Zoccolillo, M. (1993). Gender and the development of conduct disorder. *Development and Psychopathology, 5,* 65–78.

4

Treatments for Dementia

Larry Tune

Dementia refers to a large number of disorders characterized by global cognitive deficits, including impairments of recent memory, and one or more of the following: aphasia, apraxia, agnosia, and disturbance of executive functioning. The commonest dementias are Alzheimer's disease (AD), vascular dementia, dementia due to general medical conditions (including HIV dementia), head trauma, Parkinson's disease (PD), Huntington's disease, Pick's disease, Creutzfeldt-Jacob disease, substance-induced persisting dementia, and multiple etiologies. Alzheimer's disease, alone or in combination with other conditions (e.g., stroke), is easily the most common. With the exception of dementia associated with Parkinson's disease, the remaining syndromes are either so rare or heterogeneous that it is difficult to find well-controlled studies that would meet diagnostic and clinical design criteria for standards defined for this book.

The focus of this chapter is on therapeutic interventions for Alzheimer's disease. Innumerable articles investigating patient populations defined as "geropsychiatric" or "gerontopsychiatric" have been excluded. Following this discussion, there is a brief review of therapeutic interventions for Parkinson's disease.

ALZHEIMER'S DISEASE

Alzheimer's disease accounts for approximately 70% of all patients suffering with dementia and affects approximately 2.5 million individuals in North America over the age of 65. Mortimer et al. (1992) found an incidence of 1% per year in the elderly. The prevalence increases with age. Approximately 10% of all patients over the age of 65 are demented, and 33 to 50% of adults over the age of 84 suffer from dementia.

The study of therapeutic interventions in AD has been affected by both our increased understanding of the pathophysiology of AD and by progressive refinement in diagnostic criteria. Clinicopathologic studies published in the last 10 years have shown a clinical diagnostic accuracy of approximately 90%. However, recent studies have shown that the more we understand about Alzheimer's disease, the more complicated the story becomes. For example, approximately one third of autopsy-confirmed AD cases have coexisting "Lewy body dementia" with associated clinical findings of extrapyramidal symptoms and fluctuating levels of consciousness (Thal, 1994).

Other issues critical to the investigation of any drug for AD include the myriad rating instruments used to measure clinical outcome (in the accompanying tables, over 200 separate measures were used to assess clinical outcome), the absence of clinical diagnostic markers, the absence of compelling animal models for AD, and the variability in the course of illness. This is a slow, variably progressive illness in a patient population with markedly heterogeneous premorbid cognitive abilities. Most clinical trials are of relatively short duration and emphasize short-term clinical improvement as the principal outcome measure. Until recently, most investigations have excluded the possibility of slowing the rate of progression of illness. Several recent studies have focused on change in the rate of clinical deterioration, but most of these are studies of relatively short duration.

The choice of study design must be carefully considered. Three basic designs—crossover studies, randomized control parallel design, and enrichment designs (e.g., see U.S. multicenter tacrine study; Davis et al., 1992)—have all been used. All of these designs could satisfy criteria for Type 1 studies. Each has significant strengths and weaknesses, particularly the long-term studies.

Vasodilators and Metabolic Enhancement Strategies

Most early clinical trials focused on the potential roles of vasodilators or (more recently) metabolic enhancers (Tables 4.1, 4.2) in the treatment of AD. By far the most popular of these was dihydroergotoxine mesylate (Hydergine). Hydergine is one of two drugs currently approved for use in dementia (actually for use in "idiopathic decline in mental capacity"). Despite its long (more than 40 years) and frequent use, its utility in the management of dementia is still in doubt.

Many small, double-blind investigations showed significant improvement in patients with dementia. Most of these early investigations suffered from several critical flaws, including poor diagnostic criteria and outcome measures that did not focus specifically on cognition (for full review, see Hollister & Yesavage, 1984; Olin et al., 2000). One recent investigation found that two ergot derivatives, nicergoline and ergoloid mesylate, were moderately effective in the management of mild to moderate dementia (Battaglia et al., 1989).

Nootropic agents (e.g., piracetam, oxiracetam, aniracetam, pyrrolidone), derivatives of the excitatory amino acid neurotransmitter GABA, have been extensively investigated in the treatment of dementing illnesses. Animal studies have repeatedly shown these nootrophic compounds to facilitate learning and memory performance in animals. Although the exact mechanism of action is unclear, they are thought to serve as neuroprotective agents in the central nervous system (CNS) circulation. Table 4.2 summarizes several Type 2 and Type 3 studies of piracetam, oxiracetam, and vinpocetine. Most studies have failed to show significant clinical improvement with these drugs. One lingering experimental question is whether long-term nootrophic administration might affect the progression of disease (e.g., see Croisile et al., 1993).

Cholinergic Augmentation Strategies

The newer therapeutic approaches have followed our understanding of the pathophysiology of AD. The first of these, and by far the most extensively studied, focuses on selective impairments in cholinergic neurotransmission, which were first identified in 1976 (Tables 4.3–4.6). These cholinergic strategies have attempted to potentiate cholinergic neurotransmission in one of several ways: cholinergic precursor loading, acetylcholinesterase inhibition, and direct or indirect central cholinergic stimulation.

Precursor loading strategies are based on demonstrations that peripheral administration enhances brain acetylcholine levels in animal models. Few of the existing human studies, most of which involved lecithin or choline administration, show convincing clinical efficacy (Table 4.6 and 4.7, respectively). We found one Type 1 study (with significant improvement from bethanechol), eight Type 2 studies (five showing improvement), and two Type 3 studies (with one showing improvement). Two studies (one each of Types 2 and 3) of nicotinic agonists showed clinical improvement. Overall, the effects of this treatment strategy have been mixed. Many have suffered either from poor study design or small sample size.

Of these cholinergic augmentation strategies, the use of acetylcholinesterase inhibitors (Tables 4.3 to 4.5, respectively), has provided promising data. The earliest studies focused on physostigmine. Physostigmine proved to be a difficult investigational compound, largely because of its relatively brief half-life ($T\frac{1}{2}$ = 30 minutes following oral ingestion) and high rate of side effects. However, Thal et al. (1983) showed that the improvement in memory performance following multiple doses of physostigmine could persist up to 36 hours.

Several investigations have used longer acting cholinesterase inhibitors. Tacrine hydrochloride alone or in combination with lecithin is the best studied of these long-acting AChEs, especially in large-scale stud-

TABLE 4.1 Hydergine[a]

Authors	*Design*	N	*Outcome Measures*	*Length of Study*	*Measure Results*
Thompson et al. (1990)	DB, PC, random parallel group	80	DSY, WMS, SCAGS, IPSCE, GERRI	24 weeks	No significant improvement
Rouy et al. (1989)	DB, PC, random parallel group	97	SCAGS, NOISE	6 months	Significant improvement on SCAGS
Theinhaus et al. (1987)	DB, PC, random parallel group	41	IPSCE, GDS, BSRT, DSY, ZVT	12 weeks	Significant improvement on memory section of IPSCE
van Loveren-Huyben et al. (1984)	DB, PC, random parallel group	58	BDT, DS, DSY, SCAGS, BVRT, TMT, LT	24 weeks	Significant improvement on SCAGS
Hollingsworth (1980)	DB, PC, random parallel group	60	SCAGS, MSCL	3 months	Significant improvement on SCAGS
Matejcek et al. (1979)	DB, PC, random parallel group	16	EEG, SCAGS	12 weeks	Significant improvement on EEG only
Novo, Ryan, & Frazier (1978)	DB, PC, random parallel group	34	SCAGS, PNRS	16 weeks	Significant improvement on SCAGS and PNRS
Soni & Soni (1975)	DB, PC, random parallel group	78	CS	9 months	Significant improvement at 3-month evaluation only
Thibault (1974)	DB, PC, random parallel group	48	ADL, psychological, and physical states	12 weeks	Significant improvement on all three scales
Rechman (1973)	DB, PC, random crossover and parallel group	43, 60	CS	16 and 12 weeks	Significant improvement on para. group study only
McConnachie (1973)	DB, PC, random parallel group	58	ADL, physical, mood, and motor activity scales	12 weeks	Significant improvement in all but ADL
Jennings (1972)	DB, PC, random parallel group	50	CSCL, MSCL	12 weeks	Significant improvement on CSCL
Banen (1972)	DB, PC, random parallel group	78	Subtests from WAIS	12 weeks	No significant improvement on WAIS subtests
Tribolitti & Ferri (1969)	DB, PC, random parallel group	59	MSCL, "in-house" rating scales	12 weeks	Significant improvement on one subtest of MSCL

All studies were Type 1.

[a]Refer to "List of Acronyms," pp. 113–116, for definitions of abbreviations.

ies. Four Type 1 studies showed that tacrine provides a modest, clinically significant effect. Three of nine Type 2, and three of four Type 3 studies report similar findings. Most of the Type 2 and 3 studies involve relatively small samples and are of relatively short duration. None of these has demonstrated a clear effect on the course of illness. Of particular interest is the U.S. multicenter tacrine study (Davis et al., 1992), which utilized a novel enrichment strategy combining aspects of both crossover and parallel design studies. All patients were initially treated with tacrine. Those patients showing a response in the open trial, following a drug washout period, participated in a randomization trial investigating either tacrine or placebo in a double-blind, parallel group study.

Schneider and Tariot (1994) reviewed the clinical trials involving tacrine and found that individualized dosing produced greater clinical results. Clini-

TABLE 4.2 Nootropics[a]

Authors	*Drug*	*Type*	*Design*	N	*Outcome Measures*	*Length of Study*	*Measure Results*
Ruther et al. (1994)	Cerebrolysin	1	DB, PC, random parallel group	120	MMSE, SCAGS, CGI, ADL, TMT	4 weeks	Significant improvement on CGI, TMT
Croisile et al. (1993)	Piracetam	2	DB, PC, random parallel group	33	MMSE, DS, AB, VVLT, SS, CFT	1 year	No significant improvement
Green et al. (1992)	Oxiracetam	2	DB, PC, random parallel group	24	BSRT, BVRT, BNT, COWGT, TT, BDT, ROCF	3 months	No significant improvement
Bottini et al. (1992)	Oxiracetam	2	DB, PC, random parallel group	58	QOL, RT, COWGT, SS, RPMT, TT, DS, WLL	12 weeks	Significant improvement on QOL, SS, RPM, COWGT
Villardita et al. (1987)	Oxiracetam	2	DB, PC, random cross-over	40	MMSE, ACPT, VCPT, WLL, LM, DS, BTT, VFT, RCFT, RPMT, LAS, MC, GS, IADL	90 days	Significant improvement on MMSE, ACPT, BTT, VFT, IADL
Sourander et al. (1987)	Aniracetam	2	DB, PC, random parallel group	44	FTT, TMT, BD, DS, SM, BVRT, SCAGS, PB, SVT, HP, VPM, OM, TG, WLL, SM, CN, SIM, ASMC, OR	3 months	Significant improvement on WLL only

Growden et al. (1986)	Piracetam and physostigmine	2	DB, PC, random crossover	18	BPDP, DS, BS, SR, BNT, VFT, PWT, AF	2 to 3 weeks	No significant improvement
R. C. Smith et al. (1984)	Lecithin and piracetam plus lecithin	2	DB, PC, random crossover	11 & 11	BSRT, AST, DRS, PMSE	10 and 6 months	No significant improvement on lecithin; improvement on BSRT in 8/11 piracetam + lecithin
Clauss et al. (1991)	Pramiracetam	3	SB, dose finding and DB, PC, random crossover	10	ADAS-Cog, BSRT, DS, VFT, LM, VSRT	5 and 4 weeks	Significant improvement on part of VSRT
Sinforiani et al. (1990)	Acetyl-L-carnitine and piracetam	3	SB, open label	12 & 12	DS, DSY, BTT, GS, VFT, WLL	2 week IV and 90 day oral	No significant improvement for piracetam
Falsaperla, Preti, & Oliani (1990)	Oxiracetam and selegiline	3	SB, random parallel group	40	BRS, RMT, DS, SR, VFT, GS	90 days	Significant improvement on all tests with oxiracetam
Thal, Salmon, et al. (1989)	Vinpocetine	3	Open label pilot study	19	VFT, BSRT, COWGT, BNT, CCSE, CGI	52 weeks	No significant improvement
Heiss et al. (1988)	Piracetam in Alzheimer's disease and MID	3	Open label	9 & 7	RCGM in PET	2 weeks	Inc. in RCGM in AD but not MID
Branconnier et al. (1983)	Pramiracetam	3	Open label	32	BSRT, VFT, RMPT, SCAGS	4 weeks	Significant improvement on SCAGS
Delwaide, Devoitille, & Ylieff[b] (1980)	Piracetam, lysin-vasopressin, and physostigmine	3	DB, crossover	13	AVLT	Acute injection	Significant improvement with piracetam and lysin-vasopressin

[a]Refer to "List of Acronyms," pp. 113–116, for definitions of abbreviations.

[b]See also Table 4.4.

TABLE 4.3 Cholinesterase Inhibitors: Tacrine[a]

Authors	Drug	Type	Design	N	Outcome Measures	Length of Study	Measure Results
Knapp et al. (1994)	Tacrine	1	DB, PC, random parallel group	263	CIBC, ADAS-Cog, FCCA	30 weeks	Significant difference on CIBC, ADAS-Cog, FCCA
Sahakian & Coull (1993)[b]	Tacrine	1	DB, PC, random cross-over	89	MMSE, AMTS, ADL, RNCP, KOL, CANTAB	30 weeks	Significant effect on MMSE, AMTS, CANTAB-attention
Wilcock et al. (1993)	Tacrine	1	DB, PC, random cross-over	79	MMSE, ADAS-NCog, FLS, ADL, KOL, LMT, DS, IADL, CAMCOG	24 weeks	Significant improvement on KOL & CAMCOG
Farlow et al. (1992)	Tacrine	1	DB, PC, random parallel group	468	ADAS-Cog, CL-CGIC, CG-CGIC, MMSE, PDS, ADAS, ADAS-NCog	12 weeks	Significant improvement on ADAS-Cog, CL-CGIC, CG-CGIC
Maltby et al. (1994)	Tacrine and lecithin	2	DB, PC, random parallel group	41	MMSE, V&V SRT, WNA, LPRS, IADL	36 weeks	No significant difference between groups
Minthon et al. (1993)	Tacrine and lecithin	2	DB, PC, random cross-over	17	VOCT, KBD, VL, DS, RT, CFF, EEG, rCBF	26 weeks	6 patients classified as responders
Schneider et al. (1993)[c]	L-Deprenyl and tacrine or physostigmine	2	DB, PC, random cross-over	10	ADAS-Cog, MMSE	8 weeks	Significant improvement on ADAS-Cog in those receiving drug first
Gustafson (1993)[d]	Physostigmine, tacrine, and lecithin	2	DB, PC, random cross-over	10 & 17	rCBF, EEG, OBS-DS, OBS-CS, CGI, RR	2-hr iv (P) 26 weeks (T&L)	No significant improvement compared with placebo
Davis et al. (1992)	Tacrine	2	DB, PC, random parallel group	215	ADAS, CGIC, MMSE, PDS, IADL, PSMS	14 weeks	Smaller decline in ADAS-Cog

Molloy et al. (1991)	Tacrine	2	DB, PC, random cross-over	34	MMSE, MSQ, VFT, PWT, DS, LMT, CST, BVRT, BI, LS	9 weeks	No significant difference between groups
Weinstein, Teunisse, & van Gool (1991)	Tacrine and lecithin	2	DB, PC, random parallel group	12	CAMCOG, IDDD	12 weeks	No significant difference between groups
Chatiellier & Lacomblez (1990)	Tacrine and lecithin	2	DB, PC, random cross-over	67	MMSE, SGRS, MDS, LC, PVAS	8 weeks	Significant improvement on PVAS
Fitten et al. (1990)[e]	Tacrine and lecithin	2	DB, PC, random cross-over	10 & 6	MMSE, FOM, DS, TMT, NLT, ADL, IADL, NOSIE, GDS, COWGT, GERRI, ADAS	3 weeks and 10 weeks	3 weeks, no significant improvement; 10 weeks, mild improvement in some
Gauthier et al. (1990)	Tacrine and lecithin	2	DB, PC, random cross-over	52	MMSE, RDRS-II, HDS	20 weeks	Significant improvement on MMSE
Summers et al. (1986)	Tacrine	2	DB, PC, random cross-over	17	GAS, NLT, OT	6 weeks	Significant improvement on GAS, NLT, OT
Alhainen & Riekkinen (1993)	Tacrine	3	Pilot responder discrimination	25	QEEG, MMSE, ADAS-Cog, BRST, HVR, VFT, DS, TMT	7 weeks	Significant improvement on MMSE, TMT
Mellow et al. (1993)	Tacrine and TRH	3	Pilot SB, PB, crossover	6	BSRT, VFT, DS, PMT	Acute 2 days	Significant improvement on VFT
Kaye et al. (1982)[f]	Tacrine and lecithin	3	PC random crossover	10	SLT, BSRT, FR-subjects diagnosed with PDD	Acute 3 doses	No significant improvement
Summers & Viesselman (1981)	Tacrine	3	Pilot—1, 6, 24 hour post-iv	12	OT, NLT	Acute 1-hour iv	Significant improvement on OT in 6 of 12

[a]Refer to "List of Acronyms," pp. 113–116, for definitions of abbreviations.

[b]See also Eagger et al., 1991, 1992; Eagger, Levy, & Sahakain, 1992; for papers evaluating the same population.

[c]See also Table 4.9.

[d]See also Gustafson et al., 1987, for evaluation of the same population.

[e]See also Perryman & Fitten, 1993, for evaluation of the same population.

[f]See also Table 4.11.

TABLE 4.4 Cholinesterase Inhibitors: Physostigmine[a]

Authors	*Drug*	*Type*	*Design*	N	*Outcome Measures*	*Length of Study*	*Measure Results*
Gustafson (1993)[b]	Physostigmine, tacrine, and lecithin	2	DB, PC, random crossover	10 & 17	rCBF, EEG, OBS-DS, OBS-CS, CGI, RR	2-hr IV (P), 26 weeks (T&L)	No significant improvement compared with placebo
Sano et al. (1993)	Physostigmine	2	DB, PC, random crossover	29	BSRT	12 weeks	Significant difference on BSRT-Total Recall/ Intrusions
Schneider et al. (1993)[c]	L-Deprenyl and tacrine or physostigmine	2	DB, PC, random crossover	10	ADAS-Cog, MMSE	8 weeks	Significant important on ADAS-Cog in those receiving drug first
Sevush, Gutterman, & Villalon (1991)	Physiostigmine	2	DB, PC, random crossover	8	AVLT, DS, VFT	3 weeks	Significant improvement on AVLT
Harrell, Calloway, et al. (1990)	Physostigmine	2	DB, PC, random crossover	20	BSRT, COWGT, PRT, FTT	8 weeks	No significant improvement except for responder subgroup
Jenike et al. (1990)	Physostigmine	2	DB, PC, random crossover	12	DRST, BSRT, ADAS	8 days	No significant difference between groups
Thal, Salmon et al. (1989)	Physostigmine	2	DB, PC, random parallel group	16	BSRT, BICMT, MDS	12 weeks	Significant improvement on BSRT in 7/10 physostigmine subjects
Stern, Sano, & Mayeux (1988)	Physostigmine	2	DB, PC, random crossover	14	BSRT	36 weeks	Significant improvement compared with placebo
Stern, Sano, & Mayeux (1987)	Physostigmine	2	DB, PC, random crossover	22	BSRT, WAIS-R, WMS, RDT, mMMSE, CWAT, VFT	2 weeks	Significant improvement on WAIS-R Digit Span Subtest
Beller, Overall, & Swann (1985)	Physostigmine	2	DB, PC, random crossover	8	BSRT	8 days	Significant improvement on highest dose
Mohs et al. (1985)	Physostigmine	2	DB, PC, crossover	12	ADAS	6–10 days	Significant improvement in 3 subjects
Schwartz & Kohlstaedt (1986)	Physostigmine and lecithin	2	DB, PC, random crossover, & replication	11	BSRT	Acute injections	No significant improvement

Sullivan et al. (1982)	Physostigmine	2	DB, PC, random crossover	12	VPAL, NVPAL, BPDP, VRMT	Acute 30-min iv	No significant improvement
Davis & Mohs (1982)	Physostigmine	2	DB, PC, random crossover	10	DS, FFT, BSRT	Acute 30-min iv	Significant improvement in 8 subjects
Peters & Levin (1979)	Physostigmine and lecithin	2	DB, PC, random crossover	5	BSRT	Acute subQ injection	No significant improvement compared to baseline
Bierer et al. (1994)	Physostigmine and clonodine	3	SB, PC, random crossover	10	ADAS	2 weeks	No significant improvement
Beller et al. (1988)	Physostigmine	3	Open-label follow-up	5	BSRT	17 months to 3 years	4/5 BSRT scores at end same as at start
Thal et al. (1986)	Physostigmine	3	DB, PC, crossover, open-label follow-up	16 & 10	BSRT	1 week and 4–18 months	Significant improvement for responders
Muramoto, Sugishia, & Ando (1984)	Physostigmine	3	DB, SB, PC, random crossover	6	Figure copying	Acute injections	Significant improvement in 3/6 subjects
Wettstein (1983)	Physostigmine and lecithin	3	DB, PC, random crossover	8	Self-designed test battery	12 weeks	No significant improvement
Jotkowitz (1983)	Physostigmine	3	SB, PC, crossover	10	BRS	Up to 10 months	No significant improvement
Thal et al. (1983)	Physostigmine and lecithin	3	Open label, DB, PC, crossover	8	BSRT	6 days for each	Significant improvement in 6 of 8
Ashford et al. (1981)	Physostigmine	3	DB, PC, random crossover	6	BWLLT, BVRT subjects diagnosed with PDD	Acute 30-min iv	No significant improvement
Christie et al. (1981)[c]	Physostigmine and arecoline	3	DB, PC, random crossover	11 & 7	SPT	Acute 30-min iv	Significant improvement in both groups
Delwaide, Devoitille, & Ylieff (1980)[d]	Piracetam, lysin-vasopressin, and physostigmine	3	DB, crossover	13	AVLT	Acute injection	No significant improvement with physostigmine
Muramoto et al. (1979)	Physostigmine	3	DB, PC, case study	1	Figure copying, BSRT	Acute subQ injection	Significant improvement on figure copying

[a]Refer to "List of Acronyms," pp. 113–116, for definitions of abbreviations.

[b]See also Gustafson et al., 1987.

[c]See also Table 4.9.

[d]See also Table 4.2.

TABLE 4.5a Cholinesterase Inhibitors: Velnacrine[a]

Authors	*Drug*	*Type*	*Design*	N	*Outcome Measures*	*Length of Study*	*Measure Results*
Antuono (1995)	Velnacrine	1	DB, PC, random parallel group	449	ADAS-Cog, CGIC	24 weeks	Significantly less deterioration on ADAS-Cog and CGIC
Murphy et al. (1991)	Velnacrine maleate	1	DB, PC, random parallel group	105	ADAS-Cog, CGI, IADL, PGIR, ADAS-NCog	15 weeks	No significant improvment
Ebmeier et al. (1992)	Velnacrine	2	DB, PC, random parallel group (SPECT)	12 and 21	ORT, WRT, SPECT	Single dose	Significant improvement on WRT and increase in frontal SPECT
Sigfried (1993)	Velnacrine	3	DB, PC, random crossover	35	ADAS-Cog, IWRT, CGII, CRTT	3 weeks	Significant improvement on ADAS-Cog, IWRT
Dal-Bianco et al. (1991)	Galanthamine	3	Open label	18	Neuropsychological battery	2–6 months	No significant improvement

[a]Refer to "List of Acronyms," pp. 113–116, for definitions of abbreviations.

cal response occurred at higher doses (>120 mg/day). Unfortunately, adequate dosing (>120 mg/day) often resulted in significant hepatotoxicity (approximately 30% of patients). Because of this, any treatment strategy must be diligently monitored with weekly determinations of hepatic enzymes. The clinical treatment strategy should be to attempt to administer higher doses of tacrine (120 to 160 mg/day in four divided doses).

Despite the problems inherent in tacrine therapy (hepatotoxicity, the requirement for QID dosing, and side effects), several recent findings from prolonged clinical trials have proven exciting. Knopman et al. (1996), in a 2-year open-label continuation trial, found that patients taking tacrine (>80 mg/day) were significantly less likely to have entered a nursing home than age-matched patients taking either a placebo or low-dose tacrine (<80 mg/day). Second, Kaufer et al. (1996) found that tacrine (doses > 80 mg/day) had an independent, positive effect on behavioral symptoms associated with AD.

Other acetylcholinesterase inhibitors include velnacrine (a hydroxy metabolite of tacrine). The clinical effects of velnacrine are similar to those of tacrine. Three of four studies (two Type 1 studies) showed modest clinical improvement. Unfortunately, hepatotoxicity was a greater problem for velnacrine than for tacrine, affecting approximately 50% of patients.

One of the more novel cholinergic strategies is a procholinergic strategy using high-dose infusions of thyrotropin in conjunction with physostigmine (Mellow et al., 1993). One Type 1 study investigating 4-aminopyridine showed no apparent therapeutic benefit (see "Other Treatment Strategies" section). Asthana et al. (1996) found that continuous intravenous infusion of physostigmine resulted in significant short-term improvement in five of nine patients with mild-to-moderate AD.

The overall clinical results of these cholinergic augmentation strategies, especially short-term trials with cholinesterase inhibitors, have not been compelling. However, this has been confounded by (a) impractical dosing requirements, (b) a high rate of side effects (except in a relatively small percentage of AD patients), and (c) the relatively short duration of most clinical trials. The largest and best-designed studies found modest clinical improvement with tacrine, but raised serious concerns about hepatotoxicity.

The second generation of cholinesterase inhibitors is showing clinical efficacy similar to tacrine, but with less toxicity and greater ease of administration

TABLE 4.5b Second Generation Cholinesterase Inhibition[a]

Authors	*Drug*	*Type*	*Design*	N	*Outcome Measures*	*Length of Study*	*Results*
Rogers et al. (1998a)	Donepezil	1	DB, PC, randomized parallel	468	ADAS—Cog; CIBIC Plus MMSE, CDR-SB	12 weeks	Significant improvement in cognition, global function
Rodgers (1998b)	Donepezil	1	DB, PC, randomized parallel	473	ADAS—Cog; CIBIC Plus MMSE, CDR-SB	24 weeks	Significant improvement in cognition, global function
Burns et al. (1999)	Donepezil	1	DB, PC, randomized parallel	647	ADAS—Cog; CIBIC Plus MMSE, CDR-SB	24 weeks	Significant improvement in cognition, global function, ADC's
Corey-Bloom et al. (1998)	Rivastigmine	1	DB, PC, randomized parallel	699	ADAS—Cog; CIBIC Plus MMSE	26 weeks	Significant improvement in cognition, global function
Rosler et al. (1999)	Rivastigmine	1	DB, PC, randomized parallel	725	ADAS—Cog; CIBIC Plus MMSE	26 weeks	Significant improvement in cognition, global function
Agid et al. (1998)	Rivastigmine	1	DB, PC, randomized parallel	402	CIBIC, MMSE	5 months	Significant improvement in cognition, global function, ADC, behavior
Tariot et al. (2000)	Galantamine	1	DB, PC, randomized parallel	978	ADAS—Cog; CIBIC, DAD	6 months	Significant improvement in cognition, global function
Raskind et al. (2000)	Galantamine	1	DB, PC, randomized parallel	636	ADAS—Cog; CIBIC, DAD	6 months	Significant improvement in cognition, global function

[a]Refer to "List of Acronyms," pp. 113–116, for definitions of abbreviations.

(Table 4.6). Donepezil, rivastigmine, and galantamine have received approval for use in mild-to-moderate Alzheimer's disease. All three drugs cite large, multicenter, placebo-controlled trials in which significant long-term effects have been shown for cognition, activities of daily living, and behavior. Given the "history" of AChE therapy, perhaps most noteworthy in these studies was the demonstration of (a) once or twice daily dosing, (b) absence of hepatotoxicity, and (c) low incidence of side effects traditionally associated with AChE therapy.

The most exciting noncholinergic strategy focuses on reducing the accumulation of amyloid protein, the degradation of tau protein. This is an insoluble, fibrillary component of the senile plaques first described by Alzheimer in 1907. Amyloid protein accumulation is thought by many to be the central lesion in many forms of AD.

There are a number of studies that have used antiamyloid treatment strategies (Table 4.8). One approach has been to focus on the possible role of nonsteroidal anti-inflammatory drugs (NSAIDs) as a

TABLE 4.6 Lecithin and Tacrine[a]

Authors	*Drug*	*Type*	*Design*	N	*Outcome Measures*	*Length of Study*	*Measure Results*
Maltby et al. (1994)	Tacrine and lecithin	2	DB, PC, random parallel group	41	MMSE, V&V SRT, WNA, LPRS, IADL	35 weeks	No significant difference between groups
Minthon et al. (1993)	Tacrine and lecithin	2	DB, PC, random cross-over	17	VOCT, KBD, VL, DS, RT, CFF, EEG, rCBF	26 weeks	6 patients classified as responders
Gustafson (1993)[b]	Physostigmine, tacrine, and lecithin	2	DB, PC, random cross-over	10 & 17	rCBF, EEG, OBS-DS, OBS-CS, CGI, RR	2-hr IV (P), 26 weeks (T&L)	No significant improvement compared with placebo
Weinstein et al. (1991)[b]	Tacrine and lecithin	2	DB, PC, random parallel group	12	CAMCOG, IDDD	12 weeks	No significant difference between groups
Lampe et al. (1990)	TRH and lecithin	2	DB, PC, random cross-over	8	VFT, TMT, BSRT, BVRT	2 weeks	Significant improvement on part of BSRT
Chatellier & Lacomblez[b] (1990)	Tacrine and lecithin	2	DB, PC, random cross-over	67	MMSE, SGRS, MDS, LC, PVAS	8 weeks	Significant improvement on PVAS
Fitten et al. (1990)[b]	Tacrine and lecithin	2	DB, PC, random cross-over	10 & 6	MMSE, FOM, DS, TMT, NLT, OT, ADL, IADL, NOSIE, GDS, COWGT, GERRI, ADAS	3 weeks and 10 weeks	3 weeks, no significant improvement; 10 weeks, mild improvement in some
Gauthier et al. (1990)[b]	Tacrine and lecithin	2	DB, PC, random cross-over	52	MMSE, RDRS-II, HDS	20 weeks	Significant improvement on MMSE
Heyman et al. (1987)	Lecithin	2	DB, PC, random parallel group	37	MMSE, AST, VFT, BSRT, VSRT, SMT	6 months	No significant improvement
Jenike et al. (1986)[c]	Lecithin and ergoloid mesylates	2	DB, PC, random cross-over	7	DRS, DRST	10 weeks	No significant improvement
Schwartz & Kohlstaedt (1986)	Physostigmine and lecithin	2	DB, PC, random cross-over, and replication	11	BSRT	Acute injections	No significant improvement
Little et al. (1985)	Lecithin	2	DB, PC, random parallel group	51	PWT, VFT, OR, KT, IL CA, DCT	6 months	No significant improvement

Smith et al. (1984)[d]	Lecithin and piracetam plus lecithin	2	DB, PC, random crossover	11 & 11	BSRT, AST, DRS, PMSE	10 months and 6 months	No significant improvement on lecithin; improvement on BSRT in 8/11 piracetam + lecithin
Weintraub et al. (1983)	Lecithin	2	DB, PC, random crossover	13	DRS	6 months	No significant improvement
Brinkman et al. (1982)	Lecithin	2	DB, PC, random crossover	10	BSRT	6 weeks	No significant improvement
Sullivan et al. (1982)	Lecithin	2	DB, PC, random crossover	18	VPAL-NVPAL, BPDP, VRMT	16 weeks	No significant improvement
Hyman, Esslinger, & Damasio (1982)	Lecithin	2	DB, PC, random crossover	18	MMSE, DS, VFT, AST	8 weeks	No significant improvement
Pomara et al. (1982)	Lecithin	2	DB, PC, random crossover	5	BSRT	4 weeks	No significant improvement
Dysken et al. (1982)	Lecithin	2	DB, PC, random crossover	10	WRT, WLL, PALT	4 weeks	No significant improvement
Vroulis et al. (1981)	Lecithin	2	DB, PC, random crossover	18	BSRT, AST, DRS, IMCI	4–16 weeks	No significant improvement; slight improvement in 8/15
Peters & Levin (1979)[b]	Physostigmine and lecithin	2	DB, PC, random crossover	5	BSRT	Acute subQ injection	No significant improvement compared with baseline
Etienne et al. (1981)	Lecithin	2	DB, PC, crossover	11	WMS, FRT	3 months	No significant improvement
Thal et al. (1983)[b]	Physostigmine and lecithin	3	Open label and DB, PC, crossover	8	BSRT	6 days for each	Significant improvement in 6 of 8
Wettstein (1983)[b]	Physostigmine and lecithin	3	DB, PC, rand Xover	8	Self-designed test battery	12 weeks	No significant improvement
Kaye et al. (1982)[c]	Tacrine and lecithin	3	PC, random crossover	10	SLT, BSRT, FR; subjects diagnosed with PDD	Acute 3 doses	No significant improvement

[a]Refer to "List of Acronyms," pp. 113–116, for definition of abbreviations.

[b]See also Table 4.3.

[c]See also Table 4.1.

[d]See also Table 4.2.

TABLE 4.7 Muscarinic/Cholinergic Agonists[a]

Authors	Drug	Type	Design	N	Measures	Length of Study	Measure Results
Harbaugh et al. (1989)	Bethanechol chloride muscarinic agonist	1	DB, PC, random cross-over	49	DS, DSY, BDT, WMS, TMT, BSRT, VFT, BNT, MMSE	24 weeks	Significant improvement on MMSE only
Wilson et al. (1995)	Nicotine patches	2	DB, PC, random cross-over	6	DMTS, DRS, RAT	3 weeks	Significant improvement on RAT
Soncrant et al. (1993)	Arecoline muscarinic/cholinergic agonist	2	Open label and DB, PC, random crossover	9	BSRT, COWGT, VFT, DS, BVRT, VCRMT, VBCRMT, SCWIT, TT, ERDT, CALC	Approximately 2 weeks for each	Significant improvement on part of BSRT; 6/9 were responders on BSRT
Raffaele, Berardi, Asthana, et al. (1991)	Arecoline muscarinic/cholinergic agonist	2	Open label and DB, PC, random crossover	8	BSRT	Approximately 2 weeks for each	Significant improvement in open label but not on double blind
Penn et al. (1988)	Bethanechol chloride muscarinic agonist	2	DB, PC, random cross-over, and escalating dose	10 & 8	MMSE, COWGT, BSDL, BSRT	24 weeks	No significant improvement in either study
Tariot et al. (1988)	Arecoline muscarinic/cholinergic agonist	2	DB, PC, random parallel group	12	PRT, VFT, BSRT	Acute 2-hour infusions	No significant difference between groups
Mouradian et al. (1988)	RS-86 muscarinic agonist	2	DB, PC, random cross-over	7	DS, PMT, VFDT, RF, DL, WLL, RT, LMT, SM	2 weeks	No significant improvement
Davis et al. (1987)	Oxo-tremorine	2	DB, PC, random cross-over	7	WRT	Acute	No significant improvement
Hollander et al. (1987)	RS-86 muscarinic agonist	2	DB, PC, random cross-over	12	ADAS	3 weeks	6/12 had >10% improvement on ADAS
Bruno et al. (1986)	RS-86 muscarinic agonist	2	DB, PC, random cross-over	8	IMPP, PMT, VFDT, RF, DL, WLL, RT	3 weeks	No significant improvement

Wettstein & Spiegel (1984)	RS-86 muscarinic agonist	2	DB, PC, random cross-over, and parallel group	6 & 17	MMSE, WRT, PRT, WLL, VT, CP	12 and 18 weeks	Significant improvement on VT in Study 1; No significant results in Study 2
Thal et al. (1981)	Choline chloride	2	DB, PC, random cross-over	7	WLL, CP, VFT, CR, PB	12 weeks	No significant improvement
Caamano et al. (1994)	CDP-choline	3	Open label	20	MMSE, BCRS, FAST, TCD	4 weeks	Significant improvement in MMSE of EOAD subset
Jones et al. (1992)	Nicotine	3	SB, PC, crossover	70 (24 AD)	RVIP, DRMLO, CFF, FTT, DS	Acute injection	Significant improvement on parts of RVIP, DRMLO, CFF
Raffaele, Berardi, Morris, et al. (1991)	Arecoline muscarinic/cholinergic agonist	3	Open label	15	BSRT, ERDT	Acute 30-min injection	No significant improvement
Sahakian et al. (1989)	Nicotine	3	SB, PC, crossover	21	DS, FTT, CFF	Acute 7 day	Significant improvement on FTT, CFF
Newhouse et al. (1988)	Nicotine	3	SB, PC, crossover	6	COWGT, WLL	Acute 4 day	Significant decrease in intrusions
Harbaugh et al. (1984)	Bethanechol chloride muscarinic agonist	3	SB, PC, crossover pilot study	4	Subjective family response	3 months	Subjective improvement only during drug periods
Christie et al. (1981)[b]	Physostigmine and arecoline	3	DB, PC, random cross-over	11 & 7	SPT	Acute 30-min iv	Significant improvement in both groups
Renvoize & Jerram (1979)	Choline chloride	3	DB, PC, parallel group	18	BRS	2 months	No significant improvement
Ferris et al. (1979)	Choline chloride	3	Open label	14	26 cognitive tests	4 weeks	No significant improvement
C. M. Smith et al. (1978)	Choline bitartate salt	3	DB, PC, crossover	10	RPMT, DS	1 month	No significant improvement

[a]Refer to "List of Acronyms," pp. 113–116, for definitions of abbreviations.

[b]See also Table 4.4.

means of primary prevention. A second strategy, summarized below, involves treatment with estrogenlike compounds. Breitner (1996) reviewed 15 studies examining the role of either glucocorticoids or NSAIDs as a means of delaying the onset or halting the progression of AD. Of these studies, 14 of 15 suggested that both strategies are effective, decreasing the risk of developing AD or delaying the onset of AD in patient populations for which these drugs are regularly administered for other purposes (e.g., NSAIDs for treatment of arthritis or leprosy, for which the rate of AD neuropathology is significantly less than for controls). One twin study (Breitner et al., 1994) has suggested that NSAIDs reduce the risk of AD. Table 4.8 lists several of the important studies (Types 2, 3).

Again, while most of these studies lack the scientific rigor of Type 1 clinical trials, all of these mainly retrospective studies have consistently suggested a role for NSAIDs in either reducing risk or slowing progression of AD. More conclusive findings await the results of ongoing, prospective, blinded clinical trials.

Two studies are used to illustrate the reason for this current enthusiasm. McGeer et al. (1990) reviewed 7,490 charts of patients treated with NSAIDs and who suffered from AD. The overall rate of AD was 6 to 12 times lower in NSAID patients than would have been predicted in this population. Tang et al. (1996) followed a large cohort of elderly females prospectively (5 years) to assess the role of estrogen replacement therapy (ERT) in delaying/ameliorating AD. Estrogen demonstrated significant effects in both domains. However, two recent double-blind, placebo-controlled trials (Mulnard et al., 2000; Henderson et al., 2000) reveal no significant effect of estrogen therapy on disease progression in mild-to-moderate Alzheimer's disease.

Catecholamine Enhancement in Alzheimer's Disease

Several groups have investigated the other neurotransmitter abnormalities associated with AD, particularly the catecholamines. Although less compelling than the marked reductions in cholinergic neurotransmission, levels of norepinephrine and serotonin, but not dopamine, are diminished in postmortem studies of AD patients. With a few exceptions, most treatment strategies have studied the inhibition of monoamine oxidase (MAO), a major catecholaminergic (monoaminergic) degradative enzyme. Monoamine oxidase B inhibitors have been investigated on the assumption that (a) monoaminergic systems are directly involved in the pathophysiology of AD, (b) intact monoaminergic systems facilitate the effects of cholinergic medications in AD, and (c) they may effect the deposition of amyloid in patients with AD. Most published reports show clear improvements in agitation and depression, along with many measures of cognition (Table 4.9). While enthusiasm among clinicians has been dampened by concerns about side effects and the requirement that patients remain on a tyramine-free diet while on MAO inhibitors; the final story will have to await results of ongoing clinical trials.

Neuropeptide-Based Treatment Strategies

Animal studies have shown that neuropeptide treatments enhance performance on a wide variety of experimental tasks. Based on these findings, several neuropeptides have been investigated as potential treatments for AD. The most extensively studied of these are naloxone (Table 4.10), vasopressin (Table 4.11), adrenocorticotropic hormone (ACTH), and somatostatin (for review of ACTH and somatostatin, see Thal, 1994). Naloxone has been shown to have direct facilitatory effects on memory performance in animals. Unfortunately, most investigations with either naloxone (administered intravenously) or naltrexone, a long-acting, orally active opiate antagonist, have not shown any benefit for AD patients. In addition to animal data showing improvements in maze learning and amnesia induced by electroconvulsive therapy (ECT), postmortem samples from AD patients have revealed small decreases in hippocampal vasopressin levels. Most clinical studies, including one Type 1 multicenter trial, failed to demonstrate significant improvements in AD.

Novel Treatment Strategies

Acetyl-L-Carnitine/Membrane Stabilizing Agents

One of the more interesting new treatment strategies involves the use of acetyl-L-carnitine hydrochloride and other membrane "stabilizing" agents (e.g., phosphatidyl serine) as primary prevention strategy to slow the disease progression (Table 4.12 and Table 4.13). Alzheimer's disease has been associated with disturbances in membrane phospholipid turnover (Pettegrew, 1989) and membrane oxidative metabo-

TABLE 4.8 Nonsteroidal Anti-Inflammatory Drugs[a]

Authors	*Drug*	*Type*	*Design*	N	*Outcome Measures*	*Length of Study*	*Measure Results*
Rogers et al. (1993)	Indomethicin	2	DB, PC, random parallel group	28	MMSE, ADAS, BNT, TT	6 months	Significant differences across all measures
Rich et al. (1995)	NSAIDs	3	Chart review of Alzheimer's Disease Research Center	210	Duration of illness, MMSE, VFT, BNT, TT, BVRT, BDT, RNT, DRST, GIFT, PGDRS	1 year	Less decline on VFT, DRST, orientation subscale of PGDRS
Andersen et al. (1995)	NSAIDs	3	Chart review of dementia study	6,258	Relative risk for Alzheimer's disease	NA	RR .38 for NSAID users
Breitner et al. (1994)	NSAIDs, steroid/ACTH, or aspirin	3	Co-twin control	50 pairs	Age of onset of Alzheimer's disease	NA	Odds ratios for all drugs were below 1. Best for steroid/ACTH
Canadian Study of Health and Aging (1994)	NSAIDs and arthritis	3	Chart review of dementia study	793	Odds ratios of risk factors for Alzheimer's disease	NA	OR for NSAID and arthritis groups significant below 1

[a]Refer to "List of Acronyms," pp. 113–116, for definitions of abbreviations.

TABLE 4.9 Monoamine Oxidase Inhibitors[a]

Authors	*Drug*	*Type*	*Design*	N	*Outcome Measures*	*Length of Study*	*Measure Results*
Dysken et al. (1992)	Milacemide	1	DB, PC, random parallel group	228	CGI, WMS, VS, IADL, VFT	9 weeks	No significant improvement
Mangoni et al. (1991)	L-Deprenyl	1	DB, PC, random parallel group	119	BRS, DS, SS, VFT, DT, TPAT	3 months	Significant improvement on BRS, DS, SS, VFT, DT, TPAT
Marin et al. (1995)	L-Deprenyl and Physostigmine	2	DB, PC, random crossover	17	DS, VFT, WLL, CP, WR, WRT	8 weeks	No significant improvement
Burke et al. (1993)	L-Deprenyl	2	DB, PC, random parallel group	39	CDR, MMSE, BRS, GERRI	First 2 months of 15-month trial	No significant improvement over first 2 months of study
Schneider et al. (1993)[b]	L-Deprenyl and tacrine or physostigmine	2	DB, PC, random crossover	10	ADAS-Cog, MMSE	8 weeks	Sig. imp. on ADAS-Cog in those receiving drug first
Finali et al. (1991)	L-Deprenyl	2	DB, PC, random crossover	19	WLL, R-AVL	6 months	Significant improvement on some R-AVL parameters
Piccinin, Finali, & Piccirilli (1990)	L-Deprenyl	2	DB, PC, random crossover	20	TT, VFT, DS, AVLT, 7/24 Test, LC, TMT, PCT	6 months	Significant improvement on VFT, DS, LC, part of 7/24 test
Tariot, Cohen, et al. (1987)	L-Deprenyl	2	DB, PC, serial treatment	17	BPRS, BSRT, VFT, CPT, VT	8 weeks	Significant improvement on BPRS, BSRT on 10-mg dose
Tariot, Sunderland, et al. (1987)	L-Deprenyl	2	DB, PC, serial treatment	17	BSRT, VT, VFT, CPT	12 weeks	Significant improvement on free recall on BSRT
Goad et al. (1991)	Selegiline	3	Open label	8	MMSE	8 weeks	Clinically significant improvement recall and orientation
Schneider et al. (1991)	L-Deprenyl	3	Open label	14	MMSE, BSRT, COWGT, DS, NC	4 weeks	Significant improvement on BSRT
Falsaperla, Preti, & Oliani (1990)	Selegiline and oxiracetam	3	SB, random parallel group	40	BRS, RMT, DS, SR, VFT, GS	90 days	Significant improvement on all tests with selegiline
Campi, Todeschini, & Scarzella (1990)	Selegiline and acetyl-L-carnitine	3	SB, random parallel group	40	BRS, RMT, DS, SR, VFT, GS	90 days	Significant improvement on all tests with selegiline
Monteverde et al. (1990)	Selegiline and phosphatidylserine	3	SB, PC, random crossover	40	BRS, RMT, DS, SR, VFT, GS	90 days	Significant improvement on all tests with selegiline

[a]Refer to "List of Acronyms," pp. 113–116, for definitions of abbreviations.

[b]See also Tables 4.3 and 4.4.

TABLE 4.10 Naloxone/Naltrexone[a]

Authors	*Drug*	*Type*	*Design*	N	*Outcome Measures*	*Length of Study*	*Measure Results*
Henderson et al. (1989)	Naloxone	2	DB, PC, random crossover	54	MMSE, DS, FTT, VRT, VMT, VFT, BNT, modified TT, DSY	Acute injections	Significant improvement on intrusions in VMT
Tariot et al. (1986)	Naloxone	2	DB, PC, random crossover	12	COWGT, DS, BSRT, FTT, DSY, DYN, VT	Acute 3 day	No significant improvement
Hyman et al. (1985)	Naltrexone	2	DB, PC, random crossover	17	OR, DS, COWGT, VL, VMT, NC	6 weeks	No significant improvement
Pomara et al. (1985)	Naltrexone	2	DB, PC, random crossover	10	DS, TT, VFT, FTT, WLL, CNFN	Acute 4 injections	Significant improvement on TT
Tennant (1987)	Naltrexone	3	Open label and DB, PC, random crossover	6 & 3	MMSE, BRS	6 weeks	Significant improvement on MMSE, BRS
Knopman & Hartman (1986)	Naltrexone	3	Open label	10	AVLT, VFT, SD, WMS	6 weeks	Significant improvement on AVLT
Serby et al. (1986)	Naltrexone	3	Open label and DB for responders	9 & 2	BSRT, PMT, NYUMT	2 weeks each	No significant improvement
Steiger et al. (1985)	Naloxone	3	DB, PC, random crossover	16	BCRS	2 months	No significant improvement
Panella & Blass (1984)	Naloxone	3	DB, PC, random crossover	12	MMSE, MSQ, DS, BRS	Acute injections	No significant improvement
Reisberg et al. (1983a)	Naloxone	3	DB, PC, random crossover	7	BCRS, DSY, FTT, VFT, DS, PS	Acute injections	Significant improvement in all but VFT and PS
Reisberg et al. (1983b)	Naloxone	3	Open label	5	BCRS, DSY, FTT, VFT, DS, PS	Acute injections	Clinical improvement in 3/5

[a]Refer to "List of Acronyms," pp. 113–116, for definitions of abbreviations.

TABLE 4.11 Vasopressin[a]

Authors	*Drug*	*Type*	*Design*	N	*Outcome Measures*	*Length of Study*	*Measure Results*
Wolters et al. (1990)	Deglycin amide-arginine-vasopressin	1	DB, PC, random parallel group	115	SCAGS, BCRS, IADL, GAS, SLT, COC, VFT, MPM, SR, VR, MCGBRS	84 days	No significant improvement
Peabody, Davis et al., (1986)	Desamino-D-arginine-vasopressin	2	DB, PC, random parallel group	14	BSRT, LM, SV	4 weeks	No significant improvement on cognitive scales
Peabody et al. (1985)	Deglycin amide-arginine-vasopressin	2	DB, PC, random parallel group	17	BSRT, WLL	1 week	Significant improvement on parts of BSRT
Chase et al. (1982)	Lysine vasopressin	2	DB, PC, random parallel group	16	RT, TR, MPP, WLL, PMT, RF	10 days	Significant improvement on RT
Durso et al. (1982)	Lysine vasopressin	2	DB, PC, random parallel group	17	WLL, BSRT, PWT, SR, PMT, RT, RF, TR	10 days	Significant improvement on RT
Tinklenberg et al. (1982)	Deglycin amide-arginine-vasopressin	3	SB, PC, parallel group	11	BSRT, WLL	10 days	No significant improvement
Kaye et al. (1982)[b]	Desamino-D-arginine-vasopressin	3	SB, PC, crossover	7	WMS, BSRT, WLL, VFT	1 month	Significant improvement on VFT
Tinklenberg, Pfefferbaum, & Berger (1981)	Desamino-D-arginine-vasopressin	3	DB, PC, random parallel group	7	BSRT, PWT	1–2 weeks	No significant improvement
Weingartner et al. (1981)	Desamino-D-arginine-vasopressin	3	DB, PC, random crossover	7	VFT, WLL	Acute	Significant improvement on VFT

[a]Refer to "List to Acronyms," pp. 113–116, for definitions of abbreviations.

[b]See also Tables 4.3 and 4.6.

TABLE 4.12 Acetyl-L-Carnitine[a]

Authors	*Drug*	*Type*	*Design*	N	*Outcome Measures*	*Length of Study*	*Measure Results*
Spagnoli et al. (1991)	Acetyl-L-carnitine	1	DB, PC, random parallel group	130	SBI, BRS, BICMT, RPMT, VJMCT, VSMD, PRMT, SVL, BTT, TT, WAT, IBAT, GCAT, FAT	1 year	Significant decrease in deterioration on BRS, RPM, BSMD, IBAT
Pettegrew et al. (1995)	Acetyl-L-carnitine	2	DB, PC, parallel groups (3)	33	MMSE, ADAS	1 year	Significantly less deterioration on MMSE
Sano et al. (1992)	Acetyl-L-carnitine	2	DB, PC, random parallel group	30	BSRT, mMMSE, WMS, BVRT, VFT, cancellations	6 months	Significant difference on VFT, DS, cancellations
Passeri et al. (1990)	Acetyl-L-carnitine	2	DB, PC, random parallel group	60	MMSE, BRS, RCFT, VFT, CT, TPBT	3 months	Significant improvement on BRS, RCFT, CT, VFT, TPBT
Rai et al. (1990)	Acetyl-L-carnitine	2	DB, PC, random parallel group	20	KOL, DCT, NLT, VFT	24 weeks	No significant difference
Urakami et al. (1993)	Nebracetam fumarate	3		9	MMSE, GBS, HWDS	8 weeks	Significant improvement on GBS, HWDS
Sinforiani et al. (1990)	Acetyl-L-carnitine and piracetam	3	SB, open label	12 & 12	DS, DSY, BTT, GS, VFT, WLL	2-week iv and 90-day oral	Significant improvement on DSY, GS for ALC
Campi et al. (1990)	Acetyl-L-carnitine and selegiline	3	SB, random parallel group	40	BRS, RMT, DS, SR, VFT, GS	90 days	Significant improvement for selegiline on all measures
Bellagamba et al. (1990)	Acetyl-L-carnitine	3	DB, PC, random parallel group	35	DSY, RCFT, RPMT, and others	3 months	Significant improvement on DSY, RCFT, RPMT

[a]Refer to "List of Acronyms," pp. 113–116, for definitions of abbreviation.

[b]See also Table 4.4.

TABLE 4.13 Membrane Stabilizing Agents[a]

Authors	*Drug*	*Type*	*Design*	N	*Outcome Measures*	*Length of Study*	*Measure Results*
Crook et al. (1991)	Phosphatidylserine	1	DB, PC, random parallel group	149	FRT, NFA, TNR, MOR	12 weeks	Significant improvement on FRT, NFA
Amaducci & the SMID Group (1988)	Phosphatidylserine	1	DB, PC, random parallel group	142	DRS, RMT, SR, DS, BTT, TT, ST, CASE	3 months with 21-month follow-up	Significant improvement on ST, BTT, and BDS subscale
Flicker et al. (1991)	Ganglioside GM_1	2	DB, PC, random crossover	12	DS, TNR, DSY, BDT, FTT, ORT, SLT, MMSE, JLO	15 weeks	No significant improvement
Crook, Petrie, et al. (1994)	Phosphatidylserine	2	DB, PC, random parallel group	51	CGI, CRS, MAC-P	12 weeks	Significant difference on 2 CGI variables, 3 CRS variables
Ala et al. (1990)	Ganglioside GM_1	2	DB, PC, random parallel group	46	MMSE, BCRS, VFT, PB, LC, DSY, BSRT, RCFT, CD	12 weeks	No significant improvement
Delwaide et al. (1986)	Phosphatidylserine	2	DB, PC, random parallel group	35	CS, PRS	6 weeks	Significant improvement on PRS
Heiss et al. (1994)	Phosphatidylserine, pyritinol, cognitive training	3	Open label 4 parallel group combination of three "drugs"	70	MMSE, FTT, PMT, VMT, VFT, TT, RT, OT, IPT, QEEG, PET	6 months	No significant difference among the 4 groups
Monteverde et al. (1990)	Phosphatidylserine and selegiline	3	SB, PC, random crossover	40	BRS, RMT, DS, SR, VFT, GS	90 days	Significant improvement on subscales of BRS & RMT for P-serine

[a]Refer to "List of Acronyms," pp. 113–116, for definitions of abbreviations.

lism. Animal studies show that carnitine acts as a carrier of fatty acids from the cytosol into the mitochondrial matrix, in which they can be subjected to beta oxidation. Carnitine increases the activity of acetyl-CoA and choline acetyltransferase and in this way may have cholinomimetic effects. It also normalizes alterations in membrane and energy metabolism and increases both the levels and utilization of nerve growth factor (NGF) in the CNS.

Several open clinical trials (Type 2 studies without placebo controls) have been conducted. Of the 22 trials reviewed in Calvani et al. (1992), clinical improvement was found in 7 trials compared to the placebo, and 4 of 7 trials showed substantial improvement. Recently, Thal et al. (1996), in a double-blind, randomized, placebo-controlled trial (Type 1), parallel design study found significant clinical improvements on disability, attention, and apraxia over a 1-year period. They found that a subgroup of younger AD patients might benefit from this therapy, while older patients actually did poorer. Overall, there was little difference between the AD patients and the placebo controls. Both Type 1 studies of phosphatidyl serine, as well as two of four Type 2 studies, and one of two Type 3 studies, found modest positive effects.

Estrogen Replacement

The second of the antiamyloid strategies, based on (a) the preclinical observation that estrogen administration influences cholinergic function and increases binding sites of hypothalamic nicotinic acetylcholine receptors in rats and (b) recent data suggesting that estrogen has a clear role in diminishing amyloid deposition, estrogen replacement strategies have recently gained attention. Estrogen administration has been associated with modest improvements in measures of attention, memory, and concentration in pre- and postmenopausal women. Several small open trials (Fillit et al., 1986; Honjo et al., 1989; Ohkura et al., 1995) have found that estrogen replacement therapy improves psychometric test performance, as well as cortical cerebral blood flow and electroencephalogram (EEG) activity in patients with AD. Table 4.14 presents estrogen data to date.

Several recent studies have found this treatment strategy encouraging. In addition to Tang et al. (1996; see above discussion of cholinergic augmentation strategies), Schneider et al. (1996) recently reported on a 30-week, randomized, double-blind, placebo-controlled multicenter investigation of 343 female patients with AD. Women receiving estrogen replacement therapy (ERT) in addition to tacrine showed significantly greater improvement in AD symptoms than did patients receiving a placebo or tacrine alone. This suggests that prior, or continuing, treatment with estrogen may enhance response to tacrine in AD patients.

Other Treatment Strategies

A vast array of interventions have been tried for AD patients. Most strategies have been unconvincing, either because of limitations in study design or because the rationale was weak. They are summarized in Table 4.15. These unsuccessful strategies have included carbon dioxide, carbonic anhydrous inhibitors, tocopherol (vitamin E; to date, though many well-controlled, large-scale clinical trials are under way, and early results suggest a role in primary prevention), hyperbolic oxygen, and vasodilators (papaverine, cyclandelate, isosuprine, cinnizarine).

Summary for the Treating Clinician

While no cure exists for AD, the most promising, symptomatic treatments for AD subjects are the AChEs and vitamin E. The second generation of AChEs, notably donepezil, galantamine, and rivastigmine, offer demonstrable clinical efficacy and simpler dosing, minimal side effects, and negligible hepatotoxicity. At this time there are no "head-on" comparisons among these three compounds. The clinical effects are very likely due to a class effect. At the current time, it is hard to advocate one over another.

Combination trials of NSAIDs and/or estrogen replacement with AChEs are now under way. While these combinations are now not approved interventions, these trials are likely to soon change this recommendation.

DEMENTIA ASSOCIATED WITH PARKINSON'S DISEASE

Dementia is common in Parkinson's disease, but the exact pathophysiology, especially the relationship among Alzheimer's disease, Parkinson's dementia,

TABLE 4.14 Estrogen[a]

Authors	*Drug*	*Type*	*Design*	N	*Outcome Measures*	*Length of Study*	*Measure Results*
Hagino et al. (1995)	Estrogen replacement therapy	3	Open label	15 & 7	MMSE, HWDS, GBS	6 weeks and 5–28 months	Significant improvement on MMSE, HDS, GBS in Study 1 & in some subjects in Study 2
Ohkura et al. (1995)	Estrogen replacement therapy	3	Open label, case study	7	MMSE, HWDS, GBS	5–45 months	Nonsignificant improvement on MMSE and HDS in 4 cases
Weis (1987)	Estrogen and nalmefene	3	Open label	5	GDS, MMSE, BSRT, TMT, VFT, BCRS	4 weeks	No significant improvement
Brenner et al. (1994)	Estrogen replacement therapy	2	Population-based case control	107 AD, 120 cntr.	Adjusted odds ratios of estrogen replacement therapy and AD	Followed for 6 years	No association between ERT and AD
Henderson et al. (1994)	Estrogen replacement therapy	3	Population-based case control	143 AD, 92 cntr.	Likelihood of developing AD in controls and comparison of MMSE scores	NA	Significant difference in risk and MMSE scores favoring ERT
Barrett-Conner & Kritz-Silverstein (1993)	Estrogen replacement therapy	1	Population-based case control	800	Adjusted odds ratio of ERT and cognitive function (BSRT, WMS, MMSE, BRS, TMT, VFT)	Followed for 15 years	No significant effect of estrogen on cognitive function
Honjo et al. (1989)	Estrogen replacement therapy	3	Open label, parallel group	7	JST, HWDS	6 weeks	Significant improvement on JST
Fillit et al. (1986)	Estrogen replacement therapy	3	Open label	7	GDS, BRS, WAIS, MMSE, RMT, DRS	6 weeks	Significant improvement in three subjects
Mulnard et al. (2000)	Estrogen replacement	1	DB, PC	120	CG1C, CDR	1 year	No effect on sentinel events
Henderson et al. (2000)			DB, PC, parallel group	42	ADAS-Cog, CGIC, Caregiver function status	16 weeks	No effect on outcome measures

[a]Refer to "List of Acronyms," pp. 113–116, for definitions of abbreviations.

TABLE 4.15 Other Interventions[a]

Authors	Drug	Type	Design	N	Outcome Measures	Length of Study	Measure Results
Scherder et al. (1995)	Trans-Q electrical nerve stimulation	2	DB, PC, random parallel group	16	DS, VMS, VFT, EWT, FRT, PRT	6 weeks	Significant effect on recognition in EWT and on FRT, PRT
Saletu et al. (1992)	Denbufylline in AD and MID	2	DB, PC, random parallel group	45 and 51	EEG mapping, CGI, MMSE, DSY, TMT, DS, SCAGS	12 weeks	Significant improvement on CGI, MMSE, DSY, SGAGS
Tollefson (1990)	Nimodepine	1	DB, PC, random parallel group	227	BSRT, VFT, FT, CGI, ADL, RAGS, SRT, SDMT, FLNT	12 weeks	Significant improvement on parts of the BSRT
Saletu et al. (1994)	Nicergoline in SDAT and Multi-infarct dementia	1	DB, PC, random parallel group	112	CGI, MMSE, SCAGS	8 weeks	Significant improvement on CGI & MMSE for both SDAT & MID
Battaglia et al. (1989)	Nicergoline	1	DB, PC, random parallel group	315	SCAGS	6 months	Significant improvement on SCAGS
Nicergoline Study Group (1990)	Nicergoline and ergoloid mesylates	3	SB placebo followed by DB, parallel group	73 and 73	SCAGS, PP	7 months	Significant improvement on SCAGS, PP for both groups
Miller, Fong, & Tinklenberg (1993)	ORG 2766 ACTH 4-9 analog	2	DB, PC, random parallel group	40	BSRT, MMSE, DSY, ADAS, GDS, RT, PTT	16 weeks	Significant improvement on RT
Kragh-Sorensen et al. (1986)	ORG 2766 ACTH 4-9 analog	2	DB, PC, random parallel group	156	SCAGS, GAGS, LPRS, BRS	4 weeks	Significant improvement on SCAGS, LPRS & GAGS at varied doses
Soininen et al. (1985)	ORG 2766 ACTH 4-9 analog	2	DB, PC, random parallel group	77	SCAGS, GPIE, LPRS, GAS	6 months	No significant improvement
Ferris et al. (1982)	L-Dopa	3	DB, PC, random crossover	56	BSRT	16 weeks	No significant improvement
Branconnier et al. (1979)	ACTH 4-10	2	DB, PC, random crossover	18	SPPT, BGT, RT, WMS	Acute injection	No significant improvement
Davidson et al. (1988)	4-Aminopyridine	2	DB, PC, random crossover	14	ADAS	4 weeks	No significant improvement
D. F. Smith et al. (1984)	Tryptophan	2	DB, PC, random crossover	28	PGRS, GRS	4 weeks	No significant improvement
Cutler et al. (1985)	Zimeldine	2	DB, PC, random crossover	4	RT, OM, WLL	23 weeks	No significant improvement
Dehlin et al. (1985)	Alaproclate	2	DB, PC, random parallel group	40	GBS, CGI, CPRS	8 weeks	Significant improvement on subtest of GBS
Meador et al. (1993)	Thiamine 1 DB and 1 SB experiment	2 and 3	DB and SB, PC, random crossover	18 and 28	ADAS, MMSE, CGI	8 weeks	Significant improvement on ADAS in 13 DB subjects
Nolan et al. (1991)	Thiamine	2	DB, PC, random parallel group	15	BNT, MMSE, WLL	1 year	No significant improvement

(continued)

TABLE 4.15 (continued)

Authors	*Drug*	*Type*	*Design*	N	*Outcome Measures*	*Length of Study*	*Measure Results*
Blass et al. (1988)	Thiamine	2	DB, PC, random crossover	16	MMSE	6 months	Significant improvement on MMSE
Adolfsson et al. (1982)	Levodopa	2	DB, PC, random parallel group	37	DS, SIM, FOM, BGT, RT, FTT	10 weeks	No significant improvement
Lebowitz & Crook (1991)	Guanfacine	1 and 2	DB, SB, PC, random parallel group	160 and 40	MAC-S, MAC-CGI, MAC-P, LM, BVRT, PAT	4 weeks	No significant improvement
Crook, Wilner, et al. (1992)	Guanfacine	2	DB, PC, random parallel group	29	CGI, CRS, MAC-F, ALT, LMT, BVRT	13 weeks	No significant improvement
Schlegel et al. (1989)	Guanfacine	2	DB, PC, random crossover	5	PMT, SM, VFT, DS, BVRT	4 weeks	No significant improvement
Mouradian et al. (1991)	Somatostatin (Octreotide)	2	DB, PC, random crossover	14	ADAS, BSRT, DS, SM, VFT, RVL, LMT	Acute injections and iv	No significant improvement
McLachlan et al. (1991)	Desferri-oxamine	2	DB, PC, random parallel group	48	ADL, VHB	24 months	Significant decrease in rate of decline of ADL
Mellow et al. (1989)	Thyrotropin-releasing hormone	2	DB, PC, random crossover	10	VT, VFT, PRT, BSRT	Acute 3 day	No significant improvement on cognition
Lampe TH et al. (1990)	TRH and lecithin	2	DB, PC, random crossover	8	VFT, TMT, BSRT, BVRT	2 weeks	Significant improvement on part of BSRT
Peabody et al. (1986)	Thyrotropin-releasing hormone	3	DB, PC, crossover	4	DS, BSRT, TET, ZVT	Acute injection	No significant improvement
Imagawa (1990)	Coenzyme Q_{10}, vitamin B_6, and iron	3	Open label	27	HWDS	8 weeks	Significant improvement on HWDS
Mohr et al. (1986)	THIP	2	DB, PC, random crossover	6	SR, VFDT, WLL, PMT, RT, RF	2 weeks	No significant improvement
Mohr et al. (1989)	Clonidine	2	DB, PC, random crossover	8	SM, VFT, DS, OP, VL	~4 weeks	No significant improvement
Ihl, Perisic, & Dierks (1989)	Tenilsetam	3	Open label	12	RT, SLT, CGI, FJT(?)	3 months	Significant improvement on FJT & RT
Fleischhacker, Buchgeher, & Schubert (1986)	Memantine	3	SB, PC, random parallel group	20	FPB, PGRS, SCAGS, CGI, SKT	5 weeks	No significant improvement
Sano et al. (1997)	Vitamin E, vitamin E and selegeline, selegeline		DB, PC	341	CDR, MMSE, ADAS-Cog	2 years	Vitamin E reduced risk of institutionalization

[a]Refer to "List of Acronyms," pp. 113–116, for definitions of abbreviations.

TABLE 4.16 Dementia in Parkinson's Disease[a]

Authors	*Drug*	*Type*	*Design*	N	*Measures*	*Length of Study*	*Measure Results*
Sano et al. (1990)	Piracetam	2	DB, PC, random crossover	20	mMMSE, BSRT, VFT, RT, CPT	24 weeks	No significant improvement
Garcia et al. (1982)	Lecithin	2	DB, PC, random parallel group	16	VOCT, BDT, RPMT, DSY, VFT, OR	9 weeks	No significant differences between groups
Barbeau (1980)	Lecithin	3	Open label	10	KBD	3 months	Improvement in KBD

[a]Refer to "List of Acronyms," pp. 113–116, for definitions of abbreviations.

and Lewy body dementia, has yet to be fully understood. Dementia is common in Parkinson's disease, affecting approximately 30% of all PD patients (Koller & Megaffin, 1994; Pollack & Hornabrook, 1988). Age and duration of illness appear to be significant risk factors in the development of dementia. Mayeux et al. (1990) found that the incidence rate of dementia was 69/1,000 population per years of follow-up, and that the risk of dementia as a function of age in this group reached 65% by age 85 (Koller & Megaffin, 1994). This resulted in an age-specific prevalence of 21% in patients whose other PD symptoms occurred after age 70. This dementia may be genetically determined. Marder et al. (1990) found that the risk of dementia among first-degree relatives of demented patients with PD was sixfold greater than in relatives of nondemented PD patients.

Table 4.16 summarizes a limited experience with treatments for the dementia associated with PD. Both piracetam and phosphatidylserine have been tried in Type 1 studies without success. Two Type 3 studies—open clinical trials with a small number of subjects—have both proposed that the coadministration of lecithin with sinemet resulted in improved performance in measures of cognitive performance. One encouraging note is that many of the ongoing trials mentioned above for AD subjects have now been extended to patients with Lewy body dementia and dementia associated with Parkinson's disease.

List of Acronyms

AB	Aphasia battery
ACPT	Auditory Continuous Performance Test
ACTH	adrenocorticotropic hormone
AD	Alzheimer's disease
ADAS	Alzheimer's Disease Assessment Scale
ADAS-Cog	Alzheimer's Disease Assessment Scale—Cognitive Scale
ADAS-NCog	Alzheimer's Disease Assessment Scale—Noncognitive Scale
ADL	activities of daily living
AF	attentional focusing
AMTS	Abbreviated Mental Test score
ASMC	automatic speech and mental control
AST	Aphasia Screening Test
AVLT	Auditory Verbal Learning Test
BCRS	Brief Cognitive Rating Scale
BDT	Block Design subtest of the Wechsler Adult Intelligence Test
BGT	Bender-Gestalt Test
BI	Barthal Index
BICMT	Blessed Information-Concentration-Memory Test
BNT	Boston Naming Test
BPDP	Brown-Peterson Distractor Paradigm
BPRS	Brief Psychiatric Rating Scale
BRS	Blessed-Roth Scale
BS	block span
BSDL	Benton Serial Digit Learning
BSRT	Buschke Selective Reminding Task
BTT	block–tapping task
BVRT	Benton Visual Retention Test
BWLLT	Buschke Word List Learning Test
CA	cube analysis
CALC	calculations
CAMCOG	Cambridge Cognitive Examination
CANTAB	Cambridge Neuropsychological Test Automated Battery
CASE	Clifton Assessment Scale for the Elderly

CCSE Cognitive Capacity Screening Examination
CD clock drawing
CDR Clinical Dementia Rating Scale
CFF critical flicker fusion
CFT Complex Figure Test
CG-CGIC Caregiver-Rated Clinical Global Impression of Change
CGI clinical global impression
CGIC clinical global impression—change
CGII clinical global impression of improvement
CIBC clinician interview-based impression
CL-CGIC clinician-rated clinical global impression of change
CN color naming
CNFN confrontation naming
COC cross-out concentration
COWGT Controlled Oral Word Generation Test
CP constructional praxis
CPRS Comprehensive Psychopathological Rating Scale
CPT continuous performance task
CR category recognition
CRTT choice reaction time task
CS Crichton Scale
CSCL Clinical Status Checklist
CST Color Slide Test
CT Corsi's Test
CWAT Controlled Word Association Test
DAT dementia of the Alzheimer type
DB double blind
DCT Digit Copy Test
DL dichotic listening
DMTS delayed matching to sample
DRMLO delayed response matching to location order
DRS Dementia Rating Scale
DRST Delayed Recognition Span Test
DS Digit Span subtest of the Wechsler Adult Intelligence Test
DSY Digit Symbol subtest of the Wechsler Adult Intelligence Test
DYN dynometry
EEG electroencephalogram
EOAD early-onset Alzheimer's disease
ERDT Extended Range Drawing Test
ERT estrogen replacement therapy
EWT Eight Word Test
FAST functional assessment stages
FAT Finger Agnosia Test
FCCA Final Comprehensive Consensus Assessment
FFT Famous Faces Test
FLNT First and Last Names Test
FLS Functional Life Scale
FOM Fuld Object Memory
FPB Funktionspsychose-Skala-B
FR free recall of random and related words
FRT Facial Recognition Test
FTT finger-tapping task
GAS Global Assessment Scale
GBS Gottfries, Brane, and Steen Scale Test
GCAT Geometrical Constructive Apraxia Test
GDS Global Deterioration Scale
GERRI Geriatric Evaluations by Relatives Rating Instrument
GIFT Gollin Incomplete Figures Test
GPIE General Psychiatric Impression—Elderly
GRS Gerontopsychiatric Rating Scale
GS Gibson Spiral
HDS Hierarchic Dementia Scale
HP hand positions
HVR Halton's Visual Reproductions
HWDS Hasegawa's Dementia Scale
IADL instrumental activities of daily living
IBAT Ideomotor and Buccal-Facial Apraxia Test
IDDD Interview for Deterioration in Daily life in Dementia
IL incomplete letters
IMCI Information-Memory-Concentration Instrument
IMPP immediate memory for prose passages
IPSCE Inventory of Psychic and Somatic Complaints in the Elderly
IPT Incomplete Picture Task
IWRT Immediate Word Recognition Task
JLO judgment of line orientation
JST Japanese Screening Test
KBD Koh's Block Design
KOL Kendrick Object Learning
KT Kew Tests
LAS Luria Alternating Series
LC letter cancellation
LM letter matching
LMT Logical Memory test of the Wechsler Adult Intelligence Test
LPRS London Psychogeriatric Rating Scale
LS Lawton Scale
LT Labyrinth Test
MAC-CGI Memory Assessment Clinics Clinical Global Improvement Scale
MAC-P Memory Assessment Clinics Psychiatric Rating Scale

MAC-S	Memory Assessment Clinics Self-Rating Scale
MC	mental control
MCGBRS	Modified Crighton Geriatric Behavior Rating Scale
MDS	Mattis Dementia Scale
mMMSE	Modified Mini-Mental State Exam
MMSE	Mini-Mental State Exam
MOR	misplaced object recall
MPM	Modified Progressive Matrices
MPP	memory for prose passages
MSCL	Mental Status Checklist
MSQ	Mental Status Questionnaire
NC	number cancellation
NFA	name-face association
NLT	Name Learning Test
NOSIE	Nurse's Observation Scale for In-Patients
NSAID	nonsteroidal anti-inflammatory drug
NVPAL	nonverbal paired-associate learning
NYUMT	New York University Memory Task
OBS-CS	Organic Brain Syndrome—Confusion Scale
OBS-DS	OBS Disorientation Scale
OM	object memory
OP	object placement
OR	orientation
ORT	Object Recognition Task
OT	Orientation Test
PALT	Paired Associates Learning Test
PB	pegboard
PC	placebo-controlled
PCT	Picture Cancellation Task
PDD	primary degenerative dementia
PDS	Progressive Deterioration Scale
PET	positron-emission tomography
PGDRS	Psychogeriatric Dependency Rating Scales
PGRS	Plutchik Geriatric Rating Scale
PMSE	Pfeifer Mental Status Exam
PMT	Picture Memory Task
PNRS	Plutchnik Nurse's Rating Scale
PP	Polarity Profile
PRMT	Prose Memory Test
PRS	Peri Scale
PRT	Picture Recognition Task
PS	perceptual speed
PSMS	Physical Self-Maintenance Scale
PTT	Pursuit Tracking Task
PVAS	Physician Visual Analogue Scale
PWT	Paired Words Test
QEEG	Quantitative EEG
RAGS	relative's assessment of global symptomatology
RAT	Repeated Aquisition Task
RAVL	Rey Auditory Verbal Learning Test
rCBF	regional cerebral blood flow
RCFT	Rey Complex Figure Test
RCGM	regional cerebral glucose metabolism
RDRS-II	Rapid Disability Rating Scale II
RDT	Rosen Drawing Test
RF	recurring figures
RMPT	Roadmap Test
RMT	Randt Memory Test
RNCP	Rosen Noncognitive Portion
RNT	Responsive Naming Test
RPMT	Raven's Progressive Matricies Test
RR	relative reports
RT	reaction time
RVIP	raid visual information processing
SB	single blind
SBI	spontaneous behavior interview
SCAGS	Sandoz Clinical Assessment–Geriatric Scale
SCWIT	Stroop Color Word Interference Test
SDAT	senile dementia of the Alzheimer's type
SDMT	Symbol Digit Modality Test
SGRS	Stockton Geriatric Rating Scale
SIM	Similarities subtest of the Wechsler Adult Intelligence Test
SKT	Syndrom-Kurztest
SLT	shopping-list task
SM	sentence memory
SMT	Spatial Memory Test
SPECT	single-photon emission computed tomography
SPPT	Sperling's Perceptual Trace
SPT	Shepard Picture Test
SR	story recall
SRT	Standardized Roadmap Test
SS	short story
ST	Set Test
SV	sentence verification
SVL	supraspan verbal learning
SVT	Serial Visuographic Task
T & L	tacrine and lecithin
TCD	transcranial Doppler ultrasonography
TET	Time Estimation Task
TC	trigrams
THIP	4,5,6,7-tetrahydroisozalolo(5,4-c)-pyridin-3-ol
TMT	Trail Making Test
TNR	telephone number recall
TPBT	Toulouse-Pieron Barrage Test
TR	tachistoscopic recognition
TRH	thyrotropin-releasing hormone
TT	Token Test

V&V SRT	Visual and Verbal Selective Reminding Tasks
VCPT	Visual Continuous Performance Test
VCRMT	Visual Continuous Recognition Memory Task
VFDT	Visual Form Discrimination Test
VFT	Verbal Fluency Test
VJ	verbal judgment
VL	verbal learning
VMS	Visual Memory Span from WMS
VMT	Visual Memory Task
VOCT	vocabulary test
VPAL	verbal paired-associate learning
VPM	visual pattern matching
VR	visual recognition
VRMT	Verbal Recognition Memory Test
VRT	verbal reproduction task
VSMD	visual search on matrices of digits
VSRT	verbal selective reminding task
VST	visuomotor task
VT	vigilance task
VVLT	Visuo-Verbal Learning Test
WAIS-R	Wechsler Adult Intelligence Scale—Revised
WAT	word association test
WLL	word list learning
WMS	Wechsler Memory Scale
WNA	Walsh neuropsychological approach
WR	word recall
WRT	word recognition task
ZVT	Zahlen Verbindungs Test

References

Adolfsson, R., Brane, G., et al. (1982). A double-blind study with levodopa in dementia of Alzheimer type. In S. Corkin et al., *Alzheimer's disease: A report of progress in research* (Vol. 19). New York: Raven Press.

Agid, Y., Dubois, B., Anand, R., et al. (1998). Efficacy and tolerability of rivastigmine in patients with dementia of the Alzheimer type. *Current Therapeutic Research—Clinical and Experimental, 59,* 837–845.

Ala, T., Remero, S., et al. (1990). GM-1 treatment of Alzheimer's disease: A pilot study of safety and efficacy. *Archives of Neurology, 47,* 1126–1130.

Alhainen, K., & Rickkinen, P. J. (1993). Discrimination of Alzheimer's patients responding to cholinesterase inhibitors. *Acta Neurologica Scandinavica, 149,* 16–21.

Amaducci, L., & the SMID Group. (1988). Phosphaditylserine in the treatment of Alzheimer's disease: Results of a multicenter study. *Psychopharmacology Bulletin, 24*(1), 130–134.

American Psychiatric Association. (1994). *Diagnostic and statistical manual of mental disorders* (4th ed.). Washington, DC: Author.

Andersen, K., Launer, L. J., et al. (1995). Do nonsteroidal anti-inflammatory drugs decrease the risk for Alzheimer's disease. *Neurology, 45,* 1441–1445.

Antuona, P. G. (1995). Effectiveness and safety of velnacrine for the treatment of Alzheimer's disease: A double-blind, placebo controlled study. *Archives of Internal Medicine, 155,* 1766–1772.

Asthana, S., Raffaele, K. C., Bernardi, A., et al. (1996). Treatment of Alzheimer's disease by continuous influsion of physostigmine. *Alzheimer's Disease & Associated Disorders,* 9(4), 223–232.

Ashford, J. W., Soldinger, S., et al. (1981). Physostigmine and its effect on six patients with dementia. *American Journal of Psychiatry, 138*(6), 829–830.

Banen, D. M. (1972). An ergot preparation (Hydergine) for relief of symptoms of cerebrovascular insufficiency. *Journal of the American Geriatric Society, 24,* 22–24.

Barbeau, A. (1980). Lecithin in Parkinson's disease. *Journal of Neural Transmission, 16*(Suppl.), 187–193.

Barrett-Conner, E., & Kritz-Silverstein, D. (1993). Estrogen replacement therapy and cognition in older women. *Journal of the American Medical Association,* 269(20), 2637–2641.

Battaglia, A., Bruni, G., et al. (1989). Nicergoline in mild to moderate dementia: A multicenter, double-blind, placebo-controlled study. *Journal of the American Geriatrics Society,* 37, 295–302.

Bellagamba, G., Postacchini, D., et al. (1990). Acetyl-L-carnitine activity in senile dementia Alzheimer type. *Neurobiology of Aging, 11,* 345.

Beller, S. A., Overall, J. E., et al. (1988). Long-term outpatient treatment of senile dementia with oral physostigmine. *Journal of Clinical Psychiatry,* 49(10), 400–404.

Beller, S. A., Overall, J. E., & Swann, A. C. (1985). Efficacy of oral physostigmine in primary degenerative dementia: A double-blind study of response to different dose levels. *Psychopharmacology,* 87, 147–151.

Bierer, L. M., Aisen, P. S., et al. (1994). A pilot study of clonidine plus physostigmine in Alzheimer's disease. *Dementia,* 5, 243–246.

Blass, J. P., Gleason, P., et al. (1988). Thiamine and Alzheimer's disease: A pilot study. *Archives of Neurology, 45,* 833–835.

Bottini, G., Vallar, G., et al. (1992). Oxiracetam in dementia: A double-blind, placebo-controlled study. *Acta Neurologica Scandinavica, 86,* 237–241.

Branconnier, R. J., Cole, J. O., et al. (1983). The therapeutic efficacy of pramiracetam in Alzheimer's disease: Preliminary observations. *Psychopharmacology Bulletin, 19*(4), 726–730.

Branconnier, R. J., Cole, J. O., & Gardos, G. (1979). ACTH 4-10 in the amelioration of neuropsychological symptomatology associated with senile organic brain syndrome. *Psychopharmacology, 61*, 161–165.

Breitner, J. C. S. (1996). Inflammatory processes and anti-inflammatory drugs in Alzheimer's disease: A current appraisal. *Neurobiology of Aging, 17*, 789–794.

Breitner, J. C. S., Gau, B. A., et al. (1994). Inverse association of anti-inflammatory treatments and Alzheimer's disease: Initial results of a co-twin control study. *Neurology, 44*, 227–232.

Brenner, D. E., Kukull, W. A., et al. (1994). Postmenopausal estrogen replacement therapy and the risk of Alzheimer's disease: A population-based case-control study. *American Journal of Epidemiolgy, 140*(3), 262–267.

Brinkman, S. D., Pomara, N., et al. (1992). A dose-ranging study of lecithin in the treatment of primary degenerative dementia (Alzheimer disease). *Journal of Clinical Pharmacology, 2*(4), 281–285.

Bruno, G., Mohr, E., et al. (1986). Muscarinic agonist therapy of Alzheimer's disease: A clinical trial of RS-86. *Archives of Neurology, 43*, 659–661.

Burke, W. J., Ranno, A. K., et al. (1993). L-Deprenyl in the treatment of mild dementia of the Alzheimer type: Preliminary results. *Journal of the American Geriatric Society, 41*, 367–370.

Burns, A., Russell, E., & Page, S. (1999). New drugs for Alzheimer's disease. *British Journal of Psychiatry, 174*, 476–479.

Caamano, J., Gomez, M. J., et al. (1994). Effects of CDP-choline on cognition and cerebral hemodynamics in patients with Alzheimer's disease. *Methods and Findings in Experimental and Clinical Pharmacology, 16*(3), 211–218.

Calvani, M., Carta, A., et al. (1992). Action of acetyl-L-carnitine in neurodegeneration and Alzheimer's disease. *Annals of the New York Academy of Sciences, 663*, 483–486.

Campi, N., Todeschini, G. P., & Scarzella, L. (1990). Selegiline versus L-acetylcarntine in the treatment of Alzheimer type dementia. *Clinical Therapeutics, 12*(4), 306–314.

Canadian Study of Health and Aging. (1994). The Canadian Study of Health and Aging: Risk factors for Alzheimer's disease in Canada. *Neurology, 44*, 2073–2080.

Chase, T. N., Durso, R., et al. (1982). Vasopressin treatment of cognitive deficits in Alzheimer's disease. In S. Corkin et al., *Alzheimer's disease: A report of progress in research* (Vol. 19). New York: Raven Press.

Chatellier, G., & Lacomblez, L. (1990). Tacrine (tetrahydroaminoacridine: THA) and lecithin in senile dementia of the Alzheimer type: A multicenter trial. *British Medical Journal, 300*, 495–499.

Christie, J. E., Shering, A., et al. (1981). Physostigmine and arecoline: Effects of intravenous infusions in Alzheimer presenile dementia. *British Journal of Psychiatry, 138*, 46–50.

Clauss, J. J., Ludwig, C., et al. (1991). Nootropic drugs in Alzheimer's disease: Symptomatic treatment with pramiracetam. *Neurology, 41*, 570–574.

Corey-Bloom, J., Anand, R., Veach, J., et al. (1998). A randomized trial evaluating the efficacy and safety of ENA 713 (rivastigmine tartrate), a new acetylcholinesterase inhibitor, in patients with mild to moderate severe Alzheimer's disease. *International Journal of Geriatric Psychopharmacology, 1*, 55–65.

Croisile, B., Trillet, M., et al. (1993). Long-term and high-dose piracetam treatment of Alzheimer's disease. *Neurology, 43*, 301–305.

Crook, T., Petrie, W., et al. (1992). Effects of phosphatidylserine in Alzheimer's disease. *Psychopharmacology Bulletin, 28*(1), 61–66.

Crook, T., Wilner, E., et al. (1992). Noradrenergic intervention in Alzheimer's disease. *Psychopharmacology Bulletin, 28*(1), 67–70.

Crook, T. H., Tinklenberg, J., et al. (1991). Effects of phosphatidylserine on age-associated memory impairment. *Neurology, 41*, 644–649.

Cutler, N. R., Haxby, J., et al. (1985). Evaluation of zimeldine in Alzheimer's disease: Cognitive and biochemical measures. *Archives of Neurology, 42*, 744–748.

Dal-Bianco, P., Maly, J., et al. (1991). Galanthamine treatment in Alzheimer's disease. *Journal of Neural Transmission, 33*(Suppl.), 59–63.

Davidson, M., Zemishlany, Z., et al. (1988). 4-Aminopyridine in the treatment of Alzheimer's disease. *Biological Psychiatry, 23*, 485–490.

Davis, K. L., Hollander, E., et al. (1987). Induction of depression with oxotremorine in patients with Alzheimer's disease. *American Journal of Psychiatry, 144*(4), 468–471.

Davis, K. L., & Mohs, R. C. (1982). Enhancement of memory processes in Alzheimer's disease with multiple-dose intravenous physostigmine. *American Journal of Psychiatry, 139*(11), 1421–1424.

Davis, K. L., Thal, L. J., et al. (1992). A double-blind, placebo-controlled multicenter study of tacrine for Alzheimer's disease. *New England Journal of Medicine, 327*(18), 1253–1259.

Dehlin, O., Hedenrud, B., et al. (1985). A double-blind comparison of alaproclate and placebo in the treatment of patients with senile dementia. *Acta Psychiatrica Scandinavica, 71,* 190–196.

Delwaide, P. J., Devoitille, A. R., & Ylieff, M. (1980). Acute effects of drugs on memory of patients with senile dementia. *Acta Psychiatrica Belgica, 80,* 748–754.

Delwaide, P. J., Gyselynck-Mambourg, A. M., et al. (1986). Double-blind randomized controlled study of phosphatidylserine in senile demented patients. *Acta Neurologica Scandinavica, 73,* 136–140.

Durso, R., Fedio, P., et al. (1982). Lysine vasopressin in Alzheimer disease. *Neurology, 32,* 674–677.

Dysken, M. W., Fovall, P., et al. (1982). Lecithin administration in Alzheimer dementia. *Neurology,* 32, 1203–1204.

Dysken, M. W., Mendels, J., et al. (1992). Milacemide: A placebo-controlled study in senile dementia of the Alzheimer type. *Journal of the American Geriatric Society, 40,* 503–506.

Eagger, S. A., et al. (1991). Tacrine in Alzheimer's disease. *Lancet, 337,* 989–992.

Eagger, S. A., et al. (1992). Tacrine in Alzheimer's disease—Time course of changes in cognitive function and practice effects. *British Journal of Psychiatry, 16,* 36–40.

Eagger, S. A., Levy, R., & Sahakain, B. J. (1992). Tacrine in Alzheimer's disease. *Acta Neurologica Scandinavica,* 139(Suppl.), 75–80.

Ebmeier, K. P., Hunter, R., et al. (1992). Effects of a single dose of the acetylcholinesterase inhibitor velnacrine on recognition memory and regional cerebral blood flow in Alzheimer's disease. *Psychopharmacology, 108,* 103–109.

Etienne, P., Dastoor, D., et al. (1981). Alzheimer's disease: Lack of effect of lecithin treatment for 3 months. *Neurology, 31,* 1552–1554.

Falsaperla, A., Preti, P. A. M., & Oliani, C. (1990). Selegiline versus oxiracetam in patients with Alzheimer-type dementia. *Clinical Therapeutics, 12*(5), 376–384.

Farlow, M., Gracon, S. I., et al. (1992). A controlled trial of tacrine in Alzheimer's disease. *Journal of the American Medical Association, 268*(18), 2523–2529.

Ferris, S., Mann, J. J., Stanley, M., et al. (1981). Central amine metabolism in Alzheimer's disease: In vivo relationship to cognitive performance. *Neurobiology of Aging, 2,* 57–60.

Ferris, S. H., Sathananthan, G., et al. (1979). Long-term choline treatment of memory-impaired elderly patients. *Science, 205,* 1039–1040.

Fillit, H., Weinreb, H., et al. (1986). Observations in a preliminary open trial of estradiol therapy for senile dementia–Alzheimer's type. *Psychoneuroendochrinology, 11*(3), 337–345.

Finali, G., Piccirilli, M., et al. (1991). L-Deprenyl therapy improves verbal memory in amnesic Alzheimer's patients. *Clinical Neuropharmacology, 14*(6), 523–536.

Fitten, L. J., Perryman, K. M., et al. (1990). Treatment of Alzheimer's disease with short and long-term oral THA and lecithin: A double blind study. *American Journal of Psychiatry, 147*(2), 239–242.

Fleischhacker, W. W., Buchgeher, A., & Schubert, H. (1986). Memantine in the treatment of senile dementia of the Alzheimer type. *Progress in Neuro-Psychopharmacology and Biological Psychiatry, 10,* 87–693.

Flicker, C., Ferris, S. H., & Reisberg, B. (1991). Mild cognitive impairment in the elderly: Predictors of dementia. *Neurology, 41,* 1006–1009.

Garcia, C. A., Tweedy, J. R., et al. (1982). Lecithin and Parkinsonian dementia. In S. Corkin et al., *Alzheimer's disease: A report of progress in research* (Vol. 19). New York: Raven Press.

Gauthier, S., Bouchard, R., et al. (1990). Tetrahydroaminoacridine-lecithin combination treatment in patients with intermediate stage Alzheimer's disease. *New England Journal of Medicine, 322*(18), 1272–1276.

Goad, D. L., Davis, C. M., et al. (1991). The use of selegline in Alzheimer's patients with behavior problems. *Journal of Clinical Psychiatry, 52*(8), 342–345.

Green, R. C., Goldstein, F. C., et al. (1992). Treatment trial of oxiracetam in Alzheimer's disease. *Archives of Neurology, 49,* 1135–1136.

Growden, J. H., Corkin, S., et al. (1986). Piracetam combined with lecithin in the treatment of Alzheimer's disease. *Neurobiology of Aging, 7,* 296–276.

Gustafson, L. (1993). Physostigmine and tetrahydroaminoacridine treatment of Alzheimer's disease. *Acta Neurologica Scandinavica, 149,* 39–41.

Gustafson, L., Edvinson, L., et al. (1987). Intravenous physostigmine treatment of Alzheimer's disease evaluated by psychometric testing, regional cerebral blood flow (rCBF) measurement, and EEG. *Psychopharmacology,* 93, 31–35.

Hagino, N., Ohkura, T., et al. (1995). Estrogen in clinical trials for dementia of Alzheimer type. In I. Hanin et al., *Alzheimer's and Parkinson's diseases.* New York: Plenum Press.

Harbaugh, R. E., Reeder, T. M., et al. (1989). Intracerebroventricular bethanechol chloride infusion in Alzheimer's disease: Results of a collaborative double-blind study. *Journal of Neurosurgery, 71,* 481–486.

Harbaugh, R. E., Roberts, D. W., et al. (1984). Preliminary report: Intracranial cholinergic drug infusion in patients with Alzheimer's disease. *Neurosurgery, 15*(4), 514–518.

Harrell, L. E., Callaway, R., et al. (1990). The effect of long-term physostigmine administration in Alzheimer's disease. *Neurology, 40,* 1350–1354.

Harrell, L. E., Jope, R. S., et al. (1990). Biological and neuropsychological characterization of physostigmine responders and nonresponders in Alzheimer's disease. *Journal of the American Geriatric Society, 38,* 113–122.

Heiss, W. D., Hebold, I., et al. (1988). Effect of piracetam on cerebral glucose metabolism in Alzheimer's disease as measured by positron emission tomography. *Journal of Cerebral Blood Flow and Metabolism, 8,* 613–617.

Heiss, W. D., Kessler, J., et al. (1994). Long-term effects of phosphatidylserine, pyritinol, and cognitive training in Alzheimer's disease: A neuropsychological, EEG, and PET investigation. *Dementia, 5,* 88–98.

Henderson, V. W., Paganini-Hill, A., et al. (1994). Estrogen replacement therapy in older women: Comparisons between Alzheimer's disease cases and nondemented control subjects. *Archives of Neurology, 51,* 896–900.

Henderson, V. W., Paganini-Hill, A., Miller, B. L., et al. (2000). Estrogen for Alzheimer's disease in women: Randomized, double-blind, placebo-controlled trial. *Neurology, 54*(2), 295–301.

Henderson, V. W., Roberts, E., et al. (1989). Multicenter trial of naloxone in Alzheimer's disease. *Annals of Neurology, 25,* 404–406.

Heyman, A., Schmechel, D., et al. (1987). Failure of long term high-dose lecithin to retard progression of early-onset Alzheimer's disease. *Journal of Neural Transmission, 24*(Suppl.), 279–286.

Hollander, E., Davidson, M., et al. (1987). RS 86 in the treatment of Alzheimer's disease: Cognitive and biological effects. *Biological Psychiatry, 22,* 1067–1078.

Hollingsworth, S. W. (1980). Response of geriatric patients from the satellite nursing homes of Maricopa County to Hydergine therapy: A double-blind study. *Current Therapeutic Research, 27*(3), 401–410.

Hollister, L. E., & Yesavage, J. (1984). Ergoloid mesylates for senile dementias: Unanswered questions. *Annals of Internal Medicine, 100,* 894–898.

Honjo, H., Ogino, Y., et al. (1989). In vivo effects by estrone sulfate on the central nervous system—Senile dementia (Alzheimer's type). *Journal of Steroid Biochemistry, 34*(1–6), 521–525.

Hyman, B., Esllinger, P. J., & Damasio, A. R. (1982). Effect of naltrexone on senile dementia of the Alzheimer type. *Journal of Neurology, Neurosurgery, and Psychiatry, 49,* 1321–1322.

Ihl, R., Perisic, I., & Dierks, T. (1989). Effects of 3 months of treatment with tenilsetam in patients suffering from dementia of the Alzheimer type (DAT). *Journal of Neural Transmission, 1*(Sec. P-D), 84–85.

Imagawa, M. (1992). Coenzyme Q, iron, and vitamin B-6 in genetically confirmed Alzheimer's disease. *Lancet, 340* (8820), 671.

Imagawa, M. (1990). Therapy with a combination of coenzyme Q10, vitamin B6 and iron for Alzheimer's disease and senile dementia of the Alzheimer type. In K. Iqbal, D. R. C. McLachlan, et al. (Eds.), *Alzheimer's disease: Basic mechanisms, diagnosis and therapeutic strategies.* New York: Wiley.

Jenicke, M. A., Albert, M. S., et al. (1986). Combination therapy with lecithin and ergoloid mesylates for Alzheimer's disease. *Journal of Clinical Psychiatry, 47*(5), 249–251.

Jenicke, M. A., Albert, M. S., et al. (1990). Oral physostigmine treatment for patients with presenile and senile dementia of the Alzheimer type: A double-blind placebo-controlled trial. *Journal of Clinical Psychiatry, 51*(1), 3–7.

Jennings, W. G. (1972). An ergot alkaloid preparation (Hydergine) versus placebo for treatment of symptoms of cerebrovascular insufficiency: Double-blind study. *Journal of the American Geriatric Society, 20*(8), 407–412.

Jones, G. M. M., Sahakian, B. J., et al. (1992). Effects of acute subcutaneous nicotine on attention, information processing and short-term memory in Alzheimer's disease. *Psychopharmacology, 108,* 485–494.

Jotkowitz, S. (1983). Lack of clinical efficacy of chronic oral physostigmine in Alzheimer's disease. *Annals of Neurology, 14,* 690–691.

Kaufer, D. I., Cummings, J., & Christine, D. (1996). Effect of tacrine on behavioral symptoms in Alzheimer's Disease: An open label study. *Journal of Geriatric Psychiatry and Neurology, 9,* 1–6.

Kaye, W. H., Weingartner, H., et al. (1982). Cognitive effects of cholinergic and vasopressinlike agents in patients with primary degenerative dementia. In S. Corkin et al., *Alzheimer's disease: A report of progress in research* (Vol. 19). New York: Raven Press.

Knapp, M. J., Knopman, D. S., et al. (1994). A 30-week randomized controlled trial of high-dose tacrine in patients with Alzheimer's disease. *Journal of the American Medical Association, 271*(13), 985–991.

Knopman, D. S., & Hartman, M. (1986). Cognitive effects of high-dose naltrexone in patients with probable Alzheimer's disease. *Journal of Neurology, Neurosurgery, and Psychiatry, 49,* 1321–1322.

Knopman, D., Schneider, L., Davis, K., et al. (1996). Long term tacrine (Cognex) treatment: Effects on nursing home placement and mortality, Tacrine Study Group. *Neurology, 47*(1), 166–177.

Koller, W., & Megaffin, B. B. (1994). Parkinson's disease and Parkinsonism. In C. E. Coffey & J. L. Cummings (Eds.), *Textbook of geriatric neuropsychiatry* (pp. 433–456). Washington, DC: American Psychiatric Press.

Kragh-Sorensen, P., Olsen, R. B., et al. (1986). Neuropeptides: ACTH-peptides in dementia. *Progress in Neuro-Psychopharmacology and Biological Psychiatry, 10,* 479–492.

Lampe, T. H., Norris, J., et al. (1990). Therapeutic potential of thyrotropin-releasing hormone and lecithin co-administration in Alzheimer's disease. In K. Iqbal, D. R. C. McLachlan, et al. (Eds.), *Alzheimer's disease: Basic mechanisms, diagnosis and therapeutic strategies.* New York: Wiley.

Lampe, T. H., Norris, S. C., Risse, E., et al. (1991). Therapeutic potential of thyrotropin-releasing hormone and lecithin coadministration in Alzheimer's disease. In K. Equable, D. R. C. McLachlan, B. Winblad, & H. M. Wisniewski (Eds.), *Alzheimer's disease: Basic mechanisms, diagnosis, and therapeutic strategies.* New York: Wiley.

Lebowitz, B., & Crook, T. (1991). Treatment of adult-onset cognitive disorders: Results of multicenter trials. *Psychopharmacology Bulletin, 27*(1), 41–46.

Little, A., Levy, R., et al. (1985). A double-blind, placebo-controlled trial of high-dose lecithin in Alzheimer's disease. *Journal of Neurology, Neurosurgery, and Psychiatry, 48,* 736–742.

Maltby, N., Broe, G. A., et al. (1994) Efficacy of tacrine and lecithin in mild to moderate Alzheimer's disease: Double blind trial. *British Medical Journal, 308,* 879–883.

Mangoni, A., Grassi, M. P., et al. (1991). Effects of a MAO-B inhibitor in the treatment of Alzheimer's disease. *European Neurology, 31,* 100–107.

Marder, K., Flood, P., & Cote, L. (1990). A pilot study of risk factors for dementia in Parkinson's disease. *Movement Disorders, 5,* 156–161.

Marin, D. B., Bierer, L. M., et al. (1995). L-Deprenyl and physostigmine for the treatment of Alzheimer's disease. *Psychiatry Research, 58,* 181–189.

Matejcek, M., Knor, K., et al. (1979). Electroecephalographic and clinical changes in geriatric patients treated 3 months with alkaloid preparation. *Journal of the American Geriatric Society, 27,* 198–202.

Mayeux, R., Chen, J., & Mirabello, E. (1990). An estimate of the incidence of dementia in idiopathic Parkinson's disease. *Neurology, 40,* 1513–1517.

McConnachie, R. W. (1973). A clinical trial comparing "Hydergine" with placebo in the treatment of cerebrovascular insufficiency in elderly patients. *Current Medical Research and Opinion, 1*(8), 463–468.

McGeer, P. L., McGeer, E., Rodgers, J., et al. (1990). Anti-inflammatory drugs and Alzheimer's disease. *Lancet, 335,* 1037.

McLachlan, D. R. C., Dalton, A. J., et al. (1991). Intramuscular desferrioxamine in patients with Alzheimer's disease. *Lancet, 337,* 1304–1308.

Meador, K., Loring, D., et al. (1993). Preliminary findings of high-dose thiamine in dementia of the Alzheimer type. *Journal of Geriatric Psychiatry and Neurology, 6,* 222–229.

Mellow, A. M., Stephen, M. A., et al. (1993). A peptide enhancement strategy in Alzheimer's disease: Pilot study with TRH-physostigmine infusions. *Biological Psychiatry, 34,* 271–274.

Mellow, A. M., Sunderland, T., et al. (1989). Acute effects of high-dose thyrotropin releasing hormone infusions in Alzheimer's disease. *Psychopharmacology, 98,* 403–407.

Miller, T. P., Fong, K., & Tinklenberg, J. R. (1993). An ACTH 4-9 analog (ORG 2766) and cognitive performance: High-dose efficacy and safety in dementia of the Alzheimer's type. *Biological Psychiatry, 33,* 307–309.

Minthon, L., Gustafson, L., et al. (1993). Oral tetrahydroaminoacridine treatment of Alzheimer's disease evaluated clinically by regional cerebral blood flow and EEG. *Dementia, 4,* 32–42.

Mohr, E., Bruno, G., et al. (1986). GABA-agonist therapy for Alzheimer's disease. *Clinical Neuropharmacology, 9*(3), 257–263.

Mohr, E., Schlegel, J., et al. (1989). Clonidine treatment of Alzheimer's disease. *Archives of Neurology, 46,* 376–378.

Mohs, R. C., Davis, B. M., et al. (1985). Oral physostigmine treatment of patients with Alzheimer's disease. *American Journal of Psychiatry, 142*(1), 28–33.

Molloy, D. W., Guyatt, G. H., et al. (1991). Effect of tetrahydroaminoacridine on cognition, function and behavior in Alzheimer's disease. *Canadian Medical Association Journal, 144*(1), 29–34.

Monteverde, A., Gnemmi, P., et al. (1990). Selegiline in the treatment of mild to moderate Alzheimer-type dementia. *Clinical Therapeutics, 12*(4), 315–322.

Mortimer, J. A., Ebbitt, B., et al. (1992). Predictors of cognitive and functional progression in patients with probable Alzheimer's disease. *Neurology, 42*(9), 1689–1696.

Mouradian, M. M., Thin, J., et al. (1991). Somatostatin replacement therapy for Alzheimer disease. *Annals of Neurology, 30,* 610–613.

Mouradian, M. M., Mohr, E., et al. (1988). No response to high-dose muscarinic agonist therapy in Alzheimer's disease. *Neurology, 38,* 606–608.

Mulnard, R. A., Cotman, C. W., et al. (2000). Estrogen replacement therapy for treatment of mild to moderate Alzheimer disease: A randomized controlled trial. *Journal of the American Medical Association, 283*(8), 1007–1015.

Muramoto, O., Sugishia, M., et al. (1979). Effect of physostigmine on constructional and memory tasks in Alzheimer's disease. *Archives of Neurology, 36,* 501–503.

Muramoto, O., Sugishia, M., & Ando, K. (1984). Cholinergic system and constructional praxis: A further study of physostigmine in Alzheimer's disease. *Journal of Neurology, Neurosurgery, and Psychiatry, 47,* 485–491.

Murphy, M. F., Hardiman, S. T., et al. (1991). Evaluation of HP 029 (velnacrine maleate) in Alzheimer's disease. *Annals of the New York Academy of Sciences, 640,* 253–262.

Newhouse, P. A., Sunderland, T., et al. (1988). Intravenous nicotine in Alzheimer's disease: A pilot study. *Psychopharmacology, 95,* 171–175.

Nicergoline Study Group. (1990). A double-blind randomized study of two ergot derivatives in mild to moderate dementia. *Current Therapeutic Research, 48*(4), 597–612.

Nolan, K. A., Black, R. S., et al. (1991). A trial of thiamine in Alzheimer's disease. *Archives of Neurology, 48,* 81–83.

Novo, F. P., Ryan, R. P., & Frazier, E. L. (1978). Dihydroergotexine mesylate in the treatment of symptoms of idiopathic cerebral dysfunction in geriatric patients. *Clinical Therapeutics, 1*(5), 359–369.

Ohkura, T., Isse, K., et al. (1995). Long-term estrogen replacement therapy in female patients with dementia of the Alzheimer type: Seven case reports. *Dementia, 6,* 99–107.

Panella, J. J., & Blass, J. P. (1984). Lack of clinical benefit for naloxone in a dementia day hospital. *Annals of Neurology, 15*(3), 306–307.

Passeri, M., Cucinotta, D., et al. (1990). Acetyl-L-carnitine in the treatment of mildly demented elderly patients. *International Journal of Clinical Pharmacology Research, 10*(1–2), 75–79.

Peabody, C. A., Davis, H., et al. (1986). Desamino-D-arginine-vasopressin (DDAVP) in Alzheimer's disease. *Neurobiology of Aging, 7,* 301–303.

Peabody, C. A., Deblois, T. E., & Tinklenberg, J. R. (1986). Thyrotropin-releasing hormone (TRH) and Alzheimer's disease. *American Journal of Psychiatry, 143*(2), 262–263.

Peabody, C. A., Thiemann, O., et al. (1985). Desglycinamide-9-arginine-8-vasopressin (DGAVP, Organon 5667) in patients with dementia. *Neurobiology of Aging, 6,* 95–100.

Penn, R. D., Martin, E. M., et al. (1988). Intraventricular bethanechol infusion for Alzheimer's disease: Results of double-blind and escalating-dose trials. *Neurology, 38,* 219–222.

Perryman, K. M., & Fitten, L. J. (1993). Delayed matching-to-sample performance during a double-blind trial of tacrine (THA) and lecithin in patients with Alzheimer's disease. *Life Sciences, 53,* 479–486.

Peters, B. H., & Levin, H. S. (1979). Effects of physostigmine and lecithin on memory in Alzheimer's disease. *Annals of Neurology, 6,* 219–221.

Pettegrew, J. W. (1989). Molecular insights into Alzheimer's disease. *Annals of the New York Academy of Sciences, 568,* 5–28.

Pettegrew, J. W., Klunk, W. E., et al. (1995). Clinical and neurochemical effects of acetyl-L-carnitine in Alzheimer's disease. *Neurobiology of Aging, 16*(1), 1–4.

Piccinin, G. L., Finali, G., & Piccirilli, M. (1990). Neuropsychological effects of L-deprenyl in Alzheimer's type dementia. *Clinical Neuropharmacology, 13*(2), 147–163.

Pollack, M., & Hornbook, R. W. (1968). The prevalence, natural history, and dementia of Parkinson's disease. *Brain, 89,* 429–448.

Pomara, N., Goodnick, P. J., et al. (1982). A dose-response study of lecithin in the treatment of Alzheimer's disease. In S. Corkin et al., *Alzheimer's disease: A report of progress in research* (Vol. 19). New York: Raven Press.

Pomara, N., Roberts, R., et al. (1985). Multiple, single dose naltrexone administrations fail to effect overall cognitive functioning and plasma cortisol in individuals with probable Alzheimer's disease. *Neurobiology of Aging, 6*(3), 233–236.

Raffaele, K. C., Bernardi, A., Asthana, S., et al. (1991). Effects of long-term continuous infusion of the muscarinic cholinergic agonist arecoline on verbal memory in dementia of the Alzheimer's type. *Psychopharmacology, 27*(3), 315 319.

Raffaele, K. C., Berardi, A., Morris, P. P., et al. (1991). Effects of acute infusion of the muscarinic cholinergic agonist arecoline on verbal memory and visuo-spatial function in dementia of the Alzheimer's type. *Progress in Neuro-Psychopharmacology and Biological Psychiatry, 15,* 643–648.

Rai, G., Wright, G., et al. (1990). Double-blind, placebo controlled study of acetyl-L-carnitine in patients with Alzheimer's dementia. *Current Medical Research and Opinion, 11*(10), 638–647.

Raskind, M. A., Peskind, E. R., Wessel, T., et al. (2000). Galantamine in AD: A 6-month randomized, placebo-controlled trial with a 6-month extension. *Neurology, 54,* 2261–2268.

Rechman, S. A. (1973). Two trials comparing "Hydergine" with placebo in the treatment of patients suffering from cerebrovascular insufficiency. *Current Medical Research and Opinion, 1*(8), 456–462.

Reisberg, B., Ferris, S. H., et al. (1983a). Effects of naloxone in senile dementia: A double-blind trial. *New England Journal of Medicine, 308*(12), 721–722.

Reisberg, B., Ferris, S. H., et al. (1983b). Naloxone effects on primary degenerative dementia (PDD). *Psychopharmacology Bulletin, 19*(1), 45–47.

Renvoize, E. B., & Jerram, T. (1979). Choline in Alzheimer's disease. *New England Journal of Medicine, 301,* 330.

Rich, J. B., Rasmusson, D. X., et al. (1995). Nonsteroidal anti-inflammatory drugs in Alzheimer's disease. *Neurology, 45,* 51–55.

Rodgers, S., Friedhof, L., & the Donepezil Study Group. (1996). The efficacy and safety of donepezil in patients with Alzheimer's disease: Results of a U.S. Multicenter, randomized, double-blind, placebo-controlled trial. *Dementia, 7,* 293–303.

Rogers, L., Kirby, L. C., et al. (1993). Clinical trial of indomethacin in Alzheimer's disease. *Neurology, 43,* 1609–1611.

Rogers, S. L., Doody, R. S., Mohs, R. C., et al. (1998a). Donepezil improves cognition and global function in Alzheimer's disease: A 15-week, double-blind, placebo-controlled study. *Archives of Internal Medicine, 158,* 1021–1031.

Rogers, S. L., Farlow, M. R., Doody, R. S., et al. (1998b). A 24-week, double-blind, placebo-controlled trial of donepezil in patients with Alzheimer's disease. *Neurology, 50,* 136–145.

Rosler, M., Anand, R., Cicin-Sain, A., et al. (1999). Efficacy and safety of rivastigmine in patients with Alzheimer's disease: International randomized controlled trial. *British Medical Journal, 318,* 633–640.

Rouy, J. M., Douillon, A. M., et al. (1989). Ergoloid mesylates ("Hydergine") in the treatment of mental deterioration in the elderly: A 6-month double-blind, placebo-controlled trial. *Current Medical Research and Opinion, 11*(6), 380–389.

Ruther, E., Ritter, R., et al. (1994). Efficacy of the peptidic nootropic drug cerebrolysin in patients with senile dementia of the Alzheimer type (SDAT). *Pharmacopsychiatrist, 27,* 32–40.

Sahakian, B. J., & Coull, J. T. (1993). Tetrahydroaminoacridine (THA) in Alzheimer's disease: An assessment of attentional and mnemonic function using CANTAB. *Acta Neurologica Scandinavica, 149,* 29–35.

Sahakian, B., Jones, G., et al. (1989). The effects of nicotine on attention, information processing, and short-term memory in patients with dementia of the Alzheimer type. *British Journal of Psychiatry, 154,* 797–800.

Saletu, B., Anderer, P., et al. (1992). EEG mapping and psychopharmacological studies with denbufylline in SDAT and MID. *Biological Psychiatry, 32,* 668–681.

Saletu, B., Paulus, E., et al. (1994). Nicergoline in senile dementia of Alzheimer type and multi-infarct dementia: A double-blind, placebo-controlled, clinical and EEG/ERP mapping study. *Psychopharmacology, 117,* 385–395.

Sano, M., Bell, K., et al. (1992). Double-blind parallel design pilot study of acetyl levocarnitine in patients with Alzheimer's disease. *Archives of Neurology, 49,* 1137–1141.

Sano, M., Bell, K., et al. (1993). Safety and efficacy of oral physostigmine in the treatment of Alzheimer disease. *Clinical Neuropharmacology, 16*(1), 61–69.

Sano, M., Stern, Y., et al. (1990). A controlled trial of piracetam in intellectually impaired patients with Parkinson's disease. *Movement Disorders, 5*(3), 230–234.

Scherder, E. J. A., Bouma, A., & Steen, A. M. (1995). Effects of short-term transcutaneous electrical nerve stimulation on memory and affective behaviour in patients with probable Alzheimer's disease. *Behavioural Brain Research, 67,* 211–219.

Schlegel, J., Mohr, E., et al. (1989). Guanfacine treatment of Alzheimer's disease. *Clinical Neuropharmacology, 12*(2), 124–128.

Schneider, L. S., Farlow, M. R., Henderson, V. W. (1996). Effects of estrogen replacement therapy on response to tacrine in patients with Alzheimer's disease. *Neurology, 46,* 1580–1584.

Schneider L. S., & Olin, J. T. (1994). Overview of clinical trials of Hydergine in dementia. *Archives of Neurology, 51,* 787–798.

Schneider, L., Olin, J. T., & Pawluczyk, S. (1993). A double blind crossover pilot study of *l*-deprenyl (selegiline) combined with cholinesterase inhibitor in Alzheimer's disease. *American Journal of Psychiatry, 150,* 321–333.

Schneider, L. S., Pollock, V. E., et al. (1991). A pilot study of low-dose L-deprenyl in Alzheimer's disease. *Journal of Geriatric Psychiatry and Neurology, 4,* 143–148.

Schneider, L. S., & Tariot, P. N. (1994). Emerging drugs for Alzheimer's disease. *Medical Clinics of North America, 78*(4), 911–934.

Schwartz, A. S., & Kohlstaedt, E. V. (1986). Physostigmine in Alzheimer's disease: Relationship to dementia severity. *Life Sciences, 38*(11), 1021–1028.

Serby, M., Resnick, R., et al. (1986). Naltrexone and Alzheimer's disease. *Progress in Neuro-Psychopharmacology and Biological Psychiatry, 10,* 587–590.

Sevush, S., Guterman, A., & Villalon, A. V. (1991). Improved verbal learning after outpatient oral physostigmine therapy in patients with dementia of the Alzheimer type. *Journal of Clinical Psychiatry, 52*(7), 300–303.

Sigfried, K. R. (1993). Pharmacodynamic and early clinical trials with velnacrine. *Acta Neurologica Scandinavica, 149,* 26–28.

Sinforiani, E., Iannuccelli, M., et al. (1990). Neuropsychological changes in demented patients treated with acetyl-L-carnitine. *International Journal of Clinical Pharmacology Research, 10*(1–2), 69–74.

Smith, C. M., Swase, M., et al. (1978). Choline therapy in Alzheimer's disease. *Lancet, 2,* 318.

Smith, D. E., Stromgren, E., et al. (1984). Lack of effect of tryptophan treatment in demented gerontopsychiatric patients. *Acta Psychiatrica Scandinavica, 70,* 470–477.

Smith, R. C., Vroulis, G., et al. (1984). Comparison of therapeutic response to long-term treatment with lecithin versus piracetam plus lecithin in patients with Alzheimer's disease. *Psychopharmacology Bulletin, 20*(3), 542–545.

Soininen, H., Koskinen, T., et al. (1985). Treatment of Alzheimer's disease with a synthetic ACTH49 analog. *Neurology, 35,* 1348–1351.

Soncrant, T. T., Raffaele, K. C., et al. (1993). Memory improvement without toxicity during chronic, low dose intravenous arecoline in Alzheimer's disease. *Psychopharmacology, 112,* 421–427.

Soni, S. D., & Soni, S. S. (1975). Dihydrogenated alkaloids of ergotexine in non-hospitalised elderly patients. *Current Medical Research and Opinion, 3*(7), 464–468.

Sourander, L. B., Portin, R., et al. (1987). Senile dementia of the Alzheimer type treated with aniracetam: A new nootropic agent. *Psychopharmacology, 91,* 90–95.

Spagnoli, A., Lucca, U., et al. (1991). Long-term acetyl-L-carnitine treatment in Alzheimer's disease. *Neurology, 41,* 1726–1732.

Steiger, W. A., Mendelson, M., et al. (1985). Effects of naloxone in treatment of senile dementia. *Journal of the American Geriatric Society, 33,* 155.

Stern, Y., Sano, M., & Mayeux, R. (1987). Effects of oral physostigmine in Alzheimer's disease. *Annals of Neurology, 22,* 306–310.

Stern, Y., Sano, M., & Mayeux, R. (1988). Long term administration of oral physostigmine in Alzheimer's disease. *Neurology, 38,* 1837–1841.

Sullivan, E. V., Shedlack, K. J., et al. (1982). Physostigmine and lecithin in Alzheimer's disease. In S. Corkin et al., *Alzheimer's disease: A report of progress in research* (Vol. 19). New York: Raven Press.

Summers, W. K., Majovski, L. V., et al. (1986). Oral tetrahydroaminoacridine in long-term treatment of senile dementia, Alzheimer type. *New England Journal of Medicine, 315*(20), 1241–1245.

Summers, W. K., & Viesselman, J. O. (1981). Use of THA in treatment of Alzheimer-like dementia: pilot study in 12 patients. *Biological Psychiatry, 16*(2), 145–153.

Tang, M. X., Jacobs, D., Stern, Y., et al. (1996). Effect of estrogen during menopause on risk and age at onset of Alzheimer's disease. *Lancet, 348*(9025), 429–432.

Tariot, P. N., Cohen, R. M., et al. (1987). L-Deprenyl in Alzheimer's disease: Preliminary evidence for behavioral change with monoamine oxidase B inhibitors. *Archives of General Psychiatry, 44,* 427–433.

Tariot, P. N., Cohen, R. M., et al. (1988). Multiple-dose arecoline infusions in Alzheimer's disease. *Archives of General Psychiatry, 45,* 901–905.

Tariot, P. N., Solomon, P. R., Morris, J. C., et al. (2000). A 5 month, randomized, placebo-controlled trial of galantamine in AD. *Neurology, 54,* 2269–2276.

Tariot, P. N., Sunderland, T., et al. (1986). Naloxone and Alzheimer's disease: Cognitive and behavioral effects of a range of doses. *Archives of General Psychiatry, 43,* 727–732.

Tariot, P. N., Sunderland, T., et al. (1987). Cognitive effects of L-deprenyl in Alzheimer's disease. *Psychopharmacology, 91,* 489–495.

Tennant, F. S. (1987). Preliminary observations on naltrexone for the treatment of Alzheimer's type dementia. *Journal of the American Geriatric Society, 35*(4), 369–370.

Thal, L. (1994). Future directions for research in Alzheimer's disease. *Neurobiology of Aging, 15*(Suppl. 2), S71–S72.

Thal, L. J., Fuld, P. A., et al. (1983). Oral physostigmine and lecithin improve memory in Alzheimer's disease. *Annals of Neurology, 13,* 491–496.

Thal, L. J., Masur, D. M., et al. (1986). Acute and chronic effects of oral physostigmine and lecithin in Alzheimer's disease. *Progress in Neuro-Psycho-*

pharmacology and Biological Psychiatry, 10, 627–636.

Thal, L. J., Masur, D. M., et al. (1989). Chronic oral physostigmine without lecithin improves memory in Alzheimer's disease. *Journal of the American Geriatric Society, 37,* 42–48.

Thal, L. J., Rosen, W., et al. (1981). Choline chloride fails to improve cognition in Alzheimer's disease. *Neurobiology of Aging, 2,* 205–208.

Thal, L. J., Salmon, D. P., et al. (1989). The safety and lack of efficacy of vinpocetine in Alzheimer's disease. *Journal of the American Geriatric Society, 37,* 515–520.

Thibault, A. (1974). A double-blind evaluation of "Hydergine" and placebo in the treatment of patients with organic brain syndrome and cerebral arteriosclerosis in a nursing home. *Current Medical Research and Opinion, 2*(8), 482–487.

Thienhaus, O. J., Wheeler, B. G., et al. (1987). A controlled double-blind study of high-dose dihydroergotexine mesylate (Hydergine) in mild dementia. *Journal of the American Geriatric Society, 35,* 219–223.

Thompson, T. L., Filly, C. M., et al. (1990). Lack of efficacy of Hydergine in patients with Alzheimer's disease. *New England Journal of Medicine, 323*(7), 445–448.

Tinklenberg, J. R., Pfefferbaum, A., & Berger, P. A. (1981). 1-Desamino-D-arginine vasopressin (DDAVP) in cognitively impaired patients. *Psychopharmacology Bulletin, 17*(3), 206–207.

Tinklenberg, J. R., Pigache, R., et al. (1982). Desglycinamide-9-arginine-8-vasopressin (DGAVP, Organon 5667) in cognitively impaired patients. *Psychopharmacology Bulletin, 18*(4), 202–204.

Tollefson, G. D. (1990). Short-term effects of the calcium channel blocker nimodepine (Bay-e-9736) in the management of primary degenerative dementia. *Biological Psychiatry, 27,* 1133–1142.

Triboletti, F., & Ferri, H. (1969). Hydergine for treatment of symptoms of cerebrovascular insufficiency. *Current Therapeutic Research, 11*(10), 609–620.

Urakami, K., Shimomura, T., et al. (1993). Clinical effect of WEB 1881 (nebracetam fumarate) on patients with dementia of the Alzheimer type and study of its clinical pharmacology. *Clinical Neuropharmacology, 16*(4), 347–358.

Van Dyck, C. H., Newhouse, P., Falk, W. E., et al. (2000). Extended-release physostigmine in Alzheimer disease: A multicenter, double-blind, 12-week study with dose enrichment. *Archives of General Psychiatry, 57,* 157–164.

van Loveren-Huyben, C. M. S., Engelaar, H. F. J. W., et al. (1984). Double-blind clinical and psychologic study of ergoloid mesylates (Hydergine) in subjects with senile mental deterioration. *Journal of the American Geriatric Society, 32*(8), 584–588.

Villardita, C., Parini, J., et al. (1987). Clinical and neuropsychological study with oxiracetam versus placebo in patients with mild to moderate dementia. *Journal of Neural Transmission, 24*(Suppl.), 293–298.

Vroulis, G. A., Smith, R. C., et al. (1981). The effects of lecithin on memory in patients with senile dementia of the Alzheimer's type. *Psychopharmacology Bulletin, 17*(1), 127–129.

Weingartner, H., Kaye, W., et al. (1981). Vasopressin treatment of cognitive dysfunction in progressive dementia. *Life Sciences, 29*(26), 2721–2726.

Weinstein, H. C., Teunisse, S., & van Gool, W. A. (1991). Tetrahydroaminoacridine and lecithin in the treatment of Alzheimer's disease. *Journal of Neurology, 238,* 34–38.

Weintraub, S., Mesulam, M. M., et al. (1983). Lecithin in the treatment of Alzheimer's disease. *Archives of Neurology, 40,* 527–528.

Weis, B. L. (1987). Failure of nalmefene and estrogen to improve memory in Alzheimer's disease. *American Journal of Psychiatry, 144*(3), 386–387.

Wettstein, A. (1983). No effect from double-blind trial of physostigmine and lecithin in Alzheimer's disease. *Annals of Neurology, 13,* 210–212.

Wettstein, A., & Spiegel, R. (1984). Clinical trials with the cholinergic drug RS 86 in Alzheimer's disease (AD) and senile dementia of the Alzheimer type (SDAT). *Psychopharmacology, 84,* 572–573.

Wilcock, G. K., Surmon, D. J., et al. (1993). An evaluation of the efficacy and safety of tetrahydroaminoacridine (THA) without lecithin in the treatment of Alzheimer's disease. *Age and Aging, 22,* 316–324.

Wilson, A. L., Langley, L. K., et al. (1995). Nicotine patches in Alzheimer's disease: Pilot study on learning, memory and safety. *Pharmacology, Biochemistry and Behavior, 51*(2–3), 509–514.

Wolters, E. C., Riekkinen, P., et al. (1990). DGAVP (Org 5667) in early Alzheimer's disease patients: An international double-blind, placebo-controlled multicenter trial. *Neurology, 40,* 1099–1101.

5

Pharmacological Treatments for Substance Use Disorders

Charles P. O'Brien
James McKay

The treatment of substance abuse with pharmacological agents is well established, although most experts agree that, to be successful, medication interventions must be combined with psychosocial therapies. A large number of Type 1 and Type 2 controlled trials have shown that the use of the nicotine patch or nicotine chewing gum to induce and maintain smoking cessation significantly increases the abstinence rate. Combining the nicotine patch with the nicotine antagonist mecamylamine has also shown promise. Recent reviews of alcoholism treatment have agreed that disulfiram, whether provided orally or through implants, has not been more effective than placebo in reducing drinking. Several studies of SSRIs indicate that they may lead to short-term reductions in alcohol consumption in heavy drinkers. Acamprosate has shown strong initial promise by improving retention in treatment and decreasing drinking in alcoholics following initial detoxification. Studies of opioid antagonists, especially naltrexone, indicate that these drugs are particularly effective in preventing full-blown relapses in alcoholics who have had a "slip" after achieving abstinence: Of 13 randomized studies of naltrexone, 9 have yielded positive results for naltrexone over placebo. None of the studies summarized in this review has produced compelling evidence for the efficacy of medications for the treatment of cocaine dependence. Methadone maintenance treatment for heroin dependence was developed in the 1960s; it is currently the treatment of choice for this condition. The improvement in all areas of function shown by methadone patients is most often produced by a combination of the medication and psychosocial intervention. Leva-alpha-acetyl-methadol (LAAM), an alternative to methadone, is more convenient than methadone because it requires dosing only 3 times per week, yet still provides physiological stability, in contrast to methadone, which must be taken daily.

Substance use disorders affect virtually every sector of society. As a group they are among the most common of all mental disorders. Household surveys have found a lifetime prevalence rate of 15 to 18% and a 6-month prevalence rate of 6 to 7% (Robins et al., 1984; Myers et al., 1984). These rates do not include nicotine addiction, the most devastating and difficult to treat of all of the addictive disorders. Many individuals have multiple addictions; for example, alcoholics are frequently addicted to both cocaine and nicotine. There is also a good deal of overlap with other mental disorders, such as anxiety and affective disorders. While there are common properties among the disorders produced by the major drugs of abuse, there are also important differences, particularly in treatment approaches. Thus, a chapter on treatment of substance use disorders is required to consist of four distinct reviews focusing on the major drugs or drug categories: nicotine, alcohol, stimulants (cocaine), and opioids (heroin). Other drugs, such as cannabinoids, hallucinogens, and minor tranquilizers, may also be abused, but they account for a small proportion of patients needing treatment, and no effective medications for them are currently available.

The features that define substance use disorders include compulsive use of the substance in spite of interference with normal activities and adverse effects on health. Terminology in this area is confusing because *DSM-IV* describes two kinds of "dependence." The diagnosis of dependence is the overall label for the syndrome produced by compulsive drug use, and it may or may not include "physiological dependence." There is no justification for distinguishing "physiological" from "not physiological" because, in the absence of the signs of classic drug withdrawal (tremors, vomiting, etc.), we now recognize major changes in the brain that may be evident only in the patient's behavior. Tolerance and physiological dependence were emphasized in previous definitions of addiction, but modern research has shown that these are simply normal adaptive reactions to the use of many substances, including ordinary medications such as those used in the treatment of hypertension. Tolerance is simply reduced effect with repeated use of a drug, while physiological dependence refers to a state demonstrated by the appearance of physiological rebound symptoms when a drug to which the body has become adapted is suddenly withdrawn. While tolerance and physiological dependence are often present and will influence the course of treatment, they are not essential features of addiction (*dependence* in the diagnostic sense).

SUCCESS OF TREATMENT

In this chapter, we define successful treatment as significant improvement in the ability to function according to one's societal role. Total abstinence from the addicting substance is the accepted goal of treatment, but this is not often achieved. Significant reduction in substance use, so that function in society is improved, can be considered a partial treatment success. In the case of opiate addiction, transfer to a stable maintenance medication that is similar in some ways to heroin is considered successful treatment, provided that the person is able to refrain from socially and personally harmful behavior. This definition of success is commonly utilized for other chronic disorders, such as arthritis or diabetes. It is therefore a pragmatic and medically acceptable definition based on functional capacity.

DETOXIFICATION

Detoxification is simply the removal of a drug from the body. This usually occurs because of metabolism by the liver and excretion via the kidneys. If the intake of the drug is gradually lowered, detoxification can be accomplished with little risk or discomfort as the body adapts to the absence of the drug. Detoxification is often confused with treatment. In reality, detoxification is, at best, the first step in treatment. Detoxification from sedatives such as alcohol can be dangerous because of medical complications during withdrawal, but these are readily treated in any medical facility. Treatment of the addiction involves a process of rehabilitation so as to reduce the probabilities of relapse and lengthen the period of time that the person is no longer using the drug of abuse. There is no evidence that rapid detoxification under general anesthesia is any more effective in the long term than less heroic and expensive means. Although some interesting research has been done on novel ways to achieve detoxification, for the purposes of this chapter we emphasize long-term treatment.

PSYCHOACTIVE AGENTS IN THE TREATMENT OF ADDICTION

The purpose of this chapter is to review psychopharmacological treatment of substance use disorders. One might reasonably ask whether medications are ever justified in the treatment of a disorder that involves excessive use of drugs. While there is controversy about this question on philosophical grounds, empirical studies clearly show the benefits of medications when they are indicated. In addition to treating the addictive disorder itself, psychoactive medications are often indicated for accompanying psychiatric disorders. One school of thought that once had many proponents was that addicts are all more-or-less alike and have to be treated by "getting at the underlying problem" and insisting on strict freedom from all chemicals. In that earlier era, nicotine and caffeine were not usually thought of as chemicals, but all psychoactive medications prescribed by physicians were to be avoided. Subsequent data, however, have demonstrated that all addicts are not alike. Even within a single drug category such as alcohol, there are alcoholics with different needs requiring different kinds of treatment. The concept of patient-treatment matching has become popular despite a relative paucity of replicated empirical findings.

NICOTINE DEPENDENCE

Cessation of smoking may be very difficult even for smokers who strongly desire to quit, and subsequent resumption of smoking, despite long periods of abstinence, is common. Those who began smoking prior to age 21 are less likely to succeed in smoking-cessation programs. Most smokers are nicotine-dependent and experience a variable withdrawal syndrome when regular administration of nicotine is stopped. The nicotine withdrawal syndrome consists of irritability, impatience, hostility, anxiety, dysphoric or depressed mood, difficulty concentrating, restlessness, decreased heart rate, and increased appetite or weight gain.

Nicotine administration can block these withdrawal symptoms whether given intravenously, by absorption though the mucosal membranes of the mouth (chewing gum), or by absorption through the skin (patch). However, the peak nicotine levels associated with the psychoactive effects of smoking are not achieved by chewing gum or by patch administration. The widespread availability of nicotine patches and chewing gum as over-the-counter medications has enabled many smokers to give up tobacco as a source of nicotine and thus avoid the serious health risks of tobacco smoke. Most smokers can then gradually reduce their nicotine dependence over several days to several weeks. Craving for the psychoactive effects continues, however, and relapses to smoking over the ensuing months are common. Table 5.1 summarizes some significant studies and reviews showing stable, confirmed abstinence rates at 6 and 12 months. The preponderance of controlled studies shows that in addicted smokers who are motivated to quit and remain abstinent, the use of the nicotine patch or chewing gum significantly increases the abstinence rate. Current research involves efforts to enhance the success rate of these nicotine delivery systems using behavior therapy. Another approach that shows promising results involves combining the nicotine patch with the nicotine antagonist mecamylamine (Rose et al., 1994). Two other medications have been tested in clinical trials, but the results so far are inconclusive. These are clonidine, an antihypertensive medication that reduces central noradrenergic activity by stimulation of alpha-2 adrenergic auto receptors, and naltrexone, an opiate receptor antagonist discussed later as a treatment for alcoholism and for opiate dependence.

The association of smoking and depression has prompted the use of antidepressant medication in conjunction with nicotine replacement in programs for treatment of smoking addiction. Fluoxetine and other antidepressants are often recommended for depressed smokers and for those attempting to quit whose symptoms meet diagnostic criteria for depression. Three placebo-controlled studies of bupropion in nondepressed smokers (Gonzales et al., 2001; Hurt et al., 1997; Jorenby et al., 1999) showed that this antidepressant significantly improved abstinence rates. It is not clear whether bupropion inhibits nicotine craving, but there is evidence that it reduces withdrawal symptoms. (Shiffman et al., 2000).

ALCOHOL DEPENDENCE (ALCOHOLISM)

Medications that have been evaluated as treatments for alcoholism include antidipsotropic agents, serotonergic antidepressants and anxiolytic agents, and agents that reduce craving or possibly block the reinforcing effects of alcohol at the neurotransmitter level (O'Brien et al., 1995). Studies of these agents are described in Table 5.2.

Antidipsotropic Medications

Antidipsotropic medications are agents that produce an unpleasant reaction when alcohol is consumed, thereby acting as a deterrent to drinking (Fuller, 1995). The studies presented in Table 5.2 indicate that overall, disulfiram (Antabuse) provided orally or through implants is not more effective than placebo in reducing drinking. Similar conclusions were also reached in another review (Hughes & Cook, 1997). However, there is evidence that disulfiram may reduce further drinking in older patients who have relapsed but have good motivation and at least moderate social stability, and one study suggests it may be

TABLE 5.1 Treatment of Nicotine Use Disorder: Nicotine Replacement

Authors	*Study Class*	N	*Treatment Length*	*Follow-up Length*	*Results*	*Comments*
Fiore et al. (1994b)	4	5,098 17 studies	4 weeks or longer	6 months	*Double-Blind, Placebo-Controlled Trials* Abstinence rates: End of treatment / 6 months Nicotine patch: 27% / 22% Placebo: 13% / 9%	Excellent review; counseling added modestly to nicotine patch results.
Imperial Cancer Fund General Practice Research Group (1993)	1	1,686	12 weeks	—	Cessation rates Nicotine patch 19.4% Placebo patch 11.7%	No additional effect of detailed written supporting material.
Fiore et al. (1994a)	1	Study 1 = 88 Study 2 = 112	8 weeks 6 weeks	6 months	Posttreatment: Nicotine / Placebo 1. 22 mg patch—8 weeks: 59% / 40% 2. 22 mg 4 weeks then 11 mg 2 weeks: 37% / 20% 6 months / Follow-up Study 1: 34% / 21% Study 2: 18% / 7%	Higher dose patch for 8 weeks shows somewhat better results.
Richmond et al. (1994)	1	313	5 weeks	6 months	Abstinence Rates: 3 months / 6 months Nicotine patch: 48% / 33% Placebo patch: 21% / 14%	

Nicotine Patch Plus Nicotine Gum						
Kornitzer et al. (1995)	1	374	12 weeks	12 months	1. Nicotine patch + nicotine gum 2. Nicotine patch + placebo gum 3. Placebo patch + nicotine gum	This study suggests that the flexibility of nicotine gum adds significantly to the results of the patch alone.

	Abstinence Rates		
	12 weeks	24 weeks	52 weeks
1.	34.2%	27.5%	18.1%
2.	22.7%	15.3%	12.7%
3.	17.3%	14.7%	13.3%

Nicotine Patch Plus Mecamylamine						
Rose et al. (1994)	1	48	6–8 weeks	12 months	Mecamylamine 2.5–5 mg, twice daily + nicotine patch compared to placebo + nicotine patch	The addition of the nicotine antagonist improves outcome, but the nicotine-alone results are lower than those seen in most studies.

	Abstinence Rates		
	7 weeks	6 months	12 months
Mecamylamine & nicotine	58%	37.5%	37.5%
Placebo & nicotine	29%	12.5%	4.2%

Bupropion						
Hurt et al. (1997)	1	615	7 weeks	12 months		150 and 300-mg dose sig. more effective than placebo; 100 mg not effective. Less wgt gain. Long-term relapse a problem.
Jorenby et al. (1999)	1	893	9 weeks	12 months		Comparison of placebo, nic. patch, bupropion, buprop. + patch. Bupropion sig. more effective than patch alone and placebo. Best result with patch + bupropion at 12 months.

TABLE 5.2 Medications for Alcohol Dependence

Author	Study Class	N	Treatment Length	Follow-up Length	Results	Comments
Antidipsotropic medications						
Oral disulfiram						
Baekland et al. (1971)	2	232	26 weeks	—	Patients who had a better response to disulfiram were older, had longer histories of heavy drinking, were less likely to be depressed, and had higher motivation and AA contact.	Subjects were participants in an outpatient clinic.
Gerrein et al. (1973)	2	49	8 weeks	—	Better attendance and abstinence rates in supervised disulfiram, compared to nonsupervised and no disulfiram.	Statistical significance of abstinence results not provided.
Fuller & Roth (1979)	1(N)	128	12 months	—	Continuous abstinence rates higher in disulfiram than placebo (23% vs. 12%), but not statistically significant.	Outcomes similar for 1-mg and 250-mg disulfiram conditions.
Fuller et al. (1986)	1	605	12 months	—	No differences between disulfiram and placebo in total abstinence, time to first drink, psychosocial functioning.	Disulfiram was effective for patients who drank and completed all assessments.
Chick et al. (1992)	2	126	26 weeks	—	Supervised disulfiram (200 mg/day) produced better outcomes on most drinking measures than placebo.	Patients in control condition were told they were receiving placebo.
Carroll et al. (1998)	1	122	12 weeks	—	Disulfiram (modal dose 261 mg/day) produced longer durations of alcohol and cocaine abstinence and better retention than placebo.	Subjects had comorbid alcohol abuse/dependence and cocaine dependence and received one of three manualized, weekly outpatient therapies.
Implanted disulfiram						
Johnsen et al. (1987)	2(N)	21	—	20 weeks	No differences between disulfiram and placebo in self-reported drinking or liver function measures.	Wound complications in 30% of disulfiram implant group.
Johnsen & Morland (1991)	1	76	—	300 days	Disulfiram implants (1 g) did not produce better drinking outcomes than placebo implants, although improvements were observed in both conditions.	Subjects in both conditions were told they were receiving disulfiram.
Serotonergic agents						
SSRIs						
Naranjo et al. (1987)	1	39	12 weeks	—	Citalopram (40 mg/day) produced better drinking outcomes than 20 mg/day or placebo.	Subjects were male heavy drinkers; non-treatment-seeking.
Naranjo et al. (1989)	1	29	7 weeks	—	Viqualine (200 mg/day) produced better drinking outcomes than placebo. 100 mg/day was ineffective.	Subjects were male heavy drinkers; non-treatment-seeking.
Gorelick & Paredes (1992)	1	20	4 weeks	—	Small advantage to fluoxetine (80 mg/day) over placebo in first week, but not in Weeks 2–4.	Study conducted on an inpatient research ward where alcohol was available.

Naranjo et al. (1990)	1	29	4 weeks	—	Fluoxetine (60 mg/day) reduced number of drinks consumed, but not days abstinent. 40 mg/day was ineffective.	Subjects were male heavy drinkers; non-treatment-seeking.
Naranjo et al. (1992)	1	16	4 weeks	—	Citalopram (40 mg/day) increased abstinent days and decreased number drinks consumed, compared to placebo.	Alcohol-dependent subjects.
Kranzler et al. (1995)	1	101	12 weeks	—	Fluoxetine (60 mg/day) was no better than placebo in reducing alcohol consumption.	Subjects were alcohol-dependent outpatients also receiving relapse prevention.
Cornelius et al. (1997)	1	51	12 weeks	—	Fluoxetine (mean of 25 mg/day) produced lower total alcohol consumption and greater reductions in depressive symptoms than placebo.	Subjects had comorbid alcohol dependence and major depression and also received two therapy sessions per week.
Angelone et al. (1998)	1	81	16 weeks	—	Fluvoxamine (150 mg/day) and citalopram (20 mg/day) both produced higher rates of continuous abstinence than placebo but did not differ from each other. Only citalopram reduced craving.	Subjects were hospitalized for 3 weeks prior to baseline and received 8 weeks of daily outpatient cognitive behavioral therapy (CBT), followed by 8 weeks of weekly CBT.
Buspirone						
Bruno (1989)	2	50	8 weeks	—	Buspirone (20 mg/day) produced better retention than placebo. Comparisons of drinking outcomes not done due to high dropout rate in placebo condition.	Subjects were outpatients with mild to moderate alcohol abuse.
Tollefson et al. (1992)	1	51	24 weeks	—	Buspirone (30 or 60 mg/day) produced better drinking outcomes than placebo on a subjective, global measure.	Standardized measures of drinking outcomes not included. Subjects were abstinent alcoholics with comorbid anxiety disorder.
Malcolm et al. (1992)	1	67	26 weeks	—	Buspirone (45–60 mg/day) did not produce better outcomes than placebo on any drinking measures.	Subjects were anxious, alcohol-dependent male veterans.
Kranzler et al. (1994)	1	61	12 weeks	—	Buspirone (up to 52 mg/day) produced better drinking outcomes than placebo.	Subjects were alcohol-dependent with comorbid anxiety disorder and were in outpatient treatment.
Serotonin receptor antagonists						
Johnson et al. (1996)	1	423	12 weeks	—	Retanserin (2.5 or 5 mg/day) did not produce better outcomes on any of drinking, craving, or clinical status outcome measures.	Subjects also received weekly individual manual-guided cognitive behavioral therapy.
Johnson et al. (2000)	1	271	12 weeks	—	Ondansetron at three dose levels (1 μg/kg, 4 μg/kg, 16 μg/kg, 2 ×/day) produced fewer drinks per day than placebo, and 4 μg/kg dose produced more abstinent days than placebo. These results were obtained only in early-onset (<25-year-old) drinkers.	Subjects also received weekly group manual-guided cognitive behavioral therapy.

(*continued*)

TABLE 5.2 (continued)

Author	Study Class	N	Treatment Length	Follow-up Length	Results	Comments
Johnson et al. (2000)	?	21	8 weeks	—	Ondansetron (4 μg/kg, 2 ×/day) plus naltrexone (25 mg, 2 ×/day) produced fewer drinks/day and drinks/drinking day than placebo in patients with early-onset alcoholism.	Subjects also received weekly group manual-guided cognitive behavioral therapy.
Acamprosate						
Lhuitre et al. (1985)	1	85	90 days	—	Acamprosate produced lower rate of relapse than placebo.	—
Lhuitre et al. (1990)	1	365	90 days	—	Acamprosate condition had lower liver enzyme values during follow-up than placebo.	—
Paille et al. (1995)	1	538	12 months	6 months	Drinking outcomes consistently best in high-dose acamprosate (2 g/day), followed by low-dose (1.3 g/day) and placebo.	Subjects also received supportive outpatient therapy as required.
Whitworth et al. (1996)	1	455	12 months	—	Complete abstinence rates and days of abstinence favored acamprosate over placebo.	—
Sass et al. (1996)	1	272	48 weeks	48 weeks	Drinking outcomes consistently favored acamprosate over placebo. Effect of acamprosate persisted during the posttreatment follow-up period.	Subjects were also offered outpatient therapy with a behavioral orientation during the study period.
Pelc et al. (1997)	1	188	90 days	—	Acamprosate conditions (1332 and 1998 mg/day) had better outcomes on all drinking measures than placebo, and there were trends toward stronger effects at the higher dose.	Subjects entered the study following a 14-day inpatient detoxification and received supportive counseling as needed during the trial.
Poldrugo (1997)	1	246	6 months	6 months	Acamprosate (1332 or 1998 mg/day, depending on weight) produced higher abstinence rates and better retention than placebo. Similar abstinence results were obtained in the posttreatment follow-up.	Subjects entered the study following brief inpatient detoxification and received comprehensive outpatient treatment that included active linking to recovering alcoholics in the community.
Besson et al. (1998)	1	118	360 days	360 days	Acamprosate (1332 or 1998 mg/day, depending on weight) produced more abstinent days and higher abstinence rates than placebo during the trial. The best results were in patients in the acamprosate condition who also took disulfiram. Low follow-up rates in the posttreatment phase precluded analysis.	Subjects entered the study following brief inpatient detoxification and received routine outpatient counseling provided by attending physicians.
Tempesta et al. (2000)	1	330	6 months	3 months	Acamprosate (1998 mg/day) produced more abstinent days and higher abstinence rates than placebo, as well as less severe relapses. Results in the posttreatment follow-up also favored acamprosate but were not significant.	Subjects entered the study following brief inpatient detoxification and received supportive outpatient counseling (1–2 sessions/wk).

Chick et al. (2000b)	1	581	24 weeks	4 weeks	Acamprosate (1998 mg/day) did not produce better drinking outcomes than placebo, either in the full sample or in subgroup analyses.	Subjects entered the study within 5 weeks of detoxification and received usual psychosocial outpatient care during the trial.
Opioid antagonists						
Naltrexone						
Volpicelli et al. (1990, 1992)	1	70	12 weeks	—	Less craving, fewer days drinking, lower relapse rate in naltrexone (50 mg/day) group, compared to placebo. Subjects who drank at all were much less likely to progress to full relapse if they received naltrexone.	Subjects were male veterans in an intensive day hospital rehabilitation program.
O'Malley et al. (1992)	1	97	12 weeks	(see below)	Fewer days drinking, longer time to first relapse in naltrexone (50 mg/day) group, compared to placebo.	Subjects also received coping skills or supportive therapy.
O'Malley et al. (1996a)	1	97	—	26 weeks	Naltrexone led to higher abstinence rates in Month 1 (but not 2–6), lower relapse rate over all 6 months, compared to placebo.	Among subjects who drank at all, best outcomes were in naltrexone/coping-skills group.
Volpicelli et al. (1997)	1	97	12 weeks	—	On intent-to-treat analysis, rates of relapse and days drinking were not significantly different in naltrexone (50 mg/day) and placebo groups. However, liver enzyme results were better in naltrexone group, and all results favored naltrexone in more compliant patients.	Subjects also received outpatient counseling; 2 ×/week in first month, 1 ×/week in Months 2 and 3.
Oslin et al. (1997)	1	44	12 weeks	—	Naltrexone (50 mg/day) did not produce higher abstinence rates than placebo. However, among patients who drank at all, those who received naltrexone were less likely to have full relapses.	Subjects were all over 50 years of age and received weekly group therapy and case management.
Kranzler et al. (1998)	1	20	4 weeks	4 weeks	Injectable, sustained-release naltrexone (206 mg) produced fewer heavy drinking days during injection and follow-up periods than placebo injection.	Subjects also received individual coping-skills therapy (weekly, for 8 weeks).
Hersh et al. (1998)	1	64	8 weeks	—	Naltrexone (50 mg/day) did not produce better alcohol or cocaine use outcomes than placebo.	Subjects had comorbid alcohol and cocaine abuse/dependence. They also received manualized relapse prevention therapy (up to 12 ind. sessions over 8 weeks).
Anton et al. (1999)	1	131	12 weeks	—	Naltrexone (50 mg/day) produced less drinking, longer time to relapse, more time between relapses, and greater resistance to and control over alcohol-related thoughts and urges than placebo.	Subjects were abstinent a minimum of 5 days prior to study entry and received manualized cognitive behavioral therapy (weekly).

(*continued*)

TABLE 5.2 (continued)

Author	*Study Class*	N	*Treatment Length*	*Follow-up Length*	*Results*	*Comments*
Knox & Donovan (1999)	2	122	3 weeks	6 months	This study is severely flawed in that treatment was limited to a 3-wk inpatient stay, and then outpatient care was optional. No difference between naltrexone and placebo at 6-month follow-up.	Treatment of a chronic disorder by brief inpatient treatment with optional follow-up care is difficult to rationalize.
Kranzler et al. (2000)	1	183	12 weeks	—	Naltrexone (50 mg/day), nefazodone (200 mg/day), and placebo did not differ on drinking outcomes. Naltrexone did produce more adverse neuropsychiatric and gastrointestinal effects, poorer compliance, and greater treatment attrition.	Subjects were abstinent a minimum of 3 days prior to study entry and received manualized individual cognitive behavioral therapy (weekly).
Chick et al. (2000a)	1	175	12 weeks		In compliant patients, the naltrexone group consumed less alcohol, had less craving, and had improved liver function. For total sample, no difference in drinking, but improved liver function in the naltrexone group.	Very little counseling involved in this study.
Morris et al. (2001)	1	111	12 weeks		Significantly fewer relapses and less consumption of alcohol in group randomized to naltrexone.	—
Latt et al. (2001)	1	107	12 weeks		Naltrexone significantly reduced relapse rates. The effect was most marked in the first 6 weeks.	This study was specifically designed to test naltrexone in a primary-care practice without formal psychotherapy.
Krystal et al. (2001)	1	627	3 months & 12 months		No difference between naltrexone and placebo for 3 months or 12 months. Secondary analyses including medication compliance also found no effect.	This is the largest and longest study of naltrexone in alcoholism. It is the first multiclinic trial with 15 VA clinics involved. Counseling was once weekly for 16 weeks; 12-step facilitation.
Nalmefene						
Mason et al. (1994)	1	21	12 weeks	—	Nalmefene (40 mg) led to lower rates of relapse and more abstinent days than nalmefene (10 mg) or placebo. Both nalmefene conditions led to reductions in drinks per drinking day.	Subjects were alcohol-dependent, with no other substance dependence or major psychiatric disorders. Psychosocial treatment was not provided.
Mason et al. (1999)	1	105	12 weeks	—	Nalmefene (20 and 80 mg/day conditions) produced lower rates of relapse to heavy drinking and fewer number of relapses than placebo. Outcomes did not differ between the two doses.	Subjects were abstinent an average of 2 weeks prior to randomization and received manualized individual cognitive behavioral therapy (weekly).

effective in reducing alcohol and cocaine use in patients with comorbid alcohol and cocaine use disorders (Carroll et al., 1998). Disulfiram may also be more effective in preventing relapse when it is used in treatment interventions that include contracts that specify that disulfiram ingestion will be monitored by a significant other (Azrin et al., 1982; O'Farrell et al., 1985). Since poor compliance is a major obstacle to the effectiveness of disulfiram treatment, this sort of behavioral contracting may be an important component of treatment with this agent. However, the side effects of disulfiram and potential danger of disulfiram-ethanol reactions contraindicate its use in patients with a wide array of medical and psychiatric conditions and in pregnant women (Fuller, 1995; Schuckit, 1996).

Serotonergic Agents

Serotonin appears to play an important neurochemical role in the modulation of mood and impulse control and may therefore influence the development and maintenance of alcohol use disorders (Kranzler & Anton, 1994). Because several studies have suggested that individuals with alcohol use disorders may have low levels of serotonin (e.g., Gorelick, 1989; Kranzler & Anton, 1994; Roy et al., 1990), a number of serotonergic drugs have been evaluated as possible treatments for alcoholism. The agents that have received the greatest attention are selective serotonin reuptake inhibitors (SSRIs), such as fluoxetine, and buspirone, a serotonin 1A receptor partial agonist. Studies of SSRIs presented in Table 5.2 indicate that these agents may lead to short-term reductions in alcohol consumption in heavy drinkers. However, studies that have been done with alcoholics in psychosocial treatment programs have yielded mixed findings (e.g., Angelone et al., 1998; Gorelick & Paredes, 1992; Kranzler et al., 1995). On the other hand, a study with alcoholics who had comorbid major depression found that fluoxetine reduced both alcohol use and depression levels (Cornelius et al., 1997). It also appears that buspirone may be an effective treatment for alcoholics who have comorbid anxiety disorders. Finally, several studies suggest that tricyclic antidepressants may reduce both depression and alcohol use in patients with major depression (Mason et al., 1996; McGrath et al., 1996).

The efficacy of two serotonin receptor antagonists, ritanserin and ondansatron, has been examined in several studies. Ritanserin does not appear to be an effective treatment for alcohol use disorders (Johnson et al., 1996). However, ondansatron produced better alcohol use outcomes than placebo in patients with early-onset alcoholism (i.e., prior to age 25) who were receiving cognitive behavioral therapy, when used alone or in combination with naltrexone (Johnson et al., 2000).

Acamprosate

Calcium bisacetyl homotaurine (acamprosate) has shown strong initial promise in improving treatment retention and decreasing drinking in alcoholics following initial detoxification. Of the 10 studies of acamprosate presented in Table 5.2, 9 generated positive findings during the treatment phase, and some of these studies indicate that the effects of acamprosate persist to some degree during posttreatment follow-up periods. Although the action of acamprosate is not entirely clear, it appears that the drug functions as a GABA receptor agonist and that it may also lower neuronal excitability by reducing the postsynaptic efficacy of excitatory amino acid (EAA) neurotransmitters. Acamprosate produces few subjective side effects, although reports of cognitive deficits have occurred. It must be given two or three times daily, thus requiring adherence on the part of the patient.

Opioid Antagonists

Of 13 randomized studies of naltrexone in alcoholism treatment, 9 produced positive results for naltrexone over placebo. Counting the two positive trials for nalmefene, the score is 11 of 15 positive for opioid antagonist treatment. A key factor appears to be adherence to the medication regimen. Two of the studies classed as positive showed no difference from placebo on an "intent to treat" analysis, but when *a priori* standards of medication compliance were applied, naltrexone was superior to placebo. Although naltrexone needs to be taken only once daily, adherence to this medication remains an issue. Nausea is the most significant side effect, reported variously in different studies, mostly around 10 to 15%. Those studies with high dropout rates or reduced medication adherence have either not shown efficacy or shown efficacy only in those patients rated as compliant with the treatment. The largest study (Krystal et al., 2001) found no advantage for naltrexone even considering adherence to the medication regimen. Of the 15 trials, 4 were completely negative, but 1 of these involved alcoholism with cocaine abuse and another involved just a brief inpatient course of naltrexone with no outpatient continuation and thus was not a rational treatment for a chronic disorder.

The fact that not all of the clinical trials of naltrexone have been positive has supported the reluctance of those who believe that alcoholism should not be treated with a medication at all. Indeed it is surprising that most of the randomized clinical trials involving such a complex biopsychosocial disorder as alcoholism have shown a significant advantage for naltrexone over placebo. Alcoholism clearly does respond to nonmedication approaches; thus, it is expected that many of those assigned to placebo plus counseling will do well. The fact that more of those randomized to the opioid antagonist did significantly better than those on placebo in 11 of 15 trials is at least as good as the record for antidepressant medication, where placebo treatment may also equal medication (Robinson & Rickels, 2000). Perhaps the next generation of studies on alcoholics will focus on subgroups of patients who may be more likely to respond to an opioid antagonist plus counseling.

In the studies that have found effects for opioid antagonists, it appears that these medications may be particularly effective in preventing full-blown relapses in alcoholics who have had a "slip" after achieving abstinence (O'Malley et al., 1992; Oslin et al., 1997; Volpicelli et al., 1992). Initial studies of subjective response to alcohol following administration of naltrexone (King et al., 1997; Swift et al., 1994; Volpicelli et al., 1995) and retrospective reports of subjective responses to alcohol "slips" (O'Malley et al., 1996b) indicate that naltrexone may reduce the positive reinforcing stimulant effects and augment the sedative and aversive effects of alcohol (Swift, 1995).

Other studies have generated additional information about the effects of naltrexone. First, it appears that the effectiveness of naltrexone may continue beyond the period in which the drug is taken. In a 6-month posttreatment follow-up of the sample from the O'Malley et al. (1992) study, patients who received naltrexone in the initial 12-week portion of the trial were less likely to have one or more heavy drinking days during follow-up (O'Malley et al., 1996a). However, the positive effects of naltrexone over placebo were significantly larger early in the follow-up than at the end. Second, it appears that naltrexone may be particularly effective for patients with high levels of alcohol craving at intake to treatment (Jaffe et al., 1996; O'Malley, 1995; Volpicelli et al., 1995), those with poor learning ability (Jaffe et al., 1996; O'Malley, 1995), and those with a high degree of somatic symptoms (Volpicelli et al., 1995). Third, the effectiveness of naltrexone relative to placebo appears to be greater in more compliant patients (i.e., those who adhere to the treatment protocol and are compliant with taking medication; Pettinati et al., 2000; Volpicelli et al., 1997). Finally, a multicenter study concluded that naltrexone was generally safe but was discontinued in 15% of patients because of adverse events, most frequently nausea or headache (Croop et al., 1997).

COCAINE DEPENDENCE

Most efforts to identify medications that would be effective in treating patients with cocaine use disorders have been directed toward finding agents that either correct alterations in neurochemical substrates brought on by chronic cocaine use or blocking the reinforcing effects of cocaine (Kleber, 1995). Although there have been a number of promising leads, no pharmacological agent has yet generated consistent evidence of effectiveness in reducing cocaine use. In this section, we will provide a brief overview of studies of the following medications: antidepressants, dopaminergic agents, and other agents that have been evaluated in at least several studies. Details of the studies are presented in Table 5.3.

Antidepressants

Cocaine abusers frequently report anhedonia following cessation of cocaine use, and dysphoria and/or depression may play a role in the onset and maintenance of cocaine use. These observations have raised the possibility that antidepressant medications could reduce cocaine use in cocaine-dependent patients. Studies of tricyclic antidepressants indicate that, while these agents do not improve retention in treatment, they may lead to reduced cocaine use in some patients, particularly those with less severe cocaine abuse (Carroll et al., 1994; Nunes et al., 1995). Furthermore, one study found more rapid increase in cocaine abstinence in opioid dependent patients who reported regular cocaine use (Oliveto et al., 1999). However, initial studies of fluoxetine and gepirone found no evidence that these agents were more effective than placebo in improving retention or reducing cocaine use.

Dopaminergic Agents

Several agents with dopamine-agonist properties that appear relatively quickly to counteract alterations in the dopamine system caused by chronic use of cocaine have been evaluated as adjuncts to detoxification and aids in initial treatment (e.g., amantadine, bromocriptine, methylphenidate, and diethylpropion). None of these agents has shown consistent evidence of effectiveness in reducing cocaine use. However, one recent study found that amantadine was more effective than placebo in reducing cocaine use during a 4-week trial in patients with severe cocaine withdrawal symptoms at intake (Kampman et al., 2000). Another line of medications research has focused on identifying agents that block the dopamine-mediated reinforcing effects of cocaine. Unfortunately, most of these agents (e.g., neuroleptics) have serious side effects and are not likely to lead to high compliance on the part of cocaine abusers. However, there is preliminary evidence that flupenthixol, which has antidepressant effects at low doses and neuroleptic effects at high doses, may be effective in reducing cocaine use.

Other Agents

Buprenorphine, an opioid agonist/antagonist that has been shown in animal models to selectively reduce cocaine self-administration, has not been more effective than methadone in reducing cocaine use in patients who are dependent on both cocaine and opioids, with the exception of male patients in one study (Oliveto et al., 1999). Other studies of buprenorphine are in progress. Carbamazepine, an anticonvulsant agent, has been evaluated as a treatment for cocaine abuse because it reverses cocaine-induced kindling in an animal model and dopamine receptor supersensitivity that can result from long-term cocaine use (Kleber, 1995). Once again, double-blind studies have found no difference between carbamazepine and placebo in treatment retention or cocaine use outcomes.

Three studies have evaluated medications that have traditionally been used to treat abuse of other substances. In two studies, disulfiram was more effective than placebo in decreasing cocaine use, even in patients without alcohol use disorders (Carroll et al., 1998; Petrakis, 2000). In a third study, naltrexone did not produce better cocaine use outcomes in patients with comorbid alcohol and cocaine use disorders (Hersh et al., 1998). Finally, there is initial evidence that propranolol may improve treatment retention in cocaine patients (Kampman et al., 1999) and improve cocaine use outcomes in the subgroup of cocaine patients with severe cocaine withdrawal symptoms at intake to treatment (Kampman et al., 2001).

Summary and Future Directions

None of the studies summarized in this review has produced compelling evidence of the efficacy of medications in the treatment of cocaine dependence. However, a number of limitations in these studies have been noted by Kleber (1995) and others, including low statistical power, possible subtherapeutic doses of medications, and the failure to control for the amount and type of concurrent psychosocial services received. Studies with larger sample sizes, such as those by Carroll et al. (1994) and Nunes et al. (1995), identified patient-by-treatment matching effects, which underscore the importance of having adequate statistical power to examine relationships between patient characteristics and differential response to a particular medication. Moreover, there is initial evidence that medications such as propranolol and amantadine, which can reduce the dysphoria associated with initial abstinence from cocaine, may be effective with patients who have more severe withdrawal symptoms early in treatment. Future research efforts should also continue to examine the joint impact of psychosocial and psychopharmacological interventions, as there is evidence that psychosocial treatments can reduce cocaine use (Alterman et al., 1994; Carroll et al., 1994b; Higgins et al., 1993; McKay et al., 1997).

Despite the apparent lack of efficacy of pharmacotherapy interventions for cocaine dependence, preclinical evidence has shown that there are persistent changes in brain reward systems after cessation of chronic cocaine use, a finding that suggests that there are biological factors that continue after cessation of cocaine use and may increase the probability

TABLE 5.3 Medications for Cocaine Dependence

Authors	Class	N	Treatment Length	Follow-up Length	Results	Comments
Antidepressants						
Desipramine						
Gawin et al. (1989b)	1	72	6 weeks	—	Desipramine (2.5 mg/kg) produced better cocaine use outcomes and lower craving than lithium or placebo.	Subjects were cocaine-dependent and received weekly psychotherapy.
Levin & Lehman (1991)	4	200	12–168 days	—	Retention in treatment: desipramine no better than placebo. Reducing cocaine use during trial: desipramine better than placebo.	In meta-analysis, only 2 of 6 studies found advantage to desipramine in reducing cocaine use.
Weddington et al. (1991)	2	54	12 weeks	—	Trend indicated desipramine (200 mg/day) was associated with higher early dropout rate than amantadine or placebo. No group differences in cocaine use or craving.	Subjects in this single-blind study also received outpatient psychotherapy (2 ×/week). Dosage of desipramine may have been subtherapeutic.
Arndt et al. (1992)	1	59	12 weeks	26 weeks	Desipramine (250–300 mg/day) associated with higher dropout rate and worse cocaine use outcomes at 3- and 6-month follow-up than placebo. No group differences in cocaine use during the 12-week treatment phase.	Subjects were methadone-maintained male veterans who also met *DSM-III* criteria for cocaine abuse.
Kolar et al. (1992)	2	22	12 weeks	—	Desipramine (200 mg/day) produced better retention rates and higher abstinence rates at the end of the trial than amantadine or placebo.	Subjects were methadone maintenance patients who also met *DSM-III-R* criteria for cocaine dependence.
Kosten et al. (1992)	1	94	12 weeks	—	Desipramine (150 mg/day) did not produce better retention or cocaine urine toxicology results than amantadine or placebo but was associated with greater reductions in money spent for cocaine in Weeks 2 and 4 than placebo.	Subjects were methadone maintenance patients who also met *DSM-III-R* criteria for cocaine dependence.
Carroll et al. (1994a)	1	139	12 weeks	(See below)	Desipramine (300 mg/day) did not produce better retention than placebo. Reductions in cocaine use at 6 weeks (but not 12 weeks) were greater for desipramine than placebo. Patients with lower baseline severity of cocaine use also had better cocaine use outcomes on desipramine than for placebo.	Subjects also received either relapse prevention or clinical management therapy in individual session (1×/wk.).
Carroll et al. (1994b)	1	97	—	12 months	No differences in cocaine use between desipramine and placebo group during the 12-month follow-up from the above study.	Differences favoring relapse prevention over clinical management emerged in Months 6–12.
Rawson et al. (1994)	1	99	16 weeks	10 weeks	No differences between desipramine (200 mg/day) and placebo on any outcome measures.	Subjects also received a 26-week outpatient treatment package.

Oliveto et al. (1999)	1	189	13 weeks	—	Desipramine (150 mg/day) increased cocaine abstinence more rapidly than placebo in both men and women.	Subjects were opioid-dependent and reported regular cocaine use.
Imipramine						
Nunes et al. (1995)	1	113	12 weeks	—	Imipramine (150–300 mg/day) produced greater reductions in craving, cocaine euphoria, and depression, and also a trend ($p < .09$) toward higher rates of 3 consecutive cocaine-free weeks than placebo. Imipramine effect was greater among nasal users.	Subjects also received weekly individual counseling.
Fluoxetine						
Grabowski et al. (1995)	1	155	12 weeks	—	Retention was lowest in high-dose fluoxetine (40 mg/day), followed by low-dose (20 mg), and placebo. No group differences in cocaine use outcomes.	Subjects also received 1 hour of behaviorally oriented therapy per week and visited the clinic at least one other time per week.
	1(N)	21	8 weeks	—	Fluoxetine (20 mg/day) produced better cocaine outcomes than placebo in Weeks 3 and 4, but not in the other 6 weeks.	Subjects were methadone maintenance patients who were also cocaine-dependent.
Gepirone						
Jenkins et al. (1992)	1	41	12 weeks	—	No differences were found between gepirone (16 mg/day) and placebo on any outcome measures.	Subjects all received 1 week of inpatient treatment at start of study, followed by outpatient therapy.
Dopamanergic agents: Agonists						
Amantadine						
Tennant & Sagherian (1987)	1	14	10 days	—	Amantadine (100 mg/day) led to greater retention and lower withdrawal scores during detoxification than bromocriptine.	Subjects were cocaine-dependent and participating in an outpatient detoxification program.
Gawin et al. (1989c)	2	10	1 day	—	Amantadine (300 mg) did not result in reduced craving, compared to placebo.	Subjects were severe cocaine abusers in outpatient treatment.
Giannini et al. (1989)	1	30	30 days	—	Amantadine (100 mg/6 hrs) led to lower ratings of psychiatric symptoms than placebo early in withdrawal.	No measures of cocaine use were included in the study.
Weddington et al. (1991)	2	54	12 weeks	—	Amantadine (400 mg/day) did not produce better outcomes (retention, cocaine use) than placebo.	Subjects in this single-blind study also received outpatient psychotherapy (2 ×/week).
Kolar et al. (1992)	2	22	12 weeks	—	Amantadine (200 mg/day) did not produce better outcomes (retention, cocaine use) than placebo.	See above.
Kosten et al. (1992)	1	94	12 weeks	—	Amantadine (300 mg/day) did not produce better retention or cocaine urine toxicology results than placebo but was associated with greater reductions in money spent for cocaine in Weeks 2 and 4.	See above.

(*continued*)

TABLE 5.3 (continued)

Authors	*Class*	N	*Treatment Length*	*Follow-up Length*	*Results*	*Comments*
Alterman et al. (1992)	1	42	10.5 dys	2 weeks	Amantadine (200 mg/day) produced higher rates of cocaine-free urines at 2 and 4 weeks postbaseline.	Subjects were cocaine-dependent male veterans in a day hospital program.
Bromocriptine						
Moscovitz et al. (1993)	2	29	2 weeks	—	Bromocriptine (3.75 mg/day) produced a higher rate of cocaine-negative urine screens than placebo, but statistical analyses not performed.	Subjects were male veterans who were frequent cocaine users and presented for minor medical complaints at a hospital.
Methylphenidate						
Gawin et al. (1985)	3	5	2–5 weeks	—	Methylphenidate (up to 100 mg/day) appeared to increase cocaine use.	Patients did not have attention deficit disorder.
Grabowski et al. (1997)	1	24	11 weeks	—	Methylphenidate (5 mg + 20 mg sustained-release) produced similar cocaine use outcome to placebo.	Patients were cocaine-dependent and received manualized behavioral treatment (1 hr/wk).
Diethylpropion						
Alim et al. (1995)	?	50	2 weeks	—	Diethylpropion (25–75 mg/day) did not produce better craving outcomes than placebo.	Patients received medication while on an inpatient unit.
Dopamanergic agents: Antagonists						
Flupenthixol						
Gawin et al. (1989a)	3	10	Not specified	up to 62 weeks	Flupenthixol decanoate (10 or 20 mg every 2–4 weeks) appeared to enhance retention and abstinence rates.	Subjects in this open trial were poor-prognosis crack smokers who were cocaine-dependent.
Khalsa et al. (1994)	1	63	6 weeks	—	Flupenthixol and desipramine were both superior to placebo in retention, cocaine use, cocaine craving. No comparisons of the two active drugs were provided.	Patients in this preliminary report were crack cocaine users receiving minimal psychotherapy.
Other agents						
Buprenorphine						
Strain et al. (1994b)	1	164	26 weeks	—	Buprenorphine (8 mg/day) and methadone did not differ on rates of cocaine-positive urines.	Patients were new admissions to an opioid treatment program.
Strain et al. (1994a)	1	51	26 weeks	—	Buprenorphine (11 mg/day) and methadone did not differ on rates of cocaine-positive urines.	Patients were new admissions to an opioid treatment program who had used cocaine prior to admission.
Oliveto et al. (1999)	1	189	13 weeks	—	Buprenorphine (12 mg/day) increased cocaine abstinence more rapidly than methadone (65 mg/day) in men, whereas the opposite effect was obtained in women.	Subjects were opioid-dependent and reported regular cocaine use.

Carbamazepine						
Cornish et al. (1995)	1	82	10 weeks	—	Carbamazepine (200 mg) and placebo did not differ on retention, rates of cocaine-positive urines, or craving.	Patients were male, cocaine-dependent, new admissions to a VA outpatient program.
Montoya et al. (1995)	1	62	8 weeks	—	Carbmazepine (600 mg) and placebo did not differ on retention or rates of cocaine-positive urines.	Patients were cocaine-dependent and also received individual counseling 2 ×/week.
Disulfiram						
Carroll et al. (1998)	1	122	12 weeks	—	Disulfiram (modal dose 261 mg/day) produced longer durations of alcohol and cocaine abstinence and better retention than placebo.	Subjects had comorbid alcohol abuse/dependence and cocaine dependence and received one of three manualized, weekly outpatient therapies.
Petrakis et al. (2000)	1	67	12 weeks	—	Disulfiram (250 mg/day) produced greater decreases in the quantity and frequency of cocaine use than placebo. Alcohol use was minimal in both conditions.	Patients had comorbid cocaine and opioid dependence and had been on methadone for at least 3 months prior to study entry.
Propranolol						
Kampman et al. (1999)	1	65	7 weeks	—	Propranolol (100 mg/day) produced better retention than a multivitamin placebo control, but no difference on cocaine use outcomes.	Patients were primary cocaine dependent and received 2 hr/week of individual therapy.
Naltrexone						
Hersh et al. (1998)	1	64	8 weeks	—	Naltrexone (50 mg/day) did not produce better alcohol or cocaine use outcomes than placebo.	Subjects had comorbid alcohol and cocaine abuse/dependence. They also received manualized relapse prevention therapy (up to 12 sessions over 8 weeks).

of relapse (Koob, 1992). Evidence of postcocaine conditioned responses have been demonstrated in human studies showing craving and autonomic nervous system arousal in response to cocaine-related cues (Childress et al., 1987; O'Brien et al., 1988). Recently, focal changes in limbic activity as measured by cerebral blood flow have been reported in abstinent formerly cocaine-dependent patients (Childress et al., 1996), and this phenomenon has been used to screen new medications that might diminish this conditioned craving effect (Berger et al., 1995; Robbins et al., 1992). It seems reasonable to hope that a medication will ultimately be found that can ameliorate these biological effects of cocaine use and augment the effects of psychosocial interventions.

OPIOID DEPENDENCE

While the history of opiate addiction in the United States goes back more than 100 years, most of the societal response has been legal rather than medical. Physicians are heavily restricted in their ability to deal with opiate addiction as a medical problem. Most treatment consists of detoxification, that is, removal of the drug from the body by metabolism while withdrawal symptoms are being treated by another medication. Detoxification is simply a first step in a long-term relapse prevention program. Two medical approaches to aid in detoxification are available. One is the use of an opioid agonist in gradually decreasing doses over 5 to 10 days. This permits a smooth, comfortable detoxification for most patients. A long-acting medication such as methadone is preferable because it permits a smooth transition to the drug-free state. A second option is the use of a drug that blocks certain aspects of the withdrawal syndrome, such as clonidine or lofexidine.

While some opioid addicts are able to detoxify and remain drug-free, the majority relapse, even after intensive psychotherapy. More important, many heroin addicts will not even consider a drug-free treatment approach or entry into a therapeutic community. Maintenance treatment using methadone (see Table 5.4) was developed in the 1960s and consists of transferring the patient from heroin, a short-acting opiate that must be taken by injection two to four times daily, to methadone, a long-acting opioid that needs be taken only once daily by mouth. The changes produced by transfer to a long-acting opioid are significant. The treatment requires relatively little effort on the part of the patient, so it has wide appeal. This appeal is important from a public health perspective as infections associated with heroin use, such as HIV and resistant tuberculosis, threaten the general public as well as substance abusers.

Initially, most heroin addicts have poor motivation for changing their lives. When first introduced to methadone treatment, they still want to get "high" and mix other drugs with the prescribed medication. With appropriate counseling in a structured program, the patient can make the transition from thinking as a street addict to behaving as a productive citizen. Methadone substitutes for heroin, reduces drug-seeking behavior, and blocks opiate withdrawal symptoms. It stabilizes physiological systems because of its long duration of action in contrast to the short action of heroin, which produces ups and downs (Kreek, 1992). Typically, patients continue to use some heroin during the first few weeks or months on methadone. Methadone does not block the effects of heroin, but it produces cross-tolerance to heroin and all similar drugs. Thus, the effects of usual doses of heroin are diminished, and over time, the typical patient decreases heroin use further and then stops. The evidence shows that the improvement in all areas of function shown by methadone patients is produced by a combination of medication (methadone) and psychosocial intervention. When methadone dose is held constant at a level adequate for most patients (60 mg), there is an orderly relationship between the "dose" of psychotherapy and the outcome of treatment (McLellan et al., 1993). Some improvement is seen with methadone alone, but with increments in psychosocial interventions, there is significantly greater improvement as measured by illicit drug use, psychiatric symptoms, family problems, and employment. Other studies have demonstrated that patients on methadone become healthier and have lower rates of exposure to infections, including HIV (Metzger et al., 1993).

The physiological stability produced by methadone is demonstrated in several ways. Patients report fewer sleep problems and less depression. Males report improved sexual performance. While on heroin, they were in and out of withdrawal, and when they found time for sex, they frequently experienced premature ejaculations. On methadone, while sexual arousal and orgasm were reported to be slowed, the patients reported that sex was more satisfying (Mintz

TABLE 5.4 Medications for Heroin Dependence: Methadone

Authors	*Study Class*	N	*Treatment Length*	*Follow-up Length*	*Results*	*Comments*
Dole et al. (1969)	2	32	12 months	12 months	18 of 20 nonmethadone heroin users were reincarcerated vs. only 3 of 12 in methadone group. Use of heroin mainly limited to first 3 months on methadone.	Earliest methadone controlled trial randomized but not blinded.
Gunne & Gronbladh (1984)	2	34	24 months	5 years	At follow-up, 12 of 17 patients assigned to methadone were no longer using illegal drugs, while only 1 of 17 in control groups was doing well at follow-up.	Random assignment but not blinded.
Stimmel et al. (1977)	3	335	Variable	6 years	At follow-up after detoxification from methadone, 83% of those who completed treatment were narcotic-free. Including all patients, 35% were narcotic-free.	This study shows high abstinence rates for patients judged ready to detoxify from methadone.
Anglin et al. (1989)	3	99	—	2 years	Former patients followed after closing of methadone program; 54% returned to addiction, and incarceration rate was double that of comparison group.	This was not a typical outcome study, but it documented the social and economic loss when methadone treatment is cut off.
Newman & Whitehill (1978)	1	100	2.5 years	2.5 years	60% of maintenance patients remained in treatment for 2.5 years. Only 20% of detoxified patients remained in treatment for 60 days and none for entire study.	Study was a controlled randomized trial but drug-placebo differences were so great that patients all knew their assignment.

et al., 1974). Women report irregular menses while on heroin, but on methadone, there is initial suppression of menstruation and then, after about 6 to 12 months, a resumption of regular cycling. A similar stabilization is noted in the hypothalamic-pituitary-adrenal axis. Women can conceive while on methadone, and the babies are born physically dependent on the opioid. While on methadone, expectant mothers can receive good prenatal care, and the withdrawal syndrome in newborns is readily treated. While it would be preferable to have women drug-free during pregnancy, babies born to methadone-treated mothers are significantly healthier than babies born of mothers using street heroin.

Length of Methadone Treatment

Brief maintenance (extended detoxification) as defined by federal methadone regulations is up to 180 days of methadone treatment. This is enough time to give some patients a stable period during which they can organize their lives and become engaged in psychotherapy. A 6-month period is too short for most patients, however, and the duration of methadone treatment should be determined by the patient's needs and not by an arbitrary time limit. Some patients require several years of stable methadone maintenance before they can be detoxified by gradually decreasing the dose of methadone. Many others require indefinite maintenance on this medication. For these patients, methadone should be considered a type of "hormone replacement" therapy analogous to thyroxine for patients with hypothyroidism or prednisone for patients with Addison's disease. The endogenous opioid system is so complicated that a simple diagnostic test has not yet been devised that could demonstrate a primary or secondary endorphin-deficiency state, if one exists. Some data measuring spinal fluid or plasma endogenous opioids from addicts do exist, however, but they are limited to individual peptides and do not give a clear picture of the overall system (O'Brien, 1993). There are also data from nonaddict populations showing that the system can be congenitally hyperactive, resulting in babies born with stupor and respiratory depression that are reversed by opiate antagonists such as naloxone or naltrexone (Myer et al., 1990). It is theoretically possible, therefore, that other individuals could be born with congenitally *low* endogenous opioids, possibly giving them a lower threshold for pain and making them more vulnerable to becoming opioid addicts. It is also possible, but not clearly demonstrated, that years of taking exogenous opiates, such as heroin, could suppress the production of endogenous opioids or render opiate receptors relatively insensitive and create a need for lifetime methadone as "hormone replacement." This would explain why many former opioid addicts are unable to remain free of exogenous opioids despite apparently good motivation.

A hypothetical derangement of the endogenous opioid system would also be consistent with data demonstrating a protracted opioid withdrawal syndrome (Martin & Jasinski, 1969). While the acute opioid withdrawal syndrome diminishes in a matter of 5 to 10 days whether or not treatment is received, a more subtle withdrawal syndrome lasting 6 months has been described under controlled inpatient conditions. Symptoms consist of sleep disturbance and dysphoria with accompanying disturbances in appetite, blood pressure, and cortisol rhythms. These symptoms would be expected to increase the probability of heroin use if the patient were in an environment where opiates were available.

Methadone Controversies

Despite overwhelming evidence demonstrating efficacy (Table 5.4), methadone remains a controversial treatment (IOM Report, 1990). Methadone produces clear functional improvement, but it is not a cure. The patient remains physically dependent on a synthetic replacement medication and is capable of functioning normally. The general public expects methadone patients to be stuporous, but this is not the case for a properly regulated methadone patient. Tolerance develops to the sedating effects of opioids, and patients receiving methadone are quite alert (Zacny, 1995) and capable of operating motor vehicles and performing complex tasks such as teaching school or practicing law or medicine. Approximately 190,000 patients in the United States are receiving methadone as treatment for heroin addiction at present. Good programs, defined as having adequate counseling staff and using adequate doses of methadone, have success rates of 60 to 70% as indicated by significant improvement in functional status. This is remarkable, considering the typical patient arrives with little motivation for change and numerous problems. Unfortunately, methadone programs are generally underfunded, and some programs do little more than dispense methadone. While this can be of some benefit, the full impact of methadone treatment requires a structured counseling/psychotherapy program. Eventually, frequent counseling sessions become unnecessary, and patients can be trusted to take methadone at home. Legal requirements permit only limited doses to be prescribed for use at home, even for patients who have demonstrated their trustworthiness. An exception is "medical maintenance" that requires only monthly visits but is available in only a few experimental programs (Novick et al., 1988).

During the 1990s, heroin in the United States became cheaper with historically high purity. Thus, the average street heroin addict is likely to have a higher level of physiological dependence. This has necessitated higher doses of methadone in order to prevent withdrawal and to produce sufficient cross-tolerance to counter the effects of very potent heroin. Although very few treatment outcome studies have been done under these new circumstances, there is anecdotal evidence that methadone treatment may be less effective or at least more difficult in the era of cheap and potent heroin.

Other Medications for Opioid Dependence

LAAM (Table 5.5) is levo-alpha-acetylmethadol, a long-acting opioid that has been studied extensively in clinical trials prior to its approval by the Food and Drug Administration (FDA) in 1993. LAAM is similar to methadone, but its long half-life and even longer acting metabolites produce opiate effects for about 72 hours after a single daily ingestion. This makes LAAM very convenient because it requires dosing only three times per week and still provides physiological stability in contrast to methadone, which must be taken daily.

Buprenorphine (Table 5.6) belongs to another class of medications called *partial agonists*. It has been approved for the treatment of pain and has shown good efficacy as a maintenance drug in several clinical trials among heroin addicts. As a partial μ opiate agonist, buprenorphine activates opiate receptors, producing effects similar to heroin and methadone, but there is a "ceiling," so that higher doses produce no greater effect. In comparisons between high-dose methadone and buprenorphine at 8 to 32 mg per day, methadone generally had better retention and fewer opioid-positive urines. In studies so far, overdose from buprenorphine has not been seen, and if heroin or other opioids are taken, their effects are attenuated or blocked by the presence of buprenorphine. This medication is expected to receive FDA approval and to join methadone and LAAM as a third option for agonist maintenance in the treatment of heroin addicts. Based on experience from clinical trials, there are some heroin addicts who prefer methadone, others who prefer LAAM, and still others who feel that they function best while on buprenorphine. As with other classes of medications, it is helpful for the clinician to have a selection of medications from which to choose. Buprenorphine may not be appropriate for patients with a high degree of dependence due to a high daily dose of heroin.

Federal law was changed in 2000, giving physicians the possibility of treating opiate addiction in the office using schedule III–V medications. Buprenorphine is expected to fall into this range when it is approved by the FDA for the treatment of opiate addiction. Previously, treatment was limited to specially licensed programs where methadone is dispensed. Thus, appropriately trained physicians will be able to treat opioid-dependent patients in the office, thus greatly increasing treatment availability.

Opioid Antagonist Treatment

The discovery of specific opiate receptor antagonists in the early 1970s gave rise to hopes for the "perfect" medication for the treatment of heroin addiction. Naltrexone (Table 5.7) seemed to be the answer because it specifically blocks μ opiate receptors and to a lesser extent k receptors (Raynor et al., 1994), but it has little or no direct or agonist effects of its own. Naltrexone and its short-acting analogue naloxone have high affinity for opiate receptors and will displace drugs like morphine or methadone, the result being the sudden onset of withdrawal symptoms when the drug is given to people who are opioid dependent. If the heroin addict is first detoxified so that opiate receptors are gradually evacuated, naltrexone will bind to the receptors and prevent subsequent injections of heroin from having an effect. Numerous clinical trials showed that naltrexone was effective in blocking opiate receptors and safe; thus, it was approved by the FDA in 1983 for use in the rehabilitation of opiate-dependent patients. Clinical

TABLE 5.5 Medications for Heroin Dependence: LAAM

Authors	Study Class	N	Treatment Length	Follow-up Length	Results	Comments
Freedman & Czertko (1981)	2	48	4 months plus	—	Single-blind to dose, not to medication; mean dose 26 mg methad., after 16 weeks switches to LAAM, mean 24.1. LAAM patients had significantly lower positive urines than methadone, longer retention, more satisfaction.	Results favorable to LAAM, but study was conducted in low-heroin-purity era and may not be currently relevant.
Judson & Goldstein (1979)	3	179	5-week induction study	—	92 patients were slowly inducted onto LAAM; 87 were inducted rapidly. No significant difference in outcome.	Induction onto LAAM is not difficult for most patients.
Herbert et al. (1995)	3	623	64 weeks	—	Labeling assessment study required by FDA; few side effects, similar results to earlier studies.	Demonstrated usefulness of LAAM in the "real world."
Ling et al. (1976)	1	430	40 weeks	—	Random assignment among methadone (100 mg. methadone 50 mg and LAAM 80 mg.) LAAM and methadone 100 mg were superior in several respects to methadone 50 mg.	This is the pivotal efficacy study for LAAM.
Ling et al. (1978)	3	636	40 weeks	—	Random assignment, open trial. No safety problems for either drug. No difference in patient acceptance or treatment outcome. Dropouts were higher for the LAAM group.	—
Marcovici et al. (1981)	2	130	40 weeks	—	Patients were randomly assigned to LAAM or methadone. There were no significant differences in treatment retention or in drug-positive urines.	The study was not double-blind but did give a good, prospective comparison of the two medications.

TABLE 5.6 Medications for Heroin Dependence: Buprenorphine

Authors	*Study Class*	N	*Treatment Length*	*Follow-up Length*	*Results*	*Comments*
Mello & Mendelson (1980)	1	10	14 days	—	This inpatient experiment showed that buprenorphine 8 mg daily suppressed heroin self-administration 69–98%.	Buprenorphine suppresses heroin use.
Bickel et al. (1988)	1	45	90 days		Detoxification, methadone vs. buprenorphine, method was more effective in blocking opiate effects in lab, but use of street opiates not different.	No clinical difference between methadone and buprenorphine.
Johnson et al. (1992)	1	162	6 months	—	Buprenorphine 8 mg was compared to methadone 20 mg and methadone 60 mg. Low-dose methadone had lower retention rates than the other two groups. There was a trend for buprenorphine groups to have a higher percentage of opiate-free urines. There were no differences in urines positive for cocaine metabolites.	—
Bickel & Amass (1995)	5	NA	—	—	This is an excellent, up-to-date review describing pros and cons of buprenorphine medication for opiate addiction.	—
Ling et al. (1998)	1	736	16 weeks		Double-blind comparison of 1, 4, 8, 16 mg bup. 8 and 16 mg were sig. better than 1 mg.	8–16 mg appear to be optimal doses, but higher doses may be necessary in era of potent heroin.
Ling et al. (1998)	1	225	52 weeks		Double-blind comparison of 8 mg buprenorphine vs. 30 mg and 80 mg methadone. Performance of 80-mg meth. group was better than low-dose methadone or 8 mg buprenorphine.	—
Johnson et al. (2000)	2	220	17		Randomized, not blinded, comparison of LAAM, buprenorphine 16–32 mg, methadone 60–100 mg, and methadone 20 mg. Low-dose methadone significantly less effective than LAAM, bup., or high-dose methadone.	Low-dose methadone signific. less effective. Other three groups about equal.

TABLE 5.7 Medications for Heroin Dependence: Naltrexone

Authors	*Study Class*	*N*	*Treatment Length*	*Follow-up Length*	*Results*	*Comments*
Gerra et al. (1995)	1	152	3 months	6 months	Double-blind, placebo-controlled 3 months of daily medication: clonidine only, clonidine and naltrexone, clonidine and naloxone; placebos. Better results with longer duration of naltrexone treatment.	Consistent with prior studies showing high dropout rate, but good results for patients who remain longer.
Shufman et al. (1994)	2	32	—	3 months	Fewer heroin-positive urine tests, more drug-free patients, more improvement in psychological parameters in naltrexone group.	Small sample size.
Azatian et al. (1994)	6	68	—	7 weeks	Open study; only 3 of 44 (inpatient detox subject succeeded) in entering maintenance phase. A total of 27 of 68 entered maintenance, and all discontinued by 50 days.	No control group; high early dropout rate.
Lerner et al. (1992)	1	31	—	2 months	Craving reduced in naltrexone group; reports of euphoria blocked when opiates used, but no evidence of reduced drug use compared to placebo.	—
Greenstein et al. (1984)	3	327	6 months or longer	6 months	Few side effects, multiple treatment episodes, no evidence of increased nonopiate use, one third of patients opiate-free at 6-months follow-up.	—
Washton et al. (1984)	3	114	6 months	12–18 months	All patients successfully detoxified and began naltrexone; 61% completed 6 months of treatment; at 12–18-months follow-up, 64% still opiate-free.	Shows excellent results with middle-class opiate addicts.
Ling & Wesson (1984)	3	60	6 months	Variable	Physicians and other health professionals. Avg. duration of naltrexone 6 months All patients rated as much or moderately improved at 6 months	Excellent results for health care workers.
Tennant et al. (1984)	3	160	51 days (mean)		Mean treatment length 51 days; 29.5% dropped out in first week. Better results with those completely detoxified before starting naltrexone.	—
Judson et al. (1981)	2	119	12 months	End of treatment	60 mg vs. 120 mg thrice weekly. No difference between the two groups. Dramatic decrease in craving by end of first week.	Double-blind, two-dose comparison. No placebo group.
Hollister et al. (1978)	1	192	9 months	—	Very high dropout rates in both groups. No significant differences.	Multiclinic trial.
Cornish et al. (1997)	1	51	6 months	6 months	All participants volunteers from federal probation. Those randomized to control group received equivalent counseling, but no placebo. 52% completion in naltrexone vs. 33% for controls. Opioid use 8% in naltrexone vs. 30% for controls. Only 26% of naltrexone groups were reincarcerated vs. 56% for controls.	Demonstrates potential usefulness of naltrexone in a parole population.

trials, however, did not demonstrate overall efficacy because dropout rates were so high.

Currently, naltrexone is a very underutilized medication in the treatment of heroin addiction. Unlike methadone, it has no positive psychoactive effects. Few street heroin addicts show any interest in this type of treatment, and few programs encourage patients to try it. Opioid antagonists are more complicated to prescribe than methadone, and most physicians have not been trained in their use. Opioid-dependent health care workers, such as physicians, pharmacists, and nurses, often do well on naltrexone because it enables them to return to work with no risk of relapse even though they work in areas with high drug availability. There is also evidence that naltrexone is helpful in preventing relapse in parolees and probationers who have a conditional release from prison after drug-related crimes (Brahen et al., 1984; Cornish et al., 1997). The Cornish study is a randomized controlled trial in which those parolees assigned to naltrexone had significantly less opiate use and less than half the reincarceration rate of the control group. Recently, in St. Petersburg, Russia, a double-blind study in young heroin addicts found significantly less heroin use and better program retention than in the placebo group (Krupitsky et al., 2001). Of interest for the treatment of alcoholism is that the naltrexone group also reported significantly less alcohol use than the placebo group even though alcohol was not a major focus of this heroin treatment study.

Experience with naltrexone demonstrates that blocking opiate receptors does not impair normal function for most people. Studies in animals have implicated opiate receptors in a wide variety of functions, such as control of appetite, sexual behavior, and, of course, pain perception. Occasionally, normal volunteers given naltrexone report dysphoria or depression, but most former heroin addicts have few symptoms related to the blocking of opiate receptors. Some have remained on naltrexone for over 15 years with no apparent change in appetite or pain perception and no impairment of ability to experience pleasure from sources such as sex or music.

CONCLUSIONS

The studies reviewed in this chapter indicate that, at this time, there are medications with at least some degree of efficacy in the treatment of nicotine, alcohol, and opiate use disorders. On the other hand, no medication has proved consistently efficacious in the treatment of cocaine dependence. Long-term psychosocial interventions should generally be used in conjunction with pharmacotherapy when treating substance use disorders to facilitate retention and medication adherence and to address the myriad of psychological and social problems that often accompany addiction (O'Brien, 1996). It is also important to treat coexisting psychiatric disorders with appropriate psychoactive medications and psychotherapy. Additional studies are needed to examine issues such as the long-term efficacy and effectiveness of existing and new medications, matching subgroups of patients to particular medications, and potential dangers associated with severe relapse while on medications (Schuckit, 1996).

References

Alim, T. N., Rosse, R. B., Vocci, F. J., Lindquist, T., & Deutsch, S. I. (1995). Diethylpropion pharmacotherapeutic adjuvant therapy for inpatient of cocaine dependence: A test of the cocaine-agonist hypothesis. *Clinical Neuropharmacology, 18,* 183–195.

Alterman, A. I., Droba, M., Antelo, R. E., Cornish, J. W., Sweeney, K. K., Parikh, G. A., & O'Brien, C. P. (1992). Amantadine may facilitate detoxification of cocaine addicts. *Drug and Alcohol Dependence, 31,* 19–29.

Alterman, A. I., O'Brien, C. P., McLellan, A. T., August, D. S., Snider, E. C., Droba., M., Cornish, J. W., Hall, C. P., Raphaelson, A. H., & Schrade, F. X. (1994). Effectiveness and costs of inpatient versus day hospital cocaine rehabilitations. *Journal of Nervous and Mental Disease, 182*(3), 157–163.

Angelone, S. M., Bellini, L., Di Bella, D., & Catalano, M. (1998). Effects of fluvoxamine and citalopram in maintaining abstinence in a sample of Italian detoxified alcoholics. *Alcohol and Alcoholism, 33,* 151–156.

Anglin, M. D., Speckart, G. R., Booth, M. W., & Ryan, T. M. (1989). Consequences and costs of shutting off methadone. *Addictive Medicine, 14,* 307–326.

Anton, R. F., Moak, D. H., Waid, L. R., Latham, P. K., Malcolm, R. J., & Dias, J. K. (1999). Naltrexone and cognitive behavioral therapy for the treatment of outpatient alcoholics: Results of a placebo-controlled trial. *American Journal of Psychiatry, 156,* 1758–1764.

Arndt, I. O., Dorozynksy, L., Woody, G. E., McLellan,

A. T., & O'Brien, C. P. (1992). Desipramine treatment of cocaine dependence in methadone-maintained patients. *Archives of General Psychiatry, 49,* 888–893.

Azatian, A., Papiasvilli, A., & Joseph, H. (1994). A study of the use of clonidine and naltrexone in the treatment of opioid addiction in former USSR. *Journal of Addictive Disease, 13*(1), 35–52.

Azrin, N. H., Sisson, R. W., Meyers, R., & Godley, M. (1982). Alcoholism treatment by disulfiram and community reinforcement therapy. *Journal of Behavioral Therapy and Experimental Psychiatry, 13,* 105–112.

Baekeland, F., Lundwalll, L., Kissen, B., & Shanahan, T. (1971). Correlates of outcome in disulfiram treatment of alcoholism. *Journal of Nervous and Mental Disease, 153,* 1–9.

Berger, S. P., Hall, S., Michalian, J. D., Reid, M. S., Crawford, C. A., Delucchi, K., Carr, K., & Hall, S. (1996). Haloperidol antagonism of cue-elicited cocaine craving. *Lancet, 347,* 504–508.

Besson, J., Aeby, F., Kasas, A., Lehert, P., & Potgieter, A. (1998). Combined efficacy of acamprosate and disulfiram in the treatment of alcoholism: A controlled study. *Alcoholism: Clinical and Experimental Research, 22,* 573–579.

Bickel, W. K., & Amass, L. (1995). Buprenorphine treatment of opioid dependence: A review. *Experimental and Clinical Psychopharmacology,* 3(4), 477–489.

Bickel, W. K., Stitzer, M. L., Bigelow, G. E., Liebson, I. A., Jasinski, D. R., & Johnson, D. E. (1988). A clinical trial with buprenorphine: Comparison with methadone in the detoxification of heroin addicts. *Clinical Pharmacological Therapy, 43,* 72–78.

Brahen, L. S., Henderson, R. K., Copone, T., & Kordal, N. (1984). Naltrexone treatment in a jail work-release program. *Journal of Clinical Psychiatry, 45,* 49–52.

Bruno, F. (1989). Buspirone in the treatment of alcoholic patients. *Psychopathology,* 22(Suppl. 1), 49–59.

Carroll, K. M., Nich, C., Ball, S. A., McCance, E., & Rounsaville, B. J. (1998). Treatment of cocaine and alcohol dependence with psychotherapy and disulfiram. *Addiction,* 93, 713–728.

Carroll, K. M., Rounsaville, B. J., Gordon, L. T., Nich, C., Jatlaw, P., Bisignini, R. M., & Gawin, F. H. (1994a). Psychotherapy and pharmacotherapy for ambulatory cocaine abusers. *Archives of General Psychiatry, 51,* 177–187.

Carroll, K. M., Rounsaville, B. J., Nich, C., Gordon, L. T., Wirtz, P. W., & Gawin, F. H. (1994b). One year follow-up of psychotherapy and pharmacotherapy for cocaine dependence: Delayed emergence of psychotherapy effects. *Archives of General Psychiatry, 51*(12), 989–997.

Chick, J., Anton, R., Checinski, K., Croop, R., Drummond, D. C., Farmer, R., Labriola, D., Marshall, J., Moncrieff, J., Morgan, M. Y., Peters, T., & Ritson, B. (2000a). A multicentre, randomized, double-blind, placebo-controlled trial of naltrexone in the treatment of alcohol dependence or abuse. *Alcohol and Alcoholism, 35*(6), 587–593.

Chick, J., Gough, K., Falkowski, W., Kershaw, P., Hore, B., Mehta, B., Ritson, B., Roopner, R., & Torley, D. (1992). Disulfiram treatment of alcoholism. *British Journal of Psychiatry, 161,* 84–89.

Chick, J., Howlett, H., Morgan, M. Y., & Ritson, B. (2000b). United Kingdom multicentre acamprosate study (UKMAS): A 6-month prospective study of acamprosate versus placebo in preventing relapse after withdrawal from alcohol. *Alcohol and Alcoholism, 35,* 176–187.

Childress, A. R., McLellan, A. T., Ehrman, R., & O'Brien, C. P. (1987). Extinction of conditioned responses in abstinent cocaine or opioid users (Monograph). *Problems of Drug Dependence, 76,* 189–195.

Childress, A. R., Mozley, D., Fitzgerald, J., Reivich, M., Jaggi, J., & O'Brien, C. P. (1995). Limbic activation during cue-induced cocaine craving. *25th Annual Meeting of Society for Neuroscience* (767.1, p. 1956). San Diego, CA.

Cornelius, J. R., Salloum, I. M., Ehler, J. G., Jarrett, P. J., Cornelius, M. D., Perel, J. M., Thase, J. E., & Black, A. (1997). Fluoxetine in depressed alcoholics. *Archives of General Psychiatry, 54,* 700–705.

Cornish, J. W., Maany, I., Fudala, P. J., Neal, S., Poole, S. A., Volpicelli, P., & O'Brien, C. P. (1995). Carbamazepine treatment for cocaine dependence (Monograph). *Drug and Alcohol Dependence, 38,* 221–227.

Cornish, J. W., Metzger, D., Woody, G. E., Wilson, D., McLellan, A. T., Vandergrift, B., & O'Brien, C. P. (1997). Naltrexone pharmacotherapy for opioid dependent federal probationers. *Journal of Substance Abuse Treatment, 14*(6), 529–534.

Croop, R. S., Faulkner, E. B., & Labariola, D. F. (1997). The safety profile of naltrexone in the treatment of alcoholism: Results from a multicenter usage study. The Naltrexone Usage Study Group. *Archives of General Psychiatry, 54*(12), 1130–1135.

Dole, V. P., Robinson, J. W., Orraca, J., Towns, E., Searcy, P., & Caine, E. (1969). Methadone treatment of randomly selected criminal addicts. *New England Journal of Medicine, 280*(25), 1372–1375.

Fiore, M. C., Kenford, S. L., Jorenby, D. E., Wetter, D. W., Smith S. S., & Baker, T. B. (1994a). Two studies of the clinical effectiveness of the nicotine patch with different counseling treatments. *Chest, 105*(2), 524–533.

Fiore, M. C., Smith, S. S., Jorenby, D. E., & Baker, T. B. (1994b). The effectiveness of the nicotine patch for smoking cessation: A meta-analysis. *Journal of the American Medical Association, 271*(24), 1940–1947.

Freedman, R. R., & Czeretko, G. (1981). A comparison of thrice weekly LAAM and daily methadone in employed heroin addicts. *Drug and Alcohol Dependence, 8*(3), 215–222.

Fuller, R. K. (1995). Antidipsotropic medications. In R. K. Hester & W. R. Miller (Eds.), *Handbook of alcoholism treatment approaches: Effective alternatives* (2nd ed., pp. 123–133). Needham Heights, MA: Allyn & Bacon.

Fuller, R. K., Branchey, L., Brightwell, D. R., Derman, R. M., Emrick, C. D., Iber, F. L., James, K. E., Lacoursiere, R. B., Lee, K. K., Lowenstam, I., Maany, I., Neiderheiser, D., Nocks, J. J., & Shaw, S. (1986). Disulfiram treatment of alcoholism: A Veterans Administration cooperative study. *Journal of the American Medical Association, 256*, 449–1455.

Fuller, R. K., & Roth, H. P. (1979). Disulfiram for the treatment of alcoholism: An evaluation in 128 men. *Annals of Internal Medicine, 90*, 901–904.

Gawin, F. H., Allen, D., & Humblestone, B. (1989a). Outpatient treatment of "crack" cocaine smoking with flupenthixol decanoate. *Archives of General Psychiatry, 46*, 322–325.

Gawin, F. H., Kleber, H. D., Byck, R., Rounsaville, B. J., Kosten, T. R., Jatlow, P. I., & Morgan, C. (1989b). Desipramine facilitation of initial cocaine abstinence. *Archives of General Psychiatry, 46*, 117–121.

Gawin, F. H., Morgan, C., Kosten, T. R., & Kleber, H. D. (1989c). Double-blind evaluation of the effect of acute amantadine on cocaine craving. *Psychopharmacology, 97*, 402–403.

Gawin, F. H., Riordan, C., & Kleber, H. (1985). Methylphenidate treatment of cocaine abusers without attention deficit disorder: A negative report. *American Journal of Drug and Alcohol Abuse, 11*, 193–197.

Gerra, G., Marcato, A., Caccavar, R., et al. (1995). Clonidine and opiate receptor antagonists in the treatment of heroin addiction. *Journal of Substance Abuse Treatment, 12*(1), 35–41.

Gerrein, J. R., Rosenberg, C. M., & Manohar, V. (1973). Disulfiram maintenance in outpatient treatment of alcoholism. *Archives of General Psychiatry, 29*, 798–802.

Giannini, A. J., Folts, D. J., Feather, J. N., & Sullivan, B. S. (1989). Bromocriptine and amantadine in cocaine detoxification. *Psychiatry Research, 29*, 11–16.

Gonzales, D. H., Nides, M. A., Ferry, L. H., Kustra, R. P., Jamerson, B. D., Segall, N., Herrero, L. A., Krishen, A., Sweeney, A., Buaron, K., & Metz, A. (2001). Bupropion SR as an aid to smoking cessation in smokers treated previously with bupropion: A randomized placebo-controlled study. *Clinical Pharmacological Therapy, 69*(6), 438–444.

Gorelick, D. A. (1989). Serotonin reuptake blockers and the treatment of alcoholism. In M. Galanter (Ed.), *Recent developments in alcoholism* (pp. 267–281). New York: Plenum Press.

Gorelick, D. A., & Paredes, A. (1992). Effect of fluoxetine on alcohol consumption in male alcoholics. *Alcoholism: Clinical and Experimental Research, 16*, 261–265.

Grabowski, J., Roache, J. D., Schmitz, J. M., Rhoades, H., Creson, D., & Korszun, A. (1997). Replacement medication for cocaine dependence: Methylphenidate. *Journal of Clinical Psychopharmacology, 17*, 485–488.

Grabowski, J., Rhoades, H., Elk, R., Schmitz, J., Davis, C., Creson, D., & Kirby, K. (1995). Fluoxetine is ineffective for treatment of cocaine dependence or concurrent opiate and cocaine dependence: Two placebo-controlled, double blind trials. *Journal of Clinical Psychopharmacology, 15*, 163–174.

Greenstein, R. A., Arndt, I. C., McLellan, A. T., O'Brien, C. P., & Evans, B. (1984). Naltrexone: A clinical perspective. *Journal of Clinical Psychiatry, 45*(9, Sec. 2), 25–28.

Gunne, L., & Gronbladh, L. (1984). The Swedish methadone maintenance program. In G. Servan (Ed.), *Social and medical aspects of drug abuse* (pp. 205–213). Jamaica, NY: Spectrum.

Herbert, S., Montgomery, A., Fudala, P., Vocci, F., Gampel, J., Mojsiak, J., Hill, J., & Walsh, R. (1995). LAAM labeling assessment study: Retention, dosing, and side effects in a 64-week study (Monograph). *Problems of Drug Dependence, 153*, 259.

Hersh, D., Van Kirk, J. R., & Kranzler, H. R. (1998). Naltrexone treatment of comorbid alcohol and cocaine use disorders. *Psychopharmacology, 139*, 44–52.

Higgins, S. T., Budney, A. J., Bickel, W. K., Hughes, J. R., Goerg, F., & Badger, G. (1993). Achieving cocaine abstinence with a behavioral approach. *American Journal of Psychiatry, 150*, 763–769.

Hollister, L. (1978). Clinical evaluation of naltrexone treatment for opiate-dependent individuals. *Archives of General Psychiatry, 35*, 335–340.

Hughes, J. C., & Cook, C. C. H. (1997). The efficacy of disulfiram: A review of outcome studies. *Addiction, 92,* 381–395.

Hurt, R. D., Sachs, D. P., Glover, E. D., Offord, K. P., Johnston, J. A., Dale, L. C., Khayrallah, M. A., Schroeder, D. R., Glover, P. N., Sullivan, C. R., Croghan, I. T., & Sullivan, P. M. (1997). A comparison of sustained-release bupropion and placebo for smoking cessation. *New England Journal of Medicine, 337*(17), 1195–1202.

Imperial Cancer Fund General Practice Research Group. (1993). Effectiveness of a nicotine patch in helping people stop smoking: Results of a randomized trial in general practice. *British Medical Journal, 306*(6888), 1304–1308.

Institute of Medicine Report. (1990). The effectiveness of treatment. In D. R. Gerstein & H. J. Harwood (Eds.), *Treating drug problems* (pp. 132–199). Washington, DC: National Academy Press.

Jaffe, A. J., Rounsaville, B., Chang, G., Schottenfeld, R. S., Meyer, R. E., & O'Malley, S. S. (1996). Naltrexone, relapse prevention, and supportive therapy with alcoholics: An analysis of patient treatment matching. *Journal of Consulting and Clinical Psychology, 64,* 1044–1053.

Jenkins, S. W., Warfield, N. A., Blaine, J. D., Cornish, J., Ling, W., Rosen, M. I., Urschel, H., Wesson, D., & Ziedonis, D. (1992). A pilot study of gepirone vs. placebo in the treatment of cocaine dependency. *Psychopharmacology Bulletin, 28,* 21–26.

Johnsen, J., & Morland, J. (1991). Disulfiram implant: A double-blind placebo controlled follow-up on treatment outcome. *Alcoholism: Clinical and Experimental Research, 15,* 532–536.

Johnsen, J., Stowell, A., Bache-Wiig, J. E., Stendsrud, T., Ripel, A., & Morland, J. (1987). A double-blind placebo controlled study of male alcoholics given a subcutaneous disulfiram implantation. *British Journal of Addiction, 82,* 607–613.

Johnson, B. A., Ait-Daoud, N., & Prihoda, T. J. (2000a). Combining ondansetron and naltrexone effectively treats biologically predisposed alcoholics: From hypotheses to preliminary clinical evidence. *Alcoholism: Clinical and Experimental Research, 24,* 737–742.

Johnson, B. A., Jasinski, D. R., Galloway, G. P., Kranzler, J., Weinreib, R., Anton, R. F., Mason, B. J., Bohn, M. J., Pettinati, H. M., Rawson, R., & Clyde, C. (1996). Ritanserin in the treatment of alcohol dependence: A multi-center clinical trial. *Psychopharmacology, 128,* 206–215.

Johnson, B. A., Roache, J. D., Javors, M. A., DiClemente, C. C., Cloninger, C. R., Prihoda, T. J., Bordnick, P. S., Ait-Daoud, N., & Hensler, J. (2000b). Ondansetron for reduction of drinking among biologically predisposed alcoholic patients. *Journal of the American Medical Association, 284,* 963–971.

Johnson, R. E., Chutuape, M. A., Strain, E. C., Walsh, S. L., Stitzer, M. L., & Bigelow, G. E. (2000). A comparison of levomethadyl acetate, buprenorphine, and methadone for opioid dependence. *New England Journal of Medicine, 343*(18), 1290–1297.

Johnson, R. E., Jaffe, J. H., & Fudala, P. J. (1992). A controlled trial of buprenorphine treatment for opioid dependence. *Journal of the American Medical Association, 267,* 2750–2755.

Jorenby, D. E., Leischow, S. J., Nides, M. A., Rennard, S. I., Johnston, J. A., Hughes, A. R., Smith, S. S., Muramoto, M. L., Daughton, D. M., Doan, K., Fiore, M. C., & Baker, T. B. (1999). A controlled trial of sustained-release bupropion, a nicotine patch, or both for smoking cessation. *New England Journal of Medicine, 340*(9), 685–691.

Judson, B. A., Carney, T. M., & Goldstein, A. (1981). Naltrexone treatment of heroin addiction: Efficacy and safety in a double-blind dosage comparison. *Drug and Alcohol Dependence, 7*(4), 325–346.

Judson, B. A., & Goldstein, A. (1979). Leva-alpha-acetylmethadol (LAAM) in the treatment of heroin addicts: 2. Dosage schedule for induction and stabilization. *Drug and Alcohol Dependence, 4,* 461–166.

Kampman, K. M., Rukstalis, M., Ehrman, R., McGinnis, D. E., Gariti, P., Volpicelli, J. R., Pettinati, H., & O'Brien, C. P. (1999). Open trials as a method of prioritizing medications for inclusion in controlled trials of cocaine dependence. *Addictive Behaviors, 24,* 287–291.

Kampman, K. M., Volpicelli, J. R., Alterman, A. I., Cornish, J., & O'Brien, C. P. (2000). Amantadine in the treatment of cocaine-dependent patients with severe withdrawal symptoms. *American Journal of Psychiatry, 157,* 2052–2054.

Kampman, K. M., Volpicelli, J. R., Mulvaney, F., Alterman, A. I., Cornish, J., Gariti, P., Cnaan, A., Poole, S., Muller, E., Acosta, T., Luce, D., & O'Brien, C. P. (2001). Effectiveness of propranolol for cocaine dependence treatment may depend on cocaine withdrawal symptom severity. *Drug and Alcohol Dependence, 63*(1), 69–78.

Khalsa, E., Jatlow, P., & Gawin, F. (1994). Flupenthixol and desipramine treatment of crack users: Double-blind results. *NIDA Research Monograph, 141,* NIH Publication Number 94-3794, p. 438.

King, A. C., Volpicelli, J. R., Frazer, A., O'Brien, C. P. (1997). Effect of naltrexone on subjective alcohol response in subjects at high and low risk for future alcohol dependence. *Psychopharmacology, 129,* 15–22.

Kleber, H. D. (1995). Pharmacotherapy, current and potential, for the treatment of cocaine dependence. *Clinical Neuropharmacology, 18* (Suppl. 1), S96–S109.

Knox, P. C., & Donovan, D. M. (1999). Using naltrexone in inpatient alcoholism treatment. *Journal of Psychoactive Drugs, 31,* 373–388.

Kolar, A. F., Brown, B. S., Weddington, W. W., Haertzen, C. C., Michaelson, B. S., & Jaffe, J. H. (1992). Treatment of cocaine dependence in methadone maintenance clients: A pilot study comparing the efficacy of desipramine and amantadine. *International Journal of the Addictions, 27,* 849–868.

Koob, G. F. (1992). Neurobiological mechanisms in cocaine and opiate dependence. In C. P. O'Brien & J. Jaffe (Eds.), *Addictive states* (pp. 79–92). New York: Raven Press.

Kornitzer, M., Boutsen, M., Dramaix, M., Thijs, J., & Gustavsson, G. (1995). Combined used of nicotine patch and gum in smoking cessation: A placebo-controlled clinical trial. *Preventive Medicine, 24*(1), 41–47.

Kosten, T. R., Morgan, C. M., Falcione, J., & Schottenfeld, R. S. (1992). Pharmacotherapy for cocaine-abusing methadone-maintained patients using amantadine or desipramine. *Archives of General Psychiatry, 49,* 894–898.

Kranzler, H. R., & Anton, R. F. (1994). Implications of recent neuropsychopharmacologic research for understanding the etiology and development of alcoholism. *Journal of Consulting and Clinical Psychology, 62,* 1116–1126.

Kranzler, H. R., Burleson, J. A., Del Boca, F. K., Babor, T. F., Korner, P., Brown, J., & Bohn, M. J. (1994). Buspirone treatment of anxious alcoholics: A placebo-controlled trial. *Archives of General Psychiatry, 51,* 720–731.

Kranzler, H. R., Burleson, J. A., Korner, P., Del Boca, F. K., Bohn, M. J., Brown, J., & Liebowitz, N. (1995). Placebo-controlled trial of fluoxetine as an adjunct to relapse prevention in alcoholics. *American Journal of Psychiatry, 152,* 391–397.

Kranzler, H. R., Modesto-Lowe, V., & Nuwayser, E. S. (1998). Sustained-release naltrexone for alcoholism treatment: A preliminary study. *Alcoholism: Clinical and Experimental Research, 22,* 1074–1079.

Kranzler, H. R., Modesto-Lowe, V., & Van Kirk, J. (2000). Naltrexone vs. nefazodone for treatment of alcohol dependence. *Neuropsychopharmacology, 22,* 493–503.

Kreek, M. J. (1992). Rationale for maintenance pharmacotherapy of opiate dependence. In C. P. O'Brien & J. H. Jaffe (Eds.), *Addictive states* (pp. 205–330). New York: Raven Press.

Krupitsky, E. M., Zvartau, E. E., Neznanov, N. G., Burakov, A. M., Masalov, D. V., Tsoi, M. V., Didenko, T. Y., Romanova, T. N., Ivanova, E. B., Egorova, V. Y., Bespalov, Ä. Y., Martynikhin, A. V., Grinenko, A. Y., & Woody, E. (2001). A double-blind, placebo-controlled, clinical trial of naltrexone for heroin addiction in Russia: Sample characteristics and short-term follow-up. *Proceedings of the College on Problems of Drug Dependence Annual Meeting,* Scottsdale, Arizona.

Krystal, J. H., Cramer, J. A., Krol, W. F., Kirk, G. F., Rosenheck, R. A., & the Veterans Affairs Naltrexone Cooperative Study 425 Group. (2001). Naltrexone in the treatment of alcohol dependence. *Research Society on Alcoholism Meeting,* Montreal, Canada.

Latt, N. C., Jurd, S., Houseman, J., & Wutzke, S. (2001). Naltrexone in alcohol dependence: Effectiveness in a standard clinical setting. *Research Society on Alcoholism,* Montreal, Canada.

Lerner, A., Sigal, M., Bacalul, E., et al. (1992). A naltrexone double blind placebo controlled study in Israel. *Israel Journal of Psychiatry and Related Sciences, 29*(1), 36–43.

Levin, F. R., & Lehman, A. F. (1991). Meta-analysis of desipramine as an adjunct in the treatment of cocaine addiction. *Journal of Clinical Psychopharmacology, 11,* 374–378.

Lhuintre, J. P., Moore, N. D., Saligaut, C., Boismare, F., Daoust, M., Chretien, P., Tran, G., & Hillemand, B. (1985). Ability of calcium bis acetyl homotaurinate, a GABA agonist, to prevent relapse in weaned alcoholics. *Lancet, 1*(8436), 1014–1016.

Lhuintre, J. P., Moore, N. D., Tran, G., Steru, L., Lancrenon, S., Daoust, M., Parot, P., Ladure, P., Libert, C., Boismare, F., & Hillemand, B. (1990). Acamprosate appears to decrease alcohol intake in weaned alcoholics. *Alcohol and Alcoholism, 25,* 613–622.

Ling, W., Charuvastra, C., Collins, J. F., Batki, S., Brown, L. S., Kintaudi, P., Wesson, D. R., McNicholas, L., Tusel, D. J., Malkerneker, U., Renner, J. A., Santos, E., Casadonte, P., Fye, C., Stine, S., Wang, R. I. H., & Segal, D. (1998). Buprenorphine maintenance treatment of opiate dependence. A multimember, randomized clinical trial. *Addiction, 93,* 475–486.

Ling, W., Charuvastra, C., Kaim, S. C., & Klett, J. (1976). Methadyl acetate and methadone as maintenance treatments for heroin addicts. *Archives of General Psychiatry, 33,* 709–720.

Ling, W., Klett, J., & Gillis, R. D. (1978). A cooperative clinical study of methadyl acetate. *Archives of General Psychiatry, 35,* 345–353.

Ling, W., & Wesson, D. R. (1984). Naltrexone treatment for addicted health-care professionals: A collaborative private practice. *Journal of Clinical Psychiatry*, 34(9, Sec. 2), 46–52.

Malcolm, R., Anton, R. F., Randall, C. L., Johnston, A., Brady, K., & Thevos, A. (1992). A placebo-controlled trial of busipirone in anxious inpatient alcoholics. *Alcoholism: Clinical and Experimental Research, 16,* 1007–1013.

Marcovici, M., O'Brien, C. P., McLellan, A. T., & Kacio, J. (1981). A clinical, controlled study of *l*-α-acetyl-methadol in the treatment of narcotic addiction. *American Journal of Psychiatry, 138,* 234–236.

Martin, W. R., & Jasinski, D. (1969). Psychological parameters of morphine in human tolerance, early abstinence, protracted abstinence. *Journal of Psychiatry Research, 7,* 9–16.

Mason, B. J., Kocsis, J. H., Ritvo, E. C., & Cutler, R. B. (1996). A double-blind, placebo controlled trial of desipramine for primary alcohol dependence stratified on the presence or absence of major depression. *Journal of the American Medical Association,* 275, 761–767.

Mason, B. J., Ritvo, E. C., Morgan, R. O., Salvato, F. R., Goldberg, G., Welch, B., & Mantero-Antienza, E. (1994). A double-blind, placebo-controlled pilot study to evaluate the efficacy and safety of oral nalmefene HCl for alcohol dependence. *Alcoholism: Clinical and Experimental Research, 18,* 1162–1167.

Mason, B. J., Salvato, F. R., Williams, L. D., Ritvo, E. C., & Cutler, R. B. (1999). A double-blind, placebo-controlled study of oral nalmefene for alcohol dependence. *Archives of General Psychiatry, 56,* 719–724.

McGrath, P. J., Nunes, E. V., Stewart, J. W., Goldman, D., Agosti, V., Ocepek-Welikson, K., & Quitkin, F. M. (1996). Imipramine treatment of alcoholics with primary depression: A placebo-controlled clinical trial. *Archives of General Psychiatry,* 53, 232–240.

McKay, J. R., Cacciola, J., McLellan, A. T., Alterman, A. I., & Wirtz, P. W. (1997). An initial evaluation of the psychosocial dimensions of the ASAM criteria for inpatient and day hospital substance abuse rehabilitation. *Journal of Studies on Alcohol, 58,* 239–252.

McLellan, A. T., Arndt, I. O., Metzger, D., Woody, G., & O'Brien, C. P. (1993). The effects of psychosocial services in substance abuse treatment. *Journal of the American Medical Association,* 269(15), 1959–1993.

Mello, N. K., & Mendelson, J. H. (1980). Buprenorphine suppresses heroin use by heroin addicts. *Science, 207,* 657–659.

Metzger, D. S., Woody, G. E., McLellan, A. T., O'Brien, C. P., Druley, P., Navaline, H., DePhilippis, D., Stolley, P., & Abrutyn, E. (1993). Human immunodeficiency virus seroconversion among in- and out-of-treatment drugs users: An 18 month prospective follow-up. *Journal of AIDS, 6,* 1049–1056.

Mintz, J., O'Brien, C. P., & Goldschmidt, J. (1974). Sexual problems of heroin addicts when drug free, on heroin, and on methadone. *Archives of General Psychiatry, 31,* 700–703.

Montoya, I. D., Levin, F. R., Fudala, P. J., & Gorelick, D. A. (1995). Double-blind comparison of carbamazepine and placebo for treatment of cocaine dependence (Monograph). *Drug and Alcohol Dependence, 38,* 213–219.

Morris, P. L. P., Hopwood, M., Whelan, G., Gardiner, J., & Drummond, E. (2001). Naltrexone for alcohol dependence: A randomized controlled trial. *Addiction.*

Moscovitz, H., Brookoff, D., & Nelson, L. (1993). A randomized trial of bromocriptine for cocaine users presenting to the emergency department. *Journal of General Internal Medicine, 8,* 1–4.

Myer, E. C., Morris, D. L., Brase, D. A., Dewey, W. L., & Zimmerman, A. W. (1990). Naltrexone therapy of apnea in children with elevated cerebrospinal fluid b-endorphin. *Annals of Neurology, 27,* 75–80.

Myers, J. K., Weissman, M. M., Tischler, G. L., Holzer, C. E., Leaf, P. J., Orvaschel, H., Anthony, J. C., Boyd, J. H., Burke, J. D., Kramer, M., & Stoltzman, R. (1984). Six month prevalence of psychiatric disorders in three communities 1980–1982. *Archives of General Psychiatry, 41,* 959–967.

Naranjo, C. A., Kadlec, K. E., Sanhueza, P., Woodley-Remus, D. V., & Sellers, E. M. (1990). Fluoxetine differentially alters alcohol intake and other consumatory behaviors in problem drinkers. *Clinical Pharmacology and Therapeutics, 47,* 490–498.

Naranjo, C. A., Poulos, C. X., Bremner, K. E., & Lanctot, K. L. (1992). Citalopram decreases desirability, liking, and consumption of alcohol in alcohol-dependent drinkers. *Clinical Pharmacology and Therapeutics, 51,* 729–739.

Naranjo, C. A., Sellers, E. M., Sullivan, J. T., Woodley, D. V., Kadlec, K., & Sykora, J. (1987). The serotonin uptake inhibitor citalopram attenuates ethanol intake. *Clinical Pharmacology and Therapeutics, 41,* 266–274.

Naranjo, C. A., Sullivan, J. T., Kadlec, K. E., Woodley-Remus, D. V., Kennedy, G., & Sellers, E. M. (1989). Differential effects of viqualine on alcohol intake and other consumatory behaviors. *Clinical Pharmacology and Therapeutics, 41,* 266–274.

Newman, R. G., & Whitehill, W. G. (1978). Double-blind comparison of methadone and placebo maintenance treatment of narcotic addicts in Hong Kong. *Lancet, 8141*, 485–488.

Novick, D. M., Pascarelli, E. F., & Joseph, H. (1988). Methadone maintenance patients in general medical practice: A preliminary report. *Journal of the American Medical Association, 259*, 3299–3302.

Nunes, E. V., McGrath, P. J., Quitkin, F. M., Ocepek-Welikson, K., Stewart, J. K. W., Koenig, T., Wager, S., & Klein, D. F. (1995). Imipramine treatment of cocaine abuse: Possible boundaries of efficacy. *Drug and Alcohol Dependence, 39*, 185–195.

O'Brien, C. P. (1993). Opioid addiction. In A. Herz (Ed.), *Handbook of experimental pharmacology* (Vol. 104/II (63, pp. 803–823). Berlin and Heidelberg: Springer-Verlag.

O'Brien, C. P. (1996). Recent developments in the pharmacotherapy of substance abuse. *Journal of Consulting and Clinical Psychology, 64*, 677–686.

O'Brien, C. P., Childress, A. R., Arndt., I. O., McLellan, A. T., Woody, G. E., & Maany, I. (1988). Pharmacological and behavioral treatments of cocaine dependence: Controlled studies. *Journal of Clinical Psychiatry, 49*(2), 17–22.

O'Brien, C. P., Eckardt, M. J., & Linnoila, V. M. (1995). Pharmacotherapy of alcoholism. In F. E. Bloom & D. J. Kupfer (Eds.), *Psychopharmacology: The fourth generation of progress* (pp. 1745–1755). New York: Raven Press.

O'Farrell, J. J., Cutter, H. S. G., & Floyd, F. J. (1985). Evaluating behavioral marital therapy for male alcoholics: Effects on marital adjustment and communication from before to after therapy. *Behavior Therapy, 16*, 147–167.

Oliveto, A. H., Feingold, A., Schottenfeld, R., Jatlow, P., & Kosten, T. R. (1999). Desipramine in opioid-dependent cocaine abusers maintained on buprenorphine vs. methadone. *Archives of General Psychiatry, 56*, 812–820.

O'Malley, S. S. (1995). Integration of opioid antagonists and psychosocial therapy in the treatment of narcotic and alcohol dependence. *Journal of Clinical Psychiatry, 56*(Suppl. 7), 30–38.

O'Malley, S. S., Jaffe, A. J., Chang, G., Rode, S., Schottenfeld, R. S., Meyer, R. E., & Rounsaville, B. J. (1996a). Six-month follow-up of naltrexone and psychotherapy for alcohol dependence. *Archives of General Psychiatry, 53*, 217–224.

O'Malley, S. S., Jaffe, A. J., Chang, G., Schottenfeld, R. S., Meyer, R. E., & Rounsaville, B. J. (1992). Naltrexone and coping skills therapy for alcohol dependence. *Archives of General Psychiatry, 49*, 881–887.

O'Malley, S. S., Jaffe, A. J., Rode, S., & Rounsaville, B. J. (1996b). The experience of a "slip" among alcoholics on naltrexone versus placebo. *American Journal of Psychiatry, 153*, 281–283.

Oslin, D., Liberto, J. G., O'Brien, J., Krois, S., & Norbeck, J. (1997). Naltrexone as an adjunctive treatment for older patients with alcohol dependence. *American Journal of Geriatric Psychiatry, 5*, 324–332.

Paille, F. M., Guelfi, J. D., Perkins, A. C., Royer, R. J., Steru, L., & Parot, P. (1995). Double-blind randomized multicentre trial of acamprosate in maintaining abstinence from alcohol. *Alcohol and Alcoholism, 30*, 239–247.

Pelc, I., Verbanck, P., Le Bon, O., Gavrilovic, M., Lion, K., & Lehert, P. (1997). Efficacy and safety of acamprosate in the treatment of detoxified alcohol-dependent patients. *British Journal of Psychiatry, 171*, 73–77.

Petrakis, I. L., Carroll, K. M., Nich, C., Gordon, L. T., McCance-Katz, E. F., Frankforter, T., & Rounsaville, B. J. (2000). Disulfiram treatment for cocaine dependence in methadone-maintained opioid addicts. *Addiction, 95*, 219–228.

Pettinati, H. M., Volpicelli, J. R., Pierce, J. D., & O'Brien, C. P. (2000). Improving naltrexone response: An intervention for medical practitioners to enhance medication compliance in alcohol dependent patients. *Journal of Addictive Diseases, 19*, 71–83.

Poldrugo, F. (1997). Acamprosate treatment in a long-term community-based alcohol rehabilitation programme. *Addiction, 92*, 1537–1546.

Rawson, R. A., Shoptaw, M. J., & Minsky, S. (1994). Effectiveness of desipramine in treating cocaine dependence. *NIDA Research Monograph, 153*, 494.

Raynor, K., Kong, H., Chen, Y., Yasuda, K., Yu, L., Bell, G. I., & Reisine, T. (1994). Pharmacological characterization of the cloned k-, d- and m-opioid receptors. *Molecular Pharmacology, 45*(2), 330–334.

Richmond, R. L., Harris, K., & de Almeida Neta, A. (1994). The transdermal nicotine patch: Results of a randomized placebo-controlled trial. *Medical Journal of Australia, 161*(2), 130–135.

Robbins, S., Ehrman, R., Childress, A. R., & O'Brien, C. P. (1992). Using cue reactivity to screen medications for cocaine abuse: Amantadine hydrochloride. *Addictive Behaviors, 17*, 491–499.

Robins, L. N., Helzer, J. E., Weissman, M. M., Orvaschel, H., Gruenberg, E., Burke, J. D., & Regier, D. A. (1984). Lifetime prevalence of specific psychiatric disorders in three sites. *Archives of General Psychiatry, 41*, 949–958.

Robinson, D. S., & Rickels, K. (2000). Concerns about clinical drug trials. *Journal of Clinical Psychopharmacology, 20*(6), 593–596.

Rose, J. E., Behm, F. M., Westman, E. C., Levin,

E. D., Stein, R. M., & Ripka, G. V. (1994). Mecamylamine combined with nicotine skin patch facilitates smoking cessation beyond nicotine patch treatment alone. *Clinical Pharmacological Therapy, 56*(1), 86–99.

Roy, A., Virkkunen, M., & Linnoila, M. (1990). Serotonin in suicide, violence, and alcoholism. In E. F. Coccaro & D. L. Murphy (Eds.), *Serotonin in major psychiatric disorders* (pp. 187–208). Washington, DC: American Psychiatric Press.

Sass, H., Soyka, M., Mann, K., & Zieglgansberger, W. (1996). Relapse prevention by acamprosate: Results from a placebo controlled study in alcohol dependence. *Archives of General Psychiatry, 53*(8), 673–680.

Schuckit, M. A. (1996). Recent developments in the pharmacotherapy of alcohol dependence. *Journal of Consulting and Clinical Psychology, 64,* 669–676.

Shiffman, S., Johnston, J. A., Khayrallah, M., Elash, C. A., Gwaltney, C. J., Paty, J. A., Gnys, M., Evoniuk, G., & DeVeaugh-Geiss, J. (2000). The effect of bupropion on nicotine craving and withdrawal. *Psychopharmacology (Berl.), 148*(1), 33–40.

Shufman, E. N., Porat, S., Witztum, E., Gandacu, D., Bar-Hamburger, R., & Ginath, U. (1994). The efficacy of naltrexone in preventing reabuse of heroin after detoxification. *Biological Psychiatry, 35,* 935–945.

Stimmel, B., Goldeberg, J., Rotkopf, E., & Cohen, M. (1977). Ability to remain abstinent after detoxification—A six year study. *Journal of the American Medical Association, 237*(12), 1216–1220.

Strain, E. C., Stitzer, M. L., Liebson, I. A., & Bigelow, G. E. (1994a). Buprenorphine versus methadone in the treatment of opioid-dependent cocaine users. *Psychopharmacology, 116,* 401–406.

Strain, E. C., Stitzer, M. L., Liebson, I. A., & Bigelow, G. E. (1994b). Comparison of buprenorphine and methadone in the treatment of opioid dependence. *American Journal of Psychiatry, 151,* 1025–1030.

Swift, R. M. (1995). Effect of naltrexone on human alcohol consumption. *Journal of Clinical Psychiatry, 56*(Suppl. 7), 24–29.

Swift, R. M., Whelihan, W., Kuznetsov, O., Buongiorno, G., & Hsuing, H. (1994). Naltrexone-induced alterations in human ethanol intoxication. *American Journal of Psychiatry, 151,* 1463–1467.

Tempesta, E., Janiri, L., Begnamini, A., Chabac, S., & Potgieter, A. (2000). Acamprosate and relapse prevention in the treatment of alcohol dependence: A placebo-controlled study. *Alcohol and Alcoholism, 35,* 202–209.

Tennant, F. S., Rawson, R. A., Cohen, A. J., et al. (1984). Clinical experience with naltrexone in suburban opioid addicts. *Journal of Clinical Psychiatry, 34*(9, Sec. 2), 42–45.

Tennant, F. S., & Sagherian, A. A. (1987). Double-blind comparison of amantadine and bromocriptine for ambulatory withdrawal from cocaine dependence. *Archives of Internal Medicine, 147,* 109–112.

Tollefson, G. D., Montague-Clouse, J., & Tollefson, S. L. (1992). Treatment of comorbid generalized anxiety in a recently detoxified alcohol population with a selective serotonergic drug (busipirone). *Journal of Clinical Psychopharmacology, 12,* 19–26.

Volpicelli, J. R., Alterman, A. I., Hayashida, M., & O'Brien, C. P. (1992). Naltrexone in the treatment of alcohol dependence. *Archives of General Psychiatry, 49,* 876–880.

Volpicelli, J. R., Clay, K. L., Rhines, J. S., Volpicelli, L. A., Alterman, A. I., & O'Brien, C. P. (1997). Naltrexone and alcohol dependence: Role of subject compliance. *Archives of General Psychiatry, 54,* 737–742.

Volpicelli, J. R., Clay, K. L., Watson, N. T., & O'Brien, (1995). Naltrexone in the treatment of alcoholism: Predicting response to naltrexone. *Journal of Clinical Psychiatry, 56*(Suppl. 7), 39–44.

Volpicelli, J. R., O'Brien, C. P., Alterman, A. I., & Hayashida, M. (1990). Naltrexone and the treatment of alcohol dependence: Initial observations. In L. Reid (Ed.), *Opioids, bulimia, and alcohol abuse and alcoholism* (pp. 195–214). New York: Springer-Verlag.

Volpicelli, J. R., Watson, N. T., King, A. C., Sherman, C. E., & O'Brien, C. P. (1995). Effect of naltrexone on alcohol "high" in alcoholics. *American Journal of Psychiatry, 152,* 613–615.

Washton, A. M., Pottash, A. C., & Gold, M. S. (1984). Naltrexone in addicted business executives and physicians. *Journal of Clinical Psychiatry, 34*(9, Sec. 2), 39–41.

Weddington, W. W., Brown, B. S., Haertzen, C. A., Hess, J. M., Mahaffey, J. R., Kolar, A. F., & Jaffe, J. H. (1991). Comparison of amantadine and desipramine combined with psychotherapy for treatment of cocaine dependence. *American Journal of Drug and Alcohol Abuse, 17,* 137–152.

Whitworth, A. B., Fischer, F., Lesch, O. M., Nimmerichter, A., Oberbauer, H., Platz, T., Potgeiter, A., Walter, H., & Fleischhacker, W. W. (1996). Comparison of acamprosate and placebo in long-term treatment of alcohol dependence. *Lancet, 347,* 1438–1442.

Zacny, J. C. (1995). A review of the effects of opioids on psychomotor and cognitive functioning in humans. *Experimental and Clinical Psychopharmacology, 3*(4), 432–466.

6

Psychosocial Treatments for Alcohol Use Disorders

John W. Finney
Rudolf H. Moos

Of 15 psychosocial treatments examined in 3 or more studies (mostly of the Type 1 and, especially, the Type 2 varieties), those with the most evidence of effectiveness helped patients shape and adapt to their life circumstances. These cognitive behavioral treatments include social skills training and the community reinforcement approach. Two recent multisite evaluations, not included in previous reviews, suggest that 12-step treatment can be as effective as cognitive behavioral treatment. With regard to patient-treatment matching, interpersonally oriented treatment appears more effective for patients who are functioning better, whereas cognitive behavioral approaches seem to work better for more impaired patients. However, the evidence on matching is mixed, and some study findings may be attributed to multiple tests for interaction effects. Therapist characteristics may have a stronger impact on treatment outcome than type of treatment. In general, patients of therapists who are more interpersonally skilled, less confrontational, and/or more empathic experience better outcomes, although therapist characteristics may have different effects, depending on the treatment orientation. On the issue of duration and amount of treatment, an effective strategy for many patients may be to provide lower intensity treatment for a longer duration, that is, treatment sessions spread at a lower rate over a longer period. With respect to treatment setting, there is little or no difference in the outcome between inpatient and outpatient treatment for patients who are clinically eligible for treatment in either setting. Patients who are more severely impaired and/or less socially stable may experience better outcomes following treatment in inpatient or residential settings.

Grant et al. (1996) found in 1992 that 7.4% of the U.S. population 18 and older met *DSM-IV* criteria for alcohol abuse or dependence in the prior year; over 18% had met diagnostic criteria at some point in their lives. Another substantial segment of the population has less severe forms of alcohol use disorders, that is, heavy drinking associated with adverse effects on health, work, social relationships, or psychological state. The heavy toll exacted by alcohol use disorders has prompted an increase in the availability of treatment services. Weisner, Greenfield, and Room (1995) reported that the number of persons with alcohol use disorders using treatment services on a given day in the United States rose from 293,000 to 563,000 during the 1980s.

Over 300 comparative alcohol treatment trials (Miller et al., 1998) have been undertaken to evaluate the effects of different forms of treatment for alcohol use disorders. Several reviews of this research literature have been published in recent years (e.g., Finney & Monahan, 1996; Holder et al., 1991; Miller et al., 1995, 1998). Almost all of the prior studies have assumed that the outcome of treatment is a function of patients' characteristics at intake, especially the severity and chronicity of alcohol abuse and other aspects of psychosocial functioning (for an overview, see Institute of Medicine, 1989), and the treatment itself. From a broader perspective, however, treatment outcome is also influenced by life context factors prior to intake and those that occur during the treatment and posttreatment intervals (Moos, Finney, & Cronkite, 1990). We consider the relevant research evidence here in terms of the modality of treatment, therapists' characteristics, the duration and amount of treatment, and the setting of treatment. We conclude that the most effective treatments are those that help patients shape and adapt to their life circumstances.

EFFECTIVENESS OF PSYCHOSOCIAL TREATMENT

In this section, we discuss the effectiveness of psychosocial treatment modalities that have been considered in each of four reviews published in the 1990s. We also review evidence on matching patients with psychosocial treatment modalities.

Effectiveness of Treatment Modalities

Table 6.1 provides the rankings for 15 psychosocial modalities that had three or more studies addressing their effectiveness in each of the reviews by Holder et al. (1991), Miller et al. (1995), Finney and Monahan (1996), and Miller et al. (1998). Also included in Table 6.1 is the estimated cost of each modality provided by Holder et al. (1991), adjusted to 1995 dollars. There is no relationship between cost and Finney and Monahan's (1996) or Miller et al.'s (1995, 1998) modality effectiveness rankings. The Holder et al. (1991) rankings suggest that less effective modalities are more costly, although the correlation ($r = -.46$) is not statistically significant at the .05 level (see all four reviews for additional data on the relationship between cost and broader arrays of treatment modalities).

There is variation in the rankings of some modalities across the reviews. For the most part, however, the modalities that have high effectiveness rankings across these reviews fall into the general category of cognitive behavioral interventions, which focus primarily on enhancing patients' skills in coping with everyday life circumstances (including relapse-inducing situations) and on improving the match between patients' abilities and environmental demands. The relevant studies typically met the criteria for either a Type 1 study (e.g., random assignment to treatment conditions, state-of-the-art diagnostic procedures, adequate statistical power, appropriate statistical analyses) or, more frequently, Type 2 studies (those that were missing one or more of the criteria of a Type 1 study, but not of poor methodological quality overall). Two modalities that were consistently found to be effective (that is, to be superior to at least one control or, more commonly, alternative treatment condition against which they were compared on at least one drinking-related outcome variable at one or more follow-up points) are social skills training and the community reinforcement approach.

Social skills training focuses on developing assertion and communication skills. After an initial assessment to identify skill deficits, patients learn how to initiate social interactions, express their thoughts and feelings, respond appropriately to criticism from others, and so on. Treatment is usually in a group format, so that patients can role-play, receive feedback, and model the behavior of others. There is some evidence (Smith & McCrady, 1991) that patients with neuropsychological impairment may benefit less from skills training because of their greater difficulty in learning and recalling skills.

The community reinforcement approach (CRA) has been somewhat of a moving target. It initially consisted of interventions to assist with family, job-related, and legal problems, as well as a club where the former patients could go to enjoy social activities without alcohol being present. In a later version, the social club was dropped, and a buddy system, mailed daily reports to identify problems that might lead to relapse, group counseling (as opposed to previously used individual counseling), and a component to encourage patients to take Antabuse at a specific time and place and in the presence of another person were added to CRA. Still later, in an outpatient sample, the time devoted to CRA was reduced, and the buddy system and the early-warning component were dropped. Despite this variation, CRA has retained a core, broad-spectrum focus on patients' drinking behavior and their family- and job-related problems. Four of the original studies that supported the effectiveness of CRA were conducted by the same research

TABLE 6.1 Rankings by Effectiveness Indices of 15 Psychosocial Treatment Modalities Having Three or More Studies in Holder et al. (1991), Miller et al. (1995), Finney and Monahan (1996), and Miller et al. (1998)

Modality	*Holder et al. (1991)*	*Miller et al. (1995)*	*Finney and Monahan (1996)*	*Miller et al. (1998)*	*Cost*[a] *(1995 Dollars)*
Social skills training	1	1	2	2	362
Self-control training	2	8	10	6	141
Brief motivational counseling	3	2	7	1	62
Marital therapy, behavioral	4	7	3	5	688
Community reinforcement	5.5	3	1	3	660
Stress management training	5.5	12	5	11	161
Aversion, covert sensitization	7	6	8.5	8	440
Marital therapy, other	8	9	4	10	688
Cognitive therapy	9.5	5	11	7	433
Hypnosis	9.5	11	15	12	738
Aversion, electric shock	11	10	8.5	9	410
Aversion, nausea	12	4	6	4	1380
Confrontational interventions	13	13	13	12	375
Educational lectures/films	14	15	12	15	135
General counseling	15	14	14	14	738

Source: [a]The cost data are drawn from Miller et al. (1995), based on data collected by Holder et al. (1991), and were adjusted from 1987 to 1995 dollars by use of a Consumer Price Index weighting factor.

group, but more recent studies by other investigators have supported the efficacy of CRA (Abbot et al., 1998; Smith et al., 1998).

With respect to patient-CRA matching, unmarried patients were found in one study (Azrin et al., 1982) to benefit more from broad-spectrum CRA treatment, perhaps because it provided an essential source of support for these individuals with fewer social resources. For married patients, most of whom had some family support, the Antabuse assurance component alone was as effective as more intensive CRA treatment.

Behavioral marital therapy (BMT; O'Farrell et al., 1993, 1998) is another psychosocial treatment approach that consistently has been shown to be effective (see Table 6.1). BMT begins with a thorough assessment of the alcoholic patient's drinking behavior and of the marital relationship. Interventions to address drinking include behavioral contracts and Antabuse contracts. Marital interventions focus on improving the relationship and resolving marital conflicts and problems, using such procedures as increasing caring behaviors, planning joint recreational activities, enhancing communication skills, and developing behavioral change agreements. Beyond the obvious condition of being in a relatively stable relationship, research has not addressed which types of patients benefit differentially from BMT versus other treatment modalities.

Other treatments with evidence of effectiveness in some of the reviews are motivational counseling (see a later section on brief interventions), behavioral contracting, stress management training, relapse prevention training, and aversion conditioning. Again, most of these treatments tend to focus on enhancing patients' real-life coping skills and/or altering reinforcement contingencies in their natural environments.

A noteworthy feature of Table 6.1 is the low effectiveness rankings of many of the prevalent treatment approaches in the United States—educational films, confrontational interventions, and general alcoholism counseling—a pattern that has been highlighted previously in reviews by Miller and his colleagues (e.g., Miller et al., 1995). However, it is difficult to think of education as a complete treatment in itself, rather than a component of a multimodal approach. Confrontational interventions consistently fare poorly, perhaps because many individuals react negatively to pervasive criticism. General alcoholism counseling has little research support, but counseling sessions have often served as "control" conditions and may have been poorly implemented. In addition, these treatments may not focus as explicitly or intensively on helping patients cope with their life circumstances outside the treatment situation.

Table 6.1 also does not include the 12-step approach of Alcoholics Anonymous (AA). Although there is correlational evidence that links greater involvement in AA with more positive outcomes (for a review, see Emrick et al., 1993), AA was not found to be more effective than alternatives in the one or two studies covered in each of the reviews included in Table 6.1. In each trial, AA attendance was compulsory rather than voluntary.

Two recent studies, not included in the reviews summarized in Table 6.1, provide support for the efficacy and effectiveness of 12-step treatment approaches. One is Project MATCH (Project MATCH Research Group, 1997a), a randomized, multisite trial that examined the relative efficacy of a 12-step facilitation (TSF) treatment, along with that of cognitive behavioral treatment (CBT) and motivational enhancement therapy (MET). Over 900 patients received one of these three treatments as outpatient aftercare following inpatient or day hospital treatment; the other arm of the study focused on over 700 individuals who had presented at outpatient clinics or had been recruited through advertisements. No overall main effect of treatment conditions was found in either arm on two primary drinking-related outcome variables over a 12-month follow-up period (Project MATCH Research Group, 1997a). However, TSF patients were functioning somewhat better with respect to several secondary outcome variables.

A naturalistic, multisite evaluation focused on over 3,000 Department of Veterans Affairs inpatients who received traditional 12-step, cognitive behavioral, or mixed 12-step and cognitive behavioral treatment under "normal" conditions of treatment delivery. At a 1-year follow-up, there were no differences among the three groups on 9 of 11 outcome criteria (Ouimette et al., 1997). Patients in 12-step programs were significantly more likely than cognitive behavioral patients to abstain from alcohol and other drugs in the 3 months prior to follow-up, and mixed-program patients were more likely to be unemployed than patients in the other two groups. Because of the prior empirical support for cognitive behavioral treatment, the fact that 12-step patients fared as well as or better than those receiving cognitive behavioral treatment in two large-scale evaluations is important new evidence supporting the efficacy/effectiveness of 12-step approaches.

Matching Patients to Effective Treatment Modalities

Mattson and her colleagues (1994) reviewed findings with respect to matching alcohol patients to two general types of treatment: cognitive behavioral approaches that teach coping and communication skills, and interpersonal or relationship-oriented therapies. Overall, they concluded that relationship-oriented treatment is more effective for patients who are functioning better, that is, those with weaker urges to drink, good role-playing skills, and less sociopathy and psychiatric severity. Patients with antisocial personality disorders do better in cognitive behavioral than in relationship-oriented treatment. In general, the more structured cognitive behavioral approaches seem to work better for more impaired patients. Thus, programs to teach coping skills are more effective for patients who have severe psychiatric disorders or who are sociopathic. Communication skills training is particularly effective for patients who have less education, are more anxious, and have stronger urges to drink. More anxious patients fare better when given communication skills training than when given mood management training, perhaps because such patients find the new interpersonal abilities they develop in communication skills training to be especially helpful in initiating and sustaining social interactions that were previously avoided.

In contrast, Project MATCH has yielded relatively little evidence of patient-treatment matching effects. Sixteen a priori hypotheses selected on the basis of prior research evidence and theoretical support were examined with respect to two primary drinking-outcome variables in each of the two arms of the studies (64 contrasts overall). However, only one was statistically significant. Contrary to expectation, there was little difference in outcome by treatment condition among outpatients with greater psychiatric impairment. Among those lower in psychiatric severity, however, TSF patients experienced better outcomes than did patients in CBT and MET (Project MATCH Research Group, 1997a). Analyses of secondary hypotheses indicated that patients high in anger had better outcomes after MET treatment, whereas those lower in anger had better outcomes in CBT and TSF at 1- and 3-year follow-ups (Project

MATCH Research Group, 1998). Patients with more symptoms of alcohol dependence had better 1-year outcomes following TSF; patients low in dependence fared better in CBT (Project MATCH Research Group, 1997b). It was also found that patients who had high support for drinking had better outcomes following TSF than did patients in MET, an effect apparently mediated in part by patients' greater involvement in Alcoholics Anonymous (Longabaugh et al., 1998).

Although some matching findings emerged, especially in the secondary analyses of Project MATCH, the lack of more supportive evidence of patient-treatment interaction effects suggested by prior findings and theory in this methodologically rigorous trial is disconcerting. Moreover, a recent review (Moyer et al., 2001) suggests that more than 20% of the variance in the number of significant patient-treatment interaction effects found in 54 alcohol treatment studies can be accounted for by the number of tests for interaction effects conducted. The extent to which Type I error (rejecting a true null hypothesis) apparently has contributed to previously cited findings regarding patient-treatment matching effects, in combination with the largely negative findings of Project MATCH, raises serious questions about matching patients to alcohol treatment modalities. Overall, patient-treatment matching is a complex process (see Finney & Moos, 1986) and now seems more likely to apply to patients at the extremes of a matching dimension (Moyer et al., 2001). Consequently, although future research may provide better guidance, patient-treatment matching is likely to remain a combination of art and science at the level of clinical practice.

THERAPIST CHARACTERISTICS

Therapist characteristics may have a stronger impact on treatment outcome than the type of treatment applied. Supporting this assertion, Najavits and Weiss (1994) reviewed seven studies finding substantial differences in either patient retention or outcome for different therapists. Therapist differences were not attributable to variation in the characteristics of patients being treated or to therapists' training, treatment orientation, or experience. A few studies have attempted to determine why patient outcomes differ across therapists (for a review, see Najavits & Weiss, 1994); most have focused on therapists' relational style with patients. In general, patients of therapists who are more interpersonally skilled, less confrontational, and/or more empathic experience better outcomes.

Findings from the Project MATCH Research Group (1998) indicate variable effects for 80 therapists, depending on treatment condition and follow-up point. Although therapist education and experience were weakly related to the outcomes of MET and CBT patients, they were associated with negative outcomes for TSF patients. Therapists who were high on need for nurturance and low on need for aggression had patients with better outcomes in the MET condition; therapists low on need for nurturance and high on need for aggression had better patient outcomes in the TSF condition. Women patients with female therapists experienced better outcomes than with male therapists in only the TSF condition.

Not all patients will respond in the same way to the same therapist. McLachlan (1972) found that less directive and structured therapists were more successful with patients who had higher, more abstract levels of conceptual functioning; for patients at lower conceptual levels, more directive therapists had better outcomes. Hser (1995) noted that the nature of patient-therapist interactions may vary with differences in substance abuse program characteristics. For example, Hser hypothesized that therapist characteristics have more impact on patient outcomes in programs that are less highly structured.

DURATION AND AMOUNT OF TREATMENT

In this section, we consider the effectiveness of brief interventions, longer versus shorter stays in inpatient/residential treatment, and aftercare participation.

Brief Interventions

Three reviews of predominantly Type 1 and Type 2 studies have reported considerable support for the effectiveness of brief interventions. Bien et al. (1993) concluded that brief interventions were more effective than no intervention, and, in many cases, as effective as more extensive interventions. Reviewing eight randomized controlled trials comparing brief advice of 1 hour or less with a no-treatment control condition, Wilk et al. (1997) found that patients receiving interventions were about twice as likely to quit or moderate their drinking as were control patients.

Among 43 treatment approaches considered by Miller et al. (1995) and the 60 reviewed by Miller et al. (1998) in their "mesa grande," brief interventions had the highest score on the authors' effectiveness criterion. Project MATCH (Project MATCH Research Group, 1996) also found a planned four sessions of motivational enhancement treatment to be as effective as cognitive-behavioral and 12-step facilitation treatments that were offered over 12 sessions. Several points should be kept in mind when considering this evidence, however.

First, Bien et al. (1993) reported that the average study effect size favoring brief interventions over a control condition was .38. This effect size falls between what Cohen (1988) termed a "small" and a "medium" effect. However, each study's effect size was calculated for a single drinking-related outcome. The usual practice in a meta-analysis is to calculate an average effect size for all drinking-related outcomes or for different classes of drinking-related outcomes at each follow-up point (see Mattick & Jarvis, 1994). Such an approach might have yielded a smaller effect of brief intervention versus no intervention.

Second, Jonson et al. (1995) noted that the brief interventions in some of the studies reviewed by Bien et al. (1993) were considered more extended interventions in other studies. As one example, Monahan and Finney (1996) calculated that the average patient in the single-session "advice" condition in the well-known study by Edwards et al. (1977) actually received more than 30 hours of assessment and treatment during the year when other participants were receiving extended "treatment." Thirty hours typically would be classified as extended treatment.

In Project MATCH (Project MATCH Research Group, 1998), patients, on average, attended proportionately more of the 4 planned sessions of MET than they did of the 12 planned sessions of TSF and CBT. In addition, all patients received 8 hours of assessment prior to treatment and five follow-up contacts at 3-month intervals, all of which may have had therapeutic impact. Overall, the difference in treatment intensity between MET and the other two conditions was not as large as it might at first appear.

In Miller et al.'s (1995, 1998) reviews, a brief intervention that was not significantly inferior to a more extensive intervention was considered "effective"—it received an effectiveness score of +1 (the more extensive comparison intervention received a score of −2). Thus, studies finding no difference in treatment outcome constituted "positive evidence" for the effectiveness of brief interventions. This aspect of Miller et al.'s (1995) box-scoring system combines cost and effectiveness. We believe these two dimensions should remain separate so that their relationship can be determined from independent data.

Effectiveness ratings of brief interventions benefited as well from Miller et al.'s (1995, 1998) assigning modalities that were shown to be superior to a no-treatment control condition a +2, whereas modalities shown to be superior to another modality received only a +1. Studies of brief interventions in medical settings seem more likely to have no-treatment control conditions (e.g., see Wilk et al., 1997) than studies of more intensive/extensive treatment modalities. In this regard, we agree with Chambless and Hollon (1998) that "comparisons with other rival interventions can provide the most stringent tests of all" and "sit atop a hierarchy of increasingly competitive difficulty" (p. 8) with respect to evaluating treatment modalities. Finally, Edwards and Rollnick (1997) found considerable attrition in studies of brief interventions in medical settings. They concluded that results may be based on patients "most susceptible to intervention" and raised questions about the generalizability of findings to what might be expected in routine application of such interventions in primary-care settings (see also Drummond, 1997).

Even with these caveats in mind, the evidence supporting the effectiveness of low-cost brief interventions is impressive. Miller and Sanchez (1993) offered the acronym FRAMES to identify the six "active ingredients" of brief interventions they believe contribute to change in drinking behavior: *F*eedback of personal risk or impairment, emphasis on personal *R*esponsibility for change, clear *A*dvice to change, a *M*enu of alternative change options, therapeutic *E*mpathy, and enhancement of patients' *S*elf-efficacy or optimism. Bien et al. (1993) also note that many brief interventions have included ongoing follow-through contacts with patients. Overall, the FRAMES elements may help patients enhance their motivation to change their drinking behavior; ongoing contacts may supply the support needed by some individuals to maintain such change.

Studies of brief interventions have been conducted most often with clients of low to moderate severity in terms of their alcohol use disorders. Research is needed to examine the effectiveness of brief interventions among patient populations that vary more substantially in severity. At present, however, low to moderate alcohol-severity patients with positive life contexts and without severe skills deficits appear to be the best candidates for brief interventions. There also is some indication that brief interventions may be less effective for persons who have failed to respond to previous advice to reduce their alcohol consumption (Bien et al., 1993).

Length of Stay in Inpatient/ Residential Treatment

Miller and Hester (1986) and Mattick and Jarvis (1994) reviewed several randomized Type 1 and Type 2 trials comparing different lengths of inpatient or residential treatment for alcohol abuse. The consistent finding was no difference in outcome. In contrast, many correlational studies have found longer stays in treatment to be associated with better outcomes. In addition, Monahan and Finney (1996) found that amount of treatment, indexed by treatment in inpatient, residential, and day hospital settings, was related to treatment group abstinence rates across 150 treatment groups included in 100 studies. They speculated that one reason for their finding was the difference in amount of treatment received in the high and low treatment groups. On average, patients in the high-intensity treatment groups received 148 hours of treatment in comparison with 14 hours for patients in the low-intensity groups. A 10 : 1 differential at these levels of treatment intensity has not been represented in many randomized trials of treatment duration.

It may be that beneficial effects of longer stays in inpatient/residential treatment apply only to more impaired patients with fewer social resources. For example, Welte et al. (1981) found no relationship between LOS and outcome for higher social stability patients; in contrast, for patients with lower social stability, those with longer stays had better outcomes. This finding is conceptually comparable to the finding that broad-spectrum CRA treatment may be more effective for unmarried patients.

Outpatient Care Following Inpatient Treatment

Most clinicians recommend additional outpatient treatment to maintain or enhance the therapeutic gains achieved during inpatient/residential or intensive outpatient (e.g., day hospital) treatment. Outpatient treatment attempts to provide the ongoing support needed to continue a course of sobriety or to limit the course of a relapse. Ito and Donovan's (1986) review suggests a link between such "aftercare" participation and positive outcomes. A more recent randomized trial (O'Farrell et al., 1993) also linked aftercare involvement to positive outcomes. With respect to patient-treatment matching, Ito and Donovan (1986) point to evidence that aftercare is particularly beneficial for patients experiencing their first treatment episode. Most of the other evidence on patient-aftercare matching concerns the type of aftercare offered (i.e., the modality).

On a practical level, Ito and Donovan (1986) describe interventions and other nonpatient factors that can increase aftercare participation, such as reminder telephone calls, orientation lectures, and behavior contracts. Also, patients are more likely to attend aftercare when it is offered at the same facility at which they received initial treatment, or at locations closer to their residences.

Summary

These reviews indicate that an effective strategy may be to provide lower intensity treatment for a longer duration, that is, treatment sessions spread at a lower rate over a longer period (see Stout et al., 1999). The effectiveness of this strategy is suggested by the positive findings for outpatient care following inpatient treatment and for brief interventions that incorporate extended contacts with patients. More extended treatment may improve patient outcomes because it provides patients with ongoing support and the potential to discuss and resolve problems prior to the occurrence of a full-blown relapse. In this vein, brief interventions may be most effective for relatively healthy patients who have intact community support systems. Patients who have severe alcohol dependence, concomitant psychiatric disorders, and/or deficient social resources appear to be appropriate candidates for longer (and more intensive) treatment to address their multiple disorders.

TREATMENT SETTING

Choosing the setting of treatment is an important decision for treatment providers and patients, given the extent to which treatment setting drives treatment cost. Prompted by the cost differential between inpatient and outpatient treatment for alcohol abuse, three reviews of the literature on the relative effectiveness of treatment in these two types of settings were published in the 1980s (Annis, 1986; Miller & Hester, 1986; Saxe et al., 1983). After examining controlled studies employing either random assignment to treatment setting or matching inpatients and outpatients on pretreatment variables, each of these reviews concluded there was no evidence for the overall superiority of inpatient over outpatient treatment, although more severely impaired patients might be treated more effectively in inpatient or residential settings.

In a more recent review of 14 relevant studies of the Type 1 and 2 varieties by Finney, Hahn, and Moos (1996), 5 studies found inpatient treatment significantly superior to outpatient treatment on at least one drinking-related outcome variable, and 2 found day hospital treatment superior to inpatient treatment. In all but one instance in which a significant effect emerged, patients in the "superior" setting received more intensive treatment. A subsequent analysis of effect sizes yielded an average positive effect of inpatient treatment across studies that was significant although small at 3-month follow-ups, but no longer significant at 6- and 12-month follow-ups (Finney & Moos, 1996; cf. Mattick & Jarvis, 1994). Likewise, Rychtarik et al. (2000) found no differences over an 18-month follow-up interval on primary outcome variables for patients randomly assigned to inpatient, intensive outpatient, and standard outpatient treatment.

Many of the studies comparing inpatient and outpatient treatment have focused primarily on patients considered eligible for treatment in outpatient settings (Finney & Moos, 1996). Are some patients better matched to inpatient or residential treatment? Aspects of hypothesized patient-treatment setting matches have been captured in the American Society of Addiction Medicine (ASAM) Placement Criteria (Hoffmann et al., 1991). The criteria attempt to match patients to four levels of care: (a) outpatient treatment; (b) intensive outpatient/partial hospitalization treatment; (c) medically monitored intensive inpatient treatment; and (d) medically managed intensive inpatient treatment. Placement decisions are based on a patient's standing on six dimensions: (a) acute intoxication and/or withdrawal potential; (b) biomedical conditions and complications; (c) emotional/behavioral conditions or complications; (d) treatment acceptance/resistance; (e) relapse potential; and (f) recovery environment.

Although the rationales for patient-treatment setting matches are generally compelling, only a few have been subjected to research (see McKay et al., 1997). For example, Rychtarik et al. (2000) found that patients who were high in alcohol involvement did better following inpatient rather than outpatient treatment; outpatients who were low in alcohol involvement fared better than inpatients who were low in alcohol involvement. Similarly, patients with lower cognitive impairment had better outcomes following inpatient than outpatient treatment. On the other hand, Rychtarik and his colleagues (2000) found no support for the hypothesis that persons from environments that promote excessive drinking benefit more from a residential stay that provides a respite from that environment. Other suggestive evidence (see Finney et al., 1996; Miller & Hester, 1986) indicates that patients with psychiatric impairment and those with few social resources may benefit from inpatient or residential treatment, which, of course, is typically followed by outpatient care.

Overall, we believe that the best approaches for treatment providers now are those recommended in previous reviews; these (a) provide outpatient treatment for most individuals with sufficient social resources and no serious medical/psychiatric impairment; (b) use less costly intensive outpatient treatment options for patients who have failed with brief interventions or for whom a more intensive intervention seems warranted, but who do not need the structured environment of a residential setting; and (c) retain residential options for those with few social resources and/or environments that are serious impediments to recovery and use inpatient treatment options for individuals with serious medical/psychiatric conditions.

Although it is very important from a cost perspective, the setting of treatment for alcohol abuse is a distal variable in relation to patients' posttreatment functioning. Other treatment variables, such as the treatment modality, therapists' characteristics, and the amount and duration of treatment, should have a more direct impact on patient posttreatment functioning. Treatment setting can affect duration and amount of treatment (Finney et al., 1996), however, and residential settings may attract some patients (e.g., homeless individuals) who would not present for outpatient treatment.

DISCUSSION

The reviews we have considered point to the effectiveness of cognitive behavioral interventions (see also DeRubeis & Crits-Christoph, 1998). Many of the treatment modalities with evidence of effectiveness (e.g., the community reinforcement approach, behavioral marital therapy, and social skills training) address not only drinking behavior, but also patients' life contexts and their ability to cope with life contexts. This broad-spectrum approach may be necessary to achieve positive outcomes with many patients whose alcohol abuse has produced, and is perpetuated by, deficits in coping skills and problems in multiple life areas. Likewise, 12-step interventions, which have been shown to be as effective as cognitive behavioral treatment in two recent multisite evaluations, provide coping skills (Snow et al., 1994), social support over time in the form of 12-step groups and sponsors, and a general (spiritual) orientation toward life.

Regardless of the treatment applied, therapists are likely to have a significant impact on patients' post-treatment functioning. The few studies of therapist effects suggest that therapists who are interpersonally skilled, empathic, and less confrontational produce better patient outcomes, presumably because they establish better therapeutic alliances with their patients.

On the issue of duration and amount of treatment, an effective strategy for many patients may be to provide lower intensity treatment for a longer duration, that is, treatment sessions spread at a lower rate over a longer period. Although more research is needed, it seems wise at this point to restrict brief interventions to less severe patients. Longer term interventions—in some cases, in an inpatient or residential setting—should be reserved for patients with more severe, treatment-resistent alcohol use disorders, fewer social resources, and more concomitant disorders and problems. Finally, reviews indicate that the setting in which treatment is provided exerts little average effect, but patients who have serious medical/psychiatric comorbidities and those with few social resources may be better treated in inpatient and residential settings, respectively.

Although the research reviews we have summarized are valuable syntheses, they have limitations in terms of informing alcohol treatment practices (Finney, 2000). For the most part, the reviews have been of the box-score type. Box-score reviews use the proportion of relevant studies that have found a particular treatment approach to be significantly better than some alternative as the index of treatment effectiveness. This box-score method of summarizing research has significant problems.

For example, studies with low statistical power (due primarily to small patient samples) may yield nonsignificant effects, even though the magnitude of difference between treatment conditions is comparable to that in studies finding significant effects. Morley et al. (1996) calculated the average statistical power of comparative alcohol treatment studies reported between 1980 and 1992 to be .54. In other words, studies had just over a 50–50 chance of detecting a medium-size difference between treatment conditions at a statistically significant level. Another methodological problem is that many studies examine multiple drinking-related outcome variables assessed at multiple follow-up points for multiple treatment conditions. There typically is no correction in box-score reviews for the number of tests for treatment effects that were conducted in studies (but see Finney & Monahan, 1996).

Box-score reviews of the alcohol treatment research literature also suffer from the fact that most studies are comparisons of alternative treatments, not of treatment and no-treatment control conditions. Consequently, the strength of the competition against which different modalities are pitted varies from study to study. If two highly effective modalities were consistently pitted against only each other in studies, each would be found to be "ineffective" in a box-score review. Finney and Monahan (1996) adjusted their box-score effectiveness ratings for the strength of the competition, but those competition ratings themselves were box-score indices. Overall, these methodological problems make the results of box-score reviews tenuous. Although rankings for the 15 modalities in Table 6.1 in the Miller et al. (1995, 1998) reviews correlated .96, the correlations of rankings were .64 to .74 across the other pairs of reviews, indicating that 59 to 45% of the variance did not overlap.

A desirable alternative to box-score reviews is research syntheses based on effect sizes. Effect sizes index the *magnitude* of treatment effects. Syntheses based on effect sizes are less likely than box-score approaches to be distorted by low power and multiple tests. Thus, different conclusions regarding treatment effectiveness may emerge in box-score and effect-size reviews of the same set of studies.

Although an effect size synthesis is the more desirable approach, only a few reviews have used effect sizes as the index of alcohol treatment effectiveness (e.g., Bien et al., 1993; Finney & Moos, 1996). These reviews have focused on a specific pairs of treatment conditions (e.g., brief versus extended treatment and inpatient versus outpatient treatment). The reason that comprehensive reviews using effect sizes are lacking is that there is no standard comparison group to make differences in effect sizes meaningful across studies of a number of treatment modalities (cf. Mattick & Jarvis, 1993). Less than one third of the comparative alcohol treatment evaluations reported between 1980 and 1992 employed a no- or minimal-treatment comparison group (Floyd et al., 1996). Most studies compare alternative treatment conditions, none of which is common across a large number of studies. Effect sizes for a study comparing Treatment A and Treatment B and another study comparing Treatment C and Treatment D provide no information about the relative effectiveness of, say, Treatment A and Treatment D (see Finney, 2000).

Even with their limitations, box-score reviews of the results of a large number of studies can reveal important general patterns. However, because of the small number of studies of individual treatment modalities, patterns of findings across studies can change over time as more studies are considered. Moreover, quantitative syntheses can obscure important differences across studies, such as variation in treatment implementation (therapist characteristics, duration and amount of treatment, and treatment setting) and in patient characteristics, that should be considered in evaluating overall effectiveness.

Evaluating the effectiveness of alcohol treatment using study-level findings is best carried out, as are primary-treatment evaluations, by using a mixture of quantitative and qualitative analyses (that is, examining individual studies). We have attempted to provide some general guidance to treatment providers regarding effective interventions, as well as to highlight some of the issues that they need to keep in mind as they attempt to make sense of research findings and to gauge how individual studies and research syntheses should be used to shape their clinical practice.

ACKNOWLEDGMENTS Preparation of this revised chapter was supported in part by the Department of Veterans Affairs Mental Health Strategic Health Group and the Quality Enhancement Research Initiative of the Health Services Research and Development Service, and by NIAAA Grants AA08689, AA12718, and AA06699. The views expressed are those of the authors and do not necessarily reflect those of the Department of Veterans Affairs. We thank Courtney Ahrens, Paige Ouimette, Keith Humphreys, and two reviewers for their helpful comments on an earlier version of this chapter.

References

Abbot, P. J., Weller, S. B., Delaney, H. D., & Moore, B. A. (1998). Community reinforcement approach in the treatment of opiate addicts. *American Journal of Drug and Alcohol Abuse, 24*(1), 17–30.

Annis, H. M. (1986). Is inpatient rehabilitation cost effective? Con position. *Advances in Alcohol and Substance Abuse, 5*, 175–190.

Azrin, N. H., Sisson, R. W., Meyers, R., & Godley, M. (1982). Alcoholism treatment by disulfiram and community reinforcement therapy. *Journal of Behavior Therapy and Experimental Psychiatry, 13*, 105–112.

Bien, T. H., Miller, W. R., & Tonigan, J. S. (1993). Brief interventions for alcohol problems: A review. *Addiction, 88*, 315–336.

Chambless, D. L., & Hollon, S. D. (1998). Defining empirically supported therapies. *Journal of Consulting and Clinical Psychology, 66*, 7–18.

Cohen, J. (1988). *Statistical power analysis for the behavioral sciences* (2nd ed.). Hillsdale, NJ: Erlbaum.

DeRubeis, R. J., & Crits-Christoph, P. (1998). Emprically supported individual and group psychological treatments for adult mental disorders. *Journal of Consulting and Clinical Psychology, 66*, 290–303.

Donovan, D. M. (1999). Efficacy and effectiveness: Complementary findings from two multisite trials evaluation outcomes of alcohol treatments differing in theoretical orientations. *Alcoholism: Clinical and Experimental Research, 23*, 564–572.

Drummond, D. C. (1997). Alcohol interventions: Do the best things come in small packages? *Addiction, 92*, 375–279.

Edwards, A. G. K., & Rollnick, S. (1997). Outcome studies of brief alcohol intervention in general practice: The problem of lost subjects. *Addiction, 92*, 1699–1704.

Edwards, G., Orford, J., Egert, S., Guthrie, S., Hawker, A., Hensman, C., Mitcheson, M., Oppenheimer, E., & Taylor, C. (1977). Alcoholism: A controlled trial of "treatment" and "advice." *Journal of Studies on Alcohol, 38,* 1004–1031.

Emrick, C. D., Tonigan, J. S., Montgomery, H., & Little, L. (1993). Alcoholics Anonymous: What is currently known? In B. S. McCrady & W. R. Miller (Eds.), *Research on Alcoholics Anonymous: Opportunities and alternatives* (pp. 41–76). New Brunswick, NJ: Alcohol Research Documentation, Rutgers Center of Alcohol Studies.

Finney, J. W. (2000). Limitations in using existing alcohol treatment trials to develop practice guidelines. *Addiction, 95,* 1491–1500.

Finney, J. W., Hahn, A. C., & Moos, R. H. (1996). The effectiveness of inpatient and outpatient treatment for alcohol abuse: The need to focus on mediators and moderators of setting effects. *Addiction, 91,* 1773–1796.

Finney, J. W., & Monahan, S. C. (1996). The cost effectiveness of treatment for alcoholism: A second approximation. *Journal of Studies on Alcohol, 57,* 229–243.

Finney, J. W., & Moos, R. H. (1986). Matching patients with treatments: Conceptual and methodological issues. *Journal of Studies on Alcohol, 47,* 122–134.

Finney, J. W., & Moos, R. H. (1996). The effectiveness of inpatient and outpatient treatment for alcohol abuse: Effect sizes, research design issues, and explanatory mechanisms (response to commentaries). *Addiction, 91,* 1813–1820.

Floyd, A. S., Monahan, S. C., Finney, J. W., & Morley, J. A. (1996). Alcoholism treatment outcome studies, 1980–1992: The nature of the research. *Addictive Behaviors, 21,* 413–428.

Grant, B. F. (1996). *DSM-IV, DSM-III-R,* and *ICD-10* alcohol and drug abuse/harmful use and dependence, United States, 1992. *Alcoholism: Clinical and Experimental Research, 10,* 1481–1488.

Hoffmann, N. G., Halikas, J. A., Mee-Lee, D., et al. (1991). *Patient placement criteria for the treatment of psychoactive substance use disorders.* Washington, DC: American Society of Addiction Medicine.

Holder, H., Longabaugh, R., Miller, W. R., & Rubonis, A. V. (1991). The cost effectiveness of treatment for alcoholism: A first approximation. *Journal of Studies on Alcohol, 52,* 517–540.

Hser, Y. (1995). Drug treatment counselor practices and effectiveness. *Evaluation Review, 19,* 389–408.

Institute of Medicine. (1989). *Prevention and treatment of alcohol problems: Opportunities for research: Report of a study.* Washington, DC: National Academy Press.

Ito, J., & Donovan, D. M. (1986). Aftercare in alcoholism treatment: A review. In W. R. Miller & N. Heather (Eds.), *Treating addictive behaviors: Processes of change* (pp. 435–452). New York: Plenum Press.

Jonson, H., Hermansson, U., Ronnberg, S., Gyllen-Hammar, C., & Forsberg, L. (1995). Comments on brief intervention of alcohol problems: A review of a review. *Addiction, 90,* 1118–1120.

Longabaugh, R., Wirtz, P. W., Zweben, A., & Stout, R. L. (1998). Network support for drinking, Alcoholics Anonymous and long-term matching effects. *Addiction, 93,* 1313–1333.

Mattick, R. P., & Jarvis, T. J. (1993). *An outline for the management of alcohol problems: Quality assurance in the treatment of drug abuse project.* National Drug and Alcohol Research Centre.

Mattick, R. P., & Jarvis, T. (1994). In-patient setting and long duration for the treatment of alcohol dependence? Out-patient care is as good. *Drug and Alcohol Review, 13,* 127–135.

Mattson, M. E., Allen, J. P., Longabaugh, R., Nickless, C. J., Connors, G. J., & Kadden, R. M. (1994). A chronological review of empirical studies of matching alcoholic clients to treatment. *Journal of Studies on Alcohol, Supplement No. 12,* 16–29.

McKay, J. R., Cacciola, J. S., McLellan, A. T., Alterman, A. I., & Wirtz, P. W. (1997). An initial evaluation of the psychosocial dimensions of the American Society of Addiction Medicine criteria for inpatient versus intensive outpatient substance abuse rehabilitation. *Journal of Studies on Alcohol, 58,* 239–252.

McLachlan, J. F. C. (1972). Benefit from group therapy as a function of patient-therapist match on conceptual level. *Psychotherapy: Theory, Research and Practice, 9,* 317–323.

Miller, W. R., Andrews, N. R., Wilbourne, P., & Bennett, M. E. (1998). A wealth of alternatives: Effective treatments for alcohol problems. In W. R. Miller & N. Heather (Eds.), *Treating addictive behaviors* (2nd ed., pp. 203–216). New York: Plenum Press.

Miller, W. R., Brown, J. M., Simpson, T. L., Handmaker, N. S., Bien, T. H., Luckie, L. F., Montgomery, H. A., Hester, R. K., & Tonigan, J. S. (1995). What works? A methodological analysis of the alcohol treatment outcome literature. In R. K. Hester & W. R. Miller (Eds.), *Handbook of alcoholism treatment approaches: Effective alternatives* (pp. 12–44). Boston, MA: Allyn & Bacon.

Miller, W. R., & Hester, R. K. (1986). Inpatient alcoholism treatment: Who benefits? *American Psychologist, 41,* 794–805.

Miller, W. R., & Sanchez, V. C. (1993). Motivating young adults for treatment and lifestyle change. In G. Howard & P. E. Nathan (Eds.), *Issues in alcohol use and misuse by young adults*. Notre Dame, IN: University of Notre Dame Press.

Monahan, S. C., & Finney, J. W. (1996). Explaining abstinence rates following treatment for alcohol abuse: A quantitative synthesis of patient, research design, and treatment effects. *Addiction, 91*, 787–805.

Moos, R. H., Finney, J. W., & Cronkite, R. C. (1990). *Alcoholism treatment: Context, process, and outcome*. New York: Oxford University Press.

Morley, J. A., Finney, J. W., Monahan, S. C., & Floyd, A. S. (1996). Alcoholism treatment outcome studies, 1980–1992: Methodological characteristics and quality. *Addictive Behaviors, 21*, 429–443.

Moyer, A., Finney, J. W., Elworth, J. T., & Kraemer, H. C. (2001). Can methodological features account for patient-treatment matching findings in the alcohol field? *Journal of Studies on Alcohol, 62*, 62–73.

Najavits, L. M., & Weiss, R. D. (1994). Variations in therapist effectiveness in the treatment of patients with substance use disorders: An empirical review. *Addiction, 89*, 679–688.

O'Farrell, T. J., Choquette, K. A., & Cutter, H. S. G. (1998). Couples relapse prevention sessions after Behavioral Marital Therapy for male alcoholics: Outcomes during the three years after starting treatment. *Journal of Studies on Alcohol, 59*, 357–370.

O'Farrell, T. J., Choquette, K. A., Cutter, H. S. G., Brown, E. D., & McCourt, W. F. (1993). Behavioral Marital Therapy with and without additional couples relapse prevention sessions for alcoholics and their wives. *Journal of Studies on Alcohol, 54*, 652–666.

Ouimette, P. C., Finney, J. W., & Moos, R. H. (1997). Twelve step and cognitive-behavioral treatment for substance abuse: A comparison of treatment effectiveness. *Journal of Consulting and Clinical Psychology, 65*, 230–240.

Project MATCH Research Group. (1997a). Matching alcoholism treatments to client heterogeneity: Project MATCH posttreatment drinking outcomes. *Journal of Studies on Alcohol, 58*, 7–29.

Project MATCH Research Group. (1997b). Project MATCH secondary a priori hypotheses. *Addiction, 92*, 1671–1698.

Project MATCH Research Group. (1998). Therapist effects in three treatments for alcohol problems. *Psychotherapy Research, 8*, 455–474.

Rychtarik, R. G., Connors, G. J., Wirtz, P. W., Whitney, R. B., MiGillicuddy, N. B., & Fitterling, J. M. (2000). Treatment settings for persons with alcoholism: Evidence for matching clients to inpatient versus outpatient care. *Journal of Consulting and Clinical Psychology, 68*, 277–289.

Saxe, L., et al. (1983). *The effectiveness and costs of alcoholism treatment*. Washington, DC: U.S. Office of Technology Assessment.

Smith, D. E., & McCrady, B. S. (1991). Cognitive impairment among alcoholics: Impact on drink refusal skill acquisition and treatment outcome. *Addictive Behaviors, 16*, 265–274.

Smith, J. E., Meyers, R. J., & Delaney, H. D. (1998). The community reinforcement approach with homeless alcohol-dependent individuals. *Journal of Consulting and Clinical Psychology, 66*, 541–548.

Snow, M. G., Prochaska, J. O., & Rossi, J. (1994). Processes of change in Alcoholics Anonymous: Maintenance factors in long-term sobriety. *Journal of Studies on Alcohol, 55*, 362–371.

Stout, R. L., Rubin, A., Zwick, W., Zywiak, W., & Bellino, L. (1999). Optimizing the cost-effectiveness of alcohol treatment: A rationale for extended case monitoring. *Addictive Behaviors, 24*, 17–35.

Weisner, C., Greenfield, T., & Room, R. (1995). Trends in the treatment of alcohol problems in the US general population, 1979 through 1990. *American Journal of Public Health, 85*, 55–60.

Welte, J., Hynes, G., & Sokolow, L. (1981). Effect of length of stay in inpatient alcoholism treatment on outcome. *Journal of Studies on Alcohol, 42*, 483–499.

Wilk, A. I., Jenson, N. M., & Havighurst, T. C. (1997). Meta-analysis of randomized control trials addressing brief interventions in heavy alcohol drinkers. *Journal of General Internal Medicine, 12*, 274–283.

7

Pharmacological Treatments for Schizophrenia

Daniel Bradford
Scott Stroup
Jeffrey Lieberman

Schizophrenia is a chronic mental disorder with a lifetime prevalence rate of approximately 1%. The first antipsychotic drug, chlorpromazine, was introduced in 1954, followed by several similar drugs. With the later introduction of clozapine, risperidone, olanzapine, quetiapine, and ziprasidone, antipsychotic drugs have come to be classified as conventional (chlorpromazine like) or atypical (clozapine like). Both of these broad classes of medications have been demonstrated to safely improve symptoms in both the acute and chronic phases of schizophrenia. The atypical antipsychotics offer hope for enhanced efficacy in the treatment of schizophrenic psychopathology, particularly in reducing negative symptoms, with a reduced burden of extrapyramidal motor dysfunction. Because of the limited efficacy of antipsychotic medication in resolving the full range of schizophrenic psychopathology, adjunctive treatments are often used to reduce morbidity. Concomitant medications such as benzodiazepines, lithium, carbamazepine, valproic acid, antidepressants, glutamate agonists, and dopamine agonists have been used alone and in combination with antipsychotic drugs in order to improve treatment response. In this chapter, we review controlled trials of the pharmacological agents used to treat schizophrenia.

BACKGROUND

Schizophrenia is a chronic mental disorder with a lifetime prevalence rate of approximately 1%. The diagnosis is based on specific symptoms such as delusions, hallucinations, disorganization, and unusual behavior lasting for at least 1 month, in association with significant social and occupational deterioration prior to or subsequent to the psychotic symptoms. Schizophrenic psychopathology falls into two and possibly three symptom clusters: positive symptoms comprising delusions, hallucinations, and formal thought disorder; negative symptoms comprising deficits in emotional and verbal expression and in motivation; and disorganization symptoms reflected in disordered thought processes, bizarre behavior, and inappropriate affect (Liddle et al., 1994). Patients with schizophrenia frequently exhibit affective symptoms during both the psychotic and residual phases of the illness. Increasing attention is now being paid to cognitive symptoms of schizophrenia, which have been shown to relate more strongly to functional outcomes than positive symptom severity (Green, 1996; Harvey et al.; 1998). The cognitive symptoms being studied include learning and secondary memory, motor function, verbal fluency, attention, and executive functioning.

Treatment strategies need to target both the acute psychotic phase of the disorder and debilitating residual symptoms. The illness course and outcome differ among individuals, although complete symptom remission with return to premorbid status is not common. Progressive deterioration characterizes the course of a significant minority of patients, particularly in the early phase of the illness. Therefore, long-term management of schizophrenia requires prophylaxis against symptom exacerbation and relapse.

The first antipsychotic drug, chlorpromazine, was introduced in 1954, followed by several similar drugs; with the later introduction of clozapine, risperidone, olanzapine, quetiapine, and ziprasidone, antipsychotic drugs have come to be classified as conventional (chlorpromazine-like) or atypical (clozapine-like). Although there is no consensus definition of atypical antipsychotic drugs, they are generally thought to produce fewer extrapyramidal side effects (EPS) and tardive dyskinesia (TD) than conventional drugs, to have some greater efficacy (in refractory patients, against negative symptoms), and to induce only limited prolactin elevation.

Antipsychotic medications have been clearly demonstrated to be effective and safe for both the acute and chronic phases of schizophrenia. The efficacy of conventional antipsychotic drugs and their propensity to produce both acute and chronic side effects have been thoroughly studied. The newer atypical antipsychotic drugs are eagerly sought by clinicians because these agents hold out the promise of increased therapeutic efficacy with significantly less risk of extrapyramidal and neurocognitive adverse effects (Kinon & Lieberman, 1996). A landmark study by Kane et al. (1988), which compared clozapine to the chlorpromazine, demonstrated the superior efficacy of clozapine in reducing symptoms in 30% of treatment-resistant patients. More recent studies of clozapine in treatment-refractory schizophrenia have generally confirmed this finding and provided support for use of the drug in selected populations. Recent meta-analyses reported advantages of olanzapine (Duggan et al., 2001) for negative symptoms when compared to typical antipsychotics, but not for risperidone (Kennedy et al., 2001).

Concomitant medications such as benzodiazepines, lithium, carbamazepine, valproic acid, and dopamine agonists have been used alone and in combination with antipsychotic drugs in order to improve treatment response, although clear demonstration of the effectiveness of these strategies is lacking. In addition, antidepressants have been extensively used to treat depressive symptoms associated with schizophrenia.

ACUTE TREATMENT EFFECTS

Typical Antipsychotics

The introduction of the prototypical conventional antipsychotic drug chlorpromazine in the 1950s, with the subsequent development of other neuroleptic agents with similar pharmacological activity, produced a revolution in the treatment of schizophrenia. These drugs are credited with providing the first effective medical management of schizophrenia, and they constitute one of the great medical advances of the twentieth century. Early doubts about the efficacy of these compounds led to the design of rigorous clinical trials, such as the placebo-controlled double-blind study with thoughtful subject inclusion and exclusion criteria, random treatment assignment, and the use of standardized rating instruments, to prove the value of the drugs. Over 100 placebo-controlled trials have conclusively demonstrated the effectiveness of antipsychotic drugs (Davis et al., 1989). A representative sample of methodologically rigorous acute treatment trials that demonstrate the efficacy of conventional antipsychotic drugs commonly used and currently available in the United States, compared with placebo, is given in Table 7.1. Placebo-controlled studies in which antipsychotic efficacy could not be demonstrated have generally been restricted to poorly designed studies that involved doses of chlorpromazine less than 300 mg daily (Klein & Davis, 1969).

In general, the studies have found that approximately 60% of subjects treated with antipsychotic drugs, compared to 20% of placebo-treated subjects, demonstrated a nearly complete resolution of acute positive symptoms within a 6-week trial. Only 8% of medication-treated subjects showed no improvement or worsening, whereas nearly half of placebo-treated subjects did not improve or worsened (NIMH-PSC Collaborative Study Group, 1964). All symptoms associated with schizophrenia improved on antipsychotic drugs, although positive symptoms seemed to respond to a greater degree and more consistently than negative symptoms.

Unfortunately, although symptomatic improvement is clinically important and partly responsible for the deinstitutionalization of the treatment of schizophrenia, patient functioning and social reintegration have not consistently improved with the use of typical an-

TABLE 7.1 Representative Studies of Definitive Antipsychotic Drug Efficacy (vs. Placebo or Active Placebo)

Drug	Number of Studies	Reference
Typical APDs		
Chlorpromazine	8	Clark et al. (1968)
		Hollister et al. (1960)
		Casey et al. (1960a, 1960b)
		Kurland et al. (1961)
		NIMH-PSC (1964)
		Caseye et al. (1960)
		Schiele et al. (1961)
		Adelson & Epstein (1962)
Fluphenazine	2	NIMH-PSC (1964)
Haloperidol	9	Vestre et al. (1962)
		Garry & Leonard (1962)
		Azima et al. (1960)
		Samuels et al. (1961)
		Chouinard et al. (1993)
		Brandrup & Kristjansen (1961)
		Beasley et al. (1996)
		Marder & Meibach (1994)
		Okasha & Twefik (1964)
		Reese & Davies (1965)
Loxapine	3	Simpson (1970)
		Van der Velde & Kiltie (1975)
		Clark et al. (1972)
Mesoridazine	2	McIndoo (1971)
		Ritter & Tatum (1972)
Molindone	2	Gallant & Bishop (1968)
		Clark et al. (1970)
Perphenazine	3	Kurland et al. (1961)
		Adelson & Epstein (1962)
Trifluoperazine	3	Casey et al. (1960a, 1960b)
		Hollister et al. (1960)
		Adelson & Epstein (1962)
Thiothixene	4	Wolpert et al. (1968)
		Huang et al. (1987)
		Yilmaz (1971)
		Gallant et al. (1966)
Thioridazine	2	NIMH-PSC (1964)
		Schiele et al. (1961)
Atypical APDs		
Clozapine	2	Shopsin et al. (1979)
		Pickar et al. (1992)
Risperidone	2	Marder & Meibach (1994)
		Chouinard et al. (1993)
Olanzapine	2	Beasley et al. (1996a)
		Beasley et al (1996b)
Quetiapine	2	Borison et al. (1996)
		Small et al. (1997)
Ziprasidone	2	Keck et al. (1998)
		Daniel et al. (1999)

tipsychotic drugs. This disappointing observation was made soon after the introduction of these drugs into clinical practice (Schooler et al., 1967).

Further, despite the dozens of typical antipsychotic drugs that have become available to clinicians in the United States since 1954, these drugs share much the same mechanism of action and do not appear to differ in efficacy. Table 7.2 lists the efficacy demonstrated in controlled clinical trials of a representative sample of antipsychotic drugs compared to the reference drug chlorpromazine or haloperidol.

During the treatment of an acute episode of schizophrenia, the therapeutic effect of antipsychotic drugs usually is manifest within the first 1 to 3 weeks; most gains are noted within 6 to 8 weeks (Davis et al., 1989). Some patients, however, including first-episode patients (Lieberman, 1993), may require several months to achieve a full clinical response and symptom remission. When patients fail to respond to a standard course of treatment, clinicians generally employ maneuvers such as increasing the dose, switching to another antipsychotic drug, or maintaining the initial treatment for an extended trial. Little evidence from controlled clinical trials supports the efficacy of any of these strategies (Kinon et al., 1993; Levinson et al., 1990; Rifkin et al., 1991; Van Putten et al., 1990; Volavka et al., 1992), although an individual patient may show a better response to one particular drug than to another (Gardos, 1974). In addition, there are few data to support the usefulness of doses beyond the range of 400–1,000 mg daily of chlorpromazine or the equivalent dose of other antipsychotics; extremely large doses of 2,000 mg of chlorpromazine daily or its equivalent are not generally associated with greater efficacy (Bjorndal et al., 1980; Ericksen et al., 1978; McCreadie & MacDonald, 1977; Neborsky et al., 1981; Quitkin et al., 1975) and can lead to a greater incidence of side effects. The practice of administering large parenteral doses of high-potency antipsychotics within a 24-hour period ("rapid neuroleptization") has not demonstrated any gains in efficacy over standard treatment and has largely been discontinued as a therapeutic strategy.

Atypical Antipsychotics

The atypical antipsychotics offer hope for enhanced efficacy in the treatment of schizophrenic psychopathology, particularly in reducing negative symp-

TABLE 7.2 Representative Studies of Relative Antipsychotic Drug Efficacy (vs. Chlorpromazine and/or Haloperidol)

	Number of Studies				
Drug	*Superior to CPZ*	*Equal to CPZ*	*Superior to HAL*	*Equal to HAL*	*Reference*
Typical APDs					
Fluphenazine		3			Cole et al. (1964)
					NIMH-PSC (1964)
					Laskey et al. (1962)
					Hanlon et al. (1965)
Haloperidol	2				Pratt et al. (1964)
					Fox et al. (1964)
		1			Serafetinides et al. (1972)
Loxapine	1				Tuason et al. (1984)
		1			Rifkin et al. (1984)
				2	Fruensgaard et al. (1977)
					Tuason (1986)
Mesoridazine		1			Freeman et al. (1969)
Molindone				2	Binder et al. (1981)
					Escobar et al. (1985)
Perphenazine		4			Adelson & Epstein (1962)
					Hanlon et al. (1965)
					Kurland et al. (1961)
					Casey et al. (1960)
Trifluoperazine		4			Adelson & Epstein (1962)
					Schiele et al. (1961)
					Hanlon et al. (1965)
					Hollister et al. (1960)
Thiothixene		1			Rickels et al. (1978)
Thioridazine		3			Schiele et al. (1961)
					Cole et al. (1964)
					NIMH-PSC (1964)
					Laskey et al. (1962)
Atypical APDs					
Clozapine		1			Gelenberg & Doller (1979)
	4				Leon (1979)
					Shopsin et al. (1979)
					Kane et al. (1988)
					Claghorn et al. (1987)
				1	Klieser et al. (1994)
Risperidone				4	Peuskens (1995)
					Ceskova & Svestka (1993)
					Min et al. (1993)
					Borison et al. (1992)
			4		Chouinard et al. (1993)
					Marder & Meibach (1994)
					Claus et al. (1992)
					Muller-Spahn (1992)
Olanzapine			2		Beasley et al. (1996b)
					Tollefson et al. (1997)
				1	Beasley et al. (1997a)
Quetiapine		1			Peuskens & Link (1997)
				2	Arvanitis et al. (1997)
					Copolov et al. (2000)
Ziprasidone				1	Goff et al. (1998)

toms, with a reduced burden of extrapyramidal motor dysfunction. The number of double-blind studies comparing acute treatment effects of atypical antipsychotics with the effects of their typical counterparts and the studies comparing effects in treatment-refractory patients have grown dramatically in the past few years. While advantages for the atypical drugs, particularly clozapine, have been shown in many studies, it remains unclear whether the newer atypical drugs have true advantages in effectiveness and side effect profiles over typical drugs prescribed at appropriate doses. A recent meta-analysis (Geddes et al., 2000) showed a modest advantage for atypical antipsychotics in efficacy and extrapyramidal symptoms over typical antipsychotics. However, in trials where the mean dose of the drug compared to the atypical antipsychotic drug was less than the equivalent of 12 mg of haloperidol, increased efficacy for atypical drugs was not present. The advantage of atypical drugs in regard to extrapyramidal symptoms remained, but no difference in overall tolerability was demonstrated between typical and atypical antipsychotic drugs. Direct comparisons of different atypical antipsychotics are very few, so it is not entirely clear whether advantages in efficacy exist for individual drugs, even when the comparator drug is dosed appropriately.

Atypical agents currently approved by the FDA include clozapine, risperidone, olanzapine, quetiapine, and ziprasidone. The evidence supporting the use of each is briefly reviewed below.

Baldessarini and Frankenburg (1991) reviewed 14 double-blind studies from 1971 through 1988 that compared the efficacy of clozapine to a conventional neuroleptic in the treatment of schizophrenic psychopathology. Overall, these authors reported that 9% more clozapine-treated subjects improved, and mean ratings were 13% better in these clozapine patients than in those treated with a conventional antipsychotic, though the differences were not statistically significant. Rates of EPS, however, were markedly lower in clozapine-treated patients.

Unfortunately, an incidence rate of 1% for clozapine-induced agranulocytosis was reported (Alvir et al., 1993), and this has resulted in the limitation of clozapine use to refractory patients. In addition to the agranulocytosis, frequent side effects of clozapine include sedation, weight gain, hypotension, tachycardia, and a dose-dependent risk of seizures. A particularly important study, conducted by Kane et al. (1988), entered 268 patients with treatment-resistant schizophrenia into a double-blind comparison of clozapine and chlorpromazine. Treatment resistance was defined as having failed to respond to at least three prior antipsychotics, without any period of good functioning in the past 5 years, then not responding to a single-blind 6-week haloperidol lead-in trial. At 6 weeks, 30% of the clozapine-treated group but only 4% of the chlorpromazine-treated group met the a priori response criteria of a reduction greater than 20% from baseline in the Brief Psychiatric Rating Scale (BPRS) total score plus either a posttreatment clinical global impression (CGI) score of 3 (mild) or less, or a posttreatment BPRS total score of 35 or lower.

Since the initial Kane et al. study, five more double-blind comparisons of clozapine and a typical antipsychotic have been conducted (Buchanan et al., 1998; Hong et al., 1997; Kane et al., in press; Kumra et al., 1996; Rosenheck et al., 1997), along with one open-label study with random treatment assignment (Essock et al., 1996). The Kumra et al. study was a double-blind comparison of clozapine and haloperidol in treatment-refractory childhood schizophrenia. Two of the studies (Buchanan et al., 1998; Kane et al., in press) included patients who were said to be partially responsive to typical antipsychotics. Four of the six studies found a significant difference favoring clozapine. A recent meta-analysis of the seven trials comparing clozapine to a typical antipsychotic drug in treatment-refractory schizophrenia (Chakos et al., 2001) showed an advantage for clozapine with regard to total psychopathology, categorical response to treatment (the number of patients who met an arbitrary cut-off point for response), extrapyramidal symptoms, tardive dyskinesia, and study completion rates. Of note, however, is the fact that the two studies that showed the most modest advantages for clozapine (Essock et al., 1996; Rosenheck et al., 1997) were the two longest trials, with durations of 2 years and 1 year, respectively.

Nevertheless, the efficacy of clozapine among refractory patients, with no acute EPS and no risk for tardive dyskinesia, represents a landmark achievement in psychopharmacology. Furthermore, the success of clozapine has provided the impetus for an enormous research effort that has resulted in the development of several other atypical antipsychotic drugs.

Risperidone

Several double-blind studies have compared the efficacy of risperidone to that of a conventional antipsychotic; some of these studies were placebo-controlled. Muller-Spahn et al. (1992) in an international multicenter 8-week study found that risperidone at doses of 4, 8, or 12 mg was superior to haloperidol in symptom reduction, while at 16 mg it was equally efficacious.

Claus et al. (1992) in a study of 44 chronic schizophrenia patients treated with risperidone (mean dose = 2 mg) or haloperidol (mean dose = 10 mg) in a 12-week parallel group trial found a significantly greater improvement in overall psychopathology and significantly reduced need for anti-Parkinsonian medication in the risperidone-treated group.

Borison et al. (1992) conducted a randomized, parallel-group, double-blind trial of risperidone versus haloperidol and placebo in 36 patients with acute exacerbations of schizophrenia. In this study, symptom reduction occurred more rapidly with risperidone than with haloperidol. Risperidone was significantly superior to placebo, with a trend toward superiority to haloperidol. Risperidone also produced significantly fewer extrapyramidal side effects than did haloperidol.

Ceskova and Svestka (1993), however, in an 8-week double-blind comparison of risperidone (2 to 20 mg) and haloperidol (2 to 20 mg) in 62 patients with schizophrenia or schizoaffective disorder, found no differences between groups in total BPRS scores.

Chouinard et al. (1993), in a multicenter placebo-controlled study of 135 patients with chronic schizophrenia patients treated with either 2, 6, 10, or 16 mg of risperidone, 20 mg of haloperidol, or placebo, found that patients treated with risperidone at 6 mg had better scores on the total PANSS and the PANSS general psychopathology subscale than patients treated with haloperidol. Haloperidol treatment resulted in significantly more EPS than doses of 2, 6, and 16 mg of risperidone; however, 10 mg of risperidone resulted in equal amounts of EPS.

In a multicenter study of 107 patients with chronic schizophrenia patients treated with risperidone (5 to 15 mg) or perphenazine (16 to 48 mg) for 8 weeks for an acute exacerbation, Hoyberg et al. (1993) found no significant differences in total PANSS scores at end point. However, the number of patients with predominantly negative symptoms who showed a 20% drop in total PANSS scores was significantly greater in the risperidone-treated group. Side effect vulnerability was approximately equal between the groups.

Min et al. (1993) found that mean changes from baseline on the total PANSS score, the total BPRS score, and the CGI score were similar in groups treated with risperidone and those treated with haloperidol. Risperidone caused fewer extrapyramidal symptoms than haloperidol.

Marder and Meibach (1994), in a multicenter study of 388 patients with schizophrenia patients treated with one of four doses of risperidone (2, 6, 10, or 16 mg), 20 mg of haloperidol, or placebo, reported significantly greater overall clinical improvement from 6, 10, and 16 mg of risperidone than from placebo and significantly greater improvements from 6 and 16 mg of risperidone than from haloperidol, as assessed by the PANSS. Both negative and positive symptom scores were reduced significantly more with 6 and 16 mg of risperidone than with placebo, while only positive symptoms were reduced significantly more by haloperidol than by placebo. There were no significant differences found in the reduction of negative symptoms when any of the four doses of risperidone were directly compared to haloperidol. Both 16 mg of risperidone and 20 mg of haloperidol resulted in significant increases in Parkinsonian side effects compared to placebo, though not compared to other risperidone doses.

Peuskens (1995), in a multicenter parallel-group, double-blind 8-week study of 1,362 patients with schizophrenia treated with either 1, 4, 8, 12, or 16 mg of risperidone or 10 mg of haloperidol, found no significant advantage on the PANSS and in CGI assessments for any dose of risperidone compared to haloperidol. However, 1, 4, 8, and 12 mg of risperidone produced significantly lower incidence rates of EPS than haloperidol.

Blin et al. (1996) reported on 62 patients hospitalized for acute exacerbations of schizophrenia who were randomly assigned to receive risperidone (mean dose, 7.4 mg/day), haloperidol (7.6 mg/day), or methotrimeprazine (100 mg/day) for 4 weeks. The improvements in total PANSS and Clinical Global Impression Scale severity scores from baseline to the end of the study were significantly greater in the risperidone patients than in the haloperidol or methotrimeprazine groups.

Trials that compared multiple doses of risperidone to one dose of haloperidol have been criticized as potentially biasing the results toward a more favorable response from risperidone. Nevertheless, the evidence suggests that risperidone is at least equal to conventional antipsychotics in the treatment of schizophrenic psychopathology, with a lower incidence rate of EPS at lower dose ranges.

The efficacy of risperidone compared to conventional antipsychotics in the treatment of negative symptoms or in treatment refractory populations has been studied to a lesser degree. Two double-blind studies have compared risperidone to typical antipsychotics in treatment-refractory populations. Wirshing et al. (1999), in an 8-week double-blind comparison of risperidone and haloperidol, found clinical superiority of risperidone after 4 weeks of treatment, but this difference disappeared after 4 more weeks of treatment. In a 14-week study comparing clozapine, risperidone, olanzapine, and haloperidol for a rigorously defined treatment refractory sample of 157 inpatients, Volavka et al. (in press) showed risperidone to be superior to haloperidol for negative symptoms.

A recent meta-analysis by Kennedy et al. (2001) of 12 short-term and 2 long-term trials of risperidone versus a typical antipsychotic in the treatment of schizophrenia failed to show any advantage for risperidone in reducing positive or negative symptoms. The study did show an advantage for risperidone for extrapyramidal symptoms, however.

Convincing evidence that risperidone is more effective than typical antipsychotics for a wide range of symptoms in schizophrenia does not currently exist. Nevertheless, risperidone is an effective medication with a side effect profile favorable to that of typical antipsychotics.

Olanzapine

The FDA approved olanzapine in 1996 for the treatment of schizophrenia. Beasley et al. (1996) reported on the efficacy of olanzapine in a 6-week study that compared three dose ranges of olanzapine (5 ± 2.5, 10 ± 2.5, 15 ± 2.5 mg/day) to one dose level of haloperidol (15 ± 5 mg/day) and to placebo in 335 schizophrenia patients. The middle and higher doses of olanzapine as well as haloperidol were significantly superior to placebo in improving overall symptomatology and positive symptoms, as assessed by the BPRS. Only the low and high doses of olanzapine were superior to placebo in improving negative symptoms, as assessed by the SANS, while the higher dose of olanzapine was found superior to haloperidol. Despite the lack of statistically significant differences between olanzapine- and haloperidol-treated patients on BPRS total and CGI scores at the end of the study, there was a significant difference between the high-dose olanzapine group and the haloperidol group in the number of patients who demonstrated at least an 80% improvement from baseline. In addition, no acute dystonia was observed with olanzapine, and at the high dose of olanzapine, rates of Parkinsonism and akathisia were approximately one third and one half less, respectively, than those observed in the haloperidol group.

Beasley et al. (1997) in a 6-week trial involving 431 patients with schizophrenia found no significant differences between olanzapine and haloperidol with regard to reduction in positive symptoms, negative symptoms, or total psychopathology. Patients treated with olanzapine, however, had acute extrapyramidal symptoms or prolactin elevations less often than those treated with haloperidol.

Tollefson at al. (1997), in a study of 1,996 patients with schizophrenia or schizoaffective disorder, found olanzapine to be superior to haloperidol for total BPRS score and also showed statistically significant advantages for olanzapine in change in negative symptoms, extrapyramidal symptom profile, effect on prolactin levels, and categorical response rate. Following these conflicting reports, Duggan et al. (2001) reviewed the data from nine published and unpublished studies of olanzapine versus a typical antipsychotic. They found advantages for olanzapine in total psychopathology in short- or medium-term studies, for negative symptoms in short- and long-term studies, for positive symptoms in short-term studies, and for depression and extrapyramidal symptoms.

Three major studies have compared olanzapine to typical antipsychotics in treatment-refractory patients. Conley et al. (1998) reported a study very similar in design to the original Kane et al. (1988) study, which established clozapine as a treatment for refractory schizophrenia. In this 6-week trial of 84 patients randomized to either olanzapine or chlorpromazine, no differences were found between the two drugs in effects on positive or negative symptoms or total psychopathology. Breier et al. (1999) conducted a prospective, double-blind, 6-week study of 526 patients who were found to be partially responsive to typical antipsychotics. In this study, olanzapine was superior to haloperidol in reducing negative and depressive symptoms, and it produced less akathisia and fewer extrapyramidal symptoms in both last observation carried forward and completer analyses, as well as greater improvements in total symptoms and positive symptoms among completers. More patients treated with olanzapine completed the study, and fewer olanzapine-treated patients left the study due to lack of efficacy. Finally, in the Volavka et al. (in press) study mentioned above, olanzapine was found to be superior to haloperidol for total PANSS score, the study's principal measure of efficacy.

On the whole, the available evidence suggests that olanzapine may have some advantages over typical antipsychotics both in the acute treatment of psychosis and in the treatment of patients selected for prior treatment resistance to typical antipsychotics.

Sertindole

Sertindole was initially recommended by the FDA for approval but was then never officially approved. Ultimately, cardiac toxicity in some of the later trials led its manufacturer to withdraw it from the market worldwide. Unexplained sudden deaths during treatment were thought to be possibly related to dose-related lengthening in the electrocardiographic QT interval. All the studies on sertindole (Brown et al., 1997; Van Kamman et al., 1996; Zimbroff et al., 1997) reported similar EPS rates for sertindole- and placebo-treated patients. In a review of the available clinical trials on sertindole, Lewis et al. (2001) concluded that sertindole had greater antipsychotic efficacy than placebo, was better tolerated than haloperidol, and produced fewer movement disorders than either placebo or haloperidol.

Quetiapine

The FDA approved quetiapine in 1998; its efficacy has been evaluated in five methodologically rigorous clinical trials. Two 6-week double-blind, placebo-controlled studies enrolled 109 and 286 patients, respectively (Borison et al., 1996; Small et al., 1997); the first study used a mean dose of quetiapine of 307 mg, and the second used both a low-dose (mean = 209 mg) and a high-dose group (mean = 407 mg). Evidence of a benefit for the quetiapine-treated groups was shown by significant reductions in BPRS total scores, CGI scores, BPRS activation and thought disturbance subscores, and the SANS total score. However, in a randomized double-blind, 6-week study (Peuskens et al., 1997) that compared the efficacy of quetiapine to chlorpromazine among 201 patients, with doses up to 750 mg for each, no significant differences were found between groups on the BPRS total or factor scores, CGI, or SANS scores. Arvanitis et al. (1997), in a 6-week double-blind trial that compared the efficacy of five fixed doses of quetiapine (75, 150, 300, 600, or 750 mg/day) to haloperidol 12 mg and placebo in 361 schizophrenia patients, reported that all doses of quetiapine, as well as haloperidol, were superior to placebo in reducing total and positive symptom BPRS scores, but only 300 mg of quetiapine was superior to placebo in reducing SANS total scores.

Copolov et al. (2000) conducted a 6-week double-blind, randomized, parallel-group trial comparing quetiapine (mean dose of 455 mg/day) with haloperidol (mean dose of 8 mg/day) in 448 hospitalized patients. They found comparable improvements in psychopathology for the two drugs, with less EPS and less prolactin elevation in the quetiapine group.

Quetiapine did not cause EPS at greater rates than placebo in the three placebo-controlled studies. In the direct comparison with chlorpromazine, neither medication was associated with EPS. Quetiapine is effective for schizophrenic psychopathology and causes less EPS than typical antipsychotics. However, with the limited data available, claims that efficacy is greater than that of conventional antipsychotics are premature.

Ziprasidone

The FDA approved ziprasidone in February 2001 for the treatment of schizophrenia. Three major studies have shown it to be effective against positive and negative symptoms of schizophrenia, with little or no weight gain, a feature that distinguishes it from many of the current antipsychotics. Approval of the ziprasidone was delayed by the FDA in 1998 pending more data on QT-interval changes in the cardiac rhythm; it was suggested that theoretically it could cause a dangerous arrhythmia called *torsade de pointes*. The drug was approved after the manufacturer submitted further safety data, including the fact that over 4,000 patients had been treated in clinical trials with ziprasidone without evidence of torsade de pointes. The FDA does not require an EKG prior to treatment, and cardiac checkups during treatment are not mandated. To date, more than 50,000 patients have been treated with ziprasidone without evidence of cardiac toxicity.

The efficacy of ziprasidone in treating schizophrenia has been established in three major studies lasting more than 1 week: two versus placebo and one versus haloperidol. Numerous other studies have been conducted, but they have not to date been published in peer-reviewed journals. Keck et al. (1998) conducted a 4-week double-blind comparison of placebo and ziprasidone at 40 mg per day and 120 mg per day in 139 patients with schizophrenia and schizoaffective disorder. Ziprasidone at 120 mg per day produced statistically significant improvements in BPRS total and CGI-S scores. The drug did not cause movement disorders at a rate higher than placebo. Daniel et al. (1999) compared ziprasidone at 80 mg per day and 160 mg per day to placebo in a 6-week double-blind trial of 302 patients. They demonstrated the superiority of both doses to placebo in reducing the PANSS total, BPRS total, BPRS core items, CGI-S, and PANSS negative subscale scores. Ziprasidone at 160 mg per day was also shown to significantly reduce depressive symptoms in patients with clinically significant depression at baseline. The drug was well tolerated and caused movement disorders and weight gain at rates similar to placebo. In the only published study comparing ziprasidone to a typical antipsychotic, Goff et al. (1998) found ziprasidone at 160 mg per day to be superior to placebo and comparable to haloperidol in improving BPRS total, BPRS psychosis core, and CGI-S scores. Ziprasidone had a much lower propensity to cause extrapyramidal symptoms and prolactin elevation than haloperidol.

The existing evidence on ziprasidone indicates that it is an effective antipsychotic, comparable to haloperidol in treating schizophrenia. Further study and clinical experience are needed to determine if this drug has a role in treatment-refractory schizophrenia or other special populations.

Factors That Influence Antipsychotic Response

Significant efforts are under way to identify factors that may be associated with antipsychotic treatment refractoriness, since preventive measures may offer more hope than new drugs. For example, a delay in treatment of the first episode of schizophrenia (Loebel et al., 1992) and in the treatment of acute exacerbations (May et al., 1976; Wyatt, 1995) may be associated with poorer clinical outcomes. Robinson et al. (1999) reported that 87% of their sample of first-episode patients with schizophrenia or schizoaffective disorder responded to treatment within 1 year. They demonstrated that male gender, a history of obstetric complications, poorer attention at baseline, more severe hallucinations and delusions, and the development of EPS during antipsychotic treatment were associated with a significantly lower likelihood of response.

Extrapyramidal Side Effects

Antipsychotic-induced extrapyramidal side effects occur both acutely and after long-term treatment. In general, typical antipsychotics are more likely to cause EPS than atypical antipsychotics when the drugs are used at usual therapeutic doses. Commonly occurring acute EPS include akathisia, dystonia, and Parkinsonism, each having a characteristic time of onset. Akathisia typically is witnessed in a few hours to days after medication administration, dystonia within the first 96 hours, and Parkinsonism within a few days to weeks (Casey, 1993). Neuroleptic malignant syndrome (NMS), another type of acute EPS, is characterized by rigidity, hyperthermia, and autonomic instability and may be fatal if untreated; fortunately, this occurs infrequently. The increasing use of atypical antipsychotics is believed to have substantially reduced the problem of extrapyramidal side effects.

The treatment of acute EPS depends on the specific side effect (Casey, 1993). Dystonia can be quickly and successfully treated with an intramuscular injection of an anticholinergic or an antihistaminic agent. The initial treatment for Parkinsonian side effects is lowering the dose of antipsychotic. If an adequate response is not achieved, adding an anticholinergic or antihistaminic drug is usually efficacious. If symptoms persist, switching to a class of antipsychotic that produces less EPS is indicated.

Eliminating akathisia is more difficult: Lowering the antipsychotic dose is usually tried first, followed by individual trials of beta-adrenergic blockers, anti-Parkinsonian agents, and benzodiazepines (Casey, 1993). Controlled trials comparing the efficacy of the various treatments are not available.

Tardive dyskinesia (TD) is a hyperkinetic involuntary movement disorder induced by sustained exposure to antipsychotic medication; it occurs at the rate of 4% per year in the adult, nongeriatric population (Glazer et al., 1993; Kane et al., 1985; Morgenstern & Glazer, 1993). In addition to the more frequently observed orofacial and choreoathetoid signs of TD, tardive dystonias and tardive akathisia have been described. Treatment of TD has largely been unsuccessful, though there are some data from controlled trials (Adler et al., 1993) suggesting that the antioxidant vitamin E may be useful in less chronic patients. Tardive dyskinesia does not result from clozapine use and results only to a minimal extent with other atypical antipsychotics. In a double-blind, random-assignment study of 1,714 patients, Beasley et al. (1999) found a 0.52% long-term risk of TD with olanzapine treatment, compared to a 7.45% risk with haloperidol. Among a sample of geriatric patients, Jeste et al. (1999) reported a lower incidence of TD in patients treated with risperidone than in those treated with haloperidol. Atypical antipsychotics, in particular clozapine, have been used in clinical practice to treat TD, but there have been no methodologically rigorous trials to date to support this practice.

Maintenance Treatment Effects

Numerous studies have demonstrated that schizophrenic patients who have successfully responded to antipsychotic medication will experience a clinical worsening, as indicated by either symptom worsening or an increased rate of rehospitalization, when their treatment is discontinued (Davis, 1975; Kane & Lieberman, 1987). Controlled clinical trials of drug discontinuation demonstrate that after 1 year of maintenance treatment, 30% of patients will relapse on medication, while the rate is 65% in patients who have undergone placebo substitution. Even those patients who have been successfully maintained in the community for 2 to 3 years on antipsychotic drugs will demonstrate a relapse rate of 66% by 1 year after their treatment is discontinued (Hogarty et al., 1976). First-episode patients show comparable drug effects, although with lower relapse rates. During the year following their initial recovery, a relapse rate of 40% has been reported on placebo as compared to none while on medication (Kane et al., 1982). Robinson and Lieberman et al. (1999) showed that discontinuing drug therapy increased the risk of relapse almost five times in a sample of patients with first-episode schizophrenia or schizoaffective disorder. This study also showed an 82% cumulative risk of relapse for patients who had recovered from a first episode of psychosis. Those who had one relapse within 5 years had a 78% chance of having a second relapse and an 86% chance of having a third.

The benefits of maintenance antipsychotic drug treatment are tempered by the risk to the patient of long-term side effects such as the development of tardive dyskinesia. Limiting antipsychotic drug exposure has intuitive appeal for minimizing side effect risk. However, maintenance studies of the dose-response relationship for up to 1 year of continuous antipsychotic drug treatment indicate that standard drug doses (fluphenazine decanoate 12.5 to 50 mg biweekly; haloperidol decanoate 50 to 200 mg monthly) provide significantly greater prophylaxis against relapse than do doses of one half to one tenth as much (Hogarty et al., 1988; Johnson et al., 1987; Kane et al., 1983, 1986, 1993; Marder et al., 1987; Schooler et al., 1993), although the lower doses may be associated with better social adjustment and fewer extrapyramidal side effects. A targeted approach that involves slowly titrating patients off maintenance medication with reintroduction of the medication rapidly during presumptive incipient relapsing has not been found more effective than continuous administration of maintenance medication and is associated with risks of symptom exacerbation and relapse (Carpenter et al., 1990; Gaebel et al., 1993; Herz et al., 1991; Jolley et al., 1990; Schooler et al., 1993).

Only one randomized trial of an atypical antipsychotic has been conducted over more than 1 year. In this study, Essock et al. (1996) studied 227 patients with schizophrenia for 2 years; patients were randomly assigned to treatment with clozapine or usual care. Those patients treated with clozapine showed significantly greater reductions in side effects, disruptiveness, and hospitalizations, but not lower overall symptoms or improved quality of life.

Clozapine's efficacy in the maintenance phase of treatment is supported by three open-label studies. Meltzer et al. (1990) reported that among treatment-resistant schizophrenia patients, the rehospitalization rate after 1 year of clozapine treatment was reduced by 83% in comparison to the year prior to clozapine treatment. Miller et al. (1992) found that patients treated with clozapine for 2-1/2 years had fewer and shorter hospitalizations than in the previous 2-1/2 years. Breier et al. (1993) also reported that a year of clozapine treatment was superior to the previous year of conventional antipsychotics, with both fewer exacerbations of illness and fewer hospitalizations. An open mirror-image clinical study has found that during 1 year of risperidone treatment, the number of days of hospitalization was fewer than in the preceding reference period (Addington et al., 1993). There is hope that long-term trials with atypical antipsychotic drugs will demonstrate that greater efficacy, as measured by reduced rates of relapse, more global symptom remission, and improved social reintegration, accompanied by a significantly decreased risk of tardive dyskinesia, can yet be realized in the maintenance treatment of schizophrenia. A multicenter, NIMH-funded trial (Clinical Antipsychotic Trials of Intervention Effectiveness-Schizophrenia Trial) is now under way to determine the long-term (18-month) effectiveness and tolerability of the newer atypical antipsychotics relative to each other and to a typical antipsychotic.

Summary of Antipsychotic Drug Effects

Most studies of antipsychotic drugs have focused on positive symptom psychopathology; they have demonstrated that both conventional and atypical drugs are effective both acutely and prophylactically. However, the response of patients beyond positive symptoms has been less well studied and antipsychotic drug efficacy much less well demonstrated.

Other Pharmacological Treatments

Because of the limited efficacy of antipsychotic medication in resolving the full range of schizophrenic psychopathology, and the frequently occurring comorbid symptoms that arise over the course of the illness (e.g., anxiety, depression, mood lability, and motor unrest), adjunctive treatments are often used to reduce morbidity. In the section below, we review controlled trials of pharmacological agents, not classified as antipsychotics, that have been used to treat patients with schizophrenia. We report on the efficacy of these drugs when used either in combination with an antipsychotic drug or as a lone treatment, to treat both schizophrenic psychopathology and comorbid conditions. The classes of medication described are antianxiety/hypnotics, antidepressants, mood stabilizers, and dopamine agonists. In addition, we briefly review the efficacy of electroconvulsive therapy as a treatment for schizophrenic psychopathology.

The use of adjunctive pharmacological treatments in schizophrenia patients has been the subject of numerous reviews (Christison et al., 1991; Donaldson et al., 1983; Farmer & Blewett, 1993; Johns & Thompson, 1995; Lindenmayer, 1995; Meltzer, 1992; Meltzer et al., 1986; Rifkin, 1993; Siris, 1993; Wolkowitz, 1993). Given our space limitations and the large number of studies involved, where applicable recent review articles are summarized and updated with reports of subsequently published methodologically rigorous studies.

Antianxiety/Hypnotics

Benzodiazepines have been used to treat patients with schizophrenia since the early 1960s (see Table 7.3). Wolkowitz and Pickar (1991) reported on 14 double-blind studies published from 1961 to 1982 in which benzodiazepines alone were used to treat schizophrenic psychopathology. Of the 14 studies, 9, including all those after 1975, reported some positive effects; however, in almost all the studies, there was variability in response, some patients doing well while others did poorly. These authors noted that due to methodological limitations, the conclusions that may be drawn from the data are limited, though there is some evidence that benzodiazepines alone have an antipsychotic effect for at least some patients. The authors also reviewed the efficacy of benzodiazepines when used as adjunctive agents to antipsychotics. Of 16 double blind studies published from 1966 to 1989, 11 indicated some positive results, though again, in nearly all studies, some individual patients responded well and others poorly. In one of the larger studies (Csernansky et al., 1988), a double-blind comparison of alprazolam, diazepam, and placebo for the treatment of negative symptoms in outpatients with schizophrenia who had been maintained on antipsychotics, there was no sustained significant effect on negative symptoms in patients who received a benzodiazepine.

Wolkowitz and Pickar (1991) sought to determine if there were factors that would predict a clinical response to benzodiazepines. They looked at whether there was a differential efficacy among the benzodiazepines, whether the onset of the response would predict the duration of the response, and whether there was a relationship between response and dose

TABLE 7.3 Benzodiazepines

Author	*Study Design (Double Blind)*	N *Patients*	*Results*
Wolkowitz & Pickar (1991) (review article)	Benzodiazepines vs. placebo	14 studies 576 patients	9 studies reported positive results
	Benzodiazepines and neuroleptics vs. neuroleptics	16 studies 644 patients	11 studies reported positive results
Salzman et al. (1991)	2 mg IM lorazepam vs. 5 mg IM haloperidol administered to acutely psychotic patients	60	Greater number of subjects had a decrease in aggression with lorazepam
Barbee et al. (1992)	Acutely psychotic patients received either alprazolam and haloperidol or haloperidol alone	28	Combination of alprazolam and haloperidol superior to haloperidol alone in reducing aggression
Battaglia et al. (1997)	Psychotic, agitated, and aggressive patients received either lorazepam treatment, haloperidol treatment, and combination treatment	98	Combination treatment superior to either alone
Carpenter et al. (1999)	Compared diazepam with placebo and with fluphenazine in patients with symptoms thought to be prodromal of an impending relapse	53	Diazepam was superior to placebo and comparable to fluphenazine in preventing a psychotic relapse

or plasma level. The only associations with a more favorable clinical response noted were higher doses of benzodiazepines and higher plasma levels; however, the authors noted that none of the studies specifically investigated dose-response relationships.

There have been four controlled studies published since the Wolkowitz and Pickar review. Salzman et al. (1991), in a double-blind study that compared the efficacy at 2, 24, and 48 hours of 2 mg of intramuscular lorazepam to 5 mg of intramuscular haloperidol administered to 60 psychotic inpatients (26 with schizophrenia), reported that lorazepam and haloperidol both reduced aggression, agitation, and assaultive behavior; however, at 2 hours, the number of patients who showed a decrease in aggression was significantly greater with lorazepam. Barbee et al. (1992), who compared the efficacy of haloperidol with that of either alprazolam or placebo over 72 hours in 28 acutely psychotic schizophrenia patients, reported that both groups improved significantly, though the combination of haloperidol and alprazolam was more effective in controlling agitation than haloperidol alone, particularly in the first 48 hours, and lower doses of medication were needed in the combination-treated group. This study suggests that benzodiazepine augmentation may be useful in limiting the quantity of antipsychotics required for the acute treatment of schizophrenia (Bodkin, 1990). Battaglia et al. (1997) conducted a prospective, randomized, double-blind, multicenter trial of 98 psychotic, agitated, and aggressive patients, comparing lorazepam treatment, haloperidol treatment, and combination treatment. All three treatments were effective in causing significant reductions in scores on the Agitated Behavior Scale after 1 hour and on a modified Brief Psychiatric Rating Scale after 2 and 3 hours. Combination treatment with lorazepam was found to be superior to either drug alone. Carpenter et al. (1999) endeavored to determine whether diazepam could help to prevent a psychotic relapse when given for indications of disturbed sleep, increased anxiety or other dysphoric affect, agitation and irritability, increased suspiciousness, and peculiar perceptual experiences thought to be prodromal of an impending psychotic exacerbation. They conducted a double-blind, randomized clinical trial with 53 patients with schizophrenia, comparing diazepam with placebo and with fluphenazine. They found that diazepam was superior to placebo and comparable to fluphenazine in preventing a psychotic relapse.

Few studies in the literature have specifically addressed in a double-blind fashion the use of benzodiazepines to treat nonpsychotic symptoms common in people with schizophrenia. Nevertheless, there is some evidence to suggest that schizophrenia patients with anxiety, depression, hostility, irritability, and motor unrest may benefit from benzodiazepines (Wolkowitz & Pickar, 1991). A well-designed small double-blind study that looked at benzodiazepine response among six anxious schizophrenia patients over 12 weeks, with multiple crossovers (Kellner et al., 1975), concluded that some patients from this subgroup may experience reduced anxiety with adjunctive benzodiazepine use. Though benzodiazepines are frequently used as hypnotic agents in clinical practice, no controlled studies have established their efficacy in patients with schizophrenia.

Despite the evidence of a role of benzodiazepines in the treatment of at least some schizophrenia patients, there has been little recent systematic research in this area, perhaps because of the introduction of the atypical antipsychotics, the potential for dependency, and reluctance to prescribe these agents to patients with comorbid substance abuse disorders. In addition, there are reports that benzodiazepines may result in a "disinhibiting" (Karson et al., 1982) or worsening of psychopathology in some patients (Wolkowitz & Pickar, 1991). Nevertheless, at a minimum, the benzodiazepines appear to be a useful adjunct to antipsychotics in the treatment of agitated or anxious schizophrenia patients.

Antidepressants

The efficacy of antidepressant medications for the treatment of schizophrenic psychopathology, either used alone or as adjuncts to antipsychotics (see Table 7.4), was first comprehensively reviewed by Siris et al. (1978) in an analysis of the results of double-blind controlled studies. When antidepressants were used alone, only 1 of 14 studies demonstrated clearly positive findings; however, 2 of 12 studies that compared a combination of a tricyclic antidepressant and an antipsychotic to an antipsychotic alone found a superior response from the combination. Poor results were observed when a combination of an MAO inhibitor and an antipsychotic were compared to an antipsychotic alone, with only 1 of 12 studies demonstrating a clear superiority for the combination. The authors acknowledged that antidepressants do not appear indicated as a sole treatment for schizophrenia; however, they noted that the overwhelming preponderance of negative findings may have resulted from weaknesses in study design and, in particular, inadequate antidepressant dosages. In addition, the authors recommended that future research efforts be targeted to specific depressive syndromes that afflict a significant percentage of patients over the course of their illness (McGlashan & Carpenter, 1976).

Subsequent recognition that a secondary or postpsychotic depression occurs among schizophrenia patients (Siris, 1991) led to additional research interest in adjunctive antidepressant usage, the efficacy of which was reviewed in an analysis of double-blind studies by Plasky (1991). Of six placebo-controlled studies using tricyclic antidepressants in addition to an antipsychotic, two demonstrated a significant reduction in depression. The author noted that these two studies were of patients whose acute psychosis was under control and suggested that adjunctive antidepressant treatment may be successful for the treatment of depression only when the acute psychotic episode has stabilized. Furthermore, Plasky (1991) noted that in two studies of acutely psychotic patients, the antidepressants appeared to have resulted in a worsening of the psychosis, and they cautioned about premature use of antidepressant medication.

Since the above reviews, only a small number of double-blind studies have continued to examine the efficacy of antidepressants as an adjunctive medication to antipsychotics. Siris et al. (1991) studied the therapeutic efficacy of adjunctive imipramine, when added to fluphenazine decanoate and benztropine, in 27 well-stabilized patients with schizophrenia or schizoaffective disorder with negative symptoms who also met the criteria for a postpsychotic depression. The authors found that the imipramine-treated group had superior global and negative symptom ratings at 6 to 9 weeks. They explained their positive findings in this subgroup of patients as further support for a syndromal overlap of postpsychotic depression and negative symptoms (Siris et al., 1988). In a later study, Siris et al. (2000) used the same protocol in a more heterogeneous sample of 72 patients with postpsychotic episodes of depression to test the generalizability of their previous finding. They again found an improvement in negative symptoms favoring the imipramine-treated group, but the effect was somewhat smaller. The authors attributed the diminished effect size to differences in the sample because the later sample was thought to be sicker than the first yet was treated with lower antipsychotic doses.

TABLE 7.4 Antidepressants

Author	*Study Design (Double Blind)*	N *Patients*	*Results*
Siris et al. (1978) (review article)	MAO inhibitor vs. placebo	6 studies 467 patients	All reported no improvement from the MAO inhibitor
	Tricyclic antidepressants vs. placebo	8 studies 618 patients	1 study reported positive results
	Tricyclic antidepressant and neuroleptic vs. neuroleptic alone	12 studies 1,724 patients	2 studies reported positive results
	MAO inhibitor and neuroleptic vs. neuroleptic alone	12 studies 1,013 patients	1 study reported positive results
Siris et al. (1991)	Imipramine, benztropine, and fluphenazine decanoate vs. benztropine, and fluphenazine decanoate. 6-week study of negative symptom/depressed patients	27	Imipramine-treated group had superior global and negative symptom ratings at study termination
Siris et al. (2000)	Same protocol as 1991 study with a more heterogeneous sample of patients	72	Improved-negative symptom ratings in imipramine group, but smaller effect size than previous study
Silver & Nassar (1992)	Fluvoxamine, neuroleptic, and benzotropine vs. neuroleptics and benzotropine; 7-week study	30	Fluvoxamine augmentation significantly reduced negative symptoms
Siris et al. (1994)	Stable patients on fluphenazine, benzotropine, and imipramine either continued or tapered off imipramine and followed for 1 year	24	Continuous imipramine treatment prevented relapse into both depression and psychosis
Hogarty et al. (1995)	Desipramine given to stable patients maintained on neuroleptics and anti-Parkinson medication	33	Desipramine superior to placebo in reducing depression
Lee et al. (1998)	Sertraline vs. placebo when added to haloperidol over 8 weeks	36	No difference in two groups
Silver et al. (2000)	Fluvoxamine vs. placebo added to antipsychotic over	53	Fluvoxamine group has significantly better SANS scores
Berk et al. (2001)	Mirtazepine vs. placebo added to haloperidol	30	Significant reduction in PANNS negative symptoms scores in mirtazepine group

In an additional double-blind placebo-controlled study that examined the efficacy of antidepressants as an adjunctive treatment for negative symptoms in 30 schizophrenia patients, Silver and Nassar (1992) found fluvoxamine superior to placebo. The authors noted that depression and extrapyramidal symptoms did not improve, as did ratings of negative symptoms, a finding leading them to conclude that fluvoxamine's benefit was for "primary" negative symptoms. Lee et al. (1998) found no difference between sertraline and placebo when added to haloperidol in 36 patients with schizophrenia in an 8-week study. Silver et al. (2000) reported on another sample of 53 patients with schizophrenia: Patients receiving fluvoxamine in addition to antipsychotic treatment had significantly better SANS scores than those treated with antipsychotic and placebo. Berk et al. (2001) conducted a 6-week randomized placebo-controlled trial of mirtazapine and haloperidol versus placebo and haloperidol in 30 patients with schizophrenia. At the study end, there was a 42% reduction in PANSS negative symptom scores in the mirtazapine group, compared to placebo. As there was no difference between the two groups on the Hamilton Depression scale at the study end, the authors suggested that the improvement in negative symptoms was not simply an improvement in primary mood symptoms.

Two other studies also lend support to the efficacy of adjunctive antidepressant usage in the treatment of schizophrenia patients. In a randomized double-blind protocol (Siris et al., 1994) that examined 24 schizophrenic or schizoaffective patients, all of whom had been successfully treated with imipramine, fluphenazine decanoate, and benztropine for 6 months, and who were then either continued or tapered off the imipramine and followed for 1 year, continuous imipramine treatment prevented relapse into both depression and psychosis. Hogarty et al. (1995) reported on a 12-week, double-blind, placebo-controlled study of 33 depressed stable schizophrenia patients maintained on antipsychotics who had undergone prior double-blind dose reduction and treatment with anti-Parkinsonian medication; the authors found that desipramine was significantly better than placebo in reducing depression. They, like others (Plasky, 1991), concluded that the chronic depression found in schizophrenia patients, in contrast to the acute episodic forms, is responsive to antidepressant medication. Definitive conclusions cannot be drawn about antidepressant usage for schizophrenia patients, however, because of the paucity of methodologically rigorous studies available. Nevertheless, the data appear to suggest that adjunctive antidepressant treatment is warranted when a patient reports persistent symptoms of depression when not in an acute episode of illness.

Mood Stabilizers

Lithium

Lithium salts have been used both alone and as an adjunct to antipsychotics in the treatment of patients with schizophrenia (Atre-Vaidya & Taylor, 1989; Christison et al., 1991; see Table 7.5). The double-blind studies suggest that antipsychotics are superior to lithium as a treatment for acutely psychotic schizophrenia patients, although some patients may improve on lithium alone. Atre-Vaidya and Taylor (1989) reported on three studies (Carman et al., 1981; Growe et al., 1979; Small et al., 1975;) that examined lithium as an adjunct to antipsychotics for treatment-refractory patients. The three studies included 48 patients, 17 of whom had a diagnosis of schizoaffective disorder. Small et al. (1975) reported the most impressive results: 10 of 20 completers improved more with adjunctive lithium treatment than with antipsychotic medication alone; however, these authors were unable to discern any predictors of response. The other two studies reported more modest positive findings. Carman et al. (1981) reported a correlation of response with affective symptom psychosis. Wilson et al. (1993), in a study that compared haloperidol alone with the combination of haloperidol plus lithium in an 8-week trial with 21 treatment-resistant schizophrenia patients, reported no advantage for the combination. Terao et al. (1995), in a study of 21 treatment-resistant schizophrenia patients treated in an 8-week crossover design with lithium or placebo, in addition to an antipsychotic, reported that lithium patients had significantly lower anxiety and depression scores, but there was no benefit for negative symptoms. Hogarty et al. (1995), as part of a larger study, compared adjunctive lithium to placebo in 29 anxious stable schizophrenia patients and found at 12 weeks an advantage for lithium in reducing anxiety and depression. This benefit was limited to female patients, however. Schulz et al. (1999) studied 41 patients with diagnoses of either schizophrenia or schizoaffective disorder who had had only partial response to fluphenazine decanoate. Patients were randomized to either lithium or placebo for 8 weeks of treatment, with patients in the placebo group able to enter an open-label treatment with lithium for 8 weeks. This double-blind study showed no significant differences in treatment response between the lithium and placebo groups. Patients originally treated with placebo added to antipsychotic medication did show significantly greater symptom reduction in the open-label adjunctive lithium phase of the study.

A review of double-blind studies provides no convincing evidence of the efficacy of lithium as an agent adjunctive to antipsychotics for schizophrenia patients. However, because there have been reports of a benefit in some treatment-refractory patients, a trial of lithium should be considered if the patient has not adequately responded or was unable to tolerate an atypical agent (e.g., clozapine). Concern about potentially toxic interactions between an antipsy-

TABLE 7.5 Mood Stabilizers

Author	*Study Design (Double Blind)*	N *Patients*	*Results*
Atre-Vaidya (1989) (Review article)	Lithium and neuroleptic vs. neuroleptic alone	3 studies 48 patients	Positive findings reported in all 3 studies
Johnstone et al. (1988)	Study of "functional" psychoses 4 cells 1. neuroleptic 2. lithium 3. neuroleptics plus lithium 4. placebo Patients treated for 4 weeks	120 (not all schizophrenic)	No evidence that lithium is beneficial in treating psychosis
Wilson et al. (1993)	Lithium plus haloperidol vs. haloperidol in treatment-resistant patients; 8-week trial	21	No advantage for the combination
Terao et al. (1995)	Lithium plus neuroleptic vs. neuroleptic alone; 8-week crossover design	21	No benefit for lithium on negative symptoms through anxiety and depression improved.
Hogarty et al. (1995)	Lithium plus neuroleptic vs. neuroleptic alone; 12-week trial for anxious stable patients	29	Lithium beneficial in reducing anxiety in female patients only.
Schultz et al. (1999)	Lithium plus neuroleptic plus neuroleptic alone; 8-week trial for partially responsive patients	41	No significant differences in treatment response
Christison et al. (1991) (review article)	Carbamazepine (CBZ) and neuroleptic vs. neuroleptic alone	5 studies 251 patients	3 of 5 studies had reported some positive results. CBZ augmentation found superior to neuroleptic in patients with "violence, agression and paranoia" in the largest ($n = 162$ patients) study
Meszaros et al. (1991)	CBZ and neuroleptic vs. neuroleptic alone	24	Modest improvement in negative symptoms from CBZ treatment
Kunovac et al. (1991)	CBZ and neuroleptic vs. neuroleptic alone	20	Modest improvement in negative symptoms from CBC treatment
Nachoni et al. (1993)	CBZ and neuroleptic vs. neuroleptic in predominately negative symptom patients; 7-week trial	28	No difference between CBZ or placebo found.
Leucht et al. (2001)	Review and data reanalysis of 8 studies comparing CBZ plus antipsychotics and antipsychotics plus placebo		No recommendation for routine clinical use for treatment or augmentation of antipsychotic treatment of schizophrenia
Carpenter et al. (1991)	Patients withdrawn from stable neuroleptic regimen for 95 days and placed on CBZ or placebo	27	Both groups had a high rate of relapse
Linnoila et al. (1976)	Valproic acid and neuroleptic vs. neuroleptic in 2-week (each phase) crossover design	32	14 of 32 VPA treated patients had an improvement in global psychopathology
Ko et al. (1985)	Valproic acid and neuroleptic vs. neuroleptic alone in 4-week (each phase) crossover design	6	No significant differences between groups
Wassef et al. (2000)	Valproic acid as add-on treatment to haloperidol in 12 hospitalized patients with acute exacerbations of chronic schizophrenia	12	Valproic acid group had greater improvements than the placebo group on the CGI scale, the BPRS and the SANS

chotic and lithium (Cohen & Cohen, 1974) appears not to be supported by the vast majority of the published literature (Rifkin, 1993).

Carbamazepine

Christison et al. (1991) reviewed five double-blind studies published through 1989, which all added either carbamazepine (CBZ) or placebo to a stable antipsychotic regimen. The results of these studies were mixed, with modest positive results seen in three (Klein et al., 1984; Neppe, 1983; Okuma et al., 1989). The study by Okuma et al. included 162 patients, of whom 127 met the criteria for *DSM-III* schizophrenia and 35 met the criteria for schizoaffective disorder; this study was larger than the other four combined. All patients were described as treatment-resistant with "excited psychotic states." CBZ augmentation was found superior to an antipsychotic alone in patients with "violence, aggression, and paranoia"; however, the authors acknowledged that the overall differences between groups were small.

Two additional double-blind placebo studies (Kunovac et al., 1991; Meszaros et al., 1991) examined the efficacy of CBZ when added to an antipsychotic in 24 and 20 stable schizophrenia patients, respectively, and both reported a modest improvement in negative symptoms, but in another study (Nachshoni et al., 1993) of 28 predominantly negative-symptom patients, no difference was reported. Carpenter et al. (1991), using a different study design, compared the efficacy of CBZ to that of placebo after 27 patients had been withdrawn from stable antipsychotic doses and found that CBZ offered no advantage over placebo, both groups having high relapse rates off antipsychotics.

Leucht et al. (2001) reviewed eight studies, which compared CBZ plus antipsychotics and placebo plus antipsychotics in the treatment of schizophrenia. The authors concluded that carbamazepine should not be recommend for routine clinical use for treatment of schizophrenia or augmentation of antipsychotic treatment of schizophrenia. The paper qualified that conclusion by saying that a trial of CBZ may be warranted for those with a history of response to carbamazepine, or for patients with associated EEG abnormalities.

Overall, there is some evidence to support CBZ as an adjunctive agent to antipsychotics in the treatment of schizophrenia, particularly for the subpopulation of aggressive, agitated patients. Because of CBZ's ability to upregulate hepatic enzymes, plasma antipsychotic levels should be monitored regularly when CBZ is used (Christison, 1991).

Valproic Acid

Valproic acid (VPA) as an adjunct to antipsychotics has been the focus of only two controlled studies. Linnoila et al. (1976), in a double-blind crossover study of 32 chronic psychiatric patients with dyskinesias, each phase lasting 14 days, found that the combination of VPA with an antipsychotic was superior to an antipsychotic alone in reducing global psychopathology in 14 of 32 patients. Ko et al. (1985) compared adjunctive VPA to placebo in a 4-week study of 6 schizophrenia patients and found no significant differences between groups. Wassef et al. (2000) conducted a 21-day double-blind, randomized, placebo-controlled study of valproic acid as add-on treatment to haloperidol in 12 hospitalized patients with acute exacerbations of chronic schizophrenia. At study end, the valproic acid group showed greater improvements than the placebo group on the CGI scale, the BPRS, and the SANS. Definitive conclusions on the efficacy of VPA for the treatment of schizophrenia patients are premature, however, given the limited data available.

Dopamine Agonists

Dopamine agonists have been associated with an exacerbation of psychotic symptoms in 40 to 60% of schizophrenia patients; however, these agents have also been used as a treatment for patients with prominent negative symptoms (see Table 7.6). This strategy is consistent with the hypothesis that a hypodopaminergic state is responsible for the negative symptoms of the illness (Davidson, 1991). The efficacy of L-dopa has been assessed in three double-blind treatment studies (Christison, 1991), two of which used it as an adjunct to antipsychotics (Gerlach & Luhdorf, 1975; Inanaga et al., 1975). Gerlach and Luhdorf (1975), in a study of 18 schizophrenia patients with prominent negative symptoms, reported significant activation in some patients, though the overall change in level of functioning was small. Inanaga et al. (1975), in a study of 104 schizophrenia inpatients with negative symptoms, reported that there were significantly more excellent responders among the L-dopa-treated patients, though there was

TABLE 7.6 Dopamine Agonists

Author	*Study Design (Double Blind)*	N *Patients*	*Results*
Gerlach & Luhdorf (1975)	L-dopa vs. placebo added to neuroleptic in 12-week (each phase) crossover design	18	Significant "activation" in some patients, though no difference in global ratines.
Inanaga et al. (1975)	L-dopa plus neuroleptic vs. neuroleptic alone	104	Significantly more L-dopa-treated patients rated as "excellent" responders.
Brambilla et al. (1979)	L-dopa vs. placebo in 4-week (each phase) crossover design	6	2 patients much improved
Gattaz et al. (1989)	Bromocriptine plus haloperidol vs. haloperidol alone; 3-week study	30	Nonsignificant improvement at 24 hours that dissipated by 21 days.
Goldberg et al. (1991)	Dextroamphetamine administered in a single doses to haloperidol treated patients	21	Improvement on measures of affect and cognition

no difference in the number considered good or fair. Brambilla et al. (1979) studied 6 chronic patients with both positive and negative symptoms in a crossover design with placebo, each phase lasting 4 weeks, and found 2 of the patients much improved.

We could find only two other double-blind studies that assessed the efficacy of dopamine agonists in chronic schizophrenia patients. Gattaz et al. (1989), in a study of 30 schizophrenia patients who received either haloperidol plus bromocriptine or haloperidol alone, reported a nonsignificant improvement in overall functioning at 24 hours for the bromocriptine-treated group, though by 21 days no differences were observed. Goldberg et al. (1991) administered a single dose of dextroamphetamine to 21 patients with chronic schizophrenia who had been stabilized on haloperidol and found improvement with dextroamphetamine on a number of variables that reflected affect and cognition.

Dopamine agonists have been the subjects of too few controlled studies to allow us to draw definitive conclusions; however, the above studies suggest that they may represent an underutilized class of medication, particularly for the treatment of negative symptoms. Clinicians' hesitancy to use these agents due to concern about exacerbating psychotic symptoms may not be warranted if patients are maintained on antipsychotics (Perovich et al., 1989).

Glutamate Agonists

Phencyclidine (PCP) was first observed by Luby et al. (1959) to produce a syndrome similar to schizophrenic psychosis with its associated emotional withdrawal, apathy, and cognitive impairment. A later study by Anis et al. (1983) demonstrating that PCP blocks the NMDA subtype of glutamate receptors in a noncompetitive manner led to an intensified effort to understand the role of glutamine receptors in schizophrenia. Because PCP inhibits the neurotransmission of glutamate through NMDA receptors (i.e., is an NMDA antagonist), it was hypothesized that reduced glutamate activity (possibly through NMDA receptor hypofunction) caused the symptoms of schizophrenia (Javitt & Zukin, 1991). From this hypothesis, it was inferred that agents that facilitate the stimulation of NMDA receptors would be therapeutic in schizophrenia, similar to the way in which amphetamine's effects on DA supported the development of D2 antagonists as antipsychotic agents in the context of the A hypothesis of schizophrenia. In this context, three glutamate agonists have been studied to date: glycine, D-cycloserine, and D-serine (see Table 7.7).

Six double-blind studies have evaluated the use of glycine as a treatment adjunctive to antipsychotic medications. Potkin et al. (1992) studied the efficacy of glycine added to antipsychotic treatment among inpatients with limited treatment response over 6 weeks. This study, which used a relatively low dose of 15 g per day, found small improvement in the glycine ($N = 11$) group versus the placebo group ($N = 8$), but no statistically significant advantages for the glycine group on the BPRS, SANS, or SAES. In a similar study of 14 patients, but with a higher dose

TABLE 7.7 Glutamate Agonists (Adapted from Abi-Saab et al., 2001)

Author	*Study Design (Double Blind)*	N *Patients*	*Results*
Potkin et al. (1992)	Low-dose glycine, placebo-controlled, add-on for 6 weeks, type of antipsychotic not reported	18	Small improvement on CGI; no significant improvement on other measures
Javitt et al. (1994)	High-dose glycine, placebo-controlled, add-on for 8 weeks, type of antipsychotic not reported	14	Significant improvement in negative scores
Heresco-Levy et al. (1996)	High-dose glycine, placebo-controlled, add-on, crossover design for 6 weeks in each phase	7 on typical antipsychotics, 4 on clozapine	Significant improvement in PANSS total and negative symptoms scores
Potkin et al. (1999)	High-dose glycine, placebo-controlled, add-on for 12 weeks	19 on clozapine	No advantages for glycine; Patients on clozapine alone had lower positive symptoms scores
Heresco-Levy et al. (1999)	High-dose glycine, placebo-controlled, add-on, crossover for 6 weeks in each phase	15 on typical antipsychotics and 7 on clozapine	Significant improvements in negative, depressive, and cognitive symptoms
Evins et al. (2000)	High-dose glycine, placebo-controlled, add-on, parallel-group for 8 weeks	30 on clozapine	No advantages for glycine
Rosse et al. (1996)	Low-dose DCS, placebo-controlled, add-on, parallel-group for 4 weeks	13 on molindone	No advantages for DCS
Goff et al. (1999a)	Medium dose DCS, placebo-controlled, add-on, crossover for 6 weeks	17 on clozapine	No advantages for DCS; worsening of negative symptoms on DCS
Goff et al. (1999b)	Medium-dose DCS, placebo-controlled, add-on, parallel-group for 8 weeks	47 on typical antipsychotics	Advantage for DCS in negative symptoms
Tsai et al. (1998)	DS, placebo-controlled, add-on, parallel-group for 6 weeks	25 on typical antipsychotics and 4 on risperidone	Advantages for DS in positive, negative, and cognitive symptoms
Tsai et al. (1999)	DS, placebo-controlled, add-on, parallel-group for 6 weeks	20 on clozapine	No advantages for DS

(30 g per day) of glycine, Javitt et al. (1994) found significant improvements in PANSS-negative scores. Heresco-Levy et al. (1996) used an even higher dose (60 g per day) of glycine to augment typical antipsychotics ($N=7$) and clozapine ($N=4$) in patients with treatment-resistant schizophrenia. They found highly significant improvements in negative, depressive, and cognitive symptoms in the glycine group, with 73% of the patients having a 30% or better improvement in negative symptoms. Heresco-Levy et al. (1999) used an add-on, crossover design to evaluate glycine (60 g per day) in patients resistant to typical antipsychotics ($N=15$) and clozapine ($N=7$). The study found highly significant improvements in the glycine group for negative, depressive, and cognitive symptoms, the response being significantly correlated with low pretreatment glycine levels. While the aforementioned studies used samples of patients treated with either typical antipsychotic drugs or clozapine, two studies evaluated the effect of glycine

when added to the treatment regimens of patients treated with clozapine only. Interestingly, both studies (Evins et al., 2000; Potkin et al., 1999) failed to show advantages for the groups with glycine added to their treatment. Glycine has a poor CNS bioavailability, and the doses needed to effect clinical benefit (30 to 60 mg per day) are very difficult to administer.

D-cycloserine (DCS) freely crosses the blood-brain barrier and acts as a partial agonist at the glycine regulatory site on the NMDA receptor. Because of this latter feature, the substance stimulates NMDA receptor function at low doses but inhibits endogenous glycine activity at higher doses, thus lowering NMDA receptor function. The drug is effective in treating negative symptoms in a narrow therapeutic range when added to typical antipsychotic regimens, as evidenced by Goff et al. (1999a) in a study of 47 patients with a medium dose of DCS. Studies by Goff et al. (1995) and Rosse et al. (1996) established that very low or very high doses of DCS either did not improve or even worsened psychotic symptoms. Consistent with the findings with glycine, Goff et al. (1999b) demonstrated that DCS did not improve symptoms when added to clozapine treatment. The narrow therapeutic window of DCS ultimately makes it a difficult compound to use clinically.

Another glutamate agonist candidate for the treatment of schizophrenia is D-serine (DS), which is a full NMDA agonist with greater CNS bioavailability than glycine. A study by Tsai et al. (1998) evaluated the use of DS in 29 patients (25 treated with typical antipsychotics and 4 treated with risperidone) with deficit syndrome schizophrenia, finding improvements in positive, negative, and cognitive symptoms. In a later add-on study of clozapine, Tsai et al. (1999) found that symptoms did not improve in the group treated with D-serine.

Glycine, DCS, and DS each show some benefit for treatment of psychotic symptoms when dosed appropriately. Though dosing challenges with glycine and DCS may make them impractical for clinical use, studies on these compounds provide strong support for a role of glutamate in the pathophysiology of schizophrenia, as well as furthering the understanding of the pharmacological mechanism of clozapine. DS is the most promising agent in this group based on current findings. This line of research will hopefully lead to improved symptom reduction for patients with schizophrenia and clues leading to the development of other novel therapeutic agents.

Electroconvulsive Therapy

Electroconvulsive therapy (ECT), which was an acceptable treatment option for schizophrenia before the introduction of antipsychotic medication, has been the subject of few controlled studies (see Table 7.8). Information gathered from open trials suggests that ECT works best in schizophrenia patients in the early stages of their illness, in those with catatonic or affective symptoms, and in conjunction with an antipsychotic (Salzman, 1980). ECT is rarely used in the treatment of schizophrenia patients today except in the most refractory cases.

Three double-blind controlled studies of schizophrenia patients maintained on antipsychotics who received either ECT or sham ECT produced consistent results. Taylor et al. (1980), in a study of 20 patients (not all schizophrenic), found that the ECT group improved much more rapidly than the sham group, but the differences disappeared by 16 weeks. Brandon et al. (1985) in a study of 19 schizophrenia patients found ECT superior at 2 and 4 weeks, but by 12 weeks, there was no clear difference. Abraham et al. (1987), in a study of 22 patients found ECT augmentation beneficial in the first 8 weeks, but no difference between groups by 12 weeks. Interestingly, May et al. (1981), in a 5-year prospective study of 228 first-episode schizophrenia patients who received one of five treatments by random assignment (antipsychotics, ECT, psychotherapy, psychotherapy plus neuroleptic, or milieu), found that the outcomes in all groups were poor, but that the ECT-treated group fared best.

Chanpattana et al. (1999) compared flupenthixol alone, continuation electroconvulsive therapy (ECT) alone, and combined continuation ECT and flupenthixol in a 6-month single-blind study of 58 patients with treatment-resistant schizophrenia who had met response criteria after an acute phase of treatment with bilateral ECT and flupenthixol (12 to 24 mg/day). Patients treated with the combination of bilateral ECT and flupenthixol relapsed at a rate of 40% (6/15), while patients in both the bilateral-ECT-alone and the flupenthixol-alone groups relapsed at a rate of 93% (14/15). All 8 of the patients treated with the combination of the two treatments maintained therapeutic benefits at follow up of 3 to 17 months. Chanpattana et al. (2000) conducted a double-blind comparison of three different stimulus intensities (seizure threshold, two times seizure thresh-

TABLE 7.8 Electroconvulsive Therapy

Author	*Study Design (Double Blind)*	N *Patients*	*Results*
Taylor et al. (1980)	ECT vs. sham ECT; 8–12 treatments. All patients on neuroleptics	20	Improvement was rapid with ECT, no difference at 16 weeks.
Brandon et al. (1988)	ECT vs. sham ECT; 8 treatments. Most maintained on neuroleptics	22	ECT superior at 2 and 4 weeks, no difference by 12 weeks.
Abraham et al. (1987)	ECT vs. sham ECT; 8 treatments. All patients maintained on neuroleptics	22	ECT superior at 8 weeks, no difference by 12 weeks
Chanpattana et al. (1999)	Flupenthixol alone, continuation electroconvulsive therapy (ECT) alone, and combined continuation ECT and flupenthixol for 6 months after acute phase combination treatment	58	Combination of bilateral ECT and flupenthixol continuation treatment better than either alone
Chanpattana et al. (2000)	Double-blind comparison of three different stimulus intensities of bilateral ECT plus flupenthixol	62	High-dosage bilateral ECT speeds clinical response in patients with schizophrenia.

old, and four times seizure threshold) of bilateral ECT plus flupenthixol in the treatment of 62 patients with schizophrenia. They concluded that treatment with high-dosage bilateral ECT speeds clinical response in patients with schizophrenia.

Overall, given early reports of the efficacy of ECT, the few controlled studies that show a benefit, at least early in the course of treatment, and recent reports of the efficacy of combined ECT and antipsychotic treatment, ECT should remain a viable adjunctive treatment option among refractory patients.

CONCLUSIONS

Pharmacological treatment has had a profoundly positive impact on the course of schizophrenia, the vast majority of patients no longer requiring chronic institutionalization. Nevertheless, schizophrenia remains a major public health concern, patients over the course of their illness displaying varying degrees of social and vocational disability, and remaining susceptible to psychotic exacerbations even when compliant with medication. The relatively recent introduction of atypical agents has been promising, with reduced negative symptoms, reduced motor side effects, and enhanced efficacy in some refractory patients. It is hoped that the future will bring atypical agents that can specifically target desired receptors to both enhance efficacy and further limit side effects. The difficulties in the pharmacological management of patients with schizophrenia are compounded by the fact that they are also more susceptible to other psychiatric symptoms than the general population. The use of adjunctive medications to treat comorbid conditions has been examined in a limited number of methodologically rigorous studies, but targeted treatment trials with antidepressants for "postpsychotic depression" and with benzodiazepines for anxiety and agitation may offer an opportunity to limit morbidity. Early identification of schizophrenia/schizophreniform disorder and aggressive treatment with antipsychotic medication to prevent the deterioration witnessed in some patients should be of the highest priority because the overall efficacy of pharmacological treatments remains limited.

ACKNOWLEDGMENTS This work was supported by the UNC Mental Health and Neuroscience Clinical Research Center (grant #MH33127) and the Foundation of Hope

References

Abi-Saab, W., D'Souza, C., Madonick, S., & Krystal, J. (2001). Targeting the glutamate system. In A. Breier, P. Tran, J. Herrea, G. Tollefson, & F. Bymaster (Eds), *Current issues in the psychopharma-*

cology of schizophrenia. Philadelphia: Lippincott Williams & Wilkins.

Abraham, K. R., & Kulhara, P. (1987). The efficacy of electroconvulsive therapy in the treatment of schizophrenia. *British Journal of Psychiatry, 151*, 152–155.

Addington, D. E., Jones, B., Bloom, D., Chouinard, G., Remington, G., & Albright, P. (1993). Reduction of hospital days in chronic schizophrenic patients treated with risperidone: A retrospective study. *Clinical Therapy, 15*(5), 917–926.

Adelson, D., & Epstein, L. J. (1962). A study of phenothiazines with male and female chronically ill schizophrenic patients. *Journal of Nervous and Mental Disease, 134*, 543–554.

Adler, L. A., Peselow, E., Rotrosen, J., Duncan, E., Lee, M., Rosenthal, M., & Angrist, B. (1993). Vitamin E treatment of tardive dyskinesia. *American Journal of Psychiatry, 150*(9), 1405–1407.

Alvir, J. M., Lieberman, J. A., Safferman, A. Z., Schwimmer, J. L., & Schaaf, J. A. (1993). Clozapine-induced agranulocytosis. Incidence and risk factors in the United States. *New England Journal of Medicine,* 329(3), 162–167.

Anis, N. A., Berry, S. C., Burton, N. R., & Lodge, D. (1983). The dissociative anesthetics, ketamine and phencyclidine, selectively reduce excitation of central mammalian neurons by N-methyl-aspartate. *British Journal of Pharmacology, 79*, 565–575.

Arvanitis, L. A., & Miller, B. G. (1997). Multiple fixed doses of "Seroquel" (quetiapine) in patients with acute exacerbation of schizophrenia: A comparison with haloperidol and placebo. The Seroquel Trial 13 Study Group. *Biological Psychiatry*, 42(4), 233–246.

Atre-Vaidya, N., & Taylor, M. A. (1989). Effectiveness of lithium in schizophrenia: Do we really have an answer? *Journal of Clinical Psychiatry, 50*, 170–173.

Azima, H., Durost, H., & Arthurs, D. (1960). The effect of R1625 (Haloperidol) in mental syndromes: A multi-blind study. *American Journal of Psychiatry, 117*, 546–547.

Baldessarini, R. J., & Frankenburg, F. R. (1991). Clozapine. A novel antipsychotic agent [see comments]. *New England Journal of Medicine, 324*(11), 746–754.

Barbee, J. G., Mancuso, D. M., Freed, C. R., & Todorov, A. A. (1992). Alprazolam as a neuroleptic adjunct in the emergency treatment of schizophrenia. *American Journal of Psychiatry, 149*(4), 506–510.

Battaglia, J., Moss, S., Rush, J., Kang, J., Mendoza, R., Leedom, L., Dubin, W., McGlynn, C., & Goodman, L. (1997). Haloperidol, Lorazepam, or both for psychotic agitation? A multi-center, prospective, double blind, emergency department study. *American Journal of Emergency Medicine* 15(4), 335–340.

Beasley, C. M., Dellva, M. A., Tamura, R. N., Morgenstern, H., Glazer, W. M., Ferguson, K., & Tollefson, G. D. (1999). Randomized double-blind comparison of the incidence of tardive dyskinesia in patients with schizophrenia during long-term treatment with olanzapine or haloperidol. *British Journal of Psychiatry, 174*, 23–30.

Beasley, C. M., Jr., Hamilton, S. H., Crawford, A. M., Dellva, M. A., Tollefson, G. D., Tran, P. V., Blin, O., & Beuzen, J. N. (1997). Olanzapine versus haloperidol: Acute phase results of the international double-blind olanzapine trial. *European Neuropsychopharmacology*, 7(2), 125–137.

Beasley, C. M., Tollefson, G., Tran, P., Satterlee, W., Sanger, T., & Hamilton, S. (1996). The Olanzapine HGAD Study Group: Olanzapine versus placebo and haloperidol: Acute phase results of the North American double-blind olanzapine trial. *Neuropsychopharmacology, 14*, 111–123.

Berk, M., Ichim, C., & Brook, S. (2001). Efficacy of mirtazapine add on therapy to haloperidol in the treatment of the negative symptoms of schizophrenia: A double blind randomized placebo-controlled study. *International Clinical Psychopharmacology, 16*(2), 87–92.

Binder, R., Glick, I., & Rice, M. (1981). A comparative study of parenteral molindone and haloperidol in the acutely psychotic patient. *Journal of Clinical Psychiatry*, 42(5), 203–206.

Bjorndal, N., Bjerre, M., Gerlach, J., Kristjansen, P., Magelund, G., Oestrich, I. H., & Waehrens, J. (1980). High dosage haloperidol therapy in chronic schizophrenic patients: A double-blind study of clinical response, side effects, serum haloperidol, and serum prolactin. *Psychopharmacology (Berlin), 67*(1), 17–23.

Blin, O., Azorin, J. M., & Bouhours, P. (1996). Antipsychotic and anxiolytic properties of risperidone, haloperidol, and methotrimeprazine in schizophrenic patients. *Journal of Clinical Psychopharmacology, 16*(1), 38–44.

Bodkin, J. A. (1990). Emerging uses for high-potency benzodiazepines in psychotic disorders. *Journal of Clinical Psychiatry, 51*(5), 41–46, discussion 50–53.

Bondolfi, G., Dufour, H., Patris, M., May, J. P., Billeter, U., Eap, C. B., & Baumann, P. (1998). Risperidone Study Group: Risperidone versus clozapine in treatment-resistant chronic schizophrenia: A randomized double-blind study. *American Journal of Psychiatry, 155,* 499–504.

Borison, R. L., Arvanitis, L. A., & Miller, B. G. (1996). ICI 204,636, an atypical antipsychotic: Efficacy and safety in a multicenter, placebo-controlled trial in patients with schizophrenia. U.S. SEROQUEL Study Group. *Journal of Clinical Psychopharmacology, 16*(2), 158–169.

Borison, R. L., Pathiraja, A. P., Diamond, B. I., & Meibach, R. C. (1992). Risperidone: Clinical safety and efficacy in schizophrenia. *Psychopharmacology Bulletin, 28*(2), 213–218.

Brambilla, F., Scarone, S., Ponzano, M., Maffei, C., Nobile, P., Rovere, C., & Guastalla, A. (1979). Catecholaminergic drugs in chronic schizophrenia. *Neuropsychobiology, 5*(4), 185–200.

Brandon, S., Cowley, P., McDonald, C., Neville, P., Palmer, R., & Wellstood-Eason, S. (1985). Leicester ECT Trial: Results in schizophrenia. *British Journal of Psychiatry, 146,* 177–183.

Brandrup, E., & Kristjansen, P. (1961). A controlled clinical test of a new psycholeptic drug (haloperidol). *Journal of Mental Science, 107,* 778–782.

Breier, A., Buchanan, R. W., Irish, D., & Carpenter, W. T., Jr. (1993). Clozapine treatment of outpatients with schizophrenia: Outcome and long-term response patterns. *Hospital and Community Psychiatry, 44*(12), 1145–1149.

Breier, A., & Hamilton, S. H. (1999). Comparative efficacy of olanzapine and haloperidol for patients with treatment-resistant schizophrenia [see comments]. *Biological Psychiatry, 45,* 403–411.

Breier, A. F., Malhotra, A. K., Su, T.-P., Pinals, D. A., Elman, I., Adler, C. M., Lafargue, R. T., Clifton, A., & Pickar, D. (1999). Clozapine and risperidone in chronic schizophrenia: Effects on symptoms, parkinsonian side effects, and neuroendocrine response. *American Journal of Psychiatry, 156,* 294–298.

Brown, G. R., & Radford, J. M. (1977). Sertindole hydrochloride: A novel antipsychotic medication with a favorable side effect profile. *Southern Medicine Journal, 90*(7), 691–693.

Buchanan, R. W., Breier, A., Kirkpatrick, B., Ball, P., & Carpenter, W. T., Jr. (1998). Positive and negative symptom response to clozapine in schizophrenic patients with and without the deficit syndrome. *American Journal of Psychiatry, 155,* 751–760.

Carman, J. S., Bigelow, L. B., Wyatt, R. J. (1981). Lithium combined with neuroleptics in chronic schizophrenic and schizoaffective patients. *Journal of Clinical Psychiatry, 42*(3), 124–128.

Carpenter, W. R., Jr., Buchanan, R. W., Kirkpatrick, B., & Breier, A. F. (1999). Diazepam treatment of early signs of exacerbation in schizophrenia. *American Journal of Psychiatry, 156*(2), 299–303.

Carpenter, W. T., Kurg, R., Kirkpatrick, B., Hanlon, T. E., Summerfelt, T., Buchanan, R. W., Waltrip, R. W., & Breier, A. S. (1991). Carbamazepine maintenance treatment in outpatient schizophrenics. *Archives of General Psychiatry, 48,* 69–72.

Carpenter, W. T., Jr., Hanlon, T. E., Heinrichs, D. W., Summerfelt, A. T., Kirkpatrick, B., Levine, J., & Buchanan, R. W. (1990). Continuous versus targeted medication in schizophrenic outpatients: Outcome results. *American Journal of Psychiatry, 147*(9), 1138–1148.

Casey, D. E. (1993). Neuroleptic-induced acute extrapyramidal syndromes and tardive dyskinesia. *Psychiatric Clinics of North America, 16*(3), 589–610.

Casey, J. F., Bennett, I. F., Lindley, C. J., Hollister, L. E., Gordon, M. H., & Springer, N. N. (1960a). Drug therapy in schizophrenia. A controlled study of the relative effectiveness of chlorpromazine, promazine, phenobarbital, and placebo. *Archives of General Psychiatry, 2,* 210–220.

Casey, J. F., Lasky, J. J., Klett, C. J., & Hollister, L. E. (1960b). Treatment of schizophrenic reactions with phenothiazine derivatives: A comparative study of chlorpromazine, triflupromazine, mepazine, prochloperazine, perphenazine and phenobarbital. *American Journal of Psychiatry, 117,* 97–105.

Ceskova, E., & Svestka, J. (1993). Double-blind comparison of risperidone and haloperidol in schizophrenic and schizoaffective psychoses. *Pharmacopsychiatry, 26*(4), 121–124.

Chakos, M., Lieberman, J., Hoffman, E., Bradford, D., & Sheitman, B. (2001). Effectiveness of second-generation antipsychotics in patients with treatment-resistant schizophrenia: A review and meta-analysis of randomized trials. *American Journal of Psychiatry, 158,* 518–526.

Chanpattana, W., Chakrabhand, M. L., Kongsakon, R., Techakasem, P., & Buppanharun, W. (1999). Short-term effect of combined ECT and neuroleptic therapy in treatment-resistant schizophrenia. *Journal of Electroconvulsive Therapy, 15*(2), 129–139.

Chanpattana, W., Chakrabhand, M. L., Buppanharun, W., & Sackeim, H. A. (2000). Effects of stimulus intensity on the efficacy of bilateral ECT in schizophrenia: a preliminary study. *Biological Psychiatry, 48*(3), 222–228.

Chouinard, G., Jones, B., Remington, G., Bloom, D., Addington, D., MacEwan, G. W., Labelle, A., Beauclair, L., & Arnott, W. (1993). A Canadian multicenter placebo-controlled study of fixed doses of risperidone and haloperidol in the treatment of chronic schizophrenic patients. *Journal of Clinical Psychopharmacology, 13*(1), 25–40.

Christison, G. W., Kirch, D. G., & Wyatt, R. J. (1991). When symptoms persist: Choosing among alternatives somatic treatments for schizophrenia. *Schizophrenia Bulletin, 17*(2), 217–245.

Claghorn, J., Honigfeld, G., Abuzzahab, F. S., Sr., Wang, R., Steinbook, R., Tuason, V., & Klerman, G. (1987). The risks and benefits of clozapine versus chlorpromazine. *Journal of Clinical Psychopharmacology, 7*(6), 377–384.

Clark, M. L., Huber, W. K., Kyriakopoulos, A. A., Ray, T. S., Colmore, J. P., & Ramsey, H. R. (1968). Evaluation of trifluperidol in chronic schizophrenia. *Psychopharmacologia, 12*(3), 193–203.

Clark, M. L., Huber, W. K., Sakata, K., Fowles, D. C., & Serafetinides, E. A. (1970). Molindone in chronic schizophrenia. *Clinical Pharmacology Therapy, 11*(5), 680–688.

Clark, M. L., Huber, W. K., Sullivan, J., Wood, F., & Costiloe, J. P. (1972). Evaluation of loxapine succinate in chronic schizophrenia. *Diseases of the Nervous System, 33*(12), 783–791.

Claus, A., Bollen, J., De Cuyper, H., Eneman, M., Malfroid, M., Peuskens, J., & Heylen, S. (1992). Risperidone versus haloperidol in the treatment of chronic schizophrenic inpatients: A multicentre double-blind comparative study. *Acta Psychiatrica Scandinavica, 85*(4), 295–305.

Cohen, W. J., & Cohen, N. H. (1974). Lithium carbonate, haloperidol and irreversible brain damage. *Journal of the American Medical Association, 230,* 1283–1287.

Cole, J. O., Goldberg, S. C., & Klerman, G. L. (1964). Phenothiazine treatment in acute schizophrenia. *Archives of General Psychiatry, 10,* 246–261.

Conley, R. R., Tamminga, C. A., Bartko, J. J., Richardson, C., Peszke, M., Lingle, J., Hegerty, J., Love, R., Gounaris, C., & Zaremba, S. (1998). Olanzapine compared with chlorpromazine in treatment-resistant schizophrenia. *American Journal of Psychiatry, 155*(7), 914–920.

Copolov, D. L., Link, C. G., & Kowalcyk, B. (2000). A multicentre, double-blind, randomized comparison of quetiapine (ICI 204,636, 'Seroquel') and haloperidol in schizophrenia. *Psychological Medicine, 30*(1), 95–105.

Csernansky, J. G., Riney, S. J., Lombrozo, L., Overall, J. E., & Hollister, L. E. (1988). Double-blind comparison of alprazolam, diazepam, and placebo for the treatment of negative schizophrenic symptoms. *Archives of General Psychiatry, 45,* 655–659.

Daniel, D. G., Zimbroff, D. L., Potkin, S. G., Reeves, K. R., Harrigan, E. P., & Lakshminarayan, M. (1999). Ziprasidone Study Group: Ziprasidone 80mg/day and 160mg/day in the acute exacerbation of schizophrenia and schizoaffective disorder: a six-week placebo-controlled trial. *Neuropsychopharmacology, 20*(5), 491–505.

Davidson, M., Kahn, R. S., Powchik, P., Warne, P., Losonczy, M. F., Kaminsky, R., Apter, S., Jaff, S., & Davis, K. L. (1991). Changes in plasma homovanillic acid concentrations in schizophrenic patients following neuroleptic discontinuation. *Archives of General Psychiatry, 48*(1), 73–76.

Davis, J. M. (1975). Overview: Maintenance therapy in psychiatry: 1. Schizophrenia. *American Journal of Psychiatry, 132*(12), 1237–1245.

Davis, J. M., Barter, J. T., & Kane, J. M. (1989). Antipsychotic drugs. In H. I. Kaplan & B. J. Sadock (Eds.), *Comprehensive textbook of psychiatry* (5th ed.). Baltimore: Williams & Wilkins.

Donaldson, S. R., Gelenberg, A. J., & Baldessarini, R. J. (1983). The pharmacologic treatment of schizophrenia: A progress report. *Schizophrenia Bulletin, 9*(4), 504–527.

Duggan, L., Fenton, M., Dardennes, R. M., El-Dosoky, A., & Indran, S. (2001). Olanzapine for schizophrenia (Cochrane Review). *Cochrane Library,* Issue 2. Oxford: Update Software.

Ericksen, S. E., Hurt, S. W., & Chang, S. (1978). Haloperidol dose, plasma levels, and clinical response: A double-blind study. *Psychopharmacology Bulletin, 14*(2), 15–16.

Escobar, J. I., Mann, J. J., Keller, J., Wilkins, J., Mason, B., & Mills, M. J. (1985). Comparison of injectable molindone and haloperidol followed by oral dosage forms in acutely ill schizophrenics. *Journal of Clinical Psychiatry, 46*(8, Pt 2), 15–19.

Essock, S. M., Hargreaves, W. A., Covell, N. H., & Goethe, J. (1996). Clozapine's effectiveness for patients in state hospitals: Results from a randomized trial. *Psychopharmacology Bulletin, 32*(4), 683–697.

Essock, S. M., Hargreaves, W. A., Hohm, F. A., Goethe, C. L., & Hipshman, L. (1996). Clozapine eligibility among state hospital patients. *Schizophrenia Bulletin, 22,* 15–25.

Evins, A. E., Fitzgerald, S. M., Wine, L., Rosselli, R., & Goff, D. C. (2000). Placebo-controlled trial of glycine added to clozapine in schizophrenia. *American Journal of Psychiatry, 157*(5), 826–828.

Farmer, A. E., & Blewett, A. (1993). Drug treatment of resistant schizophrenia. Limitations and recommendations. *Drugs, 45*(3), 374–383.

Fox, W., Gobble, I. F., Clos, M., & Denison, E. (1964). A clinical comparison of trifluperidol, haloperidol, and chlorpromazine. *Current Therapeutic Research—Clinical and Experimental, 6*, 409–415.

Freeman, H., Oktem, M. R., & Oktem, N. (1969). A double-blind comparison of the therapeutic efficacy of mesoridazine versus chlorpromazine. *Current Therapeutic Research—Clinical and Experimental, 11*(5), 263–270.

Fruensgaard, K., Korsgaard, S., Jorgensen, H., & Jensen, K. Loxapine versus haloperidol parenterally in acute psychosis with agitation: A double-blind study. *Acta Psychiatrica Scandinavica, 56*(4), 256–264.

Gaebel, W., Frick, U., Kopcke, W., Linden, M., Muller, P., Muller-Spahn, F., Pietzcker, A., & Tegeler, J. (1993). Early neuroleptic intervention in schizophrenia: Are prodromal symptoms valid predictors of relapse? *British Journal of Psychiatry* (Suppl.), (21), 8–12.

Gallant, D. M., & Bishop, M. P. (1968). Molindone: A controlled evaluation in chronic schizophrenic patients. *Current Therapeutic Research—Clinical and Experimental, 10*(9), 441–447.

Gallant, D. M., Bishop, M. P., Bishop, G., & Steele, C. A. (1968). Thiothixene: A controlled evaluation of the intramuscular antipsychotic preparation. *Current Therapeutic Research—Clinical and Experimental, 10*(11), 561–565.

Gallant, D. M., Bishop, M. P., Timmons, E., & Gould, A. R. (1966). Thiothixene (P-4657B): A controlled evaluation in chronic schizophrenic patients. *Current Therapeutic Research—Clinical and Experimental, 8*(4), 153–158.

Gardos, G. (1974). Are antipsychotic drugs interchangeable? *Journal of Nervous and Mental Disease, 159*(5), 343–348.

Garry, J. W., & Leonard, T. J. (1962). A controlled trial in chronic schizophrenia. *Journal of Mental Science, 108*, 105–107.

Gattaz, W. F., Rost, W., Hubner, C. K., & Bauer, K. (1989). Acute and subchronic effects of low-dose bromocriptine in haloperidol-treated schizophrenics. *Biological Psychiatry, 25*(3), 247–255.

Geddes, J., Freemantle, N., Harrison P., & Bebbington, P. (2000). Atypical antipsychotics in the treatment of schizophrenia: Systemic overview and meta-regression analysis. *British Medical Journal, 32*(1), 72–73, 1371–1376.

Gelenberg, A. J., & Doller, J. C. (1979). Clozapine versus chlorpromazine for the treatment of schizophrenia: Preliminary results from a double-blind study. *Journal of Clinical Psychiatry, 40*(5), 238–240.

Gerlach, J., & Luhdorf, K. (1975). The effect of L-dopa on young patients with simple schizophrenia, treated with neuroleptic drugs: A double-blind cross-over trial with madopar and placebo. *Psychopharmacologic, 44*, 105–110.

Glazer, W. M., Morgenstern, H., & Doucette, J. T. (1993). Predicting the long-term risk of tardive dyskinesia in outpatients maintained on neuroleptic medications. *Journal of Clinical Psychiatry, 54*(4), 133–139.

Goff, D. C., Henderson, D. C., & Evins, A. E., & Amico, E. (1999b). A placebo-controlled crossover trial of D-cycloserine added to clozapine in patients with schizophrenia. *Biological Psychiatry, 45*, 512–514.

Goff, D. C., Posever, T., Herz, L., Simmons, J., Kletti, N., Lapierre, K., Wilner, K. D., Law, C. G., & Ko, G. N. (1998). An exploratory Haloperidol-controlled dose-finding study of ziprasidone in hospitalised patients with schizophrenia or schizoaffective disorder. *Journal of Clinical Psychopharmacology, 18*(4), 296–304.

Goff, D. C., Tsai, G., Levitt, J., Amico, E., Manoach, D., Schoenfeld, D. A., Hayden, D. L., McCarley, R., & Coyle, J. T. (1999a). A placebo-controlled trial of D-cycloserine added to conventional neuroleptics in patients with schizophrenia. *Archives of General Psychiatry, 56*, 21–27.

Goff, D. C., Tsai, G., Manoach, D. S., & Coyle, J. T. (1995). Dose-finding trial of D-cycloserine added to neuroleptics for negative symptoms in schizophrenia. *American Journal of Psychiatry, 152*(8), 1213–1215.

Goldberg, T. E., Bigelow, L. B., Weinberger, D. R., Daniel, D. G., & Kleinman, J. E. (1991). Cognitive and behavioral effects of the coadministration of dextroamphetamine and haloperidol in schizophrenia. *American Journal of Psychiatry, 148*(1), 78–84.

Green, M. F. (1996). What are the functional consequences of neurocognitive deficits in schizophrenia? *American Journal of Psychiatry, 153*, 321–330.

Growe, G. A., Crayton, J. W., Klass, D. B., Evans, H., & Strizich, M. (1979). Lithium in chronic schizophrenia. *American Journal of Psychiatry, 136*(4A), 454–455.

Hanlon, T. E., Michaux, M. H., Ota, K. Y., Shaffer, J. W., & Kurland, A. A. (1965). The comparative effectiveness of eight phenothiazines. *Psychopharmacologia (Berl.), 7*, 89–106.

Harvey, P. D., Howanitz, E., Parrella, M., White, L., Davidson, M., Mohs, R. C., Hoblyn, J., & Davis, K. L. (1998). Symptoms, cognitive functioning, and adaptive skills in geriatric patients with lifelong schizophrenia: A comparison across treatment sites. *American Journal of Psychiatry, 155*, 1080–1086.

Heresco-Levy, U., Javitt, D. C., Ermilov, M., Mordel, C., Silipo, G., & Lichtenstein, M. (1999). Efficacy of high-dose glycine in the treatment of enduring negative symptoms of schizophrenia. *Archives of General Psychiatry, 56*(1), 29–36.

Heresco-Levy, U., Silipo, G., & Javitt, D. C. (1996). Glycinergic augmentation of NMDA receptor-mediated neurotransmission in the treatment of schizophrenia. *Psychopharmacology Bulletin.* 32(4), 731–740.

Herz, M. I., Glazer, W. M., Mostert, M. A., Sheard, M. A., Szymanski, H. V., Hafez, H., Mirza, M., & Vana, J. (1991). Intermittent vs maintenance medication in schizophrenia. Two-year results. *Archives of General Psychiatry, 48*(4), 333–339.

Hogarty, G. E., McEvoy, J. P., Munetz, M., DiBarry, A. L., Bartone, P., Cather, R., Cooley, S. J., Ulrich, R. F., Carter, M., & Madonia, M. J. (1988). Dose of fluphenazine, familial expressed emotion, and outcome in schizophrenia. Results of a two-year controlled study. *Archives of General Psychiatry, 45*(9), 797–805.

Hogarty, G. E., McEvoy, J. P., Ulrich, R. F., DiBarry, A. L., Bartone, P., Cooley, S., Hammill, K., Carter, M., Munetz, M. R., & Perel, J. (1995). Pharmacotherapy of impaired affect in recovering schizophrenic patients. *Archives of General Psychiatry, 52*, 29–41.

Hogarty, G. E., Ulrich, R. F., Mussare, F., & Aristigueta, N. (1976). Drug discontinuation among long term, successfully maintained schizophrenic outpatients. *Diseases of the Nervous System, 37*(9), 494–500.

Hollister, L. E., Erickson, G. V., & Motzenbecker, F. P. (1960). Trifluoperazine in chronic psychiatric patients. *Journal of Clinical and Experimental Psychopathology, 21*, 15–24.

Hong, C. J., Chen, J. Y., Chiu, H. J., & Sim, C. B. (1997). A double-blind comparative study of clozapine versus chlorpromazine on Chinese patients with treatment-refractory schizophrenia. *International Clinical Psychopharmacology, 12*, 123–130.

Hoyberg, O. J., Fensbo, C., Remvig, J., Lingjaerde, O., Sloth-Nielsen, M., & Salvesen, I. (1993). Risperidone versus perhenazine in the treatment of chronic schizophrenic patients with acute exacerbations. *Acta Psychiatrica Scandinavia, 88*(6), 395–402.

Huang, C. C., Gerhardstein, R. P., Kim, D. Y., & Hollister, L. (1987). Treatment-resistant schizophrenia: controlled study of moderate- and high-dose thiothixene. *International Clinical Psychopharmacology, 2*(1), 69–75.

Inanaga, K., Nakazawa, Y., Inoue, K., Tachibana, H., Oshima, M., & Kotorii, T. (1975). Double-blind controlled study of L-dopa therapy in schizophrenia. *Japonica, 29*(2), 123–143.

Javitt, D. C., & Zukin, S. R. (1991). Recent advances in the phencyclidine model of schizophrenia. *American Journal of Psychiatry, 148*(1), 1301–1308.

Javitt, D. C., Zylberman, I., Zukin, S. R., Heresco-Levy, U., & Lindenmayer, J. P. (1994). Amelioration of negative symptoms in schizophrenia by glycine. *American Journal of Psychiatry, 151*(8), 1234–1236.

Jeste, D. V., Okamoto, A., Napolitano, J., Kane, J. M., & Martinez, R. A. (1999). Low incidence of persistent tardive dyskinesia in elderly patients with dementia treated with risperidone. *American Journal of Psychiatry, 157*(7), 1150–1155.

Johns, C. A., & Thompson, J. W. (1995). Adjunctive treatments in schizophrenia: Pharmacotherapies and electoconvulsive therapy. *Schizophrenia Bulletin, 21*(4), 607–619.

Johnson, D. A., Ludlow, J. M., Street, K., & Taylor, R. D. (1987). Double-blind comparison of half-dose and standard-dose flupenthixol decanoate in the maintenance treatment of stabilised outpatients with schizophrenia. *British Journal of Psychiatry, 151*, 634–638.

Johnstone, E. C., Crow, T. J., Frith, C. D., & Owens, D. G. (1988). The Northwick Park "functional" psychosis study: Diagnosis and treatment response. *Lancet, 2*, 119–125.

Jolley, A. G., Hirsch, S. R., Morrison, E., McRink, A., & Wilson, L. (1990). Trial of brief intermittent neuroleptic prophylaxis for selected schizophrenic outpatients: Clinical and social outcome at two years. *British Medical Journal, 301*(6756), 837–842.

Kane, J., Honigfeld, G., Singer, J., & Meltzer, H. (1988). Clozapine for the treatment-resistant schizophrenic: A double-blind comparison with chlorpromazine. *Archives of General Psychiatry, 45*(9), 789–796.

Kane, J. M., Davis, J. M., Schooler, N. R., Marder, S. R., Brauzer, B., & Casey, D. E. (1993). A one-year comparison of four dosages of haloperidol decanoate. *Schizophrenia Research, 9*, 239–240. (abstract)

Kane, J. M., & Lieberman, J. M. (1987). Maintenance pharmacotherapy in schizophrenia. In H. Y. Meltzer (Ed.), *Psychopharmacology: The third generation of progress.* New York: Raven Press.

Kane, J. M., Marder, S. R., Schooler, N. R., Wirshing, W. C., Umbricht, D., Baker, R. W., Wirshing, D. A., Safferman, A., Ganguli, R., & Borenstein, M. (2001). Clozapine and haloperidol in moderately refractory schizophrenia: A six-month double-blind comparison. *Archives of General Psychiatry, 58*, 965–972.

Kane, J. M., Rifkin, A., Quitkin, F., Nayak, D., & Ramos-Lorenzi, J. (1982). Fluphenazine vs placebo in patients with remitted, acute first episode schizophrenia. *Archives of General Psychiatry, 39*(1), 70–73.

Kane, J. M., Rifkin, A., Woerner, M., Reardon, G., Sarantakos, S., Schiebel, D., & Ramos-Lorenzi, J. (1983). Low-dose neuroleptic treatment of outpatient schizophrenics: 1. Preliminary results for relapse rates. *Archives of General Psychiatry, 40*(8), 893–896.

Kane, J. M., Woerner, M., & Lieberman, J. (1985). Tardive dyskinesia: prevalence, incidence, and risk factors. *Psychopharmacology Supplement 2*, 72–78.

Kane, J. M., Woerner, M., & Sarantakos, S. (1986). Depot neuroleptics: A comparative review of standard, intermediate, and low-dose regimens. *Journal of Clinical Psychiatry, 47*(Suppl.), 30–33.

Karson, C. N., Weinberger, D. R., Bigelow, L., & Wyatt, R. J. (1982). Clonazepam treatment of chronic schizophrenia: Negative results in a double-blind, placebo-controlled trial. *American Journal of Psychiatry, 139*(12), 1627–1628.

Keck, P., Jr., Buffenstein, A., Ferguson, J., Feighner, J., Jaffe, W., Harrigan, E. P., & Morrissey, M. R. (1998). Ziprasidone 40 and 120 mg/day in the acute exacerbation of schizophrenia and schizoaffective disorder: A 4-week placebo-controlled trial. *Psychopharmacology (Berl)140*(2), 173–184.

Kellner, R., Wilson, R. M., Muldawer, M. D., & Pathak, D. (1975). Anxiety in schizophrenia. The responses to chlordiazepoxide in an intensive design study. *Archives of General Psychiatry, 32*(10), 1246–1254.

Kennedy, E., Song, F., Hunter, R., Clarke, A., & Gilbody, S. (2001). Risperidone versus typical antipsychotic medication for schizophrenia (Cochrane Review). In *Cochrane Library*, Issue 2. Oxford: Update Software.

Kinon, B. J., Kane, J. M., Johns, C., Perovich, R., Ismi, M., Koreen, A., & Weiden, P. (1993). Treatment of neuroleptic-resistant schizophrenic relapse. *Psychopharmacology Bulletin, 29*(2), 309–311.

Kinon, B. J., & Lieberman, J. A. (1996). Mechanisms of action of atypical antipsychotic drugs: A critical analysis. *Psychopharmacology, 124*, 2–34.

Klein, D. F., & Davis, J. M. (1969). Review of the antipsychotic drug literature. In D. F. Klein & J. M. David (Eds.), *Diagnosis and drug treatment of psychiatric disorders*. Baltimore: Williams & Wilkins.

Klein, E., Bental, E., Lerer, B., & Belmaker, R. H. (1984). Carbamazepine and haloperidol vs. placebo and haloperidol in excited psychoses. A controlled study. *Archives of General Psychiatry, 41*(2), 165–170.

Klieser, E., Strauss, W. H., & Lemmer, W. (1994). The tolerability and efficacy of the atypical neuroleptic remoxipride compared with clozapine and haloperidol in acute schizophrenia. *Acta Psychiatrica Scandinavica* (Suppl.), *380*, 68–73.

Ko, G. N., Korpi, E. R., Freed, W. J., Zalcman, S. J., & Bigelow, L. B. (1985). Effect of valproicacid on behavior and plasma amino acid concentrations in chronic schizophrenic patients. *Biological Psychiatry, 20*(2), 209–215.

Kumra, S., Frazier, J. A., Jacobsen, L. K., McKenna, K., Gordon, C. T., Lenane, M. C., Hamburger, S. D., Smith, A. K., Albus, K. E., Alaghband-Rad, J., & Rapoport, J. L. (1996). Childhood-onset schizophrenia: a double-blind clozapine-haloperidol comparison. *Archives of General Psychiatry, 53*, 1090–1097.

Kunovac, J., Leposavic, L. J., Jasovic-Gasic, M., & Paunovic, V. R. (1991). Efficacy of carbamazepine as an adjuvant therapy in the treatment of positive and negative symptoms in schizophrenia. *Biological Psychiatry, 29*, 395–402. (abstract)

Kurland, A. A., Hanlon, T. E., Tatom, M. H., Ota, K. Y., & Simopoulos, A. M. (1961). The comparative effectiveness of six phenothiazine compounds, phenobarbital and inert placebo in the treatment of acutely ill patients: Global measures of severity of illness. *Journal of Nervous and Mental Disease, 133*, 1–18.

Laskey, J. J., Klett, C. J., Caffey, E. M., Bennett, J. L., Rosenblum, M. D., & Hollister, L. E. (1962). Drug treatment of schizophrenic patients. *Diseases of the Nervous System, 23*, 698–706.

Lee, M. S., Kim, Y. K., Lee, S. K., & Suh, K. Y. (1998). A double-blind study of adjunctive sertraline in haloperidol-stabilized patients with chronic schizophrenia. *Journal of Clinical Psychopharmacology, 18*(5), 399–403.

Leon, C. A. (1979). Therapeutic effects of clozapine: A 4-year follow-up of a controlled clinical trial. *Acta Psychiatrica Scandinavica, 59*(5), 471–480.

Leucht, S., McGrath, J., White, P., & Kissling, W. (2001). Carbamazepine for schizophrenia and schizoaffective psychoses (Cochrane Review). In *Cochrane Library*, Issue 2, 2001. Oxford: Update Software.

Levinson, D. F., Simpson, G. M., Singh, H., Yadalam, K., Jain, A., Stephanos, M. J., & Silver, P. (1990). Fluphenazine dose, clinical response, and extrapyramidal symptoms during acute treatment. *Archives of General Psychiatry, 47*(8), 761–768.

Lewis, R., Bagnall, A.-M., & Leitner, M. (2001). Sertindole for schizophrenia (Cochrane Review). In

Cochrane Library, Issue 2, 2001. Oxford: Update Software.

Liddle, P., Carpenter, W. T., & Crow, T. (1994). Syndromes of schizophrenia. *British Journal of Psychiatry, 165*(6), 721–727.

Lieberman, J. A. (1993). Prediction of outcome in first-episode schizophrenia. *Journal of Clinical Psychiatry, 54*(Suppl.), 13–17.

Lindenmayer, J. P. (1995). New pharmacotherapeutic modalities for negative symptoms in psychosis. *Acta Psychiatrica Scandinavica, 91*(388), 15–19.

Linnoila, M., & Viukari, M. (1979). Sodium valproate and tardive dyskinesia. *British Journal of Psychiatry, 134,* 223–224.

Linnoila, M., Viukari, M., & Hietala, O. (1976). Effect of sodium valproate on tardive dyskinesia. *British Journal of Psychiatry, 129,* 114–119.

Loebel, A. D., Lieberman, J. A., Alvir, J. M., Mayerhoff, D. I., Geisler, S. H., & Szymanski, S. R. (1992). Duration of psychosis and outcome in first-episode schizophrenia. *American Journal of Psychiatry, 149*(9), 1183–1188.

Luby, E. D., Cohen, B. D., Rosenbaum, G., Gottlieb, J. S., & Kelley, R. (1959). Study of a new schizophreniomimetic drug—Sernyl. *American Medical Association Archives of Neurological Psychiatry, 81,* 363–369.

Marder, S. R., & Meibach, R. C. (1994). Risperidone in the treatment of schizophrenia. *American Journal of Psychiatry, 151*(6), 825–835.

Marder, S. R., Van Putten, T., Mintz, J., Lebell, M., McKenzie, J., & May, P. R. (1987). Low and conventional-dose maintenance therapy with fluphenazine decanoate: Two year outcome. *Archives of General Psychiatry, 44*(6), 518–521.

May, P. R., Tuma, A. H., Yale, C., Potepan, P., & Dixon, W. J. (1976). Schizophrenia—A follow up study of results of treatment: 2. Hospital stay over two to five years. *Archives of General Psychiatry, 33,* 481–486.

May, P. R., Tuma, A. H., Dixon, W. J., Yale, C., Thiele, D. A., & Kraude, W. H. (1981). Schizophrenia: A follow-up study of the results of five forms of treatment. *Archives of General Psychiatry, 38*(7), 776–784.

McCreadie, R. G., & MacDonald, I. M. (1977). High dosage haloperidol in chronic schizophrenia. *British Journal of Psychiatry, 131,* 310–316.

McGlashan, T. H., & Carpenter, W. T. (1976). Postpsychotic depression in schizophrenia. *Archives of General Psychiatry,* 33, 231–239.

McIndoo, M. V. (1971). A controlled study of mesoridazine: an effective treatment for schizophrenia. *Southern Medical Journal, 64*(5), 592–596.

Meltzer, H. Y. (1992). Treatment of the neuroleptic-nonresponsive schizophrenic patient. *Schizophrenia Bulletin, 18*(3), 515–541.

Meltzer, H. Y., Burnett, S., Bastani, B., & Ramirez, L. F. (1990). Effects of six months of clozapine treatment on the quality of life of chronic schizophrenic patients. *Hospital and Community Psychiatry, 41*(8), 892–897.

Meltzer, H. Y., Sdommers. A. A., & Luchins, D. J. (1986). The effect of neuroleptics and other psychotropic drugs on negative symptoms in schizophrenia. *Journal of Clinical Psychopharmacology,* 6(6), 329–338.

Meszaros, K., Simhandl, C., Liechtenstein, A., Denk, E., Topitz, A., & Thau, K. (1991). Clinical efficacy of adjunctive carbamazepine in chronic schizophrenia. *Biological Psychiatry, 29,* 386–394.

Miller, D. D., Perry, P. J., Cadoret, R., & Andreasen, N. C. (1992). A two and one-half year follow-up of treatment-refractory schizophrenics treated with clozapine. *Biological Psychiatry, 31*(Suppl), 85A.

Min, S. K., Rhee, C. S., Kim, C. E., & Kang, D. Y. (1993). Risperidone versus haloperidol in the treatment of chronic schizophrenic patients: A parallel group double-blind comparative trial. *Yonsei Medical Journal,* 34(2), 179–190.

Morgenstern, H., & Glazer, W. M. (1993). Identifying risk factors for tardive dyskinesia among long-term outpatients maintained with neuroleptic medications: Results of the Yale Tardive Dyskinesia Study. *Archives of General Psychiatry, 50*(9), 723–733.

Muller-Spahn, F. (1992). Risperidone in the treatment of chronic schizophrenic patients: an international double-blind parallel-group study versus haloperidol: The International Risperidone Research Group. *Clinical Neuropharmacology, 15*(Suppl. 1, Pt. A), 90A–91A.

Nachshoni, T., Levin, Y., Levy, A., Kritz, A., & Neumann, M. (1994). A double-blind trial of carbamazepine in negative symptom schizophrenia. *Society of Biological Psychiatry, 35,* 22–26.

National Institute of Mental Health-Psychopharmacology Service Center Collaborative Study Group. (1964). Phenothiazine treatment in acute schizophrenia. *Archives of General Psychiatry, 10,* 246–261.

Neborsky, R., Janowsky, D., Munson, E., & Depry, D. (1981). Rapid treatment of acute psychotic symptoms with high- and low-dose haloperidol. Behavioral considerations. *Archives of General Psychiatry,* 38(2), 195–199.

Neppe, V. M. (1983). Carbamazepine as adjunctive treatment in nonepileptic, chronic inpatients with

EEG temporal lobe abnormalities. *Journal of Clinical Psychiatry, 44*(9), 326–331.

Okasha, A., & Twefik, G. (1964). A controlled clinical trial in chronic disturbed psychotic patients. *British Journal of Psychiatry, 110*, 56–60.

Okuma, T., Yamashita, I., Takahashi, R., Itoh, H., Otsuki, S., Watanabe, S., Sarai, K., Hazasma, H., & Inanaga, K. (1989). A double-blind study of adjunctive carbamazepine versus placebo on excited states of schizophrenic and schizoaffective disorders. *Acta Psychiatrica Scandinavica, 80*, 250–259.

Perovich, R. M., Lieberman, J. A., Fleischhacker, W. W., & Alvir, J. (1989). The behavior toxicity of bromocriptine in patients with psychiatric illness. *Journal of Clinical Psychopharmacology*, 9(6), 417–422.

Peuskens, J. (1995). Risperidone in the treatment of patients with chronic schizophrenia: A multinational, multi-centre, double-blind, parallel-group study versus haloperidol: Risperidone Study Group. *British Journal of Psychiatry, 166*(6), 712–726.

Peuskens, J., & Link, C. G. (1997, October). A comparison of quetiapine and chlorpromazine in the treatment of schizophrenia. *Acta Psychiatrica Scandinavica, 96*(4), 265–273.

Pickar, D., Owen, R. R., Litman, R. E., Konicki, E., Gutierrez, R., & Rapaport, M. H. (1992). Clinical and biologic response to clozapine in patients with schizophrenia: Crossover comparison with fluphenazine. *Archives of General Psychiatry, 49*(5), 345–353.

Plasky, P. (1991). Antidepressant usage in schizophrenia. *Schizophrenia Bulletin, 17*(4), 649–657.

Potkin, S. G., Costa, J., Roy, S., Sramek, J., Jin, Y., & Gulasekaram, B. (1992). Glycine in the treatment of schizophrenia: Theory and preliminary results. In H. Y. Meltzer (Ed.), *Novel antipsychotic drugs*. New York: Raven Press.

Potkin, S. G., Jin, Y., Bunney, B. G., Costa, J., & Gulasekaram, B. (1999). Effect of clozapine and adjunctive high-dose glycine in treatment-resistant schizophrenia. *American Journal of Psychiatry, 156*(1), 145–147.

Pratt, J. P., Bishop, M. P., & Gallant, D. M. (1964). Comparison of haloperidol, trifluperidol, and chlorpromazine in acute schizophrenic patients. *Current Therapeutic Research—Clinical and Experimental, 6*, 562–571.

Quitkin, F., Rifkin, A., & Klein, D. F. (1975). Very high dosage vs standard dosage fluphenazine in schizophrenia: A double-blind study of nonchronic treatment-refractory patients. *Archives of General Psychiatry*, 32(10), 1276–1281.

Reese, L., & Davies, B. (1965). A study of the value of haloperidol in the management and treatment of schizophrenic and manic patients. *International Journal of Neuropsychiatry, 1*, 263–265.

Rickels, K., Byrdy, H., Valentine. J., Postel, W., Norstad, N., & Downing, R. (1978). Double-blind trial of thiothixene and chlorpromazine in acute schizophrenia. *International Pharmacopsychiatry, 13*(1), 50–57.

Rifkin, A. (1993). Pharmacologic strategies in the treatment of schizophrenia. *Psychiatric Clinics of North America, 16*(2), 351–363.

Rifkin, A., Doddi, S., Karajgi, B., Borenstein, M., & Wachspress, M. (1991). Dosage of haloperidol for schizophrenia. *Archives of General Psychiatry*, 48(2), 166–170.

Rifkin, A., Rieder, E., Sarantakos, S., Saraf, K., & Kane, J. (1984). Is loxapine more effective than chlorpromazine in paranoid schizophrenia? *American Journal of Psychiatry, 141*(11), 1411–1413.

Ritter, R. M., & Tatum, P. A. (1972). Two studies of the effects of mesoridazine. *Journal of Clinical Pharmacology and New Drugs*, 12(8), 349–355.

Robinson, D., Woerner, M. G., Alvir, J. M., Bilder, R., Goldman, R., Geisler, S., Koreen, A., Sheitman, B., Chakos, M., Mayerhoff, D., & Lieberman, J. A. (1999). Predictors of relapse following response from a first episode of schizophrenia or schizoaffective disorder. *Archives of General Psychiatry, 56*(3), 241–247.

Robinson, D. G. Woerner, M. G., Alvir, J. M., Geisler, S., Koreen, A., Sheitman, B., Chakos, M., Mayerhoff, D., Bilder, R., Goldman, R., & Lieberman, J. A. (1999). Predictors of treatment response from a first episode of schizophrenia or schizoaffective disorder. *American Journal of Psychiatry, 156*(4), 544–549.

Rosenheck, R., Cramer, J., Xu, W., Thomas, J., Henderson, W., Frisman, L., Fye, C., & Charney, D. (Department of Veterans Affairs Cooperative Study Group on Clozapine in Refractory Schizophrenia). (1997). A comparison of clozapine and haloperidol in hospitalized patients with refractory schizophrenia. *New England Journal of Medicine, 337*, 809–815.

Rosse, R. B., Fay-McCarthy, M., Kendrick, K., Davis, R. E., & Deutsch, S. I. (1996). D-cycloserine adjuvant therapy to molindone in the treatment of schizophrenia. *Clinical Neuropharmacology, 19*(5), 444–450.

Salzman, C. (1980). The use of ECT in the treatment of schizophrenia. *American Journal of Psychiatry, 137*(9). 1032–1041.

Salzman, C., Solomon, D., Miyawaki, E., Glassman, R., Rood, L., Flowers, E., & Thayer, S. (1991). Parenteral lorazepam versus parenteral haloperidol for the control of psychotic disruptive behavior. *Journal of Clinical Psychiatry, 52,* 177–180.

Samuels, A. S. (1961). A controlled study of haloperidol: The effects of small dosages. *American Journal of Psychiatry, 118,* 253–260.

Schexnayder, L. W., Hirschowitz, J., Sautter, F. J., & Garver, D. L. (1995). Predictors of response to lithium in patients with psychoses. *American Journal of Psychiatry, 152,* 1511–1513.

Schiele, B. C., Vestre, N. D., & Stein, K. E. (1961). A comparison of thioridazine, trifuoperazine, chlorpromazine, and placebo: A double-blind controlled study on the treatment of chronic, hospitalized, schizophrenic patients. *Journal of Clinical and Experimental Psychopathology, 22,* 151–162.

Schooler, N. R., Goldberg, S. C., Boothe, H., & Cole, J. O. (1967). One year after discharge: Community adjustment of schizophrenic patients. *American Journal of Psychiatry, 123,* 8, 986–995.

Schooler, N. R., Keith, S. J., Severe, J. B., & Mathews, S. M. (1993). Treatment strategies in schizophrenia: Effects of dosage reduction and family management outcome. *Schizophrenia Research, 9,* 260. (abstract)

Schulz, S. C., Thompson, P. A., Jacobs, M., Ninan, P. T., Robinson, D., Weiden, P. J., Yadalam, K., Glick. I. D., & Odbert, C. L. (1999). Lithium augmentation fails to reduce symptoms in poorly responsive schizophrenic outpatients. *Journal of Clinical Psychiatry, 60*(6), 366–372.

Serafetinides, E. A., Willis, D., & Clark, M. L. (1972). Haloperidol, clopenthixol, and chlorpromazine in chronic schizophrenia. *Journal of Nervous and Mental Disease, 155*(5), 366–369.

Shopsin, B., Klein, H., Aaronsn, M., & Collora, M. (1979). Clozapine, chlorpromazine, and placebo in newly hospitalized, acutely schizophrenic patients: A controlled, double-blind comparison. *Archives of General Psychiatry, 36*(6), 657–664.

Silver, H., Barash, I., Aharon, N., Kaplan, A., & Poyurovsky, M. (2000). Fluvoxamine augmentation of antipsychotics improves negative symptoms in psychotic chronic schizophrenic patients: A placebo-controlled study. *International Clinical Psychopharmacology, 15*(5), 257–261.

Silver, H., & Nassar, A. (1992). Fluvoxamine improves negative symptoms in treated chronic schizophrenia: An add-on double-blind, placebo-controlled study. *Biological Psychiatry, 31,* 698–704.

Simhandl, C., Meszaros, K., Denk, E., Thau, K., & Topitz, A. (1996). Adjunctive carbamazepine or lithium carbonate in therapy-resistant, chronic schizophrenia. *Canadian Journal of Psychiatry, 41*(5), 317.

Simpson, G. M., & Cuculic, Z. (1976). A double-blind comparison of loxapine succinate and trifluoperazine in newly admitted schizophrenic patients. *Journal of Clinical Pharmacology, 16*(1), 60–65.

Simpson, G. M., Haher, E. J., Herkert, E., & Lee, J. H. (1973). A controlled comparison of metiapine and chlorpromazine in chronic schizophrenia. *Journal of Clinical Pharmacology, 13*(10), 408–415.

Simpson, G. M., Lament, R., Cooper, T. B., Lee, J. H., & Bruce, R. B. (1973). The relationship between blood levels of different forms of butaperazine and clinical response. *Journal of Clinical Pharmacology, 13*(7), 288–297.

Siris, S. (1993). Adjunctive medication in the maintenance treatment of schizophrenia and its conceptual implications. *British Journal of Psychiatry, 163,* 66–78.

Siris, S., Pollack, S., Bermanzohn, P., & Stronger, R. (2000). Adjunctive imipramine for a broader group of post-psychotic depressions in schizophrenia. *Schizophrenia Research, 44*(3), 187–192.

Siris, S. G. (1991). Diagnosis of secondary depression in schizophrenia: Implications for *DSM-IV. Schizophrenia Bulletin, 17*(1), 75–97.

Siris, S. G., Adam, F., Cohen, M., Mandeli, J., Aronson, A., & Casey, E. (1988). Postpsychotic depression and negative symptoms: An investigation of syndrome overlap. *American Journal of Psychiatry, 145*(12), 1532–1537.

Siris, S. G., Bermanzohn, P. C., Gonzaslez, A., Mason, S. E., White, C. V., & Shuwall, M. A. (1991). The use of antidepressants for negative symptoms in a subset of schizophrenic patients. *Psychopharmacology Bulletin, 27*(3), 331–335.

Siris, S. G., Bermanzohn, P. C., Mason, S. E., & Shuwall, M. A. (1994). Maintenance imipramine therapy for secondary depression in schizophrenia. *Archives of General Psychiatry, 51,* 109–115.

Siris, S. G., Van Kammen, D. P., & Docherty, J. P. (1978). Use of antidepressant drugs in schizophrenia. *Archives of General Psychiatry, 35,* 1368–1377.

Small, J. G., Hirsch, S. R., Arvanitis, L. A., Miller, B. G., & Link, C. G. (1997). Quetiapine in patients with schizophrenia: A high- and low-dose double-blind comparison with placebo: Seroquel Study Group. *Archives of General Psychiatry, 54*(6), 549–557.

Small, J. G., Kellams, J. J., Milstein, V., & Moore, J. (1975). A placebo-controlled study of lithium combined with neuroleptics in chronic schizophrenic patients. *American Journal of Psychiatry, 132*, 1315–1317.

Taylor, P., & Fleminget, J. J. (1980). ECT for schizophrenia. *Lancet* (no volume given), 1380–1382.

Terao, T., Oga, T., Nozaki, S., Ohta, A., Ohtsubo, Yamamoto, S., Zammi, M., & Okada, M. (1995). Lithium addition to neuroleptic treatment in chronic schizophrenia: A randomized, double-blind, placebo-controlled, cross-over study. *Acta Psychiatrica Scandinavica, 92*, 220–224.

Tollefson, G. D., Beasley, C. M., Jr., Tran, P. V., Street, J. S., Krueger, J. A., Tamura, R. N., Graffeo, K. A., & Thieme, M. E. (1997). Olanzapine versus haloperidol in the treatment of schizophrenia and schizoaffective and schizophreniform disorders: Results of an international collaborative trial. *American Journal of Psychiatry, 154*(4), 457–465.

Tsai, G., Yang, P., Chung, L. C., et al. (1998). D-Serine added to antipsychotics for the treatment of schizophrenia. *Biological Psychiatry, 44*, 1081–1089.

Tsai, G. E., Yang, P., Chung, L. C., Tsai, I. C., Tsai, C. W., & Coyle, J. T. (1999). D-serine added to clozapine for the treatment of schizophrenia. *American Journal of Psychiatry, 156*(11), 1822–1825.

Tuason, V. B. (1986). A comparison of parenteral loxapine and haloperidol in hostile and aggressive acutely schizophrenic patients. *Journal of Clinical Psychiatry, 47*(3), 126–129.

Tuason, V. B., Escobar, J. I., Garvey, M., & Schiele, B. (1984). Loxapine versus chlorpromazine in paranoid schizophrenia: A double-blind study. *Journal of Clinical Psychiatry, 45*(4), 158–163.

Van Kammen, D. P., McEvoy, J. P., Targum, S. D., Kardatzke, D., & Sebree, T. B. (1996). A randomized, controlled, dose-ranging trial of sertindole in patients with schizophrenia. *Psychopharmacology (Berlin), 124*(1–2), 168–175.

Van der Velde, C. D., & Kiltie, H. (1975). Effectiveness of loxapine succinate in acute schizophrenia: A comparative study with thiothixene. *Current Therapeutic Research—Clinical and Experimental, 17*(1), 1–12.

Van Putten, T., Marder, S. R., & Mintz, J. (1990). A controlled dose comparison of haloperidol in newly admitted schizophrenic patients [see comments]. *Archives of General Psychiatry, 47*(8), 754–758.

Vestre, N. D., Hall, W. B., & Schiele, B. C. (1962). A comparison of fluphenazine, triflupromazine and phenobarbital in the treatment of chronic schizophrenic patients: A double-blind controlled study. *Journal of Clinical Psychopathology, 23*, 149–159.

Volavka, J., Cooper, T., Czobor, P., Bitter, I., Meisner, M., Laska, E., Gastanaga, P., Krakowski, M., Chou, J. C., Crowner, M., et al. (1992). Haloperidol blood levels and clinical effects. *Archives of General Psychiatry, 49*(5), 354–361.

Volavka, J., Czobor, P., Sheitman, B., Lindenmayer, P., Citrome, L., McEvoy, J., Cooper, T., Chakos, M., & Lieberman, J. (in submission). Clozapine, olanzapine, risperidone, and haloperidol in treatment-resistant patients with schizophrenia and schizoaffective disorder. *American Journal of Psychiatry.*

Wassef, A. A., Dott, S. G., Harris, A., Brown, A., O'Boyle, M., Meyer, W. J., 3rd, & Rose, R M. (2000). Randomized, placebo-controlled pilot study of divalproex sodium in the treatment of acute exacerbations of chronic schizophrenia. *Journal of Clinical Psychopharmacology, 20*(3), 357–361.

Wilson, W. H. (1993). Addition of lithium to haloperidol in non-affective, antipsychotic non-responsive schizophrenia: A double-blind, placebo controlled, parallel design clinical trial. *Psychopharmacology, 111*, 359–366.

Wirshing, D. A., Marshall, B. D., Jr., Green, M. F., Mintz, J., Marder, S. R., & Wirshing, W. C. (2001). Risperidone in treatment refractory schizophrenia. *American Journal of Psychiatry, 156*, 1374–1379.

Wolkowitz, O. M. (1993). Rational polypharmacy in schizophrenia. *Annals of Clinical Psychiatry, 5*, 79–90.

Wolkowitz, O. M., & Pickar, D. (1991). Benzodizapines in the treatment of schizophrenia: A review and reappraisal. *American Journal of Psychiatry, 148*(6), 714–726.

Wolpert, A., Sheppard, C., & Merlis, S. (1968). Thiothixene, thioridazine, and placebo in male chronic schizophrenic patients. *Clinical Pharmacology and Therapeutics, 9*(4), 456–464.

Wyatt, R. J. (1995). Early intervention for schizophrenia: can the course of the illness be altered? *Biological Psychiatry, 38*(1), 1–3.

Yilmaz, A. H. (1971). Thiothixene in chronic schizophrenia. A clinical trial. *Hawaii Medical Journal, 30*(3), 178–182.

Zimbroff, D. L., Kane, J. M., Tamminga, C. A., Daniel, D. G., Mack, R. J., Wozniak, P. J., Sebree, T. B., Wallin, B. A., & Kashkin, K. B. Controlled, dose-response study of sertindole and haloperidol in the treatment of schizophrenia. Sertindole Study Group. *American Journal of Psychiatry, 154*(6), 782–791.

8

Psychosocial Treatments for Schizophrenia

Alex Kopelowicz
Robert Paul Liberman
Roberto Zarate

Stressors like major life events and high expressed emotion in family and residential settings can adversely affect the course of schizophrenia when individuals vulnerable to the disorder are exposed to the stressors without the protection of medication, psychosocial treatment, and natural coping ability and social support. This being so, it is not surprising that the empirical data on treatment outcomes validate a biopsychosocial view of treatment for schizophrenia, including medication, psychosocial treatments, and social support.

Literally hundreds of well-controlled and designed studies of behavior therapy and social learning/token economy programs support the value of treatments that structure, support, and reinforce prosocial behaviors in persons with schizophrenia. Over 20 randomized clinical trials (Type 1 and Type 2 studies) in different parts of the world, using structured, educational family interventions, have shown the superiority of adding family intervention to medication and customary case management for persons with schizophrenia. More than 40 well-controlled and designed studies (Type 1 and Type 2) support the efficacy of social skills training to enable persons with schizophrenia to acquire instrumental and affiliative skills to improve functioning in their communities. These empirically validated, biobehavioral treatments are most efficacious when delivered in a continuous, comprehensive, and well-coordinated manner through a service delivery system such as the consumer-oriented Program for Assertive Community Treatment (PACT).

OVERVIEW OF SCHIZOPHRENIA

Diagnosis

Schizophrenia, the most disabling of the major mental disorders, is characterized by two or more of the following: (a) delusions, (b) hallucinations, (c) disorganized speech, (d) grossly disorganized or catatonic behavior, and (e) negative symptoms. These symptoms must impair social and occupational functioning and be continuously present for at least 6 months. Since other disorders, some with known etiologies, can mimic schizophrenia, before making the diagnosis it is necessary to exclude psychoses resulting from substance abuse, medical conditions that affect the brain (e.g., tumors, Cushing's disease), pervasive developmental disorders, and mood disorders (e.g., bipolar disorder or psychotic depression). In this chapter reviewing the psychological and behavioral treatments for schizophrenia, we shall include schizoaffective disorder with schizophrenia since the two have very similar clinical features, prognoses, and responses to treatments. Because schizophrenia spectrum disorders are almost always treated with antipsychotic drugs, an inventory, evaluation, and interpretation of the literature on psychological and behavioral treatments must view the treatments as *biobehavioral*, that is, multidimensional therapies with pharmacological and psychosocial components.

Etiology and Course of Illness

While there is no definitive evidence identifying one or more causal factors in the etiology of schizophrenia, most authorities would view the extraordinary heterogeneity in psychopathology, psychosocial functioning, and course of illness in this disorder as indicating that our current ignorance of central nervous system functioning masks the likelihood that there is more than one etiology in what we see as the final common pathway of psychosis. There are sufficient data from family and adoptive studies to suggest that complex, multigenetic factors may account for approximately 60% of the etiology of schizophrenia and that schizotypal personality traits may be the genetically determined phenotype (Raine, Lencz, & Mednick, 1995). Strong evidence also supports the role of socioenvironmental factors in influencing the course of the disorder. In particular, early identification and diagnosis followed by appropriate and continuous biopsychosocial treatment have been shown to improve the long-term outcomes of persons with schizophrenia (Wyatt, 1991, 1995).

The onset of schizophrenia typically occurs during adolescence and early adulthood; however, a tiny minority of cases begin during childhood. The disorder affects males and females equally, but males are disproportionately represented in treatment facilities, presumably because their illness-linked, disruptive behavior and functioning become more visible and intolerable to families and society. The onset of the disorder is about 5 years later for females (late 20s) than males (early 20s), most likely because female hormones serve a protective function against abnormalities in neurotransmitter systems (Seeman, 1996).

The long-term course of the disorder can be divided into three groupings, although accessibility to and use of comprehensive, high-quality, and continuous treatment will increase the proportion of persons with schizophrenia who have better outcomes, regardless of the level of functioning at which they may begin their treatment odyssey. One type of course is marked by one or more psychotic episodes with relatively rapid return to premorbid functioning and good prospects for recovery. The second and most common course followed by schizophrenic patients is characterized by many years of recurrent acute psychotic relapses or exacerbations, with periods of full or partial remission and varying degrees of residual impairments in functioning. A final group of about 15% of individuals with schizophrenia fail to respond to currently available treatments and demonstrate the third form of the disorder, with prolonged and persistent psychotic symptoms with moderate to severe personal and social disabilities. The proportion of individuals with treatment-refractory schizophrenia is gradually diminishing with the advent of novel, atypical antipsychotic drugs such as clozapine.

Evidence from several countries documents that over 50% of individuals with well-diagnosed and severe forms of schizophrenia can achieve good states of remission and psychosocial functioning 20 to 30 years after their initial periods of illness (Harding, Zubin, & Strauss, 1992). A key element in recovery requires the patient and practitioner(s) to forge an informed partnership, in which the patient is not a passive recipient of treatment but is an active participant in managing symptoms, preventing or containing relapses, and pursuing long-term social, personal, and occupational goals with abundant social support and training of skills (Liberman, Kopelowicz, & Young, 1994).

The course of schizophrenia can be complicated and adversely affected by concurrent abuse of alcohol, stimulant drugs (cocaine, amphetamines), or marijuana. These agents are all well documented as stressors in the exacerbation of psychosis in individuals vulnerable to schizophrenia. The financial cost to a family with a relative who has severe mental illness (e.g., schizophrenia) and concurrent substance abuse is significantly greater than the costs to families of a relative with mental illness alone; the annual costs were $13,891 per family and $3,547 per family, respectively (Clark, 1994). The prevailing view of comorbid substance abuse in schizophrenia that patients are attempting to self-medicate their depression, or positive or negative symptoms, is not borne out by the facts. Substance abuse exacerbates rather than ameliorate psychiatric symptoms (Shaner et al., 1995).

Other factors complicating the treatment and outcome of schizophrenia are comorbidity with developmental disabilities (e.g., schizophrenic symptoms developing in adolescence in an individual who has had autism since birth), comorbidity with depression (commonly present and a risk factor for suicidality), comorbidity with anxiety disorders (the presence of obsessive compulsive disorder is a predictor of poor prognosis), and homelessness (which presents a challenge to engaging and maintaining the individual in treatment).

Environments that are high in stress—either through hostility or criticism of the person with schizophrenia or emotional overinvolvement ("high expressed emotion")—have been shown in replicated international studies to carry a significantly higher risk of relapse in individuals with schizophrenia. Since the source of stressful social environments is caregivers' lack of education about the nature and proper treatment of schizophrenia, combined with the challenging and burdensome symptoms and disability exhibited by the person with schizophrenia, treatment techniques (see below, "Structured Educational Family Interventions") have been designed and validated to improve the emotional climate in relationships that the patient has with significant others in his or her living environment. Improvements in the family emotional climate have resulted in reduced relapse rates.

Consensus among authorities in the field supports an explanatory and heuristic model of the etiology, course, and outcome of schizophrenia that incorporates *vulnerability, stress, and protective factors* (Nuechterlein et al., 1994). Vulnerability factors (e.g., genes, neurodevelopmental anomalies, abnormalities in brain neural networks and neurotransmitter systems) are relatively enduring abnormalities of individuals at risk for schizophrenia that are present before, during, and after psychotic episodes. Stressors include role expectations, daily hassles, and major life events that demand adaptive changes from the individual, challenge the individual's coping abilities, and sometimes serve as triggers for psychotic episodes (e.g., drugs of abuse, high stress in the patient's living environment, major life events, and even toxic side effects of antipsychotic medications). Personal and environmental protective factors (e.g., social skills, supportive family, judicious types and doses of antipsychotic medication embedded in comprehensive and continuous treatment services) allow a vulnerable individual to buffer the deleterious effects of stressors superimposed on vulnerability and to avoid or mitigate relapse (Ventura & Liberman, 2000).

Prevalence and Cost

Based on epidemiological studies, 2 million persons in the United States are afflicted with schizophrenia or schizoaffective disorder, representing 1.1% of the population (Regier et al., 1993). There are over 300,000 acute episodes of schizophrenia annually in the United States, and the economic cost of this disorder to the nation, in terms of treatment and lost income, is more than $30 billion per year (National Institute of Menal Health [NIMH], 1995). The lifetime loss of income for a male diagnosed as having schizophrenia late in adolescence has been calculated to be $1.25 million (Wyatt et al., 1995). An estimated 100,000 hospital beds on any given day are filled with persons with schizophrenia (Rupp & Keith, 1993).

An additional cost to society comes from the involvement of the law enforcement and correctional systems in providing crisis intervention and long-term institutionalization for persons with schizophrenia who commit criminal offenses. The lifetime prevalence of schizophrenia among prisoners in correctional facilities is 6.2% (Regier et al., 1990), and few of them receive appropriate treatment. The cost of maintaining each of California's 25,000 mentally ill prisoners with only custodial services is over $25,000 per year. State psychiatric hospitals can spend more than $125,000 per year on services for a person with schizophrenia.

Schizophrenia not only carries the risk of substantial morbidity but also has a risk of mortality. Approximately 25% of persons with schizophrenia attempt suicide, and 10% succeed (Roy, 1992). Suicidality in schizophrenia is associated with being male, having fallen from a much higher premorbid level of functioning, and experiencing depression (Caldwell & Gottesman, 1990). There is a high level of comorbidity of depression with schizophrenia (Green et al., 1990; Kessler et al., 1994). Recently, a reliable and "clinician-friendly" method has been made available to predict which persons with schizophrenia have an increased risk of suicidal ideation or behavior (Young et al., 1998). Based on initial ratings of suicidal ideation, individuals having a subsequent likelihood of suicidality can be identified, so that this is a convenient method for preventive interventions.

Approximately one third of the homeless in the United States suffer from schizophrenia, and many of them also have a substance abuse disorder (Koegel, Burnam, & Farr, 1988). The number of persons with schizophrenia and other serious mental disorders joining the ranks of the disabled with Social Security pensions has risen dramatically, by 66.4% since 1986 (Manderscheid & Sonnenschein, 1992); few of the mentally disabled ever return to work and achieve functional independence. Thus, they are a burden to society and to their families for their lifetimes. Because of advocacy by family members and practitioners, the Social Security Administration has made it easier for persons with mental disabilities, such as schizophrenia, to access incentives to work. For example, the Program for Achieving Self Support permits individuals to continue to receive Social Security pensions while earning incomes from jobs, if the funds are allocated to services and needs (e.g., a car, tuition for school) listed in a written plan that articulates goals for eventual independence. More liberal use of federally supported health insurance has also been extended to formerly disabled persons who are making an effort to return to competitive jobs. This new millennium is certain to have stronger and more consistent advocacy by persons with schizophrenia and their families to disseminate the innovations in treatment and rehabilitation, as well as to generate more favorable resources from society and the community, so that remissions of symptoms and recovery of functional capacity both improve the quality of life of schizophrenics and reduce the cost of schizophrenia to the nation (Flynn, 2000).

HISTORICAL PERSPECTIVE AND SCOPE OF LITERATURE

Empirical studies of psychological and behavioral treatments for schizophrenia were first conducted in the late 1950s and early 1960s by former students of B. F. Skinner who obtained positions in psychiatric hospitals. Lindsley, Ferster, Ayllon, and Azrin published controlled single-case studies and laboratory analogues of treatment, showing clearly that environmental antecedents and consequences could powerfully influence psychotic behaviors (Liberman, 1976). These investigators documented that presentation of reinforcement produced increases in desirable, adaptive behavior on which the reinforcement was contingent and that withdrawal of reinforcement produced decreases. By the mid-1960s, Ayllon and Azrin (1965) had established the first token economy, the application of reinforcement principles to an entire ward of patients. A book reviewing the first 10 years of behavior modification includes work done with mute and withdrawn psychotics, autistic children, retardates, and patients with bizarre behaviors (Ullman & Krasner, 1975).

The original studies were carried out with "hopeless" and treatment-refractory patients who had failed to respond to antipsychotic medications. The back wards of psychiatric hospitals were hospitable to the pioneers in behavior therapy of schizophrenia, where resistance was not as strong as in treatment settings where clinicians resided with vested interests in more traditional therapies, such as psychodynamic approaches. From 1968 to 1975, there was an exponential increase in publications devoted to the token economy and other behavior therapy approaches to individuals with chronic forms of schizophrenia (Liberman, 1976). Behavioral approaches were conducive to the growing scientific norm in psychiatry, fertilized by the empiricism of psychopharmacology. Adherents of both behavior therapy and psychopharmacology relied on empiricism to document the value of their interventions; in addition, for patients who did not respond optimally to psychopharmacology, behavior therapy offered both symptomatic and rehabilitative treatments (Liberman, Kopelowicz, & Young, 1994). These studies were Type 3, using the criteria of this book, pinpointing and measuring specific, molecular, and aberrant behaviors to modify and utilizing A-B or case control designs. They were heuristic, however, in stimulating further work that would become more rigorous and methodologically substantial.

In the early 1970s, the second generation of behaviorally oriented clinicians and researchers began to publish the results of their work with persons having schizophrenia (Fichter, Wallace, & Liberman, 1976; Liberman et al., 1973; Liberman, King, & DeRisi, 1976; Paul & Lentz, 1977). The second-generation studies focused more on strengthening prosocial behaviors than on eliminating or weakening bizarre behaviors. Some of the most disastrous effects of long-term institutionalization of persons with schizophrenia were the constriction of interpersonal responses and withdrawal from social interaction. The "good" patient in a custodial setting was quiet and unobtrusive. Enhancing the social repertoires of such patients was vital to their becoming capable of leaving the hospital and adjusting to life in the community. Competence in carrying on conversations, asking for directions, obtaining necessities, and, in general, navigating the social pathways were prerequisites for successful reentry and tenure in the community. The investigators who carried out the studies of the 1970s also recognized the limitations of generalization of treatment when treatment was conducted solely in hospitals without planning for the "transfer of training" into the community (Liberman, McCann, & Wallace, 1976).

In their landmark controlled study comparing behavior therapy with milieu and custodial therapies, Paul and Lentz (1977) prepared patients for community life by having case managers visit the cities and towns to where the improved patients would be discharged to create opportunities and encouragement by using "natural reinforcers" and caregivers so that the patients would continue to utilize their learned skills. Not only did patients who were randomly assigned to the social learning program show greater clinical improvement in all areas measured, but they also had a 98% discharge rate and significantly longer tenure in the community after discharge. A retrospective of social learning and token economy programs highlighted the empirical validation that these programs achieved as well as the reasons that few of these programs followed patients and staff as deinstitutionalization accelerated in the two decades after 1980 (Liberman, 2000).

The use of social skills training, developed and validated by Liberman and his colleagues (Liberman et al., 1975; Liberman, DeRisi, & Mueser, 1989; Wallace & Liberman, 1985), also was a step in the direction of enhanced generalization of functional improvement resulting from behavioral therapies (Benton & Schroeder, 1990; Dilk & Bond, 1996; Penn & Mueser, 1996). Social skills training utilizes the full array of social learning and behavioral principles to bring about better verbal and nonverbal social interaction. Because social skills training can be performed in any treatment setting—including naturalistic community locales—it has become a treatment of choice in the new millennium for persons with schizophrenia. Skills training fits into the "vulnerability-stress-protective factors" model of schizophrenia, which has become the most widely accepted explanation of the etiology and course of schizophrenia. Buttressing the social competence of persons who have the enduring vulnerability to schizophrenic symptoms when stressors impinge on them, social skills training confers protection against relapse as well as the functional skills to improve community adaptation and quality of life (Corrigan, Schade, & Liberman, 1992; Heinssen, Liberman, & Kopelowicz, 2000). Skills training has been effective in reducing relapse rates (Falloon et al., 1985; Hogarty et al., 1986, 1991), improving social functioning (Liberman, Mueser, & Wallace, 1986; Marder et al., 1996), and enhancing quality of life (Heinssen, Liberman, & Kopelowicz, 2000; Marder et al., 1996).

The literature on the treatment and rehabilitation of persons with schizophrenia is enormous, appearing in literally hundreds of journals devoted to psychiatry, clinical psychology, behavior therapy, psychosocial rehabilitation, and vocational rehabilitation, as well as journals dedicated to this disorder (*Schizophrenia Bulletin, Schizophrenia Research*). Books devoted to schizophrenia could fill a moderate sized library. Rather than aim for an exhaustive review of the entire literature since the early 1990s, which would be an undertaking well beyond the scope of this chapter, we have drawn from review articles, selected books, and issues of the *Schizophrenia Bulletin*.

STATUS OF TREATMENTS

Introduction

The prevailing stress-vulnerability-protective factors model of schizophrenia helps the clinician to understand the etiology, course, and treatment of this lifelong disorder. Stressors, such as major life events and high expressed emotion in family and residential settings (Snyder et al., 1994), can adversely affect the course of the disorder when individuals with the vulnerability to the characteristic symptoms and associated disabilities of the disorder (Liberman et al., 1980) are exposed to the stressors without the protection of medication, psychosocial treatment, and natural coping ability and social support (Kopelowicz & Liberman, 1995). For veteran practitioners who have long considered only biological treatments as effective in protecting schizophrenic individuals from stress-induced relapse and disability, this chapter and the evidence that supports the protective value of behavioral and psychosocial treatments (Wunderlich, Wiedemann, & Buchkremer, 1996) may serve as an antidote to the insidious biological reductionism that often characterizes the field of schizophrenia research and treatment.

On the other hand, it is essential to view treatments of schizophrenia as always occurring within a matrix that includes interventions that interact with one another at the pharmacological, behavioral, and environmental support levels. The quality, consistency, accessibility, continuity, and comprehensiveness of the services being provided to patients will inevitably affect the outcome as measured by symptoms, relapse, social functioning, and attainment of personal goals and subjective satisfaction with life. Inadequate or excessive drug treatment attenuates the benefits of behavioral interventions; lack of available encouragement and reinforcement in the person's social support system weakens the effects of skills training and adherence to medication.

Treatments of schizophrenia also tend to be *outcome specific;* that is, pharmacotherapy predominantly improves symptoms and delays relapse, skills training has its main impact on social functioning, family interventions focus on improving the emotional climate of the home and reducing the burden and stress of the illness experienced by the patient and the relative alike, and assertive community treatment reduces time in the hospital and improves stability of housing. Careful orchestration of pharmacotherapy, skills training, family psychoeducation, and community support services within the matrix of an effective means of flexibly delivering all interventions, as required by changing individual needs, can significantly improve the course and outcome of the disorder as well as promote recovery in a substantial number of persons (Liberman, Kopelowicz, & Smith, 1999).

In this review of the extant treatments for schizophrenia, we will use a multilevel and multidimensional set of criteria in rating the evidence that supports each of the treatments. While few studies incorporate a multilevel approach, the field is moving rapidly to an appreciation of the value of a comprehensive assessment of outcome, measuring changes in (a) symptoms, bizarre and intolerable behaviors, and relapse rates (psychopathology); (b) deficits in activities of community living, social competence, and social adjustment (social and instrumental role functioning); (c) self-management of illness, including medication adherence, avoiding drugs of abuse, identifying prodromal signs of relapse, and coping with persistent symptoms (illness self-management); (d) burden of the disorder on the family or other caregivers in daily contact with the patient (care burden); and (e) subjective quality of life in areas of finances, medical and psychiatric care, recreational and social activities, family life, spiritual life, work or school, and overall perceived quality of life. A multidimensional approach to the evaluation of outcome in the psychosocial or behavioral treatment of persons with schizophrenia and other disabling mental disorders is "much easier said than done" and is plagued with methodological complications. For example, multiple employment measures may be required in studying vocational rehabilitation for persons with mental disorders to properly capture the degree of independent and instrumental role functioning in a job (sheltered vs. volunteer vs. transitional vs. supported vs. competitive) and the duration, mobility, salary level, and satisfaction of the consumer and employer with the job performed (Bond & Boyer, 1988).

Similarly, multiple measures offer advantages in assessing the comprehensiveness of behavior that comprises the construct of social skills (Liberman, 1982). The efficacy of supported education or supported employment services may be reflected by changes in self-concept, subsequent vocational attainment, and educational accomplishments. Because schizophrenia is a lifelong disorder requiring lifelong services, it is not possible in a time-limited study to identify longitudinal outcomes that may be sequentially linked to a particular treatment; for instance, improvement in social skills at Time A may not have evident impact on the individual's social and community functioning at Time B because opportunities, encouragement, and reinforcement for using the learned skills may emerge in the person's environment only at Time C, many months or years later—well after the study's assessment has been completed.

There are methodological challenges to the use of a multidimensional approach to measuring change wrought by behavioral and psychosocial treatments as well. For example, since assessment measures do not typically include ethnically based response sets, differences in language, linguistic nuances, and translation of items from standardized assessments may create aberrant response patterns (Sue & Sue, 1987). Certain goals for minority clients may not be isomorphic with the rehabilitation goals of the majority population; for example, independent living status may have less relevance to clients from poverty backgrounds (who cannot afford independent housing) or from backgrounds with extended kin networks and co-residence traditions (Cook & Pickett, 1995). Moreover, rehabilitation services may be delivered to ethnic minorities by practitioners from different racial and ethnic backgrounds who do not fully understand or positively relate with the client. Outcomes from poor client-practitioner match may be suboptimal.

In any evaluative review of psychosocial treatment of schizophrenia, therefore, it is difficult to know whether good or poor outcomes derive from problems in measurement, the nature of the treatment itself, the failure of the treatment to hew faithfully to the proper model of service delivery, the failure to provide sufficient amounts of the treatment, or the fact that the client did not receive the proper combination of services for his or her phase or stage of illness. In summary, "the field of psychiatric treatment and rehabilitation of schizophrenia may have outstripped its evaluation counterpart, so that the growth of multidimensional models has occurred without accompanying ways to measure their effectiveness" (Cook, 1995, p. 5).

In addition to the importance of a multidimensional approach to validating the efficacy of treatments, it is also desirable to ensure that a particular treatment is, in fact, appropriate for the phase or stage of an individual's disorder. For example, higher doses of antipsychotic medication may be required for the acute, florid phase of illness, but lower doses usually provide a higher benefit-risk ratio for those in the maintenance or recovery phases. Similarly, while social skills training is utilitarian and of tangible benefit to persons in the reconstituting, maintenance, and recovery phases, patients in the acute psychotic stage of schizophrenia may have a diminshed capacity to learn social skills—their distractibility and overarousal may, in fact, be adversely affected by the demands of a classroom-type learning environment. The multidimensional approach to treatment evaluation is depicted in Figure 8.1, the complex cube of psychiatric rehabilitation.

While a multidimensional approach to evaluating the efficacy of treatments is only beginning to influence the work of treatment researchers, we shall endeavor to rate each treatment for schizophrenia in terms of those dimensions that have been shown to improve with the respective treatment. It is also necessary to place modalities of treatment—whether pharmacological or psychosocial—in the context of a system of mental health delivery. The various modalities that have been documented to be efficacious in schizophrenia need to be organized, financed, and delivered by an agency or group of mental health practitioners that serves as a fixed point of responsibility. The treatments must be appropriately linked to the phase or stage of a person's disorder, and they must be coordinated, comprehensive, continuous, and integrated. Very few persons with schizophrenia can be treated adequately by a single practitioner in an office practice. Therefore, the pervasive deficits and requirements for linkage to multiple human service agencies require a team approach, best exemplified by the model of assertive community treatment developed and disseminated by Stein and Test and their colleagues in Madison, Wisconsin (Stein & Santos, 1998; Stein & Test, 1985). To ensure that the reader grasps the importance of an integrative approach to the treatment of schizophrenia, in which specific treatment modalities (as shown along the horizontal axis in Figure 8.1) are imbedded in a service delivery system, the ratings of relatively well-demarcated modalities will be followed by a section on the system of mental health delivery, focusing on models of agency-based treatment teams and case management.

Almost all of the available treatment research literature is about "efficacy," not "effectiveness." Efficacy is evaluated in highly controlled, clinical research studies that are conducted in specialized research settings, using highly selected subjects, supervised by academic personnel, and often working with the aid of grant support. There are precious few studies of effectiveness, where the treatments under evaluation are being carried out with the full range of patients in ordinary clinical service systems by practitioners who may or may not demonstrate fidelity to the treatment parameters. Effectiveness is evaluated in mental health services research where the use of carefully diagnosed populations and of inflexible treatment manuals derived from clinical research is not always possible or desirable (Fensterheim & Raw, 1996).

One example is the use of antipsychotic drugs. Clinical research demonstrates clearly the lack of efficacy of multiple concurrent pharmacological agents and the hazards of using high doses. When examining the practice of neuroleptic drug prescribing in ordinary hospital and community settings, one discovers widespread polypharmacy and higher doses than are recommended by academics, whose clinical experience may be very limited. Mental health ser-

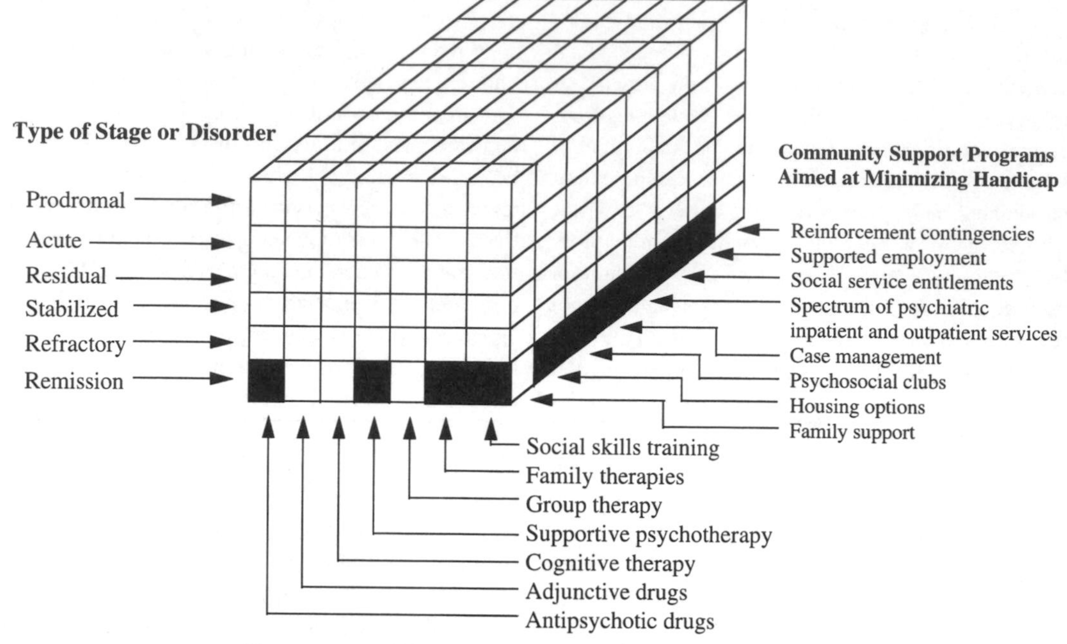

FIGURE 8.1 The complex cube of psychiatric rehabilitation reflects the three major dimensions of treatment planning and implementation. The specific modalities of assessment and intervention are displayed along the horizontal axis and keyed to the phase or stage of the individual's disorder. Whatever the array of specific treatment modalities indicated for an individual, a treatment delivery system and social support program (e.g., housing, case management, entitlements, and benefits) must be available if the treatments are to make an impact. In the graphic shown, an individual with schizophrenia that is in clinical remission is receiving maintenance antipsychotic medication, supportive psychotherapy (e.g., from his or her case manager), family intervention, and social skills training. A large number of social support services are concurrently being provided to this individual, as shown in the axis moving into the background of the figure.

vices research is only in its infancy; thus, we shall be rating treatments primarily in terms of their documented "efficacy," not "effectiveness." When effectiveness evidence is available, we shall document it in our ratings.

Individual and Group Therapy

Traditional psychodynamically oriented individual and group psychotherapy have not been shown to be efficacious in schizophrenia. In fact, there is evidence of an adverse effect of this form of psychotherapy on some persons with schizophrenia, presumably those with limited information-processing capacities (Mueser & Berenbaum, 1990). However, the supportive qualities inherent in treatment relationships of all types (e.g., with prescribing psychiatrist, nursing staff on an inpatient unit, case manager) are a necessary but not sufficient basis for delivering all types of treatments and for therapeutic change (Frank & Gunderson, 1990). In the past few decades, individual and group therapies for persons with schizophrenia have evolved from being informed by psychoanalytic theories and techniques to being inseminated by more supportive, collaborative, educational, practical, and active qualities. The qualities of the therapeutic alliance that are deemed facilitative of improvement, no matter what the specific modality may be, are delineated in the next section, on supportive therapy.

Supportive Therapy

Supportive therapy—individual, family, and group—is characterized by

- a positive, therapeutic alliance and relationship.
- a focus on reality issues, solving problems in everyday life, and practical advice.
- an active, directive, and educational role taken by the therapist, who uses her or his own life experiences and self-disclosure as a role model for the patient.
- encouragement and education of the patient and family for proper use of antipsychotic medication.

While supportive forms of individual therapy have been broadly applied by practitioners in the course of delivering pharmacotherapy or more specific psychosocial services to persons with schizophrenia, there are only three Type 1 studies attesting to its efficacy. All of these studies were well controlled, with random assignment and comparison treatments. However, the evidence for the efficacy of supportive individual therapy was ambiguous, and in one of the studies, extraordinarily high attrition limits the generality of the findings. In one study, individual supportive therapy led to worse outcomes at the 6-month point, but for those who survived past the first year and continued in supportive therapy, the relapse rates and social functioning were significantly better at the 2-year follow-up point (Hogarty, Goldberg, & Schooler, 1974). In a second study, reality-adapted supportive therapy was no better than exploratory insight-oriented therapy on most measures but did result in reduced rates of rehospitalization and improved role functioning (Gunderson et al., 1984). A third study found that a phase-specific individual therapy targeted to enhance personal and social adjustment and forestall relapse was efficacious for patients who were living with their families, but not with patients who were living alone (Hogarty et al., 1997).

Supportive group therapy is also widely used, especially with outpatients. The same principles of supportive therapy are used in these groups and may vary in emphasis from medication education to setting realistic goals, encouraging coping efforts, and socialization. There are a half dozen Type 2 empirical trials of supportive group therapy, most of which found this modality superior to control treatments (Malm, 1982).

Behavior Therapy and Social Learning Programs

Since the initial empirical demonstrations in the 1960s of the utility of laboratory-generated principles of learning for persons with schizophrenia (Ayllon & Azrin, 1968), behavior therapy has been used to manage the full spectrum of symptoms, deficits, and disturbing behaviors found in this disorder (Brenner, Hodel, & Roder, 1990; Wong et al., 1986). The majority of the hundreds of Type 3 empirical studies documenting the efficacy of reinforcement schedules, stimulus control, social modeling, shaping, and fading have used subjects longitudinally as their own controls. The designs have featured baseline periods followed by intervention, withdrawal of intervention, and return to intervention, as well as multiple baselines where each of three or four subjects has differing durations on baseline conditions before receiving the intervention. While these experimental designs lack the generality of randomized clinical trials with groups of subjects receiving different treatments, they do possess one methodological advantage, namely, capitalizing on and controlling for the vast interindividual differences in schizophrenia.

Since practitioners often have difficulty applying research results generated by standardized protocols that require all patients—no matter how different—to receive the same treatment, studies that use subjects as their own controls permit fine-tuning the intervention until it shows clear-cut effects. Furthermore, intervention effects in these individualized protocols must be dramatically enough different from baseline rates of the targeted clinical problem so that the treatment effects can be eyeballed, with little need for statistical significance. How often do we find results in the literature where the differences between treatment and control groups are statistically significant but lack clinical significance?

There have been five Type 1 studies of behavior therapy and social learning programs (token economy) for treatment-refractory patients participating in hospital or day hospital programs where social and tangible reinforcers were given to patients contingent on their engaging in prosocial behavior and activities (Baker et al., 1977; Fullerton, Cayner, & McLaughlin-Reidel, 1978; Kazdin, 1982; Menditto, Valdes, &

Beck, 1994; Paul & Lentz, 1977; Schwartz & Bellack, 1975; Spiegler & Agigian, 1976). Typically, the token economy, supplemented with structured learning of self-care and recreational and social skills, helps to organize and focus the staff-patient interactions around appropriate and functional behaviors. This approach contrasts with that in unstructured milieus, where the inevitable attention given by staff to maladaptive and dangerous behaviors inadvertently reinforces the very problems that brought the patient to the hospital in the first place.

The results of these studies have uniformly shown the efficacy of the token economy; however, because the delivery of contingent social reinforcement is a key element in the token economy, component analyses should deconstruct the multifaceted nature of this wardwide, 24-hour-per-day modality. One such study found that day hospital patients were motivated to improve their behavior by the social reinforcement accompanying the contingent tokens rather than by the tangible rewards associated with the token exchanges (Liberman et al., 1977). Generalization of improved behavior from a highly structured token economy to the more randomly programmed "real world" requires graded levels of reinforcement schedules and contingencies; hence, regressed patients who enter a token economy will require frequent reinforcement and shaping of their deficient behavior, while those whose functioning has improved to the point of discharge readiness will benefit from a "credit-card" level, wherein they have free and continuous access to privileges and rewards as long as they meet criteria for maintaining their performance at a high level.

The most rigorous and well-controlled study of the token economy randomly assigned treatment-refractory patients to a social learning program, milieu therapy, or customary custodial care (Paul & Lentz, 1977). On all measures of outcome—symptoms, activities of daily living, social behavior, discharge, tenure in the community, and cost-effectiveness—the patients in the social-learning–token-economy program fared significantly better. However, this study was conducted prior to the introduction of *DSM-III* and may have included some individuals who would not meet current criteria for schizophrenia.

Cognitive Therapy

While cognitive therapy has been well documented for efficacy in depressive and anxiety disorders, it has only recently been tested for efficacy with persons who have schizophrenia. There are several different approaches to cognitive therapy, each based on the assumption that changing an individual's thoughts, attitudes, perceptions, behavior, self-efficacy, and information-processing deficits can have favorable effects on symptoms, learning skills, and personal functioning.

These approaches can be classified into two major categories: cognitive remediation and cognitive behavior therapy. The first approach targets specific information-processing functions. The second targets psychopathological symptoms and emotional distress. Cognitive remediation can be further demarcated by the cognitive level targeted for intervention. Examples include behavioral learning techniques aimed at improving or normalizing the most elementary cognitive functions, namely, signal detection, sustained attention, verbal learning, and memory—each of which is abnormal in a large proportion of persons with schizophrenia (Green, 1993). The rationale fueling cognitive remediation is based on the hypothesis that improved cognition will facilitate the learning of broader-based and more clinically relevant functions, such as work and social skills (Liberman & Green, 1992). Cognitive remediation does appear to improve basic cognitive functions, but there is only limited scientific evidence to date to support its sustained effect or its spreading to influence clinical or social variables (Spaulding et al., 1999; Van der Gaag et al., in press). For example, in one study of attentional training using the Continuous Performance Test, subjects who received the training not only showed significantly greater improvements in measures of attention but also had significantly greater improvement in psychiatric symptoms (Medalia et al., 1998).

Cognitive remediation strategies have also been targeted directly at the deficits in social perception that have been posited to underlie social dysfunction in schizophrenia. The rationale for these interventions is that patients who are unable to correctly interpret interpersonal situations will have significant difficulty interacting effectively in these situations (Liberman et al., 1986). Typically, patients are first taught to accurately perceive various parameters associated with selected social cues, such as facial affect, verbal tone, and body language. This procedure is followed by instruction in social problem solving. Using videotaped vignettes, patients learn to identify the problem, generate a number of potential solutions to the problem, and evaluate the alternative responses that might be made for successfully dealing with the particular social situation. There is only limited evidence that this method actually results in more salutary brain functioning or social adjustment (Storzbach & Corrigan, 1996).

Another cognitive remediation approach that has received some empirical evaluation, termed *integrated psychological therapy*, consists of a sequential hierarchy of training procedures, starting with basic functions such as attention and progressing through problem solving to social skills training (Brenner et al., 1994). Results from studies of integrated psychological therapy must be viewed as tentative because of methodological limitations. Nevertheless, a recent Type 2 study found that long-stay hospitalized patients who participated fully in this program showed significantly greater problem-solving capacity than those who were in a control condition (Spaulding et al., 1999).

The second major category of cognitive therapy used for schizophrenia is cognitive behavior therapy. Cognitive behavior therapy tailors the therapeutic approach that Aaron Beck and colleagues have used with depression and anxiety to the cognitive experience of psychosis within the context of the vulnerability-stress model of schizophrenia (Garety et al., 2000). Conventional cognitive behavioral methods, such as uncovering and changing irrational, automatic thoughts and negative self-appraisals, are combined with modifications specific for the psychotic patient, including helping patients to empirically challenge delusions and teaching patients how to cope with persistent psychotic symptoms (Kingdon & Turkington, 1994). The efficacy of cognitive behavior therapy for patients with schizophrenia has now been demonstrated in several Type 2 studies. In each of these studies, cognitive behavior therapy was added to customary psychiatric care (i.e., medication plus case management) and compared either to customary care alone (Garety et al., 1994; Kuipers et al., 1997, 1998) or to an active control group (Sensky et al., 2000; Tarrier, Beckett, & Harwood, 1993; Tarrier et al., 1998, 1999). For the most part, those participants who received cognitive therapy showed a greater reduction than comparison participants in overall psychopathology as well as in certain dimensions of delusional thinking. However, many studies of this genre have used questionable methods of diagnosis, leaving open the possibility that some subjects actually had delusional disorders rather than schizophrenia (Bouchard et al., 1996). These studies also had strict selection criteria biased toward enrolling higher functioning individuals (Garety et al., 2000). It remains to be seen if the findings from these studies can be generalized to the majority of individuals with schizophrenia.

Structured Educational Family Interventions

With the growing number of international replications of the family emotional climate as one of the most powerful predictors of relapse in schizophrenia (Bebbington & Kuipers, 1994; Bertrando et al., 1992; Falloon et al., 1999; Jenkins & Karno, 1992; Kuipers & Bebbington, 1988), interventions have been designed and empirically validated that are aimed at engaging families as active participants in the treatment and rehabilitation process, while improving their coping capacities and those of their mentally ill members. A variety of terms have been coined to describe these interventions, including *family psychoeducation, behavioral family management, behavioral family therapy, family-aided assertive community treatment,* and *multiple family therapy* (Mueser, Glynn, & Liberman, 1994).

These methods have substantial elements in common, including structured and clear expectations for participation by family members and patient, outreach and other efforts to connect with the family and provide them with support, practical education about the nature of schizophrenia and how to cope with it, assisting the family to effectively utilize available treatments and community resources, teaching stress management techniques, encouraging family members to pursue their own goals and well-being without becoming emotionally overinvolved with each other, and teaching the family better means of communicating and problem solving (Strachan, 1992).

Over 20 Type 1 clinical trials have been conducted using structured educational family interventions, all of them showing the superiority of adding family intervention to medication and customary case management (Falloon et al., 1985; Goldstein et al., 1978; Hogarty et al., 1986; Leff et al., 1982, 1989; Liberman, Falloon, & Aitchison, 1984; McFarlane, Statsny, & Deakins, 1992; Randolph et al., 1994) and one showing superiority of multifamily groups compared to single-family interventions (McFarlane et al., 1995). One key feature of efficacious family interventions is their duration—a minimum of 9 months or 1 year of weekly and biweekly family sessions appears necessary for therapeutic impact.

The outcomes assessed in these studies have included relapse rates, family attitudes and emotions, social functioning, quality of life, family burden, and cost-effectiveness. In terms of relapse rates, converging evidence suggests that these structured family interventions reduce relapse by one half over that achieved with medication and case management alone. An NIMH-sponsored multihospital study of family interventions found approximately the same relapse rates in a large sample of patients as have been reported in smaller, single-site, controlled studies; however, this multisite study did not show an advantage for more intensive behavioral family management over monthly supportive and educational family sessions (Schooler et al., 1997).

Because the multisite study used family clinicians who were "second-generation" users of these methods and were not identified with the individuals who developed the techniques, one might consider the results evidence of "effectiveness" from a services research perspective. Unfortunately, this study did not use a control group receiving no family intervention, so it is difficult to interpret the significance of the results. Moreover, assessment of the families' problem-solving skills in the intensive form of intervention revealed no change from beginning to end of treatment, a finding suggesting that the treatment failed to achieve its proximal goal of improving family communication skills. Since the direct aim of treatment was not attained, it is understandable that subsequent clinical benefits would not discriminate the two types of family intervention.

Social Skills Training

Social skills training is defined by behavioral techniques or learning activities that enable persons with schizophrenia and other disabling mental disorders to acquire instrumental and affiliative skills for improved functioning in their communities (Bellack et al., 1997; Liberman, DeRisi, & Mueser, 1989). Training can be done with standardized curricula, or modules, that cover knowledge and skills that most persons with schizophrenia need for improved life functioning and management of their illness (e.g., use of antipsychotic medication, communication with mental health professionals, recognizing prodromal signs of relapse, developing a relapse prevention plan, coping with persistent psychotic symptoms, avoiding street drugs and alcohol, developing leisure skills and conversation skills). Alternatively, skills training can be individualized, with goals for improving personal effectiveness derived from each person's long-term and personalized aspirations for role functioning.

Sessions are typically conducted one to three times per week, with groups of 4 to 10 patients in office, community mental health center, day hospital, or hospital settings. Skills training requires that patients be reasonably well stabilized on their medications, be able to follow instructions and pay attention to the training process, and tolerate sessions lasting 45 to 90 minutes. Thus, social skills training is generally used with outpatients who are living in the community, where their skills can be applied (Heinssen, Liberman, & Kopelowicz, 2000). Because of the attentional requirements of the training, this modality is not suitable for patients with persistent high levels of thought disorder and distractibility, unless specially designed for this small subgroup (Massel et al., 1991; Mueser, Wallace, & Liberman, 1995). Moreover, floridly and acutely symptomatic patients may require additional efforts, but three Type 1 studies have demonstrated that they, too, may benefit from skills training if the intervention is geared to their level of cognitive capacity and symptomatology (Kopelowicz, Wallace, & Zarate, 1998; Menditto et al., 1996; Silverstein et al., 1999).

Trainers draw on behavioral learning principles and techniques such as behavioral rehearsal (role playing), social modeling, abundant positive reinforcement for incremental improvements in social skill, active coaching and prompting, in vivo exercises, and homework assignments (Corrigan, Schade, & Liberman, 1992). Skills-training techniques are also components of other structured learning modalities, such as family interventions and vocational rehabilitation (Liberman, Kopelowicz, & Smith, 1999).

Evidence for the efficacy of social skills training addresses the following outcome dimensions: acquisition, durability, and utilization of the skills in real life; improvements in social functioning; reductions in relapse rates and rehospitalization; and enhanced quality of life. More than 40 Type 1 or Type 2 studies, as well as three meta-analyses, have addressed one or more of these areas of outcome (Benton &

Schroeder, 1990; Corrigan, 1991; Dilk & Bond, 1996). Overall, there is excellent and well-replicated evidence for the efficacy of social skills training in the acquisition of the skills taught, with durability extending for at least 1 year. Generalization of the skills to real-life use, social functioning, reductions in relapse rates, and enhanced quality of life have been studied less frequently, but the limited data are positive, especially when training extends for 1 year or longer and the intervention includes a generalization component (Kopelowicz, 1998).

In three Type 1 studies, the therapeutic impact of social skills training was well documented on several dimensions of outcome. With outpatients who were all receiving maintenance doses of depot antipsychotic medication, 1 year of weekly social-skills-training sessions reduced relapse by one half, compared to those receiving medication alone (Hogarty et al., 1986). The reduction in relapse rate was the same as achieved by structured educational family intervention plus maintenance medication. Patients receiving social skills training also evinced significant improvements in social adjustment. When social skills training and family intervention were combined, 1 year relapse was zero.

In the second Type 1 study (Eckman et al., 1992), stable outpatients with chronic schizophrenia were randomly assigned to twice-weekly supportive group therapy or social skills training, where the training included medication and symptom self-management, social problem solving, and individualized personal effectiveness. While all patients received low-dose depot maintenance medication, those who experienced prodromal symptoms were randomized to receive time-limited oral antipsychotic drug or placebo during the prodromal phase.

Results indicated that the patients receiving social skills training, but not those getting supportive group therapy, significantly improved their skill levels, which were durable over a 1-year period and were found to be utilized in their real-life settings. Moreover, even patients with relatively high levels of persisting symptoms (but not severe thought disorder) learned the skills as well as those with minimal symptoms. Additionally, the patients who learned social skills showed significantly better social functioning and quality of life over the 2-year period of the study. Skills training also reduced relapse rates in the subgroup of patients who received placebo, but not time-limited oral medication, during prodromal periods, a finding suggesting that supplemental antipsychotic medication at times of prodromes or social skills training conferred similar degrees of protection against relapse on this population (Marder et al., 1996).

In the third Type 1 study (Liberman et al., 1998), the community functioning of stable outpatients with schizophrenia was compared after treatment with psychosocial occupational therapy or social skills training. Social skills training was provided by paraprofessionals for 12 hours weekly over the course of 6 months, followed by 18 months of case management geared toward facilitating the use of the learned skills in the community. Patients who received skills training showed significantly greater independent living skills during a 2-year follow-up of everyday community functioning, a finding suggesting that skills learned were utilized in the patients' natural environment. A Type 3 study that used indigenous community supporters selected by the patients rather than paraprofessionals as the "generalization aides" replicated the finding of improved interpersonal and community functioning 1 year after the 6-month skills training was completed (Tauber, Wallace, & Lecomte, 2000).

Vocational Rehabilitation

Lifelong unemployment, as well as disability pensions from the Social Security Administration, has contributed to the profound stigmatization of persons with schizophrenia, to their poor quality of life, and to the burden on their families and society. Until the early 1990s, most efforts at vocational rehabilitation were carried out in sheltered workshops or psychosocial rehabilitation clubhouses, where individuals with mental disorders had little opportunity to learn marketable skills for community employment. In addition, state-run vocational rehabilitation agencies gave short shrift to the mentally ill and infrequently coordinated their services in functional and effective ways with mental health professionals who were responsible for all other psychiatric services. Fragmentation led to futility and nihilism by rehabilitation specialists as well as psychiatric practitioners.

Fortunately, since the mid-1980s, vocational rehabilitation of individuals with schizophrenia has received increased attention (Cook & Pickett, 1995). Recent legislation, including the Americans With Disabilities Act (U.S. Department of Justice, 1998) and the Work Incentives Improvement Act of 1999, as well as federal initiatives such as the President's Task Force on Employment of Adults With Disabilities, underscores the support our society has now given to employing individuals with mental and physical disabilities. Nevertheless, a review of the recent literature reveals that, in spite of recent progress, only a small proportion of individuals with schizophrenia receives vocational rehabilitation services. Moreover, individuals with schizophrenia benefit less from vocational rehabilitation programs than individuals with other psychiatric disorders, and they continue to experience low levels of employment and vocational functioning (Lehman & Steinwachs, 1998).

A number of principles have been identified from the literature on vocational rehabilitation about what works for individuals with severe mental illness (Cook & Razzano, 2000). The first is the importance of *situational assessment* in the evaluation of vocational skills and work capacity. Situational assessment involves direct and longitudinal observation and rating of job performance and attitudes in actual or simulated work environments (Cook et al., 1994; Massel et al., 1990). Using such ratings, Rogers and colleagues (1997) were able to accurately predict the employment status of 275 patients 6 months later. The second principle is the emphasis on *rapid placement* in gainful community employment rather than lengthy vocational training. For instance, clients who were placed in jobs immediately had higher employment rates and greater job satisfaction than those receiving prevocational services prior to job placement (Bond et al., 1995).

The third principle emphasizes the importance of *ongoing, individually tailored vocational support*. Making vocational support accessible to clients on an ongoing basis after job placement is a hallmark of the supported employment model discussed below (Wehman & Moon, 1988). A related principle is *tailoring job development and support to the client's preferences*. For example, Becker and colleagues (1996) reported that 143 individuals with severe mental illness who obtained jobs in their preferred fields were twice as likely to retain their positions as those working in nonpreferred fields.

A final and perhaps overarching principle is to offer patients *competitive, supported employment* rather than sheltered or unpaid work. Supported employment is based on the following principles:

1. Vocational rehabilitation is an integral, not separate, component of psychiatric treatment and requires a team approach with specialists in job development and placement.
2. The goal of supported employment is to place an individual in competitive employment in the community, with vocational assessment and training taking place on the job. Jobs are selected and support services are provided according to the preferences and choices of the consumer.
3. Job coaching and supports from mental health and rehabilitation professionals, including ready access to psychiatric, pharmacological, and crisis services, are provided indefinitely—consistent with the long-term, stress-related nature of schizophrenia and other disabling disorders.

The development of supported employment is so new that little empirical work has been published on this innovation. However, surveys of state vocational rehabilitation agencies have found a growing number of mentally disabled persons enrolled in supported employment programs and research is slowly following practice. One Type 1 study of an approximation to supported employment (accelerated transitional employment) found that seriously mentally ill clients who were more rapidly transitioned into real jobs had almost three times more success in attaining competitive employment 15 months later than a comparison group who were transitioned gradually (Bond & Dincin, 1986). Additionally, two Type 1 studies of supported employment integrated with assertive case management teams have shown this model to result in twice the rate of competitive employment of more traditional rehabilitation services that offer extended periods of prevocational training and work adjustment. One of these studies was conducted in a rural setting (Drake et al., 1996) and the other in an inner-city environment (Drake et al., 1999), suggesting that the salutary effects of supported employment can be generalized across different treatment populations.

Another method of vocational rehabilitation, the job-finding club, deserves mention. This approach assumes that a client is ready for work but requires training and structured support in the job search process. Individuals set goals for the types of jobs they are qualified for and participate in a 1- to 2-week program that offers training in creating a résumé, finding job leads, telephoning and interacting with employers to follow up leads, going through a job interview, and maintaining motivation for a job search that may require full-time effort for many weeks.

No controlled studies with mentally ill clients have been conducted with the job-finding club, but Type 3 empirical evaluations of this approach have indicated that 19 to 61% of mentally ill clients obtain competitive employment, usually after an average of 25 days of participating in the club (Eisenberg & Cole, 1986; Jacobs et al., 1984; Jacobs, 1988; Jacobs, Collier, & Wissusik, 1992). The wide variation in outcomes appears to be a function of the population studied, with psychotic individuals faring much worse than those with less impairing disorders.

One approach to vocational rehabilitation that has become widely popular since the 1950s is the psychosocial rehabilitation center or clubhouse. This model includes programs that are based on Fountain House in New York (Beard, Propst, & Malumud, 1982; Dincin, 1975). These programs provide an accepting peer-oriented clubhouse which deemphasizes the patient role and stresses the individual's own responsibility for rehabilitation. The program typically offers a continuum of vocational opportunities, ranging from prevocational work crews, usually unpaid work opportunities within the center, to transitional employment, which consists of temporary community jobs employing patients under an arrangement between the program and a community employer. Although the long history of the clubhouse approach suggests that it has survived a trial-and-error process, empirical studies supporting its utility and efficacy are lacking (Bond, 1992).

Case Management and Treatment Teams

Since the early 1980s, well-controlled research has documented the improved outcomes and lower costs associated with brief hospitalization for acute psychotic episodes and the use of community-based alternatives to hospitalization, such as partial hospitals and intensive case management built into continuous outpatient treatment teams (Goldman, 1996; Herz, 1996). For example, 11 days of hospitalization followed by day hospital and outpatient treatment produced better symptom outcomes than 60 days of hospitalization with outpatient follow-up. Social functioning 1 and 2 years later was also better for the patients who were hospitalized briefly and then returned to their natural social and family support networks (Herz, Endicott, & Spitzer, 1977).

Thus, patients with schizophrenia and other disabling mental disorders should be discharged when the specific indications for hospitalization are no longer present (e.g., assaultiveness, florid, and disabling psychotic symptoms). In addition, clinicians should attempt to ensure that appropriate continuity of care, social and family supports, and housing are available before the patient is discharged—to avoid the "revolving-door" phenomenon of hospitalization-discharge-rehospitalization and the tragic but all too-common homelessness that afflicts so many thousands of the seriously mentally ill today.

Case management, and the treatment teams in which it is imbedded, are the "glue" that holds together and coordinates the array of biopsychosocial services that have been described above. In addition, case management provides the mechanism for ensuring that patients or clients will obtain those services appropriate for their phase of illness, tailored to the individual's symptoms, psychosocial functioning, personal goals, and environmental resources. At a minimum, case managers function as monitors of the quality of services they broker and coordinate with various agencies and practitioners to fulfill the goals of their severely mentally ill clients. In theory, each case manager is a focal point of accessibility and accountability that maximizes the effectiveness and efficiency of services (Baker & Intagliata, 1992; Intagliata, 1982).

Three main forms of case management have evolved, distinguished by the level of training and quality and amount of direct clinical services delivered to the client: *brokerage case management*, *clinical case management*, and *training in community living (TCL)*. The brokerage model of case management has been found to be relatively ineffective in fulfilling the needs of severely mentally ill individuals. For example, one Type 3 study evaluated the effects of this brokerage model of case management with 417 severely mentally ill individuals, all of whom had been hospitalized at least twice (Franklin et al., 1987). The study found that the costs and use of services increased after case management was introduced into the mental health agency, but there was no corresponding improvement in functioning or reduction in the rates and duration of subsequent hospitalizations.

In contrast, the polar opposite model of case management—the training in community living developed in the early 1980s by Stein and Test and their colleagues—has been shown to be effective in several Type 1 studies (Scott & Dixon, 1995; Stein & Test, 1985; Test, 1992). The TCL model, also known as *assertive community treatment (ACT)*, organizes the service delivery system into multidisciplinary clinical treatment teams that "serve as fixed points of responsibility for assisting patients in meeting all of their needs from the day that they enter the program to a time extending many years into the future" (Test, 1992, p. 158). Each member of the interdisciplinary team serves case management functions with a ratio of 1 : 20 (or less) for staff to clients.

Services are delivered in individuals' own environments and include direct assistance with managing their illnesses (e.g., medication, 24-hour crisis availability), modification of the environment to enhance its supportiveness (e.g., facilitating entitlements, family education, development of social networks), direct assistance with the tasks of community living (e.g., rehabilitation services including home visits), and supported employment, which is supervised by a vocational specialist on the TCL team. The full array of comprehensive and continuous services, keyed to each individual's changing needs, is provided by the team, an approach avoiding the frequent fragmentation and occasional internecine warfare among service providers who are contracted through brokerage to deliver different types of services.

The effects of TCL have been favorable, with the qualification that services may need to extend for an indefinite period of time with a frequency and intensity that match the changing needs, interests, motivation, and priorities of the patient. The originators of TCL found that 14 months of TCL services resulted in lowered rates of hospitalization, more time in independent living, and improvements in role functioning (Stein & Test, 1980). Type 1 replications of the TCL model (Hoult, 1986; Lehman et al., 1997; Rosenheck et al., 1995; Test, 1992) confirmed these results, particularly for lowered rates of hospitalization. It has been determined that for role functioning (e.g., friendships, employment) to improve, the TCL team must invest the time and effort of specialists on the team for teaching social and vocational skills and creating opportunities to use the skills in real-life situations.

From an early study of TCL, which found that erosion of the gains achieved by 14 months in TCL occurred when patients were referred to customary care in the community (Test, Knoedler, & Allness, 1985), it was thought that TCL must be available indefinitely to ensure maintenance and extension of the clinical gains (Test, 1992). However, one Type 1 study in which patients who had received TCL services for 20 months were randomly assigned to receive TCL or standard case management for 15 additional months showed very little difference between the groups at follow-up (Audini et al., 1994). One explanation for the discrepant results may be that those patients in TCL whose use of services is relatively low and who have made significant gains in functioning can be transferred to less intensive services without untoward effects. The results of one Type 3 study support this conclusion (Salyers et al., 1998).

A recent review (Mueser et al., 1998) of controlled research on TCL and its variants found that these service delivery models reduced time in the hospital and improved stability of housing, especially among persons who were high users of mental health services. These modes of organizing and delivering mental health care, however, had only moderate effects on improving symptomatology and quality of life and little effects on social functioning, arrests and time spent in jail, and vocational functioning. Studies on reducing or withdrawing these intensive methods of case management revealed some deterioration in gains made by the clients. The general principle of *treatment-specific outcomes* is valid for these intensive and outreach modes of service delivery. Thus, if improvements in social functioning are to be achieved, then the case management team will have to include specialists in social skills training. Already, there are reports that adding employment specialists to these teams has a salutary effect on improving vocational outcomes of their clientele. In summary, the TCL model is costly and labor-intensive but does have the capability to facilitate individuals' movement through the acute, stabilizing, stable, and recovery stages.

An intermediate model is clinical case management in which the case manager has clinical training and skills, functions as a primary therapist (vs. paraprofessional "enablers"), and can provide interventions that improve individuals' clinical states, role functioning, and environmental supports. While this model attempts to provide comprehensive and continuous services to clients and has been found to result in improvements in subjective quality of life and satisfaction with case management (Huxley & Warner, 1992), the clinical case manager can easily become overburdened with responsibilities and subject to burnout (Bachrach, 1992; Bond et al., 1991). Two other Type 2 studies of clinical case management have found empirical support for its efficacy, although one study was flawed by its use of historical controls and lack of randomization (Goering et al., 1988; Modrcin, Rapp, & Poertner, 1988).

Figure 8.2 depicts the tripartite model of clinical case management in the shape of a triangle. At the base of the triangle are the basic clinical skills required to form and maintain a therapeutic alliance. The left limb of the triangle comprises a clinician's technical skills in assessment and treatment. The right limb of the triangle includes the consultative, advocacy, coordinating, and liaison skills required to open up community-based resources for the client, such as housing and social service entitlements. In employing demonstrably efficacious and cost-effective methods of intensive or assertive clinical case management (Olfson, 1990; Weisbrod, Test, & Stein, 1980), it is important for practitioners to utilize the treatment methods with fidelity to the key features of the innovative model. For example, agencies that have implemented TCL with caseloads that are significantly greater than 1–20 per case manager or treatment team member have not been successful in achieving good outcomes (McGrew et al., 1994).

Dual Diagnosis: Substance Abuse and Mental Disorders

Schizophrenia and substance abuse, which are often comorbidly present in high proportions of urban and rural populations (Fowler et al., 1998; Mueser et al., 1999; RachBeisel, Scott, & Dixon, 1999), present special challenges to the treatment team and case manager in diagnosis, substance-specific interactions, psychosocial treatments, and psychopharmacology (Roberts et al., 1992). In most settings, substance abuse and schizophrenia are treated by totally different agencies, and the result is fragmented and often incompatible approaches. Even when continuity of care is ensured by a fixed point of clinical accountability for the dually diagnosed individual, poor treatment outcomes can ensue from overemphasizing the

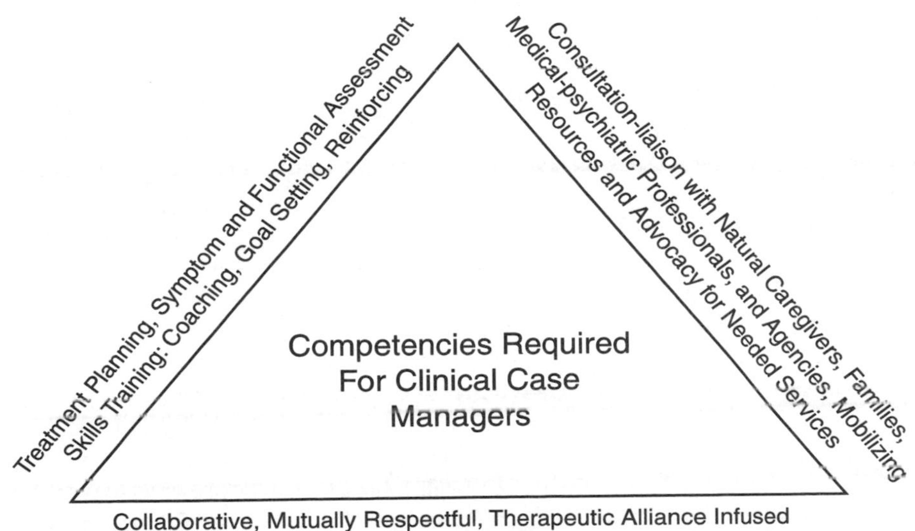

FIGURE 8.2 Competencies of clinical case managers can be organized into three major domains: (a) The bottom limb of the triangle represents relationship and personal engagement skills; (b) the left limb of the triangle represents technical biobehavioral assessment and treatment skills; and (c) the right limb of the triangle represents consultation-liaison and advocacy skills.

treatment of either disorder rather than providing a synchronous, seamless approach that leads to abstinence from substance abuse and remission of psychotic symptoms (Drake, Noordsy, & Ackerson, 1995).

In recent years, advances have been made in improving the outcome of dually diagnosed patients by the integration of mental health and substance abuse treatment services (Drake et al., 1998; Mueser et al., 1998). Two controlled studies have compared integrated treatment programs with separated ones, one a random assignment without independent assessments and the other a quasi-experimental design. In these studies, integrated treatment appeared to achieve better outcomes in terms of drug abuse, hospitalization, and more stable residences (Drake et al., 1997; Godley et al., 1994). Two studies of integrated treatment have included research controls, comparing different forms of integrated treatment. In one study of 147 dually diagnosed clients randomly assigned to three modes of treatment, those that received training with the modules of the UCLA Social and Independent Living Skills Program (Liberman et al., 1993) had greater reductions in substance abuse over 18 months than did those in 12-step or intensive case management programs (Jerrell & Ridgely, 1995). In the other study, substance abuse services were combined with assertive community treatment (ACT) or with standard case management (Drake et al., 1996). Clients assigned to ACT had better outcomes on some measures of substance abuse and quality of life, but the groups were similar in terms of reduced hospitalization and psychiatric symptoms.

It is clear, however, that despite this progress in integrating mental health and substance abuse treatments, dual disorders are often persistent over many years, and there is much room for further improvement. In addition, relatively little research has evaluated specific intervention modalities, such as individual or group treatments for dual diagnosis, and no family treatment programs have been developed and evaluated for this population.

FUTURE DIRECTIONS

It should come as no surprise that the efficacy of psychosocial treatments, requiring as they do a functional brain capable of assimilating and retaining information and skills, is attenuated by cognitive impairments that are enduring traits in most individuals with schizophrenia (Nuechterlein et al., 1994). Studies carried out in a variety of laboratories have documented the adverse influence of deficits in memory, sustained attention, and verbal learning in the capacity of individuals with schizophrenia to benefit from psychosocial interventions (Bowen et al., 1994; Corrigan et al., 1994; Kern, Green, & Satz, 1992; Mueser et al., 1991; Smith et al., 1999). These findings have generated interest in (a) determining the differential "rehabilitation readiness" of individuals with schizophrenia and (b) feasibility studies of cognitive remediation to improve information processing in the brain (Green, 1993; Green et al., 2000; Liberman & Green, 1992).

Current methods for remediating cognitive impairments in schizophrenia have utilized rather conventional behavioral techniques, such as monetary reinforcement and instructions. These techniques have not resulted in impressive durability or generalizability of treatment; hence, new strategies for remediation will undoubtedly be developed by 2010. One approach is to capitalize on the implicit or procedural learning capacity of individuals with schizophrenia. Implicit learning involves those psychomotor actions that are repetitive and overlearned and that can be employed "without thinking" or conscious awareness. Examples are riding a bicycle, catching a ball, saying nighttime prayers, or hitting a nail with a hammer. Procedural learning has been shown to be unimpaired in schizophrenia (Kern et al., 1996).

A novel and effective means of utilizing procedural or implicit learning to compensate for deficits in verbal learning and memory of persons with schizophrenia is termed *errorless learning*. In this method, the task to be learned—whether it be social or instrumental—is broken down into its constituent components, and training is done by having the individual observe a model and select the correct response, followed by prompts and reinforcement that promote similar correct responses in the subject. This method has been shown to be superior to customary trial-and-error learning in teaching persons with schizophrenia to master entry-level tasks that were identified as typical of those required in competitive employment (Kern et al., 2000).

Similarly, spatial visual learning is not as impaired in schizophrenia and can be utilized to overcome obstacles posed by verbal learning; for example, pictures of a concept, event, or interpersonal skill could be used to teach more flexible use of social skills than is currently available. These environmental adaptations have been used for years to treat patients with head injuries, and a recent Type 2 study has demonstrated the effectiveness of such compensatory strategies (termed *cognitive adaptation training*) for schizophrenia in terms of decreased symptomatology and relapse rates, as well as improved level of functioning (Velligan et al., 2000).

Assessment Guiding Treatment

The goal of psychiatric treatment and rehabilitation is to assist individuals to reduce their symptoms and relapses, improve their functioning, enhance their quality of life, and attain their personalized goals. Consequently, better methods of assessing roles, individuals, environments, and treatment effects (including both medication and psychosocial treatments) would foster research—both clinical and services research—and yield research that is more relevant to the needs of consumers and practitioners. Given the factors that influence social and instrumental role functioning, there is a pressing need to develop better means of evaluating these functional domains. Moreover, evaluation methods must be linked to *treatment planning* and *treatment monitoring and evaluation,* not existing as a separate entity. One such instrument is the Independent Living Skills Survey (ILSS). The ILSS is a comprehensive, objective, performance-focused, easy-to-administer measure of the basic functional living skills of individuals with schizophrenia (Wallace et al., 2000). The ILSS has excellent psychometric characteristics and has been successfully used to guide treatment and rehabilitation as well as to predict outcome and monitor progress in treatment.

Using instruments such as the ILSS, clinicians could allocate scarce treatment resources based on information about the complexities of the specific role(s) to which an individual aspires, the skills in the individual's current behavioral repertoire, the degree and predictability of environmental supports and rewards, and obstacles (e.g., symptoms, bizarre behaviors) that stand in the way of goal attainment in role functioning. This allocation could be the result of an algorithm that prescribes the balance of skills training and environmental modifications that maximizes the probability of improving an individual's functioning. The algorithm could itself be developed based on research investigating the process of "expert" clinicians' decision making, yielding a system that could be modeled on a computer and available to all clinicians regardless of experience and discipline. CD-ROM and virtual reality modalities will create learning opportunities for clinicians and consumers that are more cost-effective, requiring minimal staff time.

Curricula for social skills training and family intervention can be refined, standardized, and distributed in a format that allows them to be easily accessed and efficiently delivered. Developing training curricula is extremely time-consuming, and clinicians may achieve better outcomes by focusing their efforts on delivering training rather than producing it. Especially in the current era of cost containment and managed care, the use of reliable, validated, and standardized treatment programs that can be adapted to the individual will be in much demand. The modular skills-training curricula developed by Liberman and his associates at UCLA (Liberman, 2001) have proved extremely "portable" and have been translated into 16 languages and validated for efficacy and effectiveness in many countries. Each module comprises a demonstration video, which promotes procedural learning through vicarious observation of credible role models, a trainer's manual, a participant's workbook, and a user's guide. A recent adaptation of these user-friendly programs has been the development of a Friendship and Intimacy Module, aimed in part at teaching persons with schizophrenia how to engage in safe, yet satisfying, sex (Liberman et al., 2000). Other approaches to teaching persons with schizophrenia how to reduce their risk of contracting sexually transmitted diseases, including HIV and AIDS, have been shown to be promising (Carey & Carey, 1999).

Strategic Combinations of Antipsychotic Drugs and Psychosocial Treatments

As noted at the beginning of this chapter, there is complementarity in treatment-specific outcomes between antipsychotic medications and psychosocial interventions. With the advent of novel antipsychotic drugs, we shall see more opportunities for synergistic combinations of these drugs and psychosocial treatments that capitalize on the ability of these drugs to remediate neurocognitions (Green et al., 1997; Kern et al., 1999) and therefore provide a faster start for social learning programs. In one recent study, subjects randomly assigned to skills-training modules and risperidone, one of the newer antipsychotic medications, demonstrated significantly better retention in treatment and lower relapses than subjects assigned to haloperidol combined with skills training (Marder et al., 1999). In a retrospective study in Sweden (Theise et al., 1999), investigators identified 101 chronic psychotic patients from a catchment area and invited them to attend a medication clinic for optimization of their drug regimens. Seventy-five percent of the individuals had their regimens changed, primarily from conventional to newer antipsychotic agents. Of those who were placed on the newer agents, over 50% became employed. While this study was uncontrolled, it will be a harbinger of many others that will have sound methodology and will illuminate the best ways that medication and psychosocial interventions can be combined.

Early-Intervention Strategies to Promote Recovery

Substantial evidence has accumulated pointing to the relationship between the rapidity and continuity of treatment of psychotic symptoms and positive outcomes (Loebel et al., 1992; Wyatt & Henter, 1998). Taking advantage of the importance of early and continued intervention for psychosis, several investigators have mounted studies in which young persons with the early prodromal signs of schizophrenia are identified, engaged in treatment, and provided long-term services that are consonant with the individuals' personal goals and developmental stage of transition into adulthood (Johannessen et al., 2000; McGorry & Jackson, 1999). The treatments offered by these scientist-practitioners are multimodal, including group and individual therapies with supportive and cognitive behavioral features. An alternative approach has been taken by Liberman and colleagues. They have identified 10 attributes that distinguish individuals who have recovered from schizophrenia from controls who have not. Since most of these attributes—such as no substance abuse, family support, social competence, and good neurocognitive functioning—are malleable and potentially influenced by treatments, this new direction can pinpoint strategies for intervention that should optimize recovery in persons with schizophrenia (Gutkind, Liberman, Kopelowicz, & Ventura, 2001, in press).

Social System Interventions

Developing techniques to explicitly increase environmental support could be helpful. Currently, the technology for this approach to rehabilitation emphasizes low-key and permissive "psychosocial clubhouses" and "consumer-run" rehabilitation services. The Social Security Administration has established work incentives for disabled individuals, such as the Program for Achieving Self-Support. Qualified individuals can continue to receive their SSI or SSDI payments for up to 2 years while they earn money in jobs to pursue independent living or educational experiences that will enable them to become more independent and job-ready. In the future, more of these work incentives will become available as empirical data reveal the harmful effects of prolonged disability status (Liberman & Mintz, 1990; Shaner et al., 1995). As the emphasis in our society moves more toward competitive employment, techniques that will more reliably ensure job placement and training on the job are going to receive more interest from federal, state, and local governments. Not only will welfare recipients be the focal point of interest, but individuals on Social Security disability will also gain priority for conversion into economically productive citizens. Training programs for employment specialists, mental health team members, consumers, family members, and employers will become increasingly focused, structured, and empirically based. The job-finding club is one example of an approach that can be modularized to fit into existing programs with a trainer's manual, participant's workbook, and demonstration video. Another example is the Workplace Fundamentals Module, which incorporates the job club into a broader approach to job placement and job maintenance (Wallace, 1996). In keeping with the Americans With Disabilities Act, these techniques could be used to assist individuals with varying levels of skills, or to provide variations in support as an individual's skills increased with training and experience.

Dissemination and Adoption of Innovation

Empirical documentation of a treatment's efficacy rarely is sufficient to promote its dissemination and adoption by clinicians (Backer, Liberman, & Kuehnel, 1986). Even with new medications, which require only a physician's change in prescription-writing behavior, pharmaceutical firms use small armies of representatives to "teach" physicians how to use the new medication. The utilization of a psychosocial innovation—such as social skills training—is much more difficult to bring about.

Some lessons have been learned about the basic principles that can be used to overcome inertia in practitioners' behavior, for example, personal influence (e.g., demonstrating the new treatment technique and offering mentoring and apprenticeships), administrative mandates and support, congruence of the innovation with previous practices, and user-friendliness of the innovation. The social-skills-training modules in the UCLA Social and Independent Living Skills Program reflect user-friendliness insofar as they are prestructured and well-organized curricula that can be readily used by most professionals and paraprofessionals who are comfortable in working with the seriously mentally ill. Large-scale field trials in many different settings suggest that the modules are indeed user-friendly and widely adopted by clinicians (Eckman et al., 1990). In fact, within the domain of psychological and behavioral treatments for schizophrenia, the modules serve as an illustrative model for introducing efficacious and effective learning-based therapy to clinicians in a manner consistent with best practices guidelines (Heinssen, Liberman, & Kopelowicz, 2000).

References

Audini, B., Marks, M., Lawrence, R. E., Connolly, J., & Watts V. (1994). Home-based versus out-patient/in-patient care for people with serious mental illness: Phase II of a controlled study. *British Journal of Psychiatry, 165,* 204–210.

Ayllon, T., & Azrin, N. H. (1965). The measurement and reinforcement of behavior of psychotics. *Journal of the Experimental Analysis of Behavior, 8,* 357–383.

Ayllon, T., & Azrin, N. H. (1968). Reinforcer sampling: A technique for increasing the behavior of mental patients. *Journal of Applied Behavior Analysis, 1,* 13 20.

Bachrach, L. L. (1992). Case management revisited. *Hospital and Community Psychiatry, 43,* 209–210.

Backer, T. E., Liberman, R. P., & Kuehnel, T. G. (1986). Dissemination and adoption of innovative psychosocial interventions. *Journal of Consulting and Clinical Psychology, 54,* 111–118.

Baker, R., Hall, J. N., Hutchison, K., & Bridge, G.. (1977). Symptom changes in chronic schizophrenic patients on a token economy: A controlled experiment. *British Journal of Psychiatry, 131,* 381–393.

Baker, F., & Intagliata, J. (1992). Case management. In R. P. Liberman (Ed.), *Handbook of psychiatric rehabilitation* (pp. 213–243). New York: Macmillan.

Beard, J. H., Propst, R. N., & Malumud, T. J. (1982). The Fountain House model of rehabilitation. *Psychosocial Rehabilitation Journal, 5,* 47–53.

Bebbington, P., & Kuipers, L. (1994). The predictive utility of expressed emotion in schizophrenia: An aggregate analysis. *Psychological Medicine, 24,* 707–718.

Becker, D., Drake, R., Farabaugh, A., & Bond, G. R. (1996). Job preferences of clients with severe psychiatric disorders participating in supported employment programs. *Psychiatric Services, 47,* 1223–1226.

Bellack, A. S., Mueser, K. T., Gingerich, S., & Agresta, J. (1997). *Social skills training for schizophrenia.* New York: Guilford Press.

Benton, M. K., & Schroeder, H. E. (1990). Social skills training with schizophrenics: A meta-analytic evaluation. *Journal of Consulting and Clinical Psychology, 58,* 741–747.

Bertrando, P., Beltz, J., Bressi, C., & Clerici, M. (1992). Expressed emotion and schizophrenia in Italy: A study of an urban population. *British Journal of Psychiatry, 161,* 223–229.

Bond, G. (1992). Vocational rehabilitation. In R. P. Liberman (Ed.), *Handbook of psychiatric rehabilitation* (pp. 244–275). New York: Macmillan.

Bond, G., & Boyer, S. L. (1988). Rehabilitation programs and outcomes. In J. A. Ciardiello & M. D. Bell (Eds.), *Vocational rehabilitation of persons with prolonged mental illness* (pp. 231–263). Baltimore: Johns Hopkins University Press.

Bond, G. R., Dietzen, L., McGrew, J., & Miller, L. (1995). Accelerating entry into supported employment for persons with severe psychiatric disabilities. *Rehabilitation Psychology, 40,* 75–94.

Bond, G. R., & Dincin, J. (1986). Accelerating entry into transitional employment in a psychosocial rehabilitation agency. *Rehabilitation Psychology, 31,* 143–155.

Bond, G. R., Pensec, M., Dietzen, L., & McCafferty, D. (1991). Intensive case management for frequent users of psychiatric hospitals in a large city: A comparison of team and individual caseloads. *Psychosocial Rehabilitation Journal, 15,* 90–98.

Bouchard, S., Vallieres, A., Roy, M. A., & Maziade, M. (1996). Cognitive restructuring in the treatment of psychotic symptoms in schizophrenia. *Behavior Therapy, 27,* 257–278.

Bowen, L., Wallace, C. J., Glynn, S. M., Nuechterlein, K. H., Lutzger, J. R., & Kuehnel, T. G. (1994). Schizophrenics' cognitive functioning and performance in interpersonal interactions and skills training procedures. *Journal of Psychiatric Research, 28,* 289–301.

Brenner, H., Hodel, B., & Roder, V. (1990). Integrated cognitive and behavioral interventions in treatment of schizophrenia. *Psychosocial Rehabilitation Journal, 13,* 41–43.

Brenner, H. D., Roder, V., Hodel, B., Kienzle, N., Reed, D., & Liberman, R. P. (1994). *Integrated psychological therapy for schizophrenic patients.* Toronto: Hogrefe & Huber.

Caldwell, C., & Gottesman, I. (1990). Schizophrenics kill themselves too: A review of risk factors for suicide. *Schizophrenia Bulletin, 16,* 571–589.

Carey, M. P., & Carey, K. B. (1999). Behavioral research on severe and persistent mental illnesses. *Behavior Therapy, 30,* 345–353.

Clark, R. E. (1994). Family costs associated with mental illness and substance use. *Hospital and Community Psychiatry, 45,* 808–813.

Cook, J. A. (1995). Research on psychosocial rehabilitation services for persons with psychiatric disabilities. *Psychotherapy and Rehabilitation Research Bulletin, 4,* 3–5.

Cook, J. A., Bond, G., Hoffschmidt, S., Jonas, E., Razzano, L. A., & Weakland, R. (1994). Situational assessment. In Thresholds National Research and Training Center on Rehabilitation and Mental Illness, *Assessing vocational performance among persons with severe mental illness* (pp. 7–16). Chicago: Author.

Cook, J. A., & Pickett, S. A. (1995). Recent trends in vocational rehabilitation for persons with psychiatric disability. *American Rehabilitation, 20,* 2–12.

Cook, J. A., & Razzano, L. (2000). Vocational rehabilitation for persons with schizophrenia: Recent research and implications for practice. *Schizophrenia Bulletin, 26,* 87–103.

Corrigan, P. W. (1991). Social skills training in adult psychiatric populations: A meta-analysis. *Journal of Behavior Therapy and Experimental Psychiatry, 22,* 203–210.

Corrigan, P., Schade, M., & Liberman, R. P. (1992). Social skills training. In R. P. Liberman (Ed.), *Handbook of psychiatric rehabilitation* (pp. 95–126). New York: Macmillan.

Corrigan, P. W., Wallace, C. J., Schade, M. L., & Green, M. F. (1994). Learning medication self-management skills in schizophrenia: Relationships with cognitive deficits and psychiatric symptoms. *Behavior Therapy, 25,* 5–15.

Dilk, M. N., & Bond, G. R. (1996). Meta-analytic evaluation of skills training research for individuals with severe mental illness. *Journal of Consulting and Clinical Psychology, 64,* 1337–1346.

Dincin, J. (1975). Psychiatric rehabilitation. *Schizophrenia Bulletin, 1,* 131–148.

Drake, R. E., McHugo, G. J., Bebout, R. R., Becker, D. R., Harris, M., Bond, G. R., & Quimby, E. (1999). A randomized clinical trial of supported employment for inner-city patients with severe mental disorders. *Archives of General Psychiatry, 56,* 627–633.

Drake, R. E., McHugo, G. J., Becker, D. R., Anthony, W. A., & Clark, R. E. (1996). The New Hampshire study of supported employment for people with severe mental illness. *Journal of Consulting and Clinical Psychology, 64,* 391–399.

Drake, R. E., Mercer-McFadden, C., Mueser, K. T., McHugo, G. J., & Bond, G. R. (1998). Review of integrated mental health and substance abuse treatment for patients with dual disorders. *Schizophrenia Bulletin, 24,* 589–608.

Drake, R. E., Mueser, K. T., Clark, R. E., & Wallach, M. A. (1996). The course, treatment, and outcome of substance disorder in persons with severe mental illness. *American Journal of Orthopsychiatry, 66,* 42–51.

Drake, R. E., Noordsy, D. L., & Ackerson, T. (1995). Integrating mental health and substance abuse treatments for persons with chronic mental disorders. In A. F. Lehman & L. B. Dixon (Eds.), *Double jeopardy: Chronic mental illness and substance use disorders* (pp. 251–264). Chur, Switzerland: Harwood.

Drake, R. E., Yovetich, N., Bebout, R. R., Harris, M., & McHugo, G. J. (1997). Integrated treatment for dually diagnosed homeless adults. *Journal of Nervous and Mental Disease, 185,* 298–305.

Eckman, T. A., Liberman, R. P., Phipps, C. C., & Blair, K. (1990). Teaching medication management skills to schizophrenic patients. *Journal of Clinical Psychopharmacology, 10,* 33–38.

Eckman, T. A., Wirshing, W. C., Marder, S. R., Liberman, R. P., et al. (1992). Technique for training schizophrenic patients in illness self-management: A controlled trial. *American Journal of Psychiatry, 149,* 1549–1555.

Eisenberg, M. G., & Cole, H. W. (1986). A behavioral approach to job seeking for psychiatrically impaired persons. *Journal of Rehabilitation,* April/May/June, 46–49.

Falloon, I. R. H., Boyd, J. L., & McGill, C. W. (1985). Family management in the prevention of morbidity of schizophrenia. *Archives of General Psychiatry, 42,* 887–896.

Falloon, I. R. H., Held, T., Coverdale, J., Rocone, R., & Laidlaw, T. (1999). A review of long-term benefits of international studies of family interventions in schizophrenia. *Psychiatric Rehabilitation Skills, 3,* 268–290.

Fensterheim, H., & Raw, S. D. (1996). Psychotherapy research is not psychotherapy practice. *Clinical Psychological Scientist-Practitioner, 3,* 168–171.

Fichter, M. M., Wallace, C. J., & Liberman, R. P. (1976). Improving social interaction in a chronic psychotic using discriminated avoidance. *Journal of Applied Behavioral Analysis, 9,* 377–386.

Flynn, L. (2000). Blaming the wrong villain. *Psychiatric Services, 51,* 1347.

Fowler, I. L., Carr, V. J., Carter, N. T., & Lewin, T. J. (1998). Patterns of current and lifetime substance use in schizophrenia. *Schizophrenia Bulletin, 24,* 443–455.

Frank, A. K., & Gunderson, J. G. (1990). The role of the therapeutic alliance in the treatment of schizophrenia: Relationship to course and outcome. *Archives of General Psychiatry, 47,* 228–236.

Franklin, J. L., Solovitz, B., Mason, M., Clemons, J. R., & Miller, G. E. (1987). An evaluation of case management. *American Journal of Public Health, 77,* 675–678.

Fullerton, D. T., Cayner, J. J., & McLaughlin-Reidel, T. (1978). Results of a token economy. *Archives of General Psychiatry, 35,* 1451–1453.

Garety, P. A., Fowler, D., & Kuipers, E. (2000). Cognitive-behavioral therapy for medication-resistant symptoms. *Schizophrenia Bulletin, 26,* 73–86.

Garety, P. A., Kuipers, L., Fowler, D., & Chamberlain, F. (1994). Cognitive behavioural therapy for drug-resistant psychosis. *British Journal of Medical Psychology, 67,* 259–271.

Godley, S. H., Hoewing-Roberson, R., & Godley, M. D. (1994). *Final MISA report.* Bloomington, IN: Lighthouse Institute.

Goering, P. N., Wasylenki, D. A., Farkas, M., Lancee, W. J., & Ballantyne, R. (1988). What difference does case management make? *Hospital and Community Psychiatry, 39,* 272–276.

Goldman, H. H. (1996). Using cost-effectiveness data in benefit design. *Psychiatric Annals, 26,* 528–530.

Goldstein, M. J., Rodnick, E. H., Evans, J. R., May, P. R. A., & Steinberg, M. R. (1978). Drug and family therapy in the aftercare treatment of acute schizophrenia. *Archives of General Psychiatry, 35,* 169–177.

Green, M. F. (1993). Cognitive remediation in schizophrenia. *American Journal of Psychiatry, 150,* 178–187.

Green, M. F., Kern, R. S., Braff, D. L., & Mintz, J. (2000). Neurocognitive deficits and functional outcome in schizophrenia: Are we measuring the "right stuff"? *Schizophrenia Bulletin, 26,* 119–136.

Green, M. F., Marshall, B. D., & Wirshing, W. C. (1997). Does risperidone improve verbal working memory in treatment-resistant schizophrenia? *American Journal of Psychiatry, 154,* 799–804.

Green, M. F., Nuechterlein, K. H., Ventura, J., & Mintz, J. (1990). The temporal relationship between depressive and psychotic symptoms in recent-onset schizophrenia. *American Journal of Psychiatry, 147,* 179–182.

Gunderson, J. G., Frank, A. F., Katz, H. M., Vannicelli, M. L., Frosch, J. P., & Knapp, P. H. (1984). Effects of psychotherapy in schizophrenia: 2. Comparative outcome of two forms of treatment. *Schizophrenia Bulletin, 10,* 564–598.

Gutkind, D., Liberman, R. P., Kopelowicz, A., & Ventura, J. (in press). Recovery from schizophrenia: Operational criteria and factors related to recovery from schizophrenia. *Psychiatric Services.*

Harding, C. M., Zubin, J., & Strauss, J. S. (1992). Chronicity in schizophrenia revisited. *British Journal of Psychiatry, 161,* 27–37.

Heinssen, R. K., Liberman, R. P., & Kopelowicz, A. (2000). Psychosocial skills training for schizophrenia: Lessons from the laboratory. *Schizophrenia Bulletin, 26,* 21–46.

Herz, M. I. (1996). Psychosocial treatment. *Psychiatric Annals, 26,* 531–535.

Herz, M. I., Endicott, J., & Spitzer, R. L. (1977). Brief hospitalization: A two year follow-up. *American Journal of Psychiatry, 134,* 502–507.

Hogarty, G. E., Anderson, C. M., & Reiss, D. J. (1986). Family education, social skills training and maintenance chemotherapy in aftercare treatment of schizophrenia. *Archives of General Psychiatry, 43,* 633–642.

Hogarty, G. E., Anderson, C. M., Reiss, D. J., Kornblith, S. J., Greenwald, D. P., Ulrich, R. F., & Carter, M. (1991). Family psychoeducation, social skills training, and maintenance chemotherapy in the aftercare treatment of schizophrenia. 2. Two-year effects of a controlled study on relapse and adjustment. *Archives of General Psychiatry, 48,* 340–347.

Hogarty, G. E., Goldberg, S. C., & Schooler, N. (1974). Drug and sociotherapy in the aftercare of schizophrenic patients. 3. Adjustment of non-relapsed patients. *Archives of General Psychiatry, 31,* 609–618.

Hogarty, G. E., Kornblith, S. J., Greenwald, D., DiBarry, A. L., Cooley, S., Ulrich, R. F., Carter, M., & Flesher, S. (1997). Three year trials of Personal Therapy among schizophrenic patients living with or independent of family: 1. Description of study and effects on relapse rates. *American Journal of Psychiatry, 154,* 1504–1513.

Hoult, J. (1986). Community care of the acutely mentally ill. *British Journal of Psychiatry, 149,* 137–144.

Huxley, P., & Warner, R. (1992). Case management, quality of life, and satisfaction with services of long-term psychiatric patients. *Hospital and Community Psychiatry, 43,* 799–802.

Intagliata, J. (1982). Improving the quality of community care for the clinically mentally disabled: The role of case management. *Schizophrenia Bulletin, 8,* 655–674.

Jacobs, H. (1988). Vocational rehabilitation. In R. P. Liberman (Ed.), *Psychiatric rehabilitation of chronic mental patients* (pp. 245–284). Washington, DC: American Psychiatric Press.

Jacobs, H. E., Collier, R., & Wissusik, D. (1992). The Job-Finding Module: Training skills for seeking competitive community employment. In R. P. Liberman (Ed.), *Effective psychiatric rehabilitation: New directions for mental health services* (pp. 105–115). San Francisco: Jossey-Bass.

Jacobs, H. E., Kardashian, S., Kreinbring, R. K., Ponder, R., & Simpson, A. S. (1984). A skills-oriented model for facilitating employment among psychiatrically disabled persons. *Rehabilitation Counseling Bulletin, 28,* 87–96.

Jenkins, J. H., & Karno, M. (1992). The meaning of expressed emotion: Theoretical issues raised by cross-cultural research. *American Journal of Psychiatry, 149,* 9–21.

Jerrell, J. M., & Ridgely, M. S. (1995). Comparative effectiveness of three approaches to serving people with severe mental illness and substance abuse disorders. *Journal of Nervous and Mental Disease, 183,* 566–576.

Johannessen, J. O., Larsen, T. K., McGlashan, T., & Vaglum, P. (2000). Early intervention in psychosis: The TIPS project, a multi-centre study in Scandinavia. In B. Martindale & A. Bateman (Eds.), *Psychosis: Psychological approaches and their effectiveness* (pp. 210–234). London: Gaskell/Royal College of Psychiatrists.

Kazdin, A. E. (1982). The token economy: A decade later. *Journal of Applied Behavior Analysis, 15,* 431–445.

Kern, R. S., Green, M. F., Marshall, B. D., & Wirshing, W. C. (1999). Risperidone versus haloperidol on secondary memory: Can newer medications aid learning? *Schizophrenia Bulletin, 25,* 223–232.

Kern, R. S., Green, M. F., & Satz, P. (1992). Neuropsychological predictors of skills training for chronic psychiatric patients. *Psychiatry Research, 43,* 223–230.

Kern, R. S., Green, M. F., Wallace, C. J., & Goldstein, M. J. (1996). Verbal vs. procedural learning in chronic schizophrenic inpatients. *Cognitive Neuropsychiatry, 2,* 16–22.

Kern, R. S., Mitchell, S. S., Doran, D., Herrera, A. L., & Liberman, R. P. (2000). *Applications of errorless learning for vocational rehabilitation.* Symposium conducted at the International Congress of Cognitive Psychotherapy, Catania, Italy.

Kessler, R. C., McGonagle, K. A., Zhao, S., & Nelson, C. B. (1994). Lifetime and 12-month prevalence of *DSM-IIIR* psychiatric disorders in the United States: Results from the National Comorbidity Study. *Archives of General Psychiatry, 51,* 8–19.

Kingdon, D. G., & Turkington, D. (1994). *Cognitive-behavioral therapy of schizophrenia.* New York: Guilford Press.

Koegel, P., Burnam, M. A., & Farr, R. K. (1988). The prevalence of specific psychiatric disorders among homeless individuals in the inner city of Los Angeles. *Archives of General Psychiatry, 45,* 1085–1092.

Kopelowicz, A. (1998). Adapting social skills for Latinos with schizophrenia. *International Review of Psychiatry, 10,* 47–50.

Kopelowicz, A., & Liberman, R. P. (1995). Biobehavioral treatment and rehabilitation of schizophrenia. *Harvard Review of Psychiatry, 3,* 55–64.

Kopelowicz, A., Wallace, C. J., & Zarate, R. (1998). Teaching psychiatric inpatients to re-enter the community: A brief method of improving the continuity of care. *Psychiatric Services, 49,* 1313–1316.

Kuipers, L., & Bebbington, P. (1988). Expressed emotion research in schizophrenia: Theoretical and clinical implications. *Psychological Medicine, 18,* 893–909.

Kuipers, L., Fowler, D., Garety, P., Chisholm, D., Freeman, D., Dunn, G., Bebbington, P., & Hadley, C. (1998). London-East Anglia randomized controlled trial of cognitive behaviour therapy for psychosis. 3. Follow-up and economic evaluation at 18 months. *British Journal of Psychiatry, 173,* 61–68.

Kuipers, L., Garety, P., Fowler, D., Dunn, G., Bebbington, P., Freeman, D., & Hadley, C. (1997). London-East Anglia randomized controlled trial of cognitive-behavioral therapy for psychosis. I: Effects of the treatment phase. *British Journal of Psychiatry, 171,* 319–327.

Leff, J., Berkowitz, R., Shavit, N., Strachan, A., Glass, I., & Vaughn, C. (1989). A trial of family therapy versus a relatives' group for schizophrenia. *British Journal of Psychiatry, 154,* 58–66.

Leff, J., Kuipers, L., Berkowitz, R., Eberlein-Vries, R., & Sturgeon, D. (1982). A controlled trial of social intervention in the families of schizophrenic patients: Two-year follow-up. *British Journal of Psychiatry, 146,* 594–600.

Lehman, A. F., Dixon, L. B., Kernan, E., & DeForge, B. (1997). A randomized trial of assertive community treatment for homeless persons with severe mental illness. *Archives of General Psychiatry, 54,* 1038–1043.

Lehman, A., & Steinwachs, D. (1998). Patterns of usual care for schizophrenia: Initial results from the Schizophrenia Patient Outcomes Research Team (PORT) survey. *Schizophrenia Bulletin, 24,* 11–20.

Liberman, R. P. (1976). Behavior therapy for schizophrenia. In L. J. West & D. Flinn. (Eds.), *Treatment of schizophrenia* (pp. 142–169). New York: Grune & Stratton.

Liberman, R. P. (1982). Assessment of social skills. *Schizophrenia Bulletin, 8,* 62–83.

Liberman, R. P. (2000). The token economy: Images of psychiatry. *American Journal of Psychiatry, 157,* 1398.

Liberman, R. P. (2001). *Recreation for leisure, community re-entry, basic conversation skills, workplace fundamentals, symptom management, medication management modules.* Camarillo, CA: Psychiatric Rehabilitation Consultants (available from Psychiatric Rehabilitation Consultants, PO Box 2867, Camarillo, CA 93011).

Liberman, R. P., DeRisi, W. J., & Mueser, K. T. (1989). *Social skills training for psychiatric patients.* Elmsford, NY: Pergamon Press.

Liberman, R. P., Eckman, T. A., Kopelowicz, A., & Stolar, D. (2000). *Friendship and intimacy module.* Camarillo, CA: Psychiatric Rehabilitation Consultants (available from Psychiatric Rehabilitation Consultants, PO Box 2867, Camarillo, CA 93011).

Liberman, R. P., Falloon, I. R. H., & Aitchison, R. A. (1984). Multiple family therapy for schizophrenia: A behavioral, problem-solving approach. *Psychosocial Rehabilitation Journal, 7,* 60–77.

Liberman, R. P., Fearn, C. H., DeRisi, W. J., Roberts, J., & Carmona, M. (1977). The credit incentive system: Motivating the participation of patients in a day hospital. *British Journal of Social and Clinical Psychology, 16,* 85–94.

Liberman, R. P., & Green, M. F. (1992). Whither cognitive therapy for schizophrenia? *Schizophrenia Bulletin, 18,* 27–35.

Liberman, R. P., King, L. W., & DeRisi, W. J. (1976). Behavior analysis and therapy in community mental health. In H. Leitenberg (Ed.), *Handbook of behavior analysis and modification* (pp. 47–68). Englewood Cliffs, NJ: Prentice Hall.

Liberman, R. P., King, L. W., DeRisi, W. J., & McCann, M. (1975). *Personal effectiveness: Guiding people to assert themselves and improve their social skills.* Champaign, IL: Research Press.

Liberman, R. P., Kopelowicz, A., & Smith, T. E. (1999). Psychiatric rehabilitation. In B. J. Sadock & V. A. Sadock (Eds.), *Comprehensive textbook of psychiatry* (pp. 3218–3245). New York: Lippincott Williams & Wilkins.

Liberman, R. P., Kopelowicz, A., & Young, A. S. (1994). Biobehavioral treatment and rehabilitation of schizophrenia. *Behavior Therapy, 25,* 89–107.

Liberman, R. P., McCann, M. J., & Wallace, C. J. (1976). Generalization of behaviour therapy with psychotics. *British Journal of Psychiatry, 129,* 490–496.

Liberman, R. P., & Mintz, J. (1990). Psychiatric symptoms and the functional capacity for work. *Final report to the Social Security Administration on research grant to study psychiatric disability and employment outcomes.*

Liberman, R. P., Mueser, K. T., & Wallace, C. J. (1986). Social skills training for schizophrenic individuals at risk for relapse. *American Journal of Psychiatry, 143,* 523–526.

Liberman, R. P., Teigen, J., Patterson, R., & Baker, V. (1973). Reducing delusional speech in chronic paranoid schizophrenics. *Journal of Applied Behavior Analysis, 6,* 57–64.

Liberman, R. P., Wallace, C. J., Blackwell, G., Eckman, T., Vaccaro, J. V., & Kuehnel, T. C. (1993). Innovations in skills training for the seriously mentally ill. *Innovations in Research, 2,* 43–60.

Liberman, R. P., Wallace, C. J., Blackwell, G., Kopelowicz, A., Vaccaro, J. V., & Mintz, J. (1998). Skills training vs. psychosocial occupational therapy for persons with persistent schizophrenia. *American Journal of Psychiatry, 155,* 1087–1091.

Liberman, R. P., Wallace, C. J., Vaughn, C. E., Snyder, K. S., & Rust, C. (1980). Social and family factors in the course of schizophrenia: Toward an interpersonal problem-solving therapy for schizophrenics and their relatives. In J. Strauss, J. Fleck, & M. Bowers (Eds.), *Psychotherapy of schizophrenia: Current status and future directions* (pp. 21–54). New York: Plenum Press.

Loebel, A. D., Lieberman, J. A., Alvir, J. M., & Mayerhoff, D. I. (1992). Duration of psychosis and outcome in first-episode schizophrenia. *American Journal of Psychiatry, 149,* 1183–1188.

Malm, U. (1982). The influence of group therapy on schizophrenia. *Acta Psychiatrica Scandanavica, 65* (Suppl.), 65–73.

Manderscheid, R. W., & Sonnenschein, M. A. (1992). *Mental health in the United States: 1992*. Rockville, MD: U.S. Department of Health and Human Services.

Marder, S. R., Wirshing, W. C., Glynn, S. M., Wirshing, D. A., Mintz, J., & Liberman, R. P. (1999). Risperidone and haloperidol in maintenance treatment: Interactions with psychosocial treatments. *Schizophrenia Research, 36*, 288.

Marder, S. R., Wirshing, W. C., Mintz, J., McKenzie, J., Johnston-Cronk, K., Eckman, T. A., Lebell, M., & Liberman, R. P. (1996). Behavioral skills training vs. group psychotherapy for chronic schizophrenia. *American Journal of Psychiatry, 153*, 1585–1592.

Massel, H., Liberman, R., Mintz, J., Jacobs, H., Rush, T., Gianni, C., & Zarate, R. (1990). Evaluating the capacity to work in the mentally ill. *Psychiatry, 53*, 31–43.

Massel, H. K., Corrigan, P. W., Liberman, R. P., & Milan, M. (1991). Conversation skills training in thought-disordered schizophrenics through attention focusing. *Psychiatry Research, 38*, 51–61.

McFarlane, W. R., Lukens, E., Link, B., Dushay, R., Deakins, S., Newmark, M., Dunne, E. J., Horen, B., & Toran, J. (1995). Multiple-family groups and psychoeducation in the treatment of schizophrenia. *Archives of General Psychiatry, 52*, 679–687.

McFarlane, W. R., Stastny, P., & Deakins, S. (1992). Family-aided assertive community treatment. In R. P. Liberman (Ed.), *Effective psychiatric rehabilitation: New directions for mental health services* (pp. 43–54). San Francisco: Jossey Bass.

McGorry, P. D., & Jackson, H. J. (1999). *The recognition and management of early psychosis: A preventive approach*. New York: Cambridge University Press.

McGrew, J., Bond, G., Dietzen, L., & Salyers, M. (1994). Measuring the fidelity of implementation of a mental health program model. *Journal of Consulting and Clinical Psychology, 62*, 670–678.

Medalia, A., Aluma, M., Tryon, W., & Merriam, A. E. (1998). Effectiveness of attentional training in schizophrenia. *Schizophrenia Bulletin, 24*, 147–152.

Menditto, A. A., Beck, N. C., Stuve, P., & Fisher, J. A. (1996). Effectiveness of clozapine and a social learning program for severely disabled psychiatric inpatients. *Psychiatric Services, 47*, 46–51.

Menditto, A. A., Valdes, L. A., & Beck, N. C. (1994). Implementing a comprehensive social-learning program within the forensic psychiatric service of Fulton State Hospital. In P. W. Corrigan & R. P. Liberman (Eds.), *Behavior therapy in psychiatric hospitals* (pp. 61–78). New York: Springer.

Modrcin, M., Rapp, C. A., & Poertner, J. (1988). The evaluation of case management services with the chronically mentally ill. *Evaluation and Program Planning, 11*, 307–314.

Mueser, K. T., Bellack, A. S., Douglas, M. S., & Wade, J. H. (1991). Predictions of social skill acquisition in schizophrenic and major affective disorder patients from memory and symptomatology. *Psychiatry Research, 37*, 281–296.

Mueser, K. T., & Berenbaum, H. (1990). Psychodynamic treatment of schizophrenia: Is there a future? *Psychological Medicine, 20*, 253–262.

Mueser, K. T., Bond, G. R., Drake, R. E., & Resnick, S. G. (1998). Models of community care for severe mental illness: A review of research on case management. *Schizophrenia Bulletin, 24*, 37–74.

Mueser, K. T., Glynn, S. M., & Liberman, R. P. (1994). Behavior family management for serious psychiatric illness. In A. B. Hatfield (Ed.), *Family interventions for the mentally ill relatives: New directions for mental health services* (pp. 37–50). San Francisco: Jossey-Bass.

Mueser, K. T., Wallace, C. J., & Liberman, R. P. (1995). New developments in social skills training. *Behaviour Change, 12*, 31–40.

Mueser, K. T., Yarnold, P. R., Rosenberg, S. D., Swett, C., Miles, K. M., & Hill, D. (1999). Substance use disorder in hospitalized severely mentally ill psychiatric patients: Prevalence, correlates, and subgroups. *Schizophrenia Bulletin, 26*, 179–192.

National Institute of Mental Health. (1995). *1995 budget estimate*. Rockville, MD: U.S. Department of Health and Human Services.

Nuechterlein, K. H., Dawson, M. E., Ventura, J., Gitlin, M., Subotnik, K. L., Snyder, K. S., Mintz, J., & Bartzokis, G. (1994). The vulnerability/stress model of schizophrenic relapse. *Acta Psychiatrica Scandanavica, 89*, 58–64.

Olfson, M. (1990). Assertive community treatment: An evaluation of the experimental evidence. *Hospital and Community Psychiatry, 41*, 634–641.

Paul, G. L., & Lentz, R. J. (1977). *Psychosocial treatment of chronic mental patients: Milieu versus social-learning programs*. Cambridge: Harvard University Press.

Penn, D. L., & Mueser, K. T. (1996). Research update on the psychosocial treatment of schizophrenia. *American Journal of Psychiatry, 153*, 607–617.

RachBeisel, J., Scott, J., & Dixon, L. (1999). Co-occurring severe mental illness and substance use disorders: A review of recent research. *Psychiatric Services, 50*, 1427–1434.

Raine, A., Lencz, T., & Mednick, S. A. (Eds.). (1995). *Schizotypal personality*. New York: Cambridge University Press.

Randolph, E., Eth, S., Glynn, S., Paz, G., Van Vort, W., & Shaner, A. (1994). Efficacy of behavioral family management in reducing relapse in veteran schizophrenics. *British Journal of Psychiatry, 164,* 501–506.

Regier, D. A., Farmer, M. E., Lock, B. Z., Keith, S. J., & Rae, D. S. (1993). The de facto US mental and addictive disorders service system. *Archives of General Psychiatry, 51,* 492–499.

Regier, D. A., Farmer, M. E., Rae, D. S., Locke, B. Z., Keith, S. J., Judd, L. L., & Goodwin, F. K. (1990). Comorbidity of mental disorders with alcohol and other drug abuse. *Journal of American Medical Association, 264,* 2511–2518.

Roberts, L. J., Shaner, A., Eckman, T. A., Tucker, D. E., & Vacarro, J. V. (1992). Effectively treating stimulant-abusing schizophrenics: Mission impossible? In R. P. Liberman (Ed.), *Effective psychiatric rehabilitation: New directions for psychiatric services* (pp. 55–66). San Francisco: Jossey-Bass.

Rogers, E. S., Anthony, W. A., Cohen, M., & Davies, R. (1997). Prediction of vocational outcome based on clinical and demographic indicators among vocationally ready clients. *Community Mental Health Journal, 33,* 99–112.

Rosenheck, R., Neale, M., Leaf, P., Milstein, R., & Frisman, L. (1995). Multisite experimental cost study of intensive psychiatric community care. *Schizophrenia Bulletin, 21,* 129–140.

Roy, A. (1992). Suicide in schizophrenia. *International Review of Psychiatry, 4,* 205–209.

Rupp, A., & Keith, S. (1993). The costs of schizophrenia. *Psychiatric Clinics of North America, 16,* 413–423.

Salyers, M. P., Masterson, T. W., Fekete, D. M., Picone, J. J., & Bond, G. R. (1998). Transferring clients from intensive case management: Impact on client functioning. *American Journal of Orthopsychiatry, 68,* 233–245.

Schwartz, J., & Bellack, A. S. (1975). A comparison of a token economy with standard inpatient treatment. *Journal of Consulting and Clinical Psychology, 43,* 107–108.

Schooler, N. R., Keith, S. J., Severe, J. B., Matthews, S. M., Bellack, A. S., Glick, I. S., Hargreaves, W. A., Kane, J. M., Ninan, P. T., Frances, A., Jacobs, M., Lieberman, J. A., Mance, R., Simpson, G. M., & Woerner, M. G. (1997). Relapse and rehospitalization during maintenance treatment of schizophrenia: The effects of dose reduction and family treatment. *Archives of General Psychiatry, 54,* 453–463.

Scott, J. E., & Dixon, L. B. (1995). Assertive community treatment and case management for schizophrenia. *Schizophrenia Bulletin, 21,* 657–668.

Seeman, M. V. (1996). The role of estrogen in schizophrenia. *Journal of Psychiatry and Neuroscience, 21,* 123–127.

Sensky, T., Turkington, D., Kingdon, D. G., Scott, J., Siddle, R., O'Carroll, M., Scott, J., & Barnes, T. R. E. (2000). A randomized controlled trial of cognitive-behavioral therapy for persistent symptoms in schizophrenia resistant to medication. *Archives of General Psychiatry, 57,* 165–173.

Shaner, A., Eckman, T. A., Roberts, L. J., & Wilkins, J. N. (1995). Disability income, cocaine use and repeated hospitalization among schizophrenic cocaine abusers: A government-sponsored revolving door. *New England Journal of Medicine, 333,* 777–783.

Silverstein, S., Valone, C., Jewell, T., Corry, R., Ngheim, K., Saytes, M., & Portrude, S. (1999). Integrating shaping and skills training techniques in the treatment of chronic refractory individuals with schizophrenia. *Psychiatric Rehabilitation Skills, 3,* 41–58.

Smith, T. E., Hull, J. W., Romanelli, S., & Fertuck, E. (1999). Symptoms and neurocognition as rate limiters in skills training for psychotic patients. *American Journal of Psychiatry, 156,* 1817–1818.

Snyder, K. S., Wallace, C. J., Moe, K., & Liberman, R. P. (1994). Expressed emotion by residential care operators and schizophrenic residents' symptoms and quality of life. *Hospital and Community Psychiatry, 45,* 1141–1143.

Spaulding, W. D., Fleming, S. K., Reed, D., & Sullivan, M. (1999). Cognitive functioning in schizophrenia: Implications for psychiatric rehabilitation. *Schizophrenia Bulletin, 25,* 275–289.

Spiegler, M. D., & Agigian, H. (1976). *An educational-behavioral-social systems model for rehabilitating psychiatric patients.* New York: Brunner/Mazel.

Stein, L. I., & Santos, A. (1998). *Assertive community treatment of persons with severe mental illness.* New York: Norton.

Stein, L. I., & Test, M. A. (1980). Alternative to mental hospital treatment, 1. Conceptual model, treatment program, and clinical evaluation. *Archives of General Psychiatry, 37,* 392–397.

Stein, L. I., & Test, M. A. (1985). The training in community living model: A decade of experience. *New directions for mental health services* (pp. 17–27). San Francisco: Jossey-Bass.

Storzbach, D. M., & Corrigan, P. W. (1996). Cognitive rehabilitation for schizophrenia. In P. W. Corrigan & S. C. Yudofsky (Eds.), *Cognitive rehabilitation for neuropsychiatric disorders* (pp. 311–327). Washington, DC: American Psychiatric Press.

Strachan, A. (1992). Family management. In R. P. Liberman (Ed.), *Handbook of psychiatric rehabilitation* (pp. 183–212). New York: Macmillan.

Sue, S., & Sue, D. (1987). Cultural factors in the clinical assessment of Asian Americans. *Journal of Consulting and Clinical Psychology, 55,* 479–487.

Tarrier, N., Beckett, R., & Harwood, S. (1993). A trial of two cognitive-behavioral methods of treating drug-resistant residual psychotic symptoms in schizophrenia. *British Journal of Psychiatry, 162,* 524–532.

Tarrier, N., Witkowski, A., Kinney, C., McCarthy, E., Morris, J., & Humphreys, L. (1999). Durability of the effects of cognitive-behavioural therapy in the treatment of chronic schizophrenia; 12-month follow-up. *British Journal of Psychiatry, 174,* 500–504.

Tarrier, N., Yusupoff, L., Kinney, C., McCarthy, E., Gledhill, A., Haddock, G., & Morris, J. (1998). Randomised controlled trial of intensive cognitive behaviour therapy for patients with chronic schizophrenia. *British Medical Journal, 317,* 303–307.

Tauber, R., Wallace, C. J., & Lecomte, T. (2000). Enlisting indigenous community supporters in skills training programs for persons with severe mental illness. *Psychiatric Services, 51,* 1428–1432.

Test, M. A. (1992). Training in community living. In R. P. Liberman (Ed.), *Handbook of psychiatric rehabilitation* (pp. 153–170). New York: Macmillan.

Test, M. A., Knoedler, W. H., & Allness, D. J. (1985). The long-term treatment of schizophrenics in a community suppport program. In L. I. Stein & M. A. Test (Eds.), *The training in community living model: A decade of experience. New directions for mental health services* (pp. 17–27). San Francisco: Jossey-Bass.

Theise, C., Eriksson, B., & Luttovics, E. (1999). *Optimizing the treatment of patients with schizophrenia.* Abstract presented at the Eleventh Congress of the World Psychiatric Association Hamburg, Germany.

Ullman, L. P., & Krasner, L. (1975). *A psychological approach to abnormal behavior* (2nd ed.). Englewood Cliffs, NJ: Prentice Hall.

U.S. Department of Justice. (1998). *Enforcing the ADA: A status report from the Department of Justice, July–September.* Washington, DC: U.S. Department of Justice, Civil Rights Division.

Van der Gaag, M., Van den Bosch, R. J., Kern, R. S., & Liberman, R. P. (in press). Cognitive remediation in schizophrenia: A controlled clinical trial. *Schizophrenia Bulletin*

Velligan, D. I., Bow-Thomas, C. C., Huntzinger, C., Ritch, J., Ledbetter, N., Prihoda, T. J., & Miller, A. L. (2000). Randomized controlled trial of the use of compensatory strategies to enhance adaptive functioning in outpatients with schizophrenia. *American Journal of Psychiatry, 157,* 1317–1323.

Ventura, J., & Liberman, R. P. (2000). Psychotic disorders. In G. Fink (Ed.), *Encyclopedia of stress* (pp. 316–325). San Diego: Academic Press.

Wallace, C. J. (1996). *Workplace fundamentals module.* Camarillo, CA: Psychiatric Rehabilitation Consultants.

Wallace, C. J., & Liberman, R. P. (1985). Social skills training for patients with schizophrenia: A controlled clinical trial. *Psychiatry Research, 15,* 239–247.

Wallace, C. J., Liberman, R. P., Tauber, R., & Wallace J. (2000). The Independent Living Skills Survey: A comprehensive measure of the community functioning of severely and persistently mentally ill individuals. *Schizophrenia Bulletin, 26,* 631–658.

Wehman, P. H., & Moon, M. S. (1988). *Vocational rehabilitation and supported employment.* Baltimore: Paul H. Brookes.

Weisbrod, B., Test, M. A., & Stein, L. (1980). Alternatives to mental hospital treatment. II. Economic benefit-cost analysis. *Archives of General Psychiatry, 37,* 400–402.

Wong, S. E., Massel, H. K., Mosk, M. D., & Liberman, R. P. (1986). Behavioral approaches to the treatment of schizophrenia. In G. D. Burrows, T. R. Norman, & G. Rubinstein (Eds.), *Handbook of studies on schizophrenia* (pp. 79–100). Amsterdam: Elsevier.

Wunderlich, U., Wiedemann, G., & Buchkremer, G. (1996). Are psychosocial methods of intervention effective in schizophrenic patients? A meta-analysis. *Verhaltenstherapie, 6,* 4–13.

Wyatt, R. J. (1991). Neuroleptics and the natural course of schizophrenia. *Schizophrenia Bulletin, 17,* 325–351.

Wyatt, R. J. (1995). Early intervention for schizophrenia: Can the course of the illness be altered? *Biological Psychiatry, 38,* 1–3.

Wyatt, R. J., & Henter, I. D. (1998). The effects of early and sustained intervention on the long-term morbidity of schizophrenia. *Journal of Psychiatric Research, 32,* 169–177.

Wyatt, R. J., Henter, I., & Leary, M. (1995). An economic evaluation of schizophrenia—1991. *Social Psychiatry and Psychiatric Epidemiology, 30,* 196–205.

Young, A. S., Nuechterlein, K. H., Mintz, J., Ventura, J., Gitlin, M., & Liberman, R. P. (1998). Suicidal ideation and attempts in recent-onset schizophrenia. *Schizophrenia Bulletin, 24,* 629–634.

9

Pharmacological Treatments for Unipolar Depression

Charles B. Nemeroff
Alan F. Schatzberg

The treatment of unipolar major depression with antidepressant medication is well established on the basis of scores of randomized placebo-controlled trials involving thousands of patients. Tricyclic antidepressants (TCAs) were the first to be studied extensively; meta-analyses of placebo-controlled trials show them to be consistently and significantly more efficacious than a placebo. Because of a narrow safety margin and significant drug-induced adverse side effect problems, TCAs have now largely been replaced as the first-line treatment of depression by selective serotonin reuptake inhibitors (SSRIs)—fluoxetine, sertraline, paroxetine, and citalopram—and other new compounds, including venlafaxine, bupropion, and nefazodone. Each of these agents has been shown to be superior to a placebo and as effective as comparator TCAs in controlled trials. Clinical trials consistently show them to be better tolerated than TCAs, and they clearly have a wider margin of safety. However, there is a controversy concerning whether TCAs, mirtazapine, and venlafaxine are more effective than SSRIs for the treatment of the most severely ill depressed patients. Monoamine oxidase inhibitors (MAOIs), while also more effective than a placebo, are generally reserved for treatment-refractory patients. It is now generally recognized that patients with recurrent major depression benefit from continued antidepressant treatment, and there is evidence that TCAs and SSRIs are effective for the long-term management of recurrent major depression. An important issue in evaluating the antidepressant literature is to distinguish between response rated as a reduction in the level of symptoms on a rating scale and response rated as true remission from illness.

The efficacy of antidepressant medications has been well established in myriad controlled clinical trials, and in general the response of patients with unipolar depression is comparable to the success rates of treatment of major medical disorders such as coronary artery disease (by angioplasty), hypertension, and diabetes. Meta-analyses of the vast database of double-blind, placebo-controlled clinical trials have revealed a highly statistically significant effect of all of the currently available antidepressants approved by the Food and Drug Administration (FDA) for the acute management of unipolar depression. No other mental illness has received this much scrutiny. Because the FDA submission usually involves comparison to both a placebo and an already approved antidepressant, such as a tricyclic, large numbers of patients, literally thousands, have been involved in these trials.

The antidepressants currently available in the United States are usually classified by their purported neurochemical mechanism of action (e.g., see Table 9.1). Not only have all of the listed antidepressants been demonstrated to be effective in treating major

TABLE 9.1 Tricyclic and Tetracyclic Agents: Pharmacological Effects

	Reuptake Blockade		*Receptor Blockade*		
Drug	*NE*	*5-HT*	*ACh*	H_1	α_1
Imipramine	+	+	++	+	++
Desipramine	+++	0	+	0	+
Amitriptyline	±	++	++++	++++	+++
Nortriptyline	++	±	++	+	+
Doxepin	++	+	++	+++	++
Trimipramine	+	0	++	+++	++
Protriptyline	++	0	+++	+	+
Clomipramine	+	+++	++	+	++
Maprotiline	++	0	+	++	+
Amoxapine	++	0	0	±	++

Note: Based on Potter, Manji, and Rudorfer (1995). Reprinted with permission.

NE = norepinephrine; 5HT = serotonin; ACh = acetylcholine; H_1 = histamine-1; α_1 = alpha-1; + = mild effect; ++++ = marked effect.

depression, but no single antidepressant has ever been conclusively demonstrated to be more effective than any other antidepressant (Nemeroff, 1994). However, there is some controversy (see below) as to whether certain antidepressants such as venlafaxine, mirtazapine, and tricylic antidepressants (TCAs) might be more effective than the others for severe or treatment-refractory depression.

One of the important issues to discuss in this chapter is, of course, the definition of response in an antidepressant drug trial. A 50% decline in a dimensional measure of depression severity such as the Hamilton Depression Rating Scale (HAM-D) or the Montgomery-Asberg Depression Rating Scale (MADRS) is the generally accepted definition of a responder. However, many patients with severe depression (HAM-D scores, for example, greater than 28) can exhibit a 50% improvement in depression severity and therefore can be considered responders but may have considerable residual depressive symptoms (e.g., a HAM-D score of 13). Thus, patients included as responders may, in fact, be partial responders and clearly not euthymic. More stringent definitions of response include HAM-D scores of less than 7 or some other measure of euthymia. Use of the more stringent definitions of response may reveal differences in antidepressant efficacy.

Another poorly understood issue is the response of depressed patients to a placebo, which can occur in surprisingly high rates, in clinical trials comparing a placebo and an antidepressant. This is no trivial issue because novel antidepressants must be shown to be statistically superior to a placebo and as efficacious as an already approved antidepressant, usually a TCA, in order to receive FDA approval. This subject has previously been discussed in considerable detail (Schatzberg & Kraemer, 2000), but the major point to be made to the reader who is not familiar with clinical psychopharmacology trials in depression is that placebo treatment is not identical to no treatment. Patients taking part in clinical trials spend considerable periods of time with the staff (research nurses, research assistants), as well as with the trial physicians. The quantity of time spent by patients in clinical trials far exceeds the time spent by a patient treated by a mental health professional in a "standard" fee-for-service setting and certainly is greater than the time spent by those in managed-care settings. The contact with the research team, frequently lasting 3 to 6 hours per visit, clearly has effects on the patient's clinical state. Because of the availability of treatments, both psychotherapeutic and psychopharmacological, with documented efficacy, "no treatment," theoretically an appropriate comparison to a novel antidepressant, would not be approved by institutional review boards reviewing such an experimental design. This is a reasonable stance in view of the morbidity and mortality (secondary to suicide and increased risk of cardiovascular and cerebrovascular disease) in untreated depressed patients.

Another issue that has received considerable attention is the rapidity of response to antidepressants. It is generally acknowledged that antidepressants require 3 to 5 weeks before their therapeutic response is clinically evident, likely due to neurochemical effects on receptor regulation and/or gene expression. A "holy grail" in psychopharmacological research has been the search for antidepressants that work more rapidly.

This is a very complex issue, and space constraints preclude a comprehensive discussion of this controversial topic. However, it is important to note that the so-called lag time in antidepressant drug response in clinical trials is, of course, a mean of patients who respond relatively quickly, patients who respond after a few weeks, and patients who are nonresponders. In addition, the definition of response (given above) obviously has a major impact here; few patients show complete euthymia after 1 week. It has often been stated that if patients do not respond to antidepressants after 4 to 6 weeks, they should be treated for an additional 4 to 6 weeks. However, two studies (Boyer & Feighner, 1994; Nierenberg et al., 1995) have revealed that if the patient has not responded to paroxetine by 3 weeks of treatment or fluoxetine by 4 weeks of treatment, there is little likelihood that additional treatment, at that dose, will be successful.

Unfortunately, a generation of studies attempting to identify biological markers that predict treatment response to one or another antidepressant has provided no such valid predictors of either response or nonresponse to any antidepressant drug class. However, the use of positron emission tomography (PET) to label neurotransmitter transporters and receptors in vivo may provide for the first time the ability to determine whether a given patient shows, for example, a deficit in serotonin transporter binding, which might predict response to one of the selective serotonin reuptake inhibitors (SSRIs).

Other critical areas that the reader might wish to consider are issues of age, gender, and comorbid medical disorders. There is a dearth of studies of antidepressant use in children and adolescents, and what is available does little to convince one of the antidepressants' efficacy. There is widespread belief among clinicians that antidepressants are effective in this age group, but few controlled studies have demonstrated such efficacy (see DeVane & Sallee, 1996, and Fisher & Fisher, 1996, for a review). Evidence for the efficacy of only fluoxetine (Emslie et al., 1997) and puroxetine (Keller et al., 2001) in children and adolescents is available. Clearly, further studies are needed in this important area.

Similarly, there are reports of differences in efficacy of classes of antidepressant in the elderly. This controversy is described below, but surely further studies are needed in this area.

The exclusion of women of childbearing potential from clinical trials because of fears of potential teratogenic effects of antidepressants has resulted in an embarrassing lack of knowledge of pharmacokinetics and clinical efficacy in the population that has the highest prevalence rate of unipolar depression. Further studies with a focus on antidepressant–gonadal-steroid interactions are advisable.

Finally, and of paramount importance, is the documentation of antidepressant efficacy and tolerability in patients with comorbid medical disorders. Prevalence rates of unipolar depression in patients with medical disorders such as cancer, diabetes, myocardial infarction, Parkinson's disease, multiple sclerosis, and Alzheimer's disease is remarkably high (25 to 50%), and relatively few controlled treatment trials have been conducted in these populations (see Boswell, Anfinson, & Nemeroff, 1997, for a review). However, such studies are now even more vitally important to conduct because there is increasing evidence that depression is associated with an increased risk of death after myocardial infarction (Frasure-Smith, Lesperance, & Talajic, 1993, 1995) and stroke. Similarly, depression has been suggested to have a profound negative impact on patients with cancer (McDaniel, Musselman, Porter, Reed, & Nemeroff, 1995). Virtually all of the controlled treatment trials of antidepressants in patients with comorbid medical disorders, including patients with depression and comorbid stroke, cancer, Parkinson's disease, chronic obstructive pulmonary disease, multiple sclerosis, or diabetes, have clearly documented efficacy of the antidepressant.

However, because the majority of patients with medical disorders is also prescribed a variety of other medications, it is of paramount importance to prescribe antidepressant medications that are safe and, in particular, have no untoward drug-drug interactions with other prescribed medications. This is not a trivial issue because most antidepressants are bound to plasma proteins and therefore can displace other commonly prescribed drugs, such as coumadin, from their protein-binding site, increasing plasma coumadin concentrations and increasing bleeding times with potentially adverse consequences. Moreover, in recent years it has become evident that many antidepressants inhibit the activity of certain hepatic cytochrome P450 isoenzymes, which are responsible for metabolizing a wide variety of other commonly prescribed medications. Such drug-drug interactions, if not acknowledged, could lead to increases in plasma concentrations of drugs such as astemizole, a commonly prescribed antihistamine, that at high levels can exert toxic effects on the heart. These data have been comprehensively reviewed (DeVane, 1994; Ereshefsky, 1996; Nemeroff, DeVane, & Pollack, 1996).

A final area of crucial importance is maintenance treatment of depression and assessment of its efficacy compared with placebo treatment. It is generally recommended that, after a single episode of depression, patients should be treated for 6 months. If a patient has suffered more than one episode of depression, if the first episode was particularly severe (e.g., with a serious suicide attempt) or particularly difficult to treat, or if the patient has a very strong family history, long-term treatment should be considered. All of the studies that have evaluated treatment with antidepressants for 1 year or longer compared with a placebo have found highly significant beneficial effects of antidepressant treatment. Such studies have included TCAs, SSRIs, and venlafaxine. These data have been reviewed (Blacker, 1996; Hirschfeld & Schatzberg, 1994; Thase & Sullivan, 1995).

A final point should be made about the use of more than one medication to treat depression. For many years, the prevailing opinion in psychiatry has been that monotherapy for depression is highly desirable and conversely that polypharmacy is to be avoided. This is certainly not the case in other branches of medicine, in which polypharmacy is virtually the rule. Failure of a single agent to provide adequate control of hypertension, diabetes, or a neoplasm invariably leads to the use of two or three pharmacological agents. If the goal is to return the patient to complete euthymia, combination therapy of more than one psychotropic agent, as well as combination psychopharmacology and psychotherapy, may be necessary.

TRICYCLIC ANTIDEPRESSANTS

Tricyclic antidepressants were for many years the treatments of choice for major depression. They were originally introduced into the United States in the 1960s. In this country, seven TCAs are approved for treatment of major depression, and one additional compound—clomipramine—is approved for obsessive compulsive disorder (OCD) but is viewed throughout the world as an efficacious antidepressant. Two other compounds (maprotiline and amoxapine) have four-ringed structures and are variants of the tricyclic class. Amoxapine is related to the antipsychotic agent loxapine.

There is a large amount of literature demonstrating efficacy of the TCAs (Potter et al., 1998). In the United States, some of the original randomized clinical trials (RCTs) in psychiatry included imipramine or amitriptyline and showed these agents to be effective in what we now term *major depression*. Efficacy of the TCAs has been revisited in SSRI comparator trials, and the TCAs still appear to be more effective than a placebo and to be of comparable efficacy to the SSRIs. Janicak and colleagues (1993) performed meta-analyses of the TCA RCTs literature and reported these antidepressants to be overwhelmingly more effective than a placebo. For example, 50 studies that compared imipramine with a placebo reported an aggregate response rate to the TCA of 68%, compared to a 40% response rate to the placebo, a difference significant at the $p < 10^{-40}$ level.

Imipramine was used in a comparator treatment against cognitive behavior therapy in the National Institute of Mental Health (NIMH) collaborative treatment study of outpatients with major depression. That study suggested that more severely depressed patients responded better to the TCA than they did to the psychosocial treatment (Elkin et al., 1989), although other studies did not bear this out (Hollon et al., 1992).

Some investigators have argued that the TCAs are more effective than the SSRIs in the treatment of more severely depressed or melancholic inpatients in that they are more likely to induce remission within 4–6 weeks. In a study by the Danish University Antidepressant Group (DUAG, 1990), clomipramine produced significantly higher rates of remission than did paroxetine. In another report on inpatients by this group (DUAG, 1986), clomipramine was also significantly more effective than citalopram. More recently, Roose et al. (1994) reported that nortriptyline was more effective than fluoxetine in hospitalized cardiac patients with melancholia. Other studies have not borne out such differences (see below), although the perception of superior efficacy continues among some investigators.

The tricyclic antidepressants alone are less effective in major depression with psychotic features (delusional depression) or in those with so-called atypical features. In the former, TCA monotherapy has been found to be effective in only 35% of patients, in contrast to a 65% response rate in their nondelusional counterparts, a difference that is highly statistically significant (Chan et al., 1987). In delusional depressives, TCAs in combination with antipsychotics have been reported to be significantly more effective than TCAs alone (Schatzberg & Rothschild, 1992). For such patients, clinical practice now calls for combining TCAs or other antidepressants with antipsychotic agents. The presence of atypical features (hypersomnia, hyperphagia, prominent anxiety, reverse diurnal mood variation) predicts poorer responses to imipramine than to monoamine oxidase inhibitors (MAOIs) according to some RCTs (see below).

The TCAs as a class are potent inhibitors of the reuptake of norepinephrine into presynaptic neurons; they exert fewer effects on serotonin reuptake (Table 9.1). The one major exception is clomipramine, which is a potent serotonin reuptake blocker with a demethylated metabolite that is a potent norepinephrine reuptake blocker. Norepinephrine reuptake blocking effects probably account for some patients' becoming activated (increased anxiety or agitation) on these agents. Generally, such effects are dose-related and can be minimized by conservative dosing. Over time, TCAs are frequently anxiolytic in their effects.

The TCAs all have some affinity for muscarinic cholinergic receptors as antagonists (Table 9.1) and produce dry mouth, blurred vision, constipation, urinary hesitancy, memory disturbance, and tachycardia. Agents within the class vary in the degree to which they produce these side effects, with the so-called secondary tricyclics, which represent demethylated metabolites of parent tertiary TCAs, exerting more limited anticholinergic effects than their parents. Examples are nortriptyline (the metabolite of amitriptyline) and desipramine (the metabolite of imipramine).

The TCAs are also antihistaminic, with amitriptyline and doxepin being most potent at this site (Table 9.1) and being most likely to produce sedation and weight gain. These agents also block α_1 adrenergic receptors and produce orthostatic hypotension. Here, too, these side effects are mainly dose-related and can be minimized by using lower doses of drugs, particularly when initiating treatment. Some patients may, however, not be able to tolerate even the most minimal doses of these agents.

Because of their α_1 adrenergic and anticholinergic effects, the TCAs are potentially cardiotoxic in overdose and have relatively narrow safety margins (low therapeutic index). They can result in death when taken in overdose and are the number one cause of overdose death among prescription drugs in the United States. Generally, clinicians initiating treatment with a TCA begin at low doses (e.g., 50 mg of amitriptyline, imipramine, or desipramine or 25 mg of nortriptyline) to avoid side effects as much as possible and to maximize compliance. Over 7 to 10 days, doses are increased gradually to 150 mg per day of amitriptyline, imipramine, or desipramine or to 75 mg per day of nortriptyline. After 2 weeks of these doses, further gradual dosage increments can be undertaken to achieve the maximum recommended doses. Therapeutic dosage ranges are summarized in Table 9.2.

There is a relatively rich literature on the relationship of TCA plasma levels to clinical response. Generally, such relationships have been demonstrated in studies of more severely depressed patients. Glassman et al. (1977) reported a so-called sigmoidal relationship between imipramine plasma concentrations and clinical response, with maximum response rates observed at plasma levels greater than or equal to 200 ng/ml of imipramine plus desipramine. A relationship between imipramine plasma level and clinical response has not been observed for milder depressives. For nortriptyline, a so-called therapeutic window has been described, with nortriptyline blood levels less than approximately 50 ng/ml and greater than 150 ng/ml being associated with poorer response than is seen at levels between 50 and 150 ng/ml (Asberg et al., 1971). Virtually identical data are available for protriptyline. Similarly, amitriptyline is also thought to have a therapeutic window of approximately 95 to 200 ng/ml (amitriptyline and nortriptyline). Some have argued that desipramine also has a therapeutic window, but data here are more limited.

Maintenance therapy with the TCAs has been the focus of two major studies. In one, Prien et al. (1984) reported relatively low efficacy for maintenance imipramine therapy; however, in that study patients were often maintained at relatively low doses. This reflected the common practice of the day. In the more recent study of Frank et al. (1990),

TABLE 9.2 Typical Therapeutic Dosage Ranges of Tricyclic and Tetracyclic Antidepressant Drugs (Adult Patients)

Drug		
Generic Name	*Trade Name*	*Therapeutic Dose Range (mg/day)*
Imipramine	Tofranil	150–300
Desipramine	Norpramin	150–300
Amitriptyline	Elavil	150–300
Nortriptyline	Pamelor, Aventyl	50–150
Doxepin	Sinequan	150–300
Trimipramine	Surmontil	150–200
Clomipramine	Anafranil	75–200
Maprotiline	Ludiomil	75–200
Amoxapine	Asendin	200–400

imipramine was clearly demonstrated to be more effective than a placebo in 3-year maintenance therapy of recurrent unipolar depression (20% recurrence on imipramine vs. approximately 90% on the placebo). This study maintained patients at the doses to which they had responded. Moreover, lower dose versus full-dose maintenance strategies were tested in a subset of subjects (Frank et al., 1993). Full doses were significantly more effective than half doses (30% recurrence vs. 70% recurrence, respectively). Thus, maintenance therapy with TCAs appears to require continuing patients on the doses effective during acute treatment. This has now become standard practice.

MONOAMINE OXIDASE INHIBITORS

The development of the MAOIs is one of the most interesting chapters in the history of psychopharmacology. When tuberculosis was ravaging civilizations and patients infected with the tubercular bacillus were admitted to sanitoriums for long-term care, new antitubercular drugs were tested for efficacy in these settings. One such antitubercular drug, iproniazid, was noted to produce mood elevation in many patients. This led to the development of the three MAOIs currently available in the United States: phenelzine, tranylcypromine, and isocarboxizid. The last drug was unavailable for some time but is now once again available. These are all irreversible, nonselective MAOIs and, compared to newer antidepressants (see below), have a less favorable side-effect profile. Although selective and reversible MAOIs with a more favorable side-effect profile have been developed (e.g., moclobemide), they are not available for clinical use in the United States.

The MAOIs are believed to produce their therapeutic effects by preventing the degradation of monoamines, particularly serotonin, norepinephrine, and dopamine (DA), all posited to be reduced in availability in patients with unipolar depression. All of the available MAOIs have been shown to be effective in the treatment of unipolar depression and, in particular, atypical depression characterized by hypersomnia and hyperphagia (Krishnan, 1998). Table 9.3 lists the currently available MAOIs and their usual dose ranges. In addition to unipolar depression,

TABLE 9.3 Monoamine Oxidase Inhibitors

Drug		
Generic Name	*Trade Name*	*Dose Range (mg/day)*
Phenelzine	Nardil	45–90
Tranylcypromine	Parnate	10–30
Isocarboxizid	Marplan	10–30

MAOIs are also effective, like SSRIs and certain TCAs, in the treatment of panic disorder. They are also effective in the treatment of bipolar depression.

Some disadvantages of MAOIs include the necessity of dosing multiple times per day, associated with considerably poorer compliance when compared to once-a-day dosing, and the necessity of dietary constraints.

Certain foods that contain high concentrations of tyramine, an endogenous amine, such as aged meats and cheeses, chocolate, and Chianti wine, as well as over-the-counter cold medications (e.g., pseudoephedrine), are absolute contraindications in patients prescribed MAOIs because of the so-called cheese reaction, characterized by severe hypertension and possible medical sequelae such as stroke. Symptoms of this syndrome include severe headache, flushing, palpitations, and nausea.

Although not practical, the proper manner to prescribe MAOIs is to first measure baseline platelet MAO activity, begin treatment with a phenelzine or isocarboxazid, and to repeat the platelet MAO activity measurement after 3 to 4 weeks of treatment. The best treatment responses are associated with 80–90% inhibition of platelet MAO activity. Because patients vary widely as to their MAO activity, it is impossible to predict what the ideal dose of a MAOI will be for any given patient. Percentage of MAO inhibition does not appear to correlate with response to tranylcypromine.

In addition to the drug-drug and drug-food interactions noted above, MAOIs have a number of other untoward side effects, including orthostatic hypotension, sexual dysfunction, dizziness, insomnia, tachycardia, palpitations, and edema.

The MAOIs are not generally considered first-line treatments for depression because of their unfavorable side-effect profile, dietary restrictions, need for dosing multiple times per day, and the general unavailability of platelet MAO activity measurements. There is also some evidence that MAOIs may be somewhat less efficacious than TCAs, SSRIs, and some of the newer antidepressants.

SELECTIVE SEROTONIN REUPTAKE INHIBITORS

The selective serotonin reuptake inhibitors (SSRIs) have become first-line treatments (Rush et al., 1994) for most patients with major depression (Table 9.4). The first of these agents, fluoxetine, was introduced in the United States in 1988. Since then, four others have been released in the U.S. market: sertraline, paroxetine, citalopram, and fluvoxamine. Of these, fluvoxamine is approved for use in the United States only for OCD, but it is used as an antidepressant in many other countries. In this chapter, we emphasize the SSRIs approved for use in major depression in this country.

These agents work primarily by blocking the reuptake of serotonin into presynaptic neurons. They have virtually no effect to date on blocking norepinephrine reuptake (except paroxetine), and they also do not interfere with various ligands binding to muscarinic cholinergic, α_1 adrenergic, or histamine H_1 receptors. Thus, they produce little—if any—dry mouth, constipation, or urinary hesitance (anticholinergic effects), orthostatic hypotension (α_1 adrenergic blockade), or sedation and weight gain (H_1 blockade). Paroxetine is an exception in that it has weak anticholinergic potential and does produce some dry mouth, albeit less than is seen with the TCAs. It is also mildly sedating in some patients.

TABLE 9.4 Typical Antidepressant Therapeutic Dosage Ranges of Selective Serotonin Reuptake Inhibitors (Adult Patients)

Drug		
Generic Name	*Trade Name*	*Therapeutic Dose Range (mg/day)*
Fluoxetine	Prozac	20–80
Paroxetine	Paxil	20–50
Sertraline	Zoloft	50–200
Citalopram	Celexa	20–40
Fluvoxamine	Fluvoxamine	100–300

The side effects associated with increased serotonin availability and commonly seen with the SSRIs include nausea, diarrhea, insomnia, nervousness, and sexual dysfunction. The first four of these are commonly dose-dependent, so that more conservative dosing frequently avoids their occurrence. Sexual dysfunction is less clearly dose-related and can be seen even at low doses.

The initial trials failed to report high rates of sexual dysfunction (e.g., delayed ejaculation in men and anorgasmia in women) with SSRI therapy. These side effects have become apparent with wider spread long-term use. It is probable that many depressed patients are not aware of or are not bothered by sexual dysfunction in the initial weeks of treatment but do become troubled by this annoying side effect over time as they resume their normal activities. In the initial trials of fluoxetine, sexual dysfunction was noted in some 4% of subjects. Currently, estimates are that at least 30% of patients on SSRIs experience it.

Because these drugs have limited anticholinergic and noradrenergic effects, they are not cardiotoxic and are thus safe in overdoses. This represented a major step forward in treatment over the TCAs, which have a narrow safety margin (discussed above in the TCA section).

The SSRIs can be coadministered with the TCAs, but this needs to be done cautiously because, as a class, these agents generally inhibit P_{450} isoenzymes in the liver that metabolize TCAs and result in higher blood levels and increased side effects (DeVane, 1994; Nemeroff et al., 1996). Citalopram has little effect on P_{450} systems. The coprescription of SSRIs with MAOIs is contraindicated because of a risk of the serotonergic syndrome—characterized by myoclonic jerks, hyperpyrexia, and coma.

The efficacy of the SSRIs has been clearly demonstrated in numerous RCTs; these data have been reviewed elsewhere (Nemeroff, 1994). Published data are most extensive for fluoxetine, sertraline, and paroxetine, having been studied in several thousand patients. Data on citalopram are somewhat more limited.

In the eight RCTs published before the release of fluoxetine that formed the basis of the FDA submission, fluoxetine was significantly more effective than the placebo in the four placebo-controlled studies and was generally comparable to TCA in the six comparison trials (Schatzberg, 1995a). In the majority of studies, the dropout rate was lower (often significantly) for fluoxetine than for the TCA or placebo. After the FDA submission, over 5,000 papers on the drug have appeared in the archival literature. Studies have continued to show significantly greater efficacy for fluoxetine over the placebo in patients of all age groups with major depression. As noted above, a recent RCT of fluoxetine in children and adolescents with major depression has found the drug to be significantly more effective than the placebo in that age group (Emslie et al., 1997). More than 25 million patients have been treated with fluoxetine since its introduction.

Efficacy studies of paroxetine have also been reviewed in detail by our group and others (DeBattista & Schatzberg, 1995). We reviewed nearly 30 RCTs of paroxetine for major depression. Paroxetine was significantly more effective than the placebo in 8 of 11 comparison studies. Paroxetine was comparable in efficacy to the TCA in all but 5 studies, which found either the TCA or paroxetine to be more effective. Overall, dropout rates for paroxetine due to adverse events were lower in patients on paroxetine than on TCAs. An early inpatient study in Denmark reported greater efficacy with clomipramine than paroxetine, and this study has been cited in the debate on SSRI efficacy in more severely depressed patients. However, this study used a relatively low dose of paroxetine (30 mg/day).

Efficacy data for sertraline have also been reviewed in detail elsewhere (Janicak et al., 1993; Mendels, 1995). Sertraline has been reported to be more effective than a placebo in two large-scale clinical trials ($N = 545$) and to be of comparable efficacy to standard TCAs in two studies ($N = 320$). Sertraline has also been reported to be effective in the treatment of postpartum depression (Stowe, Casarella, Landry, & Nemeroff, 1995).

Citalopram has been reported to be significantly more effective than placebo in outpatients with major depression (Feighner & Overo, 1999), as well as in unipolar or bipolar melancholic depressives (Mendels et al., 1999).

As indicated above, there is an ongoing debate regarding whether the SSRIs, particularly fluoxetine, are as effective as the TCAs in the treatment of severely depressed patients, particularly in the geriatric age group. These data have been reviewed in detail elsewhere (Schatzberg, 1996). While there are occasional reports in the literature that an SSRI is less effective in these subjects, the overall data from RCTs do not bear out this conclusion. In one study, we compared desipramine and fluoxetine in a group of moderately to severely depressed patients (Bowden et al., 1993). The two drugs were of comparable efficacy; however, fluoxetine had a far more benign side-effect profile. In a small-scale study of more severely depressed inpatients, Clerc et al. (1994) reported that venlafaxine (a mixed uptake blocker) was significantly more effective at 4 to 6 weeks than fluoxetine. Thus, the debate is likely to continue for some time, although to date the data overall do not support the impression of lower efficacy.

Because fluoxetine was reported in the early trials to be "activating," some clinicians and investigators advised against using it in depressed patients with prominent anxiety. Analyses of the comparative clinical trials have revealed that the drug is as effective in anxious depressives as it is in major depressives without anxiety (Schatzberg, 1995b; Tollefson, Holman, & Sayler, 1994). Some patients may, however, require starting at a lower dose (e.g., 10 mg/day of fluoxetine). Significant SSRI efficacy in purely anxious patients (e.g., panic disorder) has been revealed in RCTs as well. Thus, the SSRIs (including fluoxetine) appear effective in both depressed and anxious patients or in those who demonstrate mixed symptoms. SSRI's are effective in the treatment of bipolar depression and less likely to cause a switch into mania than TCAS or MAIOs (Nemeroff et al., 2001).

All four SSRIs have been reported to be significantly more effective than a placebo in preventing relapse or recurrence for up to 1 year of treatment. Of patients treated with fluoxetine for 1 year, 26% experienced a relapse or recurrence, in contrast to 57% on a placebo (Montgomery et al., 1988). Similarly, 14% of patients treated with paroxetine relapsed or recurred versus 30% on a placebo (Montgomery & Dunbar, 1993). The sertraline relapse rate over 44 weeks of continuation treatment was 13%, in contrast to 46% for a placebo (Doogan & Caillard, 1992). Similarly, citalopram was significantly more effective than placebo in preventing relapse (Montgomery et al., 1993). These data are all remarkably similar and point to the efficacy of the SSRIs during continuation and maintenance treatment. Of note is that, in these longer term studies, new side effects of the SSRIs have not emerged. Thus, the relative safety of this class of agents appears to be maintained after long-term treatment.

The four SSRIs all have half-lives of at least 24 hours and can be given in a once-a-day dose. The long half-life of norfluoxetine (7 to 14 days), an active metabolite of fluoxetine, suggested that the drug can be given once or two times a week. Indeed once weekly fluoxetine has now been approved for the treatment of depression by the FDA. Such data are not available for paroxetine, citalopram, or sertraline. Paroxetine has no active metabolites and is unlikely to be effective when prescribed on a weekly or twice-weekly basis. Sertraline's demethylated metabolite has a half-life (3 days) that is much shorter than norfluoxetine's and is formed in relatively lower concentrations. This drug is also not a likely candidate for less frequent prescription.

Therapeutic antidepressant dosage ranges for the SSRIs are summarized in Table 9.4. The standard starting dose for fluoxetine, paroxetine, and citalopram is 20 mg/day; for sertraline, it is 50 mg/day. For most patients, 20 mg/day of fluoxetine is the therapeutic dose, with 40 mg/day the next most common dose. Some patients require higher doses (e.g., 60 to 100 mg/day) to respond, while others derive benefit from 10 mg/day. In double-blind studies, 20 mg/day and 40 mg/day appeared to be the most effective doses, but a 5-mg/day dose also was more effective than a placebo. (For review of dosage issues, see Schatzberg, 1995a.) Paroxetine is generally effective at doses of 20 to 30 mg/day, with a maximum recommended dose in major depression of 50 mg/day. The usual starting dose is 20 mg/day. Sertraline may be effective at 50 mg/day, but many studies report average doses of 100 to 150 mg/day. The starting dose is typically 50 mg/day. The recommended maximum dose is 200 mg/day. In elderly patients or for those with prominent anxiety or agitation, the recommended starting doses for SSRIs are 50% lower. Citalopram is effective at 20–40 mg/day, the 40-mg/day dose being used commonly by psychiatrists. To date, there are no available data that correlate antidepressant responses to SSRI plasma levels.

VENLAFAXINE (EFFEXOR)

Venlafaxine (Effexor) is a dual serotonin/norepinephrine (5HT/NE) reuptake inhibitor approved for the treatment of depression; its pharmacological and clinical properties have been reviewed (Andrews, Ninan, & Nemeroff, 1996). Because there is evidence

TABLE 9.5 Atypical Antidepressants

Drug		
Generic Name	*Trade Name*	*Dose Range (mg/day)*
Trazadone	Desyrel	300–600
Nefazadone	Serzone	400–600
Bupropion	Wellbutrin	150–450
Venlafaxine XR	Effexor XR	75–225
Mirtazapine	Remeron	30–45

that reduced availability of both NE and 5HT occurs in patients with depression and, moreover, because of evidence that both NE and 5HT reuptake blockade is associated with therapeutic efficacy in depression, an uptake blocker of both monoamines was considered of interest, especially if such a drug lacked the adverse side-effect profile of the TCAs. Venlafaxine is indeed such an agent at its higher dose range, and can be conceptualized as a TCA without the anticholinergic, antiadrenergic, and antihistaminergic effects of the TCAs. It therefore should have all of the efficacy and none of the unfavorable side effects of the TCAs.

There is indeed evidence that this is the case. Unlike TCAs, venlafaxine produces no orthostatic hypotension, is not lethal in overdose, and produces no dry mouth, constipation, blurry vision, or sedation. Its side-effect profile resembles exactly what one would predict from its postulated mechanism of action, namely, the combination of the SSRIs' side effects (nausea, headache, sexual dysfunction, and insomnia) and the NE reuptake blockers' side effects (hypertension, tachycardia, and sweating). In our clinical experience, using lower than recommended doses initially of the extended release form, such as 375 mg daily, and gradually increasing the dose every 3 to 5 days depending on emergent side effects allows the attainment of a therapeutic dose with minimal side effects. Although 75 mg is an effective dose in many patients, others require doses up to 225 mg per day or even higher (e.g., 450 mg/day; Table 9.5). Another major advantage of venlafaxine is its lack of inhibition of any of the cytochrome P_{450} hepatic isoenzymes responsible for drug-drug interactions with certain of the SSRIs (see the introductory section of this chapter). This allows for the combination of venlafaxine with TCAs and other medications in nonresponsive patients without concerns about increases in TCA plasma levels and associated toxicity.

One disadvantage of venlafaxine was originally the necessity for divided day dosing because of its short half-life, but the introduction of the sustained-release form of the drug has obviated this problem.

In contradistinction to the apparently less optimal side-effect profile of venlafaxine compared with the SSRIs is its reputation for superb efficacy in the treatment of unipolar depression, particularly in treatment-refractory patients. There is little doubt among most psychopharmacologists that venlafaxine is successful in treating a sizable proportion of patients who have failed trials with other antidepressants, including SSRIs; this has been reported in an open study (Nierenberg et al., 1994). We have treated approximately 25 patients who failed trials with other antidepressants and electroconvulsive therapy (ECT) who were venlafaxine responders. Less clear is whether venlafaxine acts more rapidly than other antidepressants, an active avenue of investigation. Because of its short half-life, venlafaxine attains steady-state plasma levels very rapidly compared with other antidepressants.

In addition to its acknowledged efficacy in treatment-refractory depression is the evidence that venlafaxine is more effective than the SSRIs in severe depression (frequently defined as the melancholic subtype or the endogenous subtype) or in hospitalized depressed patients. Two double-blind controlled studies have evaluated the efficacy of venlafaxine for severe depression. In one (Guelfi et al., 1995), venlafaxine was shown to be effective for severe depression when compared with a placebo; most impressive was the lack of any effect of the placebo in this population. In a second study (Clerc et al., 1994), fluoxetine and venlafaxine were compared in depressed inpatients; both drugs were effective, but venlafaxine was more effective than fluoxetine, and the antidepressant effect had a more rapid onset of action. Finally, Thase and colleagues (2001) have recently conducted a pooled analysis of approximately 2000 patients showing that venlafaxine is more effective than placebo or SSRI, largely fluoxetine, in attaining remission in patients with major depression.

BUPROPION (WELLBUTRIN)

Bupropion (Wellbutrin) is an amino ketone that has little effect on 5HT, NE, or DA reuptake but has been demonstrated to be effective for major depression. How it exerts its therapeutic effects via this effect on DA systems remains unclear.

Like that of the other antidepressants, the efficacy of bupropion in the treatment of major depression is comparable to that of TCAs, as well as of fluoxetine and trazodone. Because of its short half-life, bupropion was originally administered twice per day; for that reason, as well as because of a propensity for high doses of the drug to produce seizures, a slow-release form of the drug was developed, studied in clinical trials, and then released. This preparation has the advantage of once-a-day dosing and a risk of seizures no greater than that observed with other antidepressants.

Bupropion has certain advantages when compared to TCAs, including a lack of orthostatic hypertension, few cardiovascular effects, and no anticholinergic effects. Bupropion produces no sedation or cognitive impairment and, most important, in contrast to the SSRIs, produces no sexual dysfunction. In contrast to the TCAs, which are well known to produce weight gain, many patients treated with bupropion exhibit weight loss, which can in certain clinical circumstances be problematic.

Bupropion was also shown in two small studies to be effective in the treatment of bipolar depression, with little propensity to cause a switch into mania, though this was not confirmed in a subsequent study. Whether bupropion is effective in the treatment of refractory depression remains unknown.

TRAZODONE (DESYREL)

Trazodone was the first antidepressant introduced in the United States that was not lethal when taken in overdose. A triazolopyridine derivative, it is structurally unrelated to the tricyclics but is related to nefazodone (discussed in the next section). Trazodone is believed to act as an antidepressant primarily by virtue of its effects as a serotonin type 2 ($5HT_2$) receptor antagonist. Trazodone has a short half-life of 3 to 9 hours, but it can be administered once per day. In addition to antagonism of the $5HT_2$ receptor, trazodone is also known to be a weak inhibitor of serotonin reuptake, far less potent than any of the marketed SSRIs. Several trials revealed that trazodone is as effective as TCAs and fluoxetine in the treatment of major depression, though many clinicians have the impression that it is not effective in moderate to severe depression.

The major side effects include sedation, which can often limit its clinical usefulness, though frequently trazodone is combined with SSRIs to reverse SSRI-induced insomnia. Trazodone clearly has fewer anticholinergic side effects than TCAs, but its major drawback, particularly in the elderly, is orthostatic hypotension, thought to be due to α_1 adrenergic receptor blockade. Another potentially serious adverse side effect of trazodone is the fact that a small percentage of men develop priapism after trazodone use, and in a small percentage of those individuals, surgical intervention is necessary. It is also important to point out that trazodone has been associated with arrhythmias in patients with preexisting cardiac disease.

Trazodone is usually begun at a dose of 100 to 150 mg per day, increased to doses of 400 to 600 mg per day. Although such doses can be administered once per day, they are often administered in divided doses, particularly when the dose exceeds 300 mg per day.

NEFAZODONE (SERZONE)

The antidepressant nefazodone (Serzone), structurally related to trazodone, is a potent $5HT_2$ antagonist, as well as an inhibitor of both 5HT and NE reuptake (Owens, Ieni, Knight, Winders, & Nemeroff, 1995; Taylor et al., 1995). It is an effective antidepressant and has the advantages of producing no sexual dysfunction, a major advantage compared with the SSRIs, and also preserves normal sleep architecture. Like the SSRIs, nefazodone has also been shown to be effective in reducing the anxiety associated with major depression as assessed with the Covi scale.

The major disadvantages of this drug include the necessity for twice-daily dosing due to its short half-life and the necessity to titrate the dose. Although the manufacturer recommends a dose of 100 mg twice per day as the starting dose, many clinicians recommend a starting dose of 50 mg twice a day due to the sedation commonly observed with this drug. Nefazodone must be administered in a dose range of 400 to 600 mg per day to achieve maximal efficacy. In a landmark study, Keller et al. (2001) reported that nefazodone combined with cognitive-behavior therapy (CBT) is very effective in the treatment of patients with chronic depression, more effective than either treatment alone.

Nefazodone is a potent inhibitor of cytochrome P_{450} 3A4 and as such is absolutely contraindicated in patients treated with commonly used antihistamines that are metabolized by this enzyme, because of toxic cardiac events that can ensue with such drug combinations. Moreover, caution must be used when using benzodiazepines such as alprazolam, triazolam, or midazolam in combination with nefazodone because these drugs are also metabolized by cytochrome P_{450} 3A4 and exhibit markedly elevated plasma concentrations when coadministered with nefazodone.

MIRTAZAPINE (REMERON)

Mirtazapine (Remeron) is a novel antidepressant that is the newest entry into the antidepressant market in the United States. This tetracyclic is believed to act primarily as an α_2 antagonist at auto- and heteroreceptors and is also a 5HT2A and $5HT_3$ receptor antagonist. Its net effect is the increase of 5HT and NE neurotransmission (de Boer, 1996). Because of its recent introduction, most clinicians have had little clinical experience with this agent.

Its major advantages include a single daily dose, the lack of sexual dysfunction, and safety in overdose and sedating properties, which is particularly helpful in depressed patients with profound insomnia as often seen in the elderly patient. Its major side effects include marked daytime somnolence, to which patients eventually become tolerant, as well as increased appetite, weight gain, and dizziness. Of 2,796 patients in clinical trials, 2 developed agranulocytosis and 1 developed severe neutropenia. Wide-scale use post-release has not revealed an increased risk of this reaction. Its efficacy has been reported to be faster and slightly greater than that of the SSRIs in several studies (Benkert et al., 2000; Schatzberg et al., 2001), and the drug has been shown to be effective in SSRI nonresponders (Thase et al., 2001).

DISCUSSION

For all classes of antidepressants available in the United States, efficacy has been demonstrated in RCTs. The differences among these classes of agents revolve primarily around their side effects and safety. The first-generation TCAs and MAOIs are less well tolerated and are more dangerous in overdose than are the newer agents. For this reason alone, the SSRIs and other newer agents represent important steps forward in the treatment of major depression. Moreover, the TCAs are largely noradrenergic in their reuptake-blocking effects, exerting little effect on serotonin reuptake (clomipramine is a notable exception). The difference in monoamine reuptake blockade most likely accounts for a wider range of efficacy for the SSRIs (e.g., panic, OCD, bulimia, premenstrual syndrome), as well as for their demonstrated effects in milder forms of depression, such as dysthymia.

Although the various classes enjoy efficacy for major depression, a number of issues about their relative efficacy for specific subgroups or subtypes of depression remain in debate. For example, as indicated above, some argue that the TCAs are more efficacious antidepressants and are more likely to induce remission in melancholic depressives than the SSRIs. These data and the venlafaxine and mirtazapine findings suggest the need in treating severely ill patients to have drugs that exert potent noradrenergic effects. Another issue is whether the MAOIs (and perhaps the SSRIs) are more effective in atypical depressives than are the TCAs. These areas require further prospective study.

The relatively high placebo response rates in outpatient studies are of concern in some studies, with both known and investigational antidepressants failing to separate from the placebo. Research and clinical experience suggest more severely ill patients show less in the way of placebo response, but they also show less in the way of drug response. Thus, just including more severely ill patients is not a panacea. As indicated above in the introduction, we need to clarify what placebo treatment in a study actually represents and what it should include. Certainly, a great deal of supportive handholding and patient contact do not reflect a no-treatment condition but instead constitute powerful interventions. This area requires further study so that we can design better protocols to test drug efficacy.

Of related importance is that the Food and Drug Administration may approve a drug that has been shown to separate from the placebo in two studies, but that also has several so-called failed trials in which efficacy was not demonstrated. The result can be to cloud a new agent in some doubt and to undercut confidence in the drug. Thus, there is also a need to think through how much and in what types of patients efficacy should be required before approval. Although many issues remain regarding the range of efficacy for antidepressants, these drugs are certainly effective in patients with major depression, and their prescription and use have had a tremendous impact on the lives of many depressed patients.

ACKNOWLEDGMENTS The authors are supported by NIH MH-58922, MH-39415, and MH-42088 (CBN), and by NIH MH50604 and MH 47573(AFS).

References

Andrews, J. M., Ninan, P. T., & Nemeroff, C. B. (1996). Venlafaxine: A novel antidepressant that has a dual mechanism of action. *Depression, 4*, 48–56.

Asberg, M., Cronholm, B., Sjoqvist, F., et al. (1971). Relationship between plasma level and therapeutic effect of nortriptyline. *British Medical Journal, 3*, 331–334.

Benkert, O., Szegedi, A., & Kohnen, R. (2000). Mirtazapine compared with paroxetine in major depression. *Journal of Clinical Psychiatry, 61*, 656–663.

Blacker, D. (1996). Maintenance treatment of major depression: A review of the literature. *Harvard Review of Psychiatry, 4*, 1–9.

Boswell, E. G., Anfinson, T. J., & Nemeroff, C. B. (1997). Depression associated with endocrine disorders. In M. Robertson & C. Katona (Eds.), *Depression and physical illness* (pp. 255–292). Sussex, UK: Wiley.

Bowden, C. L., Schatzberg, A. F., Rosenbaum, A., et al. (1993). Fluoxetine and desipramine in major depressive disorder. *Journal of Clinical Psychopharmacology, 13*, 305–311.

Boyer, W. F., & Feighner, J. P. (1994). Clinical significance of early non-response in depressed patients. *Depression, 2*, 32–35.

Chan, C. H., Janicak, P. G., Davis, J. M., et al. (1987). Response of psychotic and nonpsychotic depressed patients to tricyclic antidepressants. *Journal of Clinical Psychiatry, 48*, 197–200.

Clerc, G. E., Ruimy, P., Verdeau-Pailles, J., et al. (1994). A double-blind comparison of venlafaxine and fluoxetine in patients hospitalized for major depression and melancholia. *International Clinical Psychopharmacology, 9*, 139–143.

Danish University Antidepressant Group (DUAG). (1986). Citalopram: Clinical effect profile in comparison with clomipramine: A controlled multicenter study. *Psychopharmacology, 90*, 131–138.

Danish University Antidepressant Group (DUAG). (1990). Paroxetine: A selective serotonin reuptake inhibitor showing better tolerance, but weaker antidepressant effect than clomipramine in a controlled multicenter study. *Journal of Affective Disorders, 18*, 289–299.

DeBattista, C., & Schatzberg, A. F. (1995). Paroxetine. In H. I. Kaplan & B. J. Sadock (Eds.), *Comprehensive textbook of psychiatry* (Vol. 2, 6th ed., pp. 2063–2069). Baltimore: Williams & Wilkins.

de Boer, T. (1996). The pharmacologic profile of mirtazapine. *Journal of Clinical Psychiatry, 57*(Suppl. 4), 19–25.

DeVane, C. L., & Sallee, F. R. (1996). Serotonin selective reuptake inhibitors in child and adolescent psychopharmacology: A review of published experience. *Journal of Clinical Psychiatry, 57*, 55–65.

DeVane, L. (1994). Pharmacokinetics of the newer antidepressants: Clinical relevance. *American Journal of Medicine*, 97(Suppl. 6A), 13–22.

Doogan, D. P., & Caillard, V. (1992). Sertraline in the prevention of depression. *British Journal of Psychiatry, 160*, 217–222.

Elkin, I., Sheat, T., Watkins, J., et al. (1989). NIMH Treatment of Depression Collaborative Research Program: 1. General effectiveness of treatments. *Archives of General Psychiatry, 46*, 971–982.

Emslie, G. J., Rush, A. J., & Weinberg, W. A., et al. (1997). A double-blind, randomized, placebo-controlled trial of fluoxetine in children and adolescents with depression. *Archives of General Psychiatry, 54*(11), 1031–1037.

Ereshefsky, L. (1996). Drug interactions of antidepressants. *Psychiatric Annals, 26*, 342–350.

Feighner, J., & Overo, K. (1999). Multicenter, placebo controlled, fixed-dose study of citalopram in moderate-to-severe depression. *Journal of Clinical Psychiatry, 60*, 1–7.

Fisher, R. L., & Fisher, S. (1996). Antidepressants for children: Is scientific support necessary? *Journal of Nervous and Mental Disease, 184*, 99–108.

Frank, E., Kupfer, D. J., Perel, J. M., et al. (1990). Three-year outcomes for maintenance therapies in recurrent depression. *Archives of General Psychiatry, 47*, 1093–1099.

Frank, E., Kupfer, D. J., Perel, J. M., et al. (1993). Comparison of full-dose versus half-dose pharmacotherapy in the maintenance treatment of recurrent depression. *Journal of Affective Disorders, 27*, 139–145.

Frasure-Smith, N., Lesperance, F., & Talajic, M. (1993). Depression following myocardial infarction: Impact on 6 month survival. *Journal of the American Medical Association, 270*, 1819–1861.

Frasure-Smith, N., Lesperance, F., & Talajic, M. (1995). Depression and 18 month prognosis after myocardial infarction. *Circulation, 91*, 999–1005.

Glassman, A. H., Perel, J. M., Shostak, M., et al. (1977). Clinical implications of imipramine plasma levels for depressive illness. *Archives of General Psychiatry, 34*, 197–204.

Guelfi, J. D., White, C., Hackett, D., et al. (1995). Effectiveness of venlafaxine in patients hospitalized for major depression and melancholia. *Journal of Clinical Psychiatry, 56*, 450–458.

Hirschfeld, R. M., & Schatzberg, A. F. (1994). Long-term management of depression. *American Journal of Medicine, 97*(Suppl. 6A), 33–38.

Hollon, S. D., DeRubeis, R., Evans, M. D., et al. (1992). Cognitive therapy and pharmacotherapy for depression: Singly and in combination. *Archives of General Psychiatry, 49*, 774–781.

Janicak, P. G., Davis, J. M., Preskorn, S. H., & Ayd, F. J. (1993). *Principles and practice of psychopharmacology*. Baltimore: Williams & Wilkins.

Keller, M. B., McCullogh, J. P., & Klein, D. N., et al. (2000). A comparison of nefazodone, cognitive behavioral analysis system of psychotherapy, and their combination for treatment of chronic depression. *New England Journal of Medicine, 342*, 1462–1470.

Keller, M. B., Ryan, N. D., & Strober, M., et al. (2001). Efficacy of paroxetine in the treatment of adolescent major depression: A randomized, controlled trial. *Journal of the American Academy of Child and Adolescent Psychiatry, 40*(7), 762–772.

Krishnan, K. R. R. (1998). Monoamine oxidase inhibitors. In A. F. Schatzberg & C. B. Nemeroff (Eds.), *Textbook of psychopharmacology* (2nd ed., pp. 239–249). Washington, DC: American Psychiatric Association Press.

McDaniel, J. S., Musselman, D. L., Porter, M. R., Reed, D. A., & Nemeroff, C. B. (1995). Depression in patients with cancer: Diagnosis, biology and treatment. *Archives of General Psychiatry, 52*, 89–99.

Mendels, J. (1995). Sertraline. In H. I. Kaplan & B. J. Sadock (Eds.), *Comprehensive textbook of psychiatry* (Vol. 2, 6th ed., pp. 2069–2073). Baltimore: Williams & Wilkins.

Mendels, J., Kiev, A., & Fabre, L. (1999). Double-blind comparison of citalopram and placebo in depressed patients with melancholia. *Depression & Anxiety, 9*, 54–60.

Montgomery, S. A., Dufour, H., Brion, S., et al. (1988). The prophylactic efficacy of fluoxetine in unipolar depression. *British Journal of Psychiatry, 153*(Suppl. 3), 69–76.

Montgomery, S. A., & Dunbar, G. (1993). Paroxetine is better than placebo in relapse prevention and the prophylaxis of recurrent depression. *International Clinical Psychopharmacology, 8*, 189–195.

Montgomery, S. A., Rasmussen, J. G. C., Tanghoj, P. (1993). A 24-week study of 20 mg. citalopram, 40 mg. citalopram, and placebo in the prevention of relapse of major depression. *International Journal of Clinical Psychopharmacology, 8*, 181–188.

Nemeroff, C. B. (1994). Evolutionary trends in the pharmacotherapeutic management of depression. *Journal of Clinical Psychiatry, 55*, 3–15.

Nemeroff, C. B., DeVane, C. L., & Pollack, B. G. (1996). Newer antidepressants and the cytochrome P450 system. *American Journal of Psychiatry, 153*, 311–320.

Nemeroff, C. B., Evans, D. L., & Gyulai, L., et al. (2001). Double-blind, placebo-controlled comparison of imipramine and paroxetine in the treatment of bipolar depression. *American Journal of Psychiatry, 158*, 906–912.

Nierenberg, A. A., Feighner, J. P., Rudolph, R., et al. (1994). Venlafaxine for treatment-resistant depression. *Journal of Clinical Psychopharmacology, 14*, 419–423.

Nierenberg, A. A., McLean, N. E., Alpert, J. E., et al. (1995). Early nonresponse to fluoxetine as a predictor of poor 8-week outcome. *American Journal of Psychiatry, 152*, 1500–1503.

Owens, M. J., Ieni, J. R., Knight, D. L., Winders, K., & Nemeroff, C. B. (1995). The serotonergic antidepressant nefazodone inhibits the serotonin transporter: In vivo and ex vivo studies. *Life Sciences, 57*, 373–380.

Potter, W. Z., Manji, A. K., & Rudorfer, M. V. (1998). Tricyclics and tetracyclics. In A. F. Schatzberg & C. B. Nemeroff (Eds.), *Textbook of psychopharmacology* (2nd ed., pp. 199–218). Washington, DC: American Psychiatric Press.

Prien, R. F., Kupfer, D. J., Mansky, P. A., et al. (1984). Drug therapy in the prevention of recurrences in unipolar and bipolar affective disorders: A report of the NIMH Collaborative Study Group comparing lithium carbonate, imipramine, and a lithium carbonate-imipramine combination. *Archives of General Psychiatry, 41,* 1096–1104.

Roose, S. P., Glassman, A. H., Attia, E., et al. (1994). Comparative efficacy of selective serotonin reuptake inhibitors and tricyclics in the treatment of melancholia. *American Journal of Psychiatry, 151,* 1735–1739.

Rush, J. A., & the Depression Guideline Panel of the Agency for Health Care Policy and Research. (1994). Synopsis of the clinical practice guidelines for diagnosis and treatment of depression in primary care. *Archives of Family Medicine, 3,* 85–92.

Schatzberg, A. F. (1995a). Fluoxetine. In H. I. Kaplan & R. J. Sadock (Eds.), *Comprehensive textbook of psychiatry* (Vol. 2, 6th ed., pp. 2056–2063). Baltimore: Williams & Wilkins.

Schatzberg, A. F. (1995b). Fluoxetine in the treatment of comorbid anxiety and depression [Monograph]. *Journal of Clinical Psychiatry, 13*(2), 2–12.

Schatzberg, A. F. (1996). Treatment of severe depression with the selective serotonin reuptake inhibitors. *Depression, 4,* 182–189.

Schatzberg, A. F., & Kraemer, H. C. (2000). Use of placebo control groups in evaluating efficacy of treatment of unipolar major depression. *Biological Psychiatry, 47,* 736–744.

Schatzberg, A., Kremer, C., Rodrigues, H., et al. (2001). Mirtazapine versus paroxetine in elderly depressed patients. *Abstracts, 41st Annual NCDEU Meeting,* Poster I-62.

Schatzberg, A. F., & Rothschild, A. J. (1992). Psychotic (delusional) major depression: Should it be included as a distinct syndrome in *DSM-IV*? *American Journal of Psychiatry, 149,* 733–745.

Stowe, Z. N., Casarella, J., Landry, J., & Nemeroff, C. B. (1995). Sertraline in the treatment of women with post-partum major depression. *Depression, 3,* 49–55.

Taylor, D. P., Carter, R. B., Eison, A. S., et al. (1995). Pharmacology and neurochemistry of nefazodone, a novel antidepressant drug. *Journal of Clinical Psychiatry,* 6(Suppl.), 3–11.

Thase, M. E., Entsuah, A. R., & Rudolph, R. L. (2001). Remission rates during treatment with venlafaxine or selective serotonin reuptake inhibitors. *British Journal of Psychiatry, 178,* 234–241.

Thase, M. E., Kremer, C., & Rodrigues, H. (2001). Mirtazapine versus sertraline after SSRI nonresponse. *Abstracts, 41st. Annual NCDEU Meeting,* Poster II-1.

Thase, M. E., & Sullivan, L. R. (1995). Relapse and recurrence of depression: A practical approach for prevention. *CNS Drugs, 4,* 261–277.

Tollefson, G. D., Holman, S. L., & Sayler, M. E. (1994). Fluoxetine, placebo, and tricyclic antidepressants in major depression with and without anxious features. *Journal of Clinical Psychiatry, 55,* 50–59.

10

Psychosocial Treatments for Major Depressive Disorder

W. Edward Craighead
Alisha B. Hart
Linda Wilcoxon Craighead
Stephen S. Ilardi

Behavior therapy (BT), cognitive behavior therapy (CBT), and interpersonal psychotherapy (IPT) have each been shown by at least two Type 1 randomized clinical trials, as well as by four meta-analytic reports in the literature, to be effective psychosocial interventions for patients meeting criteria for major depressive disorder (MDD). All three psychosocial treatments have yielded substantial reductions in scores on the two major depression rating scales (the Beck Depression Inventory and the Hamilton Rating Scale for Depression), significant decreases in percentage of patients meeting the criteria for MDD posttreatment, and substantial maintenance of effects well after treatment has ended.

The data on outcomes of psychosocial and pharmacological interventions for major depressive episodes suggest that the two treatment modes are comparable. At least one major study lends strong support for the superior effectiveness of combined psychosocial and pharmacological treatments. There are not yet adequate published data to answer the question of whether antidepressant medications, either alone or in combination with a psychosocial intervention, are superior to psychosocial interventions in the treatment of *severely* depressed patients.

Major depressive disorder (MDD) is the most commonly diagnosed psychiatric disorder among adults, with U.S. lifetime prevalence rates of 20 to 25% for women and 9 to 12% for men; point prevalence rates are approximately 6% and 3% for women and men, respectively (American Psychiatric Association [APA], 1994; Kessler et al., 1994; Regier, Kaelber, Roper, Rae, & Sartorms, 1994). These prevalence rates and gender differences are relatively constant across the *adult* life span. In addition, the prevalence of MDD has been increasing in recent birth cohorts (Lewinsohn, Hops, Roberts, Seeley, & Andrews, 1993; Weissman et al., 1996; Weissman, Fendrich, Warner, & Wickramaratne, 1992; Wickramaratne, Weissman, Leaf, & Holford, 1989), a finding suggesting that the life-time prevalence will be higher for current younger cohorts. The age of first episode of MDD has been decreasing (Burke, Burke, Regier, & Rae, 1990; Lewinsohn, Clarke, Seeley, & Rohde, 1994), so that the peak years for first onset are now between 15 and 29 years of age (Burke et al., 1990; Hankin et al., 1998). Thus, MDD is a major health problem for which it is important to develop better treatments.

Depression engenders not only extraordinary personal and family suffering but also significant societal burdens, such as an increased use of social and medical services (Johnson, Weissman, & Klerman, 1992).

There are also enormous financial costs for treatment and lost productivity due to absenteeism from work (Greenberg, Stiglin, Finkelstein, & Berndt, 1993; Wells et al., 1989).

In order to receive a diagnosis of *major depressive disorder*, a person must experience marked distress or a decrease in level of functioning. In addition, the 2 weeks before examination must be characterized by the almost daily occurrence of a dysphoric mood (sad, empty, or tearful) or a loss of interest or pleasure in almost all activities (APA, 1994). The individual must also experience at least four (only three if both dysphoric mood and loss of interest or pleasure are present) of the following seven symptoms (with the second through sixth occurring nearly every day):

1. Significant weight loss (while not trying to lose weight) or a change in appetite
2. Insomnia or hypersomnia
3. Psychomotor agitation or retardation
4. Fatigue or loss of energy
5. Feelings of worthlessness or excessive or inappropriate guilt
6. Decreased concentration or indecisiveness
7. Recurrent thoughts of death or suicidal ideation, plan, or attempt

Substantial advances have been made since the early 1970s in the successful treatment of depression. Treatments of choice now include not only somatic interventions (antidepressant medications and electroconvulsive shock) but also a number of psychosocial interventions: behavior therapy (BT; including marital therapy), cognitive behavior therapy (CBT), and interpersonal psychotherapy (IPT). This chapter reviews the evidence regarding the efficacy of these specific psychosocial treatments (including their combinations with somatic treatments), discusses the possible mechanisms of change in these therapies, and addresses numerous issues regarding the appropriate use of psychosocial treatments. This review includes only those studies that obtained information for diagnosis via a structured interview such as the Structured Clinical Interview for *DSM* (SCID; First, Spitzer, Gibbon, & Williams, 1995; Spitzer, Williams, Gibbon, & First, 1992) and employed a formal, defined diagnostic system such as the Research Diagnostic Criteria (Spitzer, Endicott, & Robins, 1978) or the *DSM*. Further, to be included, an investigation must have employed cutoff scores on standard depression severity measures, such as clinical rating scales or self-report measures, as a criterion for admission to the study. In other words, by virtue of the severity, frequency, and duration of their observed symptoms, the participants in these studies are typical of those who might seek and receive treatment by a mental health professional for an MDD. Within this book, these studies would all be considered Type 1 studies. Finally, only those therapeutic modalities that have been studied in at least two comparative Type 1 outcome trials for behavior therapy, cognitive behavior therapy, and interpersonal psychotherapy for patients between the ages of 18 and 65 years have been included in this review.

BEHAVIOR THERAPY

Description

The first behavioral treatment program of significance was developed by Lewinsohn, who built on previous behavioral formulations of depression (Ferster, 1973; Skinner, 1953; see Lewinsohn & Gotlib, 1995, for a summary of Lewinsohn's contributions). Although numerous flavors of behavior therapy have been developed for treatment of MDD, they all have in common the assumption that MDD is related to a decrease of behaviors that produce positive reinforcement. As such behavior therapies for depression have focused largely on monitoring and increasing positive daily activities, improving social and communication skills, increasing adaptive behaviors such as positive and negative assertion, increasing response-contingent positive reinforcement for adaptive behaviors, and decreasing negative life experiences.

Empirical Evidence

In a randomized clinical trial (RCT), Lewinsohn and his group demonstrated that, relative to various control groups, behavior therapy (BT) increased pleasant experiences and reduced aversive experiences, which produced concomitant decreases in depression severity (see Lewinsohn & Gotlib, 1995). This work was extended by Bellack, Hersen, and Himmelhoch (1981, 1983) and Hersen, Bellack, Himmelhoch, and Thase (1984), who demonstrated that BT was as effective as the antidepressant amitriptyline (AMI) in reducing depression over a 12-week treatment period; these effects were maintained over a 6-month follow-up period with 6 to 8 booster sessions.

Consistent with Rehm's (1977) suggestions, McLean and Hakstian (1979) added problem-solving and self-control procedures to the behavior therapy treatment package, and they conducted a 10-week clinical trial comparing this expanded behavioral treatment package to relaxation therapy, insight-oriented psychotherapy, and amitriptyline. The behavior therapy program was equal or superior to the other treatment conditions. (Although questions have been raised regarding the adequacy of the medication dosage, the results for amitriptyline were generally comparable to those obtained in other antidepressant medication studies.) These results were maintained at a 27-month follow-up, at which time the behavior therapy subjects were more socially active and productive than were participants in all the other treatment conditions (McLean & Hakstian, 1990).

Rehm's self-control therapy (1977) has been found to be superior to nonspecific psychosocial treatments and no-treatment controls (Rehm, 1990), but it has not been compared to standard antidepressant treatment. It is worth noting that the apparently essential ingredient (and perhaps the most important contribution) of this self-control therapy is the *self-monitoring* of thoughts and behaviors (Rehm, 1990), a component that is included in most other empirically supported psychosocial depression treatment protocols.

There are two recent Type 1 evaluations of BT. Jacobson and his colleagues (1996) tested the hypothesized theory of change of Beck's cognitive therapy for depression by comparing the full CBT package to its component parts—"behavioral activation" (BA) and behavioral activation plus modification of automatic dysfunctional thoughts (AT). The BA treatment was similar to the behavioral interventions previously reviewed and included such techniques as monitoring daily activities, assessment of pleasure and mastery of activities, assignment of increasingly difficult activities, imaging of behaviors to be performed, discussion of specific problems and identification of behavioral solutions to those problems, and interventions to ameliorate social skills deficits. The major finding of this study was that BA was equally effective to AT and to the full CBT package, both immediately after the 20-session treatment trial and at 6-month follow-up. Furthermore, BA performed equally well over a 2-year follow-up period, with patients across the three treatments having equivalent rates of relapse, time to relapse, and number of well weeks (Gortner, Gollan, Dobson, & Jacobson, 1998). To date, this is the only direct comparison of BT and CBT. However, Jacobson's colleagues at the University of Washington currently are conducting a follow-up replication study, in which they are comparing BA to CBT, antidepressant medication (paroxetine), and pill placebo in 400 depressed adults (Dobson et al., 2000).

Keller and colleagues (2000) randomly assigned 681 adults with chronic major depression (MDD of at least 2 years' duration, current MDD superimposed on a preexisting dysthymic disorder, or recurrent MDD with incomplete remission between episodes and a total duration of continuous illness of at least 2 years) to 12 weeks of treatment with either the cognitive behavioral analysis system of psychotherapy (CBASP), the antidepressant nefazodone, or the combination of CBASP and nefazodone. The CBASP approach (McCullough, 2000) focuses on the consequences of patients' behavior and the use of social problem solving to address interpersonal difficulties. The overall rate of response was equivalent in the CBASP and nefazodone groups, though patients receiving nefazodone had a more rapid reduction in symptoms during the first 4 weeks of treatment. Furthermore, immediately posttreatment, the combination of CBASP and nefazodone was superior to either treatment on its own. Follow-up data for this trial have not yet been published.

Behavior Marital Therapy

Another development in behavioral approaches to the treatment of depression has been the employment of behavior marital therapy (BMT) with individuals who are suffering concurrently from MDD and marital distress. Both O'Leary and colleagues' and Jacobson and colleagues' standard BMT (Beach, Sandeen, & O'Leary, 1990; Jacobson, Dobson, Fruzetti, Schmaling, & Salusky, 1991; O'Leary & Beach, 1990) have been demonstrated to be equal to individual CBT for the alleviation of depression among individuals with both MDD and marital discord. BMT was found to have the added advantage of being superior to individual CBT in the reduction of marital discord, a finding that argues for the use of

BMT with depressed patients who also are experiencing marital discord. None of these studies employed appropriate follow-up procedures to permit a determination of whether BMT confers greater prophylactic effects than individual CBT for the prevention of relapse of an MDD following successful treatment. However, given that "marital disputes" is the most frequently discussed topic among depressed patients in maintenance therapy (Weissman & Klerman, 1973) and that marital friction is an enduring problem among formerly depressed patients even when asymptomatic (Bothwell & Weissman, 1977), it seems likely that successful BMT will reduce the rate of relapse among successfully treated MDD patients in discordant marriages. Unfortunately, BMT has not been evaluated with adequate numbers of *severely* depressed patients in discordant marriages to know if these findings will be applicable to such patients or whether the presence of severe depression will necessitate treatment with antidepressants administered either alone or in tandem with BMT.

Conclusions

Although consistent findings support the efficacy of BT for depression, they have been overshadowed by subsequent outcome studies that have focused on cognitive behavior therapy and interpersonal psychotherapy as psychosocial interventions for an MDD. However, given the applicability of BT to depressed patients of all age groups (see Lewinsohn & Gotlib, 1995) and the relative efficacy, efficiency, and endurance of behavioral interventions, as well as the recent results for BA, CBASP, and BMT, it seems that this was an unwarranted and premature turn of events. From a historical perspective, it appears to have been due primarily to the sociology of science and to no small extent the exclusion of behavior therapy from the well-publicized National Institute of Mental Health (NIMH) clinical trial (Elkin, Parloff, Hadley, & Autry, 1985), rather than to the relative scientific merit and empirical outcomes of the then-available comparative treatment studies.

COGNITIVE BEHAVIOR THERAPY

Description

The most extensively evaluated psychosocial treatment for MDD is Beck's cognitive behavior therapy (CBT; Beck, Rush, Shaw, & Emery, 1979), alternatively referred to simply as cognitive therapy (CT). Cognitive behavior therapy is a short-term (16 to 20 sessions over a period of 12 to 16 weeks) directive therapy designed to change the depressed patient's negative view of the self, world, and future. The therapy begins with the presentation of the rationale, which is designed to inform the client of the therapy model and the process of therapeutic change. Following this, early CBT sessions implement strategies designed to increase active behavioral performance. The purpose of such an increase is to allow the monitoring of behaviors and their associated thoughts and feelings; behavioral changes are not posited to be directly responsible for the desired changes in depression. During the third week, expanded self-monitoring techniques are introduced in order to demonstrate the relationship between thoughts and feelings; patients are taught to evaluate their thoughts for logical errors, which include arbitrary inference, selective abstraction, overgeneralization, magnification and minimalization, personalization, and dichotomous thinking (Beck, 1976). In the middle of therapy (around Session 8 or 9), the concept of *schema*, or beliefs underlying negative and positive thoughts, is introduced, and therapy begins to focus on changing those negative schemas that are posited to have been activated, thus precipitating the MDD. Toward the end of therapy (Sessions 14–16), the focus shifts to termination and the use of cognitive strategies to prevent relapse or a future recurrence of depression.

Empirical Evidence

A number of studies have compared the effectiveness of CBT to that of several tricyclic antidepressant medications (Elkin et al., 1989; Hollon et al., 1992; Rush, Beck, Kovacs, & Hollon, 1977; Simons, Murphy, Levine, & Wetzel, 1986).[1] With the possible exception of the NIMH Treatment of Depression Collaborative Research Program (TDCRP; Elkin et al., 1989), the essential finding in all these studies is that CBT is equally effective to tricyclic antidepressant medication in alleviating MDD among outpatients[2] (see Tables 10.1 and 10.2). Similarly, CBT was as effective as a monoamine oxidase inhibitor (phenelzine), and more effective than pill placebo in the treatment of atypical depression (Jarrett et al., 1999). CBT also was equally effective to antidepressant medication when study physicians were free to pre-

TABLE 10.1 Hamilton Rating Scale of Depression Scores and Percentages "Recovered" for Major Random Clinical Trials Reviewed in this Chapter

	CBT									*IPT*		*BT*				*BMT*	
Study	1	2	3	4	5	9	10[a]	11	13	6	3	7	8	5	12	9	10[b]
N	15	19	37	16	44	12	20	36	24	17[c]	47	25	42	47	216	12	8
Pre	21.2	18.5	19.2	24.8	18.6	—	20.0	18.36	19.2	17.3	18.9	22.2	—	17.3	26.4	—	23.4
Post	5.8	6.4	7.6	8.8	6.8	—	4.5	10.25	10.7	10.2	6.9	7.0	—	6.5	15.1	—	7.2
Percentage recovered	—	63[g]	51[h]	50[h]	—	—	—	58[e], 44[h]	33[h]	—	55[h]	64[i]	—	—	33[f]	—	—

	Medications											*BT plus Medications*	*Placebo plus CM*	
Study	1	2	3	4	5	6	7	8	11	12	13	12	3	11
N	14	16	37	32[b]	—	20	14	49	36	220	43	226	34	36
Pre	22.4	19.7	19.2	24.0	—	16.8	25.5	—	16.75	26.8	20.4	27.4	19.1	17.42
Post	9.3	7.0	7.0	8.4	—	10.0	8.2	—	8.64	14.7	12.3	9.7	8.8	14.44
Percentage recovered	—	50[g]	57[h]	53[h]	—	—	43[i]	—	58[e], 42[h]	29[f]	24[h]	48[f]	29[h]	28[e], 19[h]

Source: List of studies: 1 Rush et al. (1977); 2 Murphy et al. (1984); 3 Elkin et al. (1989); 4 Hollon et al. (1992); 5 Jacobson et al. (1996); 6 DiMascio et al. (1979); 7 Bellack et al. (1981); 8 McLean & Hakstian (1979); 9 O'Leary & Beach (1990); 10 Jacobson et al. (1991); 11 Jarrett et al. (1999); 12 Keller et al. (2000); 13 Blackburn & Moore (1997).

BDI = Beck Depression Inventory; BMT = behavior marital therapy; BT = behavior therapy; CBT = cognitive behavior therapy; HRSD = Hamilton Rating Scale of Depression; IPT = interpersonal psychotherapy.

[a]Data are only for completers who met criteria for MDD and either presence or absence of marital discord.

[b]Data are only for completers who met criteria for comorbid MDD and marital discord; BMT was less effective for MDD and no marital discord.

[c]Data are only available for all patients who entered and completed at least 1 week of treatment.

[d]N = 31 for Fost.

[e]HRSD ≤ 9.

[f]HRSD ≤ 8.

[g]HRSD ≤ 7.

[h]HRSD ≤ 6.

[i]HRSD and BDI ≤ 10.

TABLE 10.2 Beck Depression Inventory Scores and Percentages "Recovered" for Major Random Clinical Trials Reviewed in this Chapter

	CBT									*IPT*		*BT*			*BMT*	
Study	1	2	3	4	5	9	10[a]	11	13	6	3	7	8	5	9	10[b]
N	18	19	37	16	44	12	20	36	24	17	47	25	42[c]	48	12	8
Pre	30.3	29.7	26.8	30.4	28.9	26	26.3	25.83	27.3	—	25.5	27.1	26.8	29.3	22	26.4
Post	5.9	9.5	10.2	7.9	9.7	6	6.5	11.72	19.0	—	7.7	7.4	9.7	8.5	5	7.0
Percentage recovered	83[d]	53[d]	65[e]	62[e]	57[g]	—	80[e]	53[e]	—	—	70[e]	64[f]	50[g]	50[g]	—	88[e]

	Medications										*Placebo plus CM*	
Study	1	2	3	4	5	6	7	8	11	13	3	11
N	14	16	36	32	—	17	14	49[c]	36	43	35	36
Pre	30.8	29.3	27.1	31.1	—	—	29.6	27.2	24.86	29.2	28.1	26.19
Post	13.0	8.9	6.5	10.5	—	—	12.8	14.2	9.67	21.5	11.0	18.94
Percentage recovered	36[d]	56[d]	69[e]	56[e]	—	—	43[f]	25[g]	69[e]	—	51[e]	28[e]

Source: List of studies: 1 Rush et al. (1977); 2 Murphy et al. (1984); 3 Elkin et al. (1989); 4 Hollon et al. (1992); 5 Jacobson et al. (1996); 6 DiMascio et al. (1979); 7 Bellack et al. (1981); 8 McLean & Hakstian (1979); 9 O'Leary & Beach (1990); 10 Jacobson et al. (1991); 11 Jarrett et al. (1999); 12 Keller et al. (2000); 13 Blackburn & Moore (1997).

BDI = Beck Depression Inventory; BMT = behavior marital therapy; BT = behavior therapy; CBT = cognitive behavior therapy; HRSD = Hamilton Rating Scale of Depression; IPT = interpersonal psychotherapy.

[a]Data are only for completers who met criteria for MDD and either presence or absence of marital discord.

[b]Data are only for completers who met criteria for comorbid MDD and marital discord; BMT was less effective for MDD and no marital discord.

[c]Data are only available for all patients who entered treatment.

[d]BDI ≤ 10.

[e]BDI ≤ 9.

[f]BDI and HRSD ≤ 10.

[g]BDI ≤ 7.

scribe the antidepressant of their choice (and free to switch medications during the treatment trial), provided they prescribed at or above established therapeutic doses (Blackburn & Moore, 1997).

Typically, 50 to 70% of MDD patients who complete a course of CBT no longer meet criteria for MDD at posttreatment, with pre-post changes from the high 20s to single digits for Beck Depression Inventory (BDI) scores and changes from the high teens/low 20s to single digits for Hamilton Rating Scale of Depression (HRSD) scores (see Tables 10.1 and 10.2). Furthermore, among the samples studied, CBT appeared to confer some enduring prophylactic effects inasmuch as only 20 to 30% of those successfully treated relapsed during the first year following treatment. Indeed, 16 weeks of CBT produced a 1-year follow-up success rate that equaled or slightly exceeded that achieved by a full year of antidepressant treatment (Evans et al., 1992), and CBT's maintenance effects were clearly superior to short-term (16 weeks) antidepressant treatment (16 weeks is not preferred but it is, unfortunately, longer than the actual average length of completed medication treatment in clinical practice; Hirschfeld et al., 1997).

Because the TDCRP study (Elkin et al., 1989) has received so much attention, including its significant role in the development of guidelines (not standards) for treatment of outpatients suffering from an MDD (Agency for Health Care Policy and Research [AHCPR], 1993; APA, 1993), it is worthy of special note. The study included 250 outpatients who were randomly assigned to one of four 16-week treatment conditions: CBT, IPT, imipramine hydrochloride plus clinical management (IMP-CM), or pill placebo plus clinical management (PLA-CM). Both the IMP-CM and the PLA-CM conditions included a "clinical management" component (20 minutes per week talking with an experienced psychiatrist), whose additive effects are not known.

The results of the TDCRP for those patients who completed treatment generally support the comparability of the three presumed active treatments in ameliorating depression at posttreatment, as measured by a Hamilton Depression Rating Scale score of 6 or less (CBT, 36%; IPT, 43%; and IMP-CM, 42%). However, only IPT and IMP-CM produced significantly greater reductions in depression than PLA-CM (21%) over the course of treatment, and then for only a few of the outcome measures. Even these acute treatment effects were not maintained at the 18-month follow-up. Thus, the percentages of patients remaining nondepressed and not receiving treatment for depression were quite low (CBT 30%, IPT 26%, IMP plus CM 19%, and PLA plus CM 20%), so that none of the active treatments was superior to the PLA-CM condition at the 18-month follow-up (Shea, Elkin, et al., 1992). These follow-up outcomes indicate that all treatments in this study had considerably weaker effects than had typically been reported in other long-term follow-up studies of these same psychotherapies. Of course, as Klein (1996) has noted, such short-term treatment (16 weeks) with antidepressant medication would not be expected to produce sustained effectiveness. It is unfortunate that this is the only clinical trial of CBT in which a pill placebo was employed; given the general discrepancies among the outcomes of this study and the other major studies demonstrating the equal effectiveness of CBT and antidepressants, it is essential that additional clinical trials, which include a pure pill-placebo control condition, be conducted. Fortunately, such trials under the direction of DeRubeis and Hollon and another by the University of Washington group are currently in progress.

Based on the original report of the TDCRP data at conferences and in print, it has been noted (Craighead, Evans, & Robins, 1992; Hollon, Shelton, & Loosen, 1991), and sustained by recent reanalyses of the original data tape (Jacobson & Hollon, 1996a), that the lack of unequivocal findings (coupled with the uniqueness of some of the exploratory findings) ensures that any interpretation of the TDCRP data is likely to be controversial. One of the major problems described in the original report of the TDCRP was "consistently significant treatment-by-site interactions for the more severely depressed and functionally impaired patients" (Elkin et al., 1989, p. 980). Even though this conclusion has been somewhat attenuated with the use of more sophisticated reanalysis of the data (Elkin et al., 1995, 1996), the general pattern of a treatment-by-site-by-severity interaction is still acknowledged, and the authors concluded, "In regard to the general efficacy of CBT in the treatment of severely depressed (and functionally impaired) outpatients . . . we believe . . . that the answer is not yet in" (Elkin et al., 1996, p. 101).

In their reanalysis of the TDCRP data on this issue, Jacobson and Hollon (1996a) underscored the importance of this site-by-treatment-by-severity interaction. They presented data illustrating that at one site CBT did as well as IMP-CM and better than PLA-CM with severely depressed patients (probably not coincidentally, this was also the site at which CBT was rated as having been done the best; see Elkin et al., 1996). At a second site, the data favored either IPT or IMP-CM over both CBT and PLA-CM, with the last two groups not significantly different from one another. At the third site, there were not enough subjects to warrant a comparison. In fact, it is ironic that so much has been made of the findings among the severely depressed patients since even across three sites there were 15 or fewer severely depressed patients per condition, and "severity" was not taken into account in the random assignment procedure except for the minimal cutoff criterion of 14 on the HRSD.

The essential point here is that the findings regarding the appropriateness of CBT alone for severely depressed patients are inconclusive from the TDCRP data. Finally, although little has been made of it, there was also a treatment by marital status confound (compounded by differential treatment effects for single and married patients), making interpretation of the data even more difficult (see Jarrett, Eaves, Grannemann, & Rush, 1991; Sotsky et al., 1991).

Consistent with general principles of good science, including the necessity of replication, definitive conclusions cannot be drawn from one study of treatments of depression. The warning of Rush and colleagues (1977) that unwarranted conclusions about the superior efficacy of CBT over tricyclics could not be drawn from one study is now equally applicable (in the reverse direction) to the TDCRP, a point well recognized by the study's investigators (Elkin et al., 1989, 1996) but not well heeded by those employing the data to create the AHCPR treatment guidelines (Depression Guideline Panel, 1993) and the APA (1993). To the extent that the TDCPR findings were the only scientific data used to formulate the guidelines' recommendation that CBT is not a treatment of choice for severe depression in the outpatient setting, the conclusion was premature, unwarranted, and unjustified; to the extent that the guidelines were based on clinical experience (as the developers of both guidelines claim; see Merriam & Karasu, 1996, and Rush, 1996), then the TDCRP data were irrelevant.

Conclusion

Given the substantial number of studies supporting the effectiveness and efficacy of CBT with patients diagnosed with an MDD, CBT appears to be a viable treatment of choice for patients with MDD[3]. It remains to be determined whether or not it must be combined with antidepressants in order to be effective with severely depressed outpatients. Given the widely varying outcomes across studies, the apparent differential competence with which the therapy was delivered across sites in a multisite study, and the superior effectiveness of CBT performed in Beck's clinic, it is particularly important that therapists delivering CBT be well trained before they undertake the therapy with patients.

INTERPERSONAL PSYCHOTHERAPY

Description

Interpersonal psychotherapy was originally developed as a time-limited (12 to 16 weeks), weekly intervention for unipolar, nonpsychotic depression (Klerman, Weissman, Rounsaville, & Chevron, 1984). The IPT model is derived in large part from Sullivan's interpersonal theory (1953) and the psychobiological theory of Meyer (1957), with its emphasis on the reciprocal relationship between biological and psychosocial facets of psychopathology. Although the IPT model "makes no assumptions about the causes of depression" (Klerman & Weissman, 1993, p. 6), it does suggest that the patient's interpersonal relations may play a significant role in both the onset and maintenance of an MDD. Accordingly, IPT focuses on the identification and amelioration of the patient's difficulties in interpersonal functioning associated with the current MDD; primary problem areas include unresolved grief, interpersonal disputes, role transitions, and interpersonal deficits (e.g., social isolation).

Empirical Evidence

As shown in Tables 10.1 and 10.2, there have been only two reported RCTs of IPT for the acute treatment of MDD in middle-aged adults. Both of these studies included long-term follow-up assessments designed to evaluate the prophylactic effects of acute

IPT treatment. In addition, there are two separate controlled studies of "maintenance" IPT following remission of the MDD.

The first RCT of IPT for the acute treatment of MDD was conducted by the treatment's originators, Weissman and Klerman and their colleagues (DiMascio et al., 1979; Weissman et al., 1979). They randomly assigned 81 patients to treatment with 16 weeks of IPT, AMI, combined IPT and AMI, or "nonscheduled" (i.e., therapy on request, up to one session per month) supportive psychotherapy control. The study's method of data analysis renders a comparison of the specific treatments with the control group difficult. However, a survival analysis indicated that all three treatments were superior to the nonscheduled control condition, and that the combination of IPT and AMI was slightly more effective than either condition alone (this last finding was only marginally significant, with $p < .10$).

The second and most frequently cited RCT of IPT is the previously summarized NIMH multisite clinical trial, the TDCRP (Elkin et al., 1989). As noted, the principal significant finding concerned the clinical rating of depression as measured by the HRSD. All groups began with a pretreatment mean of about 19, and using the criterion of a posttest score of 6 or less, both IPT (43%) and IMI-CM (42%) had a significantly greater proportion of patients who achieved the recovery criterion than was achieved in the PLA-CM (21%) condition. In a secondary data analysis (Elkin et al., 1995), IPT and IMI-CM were also found to be of comparable efficacy among the subset of patients who were severely depressed (defined as a pretreatment HRSD score of 20 or greater). However, as previously highlighted, the presence in this investigation of either a strong trend or a significant treatment-by-site-by-severity interaction (depending on the analysis) precludes the drawing of definitive conclusions from this finding (Elkin et al., 1996; Jacobson & Hollon, 1996b).

After the completion of treatment, patients in both the Weissman et al. (Weissman, Klerman, Prusoff, Sholomskas, & Padian, 1981) and the TDCRP (Elkin et al., 1989) studies were evaluated longitudinally for several months in a naturalistic follow-up design as a means of examining possible prophylactic effects achieved with the acute therapeutic interventions. In the first study, there was no prophylactic effect associated with IPT versus AMI based on a 12-month follow-up (Weissman et al, 1981); however, the authors reported significantly greater adaptive social functioning among IPT patients. The TDCRP study also found no relative prophylactic effects for IPT. Among patients who recovered during acute treatment, the percentages of patients who remained well during the 18 months of follow-up were as follows: IPT (26%), CBT (30%), IMI-CM (19%), and PLA-CM (20%) (Shea et al., 1992). Primarily because of the small number of subjects and corresponding lack of statistical power, none of these differences was statistically significant; therefore, none of the acute treatment differences was maintained over the follow-up, and none of the treatments was superior even to PLA-CM.

The IPT protocol has been employed as ongoing maintenance therapy after recovery from MDD when treated with an AMI. Klerman, DiMascio, Weissman, Prusoff, and Paykel (1974) found nearly equivalent prophylactic benefits associated with weekly maintenance IPT or AMI over an 8-month follow-up period, with relapse rates of 17% and 12%, respectively. Among a group of chronic and treatment-resistant depressed patients, Frank and her colleagues (1990) reported a significant decrease in relapse probability associated with monthly IPT maintenance sessions over a 36-month follow-up period. For this sample, however, there was a substantially larger prophylactic benefit associated with maintenance IMI, with a 36-month relapse rate of only 18% in the IMI group compared with 46% in the IPT group.

Conclusions

The data regarding IPT as a treatment alone and in combination with antidepressants for MDD are very favorable. IPT appears to be an effective and efficacious treatment both for acute treatment of an MDD and as a maintenance treatment when combined with antidepressant medication for chronic and treatment-resistant depressions.

PATIENT CHARACTERISTICS THAT MODERATE TREATMENT RESPONSE

Although each of the empirically supported interventions reviewed herein (CBT, IPT, BT) has been shown to be efficacious for a majority of depressed individuals, treatment response is highly variable from patient to patient, and a growing body of evidence documents the existence of patient characteristics that moderate treatment response. Following is a brief summary of relevant findings.

Although sorely needed, there has been very little research on patient characteristics that may moderate treatment response to BT for MDD. In one of the few relevant investigations, patients who endorsed "existential" reasons for their depression (i.e., attributed the depression to their feeling that life was meaningless) were found to respond less favorably to BT than to CBT (Addis & Jacobson, 1996).

The amelioration of dysfunctional cognitive phenomena is the sine qua non of CBT. Accordingly, one might expect the subset of depressed patients with high pretreatment levels of dysfunctional, depressotypic cognitions to be especially likely to benefit from CBT. However, the very opposite appears to be the case; that is, patients who score *low* on pretreatment measures of depressotypic cognition tend to experience the most favorable responses in CBT (reviewed in Rude & Rehm, 1991; see also Rector, Bagby, Segal, Joffe, & Levitt, 2000; Simons et al., 1995). Furthermore, MDD patients who report low levels of depressotypic cognitions appear to respond preferentially to CBT in comparison with either IPT or pill placebo (Sotsky et al., 1991), a finding consistent with the hypothesis that effective therapies capitalize on patients' preexisting strengths rather than compensate for their presenting weaknesses (Cronbach & Snow, 1977). Other patient characteristics sometimes associated with favorable outcomes in CBT include low pretreatment depression severity (Elkin et al., 1995; Organista, Munoz, & Gonzalez, 1994), absence of dysfunctional social relationships (Sotsky et al., 1991), high learned resourcefulness (Simons, Lustman, Wetzel, & Murphy, 1985; see also Burns et al., 1994), experience of intact marriage (i.e., nonsingle/nondivorced marital status; Jarrett et al., 1991; Sotsky et al., 1991), left-hemispheric verbal processing advantage (Bruder et al., 1997), and nonreduced REM latency during sleep EEG (Simons, Gordon, Monroe, & Thase, 1995).

Although Axis II personality disorder comorbidity has frequently been observed to predict poor response to various antidepressant interventions (Ilardi & Craighead, 1994/1995; Shea, Widiger, & Klein, 1992), there does not appear to be an association between personality pathology and unfavorable outcome in CBT (Hardy et al., 1995; Shea et al., 1990; Simons & Thase, 1990). In fact, in the TDCRP, comorbid Axis II pathology was predictive of poor treatment response in every treatment modality except CBT (Shea et al., 1990). If replicated, this finding would suggest CBT as a treatment of choice (alone or in combination with antidepressants) for the large subset of MDD patients with comorbid personality disorders.

In keeping with the aforementioned capitalization hypothesis (Cronbach & Snow, 1977), the TDCRP found that patients with particularly *low* levels of social dysfunction responded more favorably to IPT than to other treatment interventions (Sotsky et al., 1991). Among variables linked to an unfavorable response to IPT are Axis II comorbidity (Pilkonis & Frank, 1988; Shea et al., 1990), trait neuroticism (Frank, Kupfer, Jacob, & Jarrett, 1987), cognitive dysfunction (Blatt, Quinlan, Pilkonis, Shea, 1995; Sotsky et al., 1991), and a lifetime history of panic-agoraphobic spectrum symptoms (Frank et al., 2000). Especially high relapse-proneness following a favorable acute response to IPT has been observed among elderly (age > 70) depressed patients (Reynolds et al., 1999).

CONCLUSIONS AND FUTURE RESEARCH DIRECTIONS

Although additional research regarding the effectiveness of psychosocial interventions for MDD is still needed, adequate published data exist to permit the conclusion that three forms of psychotherapy—BT, CBT, and IPT—are efficacious interventions for depressed outpatients. This conclusion is consistent with major meta-analytic reports of psychosocial treatments for MDD (Dobson, 1989; Nietzel, Russell, Hemmings, & Gretter, 1987; Robinson, Berman, & Neimeyer, 1990). Nevertheless, the extent to which antidepressant medications (either alone or in combination with psychotherapy) may be superior to the aforementioned psychosocial interventions in the treatment of *severely* depressed patients remains unclear. Initial reports on this topic have been mixed (e.g., Elkin et al., 1995; Hollon et al., 1992; Schulberg, Pilkonis, & Houck, 1998). A recent mega-analysis (DeRubeis, Gelfand, Tang, & Simons, 1999) suggests no treatment differences for CBT versus medications or their combination for severely depressed patients. Nevertheless, no firm conclusion is warranted in the absence of additional, methodologically rigorous investigations. To that end, the field eagerly awaits the results of two large, ongoing placebo-controlled investigations of CBT versus SSRIs for the treatment of severely depressed outpatients. One is a multisite study under the direction of Hollon and DeRubeis, and the other is being conducted by the colleagues of the late Neil Jacobson at the University of Washington.

Despite the established efficacy of the above-reviewed psychotherapeutic interventions, it now seems clear that about one third of MDD patients will not respond favorably to the first treatment they receive, whether it be a somatic or psychosocial intervention. Except for the fairly consistent finding that patients with comorbid MDD and Axis II disorders tend to fare relatively poorly in all treatments (especially during posttreatment follow-up periods), there is a dearth of research identifying salient clinical and demographic features that characterize the one third of patients who are refractory to their first psychosocial treatment. Furthermore, we know very little about whether this subset of initially refractory patients may respond favorably to a second treatment, although reported crossover studies suggest that many individuals who fail on one antidepressant will experience treatment gains when switched to a different medication (see Nemeroff & Schatzberg, 1998). Psychotherapy researchers have only recently begun to employ such complex crossover designs in treatment studies for MDD (e.g., the "in-progress" follow-up study to Keller et al., 2000), so there are at present no empirical data to guide clinicians providing psychotherapy for patients who have failed to improve following an initial psychosocial intervention.

Treatment outcome research with long-term follow-up has increasingly pointed to high recurrence rates, and to the need for continued intervention beyond acute treatment (Mueller et al., 1999). Some (e.g., Andrews, 2001) have even gone so far as to argue that MDD needs to be managed like a chronic disease. Numerous clinical research efforts are under way to improve the sustainability of acute treatment gains. These approaches include a tapered schedule of psychotherapeutic "booster sessions" in the months following acute treatment (e.g., Frank et al., 1990; Jarrett et al., 1998) and prophylactic programs for recovered patients designed specifically to prevent the recurrence of the disorder (Craighead, 2000; Fava, Rafanelli, Grandi, Canestrari, & Morphy, 1998).

It is also essential that additional placebo-controlled trials be undertaken with severely depressed patients to clarify the prophylactic effects (vis-à-vis relapse and recurrence) of IPT and CBT in comparison with antidepressant medications. Not only is it important to determine the relative efficacy of these treatments with respect to short-term outcome, but it is equally significant—from both personal and public health standpoints—to know how they fare on a comparative basis in the long term. It will also be important to determine the relative short-term and long-term financial costs, including those that occur in the context of relapse and recurrence of MDD, associated with these psychosocial versus pharmacological treatment conditions.

Finally, it is suggested that future research attention be devoted to planning, developing, and evaluating treatments that simultaneously affect MDD and comorbid disorders (e.g., marital discord, Axis II personality disorders, substance abuse, physical illness). This approach has been successfully employed, for example, in the study of comorbid MDD and marital discord, and preliminary data support the efficacy of behavioral marital therapy for the subgroup of MDD patients who are also in discordant marriages. Such an approach to treatment outcome research appears likely to have a large payoff—perhaps greater than that afforded by the identification and targeting of MDD subtypes based solely on variations in presenting depressive symptomatology—and may prove especially promising with respect to the prevention of MDD recurrence in comorbid populations.

Notes

1. Additional comparative outcome trials of CBT have been conducted in other countries with different diagnostic systems. Most notable of these studies are those by Blackburn, Bishop, Glen, Whalley, and Christie (1981); Blackburn, Eunson, and Bishop (1986); Teasdale, Fennell, Hibbert, and Amies (1984); and Wilson, Goldin, and Charbonneau-Powis (1983).

2. It must be remembered that MDD patients who are suffering from psychotic features or are imminently suicidal have been excluded from all these evaluation studies comparing the effectiveness of antidepressant medications and psychosocial treatments; these patients typically are hospitalized and treated with some combination of somatic interventions (e.g., antidepressants,

neuroleptics, and electroconvulsive therapy) and psychosocial interventions.

3. Although space limitations preclude discussion, there are two topics that warrant brief mention: treatment of the elderly and treatment in inpatient settings. Several studies by Thompson and colleagues (Thompson & Gallagher, 1984; Thompson, Gallagher, & Breckenridge, 1987) and one by Steuer and colleagues (1984) demonstrated that CBT is as effective as antidepressant medication for the treatment of depression among the elderly. Thompson and colleagues (1987) also found that short-term psychodynamic psychotherapy was as effective as CBT and antidepressant medications for depression among the elderly. There is modest evidence that the presence of Axis II personality disorders predicts poor outcome among these patients (Thompson, Gallagher, & Czirr, 1988). In a study of IPT (a shortened version), Sloane, Staples, and Schneider (1985) compared the efficacy of 6 weeks of treatment with either IPT or nortriptyline (NOR) in a small sample ($N = 43$) of elderly depressed patients. By the end of treatment, there was a nonsignificant trend for a superior response to IPT; however, this trend was largely due to patients' poor tolerance of medication side effects and to a correspondingly high rate of attrition in the NOR group. Although this study is frequently cited to support the relative effectiveness of IPT, the absence of details on dependent measures and data-analytic techniques severely limits the contribution of this investigation.

There are three systematic studies of CBT with inpatients with MDDs. In a stringent test of the intervention, Thase and his colleagues (Thase, 1994; Thase, Bowler, & Harden, 1991) treated unmedicated MDD inpatients for up to 4 weeks with daily CBT. Although a large percentage of these patients responded well to CBT, not surprisingly the outcome was poorer for those inpatients whose HRSD scale scores were 25 or higher or who had hypercortisolemia. The other studies (Bowers, 1990; Miller, Norman, Keitner, Bishop, & Dow, 1989) have combined CBT with antidepressant medications, and this combination seems to reduce relapse among such patients if booster sessions of CBT are maintained following hospital discharge.

References

Addis, M. E., & Jacobson, N. S. (1996). Reasons for depression and the process and outcome of cognitive-behavioral psychotherapies. *Journal of Consulting and Clinical Psychology*, *64*, 1417–1424.

Agency for Health Care Policy and Research (AHCPR) of the Department of Human Services. (1993). New federal guidelines seek to help primary care providers recognize and treat depression. *Hospital and Community Psychiatry*, *44*, 598.

American Psychiatric Association. (1993). Practice guidelines for major depressive disorder in adults. *American Journal of Psychiatry*, *150(Suppl.4)*, 1–26.

American Psychiatric Association. (1994). *Diagnostic and statistical manual of mental disorders* (4th ed.). Washington, DC: Author.

Andrews, G. (2001). Should depression be managed as a chronic disease? *British Medical Journal*, *322*, 419–421.

Beach, S. R. H., Sandeen, E. E., & O'Leary, K. D. (1990). *Depression in marriage: A model for etiology and treatment*. New York: Guilford Press.

Beck, A. T. (1976). *Cognitive therapy and the emotional disorders*. New York: International Universities Press.

Beck, A. T., Rush, A. J., Shaw, B. F., & Emery, G. (1979). *Cognitive therapy of depression: A treatment manual*. New York: Guilford Press.

Bellack, A. S., Hersen, M., & Himmelhoch, J. (1981). Social skills training compared with pharmacotherapy and psychotherapy in the treatment of unipolar depression. *American Journal of Psychiatry*, *138*, 1562–1566.

Bellack, A. S., Hersen, M., & Himmelhoch, J. M. (1983). A comparison of social skills training, pharmacotherapy and psychotherapy for depression. *Behaviour Research and Therapy*, *21*, 101–107.

Blackburn, I. M., Bishop, S., Glen, A. I. M., Whalley, L. J., & Christie, J. E. (1981). The efficacy of cognitive therapy in depression: A treatment trial using cognitive therapy and pharmacotherapy, each alone and in combination. *British Journal of Psychiatry*, *139*, 181–189.

Blackburn, I. M., Eunson, K. M., & Bishop, S. (1986). A two-year naturalistic follow-up of depressed patients treated with cognitive therapy, pharmacotherapy and a combination of both. *Journal of Affective Disorders*, *10*, 67–75.

Blackburn, I. M., & Moore, R. G. (1997). Controlled acute and follow-up trial of cognitive therapy and pharmacotherapy in out-patients with recurrent depression. *British Journal of Psychiatry*, *171*, 328–334.

Blatt, S. J., Quinlan, D. M., Pilkonis, P. A., & Shea, M. T. (1995). Impact of perfectionism and need for approval on the brief treatment of depression: The National Institute of Mental Health Treatment of Depression Collaborative Research Program revisited. *Journal of Consulting and Clinical Psychology*, *63*, 125–132.

Bothwell, S., & Weissman, M. M. (1977). Social impairments four years after an acute depressive episode. *American Journal of Orthopsychiatry*, *47*, 231–237.

Bowers, W. A. (1990). Treatment of depressed inpatients: Cognitive therapy plus medication, relaxation plus medication, and medication alone. *British Journal of Psychiatry, 156,* 73–78.

Bruder, G. E., Stewart, J. W., Mercier, M. A., Agosti, V., et al. (1997). Outcome of cognitive-behavioral therapy for depression: Relation to hemispheric dominance in verbal processing. *Journal of Abnormal Psychology, 106,* 138–144.

Burke, K. C., Burke, J. D., Regier, P. A., & Rae, P. S. (1990). Age at onset of selected mental disorders in five community populations. *Archives of General Psychiatry, 47,* 511–518.

Burns, D. D., Rude, S., Simons, A. D., Bates, M. A., et al. (1994). Does learned resourcefulness predict the response to cognitive behavioral therapy for depression? *Cognitive Therapy and Research, 18,* 277–291.

Craighead, W. E. (2000, August). *Recurrence of major depression: Prevalence, prediction, and prevention.* Paper presented at the meetings of the American Psychological Association, Washington, DC.

Craighead, W. E., Evans, D. D., & Robins, C. J. (1992). Unipolar depression. In S. M. Turner, K. S. Calhoun, & H. E. Adams (Eds.), *Handbook of clinical behavior therapy* (2nd ed., pp. 99–116). New York: Wiley.

Cronbach, L. J., & Snow, R. E. (1977). *Aptitudes and instructional methods.* New York: Irvington.

Depression Guideline Panel. (1993). *Clinical Practice Guideline Number 5: Depression in primary care, 2: Treatment of major depression.* Rockville, MD: US Dept. of Health and Human Services, Agency for Health Care Policy and Research. AHCPR publication 93–0551.

DeRubeis, R. J., Gelfand, L. A., Tang, T. Z., & Simons, A. D. (1999). Medications versus cognitive behavior therapy for severely depressed outpatients: Mega-analysis of four randomized comparisons. *American Journal of Psychiatry, 156,* 1007–1013.

DiMascio, A., Weissman, M. M., Prusoff, B. A., Neu, C., Zwilling, M., & Klerman, G. L. (1979). Differential symptom reduction by drugs and psychotherapy in acute depression. *Archives of General Psychiatry, 36,* 1450–1456.

Dobson, K. S. (1989). A meta-analysis of the efficacy of cognitive therapy for depression. *Journal of Consulting and Clinical Psychology, 57,* 414–419.

Dobson, K. S., Dimidgian, S., Hollon, S. D., Shilling, E., Steiman, M., & McGlinchey, J. (2000, November). *The University of Washington treatments for depression study: Design, subject, assessment, and treatment evaluation considerations.* Paper presented at the annual meeting of the Association for the Advancement of Behavior Therapy, New Orleans, LA.

Elkin, I., Gibbons, R. D., Shea, M. T., & Shaw, B. F. (1996). Science is not a trial (but it can sometimes be a tribulation). *Journal of Consulting and Clinical Psychology, 64,* 92–103.

Elkin, I., Gibbons, R. D., Shea, M. T., Sotsky, S. M., Watkins, J. T., Pilkonis, P. A., & Hedeker, D. (1995). Initial severity and differential treatment outcome in the National Institute of Mental Health Treatment of Depression Collaborative Research Program. *Journal of Consulting and Clinical Psychology, 63,* 841–847.

Elkin, I., Parloff, M. B., Hadley, S. W., & Autry, J. H. (1985). NIMH treatment of depression collaborative research program: Background and research plan. *Archives of General Psychiatry, 42,* 305–316.

Elkin, I., Shea, M. T., Watkins, J. T., Imber, S. D., Sotsky, S. M., Collins, J. F., Glass, D. R., Pilkonis, P. A., Leber, W. R., Docherty, J. P., Fiester, S. J., & Parloff, M. B. (1989). National Institute of Mental Health Treatment of Depression Collaborative Research Program: General effectiveness of treatments. *Archives of General Psychiatry, 46,* 971–982.

Evans, M. D., Hollon, S. D., DeRubeis, R. J., Piasecki, J. M., Grove, W. M., Garvey, M. J., & Tuason, V. B. (1992). Differential relapse following cognitive therapy and pharmacotherapy for depression. *Archives of General Psychiatry, 49,* 802–808.

Fava, G. A., Rafanelli, C., Grandi, S., Canestrari, R., & Morphy, M. A. (1998). Six-year outcome for cognitive behavioral treatment of residual symptoms in major depression. *American Journal of Psychiatry, 155,* 1443–1445.

Ferster, C. B. (1973). A functional analysis of depression. *American Psychologist, 28,* 857–870.

First, M. B., Spitzer, R. L., Gibbon, M., & Williams, J. B. W. (1995). *Structured clinical interview for DSM-IV Axis I disorders-patient edition.* (SCID-I/P, version 2.0).

Frank, E., Kupfer, D. J., Jacob, M., & Jarrett, D. (1987). Personality features and response to acute treatment in recurrent depression. *Journal of Personality Disorders, 1,* 14–26.

Frank, E., Kupfer, D. J., Perel, T. M., Cornes, C. L., Jarrett, D. J., Mallinger, A., Thase, M. E., McEachran, A. B., & Grochocinski, V. J. (1990). Three-year out comes for maintenance therapies in recurrent depression. *Archives of General Psychiatry, 47,* 1093–1099.

Frank, E., Shear, M. K., Rucci, P., Cyranowski, J. M., Endicott, J., Fagiolini, A., Grochocinski, V. J., Houck, P., Kupfer, D. J., Maser, J. D., & Cassano,

G. B. (2000). Influence of panic-agoraphobic spectrum symptoms on treatment response in patients with recurrent major depression. *American Journal of Psychiatry, 157,* 1101–1107.

Gortner, E. T., Gollan, J. K., Dobson, K. S., & Jacobson, N. S. (1998). Cognitive-behavioral treatment for depression: Relapse prevention. *Journal of Consulting and Clinical Psychology, 66,* 377–384.

Greenberg, P. E., Stiglin, L. E., Finkelstein, S. N., & Berndt, E. R. (1993). The economic burden of depression in 1990. *Journal of Clinical Psychiatry, 54,* 405–418.

Hankin, B. L., Abramson, L. Y., Moffitt, I. E., Silva, P. A., McGee, R., & Angell, K. E. (1998). Development of depression from preadolescence to young adulthood: Emerging gender differences in a 10 year longitudinal study. *Journal of Abnormal Psychology, 107,* 128–140.

Hardy, G. E., Barkham, M., Shapiro, D. A., Stiles, W. B., Rees, A., & Reynolds, S. (1995). Impact of Cluster C personality disorders on outcomes of contrasting brief psychotherapies for depression. *Journal of Consulting and Clinical Psychology, 63,* 997–1004.

Hersen, M., Bellack, A. S., Himmelhoch, J. M., & Thase, M. E. (1984). Effects of social skill training, amtriptyline, and psychotherapy in unipolar depressed women. *Behavior Therapy, 15,* 21–40.

Hirschfeld, R. M., et al., (1997). The National Depression and Manic-Depressive Association consensus statement on the undertreatment of depression. *Journal of the American Medical Association (JAMA), 277,* 333–340.

Hollon, S. D., DeRubeis, R. J., Evans, M. D., Wiemer, M. J., Garvey, M. J., Grove, W. M., & Tuason, V. B. (1992). Cognitive therapy and pharmacotherapy for depression: Singly and in combination. *Archives of General Psychiatry, 49,* 774–781.

Hollon, S. D., Shelton, R. C., & Loosen, P. T. (1991). Cognitive therapy and pharmacotherapy for depression. *Journal of Consulting and Clinical Psychology, 59,* 88–99.

Ilardi, S. S., & Craighead, W. E. (1994/1995). Personality pathology and response to somatic treatments for major depression: A critical review. *Depression, 2,* 200–217.

Jacobson, N. S., Dobson, K. S., Fruzetti, A. E., Schmaling, K. B., & Salusky, S. (1991). Marital therapy as a treatment for depression. *Journal of Consulting and Clinical Psychology, 59,* 547–557.

Jacobson, N. S., Dobson, K. S., Truax, P. A., Addis, M. E., Koerner, K., Gollan, J. K., Gortner, E., & Prince, S. E. (1996). A component analysis of cognitive-behavioral treatment for depression. *Journal of Consulting and Clinical Psychology, 64,* 295–304.

Jacobson, N. S., & Hollon, S. D. (1996a). Cognitive-behavior therapy versus pharmacotherapy: Now that the jury's returned its verdict, it's time to present the rest of the evidence. *Journal of Consulting and Clinical Psychology, 64,* 74–80.

Jacobson, N. S., & Hollon, S. D. (1996b). Prospects for future comparisons between drugs and psychotherapy: Lessons from the CBT-versus-pharmacotherapy exchange. *Journal of Consulting and Clinical Psychology, 64,* 104–108.

Jarrett, R. B., Basco, M. R., Risser, R., Ramanan, J., Marwill, M., Kraft, D., & Rush, A. J. (1998). Is there a role for continuation phase cognitive therapy for depressed outpatients? *Journal of Consulting and Clinical Psychology, 66,* 1036–1040.

Jarrett, R. B., Eaves, G. G., Grannemann, B. D., & Rush, A. J. (1991). Clinical, cognitive, and demographic predictors of response to cognitive therapy for depression: A preliminary report. *Psychiatry Research, 37,* 245–260.

Jarrett, R. B., Schaffer, M., McIntire, D., Witt-Browden, A., Kraft, D., & Risser, R. C. (1999). Treatment of atypical depression with cognitive therapy or phemelzine: A double-blind placebo-controlled trial. *Archives of General Psychiatry, 56,* 431–437.

Johnson, J., Weissman, M. M., & Klerman, G. L. (1992). Service utilization and social morbidity associated with depressive symptoms in the community. *Journal of the American Medical Association, 267,* 1478–1483.

Keller, M. B., McCullogugh, J. P., Klein, D. N., Arnow, B., Dunner, D. L., Gelenberg, A. J., Markowitz, J. C., Nemeroff, C. B., Russell, J. M., Thase, M. E., Trivedi, M. H., & Zajecka, J. (2000). A comparison of nefazodone, the cognitive behavioral-analysis system of psychotherapy, and their combination for the treatment of chronic depression. *New England Journal of Medicine, 342,* 1462–1470.

Kessler, R., McGonagle, K., Zhao, S., Nelson, C., Hughes, M., Eshelman, S., Wittchen, H., & Kendler, K. (1994). Lifetime and 12-month prevalence of DSM-III-R psychiatric disorders in the United States. *Archives of General Psychiatry, 51,* 8–19.

Klein, D. F. (1996). Preventing hung juries about therapy studies. *Journal of Consulting and Clinical Psychology, 64,* 80–87.

Klerman, G. L., DiMascio, A., Weissman, M., Prusoff, B., & Paykel, E. S. (1974). Treatment of depression by drugs and psychotherapy. *American Journal of Psychiatry, 131,* 186–190.

Klerman, G. L., & Weissman, M. M. (1993). Interpersonal psychotherapy for depression: Background and concepts. In G. L. Klerman & M. M. Weissman (Eds.), *New applications of interpersonal psychotherapy* (pp. 3–26). Washington, DC: American Psychiatric Press.

Klerman, G. L., Weissman, M. M., Rounsaville, B. J., & Chevron, E. S. (1984). *Interpersonal psychotherapy of depression*. New York: Basic Books.

Lewinsohn, P. M., Clarke, G. N., Seeley, J. R., & Rohde, P. (1994). Major depression in community adolescents: Age at onset, episode duration, and time to recurrence. *Journal of the American Academy of Child and Adolescent Psychiatry, 33*, 809–818.

Lewinsohn, P. M., & Gotlib, I. H. (1995). Behavioral theory and treatment of depression. In E. E. Becker & W. R. Leber (Eds.), *Handbook of depression* (pp. 352–375). New York: Guilford Press.

Lewinsohn, P. M., Hops, H., Roberts, R. E., Seeley, J. R., & Andrews, J. A. (1993). Adolescent psychopathology: 1. Prevalence and incidence of depression and other DSM-III-R disorders in high school students. *Journal of Abnormal Psychology, 102*, 133–144.

McCullough, J. P. (2000). *Treatment of chronic depression: Cognitive behavioral analysis system of psychotherapy*. New York: Guilford Press.

McLean, P. D., & Hakstian, A. R. (1979). Clinical depression: Comparative efficacy of outpatient treatments. *Journal of Consulting and Clinical Psychology, 47*, 818–836.

McLean, P. D., & Hakstian, A. R. (1990). Relative endurance of unipolar depression treatment effects: Longitudinal follow-up. *Journal of Consulting and Clinical Psychology, 58*, 482–488.

Merriam, A. E., & Karasu, T. B. (1996). The role of psychotherapy in the treatment of depression: Review of two practice guidelines. *Archives of General Psychiatry, 53*, 301–302.

Meyer, A. (1957). *Psychobiology: A science of man*. Springfield, IL: Charles C Thomas.

Miller, I. W., Norman, W. H., Keitner, G. I., Bishop, S. B., & Dow, M. G. (1989). Cognitive-behavioral treatment of depressed inpatients. *Behavior Therapy, 20*, 25–47.

Mueller, T. I., Leon, A. C., Keller, M. B., Solomon, D. A., Endicott, J., Coryell, W., Warshaw, M., & Maser, J. D. (1999). Recurrence after recovery from major depressive disorder during 15 years of observational follow-up. *American Journal of Psychiatry, 156*, 1000–1006.

Nemeroff, C. B., & Schatzberg, A. F. (1998). Pharmacological treatment of unipolar depression. In P. E. Nathan & J. M. Gorman (Eds.), *A guide to treatments that work* (pp. 212–225). New York: Oxford University Press.

Nietzel, M. T., Russell, R. L., Hemmings, K. A., & Gretter, M. L. (1987). Clinical significance of psychotherapy for unipolar depression: A meta-analytic approach to social comparison. *Journal of Consulting and Clinical Psychology, 55*, 156–161.

O'Leary, K. D., & Beach, S. R. H. (1990). Marital therapy: A viable treatment for depression and marital discord. *American Journal of Psychiatry, 147*, 183–186.

Organista, K. C., Munoz, R. F., & Gonzalez, G. (1994). Cognitive behavioral therapy for depression in low-income and minority medical outpatients: Description of a program and exploratory analyses. *Cognitive Therapy and Research, 18*, 241–259.

Pilkonis, P. A., & Frank, E. (1988). Personality pathology in recurrent depression: Nature, prevalence, and relationship to treatment response. *American Journal of Psychiatry, 145*, 435–441.

Rector, N. A., Bagby, R. M., Segal, Z. V., Joffe, R. T., & Levitt, A. (2000). Self-criticism and dependency in depressed patients treated with cognitive therapy or pharmacotherapy. *Cognitive Therapy and Research, 24*, 571–584.

Regier, D. A., Kaelber, C. T., Roper, M. T., Rae, D. S., & Sartorms, N. (1994). The ICD-10 clinical field trial for mental and behavioral disorders: Results in Canada and the United States. *American Journal of Psychiatry, 151*, 1340–1350.

Rehm, L. P. (1977). A self-control model of depression. *Behavior Therapy, 8*, 787–804.

Rehm, L. P. (1990). Cognitive and behavioral theories. In B. B. Wolman & G. Stricker, (Eds.), *Depressive disorders: Facts, theories, and treatment methods* (pp. 64–91). New York: Wiley.

Reynolds, C. F., III, Frank, E., Dew, M. A., Houck, P. R., Miller, M., Mazumdar, S., Perel, J. M., & Kupfer, D. J. (1999). Treatment of 70+-year-olds with recurrent major depression: Excellent short-term but brittle long-term response. *American Journal of Geriatric Psychiatry, 7*, 64–69.

Robinson, L. A., Berman, J. S., & Neimeyer, R. A. (1990). Psychotherapy for the treatment of depression: A comprehensive review of controlled outcome research. *Psychological Bulletin, 108*, 30–49.

Rude, S. S., & Rehm, L. P. (1991). Response to treatments for depression: The role of initial status on targeted cognitive and behavioral skills. *Clinical Psychology Review, 11*, 493–514.

Rush, A. J. (1996). The role of psychotherapy in the treatment of depression: Review of two practice guidelines. *Archives of General Psychiatry, 53*, 298–300.

Rush, A. J., Beck, A. T., Kovacs, M., & Hollon, S. D. (1977). Comparative efficacy of cognitive therapy in the treatment of depressed outpatients. *Cognitive Therapy and Research, 1,* 17–36.

Schulberg, H. C., Pilkonis, P. A., & Houck, P. (1998). The severity of major depression and choice of treatment in primary care practice. *Journal of Consulting and Clinical Psychology, 66,* 932–938.

Shea, M. T., Elkin, I., Imber, S. D., Sotsky, S. M., Watkins, J. T., Collins, J. F., Pilkonis, P. A., Beckham, E., Glass, D. R., Dolan, R. T., & Parloff, M. B. (1992). Course of depressive symptoms over follow-up: Findings from the National Institute of Mental Health Treatment of Depression Collaborative Research Program. *Archives of General Psychiatry, 49,* 782–787.

Shea, M. T., Pilkonis, P. A., Beckham, E., Collins, J. F., Elkin, I., Sotsky, S. M., & Docherty, J. P. (1990). Personality disorders and treatment outcome in the NIMH Treatment of Depression Collaborative Research Program. *American Journal of Psychiatry, 147,* 711–718.

Shea, M. T., Widiger, T. A., & Klein, M. H. (1992). Comorbidity of personality disorders and depression: Implications for treatment. *Journal of Consulting and Clinical Psychology, 60,* 857–868.

Simons, A. D., Gordon, J. S., Monroe, S. M., & Thase, M. E. (1995). Toward an integration of psychologic, social, and biologic factors in depression: Effects on outcome and course of cognitive therapy. *Journal of Consulting and Clinical Psychology, 63,* 369–377.

Simons, A. D., Lustman, P. J., Wetzel, R. D., & Murphy, G. E. (1985). Predicting response to cognitive therapy of depression: The role of learned resourcefulness. *Cognitive Therapy and Research, 9,* 79–89.

Simons, A. D., Murphy, G. E., Levine, J. L., & Wetzel, R. D. (1986). Cognitive therapy and pharmacotherapy for depression. *Archives of General Psychiatry, 43,* 43–48.

Simons, A. D., & Thase, M. E. (1990). Mood disorders. In M. E. Thase, B. A. Edelstein, & M. Hersen (Eds.), *Handbook of outpatient treatment of adults: Nonpsychotic mental disorders* (pp. 91–138). New York: Plenum Press.

Skinner, B. F. (1953). *Science and human behavior.* New York: Free Press.

Sloane, R. B., Staples, F. R., & Schneider, L. S. (1985). Interpersonal therapy versus nortriptyline for depression in the elderly. In G. Burrows, T. R. Norman, & L. Dermerstein (Eds.), *Clinical and pharmacological studies in psychiatric disorders* (pp. 344–346). London: John Libbey.

Sotsky, S. M., Glass, D. R., Shea, M. T., Pilkonis, P. A., Collins, J. F., Elkin, I., Watkins, J. T., Imber, S. D. Leber, W. R., Moyer, J., & Oliveri, M. E. (1991) Patient predictors of response to psychotherapy and pharmacotherapy: Findings in the NIMH Treatment of Depression Collaborative Research Program. *American Journal of Psychiatry, 148,* 997–1008.

Spitzer, R. L., Endicott, J., & Robins, E. (1978). Research diagnostic criteria: Rationale and reliability. *Archives of General Psychiatry, 35,* 773–782.

Spitzer, R. L., Williams, J. B. W., Gibbon, M., & First, M. (1992). The structured clinical interview for *DSM-III-R* (SCID): 1. History, rationale, and description. *Archives of General Psychiatry, 49,* 624–636.

Steuer, J. L., Mintz, J., Harnmen, C. L., Hill, M. A., Jarvik, L. F., McCarley, T., Motoike, P., & Rosen, R. (1984). Cognitive-behavioral and psychodynamic group psychotherapy in treatment of geriatric depression. *Journal of Consulting and Clinical Psychology, 52,* 180–189.

Sullivan, H. S. (1953). *The interpersonal theory of psychiatry.* New York: Norton.

Teasdale, J. D., Fennell, M. J., Hibbert, G. A., & Amies, P. L. (1984). Cognitive therapy for major depressive disorder in primary care. *British Journal of Psychiatry, 144,* 400–406.

Thase, M. E. (1994). Cognitive behavior therapy of severe unipolar depression. In L. Grauhaus & J. F. Greden (Eds.), *Severe depressive disorders* (pp. 269–296). Washington, DC: American Psychiatric Press.

Thase, M. E., Bowler, K., & Harden, T. (1991). Cognitive behavior therapy of endogenous depression: 2. Preliminary findings in 16 unmedicated inpatients. *Behavior Therapy, 22,* 469–477.

Thompson, L. W., & Gallagher, D. (1984). Efficacy of psychotherapy in the treatment of late-life depression. Special Issue: Psychological treatment of unipolar depression. *Advances in Behaviour Research and Therapy, 6,* 127–139.

Thompson, L. W., Gallagher, D., & Breckenridge, J. S. (1987). Comparative effectiveness of psychotherapies for depressed elders. *Journal of Consulting and Clinical Psychology, 55,* 385–390.

Thompson, L. W., Gallagher, D., & Czirr, R. (1988). Personality disorder and outcome in the treatment of late-life depression. *Journal of Geriatric Psychiatry, 21,* 133–146.

Weissman, M. M., Bland, R. C., Canino, G. J., Faravelli, C., Greenwald, S., Hwu, H., Joyce, P. R., Karam, E. G., Lee, C., Lellouch, J., Lepine, J.,

Newman, S. C., Rubio-Stipec, M., Wells, J. E., Wickramaratne, P. J., Wittchen, H., & Yeh, E. (1996). Cross-national epidemiology of major depression and bipolar disorder. *Journal of the American Medical Association, 276,* 293–299.

Weissman, M. M., Fendrich, M., Warner, V., & Wickramaratne, P. (1992). Incidence of psychiatric disorder in offspring at high and low risk for depression. *Journal of American Academy of Child and Adolescent Psychiatry, 31,* 640–648.

Weissman, M. M., & Klerman, G. L. (1973). Psychotherapy with depressed women: An empirical study of content themes and reflection. *British Journal of Psychiatry, 123,* 55–61.

Weissman, M. M., Klerman, G. L., Prusoff, B. A., Sholomskas, D., & Padian, N. (1981). Depressed outpatients: Results 1 year after treatment with drugs and/or interpersonal psychotherapy. *Archives of General Psychiatry, 38,* 51–55.

Weissman, M. M., Prusoff, B. A., DiMascio, A., Neu, C., Goklaney, M., & Klerman, G. L. (1979). The efficacy of drugs and psychotherapy in the treatment of acute depressive episodes. *American Journal of Psychiatry, 136,* 555–558.

Wells, K. B., Stewart, A., Hays, R. D., Burnam, A., Rogers W., Daniels, M., Berry, S., Greenfield, S., & Ware, J. (1989). The functioning and well-being of depressed patients: Results from the medical outcomes study. *Journal of the American Medical Association, 262,* 914–919.

Wickramaratne, P. J., Weissman, M., Leaf, P. J., & Holford, T. R., (1989). Age, period and cohort effects on the risk of major depression: Results from five United States communities. *Journal of Clinical Epidemiology, 42,* 333–343.

Wilson, P. H., Goldin, J. C., & Charbonneau-Powis, M. (1983). Comparative efficacy of behavioral and cognitive treatments of depression. *Cognitive Therapy and Research, 7,* 111–124.

11

Psychosocial Treatments for Bipolar Disorder

W. Edward Craighead
David J. Miklowitz
Ellen Frank
Fiona C. Vajk

Whereas pharmacological interventions remain the primary treatment for bipolar disorders, adjunctive psychosocial interventions have the potential to increase adherence to medication regimens, improve quality of life, and enhance mechanisms for coping with stress. Thus, the combination of pharmacotherapy and psychosocial treatments may substantially reduce the risk of relapse and rehospitalization and increase the quality of patients' lives.

Several Type 2 and 3 studies have established that psychoeducation, designed to provide information about the disorder to bipolar patients and their families, its pharmacological treatment, and the treatment side effects, leads to greater adherence to pharmacological treatments among bipolar patients. Three Type 1 studies evaluated cognitive behavior therapy (CBT) as an ancillary treatment. These studies suggested that CBT leads to increased medication adherence, significantly fewer rehospitalizations, and improved social and occupational functioning. One Type 1 study evaluated the effectiveness of IPSRT (a combination of IPT and social rhythm therapies) for bipolar disorder. IPSRT demonstrated its greatest symptomatic effects on depressed symptomatology; this study also suggested that consistency of psychosocial interventions over time may be an important variable. Finally, several Type 1 studies have shown that marital/family therapy may be effectively combined with pharmacotherapy to reduce recurrences of the disorder and improve quality of social and occupational functioning.

Important future research topics include implementation of effectiveness studies, studies of adolescent bipolar patients, and long-term cost-effectiveness of different types of interventions.

Approximately 1.5% of the adult population experiences bipolar disorder (Kessler et al., 1994; Robins, Helzer, & Weissman et al., 1984), and for over 90% of those patients, the disorder is characterized by a recurrent course of mood fluctuation over the lifetime (*DSM-IV*; American Psychiatric Association [APA], 1994). Several studies indicate that a substantial proportion (up to 75%) experience lengthy periods of intermorbid residual symptoms despite pharmacotherapy (e.g., Gitlin, Swendsen, Heller, & Hammen, 1995; Harrow, Goldberg, Grossman, & Meltzer, 1990; Keller et al., 1986). Bipolar disorder is the sixth leading cause of disability among the physical and psychiatric disorders (Murray & Lopez, 1996).

Bipolar disorder (BPD) has a strong impact on patients' work and social functioning. Approximately one of every three patients shows deficits in work functioning 2 years after hospitalization (Coryell, Andreasen, Endicott, & Keller, 1987), only 20% work at expected levels of employment during the 6 months after an episode (Dion, Tohen, Anthony, & Waternaux, 1988), and over 50% show declines in occupational functioning over the 5 years following an episode (Coryell et al., 1993; Goldberg, Harrow, & Grossman, 1995). Rates of marital distress and family discord are higher than those of the general population (Goodwin & Jamison, 1990; Targum, Dibble, Davenport, & Gershon, 1981). The risk of suicide in bipolar patients is between 15% and 20% (*DSM-IV*; APA, 1994; Isometsae, 1993). Unfortunately, despite recent advances in the treatment of this debilitating disorder, it is estimated that fewer than one third of bipolar patients receive treatment—a lower percentage than that of any other major psychiatric disorders (Goodwin & Jamison, 1990).

The generally accepted etiology of bipolar disorder maintains that it results from biological dysregulations (with a major genetic component) that are either activated or maintained by psychosocial stressors such as negative family environments or stressful life events (see Craighead & Miklowitz, 2000). Because of the biological dysregulations associated with bipolar disorder, pharmacological treatments are the primary line of intervention. In particular, the introduction of lithium carbonate has dramatically improved both acute and prophylactic treatment (Baastrup & Schou, 1967; Goodwin & Ebert, 1973). In more recent years, anticonvulsant agents and sometimes the atypical antipsychotics have also been successfully used to treat bipolar disorder (Keck & McElroy, 1996). Thus, with the continued use of one or more of these medications, the majority of patients can now experience some level of mood stabilization.

Ironically, although patients can now benefit more from psychosocial interventions due to the mood stabilization available through pharmacotherapy, adjunctive psychosocial treatments are utilized less frequently than they were before the introduction of lithium (Zaretsky & Segal, 1994/1995). However, the 1994 NIMH Task Force concluded, "Pharmacotherapy alone does not meet the needs of many bipolar patients" (Prien & Rush, 1996). Because biological treatments have been so extensively studied, the NIMH consensus conference on bipolar disorders concluded that "perhaps the most underdeveloped area in the treatment of bipolar disorder . . . is the use of adjunct psychosocial therapies" (Potter & Prien, 1989). Although some progress has been made since the early 1990s, it is still true that the clinical outcome research literature evaluating the effectiveness of psychosocial interventions as adjuncts to medications remains woefully small.

Within the context of pharmacological interventions as the primary treatment for bipolar disorder, psychosocial interventions have been designed to increase adherence to medication regimens, decrease hospitalizations and relapses, and improve patients' quality of life. The major possible components of a multifaceted psychosocial treatment program include psychoeducation and attention to medication adherence, individual cognitive-behavioral or interpersonal therapy, and marital or family therapy. In this chapter, we review the empirical outcome data for each of these treatment components; we also summarize the relevant major ongoing Type 1 clinical trials. A separate literature on group therapy approaches to treatment of bipolar disorders has recently been reviewed elsewhere (Callahan & Bauer, 1999; Huxley, Parikh, & Baldessarini, 2000) and will not be reiterated in this chapter.

PSYCHOEDUCATION AND MEDICATION ADHERENCE

Bipolar patients frequently express resentment at how little information they receive about their disorder or their medications (Goodwin & Jamison, 1990). Yet, the few studies that do exist show a positive effect of psychoeducation for both patients and their families. The primary focus of psychoeducation is the provision of information regarding the multifaceted nature of the disorder and its successful treatment.

The issue of *medication adherence* is a particularly salient aspect of the education and treatment of bipolar disorder. Despite the high risk of relapse due to nonadherence, up to 59% of patients on long-term lithium maintenance do not adhere or only partially adhere to their prescribed medication (Goodwin & Jamison, 1990; Strakowski, Keck, McElroy et al., 1998). Because of their more limited side-effects profile, it has been presumed that adherence to the anticonvulsants will be better, but the data provide only limited support for this presumption (Lenzi, Lazzerini, Placidi, Cassano, & Akiskal, 1989). In a naturalistic 18-month prospective study of 37 adolescents whose bipolar disorder had been stabilized with lithium carbonate during inpatient hospitalization, the relapse rate among patients who discontinued medication was 92.3%, compared with 37.5% for patients who continued lithium prophylaxis without interruption (Strober, Morrell, Lampert, & Burroughs, 1990). Not only is the risk of relapse greatly increased by medication nonadherence, but there is also the possibility of discontinuation-induced refractoriness to further lithium treatment (Post, 1993). Therefore, enhancing medication adherence is one of the most important goals of ancillary psychosocial treatments.

Seltzer, Roncari, and Garfinkel (1980) evaluated the effects of psychoeducation on medication adherence among 67 psychiatric patients (44 schizophrenic, 16 bipolar, and 7 unipolar affective) who were treated with lithium, neuroleptic, or tricyclic antidepressant drugs. Within each diagnostic group, patients were divided into control and experimental groups. Patients in the experimental group were given a series of nine lectures about the nature of their disorder and its pharmacological management. "Educated" patients tended to adhere better to medication regimes at the outpatient follow-up 5 months later, and they were less fearful of medication side effects and addiction. Medication adherence was negatively related to fear of side effects and positively related to education and the resulting knowledge about the disorder and its treatment.

Peet and Harvey (1991) evaluated a more minimal psychoeducational intervention—a 12-minute videotape lecture and written handout containing factual information about lithium. Of consecutive patients attending a lithium clinic, 60 were randomly assigned to one of two groups: one group ($N = 30$) received the educational program immediately, and the other group of 30 served as a wait-list control group that was not given the program until 6 weeks later. After the wait-list control group had also received the educational program, the preintervention and postintervention data were analyzed for all 60 patients. The educational program resulted in significant increases in patients' knowledge about lithium; for example, their knowledge increased from a baseline comparable to that of social workers to a level similar to that of community psychiatric nurses. Patients' attitudes toward lithium also became more favorable after education. For all 60 patients, medication adherence improved, as measured by either self-reported tablet omissions or plasma lithium levels (Harvey & Peet, 1991). Thus, it appears that even a very minimal psychoeducational component can improve both patient attitudes and medication adherence. Unfortunately, this study did not include a long-term follow-up, so it is not possible to determine whether these gains were maintained over time, or whether this intervention led to lower relapse rates following symptom remission.

Only one study (van Gent & Zwart, 1991) has examined the effects of educating the partners of bipolar patients. The subjects in this study were 26 manic bipolar patients and their partners: 14 partners attended psychoeducation sessions without the partners being present, while the partners of the 12 remaining patients served as controls. At postintervention and at a 6-month follow-up, partners who attended psychoeducational sessions demonstrated a greater knowledge of the disorder, medications, social support, and coping strategies. However, patients' medication adherence did not change over the 12-month follow-up, compared with either the preintervention or the control group.

It is possible that patient education leads to changes only in medication adherence; however, there may be additional effects of the enhanced social support gained from education of the patient's family or spouse, such as lower rates of relapse or improved quality of life. Because of the limited size, scope, and design of the existing studies, all of which are Type 2 or Type 3 as defined in this book, the long-term effects of either patient or family psychoeducation are not yet known.

INDIVIDUAL PSYCHOTHERAPY INTERVENTIONS

Interpersonal and Social Rhythm Therapy

Interpersonal psychotherapy (IPT; Weissman, Markowitz, & Klerman, 2000) is an individual therapy that was originally developed as a treatment for major depressive disorder. The therapy is present-focused and short-term and assumes a biopsychosocial origin of depressive disorders. IPT typically focuses on one of four problem areas: grief over loss, interpersonal disputes (persistent conflicts with significant others), role transitions (changes in a person's occupational or social/family situations), and interpersonal skill deficits. IPT has been found to be effective in alleviating depressive symptoms in a major clinical trial (Elkin et al., 1989, 1995) and a 3-year maintenance trial of recurrent depressive disorders (Frank et al., 1990).

Based on modifications of IPT, interpersonal and social rhythm therapy (IPSRT) was developed by Frank and her colleagues (Frank, 1995; Frank, Kupfer, Ehlers, & Monk, 1994) as an *adjunctive* individual therapy for bipolar disorder. IPSRT was strongly influenced by the social rhythm stability hypothesis (Ehlers, Frank, & Kupfer, 1988). The major modification to IPT is that IPSRT encourages patients to recognize the impact of interpersonal events on their social and circadian rhythms. There are two goals for IPSRT: (a) to help patients to understand and renegotiate the social context associated with mood disorder symptoms, and (b) to encourage patients to recognize the impact of interpersonal events on their social and circadian rhythms, and to regularize these rhythms in order to gain control over their mood cycling. In IPSRT patients are given the Social Rhythm Metric (Monk et al., 1991), a daily self-report device on which they record their sleep/wake times, levels of social stimulation, timing of daily routines (eating, exercise, work, etc.), and daily mood. By reviewing data from this assessment device, patients gradually see how changes in their mood states can occur as a function of variable daily routines, sleep/wake cycles, and patterns of interpersonal stimulation, and reciprocally how these factors are affected by their moods. In time, patients become motivated to regulate their rhythms and find balances among these factors as a means of stabilizing their moods.

Just like IPT, as IPSRT progresses clarifying and interpretive interventions are used to help patients resolve current interpersonal problems (e.g., ongoing disputes with coworkers) and explore ways to prevent these problems from emerging in the future. The objective is to bring about an optimal balance in the patient's daily patterns of social activities, patterns of social stimulation, and sleep cycles, a balance that leads to the stabilization of mood states. A clinician may explore a bipolar patient's grief over lost hopes, aspirations, and a sense of a healthy self and may then encourage the patient to set realistic goals in the context of having a long-term, biologically based mood disorder. Like other psychosocial therapies, IPSRT includes education about bipolar disorder and strategies for improving drug adherence (Frank et al., 1994).

The University of Pittsburgh Medical Center is conducting an ongoing controlled trial of IPSRT in conjunction with lithium and other mood stabilizers (Frank, 1999; Frank et al., 1997, 1999). Patients were assigned to IPSRT or to a comparison individual therapy, intensive clinical management. Sessions of intensive clinical management were of a frequency comparable to that of IPSRT, but they consisted of 20-minute sessions (vs. 45 minutes for IPSRT) with a psychotherapist who focused on symptom management and medication adherence. Randomization occurred at two time points: during a preliminary, post-episode stabilization phase, and again during a long-term preventive phase. IPSRT or intensive clinical management sessions were held weekly during the preliminary phase (until the patient had stabilized) and biweekly and then monthly during maintenance prevention, for up to 2 years.

In the preliminary treatment phase, patients in IPSRT showed greater stabilization of their daily routines and sleep/wake cycles than those in intensive clinical management (Frank et al., 1997). Preliminary results from the preventive treatment phase indicated that patients in IPSRT and intensive clinical management did not differ in their likelihood of developing fully syndromal recurrences ($N = 86$). Clear positive effects of IPSRT were observed, however, when the patterns of subsyndromal as well as syndromal fluctuations were considered. IPSRT patients who completed a year of preventive treatment were more likely to maintain stable euthymic mood states than intensive clinical management patients. In contrast, the proportion of euthymic patients in the intensive clinical management condition decreased over the year of preventive treatment, whereas the proportion of patients with depressive symptomatology increased. IPSRT has not shown benefits over the comparison treatment in the proportion of patients experiencing manic, hypomanic, or mixed symptomatology during preventive treatment (Frank, 1999).

An interesting pattern of results emerged when the consistency of psychosocial treatment from the preliminary to the preventive phases of treatment (a function of the two-stage randomization strategy) was considered. Patients who remained in the same psychosocial treatment from the preliminary to the preventive phase had fewer syndromal recurrences than patients who switched from one modality to the other. Thus, consistency of a patient's routines, including the length, structure, and content of his or her psychosocial treatment, may protect against recurrences of BPD (Frank et al., 1999). If this is a robust finding, then consistency of adjunctive psychotherapeutic interventions may be an important consideration for bipolar patients.

Cognitive Behavior Therapy (CBT)

Since the early 1990s, there has been increased interest in the study of individual CBT used in conjunction with mood-stabilizing medications for the treatment of bipolar disorder. The primary assumption of CBT is that mood swings are in part a function of negative thinking patterns (both self-statements and core dysfunctional schemas) that can be alleviated by a combination of behavioral activation and cognitive restructuring strategies that are designed to increase the patient's engagement with the environment.

In the first study of individual therapy as an ancillary psychosocial treatment for bipolar disorder, one half of 28 newly admitted lithium-treated outpatients were randomly assigned to receive only lithium, while the other 14 received lithium and an additional preventive compliance intervention based on principles of cognitive behavior therapy (Cochran, 1984). The therapeutic program was designed to alter specific cognitions and behaviors that were hypothesized to interfere with medication adherence. The intervention consisted of six weekly individual 1-hour therapy sessions. At both posttreatment and 6-month follow-up, patients who received the intervention had significantly better medication adherence. Also, over the 6-month follow-up period, the intervention group had significantly fewer hospitalizations (2 vs. 8). Although the groups did not differ significantly in total number of relapses (9 vs. 14), patients in the intervention group had significantly fewer mood disorder episodes (5 episodes experienced by 3 intervention patients vs. 11 episodes experienced by 8 standard-treatment patients) judged to be precipitated by medication nonadherence.

In the largest scale randomized CBT study to date ($N = 69$), Perry, Tarrier, Morriss, McCarthy, and Limb (1999) compared patients who received medication management with patients who received medication management and a 7- to 12-session CBT intervention. The CBT proceeded with a different directive than Cochran's: Perry et al. (1999) taught patients to recognize emergent symptoms of BPD when they occurred and to seek appropriate medical/preventative interventions. During an 18-month follow-up period, manic relapses were significantly delayed among bipolar patients in the CBT versus the medication-only group; no differences were found in survival times to depressive relapses. CBT also had a stronger impact on social and occupational functioning than did medication management. There were no differences between the groups in medication adherence. It is notable that the effects of CBT in Perry et al.'s study were primarily on the manic pole of the illness, whereas Frank (1999) and Miklowitz, Simoneau et al. (2000) found that the effects of IPSRT and FFT, respectively, were more pronounced for depressive symptoms. Possibly, the prodromal symptoms of manic episodes are easier to identify than those of depressive episodes. Interventions aimed specifically at recognition of early symptoms and relapse prevention would therefore be expected to have a stronger impact on manic symptoms. The overall pattern of findings from these studies may suggest the wisdom of combining CBT with interpersonally oriented or family/marital psychoeducational interventions (Craighead & Craighead, 2001).

A randomized pilot study (Lam et al., 2000) further supports the short-term efficacy of CBT. This 6-month CBT program included between 12 and 20 sessions and focused on strategies for relapse prevention, sleep/wake stabilization, and behavioral activation (similar to the IPSRT approach). The investigators randomized 25 patients to CBT plus medication management or medication management alone. The 12-month follow-up data indicated that CBT was effective in reducing rates of relapse, improving medication adherence, and improving psychosocial functioning.

Although the completed studies have employed small samples, their results consistently indicate positive effects of CBT in conjunction with pharmacotherapy. The mechanisms of action of CBT treatments—whether they have a direct impact on patients' cognitive styles and core dysfunctional beliefs or whether they increase the patients' knowledge of BPD and use of illness management strategies (e.g., medication adherence, seeking emergency interventions prior to relapses, or behavioral activation)—have not been examined. Given the results of these previous studies and the allegiance to the CBT model among many community clinicians, further empirical studies are clearly warranted.

MARITAL AND FAMILY INTERVENTIONS

When a person with bipolar disorder lives in or is otherwise involved with a family, the bipolar disorder typically occurs and is maintained within a family context that reciprocally affects and is affected by the disorder (Miklowitz et al., 1988). Just as the patient needs to understand the disorder and its treatment, the family and/or spouse of the person with bipolar disorder also needs to be educated about the disorder in order to cope with its effects on interpersonal interactions and relationships.

Current successful approaches to family or marital treatment are "psychoeducational," meaning that the clinician views the dysfunction of the couple or family as largely due to a lack of the understanding, coping strategies, and interpersonal skills necessary for dealing with the disorder. Psychoeducational family and marital interventions include teaching the patient and close relatives (typically the spouse or parents) about the symptoms, course, and treatment of bipolar disorder and emphasizing strategies for relapse prevention. Psychoeducational marital and family interventions are most successfully administered concurrently with pharmacotherapy (typically mood-stabilizing medications, with or without adjunctive agents).

Marital and Family Difficulties

The marital interactions of bipolar patients are often problematic, both during patients' episodes and during well intervals. In a study of marital interactional patterns (McKnight, Nelson-Gray, & Gullick, 1989), bipolar patients' interactions with spouses during manic episodes were found to be highly active (including interruptions and conversational dominance by the manic partner). When these patients were in remission, there was a reduction in negative interactions, but this reduction was not replaced by positive interactions (such as generating positive solutions to problems). These findings indicate a need for problem-solving and communication training for couples and families in which a member suffers from bipolar disorder.

Recent research has shown that stressful family environments are predictive of the course of bipolar disorder. Specifically, if an episodic bipolar patient returns to a "high-expressed-emotion" (high-EE) family, in which one or both key relatives (parents or spouse) show critical, hostile, or emotionally overinvolved attitudes, the patient suffers twice the risk of relapse over the next 9 to 12 months of a patient who returns to a "low-EE" family, that is, a less critical, normally involved family (Miklowitz, Goldstein, Nuechterlein, Snyder, & Mintz, 1988; Miklowitz, Simoneau, Sachs-Ericsson, Warner, & Suddath, 1996; O'Connell, Mayo, Flatow, Cuthbertson, & O'Brien, 1991; Priebe, Wildgrube, & Müller-Oerlinghausen, 1989). Two of these studies further suggest that negative patient-relative verbal interactional patterns predict poor symptomatic and social functioning in 1-year community follow-ups (Miklowitz et al., 1988; O'Connell et al., 1991). Thus, the family environment plays a strong prognostic role in mood disorders (see also Butzlaff & Hooley, 1998). On the positive side, bipolar patients with high levels of social and emotional support from friends and families recover more quickly from a bipolar episode than patients with low levels of such support (Johnson, Winett, Meyer, Greenhouse, & Miller, 1999). It was data like the preceding that led to the development of family and marital interventions as adjunctive treatments to accompany pharmacotherapy for bipolar disorders.

Treatment Efficacy Studies

Several investigations have examined whether family or marital interventions, as adjunctive to pharmacotherapy, lead to improved outcomes of bipolar disorder. A group at the Cornell University Medical College (Clarkin et al., 1990; Clarkin, Hass, & Glick, 1988; Glick, Clarkin, Haas, Spencer, & Chen, 1991; Haas et al., 1988; Spencer et al., 1988) developed and tested an inpatient family intervention (IFI) for families of hospitalized psychiatric (including bipolar) patients. IFI is a brief (average of nine weekly or twice-weekly sessions) therapy involving both patients and key relatives. It focuses on helping participants cope with the hospitalization and make plans for a positive post-discharge adjustment. Similar to an outpatient crisis-oriented family program developed by Goldstein and his colleagues (Goldstein, Rodnick, Evans, May, & Steinberg, 1978) for schizophrenic patients, IFI encourages patients and family members to (a) accept that the disorder is real and probably chronic, and that medical and psychosocial treatments will be necessary after hospital discharge; (b) identify stressors both within and outside the family (e.g., aversive family interaction patterns or stressful events) that may precipitate episodes of psychiatric disorder; and (c) learn ways to modify these family patterns and cope with future stressors (Glick et al., 1991).

In a Type 2 controlled clinical trial (N = 186) with hospitalized patients with major affective, schizophrenic, and other *DSM-III* Axis I disorders, IFI was combined with standard hospital treatment (including pharmacotherapy) and compared to hospital treatment alone. At hospital discharge, the treatment effects were mostly evident in female patients with affective (including bipolar) disorders. However, the treatment effects were broader at 6-month and 18-month posthospital follow-ups: Female patients with major affective and schizophrenic disorders exhibited better global and symptomatic functioning if they had received IFI than if they had received the comparison treatment. Finally, among female patients from the affective and schizophrenic groups, family treatment was associated with improvements at 6 and 18 months in certain measures of family attitudes, including feelings of rejection held by family members toward the patient and perceptions of family burden (Clarkin et al., 1990; Glick et al., 1991; Spencer et al., 1988).

Of the 50 affective disorder patients, 21 met criteria for bipolar disorder (Clarkin et al., 1990). When the treatment effects for bipolar patients were graphed separately by gender, treatment effects were seen only among the 14 female bipolar patients; thus, the sample size is too small to allow firm conclusions about the treatment's effects on this population. Furthermore, the obtained effect seems to have been due largely to the poor showing of standardized treatment for the female bipolar patients rather than to a strong improvement among the IFI female bipolar patients. Perhaps due to lack of statistical power, the effect of treatment on global functioning for bipolar patients alone was only marginally significant at 6 months, and it was nonsignificant at 18 months. For role functioning (e.g., work performance), the effect of treatment was not significant at 6 months, but it was significant at 18 months. The trend for improved family attitudes toward the patient at 6 months was not apparent at 18 months. In short, while psychoeducational family treatment for bipolar patients may be a useful adjunctive therapy, the results from this study are equivocal and difficult to interpret.

Clarkin, Carpenter, Hull, Wilner, and Glick (1998) conducted a study of married bipolar patients randomized to standard medications only or to standard medications plus a marital intervention. The marital intervention was 25 sessions in length and focused on improving spousal communication and attitudes, educating the couple about the disorder, and enhancing adherence to drug treatments. No effects were obtained for the marital intervention on symptomatic adjustment or recurrences of the disorder during an 11-month treatment period. Patients in the marital intervention group, however, showed greater improvements in global functioning than those in the standard medication group. Medication adherence was, on average, higher in the family group throughout the 11-month period.

Miller, Keitner, Bishop, and Ryan (1991) at Brown University Medical Center have studied the families of 24 manic bipolar patients. They found that patients whose families were rated as dysfunctional during the acute period of the manic episode had twice the rate of rehospitalization over a 5-year follow-up of the other manic patients in this study. This finding led the authors to conduct a small Type 3 pilot study comparing standard treatment (including medications) to standard treatment (including medications) plus family therapy. In this study, 14 patients were randomly assigned to one of the two treatments (N = 8 for family therapy and 6 for standard treatment), which began during hospitalization and continued for 18 weeks after discharge. Each patient in the combined standard treatment–family-therapy group received 8 to 12 sessions of family therapy in addition to the standard treatment, whereas the other 6 patients received just the standard treatment. At a 2-year follow-up, there was improved family functioning among the families of those patients who had received the family therapy component. Recovery, as measured by 2 continuous months of absence of manic or depressive symptoms, was significantly greater for the standard-treatment–family-therapy condition, and rehospitalization rates were one half those of the patients who received only standard treatment. Although the study was small, it points toward family discord as a major aspect of bipolar disorder and to its amelioration as a primary goal of adjunctive psychosocial treatments; Miller and his colleagues are currently continuing study of this promising family intervention program.

In an "in-progress" randomized trial, Miller, Keitner, Ryan, and Solomon (2000) assigned 92 bipolar patients who were either manic or depressed to one of three treatment conditions: (a) standard treatment, consisting of medication plus active clinical management by a psychiatrist; (b) standard treatment plus family therapy (6 to 8 sessions over 4 months of treatment, and follow-up "booster sessions"); and (c) standard treatment plus multifamily groups, in which four to six families met together in 1 1/2-hour sessions over 6 weeks, followed by "reunion meetings" over the next 6 months. The family treatments were oriented toward education about the disorder and problem solving. The investigators attempted to build on their earlier finding that, over a 5-year follow-up, the odds of rehospitalization were twice as high among bipolar patients whose families were "dysfunctional" (as judged by observer-rated and self-report instruments) during a baseline manic episode as among patients whose families were nondysfunctional at baseline.

Preliminary results from the Miller et al. (2000) study indicate that, over the 10 months following a hospitalization, rates of recovery from an index episode (2 continuous months with a relative absence of mood disorder symptoms) are higher (32%) among patients in the two family treatment groups than among patients in the standard treatment condition (18%). Interestingly, an interaction emerged between treatment condition and the original disturbances of the family: The most dysfunctional families benefited the most from family therapy in terms of patients' recovery rates. Patients from dysfunctional families who received either form of family therapy had significantly higher recovery rates (53% for the family therapy condition, 50% for the multifamily group condition) than patients in the standard treatment condition (20%). No treatment differences in recovery rates emerged for patients who had had functional families during the pretreatment period. These findings parallel those of the following studies by Miklowitz and his colleagues, who found that the patients who benefited most from family therapy, in terms of improvements in depression scores, were those from high-EE families. It may be that disturbances in the family unit prior to treatment motivate greater efforts among patients and clinicians to make use of educational or problem-solving interventions.

Miklowitz and Goldstein (1990, 1997) developed a 9-month family-focused psychoeducational treatment (FFT) for bipolar adults recently hospitalized or treated as outpatients. FFT is delivered in 21 sessions titrated (12 weekly, 6 biweekly, and 3 monthly) over 9 months. The model is similar to Falloon, Boyd, and McGill's (1984) behavioral family management for schizophrenic disorders, although it is adapted to the needs of bipolar patients and their families.

The treatment model comprises three modules. In the first, psychoeducation, patients and relatives are given information about how to cope with bipolar disorder. This information includes didactic material about the symptoms, diagnosis, causes, and prognosis of the disorder; vulnerability and stress interactions; and risk and protective factors. It also includes a relapse prevention drill, in which participants identify the patient's prodromal signs of mania or depression and the family develops plans for how to intervene should these appear (e.g., arranging an emergency medical visit or hospitalization). Later modules of FFT (communication enhancement training and problem-solving skills training) involve teaching the patients and family members the skills for dealing with disorder-related conflicts; this teaching is accomplished by use of role-playing and behavioral rehearsal assignments.

FFT was first investigated in an initial Type 2 pilot study of nine bipolar I patients and their families (Miklowitz & Goldstein, 1990). These patients were compared with 23 historical controls, who did not receive FFT but were maintained on comparable, aggressively delivered pharmacotherapy. Relapse rates over the 9 months of treatment or follow-up were 11% (1/9) in FFT versus 61% (14/23) of the historical controls.

In a subsequent randomized study, Goldstein and colleagues at UCLA (Goldstein, Rea, & Miklowitz, 1996; Rea, Tompson, Miklowitz, Goldstein, Hwang, & Mintz, 2001) compared 9 months of clinic-based FFT to an individually focused therapy. Bipolar patients began the study during a hospitalized manic episode ($N = 53$), and they were maintained on mood-stabilizing medications. Patients in individually focused therapy received regular sessions of education, support, and problem solving, with a duration and pacing of sessions that was identical to FFT (21 weekly, biweekly, and monthly sessions). Patients in the FFT group had longer delays prior to relapsing, but only when the full 2-year study period was considered. Patients who received FFT also had a lower risk of rehospitalization than patients in individual therapy during the 2-year interval. No group differences were observed in the first year, a finding suggesting that, for some patients and families, the effects of FFT may not be "absorbed" until the full course of treatment is complete. Of particular significance for health care cost containment is that patients in FFT were less likely to be hospitalized when they did relapse than were the individually treated patients. Thus, FFT appears to have assisted patients and families to avoid a hospitalization when a relapse occurred.

More recently, Miklowitz et al. (2000) at the University of Colorado reported the results of a randomized clinical trial of FFT. Bipolar I patients ($N =$ 101) were randomized to FFT (9 months, 21 sessions, conducted in patients' homes) or a comparison condition called *crisis management* (CM), consisting of 2 sessions of home-based family education followed by 9 months of crisis intervention, delivered as needed. All patients received standard pharmacotherapy from community psychiatrists. Survival analysis indicated that patients in FFT and pharmacotherapy had greater survival rates without relapsing (71%) and longer survival times during the first study year than patients in CM plus pharmacotherapy, of whom 47% survived the first year without relapsing. Patients in FFT also had lower levels of depressive, but not manic, symptoms over the year. Preliminary data from a 2-year follow-up suggest longer term benefits of FFT for depressive symptoms (Miklowitz, Richards, George, Suddath, & Wendel, 2000).

Within the Colorado study, Simoneau, Miklowitz, Richards, Saleem, and George (1999) examined whether FFT leads to improvements in the quality of family communication and problem-solving skills, which in turn would predict symptomatic improvement. Simoneau et al. coded videotapes and transcripts of problem-solving interactions from a subset of families assessed prior to and following the 9-month FFT or CM protocols ($N = 44$). No differential effects were found for FFT (vs. CM) in reducing the frequency of negative communication behaviors (i.e., criticisms, disagreements, negative nonverbal behaviors) among patients and family members. Within the FFT group, however, positive communication behaviors among patients and relatives increased over the pre- to posttreatment period. When the family was not treated (CM), positive communication decreased slightly over the pre- to posttreatment period. Moreover, treatment-associated increases in positive interactional behaviors (particularly patients' nonverbal behaviors) predicted greater improvement over the study year in mood disorder symptoms. Thus, FFT may achieve its effects, in part, through increasing the protective, buffering influences of the family environment.

CONCLUSIONS

There still are only a handful of completed studies of psychosocial treatments for bipolar disorder. Those studies that are complete suggest an advantage in the domains of medication compliance, symptomatic stability, and psychosocial functioning for patients treated with both psychotherapy and medication over those treated with medication alone. A pressing need remains for more controlled research regarding psychosocial interventions as adjunctive treatments for this serious disorder.

A key but unanswered question concerns the stages of the disorder at which psychotherapy will be most effective with bipolar patients. Should psychotherapy begin during the acute episode and continue throughout the stabilization and maintenance phases? Alternatively, will patients who are first stabilized pharmacologically be more receptive to psychosocial treatments? What types of interventions will be most effective when patients are symptomatic versus remitted? Likewise, at what stage of the disorder will family members be most receptive to interventions targeting the family environment?

Furthermore, the disorder subtypes that will benefit most from various forms of individual, family, or group therapy need to be specified. Must bipolar patients achieve and maintain a certain level of cognitive and psychosocial functioning before they will benefit from psychosocial interventions? What interventions are most appropriate for bipolar I versus bipolar II patients, for rapid-cycling patients, or for those with and without psychotic features? Will psychosocial interventions mostly benefit the first-episode patient, or are they equally applicable to recurrent, chronic patients? Can psychosocial interventions delivered during the earliest phases of the disorder (e.g., cases where the onset occurs in childhood or adolescence) change the long-term trajectory of this debilitating illness?

Answering these questions requires controlled Type 1 clinical trials of specific, manualized treatments, including documentation of treatment integrity (adherence to the treatment protocol and competence of the therapy delivered). Such studies will require careful selection and assessment of the domains of outcome that different psychosocial interventions presumably influence (e.g., symptoms, social-occupational functioning, and family functioning). The successful investigation of these questions may broaden prevailing views of the treatment of bipolar disorder beyond purely pharmacological approaches to integrative models that provide the patient with more powerful protection against relapses and recurrences of the disorder.

Many of the preceding questions raised by the previous individual and family therapy studies are being studied in the ongoing multisite trial under the direction of Gary Sachs, sponsored by the National Institute of Mental Health, the Systematic Treatment Enhancement Program for *B*ipolar *D*isorder (STEP-*BD*). Additional important topics that future work needs to address include: the treatment of adolescents diagnosed with bipolar disorder, the cost-effectiveness of combining psychosocial treatments with pharmacotherapy, and the identification of the mediators of therapeutic change.

References

American Psychiatric Association. (1994). *Diagnostic and statistical manual of mental disorders* (4th ed.). Washington, DC: Author.

Baastrup, P. C., & Schou, M. (1967). Lithium as a prophylactic agent. *Archives of General Psychiatry, 16,* 162–172.

Butzlaff, R. L., & Hooley, J. M. (1998). Expressed emotion and psychiatric relapse: A meta-analysis. *Archives of General Psychiatry, 55,* 547–552.

Callahan, A. M., & Bauer, M. S. (1999). Psychosocial interventions for bipolar disorder. *Psychiatric Clinics of North America, 22,* 675–688.

Clarkin, J. F., Carpenter, D., Hull, J., Wilner, P., & Glick, I. (1998). Effects of psychoeducational intervention for married patients with bipolar disorder and their spouses. *Psychiatric Services, 49,* 531–533.

Clarkin, J. F., Glick, I. D., Haas, G. L., Spencer, J. H., Lewis, A. B., Peyser, J., DeMane, N., Good-Ellis, M., Harris, E., & Lestelle, V. (1990). A randomized clinical trial of inpatient family intervention: 5. Results for affective disorders. *Journal of Affective Disorders, 18,* 17–28.

Clarkin, J. F., Haas, G. L., & Glick, I. D. (Eds.). (1988). *Affective disorders and the family: Assessment and treatment.* New York: Guilford Press.

Cochran, S. D. (1984). Preventing medical noncompliance in the outpatient treatment of bipolar affective disorders. *Journal of Consulting and Clinical Psychology, 52,* 873–878.

Coryell, W., Andreasen, N. C., Endicott, J., & Keller, M. (1987). The significance of past mania or hypomania in the course and outcome of major depression. *American Journal of Psychiatry, 144,* 309–315.

Coryell, W., Scheftner, W., Keller, M., Endicott, J., Maser, J., & Klerman, G. L. (1993). The enduring psychosocial consequences of mania and depression. *American Journal of Psychiatry, 150,* 720–727.

Craighead, W. E. & Craighead, L. W. (2001). The role of psychotherapy in treating psychiatric disorders. *Medical Clinics of North America, 85,* 617–629.

Craighead, W. E., & Miklowitz, D. J. (2000). Psychosocial interventions for bipolar disorder. *Journal of Clinical Psychiatry, 61,* 58–64.

Dion, G. L., Tohen, M., Anthony, W. A., & Waternaux, C. S. (1988). Symptoms and functioning of patients with bipolar disorder six months after hospitalization. *Hospital and Community Psychiatry, 39,* 652–657.

Ehlers, C. L., Frank, E., & Kupfer, D. J. (1988). Social zeitgebers and biological rhythms: A unified approach to understanding the etiology of depression. *Archives of General Psychiatry, 45,* 948–952.

Elkin, I., Gibbons, R. D., Shea, M. T., Sotsky, S. M., Watkins, J. T., Pilkonis, P. A., & Hedeker, D. (1995). Initial severity and differential treatment outcome in the National Institute of Mental Health Treatment of Depression Collaborative Research Program. *Journal of Consulting and Clinical Psychology, 63,* 841–847.

Elkin, I., Shea, M. T., Watkins, J. T., Imber, S. D., Sotsky, S. M., Collins, J. F., Glass, D. R., Pilkonis, P. A., Leber, W. R., Docherty, J. P., Fiester, S. J., & Parloff, M. B. (1989). National Institute of Mental Health Treatment of Depression Collaborative Research Program: General effectiveness of treatments. *Archives of General Psychiatry, 46,* 971–982.

Falloon, I. R. H., Boyd, J. L., & McGill, C. W. (1984). *Family care of schizophrenia: A problem-solving approach to the treatment of mental illness.* New York: Guilford.

Frank, E. (1995). *Regularizing social routines in patients with bipolar I disorder*. Paper presented at the 34th Annual Meeting of the American College of Neuropsychopharmacology, San Juan, Puerto Rico.

Frank, E. (1999) Interpersonal and social rhythm therapy prevents depressive symptomatology in bipolar I patients. *Bipolar Disorders, 1(Suppl. 1)*, 13.

Frank, E., Hlastala, S., Ritenour, A., et al. (1997). Inducing lifestyle regularity in recovering bipolar disorder patients: results from the maintenance therapies in bipolar disorder protocol. *Biological Psychiatry, 41*, 1165–1173.

Frank, E., Kupfer, D. J., Ehlers, C. L., & Monk, T. H. (1994). Interpersonal and social rhythm therapy for bipolar disorder: Integrating interpersonal and behavioral approaches. *Behavior Therapist, 17*, 143.

Frank, E., Kupfer, D. J., Perel, J. M., Comes, C. L., Jarrett, D. J., Mallinger, A., Thase, M. E., McEachran, A. B., & Grochocinski, V. J. (1990). Three-year outcomes for maintenance therapies in recurrent depression. *Archives of General Psychiatry, 47*, 1093–1099.

Frank, E., Swartz, H. A., Mallinger, A. G., Thase, M. E., Weaver, E. V., & Kupfer, D. J. (1999). Adjunctive psychotherapy for bipolar disorder: Effects of changing treatment modality. *Journal of Abnormal Psychology, 108*, 579–587.

Gitlin, M. J., Swendsen, J., Heller, T. L., & Hammen, C. (1995). Relapse and impairment in bipolar disorder. *American Journal of Psychiatry, 152*, 1635–1640.

Glick, I. D., Clarkin, J. F., Haas, G. L., Spencer, J. H., & Chen, C. L. (1991). A randomized clinical trial of inpatient family intervention: 6. Mediating variables and outcome. *Family Process, 30*, 85–99.

Goldberg, J. F., Harrow, M., & Grossman, L. S. (1995). Course and outcome in bipolar affective disorder: A longitudinal follow-up study. *American Journal of Psychiatry, 152*, 379–385.

Goldstein, M. J., Rea, M. M., & Miklowitz, D. J. (1996). Family factors related to the course and outcome of bipolar disorder. In C. Mundt, M. J. Goldstein, K. Hahlweg, & P. Fiedler (Eds.), *Interpersonal factors in the origin and course of affective disorders* (pp. 193–203). London: Gaskell Books.

Goldstein, M. J., Rodnick, E. H., Evans, J. R., May, P. R., & Steinberg, M. R. (1978). Drug and family therapy in the aftercare of acute schizophrenics. *Archives of General Psychiatry, 35*, 1169–1177.

Goodwin, F. K., & Ebert, M. (1973). Lithium in mania: Clinical trials and controlled studies. In S. Gershon & B. Shopsin (Eds.), *Lithium: Its role in psychiatric research and treatment* (pp. 237–252). New York: Plenum Press.

Goodwin, F. K., & Jamison, K. R. (1990). *Manic-depressive illness*. New York: Oxford University Press.

Haas, G. L., Glick, I. D., Clarkin, J. F., Spencer, J. H., Lewis, A. B., Peyser, J., DeMane, N., Good-Ellis, M., Harris, E., & Lestelle, V. (1988). Inpatient family intervention: A randomized clinical trial: 2. Results at hospital discharge. *Archives of General Psychiatry, 45*, 217–224.

Harrow, M., Goldberg, J. F., Grossman, L. S., & Meltzer, H. Y. (1990). Outcome in manic disorders: A naturalistic follow-up study. *Archives of General Psychiatry, 47*, 665–671

Harvey, N. S., & Peet, M. (1991). Lithium maintenance: II. Effects of personality and attitude on health information acquisition and compliance. *British Journal of Psychiatry, 158*, 200–204.

Huxley, N. A., Parikh, S. V., & Baldessarini, R. J. (2000). Effectiveness of psychosocial treatments in bipolar disorder: State of the evidence. *Harvard Review of Psychiatry*, 8, 126–140

Isometsae, E. T. (1993). Course, outcome, and suicide risk in bipolar disorder: A review. *Psychiatr Fennica, 24*, 113–124.

Johnson, S. L., Winett, C. A., Meyer, B., Greenhouse, W. J., & Miller, I. (1999). Social support and the course of bipolar disorder. *Journal of Abnormal Psychology, 108*, 558–566.

Keck, P. E., & McElroy, S. L. (1996). Outcome in the pharmacological treatment of bipolar disorder. *Journal of Clinical Psychopharmacology, 16*(Suppl. 1), 15–23.

Keller, M. B., Lavori, P. W., Coryell, W., et al. (1986). Differential outcome of pure manic, mixed/cycling, and pure depressive episodes in patients with bipolar illness. *Journal of the American Medical Association, 255*, 3138–3142.

Kessler, R. C., McGonagle, K. A., Zhao, S., et al (1994). Lifetime and 12-month prevalence of DSM-III-R psychiatric disorders in the United States: results from the National Comorbidity Survey. *Archives of General Psychiatry, 51*, 8–19.

Lam, D. H., Bright, J., Jones, S., et al (2000). Cognitive therapy for bipolar illness: Pilot study of relapse prevention. *Cognitive Therapy Research, 24*, 503–520.

Lenzi, A., Lazzerini, F., Placidi, G. F., Cassano, G. B., & Akiskal, H. S. (1989). Predictors of compliance with lithium and carbamazepine regimens in the long-term treatment of recurrent mood and related psychotic disorders. *Pharmacopsychiatry, 22*, 34–37.

McKnight, D. L., Nelson-Gray, R. O., & Gullick, E. (1989). Interactional patterns of bipolar patients and their spouses. *Journal of Psychopathology and Behavioral Assessment, 11*, 269–289.

Miklowitz, D. J., & Goldstein, M. J. (1990). Behavioral family treatment for patients with bipolar affective disorder. Special Issue: Recent developments in the behavioral treatment of chronic psychiatric illness. *Behavior Modification, 14*, 457–489.

Miklowitz, D. J., & Goldstein, M. J. (1997). *Bipolar disorder: A family-focused treatment approach*. New York: Guilford Press.

Miklowitz, D. J., Goldstein, M. J., Nuechterlein, K. H., Snyder, K. S., & Mintz, J. (1988). Family factors and the course of bipolar affective disorder. *Archives of General Psychiatry, 45*, 225–231.

Miklowitz. D. J., Richards, J. A., George, E. L., Suddath, R., & Wendel, J. S. (2000). *Family-focused psychoeducation for bipolar disorder*. Paper presented at 34th meetings of the Association for the Advancement of Behavior Therapy, New Orleans, LA., November 16–19.

Miklowitz, D. J., Simoneau, T. L., George, E. A., Richards, J. A., Kalbag, A., Sachs-Ericsson, N., & Suddath, R. (2000). Family-focused treatment of bipolar disorder: 1-year effects of a psychoeducational program in conjunction with pharmacotherapy. *Biological Psychiatry, 48*, 582–592.

Miklowitz, D. J., Simoneau, T. L., Sachs-Ericsson, N., Warner, R., & Suddath, R. (1996). Family risk indicators in the course of bipolar affective disorder. In E. Mundt et al., *Interpersonal factors in the origin and course of affective disorders* (pp. 204–217). London: Gaskell Press.

Miller, I. W., Keitner, G. I., Bishop, D. S., & Ryan, C. E. (1991, November). *Families of bipolar patients: Dysfunction, course of illness, and pilot treatment study*. Paper presented at the meetings of the Association for the Advancement of Behavior Therapy, New York City.

Miller, I. W., Keitner, G. I., Ryan, C. E., & Solomon, D. S. (2000, June). *Family treatment of bipolar disorder*. Paper presented at the meetings of the Society for Psychotherapy Research, Braaga, Portugal.

Monk, T. H., Kupfer, D. J., Frank, E., & Ritenour, A. M. (1991). The Social Rhythm Metric (SRM): Measuring daily social rhythms over 12 weeks. *Psychiatry Research, 36*, 195–207.

Murray, C. J. L., & Lopez, A. D. (1996). *The global burden of disease: A comprehensive assessment of mortality and disability from diseases, injuries, and risk factors in 1990 and projected to 2020*. Cambridge: Harvard University Press

O'Connell, R. A., Mayo, J. A., Flatow, L., Cuthbertson, B., & O'Brien, B. E. (1991). Outcome of bipolar disorder on long-term treatment with lithium. *British Journal of Psychiatry, 159*, 123–129.

Peet, M., & Harvey, N. S. (1991). Lithium maintenance: 1. A standard education programme for patients. *British Journal of Psychiatry, 158*, 197–200.

Perry, A., Tarrier, N., Morriss, R., McCarthy, E., & Limb, K. (1999). Randomised controlled trial of efficacy of teaching patients with bipolar disorder to identify early symptoms of relapse and obtain treatment. *British Medical Journal, 16*, 149–153.

Post, R. M. (1993). Issues in the long-term management of bipolar affective illness. *Psychiatric Annals, 23*, 86–93.

Potter, W. Z., & Prien, R. F. (1989). *Report on the NIMH workshop on the treatment of bipolar disorder*. Unpublished manuscript available from R. F. Prien, NIMH, Parklawn Building, 5600 Fishers Lane, Rockville, MD 20857.

Priebe, S., Wildgrube, C., & Müller-Oerlinghausen, B. (1989). Lithium prophylaxis and expressed emotion. *British Journal of Psychiatry, 154*, 396–399.

Prien, R. F., & Rush, A. J. (1996). National Institute of Mental Health workshop report on the treatment of bipolar disorder. *Biological Psychiatry, 40*, 215–220.

Rea, M. M., Tompson, M., Miklowitz, D. J., Goldstein, M. J., Hwang, S., & Mintz, J. (2001). *Family-focused treatment vs. individual treatment for bipolar disorder: Results of a clinical trial*. Manuscript submitted for publication.

Robins, L. N., Helzer, J. E., Weissman, M. M., Orvaschel, H., Gruenberg, E., Burke, J. D., & Regier, D. A. (1984). Lifetime prevalence of specific psychiatric disorders in three sites. *Archives of General Psychiatry, 41*, 949–958.

Seltzer, A., Roncari, I., & Garfinkel, P. E. (1980). Effect of patient education on medication compliance. *Canadian Journal of Psychiatry, 25*, 638–645.

Simoneau, T. L., Miklowitz, D. J., Richards, J. A., Saleem, R., & George, E. L. (1999). Bipolar disorder and family communication: Effects of a psychoeducational treatment program. *Journal of Abnormal Psychology, 108*, 588–597.

Spencer, J. H., Glick, I. D., Haas, G. L., Clarkin, J. F., Lewis, A. B., Peyser, J., DeMane, N., Good-Ellis, M., Harris, E., & Lestelle, V. (1988). A randomized clinical trial of inpatient family intervention: 3. Effects at 6-month and 18-month follow-ups. *American Journal of Psychiatry, 145*, 1115–1121.

Strakowski, S. M., Keck, P. E., McElroy, S. L., West, S. A., Sax, K. W., Hawkins, J. M., Kmetz, G. F., Upadhyaya, V. H., Tugrul, K. C., & Bourne, M. L. (1998). Twelve-month outcome after a first hospitalization for affective psychosis. *Archives of General Psychiatry, 55*, 49–55.

Strober, M., Morrell, W., Lampert, C., & Burroughs, J. (1990). Relapse following discontinuation of lithium maintenance therapy in adolescents with bipolar I illness: A naturalistic study. *American Journal of Psychiatry, 147*, 457–461.

Targum, S. D., Dibble, E. D., Davenport, Y. B., & Gershon, E. S. (1981). The Family Attitudes Questionnaire: Patients' and spouses' views of bipolar illness. *Archives of General Psychiatry, 38*, 562–568.

van Gent, E. M., & Zwart, F. M. (1991). Psychoeducation of partners of bipolar-manic patients. *Journal of Affective Disorders, 21*, 15–18.

Weissman, M. M., Markowitz, J., & Klerman, G. L. (2000). *Comprehensive guide to interpersonal psychotherapy*. New York: Basic Books.

Zaretsky, A. E., & Segal, Z. V. (1994/1995). Psychosocial interventions in bipolar disorder. *Depression, 2*, 179–188.

12

Pharmacological Treatments for Bipolar Disorder

Paul E. Keck, Jr.
Susan L. McElroy

The vast majority of clinical trials in patients with bipolar disorders have been conducted in populations with bipolar I illness. The pharmacological management of bipolar disorder involves the treatment of acute manic, mixed, and depressive episodes, as well as the prevention of further episodes. Three medications, lithium, divalproex, and olanzapine, have been approved in the United States for the treatment of acute bipolar manic episodes. These medications appear to be associated with different clinical predictors of response. Data from randomized, double-blind, controlled trials suggest that carbamazepine, typical antipsychotics, risperidone, and ziprasidone also have efficacy in the treatment of acute mania. Other atypical antipsychotics and a number of new antiepileptic medications may have potential as antimanic agents. The pharmacological treatment of acute bipolar depression remains remarkably understudied. Data from randomized, controlled trials indicate that lithium, tricyclics, MAOIs, fluoxetine, and lamotrigine are effective antidepressants. The optimal duration of antidepressant treatment, in combination with mood stabilizers, is not known. Lithium remains the most well-studied medication for the maintenance treatment of bipolar I disorder. Less extensive data suggest that divalproex and carbamazepine are also efficacious as preventive treatments.

Bipolar disorder is a common, severe, and recurrent psychiatric illness. In the United States, lifetime population prevalence rates of bipolar I and II disorders may be as high as 2.5% (Kessler et al., 1994). In 1990, bipolar disorder was the sixth leading cause of disability worldwide and was projected to remain so in the first two decades of this century (Murray & Lopez, 1996). Bipolar disorder is characterized by disturbances in mood, cognition, and behavior and is often associated with psychotic symptoms (McElroy, Keck, & Strakowski, 1996). Untreated bipolar disorder carries substantial risks of morbidity and mortality. Morbidity is not simply limited to mood episodes themselves. For example, full recovery of functioning often lags behind remission of symptoms by many months (Dion et al., 1988; Keck et al., 1998; Strakowski et al., 1998). In addition, recurrent mood episodes may lead to progressive deterioration in functioning between episodes, and the number of episodes, in turn, may adversely affect subsequent treatment response and prognosis (Prien & Gelenberg, 1989; Swann et al., 1999). Thus, morbidity due to the illness is not limited to the acute mood episodes but may linger and lead to prolonged deficits in psychosocial and vocational functioning (Gitlin et al., 1995; Turvey et al., 1999). Bipolar disorder can also be a lethal illness. Suicide attempts are made by at least 25% of patients (Hopkins & Gelenberg, 1994), and up to one half of patients with mixed episodes are suicidal at the time of presentation for treatment (Dilsaver et al., 1994; Strakowski et al., 1996).

Bipolar disorder is a highly heritable illness (Gershon, 1989). Concordance rates for monozygotic twins for bipolar disorder range from 65% to 75% compared with concordance rates for dizygotic twins of approximately 14% (Gurling, 1995). In family studies, the lifetime prevalence rates of mood disorders (major depressive disorder and bipolar disorder) among first-degree relatives of bipolar probands are increased compared with prevalence rates for these disorders in first-degree relatives of people without psychiatric illness (Gurling, 1995).

DSM-IV delineates four types of bipolar disorders: bipolar I disorder, bipolar II disorder, cyclothymic disorder, and bipolar disorder not otherwise specified (American Psychiatric Association [APA], 1994). The *DSM-IV* criteria for manic, hypomanic, depressive, and mixed episodes are summarized in table 12.1. The criteria for bipolar I disorder require the presence of at least one manic or mixed episode; the manic or mixed episode is not better accounted for by schizoaffective disorder; is not superimposed on schizophrenia, schizophreniform disorder, delusional disorder, or psychotic disorder not otherwise specified; and is not due to a general medical condition or a substance-induced disorder. The criteria for bipolar II disorder require the presence of one or more major depressive episodes and at least one hypomanic episode, but without the occurrence of a manic or mixed episode. The criteria for cyclothymic disorder require, for at least 2 years (in children and adolescents for at least 1 year), the presence of numerous periods of hypomanic and depressive symptoms during the 2-year period; the person has not been without hypomanic or depressive symptoms for more than 2 months at a time; and no major depressive, manic, or mixed episode has been present during the first 2 years of the disturbance. The category of bipolar disorder not otherwise specified includes disorders with bipolar features that do not meet criteria for any specific bipolar disorder. For example, patients with ultrarapid cycling, who experience rapid alternation (over hours or days) between manic and depressive symptoms that do not meet the duration criteria for a manic or depressive episode, would fall into this category.

The vast majority of psychopharmacological treatment research has focused on patients with bipolar I disorder. Thus, this chapter will review the treatment of bipolar I disorder. Since the pharmacological treatment of bipolar I disorder involves the acute treatment of manic and depressive episodes, as well as maintenance treatment to prevent cycling and recurrent mood episodes, we review below studies of both acute and maintenance treatment. Finally, because studies of the pharmacological treatment of bipolar disorder vary in design, we attempt to make careful distinction between conclusions based on randomized, controlled trials and case reports, case series, or open trials.

ACUTE MANIA

Lithium

In 1970, lithium was the first drug approved by the U.S. Food and Drug Administration (FDA) for the treatment of "manic episodes of manic-depressive illness" (Goodwin & Jamison, 1990). Five controlled studies have demonstrated that lithium is superior to placebo for the treatment of acute mania (Bowden et al., 1994; Goodwin, Murphy, & Bunney, 1969; Maggs, 1963; Schou et al., 1954; Stokes et al., 1971). However, the results of these studies should be considered in light of several methodological limitations. First, only one study (Bowden et al., 1994) utilized a parallel design; the earliest four studies were crossover trials of varying duration (Goodwin et al., 1969; Maggs, 1963; Schou et al., 1954; Stokes et al., 1971). Second, two studies used nonrandom assignment to lithium or placebo (Goodwin et al., 1969; Stokes et al., 1971). Third, the diagnostic criteria used to define bipolar disorder in the early lithium studies (Goodwin et al., 1969; Maggs, 1963; Schou et al., 1954; Stokes et al., 1971) were not necessarily comparable to those of *DSM-III-R* (APA, 1987) or *DSM-IV*.

In the first placebo-controlled, crossover study, Schou and colleagues (1954) reported a definite response in 12 (40%) and a probable response in 15 (50%) of 30 patients with typical bipolar disorder based on a global impression of improvement. Response was less robust in 8 patients with atypical features (which implied a schizoaffective diagnosis), with 2 (25%) displaying a definite response and 3 (38%) displaying a probable response. In the first study to use formal rating scales and to analyze data statistically, 28 patients with mania were randomized to three consecutive 14-day periods of lithium-rest-placebo or

TABLE 12.1 Summary of *DSM-IV* Criteria for Mood Episodes Occurring in Bipolar Disorders

1. Manic Episode
   A. A distinctive period of abnormally and persistently elevated, expansive, or irritable mood, lasting at least 1 week (or any duration if hospitalization is necessary).
   B. During the period of mood disturbance three (or more) of the following symptoms have persisted (four if the mood is only irritable) and have been present to a significant degree:
      1) inflated self-esteem or grandiosity
      2) decreased need for sleep
      3) more talkative than usual or pressure to keep talking
      4) flight of ideas or subjective experience of racing thoughts
      5) distractibility
      6) increase in goal-directed activity or psychomotor agitation
      7) excessive involvement in pleasurable activities that have a high potential for painful consequences
   C. The symptoms do not meet criteria for a mixed episode.
   D. The mood disturbance is sufficiently severe to cause marked impairment in occupational functioning or in usual social activities or relationships with others, or to necessitate hospitalization to prevent harm to self or others, or there are psychotic features.
   E. The symptoms are not due to the direct physiological effects of a substance or general medical condition.
2. Major Depressive Episode
   A. Five (or more) of the following symptoms present during the same 2-week period and represent a change from previous functioning; at least one of the symptoms is either (1) depressed mood or (2) loss of interest or pleasure.
      1) depressed mood most of the day, nearly every day, as indicated by either subjective report or observation by others (note: in children and adolescents, can be irritable mood).
      2) markedly diminished interest or pleasure in all, or almost all, activities most of the day, nearly every day.
      3) significant weight loss when not dieting or weight gain, or decrease or increase in appetite nearly every day (note: in children, consider failure to make expected weight gains).
      4) insomnia or hypersomnia nearly every day.
      5) psychomotor agitation or retardation nearly every day.
      6) fatigue or loss of energy nearly every day.
      7) feelings of worthlessness or excessive or inappropriate guilt nearly every day.
      8) diminished ability to think or concentrate, or indecisiveness, nearly every day.
      9) recurrent thoughts of death, suicidal ideation, or a suicide attempt or a specific plan.
   B. The symptoms do not meet criteria for a mixed episode.
   C. The symptoms cause clinically significant distress or impairment in social, occupational or other important areas of functioning.
   D. The symptoms are not due to the direct physiological effects of a substance or a general medical condition.
   E. The symptoms are not better accounted for by bereavement.
3. Mixed Episode
   A. The criteria are met both for a Manic Episode and for a Major Depressive Episode nearly every day for at least 1 week.
   B. The mood disturbance is sufficiently severe to cause marked impairment in occupational functioning or in usual social activities or relationships with others, or to necessitate hospitalization to prevent harm to self or others, or there are psychotic features.
   C. The symptoms are not due to the direct physiological effects of a substance or a general medical condition.
4. Hypomanic Episode
   A. A distinct period of persistently elevated, expansive, or irritable mood, lasting throughout at least 4 days, that is clearly different from the usual nondepressed mood.
   B. During the period of mood disturbance, three (or more) of the following symptoms have persisted (four if the mood is only irritable) and have been present to a significant degree:
      1) inflated self-esteem or grandiosity
      2) decreased need for sleep
      3) more talkative than usual or pressure to keep talking
      4) flight of ideas or subjective experience of racing thoughts
      5) distractibility
      6) increase in goal-directed activity or psychomotor agitation
      7) excessive involvement in pleasurable activities that have a high potential for painful consequences
   C. The episode is associated with an unequivocal change in functioning that is uncharacteristic of the person when not symptomatic.
   D. The disturbance in mood and the change in functioning are observable by others.
   E. The episode is not severe enough to cause marked impairment in social or occupational functioning, or to necessitate hospitalization, and there are no psychotic features.
   F. The symptoms are not due to the direct physiological effects of a substance or a general medical condition.

(American Psychiatric Association, *DSM-IV*, 1994, pp. 327, 332, 335, 338) placebo-rest-lithium (Maggs, 1963). Results were based only on the 18 study completers. In these patients, lithium was superior to placebo during the second week of treatment.

In the first study conducted in the United States, Goodwin et al. (1969) compared the longitudinal efficacy of lithium with placebo in 12 patients with mania; 8 (67%) displayed a complete response and 1 (8%) a partial response to lithium. In the fourth study, Stokes et al. (1971) used a crossover design with alternating 7- to 10-day periods on lithium or placebo in 38 patients. The brief 7- to 10-day trial periods may have limited the opportunity for patients to display a more robust lithium response, while the equally brief placebo period may have been confounded by residual lithium effects. With these caveats in mind, Stokes et al. reported a 75% response rate (partial or full) on lithium, compared with 40% on placebo.

The only randomized, placebo-controlled, double-blind, parallel design trial of lithium used lithium as an active control in a study designed primarily to assess the efficacy of divalproex sodium in acute mania (Bowden et al., 1994). In this study, 17 (49%) of 35 patients receiving lithium displayed at least 50% improvement on the Mania Rating Scale (MRS) derived from the Schedule for Affective Disorders and Schizophrenia (SADS-C), compared with 18 (25%) of 73 patients receiving placebo. Regarding onset of action, both lithium and divalproex first separated from placebo on the MRS on Day 10 of the trial (both medications were administered via gradual titration). Pooled response rates from these five placebo-controlled studies (APA, 1987; Bowden et al., 1994; Goodwin et al., 1969; Maggs, 1963; Schou et al., 1954; Stokes et al., 1971) showed that 87 (70%) of 124 acutely manic patients experienced at least partial improvement on lithium.

Several post hoc analyses have attempted to identify predictors of lithium response. For example, subsequent analyses of data from the Bowden et al. study (1994) revealed that pure mania, or mania with predominantly elevated or elated mood, was associated with favorable lithium response (Swann et al., 1997). Patients with relatively few lifetime mood episodes were also more likely to respond to lithium than those patients with many mood episodes (Swann et al., 1999). In those studies in which response of psychotic symptoms was also assessed, lithium produced significant improvement in these symptoms as well (Bowden et al., 1994; Goodwin et al., 1969; Stokes et al., 1971). However, psychosis occurring in the absence of mood symptoms (Schou et al., 1954) and depressive symptoms during mania (Swann et al., 1997) were associated with poor lithium response.

Lithium has been compared with standard (typical) antipsychotic agents in nine controlled trials in the treatment of patients with acute bipolar mania (Garfinkel, Stancer, & Persad, 1980; Johnson, Gershon, & Hekiman, 1968; Johnson et al., 1971; Platman, 1970; Prien, Caffey, & Klett, 1972; Segal, Berk, & Brook, 1998; Shopsin et al., 1975; Spring et al., 1970; Takahashi et al., 1975). Interpretation of the results of some of these studies is limited due to the inclusion of manic patients with schizoaffective disorder; the lack of standardized rating scales for mania; lack of utilization of last observation carried forward (LOCF) analyses; and the possibility of a Type II error (failure to find a significant difference between treatments because of insufficient statistical power based on small sample size) (Johnson et al., 1968, 1971; Platman, 1970; Segal et al., 1998; Shopsin et al., 1975). Two studies also titrated lithium to serum concentrations in the low end of the therapeutic range (Shopsin et al., 1975; Takahashi et al., 1975).

In the largest and most rigorous study comparing lithium and an antipsychotic, Prien et al. (1972) compared the efficacy and safety of lithium and chlorpromazine in 255 acutely manic patients (both schizoaffective and bipolar). Response was assessed according to degree of psychomotor agitation by demarcating patients into "highly active" or "mildly active" groups. In the mildly active group, both medications produced comparable and significant improvement on the Brief Psychiatric Rating Scale (BPRS), the Inpatient Multidimensional Psychiatric Scale (IMPS), and the Psychotic Inpatient Profile (PIP). However, side effects were more frequent and severe among the chlorpromazine-treated patients. On the other hand, in the highly active group, chlorpromazine produced more rapid reduction in measures of agitation, excitement, grandiosity, hostility, and psychotic disorganization than lithium during the first week of treatment. In addition, due in part to a rapid lithium titration schedule, dropouts in the lithium-treated patients were higher (38%) than in the chlorpromazine-treated group. Nevertheless, by three weeks of treatment, both drugs were significantly and comparably effective. Prien et al. concluded that chlorpromazine was superior to lithium in ameliorating agitation in highly active patients. This finding was consistent with the results of all but one study (Spring et al., 1970). The two medications were equally effective in mildly active patients. Most studies found lithium superior to antipsychotics in the treatment of core manic symptoms.

In summary, data from the controlled trials reviewed above indicate that lithium is superior in efficacy to placebo and is relatively slow in onset of action, usually requiring a 2- to 3-week trial at therapeutic levels to reach maximum effect. These data also suggest that lithium is superior to standard antipsychotics for the normalization of mood symptoms and exerts antipsychotic effects in its own right. On the other hand, standard antipsychotics appear to have a more rapid onset of action and may therefore be more effective initially and in patients with significant agitation.

Valproate

Valproate and its divalproex formulation have been shown to be effective in the treatment of acute mania in eight controlled trials (Bowden et al., 1994; Brennan, Sandyk, & Borsook, 1994; Emrich, Von Zerssen, & Kissling, 1981; Freeman et al., 1992; Hirschfeld et al., 1999; Pope et al., 1991; Post et al., 1984; Tohen et al., 2001). Two of these trials led to FDA approval of divalproex for the treatment of acute mania in bipolar disorder (Bowden et al., 1994; Pope et al., 1991). These eight studies include comparisons of valproate with placebo in crossover trials without concomitant psychotropics (Brennan et al., 1994; Emrich et al., 1981; Post et al., 1984), with placebo in a parallel group trial of lithium-refractory or intolerant patients (Pope et al., 1991), with lithium in two parallel groups trials (Freeman et al., 1992; Hirschfeld et al., 1999), with placebo and lithium in a parallel group trial (Bowden et al., 1994), and with olanzapine in a parallel trial (Tohen et al., 2001). In the first parallel-group, double-blind, placebo-controlled study, Pope et al. (1991) studied 36 patients with bipolar disorder, manic phase (*DSM-III-R*), who were either lithium-refractory or lithium-intolerant, randomized to divalproex or placebo. Compared with the placebo-treated patients, the divalproex-treated patients displayed statistically significant improvement on all three measures used to assess response: the Young Mania Rating Scale (YMRS), the BPRS, and the Global Assessment of Functioning Scale (GAF). Of 17 patients receiving divalproex, 9 (53%) displayed greater than 50% reduction on the YMRS than 2 (10%) of 19 patients receiving placebo. There was no statistically significant difference in the frequency of side effects between the two groups. Furthermore, in responders, the onset of antimanic response to divalproex appeared rapid, with significant improvement evident within the first week of treatment despite a gradual titration schedule.

Two parallel-group, double-blind, randomized trials compared valproate with lithium (Freeman et al., 1992; Hirschfeld et al., 1999). In the first study, both drugs produced significant and comparable improvement as measured by the MRS of the SADS-C, the BPRS, and the GAF (Freeman et al., 1992). Patients with mixed mania were more likely to respond to valproic acid than to lithium. The second lithium comparison trial was designed to assess the tolerability of divalproex loading (30 mg/kg/d × 2 days, then 20 mg/kg/d) and was not powered sufficiently to detect differences in efficacy (Hirschfeld et al., 1999). Notably, there were no significant differences in adverse events among patients randomized to divalproex loading, divalproex gradual titration, or lithium gradual titration. The findings from this latter double-blind, randomized trial of divalproex (Hirschfeld et al., 1999) oral loading confirmed the findings of three other reports that divalproex loading was well tolerated (Keck et al., 1993; McElroy et al., 1993, 1996).

In the second major double-blind, placebo-controlled trial, Bowden et al. (1994) compared the efficacy of divalproex, lithium, and placebo in a 3-week trial in 176 inpatients meeting criteria for manic disorder (Research Diagnostic Criteria; Spitzer, Endicott, & Robins, 1978). The proportion of patients improving at least 50% on the MRS of the SADS-C were comparable to that for divalproex (48%) and lithium (49%) and superior to that for placebo (25%). Among divalproex responders, significant improvement was evident by Day 5 of treatment using a gradual titration schedule beginning at an initial dose of 750 mg/d. Significantly more lithium-treated patients dropped out of this study due to side effects than patients receiving divalproex or placebo. In post hoc analyses of data from this study (Bowden et al., 1994), Swann et al. found that neither the presence of depressive symptoms during mania (1997) nor the number of prior mood episodes (1999) had an adverse impact on valproate response.

Divalproex was recently compared with olanzapine in a 3-week, double-blind trial in bipolar inpatients with acute manic or mixed episodes (Tohen et al., 2001). Olanzapine was started at a dose of 15 mg/d; divalproex was started at 750 mg/d and titrated to a maximum of 2500 mg/d (and serum levels of 50 to 125 mg/L). Overall, the olanzapine-treated group displayed significantly greater improvement on the YMRS from baseline to end point compared with the divalproex group. Olanzapine was associated with significantly more common adverse events of somnolence, dry mouth, and increased appetite; divalproex, with significantly more nausea, vomiting, and diarrhea. Since these data have not yet been presented in peer-reviewed format, they must be considered preliminary.

Divalproex was compared with haloperidol in an open randomized trial in bipolar inpatients with psychotic mania (McElroy et al., 1996). In this study, 36 patients in a manic or mixed episode with psychotic features received either divalproex rapid loading (20 mg/kg/d) or halperidol (0.2 mg/kg/d) for 6 days. Divalproex and haloperidol were equally effective in reducing both manic and psychotic symptoms. The greatest rate of improvement for both drug regimens occurred over the first 3 days of treatment. Adverse events were infrequent and minor for both drugs, except for extrapyramidal side effects, which were significantly more common with haloperidol. The improvement in psychosis observed with divalproex was consistent with findings in two other studies (Bowden et al., 1994; Pope et al., 1991) and with improvement in manic psychosis produced by lithium in earlier studies.

Valproate has also been studied as treatment adjunctive to standard antipsychotics in the treatment of acute bipolar mania (Muller-Oerlinghausen et al., 1999). In a multicenter, double-blind, parallel-group, 3-week trial conducted in Europe, 136 patients receiving standard antipsychotics were randomized to valproate or placebo. By study termination, significantly more valproate-treated patients displayed a decrease in concomitant antipsychotic medications.

In summary, data from the controlled trials reviewed above indicate that valproate has a broad spectrum of efficacy in acute manic and mixed episodes (with or without psychosis) and appears to be comparable to lithium and haloperidol in overall antimanic efficacy. Further data are required to compare the efficacy of valproate with that of olanzapine.

Carbamazepine

Although 14 double-blind controlled trials have found carbamazepine to be effective in the treatment of acute mania (Keck, McElroy, & Nemeroff, 1992), only five of these studies are not confounded by the use of concomitant agents with antimanic effects (Ballenger & Post, 1978; Grossi, Sacchetti, & Vita, 1984; Lerer et al., 1987; Okuma et al., 1979; Small et al., 1991). In the only placebo-controlled trial (N = 19), which used a crossover design, Ballenger and Post (1978) reported that 63% of patients receiving carbamazepine (from 11 to 65 days) displayed significant improvement on global nursing-staff measures of depression, mania, anxiety, anger, and psychosis and on the BPRS. Patients typically experienced a relapse on placebo. In studies comparing carbamazepine with lithium, Lerer et al. (1987) found a trend toward greater improvement on the majority of BPRS items in the lithium-treated group, a trend that may have become significant with a larger sample (N = 28). Additionally, only 4 (29%) of 14 patients receiving carbamazepine were evaluated as having a good response, compared with 11 (79%) of 14 patients receiving lithium. In the second lithium comparison study, 70% of patients randomized to lithium or carbamazepine dropped out by 8 weeks of treatment because of lack of efficacy (Small et al., 1991). Of the remaining patients, 36% of carbamazepine-treated patients were rated as improved (at least partial remission of symptoms), compared with 37% of lithium-treated patients.

Carbamazepine has also been compared with chlorpromazine in two studies (Grossi et al., 1984; Okuma et al., 1979). Okuma et al. (1979) compared the two drugs in 60 acutely manic patients in a 6-week trial and reported a 66% overall rate of improvement for the carbamazepine group compared, with 54% improvement in the chlorpromazine group. In addition, carbamazepine was better tolerated. Grossi et al. (1984) reported similar results in a 3-week study (N = 37), with 55% of carbamazepine-treated and 68% of chlorpromazine-treated patients demonstrating at least partial improvement. Pooled data from these five randomized, controlled trials of carbamazepine in acute bipolar mania revealed an overall response rate to carbamazepine of 50%, compared with 56% for lithium-treated and 61% for chlorpromazine-treated control groups (differences not significant).

Typical Antipsychotics (Neuroleptics)

Prior to the introduction of lithium, antipsychotic medications were one of the few available classes of medications for the treatment of acute mania and as maintenance treatment for patients with bipolar disorder (Baldessarini, 1985). However, the emergence of lithium, valproate, and carbamazepine limited the role of typical antipsychotics in bipolar disorder to the acute treatment of psychotic mania or psychotic depression and as maintenance treatment in patients refractory to monotherapy or combination therapy with lithium, valproate, or carbamazepine (Hirschfeld et al., 1994). Despite the availability of antimanic/mood-stabilizing agents without the liabilities of antipsychotic side effects, antipsychotics remain the most commonly used adjunctive treatments for psychotic mania (Sachs et al., 2000).

There is one double-blind, placebo-controlled study of a standard antipsychotic in the treatment of acute bipolar mania (Klein, 1967). In that study, 13 patients with "manic excitement" were randomized to chlorpromazine (1200 mg/d), imipramine (300 mg/d), or placebo for 7 weeks. Response was assessed on a global outcome scale ranging from −9 (poorest outcome) to +9 (best outcome). Chlorpromazine was significantly superior to placebo and imipramine on global outcome (6.1 compared with 2.0 and −2.8, respectively). Most controlled studies of typical antipsychotics in acute mania, which evaluated chlorpromazine or haloperidol, are comparisons with lithium and were reviewed above. Four other controlled monotherapy studies found comparable efficacy when typical antipsychotics were compared with carbamazepine (Grossi et al., 1984; Okuma et al., 1979), valproate (McElroy et al., 1996), or risperidone (Segal et al., 1998).

Atypical Antipsychotics

No double-blind, randomized controlled trial of clozapine in the treatment of patients with bipolar disorder has been published. Data from a number of open trials suggest that clozapine may have acute and long-term mood-stabilizing effects in bipolar disorder, including in patients with mixed mania and/or rapid cycling refractory to treatment with mood stabilizers, typical antipsychotics, and electroconvulsive therapy (Barbini et al., 1997; Calabrese et al., 1996; Cole et al., 1993; Green et al., 2000; McElroy et al., 1991; Zarate, Tohen, & Baldessarini, 1995). The successful use of clozapine in acute mania has been reported in at least three prospective open-label studies (Barbini et al., 1997; Calabrese et al., 1996; Green et al., 2000). In the first report, 13 (87%) of 15 patients with acute mania, all of whom had failed to respond to a minimum 6-week trial of 500mg/d chlorpromazine equivalents of antipsychotic treatment in conjunction with lithium (mean serum level, 0.8 mmol/L), were rated as much or very much improved with clozapine (Green et al., 2000). In the second study, 25 acutely manic patients with *DSM-III-R* bipolar or schizoaffective disorder refractory to or unable to tolerate lithium, valproate, or carbamazepine, and at least two typical antipsychotics, received a 13-week trial of clozapine monotherapy after a 7-day washout (Calabrese et al., 1996). The mean *(SD)* peak dose of clozapine was 494 mg/d (145). Eighteen (72%) patients displayed marked improvement on the YMRS and eight (32%) had marked improvement on the BPRS, defined as 50% or greater improvement on either scale. In the third study, 30 hospitalized acutely manic patients were randomized to clozapine or chlorpromazine for a 3-week trial (Barbini et al., 1997). Although clozapine-treated patients exhibited significantly lower YMRS scores after 2 weeks of treatment, there were no significant differences between the two groups at the end of the trial. A limitation of the study was the lower mean dose of clozapine (166 mg/d) compared with chlorpromazine (310 mg/d). The authors also noted that the observed response was more rapid for patients receiving clozapine than for those receiving chlorpromazine.

Four double-blind, randomized controlled trials of olanzapine in the treatment of acute mania have been reported (Tohen et al., 1999, 2000, 2001; Berk, Ichim, & Brook, 1999). Two were placebo-controlled studies that led to the recent FDA indication for acute mania (Tohen et al., 1999, 2000). In the first placebo-controlled trial, 139 inpatients with bipolar I disorder were randomized to olanzapine ($N = 70$) or placebo ($N = 69$) for up to 3 weeks (Tohen et al., 1999). Olanzapine was begun at 10 mg/d and adjusted by 5-mg/d increments within a range of 5 to

20 mg/d; the median modal dose was 15 mg/d. The olanzapine group displayed significantly greater improvement than the placebo group on the YMRS, the CGI-BP severity of mania, and the PANSS total and positive symptom scores. Olanzapine-treated patients also displayed a significantly higher response rate (defined at 50% or greater improvement in YMRS score) of 49% than the 24% in the placebo group. However, olanzapine did not separate from placebo on the YMRS until the third week of treatment.

In the second placebo-controlled trial, 115 inpatients were randomized to olanzapine ($N = 55$) or placebo ($N = 60$) for up to 4 weeks (Tohen et al., 2000). This study used a higher olanzapine starting dose of 15 mg/d. As in the first study, the olanzapine group displayed significant improvement than the placebo group on the YMRS, CGI-BP severity of mania, and PANSS total and positive symptom scores. Unlike in the first study, these differences were evident by the end of the first week of the trial. The olanzapine group also exhibited significantly higher response (65% vs. 43%, respectively) and remission (61% vs. 36%) rates than the placebo group. In this trial, a higher proportion of patients had mixed episodes that allowed for analysis of improvement in depressive symptoms during mania. In this analysis, patients presenting with prominent depressive symptoms during mania (HAMD-21 scores ≥ 21 at baseline) showed a significant reduction in HAMD-21 total scores with olanzapine compared with placebo.

In the third controlled trial, 30 inpatients with acute mania were randomized to olanzapine ($N = 15$) or lithium ($N = 15$) for 4 weeks (Berk et al., 1999). Olanzapine was administered at a fixed dose of 10 mg/d and lithium at 800 mg/d (mean serum level, 0.7 mmol/L). There were no significant differences between the two treatment groups on any primary outcome measure, including the Mania Scale and BPRS total scores and the CGI-improvement scale. However, olanzapine-treated patients displayed significantly greater improvement than lithium-treated patients on the CGI-severity of illness scale at the end of 4 weeks. The fourth controlled trial was a double-blind, randomized, 3-week inpatient head-to-head comparison of olanzapine and divalproex described previously (Tohen et al., 2000).

To date, there are no placebo-controlled trials of risperidone monotherapy in patients with acute bipolar mania. However, there are two double-blind active comparator studies of risperidone (Sachs & Risperidone Study Group, 1999; Segal et al., 1998). In the first study, 45 inpatients were randomized to risperidone 6 mg/d ($N = 15$), haloperidol 10 mg/d ($N = 15$), lithium 800–1200 mg/d (with serum levels of 0.6–1.2 mmol/L) ($N = 15$) for up to 4 weeks (Segal et al., 1998). All three treatment groups displayed significant reductions in manic symptoms as measured by the YMRS from baseline to end point. There were no significant differences among the three treatments in reductions on the YMRS, BPRS, CGI, and GAF from baseline to end point. There were no significant differences in extrapyramidal side effects between the haloperidol and risperidone groups. The results of this study were limited by the small sample size, use of prn lorazepam throughout the 28-day trial, and relatively low lithium levels.

The second trial evaluated the efficacy of risperidone versus haloperidol and placebo as an adjunctive agent to lithium or valproate in hospitalized patients with acute mania (Sachs & Risperidone Study Group, 1999). Patients who were receiving lithium or valproate were randomized to risperidone 1–6 mg/d ($N = 52$), haloperidol ($N = 53$), or placebo ($N = 51$) for up to 3 weeks. Patients treated with risperidone or haloperidol displayed significantly greater improvement on the YMRS at 1 week, at 2 weeks, and at end point (LOCF), but not at 3 weeks of treatment. There were no significant differences between the risperidone and placebo groups in BPRS and HAMD total scores from baseline to end point. These data have been presented only in abstract form to date and thus must be regarded as preliminary.

Ziprasidone has been studied in the treatment of acute bipolar mania in one placebo-controlled trial (Keck & Ice, 2000). In this 3 week trial, 197 patients were randomized in a 2 : 1 ratio to ziprasidone (80 mg on Day 1; 160 mg/d thereafter) or placebo. Ziprasidone-treated patients displayed significantly greater improvement than placebo-treated patients on the MRS by the second day of the study. Similar significant separations of ziprasidone from placebo were observed on the CGI-severity scale at Day 4 and the PANSS positive subscale at Day 7. These differences remained significant for the remainder of the study. Ziprasidone was also significantly superior to placebo in improvement on the PANSS total score and GAF from baseline to end point. Somnolence and dizziness were the most frequently reported adverse events in association with ziprasidone. There were no significant differences between ziprasidone and placebo in measures of neurological side effects. The results of this study have not yet been published in a peer-reviewed journal. Nevertheless, these findings are consistent with an earlier report of ziprasidone's efficacy at higher doses (160 mg/d) in treating patients with schizoaffective disorder, bipolar type, who were acutely manic (Keck, Reeves, & Harrigan, 2001).

No randomized controlled trials of quetiapine in the treatment of acute bipolar mania have been reported to date. The findings of several open-label studies suggest that quetiapine may have antimanic properties (Ghaemi & Katzow, 1999; Dunayevich & Strakowski, 2000; Dunayevich et al., 2000).

New Antiepileptics

Six new antiepileptic medications—gabapentin, lamotrigine, oxcarbazepine, topiramate, tiagabine, and zonisamide—are being investigated as potential antimanic agents (McElroy & Keck, 2000; Keck & Manji, in press). No controlled trials have been reported for topiramate, tiagabine, or zonisamide.

Two controlled studies evaluated gabapentin in the treatment of bipolar mania (Pande et al., 2000; Frye et al., 2000). In the first study, 117 outpatients with bipolar I disorder who experienced breakthrough manic symptoms (defined as a YMRS total score ≥ 12) while receiving therapeutic doses of lithium, valproate, or the combination were randomized to adjunctive treatment with gabapentin 600 to 3600 mg/d ($N = 55$) or placebo ($N = 59$) (Pande et al., 2000). Patients receiving placebo displayed significantly greater improvement in YMRS total scores than patients receiving gabapentin. In the second controlled trial, 28 patients with treatment-refractory bipolar I ($N = 13$) or bipolar II ($N = 15$) disorder received 6-week crossover trials of gabapentin, lamotrigine, or placebo using the CGI-BP as the primary efficacy measure (Frye et al., 2000). The CGI-BP response rate for manic symptoms did not significantly differ among the three groups: gabapentin 20%; lamotrigine 44%; and placebo 32%. However, manic symptoms were quite low at baseline, raising the possibility that meaningful differences among the three treatments might not have been detected.

Three controlled studies have evaluated lamotrigine in bipolar patients with acute mania (Frye et al., 2000; Ichim, Berk, & Brook, 2000). The first study was described immediately above (Frye et al., 2000). In the second study, 16 outpatients with mania, hypomania, or mixed episodes who were refractory to or intolerant of lithium and who had a YMRS total score of >12, were randomized to receive lamotrigine ($N = 8$) or placebo ($N = 8$) for 8 weeks (Anand et al., 1999). Lamotrigine or placebo was either added to ongoing lithium treatment in inadequately responsive patients or administered as monotherapy to lithium-intolerant patients. Lamotrigine was initiated at 12.5 mg/d and titrated to a maximum dose of 200 mg/d. There were no significant differences between lamotrigine- and placebo-treated groups in changes in YMRS total scores and in rates of response (defined as ≥50% reduction in YMRS score from baseline to end point). Response rates were for lamotrigine 63% and 50% for placebo. Its small sample size and high placebo response rate limited this trial.

In the third controlled trial, 30 hospitalized patients with acute bipolar mania were randomized to lithium 800 mg/d (mean serum level 0.7 mmol/L) ($N = 15$) or lamotrigine 25 mg/d for Week 1, 50 mg/d for Week 2, and 100 mg/d for Week 3 ($N = 15$) for up to 4 weeks (Ichim, Berk, & Brook, 2000). Both treatment groups improved significantly on the MRS, BPRS, GAF, and CGI-improvement scales from baseline to Week 4, with no significant difference between groups. The small sample size, low lithium levels, and absence of a placebo control group limited this trial.

Oxcarbazepine, the 10-keto analogue of carbamazepine, will soon be available in the United States. This antiepileptic agent has been studied in two controlled trials as monotherapy for patients with acute bipolar mania (Muller & Stoll, 1984; Emrich et al., 1985). In the first trial, 20 patients were randomized to receive oxcarbazepine (900 to 1200 mg/d) or haloperidol (15 to 20 mg/d) for up to 2 weeks (Muller & Stoll, 1984). Both treatment groups displayed a mean reduction of 55% on the Bech-Rafaelson Mania Scale. In the second study, a placebo-controlled crossover trial, four of six patients exhibited a ≥50% on the Inpatient Multidimensional Psychiatric Scale with oxcarbazepine (Emrich et al., 1985).

Topiramate is a sulfamate-substituted monosaccharide antiepileptic agent with a number of putative mechanisms of action in epilepsy. These include blockade of voltage-gated sodium channels, antagonist activity at the kainate/AMPA glutamate receptor, enhancement of GABA activity at the $GABA_A$ receptor by binding to a nonbenzodiazepine receptor site, and carbonic anhydrase inhibition (Meldrum, 1996). Topiramate has the potentially advantageous side effect of anorexia and weight loss in some patients (Norton, Potter, & Edwards, 1997; Rosenfeld, Schaefer, & Pace, 1997). No randomized clinical trials of topiramate in the treatment of any phase of bipolar disorder have been published to date. Preliminary results from five open trials suggest that topiramate may possess antimanic properties and may be associated with weight loss in some patients (Calabrese et al., 1998; Chengappa et al., 1999; Kusumaker et al., 1997; Marcotte, 1998; McElroy et al., 2000).

Tiagabine is a selective GABA reuptake inhibitor approved for the treatment of partial seizures. There are no randomized controlled trials of tiagabine in any phase of bipolar disorder. Preliminary open trials provide contradictory data. One report suggested that tiagabine was effective as an adjunctive agent in patients with rapid cycling (Schaffer & Schaffer, 1999). However, in a second report, none of eight patients who received tiagabine alone or as adjunctive treatment for acute bipolar mania responded after a 2-week trial (Grunze et al., 1999).

Zonisamide is a sulfonamide derivative antiepileptic with several potential mechanisms of action. These include blockade of voltage-sensitive sodium channels and T-type calcium currents, modulation of gabaergic and dopaminergic systems, and free radical scavenging (Oomen & Mathews, 1999). Zonisamide (100 to 600 mg/d) was evaluated in one open trial as adjunctive treatment in 15 patients with acute bipolar mania (Kanba et al., 1994). One third of patients displayed marked global improvement and 80% at least moderate improvement.

Calcium Channel Blockers

Two recent randomized, controlled trials have helped clarify the efficacy of verapamil in the treatment of acute bipolar mania (Janicak et al., 1998; Walton, Berk, & Brook, 1996). The first study was a single-blind 28-day trial comparing verapamil with lithium in 40 patients (Walton et al., 1996). Patients receiving lithium showed significantly greater improvement on all efficacy measures (BPRS, Mania Rating Scale, CGI, GAF) than those receiving verapamil. In a 3-week, double-blind, placebo-controlled study of verapamil in 32 patients with acute mania, there were no significant differences in mean absolute change scores at end point between the two groups (Janicak et al., 1998). In contrast, two placebo-controlled, randomized trials reported that nimodipine, an L-type calcium channel blocker, was more effective than placebo as monotherapy in ultrarapidly cycling patients (Pazzaglia et al., 1993) or as adjunctive therapy to carbamazepine in patients with refractory illness (Pazzaglia et al., 1998). Based on the results of these studies, and on the limitations inherent in earlier studies of verapamil, it appears that of the calcium channel blockers, nimodipine and perhaps other L-type channel blockers are the most promising agents for patients with bipolar disorder. Further randomized, controlled trials of these agents are needed.

Thyroid Augmentation

Despite over two decades of study, there are still no controlled trials of thyroid augmentation in the treatment of any phase of bipolar disorder. Two preliminary reports suggested that high doses of thyroxine were beneficial for patients with rapidly-cycling bipolar disorder (Bauer & Whybrow, 1990). However, this strategy is associated with potential risks, and its efficacy needs to be demonstrated in more rigorous studies.

ACUTE BIPOLAR DEPRESSION

Lithium and Antidepressants

The pharmacological treatment of acute bipolar depression remains remarkably understudied. The majority of controlled trials have evaluated the efficacy of lithium in comparison to placebo or tricyclic antidepressants (Baron et al., 1975; Donnelly et al., 1976; Fieve, Platman, & Plutchik, 1968; Goodwin et al., 1969, 1972; Greenspan et al., 1979; Keck et al., 2000; Mendels, 1976; Nemeroff et al., 2001; Noyes et al., 1974; Stokes et al, 1971). All but one (Nemeroff et al., 2001) placebo-controlled study of lithium utilized crossover designs with short time intervals, ranging from 1 to 28 days of lithium or placebo treatment. These short intervals limit the interpretation of the study results because of the potential confounding effects of lingering lithium activity during the placebo period and because optimal lithium response for some patients may have required a longer trial (Zomberg & Pope, 1993). Furthermore, abrupt discontinuation of lithium may have contributed to a more rapid rate of episode recurrence than that attributable to the natural course of the illness (Suppes et al., 1991). With these limitations in mind, pooled results from five crossover studies that provided data to assess degree of response revealed that 29 (36%) of 80 patients with acute bipolar depression displayed an unequivocal response to lithium; 63 (79%) patients had at least partial improvement (Zomberg & Pope, 1993).

Two controlled studies assessed the efficacy of lithium against tricyclic antidepressants (Donnelly et al., 1978; Watanabe, Ishino, & Otsuki, 1975). In the first study, a 5-week parallel-group trial in five patients, lithium and imipramine were comparably effective (Donnelly et al., 1978). However, lithium serum concentrations were low (0.3–0.6 mmol/L) in this trial. The second study compared imipramine, lithium, and placebo in a 3-week parallel-group trial involving 29 patients (Watanabe et al., 1975). Although both lithium and imipramine were superior to placebo, the mean decrease in depression scores for the imipramine-treated patients (58%) was significantly better than for the lithium-treated patients (32%).

A number of other controlled studies examined the efficacy of tricyclics in comparison to other antidepressants (Altshuler et al., 1995; Ashberg-Wistedt, 1982; Baumhackl et al., 1989; Cohn et al., 1986; Himmelhoch et al., 1991; Kessell & Holt, 1975; Levine et al., 1995; Nemeroff et al., 2001; Sachs et al., 1994). The most recent trial compared imipramine, paroxetine, and placebo added to lithium (Nemeroff et al., 2001). Preliminary results of this large, multicenter trial found a modest 15% difference in favor of both antidepressants over placebo, although these differences were not statistically significant. A post hoc analysis indicated that response in the lithium and placebo group was associated with plasma concentrations of ≥ 0.8 mol/L. The corresponding finding was a significant difference in favor of paroxetine over placebo in patients with lower lithium levels. Two other controlled studies comparing serotonin reuptake inhibitor (SRI) antidepressants with tricyclics had significant methodological limitations (Ashberg-Wistedt, 1982; Cohn et al., 1980). In the first study, a double-blind, randomized comparison of fluoxetine and imipramine with placebo, only 64 (72%) of 89 patients remained in the trial after 3 weeks, and only 44 (49%) completed the 6-week trial because of side effects or lack of efficacy (Cohn et al., 1980). Furthermore, 7 (16%) subjects completing the study received lithium; the remainder did not. If treatment dropouts are counted as treatment failures, the response rates in this study were not significantly different for fluoxetine (60%) and imipramine (40%), and both were superior to placebo (17%). In the second SRI comparison study, four patients were randomly assigned to zimelidine or desipramine in a crossover design for 4 weeks each, but the small sample size makes this study inconclusive (Ashberg-Wistedt, 1982).

Two studies compared tricyclics with monoamine oxidase inhibitors (MAOIs) (Baumhackl et al., 1989; Himmelhoch et al., 1991). In the most methodologically rigorous of these studies, tranylcypromine had significantly greater efficacy than imipramine in 56 patients (bipolar I, N = 24; bipolar II, N = 32) treated for four weeks without lithium (Himmelhoch et al., 1991). Of 26 tranylcypromine-treated patients, 21 (81%) displayed a significant antidepressant response compared with 10 (48%) of 21 imipramine-treated patients. Response rates did not differ between bipolar I and bipolar II patients. In the second study of a MAOI, moclobemide and imipramine (administered without lithium) had comparable efficacy in a 4-week trial of 32 patients (Baumhackl et al., 1989). A greater than 50% reduction in depressive symptoms was observed in 9 (53%) of 17 patients receiving moclobemide and 9 (60%) of 15 patients receiving imipramine.

Of the three remaining controlled trials of antidepressants for the treatment of bipolar depression, one study compared maprotiline and imipramine in 14 patients treated for 6 weeks (Kessell & Holt, 1975). In this study, 6 (67%) of 9 patients in the maprotiline group responded, and 2 (40%) of 5 patients treated with imipramine responded (differences not significant). In the second study, 19 patients with bipolar depression receiving lithium were randomized to bupropion or desipramine to assess the efficacy and rate of treatment-emergent mood elevation of the two antidepressants (Sachs et al., 1994). Although both medications produced comparable response rates, patients treated with desipramine (50%) were significantly more likely to switch into hypomania or mania than patients receiving bupropion (11%). These preliminary findings require confirmation in a larger study. Finally, there was no significant difference between inositol and placebo in a subgroup of only 6 patients with bipolar depression included as part of a larger study involving patients with unipolar depression ($N = 22$) (Levine et al., 1995). Notably, inositol was superior to placebo in the larger group with major depressive disorder. Significant differences between inositol and placebo might have emerged in bipolar depression with a larger sample.

Antidepressant-induced mood switching or cycle acceleration is an important risk of antidepressant treatment in patients with bipolar depression. Unfortunately, this phenomenon has not been systematically evaluated in most of the studies reviewed above. Two studies have examined the risk of antidepressant-induced mania and cycle acceleration (Altshuler et al., 1995; Stoll et al., 1994). In the first study, life chart methodology was used to detect cycle switching in 51 patients with treatment-refractory bipolar disorder (Altshuler et al., 1995). Of these, 18 (35%) patients were rated as having an antidepressant-induced manic episode. Acceleration of cycling was also found to be associated with antidepressant treatment in 26% of patients. The second study compared patients with antidepressant-associated mania ($N = 49$) and spontaneous mania ($N = 49$) in a case control study (Stoll et al., 1994). Antidepressant-associated mania was milder in severity and briefer in duration than spontaneous mania. Among antidepressants, MAOIs and bupropion were associated with the induction of milder manic episodes than either tricyclics or fluoxetine. These findings were in agreement with the study of Sachs et al. (1994), who found a lower switch rate associated with bupropion than with desipramine in patients also on mood stabilizers, and with the results of Himmelhoch et al. (1991), who found that 21% of tranylcypromine-treated patients developed euphoric hypomania not typically requiring hospitalization, whereas 25% of imipramine-treated patients became manic, 18% with mixed episodes and 11% requiring hospitalization. Interestingly, in a meta-analysis of the rate of treatment-emergent switch into mania, with data derived from clinical trials comparing SRIs (fluoxetine, fluvoxamine, paroxetine, and sertraline), tricyclics, or placebo in 415 patients with bipolar depression, Peet (1994) reported that manic switch occurred significantly more frequently with tricyclics (11%) than with SRIs (4%) or placebo (4%).

Antiepileptics

Three controlled studies have evaluated the efficacy of carbamazepine in the treatment of patients with unipolar and bipolar depression (Kramlinger & Post, 1989; Post et al., 1986; Small, 1990). Data from these studies indicate that, like lithium, carbamazepine may be less effective for the treatment of acute depression than for acute mania. In the first of these studies, a placebo-controlled crossover study (median 45 day per treatment interval), Post et al. (1986) reported marked improvement in 12 (34%) of 35 patients (24 bipolar, 11 unipolar) with treatment-resistant depression. A trend toward greater improvement in patients with bipolar than in those with unipolar depression was observed, and the switch to placebo was associated with deterioration in carbamazepine responders. Although the finding of a 34% marked response rate was comparable with placebo response rate in parallel-design studies, this response rate was, nevertheless, impressive given the treatment-refractory nature of the cohort. In the second study, Small (1990) compared the response of 28 patients (4 bipolar, 24 unipolar) with treatment-resistant depression in a 4-week trial of lithium, carbamazepine, or their combination. All patients were then treated with both drugs for an additional 4 weeks. Of patients receiving carbamazepine or the combination, 32% displayed moderate or marked improvement compared with 13% of lithium-treated patients. These results are consistent with those of Post et al. (1986), although the cohort studied by Small had significantly fewer bipolar patients. Finally, Kramlinger and Post (1989) evaluated the antidepressant effect of lithium versus placebo augmentation of carbamazepine and found that 6 (46%) of 13 patients who had not responded to carbamazepine alone responded to lithium augmentation.

There are no controlled trials of valproate in the treatment of acute bipolar depression. In three of four open studies, valproate appeared to be more effective for the treatment of acute mania than for depression (Calabrese et al., 1992, 1999; Lambert, 1992; McElroy et al., 1988a, 1988b).

Of the other antiepileptic agents being investigated for their potential efficacy in the treatment of bipolar disorder, only lamotrigine has been studied in a randomized, controlled trial in acute bipolar depression (Calabrese et al., 1999). In this trial, 195 patients with bipolar I depression were randomized to lamotrigine monotherapy 50 mg/d, 200 mg/d, or placebo. Both lamotrigine doses were superior to placebo. Although the difference between the two doses was not significant, there was a trend toward a modest advantage for the higher dose group. Switch rates were not significantly different among the three groups: placebo, 5%; lamotrigine 50 mg/d, 3%; and lamotrigine 200 mg/d, 8%.

MAINTENANCE TREATMENT

Lithium

During the late 1960s and 1970s, 10 double-blind, placebo-controlled studies involving 514 bipolar patients demonstrated that lithium was superior to placebo in preventing recurrent affective episodes (Hopkins & Gelenberg, 1994). The average relapse rate over 1 year was 34% for lithium-treated patients compared with 81% for those receiving placebo. These data also revealed that lithium exerted greater efficacy in preventing manic than in preventing depressive episodes. Of these 10 studies, 4 were discontinuation trials (Keck et al., 2000; Maj, 2000). Since abrupt discontinuation of lithium appears to precipitate relapse (Baldessarini et al., 1997), this design may have artificially inflated the recurrence rate in patients receiving placebo. Subsequent naturalistic treatment studies of patients maintained on lithium for more than 1 year indicate that a substantial number of patients do not respond adequately to lithium prophylaxis (Harrow et al., 1990; Maj, Pirozzi, & Kemali, 1991; O'Connell et al., 1991; Peselow et al., 1991; Prien & Potter, 1990).

Identification of clinical predictors of response to lithium prophylaxis has been an important area of inquiry over the past several decades. Predictors of favorable response to lithium prophylaxis include a family history of bipolar disorder (Maj et al., 1985; Mander, 1986; Mendlewicz, Fieve, & Stallone, 1973; Prien, Caffey, & Klett, 1974) and an illness course characterized by a mania-depression-euthymia episode sequence (Faedda et al., 1991; Grof et al., 1987; Haag et al., 1986; Koukopoulos et al., 1980). Conversely, predictors of poor maintenance efficacy include rapid cycling (Dunner, Fleiss, & Fieve, 1976), multiple prior episodes (Swann et al., 1999), co-occurring alcohol or substance use disorder (Himmelhoch et al., 1980), and familial negative affective style (Miklowitz et al., 1988, 2000). With other choices for maintenance treatment becoming available, assessment for these predictors is becoming increasingly important in clinical practice (Keck & Licht, 2000; McElroy et al., 1992).

In patients successfully treated with lithium prophylaxis, the risks of discontinuing lithium appear to be substantial. For example, in a meta-analysis by Suppes et al. (1991) of 14 studies involving a total of 257 bipolar patients who discontinue lithium, the risk of recurrent affective episodes was approximately 28 times higher per month without medication than with medication. More than 50% of patients who discontinued successful lithium maintenance treatment experienced a relapse (more often of mania than of depression) within 6 months. Other studies found that the risk of recurrence is significantly lower if lithium is gradually discontinued (Baldessarini et al., 1996).

The optimal maintenance serum concentration is also directly relevant to successful lithium prophylaxis. Gelenberg et al. (1989) found that the risk of relapse was 2.6 times higher in bipolar patients randomly selected for low (0.4–0.6 mol/L) serum concentrations than in those with standard (0.8–1.0 mol/L) levels. However, patients treated with standard concentrations experienced significantly more side effects. In a second analysis of data from this study, Keller et al. (1992) reported that patients randomly assigned to the lower range of lithium levels were more likely to experience subsyndromal symptoms and that their symptoms were more likely to worsen at any time than were the symptoms of patients in the standard-level group. Furthermore, the first occurrence of subsyndromal symptoms increased the risk of full-episode relapse fourfold. These findings suggest that the optimal longitudinal management of bipolar disorder requires titration of mood stabilizer therapy to eradicate subsyndromal symptoms in order to minimize the risk of their escalation into full-syndromic relapse.

From the studies reviewed above, it is clear that a significant proportion of patients with bipolar disorder does not respond adequately to lithium maintenance treatment. In addition, patients display a wide variation of responses to lithium, ranging from remission, partial remission with varying degrees of attenuation of length and/or severity of episodes, suppression of one phase of illness but not another, no response, and, finally, relapse after initial good response (Hopkins & Gelenberg, 1994).

Valproate

Bowden et al. (2000) recently published the results of a randomized, placebo-controlled, double-blind trial of divalproex and lithium treatment of outpatients with bipolar I disorder. To enter the study, patients were required to have experienced a manic episode within 3 months and to have had a prior episode within 3 years. Patients were treated with divalproex or lithium during an initial open-label stabilization phase prior to randomization. The doses of divalproex and lithium were titrated (blindly) to target serum trough concentrations of 71 to 125 microgm/mL or 0.8–1.2 mmol/L, respectively. There was no significant difference among the three treatment groups on the primary outcome measure, time to relapse for any mood episode. This negative finding is likely to have been attributable to the inclusion of a substantial proportion of mildly ill patients and the choice of outcome measure. Among patients who responded to divalproex for acute mania and were randomized to divalproex, response was superior to placebo in the proportion of patients not terminating for relapse (71% vs. 50%), the proportion of patients who maintained a full response during the 1-year study (41% vs. 13%), and the mean number of days in maintenance treatment (209 vs. 143). In addition, patients who received divalproex were significantly less likely to display depressive symptoms than patients receiving lithium. The results of this landmark study were consistent with those in previous retrospective case series and open trials suggesting that valproate possesses efficacy as a maintenance treatment in patients receiving the drug acutely (Puzynski & Klosiewicz, 1993). Clinical features associated with response to valproate maintenance treatment in these studies included mixed mania, rapid cycling, and absence of co-occurring personality disorder (Bowden et al., 1995).

Carbamazepine

Eight controlled studies have assessed the efficacy of carbamazepine for the maintenance treatment of patients with bipolar disorder (Bellaire et al., 1988; Coxhead, Silverstone, & Cookson, 1992; Denicoff et al., 1997; Greil et al., 1997; Lusznat, Murphy, & Nunn, 1988; Okuma et al., 1981; Placidi et al., 1986; Watkins, Callendar, & Thomas, 1987). The efficacy of carbamazepine in the prevention of affective episodes has been controversial (Murphy, Gannon, & McCennis, 1989; Dardennes et al., 1995). This controversy stems in part from the heterogeneity among the early controlled maintenance studies (Bellaire et al., 1988; Coxhead et al., 1992; Lusznat et al., 1988; Okuma et al., 1981), and the availability of only one placebo-controlled maintenance trial (Okuma et al., 1981). Interpretation of this latter study is further limited by the use of rescue medications other than lithium and carbamazepine to treat breakthrough symptoms. The use of these adjunctive medications limits the degree to which relapse rates can be directly attributed to carbamazepine or placebo in this study.

Two large, prospective, double-blind, long-term maintenance studies provide new data comparing the efficacy of carbamazepine with lithium (Denicoff et al., 1997; Greil et al., 1997). In the first study (Greil et al., 1997), 144 patients were randomized to lithium ($N = 74$; mean ± SD serum level, 0.6 ± 1 mmol/L) or carbamazepine ($N = 70$, mean ± SD dose, 621 ± 186 mg/d) and followed for 2.5 years. Affective relapse, hospitalization, need for supplemental medication, and adverse events requiring treatment discontinuation were used to define treatment failure. In survival analysis, there were no significant differences between the two treatment groups in time to affective relapse or hospitalization. However, significantly more patients receiving carbamazepine required adjunctive medications for symptomatic recurrences and experienced adverse events requiring treatment discontinuation. In a post hoc analysis of predictors of response, patients with classical features (bipolar I patients without mood-incongruent delusions and comorbidity) had a lower rehospitalization rate with lithium than with carbamazepine (Greil et al., 1998). For patients with nonclassical features (mixed states, bipolar II, and NOS), a trend in favor of carbamazepine was detected.

In the second lithium comparison trial, 52 outpatients with bipolar I and II disorder were randomly assigned to an initial year of treatment with lithium or carbamazepine, crossover to the alternate medication in the second year, followed by combination treatment in the third year (Denicoff et al., 1997). Among evaluable patients, 13 (31%) of 42 lithium-treated patients relapsed within the first year compared with 13 (37%) of 35 carbamazepine-treated patients. Of the 29 remaining patients, 7 (24%) relapsed on combination treatment. As in the previous study (Greil et al., 1997), a higher percentage of patients receiving carbamazepine withdrew due to adverse events. The percentage of patients who had moderate or marked improvement on the CGI was not significantly different: 33% on lithium; 31% on carbamazepine; and 55% on the combination. Patients with rapid cycling responded significantly better to the combination (56% response) than to lithium (28%) or carbamazepine (19%).

Antipsychotics (Typical and Atypical)

There are no parallel-group, double-blind, randomized maintenance trials of standard antipsychotics in the maintenance treatment of patients with bipolar disorder. Nevertheless, these agents are commonly used, often adjunctively, during maintenance treatment in clinical practice (Keck et al., 1996; Verdoux et al., 1996). Five open studies investigated the efficacy of depot antipsychotics alone or in combination with mood stabilizers (Littlejohn, Leslie, & Cookson, 1994; Lowe & Batchelor, 1986, 1990; Naylor & Scott, 1980; White, Cheung, & Silverstone, 1993). All studies found significant reductions in the number of manic episodes and overall time affectively ill when compared with prior treatment intervals when depot antipsychotics had not been administered.

Two open, prospective, comparative maintenance studies of depot flupenthixol in patients with bipolar disorder have also been reported (Ahlfors et al., 1981; Esparon et al., 1986). In the first study, Ahlfors et al. (1981) compared flupenthixol with lithium maintenance treatment for up to 3 years in 42 patients and found that neither treatment significantly reduced the frequency of affective episodes compared with the pretreatment course of illness. These investigators also described a second group of 162 patients with bipolar disorder who were refractory to or intolerant of lithium who received open-label flupenthixol decanoate for up to 3 years (Ahlfors et al., 1981). This latter group displayed significant reductions in the frequency of manic episodes and percentage time ill due to mania, and they also displayed significant increases in the frequency of depressive episodes and percentage time ill due to depression. In the second comparison trial, Esparon et al. (1986) compared the addition of depot flupenthixol or placebo to ongoing lithium treatment in a double-blind, crossover 2-year study of 15 patients, most of whom had responded poorly to lithium. No significant difference was found between flupenthixol and placebo.

In summary, although open trials of depot antipsychotics suggest efficacy for these agents as maintenance treatments for patients with bipolar disorder, the only two prospective comparison studies, both involving flupenthixol decanoate, failed to find a significant therapeutic benefit. In addition, the apparent greater efficacy of depot antipsychotics than of prior treatments in open trials may be due to noncompliance with the earlier treatments followed by more certain drug delivery inherent in injected medications.

In addition to improved neurological and neuroendocrinological side effect profiles, atypical antipsychotics appear to differ from neuroleptics by exerting favorable effects not just on manic but also on depressive symptoms (Keck & McElroy, 1997). Thus, they may have a more useful role in the maintenance treatment of patients with bipolar disorder. Unfortunately, there are no published double-blind, randomized, controlled maintenance trials of atypical antipsychotics in patients with bipolar disorder. However, data from open trials of clozapine (Suppes et al., 1999) and olanzapine (Namj'oshi et al., 2000) suggest that atypical antipsychotics may play an important role in maintenance treatment in the future. In the clozapine trial, Suppes et al. (1999) randomized 85 patients who met *DSM-IV* criteria for schizoaffective disorder, bipolar type, or bipolar disorder with treatment-refractory illness to add-on clozapine or treatment as usual. After 1 year, patients receiving clozapine displayed significant reductions in measures of mania and psychosis, as well as global improvement, compared with patients receiving treatment as usual. In addition, total medication use decreased significantly in the clozapine group. This open-label, randomized trial confirmed earlier reports suggesting that clozapine exerted long-term mood-stabilizing effects in patients with treatment-refractory bipolar disorder. Data bearing on the efficacy of olanzapine as a maintenance treatment for bipolar disorder come from an open-label 52-week extension protocol (Namj'oshi et al., 2000) for patients who participated in the first double-blind, randomized study (Tohen et al., 1999). Overall, improvement in mania and depression ratings were sustained throughout the study period, although some patients required additional treatment with lithium or fluoxetine for breakthrough symptoms. Notably, none of the 98 patients who participated developed tardive dyskinesia during long-term treatment. There are no data regarding the efficacy of risperidone, quetiapine, or ziprasidone in the maintenance phase of bipolar disorder.

FUTURE RESEARCH AND CONCLUSIONS

Much ground has been gained in recent years in improving pharmacological treatments for patients with bipolar disorder. The number and quality of clinical trials of treatments for bipolar disorder have grown substantially. Lithium, divalproex, carbamazepine, chlorpromazine, haloperidol, risperidone, olanzapine, and ziprasidone have all been shown to have efficacy in the treatment of acute bipolar mania in randomized, double-blind clinical trials, although lithium, divalproex, and olanzapine are the most well studied. Since the early 1990s, two of these medications, divalproex and olanzapine, received indications for the treatment of acute mania. Other atypical antipsychotics, including quetiapine, aripiprazole, and iloperidone, may also have potential as antimanic agents. Open trials and several small comparison trials suggest that some of the new antiepileptics (gabapentin, lamotrigine, tiagabine, oxcarbazepine, topiramate, and zonisamide) may be potential treatments for acute mania.

The pharmacological treatment of bipolar depression remains vastly understudied. Two important placebo-controlled trials were concluded in the last several years (Calabrese et al., 1999; Nemeroff et al., 2001). However, many questions regarding the treatment of bipolar depression are unanswered. Although a variety of antidepressants with novel mechanisms of action and improved side-effect profiles are available (e.g., SSRIs, bupropion, venlafaxine, nefazodone, and mirtazapine) or in development (e.g., reboxetine and NK-1 and CRH antagonists), the vast majority of these medications have not been systematically studied in patients with bipolar depression. The optimal duration of antidepressant treatment balanced against the largely unknown probability of switch induction is also unclear from the available research.

The efficacy of new psychotropic medications as long-term mood stabilizers has been very difficult to study in recent times (Keck et al., 2000). However, this is perhaps the most important aspect of the pharmacological treatment of this recurrent illness. Maintenance studies of lithium, valproate, and carbamazepine indicate that these agents possess efficacy in this phase of illness management, but that only a minority of patients do well with treatment with any one of these agents alone. No large, prospective, randomized, controlled maintenance trial has examined the potential merits of using combinations of mood stabilizers or a mood stabilizer with an atypical antipsychotic versus a mood stabilizer alone. Although olanzapine received an indication for the treatment of acute bipolar mania, its efficacy as a maintenance treatment has not been established.

Entirely novel treatment approaches are also being studied for their potential therapeutic value in various aspects of bipolar disorder. These include omega-3 fatty acids (Stoll et al., 1999), magnesium salts (Heiden et al., 1999), transcranial magnetic stimulation (George et al., 1997), and vagal nerve stimulation (Rush et al., 2000). Randomized, controlled trials of these treatment modalities are under way. Overall, the need for alternative agents and for studies of alternative strategies with these agents remains great. Two major initiatives undertaken in the late 1990s, the Stanley Foundation Bipolar Network (Leverich et al., 2001) and the NIMH Bipolar STEP Network (Sachs et al., 2000), should help fill in important gaps in our knowledge regarding the pharmacological treatment of bipolar disorder.

Notes

The following coding system, with codes provided at the end of each reference entry, indicates the nature of the supporting evidence from each citation:

1. Randomized, prospective, clinical trial. A study must include comparison groups with random assignment, blinded assessments, clear presentation of inclusion and exclusion criteria, state-of-the-art diagnostic methods, adequate sample size to provide statistical power, and clearly described statistical methods.
2. Clinical trial. A study in which an intervention is made but some aspect of the Type I study criteria is missing.
3. Clinical study. A study that has clear methodological limitations. These studies include open treatment studies designed to obtain pilot data, naturalistic studies, and case control studies.
4. A review with secondary data analysis (e.g., meta-analysis or comparably designed trials).
5. A review without secondary data analysis designed to convey an impression of the available literature.
6. Textbook, reference manual, case reports, small case series, and opinion papers.

References

Ahlfors, U. G., Basstrup, P. C., Dencker, S. J., et al. (1981). Flupenthixol decanoate in recurrent manic depressive illness. *Acta Psychiatrica Scandinavica, 64*, 226–237. (2)

Altshuler, L. L., Post, R. M., Leverich, G. S., et al. (1995). Antidepressant-induced mania and cycle acceleration: A controversy revisited. *American Journal of Psychiatry, 152*, 1130–1138. (3)

American Psychiatric Association. (1987). *Diagnostic and statistical manual of mental disorder* (3rd ed., Rev.). Washington, DC: Author. (6)

American Psychiatric Association. (1994). *Diagnostic and statistical manual of mental disorders* (4th ed.). Washington, DC: Author. (6)

Ashberg-Wistedt, A. (1982). Comparison between zimelidine and desipramine in endogenous depression. *Acta Psychiatrica Scandinavica, 66*, 129–138. (2)

Baldessarini, R. J. (1985). *Chemotherapy in psychiatry*. Cambridge: Harvard University Press. (6)

Baldessarini, R. J., Tondo, L., Faedda, G. L., et al. (1996). Effects of the rate of discontinuing lithium maintenance treatment in bipolar disorders. *Journal of Clinical Psychiatry, 57*, 441–448. (3)

Baldessarini, R. J., Tondo, L., Floris, G., et al. (1997). Reduced morbidity after gradual discontinuation of lithium treatment for bipolar I and II disorders: A replication study. *American Journal of Psychiatry, 154*, 551–553. (3)

Ballenger, J. C., & Post, R. M. (1978). Therapeutic effects of carbarnazepine in affective illness: A preliminary report. *Journal of Community Psychopharmacology, 2*, 159–175. (2)

Barbini, B., Scherillo, P., Benedetti, F., et al. (1997). Response to clozapine in acute mania in more rapid than that of chlorpromazine. *International Journal of Clinical Psychopharmacology, 12*, 109–112. (2)

Baron, M., Gershon, E. S., & Rudy, V., et al. (1975). Lithium carbonate response in depression. *Archives of General Psychiatry, 32*, 1107–1111. (2)

Bauer, M. S., & Whybrow, P. C. (1990). Rapid cycling bipolar affective disorder 11: Treatment of refractory rapid cycling with high-dose thyroxine: An preliminary study1. *Archives of General Psychiatry, 47*, 435–440. (3)

Baumhackl, U., Biziere, K., Fischback, G., et al. (1989). Efficacy and tolerability of moclobemide compared with imipramine in depressive disorder *(DSM-III)*: An Austrian double-blind, multicentre study. *British Journal of Psychiatry, 155*(Suppl.), 78–83. (2)

Bellaire, W., Demish, K., & Stoll, K. D., et al. (1988). Carbamazepine versus lithium in prophylaxis of recurrent affective disorders. *Psychopharmacology, 96*(Suppl.), 287. (2)

Berk, J. P., Ichim, L., & Brook, S. (1999). Olanzapine compared to lithium in mania: a double-blind randomized controlled trial. *International Journal of Clinical Psychopharmacology, 14*, 339–343. (2)

Bowden, C. L., Brugger, A. M., Swann, A. C., et al. (1994). Efficacy of divalproex sodium vs. lithium and placebo in the treatment of mania. *Journal of the American Medical Association, 271*, 918–924. (1)

Bowden, C. L., Calabrese, J. R., McElroy, S. L., et al. (2000). Efficacy of divalproex versus lithium and placebo in maintenance treatment of bipolar disorder. *Archives of General Psychiatry, 57*, 481–489. (1)

Bowden, C. L., Calabrese, J. R., Wallin, B., et al. (1995). Who enters therapeutic trials? Illness characteristics of patients in clinical drug studies of mania. *Psychopharmacology Bulletin, 31*, 103–109. (4)

Brennan, M. J. W., Sandyk, R., & Borsook, D. (1994). Use of sodium valproate in the management of affective disorders: Basic and clinical aspects. In H. M. Emrich, T. Okuma, & A. A. Muller (Eds.), *Anticonvulsants in affective disorders*. Amsterdam: Excerpta Medica. (2)

Calabrese, J. R., Bowden, C. L., Sachs, G. S., et al. (1999). A double-blind placebo-controlled study of lamotrigine monotherapy in outpatients with bipolar I depression. *Journal of Clinical Psychiatry, 60*, 79–88. (1)

Calabrese, J. R., Keck, P. E., Jr., McElroy, S. L., et al. (1998, June 2). Topiramate in severe treatment refractory mania [abstract]. In *New Research Abstracts of the Annual Meeting of the American Psychiatric Association*, Toronto, CA. (3)

Calabrese, J. R., Kimmel, S. E., Woyshville, M. J., et al. (1996). Clozapine for treatment-refractory mania. *American Journal of Psychiatry, 153*, 759–764. (3)

Calabrese, J. R., Markovitz, P. J., Kimmel, S. E., et al. (1992). Spectrum of efficacy of valproate in 78 rapid-cycling bipolar patient. *Journal of Clinical Psychopharmacology, 12*(Suppl.), 53–56 (3)

Chengappa, K. N. R., Rathmore, D., Levine, J., et al. (1999). Topiramate as add-on treatment for patients with bipolar mania. *Bipolar Disorders, 1*, 42–53. (3)

Cohn, J., Collins, G., Ashbrook, E., et al. (1980). A comparison of fluoxetine, imipramine and placebo in patients with bipolar depressive disorder. *International Clinical Psychopharmacology, 3*, 313–322. (2)

Cole, J. O., Banov, M. D., Green, A., et al. (1993, May 26). Clozapine in the treatment of refractory acute mania. In *New Research Program and Abstracts of the 146th Annual Meeting of the American Psychiatric Association,* San Francisco. (3)

Coxhead, N., Silverstone, T., & Cookson, J. (1992). Carbamazepine versus lithium in the prophylaxis of bipolar affective disorder. *Acta Psychiatrica Scandinavica, 85,* 114–118. (2)

Dardennes, R., Even, C., Bange, F., et al. (1995). Comparison of carbamazepine and lithium in the prophylaxis of bipolar disorders: A meta-analysis. *British Journal of Psychiatry, 166,* 375–381. (4)

Denicoff, K. D., Smith-Jackson, E. E., Disney, E. R., et al. (1997). Comparative prophylactic efficacy of lithium, carbamazepine and the combination in bipolar disorder. *Journal of Clinical Psychiatry, 58,* 470–478. (2)

Dilsaver, S., Chen, Y.-H., Swann, A. C., et al. (1994). Suicidality in patients with pure and depressive mania. *American Journal of Psychiatry, 151,* 1312–1315. (3)

Dion, G. L., Tohen, M., Anthony, W. A., et al. (1988). Symptoms and functioning of patients with bipolar disorder six months after hospitalization. *Journal of Hospital and Community Psychiatry,* 39, 652–657. (3)

Donnelly, E. F., Goodwin, F. K., Waldman, I. N., et al. (1978). Prediction of antidepressant responses to lithium. *American Journal of Psychiatry, 135,* 552–556. (2)

Dunayevich, E., & Strakowski, S. M. (2000). Quetiapine in treatment-resistant mania: A case report [letter]. *American Journal of Psychiatry, 157,* 1341. (6)

Dunayevich, E.,Tugrul, K. C., Strakowski, S. M., et al. (in press). Quetiapine the treatment of mania: A case series. *Journal of Clinical Psychiatry,* (3)

Dunner, D. L., Fleiss, J. L., & Fieve, R. R. (1976). Lithium carbonate prophylaxis failure. *British Journal of Psychiatry, 129,* 40–44. (4)

Emrich, H. M., Dose, M., Von Zerssen, D., et al. (1985). The use of sodium valproate, carbamazepine, and oxcarbazepine in patients with affective disorders. *Journal of Affective Disorders, 8,* 243–250. (2)

Emrich, H. M., Von Zerssen, D., & Kissling, W. (1981). On a possible role of GABA in mania: therapeutic efficacy of sodium valproate. In E. Costa, G. Dicharia, & G. L. Gessa (Eds.), *GABA and benzodiazepine receptors.* New York: Raven Press.

Esparon, J., Kollaori, J., Naylor, G. J., et al. (1986). Comparison of the prophylactic action of flupenthixol with placebo in lithium treated manic-depressive patients. *British Journal of Psychiatry, 148,* 723–725. (2)

Faedda, G. L., Baldessarini, R. J., Tohen, M., et al. (1991). Episode sequence in bipolar disorder and response to lithium treatment. *American Journal of Psychiatry, 148,* 1237–1239. (4)

Fieve, R. R., Platman, S. R., & Plutchik, R. R. (1968). The use of lithium in affective disorders: Acute endogenous depression. *American Journal of Psychiatry, 125,* 79–83. (2)

Freeman, T. W., Clothier, J. L., Pazzaglia, P., et al. (1992). A double-blind comparison of valproic acid and lithium in the treatment of acute mania. *American Journal of Psychiatry, 149,* 247–250. (2)

Frye, M., Ketter, T. A., Kimbrell, T. A., et al. (2000). A placebo controlled study of lamotrigine and gabapentin monotherapy in refractory mood disorders. *Journal of Clinical Psychopharmacology, 20,* 607–614. (2)

Garfinkel, P. E., Stancer, H. C., & Persad, E. (1980). A comparison of haloperidol, lithium carbonate and their combination in the treatment of acute mania. *Journal of Affective Disorders,* 2, 279–288. (2)

Gelenberg, A. J., Kane, J. M., Keller, M. B., et al. (1989). Comparison of standard and low serum levels of lithium for maintenance treatment of bipolar disorder. *New England Journal of Medicine, 321,* 1489–1493. (1)

George, M. S., Wasserman, E. M., Kimbrell, T. A., et al. (1997). Mood improvement following daily left frontal repetitive transcranial magnetic stimulation in patients with depression: A placebo-controlled crossover trial. *American Journal of Psychiatry, 154,* 1752–1756. (2)

Gershon, E. (1989). Recent developments in genetics of manic-depressive illness. *Journal of Clinical Psychiatry, 50*(Suppl.), 4–7. (6)

Ghaemi, S. N., & Katzow, J. J. (1999). The use of quetiapine for treatment-resistant bipolar disorder: A case-series. *Journal of American Clinical Psychiatry, 11,* 137–140 (3).

Gitlin, M. J., Swendsen, J., Heller, T. L., et al. (1995). Relapse and impairment in bipolar disorder. *American Journal of Psychiatry, 152,* 1635–1640. (3)

Goodwin, F. K., & Jamison, K. R. (1990). *Manic-depressive illness.* New York: Oxford University Press. (6)

Goodwin, F. K., Murphy, D. L., & Bunney, W. E., Jr. (1969). Lithium carbonate treatment in depression and mania: a longitudinal double-blind study. *Archives of General Psychiatry, 21,* 486–496. (2)

Goodwin, F. K., Murphy, D. L., Dunner, D. L., et al. (1972). Lithium response in unipolar versus bipolar depression. *American Journal of Psychiatry, 129,* 76–79. (2)

Green, A. I., Tohen, M., Patel, J. K., et al. (2000). Clozapine in the treatment of refractory psychotic mania. *American Journal of Psychiatry, 157,* 982–986. (3)

Greenspan, K., Schildkraut, J. J., Gordon, E. K., et al. (1979). Catecholamine metabolism in affective disorders. *Journal of Psychiatry Research, 7,* 171–182. (2)

Greil, W., Kleindienst, N., Erazo, N., et al. (1998). Differential response to lithium and carbamazepine in the prophylaxis of bipolar disorder. *Journal of Clinical Psychopharmacology, 18,* 455–460. (4)

Greil, W., Sacchetti, E., Vita, A., et al. (1997). Lithium versus carbamazepine in the maintenance treatment of bipolar disorders-a randomized study. *Journal of Affective Disorders, 43,* 151–161. (2)

Grof, E., Haag, M., Grof, P., et al. (1987). Lithium response and the sequence of episode polarities: Preliminary report on a Hamilton sample. *Progressive Neuropsychopharmacology and Biological Psychiatry, 11,* 199–203. (3)

Grossi, E., Sacchetti, E., & Vita, A. (1984). Carbamazepine vs. chlorpromazine in mania: A doubleblind trial. In H. M. Emrich, T. Okuma, & A. A. Muller (Eds.), *Anticonvulsants in affective disorders.* Amsterdam: Excerpta Medica.

Grunze, H., Erfurth, A., Marcuse, A., et al. (1999). Tiagabine appears not to be efficacious in the treatment of acute mania. *Journal of Clinical Psychiatry, 60,* 759–762. (3)

Gurling, H. (1995). Linkage findings in bipolar disorder. *Natural Genetics, 10,* 8–9. (4)

Haag, M., Heidorm, A., Haag, H., et al. (1986). Response to stabilizing lithium therapy and sequence of affective polarity. *Pharmacopsychiatry, 19,* 278–279. (3)

Harrow, M., Goldberg, J. F., Grossman, L. S., et al. (1990). Outcome in manic disorders: A naturalistic follow-up study. *Archives of General Psychiatry, 47,* 665–671. (2)

Heiden, A., Frey, R., Presslich, O., et al. (1999). Treatment of severe mania with intravenous magnesium sulphate as a supplemental therapy. *Psychiatry Research, 89,* 239–246. (3)

Himmelhoch, J. M., Neil, J. F., May, S. J., et al. (1980). Age, dementia, dyskinesias, and lithium response. *American Journal of Psychiatry, 137,* 941–945. (3)

Himmelhoch, J. M., Thase, M. E., Mallinger, A. G., et al. (1991). Tranylcypromine versus imipramine in anergic bipolar depression. *American Journal of Psychiatry, 148,* 910–915. (1)

Hirschfeld, R. M., Allen, M. H., McEvoy, J. et al. (1999). Safety and tolerability of oral loading of divalproex sodium in acutely manic bipolar patients. *Journal of Clinical Psychiatry, 60,* 815–818. (2)

Hirschfeld, R. M., Clayton, P. J., Cohen, R. E., et al. (1994). Practice guideline for the treatment of patients with bipolar disorder. *American Journal of Psychiatry Monograph, 151,* 1–31. (6)

Hopkins, H. S., & Gelenberg, A. J. (1994). Treatment of bipolar disorder—How far have we come? *Psychopharmacology Bulletin, 30,* 27–37. (5)

Ichim, L., Berk, M., & Brook, S. (2000). Lamotrigine compared with lithium in mania: A double-blind randomized controlled trial. *American Journal of Clinical Psychiatry, 12,* 5–10. (2)

Janicak, P., Sharma, R., Pandey, G., et al. (1998). Verapamil for the treatment of acute mania: A double-blind, placebo-controlled trial. *American Journal of Psychiatry, 155,* 972–973. (1)

Johnson, G., Gershon, S., Burdock, E., et al. (1971). Comparative effects of lithium and chlorpromazine in the treatment of acute manic states. *British Journal of Psychiatry, 119,* 267–276. (2)

Johnson, G., Gershon, S., Hekiman, L. J. (1968). Controlled evaluation of lithium and chlorpromazine in the treatment of manic states: An interim report. *Comprehensive Psychiatry, 9,* 563–573. (2)

Kanba, S., Yagi, G., Kamijima, K., et al. (1994). The first open study of Zonisamide, a novel anticonvulsant, shows efficacy in mania. *Progressive Neuropsychopharmacology and Biological Psychiatry, 18,* 707–715. (3)

Keck, P. E., Jr., & Ice, K. (2000, May 16). A three-week, double-blind, randomized trial of ziprasidone in the acute treatment of mania. In *New Research Program Abstracts of the American Psychiatric Association Annual Meeting*, Chicago.

Keck, P. E., Jr., & Licht, R. (2000). Antipsychotic medications in the treatment of mood disorders. In P. F. Buckley & J. L. Waddinton (Eds.), *Schizophrenia and mood disorders: The new drug therapies in clinical practice.* Boston: Butterworth Heineman.

Keck, P. E., Jr., & Manji, H. (in press). Pharmacologic treatment of acute bipolar mania and maintenance treatment. In D. Charney, J. Coyle, K. Davis, & C. B. Nemeroff (Eds.), *Psychopharmacology: The fifth generation of progress.* New York: Raven Press. (5)

Keck, P. E., Jr., & McElroy, S. L. (1997). The new antipsychotics and their therapeutic potential. *Psychiatric Annals, 27,* 320–331. (5)

Keck, P. E., Jr., McElroy, S. L., & Nemeroff, C. B. (1992). Anticonvulsants in the treatment of bipolar disorder. *Journal of Neuropsychiatry and Clinical Neuroscience, 4,* 595–605. (4)

Keck, P. E., Jr., McElroy, S. L., Strakowski, S. M., et al. (1996). Factors associated with maintenance neuroleptic treatment of patients with bipolar disorder. *Journal of Clinical Psychiatry, 57,* 147–151. (3)

Keck, P. E., Jr., McElroy, S. L., Strakowski, S. M., et al. (1998). Twelve-month outcome of bipolar patients following hospitalization for a manic or mixed episode. *American Journal of Psychiatry, 155,* 646–652. (3)

Keck, P. E., Jr., McElroy, S. L., Tugrul, K. C., et al. (1993). Valproate oral loading in the treatment of acute mania. *Journal of Clinical Psychiatry, 54,* 305–308. (3)

Keck, P. E., Jr., Reeves, K. R., & Harrigan, E. P. (2001). Ziprasidone in the treatment of schizoaffective disorder: Results from two double-blind, placebo-controlled trials. *Journal of Clinical Psychopharmcology, 21,* 27–35. (2)

Keck, P. E., Jr., Welge, J. A., McElroy, S. L., et al. (2000). Placebo effect in randomized, controlled studies of acute bipolar mania and depression. *Biological Psychiatry, 47,* 748–755. (4)

Keck, P. E., Jr., Welge, J. A., Strakowski, S. M., et al. (2000). Placebo effect in randomized, placebo-controlled maintenance studies of patients with bipolar disorder. *Biological Psychiatry, 47,* 756–759. (4)

Keller, M. B., Lavori, P. W., Kane, J. M., et al. (1992). Subsyndromal symptoms in bipolar disorder: A comparison of standard and low serum levels of lithium. *Archives of General Psychiatry, 49,* 371–376. (4)

Kessell, A., & Holt, F. (1975). A controlled study of tetracyclic antidepressant-maprotiline (Ludiomil). *Medical Journal of Australia, 1,* 773–776. (2)

Kessler, R. C., McGonagle, K. A., Zhao, S., et al. (1994). Lifetime and 12-month prevalence of *DSM-III-R* psychiatric disorders in the United States. *Archives of General Psychiatry, 51,* 8–19. (1)

Klein, D. F. (1967). Importance of psychiatric diagnosis in prediction of clinical drug effects. *Archives of General Psychiatry, 16,* 118–126. (2)

Koukopoulos, A., Reginaldi, D., Laddomada, P., et al. (1980). Course of the manic-depressive cycle and changes caused by treatments. *Pharmakopsychiatrie Neuropsychopharmakologie, 13,* 156–167. (3)

Kramlinger, K. G., & Post, R. M. (1989). The addition of lithium to carbamazepine. *Archives of General Psychiatry, 46,* 794–800. (3)

Kusumaker, V., Yathain, L. N., Haslam, D. R. S., et al. (1997). Treatment of mania, mixed stat rapid cycling. *Canadian Journal of Psychiatry, 42*(Suppl. 1), 79S–86S. (3) 85.

Lambert, P. A. (1992). Acute and prophylactic therapies of patients with affective disorders using valpromide (Dipropylacetamide). In H. M. Emrich, T. Okuma, & A. A. Muller (Eds.), *Anticonvulsants in affective disorders* (pp. 33–44). Amsterdam: Excerpta Medica. (3)

Lerer, B., Moore, N., Meyendorff, E., et al. (1987). Carbamazepine versus lithium in mania: A double-blind study. *Journal of Clinical Psychiatry, 48,* 89–93. (2)

Leverich, G. S., Nolen, W., Rush, A. J., et al. (2001). The Stanley Foundation Bipolar Treatment Outcome Network: 1. Longitudinal methodology. *Journal of Affective Disorders, 56,* 652–659. (3)

Levine, J., Barak, Y., Gonzalves, M., et al. (1995). Double-blind, controlled trial of inositol treatment of depression. *American Journal of Psychiatry, 152,* 792–794. (2)

Littlejohn, R., Leslie, F., & Cookson, J. (1994). Depot antipsychotics in the prophylaxis of bipolar affective disorder. *British Journal of Psychiatry, 165,* 827–829. (3)

Lowe, M. R., & Batchelor, D. H. (1986). Depot neuroleptics and manic depressive psychosis. *International Journal of Clinical Psychopharmacology,* (Suppl.), *1,* 53–62. (3)

Lowe, M. R., & Batchelor, D. H. (1990). Lithium and neuroleptics in the management of manic depressive psychosis. *Human Psychopharmacology, 5,* 267–274. (3)

Lusznat, R. M., Murphy, D. P., & Nunn, C. M. H. (1988). Carbamazepine versus lithium in the treatment and prophylaxis of mania. *British Journal of Psychiatry, 153,* 198–204. (2)

Maggs, R. (1963). Treatment of manic illness with lithium carbonate. *British Journal of Psychiatry, 109,* 56–65. (2)

Maj, M. (2000). The impact of lithium prophylaxis on the course of bipolar disorder: A review of the research evidence. *Bipolar Disorders, 2,* 93–101. (5)

Maj, M., Arena, F., Lovero, N., et al. (1985). Factors associated with response to lithium prophylaxis in *DSM-III* major depression and bipolar disorder. *Pharmacopsychiatry, 18,* 309–313. (3)

Maj, M., Pirozzi, R., & Kemali, D. (1991). Long-term outcome of lithium prophylaxis in bipolar patients. *Archives of General Psychiatry, 48,* 772. (3)

Mander, A. J. (1986). Clinical prediction of outcome and lithium response in bipolar affective disorder. *Journal of Affective Disorders, 11,* 35–41. (3)

Marcotte, D. (1998). Use of topiramate, a new antiepileptic as a mood stabilizer. *Journal of Affective Disorders, 50,* 245–251. (3)

McElroy, S. L, Dessain, E. C., Pope, H. G., Jr., et al. (1991). Clozapine in the treatment of psychotic mood disorders, schizoaffective disorder, and schizophrenia. *Journal of Clinical Psychiatry, 52,* 411–414. (3)

McElroy, S. L., & Keck, P. E., Jr. (2000). Pharmacologic agents for the treatment of acute bipolar mania. *Biological Psychiatry, 48,* 539–557. (5)

McElroy, S. L., Keck, P. E., Jr., Pope, H. G., Jr., et al. (1988). Valproate in the treatment of rapid cycling bipolar disorder. *Journal of Clinical Psychopharmacology, 8*, 275–279. (3)

McElroy, S. L., Keck, P. E., Jr., Pope, H. G., Jr., et al. (1992). Clinical and research implications of the diagnosis of dysphoric or mixed mania or hypomania. *American Journal of Psychiatry, 149*, 1633–1644. (4)

McElroy, S. L., Keck, P. E., Jr., Stanton, S. P., et al. (1996). A randomized comparison of divalproex oral loading versus haloperidol in the initial treatment of acute psychotic mania. *Journal of Clinical Psychiatry, 59*, 142–146. (3)

McElroy, S. L., Keck, P. E., Jr., & Strakowski, S. M. (1996). Mania, psychosis, and antipsychotics. *Journal of Clinical Psychiatry, 57*, 14–26. (5)

McElroy, S. L., Keck, P. E., Jr., Tugrul, K. C., et al. (1993). Valproate as a loading treatment in acute mania. *Neuropsychobiology, 27*, 146–149. (3)

McElroy, S. L., Pope, H. G., Jr., Keck, P. E., Jr., et al. (1988). Treatment of psychiatric disorders with valproate: A series of 73 cases. *Psychiatrie Psychobiologie, 3*, 81–85.

McElroy, S. L., Suppes, T., Keck, P. E., Jr., et al. (2000). Open-label adjunctive topiramate in the treatment of bipolar disorders. *Biological Psychiatry, 47*, 1025–1033. (3)

Meldrum, B. S. (1996). Update on the mechanism of action of antiepileptic drugs. *Epilepsia, 37*, 4–11. (6)

Mendels, J. (1997). Lithium in the treatment of depression. *American Journal of Psychiatry, 134*, 373–378. (2)

Mendlewicz, J., Fieve, R. R., & Stallone, F. (1973). Relationship between effectiveness of lithium therapy and family history. *American Journal of Psychiatry, 130*, 1011–1013. (3)

Miklowitz, D. J., Goldstein, M. J., Neuechterlein, K. H., et al. (1988). Family factors and the course of bipolar affective disorder. *Archives of General Psychiatry, 45*, 225–231.

Miklowitz, D. J., Simoneau, T. L., George, E. L., et al. (2000). Family-focused treatment of bipolar disorder: One-year effects of a psychoeducational program in conjunction with pharmacotherapy. *Biological Psychiatry*. (2)

Muller, A. A., & Stoll, K. D. (1984). Carbamazepine and oxcarbazepine in the treatment of manic syndromes: Studies in Germany. In H. M. Emrich, T. Okuma, & A. A. Muller (Eds.), *Anticonvulsants in affective disorders*. Amsterdam: Excerpta Medica.

Muller-Oerlinghausen, B., Retzow, A., Henn, F. A., et al. (1999). The European Valproate Mania Study Group: Valproate as an adjunct to neuroleptic medication for the treatment of acute episodes of mania: A prospective, randomized, double-bind, placebo-controlled multicenter trial. *Journal of Clinical Psychopharmacology, 20*, 195–203. (1)

Murphy, D. J., Gannon, M. A., & McGennis, A. (1989). Carbamazepine in bipolar affective disorder. *Lancet, 2*, 1151–1152. (4)

Murray, C. J. L., & Lopez, A. D. (1996). *The global burden of disease: Summary*. Cambridge: Harvard School of Public Health. (6)

Namj'oshi, M., Rajamannar, G., Jacobs, T. G., et al. (2000, May 13–18). Clinical, humanistic and economic outcomes associated with long-term olanzapine treatment of mania. In *New Research Program Abstracts of the Annual Meeting of the American Psychiatric Association*. Chicago. (3)

Naylor, G. J., & Scott, C. R. (1980). Depot injections for affective disorders. *British Journal of Psychiatry, 136*, 105. (3)

Nemeroff, C. B., Evans, D. L., Gyulai, L., et al. (2001). A double-blind, placebo-controlled comparison of imipramine and paroxetine in the treatment of bipolar depression. *American Journal of Psychiatry, 158*, 906–912. (1)

Norton, J., Potter, D., & Edwards, K. (1997). Sustained weight loss associated with topiramate [abstract]. *Epilepsia, 38*, 58. (4)

Noyes, R., Dempsey, G. M., Blum, A., et al. (1974). Lithium treatment of depression. *Comprehensive Psychiatry, 15*, 187–193. (2)

O'Connell, R. A., Mayo, J. A., Flatow, L., et al. (1991). Outcome of bipolar disorder on long-term treatment with lithium. *British Journal of Psychiatry, 159*, 123–129. (3)

Okuma, T., Inanga, K., Otsuki, S., et al. (1979). Comparison of the antimanic efficacy of carbamazepine and chlopromazine. *Psychopharmacology, 66*, 211–217. (2)

Okuma, T., Inanaga, K., Otsuki, S., et al. (1981). A preliminary double-blind study on the efficacy of carbamazepine prophylaxis of manic depressive illness. *Psychopharmacology, 73*, 95–96. (2)

Oomen, K. J., & Mathews, S. (1999). Zonisamide: A new antiepileptic drug. *Clinical Neuropharmacology, 22*, 192–200. (5)

Pande, A. C., Crockett, J. G., Janney, C. A., et al. (2000). Gabapentin Bipolar Disorder Study Group: Gabapentin in bipolar disorder: A placebo-controlled trial of adjunctive therapy. *Bipolar Disorders, 2*, 249–255. (1)

Pazzaglia, P. J., Post, R. M., Ketter, T. A., et al. (1993). Preliminary controlled trial of nimodipine in ultra-rapid cycling affective dysregulation. *Psychiatry Research, 49*, 257–272. (2)

Pazzaglia, P. J., Post, R. M., Ketter, T. A., et al. (1998). Nimodipine monotherapy and carbamazepine augmentation in patients with refractory recurrent affective illness. *Journal of Clinical Psychopharmacology, 18,* 404–413. (2)

Peet, M. (1994). Induction of mania with selective serotonin reuptake inhibitors and tricyclic antidepressants. *British Journal of Psychiatry, 164,* 549–550. (4)

Peselow, E. D., Fieve, R. R., Difaglia, C., et al. (1991). Lithium prophylaxis of bipolar illness: The value of combination treatment. *British Journal of Psychiatry, 164,* 208–214. (3)

Placidi, G. F., Lenzi, A., Lazzerini, F., et al. (1986). The comparative efficacy and safety of carbamazepine versus lithium: A randomized, double-blind 3-year trial in 83 patients. *Journal of Clinical Psychiatry, 47,* 490–494. (2)

Platman, S. R. (1970). A comparison of lithium carbonate and chlorpromazine in mania. *American Journal of Psychiatry, 127,* 351–1153. (2)

Pope, H. G., Jr., McElroy, S. L., Keck, P. E., Jr., et al. (1991). Valproate in the treatment of acute mania: A placebo-controlled study. *Archives of General Psychiatry, 48,* 62–68. (1)

Post, R. M., Berretini, W., Uhde, T. W., et al. (1984). Selective response to the anticonvulsant carbamazepine in manic depressive illness: A case study. *Journal of Clinical Psychopharmacology, 4,* 178–185. (6)

Post, R. M., Uhde, T. W., Roy-Byme, P. P., et al. (1986). Antidepressant effects of carbamazepine. *American Journal of Psychiatry, 43,* 29–34. (2)

Prien, R. F., Caffey, E. M., Jr., & Klett, C. J. (1972). Comparison of lithium carbonate and chlorpromazine in the treatment of mania: Report of the Veterans Administration and National Institute of Mental Health Collaborative Study Group. *Archives of General Psychiatry, 26,* 146–153. (1)

Prien, R. F., Caffey, E. M., Jr., & Klett, C. J. (1974). Factors associated with treatment success in lithium carbonate prophylaxis. *Archives of General Psychiatry, 31,* 189–192. (3)

Prien, R. F., & Gelenberg, A. J. (1989). Alternatives to lithium for preventative treatment of bipolar disorder. *American Journal of Psychiatry, 146,* 840–848. (5)

Prien, R. F., & Potter, W. Z. (1990). NIMH workshop on treatment of bipolar disorder. *Psychopharmacology Bulletin, 26,* 409–427. (4)

Puzynski, S., & Klosiewicz, L. (1993). Valproic acid amide as a prophylactic agent in affective and schizoaffective disorders. *Neuropsychobiology, 20,* 151–159. (3)

Rosenfeld, W. E., Schaefer, P. A., & Pace, K. (1987). Weight loss patterns with topiramate therapy [abstract]. *Epilepsia, 38,* 60. (4)

Rush, A. J., George, M. S., Sackeim, H. A., et al. (2000). Vagus nerve stimulation (VNS) for treatment-resistant depressions: A multicenter study. *Biological Psychiatry, 47,* 276–286. (3)

Sachs, G., Risperidone Study Group. (1999, December 12–16). Safety and efficacy of risperidone vs placebo as add-on therapy to mood stabilizers in the treatment of manic phase of bipolar disorder. In *Abstracts of the 38th Annual Meeting of the American College of Neuropsychopharmacology,* Acapulco, Mexico. (1)

Sachs, G. S., Lafer, B., Stall, A., et al. (1994). A double-blind trial of bupropion versus desipramine for bipolar depression. *Journal of Clinical Psychiatry, 55,* 391–393. (2)

Sachs, G. S., Printz, D. J., Kahn, D. J., et al. (2000). *Medication treatment of bipolar disorder 2000.* Minneapolis: McGraw-Hill. (6)

Sachs, G. S., Thase, M. E., Leahy, L., et al. (2000, May 1). The systematic treatment enhancement program for bipolar disorder. In *New Research Program Abstracts of the Annual Meeting of the American Psychiatric Association.* Chicago. (3)

Schaffer, L. C., & Schaffer, C. B. (1999). Tiagabine and the treatment of refractory bipolar disorder [letter]. *American Journal of Psychiatry, 156,* 2014–2015. (6)

Schou, M., Juel-Nielson, N., Stromgren, E., et al. (1954). The treatment of manic psychoses by administration of lithium salts. *Journal of Neurology, Neurosurgery, and Psychiatry, 17,* 250–260. (2)

Segal, J., Berk, M., & Brook, S. (1998). Risperidone compared with both lithium and haloperidol in mania: A double-blind randomized controlled trial. *Journal of Clinical Neuropharmacology, 21,* 176–180. (2)

Shopsin, B., Gerson, S., Thompson, H., et al. (1975). Psychoactive drugs in mania: A controlled comparison of lithium carbonate, chlorpromazine, and haloperidol. *Archives of General Psychiatry, 32,* 34–42. (2)

Small, J. G. (1990). Anticonvulsants in affective disorders. *Psychopharmacology Bulletin, 26,* 25–36. (2)

Small, J. G., Klapper, M. H., Miktein, V., et al. (1991). Carbamazepine compared with lithium in the treatment of mania. *Archives of General Psychiatry, 48,* 915–921. (2)

Spitzer, R. L., Endicott, J., & Robins, E. (1978). Research diagnostic criteria: Rationale and reliability. *Archives of General Psychiatry, 35,* 773–782. (1)

Spring, G., Schweid, D., Gray, C., et al. (1970). A double-blind comparison of lithium and chlorpromazine in the treatment of manic states. *American Journal of Psychiatry, 126,* 1310. (2)

Stokes, P. E., Shamoian, C. A., Stoll, P. M., et al. (1971). Efficacy of lithium as acute treatment of manic-depressive illness. *Lancet, 1,* 1319–1325. (2)

Stoll, A. L., Mayer, P. V., Kolbrener, M., et al. (1994). Antidepressants associated with mania: A controlled comparison with spontaneous mania. *American Journal of Psychiatry, 151,* 1642–1645. (3)

Stoll, A. L., Severus, W. E., Freeman, M. P., et al. (1999). Omega-3 fatty acids in bipolar disorder: A preliminary double-blind, placebo-controlled trial. *Archives of General Psychiatry, 56,* 407–412. (2)

Strakowski, S. M., Keck, P. E., Jr., McElroy, S. L., et al. (1998). Twelve-month outcome following first hospitalization for affective psychosis. *Archives of General Psychiatry, 55,* 49–55. (3)

Strakowski, S. M., McElroy, S. L., Keck, P. E., et al. (1996). Suicidality in mixed and manic bipolar disorder. *American Journal of Psychiatry, 153,* 674–676. (3)

Suppes, T., Baldessarini, R. J., Faedda, G. I., et al. (1991). Risk of recurrence following discontinuation of lithium in bipolar disorder. *Archives of General Psychiatry, 48,* 1082–1088. (4)

Suppes, T., Webb, A., Paul, B., et al. (1999). Clinical outcome in a randomized one-year trial of clozapine versus treatment as usual for patients with treatment-resistant illness and a history of mania. *American Journal of Psychiatry, 156,* 1164–1169. (2)

Swann, A. C., Bowden, C. L., Calabrese, J. R., et al. (1999). Differential effects of number of previous episodes of affective disorder in response to lithium or divalproex in acute mania. *American Journal of Psychiatry, 156,* 1264–1266. (4)

Swann, A. C., Bowden, C. L., Morris, D., et al. (1997). Depression during mania: Treatment response to lithium or divalproex. *Archives of General Psychiatry, 54,* 37–42. (4)

Takahashi, R., Sakuma, A., Itoh, K., et al. (1975). Comparison of efficacy of lithium c nate and chlorpromazine in mania: Report of the collaborative study group of treatment of mania in Japan. *Archives of General Psychiatry, 32,* 1310–1318. (2)

Tohen, M., Baker, R. W., Milton, D. R., et al. (2001). Olanzapine [Abstract] versus divalproex sodium for the treatment of acute mania. *Bipolar Disorders, 3,* 60–61. (1)

Tohen, M., Jacobs, T. G., Grundy, S. L., et al. (2000). A double-blind, placebo-controlled study of olanzapine in patients with acute bipolar mania. *Archives of General Psychiatry, 57,* 841–849. (1)

Tohen, M., Sanger, T. M., McElroy, S. L., et al. (1999). Olanzapine versus placebo in the treatment of acute mania. *American Journal of Psychiatry, 156,* 702–709. (1).

Turvey, C. L., Coryell, W. H., Arndt, S., et al. (1999). Polarity sequence, depression, and chronicity in bipolar I disorder. *Journal of Nervous and Mental Disease, 187,* 181–187. (3)

Verdoux, H., Gonzales, B., Takei, N., et al. (1996). A survey of prescribing practice of antipsychotic maintenance treatment of manic-depressive outpatients. *Journal of Affective Disorders, 38,* 81–87. (3)

Walton, S., Berk, M., & Brook, S. (1996). Superiority of lithium over verapamil in mania: A randomized, controlled, single-blind trial. *Journal of Clinical Psychiatry, 57,* 543–546. (3)

Watanabe, S., Ishino, H., & Otsuki, S. (1975). Double-blind comparison of lithium and imipramine in treatment of depression. *Archives of General Psychiatry, 32,* 659–668. (2)

Watkins, S. E., Callendar, K., & Thomas, D. R. (1987). The effect of carbamazepine and lithium on remission from affective illness. *British Journal of Psychiatry, 150,* 180–182. (2)

White, E., Cheung, T., & Silverstone, T. (1993). Depot antipsychotics in bipolar affective disorder. *International Clinical Psychopharmacology, 122,* 119–122. (3)

Zarate, C. A., Jr., Tohen, M., & Baldessarini, R. J. (1995). Clozapine in severe mood disorders. *Journal of Clinical Psychiatry, 56,* 411–417. (3)

Zomberg, G. L., & Pope, H. G., Jr. (1993). Treatment of depression in bipolar disorder: New directions for research. *Journal of Clinical Psychopharmacology, 13,* 397–408. (4)

13

Psychosocial Treatments for Panic Disorders, Phobias, and Generalized Anxiety Disorder

David H. Barlow
Susan D. Raffa
Elizabeth M. Cohen

A substantial number of excellent studies, largely Type 1, have established the clinical efficacy of situational in vivo exposure for patients with panic disorder with moderate to severe agoraphobia. A substantial number of Type 1 studies have established the efficacy of cognitive behavioral treatments for persons with panic disorder; these treatments focus on education about the nature of anxiety and panic, traditional cognitive therapy, exposure to interoceptive sensations similar to physiological panic sensations, and breathing retraining. Recently, a new clinical trial (Type 1) has been reported that explores the effectiveness of separate and combined psychosocial and pharmacological treatment of panic disorder.

The treatment of choice for specific phobias is exposure-based procedures, particularly in vivo exposure; this consensus reflects a very large number of Type 1 studies of these procedures with patients with specific phobias.

The most common treatment approaches to social phobia include social skills training (SST), relaxation techniques, exposure-based methods, and multicomponent cognitive behavioral treatments, the latter, as well as exposure-based procedures, attaining the highest level of treatment efficacy in Type 1 studies.

In general, different treatment conditions for patients with generalized anxiety disorder (GAD) have not led to differential improvement rates, although most studies have shown that active treatments are superior to nondirective approaches and uniformly superior to no treatment. Recently, however, a few studies have suggested that the most successful psychosocial treatments for GAD combine relaxation exercises and cognitive therapy with the goal of bringing the worry process itself under the patient's control.

The development of empirically supported psychological treatments has been, perhaps, most evident in the appearance of effective new treatments for anxiety disorders, particularly during the last decade. Prior to 1970, anxiety disorders were a highly prevalent but ill-defined group of problems subsumed under the general headings of "anxiety neuroses or phobic neuroses." Treatment of neurosis was most often carried out in the context of long-term psychotherapy, with little or no evidence available on the efficacy of this approach (Barlow, 1988; Hayes, Barlow, & Nelson-Gray, 1999). During the late 1960s and into the 1970s, clinical trials began to establish the efficacy of exposure-based treatments for phobic disorders, specifically agoraphobia and specific phobias. In addition, early experimental analyses began to appear suggesting the efficacy of specific psychosocial treatments for obsessive compulsive disorder (e.g., Mills, Agras, Barlow, & Mills, 1973; Rachman & Hodgson, 1980).

The successful delineation of specific anxiety disorders with the appearance of the third edition of the *Diagnostic and Statistical Manual of Mental Disorders (DSM-III)* in 1980 (American Psychiatric Association [APA], 1980) led to the development of more structured and targeted psychosocial and drug treatments. From 1985 through 1995, effective and empirically supported psychosocial treatments were developed for panic disorder, generalized anxiety disorder, and social phobia, as well as posttraumatic stress disorder (Barlow, 1994; Barlow & Lehman, 1996). In addition, substantial improvements were made in the treatment of panic disorder with agoraphobia and certain varieties of specific phobia as our knowledge of the psychopathology and pathophysiology of these conditions deepened. From 1995 through 2000, additional evidence accumulated on the efficacy and effectiveness of these procedures, and major clinical trials on the separate and combined effects of these approaches and pharmacological treatments were published.

In this chapter, we review systematically the current status of the evidence regarding efficacious empirically supported treatments for panic disorder with and without agoraphobia, specific phobia, social phobia, and generalized anxiety disorder. This review is followed by a brief concluding section on future directions in treatment development and research for these disorders.

Empirical studies are evaluated according to a template recently created by the American Psychological Association to guide the development of practice guidelines (American Psychological Association Task Force on Intervention Guidelines, 1995). This template evaluates studies along two axes, one that examines the treatments' efficacy (internal validity) and a second that examines the clinical utility (effectiveness, or external validity) of the treatments being researched. This template is included in Table 13.1. In addition, the studies reviewed in this chapter are examined according to the classification system outlined in the preface of this book. The studies held to the most rigorous research standards are classified as Type 1 studies, and those that fall short of this standard of excellence are classified as Type 2 studies. Research studies conducted with more substantial methodological limitations are classified as Type 3 through Type 6 studies.

PANIC DISORDER WITH AGORAPHOBIA

Though panic attacks have been discussed in the literature over the centuries (e.g., Freud 1895/1961), they were largely ignored by the diagnostic system until the last few decades. The two diagnoses of panic disorder and agoraphobia with panic attacks were not included in the diagnostic system until the publication of *DSM-III* (APA, 1980). The most recent version of this diagnostic system, *DSM-IV* (APA, 1994), includes the related diagnoses of panic disorder without agoraphobia, panic disorder with agoraphobia, and agoraphobia without history of panic disorder.

Individuals diagnosed with panic disorder report experiencing recurrent unexpected panic attacks that consist of physical symptoms such as racing heart, shortness of breath, dizziness, sweating, and trembling or shaking. Moreover, they experience continued anxiety focused on experiencing future panic attacks and worry about consequences of the panic attacks or changes in their behavior due to the panic attacks. It is the additional anxiety about the attacks, combined with catastrophic cognitions in the face of panic, that distinguish individuals with panic disorder from nonclinical panickers (Craske & Barlow, 2001). In addition, those with agoraphobia avoid situations that trigger panic attacks, and from which escape would be difficult in the event of a panic attack, such as crowded shopping malls, restaurants, and movie theaters. Finally, individuals are diagnosed with agoraphobia without history of panic disorder when they experience agoraphobic avoidance due to anxiety focused on specific somatic symptoms, some of which may be defining symptoms of a panic attack, although they have never met criteria for a full, unexpected panic attack. It should be noted that, clinically, patients presenting with agoraphobia without history of panic disorder can be treated with protocols intended for patients with panic disorder with agoraphobia, and they will usually benefit from such treatment (Craske & Barlow, 2001).

TABLE 13.1 Overview of Template for Constructing Psychological Intervention Guidelines

Efficacy (Internal Validity)	*Clinical Utility (External Validity)*
1. Better than alternative therapy 2. Better than nonspecific therapy (RCTs) 3. Better than no therapy (RCTs) 4. Quantified clinical observations 5. Strongly positive clinical consensus 6. Mixed clinical consensus 7. Strongly negative clinical consensus 8. Contradictory evidence Note. Confidence in treatment efficacy is based on both (a) the absolute and relative efficacy of the treatment and (b) the quality of the studies on which the judgment is made, as well as their replicability. Confidence in efficacy increases from Item 8 (lowest) to Item 1 (highest).	1. Feasibility a. Patient acceptability (cost, pain, duration, side effects, etc.) b. Patient choice in face of relatively equal efficacy c. Probability of compliance d. Ease of disseminability (e.g., number of practitioners with competence, requirements for training, opportunities for training, need for costly technologies or additional support personnel, etc.) 2. Generalizability a. Patient characteristics: cultural background issues, gender issues, developmental issues, other relevant patient characteristics b. Therapist characteristics c. Issues of robustness when applied in practice settings with different time frames and the like d. Contextual factors regarding setting in which treatment is delivered 3. Costs and benefits a. Costs of delivering intervention to individual and society b. Costs of withholding effective intervention from individual and society Note: Confidence in clinical utility as reflected on these dimensions should be based on systematic and objective methods and strategies for assessing these characteristics of treatment as they are applied in actual practice. In some cases, randomized clinical trials will exist. More often, data will be in the form of quantified clinical observations (clinical replication series) or other strategies such as health economic calculations.

RCT = randomized clinical trial.

Reports on the prevalence of panic disorder, panic disorder with agoraphobia, and agoraphobia without history of panic disorder vary somewhat. The most recent epidemiological study, the National Comorbidity Survey (NCS), conducted in the United States cited a lifetime prevalence for panic disorder with or without agoraphobia at 3.5% of the population (Kessler et al., 1994). This same report noted the lifetime prevalence of agoraphobia without history of panic disorder to be 5.3% of the population. Differences between these figures and earlier epidemiological reports may be due to different geographic areas sampled, different age ranges surveyed, and the utilization of different research methods. Kessler et al. (1994) utilized a more advanced methodology than previous surveys had; consequently, the results of the National Comorbidity Survey are considered more credible than other epidemiological data currently available.

Finally, it seems that many more women than men experience these disorders. A recent meta-analysis found that three fourths of the participants in research studies on the treatment of the panic disorders are women (Gould, Otto, & Pollack, 1995). In addition, the National Comorbidity Survey found the lifetime prevalence of panic disorder and agoraphobia without history of panic disorder for women to be at least twice that listed for men (5.0% and 7.0% versus 2.0% and 3.5%, respectively) (Kessler et al., 1994). These findings replicate the sex ratio in earlier reports (e.g., Myers et al., 1984; Thorpe & Burns, 1983). The most common explanation for this marked difference in prevalence among men and women involves cultural factors. In most cultures around the world, it is more acceptable for women to report fear and to avoid various situations due to this fear. Men, however, are expected to minimize their fears and overcome avoidant tendencies regardless of the cost. Many men seem to turn to alcohol to self-medicate their anxiety and panic (Barlow, 1988, in press; Kushner, Abrams, & Borchardt, 2000).

Most individuals with panic disorder can clearly recall life stressors that occurred when they experienced the onset of their panic attacks. One study noted that 72% of patients with panic disorder reported life stress existing when their panic attacks began (Craske, Miller, Rotunda, & Barlow, 1990). Moreover, patients with panic disorder often experience other Axis I disorders concurrent with their panic disorder (Brown, Campbell, Lehman, & Grisham, 2001; Sanderson, DiNardo, Rapee, & Barlow, 1990), and studies have noted that between 25% and 75% of patients with panic disorder meet criteria for an Axis II personality disorder, most often avoidant or dependent personality disorders (Chambless & Renneberg, 1988; Reich, Noyes, & Troughton, 1987).

Our own model of etiology posits a nonspecific biological predisposition to experience stress or emotionality and possibly a separate heritability for a low threshold to experience panic attacks. Specifically, this generalized biological predisposition, combined with early development of a sense of uncontrollability over potentially threatening life events (a generalized psychological predisposition), creates a diathesis. The later experience of life stress then triggers an unexpected panic attack, and in those with biological and psychological vulnerabilities (the diathesis), anxiety becomes focused on the next possible panic attack, and panic disorder subsequently develops. Agoraphobia may then follow as a complication of panic disorder in a large proportion of these individuals, mostly women (Barlow, 1988, 2000, in press; Barlow, Chorpita, & Turovsky, 1996).

In this section, we first review the development and evaluation of in vivo exposure strategies for treating agoraphobia, followed by a description of the development and evaluation of psychosocial treatments that target panic attacks directly. We conclude with a discussion of the current status of psychosocial treatment of panic disorder with agoraphobia, as well as our view of future directions in treatment development and assessment for this disorder.

Treatment of Agoraphobia

Treatment of agoraphobia has evolved considerably over the last several decades. Initial treatments, conducted in the 1960s and 1970s, for agoraphobic avoidance consisted of systematic desensitization. This procedure involved imaginal exposure to feared situations coupled with muscle relaxation. Systematic desensitization was used at that time since it was believed that actual exposure to feared situations (situational in vivo exposure) might be too intense and would have deleterious effects. Studies conducted to examine the efficacy of systematic desensitization consistently found this approach to be largely ineffectual (Gelder & Marks, 1966; Marks, 1971). During this same era, researchers began to treat patients with agoraphobia successfully by conducting graduated in vivo exposure exercises (Agras, Leitenberg, & Barlow, 1968). In this procedure, under the supervision of a clinician, patients were expected to engage in exposure practices by which they systematically ventured away from safe places and into the situations they had been avoiding.

Situational in Vivo Exposure

During the next several years, situational in vivo exposure continued to be evaluated and was found to be more effective than no treatment or attentional control procedures (Barlow, 1988, in press; Jansson & Ost, 1982; Mavissakalian & Barlow, 1981). Situational in vivo exposure treatment routinely begins with the patients creating a hierarchy of feared situations or activities that have been consistently avoided. Examples of such items include driving out of a safety zone (which may be either several blocks or several miles from the home), shopping in a crowded mall alone, and going out to dinner in a restaurant or seeing a movie in a theater. Patients are then encouraged to repeatedly enter and remain in these feared situations, utilizing therapeutic coping procedures learned during sessions, until their anxiety diminishes. While patients with more severe agoraphobia may require the presence of their therapist during the initial exposures, most patients are able to conduct these exercises either alone or with a friend or family member who acts as a supportive coach (Barlow, 1988, in press).

Throughout the past few decades, researchers have examined the clinical efficacy of situational in vivo exposure utilizing the highest methodological standards. Nearly all of these studies fall into the top two categories of the internal validity axis (Axis 1) of the APA template; moreover, the vast majority of these studies can also be characterized as Type 1 studies according to the classification system of this volume. These studies have consistently shown evidence of the efficacy of situational in vivo exposure; the current consensus among researchers is that situational in vivo exposure is a highly effective treatment for many patients with panic disorder with agoraphobia.

Several reviews and meta-analyses conducted in the 1980s found that 60 to 75% of patients who completed situational in vivo exposure treatments showed evidence of clinical improvement (Barlow, 1988, in press; Jacobson, Wilson, & Tupper, 1988; Jansson & Ost, 1982; Munby & Johnston, 1980; Trull, Nietzel, & Main, 1988). Yet, relatively few of these patients were "cured" or completely symptom-free at the conclusion of their exposure treatment. However, clinical gains that were achieved from this approach were maintained at long-term follow-up. For example, Jansson, Jerremalm, and Ost (1986) reported maintenance of gains and some continued improvement at a 15-month follow-up. Burns, Thorpe, and Cavallaro (1986) also noted continuation of gains up to 8 years following treatment, albeit punctuated by brief setbacks.

Fava, Zielezny, Savron, and Grandi (1995) have also published long-term follow-up results of their research on exposure-based treatments for agoraphobia conducted in Bologna, Italy. This study falls into the Type 2 category due to the lack of a comparison group in the study design. However, since the efficacy of situational in vivo exposure has been proven extensively in the past, many researchers currently studying situational in vivo exposure do not view a comparison treatment group as a necessary treatment component in this type of research. Fava and his colleagues (1995) treated over 90 patients with 12 sessions of self-paced, graduated, exposure-based treatment. These 30-minute sessions were administered biweekly over a 6-month period. At the end of treatment, 87% of the patients were panic-free and considered much improved on the global clinical measures. These patients were then followed for up to 7 years after treatment, with 67% still in remission at that time.

Using survival analysis to estimate the probability that the patients would remain in remission after they successfully completed exposure treatment, results indicated that 96% of the patients remained in remission throughout the first 2 years after treatment. In addition, 77% of the patients remained in remission throughout the first 5 years after treatment and 67% for the first 7 years after the completion of exposure treatment. Study results indicated that residual agoraphobia and the presence of a personality disorder were the most significant predictors of relapse for the patients in the study.

Strategies to Improve the Effectiveness of Exposure-Based Procedures

Since the early 1990s, researchers have focused on improving the effectiveness of situational in vivo exposure-based treatments. For example, a number of studies attempted to determine whether adding relaxation training to situational in vivo exposure would improve the clinical efficacy of the situational in vivo exposure. In most of these studies, the combined treatments were no more effective than situational in vivo exposure alone (Michelson, Mavissakalian, & Marchione, 1988; Ost, Hellstrom, & Westling, 1989; Ost, Jerremalm, & Jansson, 1984). In addition, researchers have attempted to improve the efficacy of situational in vivo exposure by adding to exposure protocols cognitive therapy components such as paradoxical intention or Beck and Emery's (1985) cognitive therapy. Again, the combined treatments were most often found to be no more effective than situational in vivo exposure alone (Emmelkamp, Brilman, Kuiper, & Mersch, 1986; Emmelkamp & Mersch, 1982; Michelson et al., 1988; Ost et al., 1989; Williams & Rappaport, 1983). Finally, three controlled studies examining the effectiveness of situational in vivo exposure and breathing retraining found the combined treatment to be no more effective than situational in vivo exposure alone (Bonn, Readhead, & Timmons, 1984; De Ruiter, Rijken, Garssen, & Kraaimaat, 1989; Schmidt et al., 2000).

Michelson, Marchione, and Greenwald (1989) reported on a study comparing the effectiveness of three different treatment conditions: graded situational in vivo exposure alone, graded situational in vivo exposure plus cognitive therapy, and graded situational in vivo exposure plus relaxation training. This Type 1 study produced notable results; these authors found the treatment condition consisting of situational in vivo exposure and cognitive therapy to be the most effective of the three conditions. At posttreatment assessment, 86% of the patients receiving situational in vivo exposure plus cognitive therapy achieved high end-state functioning as compared to 73% of the situational in vivo exposure plus relaxation training group and 65% of the situational in vivo exposure alone group. In addition, follow-up comparisons continued to underscore the effectiveness of the combined situational in vivo exposure plus cognitive therapy treatment condition. Of the situational in vivo exposure plus cognitive therapy patients, 87% were considered to have achieved high end-state functioning at the 1-year follow-up assessment, while 65% of the situational in vivo exposure alone patients and 47% of the situational in vivo exposure plus relaxation training patients had achieved this same clinical status.

Many researchers have manipulated the pace of situational in vivo exposure treatment in order to show evidence of maximum therapeutic gains. Massed and intensive exposure sessions have been repeatedly compared with spaced and graduated exposure sessions. Barlow (1988, in press) discussed several advantages of spaced and graduated situation in vivo exposure. Advantages include lower attrition rates, as well as lower relapse rates (Hafoer & Marks, 1976; Jansson & Ost, 1982). In addition, gradual changes in agoraphobic avoidance are believed to be less stressful to the interpersonal system of the patient (Barlow, 1988, in press).

Yet the empirical literature does not entirely support this perspective since other studies have not found spaced and graduated situational in vivo exposures to hold such distinct advantages. For example, Chambless (1990) treated patients with agoraphobia and patients with specific phobias with either spaced exposures (conducted weekly) or massed exposures (conducted daily). The two conditions were found to be equally effective at both the posttreatment and 6-month follow-up assessments. Moreover, no differential dropout rates were found between the two conditions.

Perhaps the most striking finding regarding the effectiveness of massed, ungraded situational in vivo exposure was found in Germany. Feigenbaum (1988) treated a large number of severely agoraphobic persons with intensive, massed situational in vivo exposure. This innovative treatment consisted of massed exposures conducted throughout 4 to 10 days, during which individuals were expected to experience the situations they feared for several hours every day. Often, treatment began with therapist-assisted exposure exercises that were then followed by self-directed exposure. These patients were expected to engage in exposures such as using public transportation in a metropolitan area, taking an overnight train to a foreign city, and riding a cable car high above the Alps during the course of their intensive treatment. The progress of these patients was compared to the progress of patients who experienced more graded exposure exercises, gradually working up their hierarchy of feared situations.

While the two conditions proved to be equally effective at both the posttreatment assessment and the 8-month follow-up assessment, massed, ungraded, situational in vivo exposure proved to be superior at the 5-year follow-up assessment point. These results were later replicated with a much larger sample size (Feigenbaum, 1988). Feigenbaum and his colleagues treated over 120 patients, and over 75% were found to be symptom-free at the 5-year follow-up assessment.

In Boston, we are in the process of testing an intensive form of CBT treatment for panic disorder with moderate to severe agoraphobia. The treatment is conducted on an outpatient basis over a period of 8 days, during which participants complete an extensive self-study program as well as meeting with a therapist. The emphasis throughout the treatment is on the experience of frightening internal sensations, because of which we have called it *sensation-focused intensive therapy* (S-FIT). The first 3 days are devoted to modified standard CBT interventions, including education, cognitive restructuring, and interoceptive exposure. Participants then engage in 2 days of therapist-assisted, ungraded massed exposure, during which every effort is made to get them to the top of their fear and avoidance hierarchies in combination with aggressive symptom induction procedures. Exposure work is then conducted alone for 2 days before a final session covering relapse prevention is administered. Preliminary data on approximately 20 patients is very encouraging, and follow-up assessments ranging up to 16 months have found the gains to be maintained (Spiegel & Barlow, 2000).

Researchers have also focused their attention during treatment on the interpersonal support systems of persons with agoraphobia as a means of further improving treatment outcome. Since panic disorder with agoraphobia, at its more severe levels, produces a great deal of dependency, researchers theorized that the incorporation of spouses or partners in treatment might facilitate the treatment process. Barlow, O'Brien, and Last (1984) found that spousal involvement significantly improved treatment effectiveness for a number of women with agoraphobia. In their study, two groups of women were offered identical exposure-based treatments, but one group was asked to have their spouses accompany them to treatment sessions. While the patients in both groups showed evidence of clinical improvements, a significantly greater percentage of patients in the spouse-accompanied group were treatment responders at the posttreatment assessment (86% versus 43%, respectively). In addition, follow-up results of these same patients determined that the gap in treatment efficacy between the two groups increased during the first and second years after treatment (Cerny, Barlow, Craske, & Himadi, 1987).

Finally, Arnow, Taylor, Agras, and Telch (1985) examined the effectiveness of communication skills training with spouses or partners by adding it to a situational in vivo exposure protocol. The combined communication skills training and situational in vivo exposure treatment was found to show evidence of greater clinical improvement at both the posttreatment and the 8-month follow-up assessment. In contrast, Cobb, Mathews, Childs-Clarke, and Blowers (1984) found no additional benefit from including spouses in their treatment protocol, although procedural differences in the treatment administration might account for this finding (see Cerny et al., 1987).

Briefer Cost-Effective Modifications to Exposure-Based Procedures

Researchers have also been studying the effectiveness of more self-directed treatment protocols for agoraphobic avoidance. These studies explore the questions raised on the second axis of the APA template mentioned above; they examine the clinical utility or external validity of these treatments. For example, Ghosh and Marks (1987) conducted a study that explored the effectiveness of a 10-week self-directed exposure treatment administered in three different conditions (therapist-instructed, computer-instructed, and book-instructed). They enlisted a select group of patients to enter this study; patients with severe personality disorders or severe depression were not eligible for the protocol treatment. Patients in all three treatment conditions received the same initial introduction to treatment, which consisted of a review of the self-directed exposure program explained by a trained clinician.

After the initial assessment, the patients in the book-instructed condition (bibliotherapy) received no additional clinical appointments during the 10-week course of treatment, though they were contacted on three occasions to determine if they were engaged in the self-directed treatment program. In contrast, the patients in the computer-instructed condition had weekly 30-minute computer sessions. These were preceded by a brief 10-minute appointment with a clinician, during which the doctor merely assessed the patient's mental status. The patients in the therapist-instructed condition had weekly sessions with their psychiatrist that lasted an average of 40 minutes.

Ghosh and Marks (1987) found that patients in all three treatment conditions were significantly improved after the 10-week treatment. They found no differences among the three treatment conditions, a finding suggesting that self-directed bibliotherapy can be both a clinically effective and cost-effective treatment for agoraphobic avoidance, at least in the cases treated in this study. In contrast, Holden, O'Brien, Barlow, Stetson, and Infantino (1983) found bibliotherapy ineffective with patients with more severe levels of agoraphobia; these patients required the intervention of a therapist.

More recently, Swinson, Fergus, Cox, and Wickwire (1995) studied the efficacy of telephone-administered self-exposure instructions. This research explored the viability of a more cost-effective administration of situational in vivo exposure. They examined whether self-directed exposure would be an effective treatment modality for patients unable to attend more traditional therapy sessions conducted in person. Most of the patients enrolled in the study (over 70%) suffered from moderate or severe levels of agoraphobic avoidance. In addition, the patients had suffered from panic disorder and agoraphobia for a mean duration of approximately 13 years. The patients were offered a 10-week course of treatment that included eight telephone sessions with the therapist; the results were compared with those of patients in a wait-list control group.

The telephone-administered exposure instructions were found to be effective in reducing the agoraphobic avoidance at posttreatment in comparison to the wait-list control group; moreover, the 3- and 6-month follow-up assessments showed evidence of continued treatment gains. Finally, the clinical improvements were comparable to gains made by patients treated in the more traditional condition of individual face-to-face treatment sessions.

Treatment of Panic

Psychosocial treatments focusing on the unexpected and uncued panic attacks experienced by individuals with panic disorder were developed relatively recently. Since the publication of *DSM-III* (APA, 1980), several psychosocial treatments aimed at targeting panic attacks directly have been developed, and numerous research trials have been conducted to test their efficacy. The majority of these are cognitive behavioral treatments, and they share many commonalities. They focus on education about the nature of anxiety and panic, cognitive therapy, and some form of exposure and coping skills acquisition. Typically, different aspects of treatment are emphasized in the various protocols. A selection of the more widely utilized treatments is reviewed here. The studies reviewed in this discussion are categorized as Type 1 research since they were all conducted utilizing the highest methodological standards.

Panic Control Treatment

In the mid-1980s, Barlow and Craske (2000) developed a psychosocial treatment protocol for panic attacks, now known as the *panic control treatment* (PCT). This treatment focuses on exposing the patient to interoceptive sensations similar to physiological panic sensations. In addition to these systematized exposures, PCT includes a cognitive restructuring component directed at misconceptions about anxiety and panic, as well as "automatic" cognitions that focus on the overestimations of threat and danger associated with panic attacks. Finally, breathing retraining is incorporated into PCT; it serves to correct tendencies to hyperventilate in some panic patients and also provides a meditational calming exercise that can be effectively utilized by most patients. Panic control training has been extensively studied for several years, with good results.

In the first controlled study of PCT (Barlow, Craske, Cerny, & Klosko, 1989), three treatment conditions (PCT alone, relaxation alone, and PCT combined with relaxation) were compared to a wait-list control condition. The relaxation component consisted of progressive muscle relaxation training along with instructions to apply this relaxation in anxiety-provoking situations. At posttreatment, all three treatment conditions proved to be more effective than the wait-list control condition. Of the patients, 60% in the relaxation condition and 87% in the PCT-alone and PCT-combined-with-relaxation conditions achieved panic-free status by the conclusion of the 15-week treatment.

Craske, Brown, and Barlow (1991) reported on a 2-year follow-up of this study. These follow-up data revealed that 81% of the patients in the PCT alone condition were panic-free 2 years after acute treatment, compared to only 43% of the patients in the PCT-combined-with-relaxation condition and 36% of the patients in the relaxation-alone condition. It is believed that the patients in the PCT-combined-with-relaxation condition were not able to show evidence of greater therapeutic gains due to the abbreviated nature of treatment; that is, neither the PCT nor the relaxation therapy were presented as thoroughly in the combined treatment condition as in the two other treatment conditions.

In another study, Klosko, Barlow, Tassinari, and Cerny (1990) compared the efficacy of PCT and alprazolam to a drug placebo condition and a wait-list control condition. In this study, posttreatment assessment results showed that 87% of the patients in the PCT condition had achieved panic-free status, compared to 50% of the patients in the alprazolam condition, 36% of the patients in the placebo drug condition, and 33% of the patients in the wait-list control condition. The PCT was found to be significantly more effective than all the other three conditions (Barlow & Brown, 1995).

Recently, Schmidt et al. (2000) conducted a controlled outcome study designed to assess the necessity of breathing retraining in the context of PCT. Seventy-seven patients with panic disorder were randomly assigned to receive PCT with or without breathing retraining or to a delayed-treatment control. The findings were consistent with treatment equivalence, with 38% of the PCT group meeting the recovery criteria for high end-state functioning compared with 21% of the PCT-and-breathing-retraining group, and 0% of the wait-list group. Moreover, by the 12-month follow-up, 57% of the PCT group met the recovery criteria, compared with 37% of the combined group. This one study suggests that while breathing retraining appears not to affect initial posttreatment outcome, it may yield a poorer long-term outcome.

In yet another study, Telch et al. (1993) found PCT to be effective when administered in a group treatment format. Patients were given 8 weeks of group PCT, and their progress was compared to that of patients in a wait-list control condition. At the conclusion of treatment, 85% of the patients who had received PCT had achieved panic-free status, compared with 30% of the patients in the wait-list control condition. In addition, when a more stringent composite outcome measure (considering panic attack frequency, as well as levels of general anxiety and avoidance behavior) was utilized, 63% of the patients in the PCT condition were considered improved, compared with 9% of the patients in the wait-list control condition. At the 6-month follow-up, 79% of the patients who had received PCT had remained panic-free, and 63% were still considered clinically improved according to the composite outcome measure.

Now, results have been reported from a large multisite study that compared single and combined effects of cognitive behavioral treatment and imipramine for patients with panic disorder with no more than limited agoraphobia (Barlow, Gorman, Shear, & Woods, 2000). In this study, patients were randomly assigned to receive imipramine only, cognitive behavioral therapy only (PCT), placebo only, PCT plus imipramine, or PCT plus placebo. Patients were treated weekly for 3 months. Patients who responded to treatment were then seen in a maintenance condition monthly for 6 additional months and were then followed up for 6 months after treatment discontinuation. The results indicated that all of the treatment groups were significantly superior to placebo after the acute and maintenance phases of treatment, with some evidence that among those who responded, the drug produced a better quality of response (e.g., less depression). However, PCT plus imipramine was generally not superior to PCT plus placebo, nor did the combined treatments confer any useful advantage over the single treatments. By 6 months after the termination of treatment, significantly more patients in the imipramine-alone group and the PCT-plus-imipramine group relapsed than patients in groups receiving PCT without imipramine (PCT alone and PCT plus placebo). These results are presented in Table 13.2. This study suggests that PCT produces a more durable response than medication. Further investigation is needed of the long-term effects of adding medications to cognitive behavioral therapy, and of the most effective ways to combine medications with cognitive behavioral therapy in order to offset potential relapse.

The third edition of a comprehensive PCT treatment manual for panic disorder has recently been published. The manual is titled *Mastery of Your Anxiety and Panic -MAP3* (Barlow & Craske, 2000). This treatment manual presents clinicians with a step-by-step guide to conducting the various aspects of PCT therapy.

Cognitive Therapy

In a controlled trial of more traditional cognitive therapy, Beck, Sokol, Clark, Berchick, and Wright (1992) compared the efficacy of 12 weeks of cognitive therapy with 8 weeks of brief supportive therapy. After 8 weeks of treatment, 71% of the patients who received cognitive therapy were panic-free, compared with 25% of the patients who received supportive therapy. Moreover, at posttreatment, 94% of the patients in the cognitive therapy condition were panic-free, and at the 1-year follow-up assessment, 87% of these patients continued to be panic-free.

Clark and his colleagues have also developed a psychosocial treatment for panic disorder consisting of a unique variation of cognitive therapy (Clark, 1989; Salkovskis & Clark, 1991). This treatment also attempts to change patients' appraisals of bodily sensations and is similar to the PCT discussed above. However, Clark's approach places a greater emphasis on the cognitive therapy component of the treatment protocol.

Clark et al. (1994) conducted a randomized controlled trial comparing the effectiveness of three active treatments (cognitive therapy, applied relaxation [AR], and imipramine) to a wait-list control condition. Patients randomly assigned to one of the three active treatment conditions met weekly with a clinician throughout the first 3 months of the study; fur-

TABLE 13.2 Clinical Trials of Cognitive-Behavioral Treatments for Panic Disorder: Intent-to-Treat Analysis

Study	Length of Follow-Up (Months)	Treatment (N)	Percentage Panic-Free	Significant Comparison (Percentage Panic Free)	
				Other Treatments (Yes/No)	Wait List (Yes/No)
Craske et al. (1991)[a]	24	PCT (N = 15)	81	Yes: AR = 36% Yes: PCT & AR = 43%	
Klosko et al. (1990)	PT	PCT (N = 15)	87	No: AL = 50% Yes: PL = 36%	Yes: 33%
Newman et al. (1990)	12	CTM (N = 24) CTNM (N = 19)	87 87	—	
Cote, Gauthier, Laberge, Cormier, and Plamondon (1994)	12	CBTM (N = 13)	92	—	
		CBTNM (N = 8)	100		
Beck et al. (1992)	PT	CT (N = 17)	94	Yes: ST = 25%[b]	
Black et al. (1993)	PT	CT (N = 25)	32	Yes: FL = 68% No: PL = 20%	
Magraf and Schneider (1991)	4 weeks	CT (N = 22)	91		
Ost et al. (1993)	12	CT (N = 19)	89[c]	No: AR = 74%[c]	Yes: 5 %
Telch et al. (1993)	PT	PCT (N = 34)	85		Yes: 30%
Clark et al. (1994)	12	CT (N = 17)	76[c]	Yes: AR = 43%[c] Yes: IMI = 49%[c]	
Craske et al. (1995)	PT	CBT (N = 16)	53	Yes: NPT = 8%	
Shear et al. (1994)	6	CBT (N = 23)	45	No: NPT = 45%	
Barlow et al. (2000)	12	CBT (N = 77) CBT + PL (N = 63) PL (N = 24) IMI (N = 83) CBT = IMI (N = 65)	28*	CBT = 31.9% No: CBT + PL = 41% Yes: PL = 13% Yes: IMI = 19.7% Yes: CBT + IMI = 26	

Source: Reprinted with permission from Barlow and Lehman (1996), © 1996 American Medical Association.

Al = alprazolam; AR = applied relaxation; CBT = cognitive behavioral therapy; CBTM = cognitive behavioral therapy and medication; CBTNM = cognitive behavioral therapy without medication; CT = cognitive therapy; CTM = cognitive therapy and medication; CTNM = cognitive therapy without medication; FL = fluvoxamine; IMI = imipramine; NPT = nonprescriptive treatment; PL = pill placebo; PCT = exposure and cognitive restructuring; PT = posttreatment; ST = supportive therapy.

[a]Follow-up study of Barlow et al. (1989).

[b]At 8 weeks, which was the end of supportive therapy. At this time, 71% of CT patients were panic-free.

[c]Percentage of patients panic-free at follow-up who had received no additional treatment during the follow-up period.

*Panic-free status from rating scale.

thermore, they continued to meet with their therapist for a monthly booster session throughout the 3 months following the acute treatment phase of the study. Posttreatment results conducted after 6 months showed that all three active treatments were significantly more effective than the wait-list control condition. In fact, the cognitive therapy treatment was superior to the wait-list control condition on all panic and anxiety treatment outcome measures, while the AR condition and the imipramine treatment condition were superior to the wait-list control condition on just over half and fewer than half of the treatment outcome measures, respectively.

At posttreatment, 75% of the patients in the cognitive therapy condition were panic-free compared with 70% of the patients in the imipramine condition and 40% of the patients in the AR condition. Moreover, the 9-month follow-up results that followed the discontinuation of the imipramine treatment showed that the patients in the cognitive therapy condition had largely maintained their treatment gains. Of the patients who received cognitive therapy, 85% remained panic-free, while 60% of the patients who received imipramine and 47% of the patients who were treated with AR were panic-free.

Also, during the time between the posttreatment and 9-month follow-up, 40% of the patients in the imipramine treatment condition had sought further treatment, compared with 25% of the patients in the AR condition and 5% of the patients in the cognitive therapy condition. At the final assessment point, the cognitive therapy condition was found to be significantly more effective than either the AR or the imipramine conditions.

Alternative Treatments

A study conducted by Ost and Westling (1995) reports positive results with AR treatment. In this study, patients were randomly assigned to 12 sessions of either an AR treatment or a cognitive therapy treatment. Results showed that both treatments were equally effective. At posttreatment, 65% of the patients in the AR condition and 74% of patients in the cognitive therapy condition were panic-free. At the 1-year follow-up, 82% of the patients who had received AR treatment and 89% of the patients who had received cognitive therapy treatment were panic-free. It is interesting that, for the patients treated in this study, no relapses occurred during the 1-year postacute treatment; in fact, many of the patients who had been experiencing panic attacks at the posttreatment assessment had achieved panic-free status by the 1-year follow-up. Thus, although not as effective in studies conducted by Clark et al. (1994) or Barlow et al. (1989), AR may deserve some further consideration and evaluation.

In 1994, Shear, Pilkonis, Cloitre, and Leon developed a new approach called *emotion-focused therapy* (EFT), which focuses on interpersonal triggers for panic attacks rather than on interoceptive cues. Attrition was high in this first study, but preliminary results from this study were promising. Further evaluation by Shear and colleagues (2000) has now been completed. In this study, patients were randomly assigned to EFT, CBT, imipramine, or placebo. Treatment included approximately 3 months of weekly visits and 6 monthly maintenance sessions. This study found that EFT was less effective than either CBT or imipramine for symptoms of panic disorder. In addition, EFT results at postacute and postmaintenance were similar to those of placebo. At follow-up, EFT patients fared better than those on placebo but still less well than those treated with CBT or imipramine.

Brief Cost-Effective Treatments

Recently, attention has turned toward exploring the effectiveness for panic attacks of cognitive behavioral treatment when it is administered in a more cost-effective manner, such as with limited therapist contact. These studies explore the questions raised on the second axis of the APA template; they examine the clinical utility or external validity of these treatments. Cote, Gauthier, Laberge, Cormier, and Plamondon (1994) conducted a study in which patients were randomly assigned to receive cognitive behavioral treatment with either a standard amount of therapist contact (weekly hour-long sessions) or reduced therapist contact (bimonthly hour-long sessions with bimonthly 10-minute telephone contacts). Results of this study demonstrated that the two treatment modalities were equally effective; over 73% of the patients in both groups were both panic-free and clinically improved at the 6-month follow-up assessment. It should be noted that therapist time in the reduced-therapist-contact condition was still considerable, amounting to approximately 10 hours of contact, compared with approximately 20 hours of contact in the standard condition.

Lidren et al. (1994) examined the effectiveness of self-directed treatment utilizing a manual (bibliotherapy) for panic attacks. They found bibliotherapy to be as effective as cognitive behavioral therapy administered in a group therapy setting. Patients in both conditions were treated for 8 weeks and were compared with patients in a wait-list control condition. The patients in both of the active treatment conditions showed evidence of significant clinical improvement at posttreatment assessments, while the patients in the wait-list control condition did not. Moreover, patients in the bibliotherapy and group therapy conditions maintained their treatment gains at the 3- and 6-month follow-up assessments. In addition, an attrition rate of zero was reported for this study, pointing to the desirability of these interventions for patients suffering from panic attacks.

Craske, Maidenberg, and Bystritsky (1995) also examined the effectiveness of brief cognitive behavioral treatment. A four-session PCT protocol was compared to a four-session nondirective supportive therapy protocol. The brief PCT was found to be significantly more effective than the nondirective supportive therapy; the patients' clinical statuses were assessed by noting the frequency of their panic attacks, their degree of worry about panic attacks, and their level of phobic fear.

Finally, Clark et al. (1999) randomly assigned 43 panic disorder patients to either standard cognitive therapy consisting of up to 12 one-hour sessions in the first 3 months of treatment or brief cognitive therapy, where patients attended five sessions in addition to using between-session self-study modules. Both treatments produced significantly better results than a wait-list control.

Current Status

Table 13.2 summarizes the results of studies of psychosocial treatment for panic disorder through 2000. Nearly all of these studies are classified as Type 1; the study by Ost, Westling, and Hellstrom (1993) falls into the Type 2 category due to an absence of comparison groups. Most studies demonstrate the effectiveness of PCT or similar cognitive behavioral approaches for patients with panic disorder with no more than mild agoraphobia (compared with either no treatment or credible psychotherapeutic alternatives).

Table 13.3 summarizes the results of a comprehensive meta-analysis of treatment outcome for panic disorder with all levels of agoraphobic avoidance (Gould et al., 1995). Included in the meta-analysis were 43 controlled studies. As can be seen in the table, the cognitive behavioral treatments yielded the greatest effect size and the smallest rates of patient attrition, compared with either pharmacological treatment or treatments that combined both psychosocial and pharmacological components. Moreover, the subset of cognitive behavioral treatments that utilized interoceptive exposure yielded an even greater effect size, although most of these studies included patients with no more than mild agoraphobic avoidance.

Future Directions

Though the past decades have produced a number of empirically supported psychosocial treatment protocols for the treatment of panic disorder with and without agoraphobia, much work still lies ahead. There is a need to continue to explore the effectiveness of abbreviated treatment protocols for the panic disorders, noting which patients seem to benefit most from such treatments.

In addition, there is a need to consider and explore innovative treatment modalities. For example, the great majority of the work done during the past several years with psychosocial treatments artificially separates individuals with panic disorder into two categories: those with no more than mild agoraphobic avoidance and those with moderate to severe agoraphobia. Cognitive behavioral treatments such as PCT have been devised and utilized for the former group, while treatment for the latter group has primarily consisted of situational in vivo exposure. This demarcation is merely an artifact of the development of research studies in this area. Initially, agoraphobic avoidance was addressed by psychosocial researchers studying panic disorder with agoraphobia; a number of years later, psychosocial treatments focusing directly on panic attacks and consequent anxiety were introduced. Since pharmacological treatments focus almost exclusively on controlling panic attacks and the anxiety related to these attacks, this demarcation does not exist in most pharmacological research protocols. Clinical investigators have recently begun to attempt to reintegrate these two approaches (e.g., Barlow & Craske, 2000; Craske & Barlow, 2001), and this trend should continue.

Research on the effectiveness of combined psychosocial and pharmacological treatment conducted since the early 1990s, and prior to Barlow et al. (2000), has focused primarily on combining pharmacotherapy with exposure-based treatments for patients with moderate to severe levels of agoraphobia. Studies that have examined the effectiveness of tricyclic antidepressives such as imipramine and exposure-based procedures compared with exposure alone have, for the most part, shown evidence of superior posttreatment results for the combined treatment (Mavissakalian, 1996; Mavissakalian & Perel, 1985; Telch, Agras, Taylor, Roth, & Gallen, 1985). However, these results generally are not maintained at follow-up assessments due to the high incidence of relapse experienced by patients in the combined treatment condition after imipramine discontinuation has occurred (e.g., Mavissakalian & Michelson, 1986). The Barlow et al. (2000) clinical trial on

TABLE 13.3 Meta-Analysis of 43 Controlled Studies of Treatment of Panic Disorder with Agoraphobia

	Cognitive Behavioral Therapy	*Cognitive Therapy and Interoceptive Exposure*	*Pharmacological Treatment*	*Combination Treatment*
Effect size	.68	.88	.47	.56
Dropouts	5.6%		19.8%	22%

Source: Data from Gould et al. (1995).

panic disorder with no more than mild agoraphobia showed equivalence of monotherapies, no advantage of combining treatments, and more durability of CBT. The Clark et al. (1994) study also shows equivalence of monotherapies and greater durability of CBT. They did not test combination treatments. These results suggest that a drug may be a useful addition to CBT in more severe cases of panic disorder with substantial agoraphobia, although not in less severe cases. Finally there is plenty of room for improvement in the efficacy of these approaches, and results from all studies underscore the need to study effective maintenance strategies for this chronic condition.

Marks et al. (1993) also found that a combined treatment consisting of alprazolam, a high-potency benzodiazepine, and exposure therapy was similar in its effectiveness to either alprazolam or exposure therapy administered alone. While this result was found at the posttreatment evaluation, the effectiveness of the combined treatment did not remain at the 6-month follow-up assessment, much as in Barlow et al. (2000). Those patients who had received the combination treatment had experienced a high relapse rate after the discontinuation of the alprazolam; thus, overall gains were reduced below the point of those receiving exposure alone. Of more concern are recent reports that high-potency benzodiazepines may interfere with and detract from CBT treatment gains (Brown & Barlow, 1995; Otto, Pollack, & Sabatino, 1995).

In a recent innovation, psychosocial treatments, such as modifications of PCT, have also been utilized to help patients discontinue benzodiazepines. For example, Otto et al. (1993) conducted a study in which patients using alprazolam experienced either a slow taper of the drug or a slow taper in conjunction with 10 weeks of PCT. Results indicated that over 75% of the patients in the combined PCT-taper condition were able to discontinue their alprazolam usage, while only 25% of the slow-taper-alone condition were able to do so.

Spiegel, Bruce, Gregg, and Nuzzarello (1994) conducted a similar study. Patients were discontinued very gradually and flexibly from alprazolam. One treatment condition included 12 weekly sessions of individual PCT during the taper, while the other treatment condition involved routine supportive medical management. Nearly all patients were able to discontinue their medication usage (80% of the patients in the taper-plus-supportive-medical-management condition and 90% of the patients in the taper-plus-PCT-condition). At the 6-month follow-up, fully half of the patients in the taper-plus-supportive-medical-management condition relapsed and had begun using alprazolam again, while no patients in the taper-plus-PCT condition had done so. Results from a 3-year follow-up revealed that 33% of the patients in the PCT condition had experienced a relapse between 6 and 18 months after their treatment was discontinued. Moreover, 70% of the patients in the supportive medical management condition had experienced a relapse and required additional treatment during the 3-year follow-up period (Spiegel et al., 1994). These data suggest an innovative combination treatment, in which high-potency benzodiazepines are administered initially to those who need immediate relief or otherwise desire medication treatment, followed by psychosocial treatment such as PCT, may be quite effective for patients with panic disorder. It is possible that the future of combined treatment lies in these sequential strategies, as opposed to simultaneous administration of drug and psychosocial treatment.

Along these lines, clinical investigators have begun to examine the effectiveness of psychosocial treatments for patients who were previous nonresponders to pharmacological treatment. For example, Pollack, Otto, Kaspi, Hammerness, and Rosenbaum (1994) found that 12 weeks of group cognitive behavioral therapy helped patients who had shown evidence of an incomplete response to previous pharmacotherapy. While these patients had not shown evidence of improvement while using medication, they experienced significant improvement in global functioning, as well as panic attack frequency, after the 12-week cognitive behavioral treatment. These results suggest that there might be a select group of patients with panic disorder who may not benefit from medication treatment but then are able to show evidence of improvement when effective psychosocial treatments are administered. Of course, reversing the sequence for those who initially fail with cognitive behavioral treatments by subsequently administering an effective pharmacological treatment might produce similar results.

Finally, we now know that even those individuals doing well at follow-ups of a year or more with cognitive behavioral approaches often experience "setbacks" or other exacerbations of symptoms that occasionally progress to a full relapse (e.g., Burns et al., 1986). Often, these episodes are associated with emergent life stress or other difficulties (Brown, Antony, & Barlow, 1995). Thus, a finding that 75% of all patients treated responded to treatment at posttreatment, and 65% at a 2-year follow-up, may mask the fact that a number of these patients may have experienced significant setbacks in the months between the assessments. In view of the chronicity of panic disorder with agoraphobia, there is a need to investigate strategies to prevent exacerbations of symptoms, as well as full relapse. Based on preliminary studies demonstrating the possible value of maintenance strategies (e.g., Jansson et al., 1986; Ost, 1989) efforts are now under way in our center and elsewhere to develop more comprehensive and effective maintenance strategies for the purpose of preventing exacerbations or full relapses. Currently, a large multicenter study is under way investigating the long-term strategies for the maintenance of positive treatment results for panic disorder. In this study, all patients will receive PCT as the first line of treatment. Those who evidence treatment gains after receiving PCT then will be randomly assigned to a maintenance condition, in which they receive 6 monthly sessions of PCT. Patients who do not respond to the initial phase of PCT will be randomly assigned to receive either additional CBT sessions or a trial of paroxetine. The goal of this study is to better understand the utility of maintenance sessions for those who respond to PCT, as well as to examine the effectiveness of pharmacotherapy versus additional CBT for CBT nonresponders.

SPECIFIC PHOBIA

The *DSM-IV* diagnosis of specific phobia replaces the diagnosis of simple phobia listed in *DSM-III-R* (APA, 1987). In *DSM-IV*, a specific phobia is defined as a marked and persistent fear cued by the presence or anticipation of an object or situation. The fear must be considered excessive or unreasonable and must be associated with functional impairment or subjective distress. In addition, the specific phobia must not be better accounted for by another *DSM-IV* disorder (APA, 1994).

Five subtypes of specific phobias are included in *DSM-IV*: animal, natural environmental, blood-injection-injury, situational, and other. The "other" type serves as a catchall category for specific phobias such as choking or vomiting that do not readily fall into any of the first four subtypes. These subtypes were devised by the *DSM-IV* Anxiety Disorders Work Group as more information was gained about the heterogeneity among the specific phobias along a variety of dimensions (APA, 1996). These dimensions include age of onset, gender composition, patterns of comorbidity, and type of physiological reaction to the phobic situation, as well as other important variables such as natural course and type of treatment indicated. For example, the mean age of onset for animal, blood, storm, and water phobias tends to be early childhood, while the mean age of onset for situational height phobia is adolescence (Antony & Barlow, in press; Craske & Sipsas, 1992; Curtis, Hill, & Lewis, 1990; Marks & Gelder, 1966; Ost, 1987).

The *DSM-IV* diagnosis of specific phobia, when considered overall, is highly prevalent (Antony & Barlow, 1996). Yet, when specific phobias are given as primary diagnoses, the clinician is not likely to observe an additional clinical diagnosis. In other words, principal diagnoses of specific phobias tend to have lower rates of comorbidity than principal diagnoses of most other Axis I disorders (Brown & Barlow, 1992). In a study based on data from the NCS study (Kessler et al., 1994), Curtis et al. (1998) found that, of the 915 individuals with a lifetime history of a specific phobia, only 24.4% had a single phobia.

The remaining cases had two (26.4%), three (23.5%), four (10.4%), or more than four (17.3%) phobias.

According to the NCS, approximately 11% of the population experience a specific phobia over a lifetime (Kessler et al., 1994). Gender differences are marked, the lifetime prevalence for women being 15.7% of the population, compared with 6.7% for men. Interestingly, this gender difference in prevalence is most pronounced for the animal type of specific phobia and least apparent for height, flying, and blood-injury-injection phobias (Antony & Barlow, in press).

Treatments for Specific Phobias

A consensus has developed that the treatment of choice for specific phobias is exposure-based procedures, particularly in vivo exposure. Exposure has been shown to be effective for a wide spectrum of specific phobias. While imaginal exposure has been shown to produce fear reduction (Baker, Cohen, & Saunders, 1973) and should be used if situational in vivo exposure treatment is not feasible, in vivo exposure is generally accepted as the most powerful treatment for specific phobias (APA, 1994; Antony & Barlow, in press; Barlow, 1988, in press; Marks, 1987).

In vivo exposure treatment often appears deceptively simple, yet there are many facets to the procedure (Antony & Barlow, in press). Therapists usually initiate exposure treatment with a few office visits. During these initial sessions, the therapist gathers more specific information about the patient's feelings, thoughts, and behaviors concerning the phobic object or situation. Patients are informed that systematic, repeated in vivo exposure will allow them to become desensitized to the phobic object or situation. The clinician also lets patients know that all in vivo exposures will be predictable and under their control and teaches patients a variety of adaptive coping strategies to utilize throughout treatment. Finally, the clinician and the patient create a hierarchy of feared situations concerning the phobic object or situation and formulate a treatment plan consisting of in vivo exposure practices.

Extensive literature exists demonstrating the effectiveness of in vivo exposure treatments for specific phobias. Over the past few decades, in vivo exposure has been successfully utilized to treat most types of specific phobia (Antony & Barlow, in press). For example, clinical investigators have demonstrated the effectiveness of in vivo exposure to treat phobias of animals (e.g., Muris, Mayer, & Merckelbach, 1998; Ost, 1989; Ost, Ferebee, & Furmark, 1997; Ost, Salkovskis, & Hellstrom, 1991), heights (e.g., Bourque & Ladouceur, 1980), and flying (Beckham, Vrana, May, Gustafson, & Smith, 1990; Howard, Murphy, & Clarke, 1983; Ost, Brandberg, & Alm, 1997; Solyom, Shugar, Bryntwick & Solyom, 1973). In addition, in vivo exposure has been utilized to treat fear of dentists (Jerremalm, Jansson, & Ost, 1986b; Liddell, Di Fazio, Blackwood, & Ackerman, 1994), as well as choking phobia (McNally, 1986, 1994), with good results. In addition, blood-injury-injection phobias also have been successfully treated with in vivo exposure, although these phobias and their treatments are unique and are described below (Ost, 1989; Ost & Sterner, 1987).

Though exposure-based treatments for specific phobias are considered fairly straightforward, they are composed of many factors that may have an impact on the clinical results of treatment. These factors include the duration and temporal spacing of exposure sessions, the level of therapist involvement, and the incorporation of additional treatment components into exposure sessions. The following discussion reviews the available empirical evidence regarding these factors.

In general, it appears that massed exposure sessions result in the most robust clinical improvement (Marks, 1987). In fact, in as little as one session of therapist-guided exposure, 90% of persons with animal or injection phobias were found to be much improved or completely recovered (Ost, 1989). Ost treated over 20 patients with a specific phobia for a particular animal or injections with in vivo exposure and therapist modeling. He completed each of these sessions in less than 3 hours, with a mean session length of approximately 2 hours. Of the patients, 90% showed evidence of immediate clinical improvement, and their clinically significant improvement was retained at follow-up assessments conducted up to 4 years posttreatment. Recently, Rowe and Craske (1998) examined the benefits of an expanding-spaced exposure schedule versus massed exposure. In this model, sessions begin close together and gradually spread out as treatment progresses. They found that massed exposure led to significantly more fear reduction in a group of spider phobics. However, they also found that an expanding-spaced schedule was less likely than a massed schedule to be associated with a return of fear following treatment.

The degree of therapist involvement in exposure treatment is also considered to be an important component of the treatment. Though relatively few studies have directly examined the influence of the therapist's presence, most empirical findings point to the importance of therapist involvement during exposure treatment. For example, Ost et al. (1991) found that, while 71% of persons with spider phobia improved with therapist-assisted exposure treatment, only 6% of persons who engaged in self-directed exposures evidenced clinical improvement. In a follow-up study, Hellstrom and Ost (1995) found that the manner in which self-help treatment is disseminated affects the outcome for individuals with spider phobias. In this study, five different treatments were compared: (a) a single session of therapist-assisted exposure, (b) a spider-phobia-specific manual used in the home, (c) a spider-phobia-specific manual used in the clinic, (d) a nonspecific manual used in the home, and (e) a nonspecific manual used in the clinic. The percentage of individuals who were significantly improved were 80%, 10%, 63%, 9%, and 10%, respectively. These findings suggest that self-help manuals can be beneficial to individuals when they are used in a clinic setting.

In addition, O'Brien and Kelley (1980) found that patients who engaged in therapist-directed exposure sessions for snake phobia showed evidence of significantly greater improvement than the patients who engaged in self-directed exposure sessions. Finally, while Bourque and Ladouceur (1980) found no differences in treatment outcome when they varied the degree of therapist involvement in the exposure sessions, their results might be due to the methodological limitations of their study. In their study design, even the patients in the self-directed exposure condition were presented with the exposure rationale by their therapist prior to engaging in the self-directed exposure. Moreover, they received verbal reinforcement from their therapist immediately after they completed their self-directed exposures.

Other empirical studies have shown that certain types of specific phobias require adaptation of exposure-based procedures that incorporate additional treatment components. For example, individuals with blood-injury-injection phobia tend to have a physiological reaction that often inspires a fainting response. This physiological reaction, known as a *vasovagal syncope*, consists of an immediate increase in both heart rate and blood pressure when the person encounters the phobic stimulus, followed by a significant decrease in both heart rate and blood pressure. It is this decrease in both heart rate and blood pressure that so often induces fainting in these individuals (Page, 1994). A physical strategy that prevents the fainting response has been developed and added to exposure treatment. This coping strategy, known as *applied tension*, serves to temporarily sustain the patient's blood pressure and heart rate at an increased level, thereby eliminating the possibility of fainting.

The applied-tension technique consists of completely tensing all the large muscle groups of the body (arms, torso, and legs) for 15 seconds and then releasing the tensing for 15 seconds. Patients are expected to begin the applied-tension technique before the injection procedure (completing at least five cycles), and they are expected to continue the applied-tension technique both during and after the injection procedure to maintain an adequate blood pressure and heart rate. The applied-tension technique has been empirically validated as an additional component of exposure treatment (Ost & Sterner, 1987). In addition, Hellstrom, Fellenius, and Ost (1996) showed that a single session of applied tension along with a maintenance program of self-exposure is as effective as a five-session course of the same treatment.

Several treatment manuals for the specific phobias exist. The program developed and manualized at our center presents general information regarding the nature and treatment of specific phobias, as well as detailed treatment information for several of the most common specific phobias (Antony, Craske, & Barlow, 1995). In addition, the treatments presented in this manual incorporate additional treatment strategies to be utilized in conjunction with in vivo exposure treatments. For example, cognitive strategies used to combat cognitive distortions and anxious thought patterns and interoceptive exposure utilized to desensitize patients to the physical sensations they associate with the phobic object or situation are included as additional treatment components.

Future Directions

Though a great deal of treatment outcome research exists for specific phobias, much remains to be learned. For example, researchers have only just begun to examine differences among the specific phobia subtypes. Little is known about different characteristics of the five subtypes, and additional information in this area could improve treatments for specific phobias. Just as patients with blood-injury-injection phobias benefit from the utilization of applied tension coupled with exposure therapy, many patients with other specific phobia subtypes might respond more robustly to exposure treatments tailored specifically to their phobic object or situation. For example, studies have shown that compared to nonphobic controls, individuals with height phobias report an inflated probability of the possibility of serious injury resulting from falling from a ladder (Menzies & Clarke, 1995).

Preliminary evidence shows that, while a therapist's guidance seems necessary for patients with specific phobias to show evidence of improvement, self-directed bibliotherapy seems effective in treating panic disorder with agoraphobia (e.g., Ghosh & Marks, 1987). If subsequent research supports this finding, factors that might be relevant include differences in the disorders, as well as the differing natures of exposure treatments appropriate for each of them. For example, patients with specific phobias may need a therapist's assistance to come into initial contact with the phobic object. Also, due to the unique nature of many specific phobias, patients may need the therapist's guidance to create a diversity of in vivo exposure experiences of adequate duration and difficulty. In contrast, patients with panic disorder and agoraphobia often fear having panic attacks in many common situations; they rarely believe that there is something inherently dangerous in the situation itself. With the assistance of a manual, motivated patients suffering from panic disorder with agoraphobia may be able to create their own fear and avoidance hierarchy of common situations and to conduct effective self-directed in vivo exposures. Of course, these hypotheses are merely speculative at this time, given the limited empirical evidence regarding the effectiveness of self-directed exposure treatment for patients with either specific phobias or panic disorder with agoraphobia.

Moreover, in this era of managed care, when cost-effectiveness is considered of utmost importance, further research should be conducted to determine which of the many specific phobias can be treated in just one therapist-assisted in vivo exposure session. Though information has been gained regarding such intensive treatments for patients with certain animal and injection phobias, as well as blood phobias (Hellstrom, Fellenius, & Ost, 1996; Ost, 1989), it has yet to be determined if other common specific phobias (e.g., height) and, in particular, situational phobias such as flying or claustrophobia would respond as well to such a treatment modality.

Ost (1989) has suggested that specific phobias, such as phobias of heights, elevators, and darkness, might respond very well to therapist-assisted one-session exposure treatment. However, Ost speculates that flying phobia might require additional therapist-assisted sessions to incorporate substantial patient education regarding the flying process. In addition, Ost wonders whether claustrophobia would respond well to a one-session treatment, since it is usually not circumscribed and instead encompasses many different situations. Since situational phobias are thought to be on a continuum with panic disorder with agoraphobia, there is reason to suspect the applicability of single-session treatments. While some studies are currently under way to examine the possible effectiveness of therapist-assisted single-session exposure treatment, this is an area of research that could benefit from even further attention.

In the past few years, clinicians have begun to take advantage of technological advances in the treatment of specific phobias. For example, a number of investigators have begun to use virtual reality to expose patients to simulated situations such as heights (Rothbaum et al., 1995), flying (Rothbaum, Hodges, & Smith, 1999) and spiders (Carlin, Hoffman, & Weghorst, 1997). At this time, there is only one controlled study published on virtual reality treatments for patients with specific phobias. Rothbaum et al. (1995) treated 12 height-fearful college students using eight sessions of virtual reality exposure. Compared to eight individuals in a wait-list control condition, those who were treated with virtual reality were significantly improved. Although these preliminary findings are promising, more controlled studies with a broader range of phobias are needed (Antony & Barlow, 2001). Rothbaum, Hodges, Smith, Lee, and Price (in press) recently conducted a controlled study of virtual reality exposure (VRE) treatment for fear of flying. Forty-five patients were randomly assigned to receive either VRE treatment, standard exposure treatment (SE), or wait list (WL). The results indicated that VRE and SE were both superior to WL, with no differences between VRE and SE. VRE and SE were shown to be effective by decreases in symptoms as measured by standardized questionnaires, by the number of participants to actually fly on a real airplane following treatment, by anxiety ratings during the flight, by self-ratings of improvement, and by patient satisfaction with treatment. The gains observed in treatment were maintained at a 6-month follow-up. By 6 months posttreatment, 93% of VRE participants and 93% of SE participants had flown.

SOCIAL PHOBIA

Social phobia has recently been estimated as the most prevalent of all anxiety disorders, with a lifetime prevalence of 13.3% and a 12-month prevalence of 7.9% (Kessler et al., 1994). Moreover, social phobia is the third most prevalent of all mental disorders, exceeded only by major depressive disorder and alcohol dependence. This finding is truly remarkable, especially since social phobia was not included as a separate diagnostic category until *DSM-III* (APA, 1980).

According to *DSM-IV* (APA, 1994), individuals with social phobia fear a number of social and performance situations because of concerns that they will act in a way that will be humiliating or embarrassing or that they will visibly manifest anxiety symptoms (e.g., sweating, shaking, or blushing). For patients with social phobia, the fear and avoidance of people typically result in several areas of impairment, including occupational, academic, and social functioning (cf. Hope & Heimberg, 1993). The mean age of onset of social phobia is estimated to be 15.5 years, and onset after the age of 25 is relatively uncommon (Schneier, Johnson, Hornig, Liebowitz, & Weissman, 1992). Moreover, 69% of 361 individuals with social phobia in the large ECA (Epidemiological Catchment Area) study (Myers et al., 1984) also experienced lifetime major comorbid Axis I disorders such as specific phobia (59.0%), agoraphobia (44.9%), alcohol abuse (18.8%), major depression (16.6%), drug abuse (13.0%), dysthymia (12.5%), and obsessive compulsive disorder (11.1%) (Schneier et al., 1992). There is also recent evidence that from 22.1% to 70% of individuals with social phobia also meet criteria for avoidant personality disorder (cf. Hope & Heimberg, 1993).

Little is known about the etiology of social phobia, but numerous studies have examined the following possible factors: behavioral inhibition, genetics, biological mechanisms, developmental factors, conditioning, and cognitive models (Herbert, 1995). Barlow (1988, in press; Barlow et al., 1996; Hoffman & Barlow, in press) has hypothesized that one must be biologically and psychologically vulnerable to anxious apprehension to develop social phobia. There is evidence that genetics plays a role in social phobia. By interviewing 2,163 female twins, Kendler, Neale, Kessler, Heath, and Eaves (1992) found that probandwise concordance for social phobia was greater in monozygotic (24.4%) than dizygotic (15.3%) twin pairs. In another study examining the contribution of genetics in social phobia, first-degree relatives of social phobia probands ($N = 83$) had a significantly increased risk (16% vs. 5%; relative risk = 3.12) for social phobia compared with first-degree relatives of never mentally ill controls ($N = 231$; Fyer, Mannuzza, Chapman, Liebowitz, & Klein, 1993). This biological vulnerability may express itself in exaggerated reactivity to social evaluation situations. That is, for reasons of evolutionary significance, we are biologically vulnerable to the effects of anger, criticism, and other means of social disapproval.

As in all anxiety disorders, a generalized psychological vulnerability also exists in which individuals learn that important, personally salient events in their lives, particularly challenging or threatening events, are unpredictable and uncontrollable. In addition, research suggests that at least some patients with social phobia are predisposed to focus anxious apprehension on events involving social evaluation. Social anxiety in social evaluative situations involving performance forms the basis from which a false alarm (panic attack) develops in specific social situations. Of course, in some cases, individuals may have direct experience with a traumatic form of social rejection or humiliation, resulting in a true alarm. Another pathway to the acquisition of social phobia occurs when socially anxious individuals occasionally experience some performance deficits, even without an encounter with an alarm. Subsequent anxious apprehension in the future may lead to performance deficits, which set off the vicious cycle of anxious apprehension (Hoffman & Barlow, in press). Although the pathways of acquisition may vary, they all have biological vulnerability, psychological vulnerability, and stress/trauma in common.

Treatments for Social Phobia

Research on cognitive behavioral treatments for social phobia has substantially increased in recent years. The most common treatment approaches include social skills training (SST), relaxation techniques, exposure-based methods, and multicomponent cognitive behavioral treatments (Heimberg & Juster, 1995; Turk, Heimberg, & Hope, 2001). In this section, as above, empirical studies are evaluated according to a template recently created by the American Psychological Association to guide the development of practice guidelines (American Psychological Association Task Force on Intervention Guidelines, 1995; Barlow & Barlow, 1995). Effective treatments in this section are organized into one of the following three categories of increasing confidence in treatment efficacy: (a) better than no therapy (randomized clinical trials, RCTs); (b) better than nonspecific therapy (RCTs); and (c) better than alternative therapy (RCTs). All studies individually reviewed are Type 1 studies unless otherwise noted.

Social Skills Training

The rationale of SST is based on the concept that people with social phobias are deficient in verbal and nonverbal social skills. Heimberg and Juster (1995) pointed out that, although social skills deficits are inferred from poor social behavior, the term is often confused with *performance deficits*. They also concluded that, although nine studies have used SST as a treatment condition, some resulting in significant improvement, all but one failed to include appropriate control groups. Therefore, it is not possible to conclude that training in social skills was the component that led to positive outcomes (Heimberg & Juster, 1995). Similarly, Donahue, Van Hasselt, and Hersen (1994) concluded that the heterogeneity of the samples and the paucity of controlled comparisons do not permit definitive conclusions on SST efficacy. Because of the recognized cognitive contributions in the maintenance of social phobia, and because most individuals with social phobia have adequate social skills, therapy in recent years has targeted cognitive and behavioral interventions for the treatment of social phobia. Therefore, SST has been investigated less in recent years (Mersch, 1995).

Referring to the aforementioned template of treatment efficacy, we cannot definitively state at this time that SST is superior to even a wait-list control because of methodological limitations. This conclusion gains credence given that the only controlled study of SST, completed in 1976, found that 15 weeks of SST did not result in better clinical outcomes than a wait-list control group (Marzillier, Lambert, & Kelley, 1976).

Although SST by itself does not appear to be efficacious, there is some indication that combining SST and exposure appears to hold some promise (Turner, Beidel, Cooley, Woody, & Messer, 1994). In this pilot study of a comprehensive multicomponent treatment (which was a Type 3 study), 13 patients with severe (generalized) social phobia demonstrated significant improvements posttreatment. The authors report that 84% of those completing treatment (four dropped out) showed moderate to high end-state functioning, although pretreatment status could not be calculated because there were no pretreatment clinical global impression (CGI) ratings. Moreover, there was no control group. These preliminary findings suggest the importance of controlled clinical trials for this combined treatment. Furthermore, dismantling studies need to be conducted to explore whether the SST component itself leads to additional improvement above and beyond the gains made from the other components.

Relaxation Treatments

The effectiveness of relaxation training and other strategies targeting arousal reduction (AR) for social phobia has not yet been adequately evaluated (Heimberg & Juster, 1995; Turk, Heimberg, & Hope, 2001). Two groups of investigators have concluded that progressive muscle relaxation alone is not an effective treatment (Al-Kubaisy et al., 1992; Alstroem, Nordlund, Persson, Harding, & Ljungqvist, 1984). There has been some indication by Ost, Jerremalm, and Johansson (1981) and Jerremalm, Jansson, and Ost (1986a) that AR, including application training in which relaxation skills are used during anxiety-producing role plays (cf. Heimberg & Juster, 1995), is an effective treatment for social phobia (cf. Heimberg & Juster, 1995). Of the three controlled clinical trials conducted in this area (Alstrom et al., 1984; Jerremalm et al., 1986a; Ost et al., 1981), AR was inferior to self-instruction training, exposure, and supportive counseling and was no better than SST (Donahue et al., 1994). At this time, there is no strong body of literature to support relaxation procedures alone as an effective treatment for social phobia.

Exposure and Cognitive Therapy

There is a growing body of literature in support of a multifaceted treatment for social phobia based on exposure to feared social situations and cognitive therapy (Barlow & Lehman, 1996). Social phobia is partially maintained by the avoidance of anxiety-producing situations and the negative reinforcement that occurs as a result (Donahue et al., 1994). Barlow (1988; Hoffman & Barlow, in press) views some form of exposure as a central part of any psychosocial treatment for social phobia, and many others would agree. The essential part of exposure is to have patients repeatedly confront the situation they fear until their anxiety response habituates. The exposures can be conducted in vivo, with the stimulus encountered in the natural environment, or through imaginal exercises. Many treatment programs involve simulated social interactions in which the therapist (and confederates, if necessary) role-plays the anxiety-producing social situation. The cognitive component of treatment addresses the role of fear of negative evaluation by identifying and modifying maladaptive cognitions that occur in these situations (Donahue et al., 1994).

In an early study examining combination treatments, Butler, Cullington, Munby, Amies, and Gelder (1984) randomly assigned 45 socially phobic outpatients to one of the three following conditions: in vivo exposure plus anxiety management (AM), in vivo plus a nonspecific filler, and a wait list. The AM program consisted of distraction, relaxation, and rational self-talk. At posttreatment, both active treatment groups were superior to the wait-list controls. However, at 6-month follow-up, patients who had received the combination treatment were more improved than the in-vivo-exposure-alone group.

Mattick and Peters (1988) found that cognitive restructuring exercises may enhance the effects of exposure therapy for people with social phobia. In their study, 26 patients were randomly assigned to guided exposure, while 25 patients received guided exposure and cognitive restructuring. There were improvements in both groups at follow-up, and patients in the combined condition fared better at the 3-month follow-up.

In a subsequent study, Mattick, Peters, and Clarke (1989) randomly assigned 43 patients with social phobia to guided exposure alone, cognitive restructuring alone, guided exposure and cognitive restructuring, or a wait list. All active treatment conditions were significantly better than the wait list on a behavioral avoidance test (BAT), as well as on self-report measures of negative evaluation and irrational beliefs. Patients in the combined condition evidenced the most improvement on the BAT. The authors concluded that the exposure therapy combined with cognitive restructuring was the most effective intervention overall.

Heimberg et al. (1990) compared a treatment package called *cognitive behavioral group treatment* (CBGT), consisting primarily of in-session exposure exercises, cognitive restructuring, and homework exercises, to a credible placebo condition. This placebo condition, called *educational supportive group therapy* (ES), was a nondirective supportive group treatment that also consisted of psychoeducation about social phobia. Both groups improved significantly at posttreatment, but CBGT patients were more improved on some key measures at both posttreatment and 6-month follow-up. Moreover, a 5-year follow-up on a portion of the patients from the original study indicated that individuals who received CBGT were more likely than the ES group to be improved and to maintain their gains (Heimberg, Salzman, Halt, & Blendell, 1993). This investigation provides further support for combination treatments involving both exposure and cognitive restructuring.

To date, only a few projects have compared effective pharmacotherapy treatments to effective psychosocial treatments. In the first published study of this nature, 65 patients with social phobia were assigned randomly to one of the four following conditions: cognitive behavioral group treatment, alprazolam with instructions for self-directed exposure (EXP), phenelzine with EXP, or placebo with EXP (Gelernter et al., 1991). All treatments, including the combination of a placebo plus self-exposure instructions, were associated with substantial improvements in severe and chronic social phobia, although the results failed to demonstrate definitively the superiority of one treatment over another.

Turner, Beidel, and Jacob (1994) assigned 72 patients with social phobia randomly to receive behavior therapy (flooding), atenolol, or a placebo. On composite and improvement indices, the behavior therapy patients were significantly more improved and demonstrated superior end-state functioning. However, although beta blockers such as atenolol may minimize the somatic symptoms associated with social phobia, such as trembling (Barlow, 1988), these drugs seem incapable of reducing other difficulties associated with this disorder (Turner, Beidel, & Jacob, 1994). Other research has suggested that atenolol is not the most effective drug treatment for social phobia (Heimberg & Juster, 1995).

An important multisite (the State University of New York at Albany, Center for Stress and Anxiety Disorders, and the New York State Psychiatric Institute) collaborative project directed by Richard Heimberg and Michael Liebowitz randomly assigned 133 individuals with social phobia to one of the following four treatment conditions: CBGT, phenelzine, a psychosocial placebo (ES), and a pill placebo (Heimberg et al., 1998). Results indicated the following:

1. CBGT and phenelzine were equally effective after 12 weeks of treatment. Approximately 60% of patients completing treatment in each group showing substantial improvement. Both were superior to ES and pill placebo, which produced improvement rates of approximately 27% and 33%, respectively.
2. After 12 weeks, phenelzine was more effective than CBGT on some self-report measures.

Following the acute phase of the study, responders to this trial entered a 6-month maintenance phase and a 6-month treatment-free phase (Liebowitz et al., 1999). Of the 31 patients who completed acute treatment with phenelzine, 20 were classified as responders and were therefore eligible to enter the maintenance phase. Similarly, 21 of the 36 patients who received CBGT during the acute phase were classified as responders, eligible to enter the maintenance phase of the study. Of these patients, 6 in the phenelzine group and 7 in the CBGT group declined participation in maintenance. Following the 6-month maintenance phase, no differences were detected between the phenelzine patients (3 relapsed, 1 dropped out) and CBGT patients (2 relapsed, 1 dropped out). At this point, those patients classified as responders in the phenelzine group (10/14) and the CGBT group (11/14) were eligible to enter a 6-month treatment-free phase. Following this treatment-free phase, again, no difference was found in the dropout rates between the two groups, as each group had only one dropout. Although the relapse rate in the phenelzine group (3/14) was higher than in the CBGT group (0/14) at the end of the treatment-free phase, the difference did not reach statistical significance due to the small sample size.

Based on the empirical research, we can conclude that combined exposure and cognitive therapy treatments are superior to a wait list, a nonspecific therapy, and, in some cases, alternative therapies.

Psychological Intervention Guidelines

If we return to the psychological intervention guidelines template mentioned above, exposure-based procedures are the only treatment for social phobia that attain the highest level of treatment efficacy, "better than alternative therapy." Heimberg and Juster (1995; Turk, Heimberg, & Hope, 2001) maintain that every study with this approach demonstrates significant reductions in social phobia, compared with various control groups. Moreover, there is some evidence to support the idea that combining exposure with cognitive restructuring is even more effective that exposure alone (Butler et al., 1984; Mattick & Peters, 1988; Mattick, Peters, & Clarke, 1989).

Table 13.4 (Barlow & Lehman, 1996) indicates that combined treatments are more effective than exposure or educational supportive group psychotherapy in all but one case. In this study (Hope, Heimberg, & Bruch, 1990), CBGT and exposure alone were equally effective, and both were superior to wait-list control. One study with medication did not demonstrate the superiority of combined treatments over drug treatments. Gelernter et al. (1991) found that all treatments (CBGT, alprazolam and exposure, phenelzine and exposure, placebo and exposure) were associated with substantial improvements, although the superiority of one treatment over another was not definitively demonstrated. Heimberg et al. (1998) found that CBGT and phenelzine treatments were equally effective and superior to a placebo and educational supportive treatments.

Looking at other treatment approaches, at this time we cannot definitively state that social skills training or relaxation are better than no therapy, partially because of the methodological limitations of these studies. However, AR, which includes exposure, appears promising.

Future Directions

Clearly, more research needs to be done to evaluate the effectiveness of certain treatments compared to wait-list controls, nonspecific treatment, and alternative therapies. Given the favorable outcomes of the combined cognitive and exposure treatments, it is imperative that we, as researchers, disseminate this treatment

TABLE 13.4 Controlled Trials of Psychosocial Treatments for Social Phobia

Study	*Length of Follow-Up (Months)*	*Treatment (N)*	*Percentage Clinical Improvement of Completers (If Available)*	*Significant Comparison (Percentage Clinical Improvement)*	
				Other Treatment (Yes/No)	*Wait List (Yes/No)*
Butler et al. (1984)	6	AMT & E (N = 15)		Yes: E	Yes
Mattick and Peters (1988)	3	E & CR (N = 11)	86	Yes: E = 52%	Yes
Mattick et al. (1989)	3	E & CR (N = 25)		Yes: E	Yes
Heimberg et al. (1990)	6	CBGT (N = 20)	81	Yes: ES = 47%	
Heimberg et al. (1993)[a]	54–75	CBGT (N = 10)		Yes: ES (most)	
Hope et al. (1990)	6	CBGT (N = 13)		No: E	Yes
Gelernter et al. (1991)	2	CBGT (N = 20)		No: PH, AL, PL	
Lucas and Telch (1993)	PT	CBGT (N = 18) CBTI	61 50	Yes: ES = 24%	
Heimberg et al. (1998)	PT	CBGT (N = 28)	75	No: PH = 77% Yes: PL = 41% Yes: ES = 35%	
Liebowitz et al. (1999)[b]	6–12	CBGT (N = 14)		Yes: ES = 27% No: PH	

Source: Reprinted with permission from Barlow and Lehman (1996), © 1996 American Medical Association.

AL = alprazolam; AMT = anxiety management therapy; CBGT = cognitive behavioral group treatment; CBTI = cognitive behavioral treatment—individual; CR = cognitive restructuring; E = exposure; ES = educational supportive group psychotherapy (placebo treatment); PL = pill placebo; PH = phenelzine; PT = posttreatment.

[a]Follow-up study of Heimberg et al. (1990).

[b]Follow-up study of Heimberg et al. (1998).

to clinicians for widespread use. Barlow and Lehman (1996) stated that few attempts have been made to make these treatments more user-friendly and to present them for use by clinicians. To date, little work has been done to evaluate specific treatments beyond their original settings. Moreover, many research studies have exclusion criteria that eliminate "messy" subjects and may threaten the treatment's generalizability beyond academic clinical settings (Herbert, 1995). We do not yet know how effectively these combined treatments can be used outside experimental settings. It is generally assumed that those clients included in efficacy studies are systematically different from those who are excluded (Barlow, 1996). However, a study on the generalizability of cognitive behavioral group treatment for social phobia (Juster, Heimberg, & Engelberg, 1995) compared clients in a highly controlled efficacy study to those who refused random assignment (and the possibility of a drug condition) or who were excluded. Although the refusers and excluded clients differed systematically from the included clients on a number of variables, such as degrees of social support and socioeconomic status, all patients showed evidence of comparable clinical gain from the treatment under evaluation. We must continue to create and evaluate effective treatments for social phobia while disseminating them to practitioners and evaluating their effectiveness "in the field." Finally, ongoing multisite studies are examining if the combination of effective drug and cognitive behavioral group treatments confer any advantage over monotherapies.

GENERALIZED ANXIETY DISORDER

The diagnostic criteria for generalized anxiety disorder (GAD) have undergone substantial modification since the mid-1980s (Brown, O'Leary, & Barlow, 2001). In the past, the diagnostic category of GAD, first formulated in 1980 (APA, 1980), resulted in enormous confusion (Barlow, 1988, in press; Barlow & Wincze, 1998). This confusion was partially due to GAD's residual status, which meant that the diagnosis could not be assigned if a person met criteria for any other mental disorder (Brown et al., 2001). This convention was based on the notion that generalized anxiety was an integral part of many disorders and therefore could not be easily separated from the general clinical presentation. In *DSM-III-R* (APA, 1987), for the first time key defining features (e.g., excessive worry and persistent somatic concerns) were presented that elevated GAD beyond a strictly residual category (Brown et al., 2001). These criteria were further delineated and sharpened by *DSM-IV* (APA, 1994). The NCS study (Kessler et al., 1994) estimates the lifetime prevalence of GAD to be 5.1% and the 12-month prevalence to be 3.1% according to *DSM-III-R* criteria (APA, 1987).

As a result of changes in the diagnostic criteria and new data on prevalence, research on important characteristics of GAD, as well as empirical treatment outcome studies, has increased since the early 1990s. However, given that GAD may be the "basic" anxiety disorder in the sense that generalized anxiety is a consistent component of other anxiety disorders with the possible exception of specific phobia, treatments for GAD have still received surprisingly little attention (Barlow, 1988, 2001; Brown et al., 2001; Rapee, 1991).

Our model (Barlow, 1988, 2000, in press) of the etiology of GAD suggests that biological and psychological vulnerabilities line up to create a diathesis for chronic anxiety. Stress-related negative life events trigger neurobiological reactions such as increased corticotropin-releasing factor, activation of the hypothalamic-pituitary adrenocorticol axis, and the sense that events are proceeding uncontrollably and unpredictably. The focus of attention is shifted from the task at hand to a maladaptive self-evaluative mode, which further increases arousal. The result is increased vigilance and the narrowing of attention to the threat or challenge. This arousal-driven cognitive process continues to escalate in a negative feedback loop, resulting occasionally in performance disruption; attempts to cope, including situational avoidance, if possible; and/or a maladaptive worry process that seems to serve as a method of avoiding core negative affect (Barlow, 2000, in press; Borkovec, 1994; Craske, 1999).

Treatment of Generalized Anxiety Disorder

Until recently, clinical outcome studies have demonstrated only modest treatment gains in GAD symptomatology. These minimal treatment gains have been hypothesized to result from, among other things, high rates of comorbidity found in patients with GAD. In fact, studies have found GAD to be the most frequently assigned additional diagnosis for patients who meet criteria for another anxiety or mood disorder (cf. Brown et al., 2001). The modest treatment gains seen in patients with GAD in early studies may also have resulted from the fact that GAD tends to be chronic in nature, with patients often recalling a lifelong history of the disorder (Brown et al., 2001).

In general, different treatment conditions have not led to different improvement rates. Given the vagueness of earlier criteria, initial studies on the treatment of GAD utilized nonspecific treatment approaches such as relaxation or biofeedback, in contrast to specific treatment components directed at key features of other anxiety disorders, such as panic disorder. With the successive refinements of GAD criteria in *DSM-III-R* and *DSM-IV*, researchers now have more information regarding the key features to target in treatment. It has been only since the early 1990s that more rigorous controlled trials of treatment for GAD have been conducted, utilizing more specific treatment techniques aimed at targeting the key features of the disorder, such as cognitive therapy, behavior therapy, and combinations of several treatment components.

To properly evaluate the question of treatment choice, one must consider both the efficacy of the treatment and the clinical utility of that technique. In this section, as above, the treatment techniques reviewed focus on treatment efficacy. However, because there are fewer treatment outcome studies for GAD than for other disorders, they are organized in three categories of increasing confidence in treatment efficacy: (a) better than no therapy (randomized clinical trials, RCTs); (b) better than nonspecific therapy (RCTs); and (c) better than alternative therapy (RCTs).

Better Than No Therapy

In an early Type 2 investigation, five patients meeting *DSM-III* (APA, 1980) criteria for GAD received a treatment package consisting of EMG (electromyographic) biofeedback, relaxation, and cognitive treatment; they were compared to four GAD patients assigned to a wait list (Barlow et al., 1984). Those receiving active treatment had 18 sessions over a 14-week period. Compared to controls, the patients receiving the active treatment demonstrated a generalized improvement at posttreatment and 3-month follow-up on a variety of measures, including physiological reactivity, self-report questionnaires, and clinician ratings.

Another early controlled clinical trial for the treatment of GAD was conducted to investigate the efficacy of anxiety management (AM), a multicomponent treatment package in the form of a self-help booklet that was utilized in conjunction with therapist-conducted treatment sessions (Butler, Cullington, Hibbert, Klimes, & Gelder, 1987). In this study, 45 patients meeting research diagnostic criteria (RDC) for GAD were randomly assigned to either the AM ($N = 22$) or wait-list (WL) ($N = 23$) condition.

The treatment components included psychoeducation about anxiety, relaxation, distraction, cognitive restructuring, and exposure through graded practice. In addition, patients were encouraged to identify their strong points and engage in rewarding and pleasurable activities. Patients could stop treatment after a minimum of four sessions if they were no longer experiencing the symptoms of anxiety, if their anxiety ratings were stable for 2 weeks, and if their therapist agreed that they could control their symptoms. The average length of treatment was 8.7 sessions.

Patients were actively involved in their treatment by establishing goals and creating homework assignments, as well as scheduling more pleasurable activities and noting areas in their life in which things were going well. Some of the exercises were first practiced with the therapist in session and in addition at home. Furthermore, patients were encouraged to reduce their medication intake. During booster sessions at the end of treatment, the treatment components were reviewed, along with relapse prevention strategies.

At the end of treatment, the patients receiving AM improved significantly, compared to the wait-list controls, on every measure, including the State-Trait Anxiety Inventory, the Hamilton rating scales for anxiety and depression, and problem ratings of severity and interference. In addition, these gains were maintained or improved at 6-month follow-up. Although these results are extremely encouraging, it should be noted that patients were excluded if they had suffered from anxiety for 2 years or more, thus the patients with more chronic levels of anxiety had been eliminated.

Other studies have added a "placebo" therapy condition to examine whether improvements are caused by specific anxiety treatment techniques or are merely general therapy effects. Referring to our template of increasing treatment efficacy, we would have greater confidence in the efficacy of a certain treatment if it was shown to be superior to a nonspecific or placebo therapy. Two investigations that used both wait-list controls and a nondirective treatment condition were unable to demonstrate differential effectiveness between the active therapies and the nondirective treatments, although all treatments were superior to wait-list control groups (Blowers, Cobb, & Mathews, 1987; White & Keenan, 1992).

In one such investigation (Blowers et al., 1987), 66 patients meeting *DSM-III* criteria for GAD were assigned to one of three groups: anxiety management training (AMT), nondirective counseling (NDC), or wait-list (WL) control. All patients were assessed pretreatment, posttreatment, and at 6-month follow-up. The AMT package involved relaxation exercises and a cognitive component based on an abbreviated version of Beck and Emery's cognitive therapy (1985). Patients in the NDC condition were offered the rationale that they could be helped by understanding and becoming aware of their thoughts and feelings and would find the symptoms of anxiety to be less distressing as a result. There were few significant differences in the active treatment conditions, but both were superior to the wait-list controls according to self-report measures and clinician ratings.

Other researchers have also encountered the finding that different active treatments have not led to differential efficacy (Barlow, Rapee & Brown, 1992; Borkovec & Mathews, 1988; Durham & Turvey, 1987). In a study conducted in our center (Barlow et al., 1992), 65 patients meeting *DSM-III-R* criteria as established by the ADIS-R (Anxiety Disorders Interview Schedule–Revised) (DiNardo & Barlow, 1988) were randomized to one of four treatment groups: applied progressive muscle relaxation (REL), cognitive restructuring (COG), a combination of relaxation and cognitive restructuring (COM), or a wait list (WL). All patients in the active treatment conditions received 15 hour-long sessions conducted by senior doctoral students and staff psychologists.

Treated patients were significantly better than those in the wait-list control group. However, as stated above, differential efficacy was not found among active treatment components. Moreover, differential dropout rates were encountered among the active treatments (8% in the COM group and 38% in the REL group).

The two additional studies mentioned above also did not find a difference among treatment conditions, although they did not assign a wait-list control group. Durham and Turvey (1987) randomly assigned 41 patients to either behavior therapy or Beck's cognitive therapy and found that there were no significant differences posttreatment. At 6-month follow-up, however, there was a trend for those receiving cognitive therapy to continue to improve or maintain their gains more frequently than those patients receiving behavior therapy. In another investigation, Borkovec and Mathews (1988) randomly assigned 30 patients to one of three groups: progressive muscle relaxation (PMR) with nondirective therapy, PMR with coping desensitization, or PMR with cognitive therapy. All patients had significant improvement, but they did not differ from each other.

Better Than Nonspecific Therapy

More recently, a few controlled clinical trials have found that a certain type of treatment is better than nondirective treatment (Borkovec et al., 1987; Borkovec & Costello, 1993). In the earlier study (Borkovec et al., 1987), 30 patients who met *DSM-III* criteria according to the ADIS (Anxiety Disorders Interview Schedule) (DiNardo, O'Brien, Barlow, Waddell, & Blanchard, 1983) were randomly assigned to one of two groups: progressive muscle relaxation (PMR) with cognitive therapy (CT) or PMR with nondirective therapy (ND). Overall, all patients improved substantially at the end of treatment and also at the 6- to 12-month follow-up, as shown by clinician ratings, self-report questionnaires, and daily self-monitoring. However, the PMR and CT group was superior to the PMR and ND group on all but one posttreatment outcome measure. In addition, patients receiving cognitive therapy attributed more of their improvement to the cognitive component of treatment than patients receiving nondirective therapy did to the general psychotherapy they received. The authors concluded that cognitive therapy contains an active ingredient above and beyond the nonspecific psychotherapy treatment factors.

Better Than Alternative Therapy

A final group of studies has been conducted that compares at least two efficacious psychotherapy treatments. According to the template, demonstrated efficacy in this category results in the highest level of confidence in a given treatment. Although most investigations of this type have not resulted in significant differences emerging among active treatments (Barlow et al., 1992; Blowers et al., 1987; Borkovec & Mathews, 1988; Durham & Turvey, 1987; White & Keenan, 1992), a few empirical studies have demonstrated the superiority of one active treatment over another (Butler, Fennell, Robson, & Gelder, 1991; Durham et al., 1994).

In an empirical investigation, 57 patients meeting *DSM-III-R* criteria for GAD were randomly assigned to one of three treatment groups: cognitive behavioral treatment (CBT), behavior therapy (BT), or a wait-list control group (Butler, Fennell, Robson, & Gelder, 1991). In this controlled clinical trial, independent assessments were conducted pretreatment, posttreatment, at 6-month follow-up, and at 18-month follow-up. Treatment lasted for up to 12 sessions; patients could stop treatment after 4 sessions if they no longer experienced significant symptoms of anxiety, if their anxiety ratings were stable for at least 2 weeks, and if their therapist agreed with the patient that the patient could control anxiety symptoms effectively.

The BT package consisted of progressive muscle relaxation, reducing avoidance through graduated exposure, and building confidence by reinitiating pleasurable activities. The rationale for BT was that anxiety is maintained by avoidance of anxiety-producing situations, the person's reaction to the symptoms, and loss of confidence. The CBT package consisted of cognitive therapy as described by Beck and Emery (1985), as well as behavioral assignments. The rationale of CBT treatment was that anxiety is maintained by anxious thoughts and lack of self-confidence, which can be controlled by recognizing anxious thoughts, seeking helpful alternatives, and taking action to test these alternatives.

Results showed a superiority of CBT over BT, as demonstrated through measures of anxiety, depression, and cognition. However, the patients in the BT group improved significantly on all but one measure of anxiety and maintained their gains 6 months later. The authors (Butler et al., 1991) noted that theirs is one of the few studies in which CBT was shown to be superior to BT, and they offered several possible explanations:

1. BT cannot adequately address additional problems such as depression or social anxiety.
2. Cognitive techniques can be effectively applied to treatment reservations and low motivation.
3. CBT deals with worry, as well as somatic symptoms.
4. This study employed unusually rigorous methods of double-checking the integrity of treatment to reduce error variance and overlap between CBT and BT.

In the second study in the "Better Than Nonspecific Therapy" section above, Borkovec and Costello (1993) compared the efficacy of CBT, AR, and ND in a sample of 55 patients who met *DSM-III-R* criteria for GAD. For this study, patients in the ND condition were told that the goals of treatment were to enhance self-understanding and to discover things they could do differently to affect how they feel. All three treatments were equal in length and were reported to be highly credible to the patients. The AR and CBT treatment conditions did not differ significantly from each other but were both superior to ND at posttreatment. However, during a 1-year follow-up, 57.9% of patients receiving CBT met a high end-state functioning criterion (meaning they were close to "cured"), which was significantly better than the 33.3% of patients receiving AR who met this criterion and the 22.2% of patients receiving ND therapy who met this criterion. In addition, significantly fewer patients receiving CBT or AR than those receiving ND (61.1%) requested additional treatment (15.8% and 16.7%, respectively).

In another controlled clinical trial, 110 patients who met *DSM-III-R* criteria for GAD were randomly assigned to receive one of the following treatments over a 6-month period: 16 to 20 sessions of cognitive therapy, 8 to 10 sessions of cognitive therapy, 16 to 20 sessions of psychodynamic psychotherapy, 8 to 10 sessions of psychodynamic psychotherapy, or 8 to 10 sessions of behaviorally based anxiety management training (Durham et al., 1994). Experienced therapists conducted the cognitive therapy and psychodynamic therapy sessions, and registrars in psychiatry conducted the anxiety management sessions after a brief period of training.

Although all treatments resulted in substantial improvements, cognitive therapy was significantly more effective than analytic therapy, with about 50% of cognitive therapy patients "considerably" better at follow-up. There was no significant effect for level of contact. Although the authors made the point that significant improvements in symptoms can occur after only brief therapist training, it remains unclear whether there is a significant advantage for the experienced therapist because experienced and inexperienced therapists were conducting different types of treatment. Because therapist experience differed according to treatment type, this is considered a Type 2 study.

Cognitive behavioral therapy has also been shown to be superior to benzodiazepine medication in several controlled clinical trials (Lindsay, Gamsu, McLaughlin, Hood & Espie, 1987; Power et al., 1990; Power, Jerrom, Simpson, Mitchell, & Swanson, 1989). In one study (Power et al., 1990), 101 patients meeting *DSM-III* criteria for GAD were randomly assigned to one of the following 10-week treatment conditions: CBT, diazepam (DZ), placebo, CBT and DZ, or CBT and placebo. Posttreatment and 6-month follow-up measures indicated a superiority of all CBT treatments, especially CBT alone and the CBT/DZ combination. For more information on psychopharmacological treatments of GAD, please refer to Chapter 14 (Roy-Byrne & Cowley).

Future Directions

The more we learn about the nature of GAD, the more we should be able to improve our psychotherapeutic treatments. Additional dismantling studies should assist in determining the specific mechanisms of action in successful therapy. At this time, the most successful psychosocial treatments combine relaxation exercises and cognitive therapy with the goal of bringing the worry process itself under the patient's control (Barlow & Lehman, 1996). The results of 12 studies comparing cognitive therapy or cognitive behavioral therapy to other treatments or a wait list are summarized in Table 13.5 (Barlow & Lehman, 1996). Although one of the clinical trials (Butler et al., 1987) eliminated people who reported having anxiety for more than 2 years, the essence of GAD is that it seems to be characterological, most people reporting that they have been worriers all their lives. Thus, it is imperative that we study this population as Butler et al. (1991) did in a later project.

Until recently, most studies have not demonstrated differential rates of efficacy for active treatment techniques, although most studies have shown that active treatments are superior to nondirective approaches and uniformly superior to no treatment. Although more research in this area is still warranted, we have made substantial progress in the past decade. On the horizon is a unique treatment approach for GAD that seeks to integrate Hayes and colleagues' (1999) acceptance and commitment therapy (ACT) with traditional components of cognitive behavioral therapy, including psychoeducation, monitoring, and relaxation exercises. The new treatment, encourages acceptance and awareness of worry rather than thought challenging, and mindful action as an alternative to the habitual inaction that often results

TABLE 13.5 Controlled Trials of Cognitive Behavioral Treatments

Study	Length of Follow-Up (Months)	Treatment (N)	Percentage Clinical Improvement of Completers (If Available)	Significant Comparison (Percentage Clinical Improvement)	
				Other Treatments (Yes/No)	*Wait List (Yes/No)*
Barlow, Cohen, et al. (1984)	6	CBT (N = 5)			Yes
Blowers et al. (1987)	6	CBT (N = 20)		Yes: ND (some measures)	Yes
Borkovec et al. (1987)	6–12	CT + PR (N = 16)		Yes: ND + PR (some measures)	
Butler et al. (1987)	6	CBT (N = 22)	58.5		Yes (0%)
Borkovec and Mathews (1988)	12	CT + PR (N = 6)		No: SCD + PR	No: N + PR
Power et al. (1989)	PT	CBT (N = 10)		Yes: PL (one central measure) No: DZ (one central measure)	
Power et al. (1990)	PT	CBT (N = 21)	61.9	No: CBT + DZ = 69.8% No: CBT + PL = 55.6% Yes: DZ = 30.3% Yes: PL = 17.5%	
Butler et al. (1991)	6	CBT (N = 18)	42	Yes: BT = 5%	Yes
Barlow et al. (1992)	6	CBT (N = 29)	55		Yes
White and Keenan (1992)	6	CBT (N = 26)		No: BT, CT	Yes Yes
Borkovec and Costello (1993)	12	CBT (N = 18)	57.9	Yes: ND = 26.7% Yes: AR = 37.5%	
Durham et al. (1994)[a]	6	CT (N = 40)	>60	Yes: AP < 31% Yes: AMT < 37%	

Source: Reprinted with permission from Barlow and Lehman (1996), © 1996 American Medical Association. Adapted from Borkovec and Whisman (1996).

AMT = anxiety management training; AP = analytic psychotherapy; APL = attention placebo; AR = applied relaxation; BT = behavior therapy; CBT = cognitive behavioral therapy; DZ = diazepam; FU = follow-up; ND = nondirective therapy; PL = pill placebo; PR = progressive relaxation; PT = posttreatment; SCD = self-control desensitization.

[a]Intent-to-treat.

from the worry associated with GAD (Roemer & Orsillo, in press).

If efficacious treatments can be found for the most resistant and chronically anxious patients, then treatments should also benefit those who are on the less severe end of the anxiety continuum. Perhaps as many as 30 to 40% of the population may experience anxiety severe enough to warrant some clinical intervention (cf. Barlow, 1988, in press). In a recent survey, 33% of over 6,000 patients completing an up-to-date screening instrument in the offices of 75 physicians in a large health maintenance organization (HMO) reported elevated symptoms of anxiety and/or anxiety disorders (Fifer et al., 1994).

Additional surveys also suggest that people with anxiety difficulties are prevalent in primary-care settings (Barlow, Lerner, & Esler, 1996). In the era of rising costs of health care, developing brief, cost-effective, and perhaps self-directed treatments with proven efficacy for the treatment of anxiety in primary-care offices will be an important step, particularly since individuals with anxious symptoms, even if not fully syndromal, are impaired and at risk for the development of more severe disorders (Barlow & Lehman, 1996; Barlow, Lerner, & Esler, 1996).

CONCLUSIONS

We have reviewed the development of effective psychosocial treatments for a variety of anxiety disorders, but it is fair to say that we have reached only the first plateau of the development of these procedures. Although we now have treatments that are clearly more effective than credible alternative psychosocial interventions for most disorders, we know little about the generality of the effectiveness of these procedures. In addition to questions about the generality of effectiveness across patients, settings, and therapists of differing skills and abilities, questions have also been raised about the feasibility of these treatments, as well as their cost-effectiveness. Many of these issues are outlined succinctly in the *Template for Psychological Intervention Guidelines* referred to above (American Psychological Association Task Force on Intervention Guidelines, 1995), which provides a road map for future research. Some research along these lines is beginning to appear, suggesting, in an encouraging way, that when applied in a variety of practice settings, many of these procedures are just as effective as or more effective than as in the clinical research settings in which they were developed (Barlow, 1996; Barlow & Barlow, 1995). But most of this research lies ahead of us.

Equally important will be improving efforts to disseminate these treatments to the variety of practice settings in which they should prove useful, many of them primary-care settings, in order to meet the demands of many patients with these disorders desiring brief, effective treatments. Evidence indicates that effective psychological treatments are rarely available and much less readily available than pharmacological treatments in most settings (Barlow, 1996; Barlow, Levitt, & Bufka, 1999). Thus, it is not enough simply to develop these treatments and report on their effectiveness. Rather, it is the responsibility of those involved in treatment development to make these treatments as user-friendly as possible and to evaluate alternative methods of training and dissemination that ensure that these approaches will reach the greatest number of the people who need them.

References

Agras, W. S., Leitenberg, H., & Barlow, D. H. (1968). Social reinforcement in the modification of agoraphobia. *Archives of General Psychiatry, 19,* 423–427.

Al-Kubaisy, T., Marks, I. M., Lagsdail, S., Marks, M. P., Lovell, K., Sungur, M., & Araya, R. (1992). Role of exposure homework in phobia reduction: A controlled study. *Behavior Therapy, 23,* 599–621.

Alstroem, J. E., Nordlund, C. L., Persson, G., Harding, M., & Ljungqvist, C. (1984). Effects of four treatment methods on social phobic patients not suitable for insight-oriented psychotherapy. *Acta Psychiatrica Scandinavica, 70,* 97–110.

American Psychiatric Association. (1980). *Diagnostic and statistical manual of mental disorders* (3rd ed.). Washington, DC: Author.

American Psychiatric Association. (1987). *Diagnostic and statistical manual of mental disorders* (3rd ed., rev.). Washington, DC: Author.

American Psychiatric Association. (1994). *Diagnostic and statistical manual of mental disorders* (4th ed.). Washington, DC: Author.

American Psychiatric Association. (1996). *DSM-IV Sourcebook* (Vol. 2). Washington, DC: Author.

American Psychological Association Task Force on Psychological Intervention Guidelines. (1995, February). *Template for developing guidelines: Interventions for mental disorders and psychosocial aspects of physical disorders.* Washington, DC: Author.

Antony, M. M., & Barlow, D. H. (1996). Social and specific phobias. In D. H. Taylor & A. Tasman (Eds.), *Psychiatry*. Philadelphia: W. B. Saunders.

Antony, M. M., & Barlow, D. H. (in press). Specific phobias. In D. H. Barlow (Ed.), *Anxiety and its disorders: The nature and treatment of anxiety and panic* (2nd ed.). New York: Guilford Press.

Antony, M. M., Craske, M. G., & Barlow, D. H. (1995). *Mastery of your specific phobia*. San Antonio, TX: Graywind Psychological Corporation.

Arnow, B. A., Taylor, C. B., Agras, W. S., & Telch, M. J. (1985). Enhancing agoraphobia treatment outcome by changing couple communication patterns. *Behavior Therapy, 16*, 452–467.

Baker, B. L., Cohen, D. C., & Saunders, J. T. (1973). Self-directed desensitization for acrophobia. *Behaviour Research and Therapy, 11*, 79–89.

Barlow, D. H. (1988). *Anxiety and its disorders: The nature and treatment of anxiety and panic*. New York: Guilford Press.

Barlow, D. H. (Ed.). (1996). The effectiveness of psychotherapy: Science and policy. *Clinical Psychology: Science and Practice, 3*, 236–240.

Barlow, D. H. (2000). Unraveling the mysteries of anxiety and its disorders from the perspective of emotion theory. *American Psychologist, 55*, 1248–1263.

Barlow, D. H. (Ed.). (in press). *Anxiety and its disorders: The nature and treatment of anxiety and panic* (2nd ed.). New York: Guilford Press.

Barlow, D. H., & Barlow, D. G. (1995). Practice guidelines and empirically validated psychosocial treatments: Ships passing in the night? *Behavioral Healthcare Tomorrow, May–June*, 25–29, 76.

Barlow, D. H., & Brown, T. A. (1995). Correction to Klosko et al. (1990). *Journal of Consulting and Clinical Psychology, 63*, 830.

Barlow, D. H., Chorpita, B. F., & Turovsky, J. (1996). Fear, panic, anxiety, and disorders of emotion. In D. A. Hope (Ed.), *Nebraska symposium on motivation: Perspectives on anxiety, panic, and fear* (Vol. 43, pp. 251–328). Lincoln: University of Nebraska Press.

Barlow, D. H., Cohen, A. S., Waddell, M. T., Vermilyca, B.B., Kloska, J. S., Blanchard, E. B., & DiNardo, P.A. (1984). Panic and generalized anxiety disorders: Nature and treatment. *Behavior Therapy, 15*, 431–449.

Barlow, D. H., & Craske, M. G. (2000). *Mastery of your anxiety and panic: Client workbook for anxiety and panic*. San Antonio, TX: Graywind Psychological Corporation.

Barlow, D. H., Craske, M. G., Cerny, J. A., & Klosko, J. S. (1989). Behavioral treatment of panic disorder. *Behavior Therapy, 20*, 1–26.

Barlow, D. H., Gorman. J. M., Shear, M. K., & Woods, S. W. (2000). Cognitive-behavioral therapy, imipramine, or their combination for panic disorder: A randomized control trial. *Journal of the American Medical Association, 283*, 2529–2536.

Barlow, D. H., & Lehman, C. (1996). Advances in the psychosocial treatment of anxiety disorders: Implications for national health care. *Archives of General Psychiatry, 53*, 727–735.

Barlow, D. H., Lerner, J. A., & Esler, J. K. L. (1996). Behavioral health care in primary care settings: Recognition and treatment of anxiety disorders. In R. J. Resnick & R. H. Rozosky (Eds), *Health psychology through the life span: Practice and research opportunities* (pp. 133–148). Washington, DC: American Psychological Association Press.

Barlow, D. H., Levitt, J. T., & Bufka, L. F. (1999). The dissemination of empirically supported treatments: A view to the future. *Behaviour Research and Therapy, 37*, S147-S162.

Barlow, D. H., O'Brien, G. T., & Last, C. G. (1984). Couples treatment of agoraphobia. *Behavior Therapy, 15*, 41–58.

Barlow, D. H., Rapee, R. M., & Brown, T. A. (1992). Behavioral treatment of generalized anxiety disorder. *Behavior Therapy, 23*, 551–570.

Barlow, D. H., & Wincze, J. (1998). *DSM-IV* and beyond: What is generalized anxiety disorder? *Acta Psychiatrica Scandinavica, 98*, 23–29.

Beck, A. T., & Emery, C. (1985). *Anxiety disorders and phobias: A cognitive perspective*. New York: Basic Books.

Beck, A. T., Sokol, L., Clark, D. A., Berchick, R., & Wright, F. (1992). A crossover study of focused cognitive therapy for panic disorder. *American Journal of Psychiatry, 149*, 778–783.

Beckham, J. C., Vrana, S. R., May, J. G., Gustafson, D. J., & Smith, G. R. (1990). Emotional processing and fear measurement synchrony as indicators of treatment outcome in fear of flying. *Journal of Behavior Therapy and Experimental Psychiatry, 21*, 153–162.

Black, D. W., Wesner, R., Bowers, W., & Gabel, J. (1993). A comparison of fluvoxamine, cognitive therapy, and placebo in the treatment of panic disorder. *Archives of General Psychiatry, 50*, 44–50.

Blowers, C., Cobb, J., & Mathews, A. (1987). Generalised anxiety: A controlled treatment study. *Behaviour Research and Therapy, 25*, 493–502.

Bonn, J. A., Readhead, C. P. A., & Timmons, B. H. (1984). Enhanced adaptive behavioral response in agoraphobic patients pretreated with breathing retraining. *Lancet, 2*, 665–669.

Borkovec, T. D. (1994). The nature, functions, and origins of worry. In G. C. L. Davey & F. Tallis (Eds.), *Worrying: Perspectives on theory, assessment and treatment* (pp. 5–33). Cichester, UK: Wiley.

Borkovec, T. D., & Costello, E. (1993). Efficacy of applied relaxation and cognitive-behavioral therapy in the treatment of generalized anxiety disorder. *Journal of Consulting and Clinical Psychology, 61,* 611–619.

Borkovec, T. D., & Mathews, A. M. (1988). Treatment of nonphobic anxiety disorders: A comparison of nondirective, cognitive, and coping desensitization therapy. *Journal of Consulting and Clinical Psychology, 56,* 877–884.

Borkovec, T. D., Mathews, A. M., Chambers, A., Ebrahimi, S., Lytle, R., & Nelson, R. (1987). The effects of relaxation training with cognitive or nondirective therapy and the role of relaxation-induced anxiety in the treatment of generalized anxiety. *Journal of Consulting and Clinical Psychology, 55,* 883–933.

Borkovec, T. D., & Whisman, M. A. (1996). Psychosocial treatment far generalized anxiety disorder. In M. Mavissakalian & R. Prien (Eds.), *Long-term treatments of anxiety disorders* (pp. 171–199). Washington, DC: American Psychiatric Press.

Bourque, P., & Ladouceur, R. (1980). An investigation of various performance-based treatments with acrophobics. *Behaviour Research and Therapy, 18,* 161–170.

Brown, T. A., Antony, M. M., & Barlow, D. H. (1995). Diagnostic comorbidity in panic disorder: Effect on treatment outcome and course of comorbid diagnoses following treatment. *Journal of Consulting and Clinical Psychology, 63,* 408–418.

Brown, T. A., & Barlow, D. H. (1992). Comorbidity among anxiety disorders: Implications for treatment and *DSM-IV*. *Journal of Consulting and Clinical Psychology, 60,* 835–844.

Brown, T. A., & Barlow, D. H. (1995). Long-term outcome in cognitive-behavioral treatment of panic disorder: Clinical predictors and alternative strategies for assessment. *Journal of Consulting and Clinical Psychology, 63,* 754–765.

Brown, T. A., Campbell, L. A., Lehman, C. L., & Grisham, J. R. (2001). *Current and lifetime comorbidity of the DSM-IV anxiety and mood disorders in a large clinical sample.* Manuscript submitted for publication.

Brown, T. A., O'Leary, T. A., & Barlow, D. H. (2001). Generalized anxiety disorder. In D. H. Barlow (Ed.), *Clinical handbook of psychological disorders: A step-by-step treatment manual* (pp. 154–208). New York: Guilford Press.

Burns, L. E., Thorpe, C. L., & Cavallaro, L. A. (1986). Agoraphobia 8 years after behavioral treatment: A follow-up study with interview, self-report, and behavioral data. *Behavioral Therapy, 17,* 580–591.

Butler, C., Cullington, A., Munby, M., Amies, P., & Gelder, M. (1984). Exposure and anxiety management in the treatment of social phobia. *Journal of Consulting and Clinical Psychology, 52,* 642–650.

Butler, C., Fennell, M., Robson, P., & Gelder, M. (1991). Comparison of behavior therapy and cognitive behavior therapy in the treatment of generalized anxiety disorder. *Journal of Consulting and Clinical Psychology, 59,* 167–175.

Butler, G., Cullington, A., Hibbert, G., Klimes, I., & Gelder, M. (1987). Anxiety management for persistent generalised anxiety. *British Journal of Psychiatry, 151,* 535–542.

Carlin, A. S., Hoffman, S. G., & Weghorst, S. (1997). Virtual reality and tactile augmentation in the treatment of spider phobia: A case report. *Behaviour Research and Therapy, 35,* 153–158.

Cerny, J. A., Barlow, D. H., Craske, M. G., & Himadi, W. G. (1987). Couples treatment of agoraphobia: A two-year follow-up. *Behavior Therapy, 18,* 401–415.

Chambless, D. L. (1990). Spacing of exposure sessions in treatment of agoraphobia and simple phobia. *Behavior Therapy, 21,* 217–229.

Chambless, D. L., & Renneberg, B. (1988, September). *Personality disorders of agoraphobics.* Paper presented at World Congress of Behavior Therapy, Edinburgh, Scotland.

Clark, D. M. (1989). Anxiety states: Panic and generalized anxiety. In K. Hawton, P. Salkavskis, J. Kirk, & D. M. Clark. (Eds.), *Cognitive behavior therapy for psychiatric problems: A practical guide* (pp. 52–96). Oxford, UK: Oxford University Press.

Clark, D. M., Salkovskis, P. M., Hackmann, A., Middleton, H., Anastasiades, P., & Gelder, M. (1994). A comparison of cognitive therapy, applied relaxation, and imipramine in the treatment of panic disorder. *British Journal of Psychiatry, 164,* 759–769.

Clark, D. M., Salkovskis, P. M., Hackmann, A., Wells, A., Ludgate, J., & Gelder, M. (1999). Brief cognitive therapy for panic disorder: A randomized control trial. *Journal of Consulting and Clinical Psychology, 67,* 583–589.

Cobb, J. P., Mathews, A. M., Childs-Clarke, A., & Blowers, C. M. (1984). The spouse as co-therapist in the treatment of agoraphobia. *British Journal of Psychiatry, 144,* 282–287.

Cote, C., Gauthier, J. G., Laberge, B., Cormier, H. J., & Plamondon, J. (1994). Reduced therapist contact in the cognitive behavioral treatment of panic disorder. *Behavior Therapy, 25,* 123–145.

Craske, M. G. (1999). *Anxiety disorders: Psychological approaches to theory and treatment*. Boulder, CO: Westview Press.

Craske, M. G., & Barlow, D. H. (2001). Panic disorder and agoraphobia. In D. H. Barlow (Ed.), *Clinical handbook of psychological disorders* (3rd ed., pp. 1–59). New York: Guilford Press.

Craske, M. G., Brown, T. A., & Barlow, D. H. (1991). Behavioral treatment of panic disorder: A two-year follow-up. *Behavior Therapy*, *22*, 289–304.

Craske, M. G., Maidenberg, E., & Bystritsky, A. (1995). Brief cognitive-behavioral versus non-directive therapy for panic disorder. *Journal of Behavior Therapy and Experimental Psychiatry*, *26*, 113–120.

Craske, M. G., Miller, P. P., Rotunda, R., & Barlow, D. H. (1990). A descriptive report of features of initial unexpected panic attacks in minimal and extensive avoiders. *Behaviour Research and Therapy*, *28*, 395–400.

Craske, M. G., & Sipsas, A. (1992). Animal phobias versus claustrophobias: Exteroceptive versus interoceptive cues. *Behaviour Research and Therapy*, *30*, 569–581.

Curtis, G. C., Hill, E. M., & Lewis, J. A. (1990). *Heterogeneity of* DSM-III-R *simple phobia and the simple phobia/agoraphobia boundary: Evidence from the ECA study*. Report to the *DSM-IV* Anxiety Disorders Work Group. Ann Arbor: University of Michigan.

Curtis G. C., Magee, W. J., Eaton, W. W., Wittchen, H. U., & Kessler, R. C. (1998). Specific fears and phobias: Epidemiology and classification. *British Journal of Psychiatry*, *173*, 212–217.

De Ruiter, C., Rijken, H., Garssen, B., & Kraaimaat, F. (1989). Breathing retraining, exposure, and a combination of both in the treatment of panic disorder with agoraphobia. *Behaviour Research and Therapy*, *27*, 663–672.

DiNardo, P. A., & Barlow, D. H. (1988). *Anxiety Disorders Interview Schedule–Revised* (ADIS-R). Albany, NY: Graywind Publications/Psychological Corporation.

DiNardo, P. A., O'Brien, C. T., Barlow, D. H., Waddell, M. T., & Blanchard, E. (1983). Reliability of *DSM-III* anxiety disorder categories using a new structured interview. *Archives of General Psychiatry*, *40*, 1070–1078.

Donahue, B. C., Van Hasselt, V. B., & Hersen, M. (1994). Behavioral assessment and treatment of social phobia. *Behavior Modification*, *18*, 262–288.

Durham, R. C., Murphy, T., Allan, T., Richard, K., Treliving, L. R., & Fenton, G. W. (1994). Cognitive therapy, analytic psychotherapy and anxiety management training for generalized anxiety disorder. *British Journal of Psychiatry*, *165*, 315–323.

Durham, R. C., & Turvey, A. A. (1987). Cognitive therapy versus behavior therapy in the treatment of chronic general anxiety. *Behavior Research and Therapy*, *25*, 229–234.

Emmelkamp, P. M. G, Brilman, E., Kuiper, H., & Mersch, P. P. (1986). The treatment of agoraphobia: A comparison of self-instructional training, rational emotive therapy, and exposure in vivo. *Behavior Modification*, *10*, 37–53.

Emmelkamp, P. M. G., & Mersch, P. P. (1982). Cogni tion and exposure in vivo in the treatment of agoraphobia: Short-term and delayed effects. *Cognitive Therapy and Research*, *6*, 77–90.

Fava, G. A., Zielezny, M., Savron, G., & Grandi, S. (1995). Long-term effects of behavioural treatment for panic disorder with agoraphobia. *British Journal of Psychiatry*, *166*, 87–92.

Feigenbaum, W. (1988). Long-term efficacy of ungraded versus graded massed exposure in agoraphobics. In I. Hand & H. Wittchen (Eds.), *Panic and phobias: Treatments and variables affecting course and outcome* (pp. 83–88). Berlin: Springer-Verlag.

Fifer, S. K., Mathias, S. D., Patrick, D. L., Majonson, P. D., Lubeck, D. P., & Buesching, D. P., (1994). Untreated anxiety among adult primary care patients in a health maintenance organization. *Archives of General Psychiatry*, *51*, 740–750.

Freud, S. (1961). On the grounds for detaching a particular syndrome from neurasthenia under the description of anxiety neurosis. In J. Strachey (Ed. & Trans.), *The standard edition of the complete psychological works of Sigmund Freud* (Vol. 3, pp. 85–116). London: Hogarth Press. (Original work published 1895)

Fyer, A. J., Mannuzza, S., Chapman, T. F., Liebowitz, M. R., & Klein, D. F. (1993). A direct interview family study of social phobia. *Archives of General Psychiatry*, *50*, 286–293.

Gelder, M. G., & Marks, I. M. (1966). Severe agoraphobia: A controlled prospective trial of behavioral therapy. *British Journal of Psychiatry*, *112*, 309–319.

Gelernter, C. S., Uhde, T. W., Cimbolic, P., Arnkoff, C. B., Vittone, B. J., Tancer, M. E., & Bartko, J. J. (1991). Cognitive-behavioral and pharmacological treatments for social phobia: A controlled study. *Archives of General Psychiatry*, *48*, 938–945.

Ghosh, A., & Marks, I. M. (1987). Self-treatment of agoraphobia by exposure. *Behavior Therapy*, *18*, 3–16.

Gould, R. A., Otto, M. W., & Pollack, M. H. (1995). A meta-analysis of treatment outcome for panic disorder. *Clinical Psychology Review*, *15*, 819–844.

Hafoer, J., & Marks, I. M. (1976). Exposure in vivo of agoraphobics: Contributions of diazepam, group exposure, and anxiety evocation. *Psychological Medicine, 6,* 71–88.

Hayes, S. C., Barlow, D. H., & Nelson-Gray, R. O. (1999). *The scientist practitioner: Research and accountability in the age of managed care* (2nd ed.). Boston: Allyn & Bacon.

Hayes, S. C., Strosahl, K. D., & Wilson, K. G. (1999). *Acceptance and commitment therapy: An experiential approach to behavior change.* New York: Guilford Press.

Heimberg, R. G., Dodge, C. S., Hope, D. A., Kennedy, C. R., Zallo, L., & Becker, R. E. (1990). Cognitive-behavioral group treatment for social phobia: Comparison to a credible placebo control. *Cognitive Therapy and Research, 14,* 1–23.

Heimberg, R. G., & Juster, H. R. (1995). Cognitive-behavioral treatments: Literature review. In R. C. Heimberg, M. R. Liebowitz, D. A. Hope, & F. R. Schneier (Eds.), *Social phobia: Diagnosis, assessment and treatment* (pp. 261–309). New York: Guilford Press.

Heimberg, R. G., Liebowitz, M. R., Hope, D. A., Schneier, F. R., Holt, C. S., Welkowitz, L. A., Juster, H. R., Campeas, R., Bruch, M. A., Cloitre, M., Fallon, B., & Klein, D. F. (1998). Cognitive-behavioral group therapy versus phenelzine therapy for social phobia: 12-week outcome. *Archives of General Psychiatry, 55,* 1133–1141.

Heimberg, R. G., Salzman, D. G., Halt, C. S., & Blendell, K. A. (1993). Cognitive-behavioral group treatment for social phobia: Effectiveness at five-year followup. *Cognitive Therapy and Research, 17,* 325–339.

Hellstrom, K., Fellenius, J., & Ost, L.-G. (1996). One versus five sessions of applied tension in the treatment of blood phobia. *Behaviour Research and Therapy, 34,* 101–112.

Hellstrom, K., & Ost, L.-G. (1995). One-session therapist directed exposure vs. two forms of manual directed self-exposure in the treatment of spider phobia. *Behavior Research and Therapy, 33,* 959–965.

Herbert, J. D. (1995). An overview of the current status of social phobia. *Applied and Preventive Psychology, 4,* 39–51.

Hoffman, S. G., & Barlow, D. H. (in press). Social phobia (Social anxiety disorder). In D. H. Barlow (Ed.), *Anxiety and its disorders: The nature and treatment of anxiety and panic* (2nd ed.). New York: Guilford Press.

Holden, A. E. O., O'Brien, G. T., Barlow, D. H., Stetson, D., & Infantino, A. (1983). Self-help manual for agoraphobia: A preliminary report of effectiveness. *Behavior Therapy, 14,* 545–556.

Hope, D. A., & Heimberg, R. G. (1993). Social phobia and social anxiety. In D. H. Barlow (Ed.), *Clinical handbook of psychological disorders* (2nd ed., pp. 99–136). New York: Guilford Press.

Hope, D. A., Heimberg, R. G., & Bruch, M. A. (1990, March). *The importance of cognitive intervention in behavioral group therapy for social phobia.* Paper presented at the 10th National Conference on Phobias and Related Anxiety Disorders, Bethesda, MD.

Howard, W. A., Murphy, S. M., & Clarke, J. C. (1983). The nature and treatment of fear of flying: A controlled investigation. *Behavior Therapy, 14,* 557–567.

Jacobson, N. S., Wilson, L., & Tupper, C. (1988). The clinical significance of treatment gains resulting from exposure-based interventions for agoraphobia: A reanalysis of outcome data. *Behavior Therapy, 19,* 539–554.

Jansson, L., Jerremalm, A., & Ost, L. G. (1986). Follow-up of agoraphobic patients treated with exposure in vivo or applied relaxation. *British Journal of Psychiatry, 149,* 486–490.

Jansson, L., & Ost, L. G. (1982). Behavioral treatments for agoraphobia: An evaluative review. *Clinical Psychology Review, 2,* 311–336.

Jerremalm, A., Jansson, L., & Ost, L. G. (1986a). Cognitive and physiological reactivity and the effects of different behavioral methods in the treatment of social phobia. *Behaviour Research and Therapy, 24,* 171–180.

Jerremalm, A., Jansson, L., & Ost, L. G. (1986b). Individual response patterns and the effects of different behavioral methods in the treatment of dental phobia. *Behaviour Research and Therapy, 24,* 587–596.

Juster, H. R., Heimberg, R. C., & Engelberg, B. (1995). Self selection and sample selection in a treatment study of social phobia. *Behaviour Research and Therapy, 33,* 321–324.

Kendler, K. S., Neale, M. C., Kessler, R. C., Heath, A. C., & Eaves, L. J. (1992). The genetic epidemiology of phobias in women: The interrelationship of agoraphobia, social phobia, situational phobia, and simple phobia. *Archives of General Psychiatry, 49,* 273–281.

Kessler, R. C., MeGonagle, K. A., Zhao, S., Nelson, C. B., Hughes, M., Eshleman, S., Wittehen, H. U., & Kendler, K. 5. (1994). Lifetime and 12-month prevalence of *DSM-III-R* psychiatric disorders in the United States: Results from the national comorbidity survey. *Archives of General Psychiatry, 51,* 8–19.

Klosko, J. S., Barlow, D. H., Tassinari, R., & Cerny, J. A. (1990). A comparison of alprazolam and behavior therapy in treatment of panic disorder. *Journal of Consulting and Clinical Psychology*, *58*, 77–84.

Kushner, M. G., Abrams, K., & Borchardt, C. (2000). The relationship between anxiety disorders and alcohol use disorders: A review of major perspectives and findings. *Clinical Psychology Review*, *20*, 149–171.

Liddell, A., Di Fazio, L., Blackwood, J., & Ackerman, C. (1994). Long-term follow-up of treated dental phobics. *Behaviour Research and Therapy*, *32*, 605–610.

Lidren, D. M., Watkins, P. L., Gould, R. A., Clum, G. A., Asterino, M., & Tullach, H. L. (1994). A comparison of bibliotherapy and group therapy in the treatment of panic disorder. *Journal of Consulting and Clinical Psychology*, *62*, 865–869.

Liebowitz, M. R., Heimberg, R. G., Schneier, F. R., Hope, D. A., Davies, S., Holt, C. S., Goetz, D., Juster, H. R., Lin, S., Bruch, M., Marshall, R. D., & Klein, D. F. (1999). Cognitive-behavioral group therapy versus phenelzine in social phobia: Long-term outcome. *Depression and Anxiety*, *10*, 89–98.

Lindsay, W. R., Gamsu, C. V., McLaughlin, F., Hood, E., & Espie, C. A. (1987). A controlled trial of treatment for generalized anxiety. *British Journal of Clinical Psychology*, *26*, 3–15.

Lucas, R. A., & Telch, M. J. (1993, November). *Group versus individual treatment of social phobia*. Presented at the annual meeting of the Association for Advancement of Behavior Therapy, Atlanta, GA.

Magraf, J., & Schneider, S. (1991). *Outcome and active ingredients of cognitive-behavioral treatment for panic disorder*. Presented at the annual meeting of the Association far Advancement of Behavior Therapy, New York City.

Marks, I. M. (1971). Phobic disorders four years after treatment: A prospective follow-up. *British Journal of Psychiatry*, *129*, 362–371.

Marks, I. M. (1987). *Fears, phobias, and rituals*. New York: Oxford University Press.

Marks, I. M., & Gelder, M. G. (1966). Different ages of onset in varictics of phobia. *American Journal of Psychiatry*, *123*, 218–221.

Marks, I. M., Swinsan, R. P., Basaglu, M., Kuch, K., Nashirvani, H., O'Sullivan, G., Lelliott, P. T., Kirby, M., McNamee, G., Sengun, S., & Wickwire, K. (1993). Alprazolam and exposure alone and combined in panic disorder with agoraphobia: A controlled study in London and Toronto. *British Journal of Psychiatry*, *162*, 776–787.

Marzillier, J. S., Lambert, C., & Kelley, J. (1976). A controlled evaluation of systematic desensitization and social skills training for socially inadequate psychiatric patients. *Behaviour Research and Therapy*, *14*, 225–238.

Mattick, R. P., & Peters, L. (1988). Treatment of severe social phobia: Effects of guided exposure with and without cognitive restructuring. *Journal of Consulting and Clinical Psychology*, *56*, 251–260.

Mattick, R. P., Peters, L., & Clarke, J. C. (1989). Exposure and cognitive restructuring for social phobia: A controlled study. *Behavior Therapy*, *20*, 3–23.

Mavissakalian, M. R. (1996). Antidepressant medications for panic disorder. In M. Mavissakalian & R. Prien (Eds.), *Anxiety disorders: Psychological and pharmacological treatments* (pp. 265—284). Washington, DC: American Psychiatric Press.

Mavissakalian, M., & Barlow, D. H. (Eds.). (1981). *Phobia: Psychological and pharmacological treatment*. New York: Guilford Press.

Mavissakalian, M., & Michelson, L. (1986). Two-year follow-up of exposure and imipramine treatment of agoraphobia. *American Journal of Psychiatry*, *143*, 1106–1112.

Mavissakalian, M., & Perel, J. (1985). Imipramine in the treatment of agoraphobia: Dose-response relationships. *American Journal of Psychiatry*, *142*, 1032–1036.

McNally, R. J. (1986). Behavioral treatment of choking phobia. *Journal of Behavior Therapy and Experimental Psychiatry*, *17*, 185–188.

McNally, R. J. (1994). Choking phobia: A review of the literature. *Comprehensive Psychiatry*, *35*, 83–89.

Menzies, R. G., & Clarke, J. C. (1995). Danger expectancies and insight in acrophobia. *Behaviour Research and Therapy*, *33*, 215–221.

Mersch, P. P. A. (1995). The treatment of social phobia: The differential effectiveness of exposure in vivo and an integration of exposure in vivo, rational emotive therapy and social skills training. *Behaviour Research and Therapy*, *33*(3), 259–269.

Michelson, L., Marchione, K., & Greenwald, M. (1989, November). *Cognitive-behavioral treatments of agoraphobia*. Presented at the annual meeting of the Association for the Advancement of Behavior Therapy, Washington, DC.

Michelson, L., Mavissakalian, M., & Marchione, K. (1988). Cognitive, behavioral, and psychophysiological treatments of agoraphobia: A comparative outcome investigation. *Behavior Therapy*, *19*, 97–120.

Mills, H. L., Agras, W. S., Barlow, D. H., & Mills, J. R. (1973). Compulsive rituals treated by response prevention. *Archives of General Psychiatry*, *28*, 524–529.

Munby, J., & Johnston, D. W. (1980). Agoraphobia: The long-term follow-up of behavioral treatment. *British Journal of Psychiatry*, *137*, 418–427.

Muris, P., Mayer, B., & Merckelbach, H. (1998) Trait anxiety as a predictor of behavior therapy outcome in spider phobia. *Behavioral and Cognitive Psychotherapy, 26,* 87–91.

Myers, J. K., Weissman, M. M., Tisebler, G. L., Holzer, C. E., III, Leaf, P. J., Orvasehel, H., Anthony, J. D., Boyd, J. H., Burke, J. D., Jr., Kramer, M., & Stalzman, R. (1984). Six-month prevalence of psychiatric disorders in three communities. *Archives of General Psychiatry, 41,* 959–967.

Newman, C. F., Beck, J. S., & Beck, A. T. (1990). *Efficacy of cognitive therapy in reducing panic attacks and medication.* Presented at the annual meeting of the Association for Advancement of Behavior Therapy, San Francisco.

O'Brien, T. P., & Kelley, J. E. (1980). A comparison of self-directed and therapist-directed practice for fear reduction. *Behaviour Research and Therapy, 18,* 573–579.

Ost, L. G. (1987). Age of onset of different phobias. *Journal of Abnormal Psychology, 96,* 223–229.

Ost, L. G. (1989). One-session treatment for specific phobias. *Behaviour Research and Therapy, 27,* 1–7.

Ost, L. G., Brandberg, M., & Alm, T. (1997). One versus five sessions of exposure in the treatment of flying phobia. *Behaviour Research and Therapy, 35,* 987–996.

Ost, L. G., Ferebee, I. & Furmark, T. (1997). One session group therapy of spider phobia: Direct versus indirect treatments. *Behaviour Research and Therapy, 35,* 721–732.

Ost, L. G., Hellstrom, K., & Westling, B. E. (1989, November). *Applied relaxation, exposure in vivo, and cognitive methods in the treatment of agoraphobia.* Presented at the meeting of the Association for the Advancement of Behavior Therapy, Washington, DC.

Ost, L. G., Jerremalm, A., & Jansson, L. (1984). Individual response patterns and the effects of different behavioral methods in the treatment of agoraphobia. *Behaviour Research and Therapy, 22,* 697–707.

Ost, L. G., Jerremalm, A., & Johansson, J. (1981). Individual response patterns and the effects of different behavioral methods in the treatment of social phobia. *Behaviour Research and Therapy, 19,* 1–16.

Ost, L. G., Salkovskis, P. M., & Hellstrom, K. (1991). One-session therapist directed exposure versus self-exposure in the treatment of spider phobia. *Behavior Therapy, 22,* 407–422.

Ost, L. G., & Sterner, U. (1987). Applied tension: A specific behavioral method for treatment of blood phobia. *Behaviour Research and Therapy, 25,* 25–29.

Ost, L. G., & Westling, B. E. (1995). Applied relaxation versus cognitive behavior therapy in the treatment of panic disorder. *Behaviour Research and Therapy, 33,* 145–158.

Ost, L. G., Westling, B. E., & Hellstrom, K. (1993). Applied relaxation, exposure in vivo and cognitive methods in the treatment of panic disorder with agoraphobia. *Behaviour Research and Therapy, 31,* 383–395.

Otto, M. W., Pollack, M. H., & Sabatino, S. A. (1995). *Maintenance of remission following CBT for panic disorder: Possible deleterious effects for concurrent medication treatment.* Presented at the World Congress of Behavioural and Cognitive Therapies, Copenhagen, Denmark.

Otto, M. W., Pollack, M. H., Sachs, G. S., Teiter, S. R., Meltzer-Brody, S., & Rosenbaum, J. F. (1993). Discontinuation of benzodiazepine treatment: Efficacy of cognitive-behavioral therapy for patients with panic disorder. *American Journal of Psychiatry, 150,* 1485–1490.

Page, A. C. (1994). Blood-injury phobia. *Clinical Psychology Review, 14,* 443–461.

Pollack, M. H., Otto, M. W., Kaspi, S. P., Hammerness, P. G., & Rosenbaum, J. F. (1994). Cognitive behavior therapy for treatment-refractory panic disorder. *Journal of Clinical Psychiatry, 55,* 200–205.

Power, K. G., Jerrom, D. W. A., Simpson, R. J., Mitchell, M. J., & Swanson, V. (1989). A controlled comparison of cognitive-behaviour therapy, diazepam, and placebo in the management of generalized anxiety. *Behavioural Psychotherapy, 17,* 1–14.

Power, K. G., Simpson, R. J., Swanson, V., Wallace, L A., Feistner, A. T. C., & Sharp, D. (1990). A controlled comparison of cognitive-behaviour therapy, diazepam, and placebo, alone and in combination, for the treatment of generalised anxiety disorder. *Journal of Anxiety Disorders, 4,* 267–292.

Rachman, S. J., & Hodgson, R. S. (1980). *Obsessions and compulsions.* Englewood Cliffs, NJ: Prentice Hall.

Rapee, R. M. (1991). Generalized anxiety disorder: A review of clinical features and theoretical concepts. *Clinical Psychology Review, 11,* 419–440.

Reich, J., Noyes, R., & Troughton, E. (1987). Dependent personality disorder associated with phobic avoidance in patients with panic disorder. *American Journal of Psychiatry, 144,* 323–326.

Roemer, L., & Orsillo, S. M. (in press). Expanding our conceptualization of and treatment for generalized anxiety disorder: Integrating mindfulness/acceptance-based approaches with existing cognitive-behavioral models. *Clinical Psychology: Science and Practice.*

Rothbaum, B. O., Hodges, L. F., Kooper, R., Opdyke, D., Williford, J. S., & North, M. (1995). Effectiveness of computer-generated (virtual reality) graded exposure in the treatment of acrophobia. *American Journal of Psychiatry, 152*, 626–628.

Rothbaum, B. O., Hodges, L. F., & Smith, S. (1999). Virtual reality exposure therapy abbreviated treatment manual: Fear of flying application. *Cognitive and Behavioral Practice, 6*, 234–244.

Rothbaum, B. O., Hodges, L. F., Smith, S., Lee, J. H., & Price, L. (2000). A controlled study of virtual reality exposure therapy for the fear of flying. *Journal of Consulting and Clinical Psychology, 68*, 1020–1026.

Rowe, M. K., & Craske, M. G. (1998). Effect of an expanding-spaced vs. massed exposure schedule on fear reduction and return of fear. *Behavior Research and Therapy, 36*, 701–717.

Salkovskis, P. M., & Clark, D. M. (1991). Cognitive therapy for panic disorder. *Journal of Cognitive Psychotherapy, 5*, 215–226.

Salyam, L., Shugar, R., Bryntwick, S., & Solyam, C. (1973). Treatment of fear of flying. *American Journal of Psychiatry, 130*, 423–427.

Sanderson, W. S., DiNardo, P. A., Rapee, R. M., & Barlow, D. H. (1990). Syndrome comorbidity in patients diagnosed with a *DSM-III-R* anxiety disorder. *Journal of Abnormal Psychology, 99*, 308–312.

Schmidt, N. B., Woolaway-Bickel, K., Trakowski, J., Santiago, H., Storey, J., Koselka, M., & Cook, J. (2000). Dismantling cognitive-behavioral treatment for panic disorder: Questioning the utility of breathing retraining. *Journal of Consulting and Clinical Psychology, 68*, 417–424.

Schneier, F. R., Johnson, J., Hornig, C. D., Liebowitz, M. R., & Weissman, M. M. (1992). Social phobia: Comorbidity and morbidity in an epidemiologic sample. *Archives of General Psychiatry, 48*, 282–288.

Shear, M. K., Houck, P., Greeno, C., & Masters, B. S. (2000). *Emotion-focused psychotherapy for panic disorder: A randomized treatment study*. Manuscript in preparation.

Shear, M. K., Pilkonis, P. A., Cloitre, M., & Leon, A. C. (1994). Cognitive behavioral treatment compared with nonprescriptive treatment of panic disorder. *Archives of General Psychiatry, 51*, 395–401.

Solyom, L., Shugar, R., Bryntwick, S., & Solyom, C. (1973). Treatment of fear of flying. *American Journal of Psychiatry, 130*(4), 423–427.

Spiegel D. A., & Barlow D. H. (2000, November). Intensive treatment for panic disorder and agoraphobia. In M. G. Craske (Chair), *Brief cognitive behavioral therapy for anxiety: Intervention and prevention*. Symposium at the 34th Annual Convention of the Association for Advancement of Behavior Therapy, New Orleans.

Spiegel, D. A., Bruce, T. J., Gregg, S. F., & Nuzzarello, A. (1994). Does cognitive behavior therapy assist slow-taper alprazolam discontinuation in panic disorder? *American Journal of Psychiatry, 151*, 876–881.

Swinson, R. P., Fergus, K. D., Cox, B. J., & Wickwire, K. (1995). Efficacy of telephone-administered behavioral therapy for panic disorder with agoraphobia. *Behaviour Research and Therapy, 33*, 465–469.

Telch, M. J., Agras, W. S., Taylor, C. B., Roth, W. T., & Gallen, C. (1985). Combined pharmacological and behavioral treatment for agoraphobia. *Behaviour Research and Therapy, 23*, 325–335.

Telch, M. J., & Lucas, J. A. (1994). Combined pharmacological and psychological treatment for panic disorder: Current status and future directions. In B. E. Wolfe & J. D. Maser (Eds.), *Treatment of panic disorder: A consensus development conference* (pp. 177–197). Washington, DC: American Psychiatric Press.

Telch, M. J., Lucas, J. A., Schmidt, N. B., Hanna, H. H., Jaimcz, T. S., & Lucas, R. A. (1993). Group cognitive-behavioral treatment of panic disorder. *Behaviour Research and Therapy, 31*, 279–287.

Thorpe, C. L., & Burns, L. E. (1983). *The agoraphobic syndrome*. New York: Wiley.

Trull, T. J., Nietzel, M. T., & Main, A. (1988). The use of meta-analysis to assess the clinical significance of behavior therapy for agoraphobia. *Behavior Therapy, 19*, 527–538.

Turk, C. L., Heimberg, R. G., & Hope, D. A. (2001). Social anxiety disorder. In D. H. Barlow (Ed.), *Clinical handbook of psychological disorders: A step-by-step treatment manual* (3rd ed., pp. 114–153). New York: Guilford Press.

Turner, S. M., Beidel, D. C., Cooley, M. R., Woody, S. R., & Messer, S. C. (1994). A multicomponent behavioral treatment for social phobia: Social Effectiveness Therapy. *Behaviour Research and Therapy, 32*, 381–390.

Turner, S. M., Beidel, D. C., & Jacob, R. G. (1994). Social phobia: A comparison of behavior therapy and atenolol. *Journal of Consulting and Clinical Psychology, 62*, 350–358.

White, J., & Keenan, M. (1992). Stress control: A controlled comparative investigation of large group therapy for generalized anxiety disorder. *Behavioral Psychotherapy, 20*, 97–114.

Williams, S. L., & Rappaport, A. (1983). Cognitive treatment in the natural environment for agoraphobics. *Behavior Therapy, 14*, 299–313.

14

Pharmacological Treatments for Panic Disorder, Generalized Anxiety Disorder, Specific Phobia, and Social Anxiety Disorder

Peter P. Roy-Byrne
Deborah S. Cowley

Medication therapies for four types of anxiety disorder—panic disorder, generalized anxiety disorder, specific phobia, and social anxiety disorder—are reviewed. Of 14 placebo-controlled studies, 11 have conclusively shown that imipramine is effective for treating panic disorder. Other heterocyclics are less well studied, although three placebo-controlled trials have shown efficacy for clomipramine. The benzodiazepines alprazolam and clonazepam have been shown effective for panic disorder in 8 and 4 placebo-controlled studies, respectively. There are also controlled data indicating the efficacy of other benzodiazepines, including clonazepam, lorazepam, and diazepam. Placebo-controlled trials have shown the efficacy of the selective serotonin reuptake inhibitors (SSRIs) paroxetine (3 studies), sertraline (3 studies), fluvoxamine (6 studies), fluoxetine (1 study), and citalopram (2 studies) for panic disorder. Numerous double-blind, controlled trials have examined the efficacy of benzodiazepines for the treatment of generalized anxiety disorder. Benozodiazepines have been found superior to a placebo in most of the recent studies, and all benzodiazepines appear equally effective. Buspirone, pharmacologically unrelated to benzodiazepines, has been shown in several double-blind studies to be comparable to benzodiazepines in the treatment of generalized anxiety disorder. Three controlled trials have also shown efficacy for tricyclic antidepressants in generalized anxiety disorder. Placebo-controlled trials have also shown efficacy for antidepressants in generalized anxiety disorder including tricyclics (3 studies), extended release venlafaxine (4 studies) and most recently paroxetine (2 studies). The phobic disorders include specific and social phobias, but no pharmacological intervention has been shown to be effective for specific phobia. Double-blind, randomized trials have supported the efficacy of the monoamine oxidase inhibitors phenelzine (4 studies), meclobamide (4 studies) and broforamine (3 studies) in the treatment of social phobia. Two controlled trials found efficacy in social phobia for the benzodiazepines clonazepam and alprazolam, and seven controlled trials suggest that SSRIs fluvoxamine (2 studies), sertraline (1 study) and paroxetine (4 studies) are effective for social phobia.

Panic attacks, "generalized" or free-floating anxiety, and context-dependent fears (phobias) are the modern syndromes previously known as "neurotic anxiety" and thought at that time (before *DSM-III;* American Psychiatric Association [APA], 1980) to be poorly responsive to pharmacotherapy. However, since the early 1980s, beginning with the introduction of *DSM-III,* we have seen a growing appreciation of the important role of pharmacotherapy in the treatment of these syndromes and an accumulating body of evidence documenting the efficacy of specific classes of medication for specific anxiety disorders. This chapter reviews the clinical characteristics and pharmacotherapy of the three major anxiety disorders: panic disorder (with or without agoraphobia), generalized anxiety disorder, and phobic disorders (principally social phobia).

PANIC DISORDER

Panic attacks are sudden, unexpected bursts of extreme anxiety accompanied by at least four physical or cognitive symptoms that include palpitations; chest discomfort; shortness of breath; dizziness; sweating; numbness or tingling; hot or cold flashes; abdominal discomfort; nausea or diarrhea; depersonalization or derealization; and fear of dying, going crazy, or losing control. Panic disorder is characterized by the presence of recurrent spontaneous (i.e., unexpected) panic attacks followed by a month of persistent anxiety about having attacks, concern about the implications of attacks (often marked by hypochondriacal preoccupations), or avoidance of situations that the individual feels will bring on attacks (agoraphobia). Although as many as one third to one half of the population will experience a panic attack in their lifetimes (Norton, Cox, & Malan, 1992), only about 1 in 10 of these people will develop the recurrent attacks and accompanying chronic anxiety, bodily/illness preoccupation, or phobia avoidance that characterize panic disorder.

Panic disorder is a chronic illness with a 1-month prevalence in the general population of 1.5% and a lifetime prevalence of about 3.5% (Eaton, Kessler, Wittchen, & Magee, 1994). Twice as many women as men are affected, with peak age of onset typically in the late teens and early 20s (Eaton et al., 1994). Although there is an increased rate of the disorder in family members and greater concordance in monozygotic versus dizygotic twins, the results of genetic linkage studies thus far have been negative. Since the late 1980s, pathophysiological theories have focused on dysregulation of brain stem respiratory control centers and nearby noradrenergic and serotonergic nuclei that project to subcortical and limbic sites known to modulate emotion and its autonomic nervous system components (Papp, Coplan, & Gorman, 1992). More recently, theories have focused on the pivotal role of the amygdala, with brain stem abnormalities seen as a possible downstream effect (Roy-Byrne & Cowley, 1998). In addition, stressful life events occur at an increased rate around the time of panic onset (Roy-Byrne, Geraci, & Uhde, 1986), and panic patients have an increased tendency to amplify body sensations and an anxious experience via catastrophic and other cognitive distortions (Beck, 1988). Hence, the disorder is likely to involve a heritable biological vulnerability and a series of stressful triggers modulated perhaps by a cognitive style that may have both innate and learned origins.

Despite demonstration of the antipanic efficacy of imipramine in the early 1960s, these findings were not integrated into clinical practice in the 1960s and 1970s. Hence, treatment in the community was generally ineffective (Doctor, 1982) as inadequate doses of benzodiazepines and various forms of nonbehavioral psychotherapy were used, with disappointing results. This trend continued to a lesser degree in the 1980s, with one report documenting a surprisingly high utilization rate of nonspecific psychotherapy and low-dose benzodiazepines and surprisingly low rates (<15%) of behavioral and antidepressant treatment (Taylor et al., 1989). Although treatment rates improved in the 1990s (Swinson et al., 1992; Yonkers et al., 1996), they are still barely above 50%. Furthermore, many utilized treatments have no proven efficacy (Bandelow et al., 1995).

The mainstays of pharmacological treatment of panic disorder have been, in order of historic and chronological development, tricyclic antidepressants and monoamine oxidase inhibitors (MAOIs) in the 1960s and 1970s, high-potency benzodiazepines in the 1980s, and, more recently, in the 1990s, selective serotonin reuptake inhibitors (SSRIs). Currently, two benzodiazepines (alprazolam and clonazepam) and two SSRIs (paroxetine and sertraline) have Food and Drug Administration (FDA) approval for panic. However, other SSRIs and heterocyclic and MAOI antidepressants are also effective, highlighting the fact that there is, in general, poor concordance between established efficacy and approved indication for panic, as well as other anxiety, disorders. This review of antipanic treatments includes agoraphobia under the rubric of panic disorder since virtually all clinical medication trials have included patients with panic disorder complicated by phobic avoidance. In fact, because there is no evidence that agoraphobia exists in the absence of a history of panic attacks, *DSM-IV* (APA, 1994) precludes the diagnosis of agoraphobia in the absence of a history of panic attacks.

Tricyclic (Heterocyclic) Antidepressants

Extensive evidence supports the efficacy of tricyclic antidepressants (TCAs) in panic disorder. The initial demonstration of reduction in panic attacks, but more variable and sometimes less robust effects on anticipatory anxiety and phobic avoidance, with imipramine compared to a placebo (Klein, 1964, 1967) has been replicated many times since the late 1970s. Designs have varied in duration (6 weeks to 9 months), dosage of imipramine (i.e., whether minimally effective doses of 150 mg have been used), breadth of symptoms measured (panic, phobia, disability), sample size, proportion of sample with comorbid phobia and depression, and use of additional behavioral therapies. Of placebo-controlled trials, 11 of 14 have conclusively shown that imipramine is superior to a placebo for reduction of panic attacks (Barlow et al., 2000; Cross National Collaborative Treatment Study, 1992; Mavissakalian & Michelson, 1986; Mavissakalian & Perel, 1995; Nair et al., 1996; Schweizer, Rickels, Weiss, & Zavodnick, 1993; Sheehan, Ballenger, & Jacobsen, 1980; Taylor et al., 1990; Uhlenhuth, Matuzas, Glass, & Easton, 1989; Zitrin, Klein, & Woerner, 1978, 1983), and most that measured phobic avoidance showed similar efficacy. Three negative studies have been compromised by inadequate dosage (Evans, Kenardy, Schneider, & Hoey, 1986; Marks et al., 1983) and small sample size (Evans et al., 1986; Telch, Agras, Taylor, Roth, & Gallen, 1985). Studies using higher doses were more likely to show beneficial effects, and some studies also showed a clear dose response relationship, with daily doses of 1.5 mg/kg or greater yielding beneficial effects. More recent data (Mavissakalian & Perel, 1995) have suggested that therapeutic plasma levels are lower for phobia than for panic, explaining the occasionally observed dissociation between effects on these two different measures and further documenting the need for approximately 1.5 to 2.0 mg/kg of imipramine for phobia and 2.0 to 2.5 mg/kg for panic.

Time course of effect can only be estimated from reported mean values, which are the average of numerous, somewhat variable, individual time course profiles. Nonetheless, most studies do not show drug placebo response differences until Week 4, with maximal responses continuing for many measures to the trial's end (usually Week 8). One of the earlier studies (Zitrin et al., 1983) actually showed significant continuing improvement in phobic avoidance between Weeks 14 and 26, reinforcing Klein's original hypothesis that panic improves before phobia. Experts reviewing open trial data maintain that peak effects on panic, phobia, and anxiety measures may be delayed until 10 to 12 weeks in many patients (Lydiard & Ballenger, 1987), and controlled studies with SSRIs clearly show responses in some patients occur between Weeks 9 and 12 (Oehrberg et al., 1995). In general, antipanic effects of TCAs may, in some patients, take as long as, if not longer than, traditionally reported antidepressant effects.

Many studies show that TCAs are less well tolerated than, for example, benzodiazepines, with many patients dropping out of clinical trials both early (30% in the large Cross National Study; over 50% in some smaller studies) and late (e.g., 20% during maintenance treatment) in a recent study (Barlow et al., 2000). One direct comparison showed that imipramine was more poorly tolerated than the SSRI fluvoxamine (Bakish et al., 1996). Although these trials do not provide clear indications of the reasons, open studies (Noyes, Carvey, Cook, & Samuelson, 1989) suggest that the most common reason for early discontinuation is overstimulation/jitteriness, while for later discontinuation it is weight gain. Low initial doses, slower titration, and use of adjunctive benzodiazepines or beta blockers may attenuate early overstimulation. Elevated heart rate and blood pressure with imipramine (Taylor et al., 1990) may be a problem in older patients or those with cardiac conditions.

Few other heterocyclic agents have been studied. Desipramine was superior to a placebo for anxiety and phobia but not for panic attack frequency reduction at a mean dose of 177± mg/day in the only study of this agent performed (Lydiard et al., 1993). Open trials have also supported the efficacy of desipramine

(Kalus et al., 1991), as well as nortriptyline (Munjack et al., 1988), with estimated rates of response between 60% and 80% depending on design and sample composition. Nortriptyline's lower rate of postural hypotension and anticholinergic effects than imipramine may improve tolerability in some patients. Of other antidepressants in this class, lesser efficacy is suggested for trazodone (than for imipramine and alprazolam) (Charney et al., 1986) and maprotiline (than for fluvoxamine) (Den Boer & Westenberg, 1988). Unfortunately, these two studies were not placebo-controlled.

Benzodiazepines

The availability of high-potency benzodiazepines with the introduction of alprazolam in the mid-1980s reversed a prior tendency to view this class of medications as ineffective for panic disorder. Eight placebo-controlled, double-blind trials (Ballenger et al, 1988; Chouinard, Annable, Fontaine, & Solyom, 1982; Cross National Collaborative Treatment Study, 1992; Lydiard et al., 1992; Munjack et al., 1989; Schweizer et al., 1993; Sheehan, Raj, Harnett-Sheehan, Soto, & Knapp, 1993; Uhlenhuth et al., 1989) have found alprazolam to be superior to placebo in the treatment of panic attacks, with 55 to 75% of patients free of attacks at the end point of the study. Completer analyses showed less striking and sometimes only nonsignificant differences because of the high placebo dropout rate. Alprazolam showed similar robust effects on phobic avoidance (six of seven studies), disability (five of five studies), anticipatory anxiety (three of three studies), and generalized anxiety (seven of eight studies). Although daily mean doses of 5 to 6 mg were used in these studies, two studies of lower, 2-mg fixed doses (Lydiard et al., 1992; Uhlenhuth et al., 1989) also showed superiority to a placebo, although panic-free rates were lower than those seen with higher doses (25 to 50% vs. 55 to 75%).

The time course of effect with alprazolam is much more rapid than with tricyclic antidepressants. In general, superiority to a placebo was evident in the first week or two of treatment. While some experts suggest a superiority of these agents for phobia and anticipatory anxiety (Lydiard & Ballenger, 1987), panic attacks still appear to improve before phobia with this class of medication as well. While patients with significant primary major depression were excluded in most trials, patients meeting criteria for major depression judged secondary to panic disorder were included in some studies (mean Hamilton Depression Rating Scale [HAM-D] around 15) and in general fared as well as those without a major depression diagnosis (Ballenger et al., 1988).

The tolerability of alprazolam was in general superior to imipramine, with greater retention in studies looking at head-to-head comparisons (Cross National Collaborative Treatment Study, 1992; Schweizer et al., 1993; Uhlenhuth et al., 1989). The most common adverse effects of alprazolam were sedation or drowsiness, reported in 38 to 75%, and memory impairment, reported in up to 15% of patients. The frequent lack of patient awareness of memory effects suggests caution prescribing these agents in older patients or those needing to perform complex cognitive tasks.

Four placebo-controlled trials have also supported the efficacy of clonazepam (Tesar et al., 1991; Beauclair et al., 1994; Rosenbaum et al., 1997; Moroz & Rosenbaum, 1999) for panic disorder and demonstrated a similar rapid time course, spectrum of anxiolytic action, and side effect profile, with 1 mg being the minimal effective dose. One study demonstrated antipanic efficacy for diazepam (Dunner, Ishiki, Avery, Wilson, & Hyde, 1986), and head-to-head comparisons with alprazolam in other non-placebo-controlled studies (Charney & Woods, 1989; Schweizer et al., 1988) have shown uniform equivalence with lorazepam. The common clinical practice of using an adjunctive benzodiazepine with imipramine early in treatment has been studied using a placebo control only twice (Goddard et al., 2001; Woods et al., 1992). Although adjunctive alprazolam produced no advantage in decreasing imipramine dropouts (in fact, probably because of a rapid taper after 4 weeks of imipramine treatment, patients in this group actually did worse), this trial (Woods et al., 1992) did not mirror the usual clinical practice of tapering alprazolam slowly over months. In contrast, a study with the longer acting benzodiazepine clonazepam showed a definite benefit compared with placebo in the first 4 weeks and only minimal evidence of clinical worsening during Weeks 4 to 7 while taper was proceeding (Goddard et al., 2001).

The major public health concern regarding benzodiazepines has focused on their abuse potential, despite the fact (Nagy et al., 1989) that panic patients on long-term treatment do not escalate their doses over time (in fact, their doses go down) and that abuse of these drugs does not occur in patients without comorbid alcohol or substance abuse (Garvey &

Tollefson, 1986). There is also no evidence of tolerance to the therapeutic effects of benzodiazepines in the several long-term studies that have been done. However, virtually all studies show that discontinuation of alprazolam in panic disorder patients is associated with withdrawal symptoms, recurrent panic attacks, and failure to complete the taper in 25 to 50% of patients after as little as 6 to 8 weeks of treatment (Pecknold et al., 1988; Roy-Byrne, Dager, Cowley, Vitaliano, & Dunner, 1989). The use of a fairly rapid taper (several weeks) in all these studies fails to mirror the current clinical practice of a long, gradual taper, shown to reduce the incidence of withdrawal in one series to 7% (Pecknold, 1990). A more recent study with clonazepam (Moroz & Rosenbaum, 1999) used a longer (though still too rapid) 7-week taper and found symptomatic worsening but no deterioration beyond the original baseline symptom level (i.e., "rebound anxiety"), in contrast to the rebound anxiety noted in all alprazolam studies in at least a portion (~20%) of patients. Direct comparisons of alprazolam with imipramine (Fyer, Liebowitz, & Gorman, 1989; Rickels et al., 1993b) indicate greater taper difficulty and symptom recrudescence over the short term (1 month). However, studies showing that relapse rates after imipramine discontinuation gradually increase over 6 months (Mavissakalian & Perel, 1992b) suggest that this difference in short-term (1-month) relapse rates may merely reflect the mirror image of the time course in initial response (i.e., alprazolam more rapid, 1 to 2 weeks, and imipramine more slowly, 1 to 3 months) (Cross National Collaborate Treatment Study 1992). This suggests that much withdrawal may in fact be symptom reemergence/relapse, although this relapse is perhaps fueled by bona fide withdrawal reactions.

Monoamine Oxidase Inhibitors

In six double-blind, placebo-controlled studies, classic mixed MAO inhibitors (phenelzine, N = 5; iproniazid, N = 1) have been shown to be superior to a placebo for overall syndrome improvement (panic, anxiety, and phobia) (Lipsedge et al., 1973; Mountjoy, Roth, Garside, & Leitch, 1977; Sheehan et al., 1980; Solyom et al., 1973; Solyom, Solyom, LaPierre, Pecknold, & Morton, 1981; Tyrer, Candy, & Kelly, 1973). Unfortunately, in these older, pre-*DSM-III* studies, patients were not selected to meet diagnostic criteria for panic, there were no separate measures of panic frequency obtained, and measures of phobic avoidance or anxiety employed were different from those used in later panic studies. Of the studies, three of the six employed adjunctive exposure treatment or supportive psychotherapy, and one employed adjunctive diazepam. All these studies employed relatively low doses (usually 45 mg phenelzine). Although higher doses are now recommended by most experts, there are no data to support this. The one study comparing phenelzine to imipramine suggested that phenelzine was superior for phobic avoidance (Sheehan et al., 1980), providing the only empirical evidence to support the impression of many clinicians that this class of medications may have special efficacy for treatment of resistant patients. A number of active drug comparisons, but without placebo, have shown that the selective MAO-A inhibitors brofaromine (Van Vliet et al., 1996) and meclobamide (Kruger & Dahl, 1999) were equivalent to standard SSRIs (fluvoxamine, fluoxetine, and clomipramine), although the only placebo-controlled study (Loerch et al., 1999) failed to show efficacy for meclobamide.

The time course of MAOI effect is more difficult to estimate precisely from these older studies. Delayed effects are suggested by superior effects at 8 weeks compared with 4 weeks. Of the two studies that lasted 12 weeks, one showed greater efficacy at 12 weeks than at 6 weeks (Sheehan et al., 1980). In general, the time course of effect is likely to be comparable to that seen for other antidepressants.

These medications are well tolerated in the short term due to the absence of early overstimulation effects. However, weight gain, insomnia with paradoxical daytime sedation, sexual dysfunction, and the need to follow a special low-monoamine diet limit their acceptability for some patients. A recent placebo-controlled study showed that the selective and reversible MAO inhibitor brofaromine, which does not require a diet, is effective for panic, with a 70% response rate (Van Vliet, Westenberg, & Den Boer, 1993), confirming both open trials (Garcia Borreguero et al., 1992) and a blind comparative trial showing equivalence to clomipramine (Bakish, Saxena, Bowen, & D'Souza, 1993).

Serotonin Reuptake Inhibitors (Including Selective Serotonin Reuptake Inhibitors)

The efficacy of the TCA clomipramine in panic disorder has been supported in five double-blind, placebo-controlled studies (Broocks et al., 1998; Caillard et al.,

1999; Fahy, O'Rourke, Brophy, Scharzmann, & Sciascia, 1992; Johnston, Troyer, & Whitsett, 1988; Modigh, Westberg, & Eriksson, 1992), with one study actually showing superiority to imipramine at 12 weeks (Modigh et al., 1992) and another study showing that lower doses (60 mg) were as effective as higher doses (150 mg) (Caillard et al., 1999), consistent with an open study suggesting that a dose of 75 mg, lower than the 150 to 200 mg tricyclic doses usually required for antipanic efficacy, may be effective (Gloger et al., 1989). However, the side effect profile of this drug is far more burdensome now that newer, more tolerable SSRIs are available (Papp et al., 1997) and have largely replaced benzodiazepines as first-line medication for panic in the judgment of experts (Uhlenhuth et al., 1998).

Two of the five currently available selective SRIs (paroxetine and sertraline) are approved by the FDA for treatment of panic. Three double-blind, placebo-controlled studies (two flexible and one fixed dose) support paroxetine's short-term efficacy (Ballenger et al., 1998; Lecrubier et al., 1997; Oehrberg et al., 1995) in panic, and a long-term (36-week) extension of one of these studies (Lecrubier & Judge, 1997) showed continuing superiority to placebo. This one study showed comparable efficacy to clomipramine, with more rapid onset of effect and greater tolerability (Lecrubier et al., 1997). Three double-blind, placebo-controlled trials (two flexible and one fixed) support sertraline's efficacy (Londborg et al, 1998; Pohl et al., 1998; Pollack et al., 1998) in the acute treatment of panic disorder. These sertraline studies were unique in also showing improvements in quality of life, in addition to panic-related symptoms. Six double-blind, placebo-controlled studies demonstrate fluvoxamine's efficacy (Black et al., 1993b; deBeurs, van Balkom, Lange, Koele, & van Dyck, 1995; Den Boer & Westenberg, 1988, 1990; Hoehn-Saric, McLeod, & Hipsley, 1993; Sandmann et al., 1998), but FDA approval for treatment of panic has not been pursued. Fluoxetine's efficacy is supported by one placebo-controlled study (Michelson et al., 1988, 1999a, b) with 24-week continuation and by open case series (Louie, Lewis, & Lannon, 1993; Schneier et al., 1990). A more recent open case series has also documented efficacy for up to 26 months with once-weekly dosing with 10 to 60 mg of this long-half-life compound (Emmanual et al., 1999). Finally, two double-blind placebo-controlled trials have demonstrated antipanic efficacy for citalopram (Leinonen et al., 2000; Wade et al., 1997), 20 to 30 mg being the optimal dose. One study (Lepola et al., 1998) also showed 12-month efficacy following the acute trial. All these SSRI studies have shown effects on panic frequency, generalized anxiety, disability, and phobic avoidance, although only the sertraline studies measured all of these components.

A number of studies (deBeurs et al., 1995; Oehrberg et al., 1995) have shown that this class of medication is superior to a placebo when both are added to some form of cognitive behavioral therapy (CBT). While this contradicts other panic treatment studies, which have seemed to show drug-psychotherapy equivalence (Klosko, Barlow, Tassinari, & Cerny, 1990), a recent imipramine study (Barlow et al., 2000) did show that medication provided added benefit when combined with CBT in longer term (6-month) follow-up to acute (3-month) treatments using the Panic Disorder Severity Scale and group mean comparisons. Sample composition (i.e., severity of illness), study design (patients are sometimes rated after drugs are tapered), as well as integrity of cognitive behavioral therapy techniques, doubtless explains some of these differences. One interesting meta-analysis showed a greater effect size for serotonin antidepressants than for both tricyclics and benzodiazepines (Boyer, 1995), with the effect reduced but still maintained when only studies using high-dose imipramine or alprazolam were compared. Single studies using direct comparisons have also shown superiority to noradrenergic heterocyclics (fluvoxamine vs. maprotiline [Den Boer & Westenberg, 1990]; zimeledine vs. imipramine [Evans et al., 1986]; and clomipramine vs. desipramine [Sasson et al., 1999]). These findings suggest, but do not conclusively demonstrate, that serotonergic antidepressants may have an advantage as antipanic agents.

Studies have shown that doses of 100 to 200 mg fluvoxamine, 40 mg paroxetine, 100 to 200 mg sertraline, and 10 to 20 mg fluoxetine have been effective. Early overstimulation has been especially noted with fluoxetine in open reports (Schneier et al., 1990), prompting recommendations for low (5-mg) starting doses. Such effects have not been noted with the other SSRIs. Furthermore, the side effect burden with this class of medication has been much less severe, with much higher percentages of patients completing treatment (80 to 90%) than in studies of tricyclics (50 to 60%). However, abrupt withdrawal of

SSRIs has been associated with a withdrawal syndrome marked by irritability, nausea, dizziness, and headache in the case of both fluvoxamine (Black et al., 1993a) and paroxetine (Oehrberg et al., 1995), probably due to their relatively shorter half-life compared with fluoxetine and sertraline.

The time course of effect has been shown to be delayed as it is with tricyclics and MAO inhibitor antidepressants. In the various studies, superiority to placebo has emerged, depending on the effect and study, as early as 3 weeks and as late as 8 to 10 weeks.

Other Antidepressants

Of other "newer" antidepressants, only venlafaxine (mean dose 166 mg) has been proven effective in uncomplicated panic disorder in a placebo-controlled trial (Pollack et al., 1996). Open case series, however, suggest efficacy at lower (50 to 75 mg) doses (Geracioti, 1995; Papp et al., 1998). Nefazodone has been shown to be effective in depression, accompanied by panic attacks, only in a subanalysis of one controlled depression trial (Zajecka, 1996), consistent with open label evidence in a similar group (DeMartinis et al., 1996), as well as in uncomplicated panic (Berigan et al., 1998; Bystrisky et al., 1999). Finally, mirtazepine has been reported to be effective in open case series (Carpenter et al., 1999), and efficacy in an unpublished controlled 12-week trial is alluded to in another report (Falkai, 1999). Whether any of these agents would be more useful than the SSRIs is unknown, although the dual neurotransmitter effects of venlafaxine and mirtazepine (see below) might be an advantage.

Other Agents

Although treatment-resistant panic disorder occurs, it is relatively uncommon when adequate doses of the above medication classes have been tried in conjunction with skilled cognitive behavioral therapy. Few additional classes of medication are effective. Anticonvulsants have been reportedly effective in open trials using both valproate (Baetz & Bowen, 1998; Keck, Taylor, Tugrul, McElroy, & Bennett, 1993; Woodman & Noyes, 1994) and carbamazepine (Klein, Ubde, & Post, 1986), although the only existing placebo-controlled trial (with carbamazepine) (Ubde, Stein, & Post, 1988) failed to show drug efficacy greater than that of a placebo. One case series showed valproate combined with elonazepam effectively treated resistant panic in four patients (Ontiveros & Fontaine, 1992). Other reports indicate that patients with electroencephalogram (EEC) abnormalities might preferentially respond to anticonvulsants (McNamera & Fogel, 1990). One small placebo-controlled trial showed that the calcium channel blocker verapamil was an effective antipanic agent (Klein & Ubde, 1988), although curiously no other open reports have followed up on this preliminary finding. Another report documents the efficacy of inositol (Benjamin et al., 1995), a precursor of a key second messenger for signal transduction in certain C-protein-linked receptors. Clonidine has not been found to be effective (Ubde et al., 1989), nor has propranolol (Munjack et al., 1989), bupropion (Sheehan et al., 1983), or buspirone (Sheehan, Raj, Sheehan, & Soto, 1990). A study testing the addition of buspirone versus a placebo to cognitive therapy did show effects on generalized anxiety but not panic frequency or phobic avoidance (Cottraux et al., 1995), suggesting perhaps a role for buspirone as an adjunctive agent.

Combined augmentation treatment using multiple agents has never been studied. Anecdotal reports support combined benzodiazepine-antidepressant treatment (Ries & Wittkowsky, 1986), as well as SSRI and tricyclic combinations (Tiffon, Coplan, Papp, & Gorman, 1994). Consistent with this last combination of serotonin and norepinephrine reuptake blockers are the controlled and uncontrolled reports of venlafaxine and mirtazepine efficacy alluded to above.

Future agents that may emerge for treatment of panic include a variety of benzodiazepine partial agonists with a unique profile of activating select subreceptor families (Johnson & Lydiard, 1993). Such agents might effect symptoms without producing problems on withdrawal (i.e., discontinuation emergent symptoms). However, at this date, no agents of this kind are close to FDA approval despite years of interest and work in this area.

Predictors of Response

Although the result of both controlled and open trials are inconsistent, the presence and severity of both depression (Maddock et al., 1993) and phobic avoidance (Slaap et al., 1995) sometimes predict relatively poorer acute treatment response. This is consistent with naturalistic outcome studies (Roy-Byrne & Cowley, 1995), suggesting that these factors are associated with poorer long-term outcome.

Duration of Treatment/Chronic Treatment

All classes of agents described have been shown to retain their effectiveness over 8 to 12 months (Schweizer et al., 1993; Dager et al., 1992; Lecrubier & Judge, 1997; Michelson et al., 1996b). However, questions remain about the optimal duration of treatment following remission of panic attacks, as well as the need for continuing full doses of medication during the maintenance phase of treatment (prior to discontinuation). For tricyclics, one study suggests that after 6 months, the dose can be cut in half without symptom exacerbation over the next year (Mavissakalian & Perel, 1992a). However, with the greater tolerability of SSRIs, the advantage of decreased dose may be minimal. Nonexperimental studies with alprazolam and other benzodiazepines clearly show that patients, over time, reduce their doses by one third to one half without loss of clinical effect (Nagy et al., 1989). Suggestions that long-term benzodiazepine treatment, for anxious patients in general, is associated with cognitive deterioration have not been borne out by studies showing similar memory function in anxious patients off long-term benzodiazepines (Lucki et al., 1986).

Current consensus recommendations for treatment duration are 1 to 2 years, based on limited controlled data (APA Practice Guidelines, 1998; Ballenger et al., 1998). Many naturalistic studies have shown relapse rates between 30% and 90% following medication discontinuation after 6 to 12 months of treatment (reviewed in Roy-Byrne & Cowley, 1995). Relapse in these studies appears strongly related to illness characteristics, specifically Axis I (depression and phobic avoidance) and Axis II comorbidity.

Seven studies have examined relapse in treatment responders. Relapse rater were 46% in 2 months (Fyer et al., 1994) and 18% in 5 months (Schmeizer et al., 1993) with open imipramine discontinuation, and 45% and 65% with imipramine and clomipramine discontinuation after 10 weeks of single-blind placebo substitution (Gentil et al., 1993). Double-blind randomized studies have shown rates of 38% and 30% within 3 months of placebo substitution of imipramine (Mavissikalian & Perel, 1992b) and paroxetine (Burnham et al., 1995) and 37% within a year of imipramine discontinuation study (Mavissakalian & Perel, 1999). A single study showed a negligible 8% relapse within 6 months of placebo substitution of fluoxetine (Michelson et al., 1999b). All these studies suggest that relapse risk is likely 30 to 50% for patients with panic treated *acutely* (3 to 12 months), although one study suggested lower relapse with 18 versus 6 months of treatment (25% vs. 83%) (Mavissakalian & Perel, 1992b).

GENERALIZED ANXIETY DISORDER

Generalized anxiety disorder (GAD) is characterized by excessive worry about a number of different areas. The worry is difficult to control, occurs most of the time for at least 6 months, and is accompanied by significant distress or functional impairment, as well as by at least three of the following six symptoms: restlessness or feeling on edge, easy fatigability, concentration difficulties, irritability, muscle tension, and sleep disturbance. Since its original definition in 1980, GAD has been a problematic diagnosis with poor interrater reliability (DiNardo, Moras, Barlow, Rapee, & Brown, 1993) and high rates of psychiatric comorbidity (Brawman-Mintzer et al., 1993; Breslau & Davis, 1985). There has been an ongoing debate as to whether GAD exists as a valid, distinct disorder or is instead a prodromal, residual, or subthreshold form of other Axis I disorders or a characterological condition predisposing patients to a variety of Axis I diagnoses (e.g., Breslau & Davis, 1985; Brown, Barlow, & Liebowitz, 1994). However, it is evident that there exists a group of patients with primary or isolated, severe, generalized anxiety associated with significant functional impairment (Kessler et al., 1999).

Generalized anxiety disorder usually begins in the teens or early adulthood and is twice as common in women as in men. Data from the National Comorbidity Survey suggest that GAD has a current prevalence (in the past month) of 1.6% and a lifetime prevalence of 5.1% in the general population of the United States between the ages of 15 and 45 (Wittchen, Zhao, Kessler, & Eaton, 1994). Up to 90% of patients with GAD have a lifetime history and 60% a current history of at least one other Axis I disorder, the most common being social phobia, specific phobias, depression, dysthymia, panic disorder, and substance abuse or dependence (Brawman-Mintzer et al., 1993). GAD appears distinct from panic disorder in its familial transmission (Noyes et al., 1992) and shows heritability of about 30% in a study of female twins (Kendler, Neale, Kessler, Heath, & Eaves, 1992b).

The pathophysiology of GAD is unclear, although findings of increased muscle tension as assessed by direct measurement of muscle fiber activity using electromyogram (EMG) and of decreased "autonomic flexibility," with diminished autonomic responsivity and delayed recovery after a variety of laboratory stressors, are intriguing (Cowley & Roy-Byrne, 1991; Thayer et al., 2000). The efficacy of benzodiazepines in treating anxiety and animal studies implicating the gamma-aminobutyric acid–benzodiazepine receptor in anxiety states suggests that this receptor system may be involved in the pathophysiology of human anxiety (Ninan, Insel, Cohen, Skolnick, & Paul, 1982). Indeed, human studies indicate that patients with GAD (Cowley et al., 1991b) or high in "neuroticism" (Glue et al., 1995), a personality trait strongly associated with pathological anxiety, may be less sensitive to the effects of benzodiazepines. Furthermore, patients with GAD display altered central benzodiazepine receptor binding (Tiihonen et al., 1997), decreased peripheral benzodiazepine receptor number and mRNA (Rocca et al., 1998), and impaired benzodiazepine-induced chemotaxis (Sacerdote et al., 1999).

Historically, generalized anxiety has been treated with barbiturates, methaqualone, or, since the 1960s and 1970s, benzodiazepines. Since the early 1990s, alternative medication treatments, including buspirone and antidepressants, have been used for GAD. It should also be noted that cognitive behavioral therapy approaches specific for GAD have now been developed and appear quite effective.

Benzodiazepines

Numerous double-blind controlled trials have examined the efficacy of benzodiazepines in the treatment of generalized anxiety. For example, in 1978 Solomon and Hart reviewed 78 double-blind studies, concluding that benzodiazepines had not been shown to be superior to a placebo in the treatment of "neurotic anxiety."

Barlow (1988) reviewed eight double-blind 2 to 6 week trials performed between 1978 and 1983 and, using the Hamilton anxiety rating scale as the outcome measure, found 22 to 62% reductions in score in benzodiazepine-treated patients with generalized anxiety versus 18 to 48% decreases in placebo groups. He concluded that the effects of benzodiazepines were marginal. However, dropout rates were substantially higher in placebo groups in five of six studies supplying this information, perhaps reflecting lack of efficacy.

Two studies performed in the early 1980s suggested that patients with *DSM-III* GAD seen in primary-care settings responded equally well to diazepam and a placebo after the first week or two of treatment (Catalan et al., 1984; Shapiro et al., 1983). However, diazepam was superior to a placebo for those with the most severe anxiety (Shapiro et al., 1983).

All of these studies are difficult to interpret because treatment populations were very heterogeneous, and even since 1980, the definition of GAD has changed. As defined in *DSM-III*, for example, GAD included very mild and short-lived bouts of anxiety lasting only 1 month. More recently, with GAD requiring both persistent, hard-to-control worrying and a 6-month duration, benzodiazepines have been found superior to a placebo in acute (4- to 6-week) double-blind treatment of GAD in most (e.g., Borison, Albrecht, & Diamond, 1990; Boyer & Feighner, 1993; Cutler et al., 1993; Enkelmann, 1991; Laakman et al., 1998; Rickels et al., 1988; Rickels et al., 1993a; Rickels et al., 1997) but not all (e.g., Pecknold et al., 1989; Ross & Matas, 1987) studies. All benzodiazepines appear equally effective (Shader & Greenblatt, 1993). About two thirds of patients experience moderate-to-marked improvement of anxiety symptoms (usually assessed using Hamilton anxiety and Clinical Global Impression [CCI] ratings) with these medications, with therapeutic effects evident within the first 1 to 2 weeks. Doses are lower by approximately half than those used in treating panic disorder (usually the equivalent of 10 to 25 mg/day of diazepam). Benzodiazepines appear particularly effective for somatic anxiety symptoms (Rickels et al., 1982). Patients with minor depressive symptoms respond more poorly to most of these agents (Rickels et al., 1993a) with the possible exception of alprazolam, and a recent study (Garcia et al., 2000) demonstrated increases in negative emotions and decreases in positive emotions in both high- and low-anxiety volunteers given lorazepam.

Side effects of benzodiazepines in GAD are similar to those in panic disorder and include sedation, psychomotor impairment, anterograde amnesia (Lucki, Rickels, & Geller, 1986), and tolerance, although GAD patients may be less vulnerable than panic patients to withdrawal symptoms (Klein, Stolk, & Lenox, 1994). Of note, as with panic, dose escalation is rare in GAD patients without a history of substance abuse. For example, no dosage increases were observed in 119 anxious patients taking benzodiazepines for an average of 8 years (Rickels et al., 1986).

Azapirones

Buspirone, an azapirone anxiolytic and 5HT-lA receptor partial agonist, has been shown in several double-blind studies to be comparable to benzodiazepines, including diazepam, lorazepam, clorazepate, pam, and alprazolam, for the acute treatment of GAD (Ansseau, Papart, Gerard, von Frenckell, & Franck, 1990–1991; Cohn, Bowden, Fisher, & Rodos, 1986; Enkelmann, 1991; Feighner, Meredith, & Hendrickson, 1982; Laakman et al., 1998 Murphy, et al., 1989; Petracca et al., 1990; Rickels et al., 1982, 1988; Strand et al., 1990), yielding 30 to 50% reductions in Hamilton anxiety scale scores in 2- to 6-week trials. Other azapirones, including ipsapirone and gepirone, have also proven effective in placebo-controlled, double-blind trials (Borison et al., 1990; Boyer & Feighner, 1993; Cutler et al., 1993; Rickels et al., 1997) but are not available in the United States.

In comparison with benzodiazepines, buspirone has a delayed (2- to 4-week) onset of action, may affect cognitive anxiety symptoms to a greater extent than physical symptoms (Feighner & Cohn, 1989; Rickels et al., 1982), and has the advantage of being nonsedating and without evidence of tolerance or withdrawal symptoms. Common side effects of buspirone include nausea, dizziness, and headaches. Average therapeutic doses are 20 to 45 mg/day, although doses of up to 60 mg/day may be necessary. Buspirone displays antidepressant effects in patients with comorbid depression, usually at higher doses of 45 to 60 mg/day (Gammans et al., 1992).

In general, patients on chronic benzodiazepine treatment do not respond well when switched to buspirone (Lader & Olajide, 1987; DeMatinis, Rynn, Rickels, and Mandos, 2000). For example, in a reanalysis of treatment results in 735 patients with GAD treated with buspirone, a benzodiazepine, or a placebo, clinical improvement was similar with buspirone versus benzodiazepine treatment in those patients with no prior history of benzodiazepine treatment and in those whose benzodiazepine treatment had ended a month or more prior to the study. In those with recent benzodiazepine treatment (within the past month), there was greater attrition with buspirone treatment due to lack of efficacy and less clinical improvement than with benzodiazepine treatment (DeMartinis, Rynn, Rickels, and Mandos, 2000). However, a double-blind study (Delle Chiaie et al., 1995) of 44 GAD patients switched to buspirone versus a placebo after 5 weeks of lorazepam treatment, with lorazepam tapered during the first 2 weeks of buspirone versus placebo treatment, showed that buspirone was superior to a placebo and comparable to lorazepam in anxiolytic effects. There was no evidence of benzodiazepine withdrawal symptoms. Whether these promising results with a gradual taper of the benzodiazepine after initiation of buspirone are generalizable to patients maintained on long-term benzodiazepine treatment remains to be seen.

Antidepressants

When panic disorder and GAD initially were described as distinct anxiety disorders, panic disorder was postulated to differ from GAD in responding to antidepressant treatment. However, since the mid-1980s, several antidepressants, including venlafaxine, imipramine, trazodone, and paroxetine, have been shown in double-blind trials to be effective in treating GAD (Davidson et al., 1999; Gelenberg et al., 2000; Haskins et al., 1998; Hoehn-Saric, McLeod, & Zimmerli, 1988; Kahn et al., 1986; Rickels et al., 1993a, 2000; Rocca et al., 1997). Venlafaxine is now approved by the Food and Drug Administration for treatment of this disorder. In addition, case series support the use of clomipramine (Wingerson, Nguyen, & Roy-Byrne, 1992), mirtazapine (Goodnick et al., 1999), and nefazodone (Hedges et al., 1996) in patients diagnosed with GAD, and trials in patients with depression and comorbid anxiety suggest that fluoxetine (Versiani et al., 1999), fluvoxamine (Houck, 1998), and amitryptiline (Versiani et al., 1999) hold promise as treatments for generalized anxiety.

In an early double-blind trial, Kahn et al. (1986) reported that imipramine performed better than chlordiazepoxide in the treatment of nondepressed outpatients retrospectively diagnosed as having GAD. In a study by Hoehn-Saric et al. (1988) of nondepressed patients with GAD, imipramine was comparable to alprazolam after the first 2 weeks of treatment. Imipramine was more effective in reducing psychic anxiety symptoms such as obsessionality, dysphoria, negative anticipatory thinking, and interpersonal sensitivity, while alprazolam was superior in alleviating cardiovascular and autonomic symptoms.

Rickels et al. (1993a) compared imipramine (mean dose 143 mg/day), trazodone (mean dose 255 mg/ day), diazepam (mean dose 26 mg/day), and a placebo in 230 patients with GAD treated for 8 weeks. Although all active treatments were superior to the placebo, diazepam yielded the most improvement in anxiety ratings for the first 2 weeks, and imipramine was the most effective treatment thereafter, with 73% of patients moderately or markedly improved compared with 69% on trazodone, 66% on diazepam, and 47% on the placebo. Once more, antidepressants reduced cognitive anxiety symptoms to a greater extent than did diazepam. Patients on antidepressants also reported more side effects.

Rocca et al. (1997) compared paroxetine, imipramine, and 2′-chlordesmethyldiazepam in 81 patients with GAD. All three treatment conditions resulted in significant clinical improvement in about two thirds of patients. As in prior studies, the benzodiazepine resulted in more rapid improvement, but the antidepressants resulted in more improvement by the fourth week. In addition, paroxetine and imipramine were most effective for psychic anxiety symptoms, while 2′-chlordesmethyl-diazepam was superior for somatic symptoms. More recently, a fixed-dose study showed that both 20 mg and 40 mg of paroxetine were superior to placebo in 426 patients with GAD. (Bellow et al., 2000).

Promising observations in double-blind trials that venlafaxine was more effective than placebo in treating symptoms of anxiety in depressed outpatients (Feighner et al., 1998; Khan et al., 1998) then led to four double-blind, placebo-controlled trials, which established the efficacy of this agent in nondepressed patients with generalized anxiety disorder (Davidson et al., 1999; Gelenberg et al., 2000; Haskins et al., 1998; Rickels et al., 2000). Venlafaxine XR, in doses of 75 to 225 mg daily, yielded significantly greater decreases in anxiety than placebo within the first 2 to 3 weeks of treatment. Davidson et al. (1999) found that venlafaxine XR (75 or 150 mg/day) was more effective than buspirone (30 mg/day) throughout their 8-week study, while Gelenberg et al. (2000) showed persistent treatment gains over 28 weeks of treatment, with response rates (defined as a 40% decrease in Hamilton Anxiety score or CGI of 1 or 2) at Weeks 6 to 28 of 69% with venlafaxine XR 75 to 225 mg/day compared with 42 to 46% in the placebo group.

These studies suggest that antidepressants, and particularly imipramine, venlafaxine, and paroxetine are promising treatments for GAD. Whether all antidepressants are similarly effective in treating GAD remains to be determined.

Other Medications

Studies performed prior to 1980 showed no efficacy of beta blockers for the treatment of generalized anxiety (Hayes & Schulz, 1987). The one double-blind, placebo-controlled trial conducted more recently is more promising (Meibach, Mullane, & Binstok, 1987). This 3-week, multicenter study of propranolol (average maximum dose 189 mg/day) versus chlordiazepoxide (average dose 50 mg/day) versus a placebo in 417 outpatients with "anxiety sufficiently severe to warrant treatment with an anxiolytic agent" showed the superiority of both active drugs but fewer side effects with propranolol than with chlordiazepoxide. Surprisingly, propranolol was particularly effective in reducing psychic symptoms of anxiety. Open trials of betaxolol, a long-acting beta blocker that enters the central nervous system, in 18 inpatients and 13 outpatients with anxiety disorders (including 16 inpatients and 11 outpatients with GAD) showed marked improvement in anxiety ratings in most patients (Swartz, 1998). Nevertheless, most experts continue to feel that beta blockers are not an effective primary treatment for GAD and should be reserved for use as an adjunct, particularly in patients with prominent autonomic symptoms.

A multicenter, double-blind, 4-week trial of hydroxyzine (50 mg/day) versus a placebo in 133 GAD patients displayed significantly greater reductions in anxiety in the hydroxyzine group, although side effects were more common than in the placebo group (Ferreri, Hantouche, & Billardon, 1994). Similarly, hydroxyzine (50 mg/day) and buspirone (20 mg/day) were both superior to placebo in a more recent double-blind, multicenter, 4-week trial in a total of 244 patients with generalized anxiety disorder (Lader &

Scotto, 1998). Kava kava, an extract of the plant *Piper methysticum*, used in the South Pacific to induce relaxation and sleep, has been shown to be effective for generalized anxiety (for review, see Pittler & Ernst, 2000). For example, in three double-blind trials of anxious patients with Hamilton Anxiety scores of 19 or greater, kava kava was significantly superior to placebo in reducing anxiety (Kinzler et al., 1991; Warnecke, 1991; Volz & Kieser, 1997). Doses were 210 mg kavapyrones daily (in three divided doses), and the most common side effects were stomach upset, drowsiness, and tremor. Other treatments under investigation include cholecystokinin receptor antagonists, CRH receptor antagonists, and benzodiazepine-receptor partial agonists with anxiolytic properties but without the risks of sedation and withdrawal symptoms accompanying currently available benzodiazepines. For example, three placebo-controlled trials have suggested that abecarnil, a partial benzodiazepine-receptor agonist, is effective for GAD and less likely than benzodiazepines to produce significant discontinuation symptoms (Lydiard et al., 1997; Pollack et al., 1997; Rickels et al., 2000).

Long-Term Treatment and Outcome

Although there is extensive literature regarding acute treatment of generalized anxiety, there is less information available regarding long-term efficacy or optimal duration of treatment.

Few studies have examined results of benzodiazepine treatment beyond the first 6 weeks. Cutler et al. (1993) found lorazepam more effective than a placebo after 6 weeks, but not after 8 weeks, of treatment, primarily due to continued improvement in the placebo group. Both alprazolam and lorazepam remained superior to a placebo after 16 weeks in another study (Cohn & Wilcox, 1984). In a study of 101 GAD patients treated with cognitive behavioral treatment, a placebo, or diazepam for 10 weeks, the greatest improvement was seen in patients receiving a combination of CBT and diazepam, and diazepam alone was more effective than a placebo alone (Power, Simpson, Swanson, & Wallace, 1990). Rickels et al. (1988) showed the continued efficacy of clorazepate over a 6-month trial, with no tolerance to anxiolytic effects, but there was no placebo comparison.

Thus, benzodiazepines seem to have continued anxiolytic effects for up to 6 months, but the paucity of studies leaves without a clear answer the question of whether benzodiazepines are superior to a placebo after the initial phase of treatment.

Buspirone has been shown to yield continued efficacy over a treatment period of 3 to 6 months (Feighner, 1987; Rickels et al., 1988; Murphy et al., 1989). Venlafaxine XR yielded persistent efficacy over 28 weeks of treatment in the one study that has addressed longer term treatment with this agent (Gelenberg et al., 2000). Kava kava, in doses of 70 mg, was shown superior to placebo from the second through the sixth month of treatment in 101 outpatients with a variety of anxiety disorders, including GAD (Volz & Kiesser, 1997).

Two studies have addressed the issue of optimal duration of treatment. Rickels et al. (1983) found that 50% of patients treated with diazepam for 6 weeks had relapsed 3 months later, and 63% had relapsed after 1 year. In another trial performed by the same group (Rickels, Schweizer, & Canalosi, 1988), 45 patients with GAD who responded to 6 months of treatment with clorazepate or buspirone were then followed up 6 and 40 months after the end of the study. At 6 months, 55% of clorazepate-treated patients and 38% of those treated with buspirone reported moderate to marked anxiety. At 40 months, 34 patients were contacted, and 57% of clorazepate-treated versus 25% of buspirone-treated subjects reported moderate to severe anxiety. Although Rickels and Schweizer (1997) suggested intermittent short-term treatment for GAD, these data suggest that for many people, GAD is a chronic illness requiring treatment for longer than 6 months. The apparently better outcome with initial buspirone treatment is interesting but may be attributable to the higher dropout rate in the buspirone group during the initial treatment period, with only the most treatment-responsive patients remaining in the study.

SPECIFIC PHOBIA

Specific (formerly simple) phobias are fears and avoidance of discrete objects or situations such as spiders and heights. The treatment of choice for specific phobias is behavior therapy, specifically, systematic desensitization. Recently, successful treatment of specific phobia with fluoxetine has been reported in two patients with major depression and comorbid fear of flying (Abene & Hamilton, 1998). A small double-blind, placebo-controlled 4-week pilot study examining the efficacy of paroxetine up to 20 mg/day versus placebo for specific phobias showed significant superiority of paroxetine in reducing phobia scores on the Fear Questionnaire and Hamilton Anxiety scores (Benjamin et al., 2000). Nevertheless, in general, pharmacological treatments have not proven effective for specific phobias. In fact, use of benzodiazepines may reduce therapeutic effects of exposure treatment (Wilhelm & Roth, 1997).

SOCIAL ANXIETY DISORDER

Social anxiety disorder (previously social phobia) is defined as a fear of social or performance situations in which the person fears scrutiny by others and acting in a humiliating or embarrassing way. Feared social situations are avoided or endured with distress, and social anxiety causes significant functional impairment. Social anxiety disorder has been subdivided into a "specific" form limited to one or a few situations (most commonly, public speaking) and a "generalized" form involving fear and avoidance of multiple social situations. Some authors have argued that generalized social anxiety disorder is indistinguishable from avoidant personality disorder (see Widiger, 1992).

Social anxiety disorder is common. In the Epidemiological Catchment Area (ECA) study, the 1-month prevalence was 1.3%, and the lifetime prevalence was 2.8% (Regier et al., 1990). More recently, the National Comorbidity Survey of over 8,000 people in the United States found a 12-month prevalence of 7.9% and a lifetime prevalence of 13.3% (Kessler et al., 1994). Social anxiety disorder has an early age of onset, with a peak in childhood and the teenage years (Schneier et al., 1992b), and is more common in women than in men (Bourdon et al., 1988). It is associated with significant disability, with 22% of those with uncomplicated social anxiety disorder in the ECA study receiving public assistance and more than 50% of social phobics reporting at least moderate functional impairment due to social anxiety (Schneier et al., 1994). In up to 70% of cases, social anxiety disorder is accompanied by, and commonly precedes, other significant comorbid psychiatric disorders, such as depression, other anxiety disorders, and alcohol abuse and dependence (Schneier et al., 1992b).

A number of studies have failed to show distinctive baseline biological abnormalities in social anxiety disorder with anxiogenic challenges or in response to public speaking. However, behavioral inhibition, with autonomic arousal in response to novelty starting in infancy and shyness and introversion as a toddler, is strongly associated with later social anxiety disorder, suggesting an underlying inborn vulnerability in many individuals (Rosenbaum et al., 1991). In addition, family and twin studies suggest that social anxiety disorder is familial and has a heritable component of about 30% (Fyer et al., 1988; Kendler et al., 1992a).

Social anxiety disorder has been until recently a relatively neglected disorder. However, since the mid-1980s, behavioral and cognitive behavioral techniques have been proven effective in the treatment of this disorder (Otto, 1999), and a number of double-blind, placebo-controlled studies have examined the efficacy of psychopharmacological treatments (Versiani, 2000). Liebowitz et al. (1986, 1992) published the first open and then controlled trials of medication treatment for patients with social anxiety disorder. These trials used the beta blocker atenolol, based on prior reports of the utility of beta blockers in treating performance anxiety, and the MAO inhibitor phenelzine, based on the efficacy of this medication in treating mixed agoraphobia and social anxiety disorder and its success in treating atypical depression, which shares with social anxiety disorder the prominent symptom of interpersonal sensitivity. Since these early trials, there have been several studies using both reversible and irreversible MAO inhibitors, benzodiazepines, serotonin reuptake inhibitors, gabapentin, and beta blockers to treat social anxiety disorder.

Monoamine Oxidase Inhibitors

In 1986, Liebowitz et al. reported that 7 of 11 patients with *DSM-III* social phobia showed a "marked" response to phenelzine, while the other 4 had "moderate" improvement. Since then, four double-blind, randomized trials have supported the efficacy of phenelzine for social anxiety disorder. Liebowitz et al. (1992) treated 74 patients with social anxiety disorder with phenelzine ($N = 25$; mean dose, 75.7 mg/day), atenolol ($N = 23$; mean dose, 97.6 mg/day), and a placebo ($N = 26$). By Week 8, "response" rates (much or very much improved as assessed by an independent rater) were 64% for phenelzine, 30% for atenolol, and 23% for the placebo. The superiority of phenelzine persisted at Week 16, with a 52% response rate, versus 19% for the placebo. Patients with generalized social anxiety disorder responded better to phenelzine than to the other treatments. However, the number of patients with specific social phobias was too small to allow an analysis of the differential efficacy of atenolol and phenelzine.

Gelernter et al. (1991), in a study of 65 social phobics given phenelzine, alprazolam, a placebo, or group cognitive behavioral therapy, found that all groups improved, perhaps because all patients were encouraged to expose themselves to feared situations. Nevertheless, patients taking phenelzine were more likely than those in the other groups to display functional improvement and to fall below the mean score for the general population on the social phobia subscale of the Fear Questionnaire at the end of 12 weeks. Versiani et al. (1992) completed a double-blind trial of phenelzine ($N = 26$; mean dose, 67.5 mg/day), the reversible MAO inhibitor moclobemide ($N = 26$; mean dose, 580.7 mg/day), and a placebo ($N = 26$). After 8 weeks, phenelzine and moclobemide were both significantly more effective than the placebo, and these gains were maintained for a further 8 weeks. Responders were then maintained on active medication or changed to a placebo. Those switched to the placebo demonstrated significant increases in symptomatology that persisted for at least 5 weeks, a finding suggesting a high rate of relapse. Finally, Heimberg et al. (1998) compared 12 weeks of phenelzine, pill placebo, cognitive behavioral group treatment (CBGT), and an educational supportive group in 133 patients with social anxiety disorder. Both CBGT and phenelzine were superior to the control conditions, although response to phenelzine was more marked than CBGT response at 6 weeks.

Thus, double-blind trials to date support the efficacy of phenelzine in the treatment of social anxiety disorder. Although it has been suggested that generalized social anxiety disorder may be more responsive to MAO inhibitors than is specific social anxiety disorder, this outcome has not yet been demonstrated. Furthermore, the fact that 74% of subjects in Gelernter et al.'s (1991) study had specific social anxiety disorder would indicate that phenelzine is effective in this group. Interestingly, isolated case reports suggest that phenelzine may also be effective in the treatment of conditions related to social anxiety disorder, such as elective mutism (Golwyn & Weinstock, 1990) and social anxiety secondary to physical disfigurement (Oberlander, Schneier, & Liebowitz, 1994). Other irreversible MAO inhibitors have not been studied in double-blind trials. However, an open trial of tranylcypromine (Versiani, Mundim, & Nardi, 1988) yielded 20 "marked responders" from 29 subjects.

Irreversible MAO inhibitors such as phenelzine have significant side effects, most notably hypertensive crisis, insomnia, weight gain, and sexual dysfunction. Reversible MAO inhibitors, such as moclobemide and brofaramine, bind reversibly, are selective for the A isoenzyme of monoamine oxidase, and have fewer side effects, including a much lower rate of hypertensive crisis. The efficacy of reversible MAO inhibitors in social phobia has been demonstrated in four double-blind, placebo-controlled trials of moclobemide (International Multicenter Clinical Trial Group on Moclobemide, 1997; Noyes et al., 1997; Schneier et al., 1998; Versiani et al., 1992;) and three of brofaramine (Fablen, Nilsson, Borg, Humber, & Pauli, 1995; Lott et al., 1997; van Vliet et al., 1993). In the trial of moclobemide, phenelzine, and a placebo (Versiani et al., 1992) noted above, response rates after 8 weeks of treatment were 85%, 65%, and 15% for phenelzine, moclobemide, and placebo, respectively, but side effects were significantly more common in patients taking phenelzine (in 95%) than in those taking moclobemide (12%) or the placebo (29%). The International Multicenter Clinical Trial Group on Moclobemide (1997) demonstrated significantly greater efficacy for social anxiety with 600 mg/day moclobemide than with placebo in 578 patients. However, Schneier et al. (1998) reported response rates of only 17.5% with moclobemide versus 13.5% with placebo in a 16-week trial in 77 patients with social anxiety disorder. Another large study, of 583 patients (Noyes et al., 1997), failed to detect consistent differences between placebo and five different doses of moclobemide. However, the high placebo response rate, high dropout rate, and six different treatment groups may have yielded insufficient power to detect significant drug-placebo differences or dose-response relationships.

Three double-blind, placebo-controlled trials using brofaromine in the treatment of social anxiety disorder (Fahlen et al., 1995; Lott et al., 1997; van Vliet et al., 1992) demonstrated significant superiority of this agent relative to placebo, with doses of 150 mg/day yielding better results than the lower mean doses used in one study (Lott et al., 1997). Unfortunately, despite the promise of the reversible MAO inhibitors moclobemide and brofaromine for social anxiety disorder, the development of these medications has been discontinued in the United States. Of note, selegiline, which is a reversible MAO inhibitor in low doses, has been reported to be effective for social anxiety disorder (Simpson et al., 1998).

Beta Blockers

Despite an early, promising open study of atenolol for social phobia (Gorman et al., 1985) and several studies demonstrating the efficacy of single doses of beta blockers for treating performance anxiety in nonclinical groups such as musicians and public speakers (see Jefferson, 1995, for a review), beta blockers have not been proven effective in double-blind trials with patients with social phobia. In the study by Liebowitz et al. (1992) mentioned above, atenolol was not significantly more effective than a placebo.

Behavior therapy, primarily flooding, was superior to both a placebo and atenolol in one study (Turner, Beidel, & Jacob, 1994), while propranolol showed no advantage over a placebo in another trial in which subjects also received social skills training (Falloon, Lloyd, & Harpin, 1981).

The suggestion that beta blockers may be particularly useful for patients with discrete or specific social phobia (Liebowitz et al., 1992) has not been tested rigorously. Thus, at present, beta blockers may be useful for treating performance anxiety or discrete social phobia accompanied by prominent palpitations, tachycardia, or sweating. However, there as yet is no evidence to support their use as a primary treatment for social phobia.

Benzodiazepines

In open trials, both alprazolam, at doses of 3 to 8 mg/day, and clonazepam, 1 to 6 mg/day, have been effective in the treatment of social phobia (see Davidson, Tupler, & Potts, 1994, for a review). The only double-blind, placebo-controlled trial of alprazolam was that of Gelernter et al. (1991). Although alprazolam (mean dose 4.2 mg/day) was not superior to a placebo, this study was complicated by the inclusion of self-directed exposure in all treatment groups. Clonazepam, at an average dose of 2.4 mg/day, decreased social anxiety, interpersonal sensitivity, phobic avoidance, and disability in a 10-week double-blind study of 75 patients with social phobia (Davidson et al., 1993). Response rates were 78.3% for clonazepam and 20% for a placebo.

Use of benzodiazepines for social anxiety disorder is complicated both by their side effects (see above) and by the high rate of comorbid alcohol abuse or dependence (Schneier et al., 1992b), which may put patients at an increased risk for benzodiazepine abuse and dependence.

Serotonin Reuptake Inhibitors

There are now seven published double-blind, placebo-controlled trials of serotonin reuptake inhibitors for social anxiety disorder. Van Vliet, den Boer, and Westenberg (1994) demonstrated that fluvoxamine (150 mg/day) was superior to a placebo in reducing social and generalized anxiety after 12 weeks. Differences in phobic avoidance did not reach statistical significance, and substantial improvement (a 50% or greater decrease in Liebowitz Social Anxiety Scale score) was seen in 46% of patients on fluvoxamine versus 7% of those on the placebo. Another 12-week double-blind, placebo-controlled trial using fluvoxamine (mean dose 202 mg daily) versus placebo to treat 92 patients with social anxiety disorder (91.3% with the generalized subtype) also demonstrated superior efficacy of fluvoxamine (Stein et al., 1999). Of fluvoxamine-treated patients, 42.9%, versus 22.7% of those receiving placebo, were rated "much improved" or "very much improved" on the CGI. In a double-blind, crossover study of sertraline (50 to 200 mg/day, mean dose 133.5 mg/day) versus a placebo in 12 patients with social phobia, sertraline yielded significantly greater reductions in social anxiety and increases in social functioning than did the placebo (Katzelnick et al., 1995).

Four double-blind, placebo-controlled trials have established the efficacy of paroxetine in the treatment of social anxiety disorder (Allgulander, 1999; Baldwin et al., 1999; Stein et al., 1998; Stein, Berk et al., 1999). Stein et al. (1998) compared paroxetine (20 to 50 mg/day, mean 37 mg/day) to placebo in a 12-week trial in 187 patients with generalized social anxiety disorder. Response rates (defined as a CGI of 1 or 2) were 55% in the paroxetine group versus 23.9% in those taking placebo, and Liebowitz Social

Anxiety Scale (LSAS) scores decreased by 39.1% on paroxetine versus 17.4% on placebo. Similarly, Baldwin et al. (1999) found, in 290 patients with social anxiety disorder given 20 to 50 mg paroxetine versus placebo for 12 weeks, response rates (CGI = 1 or 2) of 65.7% versus 32.4%, respectively, and significantly greater decreases in LSAS scores with paroxetine than with placebo. Two other double-blind, placebo-controlled trials also demonstrated efficacy of paroxetine in social anxiety disorder (Allgulander, 1999; Stein, Berk et al., 1999), with differences from placebo evident by 4 to 6 weeks of treatment and only small numbers of patients in either group discontinuing treatment due to side effects.

These studies clearly establish that paroxetine, fluvoxamine, sertraline, and probably other serotinergic antidepressants are effective in the treatment of social anxiety disorder. Given their efficacy, and greater tolerability and safety compared with MAO inhibitors or benzodiazepines, SSRIs are now the first-line pharmacological treatment for social anxiety disorder (Ballenger et al., 1998).

Other Medications

Surprisingly, there have been no controlled trials of tricyclic antidepressants for patients with social phobia. Although isolated case reports suggest that they may be effective (Benca, Matuzas, & Al-Sadir, 1986), other anecdotal evidence has been cited suggesting that tricyclics are inferior to MAO inhibitors (e.g., Liebowitz et al., 1986; Versiani et al., 1988), and a recent open trial of imipramine (Simpson et al., 1998) indicated both lack of efficacy and a high dropout rate due to side effects. Open trials of buspirone appeared promising, particularly when doses exceed 45 mg/day (Munjack, Brun, & Baltazar, 1991; Schneier et al., 1993). However, two double-blind trials using buspirone showed no significant improvement with doses averaging 32 mg/day in musicians seeking treatment for performance anxiety (Clark & Agras, 1991) and no difference between buspirone 30 mg/day and placebo in 30 patients with social anxiety disorder (van Vliet et al., 1997). It remains possible that higher doses of buspirone will prove effective in controlled trials. Of note, an open trial suggests that buspirone may be an effective augmentation agent in partial responders to SSRIs (Van Ameringen et al., 1996).

A randomized, double-blind, placebo-controlled 14-week trial using flexible doses of gabapentin (900 to 3,600 mg daily in three divided doses; mean dose 2,100 mg/day) in 69 patients with social anxiety disorder (Pande et al., 1999) yielded response rates (CGI = 1 or 2) of 32% with gabapentin versus 14% with placebo. Side effects of gabapentin included dizziness, dry mouth, somnolence, nausea, flatulence, and decreased libido.

Successful treatment of social anxiety disorder with bupropion (Emmanuel, Lydiard, & Ballenger, 1991), clonidine (Goldstein, 1987), and the dopamine agonist pergolide (Villarreal et al., 2000) has also been reported. Case reports have also shown that venlafaxine (Altamura et al., 1999) and nefazodone (Van Ameringen et al., 1999; Worthington et al., 1998) are useful in the treatment of social anxiety disorder.

Long-Term Treatment

There is scant information available regarding long-term treatment of social anxiety disorder. However, this is frequently a chronic illness (Reich, Goldenberg, Vasile, Goisman, & Keller, 1994) requiring long-term treatment. In 26 patients with social phobia treated with clonazepam for an average of 11.3 months (range 1 to 29 months) by Davidson et al. (1991a), clonazepam was well tolerated, 20 patients were able to reduce their dose, and 5 discontinued their medication. Connor et al. (1998) assigned patients who had responded to 6 months of clonazepam treatment to continued treatment or to a gradual taper (0.25 mg every 2 weeks) with double-blind placebo substitution, for 5 months. Relapse rates were 0% in the continued treatment and 21% in the taper group. Continued treatment was well tolerated and somewhat more effective than gradual taper after 6 months. A trial comparing a placebo and brofaromine (Fablen et al., 1995) followed responders for 9 months. Those on brofaromine (N = 22) showed further symptomatic improvement over this period. On the placebo, 6 of 10 relapsed, versus none of 22 maintained on brofaromine.

Versiani et al. (1997) reported that, of 59 patients who responded to moclobemide and were continued on treatment for 2 years, 88% deteriorated when the medication was then discontinued. Reinstitution of moclobemide restored the therapeutic response. After another 2 years, medication was discontinued, and follow-up 6 to 24 months later found that 63% of patients had no or mild symptoms. Alcohol abuse was the strongest predictor of negative treatment outcome. Finally, Liebowitz et al. (1999) reported on a follow-up study of patients initially treated with phenelzine or cognitive behavioral group therapy (Heimberg et al., 1998). Patients responding to phenelzine or CBGT were maintained on treatment for 6 months and then followed for a 6-month treatment-free phase. Most patients maintained their gains during the maintenance phase, but relapse rates were higher in phenelzine-treated patients than in the CBGT group once treatment was discontinued. Thus, many patients with social anxiety disorder benefit from continued treatment beyond the acute phase of clinical trials.

Overall, little is known regarding optimal duration of treatment or long-term outcome of the conditions discussed in this chapter. However, all four disorders begin early in life, often in childhood or adolescence, and may be chronic in many people. Thus, further study of treatment of anxiety disorders in children and of long-term management of panic disorder, GAD, specific phobia, and social anxiety disorder is very important.

SUMMARY

Since the early 1980s, a number of pharmacological treatments have been shown effective for panic disorder, GAD, and social anxiety disorder. SSRIs are now considered by most experts to be the first-line pharmacological treatment for panic disorder based on their low rate of side effects, lack of dietary restrictions, and absence of tolerance and withdrawal symptoms. Similarly, SSRIs are an attractive first-line treatment for social anxiety disorder. The pharmacological treatments of choice for GAD are buspirone, and antidepressants, venlafaxine being the best studied. Both buspirone and antidepressants provide a promising alternative to benzodiazepines. Benzodiazepines, although effective for all of these disorders, carry with them the risk of physiological dependence and withdrawal symptoms and ineffectiveness for comorbid depression. Their greatest utility at present seems to be as an initial or adjunct medication for patients with disabling symptoms requiring rapid relief and for those unable to tolerate other medications. Chronic treatment with benzodiazepines is safe and effective but should probably be reserved for patients who are nonresponsive or intolerant to other agents. Controlled trials are necessary to determine whether patients with specific phobias respond to pharmacological agents, particularly serotonin reuptake inhibitors.

The major challenges in acute treatment of all of these disorders are to determine the most effective and also cost-effective initial combination of pharmacological and nonpharmacological treatments and to develop new anxiolytic agents with a rapid onset of action but without the risks of tolerance and withdrawal. For existing agents, particular subtypes of these disorders or types of comorbidity may respond better to some agents than to others, and studies of combination treatments may enhance efficacy, especially in patients unresponsive to or only minimally improved with single agents.

References

Abene, M. V., & Hamilton, J. D. (1998). Resolution of fear of flying with fluoxetine treatment. *Journal of Anxiety Disorders, 12,* 599–603.

Aikens, J. E., Wagner, L. I., Lickerman, A. J., Chin, M. H., & Smith, A. (1999). Primary care physician responses to a panic disorder vignette: diagnostic suspicion and clinical management. *International Journal of Psychiatry in Medicine,* 28(2), 179–188.

Allgulander, C. (1999). Paroxetine in social anxiety disorder: A randomized placebo-controlled study. *Acta Psychiatrica Scandinavica, 100,* 193–198.

Altamura, A. C., Pioli, R., Vitto, M., & Mannu, P. (1999). Venlafaxine in social phobia: A study in selective serotonin reuptake inhibitor non-responders. *International Clinical Psychopharmacology, 14,* 239–245.

American Psychiatric Association. (1980). *Diagnostic and statistical manual of mental disorders* (3rd ed.). Washington, DC: Author.

American Psychiatric Association. (1987). *Diagnostic and statistical manual of mental disorders* (3rd ed., rev.). Washington, DC: Author.

American Psychiatric Association. (1994). *Diagnostic and statistical manual of mental disorders* (4th ed.). Washington, DC: Author.

American Psychiatric Association. (1998). Practice guideline for the treatment of patients with panic disorder. *American Journal of Psychiatry, 155*(5)(Suppl), 1–34.

Ansseau, M., Papart, P., Gerard, M. A., von Frenckell, R., & Franck, C. (1990–1991). Controlled comparison of buspirone and oxazepam in generalized anxiety. *Neuropsychobiology, 24,* 74–78.

Baetz, M., & Bowen, R. C. (1998). Efficacy of divalproex sodium in patients with panic disorder and mood instability who have not responded to conventional therapy. *Canadian Journal of Psychiatry, 43*(1), 73–77.

Bakish D., Hooper, C. L., Filteau, M. J., Charbonneau, Y., Fraser, G., West, D. L., Thibaudeau, C., & Raine, D. (1996). A double-blind placebo-controlled trial comparing fluvoxamine and imipramine in the treatment of panic disorder with or without agoraphobia. *Psychopharmacology Bulletin, 32*(1), 135–141.

Bakish, D., Saxena, B. M., Bowen, R., & D'Souza, J. (1993). Reversible monoamine oxidase—A inhibitors in panic disorder. *Clinical Neuropharmacology,* (Suppl. 2), S77–S82.

Ballenger, J. C., Burrows, C. D., DuPont, R. L., et al. (1988). Alprazolam in panic disorder and agoraphobia: Results from a multicenter trial. *Archives of General Psychiatry, 45,* 413–422.

Ballenger, J. C., Davidson, J. R., Lecrubier, Y., Nutt, D. J., Baldwin, D. S., den Boer, J. A., Kasper, S., & Shear, M. K. (1998). Consensus statement on panic disorder from the International Consensus Group on Depression and Anxiety. *Journal of Clinical Psychiatry, 59*(Suppl. 8), 47–54.

Ballenger, J. C., Davidson, J. R., Lecrubier, Y., Nutt, D. J., Bobes, J., Beidel, D. C., Ono, Y., & Westenberg, H. G. (1998). Consensus statement on social anxiety disorder from the International Consensus Group on Depression and Anxiety. *Journal of Clinical Psychiatry, 59*(Suppl. 17), 54–60.

Ballenger, J. C., Wheadon, D. E., Steiner, M., Bushnell, W., & Gergel, I. P. (1998). Double-blind, fixed-dose, placebo-controlled study of paroxetine in the treatment of panic disorder. *American Journal of Psychiatry, 155*(1), 36–42.

Bandelow, B., Sievert, K., Rothemeyer, M., Hajak, G., & Ruther, E. (1995). What treatments do patients with panic disorder and agoraphobia get? *European Archives of Psychiatry and Clinical Neuroscience, 245*(3), 165–171.

Barlow, D. H. (1988). *Anxiety and its disorders.* New York: Guilford Press.

Barlow, D. H., Gorman, J. M., Shear, M. K., & Woods, S. W. (2000). Cognitive-behavioral therapy, imipramine, or their combination for panic disorder: A randomized controlled trial. *Journal of the American Medical Association, 283,* 2529–2536.

Beauclair, L., Fontaine, R., Annable, L., Holobow, N., & Chouinard, G. (1994). Clonazepam in the treatment of panic disorder: A double-blind, placebo-controlled trial investigating the correlation between clonazepam concentrations in plasma and clinical response. *Journal of Clinical Psychopharmacology, 14,* 111–118.

Beck, A. T. (1988). Cognitive approaches to panic disorder: Theory and therapy. In S. Rachman & J. D. Maser (Eds.), *Panic: Psychological perspectives* (pp. 91–109). Hillsdale, NJ: Erlbaum.

Bellew, K. M., McCafferty, J. P., Iyengar, M., Zaninelli, R. (April/May, 2000). Paroxetine for the treatment of generalized anxiety disorder: A double-blind, placebo controlled trial. Presented at the Annual Meeting of the American Psychiatric Association, Chicago, IL.

Benca, R., Matuzas, W., & Al-Sadir, J. (1986). Social phobia, MVP, and response to imipramine. *Journal of Clinical Psychopharmacology, 6,* 50–51.

Benjamin, J., Ben-Zion, I. Z., Karbofsky, E., Dannon, P. (2000). Double-blind placebo-controlled pilot study of paroxetine for specific phobia. *Psychopharmacology, 149,* 194–196.

Benjamin, J., Levine, J., Fux, M., Aviv, A, Levy, D., & Belmaker, R. H. (1995). Double-blind, placebo-controlled crossover trial of inositol treatment for panic disorder. *American Journal of Psychiatry, 152*(7), 1084–1086.

Berigan, T. R., Casas, A., & Harazin, J. (1998). Nefazodone and the treatment of panic. *Journal of Clinical Psychiatry, 59*(5), 256–257.

Black, D. W., Wesner, R., Bowers, W., & Gabel, J. (1993b). A comparison of fluvoxamine, cognitive therapy and placebo in the treatment of panic disorder. *Archives of General Psychiatry, 50,* 44–50.

Black, D. W., Wesner, R., & Gabel, J. (1993a). The abrupt discontinuation of fluvoxamine in patients with panic disorder. *Journal of Clinical Psychiatry, 54*(4), 146–149.

Borison, R. L., Albrecht, J. W., & Diamond, B. I. (1990). Efficacy and safety of a putative anxiolytic agent: Ipsapirone. *Psychopharmacology Bulletin, 26,* 207–210.

Bourdon, K. H., Boyd, J. H., Rae, D. S., Burns, B. J., Thompson, J. W., & Locke, B. Z. (1988). Gender differences in phobias: Results of the ECA community survey. *Journal of Anxiety Disorders, 2,* 227–241.

Boyer, W. (1995). Serotonin uptake inhibitors are supenor to imipramine and alprazolam in alleviating panic attacks: A meta-analysis. *International Clinical Psychopharmacology, 10,* 45–49.

Boyer, W. F., & Feighner, J. P. (1993). A placebo-controlled double-blind multicenter trial of two doses of ipsapirone versus diazepam in generalized anxiety disorder. *International Clinical Psychopharmacology, 8,* 173–176.

Brawman-Mintzer, O., Lydiard, R. B., Emmanuel, N., Paycur, R., Johnson, M., Roberts, J., Jarrell, M. P., & Ballenger, J. C. (1993). Psychiatric comorbidity in patients with generalized anxiety disorder. *American Journal of Psychiatry, 150,* 1216–1218.

Breslau, N., & Davis, C. C. (1985). *DSM-III* generalized anxiety disorder: An empirical investigation of more stringent criteria. *Psychiatry Research, 15,* 231–238.

Broocks, A., Bandelow, B., Pekrun, G., George, A., Meyer, T., Bartmann, U., Hillmer-Vogel, U., & Ruther, E. (1998). Comparison of aerobic exercise, clomipramine, and placebo in the treatment of panic disorder. *American Journal of Psychiatry, 155*(5), 603–609.

Bruce, T. J., Spiegel, D. A., & Hegel, M. T. (1999). Cognitive-behavioral therapy helps prevent relapse and recurrence of panic disorder following alprazolam discontinuation: A long-term follow-up of the Peoria and Dartmouth studies. *Journal of Consulting and Clinical Psychology, 67*(1), 151–156.

Brown, T. A., Barlow, D. H., & Liebowitz, M. R. (1994). The empirical basis of generalized anxiety disorder. *American Journal of Psychiatry, 151,* 1272–1280.

Burnham, D. B., Steiner, M. X., Gergel, I. P., et al. (1995). Paroxetine long-term and efficacy in panic disorder and prevention of relapse: A double-blind study. In *American College of Neuropsychopharmacology Annual Meeting: Abstracts of Panels and Posters.* Nashville, American College of Neuropsychopharmacology (p. 201).

Bystritsky, A., Rosen, R., Suri, R., & Vapnik, T. (1999). Pilot open-label study of nefazodone in panic disorder. *Depression and Anxiety, 10*(3), 137–139.

Caillard, V., Rouillon, F., Viel, J. F., & Markabi, S. (1999). Comparative effects of low and high doses of clomipramine and placebo in panic disorder: A double-blind controlled study: French University Antidepressant Group. *Acta Psychiatrica Scandinavica, 99*(1), 51–58.

Carpenter, L. L., Leon, Z., Yasmin, S., & Price, L. H. (1999). Clinical experience with mirtazapine in the treatment of panic disorder. *Annals of Clinical Psychiatry, 11*(2), 81–86.

Catalan, J., Gath, D., Edmonds, C., et al. (1984). The effects of non-prescribing of anxiolytics in general practice. 1. Controlled evaluation of psychiatric and social outcome. *British Journal of Psychiatry, 144,* 593–602.

Charney, D. S., & Woods, S. W. L. (1989). Benzodiazepine treatment of panic disorder: A comparison of alprazolam and lorazepam. *Journal of Clinical Psychiatry, 50,* 418–423.

Charney, D. S., Woods, S. W., Goodman, W. K., et al. (1986). Drug treatment of panic disorder: The comparative efficacy of imipramine, alprazolam and trazodone. *Journal of Clinical Psychiatry, 47,* 580–586.

Chouinard, G., Annable, L., Fontaine, R., & Solyom, L. (1982). Alprazolam in the treatment of generalized anxiety and panic disorders: A double-blind placebo-controlled study. *Psychopharmacology Berlin, 77,* 229–233.

Clark, D. B., & Agras, W. S. (1991). The assessment and treatment of performance anxiety in musicians. *American Journal of Psychiatry, 148,* 598–605.

Cohn, J. B., Bowden, C. L., Fisher, J. G., & Rodos, J. J. (1986). Double-blind comparison of buspirone and clorazepate in anxious outpatients. *American Journal of Medicine, 80,* 10–16.

Cohn, J. B., & Wilcox, C. S. (1984). Long-term comparison of alprazolam, lorazepam and placebo in patients with an anxiety disorder. *Pharmacotherapy, 4,* 93–98.

Connor, K. M., Davidson, J. R., Potts, N. L., Tupler, L. A., Miner, C. M., Malik, M. L., Book, S. W., Colket, J. T., & Ferrell, F. (1998). Discontinuation of clonazepam in the treatment of social phobia. *Journal of Clinical Psychopharmacology, 18,* 373–378.

Cottraux, J., Note, I. D., Cungi, C., Legeron, P., et al. (1995). A controlled study of cognitive behaviour therapy with buspirone or placebo in panic disorder with agoraphobia. *British Journal of Psychiatry, 167,* 635–641.

Cowley, D. S., & Roy-Byrne, P. P. (1991). The biology of generalized anxiety disorder and chronic anxiety. In R. M. Rapee & D. H. Barlow (Eds.), *Chronic anxiety* (pp. 52–75). New York: Guilford Press.

Cowley, D. S., Roy-Byrne, P. P., Hommer, D., Greenblatt, D. J., Nemeroff, C., & Ritchie, J. (1991). Benzodiazepine sensitivity in anxiety disorders. *Biological Psychiatry, 29,* 57A.

Cross National Collaborative Treatment Study. (1992). Drug treatment of panic disorder: Comparative efficacy of alprazolam, imipramine, and placebo. *British Journal of Psychiatry, 160,* 191–202.

Cutler, N. R., Sramek, J. J., Hesselink, J. M. K., Krol, A., Roeschen, J., Rickels, K., & Schweizer, E. (1993). A double-blind, placebo-controlled study comparing the efficacy and safety of ipsapirone versus lorazepam in patients with generalized anxiety disorder: A prospective multicenter trial. *Journal of Clinical Psychopharmacology, 13,* 429–437.

Dager, S. R., Roy-Byrne, P., Hendrickson, H., Cowley, D. S., et al. (1992). Long-term outcome of panic states during double-blind treatment and after withdrawal of alprazolam and placebo. *Annals of Clinical Psychiatry, 4,* 251–258.

Davidson, J. R., DuPont, R. L., Hedges, D., & Haskins, J. T. (1999). Efficacy, safety, and tolerability of venlafaxine extended release and buspirone in outpatients with generalized anxiety disorder. *Journal of Clinical Psychiatry, 60,* 528–535.

Davidson, J. R., Ford, S. M., Smith, R., et al. (1991a). Long-term treatment of avoidant personality disorder. *Comprehensive Psychiatry, 30,* 498–504.

Davidson, J. R., Ford, S. M., Smith, R. D., & Potts, N. L. S. (1991b). Long-term treatment of social phobia with clonazepam. *Journal of Clinical Psychiatry, 52*(Suppl. 11), 16–20.

Davidson, J. R., Potts, N., Richichi, E., Krishnan, R., et al. (1993). Treatment of social phobia with clonazepam and placebo. *Journal of Clinical Psychopharmacology, 13,* 423–428.

Davidson, J. R., Tupler, L. A., & Potts, N. L. S. (1994). Treatment of social phobia with benzodiazepines. *Journal of Clinical Psychiatry, 5*(Suppl. 6), 28–32.

deBeurs, E., van Balkom, A. J., Lange, A., Koele, P., & van Dyck, R. (1995). Treatment of panic disorder with agoraphobia: Comparison of fluvoxamine, placebo, and psychological panic management combined with exposure and of exposure in vivo alone. *American Journal of Psychiatry, 152*(5), 683–691.

Delle Chiaie, R., Pancheri, P., Casacchia, M., Stratta, P., et al. (1995). Assessment of the efficacy of buspirone in patients affected by generalized anxiety disorder, shifting to buspirone from prior treatment with brazepam: A placebo-controlled, double-blind study. *Journal of Clinical Psychopharmacology, 15,* 12–19.

DeMartinis, N., Rynn, M., Rickels, K., & Mandos, L. (2000). Prior benzodiazepine use and buspirone response in the treatment of generalized anxiety disorder. *Journal of Clinical Psychiatry, 61,* 91–94.

DeMartinis, N. A., Schweizer, E., & Rickels, K. (1996). An open-label trial of nefazodone in high comorbidity panic disorder. *Journal of Clinical Psychiatry, 57*(6), 245–248.

Den Boer, J. A., & Westenberg, H. C. (1988). Effect of a serotonin and noradrenaline uptake inhibitor in panic disorder: A double-blind comparative study with fluvoxamine and maprotiline. *International Clinical Psychopharmacology, 3,* 59–74.

Den Boer, J. A., & Westenberg, H. C. (1990). Serotonin function in panic disorder: A double blind placebo controlled study with fluvoxamine and ritanserin. *Psychopharmacology (Berlin), 102,* 85–94.

DiNardo, P. A., Moras, K., Barlow, D. H., Rapee, R. M., & Brown, T. A. (1993). Reliability of *DSM-IIIR* anxiety disorder categories. *Archives of General Psychiatry, 50,* 251–256.

Doctor, R. M. (1982). Major results of a large-scale pretreatment survey of agoraphobics. In R. L. DuPont (Ed.), *Phobia: A comprehensive summary of modern treatments* (pp. 203–214). New York: Brunner/Mazel.

Dunner, D. L., Ishiki, D., Avery, D. H., Wilson, L. C., & Hyde, T. S. (1986). Effect of alprazolam and diazepam on anxiety and panic attacks in panic disorder: A controlled study. *Journal of Clinical Psychiatry, 47,* 458–460.

Eaton, W. W., Kessler, R. C., Wittchen, H. U., & Magee, W. I. (1994). Panic and panic disorder in the United States. *American Journal of Psychiatry, 151*(3), 413–420.

Emmanuel, N. P., Lydiard, R. B., & Ballenger, J. C. (1991). Treatment of social phobia with bupropion. *Journal of Clinical Psychopharmacology, 11,* 276–277.

Emmanuel, N. P., Ware, M. R., Brawman-Mintzer, O., Ballenger, J. C., & Lydiard, R. B. (1999). Once-weekly dosing of fluoxetine in the maintenance of remission in panic disorder. *Journal of Clinical Psychiatry, 60*(5), 299–301.

Enkelmann, R. (1991). Alprazolam versus buspirone in the treatment of outpatients with generalized anxiety disorder. *Psychopharmacology (Berlin), 105,* 428–432.

Evans, L., Kenardy, J., Schneider, P., & Hoey, H. (1986). Effect of a selective serotonin uptake inhibitor in agoraphobia with panic attacks. *Acta Psychiatrica Scandinavica, 73,* 49–53.

Fablen, T., Nilsson, H. L., Borg, K., Humber, M., & Pauli, U. (1995). Social phobia: The clinical efficacy of tolerability of the monoamine oxidase-A and serotonin uptake inhibitor brofaromine: A double-blind placebo-controlled study. *Acta Psychiatrica Scandinavica, 92,* 351–358.

Fahy, T. J., O'Rourke, D., Brophy, J., Schazmann, W., & Sciascia, S. (1992). The Calway study of panic disorder. 1. Clomipramine and lofepramine in *DSM IIIR:* A placebo controlled trial. *Journal of Affective Disorders, 25,* 63–76.

Falkai, P. (1999). Mirtazapine: Other indications. *Journal of Clinical Psychiatry, 60*(Suppl. 17), 36–40.

Falloon, I. R. H., Lloyd, C. C., & Harpin, R. E. (1981). The treatment of social phobia: Real-life rehearsal with non-professional therapists. *Journal of Nervous and Mental Disease, 169,* 180–184.

Feighner, J. P. (1987). Buspirone in the long-term treatment of generalized anxiety disorder. *Journal of Clinical Psychiatry, 48,* 3–6.

Feighner, J. P., & Cohn, J. B. (1989). Analysis of individual symptoms in generalized anxiety—A pooled, multistudy, double-blind evaluation of buspirone. *Neuropsychobiology, 21,* 124–130.

Feighner, J. P., Entsuah, A. R., & McPherson, M. K. (1998). Efficacy of once-daily venlafaxine extended release (XR) for symptoms of anxiety in depressed outpatients. *Journal of Affective Disorders, 47,* 55–62.

Feighner, J. P., Merideth, C. H., & Hendrickson, C. A. (1982). A double-blind comparison of buspirone and diazepam in outpatients with generalized anxiety disorder. *Journal of Clinical Psychiatry, 43,* 103–108.

Ferreri, M., Hantouche, E. C., & Billardon, M. (1994). Advantages of bydroxyzine in generalized anxiety disorder: A double blind controlled versus placebo study. *L'Encephale, 20,* 785–791.

Fyer, A. J., Liebowitz, M. R., & Gorman, J. M. (1989, December 11–16). *Comparative discontinuation of alprazolam and imipramine in panic patients.* Paper presented at the 27th Annual Meeting of the American College of Neuropsychopharmacology, San Juan, Puerto Rico.

Fyer, A. J., Liebowitz, M., Saoud, J., Davies, S., & Klein, D. (1994). *Discontinuation of alprazolam and imipramine in panic patients.* Paper presented at New Clinical Drug Evaluation Unit Program 34th Annual Meeting, Marco Island, Florida.

Fyer, A. J., Mannuzza, S., Chapman, T. F., et al. (1988). A direct interview family study of social phobia. *Archives of General Psychiatry, 29,* 72–75.

Gammans, R. E., Stringfellow, J. C., Hvizdos, A. J., Seidehamel, R. J., et al. (1992). Use of buspirone in patients with generalized anxiety disorder and co-existing depressive symptoms: A meta-analysis of eight randomized controlled studies. *Neuropsychobiology, 25,* 193–201.

Garcia, C., Micallef, J., Dubeuil, D., Philippot, P., Jouve, E., & Blin, O. (2000). Effects of lorazepam on emotional reactivity, performance, and vigilance in subjects with high or low anxiety. *Journal of Clinical Psychopharmacology, 20,* 226–233.

Garcia Borreguero, D., Lauer, C. J., Ozdagler, A., Wiedemann, K., Holsboer, F., & Krieg, J. C. (1992). Brofaromine in panic disorder: A pilot study with a new reversible inhibitor of monoamine oxidaseA. *Pharmacopsychiatry, 25*(6), 261–264.

Garvey, M. J., & Tollefson, C. O. (1986). Prevalence of misuse of prescribed benzodiazepines in patients with primary anxiety disorder or major depression. *American Journal of Psychiatry, 143,* 1601–1603.

Gelenberg, A. J., Lydiard, R. B., Rudolph, R. L., Aguiar, L., Haskins, J. T., & Salinas, E. (2000). Efficacy of venlafaxine extended-release capsules in nondepressed outpatients with generalized anxiety disorder: A 6-month randomized controlled trial. *Journal of the American Medical Association, 283,* 3082–3088.

Gelernter, C. S., Ubde, T. W., Cimbolic, P., et al. (1991). Cognitive-behavioral and pharmacological treatments of social phobia: A controlled study. *Archives of General Psychiatry, 48,* 938–945.

Gentil, V., Lotufo-Neto, F., Andrade, L., Cordas, T., Bernik, M., Ramos, R., Macie, L., Miyakawa, E., & Gorenstein, C. (1993). Clomipramine, a better reference drug for panic/agoraphobia. 1. Effectiveness comparison with imipramine. *Journal of Psychopharmacology, 7,* 316–324.

Geracioti, T. D., Jr. (1995). Venlafaxine treatment of panic disorder: A case series. *Journal of Clinical Psychiatry, 56*(9), 408–410.

Gloger, S., Crunhaus, L., Gladic, D., O'Ryan, F., Cohen, L., & Codner, S. (1989). Panic attacks and agoraphobia: Low dose clomipramine treatment. *Journal of Clinical Psychopharmacology,* 9(1), 28–32.

Goddard, A. W., Brovelle, T., Almai, A., Morrissey, K. A., Clary, C. M., Jetty, P., & Charney, D. (2001). Early co-administration of clonazepam with sertraline: For panic disorder. *Archives of General Psychiatry, 58,* 681–686.

Goldstein, S. (1987). Treatment of social phobia with clonidine. *Biological Psychiatry, 22,* 369–372.

Golwyn, D. H., & Weinstock, R. C. (1990). Phenelzine treatment of elective mutism: A case report. *Journal of Clinical Psychiatry, 51,* 384–385.

Goodnick, P. J., Puig, A., DeVane, C. L., & Freund, B. V. (1999). Mirtazapine in major depression with comorbid generalized anxiety disorder. *Journal of Clinical Psychiatry, 60,* 446–448.

Gorman, J. M. (1997). The use of newer antidepressants for panic disorder. *Journal of Clinical Psychiatry,* 58(Suppl. 14), 54–58, discussion 59.

Gorman, J. M., Liebowitz, M. R., Fyer, A. J., et al. (1985). Treatment of social phobia with atenolol. *Journal of Clinical Psychopharmacology, 5,* 298–301.

Haskins, J. T., Rudolph, R., Pallay, A., & Derivan, A. T. (1998). Double-blind placebo-controlled study of once daily venlafaxine XR in outpatients with generalized anxiety disorder. *European Neuropsychopharmacology,* 8(Suppl. 1), S257.

Hayes, P. F., & Schulz, S. C. (1987). Beta-blockers in anxiety disorders. *Journal of Affective Disorders, 13,* 119–130.

Hedges, D. W., Reimherr, F. W., Strong, R. E., Halls, C. H., & Rust, C. (1996). An open trial of nefazodone in adult patients with generalized anxiety disorder. *Psychopharmacology Bulletin,* 32, 671–676.

Heimberg, R. G., Liebowitz, M. R., Hope, D. A., Schneier, F. R., Holt, C. S., Welkowitz, L. A., Juster, H. R., Campeas, R., Bruch, M. A., Cloitre, M., Fallon, B., & Klein, D. F. (1998). Cognitive behavioral group therapy versus phenelzine therapy for social phobia: 12-week outcome. *Archives of General Psychiatry, 55,* 1133–1141.

Hoehn-Saric, R., McLeod, D. R., & Hipsley, P. A. (1993). Effect of fluvoxamine on panic disorder. *Journal of Clinical Psychopharmacology, 13,* 321–326.

Hoehn-Saric, R., McLeod, D. R., & Zimmerli, W. D. (1988). Differential effects of alprazolam and imipramine in generalized anxiety disorder: Somatic versus psychic symptoms. *Journal of Clinical Psychiatry, 49,* 293–301.

Houck, C. (1998). An open-label pilot study of fluvoxamine for mixed anxiety-depression. *Psychopharmacology Bulletin, 34,* 225–227.

International Multicenter Clinical Trial Group on Moclobemide in Social Phobia. (1997). Moclobemide in social phobia. A double-blind, placebo-controlled clinical study. *European Archives of Psychiatry and Clinical Neuroscience, 247,* 71–80.

Jefferson, J. W. (1995). Social phobia: A pharmacologic treatment overview. *Journal of Clinical Psychiatry,* S(Suppl. 5), 18–24.

Johnson, M. R., & Lydiard, R. B. (1993). Future trends in the psychopharmacology of anxiety disorders. In D. L. Dunner (Ed.), *Current psychiatric therapies* (pp. 539–544). Philadelphia: Saunders.

Johnston, D. C., Troyer, I. E., & Whitsett, S. F. (1988). Clomipramine treatment of agoraphobic women. *Archives of General Psychiatry, 45,* 453–459.

Kahn, R. J., McNair, D. M., Lipman, R. S., Covi, L., Rickels, K., Downing, R., Fisher, S., & Frankenthalar, L. M. (1986). Imipramine and chlordiazepoxide in depressive and anxiety disorders. 2. Efficacy in anxious outpatients. *Archives of General Psychiatry, 43,* 79–85.

Kalus, O., Asnis, C. M., Rubinson, F., et al. (1991). Desipramine treatment in panic disorder. *Journal of Affective Disorders, 21*(4), 239–244.

Katzelnick, D. J., Kobak, K. A., Creist, J. H., Jefferson, J. W., Mantle, J. M., & Serlin, R. C. (1955). Sertraline for social phobia: A double-blind, placebo-controlled crossover study. *American Journal of Psychiatry, 152,* 1368–1371.

Keck, P. E., Jr., Taylor, V. E., Tugrul, K. C., McElroy, S. L., & Bennett, J. A. (1993). Valproate treatment of panic disorder and lactate-induced panic attacks. *Biological Psychiatry, 33*(7), 542–546.

Kendler, K. S., Neale, M. C., Kessler, R. C., et al. (1992a). The genetic epidemiology of phobias in women. *Archives of General Psychiatry, 49,* 273–281.

Kendler, K. S., Neale, M. C., Kessler, R. C., Heath, A. C., & Eaves, L. J. (1992b). Generalized anxiety disorder in women: A population-based twin study. *Archives of General Psychiatry, 49,* 267–272.

Kessler, R. C,., DuPont, R. L., Berglund, P., & Wittchen, H. U. (1999). Impairment in pure and comorbid generalized anxiety disorder and major depression at 12 months in two national sureveys. *American Journal of Psychiatry, 156,* 1915–1923.

Kessler, R. C., McConagle, K. A., Zhao, S., et al. (1994). Lifetime and 12-month prevalence of *DSM-III-R* psychiatric disorders in the United States: Results from the National Comorbidity Survey. *Archives of General Psychiatry, 51,* 8–19.

Khan, A., Upton, G. V., Rudolph, R. L., Entsuah, R., & Leventer, S. M. (1998). The use of venlafaxine in the treatment of major depression and major depression associated with anxiety: A dose-response study: Ven-lafaxine Investigator Study Group. *Journal of Clinical Psychopharmacology, 18,* 19–25.

Kinzler, E., Kromer, J., & Lehmann, E. (1991). Wirksamkeit eines Kava-Spezial-Extraktes bei Patieinten mit Angst-, Spannungs-, und Erregungszustanden nicht-psychotischer Genese. *Arzneimittelforschung, 41,* 584–588.

Klein, D. F. (1964). Delineation of two drug-responsive anxiety syndromes. *Psychopharmacologia, 5,* 397–408.

Klein, D. F. (1967). Importance of psychiatric diagnosis in prediction of clinical drug effects. *Archives of General Psychiatry, 16,* 118–126.

Klein, E., & Ubde, T. W. (1988). Controlled study of verapamil for treatment of panic disorder. *American Journal of Psychiatry, 145,* 431–434.

Klein, E., Ubde, T. W., & Post, R. M. (1986). Preliminary evidence for the utility of carbamazepine in alprazolam withdrawal. *American Journal of Psychiatry, 143,* 235–236.

Klein, F., Cohn, V., Stolk, J., & Lenox, R. H. (1994). Alprazolam withdrawal in patients with panic disorder and generalized anxiety disorder: Vulnerability and effect of carbamazepine. *American Journal of Psychiatry, 151,* 1760–1766.

Klosko, J. S., Barlow, D. H., Tassinari, R., & Cerny, J. A. (1990). A comparison of alprazolam and behavior therapy in treatment of panic disorder. *Journal of Consulting and Clinical Psychology, 58,* 77–84.

Kruger, M. B., & Dahl, A. A. (1999). The efficacy and safety of moclobemide compared to clomipramine in the treatment of panic disorder. *European Archives of Psychiatry and Clinical Neuroscience,* 249(Suppl. 1), S19–24.

Laakman, G., Schule, C., Lorkowski, G., Baghai, T., Kuhn, K., & Ehrentraut, S. (1998). Buspirone and lorazepam in the treatment of generalized anxiety disorder in outpatients. *Psychopharmacology, 136,* 357–366.

Lader, M., & Olajide, D. (1987). A comparison of buspirone and placebo in relieving benzodiazepine withdrawal symptoms. *Journal of Clinical Psychopharmacology, 7,* 11–15.

Lader, M., & Scotto, J. C. (1998). A multicentre double-blind comparison of hydroxyzine, buspirone, and placebo in patients with generalized anxiety disorder. *Psychopharmacology (Berlin) 139,* 402–406.

Lecrubier, Y., Bakker, A., Dunbar, G., & Judge, R. (1997). A comparison of paroxetine, clomipramine and placebo in the treatment of panic disorder: Collaborative Paroxetine Panic Study Investigators. *Acta Psychiatrica Scandinavica,* 95(2), 145–152.

Lecrubier, Y., & Judge, R. (1997). Long-term evaluation of paroxetine, clomipramine and placebo in panic disorder: Collaborative Paroxetine Panic Study Investigators. *Acta Psychiatrica Scandinavica,* 95(2), 153–160.

Leinonen, E., Lepola, U., Koponen, H., Turtonen, J., Wade, A., & Lehto, H. (2000). Citalopram controls phobic symptoms in patients with panic disorder: Randomized controlled trial. *Journal of Psychiatry and Neuroscience, 25*(1), 25–32.

Lepola, U. M., Wade, A. G., Leinonen, E. V., Koponen, H. J., Frazer, J., Sjodin, I., Penttinen, J. T., Pedersen, T., & Lehto, H. J. (1998). A controlled, prospective, 1-year trial of citalopram in the treatment of panic disorder. *Journal of Clinical Psychiatry,* 59(10), 528–534.

Liebowitz, M. R., Fyer, A. J., Gorman, J. M., et al. (1986). Phenelzine in social phobia. *Journal of Clinical Psychopharmacology, 6,* 93–98.

Liebowitz, M. R., Heimberg, R. G., Schneier, F. R., Hope, D. A., Davies, S., Holt, C. S., Goetz, D., Juster, H. R., Lin, S. H., Bruch, M. A., Marshall, R. D., & Klein, D. F. (1999). Cognitive-behavioral group therapy versus phenelzine in social phobia: Long-term outcome. *Depression and Anxiety, 10,* 89–98.

Liebowitz, M. R., Schneier, F., Campeas, R., Hollander, F., Hatterer, J., Fyer, A., Gorman, J., Papp, L., Davies, S., Gully, R., & Klein, D. F. (1992). Pbenelzine versus atenolol in social phobia: A placebo-controlled comparison. *Archives of General Psychiatry, 49,* 290–300.

Lipsedge, J. S., Hajjoff, J., Huggins, P., et al. (1973). The management of severe agoraphobia: A comparison of iproniazid and systematic desensitization. *Psychopharmacology, 32,* 67–80.

Loerch, B., Graf-Morgenstern, M., Hautzinger, M., Schegel, S., Hain, C., Sandmann, J., & Benkert, O. (1999). Randomised placebo-controlled trial of moclobemide, cognitive-behavioural therapy and their combination in panic disorder with agoraphobia. *British Journal of Psychiatry, 174,* 205–212.

Londborg, P. D., Wolkow, R., Smith, W. T., DuBoff, E., England, D., Ferguson, J., Rosenthal, M., & Weise, C. (1998). Sertraline in the treatment of panic disorder: A multi-site, double-blind, placebo-controlled, fixed-dose investigation. *British Journal of Psychiatry, 173,* 54–60.

Lott, M., Greist, J. H., Jefferson, J. W., Kobak, K. A., Katzelnick, D. J., Katz, R. J., & Schaettle, S. C. (1997). Brofaromine for social phobia: A multicenter, placebo-controlled, double-blind study. *Journal of Clinical Psychopharmacology, 17,* 255–260.

Louie, A. K., Lewis, T. B., & Lannon, R. A. (1993). Use of low-dose fluoxetine in major depression and panic disorder. *Journal of Clinical Psychiatry,* 54(11), 435–438.

Lucki, I., Rickels, K., & Geller, A. M. (1986). Chronic use of benzodiazepines and psychomotor and cognitive test performance. *Psychopharmacology, 88,* 426–433.

Lydiard, R. B., & Ballenger, J. C. (1987). Antidepressants in panic disorder and agoraphobia. *Journal of Affective Disorders, 13,* 153–168.

Lydiard, R. B., Ballenger, J. C., & Rickels, K. (1997). A double-blind evaluation of the safety and efficacy of abecarnil, alprazolam, and placebo in outpatients with generalized anxiety disorder: Abercarnil Work Group. *Journal of Clinical Psychiatry,* 58(Suppl. 11), 11–18.

Lydiard, R. B., Lesser, L. M., Bellenger, J. C., Rubin, R. T., Laraia, M., & DuPont, R. (1992). A fixed-dose study of alprazolam 2 mg, alprazolam 6 mg, and placebo in panic disorder. *Journal of Clinical Psychopharmacology, 12,* 96–103.

Lydiard, R. B., Morton, W. A., Emmanuel, N. P., et al. (1993). Preliminary report: Placebo-controlled, double-blind study of the clinical and metabolic effects of desipramine in panic disorder. *Psychopharmacology Bulletin, 29*(2), 183–188.

Maddock, R., Carter, C., Blacker, K., et al. (1993). Relationship of past depressive episodes to symptom severity and treatment response in panic disorder with agoraphobia. *Journal of Clinical Psychiatry,* 54, 88–95.

Marks, I. M., Gray, S., Cohen, D., Hill, R., Mawson, D., Ramm, E., & Stern, R. (1983). Imipramine and brief therapist-aided exposure in agoraphobics having self-exposure homework. *Archives of General Psychiatry, 40,* 153–162.

Mavissakalian, M., & Michelson, L. (1986). Agoraphobia: Relative and combined effectiveness of therapist-assisted in vivo exposure and imipramine. *Journal of Clinical Psychiatry, 47,* 117–122.

Mavissakalian, M., & Perel, J. M. (1992a). Clinical experiments in maintenance and discontinuation of imipramine therapy in panic disorder with agoraphobia. *Archives of General Psychiatry, 49*(4), 318–323.

Mavissakalian, M., & Perel, J. M. (1992b). Protective effects of imipramine maintenance treatment in panic disorder with agoraphobia. *American Journal of Psychiatry, 149*(8), 1053–1057.

Mavissakalian, M., & Perel, J. M. (1995). Imipramine treatment of panic disorder with agoraphobia: Dose ranging and plasma level-response relationships. *American Journal of Psychiatry, 152*(5), 673–682.

Mavissakalian, M., & Perel, J. M. (1999). Long-term maintenance and discontinuation of imipramine therapy in panic disorder with agoraphobia. *Archives of General Psychiatry, 56,* 821–827.

McNamara, M. F., & Fogel, B. S. (1990). Anticonvulsantresponsive panic attacks with temporal lobe EEC abnormalities. *Journal of Neuropsychiatry and Clinical Neurosciences,* 2(2), 193–196.

Meibach, R. C., Mullane, J. F., & Binstok, C. (1987). A placebo-controlled multicenter trial of propranolol and chlordiazepoxide in the treatment of anxiety. *Current Therapeutic Research, 41,* 65–76.

Michelson, D., Lydiard, R. B., Pollack, M. H., Tamura, R. N., Hoog, S. L., Tepner, R., Demitrack, M. A., & Tollefson, G. D. (1998). Outcome assessment and clinical improvement in panic disorder: Evidence from a randomized controlled trial of fluoxetine and placebo: The Fluoxetine Panic Disorder Study Group. *American Journal of Psychiatry, 155,* 1570–1577.

Michelson, D., Pollack, M., Lydiard, R. B., Tamura, R., Tepner, R., & Tollefson, G. (1999b). Continuing treatment of panic disorder after acute response: Randomised, placebo-controlled trial with fluoxetine. The Fluoxetine Panic Disorder Study Group. *British Journal of Psychiatry, 174,* 213–218.

Modigh, K., Westberg, P., & Eriksson, F. (1992). Superiority of clomipramine over imipramine in the treatment of panic disorder. *Journal of Clinical Psychopharmacology, 12,* 251–261.

Moroz, G., & Rosenbaum, J. F. (1999). Efficacy, safety, and gradual discontinuation of clonazepam in panic disorder: A placebo-controlled, multicenter study using optimized dosages. *Journal of Clinical Psychiatry, 60*(9), 604–612.

Mountjoy, C., Roth, M., Garside, R. F., & Leitch, I. M. (1977). A clinical trial of phenelzine in anxiety, depressive and phobic neuroses. *British Journal of Psychiatry, 31,* 486–492.

Munjack, D. J., Brun, J., & Baltazar, P. L. (1991). A pilot study of buspirone in the treatment of social phobia. *Journal of Anxiety Disorders, 5,* 87–88.

Munjack, D. J., Crocker, B., Cabe, D., et al. (1989). Alprazolam, propranolol, and placebo in the treatment of panic disorder and agoraphobia with panic attacks. *Journal of Clinical Psychopharmacology, 9,* 22–27.

Munjack, D. J., Usigli, R., Zulueta, A., et al. (1988). Nortriptyline in the treatment of panic disorder and agoraphobia with panic attacks. *Journal of Clinical Psychopharmacology, 8*(3), 204–207.

Murphy, S. M., Owen, R., & Tyrer, P. (1989). Comparative assessment of efficacy and withdrawal symptoms after 6 and 12 weeks' treatment with diazepam or buspirone. *British Journal of Psychiatry, 154,* 529–534.

Nagy, L. M., Krystal, J. H., Woods, S. W., et al. (1989). Clinical and medication outcome after short-term alprazolam and behavioral group treatment in panic disorder. *Archives of General Psychiatry, 46,* 993–999.

Nair, N. P., Bakish, D., Saxena, B., Amin, M., Schwartz, G., & West, T. E. (1996). Comparison of fluvoxamine, imipramine, and placebo in the treatment of outpatients with panic disorder. *Anxiety,* 2(4), 192–198.

Ninan, P. T., Insel, T. M., Cohen, R. M., Skolnick, P., & Paul, S. M. (1982). A benzodiazepine receptor-mediated experimental "anxiety" in primates. *Science, 218,* 1332–1334.

Norton, C. R., Cox, B. J., & Malan, J. (1992). Nonclinical panickers: A critical review. *Clinical Psychology Review, 12,* 121–139.

Noyes, R., Jr., Carvey, M. J., Cook, B. L., & Samuelson, L. (1989). Problems with tricyclic antidepressant use in patients with panic disorder or agoraphobia: Results of a naturalistic follow-up study. *Journal of Clinical Psychiatry, 50*(5), 163–169.

Noyes, R., Jr., Moroz, G., Davidson, J. R., Liebowitz, M. R., Davidson, A., Siegel, J., Bell, J., Cain, J. W., Curlik, S. M., Kent, T. A., Lydiard, R. B., Mallinger, A. G., Pollack, M. H., Rapaport, M., Rasmussen, S. A., Hedges, D., Schweizer, E., & Uhlenhuth, E. H. (1997). Moclobemide in social phobia: A controlled dose-response trial. *Journal of Clinical Psychopharmacology, 17,* 247–254.

Noyes, R., Woodman, C., Garvey, J. M., Cook, B. L., Suelzer, M., Clancy, J., & Anderson, D. J. (1992). Generalized anxiety disorder versus panic disorder: Distinguishing characteristics and patterns of comorbidity. *Journal of Nervous and Mental Disease, 180*, 369–379.

Oberlander, E. L., Schneier, F. R., & Liebowitz, M. R. (1994). Physical disability and social phobia. *Journal of Clinical Psychopharmcology, 14*, 136–143.

Oehrberg, S., Christiansen, P. E., Behnke, K., et al. Borup, A. L., Severin, B., Soegaard, J., Calberg, H., Judge, R., Ohrstrom, J. K., & Manniche, P. M. (1995). Paroxetine in the treatment of panic disorder: A randomised, double-blind, placebo-controlled study. *British Journal of Psychiatry, 167*(3), 374–379.

Ontiveros, A., & Fontaine, R. (1992). Sodium valproate and clonazepam *for* treatment-resistant panic disorder. *Journal of Psychiatric Neurosciences, 17*(2), 78–80.

Otto, M. W. (1999). Cognitive-behavioral therapy for social anxiety disorder: Model, methods, and outcome. *Journal of Clinical Psychiatry, 60*(Suppl. 9), 14–19.

Pande, A. C., Davidson, J. R., Jefferson, J. W., Janney, C. A., Katzelnick, D. J., Weisler, R. H., Greist, J. H., & Sutherland, S. M. (1999). Treatment of social phobia with gabapentin: A placebo-controlled study. *Journal of Clinical Psychopharmacology, 19*, 341–348.

Papp, L. A., Coplan, J., & Gorman, J. M. (1992). Neurobiology of anxiety. In A. Tasman & M. B. Riba (Eds.), *Review of psychiatry* (Vol. 11, pp. 307–322). Washington, DC: American Psychiatric Press.

Papp, L. A., Schneier, F. R., Fyer, A. J., Leibowitz, M. R., Gorman, J. M., Coplan, J. D., Campeas, R., Fallon, B. A., & Klein, D. F. (1997). Clomipramine treatment of panic disorder: Pros and cons. *Journal of Clinical Psychiatry, 58*(10), 423–425.

Papp, L. A., Sinha, S. S., Martinez, J. M., Coplan, J. D., Amchin, J., & Gorman, J. M. (1998). Low-dose venlafaxine treatment in panic disorder. *Psychopharmacology Bulletin, 34*(2), 207–209.

Pecknold, J. C. (1990, June 19–22). *Discontinuation studies: Short-term and long-term*. Paper presented at Panic and Anxiety: A Decade of Progress, Geneva, Switzerland.

Pecknold, J. C., Matas, M., Howarth, B. C., Ross, C., Swinson, R., Vezeau, C., & Ungar, W. (1989). Evaluation of buspirone as an antianxiety agent: Buspirone and diazepam versus placebo. *Canadian Journal of Psychiatry, 34*, 766–771.

Pecknold, J. C., Swinson, R. P., Kuch, K., et al. (1988). Alprazolam in panic disorder and agoraphobia: Discontinuation effects. *Archives of General Psychiatry, 45*, 429–436.

Petracca, A., Nisita, C., MeNair, D., Melis, C., Cuerani, C., & Cassano, C. B. (1990). Treatment of generalized anxiety disorder: Preliminary clinical experience with buspirone. *Journal of Clinical Psychiatry, 51*, 31–39.

Pittler, M. H. & Ernst, E. (2000). Efficacy of kava extract for treating anxiety: Systematic review and meta-analysis. *Journal of Clinical Psychopharmacology, 20*, 84–89.

Pohl, R. B., Wolkow, R. M., & Clary, C. M. (1998). Sertraline in the treatment of panic disorder: A double-blind multicenter trial. *American Journal of Psychiatry, 155*(9), 1189–1195.

Pollack, M. H., Otto, M. W., Worthington, J. J., Manfro, G. G., & Wolkow, R. (1998). Sertraline in the treatment of panic disorder: A flexible-dose multicenter trial. *Archives of General Psychiatry, 55*(11), 1010–1016.

Pollack, M. H., Worthington, J. J., Manfro, G. G., Otto, M. W., & Zucker, B. G. (1997). Abercarnil for the treatment of generalized anxiety disorder: A placebo-controlled comparison of two dosage ranges of abercarnil and buspirone. *Journal of Clinical Psychiatry 58*(Suppl. 11), 19–23.

Pollack, M. H., Worthington, J. J., Otto, M. W., et al. (1996). Venlafaxine for panic disorder: Results from a double-blind, placebo-controlled study. *Psychopharmacology Bulletin*, 32, 667–670.

Power, K. C., Simpson, R. J., Swanson, V., & Wallace, L. A. (1990). Controlled comparison of pharmacological and psychological treatment of generalized anxiety disorder in primary care. *British Journal of General Practice, 40*, 289–294.

Regier, D. A., Farmer, M. F., Rae, D. S., Locke, B. Z., Keigh, S. J., Judd, L. L., & Goodwin, F. K. (1990). Comorbidity of mental disorders with alcohol and other drug abuse: Results from the epidemiological catchment area (ECA) study. *Journal of the American Medical Association, 264*, 2511–2518.

Reich, J., Goldenberg, I., Vasile, R., Goisman, R., & Keller, M. (1993). A prospective follow-along study of the course of social phobia. *Psychiatry Research*, 54, 249–258.

Rickels, K., Case, W. C., Downing, R. W., et al. (1983). Long-term diazepam therapy and clinical outcome. *Journal of the American Medical Association, 250*, 767–771.

Rickels, K., Case, W. C., Schweizer, E., et al. (1986). Low-dose dependence in chronic benzodiazepine users: A preliminary report on 119 patients. *Psychopharmacology Bulletin, 22*, 407–415.

Rickels, K., DeMartinis, N., & Aufdembrinke, B. (2000). A double-blind, placebo-controlled trial of abecarnil and diazepam in the treatment of patients with generalized anxiety disorder. *Journal of Clinical Psychopharmacology, 20*, 12–18.

Rickels, K., Downing, R., Schweizer, E., & Hassman, H. (1993a). Antidepressants for the treatment of generalized anxiety disorder: A placebo-controlled comparison of imipramine, trazodone, and diazepam. *Archives of General Psychiatry, 50,* 884–895.

Rickels, K., Pollack, M. H., Sheehan, D. V., & Haskins, J. T. (2000). Efficacy of extended-release venlafaxine in nondepressed outpatients with generalized anxiety disorder. *American Journal of Psychiatry, 157,* 968–974.

Rickels, K., & Schweizer, F. (1990). The clinical course and long-term management of generalized anxiety disorder. *Journal of Clinical Psychopharmacology, 10,* 1015–1105.

Rickels, K., Schweizer, F., Canalosi, I., et al. (1988). Long-term treatment of anxiety and risk of withdrawal: Prospective comparison of clorazepate and buspirone. *Archives of General Psychiatry, 45,* 414–450.

Rickels, K., Schweizer, E., Weiss, S., & Zavodnick, S. (1993b). Maintenance drug treatment for panic disorder. 2. Short- and long-term outcome after drug taper. *Archives of General Psychiatry, 50,* 61–68.

Rickels, K., Weisman, K., Norstad, N., Singer, M., Stoltz, K., Brown, A., & Danton, J. (1982). Buspirone and diazepam in anxiety: A controlled study. *Journal of Clinical Psychiatry, 43,* 81–86.

Ries, R. K., & Wittkowsky, A. K. (1986). Synergistic action of alprazolam with tranylcypromine in drug-resistant atypical depression with panic attacks. *Biological Psychiatry, 21,* 522–526.

Rocca, P., Beoni, A. M., Eva, C., et al. (1998). Peripheral benzodiazpine receptor messenger RNA is decreased in lymphocytes of generalized anxiety disorder patients. *Biological Psychiatry, 43,* 767–773.

Rocca, P., Fonzo, V., Scotta, M., Zanalda, E., & Ravizza, L. (1997). Paroxetine efficacy in the treatment of generalized anxiety disorder. *Acta Psychiatrica Scandinavica, 95,* 444–450.

Rosenbaum, J. F., Biederman, J., Hirshfield, D. R., et al. (1991). Further evidence of an association between behavioral inhibition and anxiety disorders: Results from a family study of children from a non-clinical sample. *Journal of Psychiatry Research, 25,* 4945.

Rosenbaum, J. F., Moroz, G., & Bowden, C. L. (1997). Clonazepam in the treatment of panic disorder with or without agoraphobia: A dose-response study of efficacy, safety, and discontinuance: Clonazepam Panic Disorder Dose-Response Study Group. *Journal of Clinical Psychopharmacology, 17*(5), 390–400.

Ross, C. A., & Matas, M. (1987). A clinical trial of buspirone and diazepam in the treatment of generalized anxiety disorder. *Canadian Journal of Psychiatry, 32,* 351–355.

Roy-Byrne, P. P., & Cowley, D. S. (1995). Course and outcome in panic disorder: A review of recent follow-up studies. *Anxiety, 1,* 151–160.

Roy-Byrne, P. P., & Cowley, D. S. (1998). Search for pathophysiology of panic disorder. *Lancet, 352,* 1646–1647.

Roy-Byrne, P. P., Dager, S. R., Cowley, D. S., Vitaliano, P., & Dunner, D. L. (1989). Relapse and rebound following discontinuation of benzodiazepine treatment of panic attacks: Alprazolam versus diazepam. *American Journal of Psychiatry, 146,* 860–865.

Roy-Byrne, P. P., Geraci, M., & Ubde, T. W. (1986). Life events and the onset of panic disorder. *American Journal of Psychiatry, 143,* 1424–1427.

Sacerdote, P., Panerai, A. E., Frattola, L., & Ferrarese, C. (1999). Benzodiazepine induced chemotaxis is impaired in monocytes from patients with generalized anxiety disorder. *Psychoneuroendocrinology, 24,* 243–249.

Sasson, Y., Iancu, I., Fux, M., Taub, M., Dannon, P. N., & Zohar, J. (1999). A double-blind crossover comparison of clomipramine and desipramine in the treatment of panic disorder. *European Neuropsychopharmacology,* 9(3), 191–196.

Schneier, F. R., Goetz, D., Campeas, R., Fallon, B., Marshall, R., & Liebowitz, M. R. (1998). Placebo-controlled trial of moclobemide in social phobia. *British Journal of Psychiatry, 172,* 70–77.

Schneier, F. R., Heckelman, L. R., Garfinkel, R., Campeas, R., et al. (1994). Functional impairment in social phobia. *Journal of Clinical Psychiatry, 55,* 322–331.

Schneier, F. R., Johnson, J., Hornig, C. D., et al. (1992b). Social phobia: Comorbidity and morbidity in an epidemiological sample. *Archives of General Psychiatry, 49,* 282–288.

Schneier, F. R., Liebowitz, M. R., Davies, S. O., et al. (1990). Fluoxetine in panic disorder. *Journal of Clinical Psychopharmacology, 10*(2), 119–121.

Schneier, F. R., Sanud, J. B., Campeas, R., Fallon, B. A., et al. (1993). Buspirone in social phobia. *Journal of Clinical Psychopharmacology, 13,* 251–256.

Schweizer, E., Fox, I., Case, C., & Rickels, K. (1988). Lorazepam versus alprazolam in the treatment of panic disorder. *Psychopharmacology Bulletin, 24,* 224–227.

Schweizer, E., Rickels, K., Weiss, S., & Zavodnick, S. (1993). Maintenance drug treatment of panic disorder. 1. Results of a prospective, placebo-controlled comparison of alprazolam and imipramine. *Archives of General Psychiatry, 50,* 51–60.

Shader, R. I., & Greenblatt, D. J. (1993). Use of benzodiazepines in anxiety disorders. *New England Journal of Medicine, 328,* 1398–1405.

Shapiro, A. K., Struening, E. L., Shapiro, F., et al. (1983). Diazepam: How much better than placebo? *Journal of Psychiatry Research, 17,* 51–53.

Sheehan, D. V., Ballenger, J., & Jacobsen, C. (1980). Treatment of endogenous anxiety with phobic, hysterical, and hypochondriacal symptoms. *Archives of General Psychiatry, 37,* 51–59.

Sheehan, D. V., Davidson, J., Mansebreck, T., et al. (1983). Lack of efficacy of a new antidepressant (bupropion) in the treatment of panic disorder with phobias. *Journal of Clinical Psychopharmacology, 3,* 28–31.

Sheehan, D. V., Raj, A. B., Harnett-Sheehan, K., Soto, S., & Knapp, F. (1993). The relative efficacy of high-dose buspirone and alprazolam in the treatment of panic disorder: A double-blind placebo-controlled study. *Acta Psychiatrica Scandinavica, 88,* 1–11.

Sheehan, D. V., Raj, A. B., Sheehan, K. H., & Soto, S. (1990). Is buspirone effective for panic disorder? *Journal of Clinical Psychopharmacology, 10*(1), 3–11.

Simpson, H. B., Schneier, F. R., Campeas, R. B., Marshall, R. D., Fallon, B. A., Davies, S., Klein, D. F., & Liebowitz, M. R. (1998). Imipramine in the treatment of social phobia. *Journal of Clinical Psychopharmacology, 18,* 132–135.

Simpson, H. B., Schneier, F. R., Marshall, R. D., Campeas, R. B., Vermes, D., Silvestre, J., Davies, S., & Liebowitz, M. R. (1998). Low dose selegiline (L-Deprenyl) in social phobia. *Depression and Anxiety, 7,* 126–129.

Slaap, B. R., van Vliet, I. M., Westenberg, H. C., & den Boer, J. A. (1995). Phobic symptoms as predictors of nonresponse to drug therapy in panic disorder patients (a preliminary report). *Journal of Affective Disorders, 33*(1), 31–8.

Solyom, C., Solyom, L., LaPierre, Y., Pecknold, J. C., & Morton, L. (1981). Phenelzine and exposure in the treatment of phobias. *Biological Psychiatry, 16,* 239–247.

Solyom, L., Heseltine, C. F. D., McClure, D. J., Solyom, C., Ledgwidge, B., & Steinburg, G. (1973). Behaviour therapy versus drug therapy in the treatment of phobic neurosis. *Canadian Psychiatric Association Journal, 18,* 25–31.

Stein, D. J., Berk, M., Els, C., Emsley, R. A., Gittelson, L., Wilson, D., Oakes, R., & Hunter, B. (1999). A double-blind placebo-controlled trial of paroxetine in the management of social phobia (social anxiety disorder) in South Africa. *South African Medical Journal, 89,* 402–406.

Stein, M. B., Fyer, A. J., Davidson, J. R., Pollack, M. H., & Wiita, B. (1999). Fluvoxamine treatment of social phobia (social anxiety disorder): A double-blind, placebo-controlled study. *American Journal of Psychiatry, 156,* 756–760.

Stein, M. B., Liebowitz, M. R., Lydiard, R. B., Pitts, C. D., Bushnell, W., & Gergel, I. (1998). Paroxetine treatment of generalized social phobia (social anxiety disorder): A randomized controlled trial. *Journal of the American Medical Association, 280,* 708–713.

Strand, M., Hetta, J., Rosen, A., Sorensen, S., et al. (1990). A double-blind, controlled trial in primary care patients with generalized anxiety: A comparison between buspirone and oxazepam. *Journal of Clinical Psychiatry, 51,* 40–50.

Swartz, C. M. (1998). Betaxolol in anxiety disorders. *Annals of Clinical Psychiatry, 10,* 9–14.

Swinson, R. P., Cox, B. J., & Woszczyna, C. B. (1992). Use of medical services and treatment for panic disorder with agoraphobia and for social phobia. *Canadian Medical Association Journal, 147*(6), 878–883.

Taylor, C. B., Hayward, C., King, R., et al. (1990). Cardiovascular and symptomatic reduction effects of alprazolam and imipramine in patients with panic disorder: Results of a double-blind, placebo-controlled trial. *Journal of Clinical Psychopharmacology, 10*(2), 112–118.

Taylor, C. B., King, R., Margraf, J., et al. (1989). Use of medication and in vivo exposure in volunteers for panic disorder research. *American Journal of Psychiatry, 146*(11), 1423–1426.

Telch, M. J., Agras, S., Taylor, C. B., Roth, W. T., & Gallen, C. (1985). Combined pharmacological and behavioural treatment for agoraphobia. *Behaviour Research and Therapy, 23,* 325–335.

Tesar, C. E., Rosenbaum, J. F., Pollack, M. H., et al. (1991). Double-blind, placebo-controlled comparison of clonazepam and alprazolam for panic disorder. *Journal of Clinical Psychiatry, 52,* 69–76.

Thayer, J. F., Friedman, B. H., Borkovec, T. D., Johnson, B. H., & Molina, S. (2000). Phasic heart period reactions to cued threat and nonthreat stimuli in generalized anxiety disorder. *Psychophysiology, 37,* 361–368.

Tiffon, L., Coplan, J. D., Papp, L. A., & Corman, J. M. (1994). Augmentation strategies with tricyclic or fluoxetine treatment in seven partially responsive panic disorder patients. *Journal of Clinical Psychiatry, 55*(2), 66–69.

Tiihonen, J., Kuikka, J., Rasanen, P., et al. (1997). Cerebral benzodiazepine receptor binding and distribution in generalized anxiety disorder: A fractal analysis. *Molecular Psychiatry, 2*, 463–471.

Turner, S. M., Beidel, D. C., & Jacob, R. G. (1994). Social phobia: A comparison of behavior therapy and atenolol. *Journal of Consulting and Clinical Psychology, 62*, 350–358.

Tyrer, P., Candy, J., & Kelly, D. A. (1973). A study of the clinical effects of phenelzine and placebo in the treatment of phobic anxiety. *Psychopharmacology, 32*, 237–254.

Ubde, T. W., Stein, M. B., & Post, R. M. (1988). Lack of efficacy of carbamazepine in the treatment of panic disorder. *American Journal of Psychiatry, 145*, 1104–1109.

Ubde, T. W., Stein, M. B., Vittone, B. J., et al. (1989). Behavioral and psychologic effects of short-term and long-term administration of clonidine in panic disorder. *Archives of General Psychiatry, 46*(2), 170–177.

Uhlenhuth, E. H., Balter, M. B., Ban, T. A., & Yang, K. (1998). International study of expert judgement on therapeutic use of benzodiazepines and other psychotherapeutic medications: 5. Treatment strategies in panic disorder, 1992–1997. *Journal of Clinical Psychopharmacology, 18*(6, Suppl 2), 27S–31S.

Uhlenhuth, E. H., Matuzas, A. W., Glass, R. M., & Easton, C. (1989). Response of panic disorder to fixed doses of alprazolam or imipramine. *Journal of Affective Disorders, 17*(3), 261–270.

Van Ameringen, M., Mancini, C., & Oakman, J. M. (1999). Nefazodone in social phobia. *Journal of Clinical Psychiatry, 60*, 96–100.

Van Ameringen, M., Mancini, C., & Wilson, C. (1996). Buspirone augmentation of selective serotonin reuptake inhibitors (SSRIs) in social phobia. *Journal of Affective Disorders, 39*, 115–121.

van Vliet, I. M., den Boer, J. A., & Westenberg, H. C. M. (1994). Psychopharmacological treatment of social phobia: A double blind placebo controlled study with fluvoxamine. *Psychopharmacology, 115*, 128–134.

van Vliet, I. M., den Boer, J. A., Westenberg, H. C., & Pian, K. L. (1997). Clinical effects of buspirone in social phobia: A double-blind placebo-controlled study. *Journal of Clinical Psychiatry, 58*, 164–168.

van Vliet, I. M., den Boer, J. A., Westenberg, H. C., & Slaap, B. R. (1996). A double-blind comparative study of brofaromine and fluvoxamine in outpatients with panic disorder. *Journal of Clinical Psychopharmacology, 16*(4), 299–306.

van Vliet, I. M., Westenberg, H. C., & Den Boer, J. A. (1993). MAO inhibitors in panic disorder: Clinical effects of treatment with brofaromine: A double-bond placebo controlled study. *Psychopharmacology (Berlin), 112*(4), 483–489.

Versiani, M. (2000). A review of 19 double-blind placebo-controlled studies in social anxiety disorder (social phobia). *World Journal of Biological Psychiatry, 1*, 27–33.

Versiani, M., Amrein, R., & Montgomery, S. A. (1997). Social phobia: long-term treatment outcome and prediction of response—A moclobemide study. *International Clinical Psychopharmacology, 12*, 239–254.

Versiani, M., Mundim, F. D., & Nardi, A. E. (1988). Tranylcypromine in social phobia. *Journal of Clinical Psychopharmacology, 8*, 279–283.

Versiani, M., Nardi, A. E., Mundim, F. D., Alves, A. B., Liebowitz, M. R., & Amrein, R. (1992). Pharmacotherapy of social phobia: A controlled study with moclobemide and phenelzine. *British Journal of Psychiatry, 161*, 353–360.

Versiani, M., Ontiveros, A., Mazzotti, G., Ospina, J., Davila, J., Mata, S., Pacheco, A., Plewes, J., Tamura, R., & Palacios, M. (1999). Fluoxetine versus amitryptyline in the treatment of major depression with associated anxiety (anxious depression): a double-blind comparison. *International Clinical Psychopharmacology, 14*, 321–327.

Villarreal, G., Johnson, M. R., Rubey, R., Lydiard, R. B., & Ballenger, J. C. (2000). Treatment of social phobia with the dopamine agonist pergolide. *Depression and Anxiety, 11*, 45–47.

Volz, H-P. & Kieser, M. (1997). Kava-kava extract WS1490 versus placebo in anxiety disorders: A randomized placebo-controlled 25-week outpatient trial. *Pharmacopsychiatry, 30*, 1–5.

Wade, A. G., Lepola, U., Koponen, H. J., Pedersen, V., & Pedersen, T. (1997). The effect of citalopram in panic disorder. *British Journal of Psychiatry, 170*, 549–553.

Warnecke, G. (1991). Psychosomatische Dysfunktionen im weiblichen Klimakterium. *Fortschr Med, 109*, 119–122.

Widiger, T. A. (1992). Generalized social phobia versus avoidant personality disorder: A commentary on three studies. *Journal of Abnormal Psychology, 101*, 340–343.

Wilhelm, F. H. & Roth, W. T. (1997). Acute and delayed effects of alprazolam on flight phobics during exposure. *Behavior Research and Therapy, 35*, 831–841.

Wingerson, D., Nguyen, C., & Roy-Byrne, P. P. (1992). Clomipramine treatment for generalized anxiety disorder. *Journal of Clinical Psychopharmacology, 12*, 214–215.

Wittchen, H. U., Zhao, S., Kessler, R. C., & Eaton, W. (1994). *DSM-III-R* generalized anxiety disorder in the national comorbidity survey. *Archives of General Psychiatry, 51*, 355–364.

Woodman, C. L., & Noyes, R., Jr. (1994). Panic disorder: Treatment with valproate. *Journal of Clinical Psychiatry, 55*(4), 134–136.

Woods, S. W., Nagy, L. M., Koleszer, A. S., et al. (1992). Controlled trial of alprazolam supplements during imipraminc trcatmcnt of panic disordcr. *Journal of Clinical Psychopharmacology, 12*, 32–38.

Worthington, J. J., III, Zucker, B. G., Fones, C. S., Otto, M. W., & Pollack, M. H. (1998). Nefazodone for social phobia: A clinical case series. *Depression and Anxiety, 8*, 131–133.

Yonkers, K. A., Ellison, J. M., Shera, D. M., Pratt, L. A., Cole, J. O., Fierman, E., Keller, M. B., & Lavori, P. W. (1996). Description of antipanic therapy in a prospective longitudinal study. *Journal of Clinical Psychopharmacology 16*(3), 223–232.

Zajecka, J. M. (1996). The effect of nefazodone on comorbid anxiety symptoms associated with depression: Experience in family practice and psychiatry outpatient settings. *Journal of Clinical Psychiatry, 57*(Suppl 2), 1–14.

Zitrin, C. M., Klein, D. F., & Woerner, M. C. (1978). Behavior therapy, supportive psychotherapy, imipramine, and phobias. *Archives of General Psychiatry, 35*, 307–316.

Zitrin, C. M., Klein, D. F., Woerner, M. C., & Ross, D. S. (1983). Treatment of phobias. 1. Comparison of imipraminc hydrochloridc and placcbo. *Archives of General Psychiatry, 40*, 125–138.

15

Cognitive Behavioral Treatments for Obsessive Compulsive Disorder

Martin E. Franklin

Edna B. Foa

Cognitive behavioral therapy (CBT) involving exposure and ritual prevention (EX/RP) is a well-established treatment for obsessive compulsive disorder (OCD) in adults. Support for its efficacy is derived from many Type 1 and Type 2 studies, as well as from several meta-analytic studies and literature reviews. CBT involving EX/RP has been found superior to several control conditions and to pharmacotherapy with serotonin reuptake inhibitors (SRIs), although studies examining whether CBT plus SRI pharmacotherapy is superior to CBT alone have yielded equivocal findings. There is some preliminary evidence for the efficacy of group CBT and for family involvement in treatment, although more research is needed in both of these areas. Further research is needed to determine the role of cognitive therapy in OCD, to identify predictors of treatment outcome, and to examine the relative efficacy of CBT, SRIs, and their combination in pediatric OCD.

The symptoms that characterize what we now call *obsessive compulsive disorder* (OCD) have been recognized for centuries in many cultures (for a review see Pitman, 1994). However, it was only since the early 1970s that effective psychosocial and pharmacological therapies for OCD were developed and studied. In this chapter, we will briefly discuss diagnostic and theoretical issues, then review the literature about available treatments. We have focused primarily on the outcome of cognitive behavioral treatment (CBT) by exposure and ritual prevention (EX/RP; originally referred to as *response prevention*) because most experts consider it the treatment of choice for OCD (March et al., 1997). Notably, two recent studies that have examined the effectiveness of EX/RP outside the context of controlled research trials suggest that its benefits are not limited to the highly selected patient samples that often characterize randomized controlled trials (RCTs; Franklin, Abramowitz, Kozak, Levitt, & Foa, 2000; Rothbaum & Shahar, 2000).

DEFINITION OF OBSESSIVE COMPULSIVE DISORDER

According to the *DSM-IV* (American Psychiatric Association [APA], 1994), OCD is characterized by recurrent obsessions and/or compulsions that interfere considerably with daily functioning. Obsessions are "persistent ideas, thoughts, impulses, or images that are experienced as intrusive and inappropriate and cause marked anxiety or distress" (p. 418). Compulsions are "repetitive behaviors . . . or mental acts . . . the goal of which is to prevent or reduce anxiety or distress" (p. 418).

The updated *DSM-IV* definition of OCD is on the whole similar to the conceptualization posed in

DSM-III-R (APA, 1987) but includes several noteworthy changes based on recent thinking about the disorder. The view that obsessions and compulsions are functionally related (i.e., that compulsions are performed in order to decrease distress associated with obsessions; Foa & Tillmanns, 1980) became more prominent in the *DSM-IV* definition of OCD because of strong empirical support for this view. In the *DSM-IV* field study on OCD, 90% of participants reported that their compulsions aim to either prevent harm associated with their obsessions or reduce obsessional distress; only 10% perceived their compulsions as unrelated to obsessions (Foa et al., 1995). Accordingly, obsessions are defined in *DSM-IV* as thoughts, images, or impulses that cause marked anxiety or distress, and compulsions are defined as overt (behavioral) or covert (mental) actions that are performed in an attempt to reduce the distress brought on by obsessions or according to rigid rules.

Data from the field study also indicated that the vast majority (over 90%) of obsessive compulsives manifest both obsessions and behavioral rituals. When mental rituals are included, only 2% of the sample reported obsessions only (Foa et al., 1995). Behavioral rituals are equivalent to mental rituals (such as silently repeating prayers) in their functional relationship to obsessions: Both serve to reduce obsessional distress, prevent feared harm, or restore safety. Thus, the traditional view that obsessions are mental events and compulsions are behavioral events is not valid: Although all obsessions are indeed mental events, compulsions may be either behavioral or mental.

It has been argued that a continuum of "insight" or "strength of belief" more accurately represents the clinical picture of OCD than the previously prevailing view that *all* obsessive compulsives recognize the senselessness of their obsessions and compulsions (Kozak & Foa, 1994). The growing consensus about this issue (Foa et al., 1995; Insel & Akiskal, 1986; Lelliott, Noshirvani, Basoglu, Marks, & Monteiro, 1988) led to an important revision for the *DSM-IV* definition of OCD. Individuals who evidence obsessions and compulsions but do not recognize their senselessness now receive the diagnosis of OCD "with poor insight." The importance of the insight in OCD assessment and treatment is highlighted by a recent study (Foa, Abramowitz, Franklin, & Kozak, 1999) suggesting that individuals suffering from this subtype may be less responsive to exposure and ritual prevention, which is considered the first-line treatment for OCD.

PREVALENCE AND COURSE

Once thought to be a rare disorder, OCD is now estimated to occur in about 2.5% of the adult population in the United States (Karno, Golding, Sorenson, & Burnam, 1988). Recent epidemiological studies with children and adolescents suggest similar lifetime prevalence rates in these samples (e.g., Flament et al., 1988; Valleni-Basile et al., 1994). Slightly more than half of the adults suffering from OCD are female (Rasmussen & Tsuang, 1986), whereas a 2:1 male-to-female ratio has been observed in several pediatric clinical samples (e.g., Hanna, 1995; Swedo, Rapoport, Leonard, Lenane, & Cheslow, 1989). Age of onset of the disorder typically ranges from early adolescence to young adulthood, with earlier onset in males; modal onset in males is 13 to 15 years old and 20 to 24 in females (Rasmussen & Eisen, 1990). However, cases of OCD have been documented in children as young as age 2 (Rapoport, Swedo, & Leonard, 1992). Development of the disorder is usually gradual, but more acute onset has been reported in some cases. A subset of pediatric patients suffer from a similar clinical course of illness now referred to as Pediatric Autoimmune Neuropsychiatric Disorders Associated with Strep (PANDAS), in which patients experience dramatic-onset OCD and/or tic symptoms following strep infection (Swedo et al., 1998). Notably, these exacerbations in PANDAS are often followed by periods of relative symptom quiescence, until such time as the child is reinfected.

Although chronic waxing and waning of symptoms is typical of OCD, episodic and deteriorating courses have been observed in about 10% of patients (Rasmussen & Eisen, 1989). OCD is frequently associated with impairments in general functioning, such as disruption of gainful employment (Leon, Portera, & Weissman, 1995), and with marital and other interpersonal relationship difficulties (Emmelkamp, de Haan, & Hoogduin, 1990; Riggs, Hiss, & Foa, 1992). Adolescents identified as having OCD (Flament et al., 1988) reported in a subsequent follow-up study that they had withdrawn socially to prevent contamination and to conserve energy for obsessive compulsive behaviors (Flament et al. 1990).

ETIOLOGY AND MAINTENANCE OF OBSESSIVE COMPULSIVE DISORDER

There are several theoretical accounts of the etiology and maintenance of OCD. Mowrer's (1939, 1960) two-stage theory for the acquisition and maintenance of fear and avoidance behavior was invoked by Dollard and Miller (1950) to explain OCD. Accordingly, a neutral event comes to elicit fear after being experienced along with an event that by its nature causes distress. Distress can be conditioned to mental events (e.g., thoughts) as well as to physical events (e.g., floors, bathrooms). Once fear is acquired, escape or avoidance patterns (i.e., compulsions) develop to reduce fear and are maintained by the negative reinforcement of fear reduction. While Mowrer's theory does adequately account for fear acquisition (Rachman & Wilson, 1980), it is consistent with observations about the maintenance of compulsive rituals: Obsessions give rise to anxiety/distress, and compulsions reduce it (e.g., Roper & Rachman, 1976; Roper, Rachman, & Hodgson, 1973).

Cognitive theorists have argued that OCD is founded in ideas of exaggerated negative consequences (Carr, 1974; McFall & Wollersheim, 1979). However, clinical observations suggest that mistaken evaluation of danger and the idea that self-worth is connected with being perfect are typical of all anxiety disorders. These theories do not address the characteristics that distinguish OCD from other disorders. Salkovskis (1985) offered a more thorough cognitive analysis of OCD. He proposed that five assumptions are specifically characteristic of OCD:

1. thinking of an action is analogous to its performance
2. failing to prevent (or failing to try to prevent) harm to self or others is morally equivalent to causing the harm
3. responsibility for harm is not diminished by extenuating circumstances
4. failing to ritualize in response to an idea about harm constitutes an intention to harm
5. one should exercise control over one's thoughts (Salkovskis, 1985, p. 579)

An interesting implication of this theory is that whereas the obsessive intrusions may be seen by the patient as unacceptable, the mental and overt rituals that they prompt are acceptable.

Foa and Kozak (1985) hypothesized that individuals with obsessive compulsive disorder often conclude that a situation is dangerous based on the absence of evidence of safety, and that they fail to make inductive leaps about safety from information about the absence of danger. For example, in order to feel safe, an OCD sufferer requires a guarantee that the toilet seat is safe before sitting on it, whereas a person without OCD would sit on the toilet seat unless there was something particular about it indicating danger, such as visible brown spots on the seat. Consequently, rituals that are performed to reduce the likelihood of harm can never really provide safety and must be repeated.

The prevailing biological account of OCD hypothesizes that abnormal serotonin metabolism is expressed in OCD symptoms. The efficacy of serotonin reuptake inhibitors (SRIs) for OCD as compared to nonserotonergic compounds and to pill placebo (PBO) has provided a compelling argument for this hypothesis (Zohar & Insel, 1987). Significant correlations between clomipramine (CMI) plasma levels and improvement in OCD have led researchers to suggest that serotonin function mediates obsessive compulsive symptoms, thus lending further support to the serotonin hypothesis (Insel et al., 1985; Stern, Marks, Wright, & Luscombe, 1980). However, the studies that directly investigated serotonin functioning in obsessive compulsives are inconclusive (Joffe & Swinson, 1991). For example, serotonin platelet uptake studies have failed to differentiate obsessive compulsives from controls (Insel, Mueller, Alterman, Linnoila, & Murphy, 1985; Weizman et al., 1986). Also inconsistent with the serotonin hypothesis is the finding that clomipramine, a nonselective serotonergic medication, appears to produce greater OCD symptom reduction than selective serotonin reuptake inhibitors such as fluoxetine, fluvoxamine, and sertraline (Greist, Jefferson, Kobak, Katzelnick, & Serlin, 1995). With respect to other biological theories, research being conducted at the National Institute of Mental Health on PANDAS may shed light on the role of basal ganglia dysfunction in certain neuropsychiatric conditions, including OCD (Swedo et al., 1998). Some have even proposed that childhood onset OCD represents a phenomenologically and etiologically distinct subtype of OCD, bearing a close genetic relationship to tic disorders and possibly sharing a common or similar pathogenesis (Eichstedt & Arnold, 2001).

EARLY TREATMENTS FOR OBSESSIVE COMPULSIVE DISORDER

Until the middle of the 1960s, OCD was considered refractory to treatment. Neither psychodynamic psychotherapy nor a wide variety of pharmacotherapies had proven successful in ameliorating OCD symptoms. Early case reports employing exposure procedures (e.g., systematic desensitization, paradoxical intention, imaginal flooding, satiation) also yielded generally unimpressive results, as did several operant conditioning procedures aimed at blocking or punishing obsessions and compulsions (e.g., thought stopping, aversion therapy, covert sensitization). For a review see Foa, Franklin, and Kozak (1998).

A dramatic shift occurred when Victor Meyer (1966) reported on two patients treated successfully with a behavioral program that included prolonged exposure to obsessional cues and strict prevention of rituals (EX/RP). This treatment program was subsequently found to be very successful in 10 of 15 cases and partly effective in the remainder; after 5 years, only 2 of 15 patients in this open clinical trial had relapsed (Meyer & Levy, 1973; Meyer, Levy, & Schnurer, 1974). Another shift occurred with the finding that the tricyclic clomipramine (Anafranil) was effective in reducing OCD symptoms (e.g., Fernandez-Cordoba & Lopez-Ibor Alino, 1967). Subsequent research efforts were aimed at developing these treatments further and determining their relative efficacy.

REVIEW OF OBSESSIVE COMPULSIVE TREATMENT OUTCOME LITERATURE

In the three decades following these initial reports, the efficacy of two treatments has been established: cognitive behavioral therapy by EX/RP and pharmacotherapy with serotonin reuptake inhibitors (SRIs). We will begin by examining results from several recent meta-analytic studies and literature reviews. We will then evaluate results emerging from controlled studies of EX/RP employing a set of criteria that we label the gold standard for treatment outcome studies.

Meta-Analytic Studies and Literature Reviews

A meta-analysis was conducted by Cox, Swinson, Morrison, and Lee (1993) to examine the relative efficacy of serotonin reuptake inhibitors and behavioral treatments. Results indicated that fluoxetine, clomipramine, and exposure therapy were highly effective for ameliorating OCD symptoms, with effect sizes of 3.45, 3.25, and 2.56, respectively. Again, no differences among these treatments emerged. Only 25 treatment studies conducted between 1975 and 1991 were considered appropriate for this analysis, of which just 9 included an exposure-based behavior therapy condition. Studies were excluded if they were case studies or reported only percentages of improved patients, or if it was determined that there was insufficient information (e.g., no reporting of means and standard deviations) to calculate Cohen's *d* for conversion to Z scores. Notably, many of seminal studies of EX/RP (e.g., Foa & Goldstein, 1978; Marks et al., 1975) were excluded from this analysis.

In another meta-analysis, studies on efficacy of antidepressants, exposure-based behavior therapy, cognitive therapy, and the combination of these methods were included (van Balkom et al., 1994). The literature search for this analysis yielded 86 studies published between 1970 and 1993 that provided sufficient information to allow the calculation of effect sizes; a total of 2,569 patients were available for posttest, following a 13% dropout rate across studies. Serotonergic antidepressants, behavior therapy, cognitive therapy, and the combinations of antidepressants and behavior therapy and of placebo and behavior therapy were associated with large effect sizes for improvements in assessor-rated OCD symptoms (1.63, 1.47, 1.04, 1.99, and 1.85, respectively), depression, general anxiety, and social adjustment; behavior therapy alone and in combination with serotonergic antidepressants was significantly superior to PBO. Moreover, on some measures of OCD, behavior therapy yielded superior outcome to that of SRIs. The authors noted the lack of data on long-term efficacy.

Using a less sophisticated method, Foa and Kozak (1996) summarized both the short-term and long-term efficacy of EX/RP, focusing on rate of responding. Immediately after therapy, 83% of 330 OCD patients treated in 12 studies were identified as treatment responders. At follow-up ($M = 2.4$ years; range 3 months to 6 years), 76% of 376 OCD patients in 16 studies were responders. The 83% responder rate after CBT contrasts with the 61% rate to CMI found in the largest study of this medication (DeVeaugh-Geiss, Landau & Katz, 1989). The contrast of the 76% follow-up responder rate for CBT compared to CMI is even more striking because of high relapse rate, 89%, upon CMI discontinuation (Pato, Zohar-Kadouch, Zohar, & Murphy, 1988).

Variations in EX/RP treatment procedures are common in OCD outcome studies and may compromise our ability to compare results from one EX/RP study to another. In order to explore the degree to which these EX/RP treatment variables influenced outcome, Abramowitz (1996) conducted a meta-analytic study that included 38 trials from 24 controlled and uncontrolled studies. His results indicated that (a) therapist-assisted exposure was more effective than self-exposure; (b) studies that included strict ritual prevention instructions yielded greater improvement than those with partial or no ritual prevention instructions; and (c) imaginal and in vivo exposure in combination was superior to in vivo exposure alone.

Methodological drawbacks of the meta-analytic studies described above weaken any conclusions that can be drawn from them. First, results from uncontrolled and controlled studies were given equal weight, thereby potentially inflating the effects of EX/RP by including nonspecific treatment effects. Second, meta-analysis of EX/RP treatments is particularly problematic because studies varied greatly in how this treatment was implemented. Specifically, studies varied with respect to the setting in which treatment was conducted (inpatient vs. outpatient), length and frequency of treatment sessions, extent of therapist involvement in exposure exercises, strictness of ritual prevention rules, extent and nature of homework assignments, and inclusion of imaginal exposure. Several of these parameters have been shown to influence outcome substantially (e.g., Abramowitz, 1996; Foa et al., 1984; Rabavilas, Boulougouris, & Stefanis, 1976), accentuating the inherent problem of collapsing across disparate procedures.

"Gold Standard" OCD Treatment Outcome Studies

Given the problems with the existing meta-analytical studies, we will move on now to a review of EX/RP studies. The following study selection criteria were used: The sample comprised (a) OCD patients, (b) at least one comparison group, and (c) at least eight patients per experimental cell. The validity of each study's results will be evaluated by considering the set of criteria that defines our "ideal" treatment outcome study: (a) clearly defined inclusion/exclusion criteria, (b) reliable and valid diagnostic methods, (c) random assignment to treatment condition, (d) blind assessments by trained assessors using reliable and valid outcome measures, (e) manualized treatments, (f) measures of treatment adherence, (g) adequate sample size for statistical power, (h) appropriate statistical analyses, and (i) exposure and ritual prevention that meet acceptable clinical practice standards as suggested by expert consensus (see Kozak & Foa, 1996). Adequate planned systematic exposure was defined as involving confrontation of obsession-evoking stimuli of sufficient duration (typically 90 minutes or longer), frequency (15 to 20 sessions), and spacing (initially at least once a week, but often more frequently). Adequate ritual prevention should occur immediately after exposure and include patients' voluntary compliance with instructions to refrain from ritualizing and procedures to help the patient achieve the greatest reduction in rituals possible. Exposure and ritual prevention should also be exercised between sessions.

We will review these studies by topic in order to provide a sense of which issues in OCD treatment outcome have already been addressed adequately as well as acknowledgment of those areas that need to be addressed.

The Separate Effects of Exposure In Vivo, Imaginal Exposure, and Ritual Prevention

In early studies of the efficacy of EX/RP for OCD (e.g., Foa & Goldstein, 1978; Meyer, Levy, & Schnurer, 1974), exposure and ritual prevention were implemented concurrently, thus making it impossible to determine the contribution of each procedure alone to outcome. To address this issue, Foa et al. (1984) assigned patients with washing rituals to either treatment by exposure only, ritual prevention only, or their combination. Each treatment was conducted intensively (15 daily 2-hour sessions conducted over 3 weeks) and followed by a home visit. Blind assessors evaluated patients' symptoms at pretreatment, posttreatment, and follow-up; patients also completed self-report measures at each assessment. All treatments were effective, and gains were maintained at follow-up ($M = 12$ months, range 3 to 24 months). Assessor ratings of obsessions were reduced at posttreatment by 36% for EX, 28% for RP, and 63% for EX/RP; at follow-up, reductions from pretreatment ratings of

25% for EX, 29% for RP, and 48% for EX/RP were observed. On assessor ratings of ritual severity, the following reductions were observed: 50% for EX, 45% for RP, and 63% for EX/RP at posttreatment, and 15% for EX, 26% for RP, and 63% for EX/RP at follow-up. The combined treatment was superior to the single-component treatments on almost every symptom measure at both posttreatment and follow-up. In comparing the single-component treatments to one another, EX patients had lower ratings of anxiety than RP patients upon confrontation with feared contaminants in a posttreatment exposure test, and RP patients reported greater decreases in urge to ritualize than did EX patients, a finding suggesting that the two components affect OC symptoms differently.

Patients were allocated to groups by a serial assignment procedure to balance for level of depression, gender, and therapist. In studies with small samples (cell sizes ranged from 9 to 12), this procedure is advantageous over random assignment because it ensures across-group equality on outcome-related factors. Inclusion/exclusion criteria were clearly described, and blind assessors rated patients' symptoms using reliable and valid outcome measures. Treatments were described in detail although they were not manualized and treatment integrity was not assessed. Statistical analyses were generally appropriate, although setting a more conservative alpha level or correcting for the large number of tests may have been advisable.

In the Foa and Goldstein (1978) open clinical trial, EX/RP was accompanied by imaginal exposure (I/EX). To examine the additive effect of imaginal exposure, patients with checking rituals were treated with either 10 two-hour sessions of EX/RP delivered over 2 weeks or 10 sessions of EX/RP + I/EX (Foa, Steketee, Turner, & Fischer, 1980). Sessions were 2 hours long and consisted of either 90-minute I/EX and 30-minute in vivo EX or 2 hours of in vivo EX only. Immediately after treatment, the mean symptom reduction in the EX/RP group was 66% for obsessions and 75% for compulsions; the EX/RP + I/EX group evidenced reductions of 63% for obsessions and 70% for compulsions. No posttreatment group differences were detected on six OC symptom outcome measures. However, group differences did emerge at follow-up (*M* follow-up = 11 months, range 3 months to 2.5 years): On four out of six measures, the group receiving I/EX was less symptomatic than in pretreatment. Specifically, mean reductions in obsessions and compulsions at follow-up were 43% and 53%, respectively, for EX/RP alone and 72% and 74% for EX/RP + I/EX. Thus, imaginal exposure seems to contribute to maintenance of treatment gains. The results of this study underscore the importance of obtaining follow-up data; in the absence of these data, the effects of I/EX would not have been detected.

The Foa, Steketee, and Milby study (1980) specified inclusion/exclusion criteria, treatments were described clearly and implemented in accordance with accepted clinical practice standards, blind assessors rated symptom severity, and statistical analyses were conducted appropriately. While the design met some of our gold standard criteria, several methodological problems should be noted. Patients were assigned to condition according to order of applying for treatment rather than at random, diagnostic methods were not described, measures of treatment adherence were not included, and sample size (15) was marginal.

To further examine whether the addition of I/EX to EX/RP enhances treatment efficacy, de Araujo, Ito, Marks, and Deale (1995) replicated the Foa, Steketee, Turner, and Fischer (1980) design, but the treatment program and the patient population differed across the two studies. Patients in this study had a range of rituals, and treatment included a mean of 9 weekly 90-minute sessions of either in vivo EX or 30-minute I/EX and 60 minutes in vivo EX. At posttreatment, both groups evidenced reductions on measures of OC symptoms, including the Yale-Brown Obsessive Compulsive Scale (Y-BOCS) (46% reduction in Y-BOCS total for EX/RP group, 48% in EX/RP + I/EX), as well as on measures of depression and disability. No group differences were found either at posttreatment or at 6-month follow-up (42% reduction in Y-BOCS total for EX/RP group, 49% in EX/RP + I/EX), a finding suggesting no augmentive effect for imaginal exposure.

The de Araujo et al. (1995) study had several strengths, including utilization of random assignment to condition, blind assessors, clearly stated inclusion/exclusion criteria, adequate sample size for completer data ($N = 23$ per cell), appropriate outcome measures (Y-BOCS; Hamilton Depression, or HAM-D), and clearly described treatments. However, assessor training was not described, diagnostic methods were not explicated ("patients who met *DSM-III-R* criteria for OCD . . . "), and treatment adherence was not measured. Moreover, because in the Foa et al. (1980) study the effects of imaginal exposure were not detected until an average of 11 months posttreatment, the length of follow-up (6-months) in the de Araujo et al. (1995) study may have been insufficient to detect such effects. Also, the treatment procedure and patient samples of the two studies differ in important ways that were likely to produce different results. Specifically, treatment was conducted daily in the Foa et al. study, sessions were of 2-hour duration, and imaginal exposure was 90 minutes long; in the de Araujo et al. study, treatment was conducted weekly, sessions were 90 minutes in duration, and imaginal exposure was conducted over 30 minutes only. These procedural differences are troublesome because they reflect a general tendency in treatment research. Namely, researchers who intend to examine the replicability of a previous result do not always adhere to the procedure of the treatment they choose to examine, and therefore resultant differences in outcome are uninterpretable.

EX/RP Versus Anxiety Management Training (AMT)

One very small early study had suggested the superiority of EX/RP over relaxation using a crossover design (Marks et al., 1975), but the question of whether nonspecific factors explain the observed symptom reductions in EX/RP treatment studies was addressed recently by Lindsay and colleagues (1997). Eighteen patients were randomly assigned to intensive (daily) regimens of either EX/RP or AMT. Results on therapist-rated Y-BOCS and several self-report OCD inventories indicated that EX/RP was clearly superior to AMT, even though both groups rated their therapists as highly supportive and understanding. This study adds further evidence of the efficacy of EX/RP and suggests that having supportive and understanding therapists offering face-valid treatments with a comprehensive rationale does not result in reduced OCD symptoms in the absence of EX/RP (Lindsay et al., 1997).

Lindsay et al.'s study met several of the gold standard criteria for EX/RP outcome studies, including clearly described inclusion/exclusion and therapist ratings of OCD symptoms using the Y-BOCS, a reliable and valid outcome measure. Both treatments were manualized, although treatment integrity was not assessed. Statistical analyses were appropriate, including Bonferroni correction for multiple tests to limit Type I error. As noted by the authors, limitations included the small sample size, the failure to assess credibility of the control group, and the fact that random assignment did not equalize gender ratios. Additionally, the absence of independent evaluators to conduct symptom ratings (ratings were conducted by therapists instead) does allow for the possibility that rater bias may have affected outcome.

Individual Versus Group EX/RP

Efficacy of group and individual behavior therapy was examined in a study by Fals-Stewart, Marks, and Schafer (1993). OCD patients were randomly assigned to receive EX/RP conducted individually, group EX/RP treatment, or a psychosocial placebo (relaxation). Each of the active treatments was 2 weeks long, with sessions held twice weekly, and included daily exposure homework assignments. Results indicated significant reductions in OC symptoms at posttreatment only in the two active treatments: Mean Y-BOCS reduction was 40% for individual EX/RP, 46% for group EX/RP, and 9% in attention control. Moreover, no differences between individual and group EX/RP were detected at posttreatment or at 6-month follow-up (mean Y-BOCS reduction at follow-up = 36% for individual EX/RP, 37% for group EX/RP), although profile analysis of Y-BOCS scores collected throughout treatment indicated a faster reduction in symptoms for patients receiving individual treatment. These results offer evidence of the efficacy of group treatment, considered by the authors especially important in light of the efficiency and practicality of treatment delivery afforded by group approaches.

Fals-Stewart et al.'s (1993) study had several strengths. Diagnostic interviews were conducted by trained social workers, and outcome measures were acceptable (e.g., Y-BOCS). Sample size was more than sufficient (30 to 32 per cell), and there were only 4 dropouts from treatment following randomization. Statistical analyses were appropriate, and therapy was provided by trained social workers experienced with OCD treatment. Difficulties interpreting the study's results arose, however, from the inclusion/exclusion criteria and from the specific form of EX/RP used. Patients were excluded from the study if they were diagnosed with *any* personality disorder or with comorbid major depression with a BDI greater than 22. This exclusion criterion, together with the relatively low pretreatment Y-BOCS scores (range 19 to 22) and the fact that all 93 patients had never received previous treatment for OCD, rendered the sample atypical and limited the generalizability of findings that group and individual treatments are equally effective.

Family Involvement Versus Standard Treatment

Influenced by findings that efficacy of exposure therapy for panic disorder with agoraphobia is enhanced by partner assistance, Emmelkamp et al. (1990) examined whether such assistance would also enhance the efficacy of EX/RP for OCD. Patients who were married or living with a romantic partner were randomly assigned to receive EX/RP either with or without partner involvement in treatment. Each treatment lasted 5 weeks and consisted of eight 45- to 60-minute sessions with the therapist; exposures were not practiced in session. Patients and partners rated their symptoms at four assessment periods; independent evaluators rated patients only before and after treatment. Results indicated that OCD severity was significantly reduced immediately after treatment for both groups: A mean 33% reduction in assessor rated anxiety-discomfort was observed for the sample as a whole. No group differences were detected, and initial marital distress did not predict outcome. It is important to note that, like the results from Emmelkamp and his colleagues described earlier, while the mean pre-post symptom reduction reached statistical significance, the modest reduction may not reflect clinically significant improvement.

In the Emmelkamp et al. (1990) study, eligible patients (those with partners) were randomly assigned to treatment. Blind assessors were used, but only at two assessment periods, and training on the measures was not discussed. Inclusion/exclusion criteria were clearly described, although diagnostic methods were not. Sample size (50) was more than adequate, and there were very few treatment dropouts. Statistical analyses were conducted appropriately, although in the tabular presentation of results the group condition was collapsed. Description of treatments did not include sufficient details regarding how ritual prevention was discussed with patients, and treatment adherence data were not provided. As with previously discussed studies, no therapist-assisted exposure was included, and between-sessions exposure homework was assigned only twice per week. These diluted procedures seem to have produced only modest symptom reductions.

Mehta (1990) also examined the adjunctive role of family involvement in EX/RP treatment in a study conducted in India. In order to adapt the treatment to serve the large numbers of young unmarried people seeking OCD treatment and the "joint family system" prevalent in India, a family-based rather than spouse-based treatment approach was utilized. Patients ($N = 30$) previously nonresponsive to pharmacotherapy were randomly assigned to receive treatment by systematic desensitization and EX/RP either with or without family assistance. Sessions in both conditions were held twice per week for 12 weeks; response prevention was "gradual . . . to reduce the frequency of the target behavior until they reached a desired level" (p. 1334). In the family condition, a designated family member (parent, spouse, or adult child) assisted with homework assignments, supervised relaxation therapy, participated in response prevention, and was instructed to be supportive when patients became depressed and anxious. On the only measure of OCD symptoms, the Maudsey Obsessional Compulsive Inventory (MOCI), a greater improvement was found for the family-based intervention at posttreatment and 6-month follow-up: MOCI reductions of 56% at posttreatment and 61% at follow-up were observed in the family treatment, compared to 39% at posttreatment and 29% at follow-up for individual treatment.

In Mehta's (1990) study, patients were randomly assigned to treatment, and sample size was satisfactory. However, OC symptoms were assessed exclusively by self-report (MOCI), introducing a possible bias. Inclusion/exclusion criteria and diagnostic methods were not specified in sufficient detail. While the number of treatment sessions was sufficient, treatment descriptions were sketchy (e.g., degree to which relaxation training was emphasized), and no treatment adherence data were provided. The statistical analyses consisted of between-subjects *t* tests at each assessment occasion; a mixed-design ANOVA would have been more appropriate. Despite its shortcomings, the study does provide interesting information about the efficacy of EX/RP treatment within the context of a culture where family relationships are thought to be especially important.

Does the Addition of Cognitive Procedures Enhance Efficacy of EX/RP?

The increased interest in cognitive therapy (e.g., Beck, 1976; Ellis, 1962) prompted researchers to examine the efficacy of cognitive procedures with OCD. The impetus for this originated out of growing dissatisfaction with existing formulations of pathological anxiety and its treatment as mediated by automatic processes such as extinction (Stampfl & Levis, 1967) or habituation (Watts, 1973). An early study of cognitive therapy for OCD yielded no differences between a combination of self-instructional training (Meichenbaum, 1974) and EX/RP versus EX/RP alone (Emmelkamp, van der Helm, van Zanten, & Ploch, 1980), yet encouraged researchers to develop and test other cognitive therapies for OCD. Emmelkamp, Visser, and Hoekstra (1988) examined the efficacy of another cognitive approach, rational emotive therapy (RET), by randomly assigning patients to one of the two treatments: EX/RP or RET. Treatment consisted of 10 sessions (60 minutes each) conducted over 8 weeks; patients in both conditions were also given homework assignments. Outcome was assessed by self-report measures and by pooled ratings of OC symptom severity by therapists and patients. Both groups were improved at posttreatment: On the pooled OC symptom ratings, the RET group evidenced an average posttreatment improvement of 40% and the EX/RP, 51%. Two thirds of patients in both groups received additional treatment during follow-up, thus precluding conclusions about long-term maintenance of gains. Emmelkamp et al.'s (1988) study included random assignment, treatment manuals, and a thorough discussion of treatment integrity. But several limitations should be noted: Inclusion/exclusion criteria and diagnostic methods were not described adequately, and assessment was not blind to treatment conditions, relying on therapists' and patients' ratings. A primary difficulty lies in the treatment procedure itself: Sessions were only 60 minutes in length, were held approximately once per week, did not include therapist-assisted exposure, included only two homework assignments per week, and seem to have employed a more gradual response prevention than is typically recommended. This truncated treatment program may have been responsible for the inferior outcome of EX/RP compared to that in other studies (e.g., Foa, Kozak, Steketee, & McCarthy, 1992).

In a further comparison of cognitive therapy with EX/RP, Emmelkamp and Beens (1991) compared a program that included six sessions of RET alone followed by six sessions of RET plus self-controlled EX/RP to a program that included 12 sessions of self-controlled EX/RP. In both programs, the first six sessions were followed by 4 weeks of no treatment, after which the additional six sessions were delivered. As in Emmelkamp et al.'s (1988) study, treatment sessions were conducted approximately once per week and lasted for 60 minutes each. EX/RP sessions did not include therapist-assisted exposure, and patients were assigned twice-weekly exposure homework exercises. The RET program was equivalent to that employed in the Emmelkamp et al. (1988) study; when self-controlled EX/RP was introduced following the first six RET-only sessions, the subsequent sessions focused on irrational thoughts that occurred in response to exposure homework exercises. Assessments were conducted at seven points over 44 weeks and involved patient, therapist, and assessor ratings of five OCD targets as well as self-report measures (e.g., MOCI; Hodgson & Rachman, 1977). Immediately following the completion of six sessions of cognitive therapy without exposure and EX/RP (Week 9), mean reduction of anxiety associated with main OC problem was only 25% for RET and 23% for EX/RP. Following six more sessions (RET + EX/RP in one condition and EX/RP only in the other), both groups improved on most measures over time, and no significant group differences emerged. The authors interpreted the absence of group differences as indicating that cognitive therapy is as effective as EX/RP for OCD. This interpretation is somewhat confusing because it appeared that EX/RP was more effective on mean reduction in assessor-rated anxiety associated with main OC problem (59% for EX/RP vs. 36% for RET) yet less effective on patient-rated anxiety associated with main OC problem (26% for EX/RP vs. 53% for RET). Insufficient power to compare active treatments may have obscured between-group differences. Final follow-up data are uninterpretable because most patients received additional treatments after first follow-up.

Many of the same methodological strengths noted for Emmelkamp et al. (1988) were also evident in this study: random assignment to treatment, blind assessments, clear inclusion/exclusion criteria, use of treatment manuals, and considerable attention to treatment integrity despite the absence of formal adherence measures. Approximately 33% of the sample dropped out during treatment, a higher percentage than reported in several other studies, which negatively impacts generalizability of findings. Again, the main criticism of this study was the use of an EX/RP treatment that does not meet acceptable practice standards. In both studies, cognitive therapy was compared to a truncated version of EX/RP that may not have served as a sufficiently powerful comparison.

In a further examination of the relative efficacy of cognitive therapy and EX/RP for OCD, van Balkom et al. (1998) randomly assigned patients to (a) cognitive therapy for Weeks 1 to 16; (b) EX/RP for Weeks 1 to 16; (c) fluvoxamine for Weeks 1 to 16 plus cognitive therapy in Weeks 9 to 16; (d) fluvoxamine for Weeks 1 to 16 plus EX/RP in Weeks 9 to 16; and (e) wait list for Weeks 1 to 8. Behavioral experiments (exposures) were not introduced into the cognitive treatment until after Session 6 (Week 8). Conversely, in the first six EX/RP sessions, care was taken by the therapist to specifically avoid any discussion of disastrous consequences. The authors regarded this procedure as measuring the effects of "purer" versions of cognitive therapy and EX/RP. Cognitive therapy focused primarily on themes of danger overestimation and inflated personal responsibility. EX/RP included self-exposure, with patients determining the speed at which they worked through the fear hierarchy. Sessions in both treatment conditions lasted for 45 minutes. Results indicated that all active treatments were superior to wait list at Week 8. Additionally, after eight weeks of cognitive therapy without behavioral experiments and EX/RP without discussion of disastrous consequences, Y-BOCS reductions of 15% and 25% were observed for cognitive therapy and EX/RP, respectively. At posttreatment, all active treatments improved significantly on almost all measures, including the Y-BOCS and Beck Depression Inventory (BDI; Beck, Ward, Mendelson, Mock, & Erbaugh, 1961). However, inspection of the mean reduction in Y-BOCS scores for the EX/RP condition suggested that outcome at posttreatment (46% Y-BOCS reduction for CT; 32% for EX/RP) was inferior to that achieved in other studies (e.g., Foa et al., 1992). It should be noted that the mean posttreatment score in the EX/RP group of 17.1 would be considered sufficiently severe to meet initial severity criteria for many OCD treatment studies. The authors suggested that the lack of observed differences between the combined conditions and the monotherapies indicates that clinicians should start with either cognitive therapy or EX/RP alone rather than with combination treatments.

Random assignment to treatments, reliable and valid diagnostic procedures, clear inclusion and exclusion criteria, use of treatment manuals, attention to treatment adherence, adequate sample size, and sophisticated statistical analyses all constitute strengths of van Balkom et al.'s (1998) report. In particular, the authors used state-of-the-art reliable change indices to examine the clinical relevance of their data. However, several methodological shortcomings should be noted. No mention is made of assessor blindness or training, nor are data on treatment adherence provided. Most important, as noted above, the EX/RP version employed in this study was inadequate. First, the length of session was relatively short (45 minutes), and sessions were held once per week instead of the more frequent schedule recommended. Second, it is unclear how much homework patients were asked to complete between sessions, how long their homework exposures were, and to what extent patients complied with homework assignments. Third, discussion of negative consequences in the first six sessions is an important component of EX/RP, and banning such discussion constitutes further diluting of this treatment and its rationale (see Foa & Kozak, 1996). As would be expected, the results of this truncated treatment were at best modest, with a mean 32% reduction of OCD symptoms after 16 weeks of treatment.

Hiss, Foa, and Kozak (1994) investigated whether adding a formal relapse prevention program following intensive EX/RP enhanced maintenance of therapeutic gains. In this study, all components typically included to address relapse prevention (e.g., discussion of lapse vs. relapse, posttreatment exposure instructions, themes of guilt and personal responsibility) were removed from the 15 daily sessions of the intensive phase. All patients ($N = 20$) received the modified EX/RP, followed by either a relapse prevention treatment or a psychosocial control treatment (associative therapy). All patients were responders to EX/RP at posttreatment (defined as 50% or greater reduction in OCD symptoms). Nonparametric analyses of 6-month follow-up data indicated significantly less relapse in the relapse prevention group than in the associative therapy condition: 87% of patients in the relapse prevention condition remained improved (≥50% reduction from pretreatment), compared with 50% of the associative therapy group. On the Y-BOCS, the percentages of responders at follow-up were 75% and 33%, respectively. Interestingly, the exclusion of discussion about cognitions related to themes of personal responsibility and guilt during EX/RP somewhat attenuated the efficacy of the core treatment at 6-month follow-up in the associative therapy group specifically. The posttreatment outcome for EX/RP (66% and 60% Y-BOCS reductions for relapse prevention and associative therapy conditions, respectively) was still far superior to that reported by van Balkom et al. (1998), who also excluded cognitive interventions during the first part of their EX/RP treatment. It seems therefore that the inferior outcome in the latter study was due in the main to shorter sessions, the absence of therapist-assisted exposure, and the greater spacing of sessions.

The Hiss, Foa, and Kozak (1994) study met most of the criteria delineated earlier. Inclusion/exclusion criteria, diagnostic methods, and treatments were described clearly; treatment assignment was random; trained assessors evaluated patients using reliable and valid measures; statistical analyses were appropriate; and treatment was implemented according to accepted standards of clinical practice. Although close supervision to promote treatment integrity was discussed, treatment integrity measures were not provided.

In an attempt to further examine these seemingly disparate findings, Abramowitz, Franklin, and Foa (in press) conducted a meta-analysis in which cognitive therapies that included or did not include behavioral experiments were directly compared. Results of this meta-analysis indicated that those studies that included behavioral experiments yielded superior outcomes in comparison to those that did not. The caveats that were discussed above with respect to meta-analysis obviously apply to this study as well, but its results suggest the particular importance of the behavioral component.

EX/RP Versus Pharmacotherapy with Serotonin Reuptake Inhibitors (SRIs)

There is a vast literature supporting the relative efficacy of SRI pharmacotherapy compared to placebo for adult OCD (for a review, see Pigott and Seay, 1998). The first study that compared EX/RP to medication was conducted by Marks et al. (1980); preliminary results from this same trial had been reported earlier by Rachman et al. (1979). In a complex experimental design, 40 patients were randomly assigned to receive either clomipramine or pill placebo (PBO) for 4 weeks. Six weeks of inpatient psychological treatment (daily 45-minute sessions) followed. During the first 3 weeks of this phase, 10 patients from each medication condition received EX/RP, while the other 10 received relaxation. At Week 7, those patients who had received relaxation were switched to EX/RP, and the remaining patients continued to receive EX/RP. At the end of the 6-week psychosocial treatment period, patients were discharged from the hospital but remained on medication until Week 36, when a 4-week taper period commenced. Patients were followed for another year upon drug discontinuation. Results suggested that, compared to placebo, clomipramine produced significant improvements in mood and rituals only in those patients who were initially depressed. Compared to relaxation at Week 7, EX/RP was associated with greater reductions in rituals, but not with improvements in mood.

This study meets several of our gold standard criteria: Patients were randomly assigned to treatment conditions, blind raters assessed patients' symptoms on psychometrically acceptable measures, reasonable exclusion criteria were used, sample size (N = 40; 10 per experimental cell) was sufficient to show at least moderate-sized group differences, statistical analyses were described clearly, and the treatments were described in sufficient detail. Several methodological issues, including an overly complex experimental design, made interpretation of the findings difficult: Diagnostic methods were not described at all ("Patients were considered suitable . . . if they had handicapping obsessional-compulsive rituals," p. 6); no reference was made to assessor training on the outcome measures; no treatment adherence measures were used; and the inpatient behavior therapy condition, consisting of 45-minute daily sessions for 3 to 6 weeks (depending on treatment condition), may have employed insufficiently strict response prevention instructions ("After exposure (in session), patients were asked not to carry out rituals for the rest of the session and to resist ritualizing for a specified time thereafter," p. 8). Length of treatment session may also have been problematic, as is the lack of information regarding what patients did on the inpatient unit for 6 weeks when they were not in session. Weaknesses in the experimental design led to underestimation of changes attributable to the behavioral treatment at Week 7 (EX/RP vs. relaxation comparison), and the design did not allow for a direct comparison of clomipramine and exposure alone across the same time period. Moreover, the drug-only period was too short (4 weeks) to allow optimal assessment of the efficacy of clomipramine alone.

In a subsequent comparison of clomipramine and EX/RP in 49 obsessive compulsives (Marks et al., 1988), patients were randomized to one of four treatment conditions, three of which included CMI for approximately 6 months and one, pill placebo (PBO). One of the CMI groups received antiexposure instructions for 23 weeks, the second group had self-controlled exposure for 23 weeks, and the third group received self-controlled exposure for 8 weeks followed by therapist-aided exposure from Week 8 until Week 23; the PBO group also received self-controlled exposure for 8 weeks followed by therapist-aided exposure from Week 8 until Week 23. Inspection of the means in the PBO group at the different treatment stages revealed clear superiority for therapist-aided exposure over self-exposure. The mean reduction after 8 weeks of self-exposure was 20% for rituals and 23% for OCD-related discomfort; the mean reduction after an additional 9 sessions of therapist-aided exposure was 71% and 68%, respectively. However, in the absence of a placebo group that received therapist-aided exposure first, we cannot rule out the alternative hypothesis that order effect mediated the superiority of therapist-aided exposure. Because of confounds introduced by the complicated design, it is impossible to compare the effects of CMI with those of EX/RP.

Marks et al. (1988) provided a clear description of inclusion/exclusion criteria, employed random assignment, and utilized psychometrically acceptable outcome measures. A major problem with this study is the design adopted by the authors, which introduced major confounds. Thus, the major two questions of interest, the relative efficacy of CMI versus EX/RP and the relative efficacy of self-exposure and therapist-aided exposure, cannot be answered with certainty. Several other problems complicate interpretation of findings: Diagnostic methods were not described, treatment adherence data were not provided, treatment descriptions were sparse, and time spent on exposure homework was not reported. The latter point is especially important because of the authors' interest in the efficacy of self-exposure programs. An additional confound stems from the evaluators' ability to guess accurately 90% of the time whether patients received CMI or PBO, indicating an inadequate blinding procedure due to the evaluators' inquiry about medication side effects during assessment of OC symptoms.

With the growing interest in selective SRIs and the increased awareness of the severe side effects of CMI, Cottraux et al. (1990) compared the efficacy of another SRI, fluvoxamine (FLU) with that of EX/RP. Patients were assigned to one of three conditions: FLU with antiexposure instructions, FLU + EX/RP, and pill placebo (PBO) with EX/RP. In the antiexposure condition, patients were specifically instructed to avoid feared situations or stimuli. Treatment continued for 24 weeks, after which EX/RP was stopped and medication was tapered over 4 weeks. EX/RP treatment was provided in weekly sessions and consisted of two distinct treatment phases: self-controlled exposure between sessions and imaginal exposure during sessions for the first 8 weeks, followed by 16 weeks of therapist-guided exposure and ritual prevention. Other psychosocial interventions (e.g., couples therapy, cognitive restructuring, assertiveness training) were also provided as deemed necessary. Assessment included ratings by blind evaluators and self-report measures. At posttreatment (Week 24), reduction in assessor-rated duration of rituals per day were FLU + antiexposure 42%, FLU + EX/RP 46%, and PBO + EX/RP 25%. At 6-month follow-up, reductions in assessor-rated duration of rituals per day were FLX + antiexposure 42%, FLX + EX/RP 45%, and PBO + EX/RP 35%. While FLX + EX/RP produced slightly greater improvement in depression at posttreatment than did PBO + EX/RP, the superiority of the combined treatment for depression was not evident at follow-up. Interestingly, the FLX + antiexposure group complied minimally with therapy instructions: Most reported doing exposure on their own, thus invalidating the comparison between exposure and antiexposure with fluvoxamine.

Cottraux et al. (1990) randomly assigned patients to treatment conditions, used blind assessors, conducted appropriate nonparametric statistical analyses because of skewed distributions, provided estimates of power to detect differences on OC symptom measures, and used adequate inclusion/exclusion criteria. They did not, however, describe diagnostic methods adequately or provide treatment adherence ratings. The primary problem with this study lies in the implementation of EX/RP. EX/RP treatment description was inadequate; it was described only as "flexible," it included the use of a myriad of other techniques (e.g., couples therapy, cognitive restructuring, assertion training) on an "as-needed" basis, and ritual prevention instructions were not provided. Moreover, treatment sessions were conducted just once per week for an unspecified length of time.

In contrast to the failure to find an advantage for fluvoxamine plus EX/RP versus EX/RP alone reported by van Balkom et al. (1998), Hohagen et al. (1998) did find an advantage for EX/RP plus fluvoxamine over EX/RP plus pill placebo. Fifty-eight patients were randomly assigned to one of the two conditions, and EX/RP in both conditions involved a 3-week assessment period followed by a 4-week regimen of lengthy (3-hour minimum) thrice-weekly EX/RP. Analyses were conducted on a subset of patients (N = 49), with nine outliers dropped so that the two groups could be equated on baseline Y-BOCS severity. Results indicated that both groups improved significantly and comparably on compulsions, but that the patients who received fluvoxamine in combination with EX/RP were significantly better at posttreatment on obsessions than those who received EX/RP plus placebo. The percentage reductions on the Y-BOCS total scores were 44% for EX/RP plus PBO and 55% for EX/RP plus fluvoxamine. Additionally, subanalyses indicated that patients who suffered from secondary depression also fared better if they were receiving active medication along with EX/RP.

Hohagen et al. (1998) utilized random assignment, clearly described their inclusion/exclusion criteria, used reliable and valid assessment instruments administered by trained evaluators, manualized EX/RP treatment, and had a sufficient sample size to test their primary hypotheses. Faced with a statistical conundrum, the authors chose the relatively common method of dropping outliers in order to eliminate baseline differences in severity between the groups and then conducted all subsequent statistical analyses on the remaining subset of patients. Results using statistical methods designed for this purpose (e.g., ANCOVA) were not presented, nor did the authors indicate that they were run and equivalent to the results that were presented in the paper. Study findings provide empirical support for the use of concomitant pharmacotherapy, especially with those patients for whom obsessions predominate the clinical picture and for those with significant secondary depression.

As discussed above, previous comparisons of EX/RP and pharmacotherapy have utilized experimental designs that made direct comparisons of their relative efficacy uninterpretable (e.g., Marks et al., 1980, 1988) or examined the efficacy of antidepressant medications not known to have specific effects on OCD symptoms (e.g., Foa et al., 1992). A recently completed multicenter study conducted at the University of Pennsylvania and Columbia University endeavored to provide a clear comparison of the efficacy of CMI, intensive EX/RP, and their combination. In this study, an EX/RP program that included an intensive phase (15 two-hour sessions conducted over 3 weeks) and follow-up phase (6 brief sessions delivered over 8 weeks) was compared to CMI, EX/RP + CMI, and pill placebo (PBO). Preliminary analyses suggest that all active treatments are superior to PBO, EX/RP is more efficacious than CMI, and the combination of the two treatments is not superior to EX/RP alone (Kozak, Liebowitz, & Foa, 2000). However, the design adopted in this study may not have been appropriate for promoting an additive effect because the EX/RP program was largely completed before the effects of CMI could be realized. In the Penn-Columbia study, diagnostic status was determined by structured clinical interview, patients were randomly assigned to treatments, and assessments were conducted by trained blind evaluators. Treatments were manualized, measures of treatment adherence were included, and OCD severity was assessed on reliable and valid measures (e.g., Y-BOCS).

In summary, there is ample information about the efficacy of both SRI pharmacotherapy and EX/RP treatments, but information about their relative efficacy is scarce because most of the few studies that addressed this issue are plagued with design and procedural deficiencies. Interestingly, most of these studies failed to find clear long-term superiority for treatments that combined pharmacotherapy and EX/RP. Nevertheless, many experts advocate combined procedures as the treatment of choice for OCD (e.g, Greist, 1992).

SUMMARY AND CONCLUSIONS

Since Victor Meyer introduced treatment by exposure and response prevention in 1966, the efficacy of this treatment for OCD has been established in numerous studies. It should be noted, however, that until the middle of the 1980s, the treatment used in most outcome studies was intensive, with long therapist-assisted exposure sessions conducted daily (e.g., Foa & Goldstein, 1978; Marks et al., 1975). Rules for ritual prevention were explicit, and ritual prevention implementation was either supervised by staff members for inpatients or by designated individuals at home for outpatients (e.g., Foa et al., 1984; Meyer, Levy, & Schnurer, 1974). The results of studies using these intensive programs were extremely favorable. Increasing concerns with managed-care demands, emphasis on cost-effectiveness of treatment, and researchers' increased consciousness of developing treatment packages that can be readily disseminated may have resulted recently in reducing the number of EX/RP sessions, spacing and shortening them, and relying on instructions for self-exposure and ritual prevention. As is apparent from the above review, such attenuation resulted in the lessening of efficacy to the extent that degree of observed improvement, albeit statistically significant, often failed to reach clinical significance.

Another issue that deserves attention is the role of cognitive procedures in the treatment of OCD. Are they necessary? Are they useful? It is important to note that most cognitive experts frequently make use of behavioral experiments in treatment and that behavioral experts clearly include informal discussions of mistaken OCD beliefs. Taken together, van Balkom et al.'s study (1998) and the meta-analysis conducted by Abramowitz (1996) suggest that removing one from the other results in suboptimal outcome. Thus, the discourse about the relative advantages and disadvantages of behavioral and cognitive approaches should shift to attempts to identify which procedures are best suited for correcting identified pathological emotions or behaviors. Accordingly, the questions of interest become: Is pathological meaning underlying circumscribed fear and avoidance better modified by exposure? Is irrational guilt more amenable to change by procedures that utilize verbal discussion? Research that addresses such questions is more likely to advance our knowledge than comparison of treatments that comprise overlapping components.

With respect to other comparative studies, trials that have compared EX/RP to pharmacotherapy have yielded inconsistent findings, with differences in research methods across the various samples compromising our ability to draw firm conclusions about this issue even after 20 years of study. Hohagen and colleagues' (1998) findings suggested that there may be a subset of patients who are more likely to respond well to EX/RP if they are receiving concomitant pharmacotherapy with an SRI, which is consistent with many experts' clinical impressions as well. The few direct comparisons of medication versus EX/RP alone generally appear to favor EX/RP, which is consistent with the view of the OCD Expert Consensus Guidelines (March et al., 1997) indicating that CBT involving EX/RP ought to be the first-line treatment for most OCD cases. Studies that have examined sequencing of treatments have not been conducted yet and may be necessary to guide clinical practice with OCD patients seen in community settings.

The comparison of EX/RP and anxiety management training conducted by Lindsay et al. (1997) underscored that EX/RP procedures yield results that are above and beyond what can be expected from a good therapeutic alliance alone. We view the evidence on the whole as consistent with the message that EX/RP should be considered the treatment of choice for OCD, and that the inclusion of its essential elements (e.g., prolonged exposure, therapist-assisted exposure, strict ritual prevention goals) is likely to be necessary to maximize outcome for the majority of cases. Fals-Stewart et al.'s study (1993) suggests that group treatment may afford a more efficient means of delivering EX/RP, but further research is needed with more ill patients before this method should be recommended over individual treatment.

FUTURE DIRECTIONS

Although a great deal is already known about the efficacy of EX/RP and pharmacotherapy for OCD, some issues await further research. Several studies have indicated that OCD patients who respond to SRIs are likely to relapse when the medication is withdrawn, suggesting the need for long-term administration of this treatment. Despite this drawback of psychopharmacology, a substantial number of OCD patients prefer this treatment over EX/RP because they find the latter too frightening. Perhaps the optimal treatment for most patients should involve medication at the start followed by EX/RP implemented after medication has lessened the OCD symptoms and thereby increased the acceptability of EX/RP. A study is now under way at the University of Pennsylvania and Columbia University (Foa and Liebowitz,

PIs) in which patients who have evidenced partial response to an SRI will be randomized to either EX/RP or stress management training (SMT) so that the augmentative effects of these two cognitive behavioral approaches can be examined. Other augmentation strategies have also been evaluated, such as pharmacotherapy with an atypical neuroleptic (McDougal et al., 2000); these alternatives are important to consider with patients who have substantial residual symptoms following SRI pharmacotherapy yet will not accept or do not have access to EX/RP.

As is apparent from the above review, many variants of EX/RP programs have been utilized in outcome studies, but the effects of the different parameters on treatment outcome have not been studied systematically. Studies comparing intensive versus weekly EX/RP protocols, both consisting of treatment components believed to be important (e.g., imaginal and in vivo exposure, strict ritual prevention, therapist-assisted exposure), will help determine the degree to which outcome is compromised simply by decreasing frequency of sessions. Preliminary results of a comparison of twice-weekly EX/RP treatment to findings from an otherwise identical intensive (daily) EX/RP regimen suggest superior outcome for the intensive treatment at posttreatment but not at 3-month follow-up (Abramowitz et al., 2000), a finding that suggests the possibility that twice weekly EX/RP may be a viable alternative to intensive treatment. We also need more studies comparing therapist-aided exposure and self-exposure before advocating reduction of therapist contact. Early investigations did address some of these issues, but their methodologies were flawed, and the number of patients was too small to allow firm conclusions.

Researchers have already identified several factors that are associated with poor outcome of EX/RP and medication (e.g., presence of schizotypal personality disorder; Minichiello, Baer, & Jenike, 1987). More recent studies have also suggested that severe overvalued ideation (Foa et al., 1999) and severe depression (Abramowitz et al., 2000) may also attenuate outcome somewhat. These patient characteristics must therefore be evaluated and taken into account by EX/RP therapists. Further, given that psychiatric comorbidity appears to be the rule, studies are needed to examine the best way to treat these OCD patients. Several alternative strategies may be used, such as treating the comorbid condition, then addressing OCD, but the evidence base for the treatment of OCD patients with substantial psychiatric comorbidity remains weak.

Another area that needs to be addressed further is the treatment of pediatric OCD with EX/RP. As is typical in psychology and psychiatry, the evidence base supporting adult treatments is far advanced relative to pediatrics, although the initial pilot studies on EX/RP have been quite encouraging (Franklin et al., 1998; March, Mulle, & Herbel, 1994; Wever & Rey, 1997). A direct comparison of EX/RP and clomipramine in children and adolescents (de Haan et al., 1998) paralleled the adult findings reported by Kozak et al. (2000): EX/RP was clearly superior to clomipramine, and the posttreatment mean Children's Y-BOCS score for the EX/RP group was well into the subclinical range. Two randomized controlled trials currently under way may further advance our knowledge of the efficacy of CBT for children and adolescents with OCD: One study is comparing EX/RP to a relaxation control condition (for further details see Piacentini, 1999), and the other is a comparison of the immediate and long-term efficacy of EX/RP, sertraline, combined treatment, and pill placebo (see March, Franklin, Nelson, & Foa, 2001). When these studies are completed, future research should be brought to bear on the issue of augmentation strategies for pediatric patients who have exhibited a partial response to SRI pharmacotherapy.

Despite overwhelming evidence of its efficacy, EX/RP's availability for adults and children continues to be limited. The paucity of therapists trained in its use may be a function, at least in part, of OCD's relatively low prevalence, as it may be difficult to develop expertise in this form of treatment if OCD patients are only occasionally encountered in one's general-practice clinic. Effectiveness studies that include extensive training of front-line clinicians followed by access to expert supervision may help us to overcome this shortage of trained treatment providers. The dissemination of less intensive treatment regimens may also help to increase the use of EX/RP, as intensive therapy may be rejected on practical grounds by clinicians and patients alike. Instead of such widespread dissemination efforts, another alternative to make EX/RP more available would be to support the development of regional centers of expertise that would function as many cancer treatment centers currently do: working actively with referral sources to solicit and accept cases, providing training opportunities for those who wish to specialize, and attempting to ensure that excellent clinical care is available for patients and their families within a reasonable distance from home. It is likely that endeavors such as these will be attempted in the next decade, as it is unfortunately the case that EX/RP remains largely an ivory-tower treatment that is not easily accessed by many of those who might benefit from it most.

ACKNOWLEDGMENT This chapter was supported by NIMH grants MH45404 and MH55126. We wish to thank Nicole Dorfan for her assistance with the preparation of this manuscript.

References

Abramowitz, J. S. (1996). Variants of exposure and response prevention in the treatment of obsessive-compulsive disorder: A meta-analysis. *Behavior Therapy, 27*, 583–600.

Abramowitz, J. S., Franklin, M. E., Filip, J. C., & Foa, E. B. (2000). *Spacing of sessions in the treatment of OCD*. Presented at the 34th annual meeting of the Association for the Advancement of Behavior Therapy, New York.

Abramowitz, J. S., Franklin, M. E., & Foa, E. B. (in press). Empirical status of cognitive methods in the treatment of OCD. In M. H. Freeston & S. Taylor (Eds.), *Cognitive approaches to treating obsessions and compulsions: A clinical casebook*. Mahwah, NJ: Erlbaum.

Abramowitz, J. S., Franklin, M. E., Street, G. P., Kozak, M. J., & Foa, E. B. (2000). The effects of pre-treatment depression on cognitive-behavioral treatment outcome in OCD clinic outpatients. *Behavior Therapy, 31*, 517–528.

American Psychiatric Association. (1987). *Diagnostic and statistical manual of mental disorders* (3rd ed., rev.). Washington, DC: Author.

American Psychiatric Association. (1994). *Diagnostic and statistical manual of mental disorders*. (4th ed.). Washington, DC: Author.

Beck, A. T. (1976). *Cognitive therapy and the emotional disorders*. New York: International Universities Press.

Beck, A. T., Ward, C. H., Mendelson, M., Mock, J., & Erbaugh, J. (1961). An inventory for measuring depression. *Archives of General Psychiatry, 4*, 561–571.

Carr, A. T. (1974). Compulsive neurosis: A review of the literature. *Psychological Bulletin, 81*, 311–318.

Cottraux, J., Mollard, E., Bouvard, M., Marks, I., Sluys, M., Nury, A. M., Douge, R., & Ciadella, P. (1990). A controlled study of fluvoxamine and exposure in obsessive-compulsive disorder. *International Clinical Psychopharmacology, 5*, 17–30.

Cox, B. J., Swinson, R. P., Morrison, B., & Lee, P. S. (1993). Clomipramine, fluoxetine, and behavior therapy in the treatment of obsessive-compulsive disorder: A meta-analysis. *Journal of Behavior Therapy and Experimental Psychiatry, 24*, 149–153.

de Araujo, L. A., Ito, L. M., Marks, I. M., & Deale, A. (1995). Does imagined exposure to the consequences of not ritualising enhance live exposure for OCD? A controlled study. 1. Main outcome. *British Journal of Psychiatry, 167*, 65–70.

de Haan, E., Hoogduin, C. A. L., Buitelaar, J. K., & Keijsers, G. P. J. (1998). Behavior therapy versus clomipramine for the treatment of obsessive-compulsive disorder in children and adolescents. *Journal of the American Academy of Child and Adolescent Psychiatry, 37*, 1022–1029.

DeVeaugh-Geiss, J., Landau, P., & Katz, R. (1989). Treatment of obsessive compulsive disorder with clomipramine. *Psychiatric Annals, 19*, 97–101.

Dollard, J., & Miller, N. E. (1950). *Personality and psychotherapy: An analysis in terms of learning, thinking and culture*. New York: McGraw Hill.

Eichstedt, J. A., & Arnold, S. L. (2001). Childhood-onset obsessive-compulsive disorder: A tic-related subtype of OCD? *Clinical Psychology Review, 21*, 137–158.

Ellis, A. (1962). *Reason and emotion in psychotherapy*. New York: Lyle Stuart Press.

Emmelkamp, P. M. G., & Beens, H. (1991). Cognitive therapy with obsessive-compulsive disorder: A comparative evaluation. *Behaviour Research and Therapy, 29*, 293–300.

Emmelkamp, P. M. G., de Haan, E., & Hoogduin, C. A. L. (1990). Marital adjustment and obsessive-compulsive disorder. *British Journal of Psychiatry, 156*, 55–60.

Emmelkamp, P. M. G., van der Helm, M., van Zanten, B. L., & Ploch, I. (1980). Treatment of obsessive-compulsive patients: The contribution of self-instructional training to the effectiveness of exposure. *Behaviour Research and Therapy, 18*, 61–66.

Emmelkamp, P. M. G., Visser, S., & Hoekstra, R. J. (1988). Cognitive therapy vs. exposure *in vivo* in the treatment of obsessive-compulsives. *Cognitive Therapy and Research, 12*, 103–114.

Fals-Stewart, W., Marks, A. P., & Schafer, J. (1993). A comparison of behavioral group therapy and individual behavior therapy in treating obsessive-compulsive disorder. *Journal of Nervous and Mental Disease, 181*, 189–193.

Fernandez-Cordoba, E., & Lopez-Ibor Alino, J. (1967). Monochlorimipramine in mental patients resisting other forms of treatment. *Actas Luso-Espanolas de Neurologia y Psiquitria, 26,* 119–147.

Flament, M. F., Koby, E., Rapoport, J. L., Berg, C. J., Zahn, T., Cox, C., Denckla, M., & Lenane, M. (1990). Childhood obsessive-compulsive disorder: A prospective follow-up study. *Journal of Child Psychology and Psychiatry and Allied Disciplines, 31,* 363–380.

Flament, M. F., Whitaker, A., Rapoport, J. L., Davies, M., Zaremba, C., Kalikow, K., Sceery, W., & Shaffer, D. (1988). Obsessive compulsive disorder in adolescence: An epidemiological study. *Journal of the American Academy of Child and Adolescent Psychiatry, 27,* 764–771.

Foa, E. B., Abramowitz, J. S., Franklin, M. E., & Kozak, M. J. (1999). Feared consequences, fixity of belief, and treatment outcome in OCD. *Behavior Therapy, 30,* 717–724.

Foa, E. B., Franklin, M. E., & Kozak, M. J. (1998). Psychosocial treatments of obsessive compulsive disorder. In R. Swinson, M. Antony, S. Rachman, & M. Richter (Eds.), *Obsessive-compulsive disorder: Theory, research, and treatment* (pp. 258–276). New York: Guilford Press.

Foa, E. B., & Goldstein, A. (1978). Continuous exposure and complete response prevention in the treatment of obsessive-compulsive neurosis. *Behavior Therapy, 9,* 821–829.

Foa, E. B., & Kozak, M. J. (1985). Treatment of anxiety disorders: Implications for psychopathology. In A. H. Tuma & J. D. Maser (Eds.), *Anxiety and the anxiety disorders* (pp. 421–452). Hillsdale, NY: Erlbaum.

Foa, E. B., & Kozak, M. J. (1986). Emotional processing of fear: Exposure to corrective information. *Psychological Bulletin, 99,* 20–35.

Foa, E. B., & Kozak, M. J. (1996). Psychological treatment for obsessive-compulsive disorder. In M. R. Mavissakalian & R. F. Prien (Eds.), *Long-term treatments of anxiety disorders* (pp. 285–309). Washington, DC: American Psychiatric Press.

Foa, E. B., Kozak, M. J., Goodman, W. K., Hollander, E., Jenike, M., & Rasmussen, S. (1995). *DSM-IV* field trial: Obsessive-compulsive disorder. *American Journal of Psychiatry, 152,* 90–94.

Foa, E. B., Kozak, M. J., Steketee, G. S., & McCarthy, P. R. (1992). Treatment of depressive and obsessive-compulsive symptoms in OCD by imipramine and behavior therapy. *British Journal of Clinical Psychology, 31,* 279–292.

Foa, E. B., Steketee, G., Grayson, J. B., Turner, R. M., & Latimer, P. (1984). Deliberate exposure and blocking of obsessive-compulsive rituals: Immediate and long-term effects. *Behavior Therapy, 15,* 450–472.

Foa, E. B., Steketee, G. S., & Milby, J. B. (1980). Differential effects of exposure and response prevention in obsessive-compulsive washers. *Journal of Consulting and Clinical Psychology, 48,* 71–79.

Foa, E. B., Steketee, G., Turner, R. M., & Fischer, S. C. (1980). Effects of imaginal exposure to feared disasters in obsessive-compulsive checkers. *Behaviour Research and Therapy, 18,* 449–455.

Foa, E. B., & Tillmanns, A. (1980). The treatment of obsessive-compulsive neurosis. In A. Goldstein & E. B. Foa (Eds.), *Handbook of behavioral interventions: A clinical guide* (pp. 416–500). New York: Wiley.

Franklin, M. E., Abramowitz, J. S., Kozak, M. J., Levitt, J., & Foa, E. B. (2000). Effectiveness of exposure and ritual prevention for obsessive compulsive disorder: Randomized compared with non-randomized samples. *Journal of Consulting and Clinical Psychology, 68,* 594–602.

Franklin, M. E., Kozak, M. J., Cashman, L., Coles, M., Rheingold, A., & Foa, E. B. (1998). Cognitive behavioral treatment of pediatric obsessive compulsive disorder: An open clinical trial. *Journal of the American Academy of Child and Adolescent Psychiatry, 37,* 412–419.

Greist, J. H. (1992). An integrated approach to treatment of obsessive compulsive disorder. *Journal of Clinical Psychiatry, 53,* 38–41.

Greist, J. H., Jefferson, J. W., Kobak, K. A., Katzelnick, D. J., & Serlin, R. C. (1995). Efficacy and tolerability of serotonin transport inhibitors in obsessive-compulsive disorder: A meta-analysis. *Archives of General Psychiatry, 52,* 53–60.

Hanna, G. L. (1995). Demographic and clinical features of obsessive-compulsive disorder in children and adolescents. *Journal of the American Academy of Child and Adolescent Psychiatry, 34,* 19–27.

Hiss, H., Foa, E. B., & Kozak, M. J. (1994). Relapse prevention program for treatment of obsessive-compulsive disorder. *Journal of Consulting and Clinical Psychology, 62,* 801–808.

Hodgson, R., & Rachman, S. (1977). Obsessional compulsive complaints. *Behaviour Research and Therapy, 15,* 389 395.

Hohagen, F., Winkelman, G., Rasche-Rauchale, H., Hand, I., Konig, A., Munchau, N., Hiss, H., Geiger-Kabisch, C., Kappler, C., Schramm, P., Rey, E., Aldenhoff, J., & Berger, M. (1998). Combination of behaviour therapy with fluvoxamine in comparison with behaviour therapy and placebo: Results of a multicentre study. *British Journal of Psychiatry, 173,* 71–78.

Insel, T. R., & Akiskal, H. S. (1986). Obsessive-compulsive disorder with psychotic features: A phenomenologic analysis. *American Journal of Psychiatry, 143*, 1527–1533.

Insel, T. R., Mueller, E. A., Alterman, I., Linnoila, M., & Murphy, D. L. (1985). Obsessive-compulsive disorder and serotonin: Is there a connection? *Biological Psychiatry, 20*, 1174–1188.

Insel, T. R., Murphy, D. L., Cohen, R. M., Alterman, I. S., Kilts., C., & Linnoila, M. (1983). Obsessive-compulsive disorder: A double-blind trial of clomipramine and clorgyline. *Archives of General Psychiatry, 40*, 605–612.

Joffe, R. T., & Swinson, R. P. (1991). *Biological aspects of obsessive compulsive disorder*. Paper presented at a meeting of the *DSM-IV* Task Force on obsessive compulsive disorder.

Karno, M., Golding, J. M., Sorenson, S. B., & Burnam, M. A. (1988). The epidemiology of obsessive-compulsive disorder in five US communities. *Archives of General Psychiatry, 45*, 1094–1099.

Kozak, M. J., & Foa, E. B. (1994). Obsessions, overvalued ideas, and delusions in obsessive-compulsive disorder. *Behaviour Research and Therapy, 32*, 343–353.

Kozak, M. J., & Foa, E. B. (1996). Obsessive compulsive disorder. In V. B. Van Hasselt & M. Hersen (Eds.), *Sourcebook of psychological treatment manuals for adult disorders* (pp. 65–122). New York: Plenum Press.

Kozak, M. J., Liebowitz, M. R., & Foa, E. B. (2000). Cognitive behavior therapy and pharmacotherapy for OCD: The NIMH-Sponsored Collaborative Study. In W. Goodman, M. Rudorfer, & J. Maser (Eds.), *Obsessive compulsive disorder: Contemporary issues in treatment* (pp. 501–530). Mahwah, NJ: Erlbaum.

Lelliott, P. T., Noshirvani, H. F., Basoglu, M., Marks, I. M., & Monteiro, W. O. (1988). Obsessive-compulsive beliefs and treatment outcome. *Psychological Medicine, 18*, 697–702.

Leon, A. C., Portera, L., & Weissman, M. M. (1995). The social costs of anxiety disorders. *British Journal of Psychiatry, 166*(Supp 27), 19–22.

Lindsay, M., Crino, R., & Andrews, G. (1997). Controlled trial of exposure and response prevention in obsessive-compulsive disorder. *British Journal of Psychiatry, 171*, 135–139.

March, J. S., Frances, A., Carpenter, D., & Kahn, D. (1997). The Expert Consensus Guideline Series: Treatment of obsessive compulsive disorder. *Journal of Clinical Psychiatry, 58*, Supplement 4.

March, J. S., Franklin, M. E., Nelson, A. H., & Foa, E. B. (2001). Cognitive-behavioral psychotherapy for pediatric obsessive-compulsive disorder. *Journal of Clinical Child Psychology, 30*, 8–18.

March, J. S., Mulle, K., & Herbel, B. (1994). Behavioral psychotherapy for children and adolescents with obsessive-compulsive disorder: An open trial of a new protocol-driven treatment package. *Journal of the American Academy of Child and Adolescent Psychiatry, 33*, 333–341.

Marks, I. M., Hodgson, R., & Rachman, S. (1975). Treatment of chronic obsessive-compulsive neurosis by in vivo exposure. *British Journal of Psychiatry, 127*, 349–364.

Marks, I. M., Lelliott, P. T., Basoglu, M., Noshirvani, H., Monteiro, W., Cohen, D., & Kasvikis, Y. (1988). Clomipramine, self-exposure and therapist-aided exposure for obsessive-compulsive rituals. *British Journal of Psychiatry, 152*, 522–534.

Marks, I. M., Stern, R. S., Mawson, D., Cobb, J., & McDonald, R. (1980). Clomipramine and exposure for obsessive-compulsive rituals—1. *British Journal of Psychiatry, 136*, 1–25.

McDougal, C. J., Epperson, C. N., Pelton, G. H., Wasylink, S., & Price, L. H. (2000). A double-blind, placebo-controlled study of risperidone addition in serotonin reuptake inhibitor-refractory obsessive-compulsive disorder. *Archives of General Psychiatry, 57*, 794–801.

McFall, M. E., & Wollersheim, J. P. (1979). Obsessive-compulsive neurosis: A cognitive behavioral formulation and approach to treatment. *Cognitive Therapy and Research, 3*, 333–348.

Mehta, M. (1990). A comparative study of family-based and patients-based behavioural management in obsessive-compulsive disorder. *British Journal of Psychiatry, 157*, 133–135.

Meichenbaum, D. (1974). Self-instructional methods. In F. H. Kanfer & A. P. Goldstein (Eds.), *Helping people change*. New York: Pergamon Press.

Meyer, V. (1966). Modification of expectations in cases with obsessional rituals. *Behaviour Research and Therapy, 4*, 273–280.

Meyer, V., & Levy, R. (1973). Modification of behavior in obsessive-compulsive disorders. In H. E. Adams & P. Unikel (Eds.), *Issues and trends in behavior therapy* (pp. 77–136). Springfield, IL: Charles C Thomas.

Meyer, V., Levy, R., & Schnurer, A. (1974). The behavioural treatment of obsessive-compulsive disorders. In H. R. Beech (Ed.), *Obsessional states* (pp. 233–258). London: Methuen.

Minichiello, W. E., Baer, L., & Jenike, M. A. (1987). Schizotypal personality disorder: A poor prognostic indicator for behavior therapy in the treatment of obsessive-compulsive disorder. *Journal of Anxiety Disorders, 1*, 273–276.

Mowrer, O. H. (1939). A stimulus-response analysis of anxiety and its role as a reinforcing agent. *Psychological Review, 46*, 553–565.

Mowrer, O. H. (1960). *Learning theory and behavior.* New York: Wiley.

Pato, M. T., Zohar-Kadouch, R., Zohar, J., & Murphy, D. L. (1988). Return of symptoms after discontinuation of clomipramine in patients with obsessive-compulsive disorder. *American Journal of Psychiatry, 145*, 1521–1525.

Piacentini, J. (1999). Cognitive behavioral therapy of childhood OCD. *Child and Adolescent Psychiatric Clinics of North America, 8*, 599–617.

Pitman, R. (1994). Obsessive compulsive disorder in western history. In E. Hollander, J. Zohar, D. Marazziti, & B. Olivier (Eds.), *Current insights in obsessive compulsive disorder* (pp. 3–10). New York: Wiley.

Rabavilas, A. D., Boulougouris, J. C., & Stefanis, C. (1976). Duration of flooding sessions in the treatment of obsessive-compulsive patients. *Behaviour Research and Therapy, 14*, 349–355.

Rachman, S., Cobb, J., Grey, S., McDonald, B., Mawson, D., Sartory, G., & Stern, R. (1979). The behavioural treatment of obsessional-compulsive disorders, with and without clomipramine. *Behaviour Research and Therapy, 17*, 467–478.

Rachman, S. J., & Wilson, G. T. (1980). *The effects of psychological therapy.* Oxford, UK: Pergamon Press.

Rapoport, J. L., Swedo, S. E., & Leonard, H. L. (1992). Childhood obsessive compulsive disorder. *Journal of Clinical Psychiatry, 53*(4, Suppl), 11–16.

Rasmussen, S. A., & Eisen, J. L. (1989). Clinical features and phenomenology of obsessive compulsive disorder. *Psychiatric Annals, 19*, 67–73.

Rasmussen, S. A., & Eisen, J. L. (1990). Epidemiology of obsessive compulsive disorder. *Journal of Clinical Psychiatry, 51*(2, Suppl), 10–13.

Rasmussen, S. A., & Tsuang, M. T. (1986). Clinical characteristics and family history in *DSM-III* obsessive-compulsive disorder. *American Journal of Psychiatry, 143*, 317–322.

Riggs, D. S., Hiss, H., & Foa, E. B. (1992). Marital distress and the treatment of obsessive compulsive disorder. *Behavior Therapy, 23*, 585–597.

Roper, G., & Rachman, S. (1976). Obsessional-compulsive checking: Experimental replication and development. *Behaviour Research and Therapy, 14*, 25–32.

Roper, G., Rachman, S., & Hodgson, R. (1973). An experiment of obsessional checking. *Behaviour Research and Therapy, 11*, 271–277.

Roper, G., Rachman, S., & Marks, I. (1975). Passive and participant modelling in exposure treatment of obsessive-compulsive neurotics. *Behaviour Research and Therapy, 13*, 271–279.

Rothbaum, B. O., & Shahar, F. (2000). Behavioral treatment of obsessive-compulsive disorder in a naturalistic setting. *Cognitive and Behavioral Practice, 7*, 262–270.

Salkovskis, P. M. (1985). Obsessional compulsive problems: A cognitive behavioral analysis. *Behaviour Research and Therapy, 23*, 571–583.

Stampfl, T. G., & Levis, D. J. (1967). Essentials of implosive therapy: A learning-theory-based psychodynamic behavioral therapy. *Journal of Abnormal Psychology, 72*, 496–503.

Steketee, G. (1993). Social support and treatment outcome of obsessive compulsive disorder at 9-month follow-up. *Behavioural Psychotherapy, 21*, 81–95.

Steketee, G. S., Foa, E. B., & Grayson, J. B. (1982). Recent advances in the treatment of obsessive-compulsives. *Archives of General Psychiatry, 39*, 1365–1371.

Stern, R. S., Marks, I. M., Wright, J., & Luscombe, D. K. (1980). Clomipramine: Plasma levels, side effects and outcome in obsessive-compulsive neurosis. *Post Graduate Medical Journal, 56*, 134–139.

Swedo, S. E., Leonard, H. L., Garvey, M., Mittleman, B., Allen, A. J., Perlmutter, S., Dow, S., Zamkoff, J., Dubbert, B. K., & Lougee, L. (1998). Pediatric autoimmune neuropsychiatric disorders associated with streptococcal infections: Clinical description of the first 50 cases. *American Journal of Psychiatry, 155*, 264–271.

Swedo, S. E., Rapoport, J. L., Leonard, H. L., Lenane, M., & Cheslow, D. (1989). Obsessive-compulsive disorder in children and adolescents: Clinical phenomenology of 70 consecutive cases. *Archives of General Psychiatry, 46*, 335–341.

Valleni-Basile, L. A., Garrison, C. Z., Jackson, K. L., Waller, J. L., McKeown, R. E., Addy, C. L., & Cuffe, S. P. (1994). Frequency of obsessive-compulsive disorder in a community sample of young adolescents. *Journal of the American Academy of Child and Adolescent Psychiatry, 33*, 782–791.

van Balkom, A. J. L. M., de Haan, E., van Oppen, P., Spinhoven, P., Hoogduin, K. A. L., & van Dyk, R. (1998). Cognitive and behavioral therapies alone versus in combination with fluvoxamine in the treatment of obsessive-compulsive disorder. *Journal of Nervous and Mental Disease, 186*, 492–499.

van Balkom, A. J. L. M., van Oppen, P., Vermeulen, A. W. A., van Dyck, R., Nauta, M. C. E., & Vorst, H. C. M. (1994). A meta-analysis on the treatment of obsessive compulsive disorder: A comparison of antidepressants, behavior, and cognitive therapy. *Clinical Psychology Review*, *5*, 359–381.

Watts, F. N. (1973). Desensitization as an habituation phenomenon: II. Studies of interstimulus interval length. *Psychological Reports*, *33*, 715–718.

Weizman, A., Carmi, M., Hermesh, H., Shahar, A., Apter, A., Tyano, S., & Rehavi, M. (1986). High-affinity imipramine binding and serotonin uptake in platelets of eight adolescent and ten adult obsessive-compulsive patients. *American Journal of Psychiatry*, *143*, 335–339.

Wever, C., & Rey, J. M. (1997). Juvenile obsessive-compulsive disorder. *Australian and New Zealand Journal of Psychiatry*, *31*, 105–113.

Zohar, J., & Insel, T. R. (1987). Drug treatment of obsessive-compulsive disorder. Special Issue: Drug treatment of anxiety disorders. *Journal of Affective Disorders*, *13*, 193–202.

16

Pharmacological Treatments for Obsessive Compulsive Disorder

Darin D. Dougherty
Scott L. Rauch
Michael A. Jenike

There is overwhelming evidence of the most rigorous type (many Type 1 studies) supporting the efficacy of serotonin reuptake inhibitors (SRIs) in the treatment of obsessive compulsive disorder (OCD). Along with SRIs, behavior therapy must be considered a viable first-line therapy. The best available data from several Type 1 studies suggest that behavior therapy is at least as effective as medication in some instances and may be superior with respect to risks, costs, and enduring benefits. A variety of second-line medication treatments for OCD have been studied in a controlled or systematic fashion. Augmentation of SRIs with clonazepam or buspirone, and with high-potency neuroleptics in cases of a comorbid tic disorder, is provisionally recommended based on the marginal available data. Other augmentation strategies find very limited support at present. Alternative monotherapies, including buspirone, clonazepam, and phenelzine, have all been the subject of positive controlled or partially controlled (Type 1 and Type 2) studies. However, the quality of these data make recommendations for these strategies tentative as well, pending additional information.

DIAGNOSTIC CRITERIA AND CLINICAL CHARACTERISTICS

Obsessive compulsive disorder (OCD) is a common condition, with lifetime prevalence estimates of approximately 2 to 3% in the United States and 0.5 to 5.5% worldwide (Angst, 1994; Rasmussen & Eisen, 1994; Karno, Golding, Sorenson, & Burnam, 1988). Classified among the anxiety disorders, the hallmark signs and symptoms of OCD include intrusive unwanted thoughts (i.e., obsessions) and repetitive behaviors (i.e., compulsions) (American Psychiatric Association [APA], 1994). Classic obsessions include violent, religious, or sexual themes, as well as preoccupations with contamination, pathological doubting or uncertainty, concerns with symmetry, and a general sense that something bad will happen if a particular ritual is not performed in precisely the right manner. Classic compulsions include washing, cleaning, counting, checking, repeating, and arranging behaviors. For most, the disease manifests itself as multiple obsessions and multiple compulsions (Rasmussen & Eisen, 1994). Experiencing occasional unwanted thoughts, performing repetitive or ritualistic behaviors, and having transient feelings of anxiety are all part of normal human experience; however, in order to meet the criteria for OCD the symptoms must be sufficiently intense or frequent to cause marked distress or impair functioning. In fact, people with OCD are often severely impaired by the symptoms of their disease. Unlike psychosis, OCD is characterized by intact insight; because people with OCD recognize that their thoughts and behaviors are extreme or nonsensical, they are often embarrassed or ashamed of their condition and frightened that they may be "going crazy." In severe cases of OCD, insight can become tenuous as obsessions progress to overvalued ideas, prompting the special diagnostic designation of "OCD with poor insight" (American Psychiatric Association [APA], 1994).

The differential diagnosis of OCD includes other psychiatric disorders that are characterized by repetitive thoughts or behaviors. For instance, the obsessions of OCD are to be distinguished from the ruminations of major depression, the racing thoughts of mania, the psychotic thoughts of schizophrenia, and the preoccupation with food and body image associated with eating disorders. Likewise, the compulsions of OCD are to be distinguished from the tics of Tourette syndrome (TS), the ritualized self-injurious behaviors of borderline personality disorder, the rhythmic movements that can present in autism or mental retardation, and the stereotypes of complex partial seizures. By definition, the diagnosis of OCD should not be made if the symptoms can be attributed to another disorder or are the consequence of substance use (APA, 1994).

Although the current diagnostic scheme classifies OCD as an anxiety disorder, a variety of disorders from other categories within *DSM-IV* are also characterized by repetitive symptoms (Hollander, 1993; Hollander et al., 1996; McElroy, Phillips, & Keck, 1994). The term *obsessive compulsive spectrum disorders (OCSD)* has been coined to reflect the notion that a family of similar disorders may exist that share some common phenomenological, etiological, and perhaps pathophysiological characteristics. Such OCSDs include TS (characterized by intrusive sensations and urges, as well as a drive to perform motor and vocal tics), trichotillomania (characterized by compulsive hair pulling), and body dysmorphic disorder (characterized by a preoccupation with certain aspects of one's own appearance). It remains to be seen whether the concept of OCSDs will prove clinically useful or neurobiologically valid, as well as which disorders can be meaningfully grouped together and by what criteria. Comorbidity with OCD is common; in addition to other OCSDs, frequently coexisting conditions include major affective disorders, other anxiety disorders, and substance use disorders (Karno et al., 1988; Rasmussen & Eisen, 1994).

ETIOLOGY AND NEUROBIOLOGY

The cause of OCD remains unknown. However, family-genetic studies suggest that there may be multiple etiological subtypes (e.g., Pauls & Leckman, 1986; Pauls et al., 1995). Specifically, family-genetic studies indicate that in some cases, OCD arises sporadically, whereas in others, there exists an apparent familial relationship suggestive of an autosomal dominant mode of inheritance with incomplete penetrance. In cohorts where a familial relationship is present, in some cases the affected members present with only OCD, whereas in other pedigrees the affected individuals have OCD or a tic disorder or both. The apparent phenomenological and familial overlap between OCD and TS extends to neurobiology as well. Again, although the pathophysiology of these disorders is incompletely understood, for both OCD and TS contemporary neurobiological models implicate dysfunction in one or another of several segregated corticostriatal pathways (Baxter et al., 1990; Insel, 1992; Rapoport & Wise, 1988; Rauch & Jenike, 1993; Rauch et al., 1998). OCD seems to involve subtle structural abnormalities in the caudate nucleus, as well as functional dysregulation of neural circuits comprising orbitofrontal cortex, cingulate cortex, and the caudate. Similarly, TS seems to involve subtle structural abnormalities in the putamen. In this way, OCD can be conceptualized as a disease involving cognitive and paralimbic corticostriatal networks, while TS involves a sensorimotor corticostriatal network (see Rauch et al., 1998, for review). Recent research suggests that autoimmune processes, precipitated in some cases by beta-hemolytic streptococcal infection, may cause damage to striatal neurons in occasional sporadic childhood-onset cases of OCD and TS (Allen et al., 1995; Swedo, 1994; Swedo et al., 1994, 1998). Neurochemically, serotonergic systems have been implicated in OCD (Rauch et al., 1998), whereas dopaminergic systems have been implicated in TS (e.g., Mallison et al., 1995). This reflects the neurochemistry of the projections to the relevant striatal territories and also parallels what has been observed regarding the effective pharmacotherapy for these disorders (see Rauch et al., 1998).

OCD: A HISTORICAL PERSPECTIVE

Descriptions of probable OCD date back to the fifteenth century, and up through the 1700s, the malady was conceptualized in religious or supernatural terms (Pitman, 1994; Hunter & Macalpine, 1982). Treatments such as exorcism not withstanding, clinical reports and attempts to medically or scientifically characterize OCD did not emerge until the late 1800s, when neurologists, including Georges Gilles de la Tourette (1885), described OCD symptoms in the context of movement disorders. In the early 1900s, other clinicians contributed eloquent phenomenological descriptions of obsessive-compulsive symptoms (Janet, 1903; Meige & Feindel, 1902), but little progress was made toward effective treatment of OCD. Freud's case of the Rat Man (1909/1924) introduced the application of psychodynamic principles in attempts to both understand and relieve what he termed obsessional neurosis.

It was not until 1967 that the tricyclic antidepressant clomipramine (CMI), the first available serotonergic reuptake inhibitor (SRI), emerged as an effective treatment for OCD (Fernandez & Lopez-Ibor, 1967). Contemporaneously, behavioral therapy for OCD was emerging as a viable treatment modality and the object of formal study (Rachman et al., 1971). Interestingly, it was also in the 1960s that Ballantine and colleagues (1987) first began their pioneering efforts to systematically study the safety and efficacy of anterior cingulotomy, a neurosurgical treatment for severe treatment-refractory OCD and other psychiatric illnesses.

The subsequent quarter century has seen great development in the assessment and treatment of OCD. Several educational and self-help books written for lay audiences (e.g., Baer, 1991; Rapoport, 1989), articles appearing in the general medical literature (Jenike, 1989), and the birth of an advocacy group (OC Foundation, Inc., PO Box 70, Milford, CT 06460–0070; 203-878-5669) all contributed to a growing awareness of OCD. Whereas it had still been believed that OCD was a relatively rare disorder (~0.1% lifetime prevalence), publication of ECA study results (Karno et al., 1988) surprised much of the psychiatric and public health community by suggesting that OCD had a lifetime prevalence of 2.6%, ranking as the fourth most common psychiatric illness in the United States. In 1989, a collaborative group of investigators from Yale and Brown Universities published studies reporting on the validation of a scale for quantifying the severity of OCD symptoms (Goodman et al., 1989a, 1989b). The Yale-Brown Obsessive Compulsive Scale (Y-BOCS) has since become the gold standard measure for many of the clinical trials that followed. During this same era, the pharmaceutical industry produced a new class of compounds known as selective serotonergic reuptake inhibitors (SSRIs) that, like CMI, acted via blockade of serotonergic reuptake sites. Unlike CMI, however, these new SSRIs had much lower affinities for adrenergic and cholinergic receptors, presumably conferring upon them a more favorable side effect profile. Investigators in psychopharmacology proceeded to systematically study these new agents, as well as other novel compounds, while their psychotherapist counterparts conducted investigations of cognitive and behavioral treatments. Since the early 1990s, there have been over 1,500 reports about drug treatments and OCD published in medical sources. Moreover, during the 1990s, the decade of the brain, neuroscience advances have brought us closer to understanding the etiology and pathophysiology of OCD and related disorders.

CONTEMPORARY TREATMENT FOR OCD

Numerous reviews have been written in the last few years regarding treatment recommendations for OCD (e.g., Dominguez & Mestre, 1994; Goodman et al., 1992; Jenike 1993a, 1993b, 1998a; Jenike & Rauch, 1994; Montgomery, 1994; Rauch & Jenike, 1994; see Table 16.1). There is broad agreement among experts in the field that first-line treatments for OCD include SRIs (CMI or SSRIs) and/or behavior therapy. When these first-line interventions fail, second-line pharmacological approaches include augmentation of SRIs with additional medications or trials of alternative medications as monotherapies in place of SRIs. Third-line treatments may include experimental treatments such as unproven augmentation therapies or intravenous CMI if available (Fallon et al., 1992, 1998; Koran et al., 1997; Warneke, 1989). Finally, other nonpharmacological treatments, including neurosurgery and electroconvulsive therapy (ECT), have remained more controversial and are reserved for particular clinical situations or as treatments of last resort. In the following section, the scientific evidentiary basis for these various treatment recommendations is reviewed. Although the focus in this chapter is on psychopharmacology, the authors

TABLE 16.1 Sample Treatment Recommendations for Obsessive Compulsive Disorder

Treatment	*Dosage*	*Time Course*
First Line		
Behavior Therapy		
Exposure and response prevention		at least 20 hours
Medication: Serial SRI Trials (consider at least 2 SSRI trials and one of CMI)		
CMI	150–250 mg/day	12 weeks
Fluoxetine	40–80 mg/day	12 weeks
Sertraline	50–200 mg/day	12 weeks
Fluvoxamine	200–300 mg/day	12 weeks
Paroxetine	40–60 mg/day	12 weeks
Citalopram	40–60 mg/day	12 weeks
Second Line		
Modifications to Behavior Therapy		
Consider inpatient sessions; home visits or other in situ sessions; or cognitive therapy		
Medication: SRI Augmentation		
Clonazepam	0.5–5 mg/day	4 weeks
Buspirone	15–60 mg/day	8 weeks
Medication: Neuroleptics		
Pimozide	1–3 mg/day	4 weeks
Haloperidol	0.5–10 mg/day	4 weeks
Risperidone	0.5–6 mg/day	4 weeks
Olanzapine	2.5–15 mg/day	4 weeks
Medication: Alternative Monotherapies		
Clonazepam	0.5–5 mg/day	4 weeks
Buspirone	30–60 mg/day	6 weeks
Phenelzine	60–90 mg/day	10 weeks
Third Line		
Low-Risk Experimental or Insufficiently Studied Therapies		
Other augmentation strategies		
Intravenous CMI (if available via experimental protocol)		
ECT (if patient has comorbid major depression)		
Fourth Line		
Consider Neurosurgery (only if OCD is long-standing, severe, debilitating, and unresponsive to an exhaustive array of other treatments)		

CMI = clomipramine; SRI = serotonin reuptake inhibitor; SSRI = selective serotonin reuptake inhibitor.

wish to explicitly emphasize that most experts view behavior therapy as a critical and effective first line treatment for OCD, and that this brand of treatment is all too often overlooked or unavailable.

Measures of Symptom Severity and Treatment Response

Before reviewing the extensive database on clinical trials in OCD, it is worth considering the instruments available for measuring severity of symptoms and clinical improvement. The tools for quantifying the dependent variables in these studies as well as the thresholds that are adopted to operationalize "treatment response" profoundly impact the results and interpretations of clinical research.

As noted above, the gold standard instrument for quantifying OCD symptom severity is the Y-BOCS (Goodman et al., 1989a, 1989b), a rater-administered scale scored from 0 to 40, with high values reflecting more severe symptoms. The Y-BOCS comprises 10 elements: 5 elements about obsessions and 5 about compulsions (i.e., frequency/time consumed, interference, distress, resistance, and control over symptoms). Each element is rated from 0 to 4. Alternative contemporary rater-administered instruments include unidimensional global scales (Pato et al., 1994). The National Institute of Mental Health Global Obsessive Compulsive Scale (NIMH-GOCS; Insel et al., 1983) is a 15-point scale that has been shown to correlate with the Y-BOCS, although the descriptive anchor points of the NIMH-GOCS tend to emphasize elements of interference and resistance. Clinical global improvement (CGI; see Pato et al., 1994) scales represent another type of unidimensional rater-administered instruments that are commonly used in clinical trials, such as the 7-point CGI with anchor points including, 1 = very much improved, 4 = no change, and 7 = very much worse. The rater-administered CGI has also been shown to correlate well with the Y-BOCS and NIMH-GOCS; modified versions of the CGI can be self-administered by patients. Other self-administered instruments include the Leyton Obsessional Inventory (LOI; Cooper, 1970) and the Maudsley Obsessive Compulsive Inventory (MOCI; Rachman & Hodgson, 1980). As inventories, both consist of symptom-related and/or trait-related questions with binary response options (i.e., yes/no or true/false). Self-ratings can be particularly problematic in OCD, which, together with the fact that these scales are limited to specific symptom sets, makes them suboptimal for characterizing symptom severity or gauging clinical improvement in treatment trials (see Kim et al., 1990; Pato et al., 1994).

Typically, for studies that report a percentage of responders, criteria for response might include decrease in Y-BOCS of 25% or 35% and/or a CGI of 1 or 2. Therefore, it is important to appreciate that a substantial proportion of "responders" in these studies remain symptomatic and meaningfully affected by their residual illness.

First-Line Pharmacotherapy: SRIs

Currently, the SRIs are the first-line treatment for OCD (Dougherty & Rauch, 1997). There is overwhelming evidence from multiple randomized, double-blind, placebo-controlled studies supporting the efficacy of SRIs in the treatment of OCD (Table 16.2). Specifically, in adults, well-designed and controlled trials have demonstrated the relative efficacy of CMI versus placebo, as well as the relative efficacy of SSRIs, including fluoxetine, sertraline, paroxetine, and fluvoxamine versus placebo. Moreover, SRIs have been shown to be significantly more effective than non-SRI tricyclic antidepressants (TCAs) in placebo-controlled as well as non-placebo-controlled studies (Table 16.3). In the only randomized, double-blind, placebo-controlled study involving non-SRI TCAs, nortriptyline was not shown to be significantly more effective than placebo (Thoren et al., 1980; Table 16.2), supporting the view that non-SRI TCAs are not an effective monotherapy for OCD.

Despite a wide range of observed SRI response rates, large-scale studies have generally yielded approximately 40 to 60% responders, with mean improvement in the active treatment group of approximately 20 to 40% (see Greist et al., 1995c). In terms of the relative efficacy among SRIs, a large-scale meta-analysis of multicenter trials of SRIs was performed by Greist and colleagues (1995c) in which CMI ($N = 520$), fluoxetine ($N = 355$), sertraline ($N = 325$), and fluvoxamine ($N = 320$) were all shown to be significantly superior to placebo. This meta-analysis further indicated that CMI might have superior efficacy over SSRIs. Although the meta-analysis of Greist et al. had many strengths, including that all studies used comparable parameters and were conducted at essentially the same centers, the results should be interpreted with caution. Since there was a serial progression to the availability of these agents and to the performance of these trials, CMI was studied on an SRI-naive population, whereas each successive agent was undoubtedly tried on a cohort comprising a larger subpopulation of patients with histories of past SRI unresponsiveness. Consequently, each successive trial might well have been conducted on a more treatment-resistant population, biasing the efficacy in favor of agents studied in earlier years (i.e., CMI). In fact, a growing number of studies (see Table 16.3) and a recent comprehensive literature review (Pigott & Seay, 1999) suggest that the SRIs all have comparable efficacy.

Data regarding duration of treatment, optimal dose, and side effects are also plentiful but difficult to interpret with confidence because studies were often not designed to specifically answer these questions. The collective wisdom, purportedly supported by the data from the multicenter trials as well as anecdotal clinical experience, has been that response to SRIs is typically delayed so that an adequate trial of an SRI requires at least 10 weeks' duration. Indeed, a meaningful proportion of responders continue to emerge past the 8-week mark in these studies as well as in anecdotal clinical experience. Experts also suggest that optimal doses of SRIs for OCD may exceed those typically used for major depression

TABLE 16.2 Placebo-Controlled Trials of SRI Therapy for Obsessive Compulsive Disorder (Adults)

Treatment Conditions	N	*Comments*	*Study*
CMI versus placebo	20	CMI significantly superior to placebo	Karabanow (1977)
CMI versus placebo crossover	14	CMI significantly superior to placebo	Montgomery (1980)
CMI versus Nortriptyline versus placebo	24	CMI, but not Nortriptyline, superior to placebo	Thoren et al. (1980)
CMI versus placebo	12	CMI significantly superior to placebo	Mavissakalian et al. (1985)
CMI versus placebo	27	CMI significantly superior to placebo	Jenike et al. (1989)[a]
CMI versus placebo	32	73% improved on CMI; 6% improved on placebo	Greist et al. (1990)[a]
CMI versus placebo	239	38% average decrease in symptoms with CMI 3% average decrease in symptoms with placebo	CMI Collaborative Group, (1991)
CMI versus placebo	281	44% average decrease in symptoms with CMI 5% average decrease in symptoms with placebo	CMI Collaborative Group, (1991)
Sertraline versus placebo	87	Sertraline significantly superior to placebo	Chouinard et al. (1990)
Sertraline versus placebo	19	Sertraline significantly superior to placebo	Jenike et al. (1990a)[b]
Sertraline versus placebo	325	Sertraline significantly superior to placebo	Greist et al. (1992a)
Sertraline versus placebo	325	Sertraline significantly superior to placebo	Greist et al. (1995)
Sertraline versus placebo	167	Sertraline significantly superior to placebo	Kronig et al. (1999)
Fluvoxamine versus placebo	16	Fluvoxamine significantly superior to placebo	Perse et al. (1987)
Fluvoxamine versus placebo	42	Fluvoxamine significantly superior to placebo	Goodman et al. (1989)
Fluvoxamine versus placebo	38	Fluvoxamine significantly superior to placebo	Jenike et al. (1990b)
Fluvoxamine versus placebo	320	Fluvoxamine significantly superior to placebo	Rasmussen et al. (in press)
Fluvoxamine versus placebo	160	Fluvoxamine significantly superior to placebo	Goodman et al. (1996)
Fluoxetine versus placebo	355	Fluoxetine (20, 40, 60 mg) significantly superior to placebo	Tollefson et al. (1994a)
Fluoxetine versus placebo	217	Fluoxetine (40, 60 mg) significantly superior to placebo while 20 mg effects equal to placebo	Montgomery et al. (1993)
Paroxetine versus placebo	348	Paroxetine (40, 60 mg) significantly superior to placebo while 20 mg effects equal to placebo	Wheadon et al. (1993)

Source: Adapted from Jenike (1998a).

[a]Included under "The clomipramine collaborative study group (1991)" report above.

[b]Included under "Chouinard et al. (1990)" report above.

CMI = clomipramine.

TABLE 16.3 Non-Placebo Controlled Trials of Drug Therapy for Obsessive Compulsive Disorder (Adults)

Treatment Conditions	N	*Comments*	*Study*
CMI versus Amitriptyline	20	CMI significantly superior to Amitriptyline	Ananth et al. (1981)
CMI versus Amitriptyline	39	95% improved on CMI 56% improved on Amitriptyline	Zhao (1991)
CMI versus Clorgyline	13	CMI effective; Clorgyline ineffective	Insel et al. (1983)
CMI versus Clorgyline	12	CMI superior to Clorgyline	Zahn et al. (1984)
CMI versus Doxepin	32	78% markedly improved on CMI 36% markedly improved on Doxepin	Cui (1986)
CMI versus Fluvoxamine	6	Comparable efficacy	Den Boer et al. (1987)
CMI versus Fluvoxamine	66	Comparable efficacy	Freeman et al. (1994)
CMI versus Fluvoxamine	79	Comparable efficacy	Koran et al. (1996)
CMI versus Fluvoxamine	26	Comparable efficacy	Milanfranchi et al. (1997)
CMI versus Fluvoxamine	133	Comparable efficacy	Mundo et al. (2000)
CMI versus Fluoxetine	11	Comparable efficacy	Pigott et al. (1990)
CMI versus Fluoxetine	55	Comparable efficacy	Lopez-Ibor et al. (1996)
CMI versus Imipramine	16	CMI superior to Imipramine	Volavka et al. (1985)
CMI versus Imipramine crossover	12	CMI superior to Imipramine	Lei (1986)
CMI versus Paroxetine	406	Comparable efficacy	Zohar et al. (1996)
CMI versus Sertraline	168	Comparable efficacy (fewer dropouts with Sertraline)	Bisserbe et al. (1995)
Fluvoxamine versus Desipramine	40	Fluvoxamine superior to Desipramine	Goodman et al. (1990)
Fluvoxamine versus Paroxetine versus Citalopram	30	Comparable efficacy	Mundo et al. (1997b)
Citalopram	29	76% improved in 24-week open label trial	Koponen et al. (1997)

Source: Adapted from Jenike (1998a).

CMI = clomipramine.

(e.g., Montgomery et al., 1993), although the dose comparison studies of OCD have not always shown significant dose-dependent responses across the OCD study population (e.g., Greist et al., 1995b). As for side effects, although the meta-analysis of Greist et al. (1995c) did not find any significant difference between medication groups regarding dropout rates due to side effects, this is a relatively insensitive measure of side effect profile. Also, the aforementioned cohort effects apply for side effects as well. Subjects participating in the early CMI trials may have viewed that agent as the only available course of treatment, whereas subjects in later SSRI trials may have been aware of the wider variety of available treatments, making them less willing to endure nuisance side effects. Clearly, as with other TCAs, the risks and side effects mediated by anticholinergic and antiadrenergic mechanisms (e.g., constipation, cardiac conduction disturbances, orthostatic hypotension) are more commonly associated with CMI than with SSRIs. Furthermore, CMI is believed to pose a significant risk with regard to lowering seizure threshold. All SRIs can pose risks (e.g., serotonergic syndrome) and produce a variety of side effects (e.g., nausea, sleep disturbances, and sexual disturbances) attributable to their primary mechanism of action via serotonergic reuptake blockade (Grimsley & Jann, 1992). There is no substantive evidence that any SRI is significantly superior or inferior to any other with regard to serotonergically mediated side effects.

Though many clinicians use SRIs as a long-term treatment for OCD, few controlled studies of long-term pharmacotherapy of OCD have been conducted. While most open studies have demonstrated high relapse rates of OCD symptoms within weeks of discontinuation (Thoren et al., 1980; Pato et al., 1988), one open-label study of SRI discontinuation found that only 23% of patients relapsed within 1 year (Fontaine & Chouinard, 1989). One randomized, double-blind study incorporating substitution of desipramine for clomipramine in a crossover design found that 89% of patients in the substituted group encountered relapse during a 2-month period (Leonard et al., 1991). Some investigators have proposed using lower doses of SRIs for OCD maintenance treatment based on open-label trials (Pato et al., 1990; Ravizza et al., 1996a), and two controlled studies have demonstrated the efficacy of this approach (Mundo et al., 1997a; Tollefson et al., 1994). Thus, the data suggest that discontinuation of SRIs in patients with OCD results in a high relapse rate though there is still some debate regarding maintenance dosages of SRIs.

In addition to the above data regarding pharmacotherapy for OCD in adults, there are analogous studies in children and adolescents documenting the efficacy of CMI over non-SRI TCAs as well as placebo (see Table 16.4). To date, there are two placebo-controlled studies of SSRIs for OCD in children, which likewise support the efficacy of fluoxetine and sertraline. Also, several open trials of SSRIs have produced findings paralleling those in adults.

Second-Line Pharmacotherapy: SRI Augmentation and Alternative Monotherapies

For patients who do not derive satisfactory reduction of symptoms with SRI therapy, second-line pharmacological treatments include SRI augmentation and alternative monotherapies. It is important to appreciate that only a minority of patients with OCD do not respond favorably to SRIs and that this relatively treatment-resistant group may be quite heterogeneous, including with respect to underlying pathophysiology. Therefore, specific subsequent treatments may be very effective for some subset of this population while having only modest mean efficacy for the overall cohort. Consequently, some second-line treatment trials have focused on the number or proportion of patients who meet responder criteria rather than the mean decrease in symptom severity over the entire study population. Moreover, in some instances, attention has been focused on the clinical characteristics that might distinguish responders from nonresponders.

TABLE 16.4 Controlled Trials of SRI Therapy for Obsessive Compulsive Disorder (Children & Adolescents)

Treatment Conditions	N	*Comments*	*Study*
CMI versus Desipramine versus placebo	8 adolescents	No significant differences crossover	Rapoport et al. (1980)
CMI versus placebo crossover	14 children	CMI superior to placebo	Flament et al. (1985a & b)
CMI versus Desipramine	48	CMI superior to Desipramine; 64% of patients relapsed when Desipramine substituted for CMI	Leonard et al. (1988)
CMI substituted with Desipramine in half of subjects	26	89% receiving Desipramine relapsed 18% remaining on CMI relapsed	Leonard et al. (1991)
CMI versus placebo	61	37% average decrease with CMI 8% average decrease with placebo	DeVeaugh-Geiss et al. (1992)
Fluoxetine versus placebo	14 children	Fluoxetine superior to placebo	Riddle et al. (1992)
Sertraline versus placebo	187	Sertraline superior to placebo	March et al. (1998)

Source: Adapted from Jenike (1998a).

CMI = clomipramine.

Augmentation of SRIs

Numerous agents have been tried as augmentors in combination with SRIs for patients who were unresponsive or only partially responsive to SRIs alone (see Tables 16.5 & 16.6) (see Jenike, 1998; McDougle & Goodman, 1997). However, few controlled trials of such strategies have been conducted (see Tables 16.5 & 16.6). Despite numerous case reports suggesting that lithium might be an effective augmentor in combination with various SRIs, the only two controlled trials of lithium, added to fluvoxamine (McDougle et al., 1991) and CMI (Pigott et al., 1991), respectively, speak against the efficacy of these combinations.

Similarly, the encouraging results from case series and uncontrolled trials of buspirone augmentation (see Jenike, 1998; McDougle & Goodman, 1997) were followed by only marginal success in controlled trials. In Pigott and colleagues' (1992a) study of buspirone plus CMI, despite a 29% responder rate, there was not significant improvement over the entire cohort with respect to OCD symptoms, and 3 of 14 subjects suffered an exacerbation of >25% on measures of depression, for unclear reasons. In Grady and colleagues' (1993) double-blind crossover study of buspirone augmentation of fluoxetine, only 1 of 14 subjects showed improvement, which may have reflected the brief duration of treatment (only 4

TABLE 16.5 SRI Augmentation Therapies for Obsessive Compulsive Disorder: Controlled Trials

Augmenting Agent	*SRI*	N	*Trial*	*Results*	*Study*
Lithium	Fluvoxamine	30	2- or 4-week double-blind placebo-controlled	Very little improvement	McDougle et al. (1991)
Lithium	CMI	9	Double-blind crossover (with T3)	None	Pigott et al. (1991)
L-Triiodo-Thyronine (T3)	CMI	9	Double-blind crossover (with Lithium)	None	Pigott et al. (1999)
Buspirone	CMI	14	2-week placebo, then 10-weeks Buspirone	4/14 (29%) improved an additional 25% on Buspirone; 3/14 (21%) worsened >25% on depression scores	Pigott et al. (1992a)
Buspirone	Fluoxetine	14	Double-blind crossover with placebo; 4 weeks per treatment condition	1/14 (7%) improved significantly more with Buspirone	Grady et al. (1993)
Haloperidol	Fluvoxamine	34	Double-blind placebo-controlled, with 17 per group; 4-week trial; after failing Fluvoxamine alone	11/17 (65%) responded to Haloperidol; 0/17 to placebo; 8/8 with tics responded to Haloperidol	McDougle et al. (1994)
Clonazepam	CMI or Fluoxetine	16	Placebo-controlled, crossover; 4-week trial; after 20-week stable dose on CMI or Fluoxetine	Significant improvement in OCD on 1/3 measures for clonazepam versus placebo; Significant improvement in global anxiety as well	Pigott et al. (1992c) (see Rauch & Jenike, 1994)
Pindolol	Paroxetine	14	Double-blind, placebo-controlled; 4-week trial after ~17-week stable dose on Paroxetine	Significant ($p < .01$) improvement in Y-BOCS	Dannon et al. (2000)
Risperidone	SRI	36	Double-blind, placebo-controlled; 6-week trial after 12 weeks on SRI	50% responders; significant ($p < .001$) reduction in Y-BOCS	McDougle et al. (2000)

CMI = clomipramine; OCD = obsessive compulsive disorder; SRI = serotonin reuptake inhibitor

TABLE 16.6 SRI Augmentation Therapies for Obsessive Compulsive Disorder: Uncontrolled Trials

Augmenting Agent	*SRI*	N	*Results*	*Study*
Lithium	CMI	1	Improved	Rasmussen (1984)
Lithium	CMI	1	Improved	Feder (1988)
Lithium	CMI	1	"Clinically meaningful" improvement	Golden et al. (1988)
Lithium	CMI	10	1 improved somewhat	Hermesh et al. (1990)
Lithium	Fluoxetine	1	Improved	Howland (1991)
Lithium	Fluoxetine	7	1 improved >20%	Jenike (1991)
Buspirone	Fluoxetine	11	9 improved ≥25%	Markovitz et al. (1990)
Buspirone	Fluoxetine	10	10 on Fluoxetine plus Buspirone did better than 10 on Fluoxetine alone ($p < .05$)	Jenike et al. (1991)
Buspirone	Fluoxetine	1 child	Improved	Alessi and Bos (1991)
Tryptophan	CMI	1	Improved; relapsed when stopped; improved again when restarted	Rasmussen (1984)
Clonidine	CMI	1	Much improved	Lipsedge and Prothero (1987)
Clonidine	CMI	2	Unimpressive results	Hollander et al. (1988)
Clonidine	Fluoxetine	17	3/17 (18%) improved >20%	Jenike (1991)
CMI	Citalopram	16	Improved more than Citalopram alone	Pallanti et al. (1999)
Fenfluramine	Fluvoxamine	1	Improved; stopped due to impotence	Hollander & Liebowitz (1988)
Fenfluramine	CMI	2	Both improved	Judd (1991)
Fenfluramine	CMI	7	6/7 (86%) improved at least moderately	Hollander et al. (1990)
Trazodone	Fluoxetine	13	4/13 (31%) improved >20%	Jenike (1991)
Fluoxetine	CMI	6 adolescents	5/6 (83%) with marked improvement 1/6 (17%) with moderate improvement	Simeon et al. (1990)
Clonazepam	Fluoxetine	7	1/7 (14%) improved >20%	Jenike (1991)
Neuroleptics	Fluvoxamine	17	7/8 (88%) with tics responded;	McDougle et al. (1990)
Pimozide in 14	+/– Lithium		2/9 (22%) without tics responded	
Risperidone	Sertraline +/– CMI	5	5/5 improved >18%; 3/5 improved >50%; 43% average decrease	Jacobsen (1995)
Risperidone	Fluvoxamine	3	3/3 improved >40%; 55% average decrease	McDougle et al. (1995)
Risperidone	CMI +/– Sertraline	14	7/14 improved >35%	Ravizza et al. (1996b)
Olanzapine	Fluoxetine	10	3/10 improved >25%	Koran et al. (2000)

Source: Adapted from Rauch and Jenike (1996).

weeks in each phase). Lastly, McDougle and colleagues (1993b) found greater improvement with placebo than with buspirone in a double-blind, placebo-controlled study of buspirone augmentation of fluvoxamine for 6 weeks.

Contrary to a small case series reporting unimpressive results (Jenike, 1998a), the use of clonazepam as an augmentor with CMI or fluoxetine has been studied in a placebo-controlled fashion, suggesting significant antiobsessional efficacy, as well as a nonspecific decrease in anxiety measures (Pigott et al., 1992c; see Rauch & Jenike 1994).

The most impressive augmentation data document the benefits of adding low doses of dopamine antagonists (both conventional and atypical neuroleptics) to SRI pharmacotherapy in patients with treatment-refractory OCD (McDougle et al., 1990, 1994, 2000). Some data (McDougle et al., 1993a) initially suggested that OCD patients with comorbid tics may be less responsive to SRI monotherapy than OCD patients without tics. More recent studies have demonstrated the efficacy of SRI augmentation with neuroleptics in OCD patients with and without comorbid tics (McDougle et al., 2000). While initial studies demonstrated the efficacy of SRI augmentation with conventional neuroleptics, more recent uncontrolled studies of augmentation with atypical neuroleptics have yielded encouraging preliminary results (Jacobsen, 1995; Koran et al., 2000; McDougle et al., 1995a), as has one controlled trial of risperidone augmentation of an SRI (McDougle et al., 2000).

Pertinent negative findings include those from a controlled crossover trial of L-triiodothyronine added to CMI, which did not yield significant antiobsessional benefits (Pigott et al., 1991).

Numerous other agents have been tried in combination with SRIs, including clonidine, tryptophan, fenfluramine, pindolol, trazodone, and nortriptyline, as well as other antidepressants (see Jenike, 1998; McDougle & Goodman, 1997, for review). The small number of subjects, lack of sufficient controls, and mixed results preclude drawing even preliminary conclusions as to the potential efficacy of such strategies. If an augmenting agent is indicated for treatment of some comorbid condition (e.g., lithium for bipolar disorder, trazodone for insomnia, or clonidine for TS) and no strong contraindication is present, then a trial of the agent in combination with an SRI is easily rationalized. Anecdotally, these strategies have appeared to be of tremendous benefit in some isolated cases. No studies have sought to establish the optimal dosage or duration of treatment for any of these augmentation strategies. Therefore, current guidelines reflect the parameters used in the reported successful trials as well as anecdotal experience with OCD and other psychiatric disorders.

Alternative Monotherapies

For patients who fail to derive satisfactory response from trials of SRIs alone as well as augmentation strategies, the next recommended step is to consider alternative monotherapies in place of SRIs. In addition to uncontrolled data, positive controlled studies lend some support for trials of clonazepam, monoamine oxidase inhibitors (MAOIs), and buspirone (see Table 16.7).

In the case of clonazepam, both small case series (see Hewlett, 1993, for review) and one placebo-controlled study (Hewlett et al., 1992) support its efficacy in OCD. In light of the circumstantial evidence supporting its efficacy as an augmentor with SRIs for OCD and its well-established efficacy more generally as an anxiolytic, trials of clonazepam as an alternative monotherapy in treatment-resistant cases seem well justified. Recommendations in this context regarding dosage (i.e., 0.5 to 5 mg per day) and duration (i.e., 3 to 4 weeks) have no controlled empirical basis and are simply extrapolated from clinical experience with benzodiazepines for other anxiety disorders and these few reports in OCD.

Non-placebo-controlled studies involving the MAOI clorgyline speak against its efficacy in OCD, showing no significant decrease in OCD severity (Insel et al., 1983) and inferior efficacy in comparison to SRIs (Insel et al., 1983; Zahn et al., 1984). In contrast, small case series suggested beneficial results from the MAOI phenelzine in patients with comorbid OCD and panic disorder (Jenike et al., 1983). A non-placebo-controlled study of phenelzine versus CMI suggested significant clinical improvement in both groups and no significant difference in efficacy between the two agents (Vallejo et al., 1992). The results of Vallejo and colleagues must be interpreted with caution, however, since the study was underpowered to identify a difference between CMI and phenelzine, and suboptimal clinical measures of improvement were employed. In fact, a placebo-controlled trial of phenelzine and fluoxetine demon-

TABLE 16.7 Alternative Medications as Monotherapies for Obsessive Compulsive Disorder: Controlled Trials

Treatment Conditions	N	*Comments*	*Study*
Clorgyline versus CMI	13	Clorgyline ineffective; CMI effective	Insel et al. (1983)
Clorgyline versus CMI	12	Clorgyline inferior to CMI	Zahn et al. (1984)
Phenelzine versus CMI	30	Both effective and comparable	Vallejo et al. (1992)
Clonazepam versus CMI versus Clonidine versus active placebo crossover	25	35% average decrease with Clonazepam; Clonazepam comparable to CMI and superior to active placebo	Hewlett et al. (1992)
Buspirone versus CMI crossover	20	Both effective and comparable, >20% improvement in >55% in both groups	Pato et al. (1991)
Fluoxetine versus Phenelzine versus placebo	64	Fluoxetine group improved significantly more than Phenelzine or placebo groups	Jenike et al. (1997)
Trazodone versus placebo	21	No significant difference	Pigott et al. (1992b)

CMI = clomipramine.

strated that patients treated with fluoxetine improved significantly more than those in the placebo or phenelzine group (Jenike et al., 1997). This study did note that a subgroup of patients with symmetry obsessions did respond to phenelzine, however. Therefore, the efficacy of phenelzine as a monotherapy for OCD should be regarded as provisional. Specific recommendations regarding dosage (i.e., phenelzine 60 to 90 mg per day) have little empirical basis, reflecting extrapolation from clinical practice with MAOIs for major depression and panic disorder; duration of trials (i.e., 10 weeks) mirrors that of SRIs for OCD. In addition to the usual low tyramine diet and other precautions typically indicated in the context of an MAOI trial, it is critical to be cautious regarding the transition from serotonergic medications to an MAOI due to the risks of dangerous interactions, including serotonergic crisis. Current guidelines are based primarily on the half-life of the agents involved rather than direct empirical data related to adverse events per se. Conservative recommendations are washout periods of at least 2 weeks when transitioning from CMI or a short-half-life SSRI to an MAOI, at least 5 weeks when transitioning from fluoxetine to an MAOI, and at least 2 weeks when transitioning from phenelzine to an SRI.

Although one open trial of buspirone did not yield significant antiobsessional benefit (Jenike & Baer, 1988), a controlled trial of buspirone versus CMI suggested that both were comparably effective (Pato et al., 1991). The relatively short duration of the trial, the modest power for detecting a difference between treatments, and the absence of a placebo group make it hard to draw firm conclusions from Pato and colleagues' study. Still, given the excellent tolerability of buspirone, other circumstantial evidence of possible efficacy as an augmentor, and its general efficacy as an anxiolytic, the clinical use of buspirone as an alternative monotherapy for cases of treatment-resistant OCD seems justified pending further information. Specific recommendations regarding dosage (i.e., up to 60 mg per day) and duration of trials (i.e., 6 weeks) have little empirical basis, simply reflecting the protocol adopted in the Pato and colleagues study.

Other pertinent negative findings are worthy of mention. In contrast to promising results with risperidone as an augmentor, an open trial of the atypical antipsychotic clozapine suggests inefficacy as an antiobsessional monotherapy (McDougle et al., 1995b). Although one case report suggested antiobsessional benefit in a patient with OCD (Young et al., 1994), and another described a marked reduction in OC symptoms for a patient with schizophrenia (LaPorta, 1994), several case reports suggest that clozapine can actually precipitate OC symptoms in patients with psychotic disorders (see McDougle et al., 1995b, for review). Controlled trials have failed to demonstrate the efficacy of trazodone (Pigott et al., 1992b), clonidine (Hewlett, 1992), and diphenhydramine (Hewlett, 1992) as monotherapies for OCD.

Nonpharmacological Therapies

Behavior Therapy

It is extremely challenging to design and conduct a controlled study of psychotherapy. Among other issues, the optimal analogue to placebo treatment in medication trials is unclear. Perhaps consequently, much of the clinical research to date regarding behavior therapy for OCD has focused on determining salient elements of the therapy rather than comparing behavior therapy to other treatments or placebo (see Baer & Minichiello, 1990). The gold standard mode of behavior therapy for OCD is exposure and response prevention. This entails the patient actually being exposed to provocative stimuli (e.g., touching a "contaminated" object) and refraining from carrying out his or her usual compulsions (e.g., refraining from hand washing), that is, response prevention. It appears that in vivo exposure and response prevention represent the salient elements of effective behavior therapy regardless of setting, supervision, or addition of cognitive techniques (Emmelkamp & De Lange, 1983; Emmelkamp & Kraanen, 1977; Emmelkamp et al., 1980).

One challenge or limitation of exposure and response prevention therapy relates to generalizability of results, since gains are often specific to the symptoms explicitly addressed and sometimes limited to the settings in which the therapies are practiced (Rachman et al., 1971, 1979; Rachman & Hodgson, 1980). Although it is commonly believed that behavior therapy is more effective for compulsive rituals than obsessive thoughts, only one (Foa & Goldstein, 1978) of four behavior therapy studies (Foa & Goldstein, 1978; Foa et al., 1980, 1984; Solyom & Sookman, 1977) addressing this issue found a significantly greater improvement in compulsions versus obsessions. In all four studies, significant gains were made in both obsessions and compulsions. However, patients with pure obsessions (e.g., intrusive thoughts of sex or violence without accompanying compulsions) tended to fare worse than patients with obsessions and compulsions (e.g., contamination with cleaning or doubting with checking) (Rachman & Hodgson, 1980).

There are numerous partially controlled trials of exposure and response prevention behavior therapy that have consistently shown impressive antiobsessional efficacy in less than 1 month (see Table 16.8). Dropout rates for these studies averaged approximately 20% (Rachman & Hodgson, 1980). Still, follow-up studies suggested that treatment gains were maintained for up to 1 to 5 years after discontinuation of active treatment, although these results were confounded by occasional "booster" sessions (Marks, 1981; Marks et al., 1975; Mawson et al., 1982). The study of Boulougouris (1977) stands as a notable exception in that patients who were treated with 11 sessions of behavior therapy maintained their gains over a 2- to 5-year follow-up period in the absence of any intercurrent therapy sessions. Furthermore, a meta-analysis (Christensen et al., 1987; Quality Assurance Project, 1985) based on data from 38 studies between 1961 and 1984 found comparable effect sizes for CMI (1.7) and behavior therapy (1.8) at the end of treatment; the benefits from exposure and response prevention persisted at a mean 80-week follow-up (effect size = 1.7), whereas no such follow-up data were available for CMI. In contrast, psychosurgery resulted in an effect size of 1.4 and dropped to 1.0 at 60-week follow-up. In a separate study, Pato and colleagues (1988) showed that almost 90% of patients who received CMI therapy for OCD relapsed after discontinuation of the medication. Thus, pending well-controlled head-to-head studies, based on partially controlled data and the limited method of meta-analysis, the implication is that in comparison with CMI or psychosurgery, behavior therapy may produce the highest mean effect size and the most enduring gains following discontinuation of active treatment.

Only a small number of studies directly comparing behavior therapy and medication have been reported. Rachman and colleagues (1979) found behavior therapy to significantly outperform CMI, as well as no significant incremental benefit from the two treatments in combination. This study is limited, however, in that the CMI condition entailed relatively low doses (mean = 164 mg/day and maximum = 225 mg/day) as well as inadequate duration of CMI treatment (6 weeks). In another head-to-head comparison of behavior therapy and CMI, medication was found to be more effective for reducing obsessional doubt, whereas behavior therapy was more effective for reducing compulsive rituals (Solyom & Sookman, 1977). Currently, a large-scale, dual-site study is under way to more thoroughly address these questions (Leibowitz & Foa, unpublished communication, 1995). In practice, medication and behavior therapy are routinely used in concert, and experts in the field have long recommended this as an optimal treatment approach (e.g., Baer & Minichiello, 1998; Rauch et al., 1996). Two recent studies (Honagen, 1998; O'Connor, 1999) have demonstrated that the combination of behavioral therapy and medication is more effective than either treatment alone, while one study (van Balkom, 1998) found that the addi-

TABLE 16.8 Summary of Partially-Controlled Studies of Behavior Therapy for Obsessive Compulsive Disorder

Study	N	*Sessions*	*Responders*
Lindsay et al. (1997)	18	15 hours total	ERP more effective than placebo[a]
Rachman et al. (1971)	10	40 minutes–1 hour × 15 (10–15 hours) over 3 weeks; all inpatient	70%
Rachman et al. (1973)	5	40 minutes × 15 (10 hours) over 3 weeks; all inpatient	60%
Marks et al. (1975)	20	40 minutes–1 hour × 15 (10–15 hours) over 3 weeks; all inpatient	70%
Boulougouris (1977)	15	90 minutes × 11 (16.5 hours); all outpatient	60%
Foa et al. (1984)	32	2 hours × 15 (30 hours) over 3 weeks; 10 inpatient/22 outpatient	90%
TOTAL (mean)	82		(70%)

[a]Note that Lindsay et al. does not provide percent responders data, though it does find a significant decrease in mean Y-BOCS following behavior therapy.

Source: Adapted from Baer & Minichiello (1990) and Jenike (1993).

tion of fluvoxamine with cognitive therapy or exposure and response prevention was not superior to either cognitive therapy or exposure and response prevention alone.

Beyond exposure and response prevention, limited trials of alternative behavioral methods have supported the use of imaginal flooding for checkers (Steketee, 1982) and "thought stopping" for patients with pure obsessions (Rimm & Masters, 1974). Moreover, a recent controlled trial suggests that cognitive therapy can also be effective for OCD (Van Oppen et al., 1995). Finally, although controlled data are not currently available regarding cognitive behavior therapy for OCD in children and adolescents, preliminary findings of open trials and case reports suggest that, with age-appropriate modifications to the regimen, results can be comparable to those in adults (Franklin et al., 1998; March, 1995; March et al., 1994; Scahill et al., 1996).

Neurosurgery

Despite a large body of uncontrolled data reporting antiobsessional benefits from a variety of neurosurgical procedures (see Cosgrove & Rauch, 1995; Jenike et al., 1998b; Mindus et al., 1994, for reviews), thus far ethical factors and technical limitations have precluded the performance of sham-controlled studies to definitively establish the efficacy of these strategies. Neurosurgical treatment of OCD is reserved for patients with severe and debilitating illness who have failed an exhaustive array of other available treatment options, and who provide informed consent or assent. Currently, the most commonly employed neurosurgical treatments for OCD include anterior cingulotomy, anterior capsulotomy, subcaudate tractotomy, and limbic leukotomy. In recent prospective trials of cingulotomy and capsulotomy, approximately 45% of patients experienced symptom reduction of at least 35% (see Jenike et al., 1998b; Mindus et al., 1994). Studies directly comparing the relative efficacy and safety among the different neurosurgical approaches are also lacking. Adverse effects, in the context of contemporary techniques, include seizure and transient headache. Perhaps surprisingly, discernible adverse effects on cognition or personality are rare (Corkin, 1980; Jenike et al., 1998b; Mindus et al., 1994). With the advent of innovative surgical devices that allow functional neurosurgery without craniotomy (e.g., by gamma knife), the performance of ethical double-blind sham-controlled trials of neurosurgery for OCD is now feasible. One such study, testing the efficacy of anterior capsulotomy, is currently being conducted by a collaborative research team involving investigators from Brown University and Massachusetts General Hospital. Deep brain stimulation (DBS), which utilizes surgically implanted electrodes that may be turned on and off to stimulate or inhibit activity in surrounding brain tissue, has been used for the treatment of neurological diseases such as Parkinson's disease and intractable pain (Devinsky et al., 1994). Investigations of the efficacy of

DBS for the treatment of OCD may be useful. More definitive data are sorely needed to determine the efficacy of neurosurgical treatments.

ECT

There are no controlled data regarding the efficacy of ECT for OCD. Given the high comorbidity of major affective illness in OCD and the well-established efficacy of ECT for major depression, it is not surprising that some patients with OCD have reportedly shown clinical improvement with ETC. Several limited case series and anecdotal reports suggest that ECT may be useful in some circumstances, and such intervention would seem prudent in cases where ECT is indicated based on the presence of comorbid severe affective illness (see Jenike & Rauch, 1994). Controlled data are needed, however, before meaningful conclusions can be drawn regarding the specific antiobsessional efficacy of ECT for OCD. In this regard, important considerations include the effects of ECT on patients with OCD in the absence of major depressive disorder, the careful clinical distinction between genuine OCD versus ruminations or intrusive thoughts due to a different diagnosis, and the use of clinical instruments to tease apart antidepressant effects and antiobsessional effects and global improvement. Currently available data do not provide compelling support for the use of ECT in OCD without comorbid ECT-responsive conditions.

New Horizons and Future Treatments for Obsessive Compulsive Disorder

Future OCD treatment research can be divided into two categories: (a) initiatives to assess and optimize the use of currently available treatments and (b) initiatives to develop new treatments. As documented by the above review, there is much work to be done in establishing the efficacy of various treatments, following up on preliminary data with well-controlled prospective trials. Moreover, optimal doses and durations for various treatments need to be determined empirically and in a scientifically rigorous fashion. Clinical subtyping may uncover important predictors of treatment response (Ackerman et al., 1994; Ravizza et al., 1995), informing patients and clinicians which treatments should be tried first or avoided in particular cases. Public policy issues regarding treatment access loom large for mental health care delivery in the United States. Education of health care consumers, as well as policymakers and clinicians, will be critical to high-quality care in the years ahead. Primary-care physicians must be informed about OCD, and trends in training must be established to ensure an adequate supply of therapists with expertise in behavioral methods. Technological innovations, such as telepsychiatry, may help to provide specialized assessment and treatment to remote regions and ultimately reduce the costs of care (Baer, 1991; Baer et al., 1995).

Truly novel treatments for OCD may emerge from advances in our understanding of its pathophysiology or serendipitously. As new compounds become available that interact with the serotonergic and dopaminergic systems via specific receptor subtypes (e.g., 5HT1D, 5HT1A, or 5HT3; Swerdlow, 1995), it is likely that several will be antiobsessional candidates. Beyond monoaminergic systems, agents that modulate neuropeptidergic transmission may represent the next wave of psychopharmacological agents to be tested in OCD and related disorders. For instance, we have proposed that, based on the neurochemistry of corticostriatal pathways, substance P antagonists might serve as potent antiobsessionals (Rauch & Jenike, 1997). Such compounds are already available within the pharmaceutical industry but currently are being studied only for other indications. The hypothalamic neuropeptide oxytocin is also the subject of intensive study, because of its purported role in species-specific grooming behaviors (Leckman et al., 1994). Beyond neuropharmacology, research regarding autoimmune-mediated causes of OCD have prompted investigation of plasmapheresis to clear autoantibodies plus prophylactic antibiotic treatment to prevent subsequent infections and further damage (Allen et al., 1995; Swedo, 1994; Swedo et al., 1994). Also, transcranial magnetic stimulation (TMS), which has shown promise as an alternative treatment for major depression, has been shown to be efficacious in the treatment of OCD in one preliminary study (Greenberg et al., 1997). Finally, recent neuroimaging studies have documented consistent brain activity changes following successful treatment with either SRIs or behavior therapy (Baxter et al., 1992; Schwartz et al., 1996). Such findings underscore the potential power of neuroimaging methods in searching for predictors of treatment responsiveness.

SUMMARY

In conclusion, since the early 1970s, we have seen tremendous advances in the treatment and understanding of OCD, with an acceleration of progress during the 1990s, the decade of the brain. It is now appreciated that OCD is a common disorder, and effective treatments, including medication, behavior therapy, and neurosurgery, have emerged. There is overwhelming evidence of the most rigorous type supporting the efficacy of SRIs in the treatment of OCD. Along with SRIs, behavior therapy must be considered a viable first-line therapy. The best available data suggest that behavior therapy is at least as effective as medication in some instances and may be superior with respect to risks, costs, and enduring benefits. A variety of second-line medication treatments for OCD have been studied in a controlled or systematic fashion. Augmentation of SRIs with clonazepam or buspirone, and with high-potency neuroleptics in cases of a comorbid tic disorder, is provisionally recommended based on the marginal available data. Other augmentation strategies find very limited support at present. Alternative monotherapies, including buspirone, clonazepam, and phenelzine, have all been the subject of positive controlled or partially controlled studies. However, the quality of these data make recommendations for these strategies tentative as well, pending additional information. Beyond second-line treatments, the current data base is inadequate for making difficult treatment decisions. There is now considerable clinical experience with neurosurgery for severe, debilitating, treatment-refractory OCD. The apparent modest success rates with neurosurgery and its relative safety based on open trials would seem to pose a reasonable option for a small number of cases. Still, controlled data on neurosurgery are sorely needed. The future of OCD treatment will hopefully entail rigorous research to more clearly establish the efficacy and safety of preexisting treatment options, as well as a refined sense of which patients might respond preferentially to which interventions, at what dose, and after how long. Furthermore, we can look forward to emerging novel treatment strategies that might include modified cognitive behavior therapies; new compounds acting via serotonergic, dopaminergic, or neuropeptidergic systems; and interventions that counteract autoimmune processes.

ACKNOWLEDGMENTS Drs. Rauch and Jenike are supported in part by the David Judah Research Fund.

References

Ackerman, D. L., Greenland, S., Bystritsky, A., Morgenstern, H., & Katz, R. J. (1994). Predictors of treatment response in obsessive-compulsive disorder: Multivariate analyses from a multicenter trial of clomipramine. *Journal of Clinical Psychopharmacology, 14*, 247–254.

Alessi, N., & Bos, T. (1991). Buspirone augmentation of fluoxetine in a depressed child with obsessive-compulsive disorder. *American Journal of Psychiatry, 148*(11), 1605–1606.

Allen, A. J., Leonard, H. L., & Swedo, S. E. (1995). Case study: A new infection-triggered, autoimmune subtype of pediatric OCD and Tourette's syndrome. *Journal of the American Academy of Child and Adolescent Psychiatry, 34*, 307–311.

American Psychiatric Association. (1994). *Diagnostic and statistical manual of mental disorders* (4th ed.). Washington, DC: Author.

Ananth, J., Pecknold, J. C., van den Steen, N., & Engelsmann, F. (1981). Double-blind comparative study of clomipramine and amitriptyline in obsessive neurosis. *Progress in Neuropsychopharmacology, 5*, 257–262.

Angst, J. (1994). The epidemiology of obsessive compulsive disorder. In E. Hollander, J. Zohar, D. Marazziti & B. Olivier (Eds.), *Current insights in obsessive compulsive disorder* (pp. 93–104). Chichester, UK: Wiley.

Baer, L. (1991). *Getting control*. Boston: Little, Brown.

Baer, L., Cukor, P., Jenike, M. A., Leahy, L., O'Laughlin, J., & Coyle, J. T. (1995). Pilot study of telemedicine for patients with obsessive-compulsive disorder. *American Journal of Psychiatry, 152*, 1383–1385.

Baer, L., & Minichiello, W. E. (1990). Behavioral treatment for obsessive-compulsive disorder. In R. Noyes, Jr., M. Roth, & G. D. Burrows (Eds.). *Handbook of anxiety, Vol. 4. The treatment of anxiety*. New York: Elsevier.

Baer, L., & Minichiello, W. E. (1998). Behavior therapy for obsessive-compulsive disorder. In M. A. Jenike, L. Baer, & W. E. Minichiello (Eds.), *Obsessive-compulsive disorders: Practical management* (3rd ed., pp. 337–367). Boston: Mosby-Year Book.

Baer, L., Minichiello, W. E., Jenike, M. A., & Holland, A. (1989). Use of a portable computer program to assist behavioral treatment in a case of obsessive compulsive disorder. *Behavior Therapy and Experimental Psychiatry, 19,* 237–240.

Ballantine, H. T., Bouckoms, A. J., Thomas, E. L., & Giriunas, I. E. (1987). Treatment of psychiatric illness by stereotactic cingulotomy. *Biological Psychiatry, 22,* 807–819.

Baxter, L. R., Jr., Schwartz, J. M., Bergman, K. S., et al. (1992). Caudate glucose metabolic rate changes with both drug and behavior therapy for obsessive-compulsive disorder. *Archives of General Psychiatry, 49,* 681–689.

Baxter, L. R., Schwartz, J. M., Cuze, B. H., et al. (1990). Neuroimaging in obsessive-compulsive disorder: Seeking the mediating neuroanatomy. In M. A. Jenike, L. Baer, & W. E. Minichiello (Eds.), *Obsessive compulsive disorder: Theory and management* (2nd ed.). Chicago: Year Book Medical Publishers.

Bisserbe, J. C., Wiseman, R. L., Goldberg, M. S., et al. (1995). A double-blind comparison of sertraline and clomipramine in outpatients with OCD. *American Psychiatric Association Annual Meeting, New Research Abstracts* 173.

Boulougouris, J. C. (1977). Variables affecting the behavior modification of obsessive-compulsive patients treated by flooding. In J. C. Boulougouris & A. D. Rabavilas (Eds.), *The treatment of phobic and obsessive compulsive disorders* (pp. 73–84). Oxford: Pergamon Press.

Chouinard, G., Goodman, W., Greist, J., et al. (1990). Results of a double-blind placebo controlled trial using a new serotonin uptake inhibitor, sertraline, in obsessive-compulsive disorder. *Psychopharma cology Bulletin, 26,* 279–284.

Christensen, H., Hadzi-Pavlovic, D., Andrews, G., & Mattick, R. (1987). Behavior therapy and tricyclic medication in the treatment of obsessive-compulsive disorder: A quantitative review. *Journal of Consulting and Clinical Psychology, 55*(5), 701–711.

Clomipramine Collaborative Group. (1991). Clomipramine in the treatment of patients with obsessive-compulsive disorder. *Archives of General Psychiatry, 48,* 730–738.

Cooper, J. (1970). The Leyton obsessional inventory. *Psychiatric Medicine, 1,* 48.

Corkin, S. (1980). A prospective study of cingulotomy. In E. S. Valenstein (Ed.), *The psychosurgery debate.* San Francisco: Freeman.

Cosgrove, G. R., & Rauch, S. L. (1995). Psychosurgery. *Neurosurgical Clinics of North America, 65,* 167–176.

Cui, Y. E. (1986). A double-blind trial of clomipramine and doxepin in obsessive-compulsive disorder. *Chung Hua Shen Ching Shen Ko Tsa Chih, 19*(5), 279–281.

Dannon, P. N., Sasson, Y., Hirschmann, S., et al. (2000). Pindolol augmentation in treatment-resistant obsessive compulsive disorder: A double-blind placebo controlled trial. *European Neuropsychopharmacology, 10,* 165–169.

Den Boer, J. A., Westenberg, H. G. M., Kamerbeek, W. D. J., et al. (1987). Effect of serotonin uptake inhibitors in anxiety disorders: A double-blind comparison of clomipramine and fluvoxamine. *International Journal of Clinical Psychopharmacoloy,* 2(1), 21–32.

DeVeaugh-Geiss, J., Moroz, G., Biederman, J., et al. (1992). Clomipramine hydrochloride in childhood and adolescent obsessive-compulsive disorder—A multicenter trial. *Journal of the American Academy of Child and Adolescent Psychiatry, 31*(1), 45–49.

Devinsky, O., Beric, A., Dogali, M., (Eds.). (1994). *Electrical and magnetic stimulation of the brain and spinal cord.* New York: Raven Press.

Dominguez, R. A., & Mestre, S. M. (1994). Management of treatment-refractory obsessive compulsive disorder patients. *Journal of Clinical Psychiatry,* 55(Suppl. 10), 86–92.

Dougherty, D., & Rauch, S. L. (1997). Serotonin-reuptake inhibitors in the treatment of OCD. In E. Hollander & D. J. Stein (Eds.). *Obsessive-compulsive disorders: Diagnosis—etiology—treatment.* New York: Marcel Dekker.

Emmelkamp, P. M. G., & De Lange, I. (1983). Spouse involvement in the treatment of obsessive-compulsive patients. *Behaviour Research and Therapy, 21,* 341–346.

Emmelkamp, P. M. G., & Kraanen, J. (1977). Therapist-controlled exposure in vivo versus self-controlled exposure in vivo: A comparison with obsessive-compulsive patients. *Behaviour Research and Therapy, 15,* 491–495.

Emmelkamp, P. M. G., Van Der Helm, M., Van Zanten, B. L., & Plochg, I. (1980). Treatment of obsessive-compulsive patients: The contribution of self-instructional training to the effectiveness of exposure. *Behaviour Research and Therapy, 18,* 61–66.

Fallon, B. A., Campeas, R., Schneier, F. R., et al. (1992). Open trial of intravenous clomipramine in five treatment refractory patients with obsessive compulsive disorder. *Journal of Neuropsychiatry, 4,* 70–75.

Fallon, B. A., Liebowitz, M. R., Campeas, R., et al. (1998). Intravenous clomipramine for obsessive-compulsive disorder refractory to oral clomipramine: A placebo-controlled study. *Archives of General Psychiatry, 55*(10), 918–924.

Feder, R. (1988). Lithium augmentation of clomipramine. *Journal of Clinical Psychiatry, 49*(11), 458.

Fernandez, C. E., & Lopez-Ibor, J. J. (1967). Monochlorimipramine in the treatment of psychiatric patients resistant to other therapies. *Actas Luso Esp Neurol Psiquiatr Cienc, 26*, 119.

Flament, M. F., Rapoport, J. L., Berg, C. J., et al. (1985a). Clomipramine treatment of childhood obsessive-compulsive disorder. *Archives of General Psychiatry, 42*, 977–983.

Flament, M. F., Rapoport, J. L., Berg, C. J., et al. (1985b). A controlled trial of clomipramine in childhood obsessive-compulsive disorder. *Psychopharmacology Bulletin, 21*(1), 150–151.

Foa, E. B., & Goldstein, A. (1978). Continuous exposure and complete response prevention in the treatment of obsessive-compulsive neurosis. *Behavior Therapy, 9*, 821–829.

Foa, E. B., Steketee, G., Grayson, J. B., et al. (1984). Deliberate exposure and blocking of obsessive-compulsive rituals: Immediate and long term effects. *Behavior Therapy, 15*, 450–472.

Foa, E. B., Steketee, G., & Milby, J. B. (1980). Differential effects of exposure and response prevention in obsessive-compulsive washers. *Journal of Clinical and Consulting Psychology, 48*(1), 71–79.

Fontaine, R., & Chouinard, G. (1989). Fluoxetine in the long-term maintenance treatment of obsessive-compulsive disorder. *Psychiatric Annals, 19*, 88–91.

Franklin, M. E., Kozak, M. J., Cashman, L. A., et al. (1998). Cognitive-behavioral treatment of pediatric obsessive-compulsive disorder: An open clinical trial. *Journal of the American Academy of Child and Adolescent Psychiatry, 7*, 412–419.

Freeman, C. P. L., Trimble, M. R., Deakin, J. F. W., Stokes, T. M., & Ashford, J. J. (1994). Fluvoxamine versus clomipramine in the treatment of obsessive compulsive disorder: A multicenter, randomized, double-blind, parallel group comparison. *Journal of Clinical Psychiatry, 55*(7), 301–305.

Freud, S. (1924). Notes upon a case of obsessional neurosis [1909]. In *Collected Papers* (Vol 2). London: Hogarth Press.

Gilles de la Tourette, G. (1885). Etude sur une affection nerveuse caracterisee par de l'incoordination motrice accompagnee de echolalie et de coprolalie. *Archives of Neurology, 9*, 19–42, 158–200.

Goodman, W. K., Kozak, M. J., Liebowitz, M., & White, K. L. (1996). Treatment of obsessive-compulsive disorder with fluvoxamine: A multicentre, double-blind, placebo-controlled trial. *International Journal of Clinical Psychopharmacology, 11*, 21–29.

Goodman, W. K., McDougle, C. J., & Price, L. H. (1992). Pharmacotherapy of obsessive compulsive disorder. *Journal of Clinical Psychiatry, 53*(Suppl.), 29–37.

Goodman, W. K., Price, L. H., Delgado, P. L., et al. (1990). Specificity of serotonin reuptake inhibitors in the treatment of obsessive compulsive disorder. *Archives of General Psychiatry, 47*, 577–585.

Goodman, W. K., Price, L. H., Rasmussen, S. A., et al. (1989a). Efficacy of fluvoxamine in obsessive-compulsive disorder: A double-blind comparison with placebo. *Archives of General Psychiatry, 46*, 36–44.

Goodman, W. K., Price, L. H., Rasmussen, S. A., et al. (1989b). The Yale-Brown Obsessive Compulsive Scale (Y-BOCS), Part I: Development, use, and reliability. *Archives of General Psychiatry, 46*, 1006–1011.

Goodman, W. K., Price, L. H., Rasmussen, S. A., et al. (1989c). The Yale-Brown Obsessive Compulsive Scale (Y-BOCS), Part II: Validity. *Archives of General Psychiatry, 46*, 1012–1016.

Golden, R. N., Morris, J. E., & Sack, D. A. (1988). Combined lithium-tricyclic treatment of obsessive-compulsive disorder. *Biological Psychiatry, 23*(2), 181–185.

Grady, T. A., Pigott, T. A., L'Heureux, F., Hill, J. L., Bernstein, S. E., & Murphy, D. L. (1993). A double-blind study of adjuvant buspirone hydrochloride in fluoxetine treated patients with obsessive compulsive disorder. *American Journal of Psychiatry, 150*, 819–821.

Greenberg, B. D., George, M. S., Dearing, J., et al. (1997). Effect of prefrontal repetitive transcranial magnetic stimulation (rTMS) in obsessive compulsive disorder: A preliminary study. *American Journal of Psychiatry, 154*, 867–869.

Greist, J. H., Jefferson, J. W., Kobak, K. A., et al. (1995a). A 1-year double-blind placebo-controlled fixed dose study of sertraline in the treatment of obsessive-compulsive disorder. *International Journal of Clinical Psychopharmacology, 10*, 57–65.

Greist, J., Chouinard, G., DuBoff, E., et al. (1995b). Double-blind comparison of three doses of sertraline and placebo in the treatment of outpatients with obsessive compulsive disorder. *Archives of General Psychiatry, 52*(4), 289–295.

Greist, J. H., Jefferson, J. W., Kobak, K. A., Katzelnick, D. J., & Serlin, R. C. (1995c). Efficacy and tolerability of serotonin transport inhibitors in obsessive-compulsive disorder: A meta-analysis. *Archives of General Psychiatry, 52*(1), 53–60.

Greist, J. H., Jefferson, J. W., Rosenfeld, R., et al. (1990). Clomipramine and obsessive-compulsive disorder: A placebo-controlled double-blind study of 32 patients. *Journal of Clinical Psychiatry, 51*(7), 292–297.

Grimsley, S. R., & Jann, M. W. (1992). Paroxetine, sertraline, and fluvoxamine: New selective serotonin reuptake inhibitors. *Clinical Pharmacology, 11*, 930–957.

Hermesh, H., Aizenberg, D., & Munitz, H. (1990). Trazodone treatment in clomipramine-resistant obsessive compulsive disorder. *Clinical Neuropharmacology, 13*(4), 322–328.

Hewlett, W., Vinogradov, S., & Agras, W. (1992). Clomipramine, clonazepam, and clonidine treatment of obsessive compulsive disorder. *Journal of Clinical Psychopharmacology, 12*, 420–430.

Hewlett, W. A. (1993). The use of benzodiazepines in obsessive compulsive disorder and Tourette's syndrome. *Psychiatric Annals, 23*, 309–316.

Hollander, E. (1993). Obsessive-compulsive spectrum disorders. *Psychiatric Annals, 23*, 355–407.

Hollander, E., Kwon, J. H., Stein, D. J., et al. (1996). Obsessive-compulsive and spectrum disorders: Overview and quality of life issues. *Journal of Clinical Psychiatry, 57*(Suppl. 8), 3–6.

Honagen, F., Winkelman, G., Rasche-Rauchle, H., et al. (1998). Combination of behaviour therapy with fluvoxamine in comparison with behaviour therapy and placebo. *British Journal of Psychiatry, 173*(Suppl. 35), 71–78.

Howland, R. H. (1991). Lithium augmentation of fluoxetine in the treatment of OCD and major depression: a case report. *Canadian Journal of Psychiatry, 36*(2), 154–155.

Hunter, R., & Macalpine, I. (1982). *Three hundred years of psychiatry 1535–1860: A history presented in selected English texts*. Hartsdale, NY: Carlisle.

Insel, T. R. (1992). Toward a neuroanatomy of obsessive-compulsive disorder. *Archives of General Psychiatry, 49*, 739–744.

Insel, T. R., Murphy, D. L., Cohen, R. M., et al. (1983). Obsessive-compulsive disorder: A double-blind trial of clomipramine and clorgyline. *Archives of General Psychiatry, 40*, 605–612.

Jacobsen, F. M. (1995). Risperidone in the treatment of severe affective illness and obsessive-compulsive disorder. *Journal of Clinical Psychiatry, 56*(9), 423–429.

Janet, P. (1903). *Les obsessions et la psychasthenie* (Vol. 1). Paris: Alcan.

Jenike, M. A. (1989). Obsessive compulsive and related disorders: A hidden epidemic. *New England Journal of Medicine, 321*, 539–541.

Jenike, M. A. (1993a). Obsessive-compulsive disorder: Efficacy of specific treatments as assessed by controlled trials. *Psychopharmacology Bulletin, 29*, 487–499.

Jenike, M. A. (1993b). Augmentation strategies for treatment-resistant obsessive-compulsive disorder. *Harvard Review of Psychiatry, 1*, 17–26.

Jenike, M. A. (1998a). Drug treatment of obsessive-compulsive disorders. In M. A. Jenike, L. Baer, & W. E. Minichiello, (Eds.), *Obsessive-compulsive disorders: Practical management* (3rd ed.). Boston: Mosby-Year Book.

Jenike, M. A., & Baer, L. (1988). Buspirone in obsessive-compulsive disorder: An open trial. *American Journal of Psychiatry, 145*, 1285–1286.

Jenike, M. A., Baer, L., Minichiello, W. E., Rauch, S. L., & Buttolph, M. L. (1997). Placebo-controlled trial of fluoxetine and phenelzine for obsessive-compulsive disorder. *American Journal of Psychiatry, 154*, 1261–1264.

Jenike, M. A., Baer, L., Summergrad, P., et al. (1989). Obsessive-compulsive disorder: A double-blind, placebo-controlled trial of clomipramine in 27 patients. *American Journal of Psychiatry, 146*, 1328–1330.

Jenike, M. A., Baer, L., & Summergrad, P., et al. (1990a). Sertraline in obsessive-compulsive disorder: A double-blind comparison with placebo. *American Journal of Psychiatry, 147*, 923, 928.

Jenike, M. A., Hyman, S. E., Baer, L., et al. (1990b). A controlled trial of fluvoxamine for obsessive-compulsive disorder: Implications for a serotonergic theory. *American Journal of Psychiatry, 147*, 1209–1215.

Jenike, M. A., & Rauch, S. L. (1994). Managing the patient with treatment resistant obsessive compulsive disorder: current strategies. *Journal of Clinical Psychiatry, 55*, 11–17.

Jenike, M. A., & Rauch, S. L. (1995). ECT for OCD. *Journal of Clinical Psychiatry, 56*, 81–82.

Jenike, M. A., Rauch, S. L., Baer, L., & Rasmussen, S. A. (1998b). Neurosurgical treatments of obsessive-compulsive disorder. In M. A. Jenike, L. Baer, & W. E. Minichiello, (Eds.), *Obsessive-compulsive disorders: Practical management* (3rd ed.). Boston: Mosby-Year Book.

Jenike, M. A., Surman, O. S., Cassem, N. H., et al. (1983). Monoamine oxidase inhibitors in obsessive-compulsive disorder. *Journal of Clinical Psychiatry, 44*, 131–132.

Judd, F. K., Chua, P., Lynch, C., & Norman, T. (1991). Fenfluramine augmentation of clomipramine treatment of obsessive-compulsive disorder. *Austra-*

lian and New Zealand Journal of Psychiatry, 25(3), 412–414.

Karabanow, O. (1977). Double-blind controlled study in phobias and obsessions. *Journal of International Medical Research, 5*(Suppl. 5), 42–48.

Karno, M., Golding, J. M., Sorenson, S. B., & Burnam, A. (1988). The epidemiology of obsessive-compulsive disorder in five US communities. *Archives of General Psychiatry, 45*, 1094–1099.

Kim, S., Dysken, M., & Kuskowski, M. (1990). The Yale-Brown obsessive compulsive scale: A reliability and validity study. *Psychiatric Research, 34*, 94–106.

Koponen, H., Lepola, U., Leinonen, E., et al. (1997). Citalopram in the treatment of obsessive-compulsive disorder: An open pilot study. *Acta Psychiatrica Scandinavica, 96*, 343–346.

Koran, L. M., McElroy, S. L., Davidson, J. R. T., et al. (1996). Fluvoxamine versus clomipramine for obsessive-compulsive disorder: A double-blind comparison. *Journal of Clinical Psychopharmacology, 16*, 121–129.

Koran, L. M., Ringold, A. L., & Elliott, M. A. (2000). Olanzapine augmentation for treatment-resistant obsessive-compulsive disorder. *Journal of Clinical Psychiatry, 61*, 514–517.

Koran, L. M., Sallee, F. R., & Pallanti, S. (1997). Rapid benefit of intravenous pulse loading of clomipramine in obsessive-compulsive disorder. *American Journal of Psychiatry, 154*(3), 396–401.

Kozak, M. J., Foa, E. B., & Steketee, G. (1988). Process and outcome of exposure treatment with obsessive-compulsive: Psychophysiological indicators of emotional processing. *Behavior Therapy, 19*, 157–169.

Kronig, M. H., Apter, J., Asnis, G., et al. (1999). Placebo-controlled, multicenter study of sertraline treatment for obsessive-compulsive disorder. *Journal of Clinical Psychopharmacology, 19*, 172–176.

LaPorta, L. D. (1994). More on obsessive-compulsive symptoms and clozapine (letter). *Journal of Clinical Psychiatry, 55*, 312.

Leckman, J. F., Goodman, W. K., North, W. G., Chappell, P. B., Price, L. H., Pauls, D. L., Anderson, G. M., Riddle, M. A., McDougle, C. J., & Barr, L. C. (1994). The role of central oxytocin in obsessive-compulsive disorder and related normal behavior. *Psychoneuroendocrinology, 19*(8), 723–749.

Lei, B. S. (1986). A cross-over treatment of obsessive compulsive neurosis with imipramine and chlorimipramine. *Chung Hua Shen Ching Shen Ko Tsa Chih, 19*(5), 275–278.

Leonard, H. L., Swedo, S. E., Lenane, M. C., et al. (1991). A double-blind desipramine substitution during long-term clomipramine treatment in children and adolescents with obsessive-compulsive disorder. *Archives of General Psychiatry, 48*, 922–927.

Leonard, H. L., Swedo, S., Rapoport, J. L., et al. (1988). Treatment of childhood obsessive-compulsive disorder with clomipramine and desmethylimipramine: A double-blind crossover comparison. *Psychopharmacology Bulletin, 24*, 93–95.

Lindsay, M., Crino, R., & Andrews, G. (1997). Controlled trial of exposure and response prevention in obsessive-compulsive disorder. *British Journal of Psychiatry, 171*, 135–139.

Lipsedge, M. S., & Prothero, W. (1987). Clonidine and clomipramine in obsessive-compulsive disorder. *American Journal of Psychiatry, 144*(7), 965–966.

Lopez-Ibor, J. J., Jr., Saiz, J., Cottraux, J., et al. (1996). Double-blind comparison of fluoxetine versus clomipramine in the treatment of obsessive compulsive disorder. *European Neuropsychopharmacology, 6*, 111–118.

Mallison, R. T., McDougle, C. J., van Dyck, C. H., Scahill, L., Baldwin, R. M., Seibyl, J. P., et al. (1995). I-123-CIT SPECT imaging of striatal dopamine transporter binding in Tourette's disorder. *American Journal of Psychiatry, 152*, 1359–1361.

March, J. S. (1995). Cognitive-behavioral psychotherapy for children and adolescents with OCD: A review and recommendations for treatment. *Journal of the American Academy of Child and Adolescent Psychiatry, 34*(1), 7–18.

March, J. S., Biederman, J., Wolkow, R., et al. (1998). Sertraline in children and adolescents with obsessive-compulsive disorder: A multicenter randomized controlled trial. *Journal of the American Medical Association, 280*, 1752–1756.

March, J. S., Mulle, K., & Herbel, B. (1994). Behavioral psychotherapy for children and adolescents with obsessive-compulsive disorder: An open trial of a new protocol driven treatment package. *Journal of the American Academy of Child and Adolescent Psychiatry, 33*(3), 333–341.

Markovitz, P. J., Stagno, S. J., & Calabrese, J. R. (1990). Buspirone augmentation of fluoxetine in obsessive-compulsive disorder. *American Journal of Psychiatry, 147*(6), 798–800.

Marks, I. M. (1981). Review of behavioral psychotherapy, 1. Obsessive-compulsive disorders. *American Journal of Psychiatry, 138*, 584–592.

Marks, I. M., Hodgson, R., & Rachman, S. (1975). Treatment of chronic obsessive-compulsive neurosis by in-vivo exposure: A two-year follow-up and issues in treatment. *British Journal of Psychiatry, 127*, 349–364.

Mavissakalianm, M., Turner, S. M., Michelson, L., & Jacob, R. (1985). Tricyclic antidepressants in obsessive-compulsive disorder: Antiobsessional or antidepressant agents? *American Journal of Psychiatry, 142*, 572–576.

Mawson, D., Marks, I. M., & Ramm, L. (1982). Clomipramine and exposure for chronic obsessive-compulsive rituals. 3. Two year follow-up and further findings. *British Journal of Psychiatry, 140*, 11–18.

McDougle, C. J., et al. (1993a). The efficacy of fluvoxamine in obsessive-compulsive disorder: Effects of comorbid chronic tic disorder. *Journal of Clinical Psychopharmacology, 13*, 354–358.

McDougle, C. J., et al. (1993b). Limited therapeutic effect of addition of buspirone in fluvoxamine-refractory obsessive-compulsive disorder. *American Journal of Psychiatry, 150*, 647–649.

McDougle, C. J., Barr, L. C., Goodman, W. K., Pelton, G. H., Aronson, S. C., Anand, A., & Price, L. H. (1995). Lack of efficacy of clozapine monotherapy in refractory obsessive-compulsive disorder. *American Journal of Psychiatry, 152*(12), 1812–1814.

McDougle, C. J., Epperson, C. N., Pelton, G. H., Wasylink, S., & Price, L. H. (2000). A double-blind, placebo-controlled study of risperidone addition in serotonin reuptake inhibitor-refractory obsessive-compulsive disorder. *Archives of General Psychiatry, 57*, 794–801.

McDougle, C. J., Fleischmann, R. L., Epperson, C. N., Wasylink, S., Leckman, J. F., & Price, L. H. (1995). Risperidone addition in fluvoxamine-refractory obsessive-compulsive disorder: Three cases. *Journal of Clinical Psychiatry, 56*(11), 526–528.

McDougle, C. J., & Goodman, W. K. (1997). Combination pharmacological treatment strategies. In E. Hollander, & D. J. Stein (Eds.), *Obsessive-compulsive disorders: Diagnosis—etiology—treatment*. New York: Marcel Dekker.

McDougle, C. J., Goodman, W. K., Leckman, J. F., Lee, N. C., Heninger, G. R., & Price, L. H. (1994). Haloperidol addition in fluvoxamine-refractory obsessive-compulsive disorder: A double-blind, placebo-controlled study in patients with and without tics. *Archives of General Psychiatry, 51*, 302–308.

McDougle, C. J., Goodman, W. K., Price, L. H., et al. (1990). Neuroleptic addition in fluvoxamine refractory obsessive compulsive disorder. *American Journal of Psychiatry, 147*, 652–654.

McDougle, C. J., Price, L. H., Goodman, W. K., et al. (1991). A controlled trial of lithium augmentation in fluvoxamine-refractory obsessive compulsive disorder: lack of efficacy. *Journal of Clinical Psychopharmacology, 11*, 175–184.

McElroy, S. L., Phillips, K. A., & Keck, P. E. (1994). Obsessive compulsive spectrum disorder. *Journal of Clinical Psychiatry, 55*(Suppl.), 15–32.

Meige, H., & Feindel, E. (1907). *Tics and their treatment*. (Trans. S. A. K. Wilson). New York: William Wood.

Milanfranchi, A., Ravagli, S., Lensi, P., et al. (1997). A double-blind study of fluvoxamine and clomipramine in the treatment of obsessive-compulsive disorder. *International Journal of Clinical Psychopharmacology, 12*, 131–136.

Mindus, P., Rauch, S. L., Nyman, H., Baer, L., Edman, G., & Jenike, M. A. (1994). Capsulotomy and cingulotomy as treatments for malignant obsessive compulsive disorder: An update. In E. Hollander, J. Zohar, D. Marazziti, & B. Olivier (Eds.), *Current insights in obsessive compulsive disorder*. Chichester, UK: Wiley.

Montgomery, S. A. (1980). Clomipramine in obsessional neurosis: A placebo-controlled trial. *Pharmaceutical Medicine, 1*(2), 189–192.

Montgomery, S. A. (1994). Pharmacological treatment of obsessive compulsive disorder. In E. Hollander, J. Zohar, D. Marazziti, & B. Olivier, (Eds.), *Current insights in obsessive compulsive disorder*. Chichester, UK: Wiley.

Montgomery, S. A., McIntyre, A., Osterheider, M., et al. (1993). A double-blind placebo-controlled study of fluoxetine in patients with DSM-IIIR obsessive-compulsive disorder. *European Neuropsychopharmacology, 3*, 143–152.

Mundo, E., Bareggi, S. R., Pirola, R., et al. (1997a). Long-term pharmacotherapy of obsessive-compulsive disorder: A double-blind controlled study. *Journal of Clinical Psychopharmacology, 17*, 4–10.

Mundo, E., Bianchi, L., & Bellodi, L. (1997b). Efficacy of fluvoxamine, paroxetine, and citalopram in the treatment of obsessive-compulsive disorder: A single-blind study. *Journal of Clinical Psychopharmacology, 17*, 267–271.

Mundo, E., Maina, G., & Uslenghi, C. (2000). Multicentre, double-blind, comparison of fluvoxamine and clomipramine in the treatment of obsessive-compulsive disorder. *International Journal of Clinical Psychopharmacology, 15*, 69–76.

O'Connor, K., Todorov, C., Robillard, S., et al. (1999). Cognitive-behaviour therapy and medication in the treatment of obsessive-compulsive disorder: A controlled study. *Canadian Journal of Psychiatry, 44*, 64–71.

Pallanti, S., Quercioli, L., Paiva, R. S., & Koran, L. M. (1999). Citalopram for treatment-resistant obsessive-compulsive disorder. *European Psychiatry, 14,* 101–106.

Pato, M. T., Eisen, J. L., & Pato, C. N. (1994). Rating scales for obsessive compulsive disorder. In E. Hollander, J. Zohar, D. Marazziti, & B. Olivier (Eds.), *Current insights in obsessive compulsive disorder.* Chichester, UK: Wiley.

Pato, M. T., Hill, J. L., & Murphy, D. L. (1990). A clomipramine dosage reduction study in the course of long-term treatment of obsessive-compulsive patients. *Psychopharmacology Bulletin, 26,* 211–214.

Pato, M. T., Pigott, T. A., Hill, J. L., Grover, G. N., Bernstein, S., & Murphy, D. L. (1991). Controlled comparison of buspirone and clomipramine in obsessive-compulsive disorder. *American Journal of Psychiatry, 148,* 127–129.

Pato, M. T., Zohar-Kaduch, R., Zohar, J., et al. (1988). Return of symptoms after discontinuation of clomipramine in patients with obsessive compulsive disorder. *American Journal of Psychiatry, 145,* 1521–1525.

Pauls, D. L., Alsobrook, J. P., Goodman, W., et al. (1995). A family study of obsessive-compulsive disorder. *American Journal of Psychiatry, 152,* 76–84.

Pauls, D. L., & Leckman, J. F. (1986). The inheritance of Gilles de la Tourette's syndrome and associated behaviors: Evidence for autosomal dominant transmission. *New England Journal of Medicine, 315,* 993–997.

Perse, T. L., Greist, J. H., Jefferson, J. W., et al. (1987). Fluvoxamine treatment of obsessive-compulsive disorder. *American Journal of Psychiatry, 144,* 1543–1548.

Pigott, T. A., L'Heureux, F., Hill, J. L., Bihari, K., Bernstien, S. E., & Murphy, D. L. (1992a). A double-blind study of adjuvant buspirone hydrochloride in clomipramine-treated patients. *Journal of Clinical Psychopharmacology, 12,* 11–18.

Pigott, T. A., L'Heureux, F., Rubenstein, C. S., et al. (1992b). A double-blind, placebo controlled study of trazodone in patients with obsessive-compulsive disorder. *Journal of Clinical Psychopharmacology, 12,* 156–162.

Pigott, T. A., L'Heureux, F., Rubenstein, C. S., Hill, J. L., & Murphy, D. L. (1992c). *A controlled trial of clonazepam augmentation in OCD patients treated with clomipramine or fluoxetine.* American Psychiatry Association Annual Meeting, Washington, DC.

Pigott, T. A., Pato, M. T., Bernstein, S. E., et al. (1990). Controlled comparisons of clomipramine and fluoxetine in the treatment of obsessive-compulsive disorder. *Archives of General Psychiatry, 47,* 926–932.

Pigott, T. A., Pato, M. T., L'Heureux. F., et al. (1991). A controlled comparison of adjuvant lithium carbonate or thyroid hormone in clomipramine-treated patients with obsessive compulsive disorder. *Journal of Clinical Psychopharmacology, 11,* 242–248.

Pigott, T. A., & Seay, S. M. (1999). A review of the efficacy of selective serotonin reuptake inhibitors in obsessive-compulsive disorders. *Journal of Clinical Psychiatry, 60,* 101–106.

Pitman, R. K. (1994). Obsessive compulsive disorder in western history. In E. Hollander, J. Zohar, D. Marazziti, & B. Olivier, (Eds.), *Current insights in obsessive compulsive disorder.* Chichester, UK: Wiley.

Quality Assurance Project. (1985). Treatment outlines for the management of obsessive-compulsive disorders. *Australian and New Zealand Journal of Psychiatry, 19,* 240–253.

Rachman, S., Cobb, J., Grey, S., et al. (1979). The behavioural treatment of obsessional-compulsive disorders, with and without clomipramine. *Behaviour Research and Therapy, 17,* 467–478.

Rachman, S. J., & Hodgson, R. J. (1980). *Obsessions and compulsions.* Englewood Cliffs, NJ: Prentice Hall.

Rachman, S., Hodgson, R., & Marks, I. M. (1971). The treatment of chronic obsessive-compulsive neurosis. *Behaviour Research and Therapy, 9,* 237–247.

Rachman, S., Marks, I. M., & Hodgson, R. (1973). The treatment of obsessive-compulsive neurotics by modeling and flooding in vivo. *Behaviour Research and Therapy, 11,* 463–471.

Rapoport, J., Elkins, R., Mikkelsen, E., et al. (1980). Clinical controlled trial of chlorimipramine in adolescents with obsessive-compulsive disorder. *Psychopharmacology Bulletin, 16*(3), 61–63.

Rapoport, J. L. (1989). *The boy who couldn't stop washing.* New York: Dutton.

Rapoport, J. L., & Wise, S. P. (1988). Obsessive-compulsive disorder: Is it a basal ganglia dysfunction? *Psychopharmacology Bulletin, 24,* 380–384.

Rasmussen, S. A., & Eisen, J. L. (1994). The epidemiology and differential diagnosis of obsessive compulsive disorder. *Journal of Clinical Psychiatry, 55*(Suppl.), 5–14.

Rasmussen, S., Goodman, W. K., Greist, J. H., Jenike, M. A., Kozak, M. J., Liebowitz, M., Robinson, D. G., & White, K. L. (in press). Fluvoxamine in the treatment of obsessive compulsive disorder: A multi-center, double-blind placebo-controlled study in outpatients. *American Journal of Psychiatry.*

Rauch, S. L., Baer, L., & Jenike, M. A. (1996). Treatment-resistant obsessive-compulsive disorder: Practical strategies for management. In M. H. Pollack, M. W. Otto, & J. F. Rosenbaum (Eds.), *Challenges in Clinical Practice: Pharmacologic and Psychosocial Strategies*. New York: Guilford Press.

Rauch, S. L., & Jenike, M. A. (1993). Neurobiological models of obsessive-compulsive disorder. *Psychosomatics*, 34, 20–32.

Rauch, S. L., & Jenike, M. A. (1997). Neural mechanisms of obsessive-compulsive disorder. *Current Review of Mood & Anxiety Disorders*, 1, 84–94.

Rauch, S. L., & Jenike, M. A. (1994). Management of treatment resistant obsessive-compulsive disorder: concepts and strategies. In B. Berend, E. Hollander, D. Marazitti, & J. Zohar (Eds.), *Current insights in obsessive-compulsive disorder*. Chichester, UK: Wiley.

Rauch, S. L., Whalen, P. J., Dougherty, D., & Jenike, M. A. (1998). Neurobiologic models of obsessive-compulsive disorder. In M. A. Jenike, L. Baer, & W. E. Minichiello (Eds.), *Obsessive-compulsive disorders: Practical management* (3rd ed.). Boston: Mosby-Year Book.

Ravizza, L., Barzega, G., Bellino, S., Bogetto, F., & Maina, G. (1995). Predictors of drug treatment response in obsessive-compulsive disorder. *Journal of Clinical Psychiatry*, 56, 368–373.

Ravizza, L., Barzega, G., Bellino, S., Bogetto, F., & Maina, G. (1996a). Drug treatment of obsessive-compulsive disorder (OCD): Long-term trial with clomipramine and selective serotonin reuptake inhibitors (SSRIs). *Psychopharmacology Bulletin*, 32, 167–173.

Ravizza, L., Barzega, G., Bellino, S., et al. (1996b). Therapeutic effect and safety of adjunctive risperidone in refractory obsessive-compulsive disorder. *Psychopharmacology Bulletin*, 32, 677–682.

Riddle, M. A., Scahill, L., King, R. A., et al. (1992). Fluoxetine in the treatment of obsessive-compulsive disorder in children and adolescents. *Journal of the American Academy of Child and Adolescent Psychiatry*, 31(3), 575.

Rimm, D. C., & Masters, J. C. (1974). *Behavior therapy: Techniques and empirical findings*. New York: Academic Press.

Scahill, L., Vitulano, L. A., Brenner, E. M., et al. (1996). Behavioral therapy in children and adolescents with obsessive-compulsive disorder: A pilot study. *Journal of Child and Adolescent Psychopharmacology*, 6, 191–202.

Schwartz, J. M., Stoessel, P. W., Baxter, L. R., et al. (1996). Systematic changes in cerebral glucose metabolic rate after successful behavior modification. *Archives of General Psychiatry*, 53, 109–113.

Simeon, J. G., Thatte, S., Wiggins, D. (1990). Treatment of adolescent obsessive-compulsive disorder with a clomipramine-fluoxetine combination. *Psychopharmacology Bulletin*, 26(3), 285–290.

Solyom, L., & Sookman, D. (1977). A comparison of clomipramine hydrochloride (Anafranil) and behaviour therapy in the treatment of obsessive neurosis. *Journal of International Medical Research*, 5(Suppl. 5), 49–106.

Steketee, G., Foa, E., & Grayson, J. B. (1982). Recent advances in the behavioral treatment of obsessive-compulsives. *Archives of General Psychiatry*, 39, 1365–1371.

Swedo, S. E. (1994). Sydenham's chorea: a model for childhood autoimmune neuropsychiatric disorders. *Journal of the American Medical Association*, 272(22), 1788–1791.

Swedo, S. E., Leonard, H. L., & Kiessling, L. S. (1994). Speculations on antineuronal antibody-mediated neuropsychiatric disorders of childhood. *Pediatrics*, 93(2), 323–326.

Swedo, S. E., Leonard, H. L., Garvey, M., et al. (1998). Pediatric autoimmune neuropsychiatric disorders associated with streptococcal infections: clinical description of the first 50 cases. *American Journal of Psychiatry*, 155(2), 264–271.

Swerdlow, N. R. (1995). Serotonin, obsessive-compulsive disorder and the basal ganglia. *International Review of Psychiatry*, 7(1), 115–129.

Thoren, P., Åsberg, M., Cronholm, B., et al. (1980). Clomipramine treatment of obsessive compulsive disorder. 1. A controlled clinical trial. *Archives of General Psychiatry*, 37, 1281–1285.

Tollefson, G. D., Birkett, M., Koran, L., & Genduso, L. (1994a). Continuation treatment of OCD: Double-blind and open-label experience with fluoxetine. *Journal of Clinical Psychiatry*, 55(10 Suppl.), 69–76.

Tollefson, G. D., Rampey, A. H., Jr., Potvin, J. H., Jenike, M. A., Rush, A. J., Dominguez, R. A., Koran, L. M., Shear, M. K., Goodman, W., & Genduso, L. A. (1994b). A multicenter investigation of fixed-dose fluoxetine in the treatment of obsessive-compulsive disorder. *Archives of General Psychiatry*, 51(7), 559–567.

Vallejo, J., Olivares, J., Marcos, T., Bulbena, A., & Menchon, J. (1992). Clomiparmine versus phenelzine in obsessive-compulsive disorder: A controlled trial. *British Journal of Psychiatry*, 161, 665–670.

van Balkom, A. J., de Haan, E., van Oppen, P., et al. (1998). Cognitive and behavioral therapies alone versus in combination with fluvoxamine in the treatment of obsessive-compulsive disorder. *Journal of Nervous and Mental Disease, 186*, 492–499.

van Oppen, P., de Haan, E., van Balkom, A. J. L. M., Spinhoven, P., Hoogduin, K., & van Dyck, R. (1995). Cognitive therapy and exposure in vivo in the treatment of obsessive compulsive disorder. *Behaviour Research and Therapy, 33*, 79–390.

Volavka, J., Neziroglu, F., & Yaryura-Tobias, J. A. (1985). Clomipramine and imipramine in obsessive-compulsive disorder. *Psychiatry Research, 14*(1), 83–91.

Warneke, L. B. (1989). The use of intravenous chlorimipramine therapy in obsessive compulsive disorder. *Canadian Journal of Psychiatry, 34*, 853–859.

Wheadon, D. E., Bushnell, W. D., & Steiner, M. (1993, December). *A fixed dose comparison of 20, 40, or 60 mg of paroxetine to placebo in the treatment of OCD*. Presented at the 1993 Annual Meeting of the American College of Neuropsychopharmacology, Honolulu.

Young, C. R., Bostic, J. Q., & McDonald, C. L. (1994). Clozapine and refractory obsessive compulsive disorder: A case report (letter). *Journal of Clinical Psychopharmacology, 14*, 209–211.

Zahn, T. P., Insel, T. R., & Murphy, D. L. (1984). Psychophysiological changes during pharmacological treatment of patients with obsessive-compulsive disorder. *British Journal of Psychiatry, 145*, 39–44.

Zhao, J. P. (1991). A controlled study of clomipramine and amitriptyline for treating obsessive-compulsive disorder. *Chung Hua Shen Ching Shen Ko Tsa Chih, 24*(2), 68–70.

Zohar, J., Judge, R., et al. (1996). Paroxetine versus clomipramine in the treatment of obsessive-compulsive disorder. *British Journal of Psychiatry, 169*, 468–474.

17

Pharmacological Treatments for Posttraumatic Stress Disorder

Rachel Yehuda
Randall Marshall
Ariel Penkower
Cheryl M. Wong

This chapter provides an update into the current rationale for psychopharmacological treatment in posttraumatic stress disorder (PTSD) as well as a review of a large number of new studies in this area. Since the last volume, numerous clinical trials have been published and are reviewed. It is now clear that SSRIs are the first line treatments for PTSD, although other medications can also be utilized to augment PTSD treatment or address adjunctive symptoms. Indeed, SSRIs are the only class of medication that has shown effectiveness for all three symptom clusters in PTSD as well as global improvement. Other medications that have been tried in PTSD do not seem to target the uniform syndrome, but rather specific aspects of the disorder. Further directions for research in this area are also discussed.

BRIEF DESCRIPTION OF POSTTRAUMATIC STRESS DISORDER AS CURRENTLY DEFINED IN *DSM-IV*

The diagnosis of posttraumatic stress disorder (PTSD) first appeared in the *DSM-III* (American Psychiatric Association [APA], 1980) with the intention of describing the characteristic symptoms that occur in individuals following exposure to extremely traumatic events. Although classified as an anxiety disorder, individuals with PTSD also often exhibit features of mood, dissociative and personality disorders.

Principal Diagnostic Criteria

The first diagnostic criterion (Criterion A) for PTSD is that a person must experience, witness, or be confronted with an event that involves "actual or threatened death, serious injury, or a threat to physical integrity of self or others," and have an immediate subjective response to this experience that involves "intense fear, helplessness or horror" (APA, 1994, p. 424). In children, however, the event may include sexual trauma without an actual physical threat.

The symptoms of PTSD are then classified into three discrete clusters that constitute diagnostic criteria B through D. Intrusive symptoms (Criterion B) include (a) having recurrent and unwanted recollections of the event, (b) having distressing dreams of the event, and (c) acting and feeling as if the event were recurring (e.g., dissociative flashback). Additionally, (d) psychological and (e) physiological distress following exposure to symbolic representations of the event may also occur. Avoidant symptoms (Criterion C) reflect both behaviors indicative of actively avoiding reminders of the trauma and symptoms of generalized emotional numbing. The former include

(a) efforts to avoid thoughts, feelings or talk of the trauma; (b) efforts to avoid reminders of the trauma; and (c) inability to recall important aspects of the trauma (e.g., psychogenic amnesia). The latter symptoms are (d) markedly diminished interest in normally significant activities, (e) feelings of detachment or estrangement from others, (f) restricted range of affect, and (g) sense of a foreshortened future. Hyperarousal symptoms (Criterion D) include (a) difficulty falling or staying asleep, (b) irritability or angry outbursts, (c) difficulties with concentration, (d) hypervigilance, and (e) exaggerated startle response. Meeting diagnostic criteria for PTSD requires the concurrent presence of one intrusive symptom, three avoidant symptoms, and two hyperarousal symptoms.

In addition to the above criteria, symptoms must be present for at least 1 month (Criterion E) and must be accompanied by clinically significant impairment in social, occupational, or other areas of functioning (Criterion F). If symptoms persist more than 3 months, the diagnosis of chronic, rather than acute, PTSD is given. The diagnosis of delayed-onset PTSD 2 is given if symptoms begin at least 6 months after the traumatic event. PTSD may be diagnosed in any person, adult or child, who meets the above diagnostic criteria, regardless of other preexisting or concurrent psychopathology.

Although the *DSM-IV* uses a categorical model for defining syndromes, emerging evidence suggests that PTSD symptoms may fall in a continuum in which disability, comorbidity, and associated symptoms correlate with a number of PTSD symptoms, including sub-threshold psychopathology (Marshall et al., 2001; Stein et al., 1997; Weiss et al., 1992).

Prevalence

Recent epidemiological studies have demonstrated that PTSD is a common psychiatric condition with an estimated lifetime prevalence of between 5% and 14% in the U.S. general population (Breslau et al., 1998; Davidson et al., 1991a; Helzer et al., 1987; Kessler et al., 1995). The high frequency of PTSD primarily reflects the extraordinarily high prevalence of potentially life-threatening events in this society. Recent epidemiological studies estimated that, based on the current definition of trauma in the *DSM-IV*, 60% of citizens in the United States are exposed to at least one traumatic event during their lives (Breslau et al., 1998; Kessler et al., 1995).

In *DSM-IV*, estimates of the prevalence of PTSD among those exposed to Criterion A stressors range from 3% to 58% (APA, 1994). This wide range reflects the fact that some types of traumatic events are more likely than others to result in PTSD. Among those who have experienced torture, such as concentration camp survivors and POWs, the prevalence of PTSD is quite high, with estimates of 50 to 75% (Goldstein et al., 1987; Kilpatrick & Resnick, 1993; Kluznick et al., 1986; Yehuda et al., 1995). Among U.S. war veterans, overall estimates of lifetime PTSD are about 30%, but this rate varies considerably depending on the degree of combat exposure. In individuals who have been exposed to natural disasters such as earthquakes, volcanic eruptions, and bush fires, the prevalence of lifetime PTSD is lower with estimates ranging from 3.5% to 16% (Kessler et al., 1995; McFarlane, 1992; Shore et al., 1986, 1989). Estimates of the prevalence of PTSD in trauma survivors also varies depending on the amount of time that has elapsed between the traumatic event and assessment of PTSD. Prospective longitudinal studies have also shown that mood and other anxiety disorders may occur as a response to trauma even in the absence of PTSD (Shalev et al., 1998; Yehuda et al., 1998).

One retrospective study examining the longitudinal course of PTSD approximated that 40% of the sample continued to experience symptoms several times a week for as long as 10 years after the onset of the disorder (Kessler et al., 1995). In the portion of the sample who remitted, 3 years represented the mean length of time until remission following professional treatment. For those who received no treatment, the mean length of time until remission was over 5 years. However, for the minority of individuals who remain symptomatic, not only may symptoms of PTSD actually intensify over time, but there is an increased risk of developing secondary and chronic comorbid mood, anxiety, substance abuse, or personality disorders (Freedy et al., 1992; Friedman & Yehuda, 1995; Green et al., 1992; Kulka et al., 1990; North et al., 1994).

Etiology

By definition, exposure to a traumatic event is a necessary requirement for the development of PTSD. However, as discussed above, not everyone who is exposed to traumatic events develops PTSD. Therefore, there are other factors that influence the development or persistence of symptoms following trauma exposure. Factors that have been associated with increased risk for the development of chronic PTSD include the severity of the trauma (Foy et al., 1984; Kessler et al., 1995; March, 1993; Yehuda et al., 1992a); past history of stress, abuse, or trauma (Bremner et al., 1993; Breslau et al., 1991; Davidson et al., 1991a; Resnick et al., 1992; Zaidi & Foy, 1994); history of behavioral or psychological problems (Breslau et al., 1998; Helzer et al., 1987; Kluznick et al., 1986; Schnurr et al., 1993); comorbid psychopathology (Breslau et al., 1998; McFarlane et al., 1989; Schnurr et al., 1993); cognitive factors, including lower intelligence (McNally & Shin, 1995); genetic factors (True et al., 1993); family history of psychopathology (Davidson et al., 1985); and subsequent exposure to reactivating environmental events (Goldstein et al., 1987; Green, 2000; Kluznick et al., 1986; McFarlane, 1990; Schnurr et al., 1993; Solomon & Preager, 1992; Solomon & Smith, 1994; True et al., 1993; Yehuda et al., 1995). A recent meta-analysis of risk for PTSD differentiated three groups of risk factors: those that predict PTSD in some populations only, those that consistently predict PTSD but to varying extents, and those with consistent effects in predicting PTSD (Brewin et al., 2000). Factors in the first group include female gender, younger age, and race. Factors in the second group include low socioeconomic status, lack of education, low intelligence, other previous trauma, other adverse childhood experiences, trauma severity, lack of social support, and life stress. Factors in the third group included psychiatric history, childhood abuse, and family psychiatric history. The acknowledgment of these risk factors may have significant implications for pharmacotherapy as described in the next section.

BRIEF HISTORICAL PERSPECTIVE ON TREATMENT

Importance of Psychosocial Treatments

When first described in the *DSM-III*, PTSD was conceptualized as defining the normative symptoms that occur following exposure to extremely stressful events. Because of the emphasis on both the environmental etiology of PTSD and the psychological nature of the response, earliest formulations of treatment were psychosocial in nature.

The earliest theories of PTSD were psychodynamic. These theories emphasized that PTSD occurred when normal coping mechanisms were overwhelmed and, accordingly, when avoidance interfered with the processing of the trauma (Horowitz, 1974; Schwartz, 1990). Psychodynamic theory postulated that the symptoms of PTSD would be relieved when the individual could integrate the traumatic event into his or her overall life narrative and self-concept. The best vehicle for achieving this integration was initially thought to be trauma-focused, time-limited psychodynamic psychotherapy. The aim of psychotherapy for trauma survivors was to modify the maladaptive defenses and coping strategies used in the aftermath of the trauma by helping the patient fully process the traumatic experience, with all its implications, and emerge from the experience intact and capable of continuing to engage with others and in the world.

Behavioral theorists explained PTSD as a conditioned fear response and postulated that effective treatments involved reexposing individuals to aspects of the traumatic event through psychoeducation and systematic desensitization or the more extreme technique of "flooding" (Keane et al., 1989). Theoretically, symptoms could be relieved by applying learning principles such as habituation or extinction and monitoring the response to traumatic reminders until patients became desensitized to these stimuli (Cooper & Clum, 1989; Keane et al., 1989).

Cognitive theories were also developed in the 1980s and 1990s (Foa et al., 1989, 1991; Kilpatrick et al., 1982). These theories maintained that PTSD reflects a failure to mobilize psychological processes that underlie natural recovery (Foa, 1997). In this view, traumatic events result in negative cognitions, such as that the world is dangerous and the victim is incompetent. However, if one could repeatedly confront trauma-related stimuli (e.g., his or her own intrusive memory) and become emotionally engaged with trauma-related thoughts and feelings (e.g., by sharing the memories with others), the result would be natural recovery because the victim would have the opportunity to disconfirm the negative cognitions. In this model, chronic PTSD results from a failure to engage with the traumatic material in the aftermath of trauma. Avoidance of trauma reminders prevents exposure to information that disconfirms the dysfunctional cognitions that the world is indiscriminately dangerous and the victim is totally incompetent. Accordingly, effective therapeutic interventions encourage confrontation with trauma-related situations (in vivo) and with the trauma memories (in imagination). Therapies such as exposure therapy (Foa), cognitive reprocessing (Resick), virtual reality therapy (Rothbaum), and EMDR (Shapiro) offset the patients' tendency to avoid trauma reminders. To the extent that the feelings associated with the event can be verbalized, as is the case, specifically, with prolonged exposure, this provides the trauma survivor with the opportunity to obtain information that will correct the dysfunctional cognitions.

What all of these therapeutic approaches have in common is that they focus on the traumatic event as the direct cause of symptoms of PTSD and emphasize that the response to the traumatic event can be modified through further environmental intervention. In a sense, the more limited focus on preexisting risk factors is interesting in light of epidemiological data demonstrating that such factors are likely to be important in the development of PTSD (McFarlane & Yehuda, 2000). Nonetheless, these treatment approaches have been demonstrated to be effective and are among the first-line treatments for PTSD. More detailed recommendations can be found in two recently published treatment guidelines in PTSD: The Expert Consensus Guideline Series on the Treatment of Posttraumatic Stress Disorder, published by the *Journal of Clinical Psychiatry* (Foa et al., 1999) and the treatment guidelines developed by the International Society for Traumatic Stress Studies, entitled "Effective Treatments for PTSD" (Foa et al., 2000).

Role of Pharmacotherapy

An early view of the role of pharmacotherapy in the treatment of PTSD posited that medications should be considered adjuncts to trauma-focused psychotherapy. By helping to modulate anxiety, pharmacotherapy could allow the individual to continue in psychosocial treatment modalities. Furthermore, pharmacotherapy was considered useful in treating comorbid conditions that are not thought to be directly related to the experience of trauma but may arise either as separate illnesses or as secondary consequences of the chronic state of PTSD. For example, pharmacotherapy may be useful in treating comorbid panic attacks or depressive illness and may result in overall improvement (Marshall et al., 1994).

A second conception viewed pharmacotherapy as directly relieving the maladaptive symptoms of the disorder (Davidson, 1992; Friedman, 1988). The increasing recognition of biological alterations in PTSD since the early 1990s strengthened this view and has justified a more central role for psychopharmacology in the treatment of PTSD. Furthermore, the findings of catecholaminergic, serotonergic, hypothalamic-pituitary-adrenal-axis, and opioid involvement in PTSD have provided a cogent argument for a rational pharmacotherapy that would directly address some of the biological abnormalities and reduce symptoms. Even so, treatment guidelines recommend using pharmacotherapy in tandem with other forms of psychosocial treatment.

Past Treatment Choices

Prior to the official establishment of the diagnosis of PTSD, trauma survivors were often diagnosed as having some kind of anxiety, depressive, or psychotic disorder, depending on the predominant symptoms. Initial pharmacological approaches were based on determining the salient presenting symptoms and using the medication that would be most expected to target those symptoms. For example, flashbacks were treated with antipsychotics, and avoidant and hyperarousal symptoms were characterized more as being part of a depression or phobic response and were accordingly medicated with antidepressants and benzodiazepines. Clinical experience suggested that although antipsychotics could be used for behavioral control and severe arousal, they were not helpful for intrusive recollections and tended to worsen avoidance and numbing symptoms. Therefore, typical antipsychotic medications are contraindicated in PTSD (Davidson, 1992; Friedman, 1988). This recommendation does not extend to some of the newer antipsychotic medications, which, although not systematically tested yet, offer promise.

Rather, at the time the diagnosis of PTSD became formalized, case reports appeared supporting the efficacy of antidepressants and led to double-blind, placebo-controlled trials. Monoamine oxidase inhibitors (MAOIs) were initially recommended in PTSD because investigators noted that in double-blind, placebo-controlled trials, phenelzine particularly improved symptoms of irritability, hyperactivity, increased emotionality, depression, phobic symptoms, and hysteria as well as panic symptoms (Quitkin et al., 1979). All of these symptoms are present in PTSD patients. Tricyclic antidepressants were similarly considered because of their efficacy in panic disorder and depression. As selective serotonin reuptake inhibitors (SSRIs) became available for depression and anxiety disorders, including obsessive compulsive disorders, these agents were also tried in PTSD. As in all psychiatric disorders, the rationale for employing medications in PTSD has not tended to occur as a result of an a priori knowledge about the specific pathophysiology of this disorder but has been an empirical process based on the fundamental assumption of the similarities between PTSD and other mood and anxiety disorders. Since the pathophysiology of all psychiatric disorders remains unknown, clinical progress continues to be based on observations from clinical practice, randomized clinical trials, and theoretical extensions of presumed mechanisms of existing treatments (Marshall & Klein, 1999).

Issues in Evaluating the Efficacy of Pharmacotherapy in PTSD

It is possible to distinguish between the efficacy of medications in three separate domains: core PTSD symptoms, associated symptoms or disorders such as depression and anxiety, and global nonspecific improvement. Several issues arise in attempting to determine whether a medication has been effective in one or more of these domains. First, it is difficult to separate the nonspecific effects of a medication from the effects on the intrusive, avoidant, and hyperarousal symptoms in patients who have chronic illness. Most published reports have examined the efficacy of medications in patients with lifetime or concurrent psychiatric disorder in addition to PTSD. A second issue is that some studies have been performed on chronic PTSD patients who have generally been unresponsive to prior treatments. The response to a medication in a treatment-refractory group may not be generalizable to groups without such treatment histories. Indeed, until recently, the majority of treatment studies were conducted in combat Vietnam veterans who had received chronic treatment from the Veterans Administration (VA) and are subject to the above-mentioned considerations. Furthermore, combat veterans are not likely to be representative of the prototypical trauma survivor in many other regards. Combat veterans recruited from VA hospitals in the United States may also not be representative of veterans the world over. A recent subanalysis of a multinational trial found that combat veterans did in fact benefit from serotonin reuptake inhibitor (SRI) treatment (Martenyi et al., 2001).

Ideally, the efficacy of new psychopharmacological agents should be tested in individuals who have met diagnostic criteria for PTSD for several months or years (as opposed to decades), who are not involved in compensation or disability claims as a result of their traumatic experiences, and who do not have a history of multiple prior treatment failures. The effect of concurrent nonpsychopharmacological treatments either before or during a drug trial should also be controlled. Follow-up studies should address issues related to relapse and remission in successfully treated patients.

CURRENT TREATMENT CHOICES

Since the last edition of this book, the field of pharmacotherapy in PTSD has grown significantly. The more recent studies have been larger and better controlled. These studies have revealed important information about the efficacy of some newer medications in the treatment of PTSD overall and core symptoms. Since 2000, several large multicenter, randomized, double-blind, placebo-controlled studies have been made public (Brady et al., 2000; Davidson et al., 2001; Judge et al., 2000; Marshall et al., 2000) as well as well-conducted single-site studies (Connor et al., 1999) and smaller controlled studies within adult (Hertzberg et al., 2000a, 2000b; Malik et al., 1999) and pediatric (Robert et al., 1999) populations. The rest of the literature consists of multiple open trials, case reports, and retrospective chart reviews with many of the newer pharmacotherapeutic agents of different classes. Table 17.1 presents an updated summary of the results of case reports. Table 17.2 presents an updated summary of all medication trials in PTSD and ranks these studies according to the criteria specified in the footnote. The findings of efficacy for each class of medications is reviewed below.

Monoamine Oxidase Inhibitors

MAOIs were historically the first medications to be considered as a possible treatment for PTSD. The first published open trial of phenelzine reported a dramatic global improvement and an almost complete reduction of intrusive symptoms in five extremely symptomatic combat veterans who had not

TABLE 17.1 Updated Summary of PTSD Clinical Case Reports

Investigators	*Year*	*Class*	*Drug*	*Type of Trauma*	*Comment*
Horrigan	1996	Adrenergic agent	Guanfacine + clonidine	Exposure to domestic violence and physical abuse	Improvements in nightmares
Raskind et al.	2000	Adrenergic agent	Prazosin	Combat	Good for nightmares
Harmon & Riggs	1996	Alpha-2-agonists	Clonidine + imipramine	Severe physical or sexual abuse	Improved aggression, impulsivity, emotional outbursts, mood lability, hyperarousal, hypervigilance, generalized anxiety, oppositionality, insomnia, and nightmares; 1 boy had decrease in repetitive traumatic play; 1 girl had decrease in dissociative
Ford	1996	Anticonvulsant	Carbamazepine	Life threatened as a police officer	Cessation of nightmares, marked improvement in startle response, irritability, sleep disturbance, and depression
Brannon et al.	2000	Anticonvulsant/mood stabilizer	Gabapentin	Electrical injury with third-degree burns	Improved nightmares and anxiety
Hamner	1996	Antipsychotic	Clozapine	Combat	Led to reduction of PTSD symptoms
Burton & Marshall	1999	Atypical antidepressants	Olanzepine	Extensive history of physical and sexual abuse	Improvement in insomnia and hyperarousal
Krashin & Oates	1999	Atypical antipsychotics	Risperidone	Combat plus child abuse	Global improvement, good for flashbacks and intensive thoughts
Monnelly & Ciraulo	1999	Atypical antipsychotics	Risperidone augmentation to paraxetine and diazepam	Combat	Improvement in anger and aggression
Leyba & Wampler	1998	Atypical antipsychotics	Risperidone augmentation to VPA, clonazepam, fluoxetine, paroxetine, trazedone	Not recorded	Improvement in nightmares and flashbacks

Mellman et al.	1998	Benzodiazepine	Temazepam	Surgical	Good for sleep disturbance and improvement of acute PTSD
Bills & Kreisler	1993	Opioid agents	Naltrexone	Coal-mining accident	Good for flashbacks but no global improvement
Ibarra et al.	1994	Opioid agents	Naltrexone	Unknown	Led to feelings of rage, explosive behavior, other unpleasant symptoms, increased blood pressure
Davidson et al.	1998	Serotonergic atypical antidepressant	Nefazodone	Mixed civilian trauma	Early improvements in nightmares and sleep; improvement in all three clusters and global improvement
Davis et al.	2000	Serotonergic atypical	Nefazodone	Combat	Overall improvement and improvement in all three clusters of symptoms
Clark et al.	1999	Serotonin agent	Cyproheptadine	Combat	No improvement in nightmares and no global improvement
Gupta et al.	1998	Serotonin agent	Cyproheptadine	Mixed civilian and combat trauma	Helped with nightmares
Gupta et al.	1998	Serotonin agent	Cyproheptadine	Exposure to domestic violence	Helped with nightmares
Connor et al.	1999	SNRI	Mirtazepine	Mixed trauma types	Global improvement
Hamner & Frueh	1998	SNRI	Venlafaxine	Combat	Improvement in depression, global anxiety, nightmares, panic attacks, sleep, irritability, social avoidance
Dow & Kline	1997	SSRI	Fluoxetine	Combat	SSRI was more effective than norepinephrine agents, e.g., notriptyline/desipramine
Tohen et al.	1994	Anticonvulsant	Carbamazepine + valproate	Unknown	Both drugs well tolerated
Harsch	1985	Serotonin agent	Cyproheptadine	Unknown	Helped with nightmares
Wells et al.	1991	Serotonin agent	Buspirone	Combat	Reduced associative symptoms of anxiety, depression, as well as insomnia and flashbacks; avoidant symptoms were not improved

TABLE 17.2 Review of Clinical Drug Trials for Posttraumatic Stress Disorder

Type	*Investigators*	*Year*	*Class*	*Drug*	*Control Used*	*Duration*	*Subjects*	*Population*
1	Baker et al.	1995	Reversible MAOI	Brofaromine	Placebo	12 weeks	118 randomized	Civilians and veterans (60% combat veterans) with chronic PTSD
1	Brady et al.	2000	SSRI	Sertraline	Placebo	2-week placebo run-in, 12 weeks	187	Adults
1	Connor et al.	1999	SSRI	Fluoxetine	Placebo	12 weeks	53	Adult civilians with chronic PTSD
1	Davidson et al.	2001	SSRI	Sertraline	Placebo	1-week placebo run-in, 12 weeks	208	Adults, mixed traumas
1	Marshall	2000	SSRI	Paroxetine	Placebo	12 weeks	44	Civilians
1	Marshall	2001	SSRI	Paroxetine	Placebo	12 weeks	551	Mostly civilians
1	Martenyi et al.	2001	SSRI	Fluoxetine	Placebo	12 weeks	301	Adults, mixed traumas, 48% with combat exposure
2	Hertzberg et al.	2000	Anticonvulsant/ mood stabilizer	Lamotrigine	Placebo	12 weeks	15	Vets and civilians/ male and female
2	Hertzberg et al.	2000	SSRI	Fluoxetine	Placebo	12 weeks	12	Combat veterans with chronic PTSD
2	Hidalgo	1999	Serotonergic atypical antidepressant	Nefazodone	None	6–12 weeks	92 completers	Men and women with chronic PTSD

Comorbid Diagnosis	Concurrent Rx	N Responders	% Improvement	Placebo response	Overall Impression of Drug
None	Low dose chloral hydrate; diphenhydramine; hydroxyzine; and benzodiazepines under special conditions	35 dropouts 10 brofaromine + 6 placebo due to reported adverse events	33% max improvement in CAPS score	31% max improvement in CAPS score	Global improvement with significant improvement in caps for both brofaromine and placebo; no group differences
Major depression, anxiety disorder, alcohol dependence or abuse, substance dependence or abuse	Not recorded	Dropout rate 54/187	Greater than 30% reduction in CAPS-2 score, CGI-I score of 1 or 2, 41–45% reduction in symptom severity	Significantly less than sertraline	Improvement in all three clusters; also in quality of life/social and occupational function
Not recorded	Not recorded	11/27 fluoxetine; 1/26 placebo	Global improvement: 85%; high-end functioning: 41%	Global improvement: 62%; high-end functioning: 4%	Global and PTSD improvement
Mild to moderate anxiety and depression levels	Psychotherapy, chloral hydrate	60% response rate for sertraline, 38% for placebo	45–50% reduction in overall PTSD symptom measures; 50–53% reduction in intrusion, 47% reduction in avoidance, 40% reduction in arousal symptoms	Significantly less than sertraline	Sertraline significantly reduced avoidance/numbing symptoms but neither reexperiencing nor hyperarousal as assessed by CAPS (physician-rated). By self-report however, all three symptom clusters were reduced
Not recorded	Chloral hydrate for the first 2 weeks	14/44 dropouts overall 68% response rate	Not recorded	28% response rate	Global improvement for all symptoms
Major depressive disorder 45%, general anxiety disorder 30%, panic 15%, dysthymia 12%, agoraphobia 25%	Chloral hydrate for the first 2 weeks	Completers: placebo–65%; paroxetine 20 mg–76%; 40 mg–62%	20 mg–63%, 40 mg–57%	37% improvement	Global improvement in all symptoms including insomnia, in both men and women
			CAPS score reduced from 80 to 45	CAPS score reduced from 81–54	Fluoxetine was superior to placebo as assessed by total CAPS score
Not recorded	Not recorded	5/10 lamotrigine, 1/4 placebo, 1 lost to follow up	Not recorded	1 patient was very much improved	Overall improvement; good for intrusive and avoidance/numbing symptoms; greater response to lamotrigine than placebo
Major depression, simple phobia, obsessive compulsive disorder, alcohol/marijuana dependence	None	1 fluoxetine and 6 placebo; 1 dropout due to overactivation	Fluoxetine: 17% response	Placebo: 33% response	No global and no PTSD improvement
Major depression	None	92 responders	Mean change of 34.4% in cluster B; 28.3% for cluster C; and 34.8% for cluster D. Overall reduction in symptoms was 31.3%	N/A	Good for all three symptom clusters

(continued)

TABLE 17.2 (continued)

Type	Investigators	Year	Class	Drug	Control Used	Duration	Subjects	Population
2	Kaplan et al.	1996	Serotonin agent	Inositol	Placebo	4 weeks	17 randomized	Of 13 completers: 8 males, 5 females with mixed trauma types
2	Malik et al.	1999	SSRI	Fluoxetine	Placebo	12 weeks	16	Adults
2	Marshall et al.	1998	SSRI	Paroxetine	No control	12 weeks	17	Civilians
2	Robert et al.	1999	TCA	Imipramine	Chloral hydrate	7 days	25	Burn victims, ages 2–19; 11 females, 14 males
3	Blaha et al.	1999	SSRI	Citalopram	Outpatient therapy	Minimum of 3 weeks		Severly burned patients
3	Bouwer & Stein	1998	Combination	Cognitive therapy with sertraline, imipramine, clomipramine, fluoxetine	None	8 weeks	14	Male torture survivors
3	Brady et al.	1995	SSRI	Sertraline	None	12 weeks	9	Adults
3	Burdon et al.	1991	SSRI	Fluoxetine in combination with low dose amitriptyline or clonazepam	None	3–8 weeks with 16-month follow up	158	Veterans
3	Canive et al.	1998	Atypical antidepressants	Bupropion	None	6 weeks	17	Male combat vets with chronic PTSD
3	Clark et al.	1999	Anticonvulsant/ mood stabilizer	Divalproex	None	8 weeks	16	Male combat veterans
3	Connor et al.	1999	SNRI	Mirtazepine	None	8 weeks as single agent	6	Chronic PTSD from private practice
3	Davidson et al.	1998	Serotonergic atypical antidepressant	Nefazodone	None	12 weeks	17	Private practice civilians

Comorbid Diagnosis	Concurrent Rx	N Responders	% Improvement	Placebo response	Overall Impression of Drug
3 with general anxiety disorder, dysthymia, and explosive personality disorder	3 partial responders to prior psychotropic meds	5 dropouts	Not recorded	Overall IES 38; avoidance = –.77; intrusion = 5.72	No significant difference between inositol and placebo for the improvement score
					Overall improvement and improvement of quality of life, vitality, social function
Manic depressive disorder 53%, panic 47%, social phobia 35%	1 patient received chloral hydrate for 1 week	4/17 dropouts	65% much improved	N/A	Global improvement in all symptoms, reduced dissociative symptoms in all patients
Acute stress disorder, pain, anxiety, itching	Lorazepam, morphine, diphenhydramine, hydroxyzine, midazolam	10/12 imipramine; 5/13 chloral hydrate	6 had 100% improvement, 2 had 86%, 1 each had 88%, 65%, 38%, and no change	2 had 100%, 1 each had 83%, 63%, 60%, and 50%. 7 had no change	Improvement in acute stress disorder symptoms and in all three PTSD clusters
					Global improvement in PTSD symptoms
Major depression	Cognitive therapy	12 of 14 responders	Not recorded	N/A	Helped depression and all PTSD symptoms
Alcohol dependence, major depressive episode, cyclothymia	Valproic acid, trazodone, psychotherapy	9 of 9, with 4/9 abstinent from alcohol use	Not recorded	N/A	Global improvement; improvement of all three clusters; improvement in depression
History of drug and alcohol abuse, previous psychiatric hospitalization	Group, individual, and family therapy; crisis intervention counseling	136/158 remained in the group, individual, and family therapy for 6-month follow-up	Not recorded	N/A	Good for hyperarousal, intrusive, and depression
8 major depression; 11 prior treatment with antidepressants	No	3 dropouts due to adverse event; 10/17 very much improved	Not recorded	N/A	Overall improvement trend, not significant; hyperarousal symptoms; depressive symptoms improved
Major depression, dysthymia, dissociation disorder	Five on trazodone, one each on fluoxetine, bupropion, buspirone, lorazepam, temazepam, and nefazodone	11/13 completers; 3 stopped due to adverse event	Not recorded	N/A	Helped comorbid depression; good for intrusive and hyperarousal symptoms, not good for avoidance/numbing symptoms
6 major depression; 4 with general anxiety disorder; 1 with panic + agoraphobia	Vitamins and ibuprofen (1), atenolol, loaratidine, premarin, darvocet, midrin, cefazil, and mecclazine (5)	Improvement in 50% patients	50% or more	N/A	Global improvement on all symptom clusters
None	Private practice psychotherapy	Overall 43% response rate; 60% in completers	Not recorded	N/A	Early improvements in nightmares and sleep; improvement in all three clusters and global improvement

(continued)

TABLE 17.2 (continued)

Type	Investigators	Year	Class	Drug	Control Used	Duration	Subjects	Population
3	Davidson et al.	1998	SSRI	Fluvoxamine	None	8 weeks	15	Mixed civilian trauma
3	Davis et al.	2000	Surotonergic atypical antidepressant	Nefazodone	None	8 weeks	36	Combat veterans with chronic PTSD
3	Dow & Kline	1997	SSRI	Fluoxetine	Sertraline, Nortriptyline, Desipramine	At least 4 weeks	72	Veterans with chronic PTSD
3	Gelpin et al.	1996	Benzodiazepine	Clonazepam and alprazolam	No treatment	2–18 days post-trauma	26	13 PTSD, 13 matched trauma controls
3	Hamner & Ulmer	1998	Atypical antipsychotics	Risperidone augmentation to antidepressant	None	6 weeks	13	Vietnam veterans with PTSD and psychosis
3	Hertzberg et al.	1996	Benzodiazepine	Trazodone	None	8–12 weeks	6	Male Vietnam combat veterans
3	Hertzberg et al.	1998	Serotonergic atypical antidepressant	Nefazodone	None	12 weeks plus 4-week follow-up	10	Combat veterans
3	Humphreys et al.	1999	Cognitive/behavior + pharmacotherapy	Mixed	None	4-week inpatient, 6-month outpatient follow-up	64	Australian Vietnam vets with chronic PTSD

Comorbid Diagnosis	Concurrent Rx	N Responders	% Improvement	Placebo response	Overall Impression of Drug
Major depression, general anxiety disorder, panic disorder, dysthymia, social and simple phobia	None	9/14; 4 dropouts; 1 not included	40–50% improvement	N/A	Reduction in all PTSD symptom clusters
Major depression	Hidroxyzine, diphenhydramine, low dose benzodiazepine, individual and group psychotherapy	31 completed at least 4 weeks and 26 completed 8 weeks; most improvement occurred in first 4 weeks; 4 dropouts due to adverse events	Total CAPS score improved by 28 ± 22%, subscales improved by 28 ± 32%, 27 ± 29%, and 27 ± 29% for B, C, and D clusters respectively, HAM-A showed mean improvement of 29 ± 47%	N/A	Overall improvement and improvement in all three clusters of symptoms
Major depression	None		50% substantial improvement in overall symptoms	N/A	SSRI was more effective than norepinephrine agents, e.g. nortriptyline/desipramine
Major depression, simple phobia, social phobia, alcohol abuse, panic disorder, dysthymia	Not recorded	4/13 benzodiazepine group and 10/13 controls	Not recorded	Other than physiological arousal symptoms, no significant difference from benzodiazepine group	Helped with physiologic arousal symptoms without global improvement
Major depression, alcohol use disorder, general anxiety disorder, panic disorder	3 months stable antidepressant prescription	11 of 13 responders	Not recorded	N/A	Improvement in all three clusters and psychotic symptoms; global improvement
6 major depression; 2 with alcohol dependence in remission	3 were in ongoing psychotherapy, 1 in individual psychotherapy	4/6 much improved	Cluster B = 21%, C = 10%, D = 16%	N/A	Global improvement and all three clusters improved but intrusive and hyperarousal symptoms improved more than avoidance symptoms, sleep improved; minimum change in depression and social/occupational function
2 history of polysubstance abuse; 1 major depression in remission; 7 met criteria for a major depressive episode	Pyschotherapy	10 of 10 responders	30–50% reduction in PTSD symptoms	N/A	Global improvement and improvement in sleep and anger and all three symptom clusters. Minimum improvement in social and occupational function, no improvement in depression
Anxiety disorder, major depression, alcohol abuse, personality disorder, marijuana/benzodiazepine abuse, somatization disorder	Antidepressant (SSRI, moclobemide, venlafaxine, nefazodone, or tricyclic) and a mood stailizer (carbamazepine, sodium valproate, or lithium)	As measured by Beck Depression Inventory = 14/17; Beck Anxiety Inventory = 8/20; Penn Inventory for PTSD = 16/37; Impact of Events Scale = 12/30	Not recorded	N/A	Reduction in depression, anxiety, and PTSD symptoms

(*continued*)

TABLE 17.2 (continued)

Type	Investigators	Year	Class	Drug	Control Used	Duration	Subjects	Population
3	Looff et al.	1995	Anticonvulsant	Carbamazepine	None	17–92 days, 35 days on average	28	12 girls, 16 boys; ages 8–17; history of sexual abuse
3	Marmar et al.	1996	SSRI	Fluvoxamine	None	10 weeks	11	Male Vietnam vets with chronic PTSD
3	Nagy et al.	1996	SSRI	Fluoxetine	Placebo			
3	Neal et al.	1997	Reversible MAOI	Moclobemide	None	12 weeks	20	Adults (2/20 were women) with mixed trauma and chronic PTSD, but those with sexual and/or physical abuse were excluded due to overlap with borderline personality disorder
3	Pitman et al.	1990	Opioid agents	Naloxone	Placebo	2 sessions divided by a 2-week interval	16	8 Vietnam veterans with PTSD and 8 without
3	Rothbaum et al.	1996	SSRI	Sertraline	None	12 weeks	5 completers	Women rape victims with chronic PTSD
3	Sajatovic et al.	1999	Serotonergic atypical antidepressant	Nefazodone	None	Minimum of 4 weeks	20	Treatment-resistant patients with depression, subgroup of 11 with comorbity of PTSD
3	Shalev & Rogel-Fuchs	1992	Benzodiazepine	Clonazepam	No clonazepam			Mixed with PTSD
3	Tucker et al.	2000	SSRI	Fluvoxamine	No treatment	10 weeks	32	16 with PTSD; 16 matched controls exposed to at least 1 serious trauma
3	Zisook et al.	2000	Serotonergic atypical antidepressant	Nefazodone	None	12 weeks	19	Treatment-refractory male Vietnam veterans with PTSD

Type 1 studies: Rigorous, randomized, prospective, clinical trials with random group assignment, appropriate exclusion and inclusion criteria, state-of-the-art diagnostic methods, adequate sample size to offer statistical power and appropriate statistical analyses. Type 2 studies: Clinical Trials in which an intervention is made but some aspect of the Type 1 study requirement is missing, such as small subject number or the like. Type 3 studies: Good open trial studies or case control studies.

Comorbid Diagnosis	*Concurrent Rx*	N *Responders*	*% Improvement*	*Placebo response*	*Overall Impression of Drug*
More than half comorbid for attention deficit hyperactivity disorder, depressive disorder; oppositional defiant disorder; polysubstance abuse	4 with attention deficit hyperactivity disorder on methylphenidate or clonidine; 4 with depression on sertraline, fluoxetine or imipramine	22/28 asymptomatic and 6/28 significantly improved	Not recorded	N/A	Good for all three symptom clusters
Major depression, borderline personality disorder, avoidant personality disorder, dependent personality disorder	Psychotherapy; chloral hydrate; intermittent low dose benzodiazepines	Treatment effects observed by 4–6 weeks; 1 dropout due to adverse event	Not recorded	N/A	Global improvement and all three clusters improved
					Drug was not statistically superior to placebo
Major depression, panic disorder, personality disorder	Benzodiazepines	11/20 no longer met criteria for PTSD; adverse events minimal; one with transient eczematous rash; 6 completers	Not recorded	N/A	Global improvement and improvement in functional impairment as well
Panic disorder, obsessive compulsive disorder, major depression	Not recorded	8/8 responders with PTSD in placebo condition	In subjects with PTSD, no decrease in pain intensity rating	In subjects with PTSD, 30% decrease in pain intensity rating	Reduced stress-induced analgesia in combat veterans who were exposed to trauma-related imagery
		45 responders	CAPS decreased by 53%	N/A	Global improvement of PTSD symptoms and depression
Major depression, substance abuse, personality disorder	Antidepressants/ anxiolytics	11 of 11 responders	Of 11 with PTSD, 4 had >20% improvement on BDI; 2 had 10–20%, 5 had <10% improvement	N/A	Improvement in PTSD and depression symptoms in subjects who had both
					Clonazepam did not differ from drug-free PTSD patients in the magnitude and the habituation rate of their responses to an auditory startle
Depression secondary to PTSD	None	16 of 16 responders	Not recorded	Significantly less than fluvoxamine	Improvement in PTSD symptoms, depression symptoms, and physiologic reactivity
Multiple Axis I comorbidities	Minimal psychotherapy	18 of 19; 1 dropout due to side effect of dizziness and hypotension	32% overall drop in CAPS scores; 26% for intrusion, 33% for avoidance, 28% for arousal	N/A	Improvement in PTSD and depressive symptoms, all three clusters of symptoms improved, improvement in sleep and sexual function

responded to other medications (Hogben & Cornfield, 1981). In subsequent studies, phenelzine was also found to produce good global improvement as well as a reduction in intrusive symptoms in two open trials of combat veterans with PTSD (Davidson et al., 1987; Milanes et al., 1984).

The results from the above-mentioned trials were confirmed by a randomized placebo-controlled study by Kosten et al. (1991; preliminary results reported in Frank et al., 1988), who found phenelzine superior to placebo and imipramine. Phenelzine resulted in a 68% global improvement compared to a 45% improvement with imipramine and a 28% improvement in the placebo group. Phenelzine was particularly helpful with core symptoms of intrusion and insomnia, with a trend toward an improvement in avoidance. Scores on the Impact of Event Scale improved 45% in the phenelzine group, 25% in the imipramine group, and 5% in the placebo group. Other hyperarousal symptoms were not reported. This early study was particularly well conducted for several reasons. Veterans were chosen from a Readjustment Veterans Outreach Center and not a VA hospital. Most of the veterans were employed, and none had comorbid substance abuse or reported major Axis I diagnoses. Subjects were selected from a pool of veterans who were already receiving supportive psychotherapy at the center. Therapeutic drug levels were monitored, and an adequate time of 8 weeks was used to assess efficacy.

MAOIs may augment norepinephrine, dopamine, and serotonin neurotransmission by blocking the degradation of these agents. The global effectiveness of phenelzine on these systems may in part reflect this "broad spectrum" psychotropic activity. On the other hand, it has also been suggested that phenelzine may improve PTSD symptoms by specifically downregulating adrenergic activity in the locus coeruleus (Davidson et al., 1987), which has been postulated as playing an important role in intrusive symptoms (Charney et al., 1993).

Two groups failed to note significant improvement with phenelzine in Israeli combat veterans with PTSD. Lerer et al. (1987) reported that phenelzine did not show a dramatic effect in an open prospective trial, although some symptoms, such as sleep disturbances and intrusive thoughts, were reduced in Israeli war veterans. In considering their findings, this group speculated about sociocultural differences between Israeli and American combat veterans with PTSD (e.g., in the incidence of substance abuse and antisocial personality) and postulated that some of the differences in efficacy may be due to the fact that overall, Israeli veterans were not as globally symptomatic. In a 5-week, randomized, cross-over design, Shestatzky et al. (1988) also did not find phenelzine to be effective. However, only 10 subjects (a mix of Israeli war veterans and civilians) were studied. The small number of subjects and the limited time period makes this controlled trial a Type 2 study.

In summary, phenelzine (therapeutic dose range 45 to 90 mg) appears to be superior to imipramine for PTSD, although findings have not been replicated with placebo and in other populations, nor using contemporary clinical trials methodologies. Other disadvantages of MAOIs include the risk of hypertensive crisis from tyramine-containing foods and certain other medications. Phenelzine is also associated with many side effects. Side effects that contributed to dropout rates in the various studies included intensification of sleep disorder, dizziness, erectile failure, delayed ejaculation, delayed urination, constipation, dry mouth, blurred vision, drowsiness, behavioral inhibition, blackouts, perceptual changes, and hypomania (Davidson et al., 1987; Kosten et al., 1991). Yet this medication is a viable choice for persons who may not respond to safer and more tolerable treatments.

Tricyclic Antidepressants (TCAs)

It is difficult to generalize about TCAs because several medications have been studied, and TCAs vary in their mechanisms and spectrum of action across neurotransmitter systems. Nonetheless, TCAs, until recently, were the best studied class of medications in PTSD, with three randomized clinical trials (Davidson et al., 1990; Kosten et al., 1991; Reist et al., 1989), three open (Burdon et al., 1991; Burstein, 1984; Chen, 1991), several retrospective (Birkhimer et al., 1985; Bleich et al., 1986; Falcon et al., 1985) and case reports (Blake, 1986; Burstein et al., 1988; Shen & Park, 1983; Turchan et al., 1992) in adults, and, recently, one controlled study in pediatric burn patients (Robert et al., 1999). Generally, prospective open trials have shown moderate efficacy in intrusive and hyperarousal symptoms (Burdon et al., 1991; Burstein, 1984; Chen, 1991). Retrospective chart reviews have been more mixed, some investigators reporting efficacy of TCAs (Bleich et al., 1986; Falcon et al., 1985) and others not (Birkhimer et al., 1985; Bleich et al., 1986). In case reports, improvements in generalized anxiety, panic, and depressive symptoms have been particularly noted (Basoglu et al., 1992; Blake, 1986; Burstein et al., 1988; Pohl & Balon, 1992; Turchan et al., 1992). However, many also reported a direct reduction in sleep disturbances (Blake, 1986; Burstein et al., 1988; Turchan et al., 1992) and other intrusive or arousal symptoms. The case reports are particularly noteworthy because the majority have reported on the efficacy of TCAs in noncombat populations, such as rape victims (Pohl & Balon, 1992), motor vehicle accident victims (Blake, 1986; Burstein et al., 1988), torture survivors (Basoglu et al., 1992), survivors of plane crashes (Turchan et al., 1992), and burn victims (Blake, 1986), and have therefore provided at least some evidence for the generalizability of the effects of TCAs across populations of trauma survivors.

The two definitive and methodologically sound studies examining the efficacy of TCA are Davidson et al.'s (1990) randomized trial comparing amitriptyline to placebo in combat veterans and Kosten et al.'s (1991) randomized trial comparing imipramine to phenelzine and placebo. Both these studies used the standardized assessments available at the time for both diagnoses and symptom ratings and considered comorbidity in evaluating treatment outcome.

Amitriptyline

Davidson et al. reported modest efficacy of amitriptyline (dose range 150 to 300 mg) in combat PTSD. Overall improvement was particularly noted in veterans who did not meet diagnostic criteria for major depression. This study also made an important contribution in comparing responses at 4 and 8 weeks and demonstrating that symptom reduction was not significant at the 4-week period, at least in this sample.

Imipramine

Kosten et al. showed that imipramine (dose range 150–300 mg) was more effective than placebo (but less effective than phenelzine) in producing global symptom improvement and improvement in intrusive symptoms in combat veterans. In the pediatric study, 25 burn patients with acute stress disorder and significant pain and anxiety were treated with a 7-day trial of imipramine or chloral hydrate: 10 of the 12 patients on imipramine and 5 of the 13 patients on chloral hydrate showed improvement in all three clusters of trauma-related symptoms.

Desipramine

Reist et al. (1989) did not find significant differences between desipramine (doses no greater than 200 mg per day) and placebo in a 4-week crossover trial. In considering the insufficient power, Davidson (1992) suggested that insufficient dosing, shorter duration of treatment, and failure to evaluate the importance of comorbidity may have contributed to these negative results.

Overall, the therapeutic effects of tricyclic drugs have been modest, but clinically meaningful, particularly for hyperarousal and intrusive symptoms in many U.S. combat veterans, and in all three symptom clusters in pediatric populations with more acute illness. Although TCAs have not been directly compared in randomized clinical trials, it may be that their differential efficacy across trials in PTSD is related to slight variations in the neurotransmitter systems that they affect. Also of note in studies of TCAs is the lack of placebo response in the three controlled trials with veterans (Davidson, 1992). Although TCAs have been generally well tolerated in the above study groups, these medications have been associated with numerous anticholinergic and cardiac side effects. These medications appear to work best after an 8-week trial in trauma survivors who do not meet diagnostic criteria for other psychiatric diagnoses (Davidson et al., 1993). However, it should be noted that TCAs are effective in reducing associated symptoms of mood and anxiety in subjects with PTSD, and that they remain a reasonable choice for the treatment of PTSD, particularly for those who do not respond to newer agents such as SSRIs.

Selective Serotonin Reuptake Inhibitors

As SSRIs became popular treatments for depression and anxiety, clinicians began to consider whether these drugs might be effective for PTSD. Four large-scale, multi-center trials with sertraline, paroxetine, and fluoxetine have demonstrated drug efficacy compared to placebo (Brady et al., 2000; Davidson et al., 2001; Judge et al., 2000; Marshall et al., in press), consistent with two prior single-site studies with fluoxetine (Connor et al., 1999; van der Kolk et al.,

1994). There are also four negative controlled trials with SSRIs to date: two multi-center trials with sertraline (unpublished) and two single-site trials with fluoxetine (Hertzberg et al., 2000; Medical Economics Company [MEC], 2001; Nagy et al., 1996). All studies provided adequate dosing of active medication and were comparable to positive trials in power and design. Three of the four negative trials involved primarily U.S. war veterans as subjects, which may or may not have contributed to the lack of findings. Yet there is a general consensus that such findings reflect the treatment-refractory status of the population being studied rather than drug efficacy. Other interpretations include heterogeneity within the PTSD syndrome or differential treatment response based on other factors such as type of trauma, length of illness, or severity of trauma, or quite simply that the medications do not work universally in PTSD.

The literature on SSRIs is also qualitatively better than that on MAOIs and TCAs, largely reflecting the development of standardized clinical assessment instruments, increasing use of state-of-the-art clinical trials methodology in trials design, and broadening of subject populations to non-combat-related PTSD.

Randomized, Double-Blind, Placebo-Controlled Trials in Adults with Chronic PTSD

Sertraline Two large multi-center, 12-week, randomized, placebo-controlled trials of sertraline in chronic PTSD showed statistically significant superiority for sertraline over placebo, and two did not (MEC, 2001). When analyzed by gender, sertraline was effective for women but not for men, perhaps because of the inclusion of substantially fewer men, most of whom were combat veterans, than women. On the basis of these studies in the aggregate, sponsored by Pfizer, Inc., the FDA recognized sertraline as an effective treatment for adults with chronic PTSD.

Brady et al. (2000) reported the first 12-week, multi-center, placebo-controlled, randomized trial that included a 1-week placebo run-in involving mostly subjects with non-combat-related trauma. The dropout rate was relatively low, at 54 of 187 subjects. In the intent-to-treat analysis, sertraline response rate was 53% compared to 32% for placebo when response was defined as much improved or very much improved, plus at least a 30% reduction in symptom severity on the Clinician Administered PTSD Scale (CAPS). There was significant improvement in the symptom clusters of hyperarousal and avoidance, but not reexperiencing. Secondary measures showed improved quality of life and social and occupational function. Mean dosage was 151 mg/day at end point.

Davidson et al. (2001) reported a second 12-week, multi-center, placebo-controlled randomized trial of flexible-dosage sertraline ($N = 100$) versus placebo ($N = 108$) in adults (mostly females) with mixed trauma and chronic PTSD. Subjects had duration of illness >6 months and CAPS scores >50. The intent-to-treat analysis found a 60% response rate for sertraline versus 38% for placebo ($p = .004$). Sertraline patients experienced a 44.6% reduction in symptoms compared to a 35% reduction in symptoms for placebo patients. Most responders met criteria by Week 4. Discontinuation rate was 11% on sertraline due to adverse events, compared to 5% on placebo. Sertraline was not superior to placebo on measures of depression, general anxiety, or sleep problems. In terms of individual symptom clusters, sertraline significantly reduced avoidance/numbing symptoms but neither reexperiencing nor hyperarousal as assessed by the CAPS (physician-rated). By self-report on the Davidson Trauma Scale, however, all three symptom clusters were reduced.

A third trial that also recruited primarily individuals with non-combat-related PTSD did not find sertraline to be superior to placebo (MEC, 2001). A fourth trial also was negative but was conducted primarily in male U.S. war veterans (MEC, 2001).

Paroxetine A 12-week, fixed-dose, randomized, placebo-controlled trial that compared paroxetine (20 mg daily), paroxetine (40 mg daily), and placebo found both doses of medication were superior to placebo for adults with chronic PTSD ($N = 551$; Marshall et al., 2000). Dropout rate was relatively low (196/551). Both doses of paroxetine were superior to placebo for all three symptom clusters based on CAPS ratings (reexperiencing, avoidance, and hyperarousal). Paroxetine was also superior to placebo in ameliorating symptoms of social and occupational functioning, comorbid depressive symptoms, and insomnia. Adverse effects were consistent with published trials of paroxetine. Contrary to the authors' hypotheses, no differences in efficacy were found between paroxetine (20 mg daily) and paroxetine (40 mg daily). Most important, this is the first study to demonstrate efficacy for an SSRI in males with PTSD.

An interim report of a single-site, randomized, placebo-controlled, 10-week study also suggested superiority for paroxetine over placebo in adults with PTSD (Marshall et al., 2000) in 30 patients completing at least 5 weeks' treatment. When responders were defined by an independent assessor global improvement rating of very much improved or much improved, paroxetine appeared superior (11/16, 68%) to placebo (4/14, 28%) (chi square = 4.82, $p = .028$). On the CAPS, total score was reduced 25.1 for paroxetine and 8.5 for placebo (from 79.8 and 76.9, respectively).

Fluoxetine A 12-week, international, multi-center, randomized, placebo-controlled trial recently found fluoxetine (N = 226) superior to placebo (N = 75) in adults with chronic PTSD as assessed by total CAPS score (Martenyi et al., 2001). In the last observation carried forward (LOCF) analysis, CAPS total score was reduced from approximately 80 to 45 by fluoxetine and from 81 to 54 by placebo. This trial was conducted in Belgium, Bosnia, Croatia, Israel, South Africa, and Yugoslavia, so it was the first positive cross-cultural medication study in PTSD. The trial is also notable in that most subjects were male (81%), and 48% of subjects were exposed to a combat-related episode. Mean dose at end point was 57mg/day of fluoxetine. A subanalysis found that fluoxetine was effective for combat-related PTSD (Martenyi et al., 2001).

A single-site, 12-week, double-blind, placebo-controlled, randomized study of fluoxetine and placebo in civilians (N = 53) reported global improvement of PTSD symptoms in 11 of 27 patients treated with fluoxetine compared to 1 of 26 subjects on placebo (Connor et al., 1999). Two thirds of subjects completed the full 12 weeks (36/53). When outcome was defined as a CGI score of much or very much improved (CGI = 2 or 1), fluoxetine was superior to placebo, though both groups had high response rates (85% vs. 62%). Fluoxetine-treated patients were significantly more likely to be rated very much improved (59% vs. 19%).

In contrast, the first randomized, double-blind, placebo-controlled study of an SSRI suggested that fluoxetine was superior to placebo in civilians but not U.S. war veterans (van der Kolk et al., 1994). Two groups of PTSD patients were studied over 5 weeks of treatment: 31 war veterans and 33 civilian patients in a trauma clinic. Fluoxetine improved numbing and hyperarousal, whereas other symptoms of avoidance and intrusive symptoms did not improve. However, when each group was analyzed separately, fluoxetine was not more effective than placebo in reducing symptoms, a finding that may reflect limitations of power and length of treatment in this early study.

In the smaller controlled trials with fluoxetine, Malik et al. (1999) reported improvement of symptoms with fluoxetine, but Hertzberg et al. (2000) did not. The former study involved 16 adult civilians, and the latter included 15 U.S. combat veterans with PTSD with substantial comorbidity with depression, anxiety disorder, and history of substance use disorder. Hertzberg et al. (2000) reported a small negative 12-week, double-blind, placebo-controlled trial in 12 U.S. Vietnam veterans with chronic PTSD (mean fluoxetine dose was 48mg/day at end point). In this study, 1 of 6 fluoxetine patients and 2 of 6 placebo-treated patients were rated as much or very much improved, and dimensional measures showed essentially no change from baseline to end point. It is noteworthy that 5 of 12 subjects were receiving disability payments for PTSD; comorbidity was very high; and 6 of 12 subjects had previously failed treatment with one or more antidepressant medications.

Open Trials of SSRIs

Numerous open-label trials of SSRIs preceded the above placebo-controlled trials. Brady et al. (1995) found that in their sample of 9 patients, all of whom had comorbid alcohol dependence, 4 of the 9 patients were abstinent from alcohol during the trial. At the end of the 12-week trial, the patients showed global improvement and improvement in all three symptom clusters. They also showed improvement in depression symptoms. In another study, involving women rape victims in a trial of 12 weeks, there was a reduction of the total CAPS score by about 53% in 4 of 5 responders (Rothbaum et al., 1996), with global improvement of PTSD symptoms and depression. Kline et al. (1994) reported good preliminary results with sertraline. This open trial studied 19 treatment-refractory combat veterans for over 12 weeks. Of the 19 subjects, 12 showed good responses for symptoms of arousal, intrusion, and explosiveness. Sertraline also showed improvement in dysphoria and hopelessness.

Several open trials were published using fluoxetine, and all reported good efficacy (Burdon et al., 1991; Davidson et al., 1991b; Dow & Kline, 1997;

McDougle et al., 1991; Nagy et al., 1993; Shay et al., 1992). Davidson et al. (1991b) first suggested that fluoxetine improved avoidant and intrusive symptoms but was less effective in relieving hyperarousal symptoms. This conclusion was based on a report of five individuals with assorted types of traumatic events, ranging from childhood incest to adult motor vehicle accidents. Other promising early open trials with combat veterans treated with fluoxetine were reported by McDougle et al. (1991, N = 20), Nagy et al. (1993), Shay (1992, N = 18), and Burdon et al. (1991, N = 158). Burdon et al. also described using fluoxetine in combination with low-dose amitriptyline and clonazepam. They reported that this combination of medications was good for hyperarousal, intrusiveness, and depression.

Marshall et al. (1998) conducted a 12-week trial of paroxetine in patients with non-combat-related chronic PTSD, hypothesizing that paroxetine's anxiolytic properties might be particularly helpful in this disorder. Of these patients, 65% (11/17) were rated as very much improved by an independent evaluation, with no dropouts due to adverse effects. There was significant improvement in all three clusters, with reductions of 50% (intrusive symptoms), 50% (avoidance), and 43% (hyperarousal), as well as 43% reduction in dissociative symptoms.

Several open-label studies with fluvoxamine have also been reported (Davidson et al., 1998; DeBoer et al., 1992; Marmar et al., 1996; Tucker et al., 2000). DeBoer et al. (1992) studied 24 World War II Dutch resistance vets using fluvoxamine for 12 weeks. Fluvoxamine reduced intrusion and hyperarousal but did not reduce avoidant symptoms. This report was notably different from the other reports because subjects were not recruited from a treatment setting. Rather, they were community-dwelling individuals who were functioning well within the community. Thus, they were only moderately symptomatic to begin with and very likely did not have the characteristics typical of a clinical population.

Blaha et al. (1999) showed global improvement in posttraumatic stress symptoms after treatment with intravenous citalopram in severely burned patients. Interestingly, these patients also had better cosmetic prognosis than control burn patients who were not treated with citalopram. From the beginning of this study to the time of publication, no patient experienced PTSD. On average, the onset of effects occurred in the third week of treatment.

Bouwer and Stein (1998) found significant reduction in depression and PTSD symptoms in 14 male torture survivors after an 8-week open-label trial of combination treatment with an SSRI and cognitively oriented psychotherapy. The different medications included sertraline, imipramine, clomipramine, and fluoxetine.

Humphreys et al. (1999) examined the 2-year outcome data of an intensive treatment program for chronic PTSD. The treatment included a combined approach of cognitive behavior therapy and pharmacotherapy. The most common medication regime included an antidepressant (SSRI, moclobemide, venlafaxine, nefazodone, or tricyclic) and a mood stabilizer (carbamazepine, sodium valproate, or lithium). The subjects included 64 Australian Vietnam veterans with chronic PTSD. The results obtained demonstrate significant reduction in depression, anxiety, and PTSD symptoms, maintained at 2-years postdischarge from the residential phase of the treatment program.

SSRIs are useful medications for PTSD because they have come the closest to targeting the whole syndrome of PTSD and not just discrete symptom clusters. Side effects that have been reported for SSRIs are insomnia, sexual dysfunction, decreased libido, weight loss and appetite loss, diarrhea, headaches, and sweating, and these vary somewhat based on the specific medication. No empirical data are available at present, however, to address most fundamental practical issues such as necessary length of treatment, relapse after discontinuation, dosage for maintenance versus acute treatment response, and combination treatments with different psychotherapies.

Other Medications

Venlafaxine

One case report on the effects of venlafaxine, a dual reuptake blocker for both serotonin and norepinephrine, showed improvement in depression, global anxiety, nightmares, panic attacks, sleep, irritability, and social avoidance after 4 weeks of treatment (Hamner & Frueh, 1998). The subject was a male combat veteran refractory to sertraline, fluoxetine, amoxapine, and behavioral treatment, with comorbid major depression.

Mirtazepine

Connor et al. (1999) reported an open-label trial of mirtazepine in six chronic PTSD patients from a private practice. All six had major depression, four had GAD, and one had panic disorder with agoraphobia. Following the 8-week trial, 50% of the subjects showed global improvement. Mirtazepine is an alpha-2-antagonist that increases the release of serotonin and norepinephrine but does not block reuptake of either.

Moclobemide

One open-label trial of moclobemide showed global improvement and improvement in functional impairment as well (Neal et al., 1997). The study took place over 12 weeks with 20 adults, 2 of whom were women. The subjects had mixed trauma and chronic PTSD, but those with sexual and/or physical abuse were excluded. The 20 subjects had comorbid diagnoses of major depression, panic disorder, and personality disorder and were being treated concurrently with benzodiazepines. Following the 12-week trial, 11 out of 20 no longer met criteria for PTSD. Adverse events were minimal (one with transient eczematous rash), with 16 completers in total.

Inositol

One double-blind, placebo-controlled crossover study of inositol in subjects with mixed trauma types ($N = 17$) showed no significant difference between inositol and placebo (Kaplan et al., 1996). Inositol is an isomer of glucose that functions as a precursor in the phosphatidyl-inositol-cycle second-messenger system for several neurotransmitter receptors. Methodological limitations in this study, including inadequate power and nonstandardized assessments, make it impossible to interpret.

Reversible Inhibitor of MAO-A (RIMA)

As discussed above, both serotonin uptake inhibition and monoamine oxidase-A (MAO-A) inhibition appear to be helpful in PTSD.

Brofaromine

Brofaromine is an experimental drug that combines serotonin uptake inhibition with selective, reversible MAO-A inhibition. Furthermore, the MAO-A inhibiting properties of brofaromine are not associated with some of the safety or tolerability problems in phenelzine.

There have only been two studies examining the efficacy of this agent in PTSD (Baker et al., 1995; Katz et al., 1995). Katz et al. randomized 64 ($N = 64$) patients with mostly non-combat-related PTSD who received up to 150 mg/day of brofaromine (modal dose 100 mg/day) versus placebo. As in the trial comparing imipramine and phenelzine (Kosten et al., 1991), no subjects met criteria for major depression. Other comorbidity was not reported, and outcome was not assessed by an independent evaluator. In the intent-to-treat analysis of a dimensional symptom measure in the total group, improvement on brofaromine (42.1%) was no different from that on placebo (31.8%). In the subset of patients with chronic PTSD of at least 1 year's duration ($N = 45$), however, brofaromine's benefit was superior to placebo (48.1% vs. 29.0%, $p < .05$), and more than half no longer met criteria for PTSD (55%) compared to 26% of patients receiving placebo. This outcome suggests that at least a subset of PTSD patients may benefit from brofaromine, although more rigorous studies are needed. Adverse effects of insomnia, headache, and dry mouth appeared more common in patients on brofaromine (34% vs. 12%, 26% vs. 18%, and 23% vs. 9%, respectively), but only 1 subject discontinued the trial for these reasons.

The second 12-week, double-blind, randomized, placebo-controlled, multi-center study of brofaromine in PTSD ($N = 118$) showed no significant difference between the brofaromine and placebo treatment groups (Baker et al., 1995).

Other Serotonergic Drugs

Buspirone

There are a few preliminary reports examining the serotonin 5HT1A partial agonist buspirone. Buspirone is used as an anxiolytic and has been reported as effective in a case study describing three combat veterans (Wells et al., 1991). Buspirone (therapeutic dose range 35–60 mg) reduced associative symptoms of anxiety, depression, insomnia, and flashbacks. Avoidant symptoms were not improved with buspirone.

Cyproheptadine

The serotonin antagonist cyproheptadine has also been used to target PTSD-associated nightmares. There are three case reports and one retrospective review in which cyproheptadine was used for the treatment of traumatic nightmares (therapeutic dose 4 to 28 mg) (Brophy, 1991; Gupta et al., 1998; Harsch, 1986). However, Clark et al. (1999) reported one case study in which there was no improvement in nightmares in 16 male combat veterans after 4 weeks of cyproheptadine.

Gupta et al. (1998) reported one 9-year-old boy who had been nonresponsive to diphenhydramine and trazodone and had comorbid diagnoses of attention-deficit-hyperactivity disorder (ADHD) and obsessive-compulsive disorder (OCD). Following 4 weeks of cyproheptadine, he reported improvement in school, remission of nightmares, and improved sleep. Gupta et al. (1998) also presented a retrospective review of two males and seven females, ages 19 to 64, who reported improvement in nightmares after taking cyproheptadine for 2 to 4 weeks. The subjects had comorbid diagnoses, including chronic undifferentiated schizophrenia, bipolar disorder type I, schizoaffective disorder, and major depression. Some of the subjects were concurrently being medicated with paroxetine, haloperidol, valproate, benzotropine, lithium naltrexone, risperidone, nortriptyline, and clonazepam.

Nefazodone

Four open-label trials of nefazodone showed improvement in all three PTSD symptom clusters (Davidson et al., 1998; Davis et al., 2000; Hertzberg et al., 1998; Zisook et al., 2000). Davidson et al. (1998) reported early improvements in nightmares and sleep, improvement in all three PTSD symptom clusters, and global improvement. The study followed 17 private practice civilians over 12 weeks of nefazodone treatment. Overall, there was a 43% response rate or 60% in treatment completers by observer rating.

Hertzberg et al. (1998) studied 10 combat veterans over 12 weeks of open treatment with nefazodone. At the end of the trial, the subjects showed global improvement and improvement in sleep, anger, and all three symptom clusters. They showed minimum improvement in social and occupational function and no improvement in depression. Davis et al. (2000) studied 36 combat veterans with chronic PTSD over a treatment period of 8 weeks. Of these subjects, 31 completed at least 4 weeks and 26 completed 8 weeks, with 4 dropouts due to adverse events. The subjects exhibited the most improvement during the first 4 weeks. In the end, subjects showed global improvement and improvement in all three symptom clusters. Zisook et al. (2000) demonstrated improvement in PTSD and depressive symptoms following 12 weeks of nefazodone in a population of treatment-refractory male Vietnam veterans with PTSD. All three clusters of symptoms improved with additional improvement in sleep and sexual function. The subjects had multiple Axis I comorbidities.

Hidalgo et al. (1999) pooled the results of six open-label trials of nefazodone in the treatment of PTSD in both civilians and combat veterans. Nefazodone showed a broad spectrum of action on PTSD symptoms. There was a mean change of 34.4% in Cluster B symptoms; 28.3% for Cluster C; and 34.8% for Cluster D. The overall percentage reduction in symptoms was 31.3%. Predictors of response included age, sex, and trauma type.

One retrospective uncontrolled study of nefazodone in 20 treatment-resistant depressed patients, 11 of whom had PTSD, showed improvement in PTSD and depression symptoms in those subjects who had both (Sajatovic et al., 1999). During the course of the study, which lasted a minimum of 4 weeks, the subjects continued to take other antidepressants.

Trazodone

Hertzberg et al. (1996) showed improvement in all of the symptom clusters following an 8- to 12-week open-label trial of trazodone. This study followed six male Vietnam combat veterans. At the end of the study, all three clusters improved, but intrusive and hyperarousal symptoms improved more than avoidance symptoms. Additionally, there were improvements in sleep. There were minimum changes in depression and social/occupational function.

Other Atypical Antidepressants

Bupropion

Canive et al. (1998) found improvement in hyperarousal and depressive symptoms following a 6-week open-label trial of bupropion. The subjects were 17 male combat veterans with chronic PTSD, 8 of whom had comorbid depression. Eleven had previous treatment with antidepressants, but none were taking any medications during the study. Three subjects dropped out due to adverse events, and ten of the remainder were very much improved by the end of the trial.

Mood Stabilizers

Lithium

There is scant information about the efficacy of lithium carbonate in the treatment of PTSD, although two open trials can be found in the literature. The primary rationale for initially trying lithium in the treatment of PTSD was its mood stabilizing properties. Van der Kolk (1983) performed an open trial of lithium carbonate (therapeutic dose 300 to 1500 mg/day) in 14 treatment-refractory combat veterans who reported feeling out of control, on the verge of exploding, emotionally cut off from their families, and preoccupied by feelings of guilt. Of the 14 veterans, 8 showed good improvement with lithium carbonate, particularly for subjective feelings of control, and improvement in hyperarousal. Kitchner and Greenstein (1985) reported similar results in an open trial with five combat veterans. These studies did not utilize structured scales to assess comorbid diagnoses, or severity of PTSD symptoms. Scales were also not used to assess improvement in either global or PTSD symptoms. Information about dosing, duration of treatment, or side effects is also not available. One case study of two veterans showed improvements in irritability and anger following treatment with lithium (Forster et al., 1995). These cases are discussed in the context of evidence that lithium may be useful in other patients with disorders of impulse control. Therefore, follow-up studies should be conducted to assess the true efficacy of these agents for reducing PTSD symptoms.

Anticonvulsants

The use of anticonvulsants such as carbamazepine and valproate in PTSD has stemmed from suggestions that the behavioral and neurobiological sensitization of trauma survivors might be relieved by raising the neuronal threshold for arousal in limbic areas (Keck et al., 1992). Anticonvulsants act as mood stabilizers and enhance $GABA_{ergic}$ activity by acting on $GABA_A$ (valproate) and $GABA_B$ (carbamazepine) receptors, thereby causing an increase in chloride conductance and a resultant neuronal hyperpolarization (stabilization).

Carbamazepine

Lipper et al. (1986) specifically hypothesized that the intrusive symptoms of PTSD would respond to anticonvulsants because these symptoms would most likely be considered "kindled" or paroxysmal experiences. Indeed, Lipper et al. found that carbamazepine (therapeutic dose 600–1000 mg/day) was moderately effective for intrusive recollections, sleep impairment, and hostility in 7 out of 10 combat veterans who participated in a 5-week open trial. All the patients studied had comorbid personality disorder, and all had some history of substance abuse. None had comorbid mood disorder, and only 1 had a comorbid generalized anxiety disorder. Significant improvements were also noted in overall anxiety, somatization, hostility, psychoticism, and confusion-bewilderment (as assessed by the Profile of Mood States). Wolf et al. (1988) reported on the efficacy of carbamazepine in 10 veterans whose histories included poor impulse control, violent behavior, and angry outbursts. All veterans had comorbid substance abuse, and some had Axis II diagnoses. One of the patients had a history of partial complex seizures. All subjects had normal sleep and waking EEGs. By staff observation and patient self-report, carbamazepine was found to be helpful in improving impulse controls and angry outbursts. A single-case study also showed efficacy of carbamazepine in treating PTSD symptoms in a patient with seizure disorder. In some subjects, carbamazepine produced side effects such as ataxia, headache, rash, mental confusion, and drowsiness (Davidson, 1992).

Looff et al. (1995) reported global improvement and improvement in all three PTSD symptom clusters following treatment with carbamazepine. The study consisted of 12 girls and 16 boys, ages 8–17, all with a history of sexual abuse. More than half were comorbid for ADHD, with some subjects comorbid for depressive disorder, oppositional defiant disorder, and polysubstance abuse. Four subjects with ADHD continued taking methylphenidate or clonidine, and four subjects with depression were also on sertraline, fluoxetine, or imipramine. At the end of the study, 22 out of 28 were asymptomatic, with the remaining 6 significantly improved.

Two separate case reports showed positive effects of carbamazepine and valproate in combination. Tohen et al. (1994) presented a record review of one adult with major depression who was treated with both drugs, and both were well tolerated. Ford (1996) presented one case study of a male ex-police officer who was nonresponsive to clomipramine, trimipramine, thioridazine, and alprazolam. Improvement with addition of valproate was observed within 2 weeks after initiation. With regards to his PTSD symptoms, he reported experiencing no more nightmares and had some improvement in his intrusive symptoms, sleep and mood.

Valproate

Fesler (1991) reported improvement in hyperarousal and avoidant symptoms in a group of 16 combat veterans following an open trial with divalproex (therapeutic dose range 750 to 1750 mg/day) over several months. Most patients had past histories of mood, anxiety, substance-abuse, and thought disorder, and all but 3 were also being treated with one other medication (usually an antidepressants, anxiolytic, or neuroleptic). Of these veterans, 11 were significantly improved in quality and length of sleep, whereas 9 improved in avoidant and numbing symptoms. No improvements were noted in intrusive symptoms. Only 1 patient dropped out of the study because of adverse side effects of nausea and vomiting. Other side effects noted were vivid dreaming, sleepwalking, headache, impaired memory, slowed thinking, and vertigo. In two case reports (Ford, 1996; Tohen et al., 1994), divalproex has been reported effective in reducing irritability, temper outbursts and mood disturbance.

In one open-label trial of divalproex in 16 male combat veterans, Clark et al. (1999) found improvements in comorbid depression and improvements in intrusive and hyperarousal symptoms. There were no changes, however, in avoidance and numbing symptoms. Some of the subjects had comorbid diagnoses of major depression, dysthymia, and dissociation disorder. This study lasted for 8 weeks, during which 11 subjects continued their previous medications. These included benzodiazepines, buproprion, fluoxetine, nefazodone, and buspirone. Over the course of the trial, 3 subjects dropped out due to adverse events, and 11 of the final 13 showed positive changes.

Gabapentin

Brannon et al. (2000) reported one case study of a civilian who was being treated with gabapentin over a period of 8 weeks. The subject had not been responsive to fluoxetine or cyproheptadine in the past and was being treated with hydrochlorothiazide at the same time as the gabapentin. At the end of the 8 weeks, the subject showed improvement in nightmares and anxiety.

Lamotrigine

Hertzberg et al. (2000) showed improvements in intrusive and avoidance/numbing symptoms following a randomized, placebo-controlled, double-blind study of lamotrigine in 15 veterans, both male and female. The study took place over 12 weeks. Of the 10 subjects in the lamotrigine group, 5 showed improvements.

In summary, lithium and anticonvulsants appear helpful with impulsivity and explosiveness, whereas anticonvulsants appear to have more specific effects on intrusive symptoms and sleep. It should be noted that all observations of mood stabilizers have been made with treatment-refractory combat veterans who were specifically selected to be on these medications because of problems with impulsivity and explosiveness and may not be generalizable to the whole of trauma.

Beta Blockers and Alpha-2-agonists

Although beta blockers and alpha-2-agonists exert their actions differently, these agents are similar in their overall effect on catecholamines and in fact are both used as antihypertensives. Beta blockers, such as propranolol, are thought to exert a more peripheral attenuation of catecholaminergic neurotransmission, whereas clonidine suppresses locus coeruleus activity and reduces adrenergic tone. These drugs have been used in the treatment of panic disorder (Ravaris et al., 1991; Tanna et al., 1977). However, the use of beta blockers and alpha-2-agonists began in direct response to scientific observations regarding increased catecholamine alterations in PTSD (Southwick et al., 1999).

Propranolol

Following Kardiner's (1941) seminal depiction of "physioneurosis" in combat veterans and preliminary descriptions of increased sympathetic nervous system activation in war veterans, Kolb et al. (1984) studied propranolol (dose range 120 to 160 mg/day) in 12 Vietnam combat veterans, in an attempt to directly address sympathetic hyperarousal in PTSD. An improvement in explosiveness, nightmares, intrusive recollections, startle response, hyperalertness, impaired sleep, self-esteem, and psychosocial function was noted. Famularo et al. (1988) employed an A-B-A design (6 weeks off–6 weeks on–6 weeks off) to explore the effects of propranolol in physically or sexually abused children with acute PTSD. Propranolol treatment significantly reduced symptoms of intrusion and arousal in 8 out of 11 children. Propranolol treatment is associated with several side effects, such as depression, fatigue, forgetfulness, sexual impairment, bradycardia, hypotension, and mental confusion.

Clonidine

In the same report as mentioned above, Kolb et al. (1984) also reported good results in alleviating flashbacks and hyperarousal using clonidine (dose range 0.1–0.4 mg per day). Kinzie and Leung (1989) added clonidine to imipramine in the treatment of nine Cambodian refugees and noted sleep improvement, reduction of nightmares, and partial improvement in startle response, but no improvement in avoidant behavior. Harmon and Riggs (1996) presented seven case reports in one open-label trial of transdermal clonidine in preschool children, ages 3 to 6, each with symptoms not previously improved by behavioral interventions. The study lasted 3 to 4 weeks after dose stabilization. The children were all in milieu therapy for 4 hours per day, individual psychotherapy, and family therapy, and two were on imipramine for depression. After the course of the study, all seven children showed improvement in aggression. Impulsivity, emotional outbursts and mood lability, hyperarousal, oppositionality, insomnia, nightmares, and generalized anxiety each showed improvement in five out of seven subjects. To date, there have been no published reports of randomized, double-blind, placebo-controlled trials of clonidine. However, one such study is in progress (Southwick, personal communication). Future data may reveal that clonidine is effective for hyperarousal and reexperiencing symptoms such as nightmares and flashbacks in the subset of individuals who show evidence of increased catecholamine activity.

Guanfacine

One case report on the effect of guanfacine, an alpha-2-agonist (Horrigan, 1996), and one on the effect of prazosin, an alpha-1 adrenergic blocker (Raskind et al., 2000), found improvement in nightmares following administration of the drug. Horrigan (1996) reported on one 7-year-old girl who had experienced minimum improvement from psychotherapy for nightmares and disruptive behavior and had had a reemergence of nightmares after being treated with clonidine. Following 7 weeks of guanfacine, she showed improvement in nightmares.

Prazosin

Another case report on the effect of prazosin found improvement in nightmares as well: Raskind et al. (2000) reported four male combat veterans who similarly showed improvement in this symptom after 8 weeks of prazosin.

Although earlier studies described catecholamine alterations as possibly central to the pathophysiology of PTSD (Kosten et al., 1987; Perry, 1990; Yehuda et al., 1992b), recent studies suggest that catecholaminergic hyperactivity may be confined to a subset of trauma survivors with PTSD. Indeed, some investigators have not found increased catecholamines in PTSD subjects (Mellman et al., 1995; Murburg et al., 1995).

Benzodiazepines

Benzodiazepines were initially tried in PTSD because of their efficacy in relieving general symptoms of anxiety and were found effective in a small number of open trials.

Dunner et al. (1986) observed positive effects with alprazolam (therapeutic dose range 0.5 to 6 mg/day) in veterans with PTSD. Lowenstein et al. (1988) demonstrated improvement in five patients with multiple-personality disorder and PTSD whose symptoms responded well to clonazepam (1 to 5 mg daily). Improvement was noted in nightmares, initial insomnia, intrusive recollections, panic attacks, severe anxiety, flashbacks, and overall well-being. In a randomized, placebo-controlled, double-blind study, alprazolam showed only modest benefit for anxiety symptoms and no benefit for core PTSD symptoms. However, this was only a 5-week trial with only 10 subjects (a mixed sample of veterans and civilians).

Mellman et al. (1998) found positive results of temazepam in four case reports of men with acute stress disorder. The drug was administered 1 to 3 weeks posttrauma for a period of 7 days. Acute PTSD symptoms improved, particularly in sleep disturbance.

In an open-label trial of clonazepam and alprazolam (Gelpin et al., 1996), there were no signs of global improvement following the administration of the drug. However, there was alleviation of physiological arousal symptoms. In this study, the drug was administered 2 to 18 days posttrauma. In contrast, Shalev et al. (1992) failed to note improvements in the startle response in patients being successfully treated with clonazepam.

In addition to the modest efficacy of benzodiazepines, the use in PTSD is relatively contraindicated because of withdrawal symptoms that may be associated with discontinuation of these agents (Risse et al., 1990) as well as the high risk of developing dependence on and abuse of these agents in this treatment population.

Drugs With Other Serotonergic Activity

Atypical Antipsychotics

The atypical antipsychotic medications have recently been used as augmentation agents to treat PTSD subjects with comorbid psychosis. These newer agents have serotonergic mechanisms of action, which may account for their efficacy in treating PTSD.

Four case reports and one open-label trial of risperidone showed improvements in PTSD symptoms following administration of the drug (Eidelman et al., 2000; Hamner & Ulmer, 1998; Krashin & Oates, 1999; Leyba & Wampler, 1998; Monnelly & Ciraulo, 1999;). Krashin and Oates (1999) described two subjects, one male and one female, who suffered from combat and childhood abuse. Following the course of the medication, they reported alleviation in flashbacks and intrusive thoughts. Monnelly and Ciraulo (1999) reported a case of one male Vietnam veteran who was on risperidone augmentation for 4 months and had previously had no success with fluoxetine, paroxetine, and diazepam. Following the course of risperidone he showed improvement in anger and aggression.

Leyba and Wampler (1998) presented four males who improved in nightmares and flashbacks following risperidone use. Comorbid diagnoses included major depression, alcohol dependence, and personality disorder not otherwise specified (PD NOS). The four subjects were concurrently taking valproate, clonazepam, fluoxetine, paroxetine, and trazedone. One subject developed akathisia. Eidelman et al. (2000) found similar improvement in flashbacks in four adult inpatients with physical trauma who were suffering from acute stress disorder.

Hamner and Ulmer (1998) found improvements in all three PTSD symptom clusters and psychotic symptoms following an open-label trial of risperidone augmentation to an antidepressant. Subjects included 13 Vietnam veterans with PTSD and psychosis who had comorbid diagnoses of major depression, alcohol use disorder, GAD, and panic disorder.

One case report showed olanzapine to have positive effects on insomnia and hyperarousal in combination with fluoxetine (Burton & Marshall, 1999). Another case report of a veteran with PTSD and comorbid psychosis reported that clozapine augmentation was helpful in reduction of symptoms (Hamner, 1996).

Opioid Antagonists

Many theorists have postulated that alterations in the opioid system may be relevant to PTSD (Charney et al., 1993; Glover, 1992; van der Kolk, 1987). However, to date, there is scant evidence for this. In one study, Pitman et al. (1990) demonstrated a naloxone-reversible stress-induced analgesia in combat veterans who were exposed to trauma-related imagery. Nonetheless, the idea of treating PTSD with opiate antagonists such as nalmefene is largely grounded in this theory. Glover reported improvement in numbing and other PTSD symptoms in 8 out of 18 combat veterans after using nalmefene (therapeutic dose 200 to 400 mg/day). Other subjects either worsened or showed no improvement (Glover, 1992).

One case report of naltrexone showed improvements in flashbacks in one man and one woman (Bills & Kreisler, 1993). The woman had the comorbid diagnoses of major depression and multiple-personality disorder. Another case report on the effects of naltrexone (Ibarra et al., 1994) was of one 32-year-old man with hypertension involved in a placebo-controlled trial on the effects of blood pressure. The subject also had PTSD. Within 24 hours postingestion, he reported feelings of rage, explosive behavior, and elevated blood pressure, among other unpleasant symptoms related to his PTSD.

FUTURE VISTAS

The pharmacological literature on PTSD is relatively small, and only a few studies can legitimately be considered Type I studies. Moreover, many studies were conducted in U.S. veteran populations, a group likely to have a higher percentage of treatment-refractory individuals. However, these studies have been important in demonstrating that medications can be quite effective in treating circumscribed symptoms of PTSD, and can lead to an overall global improvement in symptomatic trauma survivors. Therefore, these studies have tended to confirm the results of open trials and clinical case reports. Future studies will need to examine other promising medications using controlled trials, and in other trauma populations.

Since there is considerable heterogeneity across clinical trials and subject populations, we can say little with confidence about how treatments compare to each other in the absence of direct randomized comparisons. We make some preliminary observations below that might be tested in clinical trials.

The fact that different medications may target different core symptoms of PTSD has been interpreted as reflecting the complex pathophysiology of this disorder (Friedman & Southwick, 1995). It may be that medications with specific effects in some neurotransmitter systems may have particular effects on those symptoms that are primarily mediated by those systems. However, since we do not know how to characterize medications by their neurotransmitter effects, this concept remains primarily theoretical. However, the fact that no one medication has yet been found to address the complex syndrome of PTSD also raises the question of whether all symptoms in PTSD should be addressed by pharmacotherapy. And if so, the question follows whether polypharmacy strategies can be rationally used to specifically target different types of symptoms in trauma survivors.

To date, it is unknown which of the core symptom clusters, if any, are most responsible for the functional impairment in PTSD. A recent study in a non-treatment-seeking group of Holocaust survivors showed that all survivors had intrusive, distressing thoughts about the Holocaust, whereas only a subset of these survivors showed impairment in social or occupational functioning and met diagnostic criteria for PTSD. Rather, overall impairment, and neurobiological dysregulation, was related to the presence of avoidant symptoms in Holocaust survivors (Yehuda et al., 1995). Thus, it is possible that individuals eventually learn to cope with some of the symptoms of PTSD through nonpharmacological strategies, whereas other symptoms lead more directly to impairment and require more direct pharmacological intervention.

The literature is unclear as to whether pharmacotherapy in PTSD results in a global improvement by relieving associated or comorbid symptoms such as depression, panic, anxiety, and impulsivity, even though comorbidity is strongly associated with degree of impairment (Blanchard et al., 1998; Marshall et al., 2001). This raises the question of whether medications in PTSD exert their effects by addressing comorbid conditions or associated features in PTSD. As many of the patients treated in this literature have chronic PTSD and a current or past history of comorbid psychiatric disorder, future studies will need to examine the effect of comorbid symptoms and diagnoses on treatment responses to various medications.

In the last edition of this book, published in 1996, we concluded that the pharmacotherapy of PTSD is in its early stages. This is still true despite the almost doubling of the number of controlled trials. Many questions still remain. One of major difficulties with the literature is that it is difficult to determine whether one can use similar strategies in the treatment of individuals who have different degrees of chronicity and/or comorbidity. The majority of early studies have tended to focus on chronically ill, treatment-refractory combat veterans with multiple presenting problems. Future studies will need to determine whether different pharmacological strategies are optimal for more acute conditions, and whether other factors, such as type of trauma and the developmental stage at which one survived traumatic events, are relevant to pharmacological intervention. Finally, since polypharamacy in PTSD is the rule rather than the exception, studies examining combinations of medication are neccessary.

Future studies must also address the interaction of psychopharmacology and psychosocial treatments.

Other questions concern the appropriate duration for pharmacotherapy. This is a difficult question because the natural history of PTSD is still unknown. The effects of discontinuing medications on PTSD symptoms must also be formally studied. Finally, future research should address the issue of whether medications can be used to prevent relapse of symptoms from one episode of PTSD, and/or for prevention of a recurrence in response to a subsequent episode.

ACKNOWLEDGMENT This work was supported by VA Merit Review Funds (RY), RO1 49555 (RY), and NIMH Grant MH01412 (RDM).

References

American Psychiatric Association. (1980). *DSM-III: Diagnostic and statistical manual of mental disorders* (3rd ed.). Washington, DC: Author.

American Psychiatric Association. (1994). *DSM-IV: Diagnostic and statistical manual of mental disorders* (4th ed.). Washington, DC: Author.

Baker, D. G., Diamond, B. I., Gillette, G., Hamner, M., Katzelnick, D., Keller, T., Mellman, T. A., Pontius, E., Rosenthal, M., Tucker, P., et al. (1995, December). A double-blind, randomized, placebo-controlled, multi-center study of brofaromine in the treatment of post-traumatic stress disorder. *Psychopharmacology (Berlin), 122*(4), 386–389.

Basoglu, M., Marks, I. M., & Sengün, S. (1992). Amitriptyline for PTSD in a torture survivor: A case study. *Journal of Traumatic Stress, 5*, 77–83.

Bills, L. J., & Kreisler, K. (1993). Treatment of flashbacks with naltrexone. *American Journal of Psychiatry, 150*, 1430.

Birkhimer, L. J., DeVane, C. L., & Muniz, C. E. (1985). Posttraumatic stress disorder: Characteristics and pharmacological response in the veteran population. *Comprehensive Psychiatry, 26*, 304–310.

Blaha, J., Svobodova, K., & Kapounkova, Z. (1999). Therapeutical aspects of using citalopram in burns. *Acta Chirurgiae Plastica, 41*(1), 25–32.

Blake, D. (1986). Treatment of acute posttraumatic stress disorder with tricyclic antidepressants. *Southern Medical Journal, 79*, 201–204.

Blanchard, E. B., Buckley, T. C., Hickling, E. J., & Taylor, A. E. (1998). Posttraumatic stress disorder and comorbid depression: Is the correlation an illusion? *Journal of Anxiety Disorders, 12*, 21–37.

Bleich, A., Siegel, B., Garb, R., & Lerer, B. (1986). Posttraumatic stress disorder following combat exposure: Clinical features and psychopharmacological treatment. *British Journal of Psychiatry, 149*, 365–369.

Bouwer, C., & Stein, D. J. (1998). Survivors of torture presenting at an anxiety disorders clinic: Symptomatology and pharmacotherapy. *Journal of Nervous and Mental Disease, 186*(5), 316–318.

Brady, K., Pearlstein, T., Asnis, G. M., Baker, D., Rothbaum, B., Sikes, C. R., & Farfel, G. M. (2000). Efficacy and safety of sertraline treatment of posttraumatic stress disorder: A randomized controlled trial. *Journal of the American Medical Association, 283*(14), 1837–1844.

Brady, K. T., Sonne, S. C., & Roberts, J. M. (1995). Sertraline treatment of comorbid posttraumatic stress disorder and alcohol dependence. *Journal of Clinical Psychiatry, 56*(11), 502–505.

Brannon, N., Labbate, L., & Huber, M. (2000). Gabapentin treatment for posttraumatic stress disorder. *Canadian Journal of Psychiatry, 45*, 84.

Bremner, J. D., Southwick, S. M., Johnson, D. R., Yehuda, R., & Charney, D. S. (1993). Childhood physical abuse and combat-related posttraumatic stress disorder in Vietnam veterans. *American Journal of Psychiatry, 150*, 235–239.

Breslau, N., Davis, G. C., Andreski, P., & Peterson, E. (1991). Traumatic events and posttraumatic stress disorder in an urban population of young adults. *Archives of General Psychiatry, 48*, 216–222.

Breslau, N., Kessler, R. C., & Chilcoat, H. D. (1998). Trauma and posttraumatic stress disorder in the community. *Archives of General Psychiatry, 55*, 626–632.

Brewin, C. R., Andrews, B., & Valentine, J. D. (2000). Meta-analysis of risk factors for posttraumatic stress disorder in trauma-exposed adults. *Journal of Consulting and Clinical Psychology, 68*, 748–766.

Brophy, M. H. (1991). Cyproheptadine for combat nightmares in post-traumatic stress disorder and dream anxiety disorder. *Military Medicine, 156*, 100–101.

Burdon, A. P., Sutker, P. B., Foulks, E. F., Crane, M. U., & Thompson, K. E. (1991). Pilot program of treatment for PTSD (letter). *American Journal of Psychiatry, 148*, 1269–1270.

Burstein, A. (1984). Treatment of post-traumatic stress disorder with imipramine. *Psychosomatics, 25*, 681–686.

Burstein, A., Ciccone, P. E., Greenstein, R. A., Daniels, N., Olsen, K., Mazarek, A., Decatur, R., & Johnson, N. (1988). Chronic Vietnam PTSD and acute civilian PTSD: A comparison of treatment experiences. *General Hospital Psychiatry, 10*, 245–249.

Burton, J. K., & Marshall, R. D. (1999). Categorizing fear: The role of trauma in clinical formulation. *American Journal of Psychiatry, 156*(5), 761–766.

Canive, J. M., Clark, R. D., Calais, L. A., Qualls, C., & Tuason, V. B. (1998). Buproprion treatment in veterans with posttraumatic stress disoder: An open study. *Journal of Clinical Psychopharamcology, 18*(5), 379–383.

Charney, D. S., Deutch, A. Y., Krystal, J. H., Southwick, S. M., & Davis, M. (1993). Psychobiologic mechanisms of posttraumatic stress disorder. *Archives of General Psychiatry, 50*, 294–305.

Chen, C. J. (1991). The obsessive quality and clomipramine treatment in PTSD (letter). *American Journal of Psychiatry, 148*, 1087–1088.

Clark, R. D., Canive, J. M., Calais, L. A., Qualls, C., Brugger, R. D., & Vosburgh, T. B. (1999). Cyproheptadine treatment of nightmares associated with posttraumatic stress disorder. *Journal of Clinical Psychopharmacology, 19*(5), 486–487.

Connor, K. M., Davidson, J. R. T., Weisler, R. H., & Ahearn, E. (1999). A pilot study of mirtazepine in post-traumatic stress disorder. *International Clinical Psychopharmacology, 14*, 29–31.

Connor, K. M., Sutherland, S. M., Tupler, L. A., Malik, M. L., & Davidson, J.R. (1991). Fluoxetine in post-traumatic stress disorder. Randomised, double-blind study. *British Journal of Psychiatry, 175*, 17–22.

Cooper, N. A., & Clum, B. A. (1989). Imaginal flooding as a supplementary treatment for PTSD in combat veterans: A controlled study. *Behavioral Therapy, 20*, 381–391.

Davidson, J. (1992). Drug therapy of post-traumatic stress disorder. *British Journal of Psychiatry, 160*, 309–314.

Davidson, J. R. T., Hughes, D. L., Blazer, D. G., & George, L. K. (1991a). Post-traumatic stress disorder in the community: An epidemiological study. *Psychological Medicine, 21*, 713–721.

Davidson, J. R. T., Kudler, H. S., Saunders, W. B., Erickson, L., Smith, R. D., Stein, R. M., Lipper, S., Hammett, E. B., Mahorney, S. L., & Cavenar, J. O. (1993). Predicting response to amitriptyline in posttraumatic stress disorder. *American Journal of Psychiatry, 150*, 1024–1029.

Davidson, J., Kudler, H., Smith, R., Mahorney, S. L., Lipper, S., Hammett, E., Saunders, W. B., & Cavenar, J. L. Jr. (1990). Treatment of posttraumatic stress disorder with amitriptyline and placebo. *Archives of General Psychiatry, 47*, 259–266.

Davidson, J., Roth, S., & Newman, E. (1991b). Fluoxetine in post-traumatic stress disorder. *Journal of Traumatic Stress, 4*, 419–423.

Davidson, J. R. T., Rothbaum, B. O., van der Kolk, B., Sikes, C. R., & Farfel, G. M. (2001). Multi-center, double-blind comparison of sertraline and placebo in the treatment of posttraumatic stress disorder. *Archives of General Psychiatry, 58*, 485–492.

Davidson, J., & Smith, R. (1990). Traumatic experiences in psychiatric outpatients. *Journal of Traumatic Stress, 3*, 459–475.

Davidson, J., Swartz, M., Storck, M., Krishnan, R. R., & Hammett, E. (1985). A diagnostic and family study of posttraumatic stress disorder. *American Journal of Psychiatry, 142*, 90–93.

Davidson, J., Walker, J. I., & Kilts, C. (1987). A pilot study of phenelzine in the treatment of post-traumatic stress disorder. *British Journal of Psychiatry, 150*, 252–255.

Davidson, J. R., Weisler, R. H., Malik, M. L., & Connor, K. M. (1998). Treatment of posttraumatic stress disorder with nefazodone. *International Journal of Clinical Psychopharmacoloy, 13*(3), 111–113.

Davis, L. L., Nugent, A. L., Murray, J., Kramer, G. L., & Petty, F. (2000). Nefazodone treatment for chronic posttraumatic stress disorder: An open trial. *Journal of Clinical Psychopharmacology, 20*(2), 159–164.

DeBoer, M., Op den Velde, W., Falger, P. J., Hovens, J. E., De Groen, J. H., & Van Duijn, H. (1992). Fluvoxamine treatment for chronic PTSD: A pilot study. *Psychotherapy and Psychosomatics, 57*, 158–163.

Dow, B., & Kline, N. (1997). Antidepressant treatment of posttraumatic stress disorder and major depression in veterans. *Annual Clinical Psychiatry, 9*(1), 1–5.

Dunner, D. L., Ishiki, D., Avery, D. H., Wilson, L. G., & Hyde, T. S. (1986). Effects of alprazolam and diazepam on anxiety and panic attacks in panic disorder: A controlled study. *Journal of Clinical Psychiatry, 47*, 458–460.

Eidelman, I., Seedat, S., & Stein, D. J. (2000). Risperidone in the treatment of acute stress disorder in physically traumatized inpatients. *Depression and Anxiety, 11*(4), 187–188.

Falcon, S., Ryan, C., Chamberlain, K., & Curtis, G. (1985). Tricyclics: Possible treatment for posttraumatic stress disorder. *Journal of Clinical Psychiatry, 46*, 385–388.

Famularo, R., Kinscherff, R., & Fenton, T. (1988). Propranolol treatment for childhood post-traumatic stress disorder, acute type: A pilot study. *American Journal of Diseases of Children, 142*, 1244–1247.

Fesler, F. A. (1991). Valproate in combat-related posttraumatic stress disorder. *Journal of Clinical Psychiatry, 52*, 361–364.

Foa, E. B. (1997). Psychological processes related to recovery from a trauma and an effective treatment for PTSD. In R. Yehuda & A. McFarlane (Eds.),

Psychobiology of PTSD. *Annals of the New York Academy of Sciences*, 410–424.

Foa, E. B., Davidson, J. R. T., & Frances, A. (Eds.). (1999). The Expert Consensus Guideline Series: Treatment of posttraumatic stress disorder. *Journal of Clinical Psychiatry, 60*, 1–76.

Foa, E. B., Keane, T. M., & Friedman, M. J. (Eds.). (2000). *Effective treatment for PTSD: Practice guidelines from the International Society for Traumatic Stress Studies*. New York: Guilford Press.

Foa, E. B., Rothbaum, B. O., Riggs, D. S., & Murdock, T. B. (1991). Treatment of posttraumatic stress disorder in rape victims: A comparison between cognitive-behavioral procedures and counseling. *Journal of Consulting and Clinical Psychology, 59*, 714–723.

Foa, E. B., Steketee, G., & Rothbaum, B. O. (1989). Behavioral/cognitive conceptualizations of post-traumatic stress disorder. *Behavior Therapy, 20*, 155–176.

Ford, N. (1996). The use of anticonvulsants in posttraumatic stress disorder: Case study and overview. *Journal of Traumatic Stress*, 9(4), 857–863.

Forster, P. L., Schoenfeld, F. B., Marmar, C. R., & Lang, A. J. (1995). Lithium for irritability in posttraumatic stress disorder. *Journal of Traumatic Stress*, 8(1), 143–149.

Foy, D. W., Sipprelle, R. C., Rueger, D. B., & Carroll, E. M. (1984). Etiology of posttraumatic stress disorder in Vietnam veterans. *Journal of Consulting and Clinical Psychology, 40*, 1323–1328.

Frank, J. B., Kosten, T. R., Giller, E. L., & Dan, E. (1988). A randomized clinical trial of phenelzine and imipramine for post traumatic stress disorder. *American Journal of Psychiatry, 145*, 1289–1291.

Freedy, J. R., Shaw, D. L., & Jarrell, M. P. (1992). Towards an understanding of the psychological impact of natural disaster: An application of the conservation resources stress model. *Journal of Traumatic Stress, 5*, 441–454.

Friedman, M. J. (1988). Toward rational pharmacotherapy for posttraumaic stress disorder: An interim report. *American Journal of Psychiatry, 145*, 281–285.

Friedman, M. J., & Southwick, S. M. (1995). Towards pharmacotherapy for PTSD. In M. J. Friedman, D. S. Charney, & A. Y. Deutch (Eds.), *Neurobiological and clinical consequences of stress: From normal adaptation to PTSD*. Philadelphia: Lippincott-Raven.

Friedman, M. J., & Yehuda, R. (1995). Post-traumatic stress disorder and comorbidity: Psychobiological approaches to differential diagnosis. In M. J. Friedman, D. S. Charney, & A. Y. Deutch (Eds.), *Neurobiological and clinical consequences of stress: From normal adaptation to PTSD*. Philadelphia: Lippincott-Raven.

Gelpin, E., Bonne, O., Peri, T., Brandes, D., & Shalev, A. Y. (1996). Treatment of recent trauma survivors with benzodiazepines: A prospective study. *Journal of Clinical Psychiatry*, 57(9), 390–394.

Glover, H. (1992). Emotional numbing: A possible endorphin-mediated phenomenon associated with post-traumatic stress disorder and other allied psychopathologic states. *Journal of Traumatic Stress, 5*, 643–675.

Goldstein, G., van Kammen, W., Shelly, C., Miller, D. J., & van Kammen, D. P. (1987). Survivors of imprisonment in the Pacific theater during World War II. *American Journal of Psychiatry, 144*, 1210–1213.

Green, B. (2000). Traumatic stress and disaster: Mental health factors influencing adaptation. In *Annual review of psychiatry*. Washington, DC: American Psychiatric Press.

Green, B. L., Goodman, L. A., Krupnick, J. L., Corcoran, C. B., Petty, R. M., Sockton, P., & Stern, N. M. (2000). Outcomes of single versus multiple trauma exposure in a screening sample. *Journal of Traumatic Stress*, 13(2), 271–286.

Green, B. L., Lindy, J. D., Grace, M. C., & Leonard, A. C. (1992). Chronic posttraumatic stress disorder and diagnostic comorbidity in a disaster sample. *Journal of Nervous and Mental Disease, 180*, 760–766.

Gupta, S., Austin, R., Cali, L. A., & Bhatara, V. (1998). Nightmares treated with cyproheptadine. *Journal of the American Academy of Child and Adolescent Psychiatry*, 37(6), 570–572.

Gupta, S., Popli, A., Bathhurst, E., Hennig, L., Droney, T., & Keller, P. (1998). Efficacy of cyproheptadine for nightmares associated with posttraumatic stress disorder. *Comprehensive Psychiatry*, 39(3), 160–164.

Hamner, M. B. (1996). Clozapine treatment for a veteran with comorbid psychosis and PTSD. *American Journal of Psychiatry*, 153(6), 841.

Hamner, M. B., & Frueh, B. C. (1998). Response to venlafaxine in a previously antidepressant treatment-resistant combat veteran with post-traumatic stress disorder. *International Journal of Clinical Psychopharmacology*, 13(5), 233–234.

Hamner, M., & Ulmer, H. (1998). *Risperidone for positive symptoms of psychosis in PTSD: A preliminary open trial*. Poster presented at the 38th Annual NCDEU Meeting in Boca Raton, FL, *Abstract No. 16*.

Harmon, R. J., & Riggs, P. D. (1996). Clonidine for posttraumatic stress disorder in preschool children.

Journal of the American Academy of Child and Adolescent Psychiatry, 35(9), 1247–1249.

Harsch, H. H. (1986). Cyproheptadine for recurrent nightmares. *American Journal of Psychiatry, 143*, 1491–1492.

Helzer, J. E., Robin, L. N., & McEvoy, L. (1987). Post-traumatic stress disorder in the general population: Findings from the Epidemiological Catchment Area Survey. *New England Journal of Medicine, 317*, 1630–1634.

Hertzberg, M. A., Feldman, M. E., Beckham, J. C., & Davidson, J. R. (1996). Trial of trazodone for post-traumatic stress disorder using a mutliple baseline group design. *Journal of Clinical Psychopharmacology, 16*(4), 294–298.

Hertzberg, M. A., Feldman, M. E., Beckham, J. C., Kudler, H. S., & Davidson, J. R. (2000). Lack of efficacy for fluoxetine in PTSD: A placebo controlled trial in combat veterans. *Annual Clinical Psychiatry, 12*(2), 101–105.

Hertzberg, M. A., Feldman, M. E., Beckham, J. C., Moore, S. D., & Davidson, J. R. (1998). Open trial of nefazodone for combat-related posttraumatic stress disorder. *Journal of Clinical Psychiatry, 59*(9), 460–464.

Hidalgo, R., Hertzberg, M. A., Mellman, T., Petty, F., Tucker, P., Weisler, R., Zisook, S., Chen, S., Churchill, E., & Davidson, J. (1999). Nefazodone in post-traumatic stress disorder: Results from six open-label trials. *International Journal of Clinical Psychopharmacology, 14*(2), 61–68.

Hogben, G. L., & Cornfield, R. B. (1981). Treatment of traumatic war neurosis with phenelzine. *Archives of General Psychiatry, 38*, 440–445.

Horowitz, M. (1974). Stress response syndromes, character style, and dynamic psychotherapy. *Archives of General Psychiatry, 31*, 768–781.

Horowitz, M. (1986). *Stress response syndromes* (2nd ed.). Northvale, NJ: Jason Aronson.

Horrigan, J. P. (1996). Guanfacine for PTSD nightmares. *Journal of the American Academy of Child and Adolescent Psychiatry, 35*(8), 975–976.

Humphreys, L., Westernik, J., Giarratano, L., & Brooks, R. (1999). An intensive treatment program for chronic posttraumatic stress disorder: 2-year outcome data. *Australian and New Zealand Journal of Psychiatry, 33*(6), 848–854.

Ibarra, P., Bruehl, S. P., McCubbin, J. A., Carlson, C. R., Wilson, J. F., Norton, J. A., & Montgomery, T. B. (1994). An unusual reaction to opioid blockade with naltrexone in a case of post-traumatic stress disorder. *Journal of Traumatic Stress, 7*(2), 303–309.

Judge, R., Martenyi, F., Brown, E., Zhang, H., & Tollefson, G. (2000). *Fluoxetine versus placebo in Post-traumatic stress disorder*. ACNP Annual Meeting, New Research Poster, San Juan, Puerto Rico.

Kaplan, Z., Amir, M., Swartz, M., & Levine, J. (1996). Inositol treatment of post-traumatic stress disorder. *Anxiety, 2*(1), 51–52.

Kardiner, A. (1941). *The traumatic neurosis of war*. New York: Paul Hoeber.

Katz, R. J., Lott, M. H., Arbus, P., Crocq, L., Lingjaerde, O., Lopez, G., Loughrey, G. C., MacFarlane, D. J., Nugent, D., Turner, S. W., Weisaeth, L., & Yule, W. (1995). Pharmacotherapy of post-traumatic stress disorder with a novel psychotropic. *Anxiety, 1*, 169–174.

Keane, T. M., Fairbank, J. A., Caddell, J. M., & Zimering, R. T. (1989). Implosive (flooding) therapy reduces symptoms of PTSD in Vietnam combat veterans. *Behavioral Therapy, 20*, 245–260.

Keane, T. M., & Wolfe, J. (1990). Comorbidity in post-traumatic stress disorder: An analysis of community and clinical studies. *Journal of Applied Social Psychology, 20* (special issue), 1776–1788.

Keck, P. E., Jr., McElroy, S. L., & Friedman, L. M. (1992). Valproate and carbamazepine in the treatment of panic and posttraumatic stress disorders, withdrawal states, and behavioral dyscontrol syndromes. *Journal of Clinical Psychopharmacology, 12*(Suppl.), 36S–41S.

Kessler, R. C., Sonnega, A., Bromet, E., Hughes, M., & Nelson, C. B. (1995). Posttraumatic stress disorder in the National Comorbidity Survey. *Archives of General Psychiatry, 52*, 1048–1060.

Kilpatrick, D. G., & Resnick, H. S. (1993). Posttraumatic stress disorder associated with exposure to criminal victimization in clinical and community populations. In J. R. T. Davidson & E. B. Foa (Eds.), *Posttraumatic stress disorder: DSM-IV and beyond*. Washington, DC: American Psychiatric Press.

Kilpatrick, D. G., Veronen, L. J., & Resick, P. A. (1982). Psychological sequelae to rape: Assessment and treatment strategies. In D. M. Dolays & R. L. Meredith (Eds.), *Behavioral medicine: Assessment and treatment strategies*. New York: Plenum Press.

Kinzie, J. D., & Goetz, R. R. (1996). A century of controversy surrounding posttraumatic stress-spectrum syndromes: The impact on DSM-III and DSM-IV. *Journal of Traumatic Stress, 9*,159–179.

Kinzie, J. D., & Leung, P. (1989). Clonidine in Cambodian patients with posttraumatic stress disorder. *Journal of Nervous and Mental Disease, 1777*, 546–550.

Kitchner, I., & Greenstein, R. (1985). Low dose lithium carbonate in the treatment of post traumatic stress disorder: Brief communication. *Military Medicine, 150,* 378–381.

Kline, N. A., Dow, B. M., Brown, S. A., & Matloff, J. L. (1994). Sertraline efficacy in depressed combat veterans with posttraumatic stress disorder (letter). *American Journal of Psychiatry, 151,* 621.

Kluznick, J. C., Speed, N., Van Valenburg, C., & Magraw, R. (1986). Forty-year follow-up of United States prisoners of war. *American Journal of Psychiatry, 143,* 1443–1446.

Kolb, L. C., Burris, B. C., & Griffiths, S. (1984). Propranolol and clonidine in the treatment of post-traumatic stress disorders of war. In B. van der Kolk, (Ed.), *Post-traumatic stress disorder: Psychological and biological sequellae.* Washington, DC: American Psychiatric Press.

Kosten, T. R., Frank, J. B., Dan, E., McDougle, C. J., & Giller, E. L. (1991). Pharmacotherapy for posttraumatic stress disorder using phenelzine or imipramine. *Journal of Nervous and Mental Disease, 179,* 366–370.

Kosten, T. R., Mason, J. W., Giller, E. L., et al. (1987). Sustained urinary norepinephrine and epinephrine elevation in posttraumatic stress disorder. *Psychoneuroendocrinology, 12,* 13–20.

Krashin, D., & Oates, E. W. (1999). Risperidone as an adjunct therapy for post-traumatic stress disorder. *Military Medicine, 164*(8), 605–606.

Kulka, R. A., Schlenger, W. E., Fairbank, J. A., Hough, R. L., Jordan, B. K., Marmar, C. R., & Weiss, D. S. (1990). *Trauma and the Vietnam War generation: Report of findings from the National Vietnam Veterans Readjustment Study.* New York: Brunner/Mazel.

Lerer, B., Bleich, A., Kotler, M., Garb, R., Hertzberg, M., & Levin, B. (1987). Posttraumatic stress disorder in Israeli combat veterans: Effect of phenlzine treatment. *Archives of General Psychiatry, 44,* 976–981.

Leyba, C. M., & Wampler, T. P. (1998). Risperidone in PTSD. *Psychiatric Service, 49*(2), 245–246.

Lipper, S., Davidson, J. R. T., Grady, T. A., Edinger, J. D., Hammett, E. B., Mahorney, S. L., & Cavenar, J. O. (1986). Preliminary study of carbamazepine in post-traumatic stress disorder. *Psychosomatics, 27,* 849–854.

Looff, D., Grimley, P., Kuller, F., Martin, A., & Shonfield, L. (1995). Carbamazepine for PTSD. *Journal of the American Academy of Child and Adolescent Psychiatry, 34*(6), 703–704.

Lowenstein, R. J., Hornstein, N., & Farber, B. (1988). Open trial of clonazepam in the treatment of posttraumatic stress symptoms in multiple personality disorder. *Dissociation, 1,* 3–12.

Malik, M. L., Connor, K. M., Sutherland, S. M., Smith, R. D., Davison, R. M., & Davidson, J. R. (1999). Quality of life and posttraumatic stress disorder: A pilot study assessing changes in SF-36 scores before and after treatment in a placebo-controlled trial of fluoxetine. *Journal of Traumatic Stress, 12*(2), 387–393.

March, J. S. (1993). What constitutes a stressor: The "Criterion A" issue. In J. R. T. Davidson & E. B. Foa (Eds.), *Posttraumatic stress disorder, DSM-IV and beyond.* Washington, DC: American Psychiatric Press.

Marmar, C. R., Schoenfeld, F., Weiss, D. S., Metzler, T., Zatzick, D., Wu, R., Smiga, S., Tecott, L., & Neylan, T. (1996). Open trial of fluvoxamine treatment for combat-related posttraumatic stress disorder. *Journal of Clinical Psychiatry, 57*(Suppl. 8), 66–70; discussion 71–72.

Marshall, R. D., Beebe, K. L., Oldham, M., & Zaninelli, R. (in press). Efficacy and safety of paroxetine treatment of chronic PTSD: A fixed-dosage, multicenter, placebo-controlled study. *American Journal of Psychiatry.*

Marshall, R. D., & Cloitre, M. (2000). Maximizing treatment outcome in PTSD by combining psychotherapy with pharmacotherapy. *Current Psychiatry Reports, 2,* 335–340.

Marshall, R. D., & Klein, D. F. (1999). Diagnostic classification of anxiety disorders: Historical context and implications for neurobiology. In D. S. Charney, E. J. Nestler, & B. S. Bunney (Eds.), *Neurobiology of mental illness.* New York and Oxford: Oxford University Press.

Marshall, R. D., Olfson, M., Hellman, F., Blanco, C., Guardino, M., & Struening, E. (2001). Comorbidity, impairment, and suicidality in subthreshold PTSD. *American Journal of Psychiatry, 158*(9), 1467–1473.

Marshall, R. D., & Pierce, D. (2000). Implications of recent findings in posttraumatic stress disorder and the role of pharmacotherapy. *Harvard Review of Psychiatry, 7*(5), 247–256.

Marshall, R. D., Printz, D., Cardenas, D., Abbate, L., & Liebowitz, M. R. (1994). Adverse events in patients with PTSD and panic attacks on fluoxetine (letter). *American Journal of Psychiatry, 152,* 1238.

Marshall, R. D., Schneier, F. R., Fallon, B. A., Knight, C. B., Abbate, L. A., Goetz, D., & Campeas, R. (1998). An open trial of paroxetine in patients with noncombat-related, chronic posttraumatic stress disorder. *Journal of Clinical Psychopharmacology, 18*(1), 10–18.

Marshall, R. D., Schneier, F., Simpson, B., Blanco, C., Beebe, K., & Liebowitz, M. (2000, November 18). *Interim report of a controlled trial of paroxetine in PTSD*. Symposium presentation, International Society for Traumatic Stress Studies, San Antonio, TX.

Martenyi, F., Brown, E., Zhang, H., Prakash, A., & Koke, S. (2001, May). *Fluoxetine vs placebo in posttraumatic stress disorder*. Poster presentation, American Psychiatric Association Annual Meeting, New Orleans.

Martenyi, F., & Metcalfe, S. (2001, May). A clinical trial of fluoxetine and placebo for combat-related PTSD. New Clinical Drug Evaluation Unit (NCDEU), Session I-81.

McDougle, C. J., Southwick, S. M., Charney, D. S., & St. James, R. L. (1991). An open trial of fluoxetine in the treatment of posttraumatic stress disorder (letter). *Journal of Clinical Psychopharmacology, 11*, 325–327.

McFarlane, A. C. (1989a). The aetiology of post-traumatic morbidity: Predisposing, precipitating, and perpetuating factors. *British Journal of Psychiatry, 154*, 221–228.

McFarlane, A. C. (1989b). The treatment of post-traumatic stress disorder. *British Journal of Medical Psychology, 62* (pt. 1), 81–90.

McFarlane, A. C. (1990). Vulnerability to posttraumatic stress disorder. In M. E. Wolf & A. D. Mosnaim (Eds.), *Posttraumatic stress disorder: Etiology, phenomenology and treatment*. Washington, DC: American Psychiatric Press.

McFarlane, A. C. (1992). Multiple diagnoses in posttraumatic stress disorder in the victims of a natural disaster. *Journal of Nervous and Mental Disease, 180*, 498–504.

McFarlane, A. C., & Yehuda, R. (2000). Clinical treatment of posttraumatic stress disorder: Conceptual challenges raised by recent research. *Australian and New Zealand Journal of Psychiatry, 34*(6), 940–953.

McNally, R. J., & Shin, L. M. (1995). Association of intelligence with severity of posttraumatic stress disorder symptoms in Vietnam combat veterans. *American Journal of Psychiatry, 152*, 936–938.

Medical Economics Company. (2001). *PDR: Physicians' Desk Reference: Supplement A* (55th edition).

Mellman, T. A., Byers, P. M., & Augenstein, J. S. (1998). Pilot evaluation of hypnotic medication during acute traumatic stress response. *Journal of Traumatic Stress, 11*(3), 563–569.

Mellman, T. A., Kumar, A., Kulick-Bell, R., Kumar, M., & Nolan, B. (1995). Nocturnal/daytime urine noradrenergic measures and sleep in combat-related PTSD. *Biological Psychiatry, 38*, 174–179.

Milanes, F. J., Mack, C. N., Dennison, J., & Slater, V. L. (1984, June). Phenelzine treatment of post-Vietnam stress syndrome. *VA Practictioner*, 40–49.

Monnelly, E. P., & Ciraulo, D. A. (1999). Risperidone effects on irritable aggression in posttraumatic stress disorder. *Journal of Clinical Psychopharmacology, 19*(4), 377–378.

Murburg, M. M., McFall, M. E., Lewis, N., & Beith, R. C. (1995). Plasma norepinephrine kinetics in patients with posttraumatic stress disorder. *Biological Psychiatry, 38*, 819–825.

Nagy, L. M., Morgan III, C. A., Southwick, S. M., & Charney, D. S. (1993). Open prospective trial of fluoxetine for posttraumatic stress disorder. *Journal of Clinical Psychopharmacology, 13*, 107–113.

Nagy, L. M., Southwick, S. M., & Charney, D. S. (1996, November 11). *Placebo-controlled trial of fluoxetine in PTSD*. Poster presentation, International Society for Traumatic Stress Studies 12th Annual Meeting, San Francisco.

Neal, L. A., Shapland, W., & Fox, C. (1997). An open trial of moclobemide in the treatment of post-traumatic stress disorder. *International Journal of Clinical Psychopharmacology, 12*(4), 231–232.

North, C. S., Smith, E. M., & Spitznagel, E. L. (1994). Posttraumatic stress disorder in survivors of a mass shooting. *American Journal of Psychiatry, 151*, 82–88.

Perry, B. D. (1994). Neurobiological Sequelae of childhood trauma: PTSD in children. In M. M. Murburg (Ed.), *Catecholamine function in posttraumatic stress disorder: Emerging concepts*. Washington, DC: American Psychiatric Press.

Perry, B. D., Southwick, S. M., Yehuda, R., & Giller, E. L. (1990). Adrenergic receptor regulation in posttraumatic stress disorder. In E. L. Giller (Ed.), *Biological assessment and treatment of posttraumatic stress disorder*. Washington, DC: American Psychiatric Press.

Pitman, R. K., van der Kolk, V. A., Orr, S. P., & Greenberg, M. S. (1990). Naloxone-reversible analgesic response to combat-related stimuli in post traumatic stress disorder. *Archives of General Psychiatry, 47*, 541–544.

Pohl, R., & Balon, R. (1992). Antidepressants, panic disorder, and PTSD (letter). *American Journal of Psychiatry, 149*, 1752–1753.

Quitkin, R. F., Rifkin, A., & Klein, D. F. (1979). Monoamine oxidase inhibitors: A review of antidepressant effectiveness. *Archives of General Psychiatry, 36*, 749–760.

Raskind, M. A., Dobie, D. J., Kanter, E. D., Petrie, E. C., Thompson, C. E., & Peskind, E. R. (2000).

The alpha1-adrenergic antagonist prazosin ameliorates combat trauma nightmares in veterans with posttraumatic stress disorder: A report of 4 cases. *Journal of Clinical Psychiatry, 61*(2), 129–133.

Ravaris, C. L., Friedman, M. J., Hauri, P. J., & McHugo, G. J. (1991). A controlled study of alprazolam and propranolol in panic-disordered and agoraphobic outpatients. *Journal of Clinical Psychopharmacology, 11,* 344–350.

Reist, C., Kauffman, C. D., Haier, R. J., Sangdahl, C., DeMet, E. M., Chicz-DeMet, A., & Nelson, J. N. (1989). A controlled trial of desipramine in 18 men with posttraumatic stress disorder. *American Journal of Psychiatry, 146,* 513–516.

Resick, P. A., & Schnicke, M. K. (1992). Cognitive processing therapy for sexual assault victims. *Journal of Consulting and Clinical Psychology, 60,* 748–756.

Resnick, H. S., Kilpatrick, D. G., Best, C. L., & Kramer, T. L. (1992). Vulnerability-stress factors in development of posttraumatic stress disorder. *Journal of Nervous and Mental Disease, 180,* 424–430.

Risse, S. C., Whitters, A., Burke, J., Chen, S., Scurfield, R. M., & Raskind, M. A. (1990). Severe withdrawal symptoms after discontinuation of alprazolam in eight patients with combat-induced posttraumatic stress disorder. *Journal of Clinical Psychiatry, 51,* 206–209.

Robert, R., Blakeney, P. E., Villarreal, C., Rosenberg, L., & Meyer, W. J. (1999). Imipramine treatment in pediatric burn patients with symptoms of acute stress disorder: A pilot study. *Journal of the American Academy of Child and Adolescent Psychiatry, 38*(7), 873–882.

Rothbaum, B. O., Ninan, P. T., & Thomas, L. (1996). Sertraline in the treatment of rape victims with posttraumatic stress disorder. *Journal of Traumatic Stress,* 9(4), 865–871.

Sajatovic, M., DiGiovanni, S., Fuller, M., Belton, J., DeVega, E., Marqua, S., & Liebling, D. (1999). Nefazodone therapy in patients with treatment-resistant or treatment-intolerant depression and high psychiatric comorbidity. *Clinical Therapeutics, 21*(4), 733–740.

Schnurr, P. P., Friedman, M. J., & Rosenberg, S. D. (1993). Premilitary MMPI scores as predictors of combat-related PTSD symptoms. *American Journal of Psychiatry, 150,* 479–483.

Schwartz, L. S. (1990). A biopsychosocial treatment approach to post-traumatic stress disorder. *Journal of Traumatic Stress, 3,* 221–238.

Shalev, A. Y., Freedman, S., Peri, T., Brandes, D., Sahar, T., Orr, S. P., & Pitman, R. K. (1998). Prospective study of PTSD and depression following trauma. *American Journal of Psychiatry, 155,* 630–637.

Shalev, A. Y., & Rogel-Fuchs, Y. (1992). Auditory startle reflex in post-traumatic stress disorder patients treated with clonazepam. *Israel Journal of Psychiatry Related Sciences, 29,* 1–6.

Shay, J. (1992). Fluoxetine reduces explosiveness and elevates mood of Vietnam combat vets with PTSD. *Journal of Traumatic Stress, 5,* 97–101.

Shen, W. W., & Park, S. (1983). The use of monoamine oxidase inhibitors in the treatment of trauamtic war neurosis: Case report. *Military Medicine, 148,* 430–431.

Shestatzky, M., Greenberg, D., & Lerer, B. (1988). A controlled trial of phenelzine in posttraumatic stress disorder. *Psychiatry Research, 24,* 149–155.

Shore, J. H., Tatum, E. L., & Vollmer, W. M. (1986). Psychiatric reactions to disaster: The Mount St. Helens experience. *American Journal of Psychiatry, 143,* 590–595.

Shore, J. H., Vollmer, W. M., & Tatum, E. L. (1989). Community patterns of post traumatic stress disorders. *Journal of Nervous and Mental Disease, 77,* 681–685.

Solomon, S., & Smith, E. (1994). Social support and perceived controls as moderators of responses to dioxin and flood exposure. In R. J. Ursano, B. G. McCaughey, & C. S. Fullerton (Eds.), *Individual and community responses to trauma and disaster: The structure of human chaos.* New York: Cambridge University Press.

Solomon, Z., & Preager, E. (1992). Elderly Israeli Holocaust survivors during the Persian Gulf War: A study of psychological distress. *American Journal of Psychiatry, 149,* 1707–1710.

Southwick, S. M., Bremner, J. D., Rasmusson, A., Morgan, C. A. 3rd, Arnsten, A., & Charney, D. S. (1999). Role of norepinephrine in the pathophysiology and treatment of posttraumatic stress disorder. *Biological Psychiatry, 46,* 1192–1204.

Southwick, S. M., Paige, S., Morgan, C. A. 3rd, Bremner, J. D., Krystal, J. D., & Charney, D. S. (1999). Neurotransmitter alterations in PTSD: Catechlomines and serotonin. *Seminars in Clinical Neuropsychiatry,* 4(4), 242–248.

Stein, M. B., Walker, J. R., Hazen, A. L., & Forde, D. R. (1997). Full and partial posttraumatic stress disorder: Findings from a community survey. *American Journal of Psychiatry, 154,* 1114–1119.

Tanna, V. T., Penningroth, R. P., & Woolson, R. F. (1977). Propranolol in the treatment of anxiety neurosis. *Comprehensive Psychiatry, 18,* 319–326.

Tohen, M., Castillo, J., Pope, H. G., & Herbstein, J. (1994). Concomitant use of valproate and carbamazepine in bipolar and schizoaffective disorders. *Journal of Clinical Pyschopharmacology, 14*(1), 67–70.

True, W. R., Rice, J., Eisen, S., Heath, A. C., Goldberg, J., Lyons, M., & Nowak, J. (1993). A twin study of genetic and environmental contributions to liaiblity for posttraumatic stress symptoms. *Archives of General Psychiatry, 50,* 257–264.

Tucker, P., Smith, K. L., Marx, B., Jones, D., Miranda, R., & Lensgraf, J. (2000). Fluvoxamine reduces physiologic reactivity to trauma scripts in posttraumatic stress disorder. *Journal of Clinical Psychopharmacology, 20,* 367–372.

Turchan, S. J., Holmes, V. F., & Wasserman, C. S. (1992). Do tricyclic antidepressants have a protective effect in post-traumatic stress disorder? *New York State Journal of Medicine,* 92, 400–402.

van der Kolk, B. A. (1983). Psychopharmacological issues in posttraumatic stress disorder. *Hospital and Community Psychiatry, 34,* 683–691.

van der Kolk, B. A. (1987). The drug treatment of posttraumatic stress disorder. *Journal of Affective Disorders, 13,* 203–213.

van der Kolk, B. A., Dreyfuss, D., Michaels, M., Shera, D., Berkowitz, R., Fisler, R., & Saxe, G. (1994). Fluoxetine in posttraumatic stress disorder. *Journal of Clinical Psychiatry, 55,* 517–522.

Weiss, D. S., Marmar, C. R., Schlenger, W. E., Fairbank, J. A., Jordan, B. K., Hough, R. L., & Kulka, R. A. (1992). The prevalence of lifetime and partial post-traumatic stress disorder in Vietnam theater veterans. *Journal of Traumatic Stress,* 365–376.

Wells, G. B., Chu, C., Johnson, R., Nasdahl, C., Ayubi, M. A., Sewell, E., & Statham, P. (1991). Buspirone in the treatment of post-traumatic stress disorder and dream anxiety disorder. *Military Medicine, 11,* 340–343.

Wolf, M. E., Alavi, A., & Mosnaim, A. D. (1988). Posttraumatic stress disorder in Vietnam veterans clinical and EEG findings: Possible therapeutic effects of carbamazepine. *Biological Psychiatry, 23,* 642–644.

Yehuda, R., Kahana, B., Schmeidler, J., Southwick, S. M., Wilson, S., & Giller, E. L. (1995). Impact of cumulative lifetime trauma and recent stress on current posttraumatic stress disorder symptoms in Holocaust survivors. *American Journal of Psychiatry, 152,* 1815–1818.

Yehuda, R., Shalev, A.,Y., & McFarlane, A. C. (1998). Predicting the development of posttraumatic stress disorder from the acute response to a traumatic event. *Biological Psychiatry, 44,* 1305–1313.

Yehuda, R., Southwick, S. M., & Giller, E. L. (1992a). Exposure to atrocities and severity of chronic posttraumatic stress disorder in Vietnam combat veterans. *American Journal of Psychiatry, 149,* 333–336.

Yehuda, R., Southwick, S., Giller, E. L., Ma, X., & Mason, J. W. (1992b). Urinary catecholamine excretion and severity of PTSD symptoms in Vietnam combat veterans. *Journal of Nervous and Mental Disease, 180,* 321–325.

Zaidi, L. Y., & Foy, D. W. (1994). Childhood abuse and combat-related PTSD. *Journal of Traumatic Stress, 7,* 33–42.

Zisook, S., Chentsova-Dutton, Y. E., Smith-Vaniz, A., Kline, N. A., Ellenor, G. L., Kodsi, A. B., & Gillin, J. C. (2000). Nefazodone in patients with treatment-refactory posttraumatic stress disorder. *Journal of Clinical Psychiatry, 61*(3), 203–208.

18

Management of Somatoform and Factitious Disorders

Gregory E. Simon

Somatoform and factitious disorders are characterized by somatic symptoms or disease fears that are out of proportion to any identifiable somatic cause and that include heightened sensitivity to noxious physical stimuli, exaggerated or irrational disease fears, and adoption of a patient role. Effective management of these conditions requires special attention to establishing and maintaining a working treatment alliance as well as to the following: (a) attending to the circumstances of referral; (b) identifying the patient's primary concerns; (c) establishing the position that all symptoms are "real"; (d) negotiating a mutually agreeable treatment goal; (e) focusing on symptom management, not diagnosis and cure; and (f) coordinating care with medical and surgical providers. Treatments for these conditions that have proven effective, in a large number of Type 1 and Type 2 studies, are remarkably similar to those commonly used in the management of anxiety and mood disorders, in part because anxiety and depression are frequent accompaniments of somatoform and factitious disorders.

GENERAL PRINCIPLES OF TREATMENT

Treatment of patients with somatoform disorders involves challenges distinct from those encountered in the management of other psychiatric disorders. While some clinical interventions (e.g., cognitive behavioral psychotherapy, antidepressant medication) are widely used, establishment of a cooperative therapeutic relationship often requires special attention. During the initial phase of treatment, providers should consider each of the issues listed below.

Attending to the Circumstances of Referral

While some patients suffering from unexplained somatic symptoms or hypochondriacal worries may directly seek mental health care, referral by a medical provider is the most common entry into treatment. Some patients may respond to such a referral with relief, but many will be skeptical or reluctant. Referral to a mental health provider may be misinterpreted as rejection or dismissal (e.g., "The doctor must think it's all in my head").

Identifying the Patient's Primary Concerns

While the presenting symptom may be straightforward, its meaning or importance should always be explored. For example, different patients presenting with medically unexplained chest pain may have quite different concerns. One may seek only pain relief and have no worries about the cause of the pain. Another may be preoccupied with fear of an impending heart attack. A third may recognize the pain as tension-related and focus primarily on workplace stresses. Effectively addressing these different concerns will require quite different therapeutic approaches.

Clearly Establishing the Position That All Symptoms Are "Real"

Patients (and many physicians) may falsely dichotomize somatic distress into the "real" symptoms and the "psychological" ones. Not only is such a dichotomy inconsistent with scientific knowledge but it also creates major barriers to effective treatment. Accepting this dichotomous view means that any symptom amenable to psychiatric or psychological intervention was not "real" to start with. One could hardly imagine a scenario less conducive to effective symptom relief and rehabilitation.

Negotiating a Mutually Agreeable Treatment Goal

Because many patients with somatoform disorders enter treatment at the urging of physicians, employers, or disability insurers, clear establishment of a collaborative relationship is essential. Treatment will certainly fail if the patient perceives the mental health provider as a judge or adversary. If the therapist has clear obligations to some other party (employer, disability agency) she or he should clearly disclose them. Negotiating a treatment goal should begin with a list of the patient's requests. Forming a working treatment alliance may require modifying unrealistic goals (e.g., complete freedom from pain, absolute certainty about medical diagnoses) into realistic ones (e.g., improved functioning and well-being despite some pain, tolerance of reasonable uncertainty about health).

Focusing on Symptom Management, Not Diagnosis and Cure

Patients with somatoform disorders often focus on a biomedical approach to somatic symptoms. Such an approach is based on a number of underlying assumptions about bodily distress (e.g., pain or discomfort signals the presence of a diagnosable disease; health is the absence of discomfort; medicine is an exact science; persistence of symptoms should prompt more vigorous diagnostic efforts). Effective treatment must shift the agenda from diagnosis and cure to symptom management and rehabilitation. Rehabilitative management is based on a very different set of assumptions about the meaning of somatic symptoms (e.g., physical symptoms are common and often have no specific medical cause; health is the ability to function and enjoy life despite bodily discomfort; persistence of symptoms is annoying and unfortunate but doesn't imply an incorrect diagnosis). The rehabilitative approach takes a long-term view of treatment and recovery.

Coordinating Care with Medical and Surgical Providers

In the management of somatoform disorders, the therapeutic relationship is rarely a dyadic one. At least one medical provider (and often several) will play as important a role in ongoing treatment as the mental health provider. For patients with more severe somatoform disorders, mental health treatment is episodic, while medical treatment is lifelong. While the mental health provider may sometimes assume a primary treatment role, she or he is more often a consultant to the patient and his or her medical physician.

TREATMENT OF COMORBID DEPRESSIVE AND ANXIETY DISORDERS

Evaluation and management of somatoform disorders should focus first on the identification and treatment of comorbid anxiety and depressive disorders. Epidemiological research in community samples (Simon & Von Korff, 1991) and primary-care samples (Kroenke et al., 1994) has demonstrated that many (if not most) somatoform disorders occur in the setting of anxiety or depressive disorders. Somatic symptoms and excessive worry about physical health appear to be core components of depression (Katon & Russo, 1989; Silver, 1987) and panic disorder (Fava et al., 1992; Sheehan et al., 1980). Effective treatment of depression (Smith, 1992) and anxiety disorders (Noyes et al., 1986; Sheehan et al., 1980) reduces somatic distress and disease fears. As reviewed below, many of the interventions found effective in the management of somatoform disorders are widely used in the management of anxiety and depressive conditions.

SOMATIZATION DISORDER

Clinical Features

Somatization disorder is a lifelong condition characterized by multiple somatic symptoms without medical explanation. *DSM-IV* diagnostic criteria require the presence of four pain symptoms, two gastrointestinal symptoms, one sexual symptom, and one pseudoneurological symptom for a formal diagnosis. Typical symptoms may vary considerably across cultures. Somatization disorder begins early in adolescence or early adulthood and is usually chronic. Specific somatic symptoms may vary over time, but affected individuals are rarely without some unexplained somatic symptoms. Community surveys have found prevalence rates of less than 0.5%, while medical clinic studies often find much higher rates. These differences may reflect differences in diagnostic methods (structured interview vs. review of medical records).

Historical Perspective

Briquet's clinical description of somatization disorder (Briquet, 1859) predates even the early psychoanalytic descriptions of hysteria (Breuer & Freud, 1957). Work by Guze and colleagues (Guze, 1967) established Briquet's syndrome as a stable and well-defined diagnostic category. More recent descriptions (Katon et al., 1991; Kroenke et al., 1994; Simon & Von Korff, 1991) have viewed somatization disorder as the most extreme manifestation of somatization, a process characterized by heightened sensitivity to somatic distress and help-seeking behavior.

Treatment Alternatives

Expert recommendations on the management of somatization disorder have typically encouraged a conservative approach (Monson & Smith, 1983; Murphy, 1982; Quill, 1985). This approach emphasizes regular contact with a caring physician, acceptance of patients' somatic symptoms as valid, avoidance of unnecessary diagnostic testing, minimal use of new medications or therapies, and a stable level of contact regardless of symptomatic exacerbations.

Smith and colleagues have evaluated one version of this approach in two randomized trials (Rost et al., 1994; Smith et al., 1986). Both studies compared usual care to an educational intervention for treating physicians (a consultation report describing somatization disorder and recommending the management plan described above). Intervention patients showed significant decreases in health care utilization and either no change or modest improvement in measures of mental and physical health status.

Two studies (Kashner et al., 1995; Lidbeck, 1997) evaluated structured group psychotherapy for somatization disorder. Group sessions included education regarding benign nature of somatic symptoms, behavioral activation, and stress management techniques. Both programs resulted in improved health outcomes compared to usual-treatment comparison groups.

Future Prospects

Recommendations regarding psychotherapeutic management of somatization disorder have changed little since the mid-1980s. Recent treatment research (reviewed below) has focused more on specific treatments for less severe somatization syndromes. Future research may examine the effect of these specific treatments (cognitive behavioral therapy and antidepressant pharmacotherapy) on classically defined somatization disorder.

UNDIFFERENTIATED SOMATOFORM DISORDER

Clinical Features

Undifferentiated somatoform disorder is characterized by one or more physical complaints that cannot be fully explained by a known medical condition. This group of disorders is much more frequent than somatization disorder (Escobar et al., 1987; Gureje et al., 1997) and accounts for the majority of somatoform disorders seen in medical practice. In any individual, the pattern of symptoms may be stable or changing over time. This category includes a wide range of somatization syndromes, including unexplained dizziness (Kroenke et al., 1993), palpitations (Barsky et al., 1994), chronic fatigue (Kroenke et al., 1988), multiple chemical sensitivity (Simon et al., 1993), fibromyalgia (Goldenberg, 1987), non-cardiac chest pain (Cormier et al., 1988), and unexplained pelvic pain (Walker et al., 1988). Wessely et al.

(1999) pointed out the significant overlap among these syndromes and questioned the validity of distinct diagnoses within this category. The boundary between these syndromes and those included in the somatoform pain category (discussed below) is also not clearly established or empirically based. Rates of comorbidity with anxiety and depressive disorders are often greater than 50% (Kroenke et al., 1994; Simon et al., 1999). While the precise etiology for many of these syndromes remains controversial, most probably involve a combination of psychophysiological hyperreactivity, exaggerated sensitivity to somatic sensation, exaggerated illness fears, and mood disturbance (White & Moorey, 1997).

Historical Perspective

Traditional views of somatization (strongly influenced by psychoanalysis) emphasized its defensive function (Adler, 1981). Somatic symptoms were viewed as masked expressions of psychological conflict or distress. Recent research supports a broader biopsychosocial model (Kirmayer & Robbins, 1991). Perception and reporting of somatic distress are determined by biological vulnerability, psychological characteristics, and social influence (i.e., relative reinforcement of somatic or emotional symptoms).

Treatment Alternatives

Over 30 randomized trials have evaluated antidepressant pharmacotherapy for various somatization syndromes, including functional gastrointestinal disorders, unexplained chest pain, chronic fatigue, and fibromyalgia. As recently reviewed by O'Malley et al. (1999), this literature strongly supports the effectiveness of antidepressants across a wide range of somatization syndromes. Probability of significant improvement is typically 50 to 75% among treated patients, approximately 30% greater than among patients treated with placebo. Benefits of antidepressant treatment are not confined to patients with co-occurring depressive disorders. Most studies evaluated tricyclic antidepressants, and a few studies have found no significant benefit from serotonin reuptake inhibitors among patients with fibromyalgia (Norregaard et al., 1995; Wolfe et al., 1994) or chronic fatigue syndrome (Vercoulen et al., 1996; Wearden et al., 1998).

Over 20 controlled trials have evaluated cognitive behavioral psychotherapy for various somatization syndromes, including functional gastrointestinal disorders, unexplained chest pain, fibromyalgia, chronic fatigue, and electric sensitivity. As recently reviewed by Kroenke and Swindle (2000), these studies strongly support the effectiveness of structured psychotherapies focused on symptom management, behavioral activation, and modifying dysfunctional illness beliefs. Probability of significant improvement is 50 to 80% for both group and individual treatments. Two studies found structured cognitive behavioral programs superior to less specific support (Payne & Blanchard, 1995) or relaxation programs (Deale et al., 1997).

Fewer systematic data are available regarding dynamic psychotherapy. In one randomized trial among patients with irritable bowel syndrome (Guthrie et al., 1993), brief dynamic psychotherapy with relaxation was found superior to an attention control condition. A second case series (Nielsen et al., 1988) describes improvement in 7 of 10 patients with unexplained somatic symptoms.

Two controlled studies have evaluated educational interventions for primary-care physicians (Morriss et al., 1999; Smith et al., 1995). Both programs led to significant improvement in patient outcomes, and one (Smith et al., 1995) reported reductions in general medical utilization.

Lipowski (1988) described an intensive inpatient program for patients with more persistent or severe somatization syndromes. Components of the program include relaxation training, behavioral activation, and pharmacotherapy. In a case series of 92 patients (Shorter et al., 1992), approximately one third were much improved and another third somewhat improved.

Future Prospects

Data from epidemiological and treatment studies suggest significant overlap between common somatization syndromes and common anxiety and depressive disorders: high rates of co-occurrence and responsiveness to both cognitive-behavioral psychotherapy and antidepressant medications. Given this overlap, it is likely that treatment research in these two areas will converge around a common set of clinical questions: predictors of differential response to pharmacotherapy or psychotherapy, benefits of single versus combined treatment, and relative benefits of specific antidepressant drugs.

CONVERSION DISORDER

Clinical Features

Conversion symptoms are abnormalities or deficits in motor or sensory function that suggest a medical or neurological illness. A diagnosis of conversion disorder should be made only after appropriate assessment has excluded a medical or neurological cause. The presence of significant medical or neurological illness does not exclude a diagnosis of conversion disorder if the conversion symptoms are not explained by medical illness. *DSM-IV* (APA, 1994) diagnostic criteria require that the onset or exacerbation of symptoms be preceded by identifiable psychological conflicts or stressors. Symptoms may be presented in dramatic or histrionic fashion or with a remarkable lack of concern ("la belle indifférence"). Conversion symptoms are reported more commonly among women, among those from lower socioeconomic classes, and among those from non-Western or less urbanized areas. Conversion disorder may be an isolated condition or part of a more generalized somatization syndrome (e.g., somatization disorder).

Historical Perspective

Descriptions of hysterical conversion syndromes predate even the Hippocratic era (Ford & Folks, 1985). Theories of etiology have progressed from ancient Egyptian beliefs about the wandering uterus through early psychoanalytic descriptions of forbidden impulses to modern concepts of dissociation.

Treatment Alternatives

The literature on management of conversion symptoms includes only case reports and case series; no data from controlled studies are available. Clinical descriptions reflect a broad range of illness duration and psychiatric comorbidity. In general, patients with longer duration of symptoms and greater psychiatric comorbidity (anxiety, depressive, and somatoform disorders) require more intensive treatment and experience poorer outcomes (Couprie et al., 1995; Crimlisk et al., 1998; Kent et al., 1995; Kotsopoulos & Snow, 1986; Turgay, 1990).

Acute and uncomplicated conversion reactions appear to respond favorably to supportive outpatient management. In a series of 100 consecutive Libyan patients with acute conversion reactions (Pu et al., 1986), approximately half recovered rapidly with support, education, and suggestion, and most of the remainder improved after brief treatment with anxiolytic or antidepressant medication. Other case reports and small case series describe good response to a single sodium amytal interview (Steibel & Kirby, 1994), lorazepam combined with hypnosis (Stevens, 1990), or suggestion and supportive management (Brooksbank, 1984; Lazarus, 1990). While these reports vary in recommendations regarding somatic treatments (amytal, anxiolytics, physical therapy, etc.), they all describe a similar psychotherapeutic approach: emotional support regarding precipitating stresses, explanation that not all physical symptoms have a definite physical cause, expectation that symptoms will resolve rapidly, and reinforcement of any improvement. All sources also agree that convincing patients of links between physical symptoms and emotional stresses or conflicts is unnecessary and may be counterproductive.

Chronic or complicated conversion reactions (e.g., those occurring in the setting of somatization disorder) appear to require more intensive behavioral treatment. Several case series (Klonoff & Moore, 1986; Speed, 1996; Sullivan & Buchanan, 1989; Watanabe et al., 1998) describe successful inpatient rehabilitation based on systematic reinforcement for symptom improvement. Rangaswami (1985) described positive results in most of 30 Indian patients treated with reinforcement and aversive stimuli.

Future Prospects

Recent reports do not suggest any significant changes in the management of conversion symptoms. It seems likely that the psychotherapeutic approaches described above will remain the recommended treatments for the foreseeable future. While some reports describe the use of anxiolytic or antidepressant medication, the literature does not suggest any specific pharmacological treatment. Controlled clinical trials in this area would be difficult to complete; acute conversion symptoms typically resolve rapidly, and persistent symptoms are relatively rare.

SOMATOFORM PAIN DISORDER

Clinical Features

Somatoform pain disorders are characterized by persistent pain that is distressing and/or disabling. *DSM-IV* (APA, 1994) criteria for diagnosis require that psychological factors have an important role in the onset, severity, exacerbation, or maintenance of the pain. Pain symptoms such as headache, back pain, and abdominal pain are common causes of suffering, lost productivity, and health care utilization. As discussed above, this category overlaps somewhat with undifferentiated somatoform disorder. Intentionally produced or feigned pain symptoms are specifically excluded from this category.

Historical Perspective

Traditional thinking has viewed pain symptoms as either "physical" (clearly attributable to a known biomedical process) or "psychogenic." *DSM-IV* criteria reflect this dualistic view. More recent writing, however, suggests that all pain complaints are both "physical" and "psychogenic" (Coderre et al., 1993). All pain symptoms are influenced by psychological factors, and even the most "psychogenic" chronic pain syndromes are probably associated with detectable pathological changes in the central nervous system.

Treatment Alternatives

This review does not consider the wide range of somatic treatments used in the management of chronic pain (e.g., analgesics, nerve blocks). Nor does it specifically discuss the management of specific pain complaints (e.g., headache, orofacial pain, back pain). Instead, this summary reviews the general management of pain conditions, with emphasis on interventions familiar to mental health providers: psychotherapy and antidepressant medications.

A 1996 Technology Assessment Panel of the U.S. National Institutes of Health found "moderate" evidence supporting the effectiveness of cognitive behavioral techniques for chronic pain. Two more recent reviews (Kroenke & Swindle, 2000; Morley et al., 1999) describe approximately 25 randomized trials supporting the efficacy of cognitive and behavioral psychotherapy for various pain syndromes in adults and children. Across various pain syndromes and treatment programs, the proportion of patients reporting significant decreases in pain-related distress and disability ranges from 30 to 60%. Both group and individual treatment have been proven effective, though more patients may prefer individual treatment (Spence, 1989). Descriptions of these proven treatment programs typically include support and validation of pain as "real," relaxation training, activity scheduling, reinforcement of non-pain behaviors, and cognitive restructuring. Most reports describe more robust effects on distress and disability than on actual pain intensity.

As summarized in several recent reviews (Ansari, 2000; Fishbain et al., 1998; Philipp & Fickinger, 1993; McQuay et al., 1996; Sindrup & Jensen, 1999), over 75 placebo-controlled trials have examined the efficacy of antidepressant drugs in the management of various pain syndromes, and most have found pharmacotherapy superior to placebo. These studies have generally found that antidepressants do reduce pain intensity, that analgesic effect is delayed, and that pain relief is not necessarily dependent on improvement in mood. Across various pain syndromes, the proportion of patients reporting significant improvement in pain and pain-related distress ranged from 35% to 60%. For tricyclic antidepressants, analgesic effects were often noted at doses lower than those typically recommended for treatment of depression (e.g., 50 to 75 mg per day of amitriptyline). Randomized trials consistently support the analgesic effects of tricyclic antidepressants across a wide range of pain syndromes, including those with a well-defined pathological source and those considered exclusively "psychogenic." Findings regarding serotonin reuptake inhibitor antidepressants have been mixed (Jung et al., 1997), especially for treatment of headache (Langemark & Olesen, 1994; Saper et al., 1994) and neuropathic pain (Max et al., 1992; Sindrup et al., 1990). A few recent case reports support the use of venlafaxine in management of neuropathic pain (Kiayias et al., 2000; Pernia et al., 2000).

Two randomized trials have examined the combined effects of antidepressants and cognitive behavioral psychotherapy. In a four-group factorial design,

Pilowsky and colleagues (Pilowsky & Graham, 1990) found that amitriptyline increased activity level and reduced pain intensity, while psychotherapy increased perceived pain but improved productivity. In a second study (Pilowsky et al., 1995), addition of cognitive behavioral therapy to amitriptyline treatment yielded only slight benefits.

Future Prospects

Strong evidence supports the effectiveness of both cognitive behavioral psychotherapies and tricyclic antidepressant pharmacotherapy across a range of pain syndromes. Future research will probably focus on specificity of action. Proven cognitive behavioral treatments include a variety of components (relaxation training, behavioral activation, cognitive restructuring), and future research may identify the specific effects of these various components. Future research on the analgesic effects of antidepressants should help to clarify the effectiveness of specific drug classes (tricyclic antidepressants, serotonin reuptake inhibitors, etc) in specific pain syndromes.

HYPOCHONDRIASIS

Clinical Features

The central feature of hypochondriasis is fear of or preoccupation with a medical illness. This fear often arises from misinterpretation of or exaggerated emphasis of a minor physical symptom or abnormality. Hypochondriacal patients are not reassured despite appropriate (and sometimes excessive) medical evaluation and reassurance. Disease worries may sometimes appear bizarre, but clearly delusional beliefs call for a separate diagnosis of paranoid disorder or other psychotic disorder. The presence of a diagnosed medical condition does not preclude a diagnosis of hypochondriasis if essential diagnostic features are present. Anxiety and depressive disorders are common comorbid conditions. Hypochondriacal patients vary in level of insight; some may recognize that medical worries are somewhat exaggerated, while others remain completely certain that their fears are well founded. Depending on the measures used, the reported prevalence of hypochondriasis among general medical outpatients ranges from 4% to 9%. Onset is typically in early adulthood, and course is often chronic or recurrent.

Historical Perspective

While the term *hypochondriasis* dates from early Greek medicine, its current usage (morbid preoccupation with health) dates from the nineteenth century (Kenyon, 1976). Early-twentieth-century writings viewed hypochondriacal fears as defenses against awareness of unwanted affect, while more recent descriptions view hypochondriasis as a cognitive process characterized by morbid disease fear and exaggerated attention to bodily sensations (Barsky & Wyshak, 1989; Kellner, 1992).

Treatment Alternatives

Kellner (1982) and Barsky et al. (1988) have described common elements of a cognitive behavioral approach to hypochondriasis: reducing attention to distressing bodily sensations, correcting misinformation and exaggerated beliefs, and addressing the cognitive processes (selective perception, misattribution, etc.) that maintain disease fears. Several controlled trials (Avia et al., 1996; Bouman & Visser, 1998; Clark et al., 1998; Fava et al., 2000; Papageorgiou & Wells, 1998; Warwick et al., 1996) have demonstrated that such an approach is clearly superior to no treatment and marginally superior to non-specific treatments (e.g., relaxation training). Fewer data are available regarding the effectiveness of other psychotherapeutic approaches. Diamond (1987) described the use of a self-psychology approach, but no systematic information on patient outcomes is available.

The literature on psychotherapy for hypochondriasis includes conflicting advice regarding the offer of reassurance. Starcevi'c (1991) discusses the therapeutic benefit of repeated and consistent reassurance in the framework of psychodynamic psychotherapy. In contrast, Salkovskis and Warwick (1986) viewed reassurance seeking as an avoidance ritual that perpetuates disease fears. They described two single-case experiments demonstrating the therapeutic benefits of a behavioral approach that restricts reassurance as a specific technique for extinguishing hypochondriacal anxiety. Kathol (1997) argued for the benefits of reassurance when accompanied by encouragement and advice to return to usual activities.

As reviewed by Fallon et al. (1996), a number of case series and uncontrolled studies support the effectiveness of antidepressants, including clomipramine (Stone, 1993), fluoxetine (Fallon et al., 1991,

1993), and imipramine (Wesner & Noyes, 1991). Reported response rates were typically 60 to 80%. A few case reports also describe the use of serotonin reuptake inhibitor antidepressants (Perkins, 1999; Wada et al., 1999) or risperidone (Cetin et al., 1999) for hypochondriacal delusions.

Future Prospects

Moderately strong evidence suggests that symptoms of hypochondriasis respond to psychotherapeutic and pharmacological treatments proven effective against phobic and obsessive compulsive disorders (cognitive behavioral psychotherapy and serotonergic antidepressants). It seems likely that these suggestive findings will be confirmed by more rigorous clinical trials. Developments in the management of hypochondriasis are likely to parallel those in the treatment of anxiety disorders. Clinicians treating hypochondriacal patients, however, must be mindful of specific issues raised by disease fears. Unlike many of the "irrational" anxieties seen in phobias or obsessive compulsive disorder, illness fears can never be dismissed with complete certainty. In addition, the behavioral patterns of hypochondriasis usually involve medical professionals and/or family members. Including these other participants in the design and practice of a behavioral treatment program is often necessary.

BODY DYSMORPHIC DISORDER

Clinical Features

Body dysmorphic disorder (BDD; previously known as *dysmorphophobia*) is defined by distressing preoccupation with an imagined defect in physical appearance or by an exaggerated or excessive concern with some physical feature. Complaints most often focus on the head or face (e.g., a "deformed" nose) but may involve any body part (e.g., asymmetry in breast size). Accurate estimates of community prevalence are not available. Bodily preoccupations typically begin in adolescence and are often chronic. Concern about physical defects sometimes reaches delusional levels; available evidence does not clearly indicate whether delusional preoccupations represent a severe form of BDD or a distinct delusional disorder. These concerns are often presented to cosmetic surgeons or dermatologists (where prevalence may be as high as 10%). Medical or surgical treatment is invariably dissatisfying and may intensify symptoms. Common associated psychiatric disorders include social phobia, obsessive compulsive disorder, depression, delusional disorder, and eating disorder.

Historical Perspective

BDD (under the name dysmorphophobia) has been described in the European psychiatric literature since the early 1900s. Early psychoanalytic descriptions (such as Freud's Wolf-Man) emphasized the unconscious meaning of bodily preoccupations. Later descriptions viewed dysmorphophobia as a variant of hypochondriasis or obsessive compulsive disorder. BDD was not included in the American psychiatric nomenclature until the publication of *DSM-III-R*.

Treatment Alternatives

Moderately strong evidence suggests that a focused form of cognitive behavioral therapy is an effective treatment for BDD. Several case series (McKay, 1999; Newell & Shrubb, 1994; Neziroglu & Yaryura, 1993; Schmidt & Harrington, 1995; Wilhelm et al., 1999) describe positive effects of either group or individual psychotherapy programs. Two small randomized trials report superior outcomes for group (Rosen et al., 1995) or individual (Veale et al., 1996) cognitive behavioral therapy when compared to a no-treatment control group. Reported response rates are typically 50 to 75%. Common elements of these psychotherapeutic treatments include identifying and challenging distorted body perceptions, interrupting of self-critical thoughts, planned exposure to anxiety-provoking situations (e.g., wearing clothing that accentuates the perceived bodily defect), and response prevention (e.g., refraining from self-inspection). One report describes the effectiveness of psychodynamic psychotherapy (Bloch & Glue, 1988), but no systematic data on the efficacy of psychodynamic or other psychotherapeutic treatments are available.

Moderately strong evidence also supports the efficacy of serotonin reuptake inhibitor (SRI) antidepressants in the treatment of BDD and related conditions. Case series and case reports describe sustained therapeutic responses to clomipramine (Fernando, 1988; Hollander et al., 1989; Sondheimer, 1988), fluoxetine (Hollander et al., 1989), and fluvoxamine

(Hollander et al., 1994; Perugi et al., 1996; Phillips et al., 1998). Approximately two thirds of patients treated with SRI antidepressants experienced moderate or marked improvement. Several reports describe failure to respond to antidepressants without potent serotonin reuptake inhibition. One randomized comparison found clomipramine superior to desipramine (Hollander et al., 1999). SRI drugs were typically prescribed at doses recommended for management of obsessive compulsive disorder (e.g., 40 to 60 mg per day of fluoxetine).

Future Prospects

The evidence summarized above suggests that BDD responds to treatments (cognitive behavioral psychotherapy and serotonin reuptake inhibitor antidepressants) that act on obsessional thinking, phobic anxiety, and phobic avoidance. It seems likely that larger randomized trials will confirm the efficacy of both pharmacotherapy and specific psychotherapies. The relative efficacy of group or individual psychotherapeutic treatments also deserves attention. Group treatments may be especially helpful, since realistic feedback about one's appearance from peers may be more powerful than feedback from a psychotherapist.

FACTITIOUS DISORDERS

Clinical Features

Factitious disorders are defined by the intentional production of signs or symptoms of disease. Symptoms may be either physical (abdominal pain, hematuria) or psychological (hallucinations, memory loss). The primary motivation for production of symptoms is a desire to assume the sick role. Because presenting symptoms represent patient's beliefs about expected symptoms, presentations range from those clearly inconsistent with any known disease to sophisticated mimics of medical or psychiatric conditions. In factitious disorder by proxy, a caregiver intentionally produces symptoms or signs of illness in a child or dependent adult. Factitious disorder is distinct from malingering, in which the primary motivation is obtaining some concrete benefit (e.g., liability award, disability pension). Conversion disorder differs from factitious disorder in that conversion symptoms are neither intentionally nor consciously produced. No reliable data are available on the prevalence or demographic pattern of factitious disorders.

Historical Perspective

The prototypical factitious disorder, Munchausen's syndrome, was first described in 1951 (Asher, 1951). Subsequent work has broadened this category and clarified the place of factitious disorders among somatoform and dissociative disorders (Taylor & Hyler, 1993).

While the *DSM-IV* (APA, 1994) clearly provides for the diagnosis of factitious disorder with psychological symptoms, this category remains ill defined. As discussed by Rogers et al. (1990), the core elements of factitious disorder are more difficult to establish in the domain of psychological symptoms. While the conscious production of somatic symptoms can sometimes be objectively demonstrated (e.g., detection of exogenous insulin in blood samples), production of psychological symptoms is much more complex. Motivations are typically complex, and it is difficult to determine whether the motivation for the behavior is to assume the sick role.

Treatment Alternatives

Most of the literature on factitious disorder discusses recognition and diagnosis. These case reports and case series describe the clinical presentation of factitious illness in specific medical areas (Folks, 1995; Schmaling et al., 1991; Sno et al., 1991; Wallach, 1994). Clinical descriptions often mention associated affective, substance use, or personality disorders (Sutherland & Rodin, 1990). Diagnosis of factitious disorder necessarily distorts the traditional doctor-patient relationship. Uncovering patient's deceptions often requires that treating physicians employ deception themselves. One example of this ethical dilemma is the use of covert videotaping in the detection of Munchausen's syndrome by proxy (Foreman & Farsides, 1993).

Systematic data on the treatment of factitious disorders are not available. The treatment literature consists entirely of case reports and small case series. These reports typically emphasize the difficulty of engaging patients with factitious disorders in any treatment plan; most abruptly discontinue treatment when discovered or confronted. While many case descriptions end with the patient's discharge against medical advice, several have described modest success (Earle & Folks, 1986; Guziec et al., 1994; Plassman, 1994; Schwarz, Harding, & Harrington, 1993; Solyom & Solyom, 1990) following long-term psychotherapeutic treatment in which focus shifted from factitious somatic symptoms to associated personality disorder. One case report (Earle & Folks, 1986) describes a positive response to antidepressant pharmacotherapy coupled with long-term psychotherapeutic treatment. Another (Prior, 1997) report describes beneficial effects of pimozide.

No clear guidance is available regarding the treatment of factitious disorder by proxy. Published reports emphasize that caregivers typically deny any responsibility for producing symptoms (Feldman, 1994) and that further fabrications of illness may persist for years (Bools et al., 1993). One case series describes successful outcome (family reunification without further induced illness) in approximately half of cases (Berg & Jones, 1999).

Future Prospects

It seems unlikely that systematic studies of the management of factitious disorders will ever be conducted. Both the relative rarity of the condition (or rarity of its recognition) and patients' resistance to treatment will preclude formal treatment trials. For the foreseeable future, treatment of patients with factitious disorders must rely on recommendations from earlier case reports filtered by clinical judgment. Future reports may help to guide treatment by clarifying the nature of associated or underlying psychiatric disorders.

SUMMARY

The evidence reviewed above suggests that distressing somatic symptoms often respond to appropriate clinical management. Treatments proven effective in the management of somatoform disorders are remarkably similar to those commonly used in the management of anxiety and affective disorders. As discussed earlier, however, establishing a working treatment alliance and maintaining treatment adherence does involve issues unique to this group of conditions.

While the discussion above is organized according to formal diagnostic categories, the evidence reviewed suggests an alternative organization according to specific target symptoms. Major symptoms common to several of the somatoform disorders include heightened sensitivity to somatic distress, exaggerated fear of disease, and adoption of a withdrawn or disabled role.

Heightened sensitivity to noxious sensations may manifest as pain complaints or as increased sensitivity to specific kinds of somatic distress (e.g., irritable bowel syndrome, fibromyalgia). The available evidence supports the effectiveness of both pharmacotherapy and appropriate psychotherapy. Strong evidence supports the effectiveness of antidepressant medications across a wide range of somatization syndromes and pain syndromes. Most data supporting the efficacy of antidepressants concerns older tricyclic drugs. Several reports describe therapeutic effects at doses one third to one half those recommended for treatment of depression. Improvement in pain or other somatic symptoms is not necessarily dependent on antidepressant effects, and some evidence suggests that tricyclic drugs may have a direct visceral analgesic effect (Cannon et al., 1994; Mertz et al., 1998). Moderately strong evidence supports the effectiveness of cognitive and behavioral psychotherapies in reducing symptom sensitivity and functional impairment. Psychotherapeutic treatments may be more effective in reducing distress and disability than in directly affecting symptom intensity.

Disease fear and disease conviction are maladaptive cognitive processes amenable to both pharmacological and psychotherapeutic treatment. Studies of hypochondriasis and body dysmorphic disorder, the two conditions most characterized by exaggerated disease fear, provide moderately strong evidence for the effectiveness of cognitive behavioral psychotherapy and antidepressant pharmacotherapy. In contrast to data on pain and somatic symptom syndromes, studies of hypochondriacal syndromes (including body dysmorphic disorder) support the use of serotonin reuptake inhibitor antidepressants over tricyclic drugs. This evidence for selective response is not surprising given the similarity of hypochondriacal syndromes to obsessive compulsive disorder and similar anxiety disorders. Similarly, the cognitive and behavioral strategies found useful in the management of hypochondriacal syndromes closely resemble those proven useful in the management of anxiety disorders (e.g., exposure and response prevention). Case series and case reports describe antidepressant doses similar to those used in management of obsessive compulsive disorder.

The adverse behavioral consequences of somatoform disorders often call for a behavioral approach. Withdrawal from usual activities and adoption of the "sick role" may occur in several of the above-described disorders and are especially prominent in conversion disorders and factitious disorders. Moderate evidence supports the effectiveness of behavioral approaches in management of illness behaviors. Components of such an approach include reducing incentives for withdrawal, positively rewarding return to normal function, and developing specific plans for reactivation. More intractable illness behavior may require inpatient behavioral management.

Because patients typically present with a mixture of somatic, cognitive, and behavioral difficulties, effective treatment must integrate a variety of active ingredients. Treatment planning should identify the target symptoms (e.g., pain, disease fear, social isolation) that cause the most distress or interference with function. True collaboration in identifying treatment priorities is essential for therapeutic success.

References

Adler, G. (1981). The physician and the hypochondriacal patient. *New England Journal of Medicine, 304,* 1394–1396.

Ansari, A. (2000). The efficacy of newer antidepressants in the treatment of chronic pain: A review of current literature. *Harvard Review of Psychiatry, 7,* 257–277.

Asher, R. (1951). Munchausen's syndrome. *Lancet, 1,* 339–341.

Avia, M. D., Ruiz, M. A., & Olivares, M. E. (1996). The meaning of psychological symptoms: Effectiveness of a group intervention with hypochondriacal patients. *Behaviour Research and Therapy, 34,* 23–31.

Barsky, A. J., Cleary, P. D., & Coeytaux, R. R. (1994). Psychiatric disorders in medical outpatients complaining of palpitations. *Journal of General Internal Medicine, 9,* 306–313.

Barsky, A. J., Geringer, E., & Wool, C. A. (1988). A cognitive-educational treatment for hypochondriasis. *General Hospital Psychiatry, 10,* 322–327.

Barsky, A. J., & Wyshak, G. (1989). Hypochondriasis and related health attitudes. *Psychosomatics, 30,* 412–420.

Berg, B., & Jones, D. P. (1999). Outcome of psychiatric intervention in factitious illness by proxy (Munchausen's syndrome by proxy). *Archives of Diseases of Children, 81,* 465–472.

Bloch, S., & Glue, P. (1988). Psychotherapy and dysmorphophobia: A case report. *British Journal of Psychiatry, 152,* 271–274.

Bools, C. N., Beale, B. A., & Meadow, S. R. (1993). Follow-up of victims of fabricated illness (Munchausen syndrome by proxy). *Archives of Diseases of Children, 69,* 625–630.

Bouman, T. K., & Visser, S. (1998). Cognitive and behavioural treatment of hypochondriasis. *Psychotherapy and Psychosomatics, 67,* 214–221.

Breuer, J., & Freud, S. (1957). *Studies on hysteria.* New York: Basic Books.

Briquet, P. (1859). Traite clinique et therapeutique de l'hysterie. Paris: Bailliere et Fils.

Brooksbank, D. J. (1984). Management of conversion reaction in five adolescent girls. *Journal of Adolescence, 7,* 359–376.

Cannon, R. O. 3rd, Quyyami, A. A., Mincemoyer, R., Stine, A. M., et al. (1994). Imipramine in patients with chest pain despite normal coronary angiograms. *New England Journal of Medicine, 19,* 1411–1417.

Cetin, M., Ebrinc, S., Agargun, M. Y., et al. (1999). Risperidone for the treatment of monosymptomatic hypochondriacal psychosis. *Journal of Clinical Psychiatry, 60.*

Clark, D. M., Saldovskis, P. M., Hackmann, A., et al. (1998). Two psychological treatments for hypochondriasis. A randomised controlled trial. *British Journal of Psychiatry, 173,* 218–215.

Coderre, T. J., Katz, J., Vaccarine, A. L., et al. (1993). Contribution of central neuroplasticity to pathological pain: Review of clinical and experimental evidence. *Pain, 52,* 259–285.

Cormier, L. E., Katon, W., Russo, J., et al. (1988). Chest pain with negative cardiac diagnostic studies: Relationship to psychiatric illness. *Journal of Nervous and Mental Disease, 176,* 351–358.

Couprie, W., Wijdicks, E. F., Rooijmans, H. G., et al. (1995). Outcome in conversion disorder: A follow-up study. *Journal of Neurology, Neurosurgery, and Psychiatry, 58,* 750–752.

Crimlisk, H. L., Bhatia, K., Cope, H., et al. (1998). Slater revisited: 6 year follow up study of patients with medically unexplained motor symptoms. *British Medical Journal, 316,* 582–586.

Deale, A., Chalder, T., Marks, I., et al. (1997). Cognitive behavior therapy for chronic fatigue syndrome: A randomized controlled trial. *American Journal of Psychiatry, 154,* 408–414.

Diamond, D. B. (1987). Psychotherapeutic approaches to the treatment of panic attacks, hypochondriasis, and agoraphobia. *British Journal of Medical Psychology, 60,* 79–84.

Earle, J. R., & Folks, D. G. (1986). Factitious disorder and coexisting depression: A report of successful psychiatric consultation and case management. *General Hospital Psychiatry, 8,* 448–450.

Escobar, J. I., Burnam, M. A., Karno, M., et al. (1987). Somatization in the community. *Archives of General Psychiatry, 44,* 713–718.

Fallon, B. A., Javitch, J. A., Hollander, E., et al. (1991). Hypochondriasis and obsessive-compulsive disorder: Overlaps in diagnosis and treatment. *Journal of Clinical Psychiatry, 52,* 437–460.

Fallon, B. A., Liebowitz, M. R., Salman, E., et al. (1993). Fluoxetine for hypochondriacal patients without major depression. *Journal of Clinical Psychopharmacology, 13,* 438–441.

Fallon, B. A., Schneier, R., Marshall, R., et al. (1996). The pharmacotherapy of hypochondriasis. *Psychopharmacology Bulletin, 32,* 607–611.

Fava, G. A., Grandi, S., Rafanelli, C., et al. (1992). Prodromal symptoms in panic disorder with agoraphobia: A replication study. *Journal of Affective Disorders, 26,* 85–8.

Fava, G. A., Grandi, S., Rafanelli, C., et al. (2000). Explanatory therapy in hypochondriasis. *Journal of Clinical Psychiatry, 61,* 317–322.

Feldman, M. D. (1994). Denial in Munchausen syndrome by proxy: The consulting psychiatrist's dilemma. *International Journal of Psychiatry in Medicine, 24,* 121–128.

Fernando, N. (1988). Monosymptomatic hypochondriasis treated with a tricyclic antidepressant. *British Journal of Psychiatry, 152,* 851–852.

Fishbain, D. A., Cutler, R. B., Rosomoff, H. L., et al. (1998). Do antidepressants have an analgesic effect in psychogenic pain and somatoform pain disorder. *Psychosomatic Medicine, 60,* 503–509.

Folks, D. G. (1995). Munchausen's syndrome and other factitious disorders. *Neurologic Clinics, 13,* 267–281.

Ford, C. V., & Folks, D. G. (1985). Conversion disorders: An overview. *Psychosomatics, 26,* 371–383.

Foreman, D. M., & Farsides, C. (1993). Ethical use of covert videoing techniques in detecting Munchausen syndrome by proxy. *British Medical Journal, 307,* 611–613.

Goldenberg, D. L. (1987). Fibromyalgia syndrome: An emerging but controversial condition. *Journal of the American Medical Association, 257,* 2782–2787.

Gureje, O., Simon, G. E., Ustun, T. B., et al. (1997). Somatization in cross-cultural perspective: A World Health Organization study in primary care. *American Journal of Psychiatry, 154,* 989–995.

Guthrie, E., Creed, F., Dawson, D., et al. (1993). A randomised controlled trial of psychotherapy in patients with refractory irritable bowel syndrome. *British Journal of Psychiatry, 163,* 315–321.

Guze, S. B. (1967). The diagnosis of hysteria: What are we trying to do? *American Journal of Psychiatry, 124,* 491–498.

Guziec, J., Lazarus, A., & Harding, J. J. (1994). Case of a 29-year old nurse with factitious disorder. *General Hospital Psychiatry, 16,* 47–53.

Hollander, E., Allen, A., Kwon, J., et al. (1999). Clomipramine vs desipramine crossover trial in body dysmorphic disorder: Selective efficacy of a serotonin reuptake inhibitor in imagined ugliness. *Archives of General Psychiatry, 56,* 1033–1099.

Hollander, E., Cohen, L., Simeon, D., et al. (1994). Fluvoxamine treatment of body dysmorphic disorder. *Journal of Clinical Psychopharmacology, 14,* 75–77.

Hollander, E., Liebowitz, M. R., Winchel, R., et al. (1989). Treatment of body dysmorphic disorder with serotonin reuptake inhibitors. *American Journal of Psychiatry, 146,* 768–770.

Jung, A. C., Staiger, T., & Sullivan, M. (1997). The efficacy of selective serotonin reuptake inhibitors for the management of chronic pain. *Journal of General Internal Medicine, 12,* 384–389.

Kashner, T. M., Rost, K., Cohen, B., et al. (1995). Enhancing the health of somatization disorder patients: Effectiveness of short-term group therapy. *Psychosomatics, 36,* 462–479.

Kathol, R. G. (1997). Reassurance therapy: What to say to symptomatic patients with benign or non-existent disease. *International Journal of Psychiatry in Medicine, 27,* 173–180.

Katon, W., Lin, E., VonKorff, M., et al. (1991). Somatization: A spectrum of severity. *American Journal of Psychiatry, 148,* 34–40.

Katon, W., & Russo, J. (1989). Somatic symptoms and depression. *Journal of Family Practice, 29,* 65–69.

Kellner, R. (1982). Psychotherapeutic strategies in hypochondriasis: A clinical study. *American Journal of Psychotherapy, 36,* 146–157.

Kellner, R. (1992). Diagnosis and treatments of hypochondriacal syndromes. *Psychosomatics, 33,* 278–279.

Kent, D. A., Tomasson, K., & Coryell, W. (1995). Course and outcome of conversion and somatization disorders: A four-year follow-up. *Psychosomatics, 36,* 136–144.

Kenyon, F. E. (1976). Hypochondriacal states. *British Journal of Psychiatry, 129,* 1–14.

Kiayias, J. A., Vlachou, E. D., & Lakka-Papadodima, E. (2000). Venlafaxine HCL in the treatment of painful peripheral diabetic neuropathy. *Diabetes Care, 23*, 699.

Kirmayer, L., & Robbins, J. M. (1991). *Current concepts of somatization: Research and clinical perspectives*. Washington, DC: American Psychiatric Press.

Klonoff, E. A., & Moore, D. J. (1986). "Conversion reactions" in adolescents: A biofeedback-based operant approach. *Journal of Behavior Therapy and Experimental Psychiatry, 17*, 179–184.

Kotsopoulos, S., & Snow, B. (1986). Conversion disorders in children: A study of clinical outcome. *Psychiatric Journal of the University of Ottowa, 11*, 134–139.

Kroenke, K., Lucas, C. A., Rosenberg, M. L., et al. (1993). Psychiatric disorders and functional impairment in patients with persistent dizziness. *Journal of General Internal Medicine, 8*, 530–535.

Kroenke, K., Spitzer, R. L., Williams, J. B. W., et al. (1994). Physical symptoms in primary care: Predictors of psychiatric disorders and functional impairment. *Archives of Family Medicine, 3*, 774–779.

Kroenke, K., & Swindle, R. (2000). Cognitive-behavioral therapy for somatization and symptom syndromes: A critical review of controlled clinical trials. *Psychotherapy and Psychosomatics, 69*, 205–215.

Kroenke, K., Wood, D. R., Mangelsdorff, A. D., et al. (1988). Chronic fatigue in primary care: Prevalence, patient characteristics, and outcome. *Journal of the American Medical Association, 260*, 929–934.

Langemark, M., & Olesen, J. (1994). Sulpiride and paroxetine in the treatment of chronic tension-type headache: An explanatory double-blind trial. *Headache, 34*, 20–24.

Lazarus, A. (1990). Somatic therapy for conversion disorder. *Psychosomatics, 31*, 357.

Lidbeck, J. (1997). Group therapy for somatization disorders in general practice: Effectiveness of a short cognitive-behavioural treatment model. *Acta Psychiatrica Scandinavica, 96*, 14–24.

Lipowski, Z. J. (1988). An inpatient programme for persistent somatizers. *Canadian Journal of Psychiatry, 33*, 275–278.

Max, M. B., Lynch, S. A., Muir, J., et al. (1992). Effects of desipramine, amitriptyline, and fluoxetine on pain in diabetic neuropathy. *New England Journal of Medicine, 326*, 1250–1256.

McKay, D. (1999). Two-year follow-up of behavioral treatment and maintenance for body dysmorphic disorder. *Behavior Modification, 23*, 620–629.

McQuay, H. J., Tramer, M., Nye, B. A., et al. (1996). A systematic review of antidepressants in neuropathic pain. *Pain, 68*, 217–227.

Mertz, H., Fass, R., Kodner A., et al. (1998). Effect of amitriptyline on symptoms, sleep, and visceral perception in patients with functional dyspepsia. *American Journal of Gastroenterology, 93*, 160–165.

Monson, R. A., & Smith, G. R. (1983). Current concepts in psychiatry: Somatization disorder in primary care. *New England Journal of Medicine, 308*, 1464–1465.

Morley, S., Eccleston, C., & Williams, A. (1999). Systematic review and meta-analysis of randomized controlled trials of cognitive behaviour therapy and behaviour therapy for chronic pain in adults, excluding headache. *Pain, 80*, 1–13.

Morriss, R. K., Gask, L., Ronalds, C., et al. (1999). Clinical and patient satisfaction outcomes of a new treatment for somatized mental disorder taught to general practitioners. *British Journal of General Practice, 49*, 263–267.

Murphy, G. E. (1982). The clinical management of hysteria. *Journal of the American Medical Association, 247*, 2559–2564.

Newell, R., & Shrubb, S. (1994). Attitude change and behavior therapy in body dysmorphic disorder: Two case reports. *Behavioral and Cognitive Psychotherapy, 22*, 163–169.

Neziroglu, F. A., & Yaryura, T. J. A. (1993). Exposure, response prevention, and cognitive therapy in the treatment of body dysmorphic disorder. *Behavior Therapy, 24*, 431–438.

Nielsen, G., Barth, K., Brit, H., et al. (1988). Brief dynamic psychotherapy for patients presenting physical symptoms. *Psychotherapy and Psychosomatics, 50*, 35–41.

Norregaard, J., Volkmann, H., & Danneskiold-Samsoe, B. (1995). A randomized controlled trial of citalopram in the treatment of fibromyalgia. *Pain, 61*, 445–449.

Noyes, R., Reich, J., Clancy, J., et al. (1986). Reduction in hypochondriasis with treatment of panic disorder. *British Journal of Psychiatry, 149*, 631–635.

O'Malley, P. G., Jackson, J. L., Santoro, J., et al. (1999). Antidepressant therapy for unexplained symptoms and symptom syndromes. *Journal of Family Practice, 48*, 980–990.

Papageorgiou, C., & Wells, A. (1998). Effects of attention training on hypochondriasis: A brief case series. *Psychological Medicine, 28*, 193–200.

Payne, A., & Blanchard, E. B. (1995). A controlled comparison of cognitive therapy and self-help support groups in the treatment of irritable bowel syndrome. *Journal of Consulting and Clinical Psychology, 63*, 779–786.

Perkins, R. J. (1999). SSRI antidepressants are effective for treating delusional hypochondriasis. *Medical Journal of Australia, 170*, 140–141.

Pernia, A., Mico, J. A., Calderon, E., et al. (2000). Venlafaxine for the treatment of neuropathic pain. *Journal of Pain and Symptom Management, 19,* 408–410.

Perugi, G., Giannotti, D., Di Vaio, S., et al. (1996). Fluvoxamine in the treatment of body dysmorphic disorder (dysmorphophobia). *International Journal of Clinical Psychopharmacology, 11,* 247–254.

Philipp, M., & Fickinger, M. (1993). Psychotropic drugs in the management of chronic pain syndromes. *Pharmacopsychiatry, 26,* 221–234.

Phillips, K. A., Dwight, M. M., & McElroy, S. L. (1998). Efficacy and safety of fluvoxamine in body dysmorphic disorder. *Journal of Clinical Psychiatry, 59,* 165–171.

Pilowsky, I., & Graham, B. C. (1990). A controlled study of psychotherapy and amitriptyline used individually and in combination in the treatment of chronic intractable "psychogenic" pain. *Pain, 40,* 3–19.

Pilowsky, I., Spence, N., Rounsefell, B., et al. (1995). Outpatient cognitive-behavioral therapy with amitriptyline for chronic non-malignant pain: A comparative study with 6-month follow-up. *Pain, 60,* 49–54.

Plassman, R. (1994). Inpatient and outpatient long-term psychotherapy of patients suffering from factitious disorders. *Psychotherapy and Psychosomatics, 62,* 96–107.

Prior, T. I. (1997). Treatment of factitious disorder with pimozide. *Canadian Journal of Psychiatry, 42,* 532.

Pu, T., Mohamed, E., Iman, K., et al. (1986). One hundred cases of hysteria in Eastern Libya: A sociodemographic study. *British Journal of Psychiatry, 148,* 606–609.

Quill, T. E. (1985). Somatization disorder: One of medicine's blind spots. *Journal of the American Medical Association, 254,* 3075–3079.

Rangaswami, K. (1985). Treatment of hysterical conditions by avoidance conditioning. *Dayalbagh Educational Institute Research Journal of Education, 3,* 53–56.

Rogers, R., Bagby, R. M., & Rector, N. (1990). Diagnostic legitimacy of factitious disorder with psychological symptoms. *American Journal of Psychiatry, 147,* 1312–1314.

Rosen, J. C., Reiter, P., & Orosan, P. (1995). Cognitive-behavioral body image therapy for body dysmorphic disorder. *Journal of Consulting and Clinical Psychology, 63,* 263–269.

Rost, K., Kashner, T. M., & Smith, G. R. (1994). Effectiveness of psychiatric intervention with somatization disorder patients: Improved outcomes at reduced costs. *General Hospital Psychiatry, 16,* 381–387.

Salkovskis, P. M., & Warwick, H. M. (1986). Morbid preoccupations, health anxiety, and reassurance: a cognitive-behavioural approach to hypochondriasis. *Behaviour Research and Therapy, 24,* 597–602.

Saper, S. J., Silberstein, S. D., Lake, A. E., et al. (1994). Double-blind trial of fluoxetine: Chronic daily headaches and migraine. *Headache, 34,* 497–502.

Schmaling, K. B., Rosenberg, S. J., Oppenheimer, J., et al. (1991). Factitious disorder with respiratory symptoms. *Psychosomatics, 32,* 457–459.

Schmidt, N. B., & Harrington, P. (1995). Cognitive-behavioral treatment of body dysmorphic disorder: A case report. *Journal of Behavior Therapy and Experimental Psychiatry, 26,* 161–167.

Schwarz, K., Harding, R., Harrington, D., et al. (1993). Hospital management of a patient with intractable factitious disorder. *Psychosomatics, 34,* 265–267.

Sheehan, D. V., Ballenger, J., & Jacobsen, G. (1980). Treatment of endogenous anxiety with phobic, hysterical, an hypochondriacal symptoms. *Archives of General Psychiatry, 37,* 51–59.

Shorter, E., Abbey, S. E., Gillies, L. A., et al. (1992). Inpatient treatment of persistent somatization. *Psychosomatics, 33,* 295–300.

Silver, H. (1987). Physical complaints are port of the core depressive syndrome: Evidence from a cross-cultural study in Israel. *Journal of Clinical Psychiatry, 48,* 140–142.

Simon, G. E. (1991). Somatization and psychiatric disorders. In Kirmayer, L. J. & Robbins J. M., *Current Concepts of Somatization* (pp. 91–121). Washington, DC: American Psychiatric Press.

Simon, G. E., Daniell, W., Stockbridge, H., et al. (1993). Immunologic, psychological, and neuropsychological factors in Multiple Chemical Sensitivity. *Annals of Internal Medicine, 119,* 97–103.

Simon, G. E., & Von Korff, M. (1991). Somatization and psychiatric disorder in the NIMH Epidemiologic Catchment Area Study. *American Journal of Psychiatry, 148,* 1494–1500.

Simon, G. E., Von Korff, M., Piccinelli, M., et al. (1999). An international study of the relation between somatic symptoms and depression. *New England Journal of Medicine, 341,* 1329–1335.

Sindrup, S. H., Gram, L. F., Brosen, K., et al. (1990). The selective serotonin reuptake inhibitor paroxetine is effective in the treatment of diabetic neuropathy syndromes. *Pain, 42,* 135–144.

Sindrup, S. H., & Jensen, T. S. (1999). Efficacy of pharmacological treatments of neuropathic pain: An update and effect related to mechanism of drug action. *Pain, 83,* 389–400.

Smith, G. R. (1992). The epidemiology and treatment of depression when it coexists with somatoform disorders, somatization, or pain. *General Hospital Psychiatry, 14*, 265–272.

Smith, G. R., Monson, R. A., & Ray, D. C. (1986). Psychiatric consultation in somatization disorder. *New England Journal of Medicine, 314*, 1407–1413.

Smith, G. R., Rost, K., & Kashner, T. M. (1995). A trial of the effect of standardized psychiatric consultation on health outcomes and costs in somatizing patients. *Archives of General Psychiatry, 52*, 238–243.

Sno, H. N., Storosum, J. G., & Wortel, C. H. (1991). Psychogenic "HIV infection." *Internation Journal of Psychiatry in Medicine, 21*, 93 98.

Solyom, C., & Solyom, L. (1990). A treatment program for functional paraplegia/Munchausen syndrome. *Journal of Behavior Therapy and Experimental Psychiatry, 21*, 225–230.

Sondheimer, A. (1988). Clomipramine treatment of delusional disorder—Somatic subtype. *Journal of the American Academy of Child and Adolescent Psychiatry, 27*, 188–192.

Speed, J. (1996). Behavioral management of conversion disorder: Retrospective study. *Archives of Physical Medicine and Rehabilitation, 77*, 147–154.

Spence, S. H. (1989). Cognitive-behavior therapy in the management of chronic, occupational pain of the upper limbs. *Behaviour Research and Therapy, 27*, 435–446.

Starcevi'c, V. (1991). Reassurance and treatment of hypochondriasis. *General Hospital Psychiatry, 13*, 122–127.

Steibel, V. G., & Kirby, J. V. (1994). The amytal interview in the treatment of conversion disorder: Three case reports. *Military Medicine, 159*, 350–353.

Stevens, C. B. (1990). Lorazepam in the treatment of acute conversion disorder. *Hospital and Community Psychiatry, 41*, 1255–1257.

Stone, A. B. (1993). Treatment of hypochondriasis with clomipramine. *Journal of Clinical Psychiatry, 54*, 200–201.

Sullivan, M. J., & Buchanan, D. C. (1989). The treatment of conversion disorder in a rehabilitation setting. *Canadian Journal of Rehabilitation, 2*, 175–180.

Sutherland, A. J., & Rodin, G. M. (1990). Factitious disorder in a general hospital setting: Clinical features and a review of the literature. *Psychosomatics, 31*, 392–399.

Taylor, S., & Hyler, S. E. (1993). Update on factitious disorders. *International Journal of Psychiatry in Medicine, 23*, 81–94.

Turgay, A. (1990). Treatment outcome for children and adolescents with conversion disorder. *Canadian Journal of Psychiatry, 35*, 585–588.

Veale, D., Gournay, K., Dryden, W., et al. (1996). Body dysmorphic disorder: A cognitive-behavioural model and pilot randomized trial. *Behaviour Research and Therapy, 34*, 717–729.

Vercoulen, J. H., Swanink, C. M., Zitman, F. G., et al. (1996). Randomised, double blind, placebo-controlled study of fluoxetine in chronic fatigue syndrome. *Lancet, 30*, 858–861.

Wada, T., Dawakatsu, S., Nadaoka, T., et al. (1999). Clomipramine treatment of delusional disorder, somatic type. *International Journal of Clinical Psychopharmacology, 14*, 181–183.

Walker, E., Katon, W., Harrop-Griffiths, G., et al. (1988). Relationship of chronic pelvic pain to psychiatric diagnosis and childhood sexual abuse. *American Journal of Psychiatry, 145*, 75–80.

Wallach, J. (1994). Laboratory diagnosis of factitious disorder. *Archives of Internal Medicine, 154*, 1690–1696.

Warwick, H. M., Clark, D. B., Cobb, A. M., et al. (1996). A controlled trial of cognitive-behavioral treatment of hypochondriasis. *British Journal of Psychiatry, 169*, 189–195.

Watanabe, T. K., O'Dell, M. W., & Togliatti, T. J. (1998). Diagnosis and rehabilitation strategies for patients with hysterical hemiparesis: A report of four cases. *Archives of Physical Medicine and Rehabilitation, 79*, 709–714.

Wearden, A. J., Moriss, R. K., Mullis, R., et al. (1998). Randomised, double-blind, placebo-controlled treatment trial of fluoxetine and graded exercise for chronic fatigue syndrome. *British Journal of Psychiatry, 172*, 485–490.

Wesner, R. B., & Noyes, R. (1991). Imipramine an effective treatment for illness phobia. *Journal of Affective Disorders, 22*, 43–48.

Wessely, S., Nimnuan, C., & Sharpe, M. (1999). Functional somatic syndromes: One or many? *Lancet, 354*, 936–939.

White, P. D., & Moorey, S. (1997). Psychosomatic illnesses are not "all in the mind." *Journal of Psychosomatic Research, 42*, 329–332.

Wilhelm, S., Otto, M. W., Lohr, B., et al. (1999). Cognitive behavior group therapy for body dysmorphic disorder: A case series. *Behaviour Research and Therapy, 37*, 71–75.

Wolfe, F., Cathey, M. A., & Hawley, D. J. (1994). A double-blind placebo controlled trial of fluoxetine in fibromyalgia. *Scandinavian Journal of Rheumatology, 23*, 255–259.

19

Treatments for Dissociative Disorders

Jose R. Maldonado
Lisa D. Butler
David Spiegel

To date, no controlled (Type 1 or Type 2) studies addressing the treatment of dissociative amnesia, dissociative fugue, or dissociative identity disorder have been reported. All the information available reflects the experience and case reports of clinicians and treatment centers. No single treatment modality has been systematically studied in these patient populations. The dissociative disorders represent a class of psychiatric disorders characterized by loss of control of integration of identity, memory, and consciousness, usually in the aftermath of single or multiple traumatic experiences. Effective treatments include psychotherapies designed to help patients work through traumatic memories, and to access and control access to dissociative states. Techniques such as hypnosis have proven helpful, along with selective use of antianxiety and antidepressant medications for comorbid conditions. Identification and modulation of dissociative symptoms, coupled with management of related posttraumatic syndromes, have been shown to be effective treatments.

Dissociative disorders can be understood as the pathological separation of aspects of mental functioning, including perception, memory, identity, and consciousness, which would normally be processed together. The lack of integration of memory results in dissociative amnesia; of identity and consciousness, dissociative fugue, and dissociative identity disorder; and of perception, depersonalization disorder. Dissociative symptoms often occur in the context of traumatic stressors and are components of the symptom pattern of acute and posttraumatic stress disorders. They should be understood as failures in integration, defects in control systems, rather than as the creation of multiple identities, memories, or perceptions. They are thought to help individuals maintain emotional equilibrium in the face of acute or chronic traumatic stressors but result in distress and dysfunction, including intrapsychic, vocational, and interpersonal disabilities.

THE DISSOCIATIVE DISORDERS: AN OVERVIEW

The incidence of dissociative symptoms and dissociative disorders (DDs) varies depending on the population under study. It has been reported that 6.3% of adults suffer from three to four dissociative symptoms (Mulder et al., 1998). Compared to controls, subjects experiencing dissociative symptoms reported higher rates of childhood sexual abuse (2.5X), physical abuse (5X), and concurrent psychiatric disorders (4X). In fact, dissociative symptoms have been reported in virtually every major psychiatric disorder and, in less severe forms, even in nonpatient ("normal") populations (Giese et al., 1997). Looking at the acute and subacute psychiatric population of a day hospital, Lussier and colleagues (1997) found a 9% incidence of a dissociative disorder. Coons (1998) reported that DDs might comprise 5 to 10% of psychiatric populations.

Dissociative disorders (DDs) have been described in many cultures and settings. An evaluation of 166 consecutive inpatients admitted to the psychiatric clinic in a university clinic in Turkey found incidence of DDs to be 10.2%, and of dissociative identity disorder (DID) to be 5.4% of the sample (Tutkun et al., 1998). Similarly, a study of 150 psychiatric outpatient subjects in Turkey (Sar et al., 2000) suggested that these disorders occurred in 12% of the sample. As in many American studies, these patients reported high rates of childhood abuse, including neglect (83.3%), emotional abuse (72.2%), physical abuse (50%), and sexual abuse (27.8%). On the other hand, a study of DID in the general (nonpsychiatric) population in Turkey yielded an incidence of 1.7% (Akyüz et al., 1999).

Friedl and Draijer (2000) reported on a study of consecutively admitted Dutch psychiatric patients ($N = 122$). In their sample, they found that 8% suffered from DDs, and 2% presented with factitious DID. Similarly, a study of 207 consecutively admitted Swiss psychiatric inpatients revealed a 5% incidence of DDs (Modestin et al., 1996). Middleton and Butler (1998) found that DID was not uncommon among Australian psychiatric patients. L. Brown and colleagues (1999) found a positive association between dissociative symptoms, child sexual abuse, and self-mutilation in an Australian psychiatric population suffering from eating disorders. Martínez-Taboas and Bernal (2000) described higher (DES) scores among 198 Puerto Rican undergraduate students who reported a history of frequent and severe traumatic experiences. In Ethiopia, Awas and colleagues (1999) described a lifetime prevalence incidence of DDs of 6.3% among 501 community subjects in a rural community.

Over the years, a number of diagnostic tests have been designed to reliably identify and diagnose the various DDs and dissociative experiences. These include the Dissociative Experiences Scale (DES; Bernstein & Putnam, 1986), the Somatoform Dissociation Questionnaires (SDQ-20 and SDQ-5; Nijenhuis et al., 1996, 1997, respectively), the Clinician-Administered Dissociative States Scale (CADSS; Bremner et al., 1998), and Steinberg's (2000) Structured Clinical Interview for *DSM-IV* Dissociative Disorder–Revised (SCID-D-R).

There are reports suggesting an association between dissociative phenomena and other psychiatric diagnostic categories. Koopman et al. (1996) described the relationship between peritraumatic dissociation and later development of acute stress disorder (ASD). Similarly, Eriksson and Lundin (1996) reported high levels of peritraumatic dissociation and subsequent dissociative symptoms in a Swedish population. They described a high incidence of emotional numbing (43%), reduction of awareness (55%), derealization (67%), depersonalization (33%), and dissociative amnesia (29%) among the survivors of the 1996 Estonia disaster. Nijenhuis and colleagues (1998, 1999) reported that "somatoform dissociation" was extreme in DID, high in other DDs, and increased in somatoform-disorder and some eating-disorder patients. Peritraumatic dissociation was highly associated with later onset of posttraumatic phenomena (Ursano et al., 1999). In fact, subjects with significant dissociation at the time of trauma were 4.12 times more likely than those without to have acute posttraumatic stress disorder (PTSD) and 4.86 times more likely to develop chronic PTSD. In this sample, time distortion was the most common peritraumatic dissociative symptom (56.6%). These findings were confirmed by Fullerton et al. (2000), who found that individuals who dissociated at the time of a traumatic event were more likely to develop both antisocial personality disorder (ASPD) and posttraumatic stress disorder (PTSD).

Dissociative disorders and, in particular, DID have been linked to personality disorders. Among patients diagnosed with borderline personality disorder (BPD), 32% had low, 42% moderate, and 26% high levels of dissociation, compared to 71% low, 26% moderate, and 3% high dissociation in the Axis II control group (Zanarini et al., 2000a, 2000b). Lewis and colleagues (1997) were able to obtain objective corroborative documentation of childhood abuse in the case of 12 murderers. In most cases, the subjects had amnesia for most of the abuse and underreported it. Dissociative symptoms have also been found to be elevated in patients suffering from some forms of eating disorders (Santonastaso et al., 1997).

Nonabused populations submitted to high levels of trauma or stress have been found to be more susceptible to the development of dissociative symptoms. For example, police officers who suffered from PTSD exhibited more dissociative symptoms than those without (Carlier et al., 1996). There have also been cases of new-onset DID following complicated medical/surgical procedures such as kidney transplantation (Fukunishi et al., 1997).

Dissociation has been linked to a number of nonpsychiatric phenomena. Greyson (2000) found that people reporting near-death experiences (NDEs) also reported significantly higher levels of dissociative symptoms. He suggested that NDEs might represent a form of nonpathological dissociative response to stress. Dissociative disorders, including depersonalization and DID, have been described after traumatic brain injury (Cantagallo et al., 1999). High levels of dissociation have also been described in a group ($N = 146$) of non-treatment-seeking former political prisoners (Maercker & Schützwohl, 1997) and hospitalized burn patients ($N = 46$) (Taal & Faber, 1997).

Several authors have theorized about the underlying mechanisms that mediate the development of dissociative disorders. Many authors have linked "all types" of childhood abuse with elevated levels of dissociative symptoms (Brunner et al., 2000; Butzel et al., 2000; Chu et al., 1999; Draijer & Langeland, 1999; Lipschitz et al., 1996; Mulder et al., 1998). These same reports suggest that the severity of dissociative symptoms is correlated with early age at onset of abuse and with more frequent abuse. The types of abuse cited ranged from physical and sexual abuse, to neglect, to stressful life events, to maternal dysfunction.

Neuropeptides and neurotransmitters, which are released during stress, have been implicated in the development of DDs (Bremner et al., 1996). These agents may interfere with the encoding of memory, possibly explaining the amnesia and delayed recall described in some cases of abuse and trauma. Bohus and colleagues (1999) found that endogenous opiates released at the time of trauma might contribute to dissociative symptoms, at least in PTSD and BPD patients.

A twin study suggested that genetic factors might influence dissociative capacity (Jang et al., 1998). A comparison of DID patients with non-DID psychiatric patients suggested that DID patients experienced greater dissociative tendencies, greater propensity for altered states of consciousness, increased projective and imaginative activity, a diminished ability to integrate mental contents and a highly unconventional view of reality (Scroppo et al., 1998). On the other hand, Grabe and colleagues (1999) found that the character traits of self-transcendence and self-directedness were significant and independent predictors of dissociation. Thus, they theorized dissociative symptoms are caused more by environmental factors than genetic predisposition, a position contradicting earlier findings.

Brenner (1996) built on the model that suggested that DID, in particular, might be a characterological variant on a continuum with other personality disorders such as narcissistic and borderline personality disorders. He theorized that DID may be seen as a "dissociative character" that utilizes primitive forms of dissociation in which splitting is enhanced by "autohypnotic defensive altered states of consciousness."

Finally, we need to recognize that there are those who propose that DDs as a group and DID in particular do not exist as true psychiatric disorder. These clinicians suggest that these disorders are a "creation of psychotherapy and the media" (Frankel, 1995, 1996; Ganaway, 1989, 1995; Gleaves, 1996; Lego, 1996; Mayer-Gross et al., 1969; McHugh, 1995a, 1995b; Spanos, 1985, 1986).

Dissociative Amnesia (Psychogenic Amnesia)

The hallmark of this disorder is the inability to recall important personal information, usually of a traumatic or stressful nature, that is too extensive to be explained by ordinary forgetfulness (American Psychiatric Association [APA], 1994). It is considered the most common of all dissociative disorders (Putnam, 1985). Amnesia is not only a disorder by itself but also a symptom found in a number of other dissociative and anxiety disorders. In fact, amnesia is one of the symptom criteria for the diagnoses of acute and posttraumatic stress disorder, somatization disorder, dissociative fugue, and dissociative identity disorder (APA, 1994). A higher incidence of dissociative amnesia has been described in the context of war and other natural and created disasters. Studies suggest a direct relationship between the severity of the exposure to trauma and the incidence of amnesia (Brown & Anderson, 1991; Chu & Dill, 1990; Kirshner, 1973; Putnam, 1985, 1993; Sargant & Slater, 1941).

Amnesic patients are usually aware of their memory loss. Dissociative amnesia can also be distinguished from amnesias of neurological origin because the capacity to learn new information is usually retained and cognition is intact. Occasionally, there may be a history of head trauma. If that is the case, the trauma is usually too slight to have physiological consequences. Because the amnesia involves primarily difficulties in retrieval rather than encoding or storage, the memory deficits exhibited are usually reversible. Once the amnesia has cleared, normal memory function is resumed (Schacter et al., 1982).

Most cases can be divided into two clinical presentations: acute and generally severe amnesia and a more chronic and insidious form. It has been suggested that the acute cases are usually associated with traumatic circumstances. The second presentation includes patients who experienced a traumatic event years prior to their presentation. The amnesia usually involves difficulties with explicit or episodic memory (Schacter & Kihlstrom, 1989; Squire, 1987), that is, memory associated with autobiographical information. In most cases, implicit or semantic memory (memory for skills, facts, concepts and vocabulary) is intact.

Until recently, the epidemiology of this disorder has been unknown. The prior lack of studies and data reflecting the incidence and prevalence of this disorder has been noted (Putnam, 1985). Nevertheless, dissociative amnesia is considered the most common of all dissociative disorders (Putnam, 1985). The disorder may be especially difficult to diagnose in childhood, where the symptoms may be obscured or mistaken for more common diagnoses such as attention deficit disorder, oppositional behavior, learning disability, mental retardation, or pervasive developmental disorder.

The etiology of amnesic disorders is presumed to be posttraumatic, since they generally occur within the "context of severe psychosocial stress" (Kluft, 1988). Extensive review of clinical cases suggests that victims of intense trauma experience dissociative symptoms during the event and afterward. Such symptoms may buffer the full impact of the traumatic experience (Putnam, 1985; Spiegel, 1984, 1986, 1988, 1990; Spiegel et al., 1988; van der Kolk & van der Hart, 1989).

At the time of overwhelming trauma, some victims experience a fragmentation of their experience. This is characterized by a polarization of their sense of self and a selective dissociation of affects and memories. Yet, even though dissociated memories may be unavailable to consciousness, there is evidence that they continue to influence conscious (and other unconscious) experiences and behavior (Hilgard, 1977; Kihlstrom, 1984). The fact that trauma victims cannot consciously recall these memories does not mean that these memories do not affect them: They are out of sight but not out of mind. In fact, many of the psychological and physiological symptoms experienced by trauma victims can be explained by the influence exerted by dissociated memories (Gabbard, 2000; Kihlstrom, 1984, 1990).

Even though there is no clear organic process underlying dissociative amnesia, Fukuzako and colleagues (1999) studied event-related evoked potentials in six patients with the disorder in both the acute stage and after recovery from the amnesic episode, and compared the results with those of matched healthy subjects. They found that P300 amplitudes recorded during the acute amnesic stage were lower than in control subjects. Similarly, they noticed that there was a significant increase in P300 amplitude after recovery from the amnesia. These findings suggest that some yet unknown biological or psychological mechanism may be the cause for the retrograde autobiographic memory loss suffered by patient with dissociative amnesia.

The duration of the disorder varies from a few days to a few years. Even though it is possible to experience a single episode of amnesia, many patients have experienced several episodes during their lifetime. This is more common if the stressors that caused the initial episode are not resolved. The spontaneous resolution of the symptoms is rather common. At times, the recovery is gradual, as a more generalized presentation becomes progressively more narrow and localized. Sometimes, patients experience spontaneous recovery without more treatment than a protective environment. At other times, more systematic treatment is necessary.

It is necessary to rule out a number of physical and psychological conditions that may mimic the amnesic deficits. Any assessment of an acute onset amnesia, regardless of the presence or absence of psychosocial stressors, should include a battery of tests that explore possible medical and neurological disorders such as epilepsy, brain malignancy, head trauma, medication side effects (e.g., of benzodiazepines), drug abuse and acute intoxication, and cardiovascular and metabolic abnormalities. Other psychiatric diagnoses to consider include other dissociative disorders, an organic brain syndrome, a factitious disorder, and malingering.

Dissociative Fugue (Psychogenic Fugue)

This disorder is characterized by "sudden, unexpected travel away from home or one's customary place of daily activities, with inability to recall some or all of one's past" (APA, 1994, p. 481). Because of the degree of amnesia involved, patients develop a sense of confusion about personal identity or assume a new identity (Riether & Stoudemire, 1988). Patients suffering from this disorder appear "normal," usually exhibiting no signs of psychopathology or cognitive deficit. Often, patients suffering from fugue states take on an entirely new (and unrelated) identity and occupation. In contrast to patients suffering from dissociative identity disorder, in fugue states the old and new identities do not alternate. The underlying motivating factor appears to be a desire to withdraw from emotionally painful experiences.

Predisposing factors may include extreme psychosocial stress such as war or natural and created disasters, personal and/or financial pressures or losses, heavy alcohol use, or intense and overwhelming stress such as assault or rape. The most common stressors triggering fugues states include marital discord, financial and occupational difficulties, and war-related factors. Of interest, it has been reported that the onset of some fugue episodes may occur during sleep or may be associated with sleep deprivation (Kluft, 1988). As in dissociative amnesia, there may be a history of head trauma associated with the onset of the condition.

Dissociative fugue patients usually wander away from home in a purposeful way, often far away and for days at a time. Fugue patients differ from those with dissociative amnesia in that the former are usually unaware of their amnesia. Only upon resumption of their former identities do they recall past memories, at which time they usually become amnesic for experiences during the fugue episode. However, not all patients experiencing dissociative fugues states develop a new identity. If patients do adopt a new identity, it is usually quiet and somewhat reclusive, doing nothing to draw attention to himself or herself (APA, 1994).

A prevalence rate of 0.2% has been described in the general population (APA, 1994). It is theorized that the prevalence of the disorder is higher during times of exposure to extreme stress, but actual data confirming this are not available. The incidence and sex ratio are not known (Kluft, 1988). Most available reports come from military personnel exposed to war and sectors of the population that have experienced major psychosocial stress or natural disasters (Putnam, 1985).

Similar to cases of acute dissociative amnesia, the onset of the disorder is usually associated with a traumatic or overwhelming event accompanied by strong emotions such as depression, grief, suicidal or aggressive impulses, and shame. Dissociative fugue is the least understood dissociative disorder, perhaps because most of these patients do not present for treatment. Usually, they do not come to the attention of medical personnel until they have recovered their identity and memory and have returned home. Typically, patients seek psychiatric attention once the fugue is over and they are seeking to recover their original identity or retrieve their memory for events that occurred during the fugue (Riether & Stoudemore, 1988). There is also only limited research into appropriate treatment modalities for this disorder.

Dissociative Identity Disorder (Multiple Personality Disorder)

Formerly known as *multiple personality disorder*, DID is defined by the presence of two or more distinct identities or personality states that recurrently take control of behavior (APA, 1994). It represents the failure to integrate various aspects of identity, memory, and consciousness. Also characteristic of this disorder are memory disturbances and amnesia (Kluft, 1991, 1996). Patients commonly suffer from gaps in personal history affecting both recent and remote memory. The amnesia is usually asymmetrical, selectively involving different areas of autobiographical information; that is, "alters" (personality states or identities) differ in the degree of amnesia for the experiences of other alters.

Characteristically, there is a primary or host personality, which carries the patient's given name. Usually, the primary personality is the one who pursues treatment. Commonly, the host is not completely aware of the presence of alters. Different personalities may have varying levels of awareness with respect to the existence of other personalities. On an average there are 2 to 4 personalities present at the time of diagnosis. Over the course of exploration and treatment, an average of 13 to 15 personalities may be discovered (Boon & Draijer, 1993; Coons, Bowman & Milstein, 1988; Kluft, 1984b, 1991, 1996; Putnam et al., 1986; Ross, Norton & Wozney, 1989).

The host personality may experience a number of symptoms that cause the patient to seek treatment or make family and spouses bring him or her to treatment. These symptoms include memory deficits, moodiness, erratic and unpredictable behavior, depression, self-mutilation, suicidal ideation or attempts, and the overt manifestation of an alternate personality. The transition from one personality to another is usually sudden and is commonly triggered by environmental factors. The "alter" identities may have different names, sexes, ages, and personal characteristics. The different personalities may reflect various attempts to cope with difficult issues and problems (Kluft, 1988). Personalities either have a name or are named after their function or description, such as "the Angry One."

The factors that can lead to the development of dissociative identity disorder are quite varied. Most authors seem to agree that physical and sexual abuse during childhood is the most commonly found etiological factor in these patients (Kluft, 1999; Spiegel, 1984). Chronic exposure to early childhood trauma has been linked to the development of a number of chronic forms of anxiety disorders like PTSD, as well as dissociative identity disorder (Coons, Bowman, & Pellow, 1989; Kluft, 1984b; Spiegel, 1984, 1986; Spiegel & Cardena, 1991). Indeed, it is very uncommon to see a patient suffering from DID who has not been exposed to intense trauma, usually physical (or sexual) abuse, to the point of also fulfilling criterion A for the diagnosis of PTSD (APA, 1994).

Dissociative identity disorder may represent the end product of a number of traumatic experiences taking place during childhood. Among the multiple traumas associated with its development, most authors agree, DID represents the long-term sequelae of severe childhood physical or sexual abuse or neglect (Braun, 1990; Bremner, Southwick, et al., 1992; Bryer et al., 1987; Coons et al., 1988; Darves Bornoz et al., 1999; Finkelhor, 1984; Goodwin, 1982; Kluft, 1984b; Pribor & Dinwiddie, 1992; Putnam, 1988; Putnam et al., 1986; Ross, 1989; Russell, 1986; Spiegel, 1984) or other severe traumatic experiences (Yehuda, Elkin, et al., 1996). In fact, a history of sexual and/or physical abuse has been reported in 70 to 97% of patients suffering from dissociative identity disorder (Coons et al., 1988; Coons & Milstein, 1992; Kluft, 1988; Putnam, 1988; Putnam et al., 1986; Ross, 1989; Ross et al., 1990b; Schultz et al., 1989). Incest is the most common form of sexual trauma (68%) reported (Putnam et al., 1986). Other forms of childhood trauma that are associated with later development of DID include physical abuse other than sexual abuse (75%), neglect, confinement, severe intimidation with physical harm, witnessing physical or sexual abuse of a sibling, witnessing the violent death of a relative or close friend, traumatic physical illness of self, and near-death experiences (Kluft, 1984b; Putnam et al., 1986). Several authors have described DID as a complex and chronic form of PTSD, usually in response to childhood physical or sexual abuse (Kluft, 1987b, 1988; Maldonado & Spiegel, 1997; Spiegel, 1984).

Factors involved in the development of DID as a defense against overwhelming trauma may include the age of the victim, the relationship between the perpetrator and the victim, the victim's natural hypnotic capacity (Bliss, 1986; Butler et al., 1996; Kluft, 1984b, 1984c, 1988; Morgan & Hilgard, 1973; Spiegel, 1984, 1986; Spiegel & Cardena, 1991; Spiegel et al., 1988), the effects of state-dependent memory (Bower, 1981), and the patient's developmental maturity at the time of trauma (Kluft 1988; Watkins & Watkins, 1982).

The actual incidence and prevalence of this disorder is unclear. The initial systematic report on the epidemiology of dissociative identity disorder estimated a prevalence of DID in the general population of 0.01% (Coons, 1984). After this initial report, several other studies looked at the prevalence of the disorder, but most of them were conducted in selected populations or inpatient psychiatric settings. These results indicated a higher prevalence (0.5 to 1.0%), but because of the specialized nature of the populations from which the data were obtained, the estimates may be biased (Bliss & Jeppsen, 1985; Boon & Draijer, 1993; Kluft, 1996; Ross, Anderson, et al., 1991; Ross, Joshi, & Currie, 1991; Saxe et al., 1993).

The findings in studies conducted in the general population are more limited but suggest a higher prevalence than initially reported by Coons (1984) but lower (about 1%) than the one described in psychiatric settings and specialized treatment units (Ross, 1991; Vanderlinden et al., 1991). Loewenstein (1994) reported that the prevalence in North America is about 1%, compared to a prevalence of 10% for all dissociative disorders as a group.

On the other hand, several authors (Frankel, 1995, 1996; Ganaway, 1989, 1995; Lego, 1996; Mayer-Gross et al., 1969; McHugh, 1995a, 1995b; Spanos et al., 1985, 1986) have suggested that the symptoms associated with DID represent an artificial construct rather than a true psychiatric disorder and that recent public interest in the diagnosis has sparked the increase in the number of reported cases. Mayer-Gross et al. (1969) described dissociative identity disorder (MPD) as an "artificial production, the product of the medical attention that they arouse" (p. 422). McHugh (1995a) described DID as "a psychiatric artifact [created out of] behavioral efforts—conscious or unconscious—on the part of patients to capture medical attention and achieve the advantages offered by the sick role" (p. 164). Ganaway (1995) argued that the proposed models suggesting exogenous traumas as the etiological factors in DID are not sufficient explanation for the large number of cases recently reported. He suggested that a more likely explanation is that DID symptoms are generated as the result of unconscious conflicts and compromises in both patient and therapist transference within the therapeutic dyad. Frankel (1996) suggested that "a restrictive phenomenological perspective does not fully appreciate the distorting potential of suggestibility and imagination on the nature of the emerging clinical picture" (p. 64). Spanos et al. (1985, 1986) has attempted to demonstrate the iatrogenic origin of DID by simulation studies with normal volunteers in the laboratory setting. While some authors insist that iatrogenesis is responsible for many cases of the disorder (Frankel, 1995, 1996; McHugh, 1995a, 1995b), this cannot account for the existence of all cases, or for the fact that patients persist with dissociative symptoms despite influence by doctors who deny the existence of the disorder (Spiegel, 1995; Spiegel & McHugh, 1995).

Nevertheless, the validity of DID as a psychiatric diagnosis has been confirmed by the use of independent measures, such as the Rorschach test (Leavitt & Labott, 1998). In fact, these authors stated that "the fact that two relatively rare sets of signs (DID and Rorschach) converge in the same small sector of the psychiatric population represents evidence of linkage that is clinically meaningful and not explainable on the basis of artificial creation" (p. 809).

Although dissociative identity disorder has been described more commonly during adolescence and young adulthood, the average age at diagnosis is 29 to 35 years (Bliss, 1980; Coons & Sterne, 1986; Horevitz & Braun, 1984; Kluft, 1984b, 1985b; Putnam et al., 1986). Recently, there has been increased awareness that the age of onset of the disorder occurs much earlier, during childhood. Limited data indicate that usually the appearance of the first alter personality occurs by age 12 (Fagan & McMahon, 1984; Hornstein et al., 1992; Kluft, 1985a, 1986b, 1991; Peterson, 1990, 1991; Putnam, 1985, 1991; Riley & Mead, 1988; Tyson, 1992). The youngest case described in the literature was 3 years old when diagnosed (Riley & Mead, 1988).

DID has been described as more common in women than men at a ratio of 3 to 9 : 1 (APA, 1994; Allison, 1974; Bliss, 1980; Bliss & Jeppsen, 1985; Coons & Sterne, 1986; Horevitz & Braun, 1984; Kluft, 1984c, 1988; Putnam et al., 1983, 1986; Solomon, 1983; Stern, 1984). Hocke and Schmidtke (1998) conducted a meta-analysis of all scientific publications on-line reporting DID. A critical review of the 120 published cases suggested that the female-to-male ratio was 5 : 4 for children and adolescents and 9 : 1 for adults. Likewise, females are reported to present more personalities (average of 15) than men (average of 8) (APA, 1994). Reports on contemporary case studies and samples indicate a total average of 13 to 15 personalities (Kluft, 1985b; Putnam et al., 1986; Ross et al., 1989c; Schultz et al., 1989). Likewise, there is a high incidence of first-degree relatives who have the disorder (Braun, 1985; Coons, 1985; Kluft, 1984a). The average time from the appearance of symptoms to an accurate diagnosis is 6 years (APA, 1994; Putnam et al., 1986).

Patients suffering from dissociative identity disorder usually present with a number of associated psychiatric and medical syndromes. Among the psychiatric symptoms, depression is the most common (85 to 88%, Putnam et al., 1986; Ross et al., 1989a), and it is the most likely reason for seeking psychiatric consultation (Bliss, 1984; Coons, 1984; Putnam et al., 1986). Other common psychiatric symptoms included insomnia (Putnam et al., 1986), suicide attempts or gestures (Bliss, 1980, 1984; Coons, 1984; Putnam et al., 1986; Ross, 1989), self-destructive behaviors (Bliss, 1980, 1984; Coons, 1984; Greaves,

1980; Putnam et al., 1986), phobias, anxiety, panic attacks (Bliss, 1984; Coons, 1984; Fraser & Lapierre, 1986; Putnam et al., 1986), substance abuse (Coons, 1984; McDowell et al., 1999; Putnam et al., 1986; Rivera, 1991), auditory and visual hallucinations (Bliss et al., 1983; Coons, 1984; Putnam et al., 1986; Ross et al., 1990b), somatization (Ross et al., 1989), and psychotic-like behavior (Coons, 1984; Ellason & Ross, 1995; Kluft, 1987a; Putnam et al., 1986; Ross & Norton, 1988; Ross et al., 1990a). In addition, some recent reports suggest that bipolar conditions may be comorbid with DID and can complicate diagnosis and treatment (Silberg & Nemzer, 1998; Wills & Goodwin, 1996; Yeager & Lewis, 1997).

DID patients experience an unusually high incidence of dissociative symptoms common to other dissociative disorders. For example, amnesia has been described as the single most common dissociative symptom in DID patients, occurring in 85 to 98% of the cases (Bliss, 1984; Coons, 1984; Putnam et al., 1986). Fugue episodes are experienced by 55% of patients, feelings of depersonalization by 53%, and derealization by 54% (Bliss, 1984; Putnam et al., 1986).

Dissociative identity disorder has been identified across all major racial groups, socioeconomic classes, and cultures. Most cases have been described in the United States and among Caucasians (Carlson, 1981). Nevertheless, there are multiple reports of DID in almost all societies, so it is a true cross-cultural diagnosis (Coons et al., 1991), although it is rare among dissociative disorders in some societies (Saxena & Prasad, 1989). Indeed, case reports have described DID among blacks (Coons & Sterne, 1986; Ludwig et al., 1972; Solomon, 1983; Stern, 1984), Asians (Putnam, 1989; Yap, 1960), Hispanics (Ronquillo, 1991; Solomon, 1983), and citizens of Canada (Horen et al., 1995; Ross et al., 1989; Ross, Anderson, et al., 1991; Ross, Joshi, & Currie, 1991; Vincent & Pickering, 1988), Ethiopia (Awas et al., 1999), India (Adityanjee et al., 1989; Varma et al., 1981), Turkey (Akyuz et al., 1999; Chodoff, 1997; Sar et al., 1997, 2000; Tutkun et al., 1998; Yargic et al., 1998), Switzerland (Eriksson & Lundin, 1996; Mihaescu, 1998; Modestin et al., 1996), Australia and New Zealand (Brown, Russell, et al., 1999; Gelb, 1993; Irwin, 1999; Middleton & Butler, 1998; Price & Hess, 1979); Puerto Rico (Martínez-Taboas & Bernal, 2000; Martínez-Taboas & Rodríguez-Cay, 1997), the Netherlands (Boon et al., 1993; Friedl et al., 2000; van der Hart, 1993; Sno & Schalken, 1999; van der Hart & Boon, 1997; Vanderlinden et al., 1991), and the Caribbean (Wittkower, 1970).

Depersonalization Disorder

Depersonalization is characterized by persistent or recurrent episodes of feelings of detachment or estrangement from oneself (APA, 1994). Commonly, individuals report feeling like an automaton or as if they are living a dream or a movie. Patients suffering this condition describe it as if they were an outside observer of their own mental processes and actions. It is different from delusional disorders and other psychotic processes, and reality testing is intact in this syndrome (APA, 1994). The phenomena associated with depersonalization are not uncommon. In fact, depersonalization is seen in a number of psychiatric and neurological disorders (Pies, 1991; Putnam, 1985).

Some of the associated psychiatric conditions include agoraphobia and panic disorder (Ambrosino, 1973; Ball, Robinson et al., 1997; Hollander et al., 1989; James, 1961; Roth, 1959 ; Simeon et al., 1997), schizophrenia (Bezzubova, 1991; Rosenfeld, 1947; Sedman & Kenna, 1963), personality disorders (Hunter, 1966; Sedman & Reed, 1963; Simeon et al., 1997; Torch, 1978), acute drug intoxication or withdrawal (Good, 1989; Guttmann & Maclay, 1936; Mathew et al., 1993; Melges et al., 1970; Moran, 1986; Simeon et al., 1997; Szymanski, 1981; Waltzer, 1972), unipolar mood disorders (Simeon et al., 1997), and psychotic mood disorders (Blank, 1954; Sedman & Reed, 1963; Tucker, Harrow, & Quinlan, 1973).

Neurological disorders involving depersonalization include epilepsy (Devinsky et al., 1989; Harper & Roth, 1962; Kenna & Sedman, 1965), Meniere's disease (Grigsby & Johnson, 1989), sensory deprivation (Horowitz, 1964; Reed & Sedman, 1964), sleep deprivation (Bliss et al., 1959), hyperventilation (Cohen, 1988), and migraine headaches. Depersonalization can even be transiently experienced by people with no psychiatric condition at all (Castillo, 1990; Edinger, 1985; Fewtrell, 1984; Kennedy, 1976; Signer, 1988; Wineburg & Straker, 1973). For this reason, it is important that the diagnosis be given only when the presence of symptoms causes severe impairment in functioning or marked distress (Criterion C, APA, 1994).

As in other dissociative disorders, the exact incidence and prevalence of this condition is unknown. On the other hand, in a study of 30 adult subjects consecutively recruited, Simeon and colleagues (1997) found that the mean age of onset was 16 years. The *symptom* of depersonalization has been described as being the third most common psychiatric symptom, after depression and anxiety (Cattell & Cattell, 1974). It is believed that, under severe stress, up to 50% of all adults have experienced at least one single brief episode of depersonalization. Likewise, about 12 to 16% of normal college students (Dixon, 1963; Myers & Grant, 1970; Trueman, 1984), nearly 30% of individuals exposed to life-threatening danger (Noyes & Kletti, 1971; Noyes et al., 1977; Shilony and Grossman, 1993), and up to 40% of hospitalized psychiatric patients have experienced transient episodes of depersonalization (APA, 1994; Brauer, Harrow, & Tucker, 1970; Noyes et al., 1977). Cases of depersonalization have been reported during childhood (Elliott et al., 1984; Fast & Chethik, 1976) and adolescence (Meares & Grose, 1978; Meyer, 1961; Shimizu & Sakamoto, 1986).

The sex distribution is unknown. Several studies have described a greater incidence in women, ranging from 2 to 4 : 1 (Mayer-Gross, 1935; Roberts, 1960). However, other studies have contradicted such findings and described no sex differences (Chee & Wong, 1990; Dixon, 1963; Sedman, 1966). There is no known familial pattern of inheritance described. Simeon et al. (1997) study findings suggest that a number of other psychiatric conditions are associated with depersonalization disorder, including depression, anxiety disorders, and avoidant, borderline, and obsessive compulsive personality disorders. Theories of the etiology of this disorder range from the completely physiological, such as anatomical defects similar to epilepsy (Ackner, 1954; Sedman, 1970), to the purely psychological, such as a defense against painful and conflictual affects (Cattell et al., 1974; Frances et al., 1977; Oberndorf, 1950; Shraberg, 1977; Simeon et al., 1997; Stamm, 1962) or the split between observing and participating ego/self (Noyes & Kletti, 1971), to combinations of both, such as the result of a preformed functional response of the brain as an adaptation to overwhelming trauma (Mayer-Gross, 1935; Shiloney & Grossman, 1993; Simeon et al., 1997; Spiegel & Cardena, 1991). In any event, exposure to traumatic experiences seems to be the common etiological factor in this disorder. The course of the illness is usually chronic, with exacerbations usually following exposure to real or perceived stress.

HISTORICAL PERSPECTIVE ON TREATMENT

Dissociative Amnesia (Psychogenic Amnesia)

Historically, the development of most treatments for amnesia has occurred in wartime. Army psychiatrists recommended a treatment consisting of removing the soldier from the front line and supplying food and rest (Brown, 1918; Kardiner & Spiegel, 1947; Spiegel, 2000). They also stressed the need to provide a therapeutic environment based on safety and support. In many instances, patients experienced spontaneous recovery of their memory upon removal from stressful or threatening situations, when feeling physically and psychologically safe, and/or upon exposure to cues from the past (i.e., family members) (Brown, 1918; Kardiner & Spiegel, 1947; Loewenstein, 1991; Riether & Stoudemire, 1988). Psychiatric intervention was based on helping the patient sort through memories during the course of an extensive history, in the context of reassurance regarding current safety.

When additional help was necessary, pharmacologically facilitated questioning was used (called *narcosynthesis* or *narcoanalysis*; Grinker & Spiegel, 1945; Horsley, 1943; Kolb, 1985; Marcos & Trujillo, 1978; Perry & Jacobs, 1982; Ruedrich et al., 1985; Tureen & Stein, 1949). Hypnosis, consisting primarily of permissive suggestions for memory recall or abreaction of the traumatic experience, was also a popular adjuvant for treatment (Brown, 1919; Brown et al., 1999; Fisher, 1945; Grinker & Spiegel, 1945).

Dissociative Fugue (Psychogenic Fugue)

As in the case of dissociative amnesia, the onset, and therefore the treatment, of dissociative fugue is associated with traumatic experiences. The initial reports of treatment for dissociative amnesia are also associated with war experiences (Abeles & Schilder, 1935; Akhtar & Brenner, 1979; Berrington, Liddell, & Foulds, 1956; Fisher, 1945; Fisher & Joseph, 1949; Horsley, 1943; Kolb, 1985; Luparello, 1970; Marcos & Trujillo, 1978; Parfitt & Carlyle-Gall, 1944;

Stengel, 1941, 1943), although the first description of it as a distinct psychiatric illness comes from France in the late nineteenth century (Hacking, 1996). The treatment approach suggested by these studies and case reports is basically the same as that outlined above for cases of dissociative amnesia. Unfortunately, most of these studies were poorly designed and consisted of case reports and collected cases. In addition, diagnostic criteria were not well developed at the time, and many reports did not distinguish well between cases of amnesia and fugue or even cases of dissociative identity disorders or dissociative disorders (Loewenstein, 1995).

No single treatment modality has been systematically studied in this patient population. Nevertheless, the literature proposes the use of permissive suggestions and psychodynamic-like approaches. Hypnosis, as described below, has been suggested to facilitate both the recovery of personal identity and traumatic factors triggering the fugue as well as integration of these memories and the self (Spiegel, 2000; Spiegel & Maldonado, 1999). Except for the use of benzodiazepines and barbiturates for drug-facilitated interviews and to reduce the anxiety associated with the treatment process, no pharmacological treatment has been described as effective in this condition.

Dissociative Identity Disorder (Multiple Personality Disorder)

In historical context, the earliest patients suffering from DID described in the literature were believed to be possessed. Treatment at the time consisted of depossession rituals or exorcisms. As in the case of other dissociative disorders, not much information is available regarding early treatments. Most of what has been reported consists of elaborate descriptions of cases, but little about treatment. The first reported case of DID dates back to the time of Paracelsus (Bliss, 1980). Gmelin reported in 1791 a patient suffering from a case of "exchange personalities" whom he treated with hypnosis (Ellenberger, 1970). In North America, Rush is recognized as the first to present case reports on patients suffering from DID (Carlson, 1981). Detailed and well known are the descriptions of Felida X (Azam, 1887) and Mary Reynolds (Mitchell, 1888), Despine's case of Estelle, and Janet's cases of Leonie and Lucie (Ellenberger, 1970), Christine Beauchamp (M. Prince, 1906), Doris Fisher (W. F. Prince, 1917), Eve (Thigpen & Cleckley, 1957), and Wilbur's case of Sybil (Schreiber, 1974).

The treatment in most of these cases consisted of the application of psychoanalytic techniques, the use of suggestion or formal hypnosis as adjuvant in order to facilitate memory retrieval and abreaction, and an emphasis on integration. The most detailed descriptions of these therapeutic techniques are those of Prince's (1917) treatment of Doris and Wilbur's treatment of Sybil (Schreiber, 1974).

Depersonalization Disorder

Because depersonalization disorder is rare, no controlled studies of therapeutic efficacy have been undertaken. The literature contains reports of a number of therapeutic modalities used for the treatment of this condition. Historical reports pertaining to the treatment of this condition are sparse and nonconclusive.

CURRENT TREATMENTS OF CHOICE

Dissociative Amnesia (Psychogenic Amnesia)

To date, there are no controlled studies addressing the treatment of dissociative amnesia. All the information available reflects the experience and case reports of clinicians and treatment centers. No single treatment modality has been systematically studied in this patient population. There are no established pharmacological treatments except for the use of benzodiazepines or barbiturates for drug-assisted interviews.

In general, most approaches to the treatment of these patients are similar to those used with patients suffering from traumatic experiences (Loewenstein, 1995) and to the treatment of dissociative fugue (Loewenstein, 1991). Before treatment is started, it is necessary to establish that the amnesia or fugue state is of dissociative origin, particularly because of the commonality of fugue states in temporal lobe epilepsy (Akhtar & Brenner, 1979; Kapur, 1991; Lishman, 1987). Lishman (1987, described in Kapur, 1991) noted that psychogenic fugues, compared to epileptic fugues, tend to persist for relatively longer periods (days or weeks), involve more purposeful and well-integrated behavior, and show less disturbance in consciousness and fewer cognitive and physical abnormalities.

The treatment is usually defined by the presentation. Those patients with acute onset of amnesia are usually treated more directly and aggressively than patients presenting with chronic amnesia. Loewenstein (1991) distinguished between classic and nonclassic presentations in amnesia and fugue. In classic presentations, the dissociative symptomatology is overt and often dramatic. In the nonclassic cases, the primary complaint does not usually involve amnesia, and the condition may be described as a "covert" dissociative disorder. Instead, this group may seek treatment for a variety of conditions, including depression or mood swings; substance abuse; sleep or eating problems; somatoform, anxiety, or panic symptoms; suicidal or self-mutilatory impulses or acts; violent outbursts; or interpersonal difficulties.

In cases of acute presentation, the initial step in the treatment is to provide a safe environment. On numerous occasions, simply removing the person from the threatening situation and providing security and protection has allowed for the spontaneous recovery of memory (Abeles & Schilder, 1935; Grinker & Spiegel, 1945; Kennedy & Neville, 1957). At times, additional help may be needed to obtain the necessary biographical information or to facilitate the patient's recall. Among the adjuvants to treatment cited, hypnosis and barbiturate- or benzodiazepine-facilitated recall are the most popular and better described.

Almost every barbiturate has been used to facilitate pharmacologically mediated interviews. Probably the most frequently used are sodium pentobarbital and sodium amobarbital. Protocols for the administration of tranquilizers (i.e., barbiturates and benzodiazepines) for this purpose have been detailed elsewhere (Baron & Nagy, 1988; Naples & Hackett, 1978; Perry & Jacobs, 1982). Depending on the agent used (i.e., half-life) and the length of the procedure, additional or continuous dosing may be required to maintain adequate disinhibition without overt sedation. The adjuvant use of caffeine (McCall, 1992) or methylphenidate (Hurwitz, 1988) has been reported in order to allow for optimal disinhibition and patient cooperation, while antagonizing oversedation.

As with the use of medication-facilitated interviews, no studies have addressed the efficacy of hypnosis in the treatment of dissociative amnesia. Nevertheless, most researchers in this area agree that hypnosis is a very useful tool for the recovery of repressed and dissociated memories. Once the amnesia has been reversed, treatment should be directed at restructuring the events and defining the factors that led to the development of the amnesia (Maldonado & Spiegel, 1997; Maldonado, Butler, et al., 1997). This stage is followed by the reinforcement of appropriate defenses and mechanisms to prevent further need for dissociation. This procedure is best done within the context of more extensive therapeutic work. From this point on, therapy would be similar to the treatment of more chronic forms of amnesia, described next.

The covert form (chronic presentation) of amnesia is that experienced by patients who have memory gaps regarding substantial periods of time in the past, most commonly described in patients suffering from childhood sexual and physical abuse. In these cases, drug-facilitated recall is generally not recommended. Hypnosis can prove very useful and effective in recovery and working through of traumatic memories. It has the advantage that it allows for a controlled recovery of traumatic experience at a pace the patient can tolerate. Extensive abreactions are not necessary, nor recommended. The hypnotic process should be used to allow the patient to access the memories and to reframe the experience. In this sense, this work is similar to the working through of memories associated with PTSD (Maldonado & Spiegel, 1994; Spiegel, 1988). An extensive description of the uses of hypnosis will be included under the treatment of dissociative identity disorder.

Loewenstein (1991) has suggested that longer-term psychotherapy is indicated for patients with nonclassic, covert amnesia, because of the complexity of the psychological response to the original traumatic event (which may have been childhood abuse, combat, or adult victimization). Therapy is then aimed at facilitating the recall and integration of dissociated material.

Dissociative Fugue (Psychogenic Fugue)

So far there are no controlled studies addressing the treatment of dissociative fugue. Current information is based on the experience of clinicians reporting on limited numbers of patients. All suggest a treatment that involves provision of rest and assurances of safety, development of a trusting therapeutic relationship, recovery of personal identity, review of triggers or factors associated with the onset of the fugue, reprocessing of traumatic material, reintegration of traumatic memories into personal history, and returning the patient to his or her previous life. Hypnosis and drug-facilitated interviews, as outlined above, have commonly been used during the stages of recovery of personal identity and memories associated with the onset of the fugue (Maldonado & Spiegel, 1997; Maldonado, Butler et al., 1997; Spiegel & Maldonado 1999). Except for the facilitation of memory retrieval (narcosynthesis) or diminution of anxiety related to the therapeutic process, no pharmacotherapeutic agents have been systematically studied in the treatment of this condition.

The treatments for acute dissociative amnesia and fugue states have been generally similar (reviewed in Loewenstein, 1991). Traditionally, hypnosis and amytal narcosynthesis were the treatments of choice for memory recovery in amnesia and fugue (Loewenstein, 1991; Riether & Stoudemire, 1988). In the case of fugue, it was urged that treatment be undertaken as quickly as possible while the repressed material was more readily accessible, before the memories had consolidated into a nucleus, a process that increases the possibility of future flight episodes (Nemiah, 1989; Reither & Stoudemire, 1988). Patients may also experience spontaneous memory recovery upon removal from the stressful situation, when exposed to cues from their past, or when they feel psychologically safe (Loewenstein, 1991; Riether & Stoudemire, 1988). In addition, psychodynamic psychotherapy may help to address the conflicts that precipitated the amnesia or fugue, thereby reducing subsequent dissociation under stress (Loewenstein, 1991; Nemiah, 1989; Riether & Stoudemire, 1988). For patients prone to frequent fugue episodes involving flight, one report (Macleod, 1999) indicated that having the patient wear a locator beacon on a neck chain allowed for tracking the patient during disappearances, ultimately curtailing his fugue episodes.

Dissociative Identity Disorder (Multiple Personality Disorder)

Treatment for DID generally involves (a) development of a therapeutic relationship based on safety and trust; (b) negotiation with the patient about cooperation with treatment; (c) development of a contract against harm to self or others; (d) history taking and understanding personality structure; (e) abreaction and working through of traumatic experiences and, frequently, repressed or dissociated material; (f) negotiating and modulating "conflicts" among aspects of identity and personality states; (g) development of mature and more appropriate, nondissociative defenses; and (h) working toward integration of alters (Braun, 1990; Maldonado & Spiegel, 1996; Spiegel, 1984; Kluft, 1984a, 1988, 1999). Techniques such as hypnosis can facilitate control over dissociative episodes and integration of traumatic memories. Efforts at development of a social network and support system are helpful. It may include working with the current family and/or the family of origin. Special efforts are often required to prevent further traumatization, and it is important to maintain appropriate protection and separation from abusive family members. Once integration has been achieved, further work is needed to deal with residual or renewed dissociative responses to external stress or internal conflicts and to further integration with society.

Even Kluft (1984c, 1986a, 1994, 1999), who has reported the best results in treatment outcomes described in the literature, warns that "the treatment of MPD [DID] can be arduous, painful and prolonged. . . . The achievement of integration is usually considered desirable, but in some cases a reasonable degree of conflict-free collaboration among the personalities is all that can be achieved" (Kluft 1988, p. 578).

In a survey of mental health workers involved in the treatment of dissociative disorder patients, Putnam (1993) discovered that the most common treatment modality used is individual psychotherapy facilitated by the use of hypnosis. The same study indicated that the average DID patient is seen twice a week for a period of about 4 years. The survey also mentions the use of several psychoactive drugs for the treatment of associated symptoms.

In the largest reported longitudinal study, Kluft (1985b) clearly established that patients suffering from DID do not experience spontaneous remission of their illness if left untreated. Likewise, reports have suggested that the treatment of the many symptoms and associated diagnoses do not help in the resolution of the problem unless the dissociation is addressed directly (Kluft 1985c; Putnam 1986). Although a number of authors have reported excellent therapeutic success, the majority of clinicians have very likely encountered more modest and limited results (Coons, 1986; Ross, 1989).

Comprehensive systematic research into the treatment of DID has yet to be conducted. Putnam (1986) enumerated a number of factors that would make such research difficult: (a) It would require complex study designs with large numbers of patients because there are an extremely large number of variables to control for, including both the usual research variables (demographics; concurrent medical, neurological, or other psychiatric pathology; amount and kind of current or past treatment), as well as variables unique to DID (such as patient type, presence or absence of specific types of alternate personalities, and age at the time of therapeutic intervention); (b) there are pragmatic difficulties of working with DID patients in a research setting, including complex transference and countertransference interactions, placebo responses, heightened sensitivity to medication side effects, and clinicians who may be wary about administering control or placebo interventions; and finally, (c) there is a lack of resources for such research. To address many of these issues, Putnam proposed a large multicenter collaborative study where researchers could investigate a number of the issues described above in a series of coordinated small-scale studies of carefully chosen overlapping questions. To our knowledge, such a program of research has yet to be initiated, even a decade and a half later.

Putnam (1986) noted, "Our current knowledge of the diagnosis and treatment of MPD is based on pragmatic clinical experience" (p. 193). Apparently, his assessment still stands. To date, only four authors have published treatment outcome data on DID patients (Coons, 1986; Ellason & Ross, 1997; Kluft, 1984c, 1986a, 1994; Ross 1989), and none of these studies employed control groups. So it is important to bear in mind that the question addressed by these studies is "Does therapy (broadly defined) work?" rather than "What kind of therapy works best?" Or as Kluft (1993) put it, "What to do until the controlled studies come?" (p. 87).

In 1984, Richard Kluft published the first report of MPD patient outcome following therapy. Of an initial pool of 171 MPD patients whom Kluft had interviewed in his practice and research or through referrals, 123 patients with clearly defined MPD had sought treatment and become subjects of follow-up study. At the time of the report, 40 patients (33% of the 123) had not achieved integration (20 patients were still in treatment, 10 had interrupted treatment, and 10 treatments had been unsuccessful), while 83 (67%) had been successfully treated to fusion. Fusion was defined on the basis of "three stable months of (1) continuity of contemporary memory, (2) absence of overt behavioral signs of multiplicity, (3) subjective sense of unity, (4) absence of alter personalities on hypnotic re-exploration, (5) modification of transference phenomena consistent with the bringing together of personalities, and (6) clinical evidence that the unified patient's self-representation included acknowledgment of attitudes and awareness which were previously segregated in separate personalities" (Kluft, 1984c, p. 12). (Meeting these criteria for 3 months was described by Kluft as *apparent fusion*.) Of this fusion group, 33 patients (27% of the entire treatment group) met the additional criterion of showing no signs of dissociation for a minimum of 27 months (which Kluft describes as *stable fusion*) and were available to undergo an extensive reassessment of the stability of their integration.

In this select sample, 32 of 33 patients reported and were independently assessed to have attained a better quality of life and global improvement. About a quarter of the sample had experienced relapse events, though only two patients (6%) were diagnosable with MPD at the time of follow-up. The average duration of treatment was 21.6 months. Kluft also noted a number of treatment trends in the group: Individuals with fewer personalities required shorter periods of treatment and were less likely to relapse, male patients had fewer personalities and briefer treatments, and persons with borderline features were more difficult to treat to the point of stable fusion. Putnam (1986, reported in Kluft, 1993) offered a further examination of Kluft's (1984c) data. His analysis demonstrated that complexity (number of personalities) correlated positively with the time needed to reach integration and predicted that about 3 months of therapy was necessary per alter. However, this ratio applied only to those patients with 18 alters or fewer.

Kluft (1984c) emphasized the need for continuity of treatment beyond initial fusion, noting that "treatment that ends at a point of apparent fusion is rarely complete or stable" (p. 24). From his overall results Kluft (1984c) concluded that "with appropriate treatment, DID patients can achieve a stable remission of the symptoms that characterize the condition, and live stable and productive lives as unified individuals" (p. 19).

Since publication of the 1984 data, Kluft has issued further treatment outcome updates on the initial sample. In 1986(b), Kluft rereported the 1984 results with the addition of 19 patients who had not, at the time of the original report, achieved integration of sufficient duration (i.e., 27 months) to be included or who had not been thoroughly reassessed at that time. In this enlarged group, patients were reassessed between 27 and 99 months after achieving integration. Although Kluft presented the data for the total sample (now 52, which included the original 33), the overall findings appear virtually identical to those reported initially for the subset. Only 21% had had relapse events, and of these, only three patients (6%) had had diagnosable DID. Overall, 94% showed clear evidence of improved function and progress in their lives. In a more recent article, a decade later, Kluft (1994) reported that 103 (84%) of the original 123 patients whose treatments were followed had achieved stable integration, and 6 remained in active treatment.

Subjects in a study by Coons (1986) were the first 20 DID patients (17 women, 3 men) the author encountered in a state psychiatric facility. All met *DSM-III-R* criteria for MPD and the additional requirement that they exhibit amnesia (thereby making this sample relatively comparable to those who would currently fulfill *DSM-IV* criteria). Hypnosis was not used to determine the diagnosis, and all patients had a history of dissociation before entering the study. Upon intake, a detailed psychiatric and collateral social history were gathered along with neurological and psychological testing.

Of the original 20 patients, 18 were located for follow-up, and further data were gathered at that time through an interview with the patient and a questionnaire completed by the therapist. The data were collected 3 to 129 months after intake (mean, 39 months). Upon follow-up, 10 of the 18 patients were still in outpatient treatment, and 8 had terminated treatment. Of those who had terminated treatment, 5 (25% of the total sample) had achieved integration defined by five of Kluft's (1982) six criteria for integration (hypnotic reexploration was not conducted). In addition, 2 patients (10%) had achieved partial integration, and 2 (10%) others had achieved integration but had subsequently redissociated. Coons noted that the unintegrated patients had experienced emotional trauma during the course of therapy at approximately twice the rate of those patients who eventually became integrated. However, this difference was not statistically significant.

Most patients in the Coons study had been seen weekly (67%), with four patients (20%) receiving two to five sessions a week. Patients had received a wide variety of concurrent therapeutic interventions, including general modalities such as psychodynamic psychotherapy (95%), psychoeducation (40%), homogeneous group therapy (35%), marital therapy (35%), and specialized incest group therapy (15%), as well as specific techniques and interventions such as hypnosis (80%), audio/video taping (75%), journal writing (55%), crisis intervention (35%), day care (20%), sodium amytal interviews (15%), and vocational therapy (15%). Coons reported that therapists rated the effectiveness of psychodynamic psychotherapy, hypnotherapy, and homogeneous group therapy very highly. No data were reported on the success of the other interventions. Somatic treatments were also quite commonly employed, including antipsychotic medication (45%), antidepressant medication (40%), anxiolytic medication (15%), and electroconvulsive therapy (ECT; 10%). No improvement or worsening of condition was reported for the majority of patients prescribed antipsychotic medications and minor tranquilizers. Antidepressants were found to be effective in half of the cases in which they were used. No data were reported on the efficacy of ECT with the two patients for whom it was used.

Coons (1986) reported that almost all of the 20 patients showed an improvement in clinical status. Both patient and therapist reports suggest that about two thirds of patients were considered moderately to greatly improved, and only one patient was definitely judged to be clinically worse at follow-up. In all cases (of those described by the 70% of therapists who returned the questionnaire), patients had accepted their diagnosis, and approximately three quarters of this sample had achieved coconsciousness.

Ross (1989) briefly described the treatment outcomes of 22 patients who entered active specific treatment at his Dissociative Disorders Clinic in Winnipeg, Canada, or who were treated by outside colleagues. Of these 22 patients, 6 (27%) had achieved integration, 5 (23%) were currently in treatment and expected to integrate, and 1 (4.5%) had reached an unstable integration and had relapsed but was expected to reach stable integration. In the remaining sample, 4 patients (18%) were still in treatment and their outcome was uncertain; 2 (9%) patients deemed treatable had left the area unintegrated; 1 patient (4.5%) had reached an unstable integration, had relapsed, and was now lost to follow-up; and 3 (14%) had dropped out unintegrated. (Interestingly, Ross reported that of the first 40 cases seen in the clinic, 27 (67.5%) met *DSM-III* criteria for borderline personality disorder; however, borderline features did not appear to be a predictor of poor outcome in those who were treated.)

Ross noted that 12 (54%) of the 22 patients had reached or were expected to reach integration, and he suggested that this may well be a conservative estimate of successful treatment outcome because this total did not include the 4 patients in treatment with uncertain outcomes and the 2 treatable (but relocated) patients who were likely to reach integration with proper treatment. With the addition of these 6 patients, 18 of 22 patients might be expected to achieve integration, resulting in an 82% successful treatment rate. In consideration of these and Kluft's findings, Ross concluded that "MPD is a treatable disorder" (1989, p. 203).

More recently, Ellason and Ross (1997) reported on a 2-year follow-up study of 135 DID individuals who had been assessed at baseline as inpatients. Of this original sample, 62 were located, and 54 were reinterviewed by phone. All but 1 of those examined were outpatients at the time of follow-up. Overall, the patients showed significant improvement at follow-up in current Axis I (particularly anxiety, somatic, and psychotic diagnoses) and II disorders; dissociative, depressive, and Schneiderian first-rank symptoms; substance abuse; and a significant reduction in the number of antidepressant and antipsychotic drugs they used. Twelve subjects were identified as having achieved integration according to Kluft's (1984) criteria in addition to no longer meeting *DSM III-R* or *DSM-IV* criteria for DID assessed through structured interview. These integrated patients, though lower in depression at baseline, showed greater improvement than nonintegrated patients in depression symptoms, secondary features of DID, and amnesia and borderline symptoms and slightly more improvement on suicidality and Dissociative Experiences Scale and Beck Depression Inventory scores. The authors noted that these findings were consistent with previous reports that DID patients may be responsive to treatment. Critics (e.g., Merskey & Piper, 1998; Powell & Howell, 1998) have noted that Ellason and Ross's study suffers from a number of methodological limitations, including the lack of a no-treatment (or wait-list) control group to determine DID's natural (untreated) course (especially given that patients were very likely their most symptomatic at the baseline assessment), lack of a standardized treatment protocol, and failure to reassess the majority of the original sample (which may signal untoward outcomes in this subset). While Ross and Ellason acknowledged the limitations of their investigation (1998a, 1998b), they noted (1998a) that "the scientific meaning of our study is not that it answers all questions for all times; rather, it establishes a methodological threshold that must now be met by competing schools of thought" (p. 1462).

Clinical Research on Individual Modalities

"The scientific literature on the treatment of multiple personality [dissociative identity disorder] is largely descriptive and prescriptive" (Kluft, 1984a, p. 51), and therefore, there has been no systematic research support for the following, which is based on case reports and the reflections of individual therapists experienced in working with DID. The virtue of these reports is that they represent the conclusions drawn by those practitioners who have led the field in the treatment of DID; their limitation is that they are based on limited samples, without proper controlled scientific scrutiny and comparison, and they may be subject to the expectations and biases of their reporters.

Homogeneous Group Therapy in DID

Although individual psychotherapy is widely considered the treatment of choice for DID, a number of experts have suggested that these patients may benefit from group therapy as a supplemental or adjunctive intervention that may enhance overall therapeutic progress (Caul, 1984; Caul et al., 1986; Coons & Bradley, 1985). Caul and colleagues (1986) observed, "Multiple personality [DID] patients rarely have had the opportunity or ability to understand the concepts of self and self in the world. Group therapy presents an opportunity for the MPD patient to participate in a sense of togetherness with other humans in a social context. The group presents a potential to learn interaction, acceptance, tolerance, patience, compassion, sharing" (p. 147). In Coons and Bradley's (1985) description of their 2-1/2-year-long group, they found that the themes of trust, negative self-worth, and dependence were especially prominent, and that the group was particularly valuable in instilling feelings of hope and universality, in offering support to members (once trust and a sense of cohesion were established), and in stimulating change through peer pressure (although the authors cautioned against pressure to premature integration). Virtually all experts seem to agree that DID patients should be included in group therapy only if they are in concomitant individual therapy (Benjamin & Benjamin, 1992; Caul, 1984; Caul et al., 1986; Coons & Bradley, 1985). As Caul and his colleagues (1986) stated, "Group process is a supplement to individual therapy for MPD patients, not a modality that could or should be used alone" (p. 149).

Family Treatments in DID

Benjamin and Benjamin (1992) observed that "it seems ironic to us that a family-based approach has been underutilized since this disorder is precisely about the failure of a healthy family process" (p. 236). Multiple authors (Benjamin & Benjamin, 1992, 1993, 1994a,b; Chiappa, 1994; Panos et al., 1990; Porter et al., 1993; Putnam, 1989; Sachs, 1986; Sachs et al., 1988; Williams, 1991) have proposed that family interventions should be an integral part of an overall treatment plan for dissociative disorders that seeks to facilitate healthy relationships within the family and to enhance the treatment of the identified DID patient. Generally, commentators propose such interventions for the current family of the patient rather than the family of origin (Benjamin & Benjamin, 1992; Chiappa, 1994), although some have reported on family treatments for the extended families of child DID patients (Sachs et al., 1988). In the latter case, the authors asserted that it is essential that the abuse in the family that precipitated dissociation in the MPD child has ceased, that the abuser be identified and be willing to admit to the abuse and to change, and that the cessation of the abuse cycle can be verified (Sachs, 1986; Sachs et al., 1988). "Any therapeutic attempt is useless unless the trauma is terminated" (Sachs et al., 1988, p. 253).

Hypnosis as a Treatment Tool

Many traumatic memories may be elicited during the course of psychotherapy without the utilization of techniques for memory enhancement. Nevertheless, the use of hypnosis can facilitate access to repressed memories that have not emerged by the use of other methods (Maldonado & Spiegel, 1995, 1997; Spiegel, 1989). Many trauma victims respond to the traumatic event by using dissociative-like defenses during or after the trauma. In instances of repeated trauma, it is likely that victims "learn" how to trigger these dissociative responses (self-hypnosis-like defenses) in order to avoid further trauma. Most patients suffering from dissociative disorders are highly hypnotizable (Butler et al., 1996; Kluft, 1984; Maldonado & Spiegel, 1994, 1995; Putnam, 1991; Spiegel, 1988, 1989; Spiegel et al., 1982, 1988; Stuntman & Bliss, 1985). If hypnotic-like states are used during traumatic experiences, it makes sense that the very entry into this same state could lead to the retrieval of memories and affects associated with the original trauma (Butler, Duran et al., 1996), as would be predicted by the theory of state-dependent memory (Bower, 1981).

What makes hypnosis one of the most helpful tools in the treatment of patients suffering from dissociative disorders is its ability to be used as both a diagnostic tool and a powerful therapeutic technique. The hypnotic state can be seen as a controlled form of dissociation (Nemiah, 1989). Hypnosis allows for the recovery and reprocessing of recovered memories at a pace the patient can tolerate (Fine, 1991; Kluft, 1989; Maldonado & Spiegel, 1995). Despite the fact that most clinicians and researchers in the treatment of dissociative disorders agree on the usefulness of hypnotic approaches in the treatment of these conditions, no systematic studies regarding their efficacy have been conducted. Properly done, this technique effectively facilitates symbolic restructuring of the traumatic experience under hypnosis. This can be coupled with the use of a grief work model (Lindemann, 1994; Spiegel, 1988). As an adaptation of the techniques used for the treatment of PTSD, hypnosis can be used to provide controlled access to the dissociated or repressed memories and then help patients restructure their memories (Maldonado & Spiegel, 1995; Spiegel, 1996).

The most serious problem in the use of hypnosis involves its possible effects on memory. There is evidence that hypnosis can distort memory in two ways, either through confabulation, the creation of pseudomemories that are reported as real (Laurence & Perry, 1983; Spiegel, 1996), or through concreting, an unwarranted increase in the confidence with which hypnotized individuals report their memories, either true or false (Diamond, 1980; McConkey, 1992; Orne, 1979; Spiegel & Scheflin, 1994). The most clearly reproducible problem is the production of confident errors, exaggerating the truth value of memories unearthed in hypnosis.

Recently, there has been concern about the creation of "false memories." Due to the heightened sense of concentration, the hypnotic process allows patients to focus so intensely on a given time or place as to facilitate memory recall. The principle of state-dependent memory (Bower, 1981) also suggests that trance states can facilitate retrieval of memories associated by creating a state of mind similar to the one experienced at the time of the trauma. Nevertheless, *therapists must be aware that not every memory recovered with the use of hypnosis (or any other method of memory enhancement) is necessarily true. Hypnosis can facilitate improved recall of both true and confabulated material* (Dywan & Bowers, 1983). Due to its very nature, suggestibility is increased in hypnosis, and information can be implanted or imagined and reported as veridical, producing the problem of "confident errors" (McConkey, 1992; Orne, 1979; Laurence & Perry, 1983).

Therapists treating patients who may have been victims of sexual abuse or incest must also be aware that the use of hypnosis may compromise a witness's ability to testify in court. Full guidelines for use of hypnosis in the forensic setting have been detailed by the Council on Scientific Affairs of the American Medical Association (AMA). These recommendations include careful debriefing of the subject before hypnosis is employed, the use of nonleading questions, complete videotaping of all contact with the patient, and careful debriefing afterward (Orne et al. 1985). More recently, and expanding on the AMA's earlier report, the American Society of Clinical Hypnosis published a manuscript providing guidelines for clinicians working with hypnosis and for the use of hypnosis in forensic psychiatry (Hammond, Garver, Mutter, et al., 1995).

Another concern is the exacerbation rather than reduction of dissociative symptoms. Ross (1989) compared a group of DID patients who had been hypnotized before and after diagnosis (31.8%), a group hypnotized only after diagnosis (48.3%), and a group of DID patients never exposed to hypnosis (17.8%) during diagnosis or treatment. He observed that the groups did not differ on the diagnostic criteria for DID, the number of personalities identified at diagnosis, or the number of personalities identified at the time of reporting. Furthermore, the three groups did not differ in basic demographic characteristics such as age, sex, or marital status. This study suggests that the use of hypnosis per se does not have a gross distorting effect on the features of the disorder.

The possibility of iatrogenic exacerbation of DID should be a concern for any therapist treating such patients, particularly the perpetuation of splitting (Fine, 1989; Ganaway, 1989; Kluft, 1989; Torem, 1989). Torem (1989) cautioned that a number of factors may contribute to a worsening of functioning and may thwart integration, such as therapists' overinvestment in one or more alters; patient suggestibility, and therapists' inadvertent suggestions; undefined boundaries and poor limit setting; patient difficulties in trusting; therapeutic misalliances; therapists' disowning of unacceptable patient behaviors; therapists' perception and communication to patients (e.g., that their condition is one of multiple individuals in one body); and an overemphasis on the patient's internal world at the expense of external reality.

Fine (1989) observed that iatrogenic creation of new alters can occur in virtually any treatment modality, and that it is often related to the unexamined and poorly understood countertransference feelings that some therapists have toward their DID patients, at times accompanied by boundary violations: "Treatment modalities differ little in their ability to create or in their ability to protect from the creation of iatrogenic alters. The key element in decreasing the incidence of iatrogenesis is the appropriate negotiating of the countertransference, maintaining clear boundaries in therapy and acknowledging and correcting mistakes rather than denying them" (p. 81; see also Ganaway, 1989).

Finally, Kluft (1989) reported on the factors inherent in the treatment process and highlighted those that contribute to the complexity in the presentation. He believes that therapists' errors in technique and/or inappropriate behaviors (related to Fine's, 1989, boundary violations) may promote the emergence of alters. On the other hand, he pointed out that the appearance of personalities during the course of treatment could also be the result of the discovery of preexisting but previously unrecognized alters.

Treatment of Dissociative Identity Disorder in Childhood

As is the case in the adult dissociative disorders literature, very little systematic research has been reported regarding treatment of dissociative disorders in childhood. According to Kluft (1986), children are easier to treat because their alters appear less invested in remaining separated. In contrast, adolescents have a more developed system of alter personalities and, like many adults, are more invested in maintaining their independence (Kluft, 1995a; Kluft & Schultz, 1993).

Cognitive Behavioral Therapy of DID

There are no controlled studies on the use of cognitive therapies in the treatment of DID or any of the DDs. Nevertheless, there are many papers and case reports suggesting the use of standard and schema-focused cognitive techniques to help patients to formulate a working conceptualization of their dissociative episodes and to develop coping skills to help manage and overcome dissociative events (Kennerley, 1996). Bryant and colleagues (1999) demonstrated that a prolonged exposure or a combination of prolonged exposure and anxiety management was effective in preventing PTSD in a group of 45 civilian trauma survivors who were experiencing ASD at the time of initial evaluation. Given the link, already discussed, between PTSD and DID, cognitive behavior therapy (CBT) may prove an efficacious technique in preventing and possibly treating DID and other DDs. More controlled studies are needed. Fine (1999) summarized the structured cognitive-behavioral-based treatment of DID. He suggested that the use of a cognitive behaviorally based technique called the *tactical integration model* promotes proficiency over posttraumatic and dissociative symptoms, is collaborative and exploratory, conveys a consistent message of empowerment to the patient, and not only fosters symptom relief but also promotes integration of all personalities and ego states into one mainstream of consciousness.

Psychopharmacology of DID

Little is known about the rational approach to the use of psychoactive substances in the treatment of DID. Putnam (1989) remarked that "until appropriate methodology [for the study of medications in DID] can be devised, the psychopharmacology of DID will remain a pragmatic art" (p. 253). He stressed that "there is no good evidence that medication of any type has a direct therapeutic effect on the dissociative process [manifested by DID patients]" (p. 253). Loewenstein (1991) attempted to summarize the general consensus and knowledge regarding the psychopharmacological aspects of DID but finally arrived at the same conclusion: "There is no known definitive pharmacotherapy for the 'core' symptoms of [DID]" (p. 721). Furthermore, he reported that "most dissociative symptoms seem relatively impervious to pharmacologic intervention" (p. 721).

To date, there has been no double-blind controlled study of psychopharmacological agents in DID patients. The few data available are limited to cases reports and small, uncontrolled samples. Treatment has been limited to control of signs and symptoms afflicting DID patients. Because of the nature of the studies and their poor design (or lack thereof), it is impossible to know if the "success" of these medications was due to improvement of a comorbid diagnosis (different from DID) or to the direct effect on controlling symptoms directly associated with DID. To complicate matters even further, several authors (Barkin et al., 1986; Braun, 1983; Kluft, 1984a; Putnam, 1984, 1986) have suggested that there is variability in response to medication related to the predominance of different personality states. This has reportedly included the same dose having varying effects or different profiles of adverse reactions.

Kluft (1984a, 1985b) described the need for maintenance of tricyclic antidepressants (TCAs) in the treatment and eventual integration of a small sample ($N = 6$) of DID patients suffering from major depression. In another study, Barkin et al. (1986) reported that polycyclic antidepressants should be used in the treatment of DID patients only when the host and a large number of alters experience symptoms of major depression. In the same sample, the authors warn about the lack of consistent therapeutic results across the alters. The same study (Barkin et al., 1986) strongly discouraged the use of (MAOIs) due to the high lethality associated with drug-drug interactions and the potential interaction with dietary tyramine. Newer selective serotonin reuptake inhibitors are effective at reducing comorbid depressive symptoms and have the advantage of far less lethality in overdose.

Almost every single author writing on the psychopharmacology of DID (Barkin et al., 1986; Kluft, 1984a, 1988; Putnam, 1989; Ross, 1989) has reported an extremely high incidence of adverse side effects following the use of neuroleptic medications. Complications include the creation of new alters in response to medication. These authors recommend trying a nonpharmacological or other psychotropic agent before risking the use of neuroleptics. These medications may be useful rarely for the control of extreme agitation or disorganization but are not helpful for maintenance use. If misdiagnosed patients are thought to be schizophrenic, neuroleptics complicate the situation by flattening affective response while not affecting key symptoms of personality fragmentation and amnesia, thereby apparently confirming the misdiagnosis.

Barkin et al. (1986) suggested that the use of benzodiazepine agents should be limited to cases where high levels of anxiety are experienced across all alters or where anxiety interferes with therapeutic work. Loewenstein et al. (1988) described the only systematic study of pharmacotherapy of DID. In this study, clonazepam was used successfully to control PTSD-like symptoms in a small sample ($N = 5$) of DID patients. After treatment, patients exhibited improvement in sleep continuity and decreased flashbacks and nightmares.

Fichtner et al. (1990) described a single case of a 21-year-old woman with active suicidal ideation. Manic depressive illness was limited to that single personality. The antiepileptic carbamazepine was used over the course of 8 months, during which the patient exhibited decreased violent behavior and improved control over dissociation (decreased switching). Mesulam (1981) and Schenk and Bear (1981) reported dissociative symptomatology in DID patients who exhibited concurrent temporal lobe abnormalities on EEG. Unfortunately, no controlled studies were done, and no follow-up of reported cases has been published. Devinsky et al. (1988) suggested that unless there are clear EEG changes, anticonvulsants (in particular, carbamazepine) should play no role in the treatment of DID and should be avoided due to the high incidence of serious side effects.

Braun (1990) proposed the use of clonidine and high-dose propranolol for the treatment of hyperarousal, anxiety, poor impulse control, disorganized thinking, and rapid or uncontrolled switching in DID patients. His open trials suggest "good outcomes" with these agents. However, no specific data about the patients or the drug trials were reported, such as the number of patients given either drug, actual success rate, comorbid diagnoses in the sample, or prevalence of adverse drug reactions.

Barkin and colleagues (1986) stated that not enough data are available but concluded that the available data suggest that most DID patients do not respond to lithium.

Electroconvulsive Therapy

Coons (1986) reported the use of ECT in 2 of his 20 patients. Unfortunately, no data were reported regarding the effects of ECT on their overall condition. Bowman and Coons (1992) reported, however, that in a prospective study of three dissociative disorder patients (one DID, two DDNOS) with severe treatment-resistant depression, ECT resulted in a 50% drop in depression scores and marked clinical improvement, the gains being maintained for at least 4 months. They cautioned, however, that ECT did not affect the dissociative condition and should only be used when depression is experienced by most of the active alters, rather than by just one. DeBattista et al. (DeBattista, Solvason, et al., 1998) reported on the use of ECT to successfully treat comorbid depression in three of four DID patients. They also noted the lack of adverse effects of the treatment on the patients' dissociative symptoms.

Eye-Movement Desensitization and Reprocessing (EMDR)

The technique known as EMDR was initially described by Shapiro (1995) and has been mostly applied to the treatment of traumatic memories, in particular PTSD (Forbes et al., 1994; Shapiro, 1995; Shapiro et al., 1994; Silver, et al. 1995; Wilson et al., 1995; Young 1995). Nevertheless, an article by Young (1994) reported on the use of EMDR for the treatment of dissociative identity disorder patients. Systematized or controlled studies are lacking. So far, most reports confirming its usefulness are anecdotal. Other studies present equivocal findings and do not confirm any specific effects of the eye movement treatment (Oswalt et al., 1993). To date, Paulsen (1995) has written the only article specifically on the use of EMDR in the treatment of dissociative disorders.

Finally, PTSD has been described as the most common comorbid disorder in DID patients, often requiring active treatment (Loewenstein, 1991). The reason is very likely the traumatic origin of both diagnoses. As a result, the discrete use of medications for the treatment of PTSD sometimes assists in controlling some of the symptoms exhibited by DID patients. A detailed discussion of the pharmacological treatment of PTSD is beyond the scope of this chapter and can be found elsewhere (Braun et al., 1990; Fesler, 1991; Frank et al., 1988; Friedman, 1988,

1991; Kitchner & Greenstein, 1985; Kolb et al., 1984; Kosten et al., 1987; Lipper, 1988; Maldonado & Spiegel, 1994; Reist et al., 1976; Shestatzky et al., 1988).

Depersonalization Disorder

To date, virtually all reports addressing the treatment of depersonalization disorder reflect the experience and case reports of clinicians and a few treatment centers. No single treatment modality has been systematically studied in this patient population.

Treatment modalities employed include paradoxical intention (Blue, 1979), record keeping and positive reward (Dollinger, 1983), flooding (Sookman & Solyom, 1978), psychodynamic psychotherapy (Allers et al., 1997; Lehman, 1974; Noyes & Kletti, 1971; Schilder, 1939; Shilony & Grossman, 1993; Torch, 1987), psychoeducation (Allers et al., 1997; Fewtrell, 1986; Torch, 1987), psychostimulants (Cattell & Cattell, 1974; Davison, 1964; Shorvon, 1946), antidepressants (Abbas et al., 1995; Fichtner et al., 1992; Hollander et al., 1989, 1990; Noyes et al., 1987; Ratliff & Kerski, 1995; Simeon et al., 1998; Walsh, 1975), antipsychotics (Ambrosino, 1973; Nuller, 1982), anticonvulsants (Stein & Uhde, 1989), benzodiazepines (Ballenger et al., 1988; Nuller, 1982; Spier et al., 1986; Stein & Uhde, 1989), and electroconvulsive therapy (Ambrosino, 1973; Davison, 1964; Roth, 1959; Shorvon, 1946).

The potential benefit of selective serotonin reuptake inhibitors for depersonalization has received some attention. In a double-blind crossover trial of 8 weeks of desipramine and 8 weeks of clomipramine (following 1 week of single-blind placebo), Simeon and colleagues (1998) found that 2 of 7 subjects in the clomipramine trial and 1 of 6 subjects in the desipramine trial showed significant improvement, while no subjects improved during the single-blind placebo period. One clomipramine responder was followed for 4 years in open maintenance treatment, and her symptoms remained in almost complete remission during that time except when attempts were made to taper or change the medication. In addition, several case reports suggest that fluoxetine may be helpful for some patients (Abbas et al., 1995; Fitchner et al., 1992; Hollander et al., 1990; Ratliff & Kerski, 1995). In Simeon et al.'s (1997) earlier examination of 30 cases of depersonalization disorder, patient reports of treatment history indicated that 70% had been treated with medications at some time in the past, but only serotonin reuptake inhibitors and benzodiazepines were reported to have been of benefit to patients in reducing their depersonalization symptoms.

Fewtrell (1986) and Torch (1987) have proposed psychoeducation as a valuable tool for treatment: "Often the patient, despite the treatment, has not ever been approached with the concept of depersonalization, and no more relief, at least in quantitative terms, will ever be noted in these individuals than that accorded by simply putting the intangible feeling into words for the first time" (Torch, 1987, p. 136; quoted in Steinberg, 1991).

Cattell and Cattell (1974; also Nemiah, 1989) suggested that classical psychoanalysis may worsen the symptoms of depersonalization due to the isolation and fantasy promoted by free association and lack of direct contact with the therapist, which may exacerbate the patient's chronic feelings of unreality. As in the case of pharmacotherapy, there are no controlled studies that confirm this assumption.

The use of hypnosis has also been described in multiple case reports. Authors have described the role of suggestibility in the etiology of the disorder and recommend the use of hypnosis as a treatment modality (Kluft, 1988; Spiegel, 1988). All of these studies were inadequately designed, including small samples, no double-blind, and no controls. Most of them were case reports.

As in the case of the other dissociative disorders, hypnosis is used to help patients understand the amount of control they have over their symptoms. Under hypnosis, patients can practice how to dissociate and therefore to reassociate. Patients are taught self-hypnotic techniques so they can achieve this sense of mastery and control on their own. Hypnosis can also be used to help access and explore traumatic memories and thoughts that may be triggering or perpetuating the depersonalization. Once these memories are accessed, patients are helped to reframe them and to develop more appropriate defenses, which may allow them to increase their sense of integration and control.

Pharmacotherapy of Depersonalization Disorder

The results reported are promising but inconclusive. For the most part, the rationale used to justify the use of medication addresses not the primary problem of depersonalization, but possible comorbid psychiatric conditions. In particular, depersonalization has been described as occurring in the context of both depression and anxiety. Most reports are limited to single cases or very limited samples. They are also limited by the lack of objective diagnostic methods or scales that may have helped to differentiate depersonalization from other comorbid diagnoses.

In considering somatic treatments for depersonalization, it is important to determine whether the complaint represents the primary condition or whether it is secondary to another disorder. In the latter case, the experiences of depersonalization may remit with successful treatment of the primary condition (Walsh, 1975). For example, depersonalization is a common complaint in depressive illnesses (Noyes et al., 1987) and anxiety conditions (Shorvon, 1946; Hollander et al., 1989, 1990; Steinberg, 1991; Fichtner et al., 1992), and several authors have reported success in treating depersonalization in patients with depression or panic disorder with antidepressants (i.e., fluoxetine: Fichtner et al., 1992; Hollander et al., 1989, 1990; desipramine: Noyes et al., 1987).

Sedman (1970) reported that depression scores improved as the symptoms of depersonalization improved. He cited this as evidence for the use of antidepressant medications. Walsh (1975), Noyes et al. (1987), and Hollander et al. (1989) all described improvement in patients with depersonalization after treatment with antidepressant medications. As in the case above, it appears that the symptoms of depression preceded the onset of the symptoms of depersonalization. Noyes et al. (1987) reported on a single case of depersonalization successfully treated with the tricyclic antidepressant desipramine, but they acknowledged that the episode of depersonalization followed an episode of depression.

Hollander et al. (1989) used a combination of imipramine and alprazolam in one patient suffering from severe depersonalization and panic attacks. They reported resolution of the panic attacks but no changes in the symptoms of depersonalization while on the antidepressant/anxiolytic combination. They then added fluoxetine (gradually increased up to 60 mg) and noted marked reduction in symptoms of depersonalization. They concluded that "panic and depersonalization may respond selectively to pharmacological agents" (p. 402) but it is impossible to tell if the success was due to the selective effectiveness of the fluoxetine or its additive effect in the combination with the previous agents.

Because of the similarity between the depersonalization symptoms associated with temporal lobe epilepsy and depersonalization disorder, Stein and Uhde (1989) attempted a single-blind therapeutic trial of carbamazepine and clonazepam in one subject. They found that carbamazepine was not effective in reducing the symptoms. On the other hand, clonazepam was able to achieve adequate control of chronic symptoms of depersonalization after 2 weeks of treatment (at doses up to 1 mg/day).

Nuller (1982) also described adequate response of depersonalization symptoms to phenazepam, another benzodiazepine derivative, at doses between 2 and 30 mg/day in 34 of 43 patients (79% of the sample). The diagnostic uniformity of the sample is not known.

The effectiveness of high-potency benzodiazepines, but the lack of effectiveness of anticonvulsants, may suggest an underlying mechanism in depersonalization disorder that makes it more similar to panic disorder than to epilepsy. Ballenger et al. (1988) and Spier et al. (1986) similarly found that the high-potency benzodiazepine alprazolam and the benzodiazepine-anticonvulsant clonazepam were effective in the treatment of panic disorder, while a conventional antiepileptic agent (i.e., carbamazepine) was not.

Shorvon (1946) and Davison (1964) found that a single intravenous administration of amphetamine was effective in "aborting" an episode of depersonalization in about 50% of cases. Unfortunately, about half of those who responded initially to amphetamine quickly relapsed.

The use of modern antidepressant medications, in particular the SSRIs, shows some promise. Hollander et al. (1990) reported on eight patients treated with fluoxetine. At doses of 5 to 80 mg per day, six patients were very much improved, and two were only minimally improved with no reported side effects. Unfortunately, there are no double blind-controlled studies on the use of SSRIs in depersonalization disorder. Therefore, it is difficult to predict efficacy at this time.

As in the case of antidepressants, neuroleptics have been used in noncontrolled, nonblind studies with equally confusing results. Ambrosino (1973) reported lack of favorable outcome with the use of neuroleptics. On the other hand, Nuller (1982) reported a moderately good response in 60% of his sample (9 out of 15) when clozapine was used in doses between 150 and 600 mg/day after 6 weeks of treatment.

Equally erratic are the results of electroconvulsive therapy applied to depersonalization disorder. Some reports claim that the majority of the patients did not improve or worsened following the use of ECT (Ambrosino, 1973; Davison, 1964; Roth, 1959; Shorvon, 1946). Only one study suggested improvement in depressive symptomatology following ECT, but this group demonstrated no benefits in the symptoms of depersonalization (Ambrosino, 1973).

The most important aspect of the treatment of depersonalization disorder is careful assessment of possible psychiatric comorbidity and treatment of those conditions.

CONCLUSION

The dissociative disorders represent a class of psychiatric disorders characterized by loss of control of integration of identity, memory, and consciousness, usually in the aftermath of single or multiple traumatic experiences. Effective treatments include psychotherapies designed to help patients work through traumatic memories and to access and control access to dissociative states. Techniques such as hypnosis have proven helpful, along with selective use of antianxiety and antidepressant medications for comorbid conditions. Identification and modulation of dissociative symptoms, coupled with management of related posttraumatic syndromes, have been shown to be effective treatments.

References

Abbas, S., Chandra, P. S., & Srivastava, M. (1995). The use of fluoxetine and buspirone for treatment-refractory depersonalization disorder (letter). *Journal of Clinical Psychiatry, 56,* 484.

Abeles, M., & Schilder, P. (1935). Psychogenic loss of personal identity. *Archives of Neurology and Psychiatry, 34,* 587–604.

Ackner, B. (1954). Depersonalization. 1. Aetiology and phenomenology. *Journal of Mental Science, 100,* 838–853.

Adityanjee, R. G. S. P., & Khandelwal, S. K. (1989). Current status of multiple personality disorder in India. *American Journal of Psychiatry, 146,* 1607–1610.

Akhtar, S., & Brenner, I. (1979). Differential diagnosis of fugue-like states. *Journal of Clinical Psychiatry, 40,* 381–385.

Akyüz, G., Dogan, O., Sar, V., Yargiç, L. I., & Tutkun, H. (1999). Frequency of dissociative identity disorder in the general population in Turkey. *Comprehensive Psychiatry, 40,* 151–159.

Allers, C. T., White, J. F., & Mullis, F. (1997). The treatment of dissociation in an HIV-infected, sexually abused adolescent male. *Psychotherapy, 34,* 201–206.

Allison, R. B. (1974). A new treatment approach for multiple personalities. *American Journal of Clinical Hypnosis, 17,* 15–32.

Ambrosino, S. V. (1973). Phobic anxiety-depersonalization syndrome. *New York State Journal of Medicine, 73,* 419–425.

American Psychiatric Association. (1994). *Diagnostic and statistical manual of mental disorders* (4th ed.). Washington, DC: Author.

Awas, M., Kebede, D., & Alem, A. (1999). Major mental disorders in Butajira, Southern Ethiopia. *Acta Psychiatrica Scandinavica, Suppl. 397,* 56–64.

Azam, E. E. (1887). *Hypnotisme, double conscience et alteration de la personnalite.* Paris: J. B. Balliere.

Ball, S., & Robinson, A. (1997). Dissociative symptoms in panic disorder. *Journal of Nervous and Mental Disease, 185,* 755–760.

Ballenger, J. C., Burrows, G. D., Dupont, R. L., & Lesser, I. M. (1988). Alprazolam in panic disorder and agoraphobia; Results from a multicenter trial. 1. Efficacy in short term treatment. *Archives of General Psychiatry, 45,* 413–422.

Barkin, R., Braun, B. G., & Kluft, R. P. (1986). The dilemma of drug therapy for multiple personality disorder. In B. G. Braun (Ed.), *Treatment of multiple personality disorder* (pp. 107–132). Washington DC: American Psychiatric Press.

Baron, D. A., & Nagy, R. (1988). The amobarbital interview in a general hospital setting, friend or foe: A case report. *General Hospital Psychiatry, 10,* 220–222.

Benjamin, L. R., & Benjamin, R. (1992). An overview of family treatment in dissociative disorders. *Dissociation, 5,* 236–241.

Benjamin, L. R., & Benjamin, R. (1993). Interventions with children in dissociative families: A family treatment model. *Dissociation, 6,* 54–65.

Benjamin, L. R., & Benjamin, R. (1994a). A group for partners and parents of MPD clients. 1. Process and format. *Dissociation, 7,* 35–43.

Benjamin, L. R., & Benjamin, R. (1994b). A group for partners and parents of MPD clients. 3. Marital types and dynamics. *Dissociation, 7,* 191–196.

Bernstein, E. M., & Putnam, F. W. (1986). Development, reliability, and validity of a dissociation scale. *Journal of Nervous and Mental Disease, 174,* 727–735.

Berrington, W. P., Liddell, D. W., & Foulds, G. A. (1956). A re-evaluation of the fugue. *Journal of Mental Science, 102,* 280–286.

Bezzubova, E. B. (1991). Clinical characteristics of vital depersonalization in schizophrenia. *Zb Neuropatol Psikhitr, 91,* 83–86.

Blank, H. R. (1954). Depression, hypomania, and depersonalization. *Psychoanalytic Quarterly,* 23, 20–37.

Bliss, E. L. (1980). Multiple personalities: A report of 14 cases with implications for schizophrenia and hysteria. *Archives of General Psychiatry,* 37, 1388–1397.

Bliss, E. L. (1984). A symptom profile of patients with multiple personalities, including MMPI results. *Journal of Nervous and Mental Disease, 172,* 197–202.

Bliss, E. L. (1986). *Multiple personality, allied disorders, and hypnosis.* New York: Oxford University Press.

Bliss, E. L., Clark, L., & West, C. (1959). Studies of sleep deprivation: Relationship to schizophrenia. *Archives of Neurological Psychiatry, 81,* 348–359.

Bliss, E. L., & Jeppsen, E. A. (1985). Prevalence of multiple personality among inpatients and outpatients. *American Journal of Psychiatry, 142,* 250–251.

Bliss, E. L., Larson, E. M., & Nakashima, S. R. (1983). Auditory hallucinations and schizophrenia. *Journal of Nervous and Mental Disease, 171,* 30–33.

Blue, F. R. (1979). Use of directive therapy in the treatment of depersonalization neurosis. *Psychological Reports, 49,* 904–906.

Bohus, M. J., Landwehrmeyer, G. B., Stiglmayr, C. E., Limberger, M. F., Böhme, R., & Schmahl, C. G. (1999). Naltrexone in the treatment of dissociative symptoms in patients with borderline personality disorder: An open-label trial. *Journal of Clinical Psychiatry, 60,* 598–603.

Boon, S., & Draijer, N. (1993). *Multiple personality disorder in the Netherlands: A study on reliability and validity of the diagnosis.* Amsterdam: Swets & Zeitlinger.

Bower, G. H. (1981). Mood and memory. *American Psychologist, 36,* 129–141.

Bowman, E. S., & Coons, P. M. (1992). The use of electroconvulsive therapy in patients with dissociative disorders. *Journal of Nervous and Mental Disease, 180,* 524–528.

Brauer, R., Harrow, M., & Tucker, G. J. (1970). Depersonalization phenomena in psychiatric patients. *British Journal of Psychiatry, 117,* 509–515.

Braun, B. G. (1983). Psychophysiologic phenomena in multiple personality and hypnosis. *American Journal of Clinical Hypnosis, 26,* 124–137.

Braun, B. G. (1985). The transgenerational incidence of dissociation and multiple personality disorder: A preliminary report. In R. P. Kluft (Ed.), *Childhood antecedents of multiple personality* (pp. 128–150). Washington, DC: American Psychiatric Press.

Braun, B. G. (1990). Multiple personality disorder: An overview. *American Journal of Occupational Therapy, 44,* 971–976.

Braun, P., Greenberg, D., Dasberg, H., & Lerer, B. (1990). Core symptoms of posttraumatic stress disorder unimproved by alprazolam treatment. *Journal of Clinical Psychiatry, 51,* 236–238.

Bremner, J. D., Krystal, J. H., Charney, D. S., & Southwick, S. M. (1996). Neural mechanisms in dissociative amnesia for childhood abuse: Relevance to the current controversy surrounding the "false memory syndrome." *American Journal of Psychiatry, 153,* 71–82.

Bremner, J. D., Krystal, J. H., Putnam, F. W., Southwick, S. M., Marmar, C., Charney, D. S., & Mazure, C. M. (1998). Measurement of dissociative states with the Clinician-Administered Dissociative States Scale (CADSS). *Journal of Trauma and Stress, 11,* 125–136.

Bremner, J. D., Southwick, S., Brett, E., Fontana, A., Rosenheck, R., & Charney, D. S. (1992). Dissociation and posttraumatic stress disorder in Vietnam combat veterans. *American Journal of Psychiatry, 149,* 328–332.

Brenner, I. (1996). The characterological basis of multiple personality. *American Journal of Psychotherapy, 50,* 154–66.

Brown, G. R., & Anderson, B. (1991). Psychiatric morbidity in adult inpatients with childhood histories of sexual and physical abuse. *American Journal of Psychiatry, 148,* 55–61.

Brown, L., Russell, J., Thornton, C., & Dunn, S. (1999). Dissociation, abuse and the eating disorders: Evidence from an Australian population. *Australian and New Zealand Journal of Psychiatry,* 33, 521–528.

Brown, P., van der Hart, O., & Graafland, M. (1999). Trauma-induced dissociative amnesia in World War I combat soldiers. 2. Treatment dimensions. *Australian and New Zealand Journal of Psychiatry,* 33, 392–398.

Brown, W. (1918). The treatment of cases of shell shock in an advanced neurological centre. *Lancet,* 197–200.

Brown, W. (1919). Hypnosis, suggestion and dissociation. *British Medical Journal, 191,* 734–736.

Brunner, R., Parzer, P., Schuld, V., & Resch, F. (2000). Dissociative symptomatology and traumatogenic factors in adolescent psychiatric patients. *Journal of Nervous and Mental Disease, 188,* 71–77.

Bryant, R. A., Sackville, T., Dang, S. T., Moulds, M., & Guthrie, R. (1999). Treating acute stress disorder: An evaluation of cognitive behavior therapy and supportive counseling techniques. *American Journal of Psychiatry, 156*, 1780–1786.

Bryer, J. B., Nelson, B. A., Miller, J. B., & Krol, P. A. (1987). Childhood sexual and physical abuse as factors in adult psychiatric illness. *American Journal of Psychiatry, 144*, 1426–1430.

Butler, L. D., Duran, R. E. F., Jasiukaitis, P., Koopman, C., & Spiegel, D. (1996). Hypnotizability and traumatic experience: A diathesis-stress model of dissociative symptomatology. *American Journal of Psychiatry, 153*(Suppl.), 42–63.

Butzel, J. S., Talbot, N. L., Duberstein, P. R., Houghtalen, R. P., Cox, C., & Giles, D. E. (2000). The relationship between traumatic events and dissociation among women with histories of childhood sexual abuse. *Journal of Nervous and Mental Disease, 188*, 547–549.

Cantagallo, A., Grassi, L., & Della Sala, S. (1999). Dissociative disorder after traumatic brain injury. *Brain Injury, 13*, 219–228.

Carlier, I. V., Lamberts, R. D., Fouwels, A. J., & Gersons, B. P. (1996). PTSD in relation to dissociation in traumatized police officers. *American Journal of Psychiatry, 153*, 1325–1328.

Carlson, E. T. (1981). The history of multiple personality disorder in the United States. *American Journal of Psychiatry, 138*, 666–668.

Castillo, R. J. (1990). Depersonalization and meditation. *Psychiatry, 53*, 158–168.

Cattell, J. P., & Cattell, J. S. (1974). Depersonalization: Psychological and social perspectives. In S. Arieti (Ed.), *American Handbook of Psychiatry* (pp. 767–799). New York: Basic Books.

Caul, D. (1984). Group and videotape techniques for multiple personality. *Psychiatric Annals, 14*, 43–50.

Caul, D., Sachs, R. G., & Braun, B. G. (1986). Group psychotherapy in treatment of multiple personality disorder. In B. G. Braun (Ed.), *Treatment of multiple personality disorder* (pp. 145–156). Washington, DC: American Psychiatric Press.

Chee, K. T., & Wong, K. E. (1990). Depersonalization syndrome—A report of 9 cases. *Singapore Medical Journal, 31*, 331–334.

Chiappa, F. (1994). Effective management of family and individual interventions in the treatment of dissociative disorders. *Dissociation, 7*, 185–190.

Chodoff, P. (1997). Turkish dissociative identity disorder. *American Journal of Psychiatry, 154*, 1179.

Chu, D. A., & Dill, D. L. (1990). Dissociative symptoms in relation to childhood physical and sexual abuse. *American Journal of Psychiatry 147*, 887–892.

Chu, J. A., Frey, L. M., Ganzel, B. L., & Matthews, J. A. (1999). Memories of childhood abuse: Dissociation, amnesia, and corroboration. *American Journal of Psychiatry, 156*, 749–755.

Cohen, S. (1988). The pathogenesis of depersonalization: A hypothesis. *British Journal of Psychiatry, 152*, 578.

Coons, P. M. (1984). The differential diagnosis of multiple personality: A comprehensive review. *Psychiatric Clinics of North America, 7*, 51–65.

Coons, P. M. (1985). Children of parents with multiple personality disorder. In R. P. Kluft (Ed.), *Childhood antecedents of multiple personality* (pp. 151–165). Washington, DC: American Psychiatric Press.

Coons, P. M. (1986). Treatment progress in 20 patients with multiple personality disorder. *Journal of Nervous and Mental Disease, 174*, 715–721.

Coons, P. M. (1998). The dissociative disorders. Rarely considered and underdiagnosed. *Psychiatric Clinics of North America, 21*, 637–648.

Coons, P. M., Bowman, E. S., Kluft, R. P., & Milstein, V. (1991). The cross-cultural occurrence of MPD: Additional cases from a recent survey. *Dissociation, 4*, 124–128

Coons, P. M., Bowman, E. S., & Milstein, V. (1988). Multiple personality disorder: A clinical investigation of 50 cases. *Journal of Nervous and Mental Disease, 17*, 519–527.

Coons, P. M., Bowman, E. S., & Pellow, T. A. (1989). Post-traumatic aspects of the treatment of victims of sexual abuse and incest. *Psychiatric Clinics of North America, 12*, 325–337.

Coons, P. M., & Bradley, K. (1985). Group psychotherapy with multiple personality disorder patients. *Journal of Nervous and Mental Disease, 173*, 515–521.

Coons, P. M. & Millstein, V. (1992). Psychogenic amnesia: A clinical investigation of 25 cases. *Dissociation, 5*, 73–79.

Coons, P. M., & Sterne, A. L. (1986). Initial and follow-up psychological testing on a group of patients with multiple personality disorder. *Psychological Reports, 58*, 43–49.

Darves Bornoz, J. M., Berger, C., Degiovanni, A., Gaillard, P., & Lépine, J. P. (1999). Similarities and differences between incestuous and nonincestuous rape in a French follow-up study. *Journal of Trauma and Stress, 12*, 613–623.

Davison, K. (1964). Episodic depersonalization: Observations on 7 patients. *British Journal of Psychiatry, 110*, 505–513.

DeBattista, C., & Solvason, H. B. (1998). ECT in dissociative identity disorder and comorbid depression. *Journal of ECT, 14*, 275–279.

Devinsky, O., Feldmann, O., Burrowes, K., & Bromfield, E. (1989). Autoscopic phenomena with seizures. *Archives of Neurology, 46*, 1080–1088.

Devinsky, O., Putnam, F. W., Grafman, J., Bromfield, E., & Theodore, W. H. (1988). *Dissociative states and epilepsy*. Unpublished manuscript.

Diamond, B. L. (1980). Inherent problems in the use of pre-trial hypnosis on a prospective witness. *California Law Review, 68,* 313–349.

Dixon, J. C. (1963). Depersonalization phenomena in a sample population of college students. *British Journal of Psychiatry, 109,* 371–375.

Dollinger, S. (1983). A case report of dissociative neurosis (depersonalization disorder) in an adolescent treated with family therapy and behavior modification. *Journal of Consulting and Clinical Psychology, 51,* 479–484.

Draijer, N., & Langeland, W. (1999). Childhood trauma and perceived parental dysfunction in the etiology of dissociative symptoms in psychiatric inpatients. *American Journal of Psychiatry, 156,* 379–385.

Dywan, S., & Bowers, K. S. (1983). The use of hypnosis to enhance recall. *Science, 222,* 184–185.

Edinger, J. D. (1985). Relaxation and depersonalization. *British Journal of Psychiatry, 146,* 103.

Ellason, J. W., & Ross, C. A. (1995). Positive and negative symptoms in dissociative identity disorder and schizophrenia: A comparative analysis. *Journal of Nervous and Mental Disease, 183,* 236–241.

Ellason, J. W., & Ross, C. A. (1997). Two-year follow-up of inpatients with dissociative identity disorder. *American Journal of Psychiatry, 154,* 832–839.

Ellenberger, H. F. (1970). *The discovery of the unconscious: The history and evolution of dynamic psychiatry*. New York: Basic Books.

Elliott, G. C., Rosenberg, M., & Wagner, M. (1984). Transient depersonalization in youth. *Social Psychology Quarterly, 47,* 115–129.

Eriksson, N. G., & Lundin, T. (1996). Early traumatic stress reactions among Swedish survivors of the m/s Estonia disaster. *British Journal of Psychiatry, 169,* 713–716.

Fagan, J., & McMahon, P. P. (1984). Incipient multiple personality disorder in children. *Journal of Nervous and Mental Disease, 172,* 26–36.

Fast, I., & Chethik, M. (1976). Aspects of depersonalization-derealization in the experience of children. *International Review of Psychoanalysis, 3,* 483–490.

Fesler, F. A. (1991). Valproate in combat-related posttraumatic stress disorder. *Journal of Clinical Psychiatry, 52,* 361–364.

Fewtrell, W. D. (1984). Relaxation and depersonalization. *British Journal of Psychiatry, 145,* 217.

Fewtrell, W. (1986). Depersonalization: A description and suggested strategies. *British Journal of Guidance and Counseling, 14,* 263–269.

Fichtner, C. G., Horevitz, R. P., & Braun, B. G. (1992). Fluoxetine in depersonalization disorder (letter). *American Journal of Psychiatry, 149,* 1750–1751.

Fichtner, C. G., Kuhlman, D. T., Gruenfeld, M. J., & Hughes, J. R. (1990). Decreased episodic violence and increased control of dissociation in a carbamazepine-treated case of multiple personality. *Biological Psychiatry, 27,* 1045–1052.

Fine, C. G. (1989). Treatment errors and iatrogenesis across therapeutic modalities in MPD and allied dissociative disorders. *Dissociation, 2,* 77–82.

Fine, C. G. (1991). Treatment stabilization and crisis prevention: Pacing the therapy of the MPD and allied dissociative disorders. *Dissociation, 2,* 77–82.

Fine, C. G. (1999). The tactical-integration model for the treatment of dissociative identity disorder and allied dissociative disorders. *American Journal of Psychotherapy, 53,* 361–376.

Finkelhor, D. (1984). *Child sexual abuse: New theory and research*. New York: Free Press.

Fisher, C. (1945). Amnesic states in war neuroses: The psychogenesis of fugue. *Psychoanalytic Quarterly, 14,* 437–468.

Fisher, C., & Joseph, E. D. (1949). Fugue with awareness of loss of personal identity. *Psychoanalytic Quarterly, 18,* 480–493.

Forbes, D., Creamer, M., & Rycroft, P. (1994). Eye movement desensitization and reprocessing in posttraumatic stress disorder: A pilot study using assessment measures. *Journal of Behavior Therapy and Experimental Psychiatry, 25,* 113–120.

Frances, A., Sacks, M., & Aronoff, M. (1977). Depersonalization: A self relations perspective. *International Journal of Psychoanalysis, 58,* 325–331.

Frank, J. B., Kosten, T. R., Giller, E. L., & Dan, E. (1988). A randomized clinical trial of phenelzine and imipramine for posttraumatic stress disorder. *American Journal of Psychiatry, 145,* 1289–1291.

Frankel, F. H. (1995). Discovering new memories in psychotherapy—Childhood revisited, fantasy, or both? *New England Journal of Medicine, 333,* 591–594.

Frankel, F. H. (1996). Dissociation: The clinical realities. *American Journal of Psychiatry, 153,* 64–70.

Fraser, G. A., & Lapierre, Y. D. (1986). Lactate-induced panic attacks in dissociative states (multiple personalities). In B. G. Braun (Ed.), *Proceedings of the international conference on multiple personality/dissociative states* (p. 124). Chicago: Rush-Presbyterian-St. Luke's Medical Center.

Friedl, M. C., & Draijer, N. (2000). Dissociative disorders in Dutch psychiatric inpatients. *American Journal of Psychiatry, 157,* 1012–1013.

Friedman, M. (1988). Toward rational pharmacotherapy for post-traumatic stress disorder. *American Journal of Psychiatry, 145,* 281–285.

Friedman, M. (1991). Biological approaches to the diagnosis and treatment of post-traumatic stress disorder. *Journal of Traumatic Stress, 4,* 67–91.

Fukunishi, I., Ogino, M., Suzuki, J., Hasegawa, A., Ohara, T., Aikawa, A., & Suzaki, M. (1997). Kidney transplantation and liaison psychiatry, part II: A case of dissociative identity disorder. *Psychiatry and Clinical Neuroscience, 51,* 305–308.

Fukuzako, H., Fukuzaki, S., Fukuzako, T., Jing, H., Ueyama, K., & Takigawa, M. (1999). P300 event-related potentials in probable dissociative generalized amnesia. *Progress in Neuropsychopharmacology and Biological Psychiatry, 23,* 1319–1327.

Fullerton, C. S., Ursano, R. J., Epstein, R. S., Crowley, B., Vance, K. L., Kao, T. C., & Baum, A. (2000). Peritraumatic dissociation following motor vehicle accidents: Relationship to prior trauma and prior major depression. *Journal of Nervous and Mental Disease, 188,* 267–272.

Gabbard, G. O. (2000). Dissociative disorders. *Psychodynamic psychiatry in clinical practice.* Washington, DC: American Psychiatric Press.

Ganaway, G. K. (1989). Historical versus narrative truth: Clarifying the role of exogenous trauma in the etiology of MPD and its variants. *Dissociation, 2,* 205–220.

Ganaway, G. K. (1995). Hypnosis, childhood trauma, and dissociative identity disorder. *International Journal of Clinical and Experimental Hypnosis, 43,* 127–144.

Gelb, J. L. (1993). Multiple personality disorder and satanic ritual abuse. *Australian and New Zealand Journal of Psychiatry, 27,* 701–708.

Giese, A. A., Thomas, M. R., & Dubovsky, S. L. (1997). Dissociative symptoms in psychotic mood disorders: An example of symptom nonspecificity. *Psychiatry, 60,* 60–66.

Gleaves, D. H. (1996). The sociocognitive model of dissociative identity disorder: A reexamination of the evidence. *Psychological Bulletin, 120,* 42–59.

Good, M. (1989). Substance induced dissociative disorders and psychiatric nosology. *Journal of Clinical Psychopharmacology, 9,* 88–93.

Goodwin, J. (1982). *Sexual abuse: Incest victims and their families.* Boston: Wright/PSG.

Grabe, H. J., Spitzer, C., & Freyberger, H. (1999). Relationship of dissociation to temperament and character in men and women. *American Journal of Psychiatry, 156,* 1811–1813.

Greaves, G. B. (1980). Multiple personality: 165 years after Mary Reynolds. *Journal of Nervous and Mental Disease, 168,* 577–596.

Greyson, B. (2000). Dissociation in people who have near-death experiences: Out of their bodies or out of their minds? *Lancet, 355,* 460–463.

Grigsby, J. P., & Johnson, C. L. (1989). Depersonalization, vertigo and Meniere's disease. *Psychological Reports, 64,* 527–534.

Grinker, R. B., & Spiegel, J. P. (1945). *Men under stress.* Philadelphia: Blakiston.

Guttmann, E., & Maclay, W. S. (1936). Mescalin and depersonalization. *International Journal of Psychoanalysis, 41,* 193–212.

Hacking, I. (1996). Les alienes voyageurs: How fugue became a medical entity. *History of Psychiatry, 7,* 425–449.

Hammond, D. C., Garver, R. B., Mutter, C. B., Crasilneck, H. B., Frischholz, E., Gravitz, M. A., Hibler, N. S., Olson, J., Scheflin, A., Spiegel, H., & Wester, W. (1995). *Clinical hypnosis and memory: Guidelines for clinicians and for forensic hypnosis.* Washington, DC: American Society of Clinical Hypnosis Press.

Harper, H., & Roth, M. (1962). Temporal lobe epilepsy and the phobic-anxiety-depersonalization syndrome. 1. A comparative study. *Comprehensive Psychiatry, 3,* 129–151.

Hilgard, E. R. (1977). *Divided consciousness: Multiple controls in human thoughts and action.* New York: Wiley.

Hocke, V., & Schmidtke, A. (1998). Multiple personality disorder in childhood and adolescence. *Journal of Child and Adolescent Psychotherapy, 26,* 273–284.

Hollander, E., Fairbanks, J., Decaria, C., & Liebowitz, M. R. (1989). Pharmacological dissection of panic and depersonalization. *American Journal of Psychiatry, 146,* 402.

Hollander, E., Liebowitz, M. R., Decaria, C., Fairbanks, J., Fallon, B., & Klein, D. F. (1990). Treatment of depersonalization with serotonin reuptake blockers. *Journal of Clinical Psychopharmacology, 10,* 200–203.

Horen, S. A., Leichner, P. P., & Lawson, J. S. (1995). Prevalence of dissociative symptoms and disorders in an adult psychiatric inpatient population in Canada. *Canadian Journal of Psychiatry, 40,* 185–191.

Horevitz, R. P., & Braun, B. G. (1984). Are multiple personalities borderline? *Psychiatric Clinics of North America, 7,* 69–88.

Hornstein, N., & Putnam, F. W. (1992). Clinical phenomenology of child and adolescent dissociative disorders. *Journal of the Academy of Child and Adolescent Psychiatry, 31,* 1077–1085.

Horowitz, M. J. (1964). Depersonalization in spacemen and submarines. *Military Medicine, 129,* 1058–1060.

Horsley, J. S. (1943). *Narcoanalysis.* New York: Oxford Medical Publications.

Hunter, R. C. A. (1966). The analysis of episodes of depersonalization in a borderline patient. *International Journal of Psychoanalysis, 47,* 32–41.

Hurwitz, T. A. (1988). Narcosuggestion in chronic conversion symptoms using combined intravenous amobarbital and methylphenidate. *Canadian Journal of Psychiatry, 33,* 147–152.

Irwin, H. J. (1999). Pathological and nonpathological dissociation: The relevance of childhood trauma. *Journal of Psychology, 133,* 157–164.

James, I. P. (1961). The phobic-anxiety-depersonalization syndrome. *American Journal of Psychiatry, 118,* 163–164.

Jang, K. L., Paris, J., Zweig, F. H., & Livesley, W. J. (1998). Twin study of dissociative experience. *Journal of Nervous and Mental Disease, 186,* 345–351.

Kapur, N. (1991). Amnesia in relation to fugue states—Distinguishing a neurological from a psychogenic basis. *British Journal of Psychiatry, 159,* 872–877.

Kardiner, A., & Spiegel, H. (1947). *War, stress and neurotic illness.* New York: Hoeber.

Kenna, J. C., & Sedman, G. (1965). Depersonalization in temporal lobe epilepsy and the organic psychoses. *British Journal of Psychiatry, 111,* 293–299.

Kennedy, R. B. (1976). Self-induced depersonalization syndrome. *American Journal of Psychiatry, 133,* 1321–1328.

Kennedy, R. B., & Neville, J. (1957). Sudden loss of memory. *British Journal of Medicine, 2,* 428–433.

Kennerley, H. (1996). Cognitive therapy of dissociative symptoms associated with trauma. *British Journal of Clinical Psychology, 35,* 325–340.

Kilhstrom, J. F. (1984). Conscious, subconscious, unconscious: A cognitive perspective. In H. S. Bowers & D. Meichenbaum (Eds.), *The unconscious reconsidered* (pp. 149–211). New York: Wiley.

Kihlstrom, J. F., & Hoyt, I. P. (1990). Repression, dissociation, and hypnosis. In J. L. Singer (Ed.), *Repression and dissociation: Implications for personality theory, psychopathology, and health.* Chicago: University of Chicago Press.

Kirshner, L. A. (1973). Dissociative reactions: An historical review and clinical study. *Acta Psychiatrica Scandinavica, 49,* 696–711.

Kitchner, L., & Greenstein, R. (1985). Low dose lithium carbonate in the treatment of post traumatic stress disorder. *Military Medicine, 150,* 378–381.

Kluft, R. P. (1982). Varieties of hypnotic interventions in the treatment of multiple personality. *American Journal of Clinical Hypnosis, 24,* 230–240.

Kluft, R. P. (1984a). Aspects of the treatment of multiple personality disorder. *Psychiatric Annals, 14,* 51–55.

Kluft, R. P. (1984b). An introduction to multiple personality disorder. *Psychiatric Annals, 14,* 19–24.

Kluft, R. P. (1984c). Treatment of multiple personality disorder: A study of 33 cases. *Psychiatric Clinics of North America, 7,* 9–29.

Kluft, R. P. (1985a). Childhood multiple personality disorder: Predictors, clinical findings, and treatment results. In R. P. Kluft (Ed.), *Childhood antecedents of multiple personality* (pp. 167–196). Washington, DC: American Psychiatric Press.

Kluft, R. P. (1985b). The natural history of multiple personality disorder. In R. P. Kluft (Ed.), *Childhood antecedents of multiple personality* (pp. 197–238). Washington, DC: American Psychiatric Press.

Kluft, R. P. (1985c). The treatment of multiple personality disorder (MPD): Current concepts. In F. F. Flach (Ed.), *Directions in psychiatry.* New York: Hatherleigh.

Kluft, R. P. (1986a). Personality unification in multiple personality disorder: A follow-up study. In B. G. Braun (Ed.), *Treatment of multiple personality disorder* (pp. 31–60). Washington, DC: American Psychiatric Press.

Kluft, R. P. (1986b). Treating children with multiple personality disorder. In B. G. Braun (Ed.), *Treatment of multiple personality disorder* (pp. 79–105). Washington, DC: American Psychiatric Press.

Kluft, R. P. (1987a). First-rank symptoms as a diagnostic clue to multiple personality disorder. *American Journal of Psychiatry, 144,* 293–298.

Kluft, R. P. (1987b). Multiple personality disorder: An update. *Hospital and Community Psychiatry, 38,* 363–373.

Kluft, R. P. (1988). The dissociative disorders. In J. A. Talbot, R. E. Hales, & S. C. Yudofsky (Eds.), *Textbook of psychiatry* (pp. 557–585). Washington, DC: American Psychiatric Press.

Kluft, R. P. (1989). Iatrogenic creation of new alter personalities. *Dissociation, 2,* 83–91.

Kluft, R. P. (1991). Clinical presentations of multiple personality disorder. *Psychiatric Clinics of North America, 14,* 605–630.

Kluft, R. P. (1993). The treatment of dissociative patients: An overview of discoveries, successes, and failures. *Dissociation, 6,* 87–101.

Kluft, R. P. (1994). Treatment trajectories in multiple personality disorder. *Dissociation, 7,* 63–75.

Kluft, R. P. (1996). Dissociative identity disorder. In L. K. Michelson & W. J. Ray (Eds.), *Handbook of dissociation: Theoretical, empirical and clinical perspectives* (pp. 337–366). New York: Plenum Press.

Kluft, R. P. (1999). Current issues in dissociative identity disorder. *Journal of Practical Psychology and Behavioral Health, 5,* 3–19.

Kluft, R. P., & Schultz, R. (1993). Multiple personality disorder in adolescence. In S. C. Fienstein & R. C. Marohn (Eds.), *Adolescent psychiatry* (pp. 259–279). Chicago: University of Chicago Press.

Kolb, L. C. (1985). The place of narcosynthesis in the treatment of chronic and delayed stress reactions of war. In S. M. Sonnenberg, A. S. Blank, & J. A. Talbott (Eds.), *The trauma of war.* Washington, DC: American Psychiatric Press.

Kolb, L., Burris, B., & Griffiths, S. (1984). Propranolol and clonidine in the treatment of the chronic post traumatic stress disorder of war. In B. A. van der Kolk (Ed.), *Post-traumatic stress disorder: Psychological and biological sequelae.* Washington, DC: American Psychiatric Press.

Koopman, C., Classen, C., & Spiegel, D. (1996). Dissociative responses in the immediate aftermath of the Oakland/Berkeley firestorm. *Journal of Trauma and Stress, 9,* 521–540.

Kosten, T. R., Mason, J. W., Giller, E. L., Ostroff R. B., & Harkness L. (1987). Sustained urinary norepinephrine and epinephrine elevation in posttraumatic stress disorder. *Psychoneuroendocrinology, 12,* 13–30.

Laurence, J. R., & Perry, C. (1983). Hypnotically created memory among highly hypnotizable subjects. *Science, 222,* 523–524.

Leavitt, F., & Labott, S. M. (1998). Rorschach indicators of dissociative identity disorders: Clinical utility and theoretical implications. *Journal of Clinical Psychology, 54,* 803–810.

Lego, S. (1996). Repressed memory and false memory. *Archives of Psychiatric Nursing, 10,* 110–115.

Lehmann, L. (1974). Depersonalization. *American Journal of Psychiatry, 131,* 1221–1224.

Lewis, D. O., Yeager, C. A., Swica, Y., Pincus, J. H., & Lewis, M. (1997). Objective documentation of child abuse and dissociation in 12 murderers with dissociative identity disorder. *American Journal of Psychiatry, 154,* 1703–1710.

Lindemann, E. (1994). Symptomatology and management of acute grief. *American Journal of Psychiatry, 151,* 155–160.

Lipper, S. (1988). PTSD and carbamazepine. *American Journal of Psychiatry, 145,* 1322–1323.

Lipschitz, D. S., Kaplan, M. L., Sorkenn, J., Chorney, P., & Asnis, G. M. (1996). Childhood abuse, adult assault, and dissociation. *Comprehensive Psychiatry, 37,* 261–266.

Lishman, A. W. (1987). *Organic psychiatry* (2nd ed.). Oxford, UK: Blackwell Scientific Publications.

Loewenstein, R. J. (1991). Psychogenic amnesia and psychogenic fugue: A comprehensive review. In A. Tasman & S. M. Goldfinger (Eds.), *American Psychiatric Press review of psychiatry* (pp. 189–222). Washington, DC: American Psychiatric Press.

Loewenstein, R. J. (1994). Diagnosis, epidemiology, clinical course, treatment, and cost effectiveness of treatment of dissociative disorders and MPD: Report submitted to the Clinton Administration Task Force on Health Care Financing Reform. *Dissociation, 7,* 3–11.

Loewenstein, R. J. (1995). Dissociative amnesia and dissociative fugue. In G. O. Gabbard (Ed.), *Treatment of psychiatric disorders* (pp. 1570–1597). Washington, DC: American Psychiatric Press.

Loewenstein, R. J., Hornstein, N., & Farber, B. (1988). Open trial of clonazepam in the treatment of posttraumatic stress symptoms in MPD. *Dissociation, 1,* 3–12.

Ludwig, A. M., Brandsma, J. M., Wilbur, C. B., Bendfeldt, F., & Jameson, D. H. (1972). The objective study of a multiple personality. Or, are four heads better than one? *Archives of General Psychiatry, 26,* 298–310.

Luparello, T. J. (1970). Features of fugue: A unified hypothesis of regression. *Journal of the American Psychoanalytic Association, 18,* 379–398.

Lussier, R. G., Steiner, J., Grey, A., & Hansen, C. (1997). Prevalence of dissociative disorders in an acute care day hospital population. *Psychiatric Services, 48,* 244–246.

Macleod, A. D. (1999). Posttraumatic stress disorder, dissociative fugue and a locator beacon. *Australian and New Zealand Journal of Psychiatry, 33,* 102–104.

Maercker, A., & Schützwohl, M. (1997). Long-term effects of political imprisonment: A group comparison study. *Social Psychiatry and Psychiatric Epidemiology, 32,* 435–442.

Maldonado, J. R., Butler, L. D., & Spiegel, D. (1998). Treatment of dissociative disorders. In P. E. Nathan & J. M. Gorman (Eds.), *Treatments that work* (pp. 423–446). New York: Oxford University Press.

Maldonado, J. R., & Spiegel, D. (1994). Treatment of post traumatic stress disorder. In S. J. Lynn & R. Rhue (Eds.), *Dissociation: Clinical, theoretical and research perspectives* (pp. 215–241). New York: Guilford Press.

Maldonado, J. R., & Spiegel, D. (1995). Using hypnosis. In C. Classen (Ed.), *Treating women molested in childhood* (pp. 163–186). San Francisco: Jossey-Bass.

Maldonado, J. R., & Spiegel, D. (1997). Trauma, dissociation and hypnotizability. In R. Marmar & D.

Bremmer (Eds.), *Trauma, memory and dissociation*. Washington, DC: American Psychiatric Press.

Maldonado, J. R., & Spiegel, D. (1996). Hypnosis. In K. Tashman & H. Lieberman (Eds.), *Psychiatry* (pp. 1475–1499). Philadelphia: Saunders.

Marcos, L. R., & Trujillo, M. (1978). The sodium amytal interview as a therapeutic modality. *Current Psychiatric Therapies, 18*, 129–136.

Martínez-Taboas, A., & Bernal, G. (2000). Dissociation, psychopathology, and abusive experiences in a nonclinical Latino university student group. *Cultural Diversity and Ethnic Minority Psychology, 6*, 32–41.

Martínez-Taboas, A., & Rodríguez-Cay, J. R. (1997). Case study of a Puerto Rican woman with dissociative identity disorder. *Dissociation, 10*, 141–147.

Mathew, R. J., Wilson, W. H., Humphreys, D., Lowe, J. V., & Weithe, K. E. (1993). Depersonalization after marijuana smoking. *Biological Psychiatry, 33*, 431–441.

Mayer-Gross, W. (1935). On depersonalization. *British Journal of Medical Psychology, 15*, 103–126.

Mayer-Gross, W., Slater, E., & Roth, M. (1969). *Clinical psychiatry*. London: Bailliere, Tindal & Cassell.

McCall, W. V. (1992). The addition of intravenous caffeine during an amobarbital interview. *Journal of Psychiatry and Neuroscience, 17*, 195–197.

McConkey, K. M. (1992). The effects of hypnotic procedures on remembering. In E. Fromm & M. R. Nash (Eds.), *Contemporary hypnosis research* (pp. 405–426). New York: Guilford Press.

McDowell, D. M., Levin, F. R., & Nunes, E. V. (1999). Dissociative identity disorder and substance abuse: The forgotten relationship. *Journal of Psychoactive Drugs, 31*, 71–83.

McHugh, P. (1995a). Dissociative identity disorder as a socially constructed artifact. *Journal of Practical Psychiatry and Behavioral Health, 1*, 158–166.

McHugh, P. R. (1995b). Witches, multiple personalities, and other psychiatric artifacts. *Nature Medicine, 1*, 110–114.

Meares, R., & Grose, D. (1978). On depersonalization in adolescence: A consideration from the viewpoints of habituation and "identity." *British Journal of Medical Psychology, 51*, 335–342.

Melges, F. T., Tinklenberg, J. R., Hollister, L. E., & Gillespie, H. K. (1970). Temporal disintegration and depersonalization during marijuana intoxication. *Archives of General Psychiatry, 23*, 204–210.

Mersky, H., & Piper, A. (1998). Treatment of dissociative identity disorder (letter). *American Journal of Psychiatry, 155*, 1462.

Mesulam, M. M. (1981). Dissociative states with abnormal temporal lobe EEG: Multiple personality and the illusion of possession. *Archives of Neurology, 38*, 178–181.

Meyer, J. E. (1961). Depersonalization in adolescence. *Psychiatry, 24*, 537–560.

Middleton, W., & Butler, J. (1998). Dissociative identity disorder: An Australian series. *Australian and New Zealand Journal of Psychiatry, 32*, 794–804.

Mihaescu, G., Vanderlinden, J., Sechaud, M., Heinze, X., Velardi, A., Finot, S. C., & Baettig, D. (1998). The Dissociation Questionnaire DIS-Q: Preliminary results with a French-speaking Swiss population. *Encephale, 24*, 337–346.

Mitchell, S. W. (1888). Mary Reynolds: A case of double consciousness. *Transactions of the College of Physicians of Philadelphia, 10*, 366–389.

Modestin, J., Ebner, G., Junghan, M., & Erni, T. (1996). Dissociative experiences and dissociative disorders in acute psychiatric inpatients. *Comprehensive Psychiatry, 37*, 355–361.

Moran, C. (1986). Depersonalization and agoraphobia associated with marijuana use. *British Journal of Medical Psychology, 59*, 187–196.

Morgan, A. H., & Hilgard, E. R. (1973). Age differences in susceptibility to hypnosis. *International Journal of Clinical and Experimental Hypnosis, 21*, 78–85.

Mulder, R. T., Beautrais, A. L., Joyce, P. R., & Fergusson, D. M. (1998). Relationship between dissociation, childhood sexual abuse, childhood physical abuse, and mental illness in a general population sample. *American Journal of Psychiatry, 155*, 806–811.

Myers, D. H., & Grant, G. (1970). A study of depersonalization in students. *British Journal of Medical Psychology, 121*, 59–65.

Naples, M., & Hackett, T. (1978). The amytal interview: History and current uses. *Psychosomatics, 19*, 98–105.

Nemiah, J. C. (1989). Dissociative disorders (Hysterical neuroses, dissociative type). In H. I. Kaplan & B. J. Sadock (Eds.), *Comprehensive textbook of psychiatry* (pp. 1028–1044). Baltimore: Williams & Wilkins.

Nijenhuis, E. R., Spinhoven, P., Van Dyck, R., Van der Hart, O., & Vanderlinden, J. (1996). The development and psychometric characteristics of the Somatoform Dissociation Questionnaire (SDQ-20). *Journal of Nervous and Mental Disease, 184*, 688–694.

Nijenhuis, E. R., Spinhoven, P., van Dyck, R., van der Hart, O., & Vanderlinden, J. (1997). The development of the somatoform dissociation questionnaire (SDQ-5) as a screening instrument for dissociative disorders. *Acta Psychiatrica Scandinavica, 96*, 311–318.

Nijenhuis, E. R., Spinhoven, P., van Dyck, R., van der Hart, O., & Vanderlinden, J. (1998). Degree of somatoform and psychological dissociation in dissociative disorder is correlated with reported trauma. *Journal of Trauma and Stress, 11,* 711–730.

Nijenhuis, E. R., van Dyck, R., Spinhoven, P., van der Hart, O., Chatrou, M., Vanderlinden, J., & Moene, F. (1999). Somatoform dissociation discriminates among diagnostic categories over and above general psychopathology. *Australian and New Zealand Journal of Psychiatry,* 33, 511–520.

Noyes, R., Hoenk, P. R., Kupperman, B. A., & Slymen, D. J. (1977). Depersonalization in accident victims and psychiatric patients. *Journal of Nervous and Mental Disease, 164,* 401–407.

Noyes, R., & Kletti, R. (1971). Depersonalization in response to life-threatening danger. *Comprehensive Psychiatry, 18,* 375–384.

Noyes, R., Kupperman, S., & Olson, S. B. (1987). Desipramine: A possible treatment for depersonalization. *Canadian Journal of Psychiatry,* 32, 782–784.

Nuller, Y. L. (1982). Depersonalization—Symptoms, meaning, therapy. *Acta Psychiatrica Scandinavica, 66,* 451–458.

Oberndorf, C. (1950). Role of anxiety in depersonalization. *International Journal of Psychoanalysis, 31,* 1–5.

Orne, M. T. (1979). The use and misuse of hypnosis in court. *International Journal of Clinical and Experimental Hypnosis,* 27, 311–341.

Orne, M. T., Axelrad, D., Diamond, B. L., Gravitz, M. A., Heller, A., Mutter, C. B., Spiegel, D., & Spiegel, H. (1985). Scientific status of refreshing recollection by the use of hypnosis. *Journal of the American Medical Association,* 253, 1918–1923.

Oswalt, R., Anderson, M., Hagstrom, K., & Berkowitz, B. (1993). Evaluation of the one-session eye-movement desensitization reprocessing procedure for eliminating traumatic memories. *Psychological Reports,* 73, 99–104.

Panos, P. T., Panos, A., & Allred, G. H. (1990). The need for marriage therapy in the treatment of multiple personality disorder. *Dissociation,* 3, 10–14.

Parfitt, D. N., & Carlyle-Gall, C. M. (1944). Psychogenic amnesia: The refusal to remember. *Journal of Mental Science,* 379, 519–531.

Paulsen, S. (1995). Eye movement desensitization and reprocessing: Its cautious use in the dissociative disorders. *Dissociation,* 8, 32–44.

Perry, J. C., & Jacobs, D. (1982). Overview: Clinical applications of the amytal interview in psychiatric emergency settings. *American Journal of Psychiatry, 139,* 552–559.

Peterson, G. (1990). Diagnosis of childhood multiple personality disorder. *Dissociation,* 3, 3–9.

Peterson, G. (1991). Children coping with trauma: Diagnosis of "dissociation identity disorder." *Dissociation,* 4, 152–164.

Pies, R. (1991). Depersonalization's many faces. *Psychiatric Times,* 8, 27–28.

Porter, S., Kelly, K. A., & Grame, C. J. (1993). Family treatment of spouses and children of patients with multiple personality disorder. *Bulletin of the Menninger Clinic,* 57, 371–379.

Powell, R. A., & Howell, A. J. (1998). Treatment outcome for dissociative identity disorder (letter). *American Journal of Psychiatry, 155,* 1304.

Pribor, E. F., & Dinwiddie, S. H. (1992). Psychiatric correlates of incest in childhood. *American Journal of Psychiatry, 149,* 52–56.

Price, J., & Hess, N. C. (1979). Behaviour therapy as precipitant and treatment in a case of dual personality. *Australian and New Zealand Journal of Psychiatry, 13,* 63–66.

Prince, M. (1906). *Dissociation of a personality.* New York: Longman, Green.

Prince, W. F. (1917). The Doris case of quintuple personality. *Journal of Abnormal Psychology, 11,* 73–122.

Putnam, F. W. (1984). The psychophysiologic investigation of multiple personality disorder. *Psychiatric Clinics of North America,* 7, 31–40.

Putnam, F. W. (1985). Dissociation as a response to extreme trauma. In R. P. Kluft (Ed.), *Childhood antecedents of multiple personality* (pp. 63–97). Washington, DC: American Psychiatric Press.

Putnam, F. W. (1986). The treatment of multiple personality: State of the art. In B. G. Braun (Ed.), *The treatment of multiple personality disorder.* Washington, DC: American Psychiatric Press.

Putnam, F. W. (1988). The disturbance of "self" in victims of childhood sexual abuse. In R. P. Kluft (Ed.), *Incest-related syndromes of adult psychopathology.* Washington, DC: American Psychiatric Press.

Putman, F. W. (1989). *Diagnosis and treatment of multiple personality disorder.* New York: Guilford Press.

Putnam, F. W. (1991). Dissociative disorders in children and adolescents: A developmental perspective. *Psychiatric Clinics of North America, 14,* 519–532.

Putman, F. W. (1993). Dissociative disorders in children: Behavioral profiles and problems. *Child Abuse and Neglect* 17, 39–45.

Putnam, F. W., Guroff, J. J., Silberman, E. K., Barban, L., & Post, R. (1986). The clinical phenomenology of multiple personality disorder: Review of 100 recent cases. *Journal of Clinical Psychiatry, 47,* 285–293.

Putnam, F. W., Post, R. M., & Guroff, J. J. (1983). *100 cases of multiple personality disorder.* Presentation at the American Psychiatric Association Annual Meeting, New York.

Ratliff, N. B., & Kerski, D. (1995). Depersonalization treated with fluoxetine (letter). *American Journal of Psychiatry, 152,* 1689–1690.

Reed, G. E., & Sedman, G. (1964). Personality and depersonalization under sensory deprivation conditions. *Perceptual and Motor Skills, 18,* 650–660.

Reist, C., Kauffman, C. D., & Haier, R. J. (1976). A controlled trial of desipramine in 18 men with post-traumatic stress disorder. *American Journal of Psychiatry, 146,* 513–516.

Riether, A. M., & Stoudemire, A. (1988). Psychogenic fugue states: A review. *Southern Medical Journal, 81,* 568–570.

Riley, R. L., & Mead, J. (1988). The development of symptoms of multiple personality disorder in a child of three. *Dissociation, 1,* 41–46.

Rivera, M. (1991). Multiple personality disorder and the social systems: 185 cases. *Dissociation, 4,* 79–82.

Roberts, W. W. (1960). Normal and abnormal depersonalization. *Journal of Mental Science, 106,* 478–493.

Ronquillo, E. B. (1991). The influence of "Espiritismo" on a case of multiple personality disorder. *Dissociation, 4,* 39–45.

Rosenfeld, H. (1947). Analysis of a schizophrenic state with depersonalization. *International Journal of Psychoanalysis, 28,* 130–139.

Ross, C. A. (1989). *Multiple personality disorder: Diagnosis, clinical features, and treatment.* New York: Wiley.

Ross, C. A. (1991). Epidemiology of multiple personality disorder and dissociation. *Psychiatric Clinics of North America, 14,* 503–518.

Ross, C. A., Anderson, G., Fleischer, W. P., & Norton, G. R. (1991). The frequency of multiple personality disorder among psychiatric inpatients. *American Journal of Psychiatry, 148,* 1717–1720.

Ross, C. A., & Ellason, J. W. (1998a). Treatment of dissociative identity disorder—Reply. *American Journal of Psychiatry, 155,* 1462–1463.

Ross, C. A., & Ellason, J. W. (1998b). Treatment outcome of dissociative identity disorder—Reply. *American Journal of Psychiatry, 155,* 1304–1305.

Ross, C. A., Joshi, S., & Currie, R. (1991). Dissociative experiences in the general population: A factor analysis. *Hospital and Community Psychiatry, 42,* 297–301.

Ross, C. A., Miller, D. S., Reagor, P., Bjornson, L., Fraser, G. A., & Anderson, G. (1990a). Schneiderian symptoms in multiple personality disorder and schizophrenia. *Comprehensive Psychiatry, 31,* 111–118.

Ross, C. A., Miller, D. S., Reagor, P., Bjornson, L., Fraser, G. A., & Anderson, G. (1990b). Structured interview data on 102 cases of multiple personality disorder from four centers. *American Journal of Psychiatry, 147,* 596–601.

Ross, C. A., & Norton, G. R. (1988). Multiple personality disorder patients with a prior diagnosis of schizophrenia. *Dissociation, 1,* 39–42.

Ross, C. A., & Norton, G. R. (1989). Suicide and parasuicide in multiple personality disorder. *Psychiatry, 52,* 365–371.

Ross, C. A., Norton, G. R., & Wozney, K. (1989). Multiple personality disorder: An analysis of 236 cases. *Canadian Journal of Psychiatry, 34,* 413–418.

Roth, M. (1959). The phobic-anxiety-depersonalization syndrome. *Proceedings of the Royal Society of Medicine, 52,* 587–595.

Ruedrich, S. L., Chu, C. C., & Wadle, C. V. (1985). The amytal interview in the treatment of psychogenic amnesia. *Hospital and Community Psychiatry, 36,* 1045–1046.

Russell, D. E. H. (1986). *The secret trauma: Incest in the lives of girls and women.* New York: Basic Books.

Sachs, R. G. (1986). The adjunctive role of social systems in the treatment of multiple personality disorder. In B. A. Braun (Ed.), *Treatment of multiple personality disorder.* Washington, DC: American Psychiatric Press.

Sachs, R. G., Frischholz, E. J., & Wood, J. I. (1988). Marital and family therapy in the treatment of multiple personality disorder. *Journal of Marital and Family Therapy, 14,* 249–259.

Santonastaso, P., Favaro, A., Olivotto, M. C., & Friederici, S. (1997). Dissociative experiences and eating disorders in a female college sample. *Psychopathology, 30,* 170–176.

Sar, V., Tutkun, H., Alyanak, B., Bakim, B., & Baral, I. (2000). Frequency of dissociative disorders among psychiatric outpatients in Turkey. *Comprehensive Psychiatry, 41,* 216–222.

Sar, V., Yargiç, L. I., & Tutkun, H. (1996). Structured interview data on 35 cases of dissociative identity disorder in Turkey. *American Journal of Psychiatry, 153,* 1329–1333.

Sargant, W., & Slater, E. (1941). Amnestic syndromes in war. *Proceedings of the Royal Society of Medicine, 34,* 757–764.

Saxe, G. N., van der Kolk, B. A., Berkowitz, R., Chinman, G., Hall, K., Liegerg, G., & Schwartz, J. (1993). Dissociative disorders in psychiatric inpatients. *American Journal of Psychiatry, 150,* 1037–1042.

Saxena, S., & Prasad, K. (1989). *DSM-III* subclassification of dissociative disorders applied to psychiatric outpatients in India. *American Journal of Psychiatry 146,* 261–262.

Schacter, D. L., & Kihlstrom, J. F. (1989). Functional amnesia. In F. Boller & J. Grafman (Eds.), *Handbook of neuropsychology* (pp. 209–231). Amsterdam: Elsevier Science.

Schacter, D. L., Wang, P. L., Tulving, E., & Freedman, M. (1982). Functional retrograde amnesia: A quantitative case study. *Neuropsychologia, 20,* 523–532.

Schenk, L., & Bear, D. (1981). Multiple personality and related dissociative phenomena in patients with temporal lobe epilepsy. *American Journal of Psychiatry, 138,* 1311–1315.

Schilder, P. (1939). The treatment of depersonalization. *Bulletin of the New York Academy of Science, 15,* 258–272.

Schreiber, F. R. (1974). *Sybil.* New York: Warner Paperbacks.

Schultz, R., Braun, B. G., & Kluft, R. P. (1989). Multiple personality disorder: Phenomenology of selected variables in comparison to major depression. *Dissociation, 2,* 45–51.

Scroppo, J. C., Drob, S. L., Weinberger, J. L., & Eagle, P. (1998). Identifying dissociative identity disorder: A self-report and projective study. *Journal of Abnormal Psychology, 107,* 272–284.

Sedman, G. (1966). Depersonalization in a group of normal subjects. *British Journal of Psychiatry, 112,* 907–912.

Sedman, G. (1970). Theories of depersonalization: A reappraisal. *British Journal of Psychiatry, 117,* 1–14.

Sedman, G., & Kenna, J. C. (1963). Depersonalization and mood changes in schizophrenia. *British Journal of Psychiatry, 109,* 669–673.

Sedman, G., & Reed, G. F. (1963). Depersonalization phenomena in obsessional personalities and in depression. *British Journal of Psychiatry, 109,* 376–379.

Shapiro, F. (1995). *Eye movement desensitization and reprocessing: Basic principles, protocols, and procedures.* New York: Guilford Press.

Shapiro, F., Vogelmann-Sine, S., & Sine, L. F. (1994). Eye movement desensitization and reprocessing: Treating trauma and substance abuse. *Journal of Psychoactive Drugs, 26,* 379–391.

Shestatzky, M., Greenberg, D., & Lerer, B. (1988). A controlled trial of phenelzine in posttraumatic stress disorder. *Psychiatry Research, 24,* 149–155.

Shilony, E., & Grossman, F. K. (1993). Depersonalization as a defense mechanism in survivors of trauma. *Journal of Traumatic Stress, 6,* 119–128.

Shimizu, M., & Sakamoto, S. (1986). Depersonalization in early adolescence. *Japanese Journal of Psychiatry, 40,* 603–608.

Shorvon, H. J. (1946). The depersonalization syndrome. *Proceedings of the Royal Society of Medicine, 39,* 779–785.

Shraberg, D. (1977). The phobic-anxiety-depersonalization syndrome. *Psychiatric Opinion, 14,* 35–40.

Signer, S. F. (1988), Mystical-ecstatic and trance states. *British Journal of Psychiatry, 152,* 296–297.

Silberg, J. L., & Nemzer, E. D. (1998). Dissociative symptoms in children. *American Journal of Psychiatry, 155,* 708–709.

Silver, S. M., Brooks, A., & Obenchain, J. (1995). Treatment of Vietnam War veterans with PTSD: A comparison of eye movement desensitization and reprocessing, biofeedback, and relaxation training. *Journal of Traumatic Stress, 8,* 337–342.

Simeon, D., Gross, S., Guralnik, O., Stein, D. J., Schmeidler, H., & Hollander, E. (1997). Feeling unreal: 30 cases of *DSM-III-R* depersonalization disorder. *American Journal of Psychiatry, 154,* 1107–1113.

Simeon, D., Stein, D. J., & Hollander, E. (1998). Treatment of depersonalization disorder with clomipramine. *Biological Psychiatry, 44,* 302–303.

Sno, H. N., & Schalken, H. F. (1999). Dissociative identity disorder: Diagnosis and treatment in the Netherlands. *European Psychiatry, 14,* 270–277.

Solomon, R. (1983). The use of the MMPI with multiple personality patients. *Psychological Reports, 53,* 1004–1006.

Sookman, D., & Solyom, L. (1978). Severe depersonalization treated with behavior therapy. *American Journal of Psychiatry, 135,* 1543–1545.

Spanos, N. P., Weekes, J. R., & Bertrand, L. D. (1985). Multiple personality: A social psychological perspective. *Journal of Abnormal Psychology, 94,* 362–376.

Spanos, N. P., Weekes, J. R., Menary, E., & Bertrand, L. D. (1986). Hypnotic interview and age regression procedures in elicitation of multiple personality symptoms: A simulation study. *Psychiatry, 49,* 298–311.

Spiegel, D. (1984). Multiple personality as a post-traumatic stress disorder. *Psychiatric Clinics of North America, 7,* 101–110.

Spiegel, D. (1986). Dissociating damage. *American Journal of Clinical Hypnosis, 29,* 123–131.

Spiegel, D. (1988). Dissociation and hypnosis in posttraumatic stress disorder. *Journal of Traumatic Stress, 1,* 17–33.

Spiegel, D. (1989). Hypnosis in the treatment of victims of sexual abuse. *Psychiatric Clinics of North America, 12,* 295–305.

Spiegel, D. (1990). Hypnosis, dissociation and trauma: Hidden and overt observers. In J. L. Singer (Ed.), *Repression and dissociation* (pp. 121–142). Chicago: University of Chicago Press.

Spiegel, D. (1995). Psychiatry disabused: Letter to the editor. *Nature Medicine, 1,* 490–491.

Spiegel D. (1996). Hypnosis and suggestion. In D. Schacter (Ed.), *Memory distortion*. Cambridge: Harvard University Press.

Spiegel, D., & Cardena, E. (1991). Disintegrated experience: The dissociative disorders revisited. *Journal of Abnormal Psychology, 100,* 366–378.

Spiegel, D., Detrick, D., & Frischholz, E. J. (1982). Hypnotizability and psychopathology. *American Journal of Psychiatry, 139,* 431–437.

Spiegel, D., Hunt, T., & Dondershine, H. E. (1988). Dissociation and hypnotizability in posttraumatic stress disorder. *American Journal of Psychiatry, 145,* 301–305.

Spiegel, D., & Maldonado, J. R. (1999). Dissociative disorders. In J. H. Talbot & S. Yudosky (Eds.), *Textbook of psychiatry* (3rd ed., pp. 711–738). Washington, DC: American Psychiatric Press.

Spiegel, D., & McHugh, P. (1995). The pros and cons of dissociative identity (multiple personality) disorder. *Journal of Practical Psychology and Behavioral. Health, 1,* 158–166.

Spiegel, D., & Scheflin, A. W. (1994). Dissociated or fabricated? Psychiatric aspects of repressed memory in criminal and civil cases. *International Journal of Clinical and Experimental Hypnosis, 42,* 411–432.

Spiegel, H. (2000). Silver linings in the clouds of war: A five-decade retrospective. In R. W. Menninger & J. Nemiah (Eds.), *American psychiatry after World War II: 1944–1994* (pp. 52–72). Washington, DC: American Psychiatric Press.

Spier, S. A., Tesar, G. E., Rosenbaum, J. F., & Woods, S. W. (1986). Treatment of panic disorder and agoraphobia with clonazepam. *Journal of Clinical Psychiatry, 47,* 238–242.

Squire, L. (1987). *Memory and brain*. New York: Oxford University Press.

Stamm, J (1967) Altered ego states allied to depersonalization. *Journal of the American Psychoanalytic Association, 12,* 762–783.

Stein, M. B., & Uhde, T. W. (1989). Depersonalization disorder: Effects of caffeine and response to pharmacotherapy. *Biological Psychiatry, 26,* 315–320.

Steinberg, M. (1991). The spectrum of depersonalization: Assessment and treatment. In A. Tasman & S. M. Goldfinger (Eds.), *American Psychiatric Press review of psychiatry* (pp. 223–247). Washington, DC: American Psychiatric Press.

Steinberg, M. (2000). Advances in the clinical assessment of dissociation: The SCID-D-R. *Bulletin of the Menninger Clinic, 64,* 146–163.

Stengel, E. (1941). On the aetiology of the fugue states. *Journal of Mental Science, 87,* 572–599.

Stengel, E. (1943). Further studies on pathological wandering (fugues with the impulse to wander). *Journal of Mental Science, 89,* 224–241.

Stern, C. R. (1984). The etiology of multiple personalities. *Psychiatric Clinics of North America, 7,* 149–160.

Stuntman, R. K., & Bliss, E. L. (1985). Posttraumatic stress disorder, hypnotizability and imagery. *American Journal of Psychiatry 142,* 741–743.

Szymanski, H. V. (1981). Prolonged depersonalization after marijuana use. *American Journal of Psychiatry, 138,* 231–233.

Taal, L. A., & Faber, A. W. (1997). Dissociation as a predictor of psychopathology following burn injury. *Burns, 23,* 400–403.

Thigpen, C. H., & Cleckley, H. (1957). A case of multiple personality. *Journal of Abnormal and Social Psychology, 49,* 135–151.

Torch, E. M. (1978). Review of the relationship between obsession and depersonalization. *Acta Psychiatrica Scandinavica, 58,* 191–198.

Torch, E. M. (1987). The psychotherapeutic treatment of depersonalization disorder. *Hillside Journal of Clinical Psychiatry, 9,* 133–143.

Torem, M. (1989). Iatrogenic factors in the perpetuation of splitting and multiplicity. *Dissociation, 2,* 92–98.

Trueman, D. (1984). Anxiety and depersonalization and derealization experiences. *Psychological Reports, 54,* 91–96.

Tucker, G. J., Harrow, M., & Quinlan, D. (1973). Depersonalization, dysphoria, and thought disturbance. *American Journal of Psychiatry, 130,* 702–706.

Tureen, L. L., & Stein, M. (1949). The base section psychiatric hospital. *Bulletin of the U.S. Army Medical Department, 9* (Suppl.), 105–137.

Tutkun, H., Sar, V., Yargiç, L. I., Ozpulat, T., Yanik, M., & Kiziltan, E. (1998). Frequency of dissociative disorders among psychiatric inpatients in a Turkish University Clinic. *American Journal of Psychiatry, 155,* 800–805.

Tyson, G. M. (1992). Childhood MPD/dissociative identity disorder. *Dissociation, 5,* 20–27.

Ursano, R. J., Fullerton, C. S., Epstein, R. S., Crowley, B., Vance, K., Kao, T. C., & Baum, A. (1999). Peritraumatic dissociation and posttraumatic stress disorder following motor vehicle accidents. *American Journal of Psychiatry, 156,* 1808–1810.

van der Hart, O. (1993). Multiple personality disorder in Europe: Impressions. *Dissociation, 6,* 102–118.

van der Hart, O., & Boon, S. (1997). Treatment strategies for complex dissociative disorders: Two Dutch case examples. *Dissociation, 5,* 157–165.

van der Kolk, B. A., & van der Hart, O. (1989). Pierre Janet and the breakdown of adaptation in psychological trauma. *American Journal of Psychiatry, 146,* 1530–1540.

Vanderlinden, J., Van Dyck, R., Vandereycken, W., & Vertommen, H. (1991). Dissociative experiences in the general population of the Netherlands and Belgium: A study with the Dissociative Questionnaire (DIS-Q). *Dissociation, 4,* 180–184.

Varma, V. K., Bouri, M., & Wig, N. N. (1981). Multiple personality in India: Comparison with hysterical possession state. *American Journal of Psychotherapy, 35,* 113–120.

Vincent, M., & Pickering, M. R. (1988). Multiple personality disorder in childhood. *Canadian Journal of Psychiatry/Revue Canadienne de Psychiatrie, 33,* 524–529.

Walsh, R. N. (1975). Depersonalization: Definition and treatment. *American Journal of Psychiatry, 132,* 873.

Waltzer, H. (1972). Depersonalization an the use of LSD; A psychoanalytic study. *American Journal of Psychoanalysis, 32,* 45–52.

Watkins, J. G., & Watkins, H. H. (1982). Ego state therapy. In L. E. Abt & I. R. Stuart (Eds.), *Newer therapies: A source book.* New York: Van Nostrand Reinhold.

Williams, M. B. (1991). Clinical work with families of MPD patients. *Dissociation, 4,* 92–98.

Wills, S. M., & Goodwin, J. M. (1996). Recognizing bipolar illness in patients with dissociative identity disorder. *Dissociation, 9,* 104–109.

Wilson, S. A., Becker, L. A., & Tinker, R. H. (1995). Eye movement desensitization and reprocessing (EMDR) treatment for psychologically traumatized individuals. *Journal of Consulting and Clinical Psychology, 63,* 928–937.

Wineburg, E., & Straker, N. (1973). An episode of acute, self-limiting depersonalization following a first session of hypnosis. *American Journal of Psychiatry, 130,* 98–100.

Wittkower, E. D. (1970). Transcultural psychiatry in the Caribbean: Past, present and future. *American Journal of Psychiatry, 127,* 162–166.

Yap, P. M. (1960). The possession syndrome: A comparison of Hong Kong and French findings. *Journal of Mental Science, 106,* 114–137.

Yargiç, L. I., Sar, V., Tutkun, H., & Alyanak. B. (1998). Comparison of dissociative identity disorder with other diagnostic groups using a structured interview in Turkey. *Comprehensive Psychiatry, 39,* 345–351.

Yeager, C. A., & Lewis, D. O. (1997). False memories of cult abuse. *American Journal of Psychiatry, 154,* 435.

Yehuda, R., & Elkin, A.. (1996). Dissociation in aging Holocaust survivors. *American Journal of Psychiatry, 153,* 935–940.

Young, W. C. (1994). EMDR treatment of phobic symptoms in multiple personality disorder. *Dissociation, 7,* 129–133.

Young, W. C. (1995). Eye movement desensitization/reprocessing: Its use in resolving the trauma caused by the loss of a war buddy. *American Journal of Psychotherapy, 49,* 282–291.

Zanarini, M. C., Ruser, T., Frankenburg, F. R., & Hennen, J. (2000a). The dissociative experiences of borderline patients. *Comprehensive Psychiatry, 41,* 223–227.

Zanarini, M. C., Ruser, T. F., Frankenburg, F. R., Hennen, J., & Gunderson, J. G. (2000b). Risk factors associated with the dissociative experiences of borderline patients. *Journal of Nervous and Mental Disease, 188,* 26–30.

20

Psychotherapy and Pharmacotherapy for Sexual Dysfunctions

Taylor Segraves
Stanley Althof

Historically, conceptualization of the etiology and treatment of sexual disorders was primarily psychological. Over the past three decades, this approach has gradually evolved into a psychobiological paradigm. The introduction of effective pharmacological therapies for both erectile disorders and rapid ejaculation has shifted many physicians from a psychobiological model to a narrower biological model. There is considerable evidence that current pharmacological therapies are frequently successful in reversing sexual dysfunction. There is less evidence concerning the long-term efficacy of such interventions for subjective sense of sexual satisfaction and couple interaction. The evidence concerning pharmacological treatment of female sexual disorders is extremely limited. Current treatments of sexual disorders by pharmacological and psychotherapeutic methods are reviewed for hypoactive sexual desire disorder, erectile dysfunction, premature ejaculation, female orgasm disorder, male orgasm disorder, dyspareunia, vaginismus, and substance-induced sexual dysfunction. Controlled studies using rigorous research requirements are limited. In the next decade, there is a pressing need for the development of biological therapies of proven efficacy for female disorders and definition of the indications for biological therapy alone, psychotherapy alone, and combined therapy. The cost-effectiveness of these approaches clearly needs to be defined.

HISTORICAL OVERVIEW OF THERAPY FOR SEXUAL PROBLEMS

Historically, the treatment of sexual dysfunctions can be divided into five eras: the psychoanalytic; the early behavioral; the Masters and Johnson; the neo–Masters and Johnson; and the current psychobiological. Prior to 1970, psychoanalytic concepts guided clinicians in their understanding and treatment of sexual problems. Sexual symptomatology was linked to discrete, unresolved, unconscious conflicts that occurred during specific developmental periods. Sexual symptoms were traced to designated constellations of conflict occurring in early childhood (Meyer, 1976). Psychoanalytic notions were heterosexist and male-centered, as was clearly evident in the construction of the controversial concept of penis envy and the psychological interpretation given to the classification of orgasm as either clitoral or vaginal.

In a classical analysis, patients were seen three to five times weekly over the course of several years. Freud's revolutionary method employed free association, dream analysis, interpretation of unconscious motives, and the recapitulation of significant emotional attachments through the transference. Because of the focus on individual intrapsychic dynamics, couples treatment was rarely undertaken. The analytic literature was replete with elegant, richly detailed descriptions of individual case histories and analysis. By contemporary standards, these often fascinating reports qualify only as untested case formulations.

In the late 1950s, behavioral therapists described promising results from treating sexual disorders by utilization of symptom-oriented direct treatment approaches (Brady, 1966; Cooper, 1969; Haslam, 1965; Lazarus, 1963; Wolpe, 1958). These interventions were loosely modeled on classical conditioning paradigms and assumed that the dysfunction was a learned (conditioned) anxiety response. The guiding principle of behavior therapy (LoPicollo & LoPicollo, 1978; Marks, 1981; Obler, 1973) was to extinguish the anxiety or performance demands that interfered with normal sexual function. The most common behavioral technique, systematic desensitization, paired relaxation with a series of carefully designed, hierarchical anxiety-provoking sexual situations, in vivo or by imagery. Like psychoanalysis, behavior therapy concentrated on individual psychotherapy and tended to ignore the dynamics of relationships. These studies, while more rigorously documented than the analytic reports, failed to dampen the prevailing enthusiasm for the treatment of sexual problems by analytic techniques.

In 1970, Masters and Johnson published their results of a study of 790 cases employing a quasi-residential blend of daily individual and couples psychotherapy. The ingredients of their treatment model consisted of physical examination, history taking, education, prescription of behavioral tasks, and counseling for intrapsychic or interpersonal issues that interfered with natural sexual function.

Their treatment was based on three fundamental postulates: (a) a sequential four-stage progression of physiological and subjective arousal in both genders; (b) the primacy of psychogenic factors, particularly learning deficits and performance anxiety in the etiology and maintenance of sexual dysfunctions; and (c) the amenability of most sexual disorders to a brief, problem-focused treatment approach (Rosen & Leiblum, 1995).

Masters and Johnson's most important contribution was the emphasis given to the deleterious effects of performance anxiety and their prescription of sensate focus exercises to alleviate this troubling state. Performance anxiety, the fear of future sexual failure based on a previous failure, is a universal experience that appears in all sexual dysfunctions, including those of organic etiology. Masters and Johnson provided clear descriptions of their treatment method and reported initial and 5-year posttreatment "failure rates" for lifelong and acquired arousal, orgasm, and pain disorders. Their work revolutionized the treatment of sexual problems and generated great enthusiasm among clinicians for their novel short-term, directive treatment methods.

By present-day standards, Masters and Johnson's outcome data can be criticized on multiple grounds, for not (a) utilizing standardized, valid, and reliable assessment measures; (b) specifying the basis for classifying cases as successes or failures; (c) employing control, waiting-list, or placebo groups; and (d) blinding the investigators to the experimental conditions. In addition, it was questionable whether their results applied to typical patient populations as they studied affluent, well-educated, and highly motivated patients. These vital concerns linger because later researchers have been unable to replicate the magnitude of the positive outcomes achieved by Masters and Johnson (Heiman & LoPiccolo, 1983; Rosen & Beck, 1988; Wright, Perreault, & Mathieu, 1977; Zilbergeld & Evans, 1980). Nonetheless, their reports revolutionized the treatment of sexual problems and generated great enthusiasm among clinicians for their treatment method.

The neo–Masters and Johnson era was heralded by the publication of Helen Singer Kaplan's widely acclaimed book *The New Sex Therapy* (1974). As a discipline, sex therapy had come of age. Kaplan integrated modifications of Masters and Johnson's treatment methods with behavioral and analytic interventions. She treated couples by addressing both partners' intrapsychic and interpersonal contributions to the initiation and maintenance of the dysfunction. She distinguished between recent and remote etiological causation, recommending direct treatment approaches for the former while reserving traditional psychodynamic methods for the latter. The more commonly seen recent etiological causes were relationship deterioration, performance anxiety, widowhood, health concerns, and aging. Examples of remote influences included pre-Oedipal separation-individuation conflicts, unresolved Oedipal struggles, paraphiliac scripts, gender identity conflicts, and adolescent masturbatory guilt. Kaplan's prolific writings did not include outcome statistics on the follow-up of her suggested treatment interventions.

Treatments for sexual dysfunction proliferated

and evolved into blends of psychodynamic, behavioral, and cognitive therapies utilizing individual, couples, and group formats (Althof, 1989; Gagnon, Leiblum, & Rosen, 1989; Leiblum, Rosen, & Pierce, 1976; Levine, 1992b; McCarthy & McCarthy, 1984; Rosen & Leiblum, 1982; Scharf, 1982; Zilbergeld, 1992). As the field matured, clinical investigators began to develop more sophisticated methodologies that included control groups, placebo treatments, randomization of experimental conditions, and standardized, valid, and reliable questionnaires. However, the majority of these research reports lacked long-term follow-up.

The middle 1980s ushered in the current psychobiological era. This epoch is distinguished by the medicalization (Tiefer, 1995) of treatment approaches, primarily for male sexual dysfunction. Sophisticated studies with adequate long-term follow-up describing the efficacy and psychological impact of oral agents, intracavernosal injection, vacuum tumescence therapy, and treatment of rapid ejaculation by serotonin reuptake inhibitors began to appear in the literature (Althof, 1995a, 1995b; Althof et al., 1995; Assalian, 1988; Barada & McKimmy, 1994; Goldstein et al., 1998; Segraves, Saran, Segraves, & Maguire, 1993). These studies turned the tide toward the blending of medical and psychological treatments for male sexual dysfunction.

In March 1998, sildenafil citrate received approval by the Federal Drug Administration (FDA) for the treatment of erectile dysfunction (Goldstein et al., 1998). Since its release, countless prescriptions have been written, making it one of the most prescribed medications in the United States. Obviously, sildenafil transformed the treatment and research landscape. Because sildenafil, transurethral systems, injections, and vacuum pumps are reversible, safe, and efficacious, the established principle of etiology guiding treatment became less meaningful. Prior to the introduction of these treatments, men diagnosed with psychogenic erectile dysfunction were treated by mental health professionals, and those with organic dysfunction were seen by urologists or other health specialists. These therapies altered the traditional role of the mental health professional, which had been to (a) assess the etiology of erectile dysfunction; (b) offer psychotherapy to men or couples with primarily psychological dysfunction; and/or (c) treat the conspicuous psychological sequelae of organic conditions (Althof & Seftel, 1995; Levine, 1992b). Once these treatments became available, the clinician's role was expanded to include identification and attenuation of the resistances to medical treatments for erectile dysfunction.

Since 1999, the medicalization of sexual dysfunction has begun to likewise influence the treatments for female sexual dysfunction. There are reports of uncontrolled, open-label trials of sildenafil for female sexual arousal disorder, testosterone patches to enhance sexual desire, and the introduction of clitoral erection devices, gels, and homeopathic remedies as well (Berman, Shuker, & Goldstein, 1999). There recently was a controlled trial of a testosterone patch for women with low desire and a history of bilateral oophorectomy (Shifren et al., 2000).

NOSOLOGY

Knowledge concerning the treatment of sexual dysfunctions and interest in this area of psychobiology have grown significantly in the last 20 to 30 years. The recent emergence of this field can be appreciated by realizing that the first two *Diagnostic and Statistical Manuals of Mental Disorders* published by the American Psychiatric Association (APA)—*DSM-I* (1952) and *DSM-II* (1968)—did not contain diagnostic terms for the sexual dysfunctions. The *DSM-III* (APA, 1980) provided a radical departure from the previous diagnostic manuals by including a section on sexual dysfunctions. These diagnoses and their criteria sets were based on the concept of a normal sexual response cycle for men and women (Schmidt, 1995) and were strongly influenced by the works of Masters and Johnson (1966) and Helen Singer Kaplan (1974). Changes in nomenclature for the psychosexual dysfunctions in the different versions of the *Diagnostic and Statistical Manuals* are listed in Table 20.1.

The current nomenclature was officially adopted by the American Psychiatric Association in 1994. Sexual dysfunctions listed in *DSM-IV* include hypoactive sexual desire disorder, sexual aversion disorder, female sexual arousal disorder, male erectile disorder, female orgasmic disorder, male orgasmic disorder, premature ejaculation, dyspareunia, and vaginismus. Two new diagnostic entities were included in *DSM-IV:* sexual dysfunction due to a general medical condition and substance-induced sexual dysfunction. The *DSM-IV* criteria sets do not specify a mini-

TABLE 20.1 Modifications in Sexual Disorders Nomenclature in the *Diagnostic and Statistical Manuals* of the American Psychiatric Association

1. *DSM-I* was published in 1952 and did not contain diagnostic terms for the psychosexual dysfunctions.
2. *DSM-II* was published in 1968. The only diagnostic entity pertaining to psychosexual disorders was *psychophysiological genitourinary disorders,* which referred to disorders of micturation, menstruation, and sexual function.
3. *DSM-III* was published in 1980. It included diagnoses for the psychosexual disorders. The term *homosexuality* was deleted, and the term *ego dystonic homosexuality* was added as a diagnostic entity. The term *inhibited sexual excitement* referred to both male erectile disorder and female arousal disorder.
4. *DSM-III-R* was published in 1987. The term *sexual aversion disorder* was added. The term *ego dystonic homosexuality* was deleted. The use of the term *inhibited* in diagnostic entities was deleted. The term *inhibited sexual excitement* was changed to *male erectile disorder* and *female arousal disorder.*
5. *DSM-IV* was published in 1994. Subjective criteria were dropped from definitions of *male erectile disorder* and *female arousal disorder.* The terms *sexual disorder secondary to a general medical condition* and *substance-induced sexual disorder* were added.

Note. DSM = Diagnostic and Statistical Manual of Mental Disorders.

mum duration or frequency of a disorder before it reaches diagnostic criteria. Instead, diagnosis is contingent on the disorder's causing marked distress or interpersonal difficulty and depends to a large degree on clinical judgment. The diagnostic entities in *DSM-IV* are listed in Table 20.2 and the changes from *DSM-III-R* are listed in Table 20.3.

Although the diagnoses in *DSM-IV* are based primarily on disturbances in discrete phases of the sexual response cycle, there is some evidence that there is considerable overlap of diagnoses (Segraves & Segraves, 1990, 1991). For example, many individuals with hypoactive sexual disorder also meet diagnostic criteria for arousal and orgasm disorders. In one pharmaceutical study, diagnostic evaluations were available for 906 subjects, 532 females and 374 males. Approximately 40% of patients diagnosed as having hypoactive sexual desire disorder also met diagnostic criteria for arousal or orgasm disorders. In the same study, only 2% of women had a solitary diagnosis of female arousal disorder. Most patients diagnosed with a female arousal disorder also met criteria for hypoactive sexual desire disorders as well as anorgasmia. This frequent overlap among diagnostic categories needs to be kept in mind when one reviews treatment outcome research, as little of this research details secondary as well as primary diagnoses. Similarly, in the clinical situation, it is often unclear which condition is primary. For example, if a patient presents for treatment with complaints of anorgasmia, as well as decreased libido, and it is un-

TABLE 20.2 *DSM-IV* Psychosexual Disorders

1. *Hypoactive sexual desire disorder:* Persistent or recurrent deficiency in or absence of sexual fantasies and desire for sexual activity.
2. *Sexual aversion disorder:* Persistent or recurrent extreme aversion to, and avoidance of, all or almost all sexual contact with a partner.
3. *Female sexual arousal disorder:* Persistent or recurrent inability to attain, or to maintain until completion of the sexual activity, an adequate lubrication and swelling response of sexual excitement.
4. *Male erectile disorder:* Persistent or recurrent inability to obtain, or to maintain until completion of the sexual activity, an adequate erection.
5. *Female orgasmic disorder:* Persistent or recurrent delay in or absence of orgasm following a normal sexual excitement phase. This diagnosis is based on the clinician's judgment that the woman's orgasmic capacity is less than would be reasonable for her age, her sexual experience, and the adequacy of sexual stimulation.
6. *Male orgasmic disorder:* Persistent or recurrent delay in or absence of orgasm following a normal excitement phase during sexual activity, with the clinician taking into account the person's age and judging the sexual stimulation to be adequate in focus, intensity, and duration.
7. *Premature ejaculation:* Persistent or recurrent ejaculation with minimal sexual stimulation before, on, or shortly after penetration and before the person wishes it.
8. *Dyspareunia:* Recurrent or persistent genital pain associated with sexual intercourse not due exclusively to vaginismus or lack of lubrication.
9. *Vaginismus:* Recurrent or persistent involuntary spasm of the masculature of the outer third of the vagina that interferes with intercourse.
10. *Sexual dysfunction due to general medical condition:* Clinically significant sexual dysfunction that results in marked distress or interpersonal difficulty; the sexual dysfunction is fully explained by the physiological effect of a general medical condition.
11. *Substance-induced sexual dysfunction:* Clinically significant sexual dysfunction that is fully explained either by substance intoxication or by medication use.

Subtypes: Lifelong versus acquired; generalized versus situational; due to psychological factors versus combined factors.

TABLE 20.3 Changes in *DSM-IV* from *DSM-III*

1. Requirement that each of the dysfunctions cause marked distress or interpersonal difficulty.
2. *Female sexual arousal disorder:* Requires that the diagnosis be made solely on lack of physiological arousal.
3. *Male erectile disorder:* Requires that the diagnosis be made solely on lack of physiological arousal.
4. *Female orgasmic disorder:* Name has been changed from *inhibited sexual orgasm.*
5. *Male orgasmic disorder:* Name has been changed from *inhibited male orgasm.*
6. *Sexual dysfunction due to general medical condition* is a new entity.
7. *Substance-induced sexual dysfunction* is a new entry.

clear which problem came first, the choice of primary diagnosis may reflect the clinician's theoretical bias as much as it reflects the presented symptomatology. A multidisciplinary team consisting primarily of clinicians in North America and Europe recently proposed a new classification system for female sexual disorders (Basson et al., 2000a). This system combines organic and psychogenic etiologies into one classification system.

EPIDEMIOLOGY

The largest study of the prevalence of sexual disorders in the United States was conducted by Laumann and colleagues (1994) and is known as the National Health Social Life Survey. This survey was a probability sample of U.S. adults, ages 18 to 59. The sample consisted of 2,968 adults. All were interviewed face to face with a structured interview. Sexual dysfunction was more prevalent among women than men. Among males, the most common problems were difficulty with orgasm (8.3%), lack of interest (15.8%), rapid ejaculation (28.8%), and erectile difficulties (9.8%). Erectile difficulties were positively correlated with age. Women complained of painful coitus (14.4%), lack of interest (33.4%), inability to reach orgasm (24.1%), and difficulty with lubrication (18.8%). Feldman et al. (1994) studied the epidemiology of erectile dysfunction and its medical and psychosocial correlates in a random sample of men aged 40 to 70 who lived in cities and towns near Boston. A self-administered sexual questionnaire was utilized. Approximately half of the population reported at least occasional problems with erections. The prevalence of erectile problems was highly correlated with age. Only 5% of men aged 40 reported total erectile failure as compared to 15% of men aged 70. Other variables associated with erectile failure were depressive symptoms, cigarette smoking, heart disease, and hypertension. A prospective study of the same sample found that the incidence of impotence was related to various cardiovascular risk factors as well as a submissive personality (Araujo et al., 2000; Johannes et al., 2000).

Pinnock and colleagues (1999) used a mailed questionnaire to study the prevalence of erectile problems in a probability sample of men over 40 in South Australia. Erectile dysfunction was correlated with age: Only 3% of men 40 to 49 reported erections insufficient for coitus, compared to 64% of men ages 70 to 79. Various cardiovascular risk factors were associated with the presence of erectile dysfunction. Similar studies of the prevalence of erectile dysfunction have occurred in Thailand, Malaysia, Japan, and Italy (Kongkan, 2000; Parazzini et al., 2000; Shirai et al., 1999). In these studies, increasing age and cardiovascular risk factors were associated with erectile dysfunction.

Hawton et al. (1994) studied a community sample of middle-aged women in the Oxford area in the United Kingdom. A semistructured interview was utilized. Questions concerned sexual frequency and orgasm frequency. Marital adjustment was the main predictor of sexual activity and satisfaction. In this sample, 17% stated that they experienced orgasm on all coital opportunities; 16% said they never experienced orgasm; 29% said that they experienced orgasm more than 50% of the time; 2% said that they never enjoyed coitus, whereas 41% said that they always enjoyed coitus. Dunn et al. (1998) sent an anonymous postal questionnaire to a stratified random sample of the adult general population in the United Kingdom. More women than men had sexual problems. The most common sexual problems in women were vaginal dryness and infrequent orgasm.

Some sexual dysfunctions may be associated with other Axis I disorders. For example, mood disorder may be associated with an increased prevalence of hypoactive sexual desire disorder and male erectile dysfunction (Kennedy et al., 1999; Thase et al., 1999). Euthymic patients with a current diagnosis of hypoactive sexual desire have an increased lifetime prevalence of mood disorder (Schreiner-Engel & Schiavi, 1989). There are also reports of decreased libido being more common in patients with schizophrenia (Aizenberge et al., 1995), anorexia nervosa (Raboch & Faltus, 1991), and anxiety disorders (Minnen & Kampman, 2000). However, most cases of sexual dysfunction do not have a clear relationship to another Axis I disorder. There also is minimal evidence of a relationship between sexual dysfunction and personality disorder or even specific personality traits (Segraves, 1989). Most clinicians assume that the immediate causes of sexual dysfunction involve anxiety about performance, a cycle of demand and negative expectancies, and self-defeating cognitions (Segraves, 1989).

WHAT CONSTITUTES A SUCCESSFUL OUTCOME FOR SEXUAL THERAPY?

Psychotherapy outcome studies are notoriously difficult to design and conduct. The challenge facing researchers is not only to design methodologically sound studies but also to design studies that demonstrate regard for the complexity of the human condition. Thus, outcomes conceived solely in terms of women's facility in achieving coital orgasm, men's prowess at delaying ejaculation, the buckling force of an erection, the blood flow through the vagina, or the frequency with which partners bring their bodies to one another employ far too narrow and mechanistic criteria for success. Sexuality outcome studies need to assess the complex interplay among biological, emotional, psychological, and relational components of individuals' and couples' lives. Thus, it is not solely how many orgasms individuals achieve but the degree of satisfaction, passion, and sense of psychological and relational well-being of two individuals.

There is also disagreement as to what constitutes success even when the solely mechanistic criteria are employed. For instance, in treating female anorgasmia, what defines success—simply achieving orgasm once, achieving orgasm from manual or oral stimulation on some arbitrary percentage basis, achieving coital orgasm with or without clitoral stimulation on some arbitrary percentage basis, or another criterion? And what constitutes success in treating erectile dysfunction—the ability to consummate intercourse or the degree of penile rigidity?

The disagreements regarding success are further complicated by the primacy conferred on intercourse as the essential determinant of success. Is intercourse to be considered the sine qua non of outcome variables or simply one alternative sexual behavior in which couples may choose to engage? To date, this controversial issue has not been scientifically resolved, and success is defined through the eyes of the researcher.

METHODOLOGICAL PROBLEMS IN SEX THERAPY OUTCOME STUDIES

Spence (1991) criticizes sex therapy outcome studies' methodologies because they (a) employ small sample sizes; (b) do not use experimental control groups (waiting-list, no-treatment, attention placebo controls); (c) lack random allocation to conditions; (d) fail to offer clear-cut definitions of diagnostic criteria to permit replication; (e) generally do not include assessments of long-term outcome; and (f) do not adequately describe the therapy method utilized.

While anxiety is theoretically regarded as causing sexual dysfunction, scientific investigations supporting this important concept are sorely lacking. A number of studies have identified the role of cognitive distraction in sexual problems (Beck, Barlow, Sakheim, & Abrahamson, 1987; Cranston-Cuebas & Barlow, 1990; Palace & Gorzalka, 1992). Rosen and Leiblum (1995) suggested that the role of anxiety in sexual dysfunction needs to be reconceptionalized. It appears that it is not anxiety per se that is responsible for initiating or maintaining sexual difficulties. In most cases, it is the alternations in perceptual and attentional processes that occur in sexually dysfunctional male and female patients.

The few studies that report long-term follow-ups have suffered from serious problems of sample attrition. Thus, the generalizations from these important studies are open to question as to whether the results mirror the sample as a whole.

Other problems with sex therapy studies involve the contamination of study populations. This is most apparent in the early reports on erectile disorder, in which men suffering from organic etiologies were incorrectly diagnosed as suffering from psychogenic erectile dysfunction. In the Masters and Johnson era, knowledge regarding the pathophysiology of erectile function was lacking, as were more accurate diagnostic tests. Men who were not likely to benefit from a psychological intervention were inappropriately included in the population under study, and the outcome statistics were biased in a negative direction.

Finally, the evolution of psychiatry's diagnostic nomenclature was inconsistent regarding the categorization of and the criteria for sexual dysfunctions throughout the successive publications *DSM-I* through *DSM-IV*. This is most obvious in reviewing disorders of desire. Prior to *DSM-III* in 1980, desire disorders were diagnosed as either arousal or orgasmic dysfunctions. Thus, the early studies on arousal and orgasm disorders included individuals who today would be considered incorrectly diagnosed. Unfortunately, this diagnostic inconsistency hampers researchers' attempts to replicate the results of earlier studies.

PSYCHOLOGICAL TREATMENT OF SEXUAL DYSFUNCTIONS: GENERAL FORMULATIONS

Masters and Johnson's innovative format of employing mixed-sex cotherapy teams working with couples in a quasi-residential, daily combination of individual and conjoint treatment was an expensive, therapist-intensive, impractical model to reproduce. Their treatment model was evaluated to ascertain if similar results could be achieved with a more conservative, conventional outpatient treatment approach. Investigators examined the impact of a single therapist versus a mixed-sex cotherapy team and weekly versus daily treatment sessions. The results indicated that couples did as well when treated on a weekly basis and by a single therapist (Clement & Schmidt, 1983; Crowe, Gillan, & Golombok, 1981; Hawton, 1985; Heiman & LoPiccolo, 1983). Two studies examined whether matching the gender of the therapist with the gender of the symptom bearer would result in improved outcome: No differences were found (Crowe et al., 1981; LoPiccolo, Heiman, Hogan, & Roberts, 1985).

Hawton (1995) cautioned that not all patients with sexual complaints are suitable candidates for sex therapy. He compiled five factors associated with positive sex therapy outcome:

1. The quality of the couple's general relationship, specifically, the female partner's pretreatment assessment of the relationship (Hawton & Catalan, 1986).
2. The motivation of the partners, particularly the male partner, for treatment (Hawton & Fagg, 1991; Whitehead & Mathews, 1986).
3. Absence of serious psychiatric disorder in either partner.
4. Physical attraction between the partners.
5. Early compliance with the treatment program homework assignments.

Researchers also examined the efficacy of individual versus group treatment formats. Group formats were advantageous because they were less costly in terms of therapist time, provided patients with the knowledge that they were not alone in their suffering, offered peer support, and allowed patients to learn from the experiences of others. In addition, competition within the group motivated patients to change behaviors and desensitized patients to discussions of their private sexual lives (Spence, 1991). Conversely, group treatment is difficult to organize and institute because it requires the bringing together of several people's schedules and the fortuitous circumstance of several appropriate patients presenting with similar complaints at the same time. Group treatment also reduces the amount of time and attention any one patient can receive, increases patients' anxiety about confidentiality, and does not allow patients to proceed at either an accelerated or a delayed pace.

Spence (1991) reported that individual treatment was slightly more advantageous than group therapy for women with primary and secondary anorgasmia. Minimal differences between group and individual therapy have been reported in the treatment of premature ejaculation (Perelman, 1977), anorgasmia (Ersner-Hershfield & Kopel, 1970), and sexual anxiety (Nemetz et al., 1978). Regardless of the efficacy of groups, it seems that the vast majority of patients are seen in individual or couples therapy.

Long-term follow-up studies demonstrated the positive sustained effect of therapy on individuals' and couples' subjective sense of sexual satisfaction and self-acceptance (DeAmicus et al., 1985). These studies also documented improved marital adjustment both immediately posttermination and over the course of follow-up. Most important, these findings also hold for patients who reported little change in sexual symptomatology posttreatment or who evidenced symptom relapse during follow-up. This may be interpreted to mean that individuals' attitudes toward their sexual lives and the quality of couples' relationships tended to be enhanced through the process of therapy and that this change tended to be sustained over time.

OUTCOME OF TREATMENTS FOR SPECIFIC SEXUAL DYSFUNCTIONS

Sexual Desire Disorders

Psychotherapy

Of men and women with disorders of sexual desire, 50 to 70% appear to achieve modest gains immediately following psychotherapy. However, a marked deterioration in function was noted at a 3-year follow-up (DeAmicus et al., 1985; Hawton, 1995). (See Table 20.4 for a summary of outcome studies for females.) Half the individuals who reported success after treatment did not maintain heightened desire 3 years later. Paradoxically, couples reported improved and sustained levels of sexual satisfaction despite the regression in levels of sexual desire.

Pharmacotherapy

There is no pharmacotherapy with established efficacy for primary hypoactive sexual desire disorder. There is substantial evidence establishing that a certain minimal level of androgen is a necessary biological component of sexual desire (Davidson, Kwan, & Greenleaf, 1982), and the use of antiandrogenic drugs such as cyproterone acetate has been demonstrated to diminish libido (Kellet, 1993). However, a relationship between individual endogenous androgen production within the normal range and sexual interest has not been demonstrated, and numerous studies have failed to demonstrate a beneficial effect of exogenous androgen in eugonadal men with erectile problems and diminished sexual desire (Segraves, 1988b). In a well-controlled study, O'Carroll and Bancroft (1984) reported that exogenous androgen administration increased the frequency of sexual thoughts but had no effect on sexual activity in eugonadal men. It is possible that androgen administration has a subtle influence on libido in eugonadal men. There is no evidence to date that this effect is clinically significant.

Abnormally low endogenous androgen levels have been proposed as one etiology for hypoactive sexual desire disorder in females (Davis, 1999; Hoeger & Guzick, 1999). There is suggestive evidence of a relationship between endogenous androgen levels in females and libido (Bancroft et al., 1991; Persky et al., 1975). However, not all investigations have replicated this finding (Dennerstein et al., 1997; Galyer et al., 1999). Numerous clinicians have reported success in case studies and clinical series using androgen therapy in women complaining of low libido (Davis, 1998; Rabo, 2000; Sarrel, 1999; Sarrel et al., 1998; Warnock et al., 1999). A well-conducted study by Sherwin and Gelfand found that estrogen-androgen replacement was more successful than estrogen replacement alone in restoring libido in women who had had oophorectomies (Gelfand, 1999; Sherwin & Gelfand, 1987). However, other studies have not demonstrated a benefit of androgen therapy in postmenopausal women (Dow et al., 1983). It is possible that androgen therapy may be effective in women who have had oophorectomies but not in women

TABLE 20.4 Psychotherapy Outcome Studies for Female Hypoactive Sexual Desire Disorder

Study	*Type of Study*	*Results Posttherapy*	*Long-Term Follow-Up Results*
DeAmicus et al. (1985)	Type 3	21/25 women self-reported improvement posttherapy.	11/25 women sustained improvement 3 years after termination of treatment. On average, the women continued to report sustained levels of sexual satisfaction in spite of regression in sexual desire.
Hawton, Catalan, Martin, & Fagg (1986); Hawton (1995)	Type 3	22/32 women self-reported improvement posttherapy.	11/32 women sustained improvement 1 to 6 years after termination of treatment.

who have experienced a nonsurgical menopause (Welling et al., 1990). There is a marked decrease in androgen after bilateral oophorectomy. Changes in androgen levels after natural menopause are less and more gradual in onset. The available evidence is compatible with the use of androgen-estrogen replacement therapy postoophorectomy. Evidence for the use of androgens in premenopausal women experiencing low libido is not established (Basson, 1999). Supraphysiological levels of androgens clearly increase libido (Shifren et al., 2000; Tuiten et al., 2000). Whether physiological doses of androgen have a meaningful effect on libido exceeding that of placebo remains to be established (Guzick & Hoeger, 2000). Controlled trials do not indicate that over-the-counter food supplements containing dihydroepiandrosterone are effective in the treatment of hypoactive sexual desire disorder (Barnhart et al., 1999). A recent study reported that sildenafil was unsuccessful in restoring sexual function in a group of women experiencing arousal disorder and hypoactive sexual desire disorder (Basson et al., 2000b). A recent single-blind multisite study found that bupropion increased various indices of libido in females with idiopathic hypoactive sexual desire disorder (Segraves et al., 2001).

Female Arousal Disorders

Female arousal disorders are typically diagnosed in women who also report desire and orgasmic difficulties. The authors of this chapter did not find any controlled studies on the treatment of arousal disorders in women independent of orgasmic or desire disorders. A recent laboratory study conducted by Palace (1995) evaluated the effects of heightened autonomic arousal feedback and genital and subjective responses in a large sample of dysfunctional women. She noted that general autonomic arousal (produced by exposure to a dangerous situation) significantly increased both physiological and subjective sexual arousal. These fascinating findings require further study regarding how heightened autonomic arousal can be achieved in a real-life sexual setting and whether the gains associated with this form of arousal are sustainable over time. Another laboratory placebo-controlled study of arousal measured by vaginal photoplethysmography found that ephedrine sulfate increased vaginal pulse amplitude response but not subjective sexual arousal to erotic films (Meston & Heiman, 1998). The significance of this study for clinical practice is unclear. In a single-blind study of six postmenopausal women with arousal problems, Rosen, Phillips, et al. (1999) found that 40 mg of phentolamine increased measures of arousal on both vaginal photoplethysmography measures and self-reported sensation of vaginal lubrication and pleasurable vaginal sensations. As previously mentioned, an uncontrolled clinical trial in women with mixed sexual complaints did not find sildenafil to be clinically useful. The possible role of vasoactive agents in the treatment of female arousal disorders is unclear. In postmenopausal women, hormone replacement therapy is usually the treatment of choice. In premenopausal women, the complaint is usually of low libido combined with lack of subjective arousal.

Erectile Dysfunction

Psychotherapy

Men with lifelong and acquired erectile dysfunctions achieved significant gains both initially and over the long term following participation in sex psychotherapy. Men with acquired disorders tended to fare better than those with lifelong problems. Masters and Johnson (1970) reported initial failure rates of 41% for primary impotence and 26% for secondary impotence. Long-term failure rates were 41% and 31% for primary and secondary dysfunctions, respectively.

There are other well-controlled investigations (DeAmicus, 1985; Hawton et al., 1992; Heiman & LoPicollo, 1983; Kilmann et al., 1987; Reynolds, 1991) that have demonstrated the efficacy of psychological interventions for erectile dysfunctions, although none of these later studies have achieved the impressive results of Masters and Johnson's original study. In an excellent review of the studies of treatment for erectile dysfunction, Mohr and Beutler (1990) wrote:

> The component parts of these treatments typically include behavioral, cognitive, systemic and interpersonal communications interventions. Averaging across studies, it appears that approximately two-thirds of the men suffering from erectile failure will be satisfied with their improvement at follow-up ranging from six weeks to six years (p. 123).

These studies utilized either a couples or a group format. The duration of couples therapy ranged between 4 and 20 weekly meetings. Group therapies met weekly for 10 to 20 meetings. All forms of intervention except biofeedback were equally effective in producing sustained change. There are few controlled reports on individual therapy for men, except for the report by Reynolds (1991), who highlighted the difficulties of treating men without partners.

All studies with long-term follow-up noted a tendency for men to suffer relapses. The most discouraging report came from Levine and Agle (1978), who treated 16 couples in a Masters and Johnson format. Posttherapy, 11 of the 16 men noted improvement in erectile function. At the 3-year follow-up, only one couple was able to sustain its gains. Hawton et al. (1992) suggested that positive treatment outcome is associated with better pretreatment communication and general sexual adjustment, especially the female partner's interest in and enjoyment of sex, the absence of a psychiatric history in the woman, and the couple's willingness to complete homework. In writing about the problem of relapse in treating all forms of sexual dysfunction, Hawton (1986) reported that recurrence of or continuing difficulty with the presenting sexual problem was commonly being reported by 75% of couples; this caused little to no concern for 34%. Patients indicated that they discussed the difficulty with the partner, practiced the techniques learned during therapy, accepted that difficulties were likely to recur, and read books about sexuality.

Pharmacotherapy

Clearly, the most acceptable pharmacotherapy for erectile dysfunction is an oral medication. Indeed, when the oral agent sildenafil was approved by the FDA in 1998, its introduction was nothing short of dramatic. Sildenafil is a Type 5 phosphodiesterase inhibitor (PDE 5) (Goldstein, 1998). The drug enhances the man's ability to achieve a natural erection given adequate psychic and physical stimulation. Unlike other interventions, such as self-injection, transurethral, or vacuum therapy, sildenafil does not induce erection irrespective of the man's degree of arousal. Although myths abound, sildenafil does not improve libido, promote spontaneous erections, or increase the size of the penis. The efficacy of sildenafil has been demonstrated in multiple double-blind, placebo-controlled, multicenter studies employing outcome measures such as penile plethysmography to measure erectile response to an erotic film and a validated 15-item self-report questionnaire known as the International Index of Erectile Function (IIEF) (Osterloh et al., 1999). In these studies, there was a significant difference between all doses of sildenafil and placebo in the ability to obtain erections sufficient for penetration and the ability to maintain them after penetration. Increasing doses of sildenafil were associated with increased erectile function. Scientifically sound studies have been conducted in men with hypertension, including those currently receiving medications for their disease, and it has also been shown to be helpful to men with Type 1 and Type 2 diabetes, spinal cord injury, post-radical prostatectomy, and depression. Depending on the etiology of the dysfunction, sildenafil efficacy ranges between 40% and 80%. The most common side effects include headache and facial flushing, seen in 10 to 20% of men; dyspepsia, seen in 5% of men; and red/blue color vision changes or blurry vision, seen in 3% of men. The headache and facial flushing may be explained by the vasodilatory effects of sildenafil on the cerebral circulation. The dyspepsia is due to the small overlap in sildenafil activity with Type 4 phosphodiesterase found at the gastroesophageal sphincter, leaving the gastroesophageal sphincter open. The visual issues are due to the slight overlap with Type 6 phosphodiesterase, which exists in the eye (retina). The drug comes in three strengths, 25, 50, and 100 mg; most men (over 60%) use the 100-mg dose.

Absolute contraindications to sildenafil use are the concomitant use of nitrate drugs. Caution has been advised in patients with retinitis pigmentosa, preexisting hypotension, and multiple antihypertensive agents (American College of Cardiology and American Heart Association Consensus Group, 1999; Tomlinson, 1999). The significance of cardiac deaths is difficult to evaluate, as the majority of men taking sildenafil have cardiovascular risk factors. A small number of cases of priapism have been reported on sildenafil. The primary action of sildenafil is peripheral. It inhibits the inactivation of cyclic guanosine monophosphate, an intracellular second messenger, by phosphodiesterase Type 5. During sexual stimulation, nitric oxide release activates gaunylate cyclase, which results in the production of cyclic guanosine monophosphate (GMP). Cyclic GMP induces calcium efflux, smooth muscle relaxation, and thus penile engorgement. Sildenafil is taken as needed, reaches maximum plasma levels 1 hour after oral dosing, and has a terminal half-life of 3 to 5 hours. To date, there is minimal information about the psychological effect of restoration of potency in men with psychogenic impotence. One 12-week study has shown that men with subsyndromal depression have an improvement in mood after the restoration of erectile function (Rosen, Seidman, et al., 1999). From this study, one cannot determine if the mood elevation is sustained. One clinician reported two cases in which the restoration of erectile function appeared to precipitate severe marital discord (Wise, 1999). Since most sildenafil prescriptions are written by physicians without training in evaluation of couple interaction, it is important to know if the case report of marital discord after restoration of erectile function is an isolated finding.

Other Type 5 phosphodiesterase inhibitors are under development and should be available in 2002. Preliminary data regarding these compounds is quite encouraging. Prior to sildenafil the only other oral agent for erectile dysfunction was yohimbine, a natural herb of an African tree bark. Yohimbine is an alpha-2 adrenergic antagonist (Morales et al., 1994). Double-blind studies have shown that yohimbine has modest efficacy, mainly in men with psychogenic erectile problems (Reid et al., 1997; Riley et al., 1989; Sondra et al., 1990; Susset et al., 1989). There are few objective, placebo-controlled studies that validate the efficacy of yohimbine.

Other pharmacotherapies for erectile dysfunction include transurethral systems (MUSE) and intracorporeal injection therapy. Both these methods employ different delivery systems to introduce vasoactive substances into the corpora cavernosa of the penis. Of the two approaches, intracavernosal injection therapy has a higher success rate in producing firm erections. The parameters of such therapy, dose regimes, and side effects are well established. The efficacy for psychogenic as well as organic erectile problems appears well established (Althof et al., 1991). There is much less research concerning the psychological benefits of this form of therapy. The three most common agents used to induce erections are papaverine hydrochloride, phentolamine, and prostaglandin E1. Although they are frequently combined, each agent can be used singly (Althof & Seftel, 1995). As one might expect, there have also been a number of reports and studies employing the triple therapy of papaverine, phentolamine, and prostaglandin E1 (Barada & McKimmy, 1994). Triple therapy appears to have superior results over the use of papaverine-phentolamine combination therapy for some conditions, such as severe arteriogenic disease (McMahon, 1991). Triple therapy has also been used in patients with psychogenic impotence (Bennett et al., 1991). Papaverine and papaverine-phentolamine injection therapy have the disadvantages of delayed corporeal fibrosis, variable efficacy, systemic reactions, and the risk of prolonged erections (Levine et al., 1989). Prostaglandin E1 has the advantages of having a reliable dose-response curve, less risk for prolonged erection, less systemic side effects, and less delayed corporeal fibrosis. It has the major disadvantage of pain at the injection site. With all agents, a proper dose is established, and the patient is instructed in self-administration and given a "home kit."

Probably the best study of intracavernosal therapy for psychogenic male erectile disorder was conducted by the Althof group (Althof et al., 1989; Turner et al., 1989). In one of their studies, 15 men with psychogenic impotence (4 lifelong, 11 acquired; average age 49; average duration of impotence 12 years) were compared to 74 men with organic impotence and 42 men with impotence of mixed etiology. All patients completed an extensive psychometric battery that included the Case Western Reserve University Sexual Functioning Questionnaire, the Dyadic Adjustment Scale, the Beck Depression Inventory, the Spielberger State Trait Anxiety Inventory, the Personal Evaluation Inventory, and a 40-item self-report scale. All patients were started on the same papaverine-phentolamine self-injection program and assessed at baseline and 1, 3, and 6 months. At the 6-month follow-up, the men with psychogenic impotence who were still participating in the self-injection program reported an average use of four times monthly and satisfactory erections after injection on 94% of the occasions. There was no evidence of psychological deterioration, no evidence of symptom substitution, and some evidence of improvement in anxiety measures. Unfortunately, only 6 of the 15 patients with psychogenic impotence completed the trial. However, the three groups did not differ in dropout rates; all groups experienced approximately a 60% dropout rate. The three major factors accounting for dropout were the idea of self-injection, worry about side effects, and concern about artificiality. The available evidence does not suggest a harmful psychosocial effect of intracavernosal therapy on psychogenic erectile problems. However, these conclusions have to be tempered by the extremely small sample that completed treatment.

Transurethral therapy came into being through the development of an innovative drug delivery system that allowed medication to be directly applied to the urethral mucosa. The major advantage of this treatment method is that it obviates the need to inject the penis to create an erection. Through vascular channels medication placed on the urethral mucosa is transferred to the corpus cavernosum, and the result is an erection. MUSE is an acronym for *medicated urethral system for erection*, which deposits a semisolid pellet of prostaglandin E1 directly on the urethral mucosa. This proprietary drug delivery system consists of a polypropylene applicator with a hollow stem 3.2 cm long and 3.5 mm in diameter. Prostaglandin E1 in one of four predetermined dose levels (125, 250, 500, or 1000 μg) is contained within the tip of the applicator. Prior to using the MUSE, patients are instructed to void so that residual urine provides a natural lubricant for the slow and gentle insertion of the stem into the urethra. A button on the crown of the applicator is depressed, depositing the pellet approximately 3 cm into the urethra. The applicator is then withdrawn. An erectile response is evident within 10 minutes and lasts for 30–60 minutes. In double-blind, placebo-controlled studies, Padma-Nathan, Hellstrom, and Kaiser (1997) reported that 43% of patients had intercourse on at least one occasion. Lewis (1998) described that, by use of an external constriction device, the Actis ring, the number of patients able to achieve intercourse improved to approximately 60%. Although this device is effective in producing a Grade 3 or 4 erection in spinal-cord-injured men with residual upper motor neuronal function, with erectile dysfunction, Bodner et al. (1999) found that erection created by MUSE was less acceptable to the 15 patients tested than the erection created by intracavernosal injection therapy. The most common side effects are penile pain 32%, urethral burning 12%, minor urethral bleeding/spotting 5%, and flu symptoms 4%. Priapism and cavernosal fibrosis were evident in less than 0.1%. Vaginal burning or itching was noted by 5.8% of the female partners, and it is recommended that a condom barrier be employed if the female partner is pregnant. Other experimental approaches include the use of transdermal nitroglycerin and/or transdermal nitroglycerin-minoxidil to induce erections (Baert, 1989; Cavailini, 1991; Owen et al., 1989). There are not enough data available on these new methods to judge their general applicability or efficacy.

Another approach to the pharmacotherapy of erectile dysfunction has been the use of dopaminergic agents. Earlier double-blind studies suggested that levodopa has efficacy in the treatment of erectile dysfunction (Benkert et al., 1972; Pierini & Nusimovich, 1981). Considerable attention is currently being given to the evaluation of apomorphine for the treatment of erectile problems. Lal and coworkers at the Montreal General Hospital observed that men being treated for alcoholism with aversive conditioning utilizing apomorphine reported spontaneous erections (Lal et al., 1987, 1991). Other clinicians have noted that patients being treated for Parkinson's disease with apomorphine reported spontaneous erections (O'Sullivan & Hughes, 1998). Three separate double-blind trials have established that subcutaneous apomorphine is effective in eliciting erections approximately 20 minutes after administration (Danjou et al., 1988; Lal et al., 1984; Segraves et al., 1991). It has been hypothesized that apomorphine acts at the level of the paraventricular nucleus of the brain (Chen et al., 1999). Early data suggests a significant improvement in erectile activity over placebo (Heaton et al., 1995; Mulhall & Goldstein, 1999). The main side effect appears to be nausea, which is counteracted with an oral antiemetic. The clinical utility of both subcutaneous and sublingual apomorphine has been limited by its propensity to cause nausea.

Phentolamine is a mixed alpha 1 and 2 antagonist. Alpha 1 adrenoceptor stimulation mediates corporus-cavernosal vasoconstriction. Postjunctional alpha-2 receptors may also subserve a part of cavernosal muscle contraction. Over 700 patients with erectile dysfunction have been studied in double-blind placebo-controlled trials studying the efficacy of oral phentolamine. In these trials the placebo response was approximately 20%, whereas phentolamine was effective in 30 to 40% of patients. The major side effects were rhinitis, headache, and dizziness (Wyllie & Anderson, 1999). Most of these studies are unpublished. It is unclear whether the pharmaceutical company involved intends to conduct future trials with this agent.

Several double-blind placebo-controlled studies have found that naltrexone, an opiate receptor antagonist, increases the frequency of early-morning erections (van Ahlen et al., 1995; Brennemann et al., 1993; Fabbri et al., 1997). Unfortunately, two out of the three studies found that naltrexone increased early-morning erections without improving erectile function in partner sexual activities.

A variety of other substances are being evaluated as possible oral erectogenic agents (Gonzalez-Cadavid & Rajfer, 1999). It appears imperative that more mental health professionals become involved in investigating which forms of therapy are best suited to which types of patients and the cost-effectiveness of different approaches. From a clinical perspective, one would suspect that certain patients with erectile difficulties might benefit from cognitive behavioral treatment combined with pharmacotherapy. This remains clinical speculation, and there is no evidence concerning the indicators for combined therapy as opposed to behavior therapy alone or pharmacotherapy alone.

Vacuum Tumescence Devices

An alternative strategy for the man who is resistant to trying or has not benefited from psychotherapy and who finds the concept of self-injection of a substance into the penis somewhat aversive is the use of the external vacuum erection device. The vacuum device is placed over the penis, and a negative pressure facilitates blood flow into the penis, producing an erection. A tension ring (rubber band) is slipped from the base of the vacuum erection device to the base of the penis, maintaining the erection. Different studies utilizing diverse patient populations have reported that between 70% and 100% of men will achieve erections using this device (Althof & Seftel, 1995; Turner et al., 1991, 1992). Dropout rates are around 20%. Side effects are minimal, and there is no evidence of significant negative psychological effects from employing this device. To date, there is insufficient evidence for the clinician to know when to employ which of the many interventions possible for erectile disorder.

Premature Ejaculation

Since the early 1970s, an array of individual, conjoint, and group therapy approaches employing behavioral strategies such as stop-start (Masters & Johnson, 1970) or squeeze techniques (Semans, 1956) have evolved as the psychological treatments of choice for rapid ejaculation (Halvorsen & Metz, 1999; Kaplan, 1971; Levine, 1992a). It is now known that the impressive initial posttreatment success rates, ranging from 60% to 95% (Hawton, 1986, 1988; Masters & Johnson, 1966), are not necessarily sustainable. Three years after treatment, success rates dwindled to 25% (Bancroft, 1976; DeAmicus et al., 1985; Hawton, 1988).

Men have resorted to wearing multiple condoms, applying desensitization ointment to the penis, repeatedly masturbating prior to intercourse, not allowing partners to stimulate them, or distracting themselves by performing complex mathematical computations while making love to overcome rapid ejaculation. These tactics, however creative, curtail the pleasures of lovemaking and are generally unsuccessful.

The prevailing opinions regarding the etiology of rapid ejaculation have typically assumed that the dysfunction was either psychological or learned, depending upon the theorist's assumptions about how the mind operates. Clinicians surmised that the lowered ejaculatory threshold stemmed from anxiety regarding unresolved fears of the vagina, hostility toward women, interpersonal conflicts with a particular partner, or conditioning patterned on early hurried sexual experiences with prostitutes or hasty lovemaking in the backseat of a car. Once established, performance anxiety was thought to maintain the rapid ejaculatory pattern. Strassberg (1987) and Godpodinoff (1989) independently speculated that a subgroup of rapid ejaculators may have a neurophysiological vulnerability and that this biological vulnerability explains some failures of psychological treatments. There is still little evidence to support this most interesting notion.

TABLE 20.5 Psychotherapy Outcome for Rapid Ejaculation

Study	*Type*	*Results*
Masters & Johnson (1970)	3	2.2% failure rate 2.7% at follow-up
Heiman & LoPiccolo (1983)	3	Ejaculatory latency of 4 to 6 minutes Loss of 2 minutes at follow-up
DeAmicus et al. (1985)	3	15/20 improved and sustained at 3-year follow-up
Hawton (1982)	3	6/8 improved; 2/8 at 1- to 6-year follow-up

Pharmacological Treatment of Premature Ejaculation

A large number of placebo-controlled, double-blind studies have demonstrated that fluoxetine, sertraline, clomipramine, and paroxetine can be used to delay ejaculatory latency in men with rapid ejaculation. Consistent findings have been obtained using a variety of outcome measures, including patient estimate of time between penetration and ejaculation, partner estimate, and patient or partner report of stopwatch readings. It appears that ejaculatory delay occurs only during active drug treatment and that sustained pharmacotherapy is necessary for most men to maintain a slower pattern of ejaculation. Chronic treatment with 20 to 40 mg paroxetine (McMahon & Touma, 1990; Waldinger et al., 1994, 1997), 25 to 50 mg clomipramine (Althof et al., 1995; Kim & Seo, 1998), 50 to 200 mg sertraline (Biri et al., 1998; Kim & Seo, 1998; McMahon, 1998; Mendels et al., 1995), and 20 mg fluoxetine (Haensel et al., 1998; Kara et al., 1996) has been shown to increase ejaculatory control in men with rapid ejaculation.

Because some patients prefer not to take medication continuously for an episodic activity, some investigators have investigated the efficacy of various drugs taken as needed. Segraves and coworkers (1993) reported on a double-blind, placebo-controlled study of 25 to 50 mg of clomipramine taken 6 hours prior to anticipated sexual activity. At the beginning of the study, all patients had ejaculatory latencies of less than 60 seconds after penetration. On 25 mg and 50 mg of clomipramine, this latency increased to an average of 6.1 minutes and 8.4 minutes, respectively. In a similar study, Strassberg et al. (1999) found that 25 mg of clomipramine taken 4 to 6 hours prior to coitus increased ejaculatory latency from less than 1 minute to an average of 3.5 minutes. Two investigators have examined the efficacy of chronic pretreatment followed by intermittent dosing as needed. Kim and Paick (1999) reported that 2 weeks of 50 mg of daily sertraline followed by 50 to 100 mg taken at the day of anticipated coitus at 5:00 P.M. resulted in significant improvement. Patients increased ejaculatory latency from an average of 23 seconds to 4 to 5 minutes of chronic and intermittent dosing. From the study design, it is impossible to determine if the chronic pretreatment was necessary for the as-needed treatment to be effective. An interesting study by McMahon and Touma (1999) examined the role of chronic pretreatment for on-demand therapy and the relative efficacy of on-demand versus daily treatment with 20 mg paroxetine. Pretreatment ejaculatory latency was approximately 24 seconds. With chronic treatment of 20 mg paroxetine daily, the average ejaculatory latency increased to 4.5 minutes. Successful patients in this group were then switched to an on-demand dosing schedule of 20 mg paroxetine taken 3 to 4 hours prior to coitus. Thirty-two percent of the previously successful patients stated that they lost ejaculatory control upon switching to an on-demand schedule. Another group of men was started on an on-demand-dosing regime of 20 mg paroxetine 3 to 4 hours prior to coitus. This group reported an increase of ejaculatory latency to 1.5 minutes, which was less than the average latency of 3.9 minutes in the group switched from chronic to on-demand dosing. The available data suggest that clomipramine can be started as an on-demand drug, whereas paroxetine and sertraline might be more effective if on-demand use was preceded by chronic dosing.

Two different investigations have compared the relative efficacy of various serotonergic antidepressants on ejaculatory control in men with rapid ejaculation. Waldinger et al. (1998) investigated the relative efficacy of 20 mg paroxetine, 20 mg fluoxetine, and 50 mg sertraline and 100 mg fluvoxamine on ejaculatory delay. In this 6-week trial, paroxetine was the most effective, followed by fluoxetine and then sertraline. Fluvoxamine was not significantly different from placebo. Kim and Seo (1998) studied the effects of 4 weeks of daily therapy with fluoxetine, sertraline, or clomipramine. Clomipramine was the most effective followed by sertraline. Fluoxetine was not statistically different from placebo. A number of investigators have investigated whether men with rapid ejaculation can be distinguished from men with good ejaculatory control on various measures, including sensory thresholds and somatosensory evoked potentials (Paick et al., 1998; Yilmaz et al., 1999; Xin et al., 1997). Findings to date have not been consistent.

SS-cream is a newly developed topical agent that is made from the extracts of nine natural products and that is applied to the glans penis 1 hour before sexual intercourse (Xin et al., 2000). In placebo-controlled, double-blind studies, this compound significantly improved ejaculation latency and sexual satisfaction. SS-cream increases the penile sensory threshold in a dose-dependent manner and has side effects that include mild local burning and mild pain.

Female Orgasmic Disorders

Spence (1991) offers a cogent summary of the dilemmas to be considered in assessing the efficacy of psychological therapy for women with orgasmic disorders. The major issue remains unresolved: Is success predicated solely on coital orgasm, or orgasm through any means, or by a subjective rating of increased satisfaction within the sexual relationship? Adding to the confusion is the media's constant reinforcement of unrealistic expectations from sexual encounters. Both men and women are led to believe that all women can easily and regularly achieve intense multiple orgasms from intercourse alone.

Several studies (Kuriansky & Sharpe, 1981; Kuriansky, Sharpe, & O'Connor, 1982; Riley & Riley, 1978; Spence, 1991) have documented the success of masturbatory training programs in facilitating orgasm in women who have never achieved orgasm. Initial success rates range between 70% and 90%, with women being treated individually, in couples, or groups, or exposed to either videotapes or written material concerning masturbatory training programs. Kuriansky and Sharpe (1981) reported that 15% of their subjects were not able to sustain orgasmic achievement at a 2-year follow-up.

Whatever the success in achieving orgasm via masturbatory training, it begins to diminish as the woman moves from self-induced orgasm to partner-induced orgasm through manual or oral stimulation or intercourse-induced orgasm without manual stimulation. Immediately posttherapy, Kuriansky reported 89% of women achieved orgasm by themselves, 21% within the "context of a partner encounter," and 16% with intercourse alone. Heiman and LoPiccolo (1983) reported a two- to threefold (35 to 40% success rate) increase in coital orgasm at a 3 month follow up. See Table 20.6 for a summary of psychotherapy outcome studies.

The long-term results for female orgasmic dysfunction differ in two significant directions from treatments of other sexual disorders. First, over time, women demonstrate an increased capacity to achieve orgasm in partner-related as well as coital encounters. Within 2 years, women achieved greater facility in achieving orgasm within the context of a partner encounter (47%) and via intercourse (26%). In addition, those women who dropped out of a treatment program also reported improved orgasmic functioning 2 years after beginning therapy. Second, the prognosis appears more positive for women with lifelong orgasmic dysfunction than for women who acquire the dysfunction after a period of normal function. These fascinating findings can be explained by (a) practice, (b) reinforcement by success, (c) decreased inhibition, and (d) increased harmony with the body and willingness to generate pleasurable internal sensations that culminate in orgasm. The worse outcome for an acquired dysfunction occurs when the problem is posited to result from psychological causes (relationship deterioration) for the appearance of the dysfunction generally were not addressed in masturbatory training programs.

Male Orgasmic Disorder

Male orgasmic disorder or delayed or absent ejaculation is found in only 3 to 8% of men (Hawton, 1982; Masters & Johnson, 1970; Spector & Carey, 1990). There are no large-scale, long-term controlled outcome studies of men in whom this is considered a purely psychogenic condition. There are two antithetical points of view for understanding this dysfunction: the inhibition model and a desire deficit model. Treatment efforts are guided by the assumptions underlying these contrary models. When seen through the lens of the inhibition mode, behaviorists assume that the man is not receiving sufficient stimulation to reach the orgasmic threshold. Dynamic clinicians who adhere to the inhibition model assume that the symptom is a conscious or unconscious expression of the man's aggression (i.e., withholding or depriving his partner of something the partner desires). Treatment efforts therefore aim to increase excitement through prolonged, intense, rough stimulation or by interpreting the man's aggressive impulses. Masters and Johnson (1970) reported a failure rate of 17.6% using a combination of sensate focus, vigorous noncoital penile stimulation, and modifications in intercourse technique. Schnellen (1968) reported that 81% of men who prior to treatment were anorgasmic were successful in reaching orgasm through vibrator stimulation.

TABLE 20.6 Psychotherapy Outcome Studies of Female Orgasm Disorder

Study	*Type*	*Outcome*	*Follow-up*
Masters & Johnson (1970)	3	Failure rate 16.6–22.8%	Failure rate 17.6%
Riley & Riley (1979)	3	90% success	
Kuriansky et al. (1982)	3	95% success	84% sustained
Heiman & LoPiccolo (1983)	3	15–40% success	Sustained
DeAmicus et al. (1985)	3	64–76% success	Sustained
Kilmann et al. (1986)	3	25% improved	Sustained

Apfelbaum (1989) presented an alternative model, suggesting that delayed ejaculation is a desire disorder disguised as a performance disorder. He criticized those employing the inhibition model, stating that intense stimulation is a demanding coercive strategy that heightens performance anxiety. His treatment efforts were aimed at having the man acknowledge his lack of both desire to have intercourse and arousal during intercourse.

Dyspareunia and Vaginismus

Dyspareunia, or painful coitus, is a common sexual complaint among women, accounting for 10 to 15% of female respondents in community-based surveys (Rosen & Leiblum, 1995). Physical factors (hymeneal scarring, infection, sexually transmitted diseases, estrogen deficiency, pelvic inflammatory disease, and vulvar vestibulitis) frequently underlie this condition; however, even if the etiology is physical, there is likely to be a conditioned psychological response that may require psychological intervention (Sarrel & Sarrel, 1989; Schover, Youngs, & Canata, 1992). In addition, psychosocial factors alone, such as relationship discord and prior sexual abuse, have been cited as etiological agents (Binik et al., 1995; Rosen & Leiblum, 1989, 1995).

Vaginismus or the persistent and recurrent involuntary spasm of the musculature of the outer third of the vagina has been characterized as a psychosomatic disorder, a phobia, a conditioned response, or a conversion reaction (Leiblum et al., 1988). A spectrum of etiological factors, such as specific trauma(s), interpersonal and intrapsychic conflict, penetration anxiety, and multiple organic pathologies, cause this dysfunction. Approximately 10 to 30% of the male partners of these women report erectile or ejaculatory dysfunctions (Levine, 1988, 1992a).

Vaginismus is typically treated through a combination of (a) banning intercourse, (b) in vivo graduated self-insertion of dilators of increasing size, (c) systematic densensitization, (d) Kegel exercises, and (e) interpretation of resistance and psychodynamic fears. Masters and Johnson (1970) reported a 100% success rate in their treatment of 29 women. Spence (1991) suggested that more treatment sessions are required when women (a) have experienced the dysfunction over extended periods of time, (b) have undergone surgery, (c) have thoughts of anatomical abnormality, and (d) have a negative attitude toward their genitals. The need for treatment sessions was related to a strong desire for pregnancy, presence of an assertive husband, and sexual knowledge on the woman's part.

Substance-Induced Sexual Disorders

The diagnostic entity of substance-induced sexual disorders (i.e., sexual disorders associated with drug intoxication and associated with the use of prescribed medication) was introduced in *DSM-IV*. A variety of chemical agents have been associated with sexual dysfunction. Most of the reports concern substances of abuse, antihypertensive agents, and psychiatric drugs.

Sexual dysfunction has been long been assumed to be related to chronic alcohol abuse. In particular, it has been assumed that chronic alcohol abuse in males is associated with erectile dysfunction (Miller & Gold, 1988; Schiavi, 1990). Although less evidence is available concerning the effects of chronic alcohol abuse in females, most clinicians assume that chronic alcohol abuse may also be detrimental to female sexual function (Rosen, 1991). There is considerable evidence that chronic alcohol abuse has deleterious effects on hypothalamic-pituitary and testicular function (Schiavi, Stimmel, Mandeli, & White, 1995). Chronic alcohol abuse is associated with damage to the central nervous system, as manifested by dementia and Wernicke-Korsakoff syndrome. Peripheral polyneuropathy is also associated with myelin and axon degeneration as a common neurological complication of chronic alcoholism. Thus, there are several mechanisms by which chronic alcohol abuse could cause sexual dysfunction.

In reality, the controlled evidence linking chronic alcohol abuse to sexual dysfunction is limited and concerns only male alcoholics. Much of the available evidence contains numerous methodological flaws. The major studies to date have either been retrospective (Lemere & Smith, 1973), lacked control groups, or had other methodological flaws, such as including patients on disulfiram treatment (Jensen, 1984) or other pharmacological agents associated with sexual dysfunction (Whalley, 1978). Studies utilizing nocturnal penile tumescence as a measure of erectile function have reported decreased erectile capacity in patients with chronic alcoholism. These studies have methodological flaws, such as studying the patient shortly after detoxification (Snyder & Karacan, 1981a, 1981b). As disulfiram treatment has been shown to decrease erectile capacity (Tan et al., 1984), it is important that studies clearly indicate whether or not patients have received this treatment.

Schiavi et al. (1995) investigated sexual function and nocturnal penile tumescence and conducted various laboratory tests, including those of testosterone, luteinizing hormone, prolactin, and liver enzymes, in 20 healthy alcoholics with at least a 10-year history of problem drinking who had been abstinent for 2 months and were in a stable sexual relationship as compared to an age-matched nonalcoholic control group. Surprisingly, they found no significant differences between the two groups in sexual function, nocturnal penile tumescence, or hormone levels. These data suggest that a history of alcoholism in the absence of significant hepatic or gonadal failure and in a period of sobriety may be compatible with normal sexual function. It should be noted that this population might represent a particular subgroup of patients with chronic alcoholism in that they were disease-free and capable of maintaining a stable sexual relationship.

Evidence concerning the effects of narcotics on sexual function has been uniform and convincing. The evidence consists of anecdotal reports, surveys, and clinical studies. All of the studies are uniform in finding diminished libido while the person is on narcotics (Abel, 1985). Retrospective studies suggest that normal libido returns during drug-free periods (Segraves, Madsen, Carver, & Davis, 1985). Cocaine and amphetamine use has been reported to cause increased libido and spontaneous erections (Abel, 1985). However, there is evidence that chronic abuse of these agents may lead to decreased libido and other sexual dysfunctions (Siegel, 1977). It is unclear whether sexuality returns to the baseline during abstinence from these agents.

A number of clinical series and case reports establish the likelihood of a high frequency of sexual disorders, including decreased libido, erectile dysfunction, and anorgasmia while individuals are on many antihypertensive agents (e.g., spironolactone, chlorthalidone, alpha methyldapa, reserpine, guanethidine, prapranolol, clonidine, verapamil, and infidipine) (Rosen & Leiblum, 1995; Segraves, 1988; Segraves et al., 1985). Unfortunately, most of these reports do not include control groups or utilize appropriate measures of sexual function.

In one of the few properly controlled studies in this area of inquiry, Rosen and Kostis (1991) compared sexual function in men randomly assigned to propranalol or a placebo for 3 months. Propranalol therapy led to a significant decrease in the frequency of full erections. Among antihypertensive drugs, alpha-blockers such as prazosin and labetalol appear to have the lowest incidence of drug-induced sexual dysfunction, although these agents may be associated with ejaculatory inhibition (Foreman et al., 1994).

Psychiatric drugs have also been reported to cause sexual problems. This is true of almost all classes of psychiatric drugs. Most of the evidence concerning the action of these drugs comes from clinical reports, and only a handful of controlled studies have been performed. Benzodiazepines have been frequently reported to cause delay in orgasm. This has been reported with chlordiazepoxide, lorazepam, diazepam, and alprazolam (Segraves, 1995a, 1995b). A double-blind controlled study by Riley and Riley (1988) demonstrated a dose-response relationship between diazepam dose and orgasmic delay. There have been reports of association of antipsychotic agents such as thioridazine, chlorpromazine, trifluoroperazine, and haloperidol with either decreased libido or erectile problems. Ejaculatory problems have been reported with thioridazine, chlorpromazine, chlorprothixine, mesoridazine, perphenazine, trifluoroperazine, and risperidone. The one double-blind controlled study in this area of inquiry utilized minimal drug dosages and is thus of little value for this review (Tennett et al., 1972). Aizenberg et al. (1996) reported that the addition of low-dose imipramine would offset sexual dysfunction induced by thioridazine. This report has not been replicated by other clinicians. Antipsychotic-induced sexual dysfunction has been reported to correlate with prolactin elevation. There has been interest in whether the newer prolactin-sparing antipsychotics would have a lower incidence of sexual dysfunction. At this point, the evidence is inconclusive, partly because of the high prevalence of sexual problems in patients with untreated schizophrenia (Aizenberg et al., 1995; Montejo et al., 1998) and partly because of methodological problems in assessment. Most reports are in agreement that risperidone causes more sexual dysfunction than olanzapine (Tran et al., 1997) and that the sexual problems with risperidone appear dose-related (Marder & Meibach, 1994). The evidence concerning the relative incidence of sexual side effects on prolactin-sparing and traditional antipsychotics is in conflict (Hummer et al., 1999; Montejo et al., 1998). There have been case reports of antipsychotic-induced sexual dysfunction being reversed by sildenafil (Segraves, 1999; Salerian et al., 2000).

Most of the antidepressants available in the United States have been reported to cause sexual dysfunction with the possible exceptions of bupropion, mintazapine, and nefazodone (Segraves, 1995a, 1995b). This phenomenon has been confirmed in double-blind studies of many of the antidepressants (Feiger et al., 1996; Harrison et al., 1985; Kowalski et al., 1985; Monteiro et al., 1987; Segraves et al., 2000). A variety of interventions have been suggested for antidepressant-induced sexual dysfunction. These include drug holidays, changing time of dose, lowering dose, waiting for tolerance to develop, and the use of antidotes. Numerous antidotes have been reported in case reports. Some of these are the addition of bupropion, mirtazapine, nefazodone, yohimbine, cyprohepatadine, amphetamine, and many other antidotes (Rosen, Seidman, et al., 1999). The only antidotes proven effective in double-blind trials are sildenafil (Hargreave, 1998) and buspirone (Landen et al., 1999).

In a controlled study of clomipramine in patients with obsessive compulsive disorder, Monteiro et al. (1987) reported that this drug significantly interfered with orgasm in all subjects who took a dose in excess of 100 mg. Many subjects experienced total anorgasmia.

FUTURE DEVELOPMENTS

The release of sildenafil has contributed to an explosion of research concerning the pharmacological treatment of human sexual disorders. A beneficial result of the search for a treatment for female sexual dysfunction has been the appreciation of the role of biological factors in female sexuality. Desire disorders are the most common female sexual complaint. This has contributed to a search for compounds that affect sexuality by acting on the central nervous system. This work will undoubtedly contribute to a better understanding of the neurophysiological substrates of human libido. Research documenting how these interventions might be optimally employed in differing psychosocial contexts will be a natural outcome of finding new pharmacological interventions for sexual difficulties. Normal sexual function involves a complicated interactive sequencing of biological, social, relational, and individual psychological events, and effective interventions will require an appreciation of the potential complexity of these different interactive influences. This appreciation is not evident in many contemporary clinical trials.

Certain areas of advance appear almost certain to occur in the near future. More effective pharmacological treatments for sexual disorders will result in refinement of our diagnostic assessment. Pharmacotherapeutic advances will undoubtedly highlight the need for a great understanding of the interaction of biological and psychosocial influences on sexual behavior. This understanding will undoubtedly lead to integrative biological psychosocial therapies and delineation of when therapies should be combined or used in isolation.

References

Abel, L. (1985). *Psychoactive drugs and sex*. New York: Plenum Press.

Ackerman, M., & Carey, M. (1995). Psychology's role in the assessment of erectile dysfunction, historical precedents, current knowledge, and methods. *Journal of Consulting and Clinical Psychology, 63,* 862–876.

Aizenberg, D., Shiloh, R., Zemishlany, Z., & Weizman, A. (1996). Low-dose imipramine for thioridazine-induced male orgasmic disorder. *Journal of Sex and Marital Therapy, 22,* 225–229.

Aizenberg, D., Zemishlany, Z., Dorfman-Etrog, P., & Weizman, A. (1995). Sexual dysfunction in male schizophrenic patients. *Journal of Clinical Psychiatry, 56,* 137–144.

Althof, S. (1989). Psychogenic impotence: Treatment of men and couples. In R. C. Rosen & S. R. Leiblum (Eds.), *Principles and practice of sex therapy: Update for the 1990s* (pp. 237–268). New York: Guilford Press.

Althof, S. E. (1995a). Pharmacological treatment for rapid ejaculation: Preliminary strategies, concerns and questions. *Sex and Marital Therapy, 10,* 247–251.

Althof, S. E. (1995b). Pharmacological treatment of rapid ejaculation. *Psychiatric Clinics of North America,* 85–94.

Althof, S., Levine, S., Corry, P., Risen, C., Stern, E., & Kurit, D. (1995). Clomipramine as a treatment for rapid ejaculation: A double-blind crossover trial of 15 couples. *Journal of Clinical Psychiatry, 56,* 402–407.

Althof, S., & Seftel, A. D. (1995). The evaluation and treatment of erectile dysfunction. *Psychiatric Clinics of North America,* 171–192.

Althof, S., Turner, L., Levine, S., Kursh, E., Bodner, D., & Resnick, M. (1989). Why do so many people drop out from auto injection therapy for impotence? *Journal of Sex and Marital Therapy, 15,* 121–129.

Althof, S., Turner, L., Levine, S., Risen, C., Bodner, D., Kursh, E., & Resnick, M. (1991). Long term use of intra cavernous therapy in the treatment of erectile dysfunction. *Journal of Sex and Marital Therapy, 17*(2), 101–112.

American College of Cardiology and American Heart Association Consensus Group. (1999). Use of sildenafil (Viagra) in patients with cardiovascular disease. *Circulation, 99,* 168–177.

American Psychiatric Association. (1952). *Diagnostic and statistical manual of mental disorders.* Washington, DC: Author.

American Psychiatric Association. (1968). *Diagnostic and statistical manual of mental disorders* (2nd ed.). Washington, DC: Author.

American Psychiatric Association. (1980). *Diagnostic acrd statistical manual of mental disorders* (3rd ed.). Washington, DC: Author.

American Psychiatric Association. (1987). *Diagnostic and statistical manual of mental disorders* (3rd ed., rev.). Washington, DC: Author.

American Psychiatric Association. (1994). *Diagnostic and statistical manual of mental disorders* (4th ed.). Washington, DC: Author.

Apfelbaum, B. (1989). Retarded ejaculation: A much misunderstood syndrome. In R. C. Rosen & S. R. Leiblum (Eds.), *Principles and practice of sex therapy: Update for the 1990s* (pp. 168–206). New York: Guilford Press.

Araujo, A. B., Johannes, C. B., Derby, C. A., & McKinlay, J. B. (2000). Relation between psychosocial risk factors and incident erectile problems: Prospective results from the Massachusetts Male Aging Study. *American Journal of Epidemiology, 152,* 533–541.

Assalian, P. (1988). Clomipramine in the treatment of premature ejaculation. *Journal of Sex Research, 24,* 231–215.

Baert, H. C. (1989). Transcutaneous nitroglycerin therapy in the treatment of impotence. *Urology International, 44,* 309–312.

Bancroft, J., & Coles, L. (1976). Three years experience in a sexual problem clinic. *British Medical Journal, 1,* 1575–1577.

Bancroft, J. J., Sherwin, B. B., Alexander, G., Davidson, D. W., & Walker, A. (1991). Oral contraceptives and the sexuality of young women. *Archives of Sexual Behavior, 20,* 121–136.

Barada, J. H., & McKimmy, R. M. (1994). *Diagnosis and management of erectile dysfunction* (pp. 229–250). Philadelphia: Saunders.

Barnhart, K. T., Freeman, E., Grisso, J. A., Rader, D. J., Sammel, M., Kapoor, S., & Nestler, J. E. (1999). The effect of dehydroepiandrosterone supplementation to symptomatic perimenopausal women on serum endocrine profiles, lipid profiles, and health related quality of life. *Journal of Clinical Endocrinology and Metabolism, 84,* 3896–3902.

Basson, R. (1999). Androgen replacement for women. *Canadian Family Physician, 45,* 2100–2107.

Basson, R., Berman, I., Burnet, A., Derogatis, L., Ferguson, D., Fourcrou, J., Goldstein, I., Graziottin, A., Heiman, J., Laan, E., Leiblum, S., Padma-Nathan, H., Rosen, R., Segraves, K., Segraves, R., Shabsign, R., Sipski, M., Wagner, E., & Whipple, B. (2000). Report of the international consensus development conference on female sexual dysfunction: Definitions and classifications. *Journal of Urology, 163,* 888–893.

Basson, R., McInnes, R., Smith, M. D., Hodgson, G., Spain, T., & Koppiker, N. (2000). Efficacy and safety of sildenafil in estrogenized women with sexual dysfunction associated with female sexual arousal disorder. *Obstetrics and Gynecology, 95*(4 Suppl 1), S-54.

Beck, J., Barlow, D., Sakheim, D. K., & Abrahamson, D. J. (1987). Shock threat and sexual arousal: The role of selective attention thought content and affective states. *Psychopharmacology, 24,* 165–172.

Benkert, O., Cronhach, G., & Kockott, G. (1982). Effect of L-dopa on sexually impotent patients. *Psychopharmacology, 23,* 91–95.

Bennett, H., Carpenter, J., & Barada, J. (1991). Improved vasoactive drug combination for pharmacological erection program. *Journal of Urology, 1,* 1564–1568.

Berman, J. R., Shuker, J. M., & Goldstein, I. (1999). Female sexual dysfunction. In C. C. Carson, R. S. Kirby, & I. Goldstein (Eds.), *Textbook of erectile dysfunction* (pp. 627–638). Oxford, ISIS.

Binik, Y., Meana, U., Khalife, S., Bergener, S., Cohen, D., & Howe, D. (1995). *Painful intercourse: A controlled study.* Paper presented at the annual meeting of the Society for Sex Therapy and Research, New York.

Biri, H., Isen, K., Sinik, Z., Onaran, M., Kupeli, B., & Bozkiri, I. (1998). Sertraline in the treatment of premature ejaculation. *International Journal of Nephrology, 30,* 611–616.

Bodner, D. R., Haas, C. A., Krueger, B., & Seftel, A. D. (1999). Intraurethral alprostadil for treatment of erectile dysfunction in patients with spinal cord injury. *Urology, 53,* 199–202.

Brady, J. P. (1996). Brevital-relaxation treatment of frigidity. *Behaviour Research and Therapy, 4,* 171–177.

Brennemann, W., Stitz, B., van Ahlen, H., Brensing, K., & Klingmuller, D. (1993). Treatment of idiopathic erectile dysfunction in men with the opiate antagonist naltrexone—a double blind study. *Journal of Andrology, 14,* 407–410.

Brindley, G. S. (1986). Maintenance treatment of erectile impotence by cavernosal unstriated muscle relaxation injection therapy. *British Journal of Psychiatry, 149,* 210–215.

Cavallini, C. (1991). Minaxidil versus nitroglycerin: A prospective double blind controlled trial intracutaneous erection facilitation for organic impotence. *Journal of Urology, 146,* 50–53.

Chen, K., Chan, J., & Chang, L. (1999). Dopaminergic neurotransmission at the paraventricular nucleus of hypothalamus in central regulation of penile erection in the rat. *Journal of Urology, 162,* 237–242.

Clement, F., & Schmidt, C. (1983). The outcome of couple therapy for sexual dysfunctions using three different formats. *Journal of Sex and Marital Therapy, 9,* 67–81.

Cranston-Cuebas, A., & Barlow, D. H. (1990). Cognitive and affective contributions to sexual functioning. *Annual Review of Sex Research, 1,* 119–161.

Cooper, A. J. (1969). Factors in male sexual inadequacy: A review. *Journal of Nervous Disease, 149,* 337–359.

Crowe, M. J., Gillan, P., & Golombok, S. (1981). Form and content in the conjoint treatment of sexual dysfunction: A controlled study. *Behavior Research and Therapy, 19,* 47–54.

Danjou, P., Alexander, L., Warat, D., Combiez, L., & Perch, A. J. (1988). Assessment of erectogenic properties of apomorphine and Yohimbine in man. *Journal of Clinical Pharmacology, 26,* 733–739.

Davidson, J. M., Kwan, M., & Greenleaf, W. (1982). Hormonal replacement and sexuality in men. *Clinics in Endocrinology and Metabolism, 11,* 599–623.

Davis, S. R. (1998). The clinical use of androgens in female sexual disorders. *Journal of Sex and Marital Therapy, 24,* 153–163.

Davis, S. R. (1999). The therapeutic use of androgens in women. *Journal of Steroid Biochemistry and Molecular Biology, 69,* 17–184.

DeAmicus, L. L., Goldberg, D. C., LoPicollo, J., Friedman, J., & Davies, L. (1985). Clinical follow-up of couples treated for sexual dysfunction. *Archives of Sexual Behavior, 14,* 467–489.

Dennerstein, L., Dudley, E. C., Hopper, J. L., & Burger, H. (1997). Sexuality, hormones, and the menopause. *Maturitas, 26,* 83–93.

Dhabuwala, C. B., Kerkar, P., & Bhutwala, A. (1990). Intracavernasus papaverine in the management of psychaizenic impotence. *Archives of Andrology, 124,* 185–191.

Dow, M., Hart, D., & Forrest, C. A. (1981). Hormonal treatment of sexual unresponsiveness in post-menopausal women: A comparative study. *British Journal of Obstetrics and Gynecology, 90,* 361–366.

Dunn, K. M., Croft, P. R., & Hackett, G. I. (1998). Sexual problems: A study of the prevalence and need for health care in the general population. *Family Practice, 15,* 519–524.

Ersner-Hershfield, R. R., & Kopel, S. (1979). Group treatment of preorgasmic women: Evaluation of partner involvement and spacing of sessions. *Journal of Consulting and Clinical Psychology, 47,* 750–759.

Fabbri, A., Jannini, E., Gnessi, L., Moretti, C., Ulisse, S., Franzese, A., Lazzari, R., Frazoli, F. F., & Fahner, E. (1987). Sexual dysfunction in male addicts: Prevalence and treatment. *Archives of Sexual Behavior, 16,* 247–256.

Feiger, A., Kiev, A., Shrivastava, R. K., Wisselink, P. G., & Wilcox, G. S. (1996). Nefazodone versus sertraline in outpatients with major depression: Focus on efficacy, tolerability, and effects on sexual dysfunction. *Journal of Clinical Psychiatry, 57*(Suppl.), 1–11.

Feldman, H. A., Goldstein, F., Hatzichristau, D. G., Krane, R. T., Segraves, M. D., & McKunlav, J. B. (1994). Impotence and its medical and psychosocial correlates. Results of the Massachusetts Male Aging Study. *Journal of Urology, 151,* 54–61.

Foreman, M., & Doherty, P. (1993). Experimental approaches for the development of pharmacological therapies for erectile dysfunction. In A. J. Riley, M. Peet, & C. Wilson (Eds.), *Sexual pharmacology* (pp. 97–113). Oxford, UK: Clarendon Press.

Gagnon, J., Rosen, R., & Leiblum, S. (1982). Cognitive and social aspects of sexual dysfunction: Sexual scripts in sex therapy. *Journal of Sex and Marital Therapy, 8,* 44–56.

Gasser, T. C., Roach, R. M., & Larsen, R. H. (1987). Intracavernous self-injection with phentaolamine and papaverine for the treatment of impotence. *Journal of Urology, 137,* 678–680.

Gayler, K. T., Conaglen, H. M., Hare, A., & Conaglen, J. V. (1999). The effect of gynecological surgery on sexual desire. *Journal of Sex and Marital Therapy, 25,* 81–88.

Gelfand, M. M. (1999). The role of androgens in surgical menopause. *American Journal of Obstetrics and Gynecology. 180,* 325–327.

Ghadirian, A. M., Choviard, G., & Annable, L. (1982). Sexual dysfunction and prolactin levels in neuroleptic treated schizophrenic outpatients. *Journal of Nervous and Mental Disease, 10,* 463–473.

Gilbert, H. W., & Gingell, J. C. (1991). The results of an intra corporeal papaverine clinic. *Sex and Marital Therapy, 4,* 49–53.

Godpodinff, J. L. (1989). Premature ejaculation: Clinical subgroups and etiology. *Journal of Sex and Marital Therapy, 15,* 130–134.

Goldstein, I., Lue, T., Padma Nathan, H., Rosen, R., Steers, W., et al. (1998). Oral sildenafil in the treatment of erectile dysfunction. *New England Journal of Medicine* 338, 1397–1404.

Goldstein, I., Lue, T., Padma-Nathan, H., Rosen, R., Steers, W., & Wicker, P. (1998). Oral sildenafil in the management of erectile dysfunction. *New England Journal of Medicine, 338,* 1397–1404.

Gonzalez-Cadavid, N. F., & Rajfer, J. (1999). Future therapeutic alternatives in the treatment of erectile dysfunction. In C. C. Carson, R. S. Kirby, & I. Goldstein (Eds.), *Textbook of erectile dysfunction* (pp. 355–364). Oxford, UK: Isis.

Guzick, D. S., & Hoeger, K. (2000). Sex, hormones, and hysterectomies. *New England Journal of Medicine, 343,* 730–731.

Haensel, S. M., Klem, T. M., Hop, W. C., & Slo, A. K. (1998). Fluoxetine and premature ejaculation. *Journal of Clinical Psychopharmacology, 18,* 72–77.

Halvorsen, J., & Metz, M. (1992). Sexual dysfunction: 2. Classification, etiology and pathogenesis. *Journal of the American Board of Family Practice, 5,* 177–192.

Hargreave, T. B. (1998). *Efficacy of sildenafil in the treatment of erectile dysfunction in patients with depression.* Glasgow: CINP.

Harrison, W., Stewart, J., Ehrhardt, A., Rabkin, J., McGrath, P., Liebowitz, M., & Quitkin, F. (1985). A controlled study of the effects of antidepressants on sexual function. *Psychopharmacology Bulletin, 21,* 85–88.

Haslam, M. (1965). The treatment of psychogenic Dyspareunia by reciprocal inhibition. *British Journal of Psychiatry, 111,* 280–282.

Hawton, K. (1982). The behavioral treatment of sexual dysfunction. *British Journal of Psychiatry, 140,* 94–101.

Hawton, K. (1995). Treatment of sexual dysfunctions by sex therapy and other approaches. *British Journal of Psychiatry, 161,* 307–314.

Hawton, K., & Catalan, J. (1986). Prognostic factors in sex therapy. *Behaviour Research and Therapy, 24,* 377–385.

Hawton, K., Catalan, J., & Fagg, J. (1992). Sex therapy for erectile dysfunction: Characteristics of couples, treatment outcome, and prognostic factors. *Archives of Sexual Behavior, 71,* 161–175.

Hawton, K., Catalan, J., Martin, P., & Fagg, J. (1986). Long-term outcome of sex therapy. *Behaviour Research and Therapy, 24,* 665–675.

Hawton, K., & Fagg, J. (1991). Low sexual desire: Sex therapy results and prognostic factors. *Behaviour Research and Therapy,* 29, 217–224.

Hawton, K., Gath, D., & Day, A. (1994). Sexual function in a community sample of middle-aged women with partners: Effect of age, marital, socioeconomic, psychiatric, gynecological and menopausal factors. *Archives of Sexual Behavior, 23,* 375–395.

Heaton, J. P., Morales, A., Adams, M. A., Johnston, D., & el-Rashidy, R. (1999). Recovery of erectile function by oral administration of apomorphine. *Urology, 45,* 200–206.

Heiman, J., & LoPicollo, J. (1983). Clinical outcome of sex therapy. *Archives of General Psychiatry, 40,* 443–449.

Hoegler, K. M., & Guzick, D. S. (1999). The use of androgens in menopause. *Clinical Obstetrics and Gynecology, 42,* 883–894.

Hummer, M., Kemmler, G., Kurz, M., Kurzthaler, I., Oberhauser, H., & Fleischacher, W. W. (1999). Sexual disturbance during clozapine and haloperidol treatment for schizophrenia. *American Journal of Psychiatry, 156,* 631–633.

Jensen, S. B. (1974). Sexual function and dysfunction in younger married alcoholics. *Acta Psychiatrica Scandinavica, 59,* 543–549.

Johannes, C. B., Araujo, A. B., Feldman, H. A., Derby, C. A., Kleinman, K. P., & McKinlay, J. B. (2000). Incidence of erectile dysfunction in men 40 to 69 years old: Longitudinal results from the Massachusetts Male Aging Study. *Journal of Urology, 163,* 460–463.

Kaplan, H. S. (1974). *The new sex therapy: Active treatment of sexual dysfunctions.* New York: Brunner/ Mazel.

Kara, H., Aydin, S., Yucel, M., Agargun, M. Y., Odabas, O., & Yilmaz, Y. (1996). The efficacy of fluoxetine in the treatment of premature ejaculation. *Journal of Urology, 156,* 1631–1632.

Kattan, S., Collins, J. P., & Mohr, Z. D. (1991). Double-blind crossover study comparing prostaglandin E1 and papaverine in patients with vasculogenic impotence. *Urology, 37,* 516–318.

Kellet, J. (1993). The nature of human sexual desire and its modification by drugs. In J. Riley, M. Peet, & C. Wilson (Eds.), *Sexual pharmacology* (pp. 100–145). Oxford, UK: Clarendon Press.

Kennedy, S. H., Dickens, S. E., Eisfeld, B. S., & Bagby, R. M. (1999). Sexual dysfunction before antidepressant therapy in major depression. *Journal of Affective Disease, 56,* 201–208.

Kilmann, P. R., Milan, R. J., Boland, J. P., Nankin, H., Davidson, E., West, M. O., Sabalis, R., Caid, C., & Devine, J. M. (1987). Group treatment of secondary erectile dysfunction. *Journal of Sex and Marital Therapy, 13,* 168–182.

Kilmann, P. R., Mills, K., Caid, C., Davidson, E., Bella, B., Milan, R., Drose, G., Boland, J., Follingstad, D., Montgomery, B., & Wanlass, R. It. (1986). Treatment of secondary orgasmic dysfunction: An outcome study. *Archives of Sexual Behavior, 15,* 211–229.

Kim, S. C., & Seo, K. K. (1998). Efficacy and safety of fluoxetine, sertraline and clomipramine in patients with premature ejaculation. *Journal of Urology, 159,* 425–427.

Kim, S. W., & Paick, J. S. (1999). Short-term analysis of the effects of as needed use of sertraline for the treatment of premature ejaculation. *Urology, 54,* 544–547.

Kongkanand, A. (2000). Prevalence of erectile dysfunction in Thailand. *Thai Erectile Dysfunction Epidemiological Study Group, 23*(Suppl. 2), 77–80.

Kowalski, G., Stanley, R. D., & Dennerstein, L. (1985). The sexual side effects of antidepressant medication: A double blind comparison of two antidepressants in a non-psychiatric population. *British Journal of Psychiatry, 147,* 413–418.

Kuriansky, J. B., & Sharpe, L. (1981). Clinical and research implications of the evaluation of women's group therapy for anorgasmia: A review. *Journal of Sex and Marital Therapy, 7,* 268–277.

Kuriansky, J. B., Sharpe, C., & O'Connor, D. (1982). The treatment of anorgasmia: Long-term effectiveness of a short-term behavioral group therapy. *Journal of Sex and Marital Therapy, 8,* 29–43.

Lal, S., Ackman, D., Thavundayil, J. X., Kieley, M. E., & Etienne, P. C. (1984). Effect of apomorphine, a dopamine receptor agonist on penile tumescence to normal subjects. *Progress in Neuropsychopharmacology, 8,* 695–699.

Lal, S., Kiely, M. E., Thavundyil, J. X., Stewart, J. D., Assalian, P., & Ackman, C. F. (1991). Effect of bromocriptine in patients with apomorphine-responsive erectile impotence: An open study. *Journal of Psychiatry and Neuroscience, 16,* 262–266.

Lal, S., Laryea, E., Thavundayil, J., Nir, N. P., Negrete, J., Ackman, D., Blundell, P., & Gardiner, R. (1987). Apomorphine-induced penile tumescence in impotent patients: Preliminary findings. *Progress in Neuropsychopharmacology Biological Psychiatry, 143,* 819–820.

Landen, M., Eriksson, F., Agren, H, & Fahlen, T. (1999). Effect of buspirone on sexual dysfunction in depressed men treated with selective serotonin reuptake inhibitors. *Journal of Clinical Psychopharmacology, 19,* 266–271.

Laumann, E. O., Paik, A., & Rosen, R. (1999). Sexual dysfunction in the United States: Prevalence and predictors. *Journal of the American Medical Association, 281,* 537–544.

Lazarus, A. A. (1963). The treatment of chronic frigidity by systematic desensitization. *Journal of Nervous and Mental Disease, 136,* 272–278.

Lee, L. M., Stevenson, R. W., & Szasz, G. (1989). Prostaglandin E1 versus phentolamine/papaverine for the treatment of erectile impotence: A double-blind comparison. *Journal of Urology, 141,* 551–553.

Leiblum, S., Pervin, L. A., & Campbell, H. C. (1983). The treatment of vaginismis. In S. R. T. Segraves, M. D. Leiblum, R. T. Segraves, & M. D. C. Rosen (Eds.), *Principles and practice of sex therapy* (pp. 167–194). New York: Guilford Press.

Leiblum, S. R., & Rosen, R. (Eds.). (1989). *Principles and practice of sex therapy: Update for the 1990s.* New York: Guilford Press.

Leiblum, S. R., Rosen, R., & Pierce, D. (1976). Group treatment format: Mixed sexual dysfunctions. *Archives of Sexual Behavior, 5,* 313–321.

Lemere, F., & Smith, J. (1973). Alcohol-induced sexual impotence. *American Journal of Psychiatry, 150,* 212–213.

Levine, S. (1988). *Sex is not simple.* Columbus: Ohio Psychology.

Levine, S. B. (1992a). Intrapsychic and interpersonal aspects of impotence: Psychogenic erectile dysfunction. In R. C. Rosen & S. R. Leiblum (Eds.), *Erectile disorders: Assessment and treatment* (pp. 198–225). New York: Guilford Press.

Levine, S. (1992b). *Sexual life: A clinician's guide.* New York: Plenum.

Levine, S. B., & Agle, D. (1978). The effectiveness of sex therapy for chronic secondary psychological impotence. *Journal of Sex and Marital Therapy, 4,* 235–258.

Levine, S., Althof, S., Turner, L., Risen, C., Bodner, D., Kursh, E. G., & Rescind, M. (1989). Side effects of self-administration of intracavernosal papaverine and phentolamine for the treatment of impotence. *Journal of Urology, 141,* 54–57.

Lewis, R. W. (1998). Tranurethral alprostadil with MUSE vs intracavernosus alprostadil: A comparative study in 103 patients with erectile dysfunction. *International Journal of Impotence Research, 10,* 61–62.

Lief, H. I. (1989). Introduction. In American Psychiatric Association, Task Force on Treatments of Psychiatric Disorders, *Treatment of psychiatric disorders* (Vol. 3, pp. 237–238). Washington, DC: American Psychiatric Press.

Loman, G. M., & Jarow, J. P. (1992). Risk factors for papaverine-induced priapism. *Journal of Urology, 147,* 1280–1281.

LoPiccolo, J., Heiman, J., Hogan, D., & Roberts, C. (1985). Effectiveness of single therapists versus cotherapy teams in sex therapy. *Journal of Consulting and Clinical Psychology, 53,* 287–294.

LoPiccolo, J., & LoPiccolo, J. (1987). *Handbook of sex therapy.* New York: Plenum.

Marder, S. R., & Meibach, R. C. (1994). Risperidone in the treatment of schizophrenia. *American Journal of Psychiatry, 151,* 825–835.

Marks, I. M. (1981). Review of behavioral psychotherapy: 2. Sexual disorders. *American Journal of Psychiatry, 138,* 750–756.

Masters, W., & Johnson, V. (1966). *Human sexual response.* London: Churchill Livingstone.

Masters, W., & Johnson, V. (1970). *Human sexual inadequacy.* Boston: Little Brown.

McCarthy, B. (1990). Cognitive-behavioral strategies and techniques in the treatment of early ejaculation. In S. R. Leiblum & R. C. Rosen (Eds.), *Principles and practice of sex therapy: Update for the 1990s* (pp. 141–167). New York: Guilford Press.

McCarthy, B., & McCarthy, E. (1984). *Sexual awareness: Sharing sexual pleasure.* New York: Carroll & Graff.

McMahon, C. G. (1991). A comparison of the response to the intracavernosal injection of a combination of papaverine and phentolamine, prostaglandin PGEI and a combination of all three in the management of impotence. *International Journal of Impotence Research, 3,* 113–121.

McMahon, C. G. (1998a). Treatment of premature ejaculation with sertraline hydrochloride. *International Journal of Impotence Research, 10,* 181–184.

McMahon, C. G. (1998b). Treatment of premature ejaculation with sertraline hydrochoride: A single-blind placebo controlled study. *Journal of Urology, 159,* 1935–1938.

McMahon, C. G., & Touma, K. (1999). Treatment of premature ejaculation with paroxetine hydrochloride. *International Journal of Impotence Research, 11,* 241–245.

McMullen, S., & Rosen, R. (1979). Self-administered masturbation training in the treatment of primary orgasmic dysfunction. *Journal of Consulting and Clinical Psychology, 47,* 912–918.

Mendels, J., Cameram, A., & Sikes, C. (1995). Sertraline treatment for premature ejaculation. *Journal of Clinical Psychopharmacology, 15,* 341–346.

Meston, C. M., & Heiman, J. R. (1998). Ephedrine-activated physiological sexual arousal in women. *Archives of General Psychiatry, 55,* 652–656.

Meyer, J. K. (1976). Psychodynamic treatment of the individual with a sexual disorder. In J. Meyer (Ed.), *Clinical management of sexual disorders.* Baltimore: Williams & Wilkins.

Miller, N. S., & Gold, M. S. (1900). The human sexual response and alcohol and drugs. *Journal of Substance Abuse Treatment, 5,* 171–177.

Minnen, A. V., & Kampman, M. (2000). The interaction between anxiety and sexual functioning in women with anxiety disorders. *Sex Relationship Therapy, 15,* 47–57.

Mohr, D. C., & Beutler, L. E. (1990). Erectile dysfunc tion: A review of diagnostic and treatment procedures. *Clinical Psychology Review, 10,* 123–150.

Monteiro, W. O., Noshivani, H. F., Marks, I. M., & Lelliott, P. T. (1987). Anorgasmia from clomipramine in obsessive-compulsive disorder: A controlled study. *British Journal of Psychiatry, 51,* 107–112.

Montejo, A. L., Llorca, G., Izquierdo, J. A., Ledesma, J., Iglesias, S. S., & Daniel, E. (1998). New antipsychotic induced sexual dysfunction: Comparative incidence of risperidone and olanzapine using a questionnaire. *APA NR*, 181–182.

Montorsi, F., McDermott, T. E., Morgan, R., Olsson, A., Schultz, A., Kirby, H. J., & Osterloh, I. H. (1999). Efficacy and safety of fixed doses of sildenafil in the treatment of erectile dysfunction in various etiologies. *Urology, 53*, 1011–1018.

Montorsi, F., Strabi, L., Guezzang, G., Gall, L., Barbieri, L., Rigatt, P., Pizini, G., & Mian, A. (1994). Effect of yohimbine-trazodone on psychogenic impotence: A randomized, double blind placebo-controlled study. *Urology, 44*, 733–736.

Morales, A., Surridge, D. H., & Marshall, P. G. (1987). Is yohimbine effective in the treatment of organic impotence? Results of a controlled trial. *Journal of Urology, 137*, 1168–1172.

Mulhall, J. P., & Goldstein, I. (1999). Oral agents in the management of erectile dysfunction. In C. C. Carson, R. S. Kirby, & I. Goldstein (Eds.), *Textbook of erectile dysfunction* (pp. 317–322). Oxford, UK: Isis.

Nemetz, G. H., Craig, K. D., & Reith, G. (1978). Treatment of female sexual dysfunction through symbolic modeling. *Journal of Consulting and Clinical Psychology, 46*, 62–73.

Obler, M. (1973). Systematic desensitization in sexual disorders. *Journal of Behavior Therapy and Experimental Psychiatry, 4*, 93–101.

O'Carroll, R. T. Segraves, M. D. F., & Bancroft, J. (1984). Testosterone for low sexual desire and erectile dysfunction in men. *British Journal of Psychiatry, 145*, 146–151.

Osterloh, I., Eardley, I., Carson, C., & Padma-Nathan, H. (1999). Sildenafil: A selective phosphodiesterase (PDE) inhibitor in the treatment of erectile dysfunction. In C. C. Carson, R. S. Kirby, & I. Goldstein (Eds.), *Textbook of erectile dysfunction* (pp. 285–308). Oxford, UK: Isis.

O'Sullivan, J. D., & Hughes, A. J. (1998). Apomorphine-induced penile erections in Parkinson's disease. *Movement Disorders, 13*, 536–539.

Owen, J. A., Saunders, F., Harris, C., Fenemore, J., Reid, J., Surridge, D., Condra, M., Padma-Nathan, H., Bennett, A., Gesundeit, N., Hellstrom, W., Henry, D., Lu, T., Moley, J., & Palace, E. (1995). Modification of dysfunctional patterns of sexual response through autonomic arousal and false physiological feedback. *Journal of Consulting and Clinical Psychology, 63*, 604–613.

Padma-Nathan, H., Hellstrom, W. J. G., & Kaiser, F. E. (1997). Treatment of men with erectile dysfunction with transurethral aprostadil. *New England Journal of Medicine, 33*, 1–7.

Paick, J. S., Jeong, H., & Park, M. S. (1998). Penile sensitivity in men with premature ejaculation. *International Journal of Impotence Research, 10*, 247–250.

Palace, E. M., & Gorzalka, B. (1992). Differential patterns of arousal in sexually functional and dysfunctional women: Physiological and subjective components of sexual response. *Archives of Sexual Behavior, 21*, 135–159.

Parazzini, F., Menchini, F. F., Bortolotti, A., Calabro, A., Chatenoud, L., Col, E., Landoni, M., Lavezzari, M., Turchi, P., Sessa, A., & Mirone, V. (2000). Frequency and determinants of erectile dysfunction in Italy. *European Urology, 37*, 43–49.

Perelman, M. (1980). Treatment of premature ejaculation. In S. R. Leiblum & L. Pervin (Eds.), *Principles and practice of sex therapy* (pp. F193–233). New York: Guilford Press.

Persky, H., Lief, H. L., & Strauss, D. (1978). Plasma testosterone level and sexual behavior in couples. *Archives of Sexual Behavior, 7*, 157–162.

Peterson, C., Prendergast, J. P., Tam, P., Teresu, A., & Place, V. (1995). Treatment of erectile dysfunction by the medicated urethral system (MUSE). *Proceedings of the American Urological Journal, 153*(Suppl. 472A).

Pierini, A. A., & Nusimovich, B. (1981). Male diabetic sexual impotence: Effect of dopaminergic agents. *Archives of Andrology, 6*, 347–350.

Pinnock, C. B., Stapleton, A. M., & Marshall, R. (1999). Erectile dysfunction in the community: A prevalence study. *Medical Journal of Australia, 171*, 353–357.

Rabo, S. (2000). Testosterone supplemental therapy after hysterectomy with or without concomitant oophorectomy: Estrogen is not enough. *Journal of Women's Health and Gender Based Medicine, 9*, 917–923.

Raboch, J., & Faltus, F. (1991). Sexuality of women with anorexia nervosa. *Acta Psychiatrica Scandinavica, 84*, 9–11.

Reid, K., Morales, A., Harris, C., Surridge, D. H., Condra, M., Owen, J., & Fenemore, J. (1987). Double-blind trial of yohimbine in the treatment of psychogenic impotence. *Lancet*, 421–324.

Reynolds, B. (1991). Psychological treatment of erectile dysfunction in men without partners: Outcome results and new direction. *Journal of Sex and Marital Therapy, 2*, 136–145.

Riley, A. J., Goodman, R. E., Kellet, J. M., & Orr, R. (1989). Double-blind trial of Yohimbine hydrochloride in the treatment of erection inadequacy. *Sexual and Marital Therapy, 4*, 17–26.

Riley, A. J., & Riley, E. J. (1978). A controlled study to evaluate directed masturbation in the management of primary orgasmic failure in women. *British Journal of Psychiatry, 133*, 404–409.

Riley, A. J., & Riley, E. J. (1988). The effect of single dose diazepam on female sexual response induced by masturbation. *Sexual and Marital Therapy, 1*, 49–53.

Riley, A. J., & Riley, E. J. (1993). Pharmacotherapy for sexual dysfunction: Current status. In A. J. Riley, M. Peet, & C. Wilson (Eds.), *Sexual pharmacology* (pp. 211–256). Oxford, UK: Clarendon Press.

Rosen, R. C. (1991). Alcohol and drug effects on sexual response: Human experiment and clinical studies. *Annual Review of Sex Research, 2*, 119–179.

Rosen, R. C. (1995). Treatment of sexual disorders in the 1990s: An integrated approach. *Journal of Clinical and Consulting Psychology, 63*, 877, 990.

Rosen, R. C., & Beck, J. G. (1988). *Patterns of sexual arousal: Psychophysiological processes and clinical applications*. New York: Guilford Press.

Rosen, R. C., & Kostis, J. B. (1991). *Sexual sequellae of antihypertensive drugs*. Paper presented at the 13th annual meeting of the Society of Behavioral Medicine, Washington, DC.

Rosen, R. C., Lane, R. M., & Menza, M. (1999). Effects of SSRIs on sexual function: A critical review. *Journal of Clinical Psychiatry, 19*, 67–85.

Rosen, R. C., & Leiblum, S. R. (1989). Assessment and treatment of desire disorders. In R. C. Rosen & S. R. Leiblum (Eds.), *Principles and practice of sex therapy: Update for the 1990s* (pp. 1–18). New York: Guilford Press.

Rosen, R., Phillips, N. A., Gendrano, N. C., & Ferguson, D. M. (1999). Oral phentolamim and female sexual arousal disorder: A pilot study. *Journal of Sex and Marital Therapy, 25*, 137–144.

Rosen, R., Riley, A., & Wagner, G. (1997). The international index of erectile dysfunction (IIEF): A multidimensional scale for assessment of erectile dysfunction. *Urology, 49*, 822–830.

Rosen, R., Seidman, S. N., Menza, M. A., Roose, S. P., & Shabsign, R. (1999). Effective treatment of erectile dysfunction improves symptoms of depression. Poster presented at World Congress of Psychiatry, Hamburg.

St. Lawrence, J., & Madakasira, S. (1992). Evaluation and treatment of premature ejaculation: A critical review. *International Journal of Psychiatry, 22*, 77–97.

Sala, M., Braida, D., Leone, M. P., Calcaterra, P., Monti, L., & Car, E. (1990). Central effect of yohimbine on sexual behavior in the rat. *Physiology and Behavior, 47*, 166–173.

Salerian, A. J., Deibler, W. E., Vittore, B. J., Geyer, S. D., Drell, L., Mirnirani, N., Mirczak, J. A., Byrd, W., Tunick, S. B., Wax, M., & Fleisher, S. (2000). Sildenafil for psychotropic induced sexual dysfunction. *Journal of Sex and Marital Therapy, 3*,

Sarosv, M. F., Hudnall, C., & Erikson, D. R. (1989). A prospective double-blind trial of intra corporeal papaverine versus prostaglandin in the treatment of impotence. *Journal of Urology, 141*, 551–553.

Sarrel, P. M. (1999). Psychosocial effects of menopause: The role of androgens. *American Journal of Obstetrics and Gynecology, 180*, 319–324.

Sarrel, P., Dobay, B., & Witta, B. (1998). Estrogen and estrogen-androgen replacement in postmenopausal women dissatisfied with estrogen only therapy. Sexual behavior and neuroendocrine responses. *Journal of Reproductive Medicine, 43*(10), 847–856.

Sarrel, P., & Sarrel, L. (1989). Dyspareunia and vaginismus. In *American Psychiatric Association Task Force on Treatments of Psychiatric Disorders* (Vol. 3, pp. 2291–2298). Washington, DC: American Psychiatric Press.

Scharf, D. E. (1985). *The sexual relationship: An object relations view of the family*. London: Routledge, Kegan, and Paul.

Schiavi, R. C. (1990). Chronic alcoholism and male sexual function. *Journal of Sex and Marital Therapy, 16*, 23–33.

Schiavi, R. C., Stimmel, B., Mandeli, J., & White, D. (1995). Chronic alcoholism and male sexual function. *American Journal of Psychiatry, 152*, 1045–1051.

Schmidt, W. C. (1995). Sexual psychopathology and *DSM-IV*. In J. Oldham & B. Riba (Eds.), *American Psychiatric Press review of psychiatry* (Vol. 14, pp. 719–733). Washington, DC: American Psychiatric Press.

Schnellen, T. (1968). Introduction of ejaculation by electrovibration. *Fertility and Sterility,19*, 566–569.

Schover, L. R., Youngs, D., & Canata, R. (1992). Psychosexual aspects of the evaluation and management of vulvovestibularis. *American Journal of Obstetrics and Gynecology, 167*, 630–638.

Schramek, P., Doringer, R., & Waldhauser, M. (1990). Prostaglandin E1 in erectile dysfunction, *British Journal of Urology, 65*, 68–71.

Schreiner-Engel, P., & Schiavi, R. (1986). Lifetime psychopathology in individuals with low sexual desire. *Journal of Nervous and Mental Disease, 174*, 646–651.

Segraves, R. T. (1978). Treatment of sexual dysfunction. *Comprehensive Therapy, 4*, 38–43.

Segraves, R. T. (1988a). Drugs and sex. In S. R. Leiblum & R. C. Rosen (Eds.), *Sexual desire disorders* (pp. 313–347). New York: Guilford Press.

Segraves, R. T. (1988b). Hormones and libido. In S. R. Leiblum & R. C. Rosen (Eds.), *Sexual desire disorders* (pp. 271–312). New York: Guilford Press.

Segraves, R. T. (1989). Effects of psychotropic drugs on human erection and ejaculation. *Archives of General Psychiatry, 46,* 275–284.

Segraves, R. T. (1991a). Diagnosis of female arousal disorder. *Sex and Marital Therapy, 6,* 9–13.

Segraves, R. T. (1991b). Hypoactive sexual desire disorder: Prevalence and comorbidity in 906 subjects. *Journal of Sex and Marital Therapy, 17,* 55–58.

Segraves, R. T. (1991c). Multiple phase sexual dysfunction. *Journal of Sex Education and Therapy, 17,* 153–156.

Segraves, R. T. (1993). Medical aspects of orgasm disorders. In W. O'Donahue & J. Geer (Eds.), *Handbook of sexual dysfunction: Assessment and treatment* (pp. 225–252). Boston: Allyn & Bacon.

Segraves, R. T. (1994a). Male erectile disorder. In American Psychiatric Association, Task Force on Treatments of Psychiatric Disorders, *Treatments of psychiatric disorders* (Vol. 3, pp. 2218–2329). Washington, DC: American Psychiatric Press.

Segraves, R. T. (1994b). Pharmacological enhancement of human sexual behavior. *Journal of Sex Education and Therapy, 17,* 283–289.

Segraves, R. T. (1995a). Antidepressant-induced orgasm disorder. *Journal of Sex and Marital Therapy, 21,* 192–201.

Segraves, R. T. (1995b). Human sexuality and aging. *Journal of Sex Education and Therapy, 21,* 88–102.

Segraves, R. T. (1995c). Psychopharmacological influences on human sexual behavior. In J. M. Oldham & M. Riba (Eds.), *American Psychiatric Press review of psychiatry* (Vol. 14, pp. 697–718). Washington, DC: American Psychiatric Press.

Segraves, R. T. (1999). Two additional uses for sildenafil in psychiatric patients. *Journal of Sex and Marital Therapy, 25,* 265–266.

Segraves, R. T., Bari, M., Segraves, K. B., & Spirnak, P. (1991). Effect of apomorphine on penile tumescence in men with psychogenic impotence. *Journal of Urology, 145,* 1174–1175.

Segraves, R., Croft, H., Kavoussi, R., Ascher, J., Batey, S., Foster, V., Bolden-Watson, C., & Metz, (2001). Bupropion sustained release for the treatment of hypoactive sexual desire disorder in non-depressed women. *Journal of Sex and Marital Therapy, 27,* 303–306.

Segraves, R. T., Kavoussi, R., Hughes, A., Batey, S., Johnston, A., Donahue, R., & Ascher, J. (2000). Evaluation of sexual functioning in depressed outpatients: A double-blind comparison of sustained-release bupropion and sertraline treatment. *Journal of Clinical Psychopharmacology, 20,* 122–128.

Segraves, R. T., Madsen, R., Carver, S. C., & Davis, J. (1985). Erectile dysfunction associated with pharmacological agents. In R. T. Segraves & H. W. Schoenberg (Eds.), *Diagnosis and treatment of erectile disturbances* (pp. 23–64). New York: Plenum.

Segraves, R. T., Saran, A., Segraves, K., & Mcguire, E. (1993). Clomipramine versus placebo in the treatment of premature ejaculation: A pilot study. *Journal of Sex and Marital Therapy, 19,* 198–200.

Segraves, R. T., & Segraves, K. B. (1990). Categorical and multi-axial diagnosis of male erectile disorder. *Journal of Sex and Marital Therapy, 16,* 208–713.

Semans, J. H. (1956). Premature ejaculation: A new approach. *Southern Medical Journal, 49,* 353–357.

Sherwin, B. B., & Gelfand, M. M. (1987). The role of androgen in the maintenance of sexual functioning in ophorectomized women. *Psychosomatic Medicine, 49,* 397–409.

Shifren, J., Braunstein, G., Simon, I., Casson, R., Buster, J., Redmond, G., Burki, R., Ginsberg, E., Rosen, R., Leiblum, S., Caramelli, K., & Mazer, (2000). Transdermal testosterone treatment in women with impaired sexual function after oophorectomy. *New England Journal of Medicine, 343,* 682–688.

Shirai, M., Marui, E., Hayashi, K., Ishii, N., & Abe, T. (1999). Prevalence and correlates of erectile dysfunction in Japan. *International Journal and Clinical Practice Supplement, 102,* 36.

Siegel, R. K. (1982). Cocaine and sexual dysfunction. *Journal of Psychoactive Drugs, 14,* 71–74.

Snyder, S., & Karacan, I. (1981a). Disulfiram and nocturnal penile tumescence in the chronic alcoholic. *Biological Psychiatry, 16,* 399–406.

Snyder, S., & Karacan, I. (1981b). Effects of chronic alcoholism on nocturnal penile tumescence. *Psychosomatic Medicine, 43,* 423–429.

Sondra, L. P., Mazo, R. T., Segraves, M. D., & Chancelar, M. D. (1990). The role of yohimbine for the treatment of erectile impotence. *Journal of Sex and Marital Therapy, 16,* 15–21.

Spector, I. P., & Carey, J. S. (1990). Incidence and prevalence of the sexual dysfunctions: A critical review of the literature. *Archives of Sexual Behavior, 9,* 389–408.

Spence, S. H. (1991). *Psychosexual therapy: A cognitive-behavioral approach.* London: Chapman & Hall.

Steers, W. D., McConnell, J., & Benson, G. S. (1984). Some pharmacological effects of yohimbine on human and rabbit penis. *Journal of Urology, 131,* 799–802.

Strassberg, D. S., de Gouveia Brazao, C. A., Rowland, D. L., Tan, P., & Slob, A. K. (1999). Clomipramine in the treatment of rapid (premature) ejaculation. *Journal of Sex and Marital Therapy, 25,* 89–101.

Strassberg, D., Kelly, M., Carroll, C., & Kirchzer, J. (1987). The psychophysiological nature of premature ejaculation. *Archives of Sexual Behavior, 16,* 327–336.

Sussett, J. C., Tessier, C. D., Wincze, J., Banal, S., Mallıtra, C., & Schwaba, M. G. (1989). Effect of yohimbine hydrochloride on erectile impotence: A double-blind study. *Journal of Urology, 141,* 1360–1363.

Tan, E. H., Johnson, R. A., Lambie, D. C., Vijayasenah, M. E., & Whiteside, E. A. (1984). Erectile impotence in chronic alcoholics. *Alcoholism: Clinical and Experimental Research, 8,* 297–301.

Task Force on Treatments of Psychiatric Disorders (Ed.). (1994). *Treatment of psychiatric disorders* (Vol. 3, pp. 2237–2238). Washington, DC: American Psychiatric Press.

Tennett, G., Bancroft, J., & Cass, J. (1972). The control of deviant sexual behavior by drugs: A double blind controlled shady of benperidol. Chlorpromazine and placebo. *Archives of Sexual Behavior,* 3, 216–271.

Thase, M. E., Reynolds, C. F., Jennings, J. R., Berman, R., Houch, P., Howell, J., Frank, E., & Kupfer, D. (1999). Diagnostic performance of NPT studies in healthy dysfunctional (impotent) and depressed men. *Psychiatric Research, 26,* 79–87.

Tiefer, L. (1995). *Sex is not a natural act and other essays.* Boulder, CO: Westview Press.

Tomlinson, J. (1999). Viagara and its use in cardiovascular disease. *Journal of Human Hypertension, 13,* 593–594.

Tran, P. U., Hamilton, S. H., Kuntz, A. J., Potvin, J. H., Andersen, S. W., Beasley, C., & Tollefson, G. (1997). Double blind comparison of olanzapine versus risperidone in the treatment of schizophrenia. *Journal of Clinical Psychopharmacology, 17,* 402–418.

Tuiten, A., van Honk, J., Koppe, S., Chaar, H., Bernaars, C., Thijsen, J., & Verbatim, J. (2000). Time course of effects of testosterone administration on sexual arousal in women. *Archives of General Psychiatry, 57,* 149–153.

Turner, L., Althof, S., & Levine, S. (1992). A 12-month comparison of the effectiveness of two treatments for erectile failure: Self-injection versus external vacuum devices. *Urology, 39,* 139–144.

Turner, L., Althof, S., Levine, S., Bodner, D., Kursh, E., & Resnick, M. (1991). Long term use of vacuum pump devices in the treatment of erectile dysfunction. *Journal of Sex and Marital Therapy, 17,* 81–93.

Turner, L., Althof, S., Levine, S., Risen, C., Bodner, D., Kursh, E., & Resnick, M. (1989). Injection of papaverine and phentolamine in the treatment of psychogenic impotence. *Journal of Sex and Marital Therapy, 15,* 163–176.

Vallance, P. (1999). Sildenafil: Desired and undesired effects. *Hospital Medicine,* 158–159.

van Ahlen, H., Piechota, H. J., Kias, H. J., Brennemann, W., & Klingmuller, D. (1995). Opiate antagonists in erectile dysfunction: A possible new treatment option? Results of a pilot study with naltrexone. *European Urology, 28,* 246–250.

Virag, R. (1982). Intracavernous injection of papaverine for erectile failure. *Lancet, 2,* 935.

Virag, R., Frydman, D., Legman, M., & Virag, H. (1984). Intracavernous injection of papaverine as a diagnostic tool and therapeutic method in erectile failure. *Angiology, 35,* 79–87.

Waldinger, M. D., Hengeveld, M. Z., & Zwindman, A. H. (1994). Paroxetine treatment of premature ejaculation: A double blind randomized placebo-controlled study. *American Journal of Psychiatry, 151,* 1377–1379.

Waldinger, M. D., Hengeveld, M. Z., & Zwindman, A. H. (1997). Ejaculation-retarding properties paroxetine in patients with primary premature ejaculation: A double blind randomized response study. *British Journal of Urology, 156,* 1631–1632.

Waldinger, M. D., Hengeveld, M. Z., Zwindman, A. H., & Olivier, (1998). Effect of SSRI antidepressant on ejaculation: A randomized placebo controlled study with fluoxetine, fluvoxamine, paroxetine, and sertraline. *Journal of Clinical Psychiatry, 18,* 274–281.

Warnock, J. K., Bundren, J. C., & Morris, D. W. (1999). Female hypoactive sexual desire disorder: Studies of physiological androgen replacement. *Journal of Sex and Marital Therapy, 25,* 175–180.

Weiss, J., Ravalli, R., & Badlani, I. (1991). Intracavernous pharmacotherapy in psychogenic impotence. *Urology, 37,* 441–443.

Welling, M., Anderson, B., & Johnson, S. (1990). Hormonal replacement therapy for menopausal women: A review of sexual outcomes and related gynecological effects. *Archives of Sexual Behavior, 19,* 119–137.

Whalley, L. J. (1978). Sexual adjustment of alcoholics. *Acta Psychiatrica Scandinavica, 58,* 281–298.

Whitehead, A., & Mathews, A. (1986). Factors related to successful outcome in the treatment of sexually unresponsive women. *Psychological Medicine, 16,* 373–378.

Wilson, C. A. (1993). Pharmacological targets for the control of male and female sexual behavior. In A. J. Riley, M. Peet, & C. Wilson (Eds.), *Sexual pharmacology* (pp. 1–58). Oxford, UK: Clarendon Press.

Wise, T. H. (1999). Psychosocial side effects of sildenafil for erectile dysfunction. *Journal of Sex and Marital Therapy, 25,* 145–150.

Wolpe, J. (1958). *Psychotherapy by reciprocal inhibition.* Stanford: Stanford University Press.

Wright, J., Perrault, R., & Mathieu, M. (1977). The treatment of sexual dysfunction. *Archives of General Psychiatry, 34,* 881–890.

Wyllie, M. G., & Anderson, K. E. (1999). Orally active agents: The potential of alpha-adrene antagonists. In C. C. Carson, R. S. Kirby, & I. Goldstein (Eds.), *Textbook of erectile dysfunction* (pp. 317–322). Oxford, UK: Isis.

Xin, Z. C., Choi, Y. D., Rha, K. H., & Choi, H. K. (1997). Somatosensory evoked potentials in apti? With primary premature ejaculation. *Journal of Urology, 158,* 451–455.

Yilmaz, U., Tatlisen, A., Turan, H., Arman, F., & Ekmekcioglu, O. (1999). The effects of fluoxetine on several neurophysiological variables in patients with premature ejaculation. *Journal of Urology, 161,* 107–111.

Zilbergeld, B. (1992). *The new male sexuality.* New York: Bantam.

Zilbergeld, B., & Evans, M. (1980). The inadequacy of Masters and Johnson. *Psychology Today,* 29–34.

21

The Paraphilias: Research and Treatment

Barry M. Maletzky

The literature on the paraphilias has been focused chiefly on theoretical, etiological, and epidemiological concerns rather than on issues of treatment. However, a trend toward treatment outcome studies is emerging. At present, there is a consensus that cognitive/behavioral therapies form the standard against which other approaches must be judged. Behavior therapies include various forms of aversive conditioning, social skills training, biofeedback, and sexual impulse control training, among others. Cognitive approaches include restructuring cognitive distortions, relapse prevention, and empathy training. Somatic treatments have also been reported, including the administration of medroxyprogesterone acetate (MPA) and cyproterone acetate (CPA); both reduce circulating testosterone. Unfortunately, large outcome evaluations of any of these treatments are still lacking.

It is an irony of semantics that those disorders we call the paraphilias are most often loveless. One can sense that as much from the rhetoric of the *Diagnostic and Statistical Manual of Mental Disorders*, fourth edition (*DSM-IV*; American Psychiatric Association [APA], 1994) as from the decades of observation, treatment, and research and the countless clinical hours spent helping patients with these disorders. This chapter attempts to summarize our understanding of the nature and treatment of this diverse cluster of disorders, but in doing so, it recognizes that far more detail will reward the inquisitive reader who consults sources in the reference list.

DEFINITIONS

Among all sexual disorders addressed in *DSM-IV*, just one subsection comprises the paraphilias. Proximate disorders, such as those of lowered sexual arousal; sexual aversions; orgasmic, erectile, and ejaculatory disorders; sexual pain disorders; and gender identity disorders are left to other authors. Typical paraphilias are listed in Table 21.1 along with their *DSM-IV* criteria, much condensed. The present scheme does not claim to be anything but one in a series of evolving concepts about these disorders that will undoubtedly be altered repeatedly in the future.

One overriding phenomenon of taxonomy seems particularly critical in classifying paraphilias: the sensitivity of human sexual response to the chances of environmental conditioning. Our sexual behavior is assuredly idiosyncratic, often unpredictable, and resistant to classification schemes. In general, however, *DSM-IV* makes the reasonable demand that paraphilias conform to several fundamental criteria:

1. That they be characterized by recurrent, intense, sexually arousing fantasies, urges, or behaviors involving *inappropriate* objects.

TABLE 21.1 *DSM-IV* Paraphilias and Their Criteria

These must be of at least 6 months' duration; cause significant distress or impair social, occupational or other important functions; and produce recurrent sexually arousing fantasies, urges, or behaviors involving:

1. Nonhuman objects
2. Suffering or humiliation of oneself or one's partner
3. Children or other nonconsenting individuals

Exhibitionism 302.4
 Fantasies, urges, or behaviors involving the exposure of one's genitals to a stranger.

Fetishism 302.81
 Fantasies, urges, or behaviors involving the use of objects, not limited to articles of female clothing, used in cross-dressing (as in transvestic fetishism) or devices designed for genital stimulation (for example, a vibrator).

Frotteurism 302.89
 Fantasies, urges, or behaviors involving touching or rubbing against a nonconsenting person.

Pedophilia 302.2
 Fantasies, urges, or behaviors involving sexual activity with a prepubescent child by a person at least 16 years old and at least 5 years older.

Sexual masochism 302.83
 Fantasies, urges, or behaviors involving the act of being humiliated, beaten, bound, or otherwise made to suffer.

Sexual sadism 302.83
 Fantasies, urges, or behaviors involving acts in which the suffering of a victim is sexually exciting.

Transvestic fetishism 302.2
 Fantasies, urges, or behaviors in a heterosexual male involving cross-dressing.

Voyeurism 302.82
 Fantasies, urges, or behaviors involving observing unsuspecting persons who are nude, disrobing, or in sexual activity.

Sexual dysfunction not otherwise specified 302.70
 Sexual dysfunctions that do not meet the above criteria.

Note. From American Psychiatric Association (1994). *Diagnostic and Statistical Manual of Mental Disorders* (4th ed.). Washington, DC: Author.

2. That they be of greater than 6 months' duration.
3. That they cause clinically significant distress or impair day-to-day function.

Such paraphilias commonly include exhibitionism, frottage, the pedophilias, sadomasochism, transvestic fetishism, and voyeurism. However, several rather common paraphilias are relegated to the category "paraphilias, not otherwise specified." No explanation is offered for this classification, which can include telephone scatologia and bestiality. Men who rape are not allocated to a category; they usually do not fit criteria for sexual sadism (Maletzky, 2000b). Another serious problem occurs when an individual has combinations of these paraphilias, a not uncommon clinical presentation. Exhibitionism, voyeurism, and telephone scatology are more often combined than not (Freund & Watson, 1980); other combinations, such as heterosexual and homosexual pedophilia, are also not uncommon (Maletzky, 1991a, Chap. 10). Most obvious by its absence is any mention of hebephilia: Many homosexual and heterosexual pedophiles prefer sexual activity with teenagers.

Several authors have recently questioned the validity of the requirement that distress or functional impairment occur (Maletzky, O'Donohue, Negev, & Hagstrom, 2000; Spitzer & Wakefield, 1999). Most offenders experience distress only upon disclosure of their crimes and not as a result of their condition. Moreover, very few manifest obvious disturbances in social, occupational, or other important areas of function. There is often no impairment in reciprocal and affectionate relationships with adults, and despite implications in *DSM-IV*, paraphilics most often do not have a personality disorder (Marshall & Hall, 1995). Nonetheless, most clinicians feel comfortable making these diagnoses based on history, regardless of distress or impairment. Unfortunately, this practice produces a rift between clinical practice and the *DSM-IV*, poses problems in forensic settings (Holmgren, 1999), and creates potential difficulties in research (Spitzer & Wakefield, 1999). However, solutions to merging clinical reality and diagnostic taxonomy have been proposed (Maletzky et al., 2000).

Even more serious problems can occur in clinical practice inasmuch as most sexual offenders[1] do not readily admit all their deviant behavior (Abel et al., 1987). Such patients cannot be readily compared for epidemiological purposes to patients with other psychiatric disorders that are more commonly egodystonic. There are very few more damaging evils to admit than molesting a child or raping a woman. The best data available prompt the conclusion that treatment providers may never know the full extent of an offender's fantasies and actual deviant behaviors. Treatment in such cases is equivalent to treating major depressive disorder by guessing about thoughts, feelings, and even behaviors particular to that patient.

The *DSM-IV* is in accord, however, with evidence that sexually abnormal behavior due to another disease process should not be included.

The largest proportion of offenders, between 55% and 90%, comprising most clinical outpatient samples, is composed of situational pedophiles (Maletzky & Steinhauser, 1998). Other classifications make a distinction between *incestuous* and *nonincestuous* offenders. Equally nonspecific and confusing are references to *child molesters*. More recently, the terms *paraphilic* (primarily attracted to deviant stimuli) and *nonparaphilic* (primarily attracted to adults) have appeared. Other artificial schemes have attempted to distinguish age differences between perpetrator and victim (over 16 years of age, 5 years' difference, etc.), which leave unresolved the problem of adolescent offenders. Within this chaotic sea, the only safe harbor may lie in distinguishing between *situational* and *predatory* offenders. A situational offender is one who would not have offended had an enticing situation not arisen. The term *predatory* refers to a behavioral pattern, whereas *preferential* implies a knowledge of motives (often hidden), while *paraphilic* implies a knowledge of arousal patterns, not always easily gleaned. Predatory behavior, more dangerous and treatment-resistant (Maletzky, 1998), includes an active search for potential victims in the community, grooming victims (befriending, buying gifts), offending against multiple victims, and, in many cases, preferring deviant sexual activity to normal sexual outlets. Table 21.2 highlights the distinctions among situational, preferential, and predatory offenders. It is the combination of preferential and predatory traits that characterizes the most dangerous of sexual offenders.

EPIDEMIOLOGY

Since sexual offenders rarely report their crimes to authorities, data on incidence and prevalence lie mostly hidden in their memories and, unfortunately, in the memories of their victims. What data are available, however, indicate that reported sexual crimes are increasing. The figures continue to astonish: Between 30% and 70% of college-age females have been victimized in some fashion (Russell, 1988). The majority of victims experience hands-on contact before the age of 16 (Lutzker, 2000); 50% of women report being victims of exhibitionism (Zverina, Lachman, Pondelickova, & Vanek, 1987). Among children, Salter (1992) estimates prevalence rates of up to 39% for girls and 30% for boys. Of even more startling impact, 44 to 55% of college males say they would use force against a woman to obtain sexual gratification if they were guaranteed no consequences (Malamuth, Haber, & Feshbach, 1990).

These guesses stem, however, largely from identified offenders. Many researchers believe that over 90% of paraphilic acts go undetected, even for the closely scrutinized pedophilias (Holmgren, 1999). If the modest figure of female molestation before the age of 18 is taken as 30%, and if there are four times the number of adults as children in North America, then approximately 5% of men have molested young girls, a finding depressingly similar to estimates derived through other means: A nationwide survey estimated that between 4% and 17% of males had molested children of one or both genders (Wang, 1999).

MODELS OF ETIOLOGY

Compared with the absence of data on the epidemiology of the paraphilias, there is a wealth of literature describing a variety of overlapping yet well-articulated theories of etiology, although most are difficult to test empirically. A review of these conceptual domains provides a background for understanding how treatment paradigms have evolved from the different ways of explaining the causes of these disorders.

TABLE 21.2 Distinctions Among Situational, Preferential, and Predatory Pedophiles

Situational Pedophile	*Preferential Pedophile*	*Predatory Pedophile*
Living with victim	Not living with victim or, if living with victim, having at least one other victim in the community	Not living with victim
Well known to victim	May be well known to some victims	Not well known to at least some victims
Single victim	Usually multiple victims	Multiple victims
Single pedophilia, usually heterosexual	Single pedophilia, either hetero- or homosexual	Single or double pedophilia, hetero- or homosexual
Frequently married or living with a woman	Often not married or living with a woman	May be married or living with a woman

Note. These categories are not mutually exclusive.

Behavioral Learning Models

Some of the earliest and most influential studies of the paraphilias stressed the primacy of early conditioning in the development of sexual deviations (e.g., Kinsey, Pomeroy, & Martin, 1948; McGuire, Carlisle, & Young, 1965; VanWyk & Geist, 1984). These efforts created laboratory equivalents of the acquisition and maintenance of sexual behavior. From these studies, a number of general principles emerged:

1. Unconditioned stimuli can elicit sexual arousal and release (orgasm).
2. Conditioned stimuli can become associated with unconditioned stimuli so they can also, eventually and with repeated pairings, produce sexual arousal and release.
3. Such sexual conditioning is robust given the physiological power of sexual release.
4. Actions increasing the probability of sexual release are highly reinforced and thus are likely to occur in the future.
5. Human sexual behavior consists of ordered sequences in a chain of behavior leading to sexual release.
6. Actions leading to aversive consequences, such as interruption of this chain, will be reduced in frequency.
7. Humans can become aroused through stimulus generalization to objects close to, but not the same as, those initially arousing.

In behavioral models, the offender is assumed to exhibit sexual arousal to deviant stimuli. While this is often true, over 30% of admitting offenders show no deviant arousal on the plethysmograph (Looman, Abracen, Maillet, & DiFazio, 1998). However, the artificial circumstances of the plethysmograph may be blamed for its lack of sensitivity and its high rate of false negatives. One difficulty in analyzing these data stems from the inclusion of undetected offenders in "normal" comparison groups.

The behavioral model has been only partly displaced as newer theories have emerged to explain paraphilias. People's own sexual experiences and the manner in which behavioral principles have been able to predict outcomes (Maletzky, 1998) have kept alive the suspicion that life's contingencies, particularly in childhood, somehow have influenced our own sexual preferences and behaviors.

Critical Stages Model

Behavior models have been augmented more recently through the addition of research on purported sensitivities in central nervous system development (Golden, Peterson-Rhone, Jackson, & Gontkovsky, 2000). Children may go through critical stages of growth in which, during crucial intervals, various aspects of sexuality develop. Situations occurring before or after these periods (as yet not clearly defined) are weaker in influencing the development of sexual preferences. For example, a young boy caught in the act of undressing by a female relative may later in life obtain some sexual satisfaction in exposing his genitals to women. Unfortunately, no objective verification of critical stages has as yet been made.

Social Learning Models

More prevalent today, and perhaps more politically acceptable, social learning models include the culture in which offenders live as an important factor in increasing the likelihood of offending. Early studies (as reviewed in Stermac, Segal, & Gillis, 1990) pointed toward family background and the influence of behavioral modeling in shaping future sexual activity. More recent work has suggested that the lack of parental (particularly paternal) care, physical punishment, and frequent or aggressive sexual activity within the family may all predispose children to begin sexual offending in late childhood or adolescence and to use aggression to obtain gratification, to show impairment of social inhibitions against the use of force, and to act impulsively regardless of long-term consequences (Marshall, Serran, & Cortoni, 2000; Smallbone & Dadds, 2000).

A number of recent surveys appear to lend credence to this model. Factors such as self-esteem (Marshall & Mazzucco, 1995), capacity for affection and empathy (Marshall & Marshall, 2000), and ability to postpone gratification (Seidman, Marshall, Hudson, & Robertson, 1994) are reduced in some offender samples compared to nonoffender populations and even to nonsexual offenders. Marshall and Barbaree (1990a) have developed this model to its current position of prominence in the North American literature. In summary, they postulate that a deficiency in forming attachment bonds in childhood leads to low self-esteem and a lack of intimacy in adult relationships.

Proponents of social learning models have relied on the anthropological and sociological literature (e.g., Gibbens & Ahrenfeldt, 1966; Quinsey, 1984), which suggests that societies with high rates of aggressive sexual behavior show high rates of nonsexual violence, greater male dominance, and a negative attitude toward women. There has also been a greater acceptance of rape myths in societies in which sexual aggression has been prominent (Burt, 1980; Felson, 2000).

However, not all evidence supports these theories. Studies controlling for sexual, as well as nonsexual, violence find no causative specifically sexual element (as reviewed in Maletzky, 2000b; McConaghy, 1993, pp. 286–290). Confounding factors of family socioeconomic class, genetic heritage, availability of pornography, and influence of peers have not been adequately controlled. While there is no doubt that social and cultural factors influence adult sexual choice, there is as yet no comprehensive proposal of mechanisms leading inalterably from a troubled background to a lifetime of deviant sexual behavior.

Compensation Theories

Following closely on social learning models, many early workers proposed a theory, commonly embraced by many nonspecialists as well, in which an offender, deprived of normal social and sexual contacts, compensates by seeking gratification through deviant means (Groth, 1979). While attractive on commonsense grounds, studies providing an empirical basis for this theory have not been forthcoming. Most pedophiles enjoy normal sexual relationships with adult female partners, as do many men who rape and those who expose (Marshall & Barbaree, 1990a). Work accomplished since the late 1980s fails to confirm this theory (Langevin & Lang, 1987) and leaves unexplained the presence in most exhibitionists of adequate social and sexual outlets (Maletzky, 2000a).

A Feminist Perspective

In its radical form, the feminist model of sexual offending considers all men potential sexual aggressors. According to this perspective, rape most certainly, and other sexual crimes more probably, is driven by men's wishes to dominate women and, by extension, children as well (as reported in Herman, 1990). Proponents of these views believe that sexual crimes may not be sexually driven but may represent latent aggressive impulses that many men harbor toward women. One benefit of these notions has been the increasing awareness of sexual offending itself and the need for public education about its harmful effects.

However, extreme positions can transpose an advantage to contrary views: Backlash to the victims' movement has been reported (Finkelhor, 1994). Sober reflection on the available data leads to conclusions that counter the belief that sexual offending is nonsexual in nature:

1. Virtually all sexual offenders in treatment report being sexually aroused by fantasies of their deviant activities and use these fantasies in masturbation.
2. Nonoffenders may share with sexual offenders an apparently endogenous predilection toward aggression and sexuality (as reviewed in Golden et al., 2000; McConaghy, 1993, pp. 343–346). Nonoffenders may differ only in keeping this predilection more successfully hidden.
3. Most offenders display a single deviant behav-

ioral pattern. The feminist model should lead to the finding of a broad range of sexual deviations within each patient.

4. Male sexual offenders display marked reductions in sexual arousal when their testosterone levels are artificially reduced with hormone therapy (Prentky, 1997).
5. Many men who rape are sexually aroused by the aggressive elements of sexuality. However, they are also aroused by normal sexual stimuli. Only a handful of men who rape are aroused by aggression in the absence of sexual cues (Abel, Barlow, Blanchard, & Guild, 1977; Seto & Barbaree, 2000).
6. A number of studies show no strong correlation between an attitude of hostility in males and propensity to act in a sexually aggressive manner (Hudson & Ward, 1997; Stermac et al., 1990).

Addiction Models

Often, the behavior of sexual offenders appears compulsive in nature. The addiction model, as summarized in Ball and Seghorn (1999), equates offenders with alcohol and drug addicts. Deviant sexual activity in this model acts as a drug substitute in filling some (unspecified) need that can be determined in therapy. Like other addicts, some offenders come from stormy backgrounds, manipulate relationships for their own advantage, and do not learn from prior negative consequences. The analogy is internally consistent and is a popular feature in discussions of sexual abuse in the media (Carnes, 1983).

However, like other commonsense notions of causative factors, addiction models have not received empirical support. Sexual offenders are notable more for their normality than for their deviancy. No single personality factor, based either on psychological testing or interviewing technique, is pathognomonic of sexual offending (Langevin & Lang, 1987; Maletzky, 1991a, Chap. 10; Marshall & Hall, 1995). Unfortunately, offenders do not respond to 12-step programs as alcoholics do, and their deviations are much more responsive to cognitive and behavioral treatment approaches than are more standard addictions (Maletzky, 1998).

The Offender as Victim

The harm of sexual abuse is most clearly reflected in the faces of its victims. Many believe that among these lurk future offenders bound to commit further abuse because they themselves were victimized. The predominant theme in this model suggests that offenders are revisiting and reliving their earlier traumas, perhaps to gain a greater measure of control over their fractured world (Groth, 1979). Others propose identification with the aggressor as a mechanism by which offenders can gain control (Justice & Justice, 1979). More recent studies have documented differences in offenders who were or were not victims as children themselves (Dhawan & Marshall, 1996). However, the majority of retrospective, prospective, and well-controlled comparisons find that fewer than 30% of offenders were victims of sexual abuse before the age of 18 (Abel et al., 1987; Maletzky, 1993). It is unlikely that the remaining 70% could not remember the abuse. The finding that these figures do not vary as a consequence of the type of offense is surprising. An exhibitionist is as likely to have been a victim as a rapist or pedophile.

Physiological Models

The Role of Sexual Hormones

Because many sexual offenders combine elements of aggression with sexual behavior, a search for a relationship between aggression and male sexual hormones has interested many researchers. A number of studies have revealed little difference in circulating testosterone among sexual offenders and both nonsexual offenders and nonoffenders (as reviewed in Hucker & Bain, 1990). Such studies, however, have typically included small numbers of subjects and have been poorly controlled. Despite decades of interest, no replicated differences of hormone levels have yet been found between sexual offenders and nonsexual offenders. It remains possible that in utero hormonal levels may contribute to the nature and intensity of sexual drive later in life, but interest in this area is just awakening.

Maternal Immunosuppression

An interesting and persistent finding in the human sexual literature is the significantly greater proportion of older than younger brothers (but not sisters) among men with a homosexual orientation (Blanchard & Bogaert, 1997; Raboch & Raboch, 1986). Several authors have proposed that, with each successive male fetus one bears, a mother may develop an increasingly robust immune response to the development of CNS structures that define masculine behaviors in her offspring (Blanchard & Klassen, 1997; Gaultieri & Hicks, 1985). More recently, three studies have documented that homosexual pedophiles, but not heterosexual offenders, have a statistically significant preponderance of older brothers as well (Bogaert, Bezeau, Kuban, & Blanchard, 1997; Lalumiére, Harris, Quinsey, & Rice, 1998; Maletzky & Steinhauser, 2000). However, only-child homosexuals and homosexual pedophiles are not unknown; if immunosuppression operates to influence homosexual choice, it must be a contributory, rather than determining, factor.

Central Nervous System Damage

Brain damage has been associated with changes in sexual behavior, typically in the expression of anomalous sexual responses previously unknown or suppressed. Studies in primates have demonstrated a possible uncovering of latent sexual aggression with destruction of portions of the temporal lobe (Kluver & Bucy, 1939) or stimulation of diencephalic structures (MacLean, 1973). Some authors have reported findings of central nervous system (CNS) damage in sexual offenders, although often these abnormalities were minor in extent (Flor-Henry & Lang, 1988). More extensive testing, including the Halstead-Reitan Battery, has revealed no statistically significant differences when adequate controls were included (Langevin et al., 1985).

While clinicians have expressed the hope that modern techniques of neuroimaging will reveal subtle abnormalities in the brain structures of offenders, there are few studies addressing this issue. Of the new imaging techniques, results only of computerized tomography (CT) scanning have been reported thus far. These results revealed no structural changes in the majority of offenders (Langevin et al., 1985). Of interest, however, is a preliminary impression that single photon emission computed tomography (SPECT) (and perhaps positron emission tomography, or PET) scans can show altered limbic activity when a subject is sexually aroused (Stoléru et al., 1999). Should costs be more readily controlled, further exploration of this intriguing impression is warranted. The common clinical opinion that CNS damage destroys control mechanisms and thus results in disinhibition and subsequent offending begs for further study.

Genetic Factors Few studies have examined the possible role of genetic factors predisposing to abuse. However, chromosomal abnormalities have been implicated in the etiology of atypical sexual behaviors (Schiavi, Thielgaard, Owen, & White, 1988) and in those with gender dysphoric disorders (Money & Pollitt, 1964). The lack of any published research investigating the genetic heritage of sexual offending in the face of ample research for other *DSM-IV* categories underscores not only the present bias against biological contributions but also the relative lack of medical researchers in this field.

Sociobiological Models

In human societies, incest is more likely with weak familial bonds and most likely without such a bond (Erickson, 1993). Among all cases of adult-child sexual contact, the overwhelming majority (between 70% and 90%) occur between males and young females whom these males did not raise from infancy (Kuehnle, Coulter, & Gamache, 2000; Maletzky, 1991a, chap. 10; 1993).

In addition, sexual "offending" is known among nonhuman primates, our closest living relatives (see Griffen & Cherfas, 1983 for a review). Examples of pedophilia, exhibitionism, and rape have been reported in many species (Maletzky, 1996). When male gorillas are thwarted in attempts to mount an adult female, they occasionally turn their attentions to an adolescent female. More often than not, female relatives of the adolescent drive off the sulking perpetrator. Quite commonly, a male chimpanzee exposes his erect penis to a female as one of the initiating behaviors that lead to coitus. Occasionally, female gorillas are unsuccessful in warding off the sexual advances of powerful males who grasp and forcefully hold them during intercourse.

A number of authors have speculated about evolutionary mechanisms gone awry as an explanation for sexual abuse (Ellis, 1993; Quinsey & Lalumiére, 1995), while others have warned against this trend as overly facile, with more cachet than substance (Krause, 1994). Although we are probably well warned not always to see, in the pool of complex human behavior, the reflections of an ape, sociobiological models are important because they open a previously neglected area of thinking about sexual abuse. For example, most male nonhuman primates display erections before attempting to mount a female; exhibitionism is the most commonly encountered human paraphilia. Primate juveniles may become attractive to some adults due to stimulus generalization and accessibility; while pedophilia is rare among apes, it is seen in nondominant males that lose females to competitors. Sexual aggression is common in apes, although it is not commonly successful. These observations suggest that the forerunners of misaligned passions may reside in phylogenetic templates for aggression in the service of sexual access.

ASSESSMENT

No single instrument, psychological, social, or physiological, has been proven to be definitive in the assessment of the sexual offender. Thus, combinations of techniques have become essential in distinguishing offending patterns that merit clinical concern. Problems in assessment have arisen because of the private nature of sexual activity, the hesitation some therapists show in inquiring about sex, and the sexual offender's frequent reluctance to divulge crucial information. In the treatment of depression, bipolar disorder, obsessive compulsive disorder, phobias, and the like, therapists and patients combine forces to defeat the identified symptoms because these arouse painful affects. However, a sexual offender may have reservations about full disclosure, in part due to legal consequences and in part due to ego preservation. Many offenders, even when presented with irrefutable evidence that they committed deviant acts, still cannot accept responsibility. Indeed, overcoming denial is believed by most therapists to be a crucial step in effective treatment.

More common than outright denial is minimization, by which offenders may claim no memory of events due to drug or alcohol abuse or attempt to camouflage the sexual intent of their actions, as, for example, by claiming sexual molestation was motivated by educational goals ("I was teaching her about sex") or that it occurred by accident ("my hand slipped"). Evaluators have thus aimed to recover information not only from reports by patients themselves, but from significant others, police reports, and presentence investigations, and also from psychological and physiological measures, in attempts to comprehend the breadth and variety of deviant sexual motivations and behaviors.

While the determination of whether an individual has offended appears straightforward, diagnostic assessment does not end at that point. The clinician will need to determine the duration and extent of offending, against whom it has occurred, how the crime has been perpetrated, what meaning it may have for the offender, and, of even greater practical significance, how the offender might best be treated. The steps of comprehensive assessment form the foundation on which a treatment plan is then based.

Review of Materials

Every effort must be made to obtain information about the offender before the first interview. Materials often available include police reports, a presentence investigation, psychological and psychiatric evaluations, psychological testing, child protection agency reports, depositions, and any testimony recorded. As offenders often distort information about their sexual activities, reviewing these documents is an essential element in assessment. Records of the present offense are crucial, but information about any prior sexual or nonsexual crimes is also relevant. Of particular interest are histories of any drug or alcohol use and any prior psychiatric treatment.

The Clinical Interview

Clinicians are uncommonly skilled in eliciting information from patients, yet the simple values of clinical history taking and mental status evaluations are often underestimated. These skills are put to a challenge in obtaining histories from sexual offenders, not the most cooperative of clients. Frequently, early sessions are reserved for trust building and reflection rather than for insightful history taking. It often can take 5 to 10 nonconfrontive sessions before patients in either individual or group therapy feel comfortable sharing the sexual details of their offenses.

Although structured clinical interviews of psychiatric patients have appeared in the literature, none have focused on the sexual offender. Most clinicians favor unstructured interviews to elicit as much information as possible while enhancing the therapist-patient relationship. While information may be gained at various times during interviews, it should be organized into a concise, yet comprehensive, report.

In many cases, 2 or 3 hours of interviewing, perhaps separated into several sessions, should prove sufficient to gain an understanding of the offender's problem areas, sexual or nonsexual, and some indication of early treatment goals. Offenders often come to these sessions in a defensive mood, isolated and angry, with self-reproach and fears of financial loss. They deserve, and will appreciate, the therapist's support.

As part of a clinical interview, the mental status examination can be helpful as the therapist's organized report of behavioral observations. Particularly noteworthy in the examination of sexual offenders are issues of awareness and orientation, understanding and empathy toward the victim, acceptance of responsibility, and any signs of a psychiatric illness predisposing the offender to act impulsively or without consideration of others' emotions. Particularly, the clinician needs to know if the offender is aware that the behavior was wrong and why. Are there faulty assumptions and distortions? What does the offender think and feel about treatment? At this point, the therapist will gain more from nonjudgmental prompts than from vigorous probes.

Self-Reports

Aside from obtaining a history of the present offenses, the therapist can ask the patient to keep a record of covert deviant acts, such as sexual urges, fantasies, and dreams, and of actual deviant behavior, such as molesting or masturbating to fantasies of deviant sexual activity. Are these reports of any value, however, given the offender's predisposition, based on self-interest, to misreport data? An exhaustive review under strictly confidential conditions (Abel et al., 1987) revealed that authorities and therapists will learn about only a small percentage of the sexual crimes that these men have committed. In the present state of knowledge, it is best to collect such data and regard them with a critical eye.

Psychological Tests

Despite frequent attempts, both historical (Gebhard, Gargon, Pomeroy, & Christenson, 1965) and modern-day (Schlank, 1995), to typify sexual offenders by standard and specialized psychological assessment tools, no single instrument or combination of instruments has yielded a clearly defined set of characteristic responses for this group or for any subgroups within it. As a corollary, an evaluator is not yet justified in predicting the probability of future acts based on any combination of tests alone. The lack of strong correlations among test results, diagnoses, and prediction of treatment response may stem from the heterogeneity of sexual offenders in general.

Summarizing a thorough review of the utility of psychological testing for sexual offenders, Marshall and Hall (1995) concluded that such instruments "however they are scored or represented, do not satisfactorily distinguish any type of sexual offender from various other groups of subjects, including, most particularly, nonoffenders" (pp. 216–217).

Corroborating Information

Since sexual offenders often distort information, a therapist would do well to seek the observations of partners, parents, and friends, even though some of these individuals may be swayed by their own loyalties. It is vital to include a corrections official, usually a probation or parole individual, in observations and recommendations about treatment as well as for dispositional planning, as this officer plays a key role in many offenders' lives. Including the official in treatment decisions reduces manipulation and ensures more complete disclosure of pertinent facts to all interested parties. In addition, scrutiny of updated police files can be helpful, although not definitive, in determining whether an offender, during or following treatment, has reoffended. Since such records are open to the public, confidentiality has generally not been an issue.

Physiological Assessments

The Penile Plethysmograph

The most widely used measure of sexual preference, the penile plethysmograph, has an extensive and varied history in its application to sexual offenders. Originally employed to test impotence, this device has become a standard for the assessment of the sexual offender. The first devices measured penile volume changes (Freund, 1963), but penile circumference is now preferred because the methodology is available, the technique feasible, its reliability reasonable (Howes, 1998), and its validity now demonstrated (Lalumiére & Quinsey, 1994).

Technical details in the application of the plethysmograph point toward a practitioner consensus, now codified in guidelines for its use in the assessment and treatment of the sexual offender (Association for the Treatment of Sexual Abusers [ATSA], 1993). Briefly, in the standard technique, a mercury-in-rubber strain gauge, thin as a rubber band (but loose, not tight), is placed by the patient, in private, onto the midshaft of his penis, which can remain covered by clothing. He is next asked to view explicit material, such as slides, movies, and videotapes of deviant and normal sexuality; to listen to tapes describing such activity; and to create his own descriptions of sexual activity as well. Penile circumference changes are recorded, usually in terms of percentage of previously determined full erection, throughout this process. Changes less than 20% of full erection are considered too minor to be of clinical import. Testing can consume several hours.

Such testing is now the standard by which other assessment techniques are judged. Of constant surprise is the fact that, under such artificial laboratory conditions and under pressure to appear normal, a majority of offenders demonstrate deviant sexual arousal. Studies vouchsafing validity, reliability, and clinical relevance have appeared since the early 1980s (as reviewed in Howes, 1998). To date, penile tumescence changes have been associated with sexual offending in predicted directions. Many child molesters, for example, show increases in circumference in reaction to stimuli depicting sexual scenes involving children, and rapists generally show increased arousal to aggressive scenes of sexual activity.

However, the limitations of circumference changes have become increasingly obvious:

1. Just over 30% of pedophiles and incest offenders show either normal plethysmographs or a "flat line," that is, no response to any stimulus. These figures jump to over 40% of rapists and exhibitionists, perhaps indicating greater heterogeneity in these populations (Looman et al., 1998; Maletzky, 1991a, Chap 2).
2. Cheating is possible and probably is the case with many offenders (Wilson, 1998):
   a. An offender might not pay attention to the stimulus, but this can be prevented by a detection task, such as requiring the patient to report a randomly presented signal in part of the stimulus display or requiring the patient to describe what he sees.
   b. Cheating could also occur through cognitive control, such as engaging in a competing, nonsexual mental task. When instructed to produce this result, subjects have been shown to affect arousal (Looman et al., 1998). To combat this, some clinicians first present sexual stimuli to generate erections, then present deviant stimuli. It is generally more difficult for an offender to lose an erection than to block its occurrence.
3. Studies purporting to demonstrate validity and reliability often include small numbers of subjects. Much larger populations should be studied, but in reality, such research would be labor-intensive and expensive. In an age of funding cutbacks, such research is unlikely in the near future.
4. The plethysmograph is insufficiently standardized. Different stimuli are used in different laboratories. Exposure times vary, as do numbers and types of stimuli used; different measures of sexual arousal are used as well. Most centers report data in terms of percentage of full erection, but other clinicians use actual millimeters of circumference change. It is as if electrocardiograms (EKGs) were conducted with electrode placements at the whim of the examiner.
5. The testing situation is highly intrusive. A small number of offenders refuse it outright, even when faced with legal consequences. Few therapists and fewer patients enjoy it. It also implies that we expect deceit.
6. The test requires the purchase of expensive equipment and is costly to administer.
7. Its use within a legal framework can be deceptive. It smacks of objectivity, and while it is one of the few physical tests that can be definitive in psychiatry, it cannot be used to prove or disprove whether an individual has or has not committed any particular act. In addition, it can lend only marginal weight to an assumption of guilt or innocence, thus bolstering or weakening any particular case. Admittedly, false negatives are common, but fortunately, false positive are rare (Lalumiére & Harris, 1998).
8. Results thus far have suffered from a sampling bias: We evaluate only those offenders who are caught.
9. Results correlate better with a history of pedophilia than with exhibitionism or rape (McConaghy, 1993, Chap. 1), perhaps because these latter offenses stem from a greater range

of causes. Other offenses, such as telephone scatologia and frotteurism, yield very low levels of any deviant arousal (Maletzky, 1993).

10. Some findings indicate that the test has greater validity in measuring type than in measuring strength of sexual interest (Howes, 1998).

In summary, the plethysmograph remains controversial in determining deviant sexual arousal in offenders, although most clinicians and researchers continue to employ it. Indeed, the greatest benefit of the plethysmograph may lie not in assessment but in treatment, as described below.

The Abel Assessment

Recently, an altogether different approach to physiological (actually, physical) assessment has been developed based on how long an individual chooses to look at visual stimuli depicting a variety of potential sexual attractors (Osborn, Abel, & Warberg, 1995). In this test, a stimulus set of slides depicting clothed targets of pedophilia, rape, exhibitionism, sadism, and a variety of other paraphilias are shown by computer to a patient, who is asked to rate how arousing the slide is. The computer measures the time each participant took to rate each slide and depress a button to advance to the next slide. The amount of time taken before proceeding to the next slide is the crucial variable. Although termed *reaction time,* this is actually a test of *viewing time;* it purports not only to measure sexual interest, but to be a less intrusive alternative to the plethysmograph.

The Abel Assessment has been validated by its originators (Abel, Hoffman, Warberg, & Holland, 1998) and by independent laboratories (Johnson & Listiak, 1999; Letourneau, 1999). Caution is advised, however, in assuming this test can replace plethysmography:

1. The original intention of the test was to measure sexual *interest;* this may comprise a different parameter than sexual *arousal.*
2. Validity and reliability results have been equivocal (Fischer & Smith, 1999; Smith & Fischer, 1999); more data are being collected (Abel, personal communication, March 2000).
3. The test is still evolving; its originators have recently altered the method of interpreting the score (Abel, 1997b).
4. Relatively small numbers of subjects have, as yet, been tested.
5. Although its originators reported a study to demonstrate that subjects could not falsify viewing times (Abel, 1997a), in fact the transparency of the test is worrisome. The data presented are not convincing; it is possible that offenders will learn the purpose of the test and be able to conceal their true interests.
6. As with the plethysmograph, this test cannot determine if an individual has ever committed a sexual crime.

Despite these cautions, the Abel Assessment contains numerous strengths, especially when compared to the plethysmograph. It employs a standardized set of visual stimuli (slides) that do not depict pornographic images, it is easy to administer, and it is far less intrusive and is more palatable to offenders, their therapists, and the public alike. Whether it will prove a valuable addition depends upon the findings of future large and collaborative research efforts.

The Polygraph

If possible, even more controversy surrounds the use of the poorly named "lie detector." During a polygraph examination, an offender is asked, among a number of questions, about engaging in sexually deviant acts at critical periods based on the offending history, while recordings are made of pulse, blood pressure, EKG, and galvanic skin response. As with the plethysmograph, the offender is in an artificial and potentially hostile environment and is aware that the reason for this test is the suspicion of dishonesty. It is an intrusive test and one not accorded full validity in the scientific and popular literature (Abrams, 1991). However, polygraphy, a field with its own literature, has been accorded an increasing measure of respect, particularly due to its value in working with sexual offenders.

Despite some similarities, the test differs from the plethysmograph in important ways. The plethysmograph measures a physiological change both more specific and more focused than the polygraph. Conclusions about the past, such as whether an individual did or did not commit a specific act, cannot be drawn from the plethysmograph, while such conclusions are frequently made based on polygraph results.

Experience with polygraph examinations of offenders is mixed (Blasingame, 1998). Some offenders fail the test and then admit culpability for some or all of their crimes. Many others pass, having conquered the machine and their own anxiety. Although it is commonly asserted that antisocial offenders often succeed on the test since they are adept at unimpassioned trickery, no definitive studies of sexual offenders are at hand.

However, in one attribute, the plethysmograph and polygraph share an important similarity—they are equally important as devised for treatment:

> A 20-year-old college student frequented a campus laundromat at odd hours. He was charged with exposing himself to several female students. He denied culpability, and several plethysmograph evaluations failed to demonstrate any deviant arousal. Following a no contest plea to charges of indecent exposure, he entered an outpatient sexual abuse clinic that required regular polygraphs. Several weeks before his first examination, the therapist explained that the staff wanted him to succeed on the polygraph and that, to help him do so, he needed to think very hard about his recent activities and tell the entire truth before undergoing the test. In a subsequent session, he confessed to several additional acts of exposing, peeking in dormitory windows, and rubbing against women on escalators and in campus activities.

In this case, the polygraph uncovered additional areas for inquiry and treatment. Overall, the polygraph has been useful in assessment and treatment. Whether bodily measures of general anxiety and arousal can be relied on to extricate truth from deception with scientific accuracy will, in all likelihood, continue to be debated into the foreseeable future.

Assessment of Risk

Part of any sexual offender assessment is the determination of risk for the patient to be at large. Such assessments are often necessary for decisions about release from an institution, the level of supervision in the community, and the need for civil commitment. Risk factors have been divided into static, or historical, variables (such as criminal history, presence of male victims, or use of force in crimes) and dynamic, or changeable, variables (such as deviant sexual arousal or the level of denial). It appears necessary to develop instruments specifically designed to predict sexual offense risk since clinical judgment alone has been demonstrated to be only slightly greater than chance (Hanson & Thornton, 2000).

Fortunately, a number of factors, mostly static, have been identified that help predict the level of risk for sexual reoffending. These factors, taken from several recent meta-analyses (Gendreau, Little, & Goggin, 1996; Hanson & Bussière, 1998) and from large and long-term clinical follow-up trials (Hanson & Harris, in press; Maletzky, 1993) have led to the construction of a variety of instruments said to provide quantitative measures of risk in any given individual (Epperson, Kaul, & Hesselton, 1998; Hanson & Thornton, 2000; Quinsey, Harris, Rice, & Cormier, 1998). Table 21.3 lists the most common of these factors.

These actuarial tools have generally proven to be more accurate than clinical judgment alone (Hanson & Thornton, 2000). However, even scales purporting to be quantitatively derived suffer from intrinsic deficits common to all prediction schemes for human behaviors:

1. Risk assessment depends on the quality of the data available; in sexual offender evaluations, historical data are often inadequate.
2. Available instruments are not capable of predicting *when* an offender might commit a new sexual crime.
3. Scales cannot take into account all conceivable intervening variables; for example, a rapist might have few predictors of reoffense yet an-

TABLE 21.3 Risk Factors in Being at Large Within the Community

Multiple victims
Multiple paraphilias
Male victims
Deviant sexual arousal (demonstrated by the plethysmograph) or interest (demonstrated by the Abel Assessment)
Offender not living with the victim(s)
Offender not well known to the victim(s)
Predatory pattern, such as victim search and grooming
Aggression used in the commission of the act(s)
Denial or marked minimization of the act(s)
Reluctance to enter treatment
Age under 30
Unstable employment history
Unstable history of relationships
Antisocial history

nounce an intention to commit a new crime; a pedophile might have low scores yet be in an environment surrounded by children, thus increasing risk by ease of access; an exhibitionist might be crippled by an accident, thus reducing his opportunity to reoffend.

4. While it is clear that an offender with *many* risk factors is at high risk and an offender with *few* factors is at low risk, the typical offender carries a *moderate* number of such factors; assessing this risk in a quantitative fashion poses a challenge, now being met by large, ongoing prospective studies (Hanson & Thornton, 2000).

TREATMENT

The foundation of treatment for the paraphilias rests on principles shared with all patient-therapist endeavors: trust and mutual respect. This is especially true given the often involuntary nature of this population. Most such patients are mandated into treatment; indeed, the majority of sexual offenders disclaim a need for treatment at all. As a consequence, many offenders view the therapist as an extension of a coercive social system rather than as a professional trying to help. They recognize that their therapist may have to report progress, or lack of it, to authorities, and this recognition creates an oppositional atmosphere, which is magnified by the inclusion in therapy of invasive testing techniques such as the plethysmograph and polygraph. However, although not an easy task, a trusting relationship between therapist and patient can be developed, even in the face of massive denial.

Institutional Versus Community-Based Treatment

While more aggressive sexual offenders, such as rapists, may receive long-term prison sentences, many men with paraphilias are not sent to prison, although they often spend short terms in jail (Bumby & Maddox, 1999). Most sexual offenders eventually are treated within the communities in which they committed their crimes. Often, "lesser" sexual offenses, such as exhibitionism or incest, result in light sentences. The decisions of disposition are usually made, often by the court and the corrections officer, before the offender is seen by a therapist. At times, however, a therapist may be asked to testify at a sentencing hearing about the dangerousness of a person's being at large. Fortunately, some data have been presented that inform these choices (Hanson & Thornton, 2000; Maletzky, 1993).

The techniques described here can be employed within either an inpatient or an outpatient setting. Inpatient venues generally include prisons, jails, halfway houses, and state institutions. Only a handful of private inpatient resources exist nationwide. Typical outpatient settings include private subspecialty clinics and community mental health centers. Unfortunately, the latter are poorly funded, even within metropolitan counties. However, more psychiatrists are expressing interest in this field and contributing to the literature, once the exclusive domain of the nonmedical specialist.

Group Versus Individual Treatment

While the majority of treatment at present is delivered in a group format, sexual behavior is idiosyncratic, and approaches to its deviations are often best provided through individual therapy. Unfortunately, such decisions are often affected more by issues of finance than of efficacy. While groups are effective vehicles for delivering some of the techniques described below, combining approaches often offers the greatest efficacy. An orientation group at the beginning of treatment can introduce offenders to concepts of therapy and can serve as a better forum in which to challenge minimization and denial. A group may also be an efficient medium within which to review principles of cognitive therapy and relapse prevention. Certain behavioral techniques can be introduced in this format as well, such as the use of the plethysmograph and the rationale behind aversive conditioning. However, offenders will benefit from individual sessions exploring specifics about deviant chains of behavior, antecedents, and consequences. In addition, most behavioral techniques, such as aversive conditioning, aversive behavior rehearsal, plethysmographic biofeedback, and orgasmic reconditioning, can be most intensively and successfully provided in individual therapy.

Nonetheless, group sessions can reduce the number of future and more costly individual sessions while providing easier and more rapid access to treatment. Several such groups have been described in the recent literature (Schlank & Shaw, 1996; Studer & Reddon, 1998).

Cognitive/Behavioral Therapy

Literature on the paraphilias has been focused chiefly on theoretical, etiological, and epidemiological concerns rather than on issues of treatment. This disparity may reflect the present state of our science, which is more descriptive than curative. However, a trend toward treatment outcome studies is emerging (Alexander, 1999; Hanson, 1997). While much of the treatment literature of the 1970s and 1980s consisted of case reports and retrospective analyses of outcomes, since the early 1990s many researchers have constructed more closely controlled studies, including some prospective and well-conceived efforts isolating crucial treatment factors (Dwyer, 1997; Day & Marques, 1998). From these, a consensus has arisen that cognitive and behavioral therapies form the standard against which other approaches must be judged.

Behavioral Approaches

A flurry of activity in the 1960s and 1970s led to the application, at times exclusive, of treatment based on a strict rendering of behaviorism. With advances in research and experience, behavioral approaches today are employed as part of a comprehensive program utilizing a broad range of empirically and clinically tested techniques, including aversive conditioning, positive conditioning, and reconditioning.

Aversive Conditioning Techniques

Electroshock Aversive therapy based on classical conditioning paradigms attempts to pair an unconditioned aversive stimulus with a deviant response in order to reduce the likelihood of that response occurring in the future. It was hoped the reduction in sexual arousal produced in the treatment laboratory would generalize to cues in the patient's real-life experience. The earliest work employed shock as the aversive stimulus, usually at a level unpleasant but not harmful (MacCulloch, Waddington, & Sanbrook, 1978). Criticisms of the application of a simple punishment model, however, were soon raised. McConaghy (1993, chap. 8), citing evidence from the 1970s and 1980s, criticized conclusions about shock aversion based on small numbers of subjects, retrospective uncontrolled data, and the use of questionable stimulus materials. In addition, electroshock is not well regarded by patients' families and the media. Moreover, its flexibility is limited as it can be introduced for only brief durations and cannot be used with stimuli that require longer intervals to build sexual arousal, such as slides and stories. As a result, electroshock aversion has not been cited in the literature extensively since the early 1980s, although nationwide surveys of current clinical practice give indications that it is still occasionally employed in combination with a variety of other techniques in outpatient programs (Knopp, Freeman-Longo, & Stevenson, 1992). It has largely been replaced by less controversial, and more effective, aversive stimuli, particularly foul odors and tastes (Maletzky, 1991a, chap. 3).

Covert Sensitization By the mid-1970s, many therapists had devised aversive procedures that were less intrusive and easier to administer and did not alienate patients' families and the public. One such technique, covert sensitization, emerged as a hopeful replacement for physically aversive procedures.

In this technique, the patient is first trained in relaxation and then, in a relaxed state, is asked to visualize scenes of deviant sexual activity followed by an aversive event. For example, a patient who typically exposed to schoolgirls from his car was asked to imagine driving by a group of girls on their way to school:

> As you see their young faces, you start to get hard. You feel your penis stiffen as you rub it. They notice you! You call the girls over to the car. They don't know what's waiting for them. As they approach the car, you take it out and begin to masturbate violently. The girls are shocked. They don't know what to do. They're just staring at it as you rub it, but suddenly there's a pain. You've got your penis stuck in your pants' zipper. You try to yank it free, but it only catches more. It's starting to bleed and you go soft. The girls are laughing and a policeman is coming over.

In such scenes, an escape associated with nonoffending is usually added:

> You are able, finally, to get your penis back in your pants. You drive off, and as you get away, you begin to relax and breathe easier.

Such scenes commonly contain three elements:

1. The buildup of deviant sexual arousal.
2. An aversive consequence.
3. An escape from aversion associated with turning away from the deviant stimulus.

Covert sensitization has won a place in almost all treatment programs (Knopp et al., 1992) because it is easy to implement, requires no expensive equipment, and enjoys the blessing of community approval. However, despite its multiple advantages, this technique has not produced as robust a response as desired. Some patients demonstrate reductions in deviant arousal but no actual behavior change. Others have modest responses and complain that the procedure lacks sufficient power (Maletzky, 1998).

Assisted Covert Sensitization Because of these concerns, an augmented procedure has been devised. After the buildup of sexual arousal in a deviant scene and at the point where aversive imagery begins, a foul odor is also introduced via an opened vial or an automated odor pump (Maletzky, 1991a, Appendix D) and is continuously presented until the escape portion is reached:

> You pick up a young boy, 13 or 14, outside a videogame store. You offer to take him home and he accepts. As you park by his house, you put your arm around his shoulder and he doesn't resist. Pretty soon, you reach down to feel his crotch. You slowly unzip his fly, pull his penis out, and start stroking it back and forth. As you start to suck on his penis, suddenly there's a foul odor. It's like rotting flesh, putrid and nauseating. You glance down and see there's a sore on the underside of his penis, red and full of pus, and it's broken. Some of the blood and pus has gotten into your mouth and down your throat. It's nauseating. You can feel the pus in the back of your throat, and you gag. Food comes up in your throat and your mouth. You're going to vomit. You vomit all over him and yourself. You've got to get out of there. You leave the car and get a rag to clean yourself off. As you get away from him, that smell goes away, and you can deeply breathe the fresh air.

As can be seen, this procedure is not simply aversive olfactory conditioning because no real conditioned stimulus is employed; it is, rather, imagined, although the consequences of the unconditioned stimuli are real.

Although ammonia has often been suggested as the aversive stimulus (as reviewed in Barbaree & Seto, 1997), it may produce a painful response rather than a nauseous one. Rotting tissue has been more effective, perhaps because it travels via the first (olfactory) nerve to limbic areas thought to be important in the perception of sexual pleasure. A number of studies have demonstrated that the response of nausea is more powerful than that of pain for reducing harmful consummatory behaviors such as overeating (Kennedy & Foreyt, 1968), smoking (Lichtenstein & Kruetzer, 1969), and sexual response (Maletzky & George, 1973). While the covert stimuli can be modeled after real-life situations, this is a difficult task for the treatment of men who expose or rape, as scenes of such activities may not trigger arousal in some men, especially in a laboratory setting. In addition, stimuli arousing to an exhibitionist, for example, may not be deviant at all, such as passing by an attractive woman at night in an isolated location. Despite these drawbacks, variations on this technique have been employed in the majority of cognitive behavioral treatment programs in recent years (Alexander, 1999).

Minimal Arousal Conditioning Jensen, Laws, and Wolfe (1994) and Gray (1995) found sexual arousal too powerful for deconditioning in some patients. These authors placed the aversive stimulus earlier in the response chain, when minimal arousal was present and before intense sexual pleasure was attained. This point could then be advanced in the sexual chain increasingly closer to sexual release. While this procedure has not enjoyed extensive use, it is promising for offenders whose arousal levels are too high to allow typical aversion paradigms.

Aversive Behavioral Reversal Sometimes inaccurately called *shame therapy* (Serber, 1970), this technique has enjoyed fame and notoriety as much for its reported efficacy as for its apparent simplicity (Wickramaserkera, 1980). While reported to be markedly effective, its present-day use is considered insensitive and possibly unethical, although not absolutely contraindicated:

> A 23-year-old graduate student could not stop his compulsive exposing to attractive coeds on campus. Arrested twice by campus police, he was threatened with expulsion from school unless he

obtained therapy. He gave consent for a procedure in which he exposed to clinic staff for 3 minutes on each of three occasions. The staff was instructed to offer no response but merely to watch silently. Following the first session, he reported that he lost all urges to expose. He had not reexposed on 11-year follow-up.

Theoretically, this procedure is thought to produce such an aversive situation that it renders future exposing unlikely. Although attractive because of its reported efficacy, limitations include the difficulty of obtaining consent, the problems in soliciting staff members to participate, the possibility of adverse effects on staff, and, in the main, its terribly aversive nature. While submitting offenders to mental anguish might be considered by some a due reward, other, less aversive, yet equally effective, techniques exist. It would be difficult to condone its use, a paradox in that its major advances are also its unfortunate drawbacks.

Variations on this theme, however, can be employed as part of a comprehensive treatment program. A patient might be asked to expose to himself in a mirror and record his observations on tape. He might expose in front of a videotape camera, then view the tape in private or with staff or family. A pedophile might be asked to show, with a life-size doll, what he had done sexually to a child. This may also be videotaped for viewing. Faced with the reality of their own behaviors, some offenders may recoil at the images of their offenses, and this reaction may reduce the likelihood of reoffending in the future (Maletzky, 1998).

Vicarious Sensitization This novel technique, recently introduced for the treatment of a variety of sexual offenses, contains elements of cognitive restructuring, empathy training, and aversive conditioning. In this procedure, originally crafted for adolescent offenders (Weinrott & Riggan, 1996), an offender views a series of videotapes depicting adverse outcomes of deviant behaviors, both likely and improbable. Table 21.4 provides summaries of typical scenarios, depicted on screen by professional actresses and actors. Although it may appear that this technique is cerebral and thus a form of cognitive therapy, the effect on viewers is often visceral. Many offenders complain of nausea while viewing these tapes.

TABLE 21.4 Vicarious Sensitization Videotape Vignettes

- An experienced inmate describes the brutal rape of a young male sexual offender in prison; the offender is chased across the prison yard.
- Neighbors, outraged about an offender's sexual abuse of several girls in their community, chase and corner him, force him to undress, and subject him to cruel ridicule.
- A victim describes the revenge she would like to perpetrate on her offender while, on-screen, scenes are shown of an actual surgical castration and phallectomy.
- An adolescent offender is shunned by several groups of high school girls, who whisper about him, point, and make jokes; he complains that he cannot get a date to friends, who remain unsupportive.
- Several victims are shown in various states of psychological disarray due to their sexual abuse; for example, a young girl cuts her wrists, and an older woman requires electroconvulsive therapy after being raped.

New equipment developed over the past several years has rendered this technique potentially even more effective. These scenarios are now presented to the offender through a dedicated headset, thus eliminating distractions. Moreover, the scenes have been expanded and can thus be more specifically tailored to fit the offender's pattern of deviant behaviors. In addition, the aversive consequences depicted visually can be programmed to be presented following tape-recorded scenes of the patient's own offending, so that this paradigm is altered to fit a classical conditioning model. Although vicarious sensitization has been applied mainly to adolescents thus far, its scenarios flow naturally from a variety of sexual crimes, and results in adult offenders are promising (Weinrott, personal communication, March 2000).

Positive Conditioning Techniques

While therapists commonly employ the positive reinforcement of appropriate arousal as described in some of the techniques above, a variety of positive approaches stand on their own as important contributions to the treatment of offenders, including social skills training and alternative behavior completion.

Social Skills Training Most therapists believe that the large array of techniques called *social skills training* forms a crucial element of an offender treatment program. McFall (1990) outlined an assessment procedure for social skills deficits and proposed an individualized treatment approach based on an information-processing analysis of social skills. A variety of such techniques have been helpful for offenders and nonoffenders alike. Female therapists may be particularly effective in applying these approaches with male offenders. Although not easily researched, methods such as cue-assisted learning, psychodrama, assertiveness training, and *in vivo* relaxation techniques are important components in the therapeutic arsenals of most treatment programs.

Alternative Behavioral Completion Based on work with the treatment of compulsive gamblers, McConaghy (1993, Chap. 8) outlined a procedure reported as helpful for a variety of offenders. A patient listens to descriptions of typical offending situations, including entry into the behavioral chain leading to offending. However, in the image, the patient successfully tolerates the stimuli causing urges to offend, completes the chain without doing so, and then leaves the scene in a relaxed state:

> As you drive home one night, you notice an attractive woman driver on your right in a van. She can see into your car. You slow down and drive parallel with her as you begin to get aroused. You want to rub your penis and take it out to show it to her; the urge this time is weaker than before, and you drive past her quickly without exposing. You feel good about yourself for being able to stay in control.

This technique is similar to one that others have termed *success imagery* and is based on techniques of desensitization already shown to be effective in reducing social anxieties. If proven effective in larger trials, it may indicate that offending carries with it not only pleasurable feelings but anxious ones as well.

Reconditioning Techniques

A number of techniques appear to stand midway between aversive conditioning and purely cognitive approaches, perhaps combining elements of both; these include plethysmographic biofeedback, masturbation techniques, and sexual impulse control.

Plethysmographic Biofeedback Although debate surrounds the use of the plethysmograph as an assessment technique, its use in treatment is both less controversial and less publicized. Several authors (Maletzky 1991a, Chap. 4; McConaghy 1993, Chap. 8) have mentioned this potentially important and innovative approach. In this technique, the plethysmograph is automatically connected to an external light or sound device to provide feedback to the patient about his arousal level. Commonly, a bank of colored vertical lights is employed (Maletzky, 1991a, Appendix D), although an escalating sound can be used as well. Red lights can be used to denote higher levels of arousal, orange to denote intermediate levels, and green to denote low levels. The offender's task during any session might be to keep out of the red area when exposed to deviant stimuli or to keep in the red area with normal stimuli. This technique teaches self-control and conveys the important message that the offender *can* control arousal.

Masturbation Techniques Many clinicians believe that pleasure in masturbation and climax are important reinforcers of sexual behavior. Pairing fantasies of deviant sexual imagery with this pleasure repeatedly reinforces deviant arousal. Admonitions to offenders to discontinue these pairings probably go unheeded. Additional techniques are needed to recondition the powerful arousal associated with offending: fantasy change and satiation.

In fantasy change (Maletzky, 1986), an offender is asked to masturbate to deviant fantasies until the point of ejaculatory inevitability, and at that moment to switch to nondeviant fantasies. As treatment progresses, the patient is asked to make that switch earlier and earlier in the masturbatory chain until he is masturbating exclusively to nondeviant fantasies. Many therapists request that the offender tape-record these sessions in order to (partially) guarantee compliance.

In satiation (Barbaree & Seto, 1997; Laws & Marshall, 1991), the offender is asked to masturbate to ejaculation using only nondeviant fantasies. Following climax, he is asked to continue masturbating, this time to deviant fantasies, for periods of time varying from 30 to 60 minutes. Again, therapists request that tape recordings be made to ensure that this homework is completed. (Actual observation of masturbatory behavior is contraindicated as overly intrusive.) This technique pairs deviant imagery with the period of minimal sexual arousal: Having to masturbate following ejaculation may be an aversive practice. Some therapists believe that simple verbal satiation produces results equal to forced masturbation (Laws, 1995). Boredom, fatigue, and deconditioning all may play some active role.

Sexual Impulse Control Training Regardless of their origins, paraphilias represent the end of a journey of many steps. Constructing obstacles early in this chain may be more effective than designing interventions closer to the sexual pleasure of release. Under the rubric of sexual impulse control (Maletzky, 1991a, Chap. 7), a loose band of techniques attempts to construct such obstacles.

For example, a pedophile might be asked to begin masturbating to pedophilic fantasies, then stop before ejaculation, or to read about and look at pictures of pedophilic situations, then abstain from masturbation or intercourse for at least 24 hours. Partial verification of completing these homework assignments can occur either by asking the offender to tape-record masturbation sessions or by interviewing a partner (neither is proof positive). Some therapists have asked an offender to approach deviant situations, then smell a foul odor or chew a bitter tablet. Needless to say, these last methods are best used after verifying that arousal has been reduced or that the patient is well advanced in a treatment program.

Cognitive Approaches

A diverse and varied collection of cognitive techniques is widely applied to offenders to reduce the likelihood of repeated deviant behavior. Since many of these methods appear to be at least somewhat effective (McGrath, Cann, & Konopasky, 1998; Swaffer, Hollin, Beech, Beckett, & Fisher, 2000), Quinsey and Earls (1990) suggested that all of them may act in a general, rather than a specific, fashion. At present, it appears unlikely that any such technique can be isolated and tested in a prospective double-blind fashion due to ethical concerns about withholding treatment.

While cognitive therapies are not easily categorized and broad overlap between categories exists, most therapists agree that, within the cognitive approaches, three domains can be identified: recognition and correction of cognitive distortions, relapse prevention, and empathy training.

Restructuring Cognitive Distortions Based in part on the work of Yochelson and Samenow (1977) and unfortunately described as *thinking errors*, a set of typical distortions (actually assumptions and justifications) has come to be widely recognized in many offenders; examples of frequently used distortions in several paraphilias are presented in Table 21.5. Identification of a distortion is only the first step in treatment. The next, and perhaps more difficult step, is skillfully presenting it as such to the offender. Many patients are reluctant to endorse a distortion once it is pointed out since, to most, it is patently false. In these tasks, question-and-answer techniques, psychodrama, illustration by example, and role reversal have all been helpful in treatment (Murphy, 1990; Schlank & Shaw, 1997).

Simply labeling these as errors rarely leads to significant behavioral change. Incorporating corrections of these distortions into a habit of thinking by frequent conscious repetition can, however, be helpful. In discussing these, a therapist encourages the offender to give self-corrective messages often enough for them to become innate, reflexive, and automatic responses.

Relapse Prevention Based on a treatment approach to addictive behaviors (Marlatt & Gordon 1985), relapse prevention has been extended to include treatment for many sexual offenders (Laws, 1999; Pithers, 1990). Central to relapse prevention is the concept of behavioral chains and cycles. Offending is conceived of as the culmination of a chain beginning with seemingly innocuous behavior, then gathering momentum in a cascade of behaviors that result in the offending act. In chains ending with a pleasurable act, it is much more likely that interventions will be successful early rather than late in the behavioral chain.

Relapse prevention begins with self-awareness and self-scrutiny. The offender is asked to keep a record of lapses and their triggers to be better able to identify dangerous situations. Next, stimulus control procedures can be put into place:

> A young, married exhibitionist would frequently "forget" something in his office and return at night after supper to retrieve it. Often, when doing so, he would drive through parking lots and look for isolated women. As part of treatment, he was required to always notify his wife of his whereabouts. She would call him toward the end of the day to remind him to be sure to take any work he needed home with him.

A lapse, such as entering a dangerous situation, is not a defeat but an opportunity to learn which stimuli control which behaviors. A relapse is a failure,

TABLE 21.5 Examples of Distortions, Assumptions, and Justifications in Sexual Paraphilias

Category	*Pedophilia*	*Exhibitionism*	*Rape*
Misattributing blame	"She started it by being too cuddly." "She would always run around half-dressed."	"She kept looking at me like she was expecting it." "The way she was dressed, she was asking for it."	"She was saying no, but her body said yes." "I was always drinking when I did it."
Minimizing or denying sexual intent	"I was just teaching her about sex . . . better from her father than someone else."	"I was just looking for a place to pee." "My pants just slipped down."	"I was just trying to teach her a lesson; she deserved it."
Debasing the victim	"She'd had sex before with her boyfriend." "She always lies."	"She was just a slut anyway."	"The way she came on to me at the party, she deserved it." "She never fought back; she must have liked it."
Minimizing consequences	"She's always been real friendly to me, even afterward." "She was messed up even before it happened."	"I never touched her, so I couldn't have hurt her." "She smiled, so she must have liked it."	"She'd had sex with hundreds of guys before. It was no big deal."
Deflecting censure	"This happened years ago. Why can't everyone forget about it?"	"It's not like I raped anyone."	"I only did it once."
Justifying the cause	"If I wasn't molested as a kid, I'd never have done this."	"If I knew how to get dates, I wouldn't have to expose."	"If my girlfriend gave me what I want, I wouldn't be forced to rape."

although that does not preclude learning from it as well. The patient and the therapist need to review situations of heightened risk and to problem-solve alternative escape strategies; the patient thus accumulates sufficient skills to avoid offending in the future. Several workbooks, complete with exercises and homework assignments, have proven of benefit for the offender in internalizing these concepts (Freeman-Longo & Bays, 1989).

Empathy Training Although rarely conceptualized as a series of therapies, empathy training can be arbitrarily divided into five segments: (a) identification of the victim, (b) identification of the victimizing act, (c) identification of the harm, (d) role reversal, and (e) development of empathy.

Put into practice, these techniques can begin with identification of the victim and how she or he was selected. Even supposedly nuisance acts, such as obscene telephone calling or exhibitionism, are associated with long-term effects in victims (Cox & Maletzky, 1980). Psychodramatic techniques, such as role reversal, can be employed in identifying victimization. Videotapes of victims describing their experiences can be helpful in this regard. These techniques lead naturally to a discussion of offending as a victimizing act, with lasting impressions. Offenders need to be able to identify the harm they have caused and its lasting effects. Guilt induction is not the goal; emotional, as opposed to intellectual, acceptance should occur. Employing role reversal, the offender can try to imagine how a victim might feel, not only during the offending act but thereafter, as the residue of trauma persists. From such methods, the development of empathy will hopefully emerge.

The usefulness of these techniques has been reviewed by Fernandez, Anderson, and Marshall (1999). Almost all clinical programs currently include such techniques (Knopp et al., 1992); however, they do not lend themselves well to controlled research.

Biological Approaches

In work demonstrating some biological abnormalities in sexual offenders (Lang, Langevin, Bain, Frenzel, & Wright, 1989; Williams, 1999), therapists have expressed the hope that somatic treatments might prove helpful. While surgical approaches are too drastic to be considered in America, several medications have been demonstrated to reduce sexual drive in males and hence to afford some protection against reoffending among offenders treated in a community setting. However, despite promising leads, no controlled study of the use of medications by sexual offenders has been published. Nonetheless, the renewed interest in this area offers hope of continuing advances.

Hormonal Treatment

Medroxyprogesterone acetate (MPA), also known as depo-Provera, and cyproterone acetate (CPA) are the two medications most studied for the treatment of sexual offenders. Each may act in different ways to reduce circulating testosterone by either increasing its metabolism in the liver (MPA) or blocking cellular adhesion of normal circulating testosterone (CPA). In the United States, MPA is used, while CPA, not approved by the Food and Drug Administration (FDA) due to rare liver reactions, is used in Canada and on the European continent. Both reduce circulating testosterone levels, but controversy exists about how to measure effective doses. While some physicians aim to reduce testosterone to prepubertal levels (less than 50 ng/dL), others aim for a reduction to 30 to 50% of pretreatment levels. Clinical studies find both criteria adequate in markedly reducing the risk of reoffense (as reviewed in Prentky, 1997).

Both substances can be administered in long-acting depo form, especially helpful for offenders in mandated treatment. Intramuscular doses have ranged from 400 mg per week to 200 mg twice per month for MPA and 300 to 600 mg every 10 days to 3 weeks for CPA. More recently, leuprolide (Lupron), a gonadotropin agonist, has also been suggested as it also lowers testosterone; recommended doses are 7.5 mg IM every 3 to 4 weeks (Krueger & Kaplan, 2001).

There is little doubt that such hormones reduce male sexual drive, as demonstrated by a reduction in frequency of erections, self-initiated sexual behaviors, and sexual fantasies, as well as a consequent decrease in the frequencies of masturbation and intercourse. Rates of reoffense on hormones are very low. Many offenders comment parenthetically that there is a concomitant reduction in aggression as well (Maletzky, 1991b). Side effects of these agents have included mild weight gain, headaches, muscle cramping, and, rarely, blood clots, particularly in leg veins.

As expected, most offenders treated with hormones show a rapid return to deviant arousal following the discontinuance of medication (Berlin & Meinecke, 1981). Thus, it is obligatory to combine hormonal treatment with cognitive and behavioral methods in a multimodal approach. In such programs, the hormone is tapered, then discontinued while the offender is still under supervision so that progress without the drug can be monitored.

In a review of depo-Provera's use in a large outpatient sample, Maletzky (1991b) found that only 1.9% of all offenders required the medication. Among these were the most severe and dangerous offenders. A substantial portion had suffered CNS damage and demonstrated poor impulse control. Data are now being collected in an ongoing series of men mandated by the state to receive depo-Provera in an attempt to further define reoffense risk and factors specifically predictive of the need for hormonal treatment (Maletzky & Field, 2000).

Psychotropic Medications

A number of other medications have been proposed for the treatment of sexual offenders. While neuroleptic medications, particularly thioridazine, have been employed in the past, newer serotonin reuptake inhibitors are now most often mentioned for use in treatment-resistant paraphilias. The drug most discussed is fluoxetine (Kafka, 1995), although clomipramine was actually the first antidepressant used to reduce deviant sexual arousal (Casal-Ariet & Cullen, 1993). While these psychotropic medications reduce sexual drive, they can also produce side effects such as nausea and agitation.

Since both fluoxetine and clomipramine have been of some benefit in the treatment of obsessive compulsive disorder, and since sexual offending is often obsessive in thought and compulsive in deed, some clinicians have expressed the hope that such agents will reduce the pressure of deviant fantasies and preoccupations. However, at present, it appears these medications simply reduce overall sexual drive rather than target only deviant fantasies (Greenberg & Bradford, 1997). In addition, no psychotropic medication has been proven as powerful in clinical practice as the hormones MPA and CPA in reducing sexual drive. Currently, the use of these hormones is considered the first medical approach for treating offenders dangerous to be at large until, hopefully, cognitive and behavioral methods take hold.

EFFICACY OF TREATMENT TECHNIQUES

The literature on treatment outcome for the sexual offender contains a number of review articles. One widely quoted study reached the pessimistic conclusion that inadequate controls and variable rating instruments precluded any judgment about efficacy (Furby, Weinrott, & Blackshaw, 1989). More recent reports offer a different and more sanguine view—that newer and more sufficient documentation combined with clinical experience warrants a less gloomy outlook (Alexander, 1999; Marshall & Barbaree, 1990b; Sawyer, 1999). Problems noted in such reviews include short duration of follow-up and varying exclusion criteria. The use of no-treatment control groups has been believed to be unethical. However, an ongoing outcome project in California (Marques, 1994) hopes to avoid this problem through the use of untreated institutionalized offender volunteers.

Outcome studies have often grouped various types of sexual offenders together, despite evidence that treatment results can be heavily influenced by taxonomy (Marshall & Barbaree, 1990b) and diagnosis (Maletzky, 1993). Early studies indicated that, in the absence of treatment, by 6 years following discovery 41% of offenders had reoffended, including 57% of repeat offenders in the original group (Frisbie & Dondis, 1965). High rates of recidivism, up to 67%, have been shown for exhibitionists using electroshock aversion alone (Rooth & Marks, 1974). Somewhat better rates were obtained for exhibitionists by Evans at 1 year (1967) and 3 years (1970) posttreatment: Covert sensitization alone proved effective in the majority (61%) of patients. However, adding aversive odor to covert sensitization reduced relapse rates to just under 25%.

Among approaches attempting to treat offenders, medical treatment, at first ignored in the psychological literature, appears at once intriguing and limited. The antiandrogens MPA and CPA have long been employed for sexual offenders deemed too dangerous to be at large. Placebo-controlled studies have not been reported due to ethical concerns, but large case reports indicate a very low rate of recidivism among offenders taking these medications (Laschet & Laschet, 1975; Maletzky, 1991b). Unfortunately, relapse following termination of antiandrogens has been high (Berlin & Meinecke, 1981). These treatments might best be reserved for those at highest risk to reoffend and, in the main, be used over a period of time during which behavioral and cognitive elements in treatment are beginning to exert some effect.

There have been no large outcome evaluations of a single treatment technique for offenders. Multifaceted approaches have been described, and retrospective reviews have been published. All have been Type 3 studies. These are open trials, following patients throughout treatment and follow-up, subjecting offenders to a combination of cognitive/behavioral techniques, and measuring changes over time in treatment with standardized instruments. The strengths of these studies derive from their large numbers, clear presentation of inclusion criteria, rigid adherence to a commonly approved diagnostic scheme, sophisticated statistical methods, and, in many cases, long follow-up periods. Weaknesses are apparent in their lack of double-blind techniques and, especially, their lack of comparison groups.

It should come as little surprise that there has been thus far an absence of Type 1 studies (double-blind, controlled trials) or even Type 2 studies (lacking but one element of a Type 1 study). It has been difficult to isolate single techniques and subject one group of offenders to them while substituting an active placebo treatment for a control group, especially in outpatient practice.

These practical problems are compounded by the lack of funding and interest in sexual offending in government- and university-based psychiatry and psychology programs. Hence, we must await improved circumstances to be able to state with scientific rigor which treatments work and which are likely to fail.

Even with the sparse data now available, a major problem in evaluating treatment programs is the lack of a comparison group with an expected rate of recidivism. Such data have not been collected from the same populations as those under treatment. Outcome studies have typically combined a variety of populations, including those known to have widely differing prognoses, such as incest offenders and men who rape. Follow-up periods have apparently been adequate compared to outcome analyses in other *DSM-IV* categories, but sexual offending can have a lifetime potential, and follow-ups under 2 years may be of practical insignificance (Marshall & Barbaree, 1990b). Finally, all the outcome studies to be further discussed have combined elements of cognitive and behavioral treatment rather than isolated single treatment factors. Such combinations represent the standard treatment approach offered in the modern day; hence, a value in these studies is clinical relevance—they represent what one can probably expect the results of treatment to be. Unfortunately, they do not allow us to state definitely that any one of the techniques employed, or even their conjoint use, has without a shadow of a doubt led to the improvements reported.

Institutional Programs

Just four programs have reported treatment results in a sufficiently systematic form to allow them to be regarded as well tested. The first of these programs reported on sexual offenders incarcerated in a penitentiary. In one of the few comparison trials with a crossover design, Marshall and Williams (1975) studied child molesters and rapists in sufficient numbers (101) to reach meaningful statistical significance. They found a program combining early elements of cognitive and behavioral treatment significantly more effective than a traditional psychotherapy program. Of interest is the opportunity afforded by colleagues (Davidson, 1979, 1984) to follow these men over a period of 9 years and compare data for untreated offenders in the same institution. Davidson used sophisticated methods of calculating recidivism, including the portion of those at risk to reoffend, and found that treated offenders reoffended at a rate of approximately 15% compared to over 50% of those treated with traditional psychotherapy. However, further analysis revealed better outcomes for incest offenders (8% recidivism) than for men who molested girls (10.9%) or boys (13.3%) outside their families.

In a series of reports, Quinsey (1983; Quinsey, Chaplin, & Carrigan, 1980; Whitman & Quinsey, 1981) described treatment outcome from a Canadian maximum security hospital. This mixed population of child molesters, pedophiles, and rapists was composed of refractory offenders. Data, obtained from official police records, indicated a 20% recidivism rate over a 6-year period. Unfortunately, these data are difficult to evaluate due to a lack of anticipated reoffense rates in a similar population, although many of these offenders were in high-risk categories, such as preferential pedophiles and men who rape.

In the United States, the Sexual Offender Unit at Oregon State Hospital has been described by Smith (1984) and evaluated by Freeman-Longo (1984). This unit housed a variety of offenders deemed too dangerous to be at large and in need of institutional treatment. However, it excluded any inmate who declined to enter a treatment program, perhaps eliminating offenders who were more difficult to treat. While outcome data were encouraging as no patient who successfully completed the program reoffended, just 20 such offenders successfully completed treatment and follow-up over 3 years. In addition, a significant proportion of the total failed to complete treatment, and these were returned to correctional facilities. Follow-up data on these offenders would have been instructive.

An ongoing evaluation project has recently been described by Proulx and colleagues (1999) using data from another Canadian maximum security psychiatric facility. These authors followed 102 child molesters and 70 rapists for up to 13 years and found that treated offenders demonstrated lower recidivism rates than those who dropped out of treatment. Of interest were the lower overall *nonsexual* criminal rates as well.

Table 21.6 provides an overview of institutional outcome research. It is apparent that shortcomings in methodology, particularly by contamination with mixed populations, and lack of broad-based outcome measures, limit confidence in the application of these techniques. However, these programs, in attempting to treat the most serious offenders, showed a general trend in favor of treatment as opposed to no treatment, so that more extensive controlled studies would seem indicated in such populations.

Outpatient Programs

All seven of the programs reporting outcome data on outpatient sexual offenders employed the same cognitive and behavioral techniques already described for the inpatient populations. While these studies suffered the same deficiencies as those of the inpatient programs described above, they generally included larger numbers of subjects, a broader base of diagnostic groups, and a wider range of assessment techniques. Data for all seven studies are summarized in Table 21.7.

Wolfe (1984) excluded physically violent offenders and those with nonsexual criminal histories but did include most offenders commonly treated in outpatient settings. He reported results of treatment for 67 molesters of girls, 17 molesters of boys, 3 rapists,

TABLE 21.6 Outcome Data for Inpatient Programs for Sexual Offenders

Program	Types (and Numbers) of Offenders[a]	Percent Reoffending	Types of Assessment	Length of Follow-up	
				Range	Mean
Kingston Sexual Behavioral Clinic (Marshall & Barbaree, 1990b)	Incest (50) CMg (63) CMb (37)	8.0 17.5 13.5	Official police reports	1–9 years	2.5 years
Oak Ridge Mental Health Center, Ontario, Canada (Quinsey, 1983; Quinsey et al., 1980; Whitman & Quinsey, 1981)	Incest (76) CMg (59) CMb (40) Rapists (33)	11.8 16.9 22.5 27.2	Official police reports	1–6 years	3 years
Oregon State Hospital Sex Offender Unit (Freeman-Longo, 1984; Smith, 1984)	Incest (3) CMg (10) CMb (4) Rapists (3)	0 0 0	Official police reports, penile plethysmograph	6 months–3 years	1.5 years
Institute Phillippe Pinel de Montreal (Proulx et al., 1999)	CMg & b (102) Rapists (70)	5.7 35.0	Official police reports, penile plethysmograph	1 month–13 years	4.7 years

[a]CMg = men who molested nonfamilial girls; CMb = men who molested nonfamilial boys.

and 27 exhibitionists, scrutinizing probation records for 28 months after termination of treatment. Surprisingly, molesters of boys (not further defined as pedophilic) and rapists had no reoffenses, while molesters of girls reoffended at a 4.5% rate and exhibitionists at a 14.8% rate. Wolfe continues to collect data, and subsequent reports are expected.

In a review of another highly regarded clinic's outcome data, Abel, Mittelman, Becker, Rathner, and Rouleau (1988) reported, among 98 molesters of boys or girls (not differentiating the two), a reoffense rate of 12.2%. Unfortunately, these data come only from self-report and are hence suspect. In fairness, Abel's group went to great lengths to ensure confidentiality in data collection (Abel et al., 1987), and thus self-interest may have been minimized. Nonetheless, these data suffer from a lack of additional assessment techniques.

Marshall and Barbaree (1990b) reported outcomes from their cognitive and behavioral treatment program in Ontario, Canada. Of note is their inclusion of a comparison of self-reports, official police records, and official children's agencies' reports. The last yielded the highest rates of recidivism, 2.4 times greater than the other methods, catching some offenders who were not detected by self-report or police records. These researchers treated 48 incest offenders, 49 molesters of girls, 29 molesters of boys, and 44 exhibitionists, with relapse rates ranging from 8% for incest to nearly 50% for exhibitionists. In a positive departure from the norm, this study included a no-treatment control group, although comparison is difficult as this group included offenders who simply chose to refuse treatment for a variety of reasons; hence, the results were biased in favor of treatment. Still, outcome was significantly better for treated offenders in all groups but one: exhibitionists. Follow-ups ranged from 12 to 125 months.

In the largest group of patients yet reported (Maletzky, 1998), over 7,000 offenders were followed from 1973 through 1998, with average follow-ups of 11 years. This clinic, employing the usual panoply of cognitive and behavioral techniques, has attempted to follow annually all offenders assessed and treated, employing a range of assessment techniques, including self-reports, reports of significant others, the penile plethysmograph, the polygraph, and official nationwide police reports. Data are now (2000) available on over 8,000 offenders followed for at least 1 year and are presented in Table 21.8, along with the stringent requirements for any patient to be rated a success. Outcome varied with the initial diagnosis, ranging from an absence of reoffense for 95.6% of men who molested girls to 75.5% for men who raped. In contrast to the findings of Wolfe (1984), exhibitionists enjoyed among the highest success rates (95.4%), while in contrast to the findings of Marshall and Barbaree (1990b), men who molested

TABLE 21.7 Outcome Data for Outpatient Programs for Sexual Offenders

Program	*Types (and Numbers) of Offenders*[a]	*Percentage Reoffending*	*Types of Assessment*	*Length of Follow-up*	
				Range	*Mean*
Northwest Treatment Associates (Wolfe, 1984)	CMg (67) CMb (17) E (27) Rapists (3)	4.5 0 0 14.8	Probation reports	6–28 months	13.5 months
New York State Institute (Abel et al., 1988)	CMgb (98)	12.2	Self-reports	12–125 months	2 years
Kingston Sexual Behavior Clinic (Marshall & Barbaree, 1990b)	Incest (48) CMg (49) CMb (29) E (44)	8.0 17.9 13.3 47.8	Official police records, Children's Services Agencies' records		
The Sexual Abuse Clinic (Maletzky, 1993, and updated through 1998)	Sg (2,196) Sgb (765) Pbg (1,011) Pgb (1,251) E (1,604) Rapists (448)	4.2 7.6 9.3 15.8 7.4 15.6	Self-reports, penile plethysmograph, polygraph, official police records	1–25 years	11 years
Program in Human Sexuality, University of Minnesota (Dwyer, 1997)	CMg (27) CMb (11) Pgg & Pbb (115)	8 18 5 2	Personal interview, anonymous questionnaire, official police records	6 months–17 years	3.5 years
Utah Department of Corrections (Berch, Kramer, & Erickson, 1997)	Types not defined (408)	17	Official police records	1–10 years	Data unavailable
Project Pathfinder (Sawyer, 1999)	Sg & b (24) Pg & b (56) Rapists (12)	2.1 (types not specified)	Self-reports	1–60 months	Data unavailable

[a]CMg = men who molested nonfamilial girls; CMb = men who molested nonfamilial boys; Sg = situational offenders with girl victims; Sbb = situational offenders with boy victims; Pgg = predatory offenders with girls; Pbb = predatory offenders with boys; E = exhibitionists.

boys did not do as well (although 80% did not reoffend). Strengths in this line of research include the large numbers of subjects, the use of clinically relevant treatment techniques, stringent outcome criteria, and careful and extensive use of a variety of assessment techniques to cross-validate results. Because this research is so clinically based, however, it suffers from a lack of adequate comparison groups. It is potentially dangerous to allow an untreated control group to remain at large in the community. One possible solution, although imperfect, would be to include as a comparison group men sentenced to an institution who did not undergo treatment.

Dwyer (1997) reported on recidivism rates over a 17-year period in 180 offenders. Following completion of a cognitive and behavioral program, subjects were seen at 6 months and then annually. Data consisted of a personal interview and an anonymous questionnaire, but self-reports were cross-validated with official records searches. Among these offenders, 64% were preferential pedophiles, 21% child molesters, and 15% exhibitionists. No rapists were included. Just 5% of pedophiles, 11% of child molesters, and 2% of exhibitionists reoffended. An overall recidivism rate of 9% was gleaned from the data, a record matching that reported by Maletzky (1998) over the same time periods and with similar treatment techniques. While this research must be ac-

TABLE 21.8 Treatment Outcome for Paraphilias (N = 8,156)

Category	N	*Percentage Meeting Criteria for Success*[a]
Situational pedophilia, heterosexual	3,312	95.6
Predatory pedophilia, heterosexual	1,064	88.3
Situational pedophilia, homosexual	917	91.8
Predatory pedophilia, homosexual	796	80.1
Exhibitionism	1,230	95.4
Rape	643	75.5
Voyeurism	83	93.9
Public masturbation	77	94.8
Frotteurism	65	89.3
Fetishism	33	94.0
Transvestic fetishism	14	78.6
Telephone scatologia	29	93.1
Zoophilia	23	95.6

[a]A treatment success was defined as an offender who:

1. Completed all treatment sessions. (Any offender who dropped out of treatment, even if the offender met other criteria for success, was counted as a treatment failure.)
2. Reported no covert or overt deviant sexual behavior at the end of treatment or at any follow-up session.
3. Demonstrated no deviant sexual arousal, defined as greater than 20% on the penile plethysmograph, at the end of treatment or at any follow-up session.
4. Had no repeat legal charges for any sexual crime at the end of treatment or at any follow-up session.

For Categories 2, 3, and 4, follow-up sessions occurred at 6, 12, 24, 36, 48, and 60 months after the end of active treatment.

corded clinical significance due to the large number of subjects and long follow-ups, criteria for inclusion as a Type 1 or a Type 2 study are lacking, as is true of all seven of these outpatient studies and the four inpatient reports cited above.

Finally, two recent outcome studies have been reported for outpatient programs in the United States. Berch, Kramer, and Erickson (1997) searched official police reports to glean recidivism data for 408 offenders completing a community-based cognitive and behavioral program and determined an overall reoffense rate of 17% from 1 to 10 years. Unfortunately, they did not report the data by diagnostic subtype; thus, interpretation of the results is limited. Sawyer (1999) provided data on 24 situational molesters of girls and boys, 56 pedophiles (type unspecified), and 12 rapists. While reoffense rates were very low (2.1%), outcome was assessed by self-report only, a factor limiting confidence in such favorable results.

In summary, only Type 3 studies (and some of these may be considered more nearly Type 5) have been accomplished to date regarding treatment outcomes employing cognitive and behavioral treatment techniques for the sexual offender. While it does appear that a combination of these approaches has markedly reduced the rate of reoffense (and, when measured, deviant sexual arousal), the difficulty in conducting controlled trials combines with the lack of funding to pose significant obstacles to well-designed research in this field. However, double-blind studies cannot be the sole factor influencing clinical practice. It appears that combinations of the cognitive and behavioral therapies described above have been very successful in reducing the risk of reoffense.

FUTURE DIRECTIONS AND CONCLUSIONS

Estimates of the prevalence of sexual offending are so variable that epidemiological studies would be helpful in assessing the scope of this problem. Of equal importance, we need to assess the occurrence of a variety of paraphilias to understand how each might be a part of, distinct from, or preparatory to, the other. In addition, special populations of offenders have not enjoyed much attention thus far in the scientific literature. Female exposers and molesters are known (Mathews, Hunter, & Vuz, 1997), and further reports would be welcome. The same is true of those offenders who are developmentally disabled (Coston & Lakey, 1999). Treatment programs specifically designed for adolescent offenders (Page, 1995) are just now being increasingly reported (Schmidt & Heinz, 1999).

A variety of factors impede our ability to generalize about treatment effectiveness. Inclusion criteria vary, yet are known to influence outcome. For example, exhibitionists with central nervous system damage have greater rates of reoffending; yet many programs exclude such patients. In addition, treatment refusals and high dropout rates are not uncommon. One report cites refusal rates of 67% for electrical aversion and 63% for aversive behavior rehearsal (Maletzky, 1991a, Chap. 3). If a patient begins treatment, then drops out, his next victim may not be cheered by the fact that he is not counted among a clinic's failures.

Sometimes, statistics tell just half the tale. Practical issues of treatment expense, refusal, dropout rates, sources of referral, program reputation, ease of access, and inclusion criteria all combine to contribute to patient outcome. If a comprehensive cognitive and behavioral treatment program directed by doctoral-level clinicians treats one offender for $3,000 and reports a success rate of 90%, is this program to be preferred over a simpler program using a single treatment technique, costing $1,000, and yielding a 75% success rate? If 100 pedophiles are treated with a 75% success rate, at least 75 victims are saved. If 10 are treated with a 90% success rate, just nine victims are spared.

At present, assessment techniques are frankly inadequate. Physiological measurement tools for the paraphilias are based on conjecture, not empirical studies of reliability and validity. Confidential surveys should not be a substitute for measurement, but our sole physiological device, the plethysmograph, is faulty in several directions: It produces too many false negatives to be useful diagnostically, and it produces occasional but sufficient false positives to render it suspect for forensic purposes. Novel assessment measures, such as the Stroop Color Test (Greco, 1993) and the Hanson Sex Attitudes Questionnaire (Hanson, Gizzarelli, & Scott, 1994), are unlikely to offer robust validity. The Abel Assessment (Abel et al., 1998) offers a promising approach for future research.

Physiological reactions may in the future detect sexual intent. Finite chemical changes occur on arousal (George, 1995), although rapid and inexpensive detection is problematic. Perhaps patterns of central nervous system activity will in the future reveal sexual excitement. This is no longer far-fetched fantasy: Several medical centers are at work on imagery techniques such as PET that are said to be able to detect a specific neural firing pattern on sexual arousal.

Due to financial and ethical constraints, it is unlikely that controlled double-blind studies of treatment outcome will occur soon. Large, clinically based studies, however, can be as valuable as those that are more tightly controlled and can point the way to improving technologies. In addition, making treatment affordable should be made a priority by teaching, encouraging, and exhorting governmental agencies to staff and maintain sexual offender treatment programs. Fewer than 10% of county and state community-based mental health treatment facilities now offer such programs (Peterson & Barnes, 1999). The majority of offenders will, in all likelihood, never be treated because of lack of funding even if their crimes are disclosed. Tragically, many may be incarcerated, then released, never to participate in tests of how effective treatment might have been.

Clinicians and researchers also have both an obligation and an opportunity to provide education to a variety of audiences in order to reduce the damages caused by offending. Chief among these damages is the real trauma suffered by a victim, harm sometimes regarded lightly, even in public discourse. In addition, we need to address the prevention of sexual offending as thoroughly as we advocate its treatment. While public education is not a panacea, it could inform potential offenders and victims of the harm such offending causes, document the number of otherwise law-abiding individuals who carry it out, and explain the potential of treatment to reduce its likelihood. Perhaps this will increase the motivation of some offenders to obtain treatment who would otherwise have been too afraid or too ashamed or who wish to stop offending but cannot. With an increase in the numbers of sexual offenders entering treatment, we should be better able to understand the causes of such aggressive acts, the best ways to prevent them, and, perhaps, the very nature of these offenses, a veritable shopping list of humankind's darkest passions.

Note

1. Several semantic problems must be solved in any article about the paraphilias: (a) An *offender* may be different from a *patient*, but the commonly employed term *offender* is used here as it proves easier to access the literature employing that term; (b) over 95% of identified offenders have thus far been male. Use of the male pronoun is a convention widely tolerated in technical literature in this field. Female offenders are identified as such in the text.

References

Abel, G. G. (1997a). *Abel Assessment for Sexual Interest: Judges' product information*. Atlanta: Abel Screening.

Abel, G. G. (1997b). *Memorandum, 11/12/97*. Atlanta: Abel Screening.

Abel, G. G., Barlow, D. H., Blanchard, E. B., & Guild, D. (1977). The components of rapists' sexual arousal. *Archives of General Psychiatry, 34,* 895–903.

Abel, G. G., Becker, J. V., Mittelman, M. S., Cunningham-Rathner, J., Rouleau, J. L., & Murphy, W. D. (1987). Self-reported sex crimes of nonincarcerated paraphiliacs. *Journal of Interpersonal Violence, 2,* 3–25.

Abel, G. G., Hoffman, J., Warberg, B., & Holland, C. L. (1998). Visual reaction time and plethysmography as measures of sexual interest in child molesters. *Sexual Abuse: A Journal of Research and Treatment, 10,* 81–95.

Abel, G. G., Mittelman, M. S., Becker, J. V., Rathner, J., & Rouleau, J. L. (1988). Predicting child molesters' response to treatment. *Annals of the New York Academy of Sciences, 528,* 223–234.

Abrams, S. (1991). The use of polygraphy with sex offenders. *Annals of Sex Research, 4,* 239–263.

Alexander, M. A. (1999). Sexual offender treatment efficacy revisited. *Sexual Abuse: A Journal of Research and Treatment, 11,* 101–116.

American Psychiatric Association. (1994). *Diagnostic and statistical manual of mental disorders* (4th ed.). Washington, DC: Author.

Association for the Treatment of Sexual Abusers (ATSA). (1993). *The ATSA practitioners' handbook.* Portland, OR: Author.

Ball, C. J., & Seghorn, T. K. (1999). Diagnosis and treatment of exhibitionism and other sexual compulsive disorders. In B. K. Schwartz (Ed.), *The sex offender: Theoretical advances, treating special populations and legal development* (pp. 28-1 to 28-16). Kingston, NJ: Civic Research Institute.

Barbaree, H. E., & Seto, M. C. (1997). Pedophilia: Assessment and treatment. In D. R. Laws & W. O'Donohue (Eds.), *Sexual deviance: Theory, assessment, and treatment* (pp. 175–193). New York: Guilford.

Berch, L. L., Kramer, S. P., & Erickson, S. (1997). A discriminent analysis of predictive factors in sex offender recidivism. In B. K. Schwartz & H. R. Cellini (Eds.), *The sex offender: New insights, treatment innovations, and legal developments* (pp. 15-1 to 15-15). Kingston, NJ: Civic Research Institute.

Berlin, F. S., & Meinecke, C. F. (1981). Treatment of sex offenders with antiandrogenic medication: Conceptualization, review of treatment modalities and preliminary findings. *American Journal of Psychiatry, 138,* 601–607.

Blanchard, R., & Bogaert, A. F. (1997). Additive effects of older brothers and homosexual brothers in the prediction of marriage and cohabitation. *Behavior Genetics, 27,* 45–54.

Blanchard, R., & Klassen, P. (1997). H-Y antigen and homosexuality in men. *Journal of Theoretical Biology, 185,* 373–378.

Blasingame, G. D. (1998). Suggested clinical uses of polygraphy in community-based sexual offender treatment programs. *Sexual Abuse: A Journal of Research and Treatment, 10,* 37–45.

Bogaert, A. F., Bezeau, S., Kuban, M., & Blanchard, R. (1997). Pedophilia, sexual orientation, and birth order. *Journal of Abnormal Psychology, 106,* 331–335.

Bradford, J. M. W. (1990). The antiandrogen and hormonal treatment of sex offenders. In W. L. Marshall, D. R. Laws, & H. E. Barbaree (Eds.), *Handbook of sexual assault: Issues, theories, and treatment of the offender* (pp. 297–310). New York: Plenum.

Bumby, K. M., & Maddox, M. C. (1999). Judges' knowledge about sexual offenders. *Sexual Abuse: A Journal of Research and Treatment, 11,* 305–315.

Burt, M. R. (1980). Cultural myths and support for rape. *Journal of Personality and Social Psychology, 38,* 217–230.

Carnes, P. (1983). *The sexual addiction.* Minneapolis: ComCare.

Casal-Ariet, C., & Cullen, K. (1993). Exhibitionism treated with clomipramine. *American Journal of Psychiatry, 150,* 1273–1274.

Colson, C. E. (1972). Olfactory aversion therapy for homosexual behavior. *Journal of Behavior Therapy and Experimental Psychiatry, 3,* 185–187.

Coston, L., & Lakey, J. F. (1999). Creative therapy with intellectually disabled male adolescent sex offenders. In B. K. Schwartz (Ed.), *The sex offender: Theoretical advances, treating special populations, and legal developments* (pp. 20-1 to 20-7). Kingston, NJ: Civic Research Institute.

Cox, D. J., & Maletzky, B. M. (1980). Victims of exhibitionism. In D. J. Cox & R. J. Daitzman (Eds.), *Exhibitionism: Description, assessment, and treatment* (pp. 289–293). New York: Garland Press.

Damon, P. P. (1994). *Tough issues, hard facts: The report of the National Council on Crime and Delinquency.* Washington, DC: U.S. Government Printing Office.

Davidson, P. (1979, May). *Recidivism in sexual aggressors: Who are the bad risks?* Paper presented at the National Conference on the Evaluation and Treatment of Sexual Aggressors, New York.

Davidson, P. (1984, March). *Outcomes data for a penitentiary-based treatment program for sex offenders.* Paper presented at the Conference on the Assessment and Treatment of the Sex Offender, Kingston, Ontario, Canada.

Day, D. M., & Marques, J. K. (1998). A clarification of SOTEP's method and preliminary findings. *Sexual Abuse: A Journal of Research and Treatment, 10,* 162–166.

Dhawan, S., & Marshall, W. L. (1996). Sexual abuse histories of sexual offenders. *Sexual Abuse: A Journal of Research and Treatment, 8,* 7–15.

Dwyer, S. M. (1997). Treatment outcome study: 17 years after sexual offender treatment. *Sexual Abuse: A Journal of Research and Treatment, 9,* 149–160.

Ellis, L. (1993). Rape as a biosocial phenomenon. In G. C. Nagayama Hall, R. Hirschman, J. N. Graham, & M. S. Zaragoza (Eds.), *Sexual aggression: Issues in etiology, assessment and treatment* (pp. 17–41). Washington, DC: Taylor & Francis.

Epperson, D. L., Kaul, J. D., & Hesselton, D. (1998, October). *Final report of the development of Minnesota Sex Offender Screening Tool-Revised (MsSOST-R).* Paper presented at the Annual Research and Treatment Conference of the Association for the Treatment of Sexual Abusers, Vancouver, BC.

Erickson, M. T. (1993). An evolutionary perspective of incest avoidance. *American Journal of Psychiatry, 150,* 411–416.

Evans, D. R. (1967). An exploratory study into the treatment of exhibitionism by means of emotive imagery and aversive conditioning. *Canadian Psychologist, 8,* 162.

Evans, D. R. (1970). Subjective variables and treatment effects in aversive therapy. *Behaviour Research and Therapy, 8,* 141–152.

Felson, R. B. (2000). A social psychological approach to interpersonal aggression. In V. B. Van Hasselt & M. Hersen (Eds.), *Aggression and violence: An introductory text* (pp. 9–22). Needham Heights, MA: Allyn & Bacon.

Fernandez, Y. M., Anderson, M. A., & Marshall, W. L. (1999). The relationship among empathy, cognitive distortions, and self-esteem, in sexual offenders. In B. K. Schwartz (Ed.), *The sex offender: Theoretical advances, treating special populations, and legal developments* (pp. 4-1 to 4-12). Kingston, NJ: Civic Research Institute.

Finkelhor, D. (1994). The "backlash" and the future of child protection advocacy: Insights from the study of social issues. In J. E. B. Myer (Ed.), *The backlash: Child protection under fire* (pp. 113–137). Thousand Oaks, CA: Sage Press.

Fischer, L., & Smith, G. (1999). Statistical adequacy of the Abel Assessment for Interest in Paraphilias. *Sexual Abuse: A Journal of Research and Treatment, 11,* 195–205.

Flor-Henry, P., & Lang, R. (1988). Quantitative EEG analysis in genital exhibitionists. *Annals of Sex Research, 1,* 49–62.

Freeman-Longo, R. E. (1984). The Oregon State Hospital Sex Offender Unit: Treatment outcome. In F. H. Knopp (Ed.), *Retraining adult sex offenders: Methods and models* (pp. 185–209). Syracuse, NY: Safer Society Press.

Freeman-Longo, R. E., & Bays, L. (1989). *Who am I and why am I in treatment?* Orwell, VT: Safer Society Press.

Freund, K. (1963). A laboratory method of diagnosing predominance of homo- or hetero-erotic interest in the male. *Behaviour Research and Treatment, 12,* 355–359.

Freund, K., & Watson, R. (1980). Mapping the boundaries of courtship disorder. *Journal of Sex Research, 27,* 589–606.

Frisbie, L. U., & Dondis, E. H. (1965). *Recidivism among treated sex offenders.* California Mental Health Research Monograph No. 5. Sacramento, CA: Department of Mental Health.

Furby, L., Weinrott, M. R., & Blackshaw, L. (1989). Sex offender recidivism: A review. *Psychological Bulletin, 105,* 3–30.

Gaultieri, T., & Hicks, R. E. (1985). An immunoreactive theory of selective male affliction. *Behavioral and Brain Sciences, 8,* 427–441.

Gebhard, P. H., Gargon, J. H., Pomeroy, W. B., & Christenson, C. V. (1965). *Sex offenders: An analysis of types.* New York: Harper & Row.

Gendreau, P., Little, T., & Goggin, C. (1996). A meta-analysis of the predictors of adult offender recidivism: What works. *Criminology, 3,* 575–607.

George, M. S. (1995). The clinical use of SPECT in depressive disorders. In M. A. Schuckit (Chairperson), *Difficult differential diagnoses in psychiatry: The clinical use of SPECT* (pp. 542–544). *Journal of Clinical Psychiatry, 56,* 539–546.

Gibbens, T. C. N., & Ahrenfeldt, R. H. (1966). *Cultural factors in delinquency.* London: Tavistock Press.

Golden, C. J., Peterson-Rhone, A., Jackson, M. L., & Gontkovsky, S. T. (2000). Neuropsychological factors in violence and aggression. In V. B. Van Hasselt & M. Hersen (Eds.), *Aggression and violence: An introductory text* (pp. 40–53). Needham Heights, MA: Allyn & Bacon.

Gray, S. R. (1995). A comparison of verbal satiation and minimal arousal conditioning to reduce deviant arousal in the laboratory. *Sexual Abuse: A Journal of Research and Treatment, 7,* 143–153.

Greco, E. (1993). The emotional Stroop Test: A review of the literature. *Psichiatrica e Psicoterapia Analitica, 12*, 219–223.

Greenberg, D. M., & Bradford, J. M. W. (1997). Treatment of the paraphilic disorders: A review of the role of the selective serotonin reuptake inhibitors. *Sexual Abuse: A Journal of Research and Treatment, 9*, 349–360.

Griffen, J., & Cherfas, J. (1983). *The monkey puzzle: Reshaping the evolutionary tree*. New York: Pantheon Press.

Groth, N. A. (1979). *Men who rape: The psychology of the offender*. New York: Plenum.

Hanson, R. K. (1997). How to know what works with sexual offenders. *Sexual Abuse: A Journal of Research and Treatment, 9*, 129–145.

Hanson, R. K., & Bussière, M. T. (1998). Predicting relapse: A meta-analysis of sexual offender recidivism studies. *Journal of Consulting and Clinical Psychology, 66*, 348–362.

Hanson, R. K., Gizzarelli, R., & Scott, H. (1994). The attitudes of incest offenders: Sexual entitlement and acceptance of sex with children. *Criminal Justice and Behavior, 21*, 187–202.

Hanson, R. K., & Harris, A. J. N. (in press). Where should we intervene? Dynamic predictors of sex offense recidivism. *Criminal Justice and Behavior*.

Hanson, R. K., & Thornton, D. (2000). *Static 99: Improving actuarial risk assessments for sex offenders*. Ottawa, Ontario: Public Works and Government Services, Canada.

Herman, J. L. (1990). Sex offenders: A feminist perspective, In W. L. Marshall, D. R. Laws, & H. E. Barbaree (Eds.), *Handbook of sexual assault: Issues, theories, and treatment of the offender* (pp. 177–193). New York: Plenum.

Heston, L. L., & Shields, J. (1968). Homosexuality in twins. *Archives of General Psychiatry, 18*, 149–160.

Holmgren, B. K. (1999). Forging new alliances—Proposals for change in managing sex offenders within the criminal justice system. In B. K. Schwartz (Ed.), *The sex offender: Theoretical advances, treating special populations and legal developments* (pp. 37-1 to 37-20). Kingston, NJ: Civic Research Institute.

Howes, R. J. (1998). Plethysmographic assessment of incarcerated sexual offenders: A comparison with rapists. *Sexual Abuse: A Journal of Research and Treatment, 10*, 183–194.

Hucker, S. J., & Bain, J. (1990). Androgenic hormones and sexual assault. In W. L. Marshall, D. R. Laws, & H. E. Barbaree (Eds.), *Handbook of sexual assault: Issues, theories, and treatment of the offender* (pp. 93–102). New York: Plenum.

Hudson, S. M., & Ward, T. (1997). Rape: Psychopathology and theory. In D. R. Laws & W. T. O'Donohue (Eds.), *Sexual deviance: Theory, assessment, and treatment* (pp. 332–355). New York: Guilford Press.

Jensen, S., Laws, D. R., & Wolfe, R. (1994, November). *Reduction of sexual arousal: What to do and not to do*. Symposium presented at the annual conference of the Association for the Treatment of Sexual Abusers, San Francisco.

Johnson, S. A., & Listiak, A. (1999). The measurement of sexual preference—A preliminary comparison of phallometry and the Abel Assessment. In B. K. Schwartz (Ed.), *The sex offender: Theoretical advances, treating special populations, and legal developments* (pp. 26-1 to 26-20). Kingston, NJ: Civic Research Institute.

Justice, B., & Justice, R. (1979). *The broken taboo*. New York: Human Sciences Press.

Kafka, M. (1995, October). *Hypersexual desire in males: An operational definition and clinical implications for men with paraphilias and paraphilic-related disorders*. Paper presented at the annual conference of the Association for the Treatment of Sexual Abusers, New Orleans.

Kennedy, W. A., & Foreyt, J. (1968). Control of eating behaviors in obese patients by avoidance and conditioning. *Psychological Reports, 23*, 571–573.

Kinsey, A. C., Pomeroy, W. B., & Martin, C. E. (1948). *Sexual behavior in the human male*. Philadelphia: Saunders.

Kluver, H., & Bucy, P. E. (1939). Preliminary analysis of functions of the temporal lobe in monkeys. *Archives of Neurology and Psychiatry, 42*, 979–1000.

Knopp, F. H., Freeman-Longo, R. E., & Stevenson, W. F. (1992). *Nationwide survey of juvenile and adult sex offender treatment programs and models*. Orwell, VT: Safer Society Press.

Krause, B. (1994). Rethinking Oepidus. *American Journal of Psychiatry, 151*, 296–297.

Krueger, R. B., & Kaplan, M. S. (2001). depot-Leuprolide acetate for treatment of paraphilias: A report of twelve cases. *Archives of Sexual Behavior, 30*, 409–421.

Kuehnle, K., Coulter, M., & Gamache, M. (2000). Incest. In V. B. Van Hasselt & M. Hersen (Eds.), *Aggression and violence: An introductory text* (pp. 92–115). Needham Heights, MA: Allyn & Bacon.

Lalumiére, M. L., & Harris, G. T. (1998). Common questions regarding the use of phallometric testing with sexual offenders. *Sexual Abuse: A Journal of Research and Treatment, 10*, 227–237.

Lalumiére, M. L., Harris, G. T., Quinsey, V. L., & Rice, M. E. (1998). Sexual deviance and number of older brothers among sexual offenders. *Sexual Abuse: A Journal of Research and Treatment, 10,* 5–15.

Lalumiére, M. L., & Quinsey, V. L. (1994). The discriminability of rapists from nonsex offenders using phallometric measures. *Criminal Justice and Behavior, 21,* 150–175.

Lang, R. A., Langevin, R., Bain, J., Frenzel, R., & Wright, P. (1989). Sex hormones profiles in genital exhibitionists. *Annals of Sex Research, 2,* 67–75.

Langevin, R., Bain, J., Ben-Aron, M., Coulthard, R., Day, D., Handy, L., Heasman, G., Hucker, S. J., Purins, J. E., Roper, V., Russon, A., Webster, C. D., & Wortzman, G. (1985). Sexual aggression: Constructing a predictive equation. In R. Langevin (Ed.), *Erotic preference, gender identity, and aggression in men* (pp. 39–76). Hillsdale, NJ: Erlbaum.

Langevin, R., & Lang, R. A. (1987). The courtship disorders. In G. D. Wilson (Ed.), *Variant sexuality: Research and theory* (pp. 202–228). London: Croon Helm.

Laschet, V., & Laschet, L. (1975). Antiandrogens in the treatment of sexual deviations in men. *Journal of Steroid Biochemistry, 6,* 831–826.

Laws, D. R. (1995). Verbal satiation: Notes on procedure with speculations on its mechanism of effect. *Sexual Abuse: A Journal of Research and Treatment, 7,* 155–166.

Laws, D. R. (1999). Harm reduction or harm facilitation? *Sexual Abuse: A Journal of Research and Treatment, 11,* 233–241.

Laws, D. R., & Marshall, W. L. (1991). Masturbatory reconditioning with sexual deviates: An evaluative review. *Advances in Behavior Research and Therapy, 13,* 13–25.

Laws, D. R., & Serber, M. (1975). Measurement and evaluation of assertive training with sexual offenders. In R. E. Hosford & C. S. Moss (Eds.), *The crumbling walls: Treatment and counseling of prisoners* (pp. 165–172). Champaign: University of Illinois Press.

Leitenberg, H., Greenwald, E., & Tarran, M. J. (1989). The relation between sexual activity among children during preadolescence and/or early adolescence and sexual behavior and sexual adjustment in young adulthood. *Archives of Sexual Behavior, 18,* 199–243.

Letourneau, E. J. (1999, September). *A comparison of the penile plethysmograph with the Abel Assessment for Sexual Interest on incarcerated military sex offenders.* Paper presented at the Annual Research and Treatment Conference of the Association for the Treatment of Sexual Abusers, Lake Buena Vista, FL.

Lichtenstein, E., & Kruetzer, C. S. (1969). Investigation of diverse techniques to modify smoking: A follow-up report. *Behaviour Research and Therapy, 7,* 139–140.

Looman, J., Abracen, J., Maillet, G., & DiFazio, R. (1998). Phallometric nonresponding in sexual offenders. *Sexual Abuse: A Journal of Research and Treatment, 10,* 325–336.

Lutzker, J. R. (2000). Child abuse. In V. B. Van Hasselt & M. Hersen (Eds.), *Aggression and violence: An introductory text* (pp. 54–66). Needham Heights, MA: Allyn & Bacon.

MacCulloch, M. J., Waddington, T. L., & Sanbrook, J. E. (1978). Avoidance latencies reliably reflect sexual attitude during aversion therapy for homosexuality. *Behavior Therapy, 9,* 562–577.

MacLean, P. D. (1973). New findings on brain function and sociosexual behavior. In J. Zubin & J. Money (Eds.), *Contemporary sexual behavior: Critical issues in the 1970s* (pp. 53–75). Baltimore: Johns Hopkins University Press.

Malamuth, N. W., Haber, S., & Feshbach, S. (1990). Testing hypotheses regarding rape: Exposure to sexual violence, sex differences and the "normality" of rapists. *Journal of Research in Personality, 14,* 121–137.

Maletzky, B. M. (1980). "Assisted" covert sensitization. In D. J. Cox & R. J. Daitzman (Eds.), *Exhibitionism: Description, assessment, and treatment* (pp. 187–251). New York: Garland Press.

Maletzky, B. M. (1986). Orgasmic reconditioning. In A. S. Bellack & M. Hersen (Eds.), *Dictionary of behavior therapy techniques* (pp. 57–58). New York: Pergamon Press.

Maletzky, B. M. (1987, October). *Data generated by an outpatient sexual abuse clinic.* Paper presented at the Annual Conference of the Association for the Treatment of Sexual Abusers, Newport, OR.

Maletzky, B. M. (1991a). *Treating the sexual offender.* Newbury Park, CA: Sage.

Maletzky, B. M. (1991b). The use of medroxyprogesterone acetate to assist in the treatment of sexual offenders. *Annals of Sex Research, 4,* 117–129.

Maletzky, B. M. (1992, November). *Factors associated with success in a behavioral/cognitive outpatient treatment program for the sexual offender.* Paper presented at the annual conference of the Association for the Treatment of Sexual Abusers, Portland, OR.

Maletzky, B. M. (1993). Factors associated with success and failure in the behavioral and cognitive treatment of sexual offenders. *Annals of Sex Research, 6,* 241–258.

Maletzky, B. M. (1996). Evolution, psychopathology, and sexual offending: Aping our ancestors. *Aggression and Violent Behavior: A Review, 1*, 309–373.

Maletzky, B. M. (1997). Exhibitionism: Assessment and treatment. In D. R. Laws & W. O'Donohue (Eds.), *Handbook of sexual deviance*. New York: Guilford.

Maletzky, B. M. (1998, October). *Treatment outcome, technique efficacy, and assessment of risk: A five to twenty-five year follow-up of 7,500 sexual offenders*. Paper presented at the Seventeenth Annual Research and Treatment Conference of the Association for the Treatment of Sexual Abusers, Vancouver, BC.

Maletzky, B. M. (2000a). Exhibitionism. In M. Hersen & M. Biaggio (Eds.), *Effective brief therapy: A clinician's guide* (pp. 235–257). New York: Plenum.

Maletzky, B. M. (2000b). Sexual assault. In V. B. Van Hasselt & M. Hersen (Eds.), *Aggression and violence: An introductory text* (pp. 152–197). Needham Heights, MA: Allyn & Bacon.

Maletzky, B. M., & Field, G. (2000). *Antiandrogens employed to assist cognitive/behavioral treatment for the sexual offender: A follow-up of incarcerated offenders*. Manuscript submitted for publication.

Maletzky, B. M., & George, F. S. (1973). The treatment of homosexuality by "assisted" covert sensitization. *Behaviour Research and Therapy, 11*, 655–657.

Maletzky, B. M., O'Donohue, W. T., Negev, L. G., & Hagstrom, A. H. (2000). *Problems with the DSM-IV diagnosis of pedophilia*. Manuscript submitted for publication.

Maletzky, B. M., & Steinhauser, C. (1998). Community-based treatment programs for sexual offenders. In W. L. Marshall, S. M. Hudson, T. Ward, & Y. M. Fernandez (Eds.), *Sourcebook of treatment programs with sexual offenders* (pp. 105–116). New York: Plenum Press.

Maletzky, B. M., & Steinhauser, C. (2000). *An excess of older brothers among men who molest male children*. Manuscript submitted for publication.

Marlatt, G. A., & Gordon, J. R. (Eds.). (1985). *Relapse prevention*. New York: Guilford Press.

Marques, J. U. (1994, November). *New outcome data from California's Sex Offender Treatment and Evaluation Project*. Paper presented at the annual conference of the Association for the Treatment of Sexual Abusers, San Francisco.

Marshall, W. L. (1989). Pornography and sexual offenders. In D. Zillman & J. Bryan (Eds.), *Pornography: Recent research, interpretations, and policy considerations* (pp. 185–214). Hillsdale, NJ: Erlbaum.

Marshall, W. L., & Barbaree, H. E. (1990a). An integrated theory of the etiology of sexual offending. In W. L. Marshall, D. R. Laws, & H. E. Barbaree (Eds.), *Handbook of sexual assault: Issues, theories, and treatment of the offender* (pp. 257–275). New York: Plenum.

Marshall, W. L., & Barbaree, H. E. (1990b). Outcome of comprehensive cognitive/behavioral treatment programs. In W. L. Marshall, D. R. Laws, & H. E. Barbaree (Eds.), *Handbook of sexual assault: Issues, theories, and treatment of the offender* (pp. 363–385). New York: Plenum.

Marshall, W. L., & Hall, G. C. N. (1995). The value of the MMPI in deciding forensic issues in accused sexual offenders. *Sexual Abuse: A Journal of Research and Treatment, 7*, 205–219.

Marshall, W. L., Jones, R., Ward, T., Johnston, P., & Barbaree, H. G. (1991). Treatment outcome with sex offenders. *Clinical Psychology Review, 11*, 465–485.

Marshall, W. L., & Marshall, L. E. (2000). Child sexual molestation. In V. B. Van Hasselt & M. Hersen (Eds.), *Aggression and violence: An introductory text* (pp. 67–91). Needham Heights, MA: Allyn & Bacon.

Marshall, W. L., & Mazzucco, A. (1995). Self-esteem and parental attachments in sexual offenders. *Sexual Abuse: A Journal of Research and Treatment, 7*, 279–285.

Marshall, W. L., Serran, G. A., & Cortoni, F. A. (2000). Childhood attachments, sexual abuse, and their relationship to adult coping in child molesters. *Sexual Abuse: A Journal of Research and Treatment, 12*, 17–26.

Marshall, W. L., & Williams, D. 1975). A behavioral approach to the modification of rape. *Quarterly Bulletin of the British Association for Behavioral Psychotherapy, 4*, 78.

Mathews, R., Hunter, J. A., & Vuz, J. (1997). Juvenile female sexual offenders: Clinical characteristics and treatment issues. *Sexual Abuse: A Journal of Research and Treatment, 9*, 187–199.

McConaghy, N. (1993). *Sexual behavior: Problems and management*. New York: Plenum.

McFall, R. M. (1990). The enhancement of social skills. In W. L. Marshall, D. R. Laws, & H. E. Barbaree (Eds.), *Handbook of sexual assault: Issues, theories, and treatment of the offender* (pp. 311–330). New York: Plenum.

McGrath, M., Cann, S., & Konopasky, N. (1998). New measures of defensiveness, empathy, and cognitive distortions for sexual offenders against children. *Sexual Abuse: A Journal of Research and Treatment, 10*, 25–36.

McGuire, R. J., Carlisle, J. M., & Young, B. G. (1965). Sexual deviations as conditioned behavior: A hypothesis. *Behaviour Research and Therapy, 2*, 185–190.

Money, J., & Pollitt, E. (1964). Cytogenic and psychosexual ambiguity. *Archives of General Psychiatry, 11*, 589–595.

Murphy, W. D. (1990). Assessment and modification of cognitive distortions in sex offenders. In W. L. Marshall, D. R. Laws, & H. E. Barbaree (Eds.), *Handbook of sexual assault: Issues, theories, and treatment of the offender* (pp. 331–342). New York: Plenum.

Osborn, C., Abel, G. G., & Warberg, B. W. (1995, October). *The Abel Assessment: Its comparison to plethysmography and resistance to falsification.* Paper presented at the annual conference of the Association for the Treatment of Sexual Abusers, New Orleans.

Page, J. (1995, October). *Development and adaptation of material for the adolescent sex offender.* Paper presented at the annual conference of the Association for the Treatment of Sexual Abusers, New Orleans.

Peterson, K. D., & Barnes, J. M. (1999). Proactivity in the public domain—Legislative advocacy and dealing with the media. In B. K. Schwartz (Ed.), *The sex offender: Theoretical advances, treating special populations, and legal developments* (pp. 7-1 to 7-9). Kingston, NJ: Civic Research Institute.

Pithers, W. D. (1990). Relapse prevention with sexual aggressors. In W. L. Marshall, D. R. Laws, & H. E. Barbaree (Eds.), *Handbook of sexual assault: Issues, theories, and treatment of the offender* (pp. 343–361). New York: Plenum.

Prentky, R. A. (1997). Arousal reduction in sexual offenders: A review of antiandrogen interventions. *Sexual Abuse: A Journal of Research and Treatment, 9*, 335–347.

Proulx, J., Ouimet, M., Pellerin, B., Paradis, Y., McKibben, A., & Aubot, J. (1999). Posttreatment recidivism rates in sexual aggressors—A comparison between dropout and nondropout subjects. In B. K. Schwartz (Ed.), *The sex offender: Theoretical advances, treating special populations, and legal developments* (pp. 15-1 to 15-13). Kingston, NJ: Civic Research Institute.

Quinsey, V. L. (1983). Prediction of recidivism and the evaluation of treatment programs for sex offenders. In S. N. Verdun-Jones & A. A. Keltner (Eds.), *Sexual aggression and the law* (pp. 27–40). Burnaby, BC: Criminology Research Center Press.

Quinsey, V. L. (1984). Sexual aggression: Studies of offenders against women. In D. Weisstub (Ed.), *Law and mental health: International perspectives* (Vol. 1, pp. 84–121). New York: Pergamon Press.

Quinsey, V. L., Chaplin, T. C., & Carrigan, W. F. (1980). Biofeedback and signalled punishment in the modification of inappropriate age preferences. *Behavior Therapy, 11*, 567–576.

Quinsey, V. L., & Earls, C. M. (1990). The modification of sexual preferences. In W. L. Marshall, D. R. Laws, & H. E. Barbaree (Eds.), *Handbook of sexual assault: Issues, theories, and treatment of the offender* (pp. 279–295). New York: Plenum.

Quinsey, V. L., Harris, G. T., Rice, M. E., & Cormier, C. A. (1998). *Violent offenders: Appraising and managing risk.* Washington, DC: American Psychological Association.

Quinsey, V. L., & Lalumiere, M. L. (1995). Evolutionary perspectives on sexual offending. *Sexual Abuse: A Journal of Research and Treatment, 7*, 301–315.

Raboch, J., & Raboch, J. (1986). Number of siblings and birth order of sexually dysfunctional males and sexual delinquents. *Journal of Sex and Marital therapy, 12*, 73–76.

Rooth, G., & Marks, I. M. (1974). Persistent exhibitionism: Short-term response to aversion, self-regulation, and relaxation treatments. *Archives of Sexual Behavior, 8*, 227–248.

Russell, D. E. H. (1988). The incidence and prevalence of intrafamilial and extrafamilial sexual abuse of female children. In L. E. A. Walker (Ed.), *Handbook on sexual abuse of children* (pp. 19–36). New York: Springer.

Salter, A. C. (1992). Epidemiology of child sexual abuse. In W. T. O'Donohue & J. H. Gear (Eds.), *Sexual abuse of children: Theory and research* (Vol. 1, pp. 108–138). Hillsdale, NJ: Erlbaum.

Sawyer, S. P. (1999). Measuring treatment efficacy through long-term follow-up. In B. K. Schwartz (Ed.), *The sex offender: Theoretical advances, treating special populations, and legal developments* (pp. 24-1 to 24-13). Kingston, NJ: Civic Research Institute.

Schiavi, R. C., Thielgaard, A., Owen, D. R., & White, D. (1988). Sex chromosome anomalies, hormones, and sexuality. *Archives of General Psychiatry, 45*, 19–24.

Schlank, A. M. (1995). The utility of the MMPI and the MSI in identifying a sexual offender typology. *Sexual Abuse: A Journal of Research and Treatment, 7*, 185–194.

Schlank, A. M., & Shaw, T. (1996). Treating sexual offenders who deny their guilt: A pilot study. *Sexual Abuse: A Journal of Research and Treatment, 8*, 21–29.

Schlank, A. M., & Shaw, T. (1997). Treating sexual offenders who deny—A review. In B. K. Schwartz & H. R. Cellini (Eds.), *The sex offender: New insights, treatment, innovations, and legal developments* (pp. 6-1 to 6-7). Kingston, NJ: Civic Research Institute.

Schmidt, F., & Heinz, L. (1999). Treatment success of a community-based program for young adolescent sex offenders. In B. K. Schwartz (Ed.), *The sex offender: Theoretical advances, treating special populations, and legal developments* (pp. 18-1 to 18-9). Kingston, NJ: Civic Research Institute.

Seidman, B., Marshall, W. L., Hudson, S. M., & Robertson, R. J. (1994). An examination of intimacy and loneliness in sex offenders. *Journal of Interpersonal Violence, 9*, 518–534.

Serber, M. (1970). Shame aversion therapy. *Journal of Behavior Therapy and Experimental Psychiatry, 1*, 213–215.

Seto, M. C., & Barbaree, H. E. (2000). Paraphilias. In V. B. Van Hasselt & M. Hersen (Eds.), *Aggression and violence: An introductory text* (pp. 198–213). Needham Heights, MA: Allyn & Bacon.

Smallbone, S. W., & Dadds, M. R. (2000). Attachment and coercive sexual behavior. *Sexual Abuse: A Journal of Research and Treatment, 12*, 3–15.

Smith, G., & Fischer, L. (1999). Assessment of juvenile sexual offenders: Reliability and validity of the Abel Assessment for Interest in Paraphilias. *Sexual Abuse: A Journal of Research and Treatment, 11*, 209–216.

Smith, R. (1984). The Oregon State Hospital Sex Offender Unit: Program description. In F. H. Knopp (Ed.), *Retraining adult sex offenders: Methods and models* (pp. 185–209). Syracuse, NY: Safer Society Press.

Spitzer, R. L., & Wakefield, J. C. (1999). *DSM-IV* diagnostic criterion for clinical significance: Does it help solve the false positives problem? *American Journal of Psychiatry, 156*, 1856–1864.

Stermac, L. E., Segal, Z. V., & Gillis, R. (1990). Social and cultural factors in sexual assault. In W. L. Marshall, D. R. Laws, & H. E. Barbaree (Eds.), *Handbook of sexual assault: Issues, theories, and treatment of the offender* (pp. 143–159). New York: Plenum.

Stoléru, S., Grégoire, M. C., Gérard, D., Decety, J., Lafarge, E., Cinotti, L., Lavenne, F., LeBars, D., Verney-Mavry, E., Rada, H., Collet, L., Mazoyer, B., Forest, M. G., Magnin, F., Spira, A., & Comar, D. (1999). Neuroanatomical correlates of visually evoked sexual arousal in human males. *Archives of Sexual Behavior, 28*, 1–21.

Studer, L. H., & Reddon, J. R. (1998). Treatment may change risk prediction for sexual offenders. *Sexual Abuse: A Journal of Research and Treatment, 10*, 175–181.

Swaffer, T., Hollin, C., Beech, A., Beckett, R., & Fisher, D. (2000). An explanation of child sexual abusers' sexual fantasies before and after treatment. *Sexual Abuse: A Journal of Research and Treatment, 12*, 61–68.

Van Wyk, P. H., & Geist, C. S. (1984). Psychosocial development of heterosexual, bisexual, and homosexual behavior. *Archives of Sexual Behavior, 13*, 505–544.

Wang, C. (1999). *Current trends in child abuse reporting and fatalities: The results of the 1997 annual fifty state survey*. Chicago: Prevent Child Abuse America.

Weinrott, M. R., & Riggan, M. (1996). *Vicarious sensitization: A new method to reduce deviant arousal in adolescent offenders*. Manuscript submitted for publication.

Whitman, W. P., & Quinsey, V. L. (1981). Heterosocial skill training for institutionalized rapists and child molesters. *Canadian Journal of Behavioral Science, 13*, 105–114.

Wickramaserkera, I. (1980). Aversive behavioral rehearsal: A cognitive-behavioral procedure. In D. J. Cox and R. J. Daitzman (Eds.), *Exhibitionism: Description, assessment and treatment* (pp. 123–149). New York: Garland Press.

Williams, S. (1999). Alcohol's possible covert role: Brain dysfunction, paraphilias, and sexually aggressive behaviors. *Sexual Abuse: A Journal of Research and Treatment, 11*, 147–158.

Wilson, R. J. (1998). Psychophysiological signs of faking in the phallometric test. *Sexual Abuse: A Journal of Research and Treatment, 10*, 113–126.

Wolfe, R. (1984). Northwest Treatment Associates: A comprehensive, community-based evaluation and treatment program for adult sex offenders. In F. H. Knopp (Ed.), *Retraining adult sex offenders: Methods and models* (pp. 85–101). Syracuse, NY: Safer Society Press.

Wyatt, G. T. (1985). The sexual abuse of Afro-American and white American women in childhood. *Child Abuse and Neglect, 9*, 507–519.

Yochelson, S., & Samenow, S. E. (1977). *The criminal personality: Vol. 2. The change process*. New York: Jason Aronson.

Zverina, J., Lachman, M., Pondelickova, J., & Vanek, J. (1987). The occurrence of atypical sexual experience among various female patient groups. *Archives of Sexual Behavior, 16*, 325–326.

22

Treatments for Eating Disorders

G. Terence Wilson
Christopher G. Fairburn

The relative paucity of research on outcomes of treatment for anorexia nervosa (AN) contrasts sharply with the quantity and quality of research on outcomes of treatment for bulimia nervosa (BN). Because the literature on the treatment of AN contains a number of uncontrolled follow-up studies of various treatment programs, it is impossible to generalize from one clinical setting to another, to make comparisons among the studies, or to identify effective treatments.

A large number of good-to-excellent outcome studies (Type I and Type 2) suggest that several different classes of antidepressant drugs produce significantly greater reductions in the short term for binge eating and purging in BN patients than a placebo treatment. The long-term effects of antidepressant medication on BN remain untested. A very substantial number of well-designed studies (Type I and Type 2) have shown that manual-based cognitive behavioral therapy (CBT) is currently the first-line treatment of choice for BN; roughly half of patients receiving CBT cease binge eating and purging. Well accepted by patients, CBT is the most effective means of eliminating the core features of the eating disorder and is often accompanied by improvement in comorbid psychological problems such as low self-esteem and depression; long-term maintenance of improvement is reasonably good. There is little evidence that combining CBT with antidepressant medication significantly enhances improvement in the core features of BN, although it may aid in treating comorbid anxiety and depression.

Although controlled studies of their long-term effectiveness are lacking, several different psychological treatments appear equally effective in reducing the frequency of binge eating in the short term in binge-eating disorder (BED). These treatments include CBT, interpersonal therapy, behavioral weight loss programs, and guided self-help based on coginitive-behavioral principles. There is currently little evidence that antidepressant medication is effective for treating binge eating in BED patients.

There are two generally recognized eating disorders, bulimia nervosa (BN) and anorexia nervosa (AN). BN has been the subject of much research, while there have been relatively few studies of the treatment of AN. In clinical practice, many patients present with an "atypical eating disorder" (or an "eating disorder not otherwise specified") (Fairburn & Walsh, in press). These disorders resemble AN or BN but do not meet their diagnostic criteria because of their atypical form. Their treatment has not been studied other than in some preliminary studies of a provisional subgroup labeled *binge-eating disorder* (BED).

In this chapter, we review the research on the treatment of BN, AN, and BED, focusing on published and "in-press" randomized controlled treatment trials (RCTs). The treatment of obesity is not addressed since obesity is not an eating disorder, although it may cooccur with one.

BULIMIA NERVOSA

Bulimia nervosa mainly occurs among young adult women, although it is also seen in adolescence and middle age. It is characterized by a severe disturbance of eating in which determined attempts to restrict food intake are punctuated by episodes of uncontrolled overeating. These binges are commonly followed by self-induced vomiting or the misuse of laxatives, although some patients do not "purge." The effects of these behaviors on body weight tend to cancel each other out, with the result that most patients have a weight that is within the normal range. There are extreme concerns about shape and weight similar to those seen in AN, with self-worth being judged largely or even exclusively in terms of shape or weight or both. There is also a high level of psychosocial impairment. BN is associated with high rates of psychiatric comorbidity, including depression, anxiety disorders, substance abuse, and personality disorders (Bushnell et al., 1994; Lilenfeld et al., 1997). Among cases that present for treatment, the disorder tends to run a chronic, unremitting course (Fairburn et al., 1995), and this is also true of cases in the community (Fairburn et al., 2000). For this reason, short-lived treatment effects are of limited clinical significance.

Pharmacological Treatment

A number of different drugs have been investigated as possible treatments for BN. These drugs have included the anticonvulsant phenytoin, the opiate antagonist naltrexone, and the appetite suppressant fenfluramine (Mitchell & de Zwaan, 1993). The most intensively studied and commonly used drugs for BN are antidepressants.

Antidepressant Medication

The antidepressant drugs studied have included tricyclic drugs, monoamine oxidase inhibitors, and selective serotonin uptake inhibitors (SSRIs). Reviews of the literature have featured both meta-analysis and more traditional evaluations of individual studies.

In their meta-analysis, Whittal, Agras, and Gould (1999) included nine double-blind, placebo-controlled studies of antidepressant medication (Agras, Dorian, Kirkley, Arnow, & Bachman, 1987; Barlow, Blouin, Blouin, & Perez, 1988; Fluoxetine Bulimia Nervosa Collaborative Study Group, 1992; Goldstein et al., 1995; Kennedy et al., 1988, 1993; Walsh et al., 1988, 1991; Wilson, Fairburn, & Agras, 1997). The total number of patients in these studies was 870. The four outcome measures were frequency of binge eating, frequency of purging, depression, and what they labeled eating attitudes (i.e., self-reported dietary restraint, overconcern about body shape, and overconcern about body weight). Whittal et al. (1999) calculated within-treatment effect sizes (ESs), namely, posttreatment outcome minus pretreatment outcome divided by the pooled standard deviations. Weighted for sample sizes, the overall ESs were as follows: 0.66 for binge eating; 0.39 for purging; 0.73 for depression; and 0.71 for eating attitudes. Comparison of these ESs with those of CBT are discussed below.

In a traditional review of the evidence on antidepressant medication for BN, Devlin and Walsh (1995) listed 14 studies (Agras et al., 1987; Alger et al., 1991; Barlow et al., 1988; Blouin et al., 1988; Fluoxetine Bulimia Nervosa Collaborative Study Group, 1992; Horne et al., 1988; Hughes et al., 1986; Kennedy et al., 1988, 1993; Mitchell & Groat, 1984; Pope, Hudson, Jonas, & Yurgelun-Todd, 1983; Pope, Keck, McElroy, & Hudson, 1989; Walsh et al., 1988, 1991). These studies yielded a mean reduction in binge eating of 61.4% (range = 31 to 91%), with an average remission rate of 22% (range = 10 to 35%). The comparable figures for purging were a mean reduction of 58.9% (range = 34 to 91%), with an average remission rate of 34% (range = 23 to 44%). Several of the studies did not report remission rates. For example, only four studies reported remission rates for purging. In some instances, median reductions in binge eating and purging were reported, and in others, the reduction rates were derived from examination of the graphs in the original articles. The average attrition rate was 27% (range = 13 to 42%).

A major problem with all tallies of this nature is that averages compiled from studies differing widely in procedures, measurement, and methodological rigor can be misleading. The extreme variability in outcome among these studies is noteworthy. For example, one of the studies obtained a striking average reduction of 91% in purging, with a 68% remission rate after only 6 weeks of treatment with desipramine (N = 13), a rate virtually twice that of any other study using a tricyclic antidepressant (Hughes, Wells, Cunningham, & Ilstrup, 1986). Devlin and Walsh (1995) issued another important caveat. Patients' response to a pill placebo has varied widely across the studies, indicating substantial differences in patients' responsiveness.

Finally, a small study by Walsh et al. (2000) randomized nonresponders to cognitive behavior therapy or interpersonal psychotherapy (see below) and to either fluoxetine or pill placebo for 8 weeks of treatment. The frequency of binge eating increased in the placebo condition but declined significantly in the active medication treatment from 5.5 to 0.6 episodes per week. A similar pattern was found for purging.

Conclusions

Several conclusions can be drawn from the antidepressant drug studies to date.

1. *Antidepressant drugs are more effective than a pill placebo in reducing binge eating and purging.*

2. *With one exception, there have been no systematic dose response studies.* The exception showed that 60 mg/day but not 20 mg/day of fluoxetine was more effective than a pill placebo (Fluoxetine Bulimia Nervosa Collaborative Study Group, 1992).

3. *Different classes of antidepressant drug seem to be equally effective.* The data on fluoxetine (Fluoxetine Bulimia Nervosa Collaborative Study Group, 1992) are comparable to those on tricyclic antidepressants. However, there have been no direct comparisons of different drugs within the same study. At present, fluoxetine (60 mg daily) would appear to be the drug of choice because it produces fewer side effects than tricyclics.

4. *Patients who fail to respond to an initial antidepressant drug may respond to another.* This was found in an open-label study (Mitchell et al., 1989). It has been replicated in a controlled study in which treatment with desipramine (for 8 weeks) was followed by treatment with fluoxetine (60 mg/day for 8 weeks) if the patient's binge frequency had not declined by at least 75% or they experienced intolerable side effects (Walsh et al., 1997). This two-stage regime was designed to more closely approximate actual clinical practice than conventional single-drug protocols. Of the patients randomized to active medication, two thirds were sequentially administered the two drugs. Their average reduction in binge frequency was 69%, and 29% ceased binge eating. This reduction compares with 47% and 13%, respectively, among patients treated with desipramine alone in an earlier placebo controlled study conducted at the same center with a similar patient population (Walsh, Hadigan, Devlin, Gladis, & Roose, 1991).

5. *The long-term effects of antidepressant medication remain largely untested.* This is a serious deficiency of the research to date. Pope, Hudson, Jonas, and Yurgelun-Todd (1985) reported their experience over 2 years with 20 patients who were initially treated with imipramine. They found that most patients had to be kept on medication to maintain the initial treatment effects.

Walsh et al. (1991) required that patients in their study of desipramine versus placebo show a minimum reduction of 50% in binge eating after 8 weeks in order to be entered into a 16-week maintenance phase. Only 41% (29 of 71 patients) met this criterion. Of these patients, 8 declined to participate in the maintenance phase because of lack of interest, intolerable side effects, or other problems. Therefore, just 21 patients entered the study maintenance phase. Eleven (52.4%) patients completed the 16 weeks, six (28.6%) of whom relapsed (i.e., binged more than 50% of their baseline binge frequency), two (9.5%) dropped out to seek treatment elsewhere, and two (9.5%) were discontinued due to intolerable side effects. Patients who completed the full 16 weeks of maintenance failed to show statistically significant improvement over this period. These results indicate that even over this modest period of follow-up, the outcome is poor among those who remain on active medication. Similar results were obtained by Pyle et al. (1990), as described below.

The only other study of the longer term effects of antidepressant drugs was by Agras et al. (1994), described below. They found that 6 months of treatment with desipramine produced lasting improvement even after the medication was withdrawn. In contrast, treatment with desipramine for only 4 months was associated with substantial relapse. This curious finding requires replication. The mechanism(s) whereby 6 but not 4 months of treatment with desipramine reduces the probability of relapse is far from clear.

6. *Few drug studies have evaluated the effects of antidepressant medication on aspects of BN other than binge eating and purging.* There is evidence that

antidepressant drugs do not produce improvement in patients' eating between binge-eating–purging episodes. One study found that desipramine actually increased rather than decreased dietary restriction between episodes of binge eating (Rossiter, Agras, Losch, & Telch, 1988). This failure to moderate the dieting of these patients may account for the poor maintenance of change with antidepressant medication since the extreme and rigid form of dieting seen in BN is thought to encourage binge eating (Polivy & Herman, 1993; Fairburn, 1997a).

7. *Consistent predictors of a positive response to antidepressant medication have yet to be identified.* Pretreatment levels of depression appear not to be related to treatment outcome (Agras et al., 1987; Walsh et al., 1988, 1991).

8. *The mechanism(s) whereby antidepressant medication exerts its effects is unknown.* Its effects cannot be mediated by reductions in depression, since pretreatment levels of depression are unrelated to outcome. The apparent comparability of different classes of antidepressant drugs suggests some mechanism common to these agents.

Psychological Treatments

Cognitive Behavioral Therapy

The most intensively studied treatment for BN is cognitive behavioral therapy (CBT). The use of CBT derives directly from Fairburn's first formulation of this approach in Oxford (Fairburn, 1981) and the publication of a detailed treatment manual in 1985 (Fairburn, 1985). Although there are differences in the ways in which cognitive behavioral treatment has been implemented across different clinical and research settings, all are derived from the Oxford approach.

Manual-based CBT for BN is based on a model that emphasizes the critical role of both cognitive and behavioral processes in the maintenance of the disorder. It is described in detail by Fairburn (1997a). Of primary importance is the extreme personal value that is attached to an idealized body shape and low body weight and the associated low self-esteem. This results in an extreme and rigid restriction of food intake, which in turn makes patients physiologically and psychologically susceptible to periodic episodes of loss of control over eating (i.e., binge eating). These episodes are in part maintained by negative reinforcement since they temporarily reduce negative affect. Purging and other extreme forms of weight control are used in an attempt to compensate for the effects on weight of binge eating. Purging itself helps maintain binge eating by temporarily reducing the anxiety about potential weight gain and by disrupting the learned satiety that regulates food intake. In turn, binge eating and purging cause distress and lower self-esteem, thereby reciprocally fostering the conditions that will inevitably lead to more dietary restraint and binge eating. It follows from this model that treatment must address more than the presenting behaviors of binge eating and purging. The extreme dietary restraint must be replaced with a more normal pattern of eating, and the dysfunctional thoughts and attitudes about body shape and weight must also be addressed.

To achieve these goals, manual-based CBT for BN uses an integrated sequence of cognitive and behavioral interventions. The treatment is conducted on an outpatient basis and is suitable for all patients but the small minority (less than 5%) who require hospitalization. A detailed manual has been published (Fairburn, Marcus, & Wilson, 1993), together with a recent supplement in which certain aspects of its implementation are reviewed (Wilson, Fairburn, & Agras, 1997).

The Whittal et al. (1999) meta-analysis described above also included 26 studies that evaluated CBT. The total number of patients was 460. The studies that were included compared CBT variously with no treatment, delayed treatment, or an alternative form of psychological treatment. As in the meta-analysis of antidepressant medication, each ES reflected within-treatment change using the formula described above. The respective ESs were as follows: binge eating = 1.28; purging = 1.22; depression = 1.31; and eating attitudes = 1.35.

Hay and Bacaltchuk (2000) compiled a systematic, quantitative review of psychotherapy for BN for the Cochrane Library. The rigorous search strategy they used identified 21 controlled studies of BN, 15 of which were limited to the purging subtype of BN. Specifically, what they identified as CBT was compared with no treatment, delayed treatment, some alternative form of psychotherapy, or a self-help form of CBT. Relative risk analyses were used to assess remission from binge eating and standardized mean differences for continuous outcome variables. The analyses showed that CBT was significantly superior to delayed treatment in producing remission from binge eating, and that it approached statistical significance from other psychotherapies. CBT was significantly more effective than comparison psychotherapies in reducing depression.

The strengths of this Cochrane review of controlled studies of BN are offset by several limitations. All of the studies were coded for methodological quality. The criteria were the effectiveness of randomization, control of selection bias after randomization, and blinding of posttreatment assessment. As important as the methodological criteria in this review are, they are also limited. Vitally important methodological considerations were not covered in this quantitative review. For example, little if any attention is devoted to the adequacy of the CBT treatment. Indeed, at least one study is included that evaluates a form of treatment that cannot be viewed as CBT (Bachar, Latzer, Kreitler, & Berry, 1999). Nor is the adequacy of assessment evaluated. As we discuss below, studies vary widely not only in the adequacy of the method of assessment (e.g., interview versus patient self-report), but also in the length of assessment period (e.g., 1 week versus 4 weeks). Finally, unlike Whittal et al. (1999), Hay and Bacaltchuk (2000) did not report data on purging, dietary restraint, or attitudes about body shape and weight. No assessment of BN can be complete without assessing these defining features of the disorder.

Both Whitall et al. (1999) and Hay and Bacaltchuk (2000) emphasized the methodological variability of studies they included in their analyses. In view of the likely limitations of meta-analysis in general (LeLorier et al., 1997) and the shortcomings of the Hay and Bacaltchuk (2000) review, we focus next on the details of specific comparative outcome studies of CBT.

Comparisons of CBT with Antidepressant Medication

Whittal et al. (1999) compared the ESs of CBT and antidepressant medications in their meta-analysis. These planned comparisons results showed that CBT was significantly more effective than antidepressant drugs on each of their four outcome measures.

Whittal et al. (1999) also examined four studies that evaluated the effects of CBT combined with antidepressant medication (Agras et al., 1992; Goldbloom et al., 1997; Leitenberg et al., 1994; Walsh et al., 1997). Planned comparisons showed that the ESs of the combined treatment were significantly greater than medication alone for both binge and purge frequencies. The combined treatment was more effective than CBT alone for binge eating but not purging. In addition, Whittal et al. (1999) included in their meta-analysis three other studies that directly evaluated the relative and combined effectiveness of CBT and antidepressant medication (Beaumont et al., 1997; Fichter et al., 1991; Mitchell et al., 1990). In view of the marked differences and uneven methodological quality among these seven studies, the following is a critical evaluation of the findings of each study.

Mitchell et al. (1990) found that medication (imipramine) alone ($N = 45$) was superior to placebo ($N = 29$), but inferior to intensive group psychological treatment (mainly cognitive behavioral in nature) combined with either drug ($N = 48$) or placebo ($N = 33$). The two conditions with psychological treatment showed mean percentage reductions in binge eating of 89% and 92%; 51% of the patients were in remission during the last 2 weeks of treatment, and an additional 35% averaged one or fewer binges. Adding imipramine to the psychological treatment had no effect other than to produce greater reductions in symptoms of depression and anxiety. In this case, it is possible that the major improvement in frequency of binge eating and purging produced by the intensive psychological treatment precluded detecting a medication effect. All patients who had responded to treatment (defined as no more than two binge-purge episodes during the final 2 weeks) were assigned to a 4-month maintenance program and were followed up at 6 months (Pyle et al., 1990). Only 9 of 54 patients (17%) who received drug treatment could be classified as responders. Of these 9, just 2 maintained their improvement at 6 months. The psychological treatment, by contrast, showed good maintenance of change at follow-up.

Agras et al. (1992) found that CBT alone ($N = 23$) and combined treatment were equally effective in reducing the frequency of binge eating and purging in a sample of 77 BN patients. Medication (desipramine) was administered for either 16 or 24 weeks. The combined treatment with medication for 24 weeks was superior to CBT alone on only a single self-report measure of hunger. This combined group, but not CBT alone, showed significantly greater reduction in binge eating and purging than the 16-

week medication group at the 32-week assessment. Accordingly, this study is often taken as showing the superiority of combined treatment. A careful look at the data, however, suggests caution in drawing such a conclusion. CBT alone was administered for only 15 weeks (with three additional "booster" sessions), so it is difficult to compare it with 24 weeks of combined treatment. Moreover, the data failed to show differences between CBT alone and either combined condition except for a composite measure of disinhibition and hunger from the Stunkard and Messick (1985) Eating Inventory. A 1-year follow-up showed the following remission rates from binge eating and purging: 18% of patients who had received 16 weeks of drug treatment; 67% of the 24-week drug treatment; 54% of the CBT group; and 78% of the combined CBT and 24-week medication treatment. As mentioned earlier, the finding that 24 weeks of desipramine was substantially more effective than 16 weeks of desipramine treatment is difficult to explain.

In Germany, Fichter et al. (1991) compared a 35-day trial of fluoxetine (35 mg/day) with a placebo in 40 BN patients who were concurrently participating in an inpatient program of intensive behavioral therapy focused on the modification of abnormal eating and emotional expression, as well as social skills training. There were no dropouts. Both the fluoxetine and the placebo treatments were associated with statistically and clinically significant reductions in frequency of binge eating and attitudes toward eating. Similarly, both treatments resulted in significant improvement on self-rating scales of associated psychopathology. On none of these measures was fluoxetine significantly more effective than placebo. The only treatment-by-time interaction was for body weight, with fluoxetine producing a greater weight loss. A common interpretation of these findings is that the intensive behavioral treatment program produced a ceiling effect that made it impossible to show a treatment effect for fluoxetine (Fichter et al., 1991; Mitchell & de Zwaan, 1993). This interpretation seems implausible. Fichter et al.'s data show that fluoxetine resulted in a mean reduction in "binge attacks" of only 47% and in "urge to binge" of 46%, which would seem to leave ample room for a differential treatment effect to emerge.

A fourth study compared CBT with desipramine and a combination of the two treatments (Leitenberg et al., 1994). CBT was superior to desipramine, but the small size (only seven patients in each treatment) makes the findings difficult to interpret.

The fifth study in this series randomly assigned 120 patients either to antidepressant medication or a pill placebo (Walsh et al., 1997). Half the patients also received 20 individual sessions of CBT, and the other half, a form of supportive psychotherapy (SPT) over a 16-week interval. Patients randomized to receive active medication first received desipramine for 8 weeks. If the patient's binge frequency had not declined by at least 75% or if they experienced intolerable side effects, the desipramine was replaced by fluoxetine (60 mg/day) for the next 8 weeks. Patients randomized to placebo first received desipramine placebo and, following the same criteria, were then given fluoxetine placebo. As mentioned earlier, this two-stage drug treatment was designed to more closely approximate actual clinical practice than conventional single-drug protocols. CBT was adapted from Fairburn's (1985) manual. The Eating Disorder Examination (EDE; Fairburn & Cooper, 1993) was the main measure of outcome. Comprehensive and valid, the EDE is widely viewed as the gold standard for assessing eating disorders (Wilson, 1993).

Although medication was not statistically superior to placebo in reducing binge eating as measured by the EDE (which assesses binge eating over 4 weeks), it was significantly more effective than placebo in terms of patients' self-monitoring over the last 2 weeks of therapy. Differences between medication and placebo failed to reach statistically significant levels on either the EDE or self-monitoring measure of vomiting frequency. Medication also produced significantly greater reductions in depression and body weight (a mean of 3.5 versus 0.6 pounds).

CBT was significantly superior to SPT in reducing both 2-week self-monitoring and 4-week EDE measures of binge eating and vomiting. There was no difference on depression, but CBT resulted in a slight but statistically significant increase in body weight (a mean of 1.24 versus 0.2 pounds). There were no statistically significant interactions between drug and psychological treatments. Two planned comparisons revealed that adding CBT to antidepressant medication produced a significantly greater improvement in vomiting frequency (and a trend in binge-eating frequency) than medication only, whereas combining SPT with medication had no incremental benefit. Although the difference was not statistically significant, the drug-plus-CBT condition had a higher remission rate for binge eating and vomiting (50%) than placebo plus CBT (24%). A larger sample size might have resulted in a significant difference in favor of the combined treatment.

The sixth study, from Toronto, compared 16 weeks of individual CBT and fluoxetine (60 mg) and a combined CBT/fluoxetine treatment (Goldbloom et al., 1997). The combined treatment was significantly more effective than fluoxetine only in reducing frequency of binge eating and purging but did not differ from CBT only. Although these findings suggest that adding antidepressant medication to CBT has no significant incremental benefit, they must be interpreted cautiously. The attrition rate was unusually high. Of the 76 patients enrolled in the study, 33 (43%) failed to complete treatment. No follow-up was reported.

Beaumont et al. (1997) compared intensive nutritional counseling combined with either fluoxetine (60 mg) or pill placebo for 8 weeks of individual treatment. The nutritional counseling used by this Australian group shared some of the educational and behavioral features of CBT, such as self-monitoring and self-control techniques (e.g., stimulus control), but lacked the systematic cognitive focus and techniques of CBT. The two treatments showed equivalent, clinically significant reductions in binge eating and purging at the end of 8 weeks. The only advantage for the active drug was on the restraint and shape and weight concern subscales of the EDE. A 3-month follow-up showed that the improvement in binge eating and purging was maintained, but that the fluoxetine was no longer superior to pill placebo on the EDE subscales.

Conclusions

The results of the comparisons of CBT and antidepressant drugs suggest the following conclusions:

1. *CBT seems more acceptable to patients than antidepressant medication.* Patients with BN appear reluctant to take antidepressant medication and seem to prefer psychological treatment (Mitchell et al., 1990). Leitenberg et al. (1994) reported that 15% of potential subjects for their study rejected participation in the medication-only treatment condition.

2. *The dropout rate is lower with CBT than with pharmacological treatments.* In the Mitchell et al. (1990) study, the dropout rates for imipramine with and without group psychological treatment were 25% and 42.6%, respectively. The comparable rates for patients who received the pill placebo with and without psychological treatment were 14.7% and 16.1%. Agras et al. (1992) had only one CBT patient dropout, a rate of 4.3%, compared with 17% for desipramine. Leitenberg et al. (1994) reported a 14% dropout rate in their CBT condition, versus 57% in the desipramine-only treatment. In the Whittal et al. (1999) meta-analysis, the dropout rate for CBT (18.6%) was lower than for drug treatment (25.4%), although the difference was not significant.

3. *CBT seems to be superior to treatment with a single antidepressant drug* (Agras et al., 1992; Leitenberg et al., 1994; Whittal et al., 1999).

4. *Combining CBT with antidepressant medication is significantly more effective than medication alone* (Agras et al., 1992; Leitenberg et al., 1994; Mitchell et al., 1990; Walsh et al., 1997; Whittal et al., 1999).

5. *Combining CBT and antidepressant medication produces few consistent benefits over CBT alone.*

6. *CBT plus medication has not been shown to be superior to CBT plus a pill placebo* (Fichter et al., 1991; Mitchell et al., 1990; Walsh et al., 1997).

7. *The combination of CBT and antidepressant medication may be more effective than CBT alone in reducing anxiety and depressive symptoms.* Mitchell et al. (1990) found that a combination of imipramine and intensive group psychological treatment, which was largely cognitive behavioral in nature, was significantly superior to group therapy plus pill placebo in reducing anxiety and depression. Similarly, Walsh et al. (1997) reported that antidepressant medication was significantly more effective than placebo in reducing depressive symptoms averaging over the CBT and supportive psychotherapy treatments in that study.

8. *Longer term maintenance of change appears to be better with CBT than with antidepressant drugs.* As mentioned earlier, in the Pyle et al. (1990) follow-up of the Mitchell et al. (1990) study, there was poor maintenance of change among those who received drug treatment, whereas it was good among those who received psychological treatment. Similarly, Agras, Rossiter, et al. (1994) found that 4 months of desipramine was followed by a high relapse rate, but

one that was prevented when the drug was combined with CBT. The findings of the comparative psychological treatment studies (see below) also suggest that maintenance of change is good with CBT.

Comparisons of CBT with Alternative Psychological Treatments

CBT has proved consistently superior to comparison treatments designed to control for the so-called nonspecifics of psychological treatment, such as the provision of a credible therapeutic rationale, the therapeutic relationship, and nondirective therapeutic exploration of intrapsychic issues. In the first of four studies within this category, Kirkley, Schneider, Agras, and Bachman (1985), based on a small sample of 28 participants, found that CBT administered in a group setting was superior to supportive psychotherapy with self-monitoring, although this difference was no longer present at 4-month follow-up. In the second study by the same group of investigators, CBT conducted on an individual basis (N = 17) was found to be more effective than supportive psychotherapy with self-monitoring (N = 16), both at the end of treatment and at a 6-month follow-up (Agras, Schneider, Arnow, Raeburn, & Telch, 1989).

A third study compared CBT with two alternative treatments in a sample of 47 participants. One was behavior therapy, a truncated form of CBT as discussed below. The other was what the authors called a nonspecific self-monitoring treatment, a nondirective intervention designed to serve as a face-valid comparison condition (Thackwray, Smith, Bodfish, & Meyers, 1993). CBT produced significantly greater improvement on binge eating and purging than the nonspecific self-monitoring condition at both posttreatment and a 6-month follow-up. A puzzling feature of this study is the remarkably high rate of success that was achieved. Following brief individual treatment of only eight sessions, 92% of patients in CBT and 69% in the nonspecific self-monitoring condition had ceased binge eating and purging. No other study of CBT has produced such impressive success rates. The remission rates at 6-month follow-up were 69% and 15%, respectively, indicating that the improvements obtained in the self-monitoring condition were short-lived.

The fourth study (Walsh et al., 1997) has already been mentioned in the context of its antidepressant arm. It compared CBT with supportive psychotherapy (SPT) in patients who concurrently received either antidepressant medication or a pill placebo. The SPT treatment was adapted from the Fairburn, Kirk, O'Connor, and Cooper (1986) focal psychotherapy condition but differed in that it eliminated elements that overlapped with the putative active therapeutic ingredients of CBT, such as the self-monitoring of eating and the circumstances preceding binge eating. It was also less focal in nature, the emphasis being on patient self-exploration and understanding. SPT was primarily designed to control for nonspecific therapeutic influences inherent in CBT. The strengths of this study include the fact that both treatments were manual-based and closely supervised and the EDE was used as a primary outcome measure. Posttreatment results showed that CBT was more effective than SPT despite the fact that the two treatments created comparable expectations of improvement and resulted in equally favorable ratings of the therapeutic relationship. CBT resulted in mean reductions of 84.7% and 84.6% in frequency of binge eating and vomiting as measured by the EDE. The comparable results for SPT were 61.7% and 50.7%, respectively. On the self-monitoring measure, CBT resulted in reductions of 72% on binge eating and 69% on vomiting. The parallel numbers for SPT were 51.8% and 46.4%. CBT was also significantly better on the EAT (Garner, Olmsted, Bohr, & Garfinkel, 1982), a self-report measure of eating disorder features.

Controlled studies have also compared CBT with other forms of psychotherapy. Garner and colleagues compared CBT with supportive-expressive psychotherapy (SET) in the treatment of 60 patients (Garner et al., 1993). Both treatments produced substantial improvements by the end of treatment. The two treatments were equally effective in reducing binge eating, but CBT was significantly superior to SET in decreasing purging, lessening dietary restraint, and modifying dysfunctional attitudes to shape and weight. CBT produced greater improvement in depression, self-esteem, and general psychological distress. CBT also produced more rapid improvement than SET. No follow-up data were reported.

In the first of two related outcome studies, Fairburn et al. (1986) assigned 24 patients either to CBT or to an adaptation of a form of brief focal psychotherapy (Rosen, 1979). The rationale for the latter treatment was that BN is maintained by a variety of ongoing problems (mostly of an interpersonal nature) and that to overcome the eating disorder, the client has to identify and resolve these problems. The focal psychotherapy included the self-monitoring of binge eating, since binges are often triggered by interpersonal problems and therefore can serve as a useful marker of such problems. Both treatments produced striking improvements in the core symptomatology of BN at posttreatment and over a 1-year closed follow-up. CBT produced a 90% reduction in binge eating and a 93% reduction in purging at posttreatment. Beyond the specific eating-disorder psychopathology, CBT was more effective than the focal psychotherapy in its effects on patients' social adjustment and overall clinical state.

The second study from the Oxford group (Fairburn et al., 1991; Fairburn, Jones, et al., 1993) yielded several important findings. It is also one of the best controlled studies to date. In this study, CBT was compared with two alternative treatments; the first was behavior therapy (BT), comprising the CBT treatment minus cognitive restructuring, and the behavioral and cognitive methods for modifying abnormal attitudes about weight and shape; and the second treatment was an adaptation of interpersonal psychotherapy (IPT) (described in more detail later). In the latter treatment, little attention was paid to the eating disorder per se. Each condition comprised 25 patients. All three treatments were manual-based, and their implementation was closely monitored. For the first time in the field, the EDE was used as the main measure of outcome.

At posttreatment, the three therapies were equally effective in reducing binge eating. The mean reductions were 71% for CBT, 62% for BT, and 62% for IPT. However, CBT was significantly more effective than IPT in reducing purging, dietary restraint, and attitudes to shape and weight, and superior to BT on the latter two variables, despite equivalent ratings of suitability of treatment and expectations of outcome. This pattern of results shows that CBT had specific effects on different measures of outcome consistent with its theoretical rationale. As in the previous study by the Oxford group, treatment was followed by a 1-year "closed" follow-up (i.e., it was treatment-free). It showed that the effects of CBT were well maintained and significantly superior to BT but equal to IPT (Fairburn, Jones, et al., 1993). Of CBT patients 36%, and 20% of BT patients and 44% of IPT patients, had ceased both binge eating and purging. The patients were followed up once more after an average of 5.8 (*SD* ± 2.0) years, thereby providing a unique perspective of the long-term impact of these three treatments. There was a clear difference between them, even after this long period of time. Those patients who had received CBT or IPT were doing equally well, with 63% and 72%, respectively, having no *DSM-IV* eating disorder compared with 14% among those who had received BT (Fairburn et al., 1995).

In a reproduction of the Oxford CBT comparison (Fairburn, Jones, et al., 1993), Agras, Walsh, Fairburn, Wilson, and Kraemer (2000) compared the same CBT and IPT treatments in a much larger sample size of 220 patients. The findings essentially replicated those of the Fairburn, Jones, et al. (1993) study. At posttreatment, CBT was significantly superior to IPT in the number of patients who had ceased all binge eating and purging over the preceding 4 weeks as assessed by the EDE. The proportions were 29% versus 6% in the intent-to-treat analysis, and 45% versus 8% in the analysis of only those patients who completed treatment. Percentage reductions in frequency of binge eating and purging for completers were 86% and 84% for CBT versus 51% and 50% for IPT. CBT was also significantly superior to IPT in reducing dietary restraint, but not in modifying dysfunctional attitudes about body shape and weight. There were no differences between the two treatments on measures of associated psychopathology (e.g., depression, self-esteem, and interpersonal functioning). At follow-up at 4 and 8 to 12 months, there were no statistically significant differences between the two therapies in terms of remission from binge eating and purging over the preceding 4 weeks. The differential time course of the effects of CBT and IPT once again suggests that these two treatments operate via different mechanisms.

Although there is evidence that CBT and IPT operate via different mechanisms, the posttreatment course of patients in the two treatments was not dissimilar. For example, 66% of those who had recovered with CBT at the end of treatment remained recovered at follow-up, compared with 57% (4 of 7) of those treated with IPT. For those remitted at the end of CBT, 29% (6 of 21) recovered, compared with 33% (8 of 24) for the IPT group. Of the remaining participants, 7% (4 of 57) had recovered at follow-up in the CBT group, compared with 9% (7 of 79) in the IPT group. The percentages in each category at the end of treatment were similar for both treatments. These findings suggest that the absence of a statistically significant difference between CBT and IPT over follow-up may be more a function of their differential posttreatment status (such as a regression toward the mean effect) than of any delayed "catch-up" property of IPT.

The Agras, Walsh, et al. (2000) study had several distinctive methodological strengths. First, in contrast to virtually all previous controlled studies of the treatment of BN, it had sufficient statistical power to detect differences between the two therapies. Second, the quality of the two therapies was rigorously controlled by use of manual-based treatment protocols. The study was conducted at two sites in the United States (Stanford and Columbia), where the therapists were closely monitored on a weekly basis throughout the study by two experienced supervisors. In addition, each treatment was independently and continually monitored by the investigator (Fairburn) who had originally developed each protocol and conducted the earlier study at Oxford. Third, assessment was detailed and comprehensive, using the EDE interview.

Laessle et al. (1991) randomly assigned 55 patients either to what they called a nutritional management (NM) treatment or stress management (SM). The former closely approximated the behavioral components of CBT; the latter included standard cognitive behavioral strategies such as active coping and problem solving but never focused directly on the modification of eating or attitudes about weight and shape. The results showed marginally significant but consistent differences in favor of NM at both posttreatment and 1-year follow-up. NM produced significantly more rapid changes in eating behavior and purging than SM.

Comparison of CBT with Behavioral Treatment

Other studies have dismantled CBT, comparing the complete treatment with its behavioral component. Unlike Fairburn et al.'s (1993) manual-based CBT, the behavioral treatments in these studies have not focused on modifying problematic thoughts about dieting and abnormal attitudes about body shape and weight. Nor have they included the cognitive procedures of CBT, such as cognitive restructuring.

In the first of these studies, Freeman, Barry, Dunkeld-Turnbull, and Henderson (1988) compared CBT ($N = 32$) with behavior therapy (BT) ($N = 30$), group psychotherapy ($N = 30$), and a waiting-list control condition ($N = 20$). There were no between-group differences among the three treatments, although all were superior to the waiting-list control. No follow-up data were provided. A second study pitted a brief, eight-session CBT treatment against its behavioral component and a waiting-list control (Wolf & Crowther, 1992). Both treatments were administered on a group basis. The results showed that both treatments were comparably superior to the waiting-list control. A 3-month follow-up indicated that the behavioral treatment was associated with better maintenance of reduction in binge eating than the CBT treatment. It must be noted that caution is warranted when interpreting the results of brief treatments like this since it is highly unlikely that the cognitive components of the full Fairburn et al. (1993) manual can be effectively implemented in so abbreviated a program. The Wolf and Crowther (1992) study is also weakened by the fact that the same single therapist administered both treatments and conducted the posttreatment assessment.

The failure of the foregoing two studies to show that CBT was superior to BT contrasts markedly with the results from the Fairburn et al. (1991, 1993, 1995) study described above. In that study, CBT was more effective than BT at posttreatment on measures of dietary restraint and attitudes about body shape and weight. The superiority of CBT became even more evident at the 1- and 6-year follow-ups. Whereas CBT was associated with good maintenance of change, patients in the BT treatment fared poorly, with 48% dropping out or being withdrawn from the study because of lack of improvement during the closed 1-year follow-up (Fairburn, Jones, et al., 1993). As mentioned, the outcome of the BT patients remained poor at the 6-year follow-up: Fairburn et al. (1995) argued that it was likely to reflect the natural outcome of clinic cases not exposed to an effective treatment.

The discrepancy between the findings of the Fairburn et al. (1991) study and those by Freeman et al. (1988) and Wolf and Crowther (1992) can probably be attributed to the lack of systematic follow-up in the former study and the brevity of the CBT in the latter. The crucial importance of systematic follow-up is demonstrated by the findings of the Fairburn, Jones, et al. study (1993), which revealed differential effects over time of the three treatments.

Similar findings emerged from the study by Thackwray et al. (1993). At posttreatment, they found that CBT and BT were equally successful. At 6-month follow-up, however, CBT was superior to BT. Of patients who had received CBT, 69% remained abstinent from binge eating and purging, compared with only 38% of those treated with BT.

The importance of following up these patients is also illustrated by the findings of the well-designed study by Cooper and Steere (1995). They compared a modified version of Fairburn et al.'s (1993) manual-based CBT with a more narrowly focused behavioral treatment that excluded the cognitive components of the treatment. In place of the emphasis on cognitive restructuring in Stage 2 of the manual, Cooper and Steere (1995) substituted eight sessions of exposure and response prevention treatment based on Leitenberg and Rosen's (1985) behavioral treatment. This necessitated omitting from the CBT condition procedures designed to tackle dieting in order to minimize overlap between the treatments. Patients in both treatment conditions received the first eight sessions of CBT as well as the final three sessions on relapse prevention. Thus, this study provided the most searching test to date of the merits of CBT versus a more purely behavioral treatment.

Of the original 31 patients, 1 in each treatment dropped out, and 2 were withdrawn because of severe depression. The posttreatment analyses were conducted on the completers (CBT: N = 13; behavioral treatment: N = 14) with the EDE being the main measure of outcome. Both treatments produced clinically significant improvements with no between-group differences. CBT produced a mean percentage reduction of 78% in binge eating and 82.8% in purging. The comparable figures for the behavioral treatment were 78.7% and 91.1%. CBT resulted in remission rates of 46% and 54% in binge eating and purging, respectively. The comparable percentages for the behavioral treatment were 50% and 46%. Both treatments also resulted in significant improvements in dietary restraint and attitudes toward shape and weight. A 1-year follow-up of 25 of the patients (during which no patient received additional therapy) showed that whereas patients who had been treated with CBT maintained their improvements, those who had received the behavioral treatment showed significant relapse. For example, of the seven CBT patients who had ceased purging, only one relapsed. Of the six behavioral patients who had ceased purging, five relapsed. CBT was significantly superior to the behavioral treatment on purging, with near-significant trends on binge eating, dietary restraint, and attitude to eating. These findings, taken together with those from the second Oxford trial, indicate that the cognitive component of CBT is needed if treatment effects are to persist.

Conclusions

Several conclusions can be drawn from these comparisons of CBT with alternative psychological treatments.

1. *CBT is more effective than credible comparison treatments that control for the nonspecifics of therapy.*

2. *CBT is superior to behavioral versions of the treatment that omit cognitive restructuring and the focus on modifying attitudes toward body shape and weight.*

3. *CBT is significantly more effective than, or at least as effective as, any form of psychotherapy with which it has been compared.*

4. *CBT produces a clinically significant degree of improvement.* One measure of the clinical importance of treatment-induced change is the extent to which patients engage in normative levels of behavior after treatment. Fairburn et al. (1995) reported that at their 5.8-year follow-up, 74% of patients who had received CBT had global scores on the EDE within 1 standard deviation of the mean for young women in that community.

5. *CBT reliably produces changes across all four of the specific features of BN, namely, binge eating, purging, dietary restraint, and abnormal attitudes about body shape and weight.*

6. *CBT is comparatively quick-acting.* It produces more rapid improvement than supportive psychotherapy (Wilson, Loeb, et al., 1999), SET (Garner et al., 1993), stress management therapy (Laessle et al., 1991), and IPT (Fairburn et al., 1991; Wilson, Fairburn, Agras, Walsh, & Kraemer, 2001).

7. *CBT affects both the specific and the general psychopathology of BN.* Most studies have shown significant improvements in depression, self-esteem, social functioning, and measures of personality disturbance.

8. *CBT is associated with good maintenance of change at 6-month and 1-year follow-up* (e.g., Agras, Rossiter, et al., 1994; Fairburn, Jones, et al., 1993). The strongest findings have come from the Oxford

group. After a 1-year follow-up, binge eating and purging (as assessed by the EDE) had declined by over 90%. Thirty-six percent of patients had ceased all binge eating and purging. Given that the follow-up was "closed," this ensured that patients seeking additional or different treatment did not confound evaluation of maintenance of change (Fairburn, Jones, et al., 1993). The subsequent 6-year follow-up showed that the effects of CBT were maintained (an abstinence rate of 50%) (Fairburn et al., 1995). The 11-year follow-up of the Mitchell et al. (1990) study found that 67.6% of the original CBT-plus-medication group and 70.8% of the CBT-plus-placebo group were in partial or full remission (Keel, personal communication, January 25, 2001).

The good maintenance of change following CBT contrasts markedly with the natural course of the disorder, which is characterized by chronicity in the long term and flux in the short term (Fairburn et al., 2000; Keller, Herzog, Lavori, Bradburn, & Mahoney, 1992).

9. *Reliable pretreatment predictors of response to CBT have proved elusive.* Numerous pretreatment patient characteristics have emerged as predictor variables, including past history of anorexia nervosa or previous low body weight, low self-esteem, comorbid personality disorders, and severity of core eating-disorder symptoms. The results across studies have been inconsistent, however, and of limited clinical value (Agras, Crow, et al., 2000). Perhaps the most consistent finding has been that comorbid personality disorders are a negative prognostic factor. This seems especially true of borderline personality disorder (Coker, Vize, Wade, & Cooper, 1993; Fairburn, Peveler, et al., 1993; Rossiter, Agras, Telch, & Schneider, 1993). Even here, however, contradictory findings exist (Davis, Olmsted, & Rockert, 1992).

Recent research has shown that much of the overall improvement achieved with CBT is evident after the first few weeks of treatment (Wilson, Loeb, et al., 1999), and that failure to respond early is a statistically and clinically significant predictor of ultimate outcome. Using a signal detection analysis, Agras, Crow, et al. (2000) showed that reduction in purging at Session 6 provided a better prediction of outcome than any pretreatment variable.

Few studies have examined posttreatment predictors of longer term outcome. Available evidence suggests that both behavioral and attitudinal change during treatment are linked to longer term functioning. In a test of the cognitive model on which CBT is based, Fairburn, Peveler, et al. (1993) found that among patients who had recovered in terms of behavioral change, 9% of those with the least dysfunctional concern with body shape and weight disturbance relapsed, compared with 29% and 75% among those with moderate and severe degrees of concern about body shape and weight. In a study of 143 BN patients who had received group CBT treatment, Mussell et al. (2000) found that symptom remission (total absence of binge eating and purging) during the final 2 weeks of treatment was the best predictor of outcome at a 6-month follow-up.

The Status of Other Psychological Treatments

Interpersonal Psychotherapy

Other than CBT, the psychological treatment with most support is interpersonal psychotherapy (IPT). It was originally devised by Klerman, Weissman, Rounsaville, and Chevron (1984) as a short-term treatment for depression. IPT is a focal psychotherapy, the main emphasis of which is to help patients identify and modify current interpersonal problems. The treatment is both nondirective and noninterpretive and, as adapted for BN (Fairburn, 1997b), pays little attention to the patient's eating disorder. It is therefore very different from CBT. The findings of two major studies, discussed above, showed IPT was significantly less effective than CBT at posttreatment (Agras, Walsh, et al., 2000; Fairburn et al., 1991). However, neither at 1 year (Agras, Walsh, et al., 2000; Fairburn, Jones, et al., 1993) nor at 6-year follow-up (Fairburn et al., 1995) was there any statistical difference between the two treatments. The consistent difference in their time course suggests that each treatment had specific effects, probably through the operation of different mechanisms.

In the Fairburn, Jones, et al. (1993) study, IPT was significantly more effective than the behavioral treatment that was equivalent in therapist contact and ratings of suitability and expectancy, indicating a specific effect of IPT. The Agras, Walsh, et al. (2000) study lacked a third comparison treatment that controlled for nonspecific influences, making it impossible to conclude that IPT had specific effects.

Psychodynamic Therapy

Controlled studies of the effectiveness of psychodynamic therapies are lacking. The exception is Garner et al.'s (1993) comparison of CBT with supportive-expressive psychotherapy (SET). Although equally effective in reducing binge eating, SET was inferior to CBT on other measures of BN as well as associated psychopathology. The absence of a no-treatment control group makes it difficult to interpret the binge-eating result. The lack of follow-up data is another limitation of this study. Despite the absence of data to support the use of psychodynamic psychotherapy in the treatment of BN, it remains popular in the United States.

Family Therapy

A family approach to treating eating disorders has a long clinical tradition (Vandereycken, Kog, & Vanderlinden, 1989). Yet only a single controlled study has evaluated the effectiveness of a family therapy approach (Russell, Szmukler, Dare, & Eisler, 1987). This study was marked by a high dropout rate (44%) and an unusually poor outcome (only a 9% abstinence rate), especially in adult patients. (It should be remembered that most patients with BN are adults.) However, since the patients in this study may have been a particularly recalcitrant group, given that they had been referred to a specialist treatment center, the generalizability of these findings could be questioned.

Less Intensive Treatments: Self-Help

Manual-based CBT was designed for use within specialist settings. It is time-consuming (involving about 20 sessions over 5 months), and for it to be executed optimally, training is required. Since there are unlikely ever to be sufficient specialist treatment resources for those with eating disorders, there is a need to develop simpler and briefer forms of CBT suitable for widespread use (Fairburn & Carter, 1997).

Attempts to do this are at an early stage (Wilson, Vitousek, & Loeb, 2000). Treasure et al. (1994, 1996) compared CBT with a type of self-help treatment (based on an eclectic self-manual) supplemented, if necessary, with sessions of CBT. The total sample size was 110. However, the findings are difficult to interpret for a number of reasons, including the use of an unusual patient sample (cases of BN and "atypical BN" from a tertiary referral center), a complex staged design, and a poor response rate at follow-up. However, it is clear from the data that some patients obtained lasting benefit from the self-help condition, a finding confirming that a subgroup of patients respond to minimal interventions of this type.

A subsequent study using the same self-help manual in Germany compared guided self-change (GSC), consisting of the self-help manual plus 8 fortnightly sessions of individual CBT, with 16 weekly sessions of CBT in a sample of 62 patients (Thiels, Schmidt, Treasure, Garthe, & Troop, 1998). Dropout rate was higher for GSC (29%) than CBT (12.9%). At posttreatment, using an intent-to-treat analysis, there were no differences between the two treatments on the subscales of the EDE. Full CBT was superior to GSC in terms of abstinence from both binge eating and vomiting (GSC = 12.9%; CBT = 54.8%). However, these figures are based only on the week preceding assessment, which is too short a period to obtain a valid measure of response. Follow-up evaluation (a mean of 43 weeks) included 77% of the sample, with comparable attrition rates across conditions. In a completer analysis, abstinence rates at follow-up were 71% (CBT) and 70% (GSC) for binge eating, and 71% (CBT) and 61% (GSC) for vomiting. These unusually high abstinence rates are likely to be attributable at least in part to the fact that assessment was based only on the preceding week.

Mitchell et al. (2001) evaluated the effects of a self-help manual in a 16-week placebo-controlled study of fluoxetine. Ninety-one BN patients were randomized to one of four conditions: pill placebo; fluoxetine; placebo plus self-help manual; and fluoxetine plus manual. Significant main effects on reduction of binge eating were found for both fluoxetine and the self-help manual with no interaction. The abstinence rates for binge eating and purging were 9% for pill placebo, 16% for fluoxetine, 24% for placebo plus manual, and 26% for fluoxetine plus manual. The low abstinence result for fluoxetine is consistent with previous research on BN, as noted above. These preliminary data indicate that medication combined with a self-help manual may be more effective than medication alone.

The methodological limitations of the existing research on self-help demand caution in evaluating the results. Future studies should include larger sample sizes, state-of-the-art evaluation of treatment outcome (e.g., the EDE), and longer follow-up.

Less Intensive Treatments: Psychoeducation in Groups

The goal of psychoeducation is the normalization of eating and body image concerns through didactic instruction. The content consists of education and cognitive behavioral change strategies. Its advantages are that it is less costly than specialized therapy and more readily disseminable.

Davis, Olmsted, and Rockert (1990) developed a psychoeducation program (N = 15) comprising five 90-minute group sessions that produced significantly greater improvement than a wait-list control (N = 26). Compared with a longer course of 19 sessions of individual CBT, they found that the program was less effective overall (Olmsted et al., 1991). The abstinence rates for both binge eating and vomiting were 30% for CBT and 17% for psychoeducation. However, with the subset of patients with less severe specific eating-disorder symptoms and associated psychopathology, the group psychoeducational program was equally effective. Higher frequency of vomiting and comorbid depression were significant predictors of poor treatment outcome.

In a subsequent sequential design study, patients who completed the group psychoeducation program were randomly assigned either to a 16-week trial of individual CBT or to no additional treatment (Davis, McVey, Heinmaa, Rockert, & Kennedy, 1999). The combined treatment resulted in greater improvement in binge-eating and purging frequencies and a higher abstinence rate (43.2% vs. 10.5%) than group psychoeducation alone at posttreatment. This pattern was maintained at follow-up. However, there were no significant differences between the treatments on measures of dietary restraint, shape and weight concern, or associated psychopathology such as depression. This study allows only the conclusion that subsequent therapeutic contact produces improvement beyond that obtained with group psychoeducation. It does not speak to the specific value of CBT as a second-stage treatment.

Collectively, these findings suggest that group psychoeducation may be effective for at least a subset of BN patients. As with self-help strategies, future studies should include longer follow-up.

Summary

Research Implications

The methodological quality of treatment outcome studies is uneven, although research has become increasingly rigorous. Assessment of outcome is problematic in many studies. Too few studies, especially those of antidepressant medication, have used valid interview-based methods that provide a comprehensive picture of eating-disorder psychopathology. Whether the window of assessment is 4 weeks (as in the EDE) or only 1 week will significantly influence the results.

Too many studies report only completer analyses, which are likely to inflate success rates. Intent-to-treat analyses provide a more conservative and clinically useful measure and should be routinely reported.

Finally, it is now imperative that follow-up evaluations of acute treatment effects be conducted. The absence of well-controlled follow-up of short-term drug effects remains a serious shortcoming.

Clinical Implications

Manual-based CBT is currently the first-line treatment of choice for BN. Well accepted by patients, it is the most effective means of eliminating the core features of the eating disorder and is usually accompanied by improvement in comorbid psychological problems such as low self-esteem and depression. Longer term maintenance of improvement appears to be good, although additional studies are needed. Early response to CBT is the best predictor of treatment outcome.

Antidepressant medication is another effective treatment, although its acute effects are inferior to those obtained with CBT. In the longer term, antidepressant medication appears to be associated with a high rate of relapse, although more data are needed. Medication is sometimes effective in cases where CBT has failed.

IPT is a promising alternative to CBT. It is not statistically different from CBT at 1-year follow-up. CBT should be preferred to IPT on the following grounds: First, numerous well-controlled studies in different countries have demonstrated the efficacy of manual-based CBT. The evidence for IPT derives from only two studies. Second, CBT is significantly quicker in producing improvement. Third, early response to treatment with CBT provides a clinically useful predictor of outcome. Predictors of success with IPT are lacking. The only advantage for IPT might be that it appears to be more acceptable and hence disseminable among clinical practitioners trained in traditional psychotherapeutic approaches (Wilson, 1998).

ANOREXIA NERVOSA

Anorexia nervosa (AN) is the least common of the eating disorders. It affects a younger age group than BN, most cases being women aged between 10 and 30. Estimates of the prevalence of the disorder among adolescent girls (11 to 18 years), the group most at risk, average about 0.3% (Hoek, in press). Like BN, AN is uncommon among men (about 10% of cases are male).

Three features are required to make a diagnosis of anorexia nervosa. The first is the presence of a characteristic set of attitudes concerning shape and weight. Various expressions have been used to describe these attitudes, including a "relentless pursuit of thinness" and a "morbid fear of fatness." The essential feature is that these people judge their self-worth almost exclusively in terms of their shape and weight. The second diagnostic feature is the active maintenance of an extremely low weight. The definition of what constitutes "low" varies: A widely used threshold is having a body mass index (BMI) below 17.5. The low weight is achieved by a variety of means, including marked dietary restriction, excessive exercising and, in some, self-induced vomiting or the misuse of laxatives or diuretics. The third diagnostic feature has limited clinical significance; it is amenorrhoea (in postmenarchal females who are not taking an oral contraceptive).

In addition to these diagnostic features, the specific psychopathology (i.e., eating disorder psychopathology) of AN includes preoccupation with thoughts about food, eating, shape and weight; ritualistic eating habits; extreme dissatisfaction with body shape and weight; and repeated body checking (or its active avoidance). The general psychopathology is characterized by mild to moderate depressive and anxiety symptoms, obsessional features, pronounced perfectionism, low self-esteem, and social withdrawal. AN is also associated with many physical abnormalities, including marked hormonal changes and impaired cardiovascular function. These are now thought to be secondary to the disturbed eating and low weight. One further feature is important: These patients do not necessarily view themselves as being in need of treatment. Indeed, aspects of the disorder they view positively, particularly their ability to severely restrict their food intake.

In principle, there are three aspects to the treatment of AN. The first is engaging patients in treatment and maintaining their motivation thereafter; the second is establishing healthy eating habits and a normal weight; and the third is ensuring that progress is maintained in the future. With most patients, treatment is exclusively on an outpatient basis, although with some, a period of full or partial hospitalization is also required. Thus, outpatient treatment occurs in two main contexts: It is either a complete treatment in its own right or a sequel to hospitalization when treatment is sometimes described as *relapse prevention*.

Research on Treatment

AN has been the subject of few RCTs, for four main reasons. First, AN is rare, so it is difficult to recruit enough patients for an adequately powered RCT. Second, treatment takes a long time: 12 months is a typical figure, and 6 to 12 months' posttreatment follow-up is needed to determine whether the changes are maintained. This means that studies of AN take many years to complete. Third, as mentioned already, many of these patients are difficult to engage in treatment, and recruiting them into a treatment trial is even more problematic. Fourth, some patients are so seriously ill when first seen that their state precludes them being entered in a controlled trial. Partly because of these difficulties, there have been rather more studies of specific aspects of the treatment of AN, particularly the effects of different behavioral regimes and drug treatments on the rate of weight gain in hospital.

Inpatient Versus Outpatient Management

There has been one study in which inpatient and outpatient management have been compared. In this ambitious study from St. George's Hospital in London, 90 patients were randomly assigned to one of four conditions (Crisp et al., 1991):

- Group 1 (N = 30)—inpatient treatment until normal weight was restored, followed by 12 sessions of individual outpatient therapy. Inpatient treatment was multifaceted, including weight restoration, individual therapy, family therapy, dietary counseling, and occupational therapy. The average duration of hospitalization was 20 weeks.
- Group 2 (N = 20)—12 sessions of outpatient individual and family psychotherapy.
- Group 3 (N = 20)—10 sessions of outpatient group psychotherapy for patients and parents.
- Group 4 (N = 20)—no treatment.

Groups 2 and 3 received dietary counseling during four sessions of their treatment. Of the 30 patients assigned to inpatient treatment, 18 (60%) accepted. Of the 20 assigned patients, 18 (90%) accepted outpatient individual treatment, and 17 (85%) of the 20 assigned patients accepted outpatient group treatment. Patients assigned to the no-treatment condition were referred back to their local physician. In practice, only 6 received no treatment of any kind, the others receiving either outpatient or inpatient treatment elsewhere during the course of the study.

Dropouts occurred in all treatment conditions, although the rates for each treatment were not specified, so that the interpretation of the results was complicated. Attrition was most marked in the outpatient group treatment (Group 3), in which the mean number of sessions attended was only 5, compared with 8.25 in the individual and family treatment (Group 2). Among those who completed treatment, the mean weight gains at follow-up 1 year after initial assessment were 9.6 kg, 9.0 kg, and 10.2 kg for the three active treatment conditions, respectively, all of which were significantly greater than that for the control condition (Group 4). Patients in all four treatment conditions showed improved sexual adjustment and social functioning, with no clear between-group differences.

Thus, two striking findings emerged from this study. First, brief outpatient treatment was as effective as a much longer and intensive combination of inpatient and outpatient treatment. This is a finding in need of explanation and replication. Second, all three treatments were associated with a clinically significant amount of weight gain at 1-year follow-up. Crisp et al. (1991) emphasized that their preferred clinical practice would have been to follow inpatient treatment with four times as many outpatient sessions over a period of 2 years. The added value of such intensive (and expensive) treatment remains to be demonstrated.

A 2-year follow-up of patients in Groups 2 and 4 showed that those who had received outpatient individual and family therapy had gained significantly more weight and showed greater improvement in social and psychosexual functioning than those in the control condition (Gowers et al., 1994). The mean weight of the former group was 94.5% of what would be normally expected, compared with 83% in the control group, and their respective mean BMIs were 20.1 and 17.8. Twelve of the Group 2 patients versus four of the Group 4 patients were judged to have a good clinical outcome. This is a surprisingly good outcome, which is inconsistent with other clinical reports of longer term outcome. On the other hand, the findings from certain psychological treatment studies (see below) also suggest that positive results can be obtained with relatively brief treatments.

Inpatient Behavioral Programs

The findings from various early single-case experimental designs suggested that certain behavioral procedures facilitate weight gain when implemented within the broader context of an inpatient treatment program (Agras & Kraemer, 1984). Different elements of these programs have since been manipulated to determine their effect on the rate of weight gain (see Touyz & Beumont, 1997). For example, in the study with probably the greatest clinical relevance, Touyz and colleagues (1984) treated two successive cohorts of patients (N = 31 and 34) using two different behavioral programs. The first was a traditional strict-bed-rest program with individualized reinforcers for each 0.5 kg of weight gained. The second was a simple "lenient and flexible" regime. The rates of weight gain with the two programs were equivalent (0.21 kg and 0.20 kg mean daily weight gain), and similar proportions of patients reached their target weight (80.0% and 82.3%, respectively). In a subsequent report, Touyz and colleagues (1987) described obtaining a mean daily weight gain of 0.16 kg with a program that was even more flexible than their original one.

Overall, it seems from these studies that the traditional operant weight restoration programs advocated in the 1960s and 1970s may have been unnecessarily cumbersome, rigid, and restrictive.

Drug Treatment

Various drugs have been investigated as treatments for AN, the majority of studies focusing on their effect on rate of weight gain. The drugs studied are as follows:

- Antidepressant drugs (amitriptyline, clomipramine, fluoxetine, lithium)
- Antipsychotics (pimozide, sulpiride)
- Others (cyproheptadine, tetrahydrocannabinol, clonidine, cisapride)

The findings of individual studies will not be described since, with just one exception, no statistically significant differences emerged. The one significant difference (favoring cyproheptadine) was modest in clinical terms (Halmi et al., 1986).

These studies have had various limitations (Attia et al., 1998). First, with few exceptions, they have had small sample sizes (generally fewer than 25 patients in total); second, they have often used low doses of the drug in question; and third, they have typically involved inpatients who have also been participating in a multicomponent weight restoration program. Although all three of these limitations have militated against detecting a drug effect, the consistency with which negative findings have been obtained suggests that drug treatment does not enhance inpatient weight restoration.

There has been controlled study of drug treatment following weight restoration (i.e., using a "relapse prevention" design). In this study, 35 patients with AN were randomly assigned to fluoxetine ($N =$ 16) or placebo ($N = 19$) after weight gain in the hospital (Kaye et al., in press). They were then followed as outpatients for 1 year. The great majority of those on placebo did poorly and dropped out of treatment (84%), whereas this was true of 37% of those on fluoxetine. Many methodological problems complicate the interpretation of this study, but its findings are of potential importance given the high rate of relapse following inpatient weight restoration. This said, a retrospective controlled study of the influence of fluoxetine on the course of patients following hospitalization revealed no evidence of a beneficial effect (Strober et al., 1997).

Family Therapy

Dysfunctional family relationships have been implicated in the development and maintenance of AN (Vandereycken, in press), and family therapy enjoys considerable clinical popularity, particularly with adolescent patients. Family therapy is the most studied of the psychological treatments for AN.

The combination of individual and family therapy has been evaluated in two studies from St. George's Hospital. In the first, the combination was compared with dietary advice (coupled with four 15-minute sessions with a psychotherapist) in 30 outpatients with AN (Hall & Crisp, 1987). Both groups improved substantially. The same combination of treatments was one condition (Group 2) in the large St. George's study mentioned earlier (Crisp et al., 1991). As noted, these patients also did well, their outcome at 1-year being comparable to that obtained with inpatient treatment followed by individual outpatient psychotherapy. Their outcome at 2-year follow-up was also favorable (Gowers et al., 1994). Both studies had adolescent and adult patients in their samples.

Family therapy on its own has been the subject of a series of studies from the Maudsley Hospital in London (Dare, in press). In the first study, family therapy was compared with individual supportive psychotherapy in 57 patients who had received inpatient weight restoration as the initial phase of their treatment (Russell, Szmukler, Dare, & Eisler, 1987). These patients were divided into three groups prior to randomization based on two variables suspected of influencing prognosis: age at onset and duration of disorder. Thus, the study comprised three separate small RCTs (plus one on BN). The two psychological treatments lasted 1 year, and the average number of sessions attended was 11 and 16 in the family therapy and individual therapy conditions, respectively. For those AN patients with an early age of onset (before 19 years) and short duration of disorder (less than 3 years at presentation)—their average age at entry into the study was 16.6 years—family therapy was significantly more effective than individual psychotherapy both at posttreatment (Russell et al., 1987) and at 5-year follow-up (Eisler & Dare, 1997). In contrast, with patients with a later age of onset (after 19 years)—their average age at entry into the study was 27.7 years—the results favored individual supportive psychotherapy. Overall, outcome was relatively poor; for example, the mean posttreatment weight of the early-onset–short-duration group was 86% of average body weight, and that of the later-onset group was 76% of average body weight.

Subsequent research by the Maudsley group has focused on the patient group that responded preferentially to family therapy, namely, adolescents with AN. It has studied family therapy as an entire outpatient-based treatment rather than as a treatment following an initial period in the hospital, and it has concentrated on evaluating two different methods of implementing family therapy. One has involved the entire family being seen together ("conjoint family therapy"), while the other involves the parents being seen as a couple but separately from their daughter ("separated family therapy"). In a pilot study involving 18 patients treated over 6 months (le Grange et al., 1992) and in a larger trial involving 40 patients treated over 1 year (Eisler & Dare, 2000), the two treatments were found to be largely comparable in their effects, with many patients responding well. In the larger study, the mean posttreatment BMI was 18.5, with 76% of those who received separated family therapy achieving 85% average body weight, compared with 47% of those who received conjoint family therapy ($p = .06$). A more fine-grained analysis suggested that conjoint family therapy had a greater effect than separated family therapy on general psychiatric symptoms, but this finding must be viewed with caution since the differences were small and there was no adjustment for multiple statistical testing. The two treatments had equivalent effects on measures of family functioning, but with families in which there were high levels of criticism, separated family therapy was more effective.

There has been one other controlled study of family therapy. Robin, Siegel, and Moye (1995) compared behavioral family therapy with ego-oriented individual therapy in a sample of 22 adolescent girls who had developed AN within the previous 12 months. Like the patients studied more recently by the Maudsley group, such patients would be expected to have a good outcome. The two treatments were conducted on an outpatient basis for a period of 12 to 18 months and were combined with dietary advice. (Eight patients were briefly hospitalized at the outset of the study to ensure that they started at 80% or more of target weight.) The family therapy consisted of parental control over eating, cognitive restructuring, problem solving, and communication training. The individual therapy emphasized building ego strength, adolescent autonomy, and insight. It should be noted that the parents of patients in the individual therapy condition met separately with the therapist on a bimonthly basis making the treatment somewhat similar to "separated family therapy." While both treatments were successful at restoring body weight (the mean posttreatment BMIs in the two conditions were 20.1 and 19.0, respectively), family therapy was superior to individual therapy at both posttreatment and 1-year follow-up. In all other respects, the treatments were comparable in their effects (although due to the modest sample size, the study was vulnerable to Type II error). Unfortunately, it is not possible to tell from this study whether the superiority of the family therapy condition was due to its cognitive behavioral orientation or more generally to an advantage of conjoint family therapy.

Cognitive Behavior Therapy

As described above, cognitive behavior therapy (CBT) has been extensively investigated as a treatment for BN, and there is strong evidence supporting its use. With little modification, the theory on which CBT is based, the cognitive behavioral theory of the maintenance of BN (Fairburn et al., 1986; Fairburn, 1997a), applies equally well to the maintenance of AN. In particular, the core mechanisms that maintain AN are likely to be very similar to those operating in BN (Fairburn, 1997a). It is therefore reasonable to expect that CBT, suitably adapted, would be a useful treatment for AN (Vitousek, in press).

In practice, there has been little empirical work on CBT for AN. Two small controlled trials have been published, both of which involved brief forms of CBT. Both focused on the treatment of adult patients. In the first, Channon, De Silva, Helmsley, and Perkins (1989) compared individual outpatient CBT with strictly behavioral treatment and a control treatment that was eclectic in nature and focused mainly on weight restoration and monitoring. No between-treatment differences were found, but the sample size of only eight patients per condition meant that the study was seriously underpowered. In the second study, by Serfaty, Turkington, Heap, Ledsham, and Jolley (1999), 35 patients fulfilling a broad definition of AN were randomized to 20 weekly sessions of CBT ($N = 25$) or dietary counseling ($N = 10$). Two patients dropped out of CBT, compared to all 10 of those allocated to dietary counseling. On a variety of indices, the patients in the CBT condition improved, although they remained significantly underweight at 6 months postentry (mean BMI = 17.8). From these two studies, it is impossible to assess the true value of CBT.

There is one other study of possible relevance to the effects of CBT. Treasure and colleagues (1995) evaluated the effects of a simple behavioral treatment (components of which form part of CBT) with "cognitive analytic therapy," which "integrates psychodynamic factors with behavioural ones and focuses on interpersonal and transference issues" (p. 365). The patients were older patients with AN (mean age 25 years) who would be presumed to have a relatively poor prognosis. Both treatments were administered on an outpatient basis and involved 20 weekly sessions. Thirty patients entered the study, and ten from each condition completed treatment (i.e., there was a 33% dropout rate). Both groups of treatment completers gained weight, with 40% and 50%, respectively, reaching 85% average body weight. Their mean posttreatment BMIs were 17.2 and 18.2, respectively. There were no differential treatment effects, but this is not surprising given the small sample size. The question that arises from this study is whether full CBT would be any more effective than a simple behavioral treatment of the type that these investigators studied.

Summary

Research Implications

The dropout rate from outpatient treatment for AN is high. Clinical experience suggests that few of these patients are likely to be treatment responders. The response rates reported in most trials, which are generally based on treatment completers, inflate the true response rate since they ignore those who dropped out. Improved methods are needed for engaging and retaining patients in treatment.

The research on treatment outcome in AN contrasts sharply with the quantity and quality of studies of BN discussed earlier. This unsatisfactory state of affairs is probably attributable in part to the low incidence of the disorder, and in part to the clinical and methodological difficulties inherent in studying the treatment of AN. Nevertheless, there is an urgent need for good studies of the treatment of the disorder using designs and the measures of the type successfully employed in research on BN. These studies will have to involve collaboration across multiple treatment centers in view of the rarity of the disorder. As matters stand, it is virtually impossible to construct evidence-based clinical recommendations regarding treatment.

In many countries, the majority of patients with AN are managed exclusively on an outpatient basis. Systematic research is needed on the advantages and disadvantages of inpatient, day-patient treatment, and outpatient treatment.

Clinical Implications

Clinical experience and research evidence support the use of family therapy in the treatment of adolescents with AN. The method most extensively studied involves parent-directed refeeding of the patient; support for the two parents; and support for the patient in gradually taking back control over her life (Eisler & Dare, 2000). This can be done with the family seen together or with the parents and patient being seen apart. Other permutations are also possible, but they have yet to be evaluated. There is also interest in treating groups of families together (Scholz & Asen, 2001). On the other hand, it must not be forgotten that it has not been adequately established that family therapy has a specific beneficial effect. Further comparisons of family therapy with appropriate alternative treatments are warranted.

There are good reasons to think that, given its utility in the treatment of BN, CBT might benefit patients with AN. This has yet to be determined. CBT might be particularly well suited to the treatment of adult patients with AN for whom family therapy appears not be indicated (Russell et al., 1987).

It is well known that inpatient treatment comprising dietary counseling and behavioral elements can effectively restore body weight in most cases of AN. It is now clear that the behavioral component of hospital treatment can be simpler and much less restrictive than the regimes commonly advocated in the 1960s and 1970s (Touyz & Beumont, 1997). On the other hand, there is no reason to think that drug treatment enhances the rate of weight regain in the hospital. Indeed, at present, there is no specific role for pharmacotherapy in the treatment of AN.

BINGE-EATING DISORDER

Binge-eating disorder (BED) is characterized by recurrent episodes of binge eating in the absence of the extreme methods of weight control seen in BN. Thus, there is no regular purging and no overexercising, nor is there extreme and rigid dieting. Rather, the binge eating occurs against a background of a general tendency to overeat. The disorder is accompanied by concerns about shape and weight that are similar to those seen in BN (Wilfley, Schwartz, Spurrell, & Fairburn, 2000). Like BN, BED is associated with shame and self-recrimination and some degree of psychosocial impairment.

The prevalence of BED in the general population is 1.5 to 2.0%, (Bruce & Agras, 1992; Gotestam & Agras, 1995), a figure similar to that of BN. BED differs from BN in a number of important respects. BED appears to affect an older age group than BN, many patients being in their 40s. Male cases are not uncommon in BED (Spitzer et al., 1993), whereas BN predominantly afflicts women. Unlike BN, BED is also significantly associated with obesity (Bruce & Agras, 1992; Striegel-Moore, Wilfley, Pike, Dohm, & Fairburn, 2000). As in BN, comorbid psychiatric disorders are common. As many as 75% of BED patients report a lifetime history of a psychiatric disorder, over half having suffered from MDD, and in some studies, 20% of the patients were diagnosed with current MDD (Wilfley, Friedman, et al., 2000; Yanovski, Nelson, Dubbert, & Spitzer, 1993).

Research has focused not only on adaptations of pharmacological and psychological treatments for BN, but also on behavioral weight loss interventions for obesity.

Pharmacological Treatments

Appetite Suppressant Medication

Appetite suppressants are a logical class of drug to evaluate in the treatment of BED given the obvious overeating and association with obesity. In an 8-week, double-blind, placebo-controlled evaluation of d-fenfluramine (Stunkard, Berkowitz, Tanrikut, Reiss, & Young, 1996), 50 obese patients with BED participated in a 4-week placebo washout phase. Twenty-two patients improved to the point where they no longer met criteria for BED. The remaining 28 were randomized to d-fenfluramine or placebo. Three patients dropped out of the drug treatment, one from placebo. Analyses of the data from the 12 patients in each group who completed the 8-week treatment showed that d-fenfluramine was significantly more effective than placebo in reducing binge eating. No other statistically significant differences were found on a variety of measures including body weight. The strong placebo response is noteworthy. Stunkard et al. (1996) pointed out that Alger, Schwalberg, Bigaouette, Michalek, and Howard (1991) reported a 68% decrease in binge eating in their placebo patients. (The subsequent finding that fenfluramine is associated with cardiac valvular insufficiency led to its withdrawal from the market in September 1997; Jick, 2000).

Antidepressant Medication: Tricyclic Antidepressants

Two studies have evaluated the effects of desipramine. Using a 12-week, double-blind design, McCann and Agras (1990) compared desipramine ($N = 10$) with a pill placebo ($N = 13$) in the absence of any counseling regarding nutrition, weight loss, or psychological concerns. The average dose of desipramine was 188 mg/day. The desipramine resulted in a mean reduction in binge eating of 63%, whereas there was a 16% increase in binge eating in the placebo condition. The remission rates were 60% and 15%, respectively. The active drug was associated with a significant reduction in hunger ratings and increased dietary restraint, although there was no significant weight loss. Discontinuation of the drug after the 12-week treatment produced rapid relapse.

A second study by the Stanford group evaluated the effects of a trial of desipramine (285 mg/day) during the last 6 months of a 9-month cognitive behavioral treatment for binge eating and weight loss in obese BED patients (Agras, Telch, et al., 1994). The participants were 108 women with a BMI of 27 or more. The drug failed to improve on either the reduction of binge eating or weight loss at posttreatment. Consistent with previous findings, desipramine significantly reduced disinhibition and hunger ratings as measured by the Stunkard and Messick (1985) Eating Inventory.

Imipramine was tested in two small studies. Alger et al. (1991) compared imipramine (200 mg/day) with a pill placebo in obese binge eaters in an 8-week study of 41 obese binge eaters and 28 patients who met *DSM-III-R* criteria for bulimia nervosa. Clinical samples of obese binge eaters overlap with the diagnosis of BED but may not meet all of the provisional research diagnostic criteria. Imipramine was not significantly superior to placebo in reducing the frequency of binge eating. In the second study, Laederach-Hofmann et al. (1999) randomly assigned 31 obese BED patients to either a low dose of imipramine (75 mg/day) or pill placebo with concurrent diet counseling and psychological support over an 8-week period. All patients continued to receive diet counseling and psychological support for 6 months following the discontinuation of medication after 8 weeks. Imipramine resulted in significantly greater reduction in binge frequency and weight loss than placebo at posttreatment and 32-week follow-up. Only one patient in each condition dropped out of treatment.

Antidepressant Medication: Selective Serotonin Reuptake Inhibitors (SSRIs)

Four controlled studies have evaluated the effects of an SSRI. Marcus et al. (1990) evaluated the effectiveness over 52 weeks of fluoxetine (60 mg/day) versus a pill placebo in a double-blind study of obese binge eaters ($N = 22$) and non-binge eaters ($N = 23$). The fluoxetine treatment resulted in a significantly greater weight loss but reduced neither binge eating nor depressed mood in the binge eaters.

Two studies have evaluated the use of fluvoxamine. The de Zwaan and Mitchell (1992) study compared fluvoxamine (100 mg/day) with a pill placebo in BED patients who were concurrently treated with either CBT or dietary management. There was no evidence for any effect of the fluvoxamine on binge eating. All treatment groups showed a modest and comparable weight loss during treatment, followed by weight regain at 1-year follow-up. In a second study 85 obese BED patients were randomized to the drug (mean dose = 265 mg/day) or pill placebo for a period of 9 weeks (Hudson et al., 1998). Posttreatment results showed that fluvoxamine drug was significantly superior to placebo in reducing binge eating over the course of the study using a randomized regression analysis. The remission rates were 45% and 24% for completers in the two conditions. However, there was no significant difference between fluvoxamine and pill placebo for either binge-eating frequency or depression in intent-to-treat analyses of response categories (i.e., remission, marked improvement, moderate response, no response). There was a significantly higher dropout rate in the fluvoxamine condition (31%) versus placebo (10%).

McElroy et al. (2000) compared sertraline with a pill placebo in a small 6-week study of 34 BED patients, 8 of whom withdrew from treatment. The active drug resulted in a significantly more rapid reduction in binge eating than the placebo condition. The remission rates were 39% and 13% for sertraline and placebo, respectively.

Conclusions

The findings on antidepressant medication are mixed at best. Five of the studies reviewed here failed to show the superiority of the active drug in comparison with a pill placebo. This pattern contrasts sharply with that of the BN literature, where, as detailed earlier in this chapter, antidepressant medication has been shown to be consistently more effective than placebo in the short term.

Specialized Psychological Treatments

Cognitive Behavioral Therapy

CBT has also been evaluated as a treatment for BED. Given the success of CBT with BN, it is not surprising that this approach has been adapted for treating patients with BED.

The first controlled study evaluated 10 weekly sessions of group CBT compared with a waiting-list (WL) control group in 44 patients who reported recurrent binge eating without purging (Telch, Agras, Rossiter, Wilfley, & Kenardy, 1990). The selection criteria closely resemble what *DSM-IV* subsequently designated as BED. The average BMI of these patients was 32.6, with a range of 22.2–42.6. At posttreatment, CBT patients who completed the treatment program showed a mean reduction in binge-eating episodes of 94%, with a 79% remission rate over the last week of therapy. Replication of the same CBT treatment with the WL controls produced similar results, namely, a mean reduction of 85% and a remission rate of 73%. A 10-week follow-up revealed significant relapse in patients treated with CBT, although binge-eating frequency was still below pretreatment levels.

A second Stanford study evaluated the effects of 12 weekly group sessions of CBT versus a waiting-list condition in 40 obese patients with BED (Agras et al., 1995). The treatment used in the Telch et al. (1990) study was modified to include a systematic exercise program plus education in choosing low-fat foods as a means of controlling weight. CBT resulted in an 84% reduction in mean frequency of binge eating, with a 55% remission rate. The corresponding outcomes for the WL condition were 8% and 9%. Weight remained unchanged in CBT but increased by 4.1 kg in the WL group.

A third study by the same group of investigators randomized 46 individuals with BED to 12 weeks of the same group CBT treatment or a waiting-list control condition (Eldredge et al., 1997). Responders went on to a behavioral weight loss protocol, while nonresponders received an additional 12 sessions of CBT focused on their remaining problems. The dropout rate was 19% for CBT and 20% for the wait-list control condition. CBT proved significantly more effective in reducing the frequency of binge-eating days at posttreatment. Extended CBT for the nonresponders was associated with further reductions in binge eating, with 43% of the initial nonresponders no longer meeting BED criteria by the end of the second phase of CBT. There was little incremental value to continuing beyond the 20th session of CBT. The absence of a control condition makes it impossible to attribute this trend to CBT.

Two studies have compared CBT with interpersonal psychotherapy (Wilfley et al., 1993; Wilfley et al., 2001) and are discussed in the next section. Suffice it to note here that neither study revealed any difference between these two forms of specialized psychological therapy across a wide range of measures.

CBT has also been compared with behavioral weight loss (BWL) treatment. Wing and Fairburn (1995) compared an adaptation of CBT for BN with a behavioral weight loss treatment (BWL) and a delayed treatment condition (DT) in a sample of 115 BED patients. Both treatments lasted 6 months and were administered on a one-to-one basis. Publication of the results of this well-designed study has been limited to a brief abstract. It suggests that at posttreatment, both CBT and BWL produced significantly greater reductions in days on which binge eating occurred during the previous month than DT. Unlike CBT, BWL also resulted in substantial weight loss. A fuller report on this study is awaited.

The results of a second study of group CBT versus BWL, using a more complicated experimental design (Agras et al., 1994), is discussed below.

In a related study, Nauta, Hospers, Kok, and Jansen (2000) compared a form of cognitive therapy (CT) with behavioral treatment (BT) in the treatment of 37 overweight or obese BED patients. The CT, administered in 15 weekly group sessions, was a derivative of Beck's (1976) treatment, in which the primary focus was on identifying and challenging "dysfunctional cognitions about shape, weight, eating, dieting or negative self-schemas" (p. 445). BT was aimed at developing healthy, regular eating patterns; increasing exercise; and restricting caloric consumption to a range of 1,500 and 1,800 kcal a day. The dropout rate was a low number of 3 patients in each group. The two treatments produced comparable reductions in binge eating at posttreatment in intent-to-treat analyses. However, at 6-month follow-up, the abstinence rate in the CT group (86%) was significantly higher than in the BT group (44%). CT also resulted in greater improvement in dysfunctional concerns about shape, weight, and eating and in self-esteem than BT. Although BT produced greater weight loss at posttreatment than CT, there was no difference at follow-up because of rapid weight regain in the BT patients.

Interpersonal Psychotherapy

Wilfley et al. (1993) studied the efficacy of a group adaptation of the IPT treatment, originally applied to BN by Fairburn et al. (1991), in a sample of 56 patients. The comparison treatments were CBT, as noted above, and a waiting-list control (WL) condition. At the 16-week posttreatment assessment, IPT resulted in a 71% reduction in the number of days binged with a remission rate of 44%. The comparable figures for CBT were 48% and 28%, and for the WL condition, they were 10% and 0%. Both IPT and CBT were significantly more effective than the WL condition, but they did not differ from each other. The same pattern held true for disinhibited eating, as measured by the Stunkard and Messick (1985) Eating Inventory, and by measures of self-esteem and depression. IPT had an attrition rate of 11% compared with 33% in CBT, although this difference was not statistically significant. The two therapies did not differ from each other at 1-year follow-up. Patients showed a significant increase in binge eating over follow-up, although the rates remained below pretreatment levels.

Wilfley and her colleagues (2001) completed a second comparison of group CBT and IPT in the largest controlled study to date. The sample consisted of 162 overweight or obese men and women who met the *DSM-IV* criteria for BED and whose weight ranged from a BMI of 27 to 48. Treatment involved 20 sessions of group CBT or IPT. Comprehensive and rigorous assessment of treatment effects, including the use of the EDE, was completed at follow-ups of 4, 8, and 12 months. Integrity checks revealed that both therapies were administered faithfully in accordance with their specifications. Ratings of nonspecific features of the therapies (e.g., empathy of the therapist) were highly positive and did not differ across treatments.

The dropout rates were 9.9% and 8.6% for CBT and IPT, respectively. An impressive 82% of patients completed all three follow-up assessments. Using intent-to-treat analyses, posttreatment abstinence rates were 79% for CBT and 73% for IPT. At 12-month follow-up, the abstinence rates were 59% and 62%. Both therapies produced significant reductions in concerns about shape, weight, and eating as measured by the EDE, as well as in psychiatric symptoms. Both treatments were also associated with a statistically significant but clinically small reduction in BMI, the most weight loss occurring in patients who had ceased binge eating at posttreatment. The two treatments did not differ in their effects on any variable at any time point except with respect to dietary restraint at posttreatment. Despite the clinically important changes in binge eating and associated psychopathology, the absence of some form of control or comparison condition precludes drawing definitive conclusions about the specific efficacy of either CBT or IPT.

Wilfley, Friedman, et al. (2000) also conducted a detailed analysis of the comorbid psychopathology of BED patients in this treatment outcome study. Despite the relatively large sample, few significant findings emerged. The presence of Axis I disorders was unrelated to the severity of the eating disorder at baseline. Nor did it predict outcome at posttreatment or follow-up. Axis II psychopathology, however, was significantly related to severity of binge eating at baseline. The presence of cluster B personality disorders predicted treatment outcome at 1-year follow-up, but not at the end of treatment.

Finally, group IPT has been evaluated as a treatment for those BED patients who failed to respond to CBT (Agras et al., 1995). Nonresponders to group CBT were given an additional 12 sessions of IPT delivered in a group format. Results showed that the secondary treatment produced no further improvement in binge eating or weight loss.

Conclusions

The research on CBT and IPT has included the most rigorously controlled studies of the treatment of BED to date. Comprehensive and valid assessment using the EDE and conservative intent-to-treat analyses of outcome has shown clinically significant improvement in binge eating and associated eating disorders at both posttreatment and follow-up. The abstinence rates in the best controlled of these studies (Wilfley et al., 2001) were substantially higher than those obtained in BN (e.g., Agras, Walsh, et al., 2000).

In marked contrast to studies of BN (Agras, Walsh, et al., 2000; Fairburn, Jones, et al., 1993), CBT and IPT for BED appear to produce virtually identical results at all time points across all measures of binge-eating and eating-disorder psychopathology (Wilfley et al., 1993, 2001). This latter finding is part of a broader pattern of nonspecificity in treatment response in BED.

Neither CBT nor IPT produce clinically significant weight loss despite reductions in binge eating, although some data indicate that cessation of binge eating is associated with the greater weight loss.

Both CBT and IPT are significantly more effective than wait-list controls. However, neither of these specialized therapies has been shown to be superior to a credible comparison treatment that controls for nonspecific therapeutic influences. The lack of such studies is all the more telling, given the evidence of nonspecific treatment effects and the high placebo response rate in drug studies. Research has failed to identify reliable predictors of treatment outcome.

Behavioral Weight Loss Treatments

Behavioral weight loss (BWL) programs have also been used to treat binge eating in overweight and obese BED patients. This form of treatment focuses on restricting caloric intake, improving nutrition, and increasing physical activity.

Moderate Caloric Restriction

As noted above, Marcus et al. (1995) found that both BWL and CBT produced striking and equal reductions in binge eating in obese BED patients. Similarly, Nauta et al. (2000) showed that a group BWL program resulted in improvement in binge eating comparable to that of a cognitive treatment aimed at binge eating. In this study, however, a 6-month follow-up indicated that the cognitive treatment was superior because it produced continued improvement in abstinence for binge eating.

Using an additive experimental design, Agras et al. (1994) compared a 9-month behavioral weight loss program (BWL) with the two alternative treatments: One was an initial 3-month CBT treatment aimed at reducing binge eating, followed by the weight control program (CBT/BWL); the other was a combined CBT and behavioral weight loss program, supplemented by the addition of desipramine over the last 6 months of treatment (CBT/BWL/D), as noted earlier. Although the CBT treatment produced significantly greater reduction in binge eating at the 12-week stage, there were no significant differences among the three treatments at the end of 9 months on either binge-eating frequency or weight loss. At posttreatment, 41% in the CBT/BWL/D treatment, 37% in the CBT/BWL treatment, and 19% in the BWL treatment had ceased binge eating. Weight losses for these three treatments were 6.0 kg, 1.6 kg, and 3.7 kg, respectively. Although patients who ceased binge eating lost more weight than their counterparts who did not at the 3- and 6-month assessments, this difference had disappeared by the end of treatment. Wilfley et al. (2001) similarly found that obese binge eaters who stop binge eating lost more weight than those who did not.

In contrast to studies of CBT and IPT for BED, assessment of eating-disorder psychopathology in most studies of BWL has been problematic. For example, most studies have relied on the Binge Eating Scale [BES] (Gormally, Black, Daston, & Rardin, 1982), which does not assess binge-eating frequency and has low convergence with the interview-based EDE (Greeno, Marcus, & Wing, 1995). Nonetheless, these studies have consistently shown that BWL reduces binge eating. Porzelius, Houston, Smith, Arfken, and Fisher (1995) found no significant differences on BES scores between BWL and a group CBT program designed to reduce binge-eating treatment at posttreatment and 1-year follow-up.

BWL has also resulted in improvements in measures of depression (Gladis et al., 1998; Sherwood, Jeffery, & Wing, 1999; Yanovski, Gormally, Lesser, Gwirtsman, & Yanovski, 1994). Foster, Wadden, Kendall, Stunkard, and Vogt (1996) showed that BWL produced improvement in depressive symptoms at 1-year follow-up despite total weight regain, although other research has indicated that depression returns commensurate with weight regain (Wadden, Stunkard, & Liebschutz, 1988).

BWL produces significant weight loss in obese BED patients, at least in the short term (Agras et al., 1994; Marcus et al., 1995; Nauta et al., 2000). Most studies have shown that obese binge eaters and obese non-binge eaters respond equally well to BWL treatment in terms of short-term weight loss (Gladis et al., 1998; Sherwood et al., 1999), whereas others have found that comorbid BED results in a less favorable outcome (Yanovski, Gormally, et al., 1994).

Severe Caloric Restriction

Reduction of dietary restraint is an important goal of CBT for BN (Fairburn et al., 1993). Extrapolating from these findings, several clinical investigators have warned against using treatments involving either moderate or severe caloric restriction in obese BED patients on the grounds that they might encourage binge eating (e.g., Garner & Wooley, 1991). The findings from the three studies summarized in the preceding section fail to support this prediction as it applies to moderate caloric restriction. The research on the effects of very-low-calorie diets (VLCD) similarly provides no support for this assertion.

Telch and Agras (1993) identified binge eating in 20 obese patients who participated in a combined VLCD and behavioral weight loss program for obesity. The patients are very likely to have met the criteria for BED. During the 3 months of the VLCD, the frequency of binge eating declined substantially. Over the course of a subsequent 9-month phase of refeeding and behavioral treatment, the frequency of binge eating began to return to its baseline level but was no different from its rate of occurrence in those obese patients who had not reported binge eating prior to treatment. In a study of obese women with ($N = 21$) and without ($N = 17$) BED, Yanovski and Sebring (1994) found that a VLCD treatment resulted in significant reduction in the frequency and severity of binge eating by the end of treatment.

Conclusions

In general, the methodology of studies of BWL has not been as rigorous as that of research on the specialized therapies of CBT and IPT. One consistent problem has been the failure to use state-of-the-art assessment of eating-disorder psychopathology such as the EDE. A second limitation is the lack of long-term follow-up. Treatment-induced weight loss is inexorably regained over follow-up, and the impact of this relapse in weight control on BED and associated psychopathology remains to be adequately studied.

Available evidence shows that the results of BWL are comparable to those of specialized therapies in reducing binge eating and associated eating-disorder psychopathology. Despite warnings to the contrary (Garner & Wooley, 1991), there is no evidence to date that the dietary restriction that is an integral part of BWL either initiates or exacerbates binge eating (Howard & Porzelius, 1999; National Task Force, 2000). The probable explanation for these findings is that BED patients differ from those with BN. In BN, binge eating represents periodic breakdowns in otherwise excessive dietary control. BED patients, however, show little dietary restriction between binge-eating episodes (Yanovski & Sebring, 1994). Moreover, in marked contrast to BN, binge eating precedes dieting in over 50% of obese binge eaters (Mussell et al., 1995; Wilson, Nonas, & Rosenblum, 1993).

BWL appears to have similar results in producing weight loss in both obese BED and obese non-BED patients, at least in the short term. As in the treatment of obesity as a whole, the challenge is to develop methods for maintaining the weight lost during treatment.

Less Intensive Treatments

Self-Help Strategies

As in the treatment of BN, a cognitive behavioral self-help treatment may be a cost-effective alternative to full CBT. Carter and Fairburn (1998) compared a pure self-help treatment (PSH), in which BED subjects were mailed a self-help book (Fairburn, 1995) and advised to follow its recommendations, with one in which they also received up to eight, 25-minute supportive sessions (guided self-help, or GSH). There were 24 participants in each condition. The therapist's role was to encourage the patients to follow the advice in the self-help book (which was a direct translation of full CBT). A primary aim of this study was to evaluate self-help as it would be used in primary-care settings or in the general community. Thus, the guided self-help treatment was conducted by nonspecialist therapists with no formal clinical qualifications. Treatment lasted 12 weeks. Both treatments were compared with a delayed-treatment control condition (DT). Wait-list control patients were randomized at 12 weeks to one of the two treatment conditions and were included in the longer term comparisons of the two self-help groups. Patients were followed up for 6 months.

The two interventions produced significant and lasting improvements in binge eating. The remission rates for PSH and GSH were 43% and 50%, respectively, in intent-to-treat analyses. Both were superior to the control group but were similar to one another in reducing binge-eating frequency and general psychopathology over the 12 weeks. Binge-eating results for the full sample across the 9 months of the study, however, favored guided self-help. Patients who demonstrated more knowledge of the manual's psychoeducational material at posttreatment fared better at 6-month follow-up.

Loeb, Wilson, Gilbert, and Labouvie (2000) compared guided and unguided use of the Fairburn (1995) self-help manual in a randomized trial with 40 female binge eaters, 83% of whom met diagnostic criteria for BED. In contrast to the Carter and Fairburn (1998) study, these experimental conditions were designed to mimic the two least intensive interventions in a stepped-care-based specialty treatment setting. The guided-self-help (GSH) therapists were well-experienced in the treatment of eating disorders. In addition, patients in the unguided-self-help (USH) condition maintained regular contact with the clinic by mailing weekly self-monitoring forms. If records revealed major problems or if no records were received, participants were telephoned. Over the 3 months, both the USH and the GSH groups experienced significant reductions in binge-eating frequency, shape and weight concerns, other symptoms of eating-related psychopathology, and general psychopathology. In intent-to-treat analyses, binge-eating remission rates were 30% for USH and 50% for GSH. Similar to the results obtained by Carter and Fairburn (1998), the GSH condition was superior to USH in reducing binge eating and its associated symptomatology, such as dietary restraint. A limitation of this study is the lack of adequate long-term follow-up.

Psychoeducation in Groups

Little is known about psychoeducation for BED. In the sole controlled trial, 61 women with BED were randomized to one of three 8-week group interventions or to a waiting-list control condition (WL) (Peterson et al., 1998). The three active treatments all consisted of psychoeducation plus group discussion. In the therapist-led condition, a specialty therapist led both components. In the partial self-help condition, the psychoeducational component was administered by videotape followed by a therapist-led discussion. In the full self-help condition, the psychoeducational videotape was followed by a group-led discussion. The three treatments were all superior to the control condition but did not differ from each other. The abstinence rates were 69%, 68%, and 87%, respectively. Definitive conclusions about the value of psychoeducation for BED must await additional research.

Summary

Research Implications

Research on the treatment of BED is at an early stage. Sample sizes in most studies have been small. Other methodological shortcomings include limited assessment of outcome. Assessment of binge eating and associated eating-disorder psychopathology is typically limited. It has been a common practice in these drug studies to assess binge eating for a period of no more than the preceding week. Assessment using a comprehensive and valid measure of BED, such as the EDE, which also covers a more extensive 4-week period, is a research priority. The lack of long-term evaluation is a major problem, especially given the high rate of spontaneous remission in a study of the natural course of BED (Fairburn et al., 2000).

No treatment has proved differentially effective. In view of this nonspecificity in treatment response, future comparative outcome studies need to control for nonspecific therapeutic influences and the passage of time in the short and long term.

Clinical Implications

Based on current research, the recommended treatment of most overweight or obese BED patients is BWL (Gladis et al., 1998; Wilson & Fairburn, 2000). First, it appears to be as effective as specialized therapies for BED (CBT and IPT) in reducing binge eating and other eating-disorder psychopathology. Second, it produces weight loss, at least in the short term. Third, it is more disseminable than either CBT or IPT because it does not require the same professional training and expertise. BWL can be administered by a wider range of different health care professionals.

GSH, using a cognitive behavioral self-help program, can also be recommended as a less costly and more efficient treatment than CBT or IPT. Initial results with GSH are promising and encourage future studies with larger samples and longer follow-ups. BED patients who do not respond to BWL or GSH should be referred for more intensive treatment with either CBT or IPT.

Evidence on antidepressant medication is mixed at best. These drugs cannot be recommended as the first treatment for BED, although they may prove useful in treating serious psychiatric comorbidity in specific cases.

CLINICAL UTILITY OF RESEARCH FINDINGS

This chapter is based on the findings of randomized control trials (RCTs). Critics of RCTs have questioned their relevance to clinical practice, arguing that they do not reflect psychological therapy as it is implemented in the field (Seligman, 1995). This skepticism about the clinical value of RCTs may partly explain why CBT has not been adopted more widely by practitioners (Crow, Mussell, Peterson, Knopke, & Mitchell, 1999; Wilson, 1999).

RCTs are designed to establish the causal effect of a specific treatment under controlled conditions. These investigations, in which it is essential to establish internal validity by eliminating alternative explanations of the results, are now commonly referred to as *efficacy studies*. Of course, we also need so-called effectiveness studies to evaluate external validity, or the generalizability of the findings of efficacy studies to diverse settings; therapists with varying degrees of experience and expertise; and heterogeneous patient groups. RCTs can—and should—be adapted to investigate questions of clinical utility as Jacobson and Christensen (1996) argued.

A common objection to RCTs is that they allegedly select patients for one diagnosis only, using a large number of exclusion criteria, whereas in "real-world" clinical practice, patients have multiple problems (Seligman, 1995). The inclusion and exclusion criteria for patients vary from study to study. But even a cursory examination of the major RCTs on BN and BED will show that they include patients with a severe eating disorder, high rates of psychiatric comorbidity, and frequent histories of previously failed therapy (Wilson, 1998). In their quantitative review, Hay and Bacaltchuk (2000) concluded that the nature of RCTs of CBT "increases the generalizability of the findings, supporting the effectiveness as well as efficacy of [treatment]" (p. 11). One of the features of the RCTs that led them to this conclusion were the relatively low exclusion rate of patients.

An analysis by Mitchell, Maki, Adson, Ruskin, and Crow (1997) directly examined the selectivity of exclusion criteria in a number of RCTs on BN. These exclusion criteria were applied to a series of patients seeking treatment at a university-based clinic. Of the patients, 21.6% would have been excluded from 39% of the RCTs because of age (greater than 30 years); 16% from 32% of the studies because of weight (>110% of expected body weight); and 26% from 54% of the studies because of active psychotropic drug use.

Discussions of the limited external validity of RCTs often overlook the marked heterogeneity of clinical service settings to which research results are generalized. The crucial question in evaluating any research finding is how closely the study sample and methods (therapists and therapies) resemble the situation to which one wants to generalize (Kazdin & Wilson, 1978). Mitchell et al.'s (1997) sample of patients were treated in a specialty outpatient treatment clinic at the University of Minnesota. It can be argued that this hospital/facility clinic, well-known as a major clinical research center for eating disorders and substance abuse, might draw an unrepresentative sample of cases. Most practitioners, however, do not predominantly see BN patients who are drug- or alcohol-dependent, suicidal, or psychotic.

Studies of anxiety disorders have directly evaluated the application in routine clinical service settings of the same manual-based therapy that had been tested in RCTs (e.g., Franklin, Abramowitz, Kozak, Levitt, & Foa, 2000; Wade et al., 1998). The results, using the same measure of outcome as in the RCTs, were very similar. Research of this kind is needed with eating disorders. In the meantime, there is good reason to believe that the findings of RCTs have external validity and should guide clinical practice.

ACKNOWLEDGMENT CGF is grateful to the Wellcome Trust for their personal support.

References

Agras, W. S., Crow, S. J., Halmi, K. A., Mitchell, J. E., Wilson, G. T., & Kraemer, H. C. (2000). Outcome predictors for the cognitive-behavioral treatment of bulimia nervosa: Data from a multisite study. *American Journal of Psychiatry, 157*, 1302–1308.

Agras, W. S., Dorian, B., Kirkley, B. G., Arnow, B., & Bachman, J. (1987). Imipramine in the treatment of bulimia: A double-blind controlled study. *International Journal of Eating Disorders, 6*, 29–38.

Agras, W. S., & Kraemer, H. (1984). The treatment of anorexia nervosa: Do different treatments have different outcomes. In A. J. Stunkard & E. Stellar (Eds.), *Eating and its disorders* (pp. 193–208). New York: Raven Press.

Agras, W. S., Rossiter, E. M., Arnow, B., Schneider, J. A., Telch, C. F., Raeburn, S. D., Bruce, B., Perl, M., & Koran, L. M. (1992). Pharmacologic and cognitive-behavioral treatment for bulimia nervosa: A controlled comparison. *American Journal of Psychiatry, 149*, 82–87.

Agras, W. S., Rossiter, E. M., Arnow, B., Telch, C. F., Raeburn, S. D., Bruce, B., & Koran, L. (1994). One-year follow-up of psychosocial and pharmacologic treatments for bulimia nervosa. *Journal of Clinical Psychiatry, 55*, 179–183.

Agras, W. S., Schneider, J. A., Arnow, B., Raeburn, S. D., & Telch, C. F. (1989). Cognitive-behavioral and response-prevention treatments for bulimia nervosa. *Journal of Consulting and Clinical Psychology, 57*, 215–221.

Agras, W. S., Telch, C. F., Arnow, B., Eldredge, K., Detzer, M. J., Henderson, J., & Marnell, M. (1995). Does interpersonal therapy help patients with binge eating disorder who fail to respond to cognitive-behavioral therapy? *Journal of Consulting and Clinical Psychology, 63*, 356–360.

Agras, W. S., Telch, C. F., Arnow, B., Eldredge, K., Wilfley, D. E., Raeburn, S. D., Henderson, J., & Marnell, M. (1994). Weight loss, cognitive-behavioral, and desipramine treatments in binge eating disorder. An additive design. *Behavior Therapy, 25*, 209–224.

Agras, W. S., Walsh, B. T., Fairburn, C. G., Wilson, G. T., & Kraemer, H. C. (2000). A multicenter comparison of cognitive-behavioral therapy and interpersonal psychotherapy for bulimia nervosa. *Archives of General Psychiatry, 57*, 459–466.

Alger, S. A., Schwalberg, M. D., Bigaouette, J. M., Michalek, A. V., & Howard, L. J. (1991). Effect of tricyclic antidepressants and opiate agonist on binge-eating behavior in normal weight bulimic and obese, binge-eating subjects. *American Journal of Clinical Nutrition, 53*, 865–871.

American Psychiatric Association. (1987). *Diagnostic and statistical manual of mental disorders* (3rd ed., rev.). Washington, DC: Author.

American Psychiatric Association. (1994). *Diagnostic and statistical manual of mental disorders* (4th ed.). Washington, DC: Author.

Attia, E., Haiman, C., Walsh, B. T., & Flater, S. R. (1998). Does fluoxetine augment the inpatient treatment of anorexia nervosa? *American Journal of Psychiatry, 155*, 548–551.

Bachar, E., Latzer, Y., Kreitler, S., & Berry E. M. (1999). Empirical comparison of two psychological therapies. *Journal of Psychotherapy Practice and Research, 8*, 115–128.

Barlow, J., Blouin, J., Blouin, A., & Perez, E. (1988). Treatment of bulimia with desipramine: A double-blind crossover study. *Canadian Journal of Psychiatry, 33*, 129–133.

Beaumont, P. J. V., Russall, J. D., Touyz, S. W., Buckley, C., Lowinger, K., Talbot, P., & Johnson, G. F. S. (1997). Intensive nutritional counseling in bulimia nervosa: A role for supplementation with fluoxetine? *Australian and New Zealand Journal of Psychiatry, 31*, 514–524.

Beck, A. T. (1976). *Cognitive therapy and the emotional disorders*. New York: International Universities Press.

Blouin, A. G., Blouin, J. H., Perez, E. L., Bushnik, T., Zuro, C., & Mulder, E. (1988). Treatment of bulimia with fenfluramine and desipramine. *Journal of Clinical Psychopharmacology, 8*, 261–269.

Brody, M. L., Walsh, B. T., & Devlin, M. J. (1994). Binge eating disorder: Reliability and validity of a new diagnostic category. *Journal of Consulting and Clinical Psychology, 62*, 381–386.

Bruce, B., & Agras, W. S. (1992). Binge eating in females: A population-based investigation. *International Journal of Eating Disorders, 12*, 365–373.

Bushnell, J. A., Wells, J. E., McKenzie, J. M., Hornblow, A. R., Oakley-Browne, M. A., & Joyce, P. R. (1994). Bulimia comorbidity in the general population and in the clinic. *Psychological Medicine, 24*, 605–611.

Carter, J. C., & Fairburn, C. G. (1998). Cognitive-behavioral self-help for binge eating disorder: A controlled effectiveness study. *Journal of Consulting and Clinical Psychology, 66*, 616–623.

Channon, S., De Silva, P., Helmsley, D., & Perkins, R. (1989). A controlled trial of cognitive behavioural and behavioural treatment of anorexia nervosa. *Behaviour Research and Therapy, 27*, 529–535.

Coker, S., Vize, C., Wade, T., & Cooper, P. J. (1993). Patients with bulimia nervosa who fail to engage in cognitive behavior therapy. *International Journal of Eating Disorders, 13*, 35–40.

Cooper, P. J., & Steere, J. (1995). A comparison of two psychological treatments for bulimia nervosa: Implications for models of maintenance. *Behaviour Research and Therapy, 33*, 875–886.

Crisp, A. H., Norton, K., Gowers, S., Halek, C., Bowyer, C., Yeldham, D., Levett, G., & Bhat, A. (1991). A controlled study of the effect of therapies aimed at adolescent and family psychopathology in anorexia nervosa. *British Journal of Psychiatry, 159*, 325–333.

Crow, S. J., Mussell, M. P., Peterson, C. B., Knopke, A., & Mitchell, J. E. (1999). Prior treatment received by patients with bulimia nervosa. *International Journal of Eating Disorders, 25*, 39–44.

Dare, C., & Eisler, I. (in press). Family therapy in the treatment of anorexia nervosa and bulimia nervosa. In C. G. Fairburn & K. D. Brownell (Eds.), *Eating disorders and obesity: A comprehensive handbook* (2nd ed.). New York: Guilford Press.

Davis, R., McVey, G., Heinmaa, M., Rockert, W., & Kennedy, S. (1999). Sequencing of cognitive-behavioral treatments for bulimia nervosa. *International Journal of Eating Disorders, 25*, 361–374.

Davis, R., Olmsted, M. P., & Rockert, W. (1990). Brief group psychoeducation for bulimia nervosa. *Journal of Consulting and Clinical Psychology, 58*, 882–885.

Davis, R., Olmsted, M. P., & Rockert, W. (1992). Brief group psychoeducation for bulimia nervosa 2. *International Journal of Eating Disorders, 11*, 205–211.

Devlin, M. J., & Walsh, T. (1995). Medication treatment for eating disorders. *Journal of Mental Health, 4*, 459–469.

de Zwaan, M., & Mitchell, J. E. (1992). Binge eating in the obese: Special Section: Eating disorders. *Annals of Medicine, 24*, 303–308.

Eisler, I., & Dare, C. (1997). Family and individual therapy in anorexia nervosa: A 5-year follow-up. *Archives of General Psychiatry, 54*, 1025–1030.

Eisler, I., & Dare, C. (2000). Family therapy for adolescent anorexia nervosa: The results of a controlled comparison of two family interventions. *Journal of Child Psychology and Psychiatry, 41*, 727–736.

Eldredge, K. L., Agras, W. S., Arnow, B., Telch, C. F., Bell, S., Castonguay, L., & Marnell, M. (1997). The effects of extending cognitive-behavioral therapy for binge eating disorder among initial treatment nonresponders. *International Journal of Eating Disorders, 21*, 347–352.

Fairburn, C. G. (1981). A cognitive behavioural approach to the management of bulimia. *Psychological Medicine, 11*, 707–711.

Fairburn, C. G. (1985). Cognitive-behavioral treatment for bulimia. In D. M. Garner & P. E. Garfinkel (Eds.), *Handbook of psychotherapy for anorexia nervosa and bulimia* (pp.160–192). New York: Guilford Press.

Fairburn, C. G. (1995). *Overcoming binge eating*. New York: Guilford Press.

Fairburn, C. G. (1997a). Eating disorders. In D. M. Clark & C. G. Fairburn (Eds.), *The science and practice of cognitive behaviour therapy* (pp. 209–242). Oxford: Oxford University Press.

Fairburn, C. G. (1997b). Interpersonal psychotherapy for bulimia nervosa. In D. M. Garner & P. E. Garfinkel (Eds.), *Handbook of treatment for eating disorders* (pp. 278–294). New York: Guilford Press.

Fairburn, C. G., & Carter, J. C. (1997). Self-help and guided self-help for binge eating problems. In D. M. Garner & P. E. Garfinkel (Eds.), *Handbook of treatment for eating disorders* (pp. 494–500). New York: Guilford Press.

Fairburn, C. G., & Cooper, Z. (1993). The eating disorder examination. In C. G. Fairburn & G. T. Wilson (Eds.), *Binge eating: Nature, assessment, and treatment* (pp. 317–360). New York: Guilford Press.

Fairburn, C. G., Cooper, Z., Doll, H. A., Norman, P., & O'Connor, M. (2000). The natural course of bulimia nervosa and binge eating disorder in young women. *Archives of General Psychiatry, 57*, 659–665.

Fairburn, C. G., Hay, P. J., & Welch, S. L. (1993). Binge eating and bulimia nervosa: Distribution and determinants. In C. G. Fairburn & G. T. Wilson (Eds.), *Binge eating: Nature, assessment, and treatment* (pp. 123–143). New York: Guilford Press.

Fairburn, C. G., Jones, R., Peveler, R. C., Carr, S. J., Solomon, R. A., O'Connor, M. E., Burton, J., & Hope, R. A. (1991). Three psychological treatments for bulimia nervosa. *Archives of General Psychiatry, 48*, 463–469.

Fairburn, C. G., Jones, R., Peveler, R. C., Hope, R. A., & O'Connor, M. (1993). Psychotherapy and bulimia nervosa: The longer-term effects of interpersonal psychotherapy, behaviour therapy and cognitive behaviour therapy. *Archives of General Psychiatry, 50*, 419–428.

Fairburn, C. G., Kirk, J., O'Connor, M., & Cooper, P. J. (1986). A comparison of two psychological treatments for bulimia nervosa. *Behaviour Research and Therapy, 24*, 629–643.

Fairburn, C. G., Marcus, M. D., & Wilson, G. T. (1993). Cognitive behaviour therapy for binge eating and bulimia nervosa: A comprehensive treatment manual. In C. G. Fairburn & G. T. Wilson (Eds.), *Binge eating: Nature, assessment and treatment* (pp. 361–404). New York: Guilford Press.

Fairburn, C. G., Norman, P. A., Welch, S. L., O'Connor, M. E., Doll, H. A., & Peveler, R. C. (1995). A prospective study of outcome in bulimia nervosa and the long-term effects of three psychological treatments. *Archives of General Psychiatry, 52*, 304–312.

Fairburn, C. G., Peveler, R. C., Jones, R., Hope, R. A., & Doll, H. A. (1993). Predictors of twelve month outcome in bulimia nervosa and the influence of attitudes to shape and weight. *Journal of Consulting and Clinical Psychology, 61*, 696–698.

Fairburn, C. G., & Walsh, B. T. (in press). Atypical eating disorders (eating disorders not otherwise specified). In C. G. Fairburn & K. D. Brownell (Eds.), *Eating disorders and obesity: A comprehensive handbook* (2nd ed.). New York: Guilford Press.

Fichter, M. M., Leibl, K., Rief, W., Brunner, E., Schmidt-Auberger, S., & Engel, R. R. (1991). Fluoxetine versus placebo: A double-blind study with bulimic inpatients undergoing intensive psychotherapy. *Pharmacopsychiatry, 24*, 1–7.

Fluoxetine Bulimia Nervosa Collaborative Study Group. (1992). Fluoxetine in the treatment of bulimia nervosa: A multicenter, placebo-controlled, double-blind trial. *Archives of General Psychiatry, 49*, 139–147.

Foster, G. D., Wadden, T. A., Kendall, P. E., Stunkard, A., & Vogt, R. A. (1996). Psychological effects of weight loss and regain: A prospective evaluation. *Journal of Consulting and Clinical Psychology, 64*, 752–757.

Franklin, M. E., Abramowitz, J. S., Kozak, M. J., Levitt, J. T., & Foa, E. B. (2000). Effectiveness of exposure and ritual prevention for obsessive-compulsive disorder: Randomized compared with nonrandomized samples. *Journal of Consulting and Clinical Psychology, 68*, 594–602.

Freeman, C. P. L., Barry, F., Dunkeld-Turnbull, J., & Henderson, A. (1988). Controlled trial of psychotherapy for bulimia nervosa. *British Medical Journal, 296*, 521–525.

Garner, D. M., Olmsted, M. P., Bohr, Y., & Garfinkel, P. E. (1982). The eating attitudes test: Psychometric features and clinical correlates. *Psychological Medicine, 12*, 871–878.

Garner, D. M., Rockert, W., Davis, R., Garner, M. V., Olmsted, M. P., & Eagle, M. (1993). Comparison of cognitive-behavioral and supportive-expressive therapy for bulimia nervosa. *American Journal of Psychiatry, 150*, 37–46.

Garner, D. M., & Wooley, S. C. (1991). Confronting the failure of behavioral and dietary treatments for obesity. *Clinical Psychological Review, 11*, 729–790.

Gladis, M. M., Wadden, T. A., Vogt, R., Foster, G., Kuehnel, R. H., & Bartlett, S. J. (1998). Behavioral treatment of obese binge eaters: Do they need different care? *Journal of Psychosomatic Research, 44*, 375–384.

Goldbloom, D. S., Olmsted, M., Davis, R., Clewes, J., Heinmaa, M., Rockert, W., & Shaw, B. (1997). A randomized controlled trial of fluoxetine and cognitive behavioral therapy for bulimia nervosa. *Behaviour Research and Therapy, 35*, 803–811.

Goldstein, D. J., Wilson, M. G., Thompson, V. L., Potvin, J. H., Rampey, A. H., & the Fluoxetine Bulimia Nervosa Research Group. (1995). Long-term fluoxetine treatment of bulimia nervosa. *British Journal of Psychiatry, 166*, 660–666.

Gormally, J., Black, S., Daston, S., & Rardin, D. (1982). The assessment of binge eating severity among obese persons. *Addictive Behaviors, 7*, 47–55.

Gotestam, K. G., & Agras, W. S. (1995). General population-based epidemiological study of eating disorders in Norway. *International Journal of Eating Disorders, 18*, 119–126.

Gowers, S., Norton, K., Halek, C., & Crisp, A. H. (1994). Outcome of outpatient psychotherapy in a random allocation treatment study of anorexia nervosa. *International Journal of Eating Disorders, 15*, 165–178.

Greeno, C. G., Marcus, M. D., & Wing, R. R. (1995). Diagnosis of binge eating disorder: Discrepancies between a questionnaire and clinical interview. *International Journal of Eating Disorders, 17*, 153–160.

Hall, A., & Crisp, A. H. (1987). Brief psychotherapy in the treatment of anorexia nervosa. *British Journal of Psychiatry, 151*, 185–191.

Halmi, K. A., Eckert, E., LaDu, T. J., & Cohen, J. (1986). Anorexia nervosa: Treatment efficacy of cyproheptadine and amitriptyline. *Archives of General Psychiatry, 43*, 177–181.

Hay, P. J., & Bacaltchuk, J. (2000). Psychotherapy for bulimia nervosa and bingeing (Cochrane Review). In *The Cochrane Library*, Issue 4. Oxford: Update Software.

Hoek, H. W. (in press). Distribution of eating disorders. In C. G. Fairburn & K. D. Brownell (Eds.), *Eating disorders and obesity: A comprehensive handbook* (2nd ed.). New York: Guilford Press.

Horne, R. L., Ferguson, J. M., Pope, H. G., Hudson, J. I., Lineberry, C. G., Ascher, J., & Cato, A. (1988). Treatment of bulimia with bupropion: A multicenter controlled trial. *Journal of Clinical Psychiatry, 49*, 262–266.

Howard, C. E., & Porzelius, L. K. (1999). The role of dieting in binge eating disorder: Etiology and treatment implications. *Clinical Psychology Review, 19*, 25–44.

Hudson, J. I., McElroy, S. L., Raymond, N. C., Crow, S., Keck, P. E., Carter, W. P., Mitchell, J. E., Strakowski, S. M., Pope, H. l. G., Coleman, B. S., & Jonas, J. M. (1998). Fluvoxamine in the treatment of a binge-eating disorder: A multicenter placebo-controlled, double-blind trial. *American Journal of Psychiatry, 155*, 1756–1762.

Hughes, P. L., Wells, L. A., Cunningham, C. J., & Ilstrup, D. M. (1986). Treating bulimia with desipramine: A double-blind, placebo-controlled study. *Archives of General Psychiatry, 43*, 182–186.

Jacobson, N. S., & Christensen, A. (1996). Studying the effectiveness of psychotherapy: How well can clinical trials do the job? *American Psychologist, 51*, 1031–1039.

Jick, H. (2000). Heart valve disorders and appetite-suppressant drugs. *Journal of the American Medical Association, 283*, 1647–1778.

Kaye, W. H., Nagata, T., Weltzin, T. E., Hsu, G. L. K., Sokol, M. S., McConaha, C., Plotnicov, K. H., Weise, J., & Deep, D. (in press). Double-blind placebo-controlled administration of fluoxetine in restricting and restricting-purging-type anorexia nervosa. *Society of Biological Psychiatry.*

Kazdin, A. E., & Wilson, G. T. (1978). *Evaluation of behavior therapy: Issues, evidence, and research strategies*. Cambridge, MA: Ballinger.

Keller, M. B., Herzog, D. B., Lavori, P. W., Bradburn, I. S., & Mahoney, E. M. (1992). The naturalistic history of bulimia nervosa: Extraordinarily high rates of chronicity, relapse recurrence, and psychosocial morbidity. *International Journal of Eating Disorders, 12*, 1–10.

Kennedy, S. H., Goldbloom, D. S., Ralevski, E., Davis, C., D'Souza, J., & Lofchy, J. (1993). Is there a role for selective MAO-inhibitor therapy in bulimia nervosa? A placebo-controlled trial of brofaromine. *Journal of Clinical Psychopharmacology, 13*, 415–422.

Kennedy, S. H., Piran, N., Warsh, J. J., Prendergast, P., Mainprize, E., Whynot, C., & Garfinkel, P. E. (1988). A trial of isocarboxazid in the treatment of bulimia nervosa. *Journal of Clinical Psychopharmacology, 8*, 391–396.

Kirkley, B. G., Schneider, J. A., Agras, W. S., & Bachman, J. A. (1985). Comparison of two group treatments for bulimia. *Journal of Consulting and Clinical Psychology, 53,* 43–48.

Klerman, G. L., Weissman, M. M., Rounsaville, B. J., & Chevron, E. S. (1984). *Interpersonal Psychotherapy of depression.* New York: Basic Books.

Laederach-Hoffman, K., Graf, C., Horber, F., Lippuner, K., Lederer, S., Michel, R., & Schneider, M. (1999). Imipramine and diet counseling with psychological support in the treatment of obese binge eaters: A randomized, placebo-controlled double-blind study. *International Journal of Eating Disorders, 26,* 231–244.

Laessle, R. G., Beumont, P. J. V., Butow, P., Lennerts, W., O'Connor, M., Pirke, K. M., Touyz, S. W., & Waadi, S. (1991). A comparison of nutritional management with stress management in the treatment of bulimia nervosa. *British Journal of Psychiatry, 159,* 250–261.

le Grange, D., Eisler, I., Dare, C., & Russell, G. F. M. (1992). Evaluation of family treatments in adolescent anorexia nervosa: A pilot study. *International Journal of Eating Disorders, 12,* 347–358.

Leitenberg, H., & Rosen, J. C. (1985). Exposure plus response prevention treatment of bulimia. In D. M. Garner & P. E. Garfinkel (Eds.), *Handbook of psychotherapy for anorexia nervosa and bulimia* (pp. 193–209). New York: Guilford Press.

Leitenberg, H., Rosen, J. C., Wolf, J., Vara, L. S., Detzer, M. J., & Srebnik, D. (1994). Comparison of cognitive-behavior therapy and desipramine in the treatment of bulimia nervosa. *Behaviour Research and Therapy, 32,* 37–46.

LeLorier, J., Gregoire, G., Benhaddad, A., Lapierre, J., & Derderian, F. (1997). Discrepancies between meta-analyses and subsequent large randomized, controlled trials. *New England Journal of Medicine, 337,* 536–542.

Lilenfeld, L. R., Kaye, W. H., Greeno, C. G., Merikangas, K. R., Plotnicov, K., Pollice, C., Rao, R., Strober, M., Bulik, C. M., & Nagy, L. (1997). Psychiatric disorders in women and bulimia nervosa and their first-degree relatives: Effects of comorbid substance dependence. *International Journal of Eating Disorders, 22,* 253–264.

Loeb, K. L., Wilson, G. T., Gilbert, J. S., & Labouvie, E. (2000). Guided and unguided self-help for binge eating. *Behaviour Research and Therapy, 38,* 259–272.

Marcus, M. D., Wing, R. R., Ewing, L., Kern, E., Gooding, W., & McDermott, M. (1990). A double-blind, placebo-controlled trial of fluoxetine plus behavior modification in the treatment of obese binge eaters and non-binge eaters. *American Journal of Psychiatry, 147,* 876–881.

Marcus, M. D., Wing, R. R., & Fairburn, C. G. (1995). Cognitive behavioral treatment of binge eating vs. behavioral weight control on the treatment of binge eating disorder. *Annals of Behavioral Medicine, 17,* S090.

McCann, U. D., & Agras, W. S. (1990). Successful treatment of nonpurging bulimia nervosa with desipramine: A double-blind, placebo-controlled study. *American Journal of Psychiatry, 147,* 1509–1513.

McElroy, S. L., Casuto, L. S., Nelson, E. B., Lake, K. A., Soutullo, C. A., Keck, P. E., Jr., & Hudson, J. I. (2000). Placebo-controlled trial of sertraline in the treatment of binge eating disorder. *American Journal of Psychiatry, 157,* 1004–1006.

Mitchell, J. E., & de Zwaan, M. (1993). Pharmacological treatments of binge eating. In C. G. Fairburn & G. T. Wilson (Eds.), *Binge eating: Nature, assessment and treatment* (pp. 250–269). New York: Guilford Press.

Mitchell, J. E., Fletcher, L., Hanson, K., Mussell, M. P., Seim, H., Crosby, R., & Al-Banna, M. (2001). The relative efficacy of fluoxetine and manual-based self-help in the treatment of outpatients with bulimia nervosa. *Journal of Clinical Psychopharmacology, 21,* 298–304.

Mitchell, J. E., & Groat, R. (1984). A placebo-controlled, double-blind trial of amitriptyline in bulimia. *Journal of Clinical Psychopharmacology, 4,* 186–193.

Mitchell, J. E., Maki, D. D., Adson, D. E., Ruskin, B. S., & Crow, S. (1997). The selectivity of inclusion and exclusion criteria in bulimia nervosa treatment studies. *International Journal of Eating Disorders, 22,* 219–230.

Mitchell, J. E., Pyle, R. L., Eckert, E. D., Hatsukami, D., Pomeroy, C., & Zimmerman, R. (1989). Response to alternative antidepressants in imipramine nonresponders with bulimia nervosa. *Journal of Clinical Psychopharmacology, 9,* 291–293.

Mitchell, J. E., Pyle, R. L., Eckert, E. D., Hatsukami, D., Pomeroy, C., & Zimmerman, R. (1990). A comparison study of antidepressants and structured intensive group psychotherapy in the treatment of bulimia nervosa. *Archives of General Psychiatry, 47,* 149–157.

Mussell, M. P., Mitchell, J. E., Crosby, R. D., Fulkerson, J. A., Hoberman, H. M., & Romano, J. L. (2000). Commitment to treatment goals in prediction of group cognitive-behavioral therapy treatment outcome for women with bulimia nervosa. *Journal of Consulting and Clinical Psychology, 68,* 434–437.

Mussell, M. P., Mitchell, J. E., Weller, C. L., Raymond, N. C., Crow, S. J., & Crosby, R. D. (1995). Onset of binge eating, dieting, obesity, and mood disorders among subjects seeking treatment for binge eating disorder. *International Journal of Eating Disorders, 17,* 395–402.

National Task Force on the Prevention and Treatment of Obesity. (2000). Dieting and the development of eating disorders in overweight and obese adults. *Archives of Internal Medicine, 160,* 2581–2589.

Nauta, H., Hospers, H., Kok, G., & Jansen, A. (2000). A comparison between a cognitive and a behavioral treatment for obese binge eaters and obese non-binge eaters. *Behavior Therapy, 31,* 441–462.

Olmsted, M. P., Davis, R., Garner, D. M., Eagle, M., Rockert, W., & Irvine, M. J. (1991). Efficacy of a brief group psychoeducational intervention for bulimia nervosa. *Behaviour Research and Therapy, 29,* 71–84.

Peterson, C. B., Mitchell, J. E., Engbloom, S., Nugent, S., Mussell, M. P., & Miller, J. P. (1998). Group cognitive-behavioral treatment of binge eating disorder: A comparison of therapist-led versus self-help formats. *International Journal of Eating Disorders, 24,* 125–136.

Polivy, J., & Herman, C. P. (1993). Etiology of binge eating: Psychological mechanisms. In C. G. Fairburn & G. T. Wilson (Eds.), *Binge eating: Nature, assessment and treatment* (pp. 173–205). New York: Guilford Press.

Pope, H. G., Hudson, J. I., Jonas, J. M., & Yurgelun-Todd, D. (1983). Bulimia treated with imipramine: A placebo-controlled, double-blind study. *American Journal of Psychiatry, 140,* 554–558.

Pope, H. G., Hudson, J. I., Jonas, J. M., & Yurgelun-Todd, D. (1985). Antidepressant treatment of bulimia: A two-year follow-up study. *Journal of Clinical Psychopharmacology, 5,* 320–327.

Pope, H. G., Keck, P. E., McElroy, S. L., & Hudson, J. I. (1989). A placebo-controlled study of trazodone in bulimia nervosa. *Journal of Clinical Psychopharmacology, 9,* 254–259.

Porzelius, L. K., Houston, C., Smith, M., Arfken, C., & Fisher, E., Jr. (1995). Comparison of a standard behavioral weight loss treatment and a binge eating weight loss treatment. *Behavior Therapy, 26,* 119–134.

Pyle, R. L., Mitchell, J. E., Eckert, E. D., Hatsukami, D. K., Pomeroy, C., & Zimmerman, R. (1990). Maintenance treatment and 6-month outcome for bulimic patients who respond to initial treatment. *American Journal of Psychiatry, 147,* 871–875.

Robin, A. L., Siegel, P. T., & Moye, A. (1995). Family versus individual therapy for anorexia: Impact on family conflict. *International Journal of Eating Disorders, 17,* 313–322.

Rosen, B. (1979). A method of structured brief psychotherapy. *British Journal of Medical Psychology, 52,* 157–162.

Rossiter, E. M., Agras, W. S., Losch, M., & Telch, C. F. (1988). Dietary restraint of bulimic subjects following cognitive-behavioral or pharmacological treatment. *Behaviour Research and Therapy, 26,* 495–498.

Rossiter, E. M., Agras, W. S., Telch, C. F., & Schneider, J. A. (1993). Cluster B personality disorder characteristics predict outcome in the treatment of bulimia nervosa. *International Journal of Eating Disorders, 13,* 349–358.

Russell, G. F. M., Szmukler, G. I., Dare, C., & Eisler, I. (1987). An evaluation of family therapy in anorexia nervosa and bulimia nervosa. *Archives of General Psychiatry, 44,* 1047–1056.

Scholz, M., & Asen, E. (2001). Multiple family therapy with eating disordered adolescents: Concepts and preliminary results. *European Eating Disorders Review, 9,* 33–42.

Seligman, M. E. P. (1995). The effectiveness of psychotherapy. *American Psychologist, 50,* 965–974.

Serfaty, M. A., Turkington, D., Heap, M., Ledsham, L., & Jolley, E. (1999). Cognitive therapy versus dietary counselling in the outpatient treatment of anorexia nervosa: Effects of the treatment phase. *European Eating Disorders Review, 7,* 334–350.

Sherwood, N. E., Jeffery, R. W., & Wing, R. R. (1999). Binge status as a predictor of weight loss treatment outcome. *International Journal of Obesity, 23,* 485–593.

Spitzer, R. L., Yanovski, S., Wadden, T., Wing, R., Marcus, M. D., Stunkard, A., Devlin, M., Mitchell, J., Hasin, D., & Horne, R. L. (1993). Binge eating disorder: Its further validation in a multisite study. *International Journal of Eating Disorders, 13,* 137–154.

Striegel-Moore, R. H., Wilfley, D. E., Pike, K. M., Dohm, F. A., & Fairburn, C. G. (2000). Recurrent binge eating in black American women. *Archives of Family Medicine, 9,* 83–87.

Strober, M., Freeman, R., DeAntonio, M., Lampert, C., Diamond, J. (1997). Does adjunctive fluoxetine influence the post-hospital course of restrictor-type anorexia nervosa? A 24-month prospective, longitudinal follow up and comparison with historical controls. *Psychopharmacology Bulletin, 33,* 425–431.

Stunkard, A. J., Berkowitz, R., Tanrikut, C., Reiss, E., & Young, L. (1996). d-Fenfluramine treatment of binge eating disorder. *American Journal of Psychiatry, 153,* 1455–1459.

Stunkard, A. J., & Messick, S. (1985). The three-factor eating questionnaire to measure dietary restraint and hunger. *Journal of Psychosomatic Research, 29,* 71–83.

Telch, C. F., & Agras, W. S. (1993). The effects of a very low calorie diet on binge eating. *Behavior Therapy, 24,* 177–194.

Telch, C. F., Agras, W. S., Rossiter, E. M., Wilfley, D., & Kenardy, J. (1990). Group cognitive-behavioral treatment for the non-purging bulimic: An initial evaluation. *Journal of Consulting and Clinical Psychology, 58,* 629–635.

Thackwray, D. E., Smith, M. C., Bodfish, J. W., & Meyers, A. W. (1993). A comparison of behavioral and cognitive-behavioral interventions for bulimia nervosa. *Journal of Consulting and Clinical Psychology, 61,* 639–645.

Thiels, C., Schmidt, U., Treasure, J., Garthe, R., & Troop, N. (1998). Guided self-change for bulimia nervosa incorporating use of a self-care manual. *American Journal of Psychiatry, 155,* 947–953.

Touyz, S. W., & Beumont, P. J. V. (1997). Behavioral treatment to promote weight gain in anorexia nervosa. In D. M. Garner & P. E. Garfinkel (Eds.), *Handbook of treatment for eating disorders* (2nd ed., pp. 361–371). New York: Guilford Press.

Touyz, S. W., Beumont, P. J. V., & Dunn, S. M. (1987). Behaviour therapy in the management of patients with anorexia nervosa: A lenient, flexible approach. *Psychotherapy and Psychosomatics, 48,* 151–156.

Touyz, S. W., Beumont, P. J .V., Glaun, D., Philips, T., & Cowie, I. (1984). A comparison of lenient and strict operant conditional conditioning programmes in refeeding patients with anorexia nervosa. *British Journal of Psychiatry, 144,* 517–520.

Treasure, J., Schmidt, U., Troop, N., Tiller, J., Todd, G., Keilen, M., & Dodge, E. (1994). First step in managing bulimia nervosa: Controlled trial of therapeutic manual. *British Medical Journal, 308,* 686–689.

Treasure, J., Schmidt, U., Troop, N., Tiller, J., Todd, G., & Turnbull S. (1996). Sequential treatment for bulimia nervosa incorporating a self-care manual. *British Journal of Psychiatry, 168,* 94–98.

Treasure, J., Todd, G., Brolly, J., Nehmed, A., & Denman, F. (1995). A pilot study of a randomised trial of cognitive analytical therapy vs. educational behavioral therapy for adult anorexia nervosa. *Behaviour Research and Therapy, 33,* 363–367.

Vandereycken, W. (in press). History of anorexia nervosa and bulimia nervosa. In C. G. Fairburn & K. D. Brownell (Eds.), *Eating disorders and obesity: A comprehensive handbook* (2nd ed.). New York: Guilford Press.

Vandereycken, W., Kog, E., & Vanderlinden, J. (Eds.). (1989). *The family approach to eating disorders.* New York: PMA Publishing.

Vitousek, K. (in press). Cognitive behaviour therapy in the treatment of anorexia nervosa. In C. G. Fairburn & K. D. Brownell (Eds.), *Eating disorders and obesity: A comprehensive handbook* (2nd ed.). New York: Guilford Press.

Wadden, T. A., Stunkard, A. J., & Liebschutz, J. (1988). Three-year follow-up of the treatment of obesity by very low calorie diet, behavior therapy, and their combination. *Journal of Consulting and Clinical Psychology, 56,* 925–928.

Wade, W. A., Treat, T. A., & Stuart, G. L. (1998). Transporting an empirically supported treatment for panic disorder to a service clinic setting: A benchmarking strategy. *Journal of Consulting and Clinical Psychology, 66,* 231–239.

Walsh, B. T., Agras, W. S., Devlin, M. J., Fairburn, C. G., Wilson, G. T., Kahn, C., & Chally, M. K. (2000). Fluoxetine in bulimia nervosa following poor response to psychotherapy. *American Journal of Psychiatry, 157,* 1332–1333.

Walsh, B. T., Gladis, M., Roose, S. P., Stewart, J. W., Stetner, F., & Glassman, A. H. (1988). Phenelzine vs placebo in 50 patients with bulimia. *Archives of General Psychiatry, 45,* 471–475.

Walsh, B. T., Hadigan, C. M., Devlin, M. J., Gladis, M., & Roose, S. P. (1991). Long-term outcome of antidepressant treatment for bulimia nervosa. *American Journal of Psychiatry, 148,* 1206–1212.

Walsh, B. T., Wilson, G. T., Loeb, K. L., Devlin, M. J., Pike, K. M., Roose, S. P., Fleiss, J., & Waternaux, C. (1997). Medication and psychotherapy in the treatment of bulimia nervosa. *American Journal of Psychiatry, 154,* 523–531.

Whittal, M. L., Agras, W. S., & Gould, R. A. (1999). Bulimia nervosa: A meta-analysis of psychosocial and pharmacological treatments. *Behavior Therapy, 30,* 117–135.

Wilfley, D. E., Agras, W. S., Telch, C. F., Rossiter, E. M., Schneider, J. A., Cole, A. G., Sifford, L. A., & Raeburn, S. D. (1993). Group cognitive-behavioral therapy and group interpersonal psychotherapy for the nonpurging bulimic: A controlled comparison. *Journal of Consulting and Clinical Psychology, 61,* 296–305.

Wilfley, D. E., Friedman, M. A., Dounchis, J. Z., Stein, R. I., Welch, R., & Ball, S. A. (2000). Comorbid psychopathology in binge eating disorder: Relation to eating disorder severity at baseline and following treatment. *Journal of Consulting and Clinical Psychology, 68,* 296–305.

Wilfley, D. E., Schwartz, M. B., Spurrell, E. B., & Fairburn, C. G. (2000). Using the Eating Disorder Examination to identify the specific psychopathology of binge eating disorder. *International Journal of Eating Disorders, 27,* 259–269.

Wilfley, D. E., Welch, R. Robinson, Stein, R. I., Spurrell, E. B., Cohen, L. R., Ceylonese, B. E., Dounchis, Jennifer Zoler, Frank, M. A., Wiseman, C. V., & Matt, G. E. (2001). *A randomized comparison of group cognitive-behavioral therapy and group interpersonal psychotherapy for the treatment of binge eating disorder.* Unpublished manuscript, University of California, San Diego.

Wilson, G. T. (1993). Assessment of binge eating. In C. G. Fairburn & G. T. Wilson (Eds.), *Binge eating: Nature, assessment, and treatment* (pp. 227–249). New York: Guilford Press.

Wilson, G. T. (1998). Manual-based treatment and clinical practice. *Clinical Psychology: Science and Practice, 5,* 363–375.

Wilson, G. T. (1999). Cognitive behavior therapy for eating disorders: Progress and problems. *Behaviour Research and Therapy, 37,* 579–596.

Wilson, G. T., & Fairburn, C. G. (2000). The treatment of binge eating disorders. *European Eating Disorders Review, 8,* 351–354.

Wilson, G. T., Fairburn, C. G., & Agras, W. S. (1997). Cognitive-behavioral therapy for bulimia nervosa. In D. M. Garner & P. Garfinkel (Eds.), *Handbook of treatment for eating disorders* (pp. 67–93). New York: Guilford Press.

Wilson, G. T., Fairburn, C. G., Agras, W. S., Walsh, B. T., & Kraemer, H. (2001). *Cognitive behavior therapy for bulimia nervosa: Time course and mechanisms of change.* Unpublished manuscript. Rutgers University.

Wilson, G. T., Loeb, K. L., Walsh, B. T., Labouvie, E., Petkova, E., Liu, X., & Waternaux, C. (1999). Psychological versus pharmacological treatments of bulimia nervosa: Predictors and processes of change. *Journal of Consulting and Clinical Psychology, 67,* 451–459

Wilson, G. T., Nonas, C., & Rosenblum, G. D. (1993). Assessment of binge-eating in obese patients. *International Journal of Eating Disorders, 13,* 25–34.

Wilson, G. T., Vitousek, K., & Loeb, K. L. (2000). Stepped-care treatment for eating disorders. *Journal of Consulting and Clinical Psychology, 68,* 564–572.

Wolf, E. M., & Crowther, J. H. (1992). An evaluation of behavioral and cognitive-behavioral group interventions for the treatment of bulimia nervosa in women. *International Journal of Eating Disorders, 11,* 3–16.

Yanovski, S. Z., Gormally, J. F., Lesser, M. S., Gwirtsman, H. E., & Yanovski, J. A. (1994). Binge eating disorder affects outcome of comprehensive very-low-calorie diet treatment. *Obesity Research, 2,* 205–212.

Yanovski, S. Z., Nelson, J. E., Dubbert, B. K., & Spitzer, R. L. (1993). Association of binge eating disorder and psychiatric comorbidity in obese subjects. *American Journal of Psychiatry, 150,* 1472–1479.

Yanovski, S. Z., & Sebring, N. G. (1994). Recorded food intake of obese women with binge eating disorders before and after weight loss. *International Journal of Eating Disorders, 15,* 135–150.

23

Effective Treatments for Selected Sleep Disorders

Peter D. Nowell

Daniel J. Buysse

Charles Morin

Charles F. Reynolds III

David J. Kupfer

Nearly one third of adults report at least occasional insomnia within a 1-year time period, and up to 50% report insomnia during their lives. There is evidence that multiple psychological and medical consequences are associated with insomnia. In the fourth edition of the *Diagnostic and Statistical Manual of Mental Disorders* (*DSM-IV*; American Psychiatric Association [APA], 1994), insomnia is subcategorized: primary insomnia; insomnia related to another mental disorder; sleep disorder due to a general medical condition; and substance-induced sleep disorder, insomnia type. Benzodiazepines, zolpidem, and zaleplon are effective pharmacological agents, while melatonin, delta-sleep-inducing peptide (DSIP), and orexins are interesting experimental agents. Of the behavioral strategies, stimulus control, sleep restriction, relaxation, and cognitive behavioral therapy are effective.

INSOMNIA

In this chapter, we review the treatment literature concerning the fourth edition of the *Diagnostic and Statistical Manual of Mental Disorders* (*DSM-IV*; American Psychiatric Association [APA], 1994) insomnia disorders. We first present the prevalence of insomnia symptoms and the distress and impairments that are associated with them. We then discuss the *DSM-IV* diagnostic criteria that define specific insomnia disorders. We focus much of this chapter on the research methodology for insomnia and its relevance for interpreting the results of specific outcome studies. The clinical practice that emerges from these studies is best appreciated in relationship to the details of the research designs involved. This emphasis on how we identified and selected treatment studies and our discussion of clinical trial design will provide the reader with an appreciation of the complexity, as well as the limitations, behind summary findings such as "Medication is effective for the treatment of insomnia." The chapter concludes with treatment recommendations supported by the reviewed literature and a discussion of the possible direction of future research of insomnia disorders and their management.

Scope of Insomnia

One in three adults experiences some type of sleep problem. One in four reports at least occasional insomnia within a 1-year time period, and up to 50% of adults report insomnia sometime in their lives. Approximately 1 in 10 adults reports chronic insomnia, and 1 in 10 considers insomnia to be a serious problem (Ancoli-Israel & Roth, 1999; Foley et al., 1999;

Simon & Von Korff, 1997). Despite this prevalence, only a minority of patients with insomnia presents to health care providers specifically for their sleep complaint (Ancoli-Israel & Roth, 1999). Instead, between 10% and 20% of patients with insomnia use nonprescription drugs, aspirin, or alcohol for their sleep difficulties (Mellinger et al., 1985; Welstein et al., 1983). Prescription sleeping pills have been reported to be used by about 5% of the population, with about 0.5% of the population using them for over 1 year (Mellinger et al., 1985). The annual cost for the management of insomnia in the United States is estimated in the billions (Margolis, 1999; Stoller, 1994; Walsh & Engelhardt, 1999).

Demographic and Natural History of Insomnia

Insomnia complaints increase with age (Gallup Organization, 1991; Mellinger et al., 1985; Morin & Gramling, 1989). The annual incidence of insomnia among the elderly is estimated at 5% (Foley et al., 1999). Women report insomnia more than men (Karacan et al., 1983; Mellinger et al., 1985). Older men demonstrate more disrupted sleep on polysomnography (PSG) than do older women (Reynolds et al., 1986). Divorced, widowed, or separated individuals are more likely to report insomnia than are married individuals, and insomnia is reported more often in people of lower socioeconomic status than in those of upper socioeconomic status (Karacan et al., 1976; Karacan & Williams, 1983). In a prospective study of rural elderly subjects, approximately one in three reported either difficulty falling asleep, difficulty staying asleep, or early-morning awakening (Ganguli et al., 1996).

Transient symptoms of insomnia are reported more often than are persistent ones. However, prevalence estimates become complicated when insomnia syndromes are defined only by descriptions of duration such as acute insomnia or chronic insomnia. For example, a 7-year longitudinal study of young adults found that 15% reported occasional episodes of transient insomnia, 16% reported recurrent episodes of transient insomnia, and 9% reported chronic insomnia (Angst et al., 1989; Vollrath et al., 1989). It is unclear whether the recurrent forms of transient insomnia would be classified as acute or chronic in cross-sectional studies or surveys. Also, a boundary that separates acute insomnia from chronic insomnia has not been empirically demonstrated. Depending on the study or the classification scheme, this boundary may vary from 1 to several weeks. Many of the epidemiological and demographic data presented above most likely reflect the symptom of insomnia as it presents in various acute, recurrent, and chronic forms.

Longitudinal studies provide information on the evolution and stability of insomnia symptoms over time. Follow-up of young adult subjects over 2 to 7 years revealed that half of those with occasional episodes of transient insomnia had developed recurrent or persistent insomnia (Angst et al., 1989). In another study, most patients diagnosed with chronic insomnia continued to suffer from symptoms of insomnia 64 months later (Mendelson, 1995). In a third study, approximately 2 of 3 rural elderly subjects who reported insomnia symptoms at baseline continued to report them at 2-year follow-up (Ganguli et al., 1996). Efforts to subtype insomnia by sleep onset insomnia difficulties or sleep maintenance difficulties demonstrated little stability over time (Hohagen et al., 1994).

Morbidity and Comorbidity

In addition to the high prevalence of insomnia symptoms, there is evidence suggesting multiple psychological and medical consequences associated with insomnia. In general, patients report elevated levels of distress, anxiety, depression, and medical illness compared with asymptomatic individuals (Healey et al., 1981; Kuppermann et al., 1995; National Institute of Health, 1984; Roth & Ancoli-Israel, 1999; Schwartz et al., 1999; Zammit et al., 1999). Patients with insomnia more often receive elevated scores on self-report psychological inventories (Hauri & Fisher, 1986; Kales et al., 1983), and they have been shown to demonstrate higher cognitive arousal that interferes with sleep in some, but not all, studies (Haynes et al., 1985; Lichstein & Rosenthal, 1980). Patients with insomnia are at an increased risk for developing psychiatric disorders within a 1-year time period (Charon et al., 1989; Ford & Kamerow, 1989), and a comorbid psychiatric diagnosis is seen in the majority of patients complaining of insomnia (Jacobs et al., 1988; Tan et al., 1984). Chronic insomnia has been demonstrated to increase the risk of panic disorder and alcohol abuse (Weissman et al., 1997). In one study, poor sleepers in the navy received fewer promotions, remained at lower pay grades, had higher rates of attrition, and had more frequent hospitalizations than good sleepers in the navy (Johnson & Spinweber, 1983). Chronic insomnia has been reported to lead to deterioration of mood, motivation, attention, concentration, and level of energy. Interpersonal and occupational problems may develop as a result of concern with sleep, increased irritability, and poor concentration (Mendelson et al., 1984a, 1984b; Roth & Ancoli-Israel, 1999; Seidel et al., 1984; Stepanski et al., 1989).

Patients with insomnia demonstrate physiological correlates of high arousal, such as increased muscle tension and greater autonomic reactivity to stress (Bonnet & Arand, 2000; Haynes et al., 1985; Mendelson et al., 1984a), and they have an increase in stress-related illnesses such as headaches and gastrointestinal upset (Gislason & Almqvist, 1987; Moldofsky, 1989; Partinen, 1988; Vollrath et al., 1989; Whorwell et al., 1986). It has been suggested that such psychophysiological arousal comes to be associated with the patient's sleeping environment, and that this negative conditioning explains why patients with insomnia often sleep better in unexpected or unfamiliar sleep environments where these conditioned cues are absent. This is in contrast to subjects without insomnia, who tend to sleep more poorly in unfamiliar surroundings (Hauri & Fisher, 1986; Kales et al., 1983; Nowell et al., 1997a). However, negative conditioning has been difficult to demonstrate empirically (Edinger et al., 1997a, 1997b). It has been suggested that higher cognitive arousal during sleep may lead to alterations in information processing and memory that may be a risk factor for the development of chronic insomnia symptoms (Perlis et al., 1997). Despite reports of poor or limited sleep and of daytime fatigue, most patients with insomnia have not been shown to have excessive daytime sleepiness (Bonnet & Arand, 2000; Mendelson et al., 1984a; Seidel et al., 1984; Seidel & Dement, 1982; Stepanski et al., 2000; Sugarman et al., 1985).

In summary, the principal risk factors increasing insomnia prevalence include gender (female), older age, medical illness, psychiatric disorders, some personality traits (e.g., anxiety-prone, worrisome cognitive style) (Kales et al., 1976), and shift work. The consequences of untreated insomnia include decreased health and well-being; increased disabilities; increased area of health care services; increased absenteeism and accidents; and decreased job performance.

DSM-IV INSOMNIA DIAGNOSES

The preceding discussion focused on the symptoms of insomnia. One of the goals of psychiatric classifications has been to improve the reliability of diagnoses. Insomnia symptoms have been classified in different ways by several systems, such as the Diagnostic Classification of Sleep and Arousal Disorders (DCSAD; Association of Sleep Disorders Centers, 1979), the International Classification of Sleep Disorders (ICSD; Diagnostic Classification Steering Committee, Thorpy, 1990), and the International Classification of Diseases (ICD). In the *DSM-IV* (APA, 1994), the symptoms of insomnia have been combined with other symptoms to define syndromes grouped by presumed etiology. These diagnostic criteria have demonstrated moderate interrater reliability from unstructured diagnostic interviews (Buysse et al., 1994). The following overview describes these *DSM-IV* insomnia diagnoses.

The essential diagnostic feature of *primary insomnia* is a complaint of difficulty initiating or maintaining sleep or of nonrestorative sleep; the complaint lasts for at least 1 month and causes clinically significant distress or impairment in social, occupational, or other important areas of functioning. The disturbance in sleep does not occur exclusively during the course of another sleep disorder or mental disorder and is not due to the direct physiological effects of a substance or a general medical condition.

Insomnia related to another mental disorder describes insomnia that is judged to be related temporally and causally to another mental disorder. Because sleep disturbances are common features of other mental disorders, an additional diagnosis of insomnia related to another mental disorder is made only when the sleep disturbance is a predominant complaint and is sufficiently severe to warrant independent clinical attention. Most commonly, mood and anxiety disorders are considered when a chronic insomnia syndrome is being evaluated.

Sleep disorder due to a general medical condition, insomnia type, requires a prominent disturbance in sleep that is severe enough to warrant independent clinical attention and evidence from the history, physical examination, or laboratory findings that the sleep disturbance is the direct physiological consequence of a general medical condition. Most commonly, pain syndromes are considered when chronic insomnia is being evaluated.

Substance-induced sleep disorder, insomnia type, results from the direct physiological effects of a substance (e.g., a drug of abuse, a medication, or toxin exposure). This diagnosis should be made instead of a diagnosis of substance intoxication or substance withdrawal only when the symptoms are in excess of those usually associated with the intoxication or withdrawal syndrome and when the symptoms are sufficiently severe to warrant independent clinical attention. Most commonly, caffeine, nicotine, and alcohol are considered when chronic insomnia is being evaluated. The list of medications reported to cause insomnia is lengthy, but among the more common agents to be considered are antidepressant medications and stimulant medications. Dyssomnia not otherwise specified (NOS) describes insomnias that do not meet criteria for other specific *DSM-IV* dyssomnia diagnoses. Restless legs syndrome that results in insomnia would be diagnosed as dyssomnia NOS.

REVIEW OF EFFECTIVE TREATMENTS

Source of Evidence

The most rigorous evidence for treatment efficacy in chronic insomnia derives from well-designed clinical trials. Such trials would ideally include a prospective design, adequate sample sizes, reliable diagnostic methods, well-defined inclusion and exclusion criteria, randomized treatment assignment, placebo-controlled groups, and blinded assessments.

Establishing a Diagnosis

Reliable diagnostic methods and well-defined inclusion and exclusion criteria improve the internal validity of the trial. However, operationalizing such standards for patients with insomnia has varied widely across studies. The use of a structured psychiatric sleep disorders interview to assign *DSM-III-R* (APA Task Force on Laboratory Tests in Psychiatry, 1987) sleep diagnoses (Schramm et al., 1995) has been a step toward improving trial design, but no such instrument exists for *DSM-IV*. The *DSM-IV* field trial in insomnia delineated clinical factors contributing to the differential diagnosis of primary insomnia and insomnia related to a mental disorder (Nowell et al., 1997b).

Inclusion Criteria

Patients with clinically established insomnia diagnoses often, though not always, demonstrate disrupted continuity measures on a polysomnogram (PSG) (Coates et al., 1981; Mendelson et al., 1984a; Seidel et al., 1984; Sugarman et al., 1985). Patients with insomnia also demonstrate more variability in sleep measures than do patients without insomnia complaints (Frankel et al., 1976; Roehrs et al., 1985). Many treatment studies use the results of polysomnography as inclusion or exclusion criteria by "confirming" an insomnia diagnosis, by establishing a baseline "severity" for inclusion, or by documenting a different illness for the cause of the insomnia complaint (e.g., obstructive sleep apnea). However, none of the classification systems currently requires the results of polysomnography as a minimal criterion in establishing an insomnia diagnosis. Furthermore, the American Sleep Disorders Association has published practice guidelines addressing the role of PSG in the evaluation of insomnia (Reite et al., 1995). Essentially, polysomnography is not recommended in the clinical assessment of insomnia unless certain conditions are met, such as suspicion of a different primary sleep disorder as the cause of the insomnia symptom, an insomnia that follows an unusual treatment course, or treatment nonresponse. Consequently, while PSG may provide information that is potentially useful when evaluating insomnia (Coleman, 1982), it is not considered essential to establish or confirm a diagnosis. Its ability to document the severity of an insomnia disorder or to measure outcomes in chronic insomnia remains to be established despite its widespread use for these purposes.

Outcome Measures

There is a poorly defined relationship between subjective complaints of insomnia and objective measures of good and bad sleep (Akerstedt et al., 1994; Barnes et al., 1983; Buysse et al., 1989; Carskadon et al., 1976). Some researchers have suggested that alterations in the perception of sleep might be one of the primary deficits resulting in insomnia (Mendelson et al., 1984a). Accordingly, measures of subjective appraisals about sleep might be a more valid assessment of treatment effects than would polysomnographic changes in sleep. Moreover, studies with inclusion and exclusion criteria or outcome measures that rely solely on PSG variables may not generalize to studies with subjects who are defined by clinical measures alone. As a result, recent research has included both subjective and objective measures while emphasizing one or the other, depending on the study.

In addition to issues of subjective or objective outcome measures, little consensus exists as to which type of outcome measures will classify patients as "responders." Improved sleep efficiency, relief of subjective distress, reduced daytime impairment, or a combination of these (or other) measures may reflect treatment response. In general, studies have focused on sleep continuity measures and global subjective evaluations. Whether one obtains these outcome measures from the sleep laboratory or from actigraphy (ambulatory monitoring of sleep and wake states based on motion) adds additional complexities to the interpretation of treatment studies.

Control Groups

There is a large night-to-night variability in sleep measures in patients with insomnia (Frankel et al., 1976). Patients selected for extremes of continuity disturbance demonstrate improvement over time that reflects regression toward the mean rather than the effects of treatment (Roehrs et al., 1985). Even after taking extremes of selection into account, patients with insomnia tend to demonstrate improvement over time that has been explained as resulting from the demand characteristics of the experiment (Carr-Kaffashan & Woolfolk, 1979; Lacks et al., 1983; Steinmark & Borkovec, 1974). These effects can be seen in within-subject analysis of wait-list groups, sham treatment groups, and placebo groups (Elie et al., 1999). On one hand, these factors taken together suggest that valid control group and between-group comparisons are needed to isolate the effects of treatment from other factors. On the other hand, the improvements that result from nonspecific effects of treatment protocols such as self-monitoring or support tend to be modest in magnitude and not sustained relative to the chronicity of the disorder overall.

Treatment and the Course of Insomnia

A final issue in evaluating outcomes in chronic insomnia concerns the benefits of treatment in relationship to the natural history of the illness. Most studies have addressed an acute intervention and its immediate response, that is, several nights of medication and the resulting changes in sleep continuity on those nights. There is little information about acute interventions and their ability to produce sustained effects over time. For instance, what benefits from 1 month of treatment are expected to be maintained over a 1-year follow-up period? Likewise, few studies have assessed the benefits of maintenance interventions such as low-dose medication on a nightly basis for 1 year and its cumulative effects on insomnia. Usually, behavioral treatments are compared to acute, short-term medication trials. In general, such behavioral interventions have a more durable impact on outcome when the longitudinal course of the disorder is considered (Morin et al., 1999a); however, more studies are need to resolve the issue in more detail.

PHARMACOLOGICAL AGENTS

A wide variety of agents have been used for the treatment of insomnia (see Table 23.1). This review focuses on agents that are commonly used in the United States and that have been established as efficacious based on randomized, controlled clinical trials. Agents related to gamma-aminobutyric acid, antidepressants, tryptophan, antihistamines, delta-sleep-inducing peptide (DSIP), and melatonin are discussed. Agents such as benzodiazepines (Greenblatt, 1992), imidazopyridines, pyrazolopyrimidines, or cyclopyrrolones are believed to work via GABA modulation. These agents can be classified by receptor pharmacology, that is, specificity for the benzodiazepine receptor, or by pharmacokinetics (e.g., absorption, distribution, or metabolism).

Antidepressant agents studied in the treatment of primary insomnia have included imipramine, trimipramine, and trazodone. Their mechanism of action may include serotonin regulation, histamine regulation, alpha-adrenergic receptor action, or anticholin-

TABLE 23.1 Summary of Clinical Efficacy Trials in Chronic Insomnia

Intervention	*No. of Studies*	*Pooled* N	*Usual Dose (mg)*	*Dose Range (MG)*	*Duration Range (Days)*
Chloral hydrate	2	131	500	250–500	1–2
Delta peptide	1	16	25 nmol/Kg iv	N/A	3
Diphenhydramine	2	255	50	50	7–14
Doxepin (Hajak et al., 1996)	1	10	25	25–50	1
Estazolam	5	616	1 or 2	1–2	7–28
Flurazepam	22	1,372	15 or 30	15–30	2–28
Melatonin (Dawson et al., 1998; Hughes et al., 1998)	4	45	Not established	1 mg–75 mg/os	1–14
Midazolam	9	373	15	5–30	1–84
Oxazepam	6	219	15	15–50	1–11
Quazepam	10	446	15 or 30	15–60	3–14
Temazepam	9	540	30	7.5–30	3–84
Triazolam	24	2,801	0.25	0.125–1.0	1–35
Tryptophan	3	155	Not established	1–3 grams	6–28
Zolpidem (Dujardin et al., 1998)	48	789	5 or 10	1–20	14–28
Zopiclone	18	2,148	7.5	5–7.5	1–42
Zaleplon (Elie et al., 1999)	1	615	10	5–20	28
Behavioral[a]	33	1,324	5 hours	1–20 hours	1–16 weeks

[a]See text for specific interventions; time parameters based on Morin, Culbert, and Schwartz (1994).

ergic changes. Tryptophan is a dietary amino acid and a precursor of serotonin.

Antihistamines are available in many over-the-counter preparations and antagonize receptors for histamine, a modulator for wakefulness. Delta-sleep-inducing peptide has been isolated and used experimentally in sleep research, but its clinical applications remain to be further clarified. Melatonin is a naturally occurring hormone produced by the pineal gland, which has received considerable attention for its effects on circadian rhythms. Its effects on chronic insomnias unrelated to circadian disturbances have received less attention, though this has been improving in recent years (Mendelson, 1997; Roth & Richardson, 1997; Sack et al., 1997).

BEHAVIORAL INTERVENTIONS

Both nonspecific and specific behavioral treatments have been studied in patients with insomnia (Guilleminault et al., 1995).

Stimulus control therapy consists of a set of instructional procedures designed to curtail sleep-incompatible behaviors and to regulate sleep-wake schedules. This method targets both negative conditioning and circadian factors. These procedures are (Bootzin & Perlis, 1992).

1. Go to bed only when sleepy.
2. Use the bed and bedroom only for sleep and sex (i.e., no reading, television watching, eating, or working during the day or at night).
3. Get out of bed and go into another room whenever you are unable to sleep for 15 to 20 minutes, and return only when sleepy again.
4. Arise in the morning at the same time regardless of the amount of sleep during the previous night.
5. Do not nap during the day.

Sleep restriction therapy consists of prescribing an initial restricted duration of time at night during which a patient has an opportunity to attempt sleep. The amount of the restriction is determined from 2-

week sleep diaries. Once a patient's sleep becomes more efficient, then the allowable time in bed is increased gradually to allow for the greatest total amount of sleep time while preserving the newly achieved capacity for more efficient sleep (Spielman et al., 1987). This method uses the homeostatic regulation of sleep to allow a sleep debt to facilitate sleep initiation and maintenance.

Relaxation therapies are designed to alleviate somatic or cognitive arousal; they consist of techniques such as progressive muscular relaxation, autogenic training, and biofeedback (Freedman & Papsdorf, 1976; Hauri, 1981).

Sleep hygiene education is concerned with health practices such as diet, exercise, and substance use and with environmental factors such as light, noise, and temperature that may be either detrimental or beneficial to sleep (Borkovec & Fowles, 1973; Hauri, 1981).

Cognitive behavioral treatment for insomnia targets maladaptive cognitions that perpetuate insomnia. These behavioral interventions have been used as single interventions or, more typically, as combined or multimodal approaches (Morin et al., 1999a).

GENERAL METHODS OF LITERATURE REVIEW

A review of the published literature was conducted by MEDLINE for the period 1966–1995 for the first edition of this book. The medical subject heading (MeSH) "insomnia" restricted to "drug therapy" produced 1,291 citations. These 1,291 citations crossed, with "double-blind" and with "placebos," produced a final 215 citations in the English language that were further reviewed. Likewise, the MeSH "insomnia" restricted to "behavioral therapy" resulted in a final 116 citations in the English language that were further reviewed. The *Journal of Sleep Research* (not indexed in MEDLINE) was reviewed manually from Volume 1 to Volume 4, June 1995. Abstracts were not reviewed.

For the second edition of this volume, a review of the published literature was conducted by MEDLINE for the period 1995–July 2000. The medical subject heading (MeSH) has changed from "insomnia" to "sleep initiation and maintenance disorders." The search was "exploded" to include subterms and "focused" to restrict to articles primarily concerned with sleep initiation and maintenance disorders. The MeSH heading was restricted to "drug therapy," "human," and "English" and produced 134 citations. Likewise, the MeSH heading was restricted to "behavioral therapy" with similar restrictions to produce 24 citations. The *Journal of Sleep Research* is now indexed in MEDLINE. Abstracts were not reviewed.

The *DSM-IV* was published in 1994, and as a result, insomnia studies prior to its release used diagnostic criteria available at the time. Efforts to classify earlier studies by *DSM-IV* diagnoses revealed several problems. Inclusion criteria that failed to address daytime impairment or fatigue were difficult to classify as primary insomnia because the only remaining inclusion criterion for primary insomnia is "clinically significant distress." When subjects are drawn from university and community volunteers or from patients in institutionalized settings, the remaining criterion of "clinically significant" becomes more ambiguous. This ambiguity is compounded by differences that may exist between help-seeking patients with insomnia and non-help-seeking subjects with sleep difficulties (Stepanski et al., 1989). Another problem in classifying primary insomnia resulted from the lack of documentation in many studies regarding the method used to evaluate psychiatric disorders or substance use disorders. Likewise, there rarely was information to exclude circadian rhythm disorders in subjects with insomnia.

There were several difficulties in trying to classify insomnia related to another mental disorder. In studies of patients drawn from medically or psychiatrically ill populations, there was little documentation that clarified whether the insomnia syndrome was considered causally related to the primary illness and to what extent the insomnia complaint exceeded a threshold for sleep disturbance commonly associated with the primary illness. In many cases, insomnia appeared to be a symptom available for treatment that was part of the expected course of the illness. For example, studies of patients with depression and poor sleep seldom clarified what criteria were used to determine whether the insomnia difficulty was to be considered an independent sleep disorder.

Several problems emerged in trying to include or exclude studies based on research design. Randomized, double-blind, placebo-controlled trials were sought, but few studies clearly met all criteria. Double-blind conditions and placebo-controlled groups are difficult to provide, generally, in studies of behavioral interventions. The use of placebo controls may be easier to implement in pharmacological studies, but the actual degree of blinding achieved in studies of hypnotics may limit such design efforts (Morin et al., 1995). Wait-list control groups or control groups given "pseudo" or "partial" behavioral interventions may represent analogies to placebo-controlled conditions of hypnotic trials. However, strategies for behavioral interventions that would be equivalent to blinding or masking procedures remain to be investigated. To balance these design factors, we retained for review the medication studies that used a placebo control group and double-blinded evaluation and behavioral studies that used a waiting list or pseudobehavioral intervention for a control group. All studies used prospective designs.

Another difficulty in selecting adequate studies was interpreting a report of a positive finding. In general, time to fall asleep, time awake in bed, number of awakenings, total sleep time, global subjective report, and daytime impairment were considered measures of treatment response. However, most studies reported on one or another measure, and in many cases, one measure improved when another did not. Thus, studies with a positive result based on a reduced sleep latency may have had a negative result based on changes in total sleep time. Because there is no gold standard for determining treatment response, we considered the authors' report of positive treatment outcome the conclusion of the study. It should be noted, however, that the overwhelming reporting of positive outcomes, despite large variations in subject numbers, in inclusion and exclusion criteria, in outcome measures, and in definitions of response, raises the possibility of publication bias and reporting that enhances the apparent effects of treatment.

In addition to the primary references reviewed, there have been four meta-analyses and reviews of meta-analyses published since the first edition of this volume, as well as several focused consensus papers on practice guidelines. Two meta-analyses focused on medications, and two focused on behavioral treatment (Holbrook et al., 2000; Greenwood, 1995; Morin et al., 1999b; Murtagh & Nowell et al., 1997b). One consensus paper reviewed the efficacy and safety data for triazolam guidelines (Bunney et al., 1999). One practice guideline paper from the American Academy of Sleep Medicine focused on nonpharmacological treatment of chronic insomnia (Chesson et al., 1999). Another consensus paper from the National Heart, Lung, and Blood Institute focused on chronic insomnia in primary care (Walsh et al., 1999). Both meta-analyses for nonpharmacological interventions demonstrated effectiveness on outcomes of sleep onset latency and total sleep time by sleep diary measures. Effectiveness varied by type of intervention. Both meta-analyses for pharmacological interventions demonstrated efficacy on outcomes of total sleep time. However, they differed on whether medications demonstrated efficacy on sleep onset latency. The difference may be attributed to differences in methodologies. One analysis pooled benzodiazepines and zolpidem and limited the analysis to studies of *DSM-IV* primary insomnia in patients under the age of 65. The other examined benzodiazepines alone and included a broader definition of chronic insomnia in broader age groups. It is unclear to what extent diagnostic specificity (Dashevsky & Kramer, 1998) may be related to outcomes such as sleep onset latency relative to different interventions in adult versus elderly populations.

CONCLUSIONS

Table 23.1 summarizes the clinical efficacy trials for chronic insomnia. Given the limitations, what conclusions can be drawn regarding the effective treatments for *DSM-IV* insomnia diagnoses as supported by the available clinical trials?

1. *The subjective symptoms and objective signs of chronic insomnia respond to acute behavioral and pharmacological interventions*. Typically, both behavioral and pharmacological interventions reduce sleep onset by 15 to 30 minutes from pretreatment levels or close to an absolute duration of 30 minutes. The number of awakenings typically decreases to an absolute level of one to three per night. On average, both behavioral and pharmacological interventions increase total sleep time about 15 to 45 minutes, pharmacological agents acting more reliably in the short term and behavioral interventions producing more sustained effects. The majority of patients report improved sleep quality after treatment. While there is little support for choosing one medication over another based solely on efficacy, tailoring an agent with rapid-acting properties for sleep onset difficulties or a longer acting agent for sleep maintenance difficulties does have empirical support. Subjective measures,

taken as a whole, seem to correlate with the direction of objective measure, but the magnitude differs considerably and inconsistently.

2. *Effective pharmacological agents include benzodiazepines, zolpidem, and zupiclone. Effective behavioral interventions include stimulus control, sleep restriction, relaxation strategies, and cognitive behavioral therapy for acute management.* Of the medications, antihistamines and tryptophan have the least clear benefit, while melatonin and DSIP agents remain experimental. Of the behavioral strategies, sleep hygiene and paradoxical intention have the least clear benefit, while the remaining interventions provide acute beneficial effects, albeit less consistently than pharmacological agents.

Benzodiazepines, as a class, have been the most extensively studied hypnotic agents, both in terms of individual trials and in terms of patient numbers. In addition, benzodiazepines have been studied for more than 20 years with very different strategies. While the heterogeneity of trial design and outcome measures presents certain limits in combining findings to identify exactly what responds to treatment, this diversity can be useful in the sense that the vast majority of these studies (roughly 90%) report clinically significant results despite the heterogeneity of designs.

Zolpidem studies, while fewer in trial and patient numbers, have the advantage of being studied more recently with designs that have improved through development of strategies to evaluate benzodiazepines. As a result, zolpidem has been compared both to the gold standard of benzodiazepines and to placebo conditions. Most of the studies have also included subjective measures like sleep quality, sleep quantity, and daytime functioning, as well as objective measures such as polysomnography. These studies, despite a diversity of assessment instruments and definitions of response, have also reported positive responses in almost all cases.

Diphenhydramine is a common agent in over-the-counter sleep preparations, yet our literature search identified only one placebo-controlled, double-blind clinical trial for patients with chronic insomnia (Rickels et al., 1983) and none for hydroxazine, another antihistamine available in hospital formularies. Other antihistamine studies identified failed to use a placebo control, and the characterization of the insomnia syndromes made generalizability difficult (Kudo & Kurihara, 1990). While the study by Rickels et al. found support for the use of diphenhydramine at a 50-mg dose, additional well-designed trials would seem an important public health issue given the widespread availability of this agent.

Melatonin deserves mention because, unlike the other hypnotics reviewed, it is a naturally occurring hormone; because it affects circadian rhythms, which represent a potential mechanism of action distinct from the hypnotics; and because, like diphenhydramine, it is available in over-the-counter preparations. In evaluating the effects of melatonin, it is important to remember that the insomnia syndromes reviewed in this chapter are different from the sleep changes attributed to distinct disruptions of circadian systems such as shift work, jet lag, or delayed sleep phase syndrome. Our literature search identified two randomized, placebo-controlled clinical trials for patients with chronic insomnia (James et al., 1989; MacFarlane et al., 1991). Both trials used supraphysiological doses of melatonin, and the results are difficult to interpret in that some subjective measures, like total sleep time, worsened, while others, like sleep quality, improved. There were no objective improvements on polysomnography. The role of melatonin in poor sleep continues to be evaluated, with more promising results in types of insomnia not specified by the *DSM-IV* (e.g., patients with "deficient" melatonin levels, which predict a better response to melatonin replacement) (Garfinkel et al., 1995).

Morin et al. (1994), using sleep onset, maintenance, or mixed insomnia, performed a meta-analysis of nonpharmacological interventions that included stimulus control, sleep restriction therapy, relaxation therapies, and sleep hygiene education. The 59 treatment studies involved 2,102 patients. Psychological interventions averaging 5 hours of therapy time produced reliable changes in sleep latency and time awake after sleep onset. Stimulus control and sleep restriction were the most effective single-therapy procedures. After stimulus control and sleep restriction, relaxation was most effective for sleep onset reductions, and biofeedback was most effective for wake-after-sleep onset reductions. While our literature review focused on insomnia syndromes defined in *DSM-IV* and included only studies with control groups, generally we obtained similar results. A qualitative literature review makes summary conclusions more difficult without the support of quantitative methods such as meta-analysis to help make finer distinctions among treatments, such as discriminating stimulus control, sleep restriction therapy, and relaxation therapies from the less helpful sleep hygiene education and other behavioral approaches. Accordingly, we performed a quantitative review of the literature to evaluate the efficacy of benzodiazepines and zolpidem in chronic insomnia. The authors concluded that benzodiazepines and zolpidem produced reliable improvements in commonly measured parameters of sleep in patients with chronic primary insomnia. However, relative to the chronic and recurring course of insomnia, both the limited duration of the treatments studied and the lack of follow-up data from controlled trials (with the notable exception of Morin et al., 1999) represent challenges for developing evidence-based guidelines for the use of hypnotics in the management of chronic insomnia (Nowell et al., 1997b).

RECOMMENDATIONS

Identifying the disorder is the starting point in determining a treatment strategy for insomnia (Kupfer & Reynolds, 1997; Walsh, et al., 1999). Despite the prevalence of insomnia symptoms, insomnia remains relatively underdiagnosed and undertreated. Clinicians need basic knowledge of sleep medicine and need to recognize the importance of sleep-related symptoms in the delivery of general medical treatment. Patients need to be educated about the relevance of sleep disorders to their general health. A clinical history is the cornerstone of establishing an insomnia diagnosis and planning treatment. In addition to an initial clinical evaluation, procedures such as patient self-monitoring with a sleep diary, consultation with a sleep specialist, psychological testing, psychiatric evaluation, or polysomnography may provide more diagnostic and treatment information (Chesson et al., 2000; Sateia et al., 2000). Polysomnography is often not indicated for routine evaluation of the young patient with chronic insomnia. It remains to be more clearly determined whether PSG is routinely indicated in the elderly patient with insomnia (American Sleep Disorders Association, 1995; Reite et al., 1995; Vgontzas et al., 1995). In summary, basic knowledge of sleep medicine and a clinical history are generally sufficient to establish an insomnia diagnosis and to develop an effective treatment strategy. The chronic insomnias other than primary insomnia require treatment of the underlying illness (e.g., major depression). However, insomnia-specific treatment may still be necessary and useful to improve sleep (Currie et al., 2000; Dashevsky & Kramer, 1998; Lichstein et al., 2000).

Sleep hygiene, health habits, substance and medication use, beliefs and expectations about sleep, psychiatric and medical status, and provider preference all play a role in treatment planning. A sleep diary has an educational and a potential therapeutic role. The role of bibliotherapy or patient-directed education and treatment remains to be researched, although one trial provided promising results (Mimeault & Morin, 1999) another demonstrated superior outcomes for therapist involvement (Riedel et al., 1995).

Primary insomnia is best approached in a problem-solving format that unfolds over time as patients identify and modify various factors and track the effects on symptoms such as sleep quality and daytime impairment. Unfortunately, attempts to match patient variables to tailored treatments have not demonstrated robustly superior outcomes (Espie et al., 1989; Lilie & Lahmeyer, 1991; Sanavio, 1988). Nonetheless, it is still generally accepted that different patients with primary insomnia will require different treatment components. In general, a behavioral approach of stimulus control therapy, sleep restriction therapy, or cognitive behavioral therapy for insomnia would serve as a first-line intervention. A valuable component of cognitive behavioral treatment is conceptualizing primary insomnia as a chronic illness and working with patients to develop skills to manage symptom recurrence. A benzodiazepine or an imidazopyridine (e.g., zolpidem or zaleplon) may be used as an adjuvant intervention; however, there are inadequate data at this point concerning the risks and benefits of prescribing hypnotic medications for more than 4 weeks.

While dose effect studies are available for most of the medications discussed in this chapter, guidelines for each particular agent and particular patient demographics (e.g., the elderly, patients with liver dysfunction) should be directed toward standard pharmacology texts. As a rule, the lowest effective dose should be used. The efficacy of combined behavioral and pharmacological approaches as compared to single-intervention approaches has not been sufficiently addressed in the research literature. Moreover, the 4-week time frame for medication interventions requires empirical assessment because many patients are likely to have persistent symptoms and to require treatment for a longer term. While intermittent dosing strategies have been used to avoid chronic nightly exposure to benzodiazepines, our search identified only one randomized, placebo-controlled trial for patients with insomnia designed to evaluate an every-other-night regime (Scharf, 1993). This particular study used quazepam, which has a long half-life and makes generalizations to other agents difficult.

DIRECTIONS FOR THE FUTURE

Research is required regarding preventive strategies, maintenance treatments, long-term management strategies, multimodal behavioral interventions, and combined pharmacological and behavioral approaches. While studies of behavioral interventions have been more sensitive to long-term gains and follow-up assessments, longitudinal studies are greatly needed, especially for pharmacological interventions, given that the vast majority of medication trials have lasted less than 1 month. Substantial research is needed to relate specific diagnoses to differential treatment strategies (Bonnet & Arand, 1999). There has been a trend toward improved clinical trial design, but researchers need to be particularly sensitive to reliable diagnostic inclusion criteria for future clarification of this issue. The role of established agents used in novel ways (e.g., estrogens, Polo-Kantola et al., 1998; or bright light, Cooke et al., 1998; Guilleminault et al., 1995; Murphy & Campbell, 1996), and of novel agents such as orexins (Piper et al., 2000) or low-energy emission therapy (Pasche et al., 1996) or passive body heating (Dorsey et al., 1996) will be important in improving outcomes and also in clarifying etiologies and modifying factors in the initiation and maintenance of insomnia disorders. Consensus on which outcome variables constitute treatment response, relapse, and recurrence remains to be achieved. The role of multimodal or combined treatments needs further research (Hauri, 1997; Morin et al., 1999a; Riedel et al., 1998; Verbeek et al., 1999).

Efficacy is, of course, one of the most significant aspects in selecting a particular intervention and has been the organizing feature of this review. Side effects of treatment, however, present a major factor in addition to efficacy when choosing one intervention over another. Increases in postmarketing surveillance studies will be helpful in this regard (Ganzoni et al., 1995; Hajak & Bandelow, 1998). The basic concerns with benzodiazepines and zolpidem or zaleplon are daytime sedation; psychomotor effects such as memory disturbances and incoordination; tolerance, abuse, and dependence; and discontinuation syndromes ranging from rebound insomnia to withdrawal delirium and seizures. In general, high-potency benzodiazepines such as triazolam are associated with a greater risk of amnesic effects, and agents with a rapid onset of action such as diazepam are associated with a greater abuse potential. Likewise, higher doses and longer exposure to these agents increase the likelihood of tolerance, dependence, and discontinuation syndromes. However, these generalities are not without controversy. A detailed account is beyond the scope of this chapter, and the interested reader is referred to excellent reviews by Woods and Winger (1995a, 1995b).

Additional considerations include a multitude of other factors, including interaction with other illnesses and medications, ease of application, cost, consumer's preference, and applicability to special populations such as the elderly or the institutionalized. Health services research and outcome studies are needed to determine how well the interventions established in clinical trials perform in various settings, such as primary-care settings (Baillargeon et al., 1998) and sleep centers, or as implemented by various providers, such as family practitioners or sleep disorder specialists. This point is worth emphasizing because most patients with insomnia are seen in primary-care settings in which providers may be less likely to implement behavioral treatments. Thus, interventions developed in tertiary settings need to be transferred adequately to community settings in order to deliver optimal treatment to the majority of patients with insomnia. With all these issues, however, the principles outlined above, such as reliable diagnoses and adequate trial design, continue to be essential factors from which treatment and assessment decisions can be appropriately evaluated.

References

Akerstedt, T., Hume, K., Minors, D., & Waterhouse, J. (1994). The subjective meaning of good sleep, an intraindividual approach using the Karolinska Sleep Diary. *Perceptual and Motor Skills*, 79, 287–296.

American Psychiatric Association. (1987). *Diagnostic and statistical manual of mental disorders* (3rd ed.). Washington, DC: American Psychiatric Association.

American Psychiatric Association. (1994). *Diagnostic and statistical manual of mental disorders* (*DSM-IV*; 4th ed.). Washington, DC: Author.

American Sleep Disorders Association. (1995). Practice parameters for the use of polysomnography in the evaluation of insomnia: Standards of Practice Committee of the American Sleep Disorders Association. *Sleep, 18*, 55–57.

Ancoli-Israel, S., & Roth, T. (1999). Characteristics of insomnia in the United States: Results of the 1991 National Sleep Foundation Survey, 1. *Sleep, 22* (Suppl. 2), S347–S353.

Angst, J., Vollrath, M., Koch, R., & Dobler-Mikolam, A. (1989). The Zurich Study. 7. Insomnia: symptoms, classification and prevalence. *European Archives of Psychiatry and Clinical Neuroscience, 238*, 285–293.

APA Task Force on Laboratory Tests in Psychiatry. (1987). The dexamethasone suppression test: An overview of its current status in psychiatry. *American Journal of Psychiatry, 144*, 1253–1262.

Baillargeon, L., Demers, M., & Ladouceur, R. (1998). Stimulus-control: nonpharmacologic treatment for insomnia. *Canadian Family Physician, 44*, 73–79.

Barnes, R. F., Veith, R. C., Borson, S., Vershey, J., Raskind, M. A., & Halter, J. B. (1983). High levels of plasma catecholamines in dexamethasone-resistant depressed patients. *American Journal of Psychiatry, 140*, 1623–1625.

Bonnet, M. H., & Arand, D. L. (1999). The use of lorazepam TID for chronic insomnia. *International Clinical Psychopharmacology, 14*(2), 81–89.

Bonnet, M. H., & Arand, D. L. (2000). Activity, arousal, and the MSLT in patients with insomnia. *Sleep, 23*(2), 205–212.

Bootzin, R. R., & Perlis, M. L. (1992). Nonpharmacologic treatments of insomnia. [Review]. *Journal of Clinical Psychiatry*, 53(Suppl. 37–41).

Borkovec, T. D., & Fowles, D. C. (1973). Controlled investigation of the effects of progressive and hypnotic relaxation on insomnia. *Journal of Abnormal Psychology, 82*(1), 153–158.

Bunney, W. E., Jr., Azarnoff, D. L., Brown, B. W., Jr., Cancro, R., Gibbons, R. D., Gillin, J. C., Hullett, S., Killam, K. F., Kupfer, D. J., Krystal, J. H., Stolley, P. D., French, G. S., & Pope, A. M. (1999). Report of the Institute of Medicine Committee on the Efficacy and Safety of Halcion [see comments]. *Archives of General Psychiatry, 56*(4), 349–352.

Buysse, D. J., Reynolds, C. F., Hauri, P. J., Roth, T., Stepanski, E. J., Thorpy, M. J., Bixler, E. O., Kales, A., Manfredi, R. L., Vgontzas, A. N., Mesiano, D. A., Houck, P. R., & Kupfer, D. J. (1994). Diagnostic concordance for DSM-IV sleep disorders: A report from the APA/NIMH DSM-IV field trial. *American Journal of Psychiatry, 151*(9), 1351–1360.

Buysse, D. J., Reynolds, C. F., Monk, T. H., Berman, S. R., & Kupfer, D. J. (1989). The Pittsburgh Sleep Quality Index (PSQI): A new instrument for psychiatric research and practice. *Psychiatry Research, 28*, 193–213.

Carr-Kaffashan, L., & Woolfolk, R. L. (1979). Active and placebo effects in treatment of moderate and severe insomnia. *Journal of Consulting and Clinical Psychology, 47*(6), 1072–1080.

Carskadon, M. A., Dement, W. C., Mitler, M. M., Guilleminault, C., Zarcone, V. P., & Spiegel, R. (1976). Self-reports versus sleep laboratory findings in 122 drug-free subjects with complaints of chronic insomnia. *American Journal of Psychiatry, 133*(12), 1382–1388.

Charon, F., Dramaix, M., & Mendlewicz, J. (1989). Epidemiological survey of insomniac subjects in a sample of 1,761 outpatients. *Neuropsychobiology, 21*(3), 109–110.

Chesson, A. L., Jr., Anderson, W. M., Littner, M., Davila, D., Hartse, K., Johnson, S., Wise, M., & Rafecas, J. (1999). Practice parameters for the nonpharmacologic treatment of chronic insomnia: An American Academy of Sleep Medicine report: Standards of Practice Committee of the American Academy of Sleep Medicine. *Sleep, 22*(8), 1128–1133.

Chesson, A. L., Littner, M., Davila, D., Anderson, W. M., Grigg-Damberger, M., Hartse, K., Johnson, S., & Wise, M. (2000). Practice parameters for the use of light therapy in the treatment of sleep disorders. *Sleep, 22*(5), 641–660.

Coates, T. J., George, J. M., Killen, J. D., Marchini, E., Hamilton, S., & Thorensen, C. E. (1981). First night effects in good sleepers and sleep-maintenance insomniacs when recorded at home. *Sleep, 4*(3), 293–298.

Coleman, R. M. (1982). Periodic movements in sleep (nocturnal myoclonus) and restless legs syndrome. In C. Guilleminault (Ed.), *Sleeping and waking disorders: Indications and techniques* (pp. 225–244). Boston: Butterworths.

Cooke, K. M., Kreydatus, M. A., Atherton, A., & Thoman, E. B. (1998). The effects of evening light exposure on the sleep of elderly women expressing sleep complaints. *Journal of Behavioral Medicine, 21*(1), 103–114.

Currie, S. R., Wilson, K. G., Pontefract, A. J., & deLaplante, L. (2000). Cognitive-behavioral treatment of insomnia secondary to chronic pain. *Journal of Consulting and Clinical Psychology, 68,* 407–416.

Dashevsky, B. A., & Kramer, M. (1998). Behavioral treatment of chronic insomnia in psychiatrically ill patients. *Journal of Clinical Psychiatry,* 59(12), 693–699.

Dawson, D., Rogers, N. L., Van Den Heuvel, C. J., Kennaway, D. J., & Lushington, K. (1998). Effect of sustained nocturnal transbuccal melatonin administration on sleep and temperature in elderly insomniacs. *Journal of Biological Rhythms, 13*(6), 532–538.

Dorsey, C. M., Lukas, S. E., Teicher, M. H., Harper, D., Winkelman, J. W., Cunningham, R., & Satlin, A. (1996). Effects of passive body heating on the sleep of older female insomniacs. *Journal of Geriatric Psychiatry and Neurology,* 9, 83–90.

Dujardin, K., Guieu, J. D., Leconte-Lambert, C., Leconte, P., Borderies, P., de L & Giclais, B. (1998). Comparison of the effects of zolpidem and flunitrazepam on sleep structure and daytime cognitive functions: A study of untreated unsomniacs. *Pharmacopsychiatry, 31*(1), 14–18.

Edinger, J. D., Fins, A. I., Sullivan, R. J., Marsh, G. R., Dailey, D. S., Hope, T. V., Young, M., Shaw, E., Carlson, D., & Vasilas, D. (1997a). Do our methods lead to insomniacs' madness? Daytime testing after laboratory and home-based polysomnographic studies. *Sleep,* 20(12), 1127–1134.

Edinger, J. D., Fins, A. I., Sullivan, R. J., Marsh, G. R., Dailey, D. S., Hope, T. V., Young, M., Shaw, E., Carlson, D., & Vasilas, D. (1997b). Sleep in the laboratory and sleep at home: comparisons of older insomniacs and normal sleepers. *Sleep,* 20(12), 1119–1126.

Elie, R., Ruther, E., Farr, I., Emilien, G., & Salinas, E. (1999). Sleep latency is shortened during 4 weeks of treatment with zaleplon, a novel nonbenzodiazepine hypnotic. Zaleplon Clinical Study Group. *Journal of Clinical Psychiatry,* 60(8), 536–544.

Espie, C. A., Brooks, D. N., & Lindsay, W. R. (1989). An evaluation of tailored psychological treatment of insomnia. *Journal of Behavior Therapy and Experimental Psychiatry,* 20(2), 143–153.

Foley, D. J., Monjan, A., Simonsick, E. M., Wallace, R. B., & Blazer, D. G. (1999). Incidence and remission of insomnia among elderly adults: An epidemiologic study of 6,800 persons over three years. *Sleep,* 22(Suppl. 2), S366–S372.

Ford, D. E., & Kamerow, D. B. (1989). Epidemiologic study of sleep disturbances and psychiatric disorders. *Journal of the American Medical Association, 262,* 1479–1484.

Frankel, B. L., Coursey, R. D., Buchbinder, R., & Snyder, F. (1976). Recorded and reported sleep in chronic primary insomnia. *Archives of General Psychiatry,* 33(5), 615–623.

Freedman, R., & Papsdorf, J. D. (1976). Biofeedback and progressive relaxation treatment of sleep-onset insomnia: A controlled, all-night investigation. *Biofeedback and Self Regulation, 1*(3), 253–271.

Friedman, L., Benson, K., Noda, A., Zarcone, V., Wicks, D. A., O'Connell, K., Brooks, J. O., 3rd, Bliwise, D. L., & Yesavage, J. A. (2000). An actigraphic comparison of sleep restriction and sleep hygiene treatments for insomnia in older adults. *Journal of Geriatric Psychiatry and Neurology, 13*(1), 17–27.

Gallup Organization. (1991). *Sleep in America.* Princeton, NJ: Gallup Organization.

Ganguli, M., Reynolds, C. F., & Gilby, J. E. (1996). Prevalence and persistence of sleep complaints in a rural older community sample: The MoVIES project. *Journal of the American Geriatrics Society,* 44, 778–784.

Ganzoni, E., Santoni, J. P., Chevillard, V., Sebille, M., & Mathy, B. (1995). Zolpidem in insomnia: A 3-year post-marketing surveillance study in Switzerland. *Journal of International Medical Research,* 23(1), 61–73.

Garfinkel, D., Laudon, M., Nof, D., & Zisapel, N. (1995). Improvement of sleep quality in elderly people by controlled-release melatonin [see comments]. *Lancet,* 346(8974), 541–544.

Gislason, T., & Almqvist, M. (1987). Somatic diseases and sleep complaints: An epidemiological study of 3,201 Swedish men. *Acta Medica Scandinavica, 221*(5), 475–481.

Greenblatt, D. J. (1992). Pharmacology of benzodiazepine hypnotics. [Review]. *Journal of Clinical Psychiatry,* 53(Suppl. 7–13).

Guilleminault, C., Clerk, A., Black, J., Labanowski, M., Pelayo, R., & Claman, D. (1995). Nondrug treatment trials in psychophysiologic insomnia. *Archives of Internal Medicine, 155*(8), 838–844.

Hajak, G., & Bandelow, B. (1998). Safety and tolerance of zolpidem in the treatment of disturbed sleep: A post-marketing surveillance of 16944 cases. *International Clinical Psychopharmacology, 13*(4), 157–167.

Hajak, G., Rodenbeck, A., Adler, L., Huether, G., Bandelow, B., Herrendorf, G., Staedt, J., & Ruther, E. (1996). Nocturnal melatonin secretion and sleep after doxepin administration in chronic primary insomnia. *Pharmacopsychiatry,* 29, 187–192.

Harvey, A. G. (2000). Sleep hygiene and sleep-onset insomnia. *Journal of Nervous and Mental Disease, 188*(1), 53–55.

Hauri, P. (1981). Treating psychophysiologic insomnia with biofeedback. *Archives of General Psychiatry, 38*(7), 752–758.

Hauri, P., & Fisher, J. (1986). Persistent psychophysiologic (learned) insomnia. *Sleep, 9*, 38–53.

Hauri, P. J. (1997). Can we mix behavioral therapy with hypnotics when treating insomniacs? *Sleep, 20*(12), 1111–1118.

Haynes, S. N., Fitzgerald, S. G., Shute, G., & O'Meary, M. (1985). Responses of psychophysiologic and subjective insomniacs to auditory stimuli during sleep: A replication and extension. *Journal of Abnormal Psychology, 94*(3), 338–345.

Healey, E. S., Kales, A., Monroe, L. J., Bixler, E. O., Chamberlin, K., & Soldatos, C. R. (1981). Onset of insomnia: Role of life-stress events. *Psychosomatic Medicine, 43*, 439–451.

Hohagen, F., Montero, R. F., Weiss, E., Lis, S., Schonbrunn, E., Dressing, H., Riemann, D., & Berger, M. (1994). Treatment of primary insomnia with trimipramine: An alternative to benzodiazepine hypnotics? *European Archives of Psychiatry and Clinical Neuroscience, 244*(2), 65–72.

Holbrook, A. M., Crowther, R., Lotter, A., Cheng, C., & King, D. (2000). Meta-analysis of benzodiazepine use in the treatment of insomnia. *Canadian Medical Association Journal, 162*(2), 225–233.

Hughes, R. J., Sack, R. L., & Lewy, A. J. (1998). The role of melatonin and circadian phase in age-related sleep-maintenance insomnia: Assessment in a clinical trial of melatonin replacement. *Sleep, 21*, 52–68.

Jacobs, E. A., Reynolds, C. F., Kupfer, D. J., Lovin, P. A., & Ehrenpreis, A. B. (1988). The role of polysomnography in the differential diagnosis of chronic insomnia. *American Journal of Psychiatry, 145*(3), 346–349.

James, S. P., Sack, D. A., Rosenthal, N. E., & Mendelson, W. B. (1989). Melatonin administration in insomnia. *Neuropsychopharmacology, 3*(1), 19–23.

Johnson, L. C., & Spinweber, C. L. (1983). Good and poor sleepers differ in Navy performance. *Military Medicine, 148*(9), 727–731.

Kales, A., Caldwell, A. B., Preston, T. A., Healey, S., & Kales, J. D. (1976). Personality patterns in insomnia: Theoretical implications. *Archives of General Psychiatry, 33*(9), 1128–1124.

Kales, A., Caldwell, A. B., Soldatos, C. R., Bixler, E. O., & Kales, J. D. (1983). Biopsychobehavioral correlates of insomnia. 2. Pattern specificity and consistency with the Minnesota Multiphasic Personality Inventory. *Psychosomatic Medicine, 45*(4), 341–356.

Karacan, I., Thornby, J. I., Anch, M., Holzer, C. E., Warheit, G. J., Schwab, J. J., & Williams, R. L. (1976). Prevalence of sleep disturbance in a primarily urban Florida County. *Social Science and Medicine, 10*(5), 239–244.

Karacan, I., Thornby, J. I., & Williams, R. L. (1983). Sleep disturbance: A community survey. C. Guilleminault & E. Lugaresi (Eds.), *Sleep/wake disorders: Natural history, epidemiology, and long-term evolution* (pp. 37–60). New York: Raven Press.

Karacan, I., & Williams, R. L. (1983). Sleep disorders in the elderly. *American Family Physician, 27*(3), 143–152.

Kudo, Y., & Kurihara, M. (1990). Clinical evaluation of diphenhydramine hydrochloride for the treatment of insomnia in psychiatric patients: A double-blind study. *Journal of Clinical Pharmacology, 30*(11), 1041–1048.

Kupfer, D. J., & Reynolds, C. F. (1997). Management of insomnia. *New England Journal of Medicine, 336*(5), 341–346.

Kuppermann, M., Lubeck, D. P., Mazonson, P. D., Patrick, D. L., Stewart, A. L., Buesching, D. P., & Fifer, S. K. (1995). Sleep problems and their correlates in a working population. *Journal of General Internal Medicine, 10*(1), 25–32.

Lacks, P., Bertelson, A. D., Sugerman, J., & Kunkel, J. (1983). The treatment of sleep-maintenance insomnia with stimulus-control techniques. *Behaviour Research and Therapy, 21*(3), 291–295.

Lichstein, K. L., & Rosenthal, T. L. (1980). Insomniacs' perception of cognition versus somatic determinants of sleep disturbance. *Journal of Abnormal Psychology, 89*(1), 105–107.

Lichstein, K. L., Wilson, N. M., & Johnson, C. T. (2000). Psychological treatment of secondary insomnia [in process citation]. *Psychology and Aging, 15*(2), 232–240.

Lilie, J. K., & Lahmeyer, H. (1991). Psychiatric management of sleep disorders. [Review]. *Psychiatric Medicine, 9*(2), 245–260.

Linsen, S. M., Zitman, F. G., & Breteler, M. H. (1995b). Defining benzodiazepine dependence: The confusion persists. *European Psychiatry, 10*, 306–311.

MacFarlane, J. G., Cleghorn, J. M., Brown, G. M., & Streiner, D. L. (1991). The effects of exogenous melatonin on the total sleep time and daytime alertness of chronic insomniacs: A preliminary study. *Biological Psychiatry, 30*(4), 371–376.

Margolis, N. (1999). Prevalence, costs, and consequences of insomnia: Reference bibliography: 1993–1998. *Sleep, 22*(Suppl. 2), S409–S412.

Mellinger, G. D., Balter, M. B., & Uhlenhuth, E. H. (1985). Insomnia and its treatment: Prevalence and correlates. *Archives of General Psychiatry*, 42, 225–232.

Mendelson, W. B. (1995). Long-term follow-up of chronic insomnia. *Sleep*, *18*(8), 698–701.

Mendelson, W. B. (1997). A critical evaluation of the hypnotic efficacy of melatonin. *Sleep*, *20*(10), 916–919.

Mendelson, W. B., Garnett, D., Gillin, J. C., & Weingartner, H. (1984a). The experience of insomnia and daytime and nighttime functioning. *Psychiatry Research*, *12*(3), 235–250.

Mendelson, W. B., Garnett, D., & Linnoila, M. (1984b). Do insomniacs have impaired daytime functioning? *Biological Psychiatry*, *19*(8), 1261–1264.

Mimeault, V., & Morin, C. M. (1999). Self-help treatment for insomnia: Bibliotherapy with and without professional guidance. *Journal of Consulting and Clinical Psychology*, *67*(4), 511–519.

Moldofsky, H. (1989). Sleep and fibrositis syndrome. [Review]. *Rheumatic Diseases Clinics of North America*, *15*(1), 91–103.

Morin, C. M., Colecchi, C., Brink, D., Astruc, M., Mercer, J., & Remsberg, S. (1995). How "blind" are double-blind placebo-controlled trials of benzodiazepine hypnotics? *Sleep*, *18*(4), 240–245.

Morin, C. M., Colecchi, C., Stone, J., Sood, R. K., & Brink, D. (1999a). Behavioral and pharmacological therapies for late-life insomnia: A randomized controlled trial. *Journal of the American Medical Association*, *281*(11), 991–999.

Morin, C. M., Culbert, J. P., & Schwartz, S. M. (1994). Nonpharmacological interventions for insomnia: A meta-analysis of treatment efficacy. *American Journal of Psychiatry*, *151*(8), 1172–1180.

Morin, C. M., & Gramling, S. E. (1989). Sleep Patterns and Aging: Comparison of older adults with and without insomnia complaints. *Psychology and Aging*, 4, 290–294.

Morin, C. M., Hauri, P. J., Espie, C. A., Spielman, A. J., Buysse, D. J., & Bootzin, R. R. (1999b). Nonpharmacologic treatment of chronic insomnia. *Sleep*, *22*(8), 1134–1156.

Murphy, P. J., & Campbell, S. S. (1996). Enhanced performance in elderly subjects following bright light treatment of sleep maintenance insomnia. *Journal of Sleep Research*, 5, 165–172.

Murtagh, D. R. R., & Greenwood, K. M. (1995). Identifying effective psychological treatments for insomnia: A meta-analysis. *Journal of Consulting and Clinical Psychology*, *63*(1), 79–89.

National Institute of Health. (1984). Drugs and insomnia: NIH Consensus Development Conference. [Review]. *National Institutes of Health Consensus Development Conference Summary*, *4*(10), 1–9.

Nowell, P. D., Buysse, D. J., Reynolds, C. F., Hauri, P. J., Roth, T., Stepanski, E. J., Thorpy, M. J., Bixler, E., Kales, A., Manfredi, R. L., Vgontzas, A. N., Stapf, D., Houck, P. R., & Kupfer, D. J. (1997a). Clinical factors contributing to the differential diagnosis of primary insomnia and insomnia related to mental disorders. *American Journal of Psychiatry*, *154*(10), 1412–1415.

Nowell, P. D., Mazumdar, S., Buysse, D. J., Dew, M. A., Reynolds, C. F., & Kupfer, D. J. (1997b). Benzodiazepines and zolpidem for chronic insomnia: A meta-analysis of treatment efficacy. *Journal of the American Medical Association*, *278*(24), 2170–2177.

Partinen, M. (1988). Stress and the heart: The sleep factor. *Stress Medicine*, *4*, 253–363.

Pasche, B., Erman, M., Hayduk, R., Mitler, M. M., Reite, M., Higgs, L., Kuster, N., Rossel, C., Dafni, U., Amato, D., Barbault, A., & Lebet, J. P. (1996). Effects of low energy emission therapy in chronic psychophysiological insomnia. *Sleep*, *19*(4), 327–336.

Perlis, M. L., Giles, D. E., Mendelson, W. B., Bootzin, R. R., & Wyatt, J. K. (1997). Psychophysiological insomnia: The behavioural model and a neurocognitive perspective. [Review] [115 refs]. *Journal of Sleep Research*, *6*(3), 179–188.

Piper, D. C., Upton, N., Smith, M. I., & Hunter, A. J. (2000). The novel brain neuropeptide, orexin-A, modulates the sleep-wake cycle of rats. *European Journal of Neuroscience*, *12*(2), 726–730.

Polo-Kantola, P., Erkkola, R., Helenius, H., Irjala, K., & Polo, O. (1998). When does estrogen replacement therapy improve sleep quality? *American Journal of Obstetrics and Gynecology*, *178*(5), 1002–1009.

Reite, M., Buysse, D. J., Reynolds, C. F., & Mendelson, W. (1995). The use of polysomnography in the evaluation of insomnia. *Sleep*, *18*(1), 58–70.

Reynolds, C. F., Kupfer, D. J., Hoch, C. C., Stack, J. A., Houck, P. R., & Sewitch, D. E. (1986). Two-year follow up of elderly patients with mixed depression and dementia: Clinical and EEG sleep findings. *Journal of the American Geriatrics Society*, 34, 793–799.

Rickels, K., Morris, R. J., Newman, H., Rosenfeld, H., Schiller, H., & Weinstock, R. (1983). Diphenhydramine in insomniac family practice patients: A double-blind study. *Journal of Clinical Pharmacology*, 23(5–6), 234–242.

Riedel, B. W., Lichstein, K. L., & Dwyer, W. O. (1995). Sleep compression and sleep education for older insomniacs: Self-help versus therapist guidance. *Psychology and Aging, 10*(1), 54–63.

Riedel, B., Lichstein, K., Peterson, B. A., Epperson, M. T., Means, M. K., & Aguillard, R. N. (1998). A comparison of the efficacy of stimulus control for medicated and nonmedicated insomniacs. *Behavior Modification*, 22(1), 3–28.

Roehrs, T., Vogel, G., Vogel, F., Wittig, R., Zorick, F., Paxton, C., Lamphere, J., & Roth, T. (1985). Eligibility requirements in hypnotic trials. *Sleep*, 8(1), 34–39.

Roth, T., & Ancoli-Israel, S. (1999). Daytime consequences and correlates of insomnia in the United States: Results of the 1991 National Sleep Foundation Survey, 2. *Sleep*, 22(Suppl. 2), S354–S358.

Roth, T., & Richardson, G. (1997). Commentary: Is melatonin administration an effective hypnotic? [Review] [7 refs]. *Journal of Biological Rhythms, 12*(6), 666–669.

Sack, R. L., Hughes, R. J., Edgar, D. M., & Lewy, A. J. (1997). Sleep-promoting effects of melatonin: At what dose, in whom, under what conditions, and by what mechanisms? *Sleep*, *20*(10), 908–915.

Sanavio, E. (1988). Pre-sleep cognitive intrusions and treatment of onset-insomnia. *Behaviour Research and Therapy*, 26(6), 451–459.

Sateia, M. J., Doghramji, K., Hauri, P. J., & Morin, C. M. (2000). Evaluation of chronic insomnia: An American Academy of Sleep Medicine review. [Review] [414 refs]. *Sleep*, 23(2), 243–308.

Scharf, M. B. (1993). Feasibility of an every-other-night regimen in insomniac patients: Subjective hypnotic effectiveness of quazepam, triazolam, and placebo [see comments]. *Journal of Clinical Psychiatry*, 54(1), 33–38.

Schramm, E., Hohagen, F., Kappler, C., Grasshoff, U., & Berger, M. (1995). Mental comorbidity of chronic insomnia in general practice attenders using DSM-III-R. *Acta Psychiatrica Scandinavica, 91*(1), 10–17.

Schwartz, S., McDowell, A. W., Cole, S. R., Cornoni-Huntley, J., Hays, J. C., & Blazer, D. (1999). Insomnia and heart disease: A review of epidemiologic studies. *Journal of Psychosomatic Research, 47*(4), 313–333.

Seidel, W. F., & Dement, W. C. (1982). Sleepiness in insomnia: Evaluation and treatment. *Sleep*, *5*(Suppl. 2), S182–S190.

Seidel, W. F., Roth, T., Roehrs, T., Zorick, F., & Dement, W. C. (1984). Treatment of a 12-hour shift of sleep schedule with benzodiazepines. *Science*, *224*, 1262–1264.

Simon, G. E., & Von Korff, M. (1997). Prevalence, burden, and treatment of insomnia in primary care. *American Journal of Psychiatry, 154*(10), 1417–1423.

Spielman, A. J., Saskin, P., & Thorpy, M. J. (1987). Treatment of chronic insomnia by restriction of time in bed. *Sleep, 10*, 45–56.

Steinmark, S. W., & Borkovec, T. D. (1974). Active and placebo treatment effects on moderate insomnia under counterdemand and positive demand instructions. *Journal of Abnormal Psychology, 83*(2), 157–163.

Stepanski, E., Koshorek, G., Zorick, F., Glinn, M., Roehrs, T., & Roth, T. (1989). Characteristics of individuals who do or do not seek treatment for chronic insomnia. *Psychosomatics*, *30*(4), 421–427.

Stepanski, E., Zorick, F., Roehrs, T., & Roth, T. (2000). Effects of sleep deprivation on daytime sleepiness in primary insomnia. *Sleep*, *23*(2), 215–219.

Stoller, M. K. (1994). Economic effects of insomnia. [Review]. *Clinical Therapeutics, 16*(5), 873–897; discussion 854.

Sugarman, J. S., Stern, J. A., & Walsh, J. K. (1985). Daytime alertness in subjective and objective insomnia: Some preliminary findings. *Biological Psychiatry, 20*, 741–750.

Tan, T. L., Kales, J. D., Kales, A., Soldatos, C. R., & Bixler, E. O. (1984). Biopsychobehavioral correlates of insomnia. 4. Diagnosis based on *DSM-III*. *American Journal of Psychiatry, 141*, 357–362.

Verbeek, I., Schreuder, K., & Declerck, G. (1999). Evaluation of short-term nonpharmacological treatment of insomnia in a clinical setting. *Journal of Psychosomatic Research*, 47(4), 369–383.

Vgontzas, A. N., Kales, A., Bixler, E. O., & Manfredi, R. L. (1995). Usefulness of polysomnographic studies in the differential diagnosis of insomnia. *International Journal of Neuroscience*, 82, 47–60.

Vollrath, M., Wicki, W., & Angst, J. (1989). The Zurich Study. 8. Insomnia: Association with depression, anxiety, somatic syndromes, and course of insomnia. *European Archives of Psychiatry and Clinical Neuroscience*, 239(2), 113–124.

Walsh, J. K., Benca, R. M., Bonnet, M. H., Buysse, D. J., Ricca, J., Hauri, P. J., Morin, C. M., Roth, T., & Simon, R. D. (1999). Insomnia: Assessment and management in primary care. NIH Publication No. 98-4088. *American Family Physician*, 59(11), 3029–3038.

Walsh, J. K., & Engelhardt, C. L. (1999). The direct economic costs of insomnia in the United States for 1995. *Sleep*, 22(Suppl. 2), S386–S393.

Weissman, M. M., Greenwald, S., Nino-Murcia, G., & Dement, W. C. (1997). The morbidity of insomnia uncomplicated by psychiatric disorders. *General Hospital Psychiatry*, 19(4), 245–250.

Welstein, L., Dement, W. C., Redington, D., Guilleminault, C., & Mitler, M. M. (1983). Insomnia in the San Francisco Bay area: A telephone survey. In C.

Guilleminault & E. Lugaresi (Eds.), *Sleep/wake disorders: Natural history, epidemiology, and long-term evolution* (pp. 73–85). New York: Raven Press.

Whorwell, P. J., McCallum, M., & Creed, F. H. (1986). Non-colonic features of irritable bowel syndrome. *Gut*, *27*, 37–40.

Woods, J. H., & Winger, G. (1995a). Current benzodiazepine issues. [Review]. *Psychopharmacology*, *118*(2), 107–115; discussion 118.

Zammit, G. K., Weiner, J., Damato, N., Sillup, G. P., & McMillan, C. A. (1999). Quality of life in people with insomnia. *Sleep*, *22*(Suppl. 2), S379–S385.

24

Psychological Treatments for Personality Disorders

Paul Crits-Christoph

Jacques P. Barber

A Type 2 randomized clinical trial (RCT) of psychosocial treatment for avoidant personality disorder (APD) compared three group-administered behavioral interventions (graded exposure, standard social skills training, intimacy-focused social skills training) with a wait-list control; while all three treatments were more efficacious than the control condition, no differences among the treatments were identified after either the 10-week treatment or at follow-up. For the treatment of borderline personality disorder, a Type I RCT compared partial hospitalization involving group and individual psychoanalytic psychotherapy for 18 months to standard psychiatric care and found that patients in the partial hospitalization group improved significantly more than controls in terms of decreased number of suicidal attempts, acts of self-harm, psychiatric symptoms, inpatient days, and social and interpersonal functioning at 6 months and at 18 months. A Type 2 RCT of psychological treatment for borderline personality disorder (BPD) randomly assigned 44 women demonstrating parasuicidal behavior to either dialectical behavioral therapy (DBT; consisted of weekly group and individual sessions for a year) or treatment as usual in the community; DBT resulted in lower attrition, fewer and less severe episodes of parasuicidal behavior, and fewer days of hospitalization than the control condition, but no differences in depression, hopelessness, or suicidal ideation. Another Type 2 RCT compared DBT to treatment as usual for drug-dependent women with borderline personality disorder. DBT patients had significantly greater reductions in drug abuse throughout the 1-year treatment and at follow-up than did control patients. No RCTs of psychological treatment for other personality disorders have been reported. A Type 2 RCT of psychological treatment for mixed PDs (excluding Cluster A disorders) randomly assigned 81 patients to two forms of brief dynamic therapy averaging 40 weeks and wait-list control condition averaging 15 weeks; the two forms of brief dynamic therapy yielded substantial symptomatic improvements at both the end of treatment and a 1.5-year follow-up. Several substantial review articles have found a consistent adverse impact of PDs on outcomes of treatment for a wide range of Axis I disorders.

The American Psychiatric Association's *DSM* defined personality traits in terms of enduring patterns of thinking about, perceiving, and relating to the environment and oneself (American Psychiatric Association [APA], 1994). A personality disorder (Axis II diagnosis) is present when such personality traits result in impairment in social or occupational functioning or distress to the person. The *DSM-IV* described 10 specific Axis II diagnoses. These are grouped into three clusters: (a) the "odd" cluster (paranoid, schizoid, and schizotypal); (b) the dramatic cluster (histrionic, narcissistic, antisocial, and borderline); and (c) the anxious cluster (avoidant, dependent, and obsessive compulsive). The final personality disorder, Personality Disorder Not Otherwise Specified (NOS), is not in a cluster. This disorder is defined as either (a) the pattern meets general criteria for a personality disorder and traits of several personality disorders are evident, but the criteria for any one specific disorder are not met, or (b) the pattern meets the general criteria for a personality disorder, but the type of personality disorder is not included in the classification. In terms of this latter criteria, two personality disorders, passive aggressive and depressive, are listed in the appendix as potential diagnoses requiring further study but can be used to assign a personality disorder NOS diagnosis.

Although personality disorders (PDs) are relatively common compared to many other psychiatric disorders, precise estimates of the prevalence of different personality disorders are hard to obtain. The primary problem is assessment. Strides have been made in the development of structured clinical interviews for assessing Axis II disorders, but to date, these instruments have displayed modest and variable convergence (Clark, Livesley, & Morey, 1997; Perry, 1992) among themselves or with other measures. Poor convergent validity in assessing personality disorders suggest that one cannot necessarily treat similarly results from studies which use different instruments, thus limiting the validity of these measures (Perry, 1992). More recently, advances have been reported in the reliability of these measures. Maffei et al. (1997), for example, reported acceptable interrater reliability coefficients of .49 to .98 (Kappas) for *DSM-IV* categorical diagnoses, and excellent intraclass correlation coefficients from .90 to .98 for dimensional judgments. With the measurement limitations in mind, Weissman (1993) reviewed studies of the epidemiology of personality disorders. Early studies (pre-*DSM-III*) yielded overall rates of 6 to 10% of the population manifesting some type of a personality disorder. Studies of *DSM-III* or *III-R* have yielded rates of 10–13.5%. In terms of specific personality disorders, the *DSM-III* and *III-R* studies have found the prevalence of paranoid personality disorder to range from 0.4% to 1.8%; schizoid, 0.5% to 0.9%; schizotypal, 0.6 to 5.6%; histrionic, 1.3% to 3.0%; narcissistic, 0% to 0.4%; borderline, 1.1% to 4.6%; antisocial, 0.2% to 3.7% (although there may be cultural variability in such rates; see Hwu, Yeh, & Chang, 1989); avoidant, 0% to 1.3%; dependent, 1.6% to 6.7%; obsessive compulsive, 1.7% to 6.4%; and passive aggressive 0% to 3.0% (Weissman, 1993). We found no general study of the prevalence of *DSM-IV* Axis II disorder in a general patient or normative population. There is also an extensive amount of comorbidity with personality disorders, that is, having one disorder tends to be associated with having one or more additional Axis II diagnoses. For example, Widiger and Rogers (1989) reported that the average number of multiple diagnoses was 85% in a group of 568 patients. In some disorders, like borderline personality disorder, comorbidity rate ranges from 90% to 97% (Gunderson, Zanarini, & Kisiel, 1991).

A recent epidemiological study (Samuels, Nestadt, Romanoski, Folstein, & McHugh, 1994) of 810 adults in the community found an overall rate of 5.9% with *DSM-III* personality disorders, slightly lower than previous estimates. The subjects with Axis II diagnoses had higher rates of alcohol and drug use disorders, suicidal thoughts and attempts, and general life events in the past year. However, only one fifth of those people with an Axis II diagnosis were receiving treatment.

Comorbidity of Axis II with Axis I disorders is especially important for treatment planning, but few adequate studies of the epidemiological rates of such comorbidity have been done. Ruegg and Frances (1995) reviewed the literature on comorbidity of Axis I and II disorders, and found that methodological problems, particularly the use of convenience samples from treatment centers rather than randomly selected community samples, limit the conclusions that can be drawn at this time. However, the studies that have been done show high rates of comorbidity. For example, Skodol et al. (1999) reported on cooccurrence rates of mood and personality disorders in the collaborative longitudinal personality disorders study. Of the 571 patients with Axis II diagnoses, 61.3% had a current mood disorder. More specifically, 39% had a current major depressive disorder (MDD), and 74% had a lifetime MDD. MDD most often coocurred with avoidant (32%), borderline (31%), depressive (29%), and obsessive compulsive (24%) personality disorder. Of patients with bulimia, in two studies, 39% (Fahy, Eisler, & Russell, 1993) and 38% (Ames-Frankel et al., 1992) had personality disorders. Ruegg and Frances (1995) reported that large percentages of patients with anxiety disorders (36 to 76%; six studies) and mood disorders (36 to

65%; eight studies) also have a personality disorder. Patients with obsessive compulsive disorder were found to have high rates of compulsive personality disorder and other personality disorders, particularly avoidant (Ruegg & Frances, 1995). Zimmerman and Mattia (1999) found that borderline personality disorder patients were more likely to have multiple Axis I disorders than patients without borderline personality disorder. These differences were found across mood, anxiety, substance use, eating, and somatoform disorder categories.

Comorbidity of Axis II with substance use disorders has been studied extensively and has been found to be particularly high. Weiss, Mirin, Griffin, Gunderson, and Hufford (1993) found that 74% of hospitalized cocaine-dependent patients had at least one Axis II diagnosis. Similarly, Haller, Knisely, Dawson, and Schnoll (1993) found that 75% of perinatal substance abusers also received an Axis II diagnosis. In a sample of outpatient cocaine-dependent patients who participated in the pilot phase of a large multisite treatment study, Barber et al. (1996) found that 48% of the patients had at least one personality disorder and 18% had two or more. Of those with a personality disorder, 65% had a Cluster B disorder, antisocial and borderline personality disorders being the most common. Men were significantly more likely to be diagnosed with antisocial personality disorder than women. Patients with personality disorders were significantly more likely to receive another Axis 1 diagnosis and to have more severe psychiatric symptoms than patients without personality disorders. However, the groups did not differ on other measures of drug use severity or demographic variables. While lower than many studies in that population, 47% is not inconsistent with studies that required a similar drug-free period prior to diagnostic assessment (e.g., Nace et al., 1991; Pettinati, 1990) and/or scored as present only diagnostic criteria that were met when the patients were not using drugs (e.g., Weiss et al., 1993). Dinwiddie, Reich, and Cloninger (1992) found that injecting drugs increased the odds of a diagnosis of comorbid antisocial personality disorder 21-fold, and that the diagnosis of antisocial personality disorder increased the odds of injecting drugs by 27-fold. Swartz, Blazer, George, and Winfield (1990) described data on comorbidity of borderline personality disorder with Axis I disorders using a community-based sample, the Epidemiologic Catchment Area program. Individuals with borderline personality disorder were found to frequently have generalized anxiety disorder (56%), major depression (41%), agoraphobia (37%), social phobia (35%), posttraumatic stress disorder (34%), and alcohol abuse/dependence (22%), among others.

Little is known about the etiology of personality disorders. A number of studies have documented high rates of physical and sexual abuse or other trauma during childhood in patients later diagnosed having borderline personality disorder (Herman, Perry, & van der Kolk, 1989; Ogata et al., 1990; Westen, Lundolph, Misle, Ruffins, & Block, 1990). Recently, Fossati, Madeddu, and Maffei (1999) conducted a meta-analysis of the relationship between childhood sexual abuse and borderline personality disorder based on 21 studies. They found a moderate correlation of .28. Because the correlation was modest and because they found that larger effect sizes were related to smaller, less representative samples, the authors concluded that their results do not support the view that childhood sexual abuse is a major psychological risk factor or causal antecedent of borderline personality disorder. Paris (2000) recently concluded that "none of the risk factors for borderline personality disorder fully explain its development" (p. 86).

Other studies have found evidence for familial transmission of borderline personality disorder (Baron, Gruen, Asnis, & Lord, 1985; Loranger, Oldham, & Tullis, 1982) and schizotypal personality disorder (Baron et al., 1985). Twin studies have supported a genetic component for schizotypal personality disorder, but not borderline personality disorder (Torgersen, 1984). There is also a rich literature on the childhood precursor (most important, presence of conduct disorder in childhood and behavioral disinhibition) of antisocial personality disorder (Paris, 2000).

HISTORICAL PERSPECTIVE

Early psychoanalytic writings devoted a considerable amount of attention to the treatment of "characterological" problems (Alexander, 1930; Fenichel, 1945). Although some of this literature informs modern approaches, particularly modern psychodynamic approaches, it is difficult to know the relevance of these early writings to the current classification system for psychiatric disorders. For example, the distinction between obsessive compulsive disorder and obsessive compulsive personality disorder was not made in early writings on "obsessive compulsive" character, and this distinction is likely to be important for treatment selection.

Within the psychodynamic literature, there has been voluminous writing on the nature and treatment of narcissistic and borderline personality types in particular (Kernberg, 1984; Kohut, 1984; see review by Aronson, 1989). Even in these more recent writings, however, there has remained a lack of use of a consensual definition of the target patient population. As a consequence of the varying definitions of "characterological" conditions, the research literature on the treatment of personality disorders begins with the advent of the *DSM-III* and *DSM-III-R* classification system for Axis II disorders.

This is not to say that the *DSM* definition of personality pathology is not without problems. A number of authors have described various problems with the *DSM* classification, including lack of discrimination of many of the *DSM* criteria (Svrakic & Divac-Jovanovic, 1994), problems in distinguishing normal from deviant personality (Livesly, Schroeder, Jackson, & Jang, 1994), and general lack of empirical support (Widiger, 1993). Alternatives to the *DSM* system have been recently reviewed by Dyce (1994). These alternatives include interpersonal circumplex models, neurobiological learning theory, biosocial learning theory, and the five-factor model of personality. Although these alternatives appear promising, they have not yet been developed to the point where they have guided treatment research. It seems likely that the *DSM* system will not be modified or replaced until adequate data justifying an alternative system exist.

REVIEW OF TREATMENT OUTCOME LITERATURE

Despite the relatively high prevalence of Axis II disorders, there have been very few outcome studies using patients with these disorders. Perry, Banon, and Ianni (1999) recently published the first meta-analysis on the effectiveness of psychotherapy for personality disorders. They found 15 studies that have made an attempt to systematically diagnose their patients and evaluate outcome. Since most of these studies were not randomized trials, Perry et al. calculated within treatment change effect sizes that ranged between 1.1 and 1.3, depending on the measure. In addition, they compared results from four studies that reported the percentage of patients who no longer met Axis II criteria at follow-up to studies that have examined the natural history of recovery of borderline personality disorder patients. They showed that in comparison to the natural history of the latter, personality disorder patients who received psychotherapy had a sevenfold faster rate of recovery. Unfortunately, only half the patients in the four studies had a diagnosis of borderline personality disorder, thus the validity of the comparison was limited.

Below, we summarize the existing literature on the treatment of personality disorders, using the Type 1 to Type 6 classification of studies employed in this volume. Our emphasis is on Type 1 and Type 2 studies that involve patients meeting *DSM-III, III-R,* or *IV* criteria. Type 3 through Type 6 studies, including any study using pre-*DSM-III* criteria, are mentioned only when no Type 1 or 2 studies are available. Wherever possible, we report the response rates for each treatment as indicated by the percentage of patients that no longer qualify for an Axis II diagnosis at the end of treatment or follow-up assessment.

Avoidant Personality Disorders

The only randomized controlled trial on *DSM-III* avoidant personality disorder compared graded exposure, standard social skills training, intimacy-focused social skills training, and a wait-list control (Alden, 1989). The behavioral treatments were all administered in group format. All of the active treatments were better than the wait list, but no differences among the behavioral treatments were found at the end of the 10-week treatment period or at follow-up. Examination of the clinical significance of the outcomes revealed that although positive changes had occurred in the active treatment conditions, patients were not functioning at the level of normative comparison samples. This study, however, had minimal statistical power for detecting differences among the treatments (fewer than 20 patients per group).

One Type 3 study (not controlled) has been reported on *DSM-III-R* avoidant personality disorder (Renneberg, Goldstein, Phillips, & Chambless, 1990). This study evaluated an intensive (four full days) group behavioral treatment program with 17 patients. The treatment included group systematic desensitization, behavioral rehearsal, and self-image work.

Outcome was evaluated at posttreatment and 1-year follow-up. The results evidenced positive changes, especially in terms of fear of negative evaluation. Gains were maintained over the follow-up period.

In a comparative study without a control group, Stravynski, Lesage, Marcouiller, and Elie (1989) compared social skills training with group discussion plus homework in a crossover design for patients with *DSM-III* avoidant personality disorder. Although significant improvements on most measures were found in general, no differences between the treatment modalities were found, so the centrality of skills acquisition as the mechanism of action of social skills training is questionable. Treatment, however, may have been too brief (five sessions of each modality) to allow detection of an effect. More recently, Stravynski, Belisle, Marcouiller, and Lavallee (1994) examined whether a combination of office-based and in vivo treatment (real-life interactions with people in shopping malls, a cafeteria, etc.) enhanced the outcome of office-based social skills training for 28 patients with *DSM-III* avoidant personality disorder. Outcomes were generally equal in the two conditions, although the in vivo condition had a greater attrition rate.

Because avoidant personality disorder appeared to be equally responsive to different kinds of behavioral treatments, Alden and Capreol (1993) examined the hypothesis that different kinds of interpersonal problems would moderate treatment response to various therapies. To test this hypothesis, data from the Alden (1989) project described above were used. Several findings emerged. Avoidant personality disorder patients who had greater problems related to distrustful and angry behavior benefited more from structured exercises that required them to approach and talk to others (graded exposure). Patients with problems resisting others' demands benefited from both graded exposure and social skills training but were particularly responsive to intimacy-focused social skills training. The results suggest that a comprehensive assessment of interpersonal problems may be important in planning what type of treatment intervention is most likely to be beneficial to patients with avoidant personality disorder

In a quantitative case study, Coon (1994) reported on the successful treatment of avoidant personality disorder using a schema-focused cognitive therapy. Positive outcomes were evidenced not only at termination but also at 1-year follow-up.

In an uncontrolled pilot (Type 3) study of 52 weeks of supportive expressive dynamic therapy, Barber, Morse, Krakauer, Chittams, and Crits-Christoph (1997) showed that by the end of treatment (up to 52 sessions), 61% of carefully diagnosed avoidant personality disorder patients had lost their avoidant personality disorder diagnosis.

Obsessive Compulsive Personality Disorder

Barber et al. (1997) also conducted an open trial of SE for obsessive compulsive personality disorder (Type 3 study). Obsessive compulsive personality disorder patients lost their personality disorder diagnoses significantly faster than did avoidant personality disorder patients. By the end of treatment, 39% of avoidant personality disorder patients still retained their diagnosis, while only 15% of obsessive/compulsive personality disorder patients (1 out of 13) did so. Most obsessive compulsive personality disorder patients lost their diagnoses, assessed via the SCID II, within the first 17 sessions of treatment. Both avoidant personality disorder and obsessive compulsive personality disorder patients improved significantly across time on measures of personality disorders, depression, anxiety, general functioning, and interpersonal problems.

Borderline Personality Disorder

Linehan, Hubert, Suarez, Douglas, and Heard (1991) reported on 44 women who evidenced parasuicidal behavior and were diagnosed as having borderline personality disorder. They were randomized to either dialectical behavior therapy (DBT) or treatment as usual in the community. The dialectical behavior therapy is actually a complex treatment modality that is more accurately described as eclectic rather than a traditional behavior therapy per se. The treatment consists of weekly group and individual sessions for 1 year. The group component is psychoeducational, teaching interpersonal skills, distress tolerance/reality acceptance, and emotion regulation skills. The individual therapy sessions involve directive, problem-solving techniques as well as supportive techniques such as empathy and acceptance. Behavioral goals serve as the focus of the individual sessions and are addressed in a sequential order, but previous goals are readdressed if the problem returns. These goals include decreasing suicidal behaviors, decreasing therapy-interfering behaviors, decreasing behaviors that interfere with quality of life, increasing behavioral skills, decreasing behaviors related to posttraumatic stress, increasing respect for self, and achieving individual goals. The basis treatment strategies of DBT are organized into four categories: (a) dialectical strategies, (b) core strategies, (c) stylistic strategies, and (d) case management strategies. Dialectical strategies include a range of techniques that allow the therapist to hold both sides of important polarities, with the hope that a new synthesis and flexibility will arise out of the opposing positions. The core strategies consist of acceptance (validation) strategies and problem-solving strategies. Stylistic strategies involve the form and style of therapeutic communications. Two styles are balanced: reciprocal communication strategies (responsiveness, self-disclosure, warm engagement, and genuineness) and irreverent communication strategies that are intended to keep the patient off-balance. The case management strategies involve interactions between the therapist and the community (e.g., consultants, family members, significant others). More details about DBT can be found in the published treatment manual (Linehan, 1993).

The Linehan et al. (1991) study found that DBT resulted in relatively fewer and less severe episodes of parasuicidal behavior and fewer days of hospitalization than treatment as usual, but no differences in depression, hopelessness, or suicidal ideation were found. The attrition rate for DBT (16.7%) was much lower than the attrition rate for treatment as usual (58.3%). Treatment gains were, for the most part, maintained relative to the control condition during the 1-year follow-up by Linehan, Heard, and Armstrong (1993). Although this important study yielded very promising information on DBT as a treatment for parasuicidal patients with borderline personality disorder, several aspects of the study lead to a Type 2 classification. These limitations include the fact that the therapists in the treatment-as-usual condition were not equated with the DBT therapists in terms of their experience in treating patients with borderline personality disorder and the fact that 27% of the control patients never actually began therapy, although they had been referred to a therapist.

DBT has also been extended to the treatment of inpatients with a diagnosis of borderline personality disorder (Barley et al., 1993). The implementation of DBT on an inpatient unit decreased the rates of incident reports of self-inflicted injuries and overdoses. No information on the assessment of patient diagnosis, however, was presented in that report. Linehan et al. (1999) recently reported on a randomized clinical trial comparing DBT to treatment as usual (TAU) for drug-dependent women with borderline personality disorder. DBT patients had significantly greater reductions in drug abuse throughout the 1-year treatment and at follow-up than did TAU patients. (Additional ongoing studies of DBT that have not yet been published are described in Koerner and Linehan, 2000. Among those studies, one finds an ongoing replication of Linehan's original study using a "treatment by expert in the community control group.")

Psychodynamic therapy was evaluated as a treatment of borderline personality disorder by Stevenson and Meares (1992) (Type 3 study). The treatment was, broadly speaking, based on self-psychology. Therapy had a maturational goal accomplished through helping the patients discover and elaborate their inner life, with empathy and attention to disruptions in empathy central aspects of the process of therapy (Meares, 1987). Thirty patients with *DSM-III* borderline personality disorder were treated with twice-per-week therapy for 1 year. Outcome was assessed 1 year after termination of treatment. Substantial reductions in violent behavior, drug use, medical visits, episodes of self-harm, time away from work, and symptoms were evident. Thirty percent of patients no longer met criteria for borderline personality disorder. Improvement was maintained over 1 year and continued over 5 years with substantial saving in health care costs (Stevenson & Meares, 1999).

Munroe-Blum and Marziali (1995) compared open-ended individual psychodynamic therapy with a manualized interpersonal group therapy for 110 patients with borderline personality disorder (Type 1 study). The group treatment lasted 30 sessions. No differences at 1 year (termination) or 2 years were found, although patients in general benefited from both treatments. More recently, Bateman and Fonagy (1999) reported on the treatment of borderline personality disorder patients randomized to either partial hospitalization ($N = 19$) or to standard care ($N = 19$) (Type 1 study). The treatment included individual and group psychoanalytic psychotherapy for a maximum of 18 months. Results indicated that patients in the partial hospitalization group improved significantly more than controls in decreased number of suicidal attempts, acts of self-harm, psychiatric symptoms, inpatient days, and better social and interpersonal functioning at 6 months and at 18 months.

A recently manualized form of dynamic therapy, transference-focused therapy (Kernberg et al., 1989), has yet to be empirically validated and needs to be compared to existing approaches such as DBT. Furthermore, such a study needs to be conducted in a setting different from the one where these treatments were developed. A randomized clinical trial comparing dynamic therapy (based on object relations theorists, such as Kernberg), DBT, and treatment as usual has recently begun at the Karolinska Institute in Stockholm, Sweden.

Other Personality Disorders

No controlled treatment outcome studies have yet been performed for histrionic, dependent, schizotypal, schizoid, narcissistic, passive aggressive, antisocial, or paranoid personality disorder. A case study with quantitative outcome data has been published showing positive effects of cognitive therapy for a paranoid personality disorder patient (Williams, 1988).

Mixed Axis II Samples

There has been one controlled study using a sample of mixed personality disorders (Winston et al., 1991, 1994). This study randomized 81 patients with personality disorders to two forms of brief dynamic therapy, one more cognitively oriented (brief adaptive therapy) and one more oriented toward confronting defenses and eliciting affect (modeled after Davanloo, 1980), and to a wait-list control condition. The sample consisted mostly of Cluster B and C personality disorder types, as well as patients diagnosed as Personality Disorder Not Otherwise Specified (mostly with Cluster C features). However, paranoid, schizoid, schizotypal, narcissistic, and borderline personality disorders were excluded. Treatment lasted on average 40 weeks, although the wait list was on average only 15 weeks. Because of this confound of treatment condition with time, this study is classified as a Type 2 study. The results showed that both forms of brief dynamic therapy produced substantial improvements across multiple outcome measures, including general psychiatric symptoms, social adjustment, and target complaints. At follow-up assessments, obtained at 1.5 years on average after the end of therapy, the gains in improvement were maintained on target complaints (the only outcome measured).

In another study by the same group, Hellerstein et al. (1998) described the results of a study involving mixed personality disorder patients who received 40 sessions of supportive therapy ($N = 24$) or short-term dynamic psychotherapy ($N = 25$). Thirty-five percent of the patients dropped out of treatment. There were no differences between the treatment modalities at midphase (Week 20), termination, or 6-month follow-up. However, within-group effect sizes (intake to termination) were large on all outcome measures.

Hardy et al. (1995) reported on the 27 Cluster C personality disorder patients from the 114 depressed patients included in the Sheffield 2 study (Shapiro et al., 1994). Clusters A and B were not assessed in that study. In this Type 2 study, employed white-collar patients received either 8 or 16 sessions of either cognitive or psychodynamic psychotherapy. At the end of treatment, Cluster C personality disorder patients continued to display significantly more severe symptoms than non-Cluster-C personality disorder patients if they had received dynamic therapy, but not if they had received CT. Karterud et al. (1992) presented the results of the effectiveness of day hospital community treatment for decompensated personality disorder patients. In this Type 3 study, 97 patients were prospectively followed; 74 had a personality disorder diagnosis (34 were borderline personality disorder, 13 were schizotypal personality disorder, and 27 had other personality disorders, two thirds of which were cluster C personality disorder). All but the schizotypal personality disorder patients improved significantly on the Symptom Checklist-90 (SCL-90) and Health Sickness Rating Scale at discharge (mean stay was 171 days with a s.d. of 109).

Monsen, Odland, Faugli, Daae, and Eilertsen (1995) reported on the results of treating 25 patients (23 of whom had a diagnosis of a personality disorder) with psychodynamic therapy based on object relations theory and self-psychology. Treatment lasted on average a little bit more than 2 years. Patients were assessed at termination and again 5 years after termination. At the end of treatment, substantial change was found on measures of symptoms, affect consciousness, and defenses. In addition, 75% of the patients who had had an Axis I disorder at intake no longer qualified for an Axis I disorder at termination. Seventy-two percent of the patients with Axis II disorders no longer qualified for the disorder at termination. The gains were maintained at the 5-year follow-up.

Høglend (1993) studied 15 patients with personality disorders in comparison to 30 patients without Axis II disorders (Type 2 study). The treatment was psychodynamic therapy of brief to moderate length (9 to 53 sessions) that was based upon the approaches of Sifneos (1979) and Malan (1976). At termination, the Axis II patients evidenced less change than the patients without Axis II diagnoses, but at 4-year follow-up, there was no difference. For the Axis II patients, the number of treatment sessions was significantly related to the acquisition of insight and dynamic change at follow-up. Thus, length of treatment appeared to be a crucial factor in producing positive outcomes for the Axis II patients (but not the patients without personality disorders).

Axis II as Moderator of Treatment of Axis I Disorders

Reich and Vasile (1993) reviewed studies of the relation of personality traits and Axis II personality disorders to the outcome of treatments (both psychosocial and psychopharmacological) designed to benefit Axis I conditions. This review of 17 studies built upon an earlier review of 21 studies (Reich & Green, 1991) and found a consistent adverse impact of personality pathology on the treatment outcome of a wide range of Axis I disorders. Examination of the studies in these two reviews, plus some more recent studies that investigate specific personality disorders and specific psychosocial treatments, reveals the following findings: (a) Antisocial personality disorder (without a co-occurring diagnosis of depression) predicted poor outcome from cognitive therapy and psychodynamic therapy for opiate addiction (Woody, McLellan, Luborsky, & O'Brien, 1985). (b) Avoidant personality disorder was associated with relatively poorer outcome for agoraphobia from exposure therapy (Chambless, Renneberg, Goldstein, & Gracely, 1992) or from exposure therapy and additional anxiety management and group and individual therapy (Chambless, Renneberg, Gracely, Goldstein, & Fydich, 2000). (c) Schizotypal personality disorder is associated with poor outcome of behavior therapy for obsessive compulsive disorder (Minichiello, Baer, & Jenike, 1987). (d) Presence of a personality disorder predicted poor outcome of cognitive behavioral group therapy for social anxiety (Turner, 1987) and panic disorders (Mennin & Heimberg, 2000). (e) Patients with personality disorders show slower response to imipramine plus interpersonal psychotherapy for recurrent unipolar depression (Frank, Kupfer, Jacob, & Jarrett, 1987). And (f) patients with a diagnosis in the anxious cluster of personality disorders evidenced much poorer outcome with imipramine plus interpersonal therapy for recurrent unipolar depression (Pilkonis & Frank, 1988).

Presence of a personality disorder, however, does not always uniformly lead to poor outcome. For example, Longabaugh et al. (1994) investigated the extent to which antisocial personality disorder moderated the treatment of alcohol abuse; 31 patients with antisocial personality disorder were compared to 118 nonantisocial personality disorder alcohol abusers randomly assigned to either a group extended cognitive behavioral treatment (including stimulus control, rearranging consequences, restructuring cognitions, assertion training, problem solving for alternatives to drinking, and dealing with slips/relapses) or to relationship-enhanced cognitive behavioral treatment (involving functional analysis, enhancing reinforcements in relationships with partners, using partners' relationship to reinforce abstinence, and educational/didactic sessions for partners). A significant interaction was found for antisocial personality disorder by treatment modality for the average number of drinks consumed on a drinking day, with patients with antisocial personality disorder in the extended cognitive behavioral treatment having the fewest drinks (about two on a drinking day) and patients with antisocial personality disorder in the relationship enhancement condition having the most (about eight). Nonantisocial personality disorder patients had an intermediate level of drinking on a drinking day in both treatment conditions. This interaction, however, was not found for the percentage of days abstinent. At 13- to 18-month follow-up, a main effect for antisocial personality disorder emerged, with antisocial personality disorder patients showing more days abstinent than nonantisocial personality disorder patients.

Barber and Muenz (1996) reported on how features of two personality disorders, avoidant and obsessive compulsive, interact with type of psychotherapy in the treatment of depression. Using data from the Treatment of Depression Collaborative Study (Elkin et al., 1989), Barber and Muenz (1996) found that interpersonal psychotherapy produced better outcomes for depressed patients with features of obsessive compulsive personality disorder, but cognitive therapy produced better outcomes with depressed patients who also had features of avoidant personality disorder (Type 2 study).

In the treatment of public speaking anxiety among patients with social phobia, the presence of avoidant personality disorder did not predict outcome (i.e., treatment was equally successful in those with and without avoidant personality disorder) in one study (Hofmann, Newman, Becker, Taylor, & Roth, 1995).

There may be ways in which standard treatment can be enhanced or improved to more effectively treat Axis I patients who have a comorbid Axis II condition. For example, a quantitative case study by Walker, Freeman, and Christensen (1994) used restricted environmental stimulation to successfully enhance the exposure treatment of obsessive compulsive disorder (OCD) in a patient with schizotypal personality disorder. Although this treatment focused on the OCD and not the schizotypal personality disorder per se, the restricted environmental stimulation therapy was incorporated because of the attentional problems found in patients with schizotypal personality. Thus, this treatment may have other applications for schizotypal personality disorder as a means of increasing attentional focus.

SUMMARY OF RECOMMENDATIONS BASED UPON TREATMENT OUTCOME LITERATURE

It is obvious that the systematic study of treatment efficacy with personality disorders is in its infancy. With few Type 1 studies published yet, it is difficult to make recommendations with a high degree of confidence. Linehan's dialectical behavior therapy appears to be a promising treatment for parasuicidal patients with borderline personality disorders. Recent results from the United Kingdom also seem to indicate that psychodynamically oriented treatment is also effective for borderline personality disorder. Behavior therapy is promising in the treatment of avoidant personality disorder, but the specific form of behavior therapy may need to be tailored to patients' types of interpersonal problems, with graded exposure better when distrust is an issue and intimacy-focused social skills training preferable when resisting others' demands is the major interpersonal problem in patients with avoidant personality disorder. A structured cognitive behavioral treatment appears to be best for patients with antisocial personality disorder. Psychodynamic therapy, particularly longer term, appears useful for the treatment of mixed personality disorders (based upon a controlled trial and two uncontrolled trials). One clear recommendation can be made based upon a consistent finding across many studies: Standard brief treatments for Axis I conditions often fail when Axis II pathology is also present, and therefore, the clinician should be alert to the presence of a comorbid Axis II disorder and reevaluate the selection of treatment modality if progress is not made within the period of brief therapy. Consistent with this recommendation are the results of Kopta et al. (1994), who found that characterological symptoms that are typical of personality disorders improve slowly, with only 59% of outpatients achieving clinically significantly change on such symptoms after 52 treatment sessions.

FUTURE DIRECTIONS IN THE TREATMENT OF PERSONALITY DISORDERS

The studies reviewed above begin to point to some promising likely developments in the treatment of personality disorders. First, we can predict that modification is apt to be needed of the existing Axis I treatments to take into account the Axis II pathology. These modifications will include the lengthening of brief treatments and greater attention to the longstanding rigid belief systems and maladaptive interpersonal patterns of Axis II patients, rather than a focus on symptoms or recent triggers only. A second major direction will be the matching of patients to treatment modalities. This matching may occur at the level of the personality disorder syndrome, such as Barber and Muenz's (1996) finding that depressed patients with features of avoidant personality disorder do better in cognitive therapy but depressed patients with features of obsessive compulsive personality disorders fare better in interpersonal therapy. These authors have shown that using these two diagnostic categories (either dimensionally or categorically) could be helpful in matching patients to either cognitive or interpersonal psychotherapy. Alternatively, matching patients to treatment may occur in regard to other patient attributes that either underlie the distinctions between personality disorders or are other salient patient variables not captured in the current system. For example, Beutler, Mohr, Grawe, and Engle (1991) suggested that impulsivity/external coping style and resistance/reactance are two important dimensions for which there is preliminary evidence for the matching of patients to treatments. Thus, rather than use the diagnosis of antisocial personality disorder as a basis for recommending a more structured treatment modality, the underlying dimensions of impulsivity and low socialization that characterize but do not uniquely define antisocial personality disorder might be more salient for treatment selection. Whether these patient dimensions will be examined in addition to the *DSM* categories or will eventually replace them in some form remains to be seen.

Another direction for the future is the movement toward psychotherapy integration. In fact, Linehan's dialectical behavior therapy already integrates techniques from a wide variety of approaches. With personality disorders, such integration might be especially necessary because of the diverse set of problems that characterize these patients. Thus, a successful treatment might need elements of exposure therapy, understanding and modification of long-standing cognitive/interpersonal patterns, practice in new behaviors, and attention to disruptions in the therapeutic relationship (transference). Psychosocial and psychopharmacological interventions will also be examined in combination for personality disorders as a way of managing the symptoms while also treating the underlying psychological processes. Significant advances in the treatment of personality disorders can be expected to have important public health impacts, given the prevalence of these disorders and the impairment in social and occupational functioning associated with them.

ACKNOWLEDGMENTS The preparation of this manuscript was funded in part by National Institute of Mental Health grants P30-MH-45178, K02-MH00756, and RO1-MH40472. Address reprint request to Paul Crits-Christoph, Ph.D., Room 650, 3535 Market St. Philadelphia, PA 19104.

References

Alden, L. E. (1989). Short-term structured treatment for avoidant personality disorder. *Journal of Consulting and Clinical Psychology, 57,* 756–764.

Alden, L. E., & Capreol, M. J. (1993). Avoidant personality disorder: Interpersonal problems as predictors of treatment response. *Behavior Therapy, 24,* 357–376.

Alexander, F. (1930). The neurotic character. *International Journal of Psychoanalysis, 11,* 292–280.

American Psychiatric Association. (1994). *Diagnostic and statistical manual of mental disorders* (4th edition). Washington, DC: Author.

Ames-Frankel, J., Devlin, M. J., Walsh, B. T., Strasser, T. J., Sadik, C., Oldham, J. M., & Roose, S. P. (1992). Personality disorder diagnoses in patients with bulimia nervosa: Clinical correlates and changes with treatment. *Journal of Clinical Psychiatry, 53,* 90–96.

Aronson, T. A. (1989). A critical review of psychotherapeutic treatments of the borderline personality: Historical trends and future directions. *Journal of Nervous and Mental Disease, 177,* 511–527.

Barber, J. P., Frank, A., Weiss, R. D., Blaine, J., Siqueland, L., Moras, K., Calvo, N., Chittams, J., Mercer, D., & Salloum, I. (1996). Prevalence of personality disorder diagnoses among cocaine/crack dependents in the NIDA study. *Journal of Personality Disorders, 10,* 297–311.

Barber, J. P., Morse, J. Q., Krakauer, I., Chittams, J., & Crits-Christoph, K. (1997). Change in obsessive-compulsive and avoidant personality disorders following time-limited supportive-expressive therapy. *Psychotherapy, 34,* 133–143.

Barber, J. P., & Muenz, L. R. (1996). The role of avoidance and obsessiveness in matching patients to cognitive and interpersonal psychotherapy: Empirical findings from the Treatment for Depression Collaborative Research Program. *Journal of Consulting and Clinical Psychology, 64,* 951–958.

Barley, W. D., Buie, S. E., Peterson, E. W., Hollingsworth, A. S., Griva, M., Hickerson, S. C., Lawson, J. E., & Bailey, B. J. (1993). Development of an inpatient cognitive-behavioral treatment program for borderline personality disorder. *Journal of Personality Disorders, 7,* 232–240.

Baron, J., Gruen, R., Asnis, L., & Lord, S. (1985). Familial transmission of schizotypal and borderline personality disorders. *American Journal of Psychiatry, 142,* 927–934.

Bateman, A., & Fonagy, P. (1999). Effectiveness of partial hospitalization in the treatment of borderline personality disorder: A randomized controlled trial. *American Journal of Psychiatry, 156,* 1563–1569.

Beutler, L. E., Mohr, D. C., Grawe, K., & Engle, D. (1991). Looking for differential treatment effects: Cross-cultural predictors of differential psychotherapy efficacy. *Journal of Psychotherapy Integration, 1*, 121–141.

Chambless, D. L., Renneberg, B., Goldstein, A., & Gracely, E. J. (1992). MCMI-diagnosed personality disorders among agoraphobic outpatients: Prevalence and relationship to severity and treatment outcome. *Journal of Anxiety Disorders, 6*, 193–211.

Chambless, D. L., Renneberg, B., Gracely, E. J., Goldstein, A., & Fydich, T. (2000). Axis I and II comorbidity in agoraphobia: Prediction of psychotherapy outcome in a clinical setting. *Psychotherapy Research, 10*, 279–295.

Clark, L. E., Livesley, J., & Morey, L. (1997). Special feature: Personality disorder assessment: The challenge of construct validity. *Journal of Personality Disorders, 11*, 205–231.

Coon, D. W. (1994). Cognitive-behavioral interventions with avoidant personality: A single case study. *Journal of Cognitive Psychotherapy: An International Quarterly, 8*, 243–253.

Davanloo, H. (1980). *Short-term dynamic psychotherapy*. New York: Jason Aronson.

Dinwiddie, S. H., Reich, T., & Cloninger, C. R. (1992). Psychiatric comorbidity and suicidality among intravenous drug users. *Journal of Clinical Psychiatry, 53*, 364–369.

Dyce, J. A. (1994). Personality disorders: Alternatives to the official diagnostic system. *Journal of Personality Disorders, 8*, 77–88.

Elkin, I., Shea, T., Watkins, J. T., Imber, S. D., Sotsky, S. M., Collins, J. F., Glass, D. R., Pilkonis, P. A., Leber, W. R., Docherty, J. P., & Parloff, M. B. (1989). NIMH Treatment of Depression Collaborative Research Program: General effectiveness of treatments. *Archives of General Psychiatry, 46*, 971–982.

Fahy, T. A., Eisler, I., & Russell, G. F. (1993). Personality disorder and treatment response in bulimia nervosa. *British Journal of Psychiatry, 162*, 765–770.

Fenichel, O. (1945). *The psychoanalytic theory of neurosis*. New York: Norton.

Fossati, A., Madeddu, F., & Maffei C. (1999). Borderline personality disorder and childhood sexual abuse: A meta-analytic study. *Journal of Personality Disorders, 13*, 268–280.

Frank, E., Kupfer, D. J., Jacob, M., & Jarrett, D. (1987). Personality features and response to acute treatment in recurrent depression. *Journal of Personality Disorders, 1*, 14–26.

Gunderson, J. G., Zanarini, M. C., & Kisiel, C. L. (1991). Borderline personality disorder: A review of data on *DSM-III-R* descriptions. *Journal of Personality Disorders, 5*, 340–352.

Haller, D. L., Knisely, J. S., Dawson, K. S., & Schnoll, S. H. (1993). Perinatal substance abusers: Psychological and social characteristics. *Journal of Nervous and Mental Disease, 181*, 509–513.

Hardy, G. E., Barkham, M., Shapiro, D. A., Stiles, W. B., Rees, A., & Reynolds, S. (1995). Impact of Cluster C personality disorders on outcomes of contrasting brief psychotherapies for depression. *Journal of Consulting and Clinical Psychology, 63*, 997–1004.

Hellerstein, D. J., Rosenthal, R. N., Pinsker, H., Samstag, L. W., Muran, J. C., & Winston, A. (1998). A randomized prospective study comparing supportive and dynamic therapies. *Journal of Psychotherapy Practice and Research, 7*, 261–271.

Herman, J. L., Perry, J. C., & van der Kolk, B. A. (1989). Childhood trauma in borderline personality disorder. *American Journal of Psychiatry, 146*, 490–495.

Hofmann, S. G., Newman, M. G., Becker, E., Taylor, C. B., & Roth, W. T. (1995). Social phobia with and without avoidant personality disorder: Preliminary behavior therapy outcome findings. *Journal of Anxiety Disorders, 9*, 427–438.

Høglend, P. (1993). Personality disorders and long-term outcome after brief dynamic psychotherapy. *Journal of Personality Disorders, 7*, 168–181.

Hwu, H. G., Yeh, E. K., & Chang, L. Y. (1989). Prevalence of psychiatric disorders in Taiwan defined by the Chinese Diagnostic Interview Schedule. *Acta Psychiatrica Scandinavica, 79*, 136–147.

Karterud, S., Vaglum, S., Friis, S., Irion, T., Johns, S., & Vaglum, P. (1992). Day hospital therapeutic community treatment for patients with personality disorders: An empirical evaluation of the containment function. *Journal of Nervous and Mental Disease, 180*, 238–243.

Kernberg, O. (1984). *Severe personality disorders: Psychotherapeutic strategies*. New Haven: Yale University Press.

Kernberg, O., Selzer, M. A., Koenigsberg, H. W., Carr, A. C., & Appelbaum, A. H. (1989). *Psychodynamic psychotherapy of borderline patients*. New York: Basic Books.

Koerner, K., & Linehan, M. M. (2000). Research on dialectical behavior therapy for patients with borderline personality disorder. *Psychiatric Clinics of North America, 23*, 151–167.

Kohut, H. (1984). *How does analysis cure?* Chicago: University of Chicago Press.

Kopta, S. M., Howard, K. I., Lowry, J. L., & Beutler, L. E. (1994). Patterns of symptomatic recovery in psychotherapy. *Journal of Consulting and Clinical Psychology, 62*, 1009–1016.

Linehan, M. M. (1993). *Cognitive-behavioral treatment of borderline personality disorder*. New York: Guilford Press.

Linehan, M. M., Heard, H. L., & Armstrong, H. E. (1993). Naturalistic follow-up of a behavioral treatment for chronically parasuicidal borderline patients. *Archives of General Psychiatry, 50,* 971–974.

Linehan, M. M., Hubert, A. E., Suarez, A., Douglas, A., & Heard, H. L. (1991). Cognitive-behavioral treatment of chronically parasuicidal borderline patients. *Archives of General Psychiatry, 48,* 1060–1064.

Linehan, M. M., Schmidt H., Dimeff, L. A., Craft, J. C., Kanter, J., & Comtois, K. A. (1999). Dialectical behavior therapy for patients with borderline personality disorder and drug-dependence. *American Journal on Addictions, 8,* 279–292.

Livesly, W. J., Schroeder, M. L., Jackson, D. N., & Jang, K. L. (1994). Categorical distinctions in the study of personality disorder: Implications for classification. *Journal of Abnormal Psychology, 103,* 6–17.

Longabaugh, R., Rubin, A., Malloy, P., Beattie, M., Clifford, P. R., & Noel, N. (1994). Drinking outcomes of alcohol abusers diagnosed as antisocial personality disorder. *Alcoholism: Clinical and Experimental Research, 18,* 778–785.

Loranger, A., Oldham, J., & Tullis, E. (1982). Familial transmission of *DSM-III* borderline personality disorder. *Archives of General Psychiatry, 39,* 795–799.

Maffei, C., Fossati, A., Agostoni, I., Barraco, A., Bagnato, M., Deborah, D., Namia, C., Novella, L., & Petrachi, M. (1997). Interrater reliability and internal consistency of the Structured Clinical Interview for *DSM-IV* Axis II personality disorders (SCID-II), version 2.0. *Journal of Personality Disorders, 11,* 279–284.

Malan, D. H. (1976). *The frontier of brief psychotherapy.* New York: Plenum Press.

Meares, R. (1987). The secret and the self: On a new direction in psychotherapy. *Australian and New Zealand Journal of Psychiatry, 21,* 545–559.

Mennin, D. S., & Heimberg, R. G. (2000). The impact of comorbid mood and personality disorders in the cognitive-behavioral treatment of panic disorder. *Clinical Psychology Review, 20,* 339–357.

Minichiello, W. E., Baer, L., & Jenike, M. A. (1987). Schizotypal personality disorder: A poor prognostic indicator for behavior therapy in the treatment of obsessive-compulsive disorder. *Journal of Anxiety Disorders, 1,* 273–276.

Monsen, J., Odland, T., Faugli, A., Daae, E., & Eilertsen, D. E. (1995). Personality disorders: Changes and stability after intensive psychotherapy focusing on affect consciousness. *Psychotherapy Research, 5,* 33–48.

Munroe-Blum, H., & Marziali, E. (1995). A controlled trial of short-term group treatment for borderline personality disorder. *Journal of Personality Disorders, 9,* 190–198.

Nace, E. D., Davis, C. W., & Gaspari, J. P. (1991). Axis II comorbidity in substance users. *American Journal of Psychiatry, 148,* 118–120.

Ogata, S. N., Silk, K. R., Goodrich, S., Lohr, N., Westen, D., & Hill, E. M. (1990). Childhood sexual and physical abuse in adult patients with borderline personality disorder. *American Journal of Psychiatry, 147,* 1008–1013.

Paris, J. (2000). Childhood precursors of borderline personality disorders. *Psychiatric Clinics of North America, 23,* 77–88.

Perry, J. C. (1992). Problems and considerations in the valid assessment of personality disorders. *American Journal of Psychiatry, 149,* 1645–1653.

Perry, J. C., Banon, E., & Ianni, F. (1999). Effectiveness of psychotherapy for personality disorders. *American Journal of Psychiatry, 156,* 1312–1321.

Pettinati, H. (1990). Diagnosing personality disorders in substance abuse. In L. S. Harris (Ed.), *Problems of drug dependence, 1990: Proceedings of the 52nd Annual Scientific Meeting, The Committee on Problems of Drug Dependence, Inc.* National Institute on Drug Abuse Research Monograph Series, 105. Rockville, MD: U.S. Department of Health and Human Services (pp. 236–242).

Pilkonis, P. A., & Frank, E. L. (1988). Personality pathology in recurrent depression: Nature, prevalence, and relationship to treatment response. *American Journal of Psychiatry, 145,* 435–441.

Reich, J. H., & Green, A. I. (1991). Effect of personality disorders on outcome of treatment. *Journal of Nervous and Mental Disease, 179,* 74–82.

Reich, J. H., & Vasile, R. G. (1993). Effect of personality-disorders on the treatment outcome of Axis-I conditions—An update. *Journal of Nervous and Mental Disease, 181,* 475–484.

Renneberg, B., Goldstein, A. J., Phillips, D., & Chambless, D. L. (1990). Intensive behavioral group treatment of avoidant personality disorder. *Behavior Therapy, 21,* 363–377.

Ruegg, R., & Frances, A. (1995). New research on personality disorders. *Journal of Personality Disorders, 9,* 1–48.

Samuels, J. F., Nestadt, G., Romanoski, A. J., Folstein, M. F., & McHugh, P. R. (1994). DSM-III personality disorders in the community. *American Journal of Psychiatry, 151,* 1055–1062.

Shapiro, D. A., Barkham, M., Rees, A., Hardy, G. E., Reynolds, S., & Startup, M. (1994). Effects of treatment duration and severity of depression on the effectiveness of cognitive-behavioral and psychodynamic-interpersonal psychotherapy. *Journal of Consulting and Clinical Psychology, 62*, 522–534.

Sifneos, P. E. (1979). *Short-term dynamic psychotherapy*. New York: Plenum Press.

Skodol, A. E., Stout, R. L., McGlashan, T. H., Grilo, C. M., Gunderson, J. G., Shea, M. T., Morey, L. C., Zanarini, M. C., Dyck, I. R., & Oldham, J. M. (1999). Co-occurrence of mood and personality disorders: A report from the Collaborative Longitudinal Personality Disorders Study (CLPS). *Depression and Anxiety, 10*, 175–182.

Stevenson, J., & Meares, R. (1992). An outcome study of psychotherapy for patients with borderline personality disorder. *American Journal of Psychiatry, 149*, 358–362.

Stevenson, J., & Meares, R. (1999). Psychotherapy with borderline patients: 2. A preliminary cost benefit study. *Australian and New Zealand Journal of Psychiatry, 33*, 473–477.

Stravynski, A., Belisle, M., Marcouiller, M., & Lavallee, Y. (1994). The treatment of avoidant personality disorder by social skills training in the clinic or in real-life settings. *Canadian Journal of Psychiatry, 39*, 377–383.

Stravynski, A., Lesage, A., Marcouiller, M., & Elie, R. (1989). A test of the therapeutic mechanism in social skills training with avoidant personality disorder. *Journal of Nervous and Mental Disease, 177*, 739–744.

Svrakic, D., & Divac-Jovanovic, M. (1994). Personality disorders: Model for conceptual approach and classification: 2. Proposed classification. *American Journal of Psychotherapy, 48*, 562–580.

Swartz, M., Blazer, D., George, L., & Winfield, I. (1990). Estimating the prevalence of borderline personality disorder in the community. *Journal of Personality Disorders, 4*, 257–272.

Torgersen, S. (1984). Genetic and nosological aspects of schizotypal and borderline personality disorders. *Archives of General Psychiatry, 41*, 546–554.

Turner, R. M. (1987). The effects of personality disorder diagnosis on the outcome of social anxiety symptom reduction. *Journal of Personality Disorders, 1*, 136–144.

Walker, W. R., Freeman, R. F., & Christensen, D. K. (1994). Restricting environmental stimulation (REST) to enhance cognitive behavioral treatment for obsessive compulsive disorder with schizotypal personality disorder. *Behavior Therapy, 25*, 709–719.

Weiss, R. D., Mirin, S. M., Griffin, M. L., Gunderson, J. G., & Hufford, C. (1993). Personality disorders in cocaine dependence. *Comprehensive Psychiatry, 34*, 145–149.

Weissman, M. M. (1993). The epidemiology of personality disorders: A 1990 update. *Journal of Personality Disorders, 7*, 44–62.

Westen, D., Lundolph, P., Misle, B., Ruffins, S., & Block, J. (1990). Physical and sexual abuse in adolescent girls with borderline personality disorder. *American Journal of Orthopsychiatry, 60*, 55–66.

Widiger, T. (1993). The *DSM-III-R* categorical personality disorder diagnoses: A critique and an alternative. *Psychological Inquiry, 4*, 75–90.

Widiger, T., & Rogers, J. H. (1989). Prevalence and comorbidity of personality disorders. *Psychiatric Annals, 19*, 132–136.

Williams, J. G. (1988). Cognitive intervention for a paranoid personality disorder. *Psychotherapy, 25*, 570–575.

Winston, A., Laikin, M., Pollack, J., Samstag, L. W., McCullough, L., & Muran, J. C. (1994). Short-term psychotherapy of personality disorders. *American Journal of Psychiatry, 151*, 190–194.

Winston, A., Pollack, J., McCullough, L., Flegenheimer, W., Kestenbaum, R., & Trujillo, M. (1991). Brief psychotherapy of personality disorders. *Journal of Nervous and Mental Disease, 179*, 188–193.

Woody, G. E., McLellan, A. T., Luborsky, L., & O'Brien, C. P. (1985). Sociopathy and psychotherapy outcome. *Archives of General Psychiatry, 42*, 1081–1086.

Zimmerman, M., & Coryell, W. H. (1990). Diagnosing personality disorders in the community: A comparison of self-report and interview measures. *Archives of General Psychiatry, 47*, 527–531.

Zimmerman, M., & Mattia, J. I. (1999). Axis I diagnostic comorbidity and borderline personality disorder. *Comprehensive Psychiatry, 40*, 245–252.

25

Pharmacological Treatments for Personality Disorders

Harold W. Koenigsberg
Ann Marie Woo-Ming
Larry J. Siever

The use of medication to treat personality (Axis II) disorders derives from the recent confluence of anecdotal experience, a growing body of controlled studies, and emerging evidence of the presence of psychobiological traits that may underlie the personality disorders. Personality disorders are commonly divided into three clusters: Cluster A disorders (odd cluster), Cluster B disorders (dramatic cluster), and Cluster C disorders (anxious cluster). For Cluster A disorders, mainly involving schizotypal disorder, two Type 1, three Type 2, and two Type 3 studies are available. These suggest that antipsychotic medications may be useful for some aspects of these disorders. For borderline personality disorder (BPD) (a Cluster B disorder), noradrenergic agents tend to improve mood but not irritability or dyscontrol, whereas serotonergic agents may act to decrease impulsivity. There are inconsistent data about the utility of antipsychotic agents and anticonvulsants. There are very few pharmacological studies on the Cluster C disorders. Case reports and two double-blind studies suggest that antidepressants may be helpful for the avoidant personality disorder.

The pharmacotherapy of personality disorders represents a relatively new frontier of psychopharmacology. Traditionally, personality-disordered patients have been treated with psychotherapy and have not been thought responsive to pharmacological intervention. However, advances in the field since the early 1980s have challenged that perspective. A biological approach to the personality disorders questions the traditional separation of Axis I and Axis II diagnoses. However, clinical research investigations seeking to clarify the biological substrates of those disorders also pose some logistical difficulties. What follows is a summary of some of these methodological problems and a description of the more well-documented clinical strategies in current use.

Attempts to systematically investigate biological etiologies and treatments for these disorders have been in part limited by the overlap in symptomatology among the various personality disorder diagnoses. Other conceptual problems include (a) the significant clinical heterogeneity even within one personality disorder diagnosis, (b) the relationship between Axis I and Axis II disorders, and (c) limited reliability assessment of the diagnoses of personality disorders.

CLINICAL HETEROGENEITY AND OVERLAP OF AXIS II DISORDERS

Within each Axis II category, many combinations of clinical presentations are possible, and it is possible to have a clinically heterogeneous group of patients in any one study even though the patients may technically meet criteria for the same personality disorder. For example, some schizotypal patients have marked borderline features, while others appear more emotionally restricted. Different Axis II diagnoses may share similar criteria under the current (fourth-edition) *Diagnostic and Statistical Manual of Mental Disorders,* (*DSM-IV*; American Psychiatric Association [APA], 1994) categorization, and often, patients meet criteria for more than one type of personality disorder (Hyler et al., 1990), adding to the potential for clinical heterogeneity within a given study sample.

RELATIONSHIP BETWEEN AXIS I AND AXIS II DISORDERS

Overlap in symptomatology also exists between the Axis I and Axis II disorders. For example, in the Cluster B disorders in which depressive and labile mood are often found, distinction between these Axis II symptoms and the symptoms of bipolar spectrum disorders, dysthymia, or major depression is often unclear. In the Cluster C disorders, avoidant personality disorder shares many criteria of Axis I's social phobia disorder, and some authors feel that they are actually the same disorder.

Frequent comorbidity is seen between Axis I and Axis II syndromes; for example, up to 50% of patients with borderline personality disorder (BPD) or schizotypal personality disorder (SPD) are found to have concurrent diagnoses of a depressive disorder. Thus, evaluating a personality-disordered patient's response to drug treatment can be confounded by drug effects on a comorbid Axis I disorder.

RELIABILITY OF ASSESSMENT TOOLS

Methodological problems in designing studies of personality-disordered patients include limited reliability assessment of the diagnoses and limited longitudinal stability in this population. Our assessment instruments have questionable efficacy, as seen by mediocre retest and intratest reliability (Gitlin, 1993). Many of these difficulties are related to our limited understanding of how a personality disorder trait differs from adaptive personality traits. Measuring or standardizing change in a personality disorder symptom poses a challenge, given the "persistently transient" nature of many of these symptoms (e.g., mood lability in the borderline patient). Because of the environmental responsiveness of the symptoms, a cardinal feature of most of these disorders, nonpharmacological variables such as the milieu of the research setting and interactions with the research team should ideally be consistent.

Due to the episodic nature of some personality traits, such as mood lability, studies spanning a greater length of time would ideally allow investigation of these traits over their natural course. However, chaotic interpersonal relationships or suspiciousness of others may interfere with the sometimes lengthy treatment alliance required to complete a research study and lead to high dropout rates.

THE NEED FOR MULTIPLE APPROACHES TO DEFINING AND TREATING PERSONALITY DISORDERS

Attempts to avoid the overlap in diagnoses inherent in *DSM-IV* categorization have led to dimensional models of personality disorders in the context of which psychobiological findings can be understood. This approach is based on studies of biological correlates of these dimensions, and family studies that point to the heritability of these dimensions (Trestman, deVegvar, & Siever, 1995). The model presumes that the target dimensions of personality can be conceptualized in terms of cognitive and perceptual distortions, affective lability and impulsivity/aggression, and anxiety. These three categories correspond to the odd, dramatic, and anxious clusters, respectively, in *DSM-IV*. One challenge in studying a particular personality dimension is that abnormalities in more than one neurotransmitter system may converge to provide the substrate for a specific dimension. Also, targeting one core dimension still leaves unaddressed the complex clinical syndrome that encompasses a personality disorder. Finally, in defining a core dimension in the personality-disordered patient, a distinction must be made between a trait and a state symptom. Despite these hurdles, the dimensional approach allows consideration of the fluidity that is clinically recognized between Axis I and Axis II symptoms and provides a framework for inquiry into the interrelationships of types of behavior, their modulatory neurotransmitters, and pharmacological interventions.

In summary, descriptive (i.e., Axis II categories) and biological approaches can be used for investigating psychopharmacological treatments for personality disorders. A descriptive approach allows a more clinical conceptualization of the personality disorders but may not allow for meaningful measurements of change in response to medication, given the broad overlap of symptoms within Axis II, comorbidity with Axis I disorders, and an incomplete distinction between state and trait phenomena. A dimensional approach allows for more precise "targeting" of the phenomena to be examined yet may fail to wholly capture the complex entity of human personality. Although each approach has recognized limitations, each can also offer valuable frameworks within which these disorders can be further investigated.

We now turn to a review of the pharmacological treatments of personality disorders and the psychobiological findings that prompted the use of such treatments.

CLUSTER A DISORDERS (ODD CLUSTER)

Schizotypal personality disorder has been the most carefully studied of the odd cluster (Cluster A) disorders. Clinical, genetic, and psychophysiological studies have established its place within the schizophrenia spectrum disorders. Phenomenologically, the SPD patient can be described as having both the deficit-like and psychotic-like symptoms seen in schizophrenia, but in an attenuated form. Family studies have revealed significantly higher rates of SPD in the relatives of schizophrenic patients than in relatives of control patients (Silverman et al., 1993), and siblings of probands with schizophrenia have been found to be at higher risk for both SPD and schizophrenia if either one or both parents had SPD (Baron, Gruen, & Asnis, 1985).

Psychophysiological testing reveals abnormal performance on smooth-pursuit eye movements, backward masking tests, and continuous-performance tasks associated with both schizophrenia and SPD (Siever, 1991). Recent MRI studies have identified structural similarities in these two disorders, and functional imaging has identified similarities in regional brain activity during cognitive task performance in both (Kirrane & Siever, 2000). These findings have strengthened the concept of a spectrum of schizophrenia-like disorders that span both Axis I and II categories. Psychobiological investigations into SPD, based on a dimensional model of symptoms, have also supported the relationship between SPD and schizophrenia and provide a logical starting point for psychopharmacological interventions for this personality disorder.

Schizotypal personality disorder can be characterized by disturbances in the cognitive and perceptual domains, manifested by impairment in attending to the environment, discriminating among stimuli, or processing information. Clinically, this disturbance may translate into psychotic-like symptoms (such as magical thinking, ideas of reference, or perceptual distortion), deficitlike symptoms (such as poor interpersonal relatedness or social detachment), and cognitive disorganization (such as deficient performance on cognitive, psychophysiological, and attentional testing).

Psychotic-Like Symptoms in Schizotypal Personality Disorder

The commonalities of SPD and schizophrenia and the role of dopamine in psychotic symptoms spurred interest in dopaminergic function in SPD. Cerebrospinal-fluid homovanillic acid (HVA; the major dopamine metabolite) concentrations in SPD patients correlated significantly with psychotic-like symptoms and were significantly elevated over levels in other types of personality-disordered patients in one study from our center (Siever, 1991). Similarly, plasma HVA concentrations correlated significantly with psychotic-like symptoms in SPD and were elevated over those in normal subjects in an overlapping sample (Siever et al., 1991).

These findings suggest the possibility that dopamine antagonism might be beneficial in these disorders. Given the known efficacy of antipsychotic medications in the schizophrenia spectrum disorders, their effect on SPD psychotic-like symptoms has also been investigated (see Table 25.1). However, the majority of these studies primarily targeted subjects with borderline personality disorder and described findings for patients who also met criteria for SPD. The single study involving only SPD patients (Hymowitz et al., 1986) did find an improvement in psychotic-like symptoms following treatment with haloperidol; however, a single-blind study was used. The three

TABLE 25.1 Antipsychotic Studies: Borderline Personality Disorder and Schizotypal Personality Disorder

Study	*Diagnosis*	*Study Design*	*Comment*
Goldberg et al. (1986)	N = 50 BPD and/or SPD patients (BPD with at least one prior psychotic episode).	Type 1 study: thiothixene (average 8.6 mg); 12 weeks; double-blind, placebo-controlled.	Thiothixene led to improvement of psychotic-like/obsessive/phobic anxiety symptoms; no effect on depression.
Cowdry & Gardner (1988)	N = 16 female BPD outpatients, all characterized as "seriously ill with severe dysphoria in setting of rejection, and dyscontrol behavior such as assaultiveness, cutting, overdose"; of these, 6 patients were also SPD.	Type 1 study: tranylcypromine, trifluoperazine, carbamazepine, alprazolam; 6 weeks; double-blind, placebo-controlled.	Tranylcypromine led to improved global and mood scores, improved impulsivity, but no effect on behavioral dyscontrol; trifluoperazine showed a trend toward broad symptomatic improvement; carbamazepine showed improvement of impulsivity and behavioral dyscontrol; alprazolam led to increases in suicidality and dyscontrol.
Soloff et al. (1989)	N = 90 inpatients with BPD, mixed BPD/SPD symptoms, and a small number of SPD patients.	Type 2 study: amitriptyline (100–175 mg) or haloperidol (4–16 mg); 5 weeks; placebo-controlled.	Haloperidol led to global improvements, including in hostile depression and impulsive ward behavior, especially if patient had severe schizotypal symptoms, hostility, or suspiciousness. AMI not as effective as haloperidol for anxiety and hostility; not effective on core depressive symptoms.
Serban & Siegel (1984)	N = 52 outpatients with SPD (14), BPD with prior psychotic episode (16), mixed BPD/SPD (16).	Type 2 study: haloperidol or thiothixene (4–12 mg); 6 weeks to 3 months; double-blind	Thiothixene > haloperidol led to moderate to marked improvements in all patients for general symptoms, paranoid ideation, anxiety, ideas of reference, and depression, regardless of diagnosis.
Hymowitz et al. (1986)	N = 17 SPD outpatients.	Type 2 study: haloperidol (up to 12 mg; average 3.6 mg); 6 weeks; single-blind, 2-week placebo washout	Drug led to mild to moderate improvement in ideas of reference, social isolation, odd communication, and thought disorder; also GAS scores increased.
Jensen & Andersen (1989)	N = 5 SPD, 5 BPD inpatients.	Type 3 study: amoxapine (up to 300 mg); 3-week minimum; open-label, no placebo; oxazepam prn agitation (36–42 mg QD)	SPD subjects showed broad improvement in BPRS (schizophrenia subscale) and HDRS scores. BPD subjects showed no improvement.
Benedetti et al. (1998)	N = 12 inpatients with BPD and severe psychotic-like symptoms; 2 met criteria for SPD.	Type 3 study: clozapine (up to 100 mg/d, average 43 mg/d); open-label, 16-week study.	Broad symptomatic improvement in pychotic-like symptoms, impulsivity, affective instability, depression, suicidality.

TABLE 25.1 (continued)

Study	*Diagnosis*	*Study Design*	*Comment*
Chengappa et al. (1999)	N = 7 inpatients with BPD, 6 with Axis I psychotic disorders.	Clozapine; chart audit with mirror-image design; mean dose 421 mg/day.	Decrease in number of seclusion and restraint incidents, modest improvement in GAF.
Schulz et al. (1999)	N = 11 community-based referrals meeting criteria for BPD and dysthymia (7 of whom also met SPD criteria).	Type 3 study: olanzapine (up to 10 mg; average 7.7 mg); open-label, no placebo; 8-week study.	Olanzapine led to improvment in global scores on BPRS, BDHI, BIS11, GAF, SCL-90.
Koenigsberg et al. (2001)	N = 23 community and clinic referrals meeting criteria for SPD (only 20% also meet BPD criteria).	Type 2 study: risperidone (up to 2 mg); 9 weeks; double-blind, placebo-controlled, 2-week placebo washout.	Risperidone led to significantly lower PANSS general score by Week 3 and PANSS positive score by Week 7, with trend in PANSS negative score by Week 9.

Note. AMI = amitriptyline; BPD = borderline personality disorder; BDHI = Buss-Durkee Hostility Inventory; BIS11 = Baratt Impulsivity Scale, version 11; BPRS = Brief Psychiatric Rating Scale; GAF = Global Assessment of Function; HDRS = Hamilton Depression Rating Scale; PANSS = Positive and Negative Syndrome Scale; SCL-90 = Hopkins Symptom Check List 90; SPD = schizotypal personality disorder.

double-blind, placebo-controlled studies of mixed populations of SPD and BPD patients (Cowdry & Gardner, 1988; Goldberg et al., 1986; Soloff et al., 1989) showed an association between low-dose antipsychotic use and broad improvements in symptomatology, including scales of psychoticism, anxiety, depression, hostility, and rejection sensitivity. However, one study (Cowdry & Gardner, 1988) involved patients characterized by severe affective instability so that the applicability of these findings to the more typically emotionally constricted SPD subjects is in question. Other non-placebo-controlled studies (Jensen & Andersen, 1989; Serban & Siegel, 1984) described moderate, global improvements in mixed BPD and SPD populations with the use of antipsychotic medication.

The atypical antipsychotic medications are attractive candidates for the treatment of SPD because of their low incidence of side effects and the possibility that they may particularly target negative symptoms (Javitt, 1999; Lane et al., 1999). A favorable side effect profile is especially important for medications used to treat SPD because this disorder is characterized by a tendency toward somatic preoccupation, which can lead to an unusual sensitivity to side effects. One open-label study of the atypical antipsychotic olanzapine in the treatment of dysthymic borderline patients, most of whom also met criteria for SPD, has been published (Schultz et al., 1999). The authors reported robust improvement over the 8-week treatment period in global scores on the five rating scales they employed (see Table 25.1). Our group (Koenigsberg et al., 2001) completed a 9-week placebo-controlled double-blind study of low-dose risperidone in the treatment of nondepressed SPD patients, only 20% of whom had comorbid BPD. We found statistically significant reductions in Positive and Negative Syndrome (PANNS) general score by Week 3 and PANSS positive score by Week 7 in the risperidone group compared to the placebo-treated group.

Conversely, a state of dopamine agonism might be expected to exacerbate the psychotic-like symptoms of SPD. Indeed, a study of eight SPD/BPD and eight BPD patients selected by virtue of affective lability showed that, when administered amphetamine, SPD subjects had significantly increased Brief Psychiatric Rating Scale scores of thought disturbance and self-rated psychoticism compared to BPD subjects (Schulz, Cornelius, Schulz, & Soloff, 1988). The authors concluded that this finding supported the hypothesis that SPD is included in the psychotic spectrum disorders. In contrast, 20 patients selected solely on the basis of meeting SPD criteria demonstrated no increase in psychotic-like symptoms with amphetamine administration (Siever et al., unpublished, 1994). Thus, it may be that certain SPD subjects with hyperdopaminergic states may be more responsive to treatment with dopa-antagonist agents and may respond negatively to dopamine agonism, while those with normal or reduced dopaminergic activities (see below) may respond beneficially to dopamine agonism.

Thus, it appears that schizotypal symptomatology in mixed BPD/SPD populations is responsive, in modest and generalized ways, to low-dose antipsychotic medication. Given the state of dopamine antagonism induced by these medications and correlations between increased plasma and cerebrospinal fluid (CSF) HVA and psychotic-like symptoms in SPD, it is tempting to hypothesize that psychotic-like symptoms in SPD would be particularly responsive to antipsychotic medications. Future trials with primarily SPD subjects in double-blind, placebo-controlled settings would help to refine further the role for these agents in SPD.

Deficit-Like Symptoms and Cognitive Disorganization in Schizotypal Personality Disorder

Neurobiological studies of the deficit-like symptoms of SPD have investigated their relationship to psychophysiological testing, neuroanatomy, and monoaminergic indices. Abnormal performance on smooth-pursuit eye movements, backward masking tests, and continuous-performance tasks correlate with deficit symptoms of SPD (Siever, 1991). Cognitive disorganization, as measured by performance on psychological testing, has also been described among SPD patients. These subjects have been shown to make significantly increased numbers of errors on the Wisconsin Card Sort Test (WCST) and California Verbal Learning Test compared to normal subjects and other non–Cluster A personality-disordered patients (Bergman et al., 1998). These indices suggest roles for the frontal and temporal cortices in the deficit symptoms of SPD.

Correlations between neurotransmitter levels and deficit-like symptoms in SPD have been investigated. Whereas increased plasma HVA levels have been shown to correlate with psychotic-like symptoms in personality-disordered patients, decreased plasma HVA levels may be associated with deficit-like symptoms in relatives of schizophrenic patients and cognitive deficits in SPD patients (Siever, Kalus, & Keefe, 1993). Investigations of cholinergic indices in schizophrenic patients have yielded mixed results (Karson, Casanova, Kleinman, & Griffin, 1993; Tandon & Greden, 1989); however, preliminary data from our laboratory suggest that the cholinergic agent physostigmine may improve visuospatial delayed-response attentional performance in SPD patients.

Thus, an interrelationship may exist among deficit-like symptoms, cognitive deficits as measured by psychological and psychophysiological tests, and decreased plasma HVA concentrations.

The above findings raise the possibility that dopaminergic agents may lead to improvement of deficit symptoms and cognitive disorganization in SPD subjects. One double-blind, placebo-controlled study of amphetamine in SPD/BPD patients found that in addition to worsening of psychotic-like symptoms among the SPD group, all subjects had increased activation scores on the Brief Psychiatric Rating Scale (BPRS) in response to amphetamine (Schulz et al., 1988). This finding might suggest an improvement in such deficit symptoms as anergia and withdrawal. Further, a preliminary study of amphetamine use in SPD patients showed improved performance on the Wisconsin Card Sort Test (Siever et al., 1995). Our group is currently studying the effect of the mixed dopamine D1/D2 agonist pergolide on cognitive function in SPD patients.

The monoamine oxidase inhibitor (MAOI) tranylcypromine has been associated with broad-based behavioral effects in one mixed BPD/SPD group (see Table 25.1). Among the changes observed was an increased capacity for pleasure. While this may reflect an improvement in deficit-like symptoms, the effect of comorbidity of affective symptoms for both groups is unclear in the study. The continued investigation of catecholaminergic agents for SPD patients would be of value, with special focus on their effect on cognitive performance, as well as deficit-like symptoms. At present, our group is investigating the use of the alpha-1 agonist guanfacine to treat cognitive impairments in SPD patients.

Treatment of Comorbid Diagnoses in Schizotypal Personality Disorder

The use of antidepressant agents for SPD has a basis in the observation that high rates of comorbidity exist between SPD and the depressive disorders: 30 to 50% of SPD patients seen in clinical settings have been found to have a concurrent major depressive disorder, and 50% of patients have a history of major depressive disorder (Kaplan & Sadock, 1995). So far, however, trials with antidepressant agents have been conducted only in groups of mixed BPD/SPD patients (see Tables 25.1 and 25.2). The use of fluoxetine, up to 80 mg over a 12-week period, was investigated in a mixed group and was found to decrease obsessive symptoms, rejection sensitivity, depressive symptoms, anxiety, and psychoticism (Markovitz et al., 1991). These improvements occurred regardless of whether subjects had a concurrent diagnosis of major depressive disorder. Such findings are limited by the fact that the study was open-label and again by the heterogeneity of the subjects.

There have been attempts to "distinguish pharmacologically" between affective and psychotic-like symptoms, primarily in BPD groups with some SPD patients included. In one large, mixed sample, amitriptyline led to a significant improvement in anxiety and hostility in the whole group, although less effectively than haloperidol (Soloff et al., 1989). Tranylcypromine was used in a primarily BPD group with a small subset of SPD patients and was found to decrease significantly a broad array of symptoms, including depressive scores, anxiety, rejection sensitivity, and impulsivity (Cowdry & Gardner, 1988). However, the generalized response of symptoms has failed to elucidate a differential response of affective symptoms or psychotic-like symptoms to antidepressants in these patient populations.

Thus, in order to determine the efficacy of antidepressants for SPD symptomatology, replication studies using double-blind, placebo-controlled methods in homogeneous groups of SPD patients are needed.

CLUSTER B (DRAMATIC CLUSTER)

The disorders seen in Cluster B (dramatic cluster) have been defined dimensionally as being characterized by impulsivity/aggression and affective/lability. The prototype diagnoses involving these traits are borderline personality disorder and antisocial personality disorder. There are numerous investigations into the neurobiological substrates that may underlie each of these dimensions and corresponding implications for pharmacological management of the disorders that incorporate these dimensions.

Psychobiology of Impulsivity/Aggression

Impulsivity/aggression has been associated with a number of determinants, including familial inheritance, disturbances of the serotonergic and noradrenergic systems, and nonspecific cerebral dysfunction.

Family Studies of Impulsivity/Aggression

First-degree relatives of BPD patients have been shown to have significantly greater prevalences of both impulsive/aggressive behaviors and affective/lability than relatives of other personality-disordered or schizophrenic patients (Silverman & Pinkham, 1991). Furthermore, relatives of borderline probands appear to be at greater risk for BPD than the relatives of normal control subjects (Baron et al., 1985). Although such findings do not distinguish the role of environmental and genetic influences on familial inheritance, preliminary results from a twin study show that individual BPD criteria may be genetically determined. These criteria include instability in relationships, impulsivity, anger, and affective instability (Torgersen, 1992).

Serotonergic and Noradrenergic Indices in Impulsivity/Aggression

Diminished serotonergic indices have been implicated in impulsive/aggressive behavior directed toward the self (i.e., suicide attempts) and others. This association exists across diagnostic categories, lending support to the conceptualization of impulsivity/aggression as a dimensional trait. For example, decreased CSF 5-hydroxyindoleacetic acid (5-HIAA) levels have been shown to correlate inversely with a history of aggressive behavior and with rating scales of aggressive behavior. Decreased CSF 5-HIAA levels are also associated with depressed patients who have made suicide attempts, compared to the levels in depressed patients who have never attempted suicide or to the levels in healthy controls (Brown et al., 1982).

Central serotonergic function is also diminished in association with impulsivity/aggression in affective disorders, BPD, and other personality disorders. Decreased central 5-hydroxytryptophan (5-HT) function appears to be associated with self- and other-directed aggression in personality-disordered patients and to be associated with a history of suicide attempts in patients with major depression. One study compared

TABLE 25.2 Pharmacology of Borderline Personality Disorder: Antidepressant and Antipsychotic Agents

Study	*Diagnosis*	*Study Design*	*Comment*
Sheard et al. (1976)	N = 66 inmates characterized by extreme impulsivity, aggression, and hostility.	Type 2 study: lithium versus placebo.	Decrease in number of major prison infractions.
Links et al. (1990)	N = 15 BPD.	Type 1 study: lithium versus desipramine; double-blind, placebo-controlled.	Lithium led to decrease in therapist's perception of patient irritability, anger, and suicidal symptoms; trend for desipramine to have no effect or to worsen symptoms of anger/suicide and to be less effective than lithium in decreasing depression scores.
Coccaro & Kavoussi (1995)	N = 40 PD patients with histories of impulsive aggression.	Type 1 study: fluoxetine 20–60 mg; double-blind, placebo-controlled; 12 weeks.	Overt aggression scores reduced at Weeks 4, 10, 12, and end point; irritability scores reduced at Weeks 6–12 and end point.
Salzman et al. (1995)	N = 22 patients recruited from the community (13 met BPD criteria, and 9 had BPD traits); mild to moderate severity.	Type 1 study: fluoxetine 20–60 mg; double-blind, placebo-controlled; 13 weeks including 1-week placebo lead-in.	Anger and depression declined significantly more in the fluoxetine group than in the placebo group. Measures included PDRS anger and depression, POMS anger and depression, OAS anger against objects, and HAM-D scales.
Norden (1989)	N = 12 BPD patients, all except one with histories of suicidality.	Type 3 study: fluoxetine; open-label.	Very much or much improved; irritability and suicidality among the most responsive symptoms.
Coccaro et al. (1990)	N = 2 BPD; N = 1 antisocial PD.	Type 3 study: fluoxetine; open-label; 6 weeks.	Initial decrease in impulsivity-aggression scores for all 3 patients.
Cornelius, Soloff, Perel, & Ulrich (1991)	N = 5 BPD inpatients who had failed phenelzine and at least one neuroleptic.	Type 3 study: fluoxetine; open-label.	Decreases in impulsivity and suicidality.
Markovitz et al. (1991)	N = 22 outpatients: 8 BPD, 10 BPD/SPD with mixed symptoms, 4 SPD; 13 patients also with MDD.	Type 3 study: fluoxetine; open-label; 20–80 mg over 12 weeks.	Decrease in 50% of patients' self-mutilatory behavior; significant decrease in depression, rejection sensitivity, psychoticism, anxiety, and obsessive compulsive symptoms regardless of comorbid diagnosis of MDD.
Soloff et al. (1986)	N = 52, BPD inpatients.	Type 2 study: amitriptyline; placebo-controlled.	AMI nonresponders showed significantly more impulsive/assaultive behavior than placebo nonresponders; AMI responders showed improvement in impulsive behavior and depression scores.

TABLE 25.2 (continued)

Study	*Diagnosis*	*Study Design*	*Comment*
Soloff et al. (1993)	N = 92 BPD and mixed BPD/SPD features.	Type 1 study: comparison of haloperidol and phenelzine; double-blind, placebo-controlled.	Phenelzine less effective than haloperidol in decreasing impulsivity/hostile-belligerence; phenelzine did not improve atypical depresssive symptoms but did decrease scores on Buss-Durkee Hostility Inventory.
Parsons et al. (1989)	All patients had symptoms of atypical depression. Group 1: N = 40 patients with > 5 *DSM-III* BPD criteria; N = 61 patients with > 4 criteria. Group 2: N = 19 patients, BPD to a considerable extent; N = 29 patients BPD to only some extent as measured by the Personality Assessment Form.	Type 1 study: double-blind, placebo-controlled; random assignment to phenelzine 60 mg or imipramine 200 mg for 3–6 weeks each medication.	BPD patients with symptoms of atypical depression had significant improvement in CGI scores due to phenelzine, as compared to imipramine and placebo; imipramine felt to be minimally effective.

Note. AMI = amitriptyline; BPD = borderline personality disorder; CGI = Clinical Global Impression; HAM-D = Hamilton Depression Rating Scale; OAS = McLean Hospital Overt Aggression Scale; PDRS = Personality Disorders Rating Scale; POMS = Profile of Mood States; MDD = major depressive disorder; SPD = schizotypal personality disorder.

subjects with major affective disorder (acute or remitted depression or bipolar type), personality disorders, and normal controls on subscales of impulsivity, history of alcohol abuse, and history of suicide attempts (Coccaro et al., 1990). Central serotonergic function was assessed with fenfluramine; a blunted prolactin response to fenfluramine is thought to reflect decreased central serotonergic function. Results showed that among all the personality-disordered patients, those with BPD had significantly blunted peak prolactin response compared to the others, and that this was due to the impulsive/aggressive features of this disorder. Similarly, among all (PD) patients, impulsive/aggressive scores were negatively correlated with peak prolactin values. For subjects with PD or major depression, a history of a suicide attempt was associated with a significant blunting of prolactin when these patients were compared to patients who had never attempted suicide. More recently, PET has made it possible to measure cerebral glucose metabolic rates in those frontal regions believed to play a role in inhibiting impulsive behavior. Our group (Siever et al., 1999) has reported a decreased activation of the orbital and ventromedial frontal cortices in response to fenfluramine in impulsive/aggressive personality-disordered patients compared to controls. This observation demonstrates the presence of blunted serotonergic activity in relevant brain regions in impulsive/aggressive patients.

Noradrenergic function, in contrast to serotonergic indices, may be elevated in association with impulsivity/aggression across such diagnostic categories as pathological gambling, major affective disorders, and personality disorders. The CSF and plasma levels of the norepinephrine metabolite 3-methoxy-4-hydroxy-phenylglycol were found to be increased and associated with extroversion scores in pathological gamblers. The scores also correlated positively with urine concentrations of vanillylmandelic acid, a norepinephrine metabolite, and the sum of urinary output of norepinephrine and its major metabolites (Roy, De Jon, & Linnoila, 1989).

Cerebral Dysfunction in Impulsivity/Aggression

Electroencephalogram (EEG) measures have been the focus of several investigations into cerebral dysfunction as another possible biological substrate of impulsivity and aggression. The results have been equivocal. For example, episodic/dyscontrol patients (defined as having impulsive, aggressive, and violent behavior) were shown in one study to have a significant increase in nonspecific EEG changes when contrasted with subjects with depression or headaches (Drake, Hietter, & Pakalnis, 1992). However, a comparison of BPD and other personality-disordered patients has shown no significant differences in the number of EEG abnormalities, and no associations between EEG abnormalities and impulsivity (Cornelius et al., 1986).

Further evidence for generalized cerebral dysfunction in impulsive/aggressive traits was found in a study of neurological soft signs in BPD and antisocial PD patients (Stein, Hollander, Cohen, & Frenkel, 1993). Compared to control subjects, the personality-disordered patients displayed a significantly greater number of left-sided neurological soft signs. Among the patients, nine were identified as "aggressive" based on the Brown-Goodwin lifetime aggression scale. Compared to the nonaggressive PD patients, those with aggression showed significantly greater right-sided soft signs. Patients also underwent neuropsychological testing. Left-sided neurological soft signs were found to correlate with errors on Trails A and B tests, as well as on the Matching Familiar Faces Test, which may indicate an impairment of complex information processing. Right-sided soft signs correlated with errors on the Wisconsin Card Sort Test, a measure of frontal lobe functioning. Thus, in this study, lateralized neurological soft signs that correlated with specific neuropsychological deficits were found to be significantly associated with impulsive/aggressive traits in personality-disordered patients.

Psychobiology of Affective Lability

The cluster of traits thought to define affective instability in BPD subjects includes marked shifts between baseline and depressed moods, irritability, and anxiety that may persist from a few hours to a few days (Steinberg, Trestman, & Siever, 1994). Knowledge of the biological correlates of Axis I mood disorders provided a foundation for investigations into the psychobiology of affective-related traits in personality-disordered patients. However, the state-dependent markers associated with major affective disorder, such as blunted thyroid-stimulating-hormone (TSH) response to thyrotropin-releasing hormone (TRH) and lack of plasma cortisol suppression in response to dexamethasone, have not been found to correlate consistently with affective-related traits in personality-disordered patients (Coccaro & Siever, 1995). Noradrenergic and cholinergic systems, which appear to play pivotal roles in Axis I mood disorders, have also been a logical area of study for the personality disorders.

Cholinergic agents are known to create a depressive-like picture in animal and human studies and can increase the rapid-eye-movement-sleep latency associated with depression (Steinberg et al., 1994). Physostigmine, a centrally active cholinergic agent, has been shown to produce greater depressive responses in BPD subjects than in normal controls (Steinberg et al., 1995). The depressive responses correlated with affective instability, and results were independent of past or present history of major depressive disorder. Thus, the dysphoric response seen with physostigmine infusion in BPD subjects appears to be specifically associated with affective lability and not due to comorbid major depression.

The role of noradrenergic and dopaminergic systems in affective/lability has been investigated with dextroamphetamine (d-Amp), which releases and prevents reuptake of norepinephrine and dopamine. Following administration of d-Amp, a significant correlation between dysphoric/irritable mood response to the drug and measures of lifetime history of mood instability was observed in healthy volunteers (Kavoussi & Coccaro, 1993). However, neither of these variables correlated with plasma levels of homovanillic acid or 3-methoxy-4-hydroxyphenylglycol, metabolites of dopamine and norepinephrine, respectively. Irritability, another symptom associated with affective lability, has been shown to correlate with increased growth-hormone (GH) response to clonidine in personality-disordered patients and normal controls (Coccaro et al., 1991). The growth hormone response to clonidine is thought to reflect activity of postsynaptic alpha-2 adrenergic receptors. Thus, increased responsiveness of the central adrenergic system may be involved in affective instability in BPD and other personality-disordered subjects.

In summary, initial investigations have suggested that excessive cholinergic availability plays a role in the transient dysphoria seen in borderline patients, and that a hyperresponsive noradrenergic system contributes to irritability/mood instability among healthy volunteers and personality-disordered subjects.

Pharmacology of Borderline Personality Disorder: Antidepressant Agents

The investigation of antidepressant agents for the treatment of borderline symptomatology poses particular methodological challenges. First, the rates of comorbidity between BPD and Axis I depressive disorders may be as high as 50%. Although there is evidence that the affective picture in BPD can be conceptualized as a distinct entity from comorbid Axis I depressive disorders (Kavoussi & Coccaro, 1993; Koenigsberg et al., 1999; Silverman & Pinkham, 1991), the depressive symptomatology of BPD may be so heterogeneous as to defy further definition. In studies of antidepressant effects on symptoms or traits of BPD, it is important to acknowledge that we are limited in our knowledge of how dimensions or symptom clusters overlap and impinge on each other. For example, a drug's effect on depressive symptoms may in turn affect impulsive/aggressive traits.

With these caveats in mind, a summary of antidepressant trials for BPD patients can be found in Table 25.2.

The clinical effects of antidepressant agents on BPD symptomatology are consistent with biological findings that associate increased noradrenergic responsiveness with affective lability and decreased serotonergic indices with impulsivity.

There is a trend for noradrenergic agents to improve mood but to be inconsistent in treating irritability and dyscontrol in BPD. Amitriptyline, for example, while significantly decreasing depression scores and impulsive behaviors in a group of BPD patients, was found to paradoxically worsen impulsivity, assaultiveness, paranoid ideation, and global functioning in a subset of patients compared to normal controls (Soloff et al., 1986). The authors concluded that the paradoxical worsening of the amitriptyline nonresponders was due to its effect on impulsive behaviors rather than on depressive symptoms. Desipramine was also shown to have no effect or actually to worsen anger and suicidality in comparison to lithium among a cohort of borderline subjects (Links, Steiner, Boiago, & Irwin, 1990). Similarly, the noradrenergic agent maprotiline may be associated with an increase in suicide-provoking potential in patients with histories of repeated suicidal behavior (Montgomery et al., 1992). The monoamine oxidase inhibitor phenelzine has been shown to have a good effect on BPD patients with atypical depressive features such as leaden paralysis, rejection sensitivity, and mood reactivity (Parsons et al., 1989). Tranylcypromine was also found to improve physician-rated mood scores, impulsivity, and global functioning in a cohort of primarily BPD patients, yet no improvement of behavioral dyscontrol was noted (Cowdry & Gardner, 1988).

Thus, although these medications were found to improve depressive features and, in the case of amitriptyline responders, impulsive behavior, there may also be the risk of worsening anger and impulsivity in a subset of BPD patients (amitriptyline and desipramine), worsening suicidality in other patients (maprotiline), or having no effect on dyscontrol (tranylcypromine).

In contrast, serotonergic agents such as fluoxetine may act to decrease impulsivity among borderline patients. Other symptoms, such as anger, suicidality, and irritability, have also been improved with these agents. Fluoxetine was shown to be effective in decreasing impulsive aggression (Coccaro & Kavoussi, 1995) and depression scores and improving a broad array of symptoms such as rejection sensitivity, anxiety, psychoticism, and obsessive compulsive symptoms in BPD subjects, in a double-blind, placebo-controlled study. A second controlled study (Salzman et al., 1995) found that fluoxetine had a clinically and statistically significant effect in reducing anger and depression in a sample of patients with mild to moderately severe BPD. The effect on anger was independent of the antidepressant effect of the fluoxetine. A trend toward decreased self-mutilatory behavior was also noted (Markovitz et al., 1991). It must be stressed that all except two of the fluoxetine studies have been open-label; further controlled trials are needed to establish its efficacy for BPD subjects. Lithium, which may act as a serotonin agonist, has been shown to be effective in decreasing impulsivity and aggression in a sample of highly impulsive prison inmates (Sheard, Marini, Brideges, & Wagner, 1976).

Lithium has also been shown to decrease therapists' perceptions of irritability, suicidality, and angry behavior in a cohort of borderline subjects. Interestingly, there was a clear trend in this study for lithium to be more effective than desipramine (a noradrenergic agent) in decreasing anger and suicidality, as well as depression (Links et al., 1990). This observation supports the hypothesis that hyperresponsivity of noradrenergic systems may contribute to affective lability in borderline subjects.

Thus, it appears that for features of impulsivity, aggression, and depressive spectrum symptomatology, serotonergic agents such as fluoxetine and lithium would be reasonable first-line agents. Noradrenergic agents such as the tricyclic antidepressants or MAOIs are less desirable; although they may have an effect on depressive or atypical depressive features, results have been inconsistent in the trials conducted so far. If they are used, patients should be carefully monitored for the appearance of increased impulsivity.

Pharmacology of Borderline Personality Disorder: Antipsychotic Agents

Studies of antipsychotic medication use for BPD (Tables 25.1 and 25.2) have shown global, but modest, improvement in symptoms. Among the symptoms described, improvements have been shown in depression, suicidal ideation, rejection sensitivity, and psychotic-like symptoms including paranoid ideation, ideas of reference, and derealization. One study also noted an effect for haloperidol in reducing impulsive ward behavior (Soloff et al., 1989).

Thus, traditional antipsychotic agents may be a reasonable choice if patients are unable to tolerate or do not respond to lithium or fluoxetine. Although one study of BPD and SPD subjects found no difference in response to neuroleptics among diagnoses (Serban & Siegel, 1984), another study found that, in the sample of BPD and/or SPD subjects, those who did respond to thiothixene were likely to be more severely ill at baseline, with psychoticism, illusions, ideas of reference, phobic anxiety, and obsessive compulsivity (Goldberg et al., 1986). Further, schizotypal symptoms, hostility, and suspiciousness seemed to predict a good response to haloperidol in another study (Soloff et al., 1989). Thus, it may be reasonable to choose an antipsychotic medication for a borderline patient who has a predominance of psychotic-like features, such as transient paranoid ideation. Consideration of extrapyramidal side effects, including tardive dyskinesia, must also be weighed before instituting a trial with these agents.

Two open-label studies have examined the effect of the atypical antipsychotic medication, clozapine. In a study of 12 BPD inpatients with severe psychotic-like symptoms (Benedetti et al., 1998), low-dose clozapine treatment was associated with a decrease in psychotic-like symptoms, suicide attempts, physical fights, and depression. A retrospective mirror-image open-label chart-review study (Chengappa et al., 1999) of the treatment of seven inpatients meeting criteria for BPD, six of whom had Axis I psychotic disorders, found a decrease in self-mutilation, seclusion, and use of antianxiety medications and an increase in GAF score. It is not possible to determine whether the improvements were due to the effect of clozapine on BPD or on the Axis I disorder. Because of the risk of agranulocytosis, it is prudent to reserve trials of clozapine at present for the most severely symptomatic BPD patients who also have psychotic symptoms. These findings, however, suggest that safer atypical antipsychotic medications such as risperidone or olanzepine may have a role in the treatment of BPD, and more research is called for to study these medications.

Pharmacology of Borderline Personality Disorder: Mood-Stabilizing Agents

Several case reports describe the efficacy of both carbamazepine (CBZ) and valproic acid (VPA) for episodic dyscontrol and violence and dyscontrol in organic mental syndromes or dementia (Giakas, Seibyl, & Mazure, 1990; Keck, McElroy, & Friedman, 1992).

The use of CBZ for patients with behavioral dyscontrol/impulsivity or borderline patients has yielded mixed results in placebo-controlled trials. Carbamazepine has been found to decrease assaultiveness and depression significantly in patients with frontal lobe dysfunction (Foster, Hillbrand, & Chi, 1989) and was initially found to improve impulsivity and behavioral dyscontrol among borderline patients (Cowdry & Gardner, 1988). However, this finding was not replicated in a later study, which suggested that CBZ has no effect on dyscontrol and is in fact associated with an increase in impulsive, violent behavior in some borderline subjects (De Ia Fuente & Lotstra, 1994). In comparison to propranolol, use of CBZ may be associated with a decrease in aggression in patients with intermittent explosive disorder (Mattes, 1990), although both medications tend to lead to fewer aggressive outbursts. In this study, however, subjects also received antipsychotic agents, other anticonvulsants, and antidepressants, so the applicability of the findings is limited.

An open-label 8-week trial (Stein et al., 1995) of valproate in 11 patients meeting *DSM-III-R* criteria for BPD showed an overall improvement in half the sample, with modest beneficial effects on anger, impulsivity, irritability, and rejection sensitivity. Three of the patients dropped out. Recently, the preliminary results of a 10-week, double-blind, placebo-controlled study of valproate in treating *DSM-IV* BPD patients was published (Hollander et al., 2001). Of the 16 BPD patients who were randomly assigned to treatment, 6 of the 12 assigned to active treatment dropped out, and all 4 of those assigned to placebo dropped out. Patients dropped out because of either lack of efficacy or an impulsive decision, but not because of side effects. Among the 6 patients who completed treatment, there was a significant improvement in the Clinical Global Impressions (CGI) score and the Global Assessment Scale (GAS) score. These studies suggest that the efficacy of valproate may be limited by high rates of dropout in this population. Further studies are called for to develop approaches to minimizing early termination in treating BPD patients with valproate and to obtain data on larger samples.

A case report series (Pinto & Akiskal, 1998) describes the open-label use of lamotrigine, the anticonvulsant and putative mood stabilizer, in eight severely disabled BPD patients who did not meet criteria for any concurrent major mood disorder. Three of the eight patients showed a dramatic improvement, with disappearance of suicidal, impulsive sexual, and drug-taking behaviors, and no longer met BPD criteria at an average follow-up of 1 year.

In summary, the use of anticonvulsants for BPD is in the investigatory phase. Anecdotal reports suggest that CBZ, VPA, and lamotrigine may be useful for a wide array of syndromes involving episodic aggression; however, two double-blind, placebo-controlled studies (Cowdry & Gardner, 1988; De la Fuente & Lotstra, 1994) disagree as to whether CBZ is effective for borderline personality patients, and dropout rates with valproate have been high. Further controlled trials are needed to define the effect of these agents on impulsivity, aggression, and affective lability in BPD subjects.

CLUSTER C (ANXIOUS CLUSTER)

The psychobiology of anxiety (Cluster C) has been investigated in greater depth recently. The guiding principle for much of the research is the assumption that the biological factors regulating anxiety provide a common basis for the anxiety spectrum disorders, superseding Axis I and Axis II distinctions.

This assumption is supported by the comorbidity seen clinically between avoidant personality disorder (APD) and social phobia (SP). A number of authors have demonstrated the high rates of association between these two disorders (Schneier, Spitzer, & Gibbon, 1991; Stein & Hollander, 1993). Specifically, generalized social phobia, which involves pervasive fear in most social situations, is felt to be more closely linked to APD than discrete social phobia, which involves fear in one or two specific social situations. One recent study of 50 patients diagnosed with SP found rates of APD in 89% of patients diagnosed with generalized social phobia (Schneier et al., 1991). Some investigators feel that these findings suggest that APD and SP are variations of a similar underlying pathophysiology.

Thus, a review of the psychobiology of anxiety spectrum personality disorder may be best represented by studies of SP and APD. Early studies have established the role of the noradrenergic system in arousal and anxiety. Investigations of the growth hormone (GH) response to clonidine, a marker of postsynaptic alpha-2 adrenergic function, have consistently shown a blunted GH response in panic disorder patients (Uhde, 1994).

A logical outgrowth of these findings was to study the clonidine-GH response in patients with social phobia. Two studies, one using intravenous clonidine and one using oral clonidine, found contrasting results. The first study of GH response to intravenous clonidine in normal controls, SP patients, and panic disorder patients found significant blunting in SP patients compared to normal controls. There was no difference in the blunting between SP subjects and the panic disorder group (Uhde, 1994). The second study found no GH response difference for 21 subjects with SP when compared to 22 healthy controls in a double-blind, placebo-controlled study (Tancer, 1993). Thus, replication studies are needed to establish whether the clonidine-GH response is an index of abnormal noradrenergic activity in social phobia.

There have been few other positive findings with the use of chemical probes or challenge studies to define a biological basis for social phobia. Studies using lactic acid, norepinephrine, and caffeine (chosen because of their use as chemical probes in panic disorder) failed to induce symptoms of social phobia in patients with social phobia (Tancer, 1993). Investigations into the hypothalamic-pituitary-adrenal axis, via measures of urinary free cortisol and response to the dexamethasone suppression test, showed no abnormalities (Uhde, 1994). Challenge studies examining neurotransmitter systems revealed no abnormality in prolactin response to l-dopamine or fenfluramine; however, an increased cortisol response to fenfluramine differentiated social phobia patients from normal controls in one study (Uhde, 1994). Thus, the serotonergic system may play a role in the etiology of fear and avoidance responses of SP subjects. Interestingly, in contrast to impulsive borderline patients, avoidant-personality-disordered patients demonstrate some suggestions of increased serotonergic activity and reduced noradrenergic activity.

Pharmacotherapy Trials for Social Phobia and Avoidant Personality Disorder

There have been few pharmacotherapy trials involving the anxious cluster disorders. There are a limited number of controlled studies looking at avoidant personality traits in patients with SP, while the use of medications for APD alone has been documented only in reports.

The MAOI phenelzine has been shown, in two controlled trials, to decrease avoidant personality features significantly for patients with SP (Davidson et al., 1993; Versiani et al., 1992). Among the changes seen with phenelzine treatment were decreases in anxiety and avoidance in work and social settings. The reversible MAOI moclobemide has also been shown to be effective in reducing avoidant traits and social phobia symptoms (Versiani et al., 1992). The benzodiazepines clonazepam and alprazolam have also been found to decrease measures of avoidance in SP patients (Davidson et al., 1993; Reich, Noyes, & Yates, 1989). These studies are reviewed in greater depth in the chapter on pharmacological treatments of anxiety disorders.

Selective serotonin reuptake inhibitors have been shown to be effective in the treatment of SP in double-blind, placebo-controlled studies. In a 12-week multisite study of 93 patients with SP (Stein et al., 1999), paroxetine was shown to produce a significant improvement in symptoms as measured by the Liebowitz Social Anxiety Scale (LSAS) total score and in global improvement on the Clinical Global Impression Scale compared to placebo. In an open-label trial (Stein et al., 1996), patients with generalized social phobia who were treated with paroxetine (at a mean dose of 47.9 mg/day) had significant decreases in LSAS scores and Duke Social Phobia Scale ratings over an 11-week period. In a follow-on placebo-controlled, double-blind, discontinuation study of 16 responders to the initial study, the authors found that 1 of 8 patients randomized to paroxetine at the same dose relapsed over a 12-week period, compared to 5 of 8 patients randomized to a taper to placebo.

Case reports have described the usefulness of the MAOIs phenelzine and tranylcypromine for subjects with APD: After 4 to 6 weeks of treatment, patients experienced marked improvement in their abilities to socialize. These gains were maintained at a 1-year follow-up when the patients continued to take the medications (Deltito & Stam, 1989). Two case reports document the efficacy of fluoxetine for APD (Deltito & Stam, 1989; Goldman & Grinspoon, 1990). Within several weeks of initiating treatment, subjects reported decreases in social sensitivity and improvements in socialization, self-confidence, and assertiveness. Doses ranged from 1 mg po every other day to 40 mg of fluoxetine per day. Further controlled studies with well-defined groups of APD and other anxious cluster subjects are needed to establish the clinical indications for pharmacotherapy in this group of patients.

CONCLUSION

The search for pharmacological treatments for personality-disordered patients has led to an exciting expansion of our views of the Axis II disorders. Attempts to find a biological dimension that could be targeted by such treatments have enhanced the notion of a fluid boundary between Axis I and Axis II symptomatology. Future research should be aimed toward clearer descriptions, either categorically or psychobiologically, of personality disorders. Controlled clinical trials are needed to create and test hypotheses concerning the efficacy of medications in these disorders.

References

American Psychiatric Association. (1994). *Diagnostic and statistical manual of mental disorders* (4th ed.). Washington, DC: Author.

Baron, M., Gruen, R., & Asnis, L. (1985). Familial transmission of schizotypal and borderline personality disorders. *American Journal of Psychiatry, 142,* 927–933.

Benedetti, F., Sforzini, L., Colombo, C., Maffei, C., & Smeraldi, E. (1998). Low-dose clozapine in acute and continuation treatment of severe borderline personality disorder. *Journal of Clinical Psychiatry, 59,* 103–107.

Bergman, A. J., Harvey, P. D., Lees-Roitman, S., Mohs, R. C., Marder, D., Silverman, J. M., & Siever, L. J. (1998). Verbal learning and memory in schizotypal personality disorder. *Schizophrenia Bulletin, 24,* 635–641.

Brown, G. L., Ebert, M. H., Goyer, P. F., et al. (1982). Aggression, suicide and serotonin: Relationships to CSF amine metabolites. *American Joumal of Psychiatry, 139,* 741–746.

Chengappa, K. N. R., Ebeling, T., Kang, J. S., Levine, J., & Parepally, H. (1999). Clozapine reduces severe self-mutilation and aggression in psychotic patients with borderline personality disorder. *Journal of Clinical Psychiatry, 60,* 477–484.

Coccaro, E. F., Astill, J. L., Herbert, J. A., et al. (1990). Fluoxetine treatment of impulsive aggression in *DSM-III-R* personality disorder patients. *Journal of Clinical Psychopharmacology, 10,* 373–375.

Coccaro, E. F., & Kavoussi, R. J. (1995, May 20–25). *Fluoxetine in aggression in personality disorders* [New Research Abstracts]. Presented at the American Psychiatric Association 148th annual meeting, Miami.

Coccaro, E. F., Lawrence, T., Trestman, R. L., et al. (1991). Growth hormone response to IV clonidine challenge correlates with behavioral irritability in psychiatric patients and healthy volunteers. *Psychiatric Research, 39,* 129–139

Coccaro, E. F., & Siever, L. J. (1995). The neuropsychopharmacology of personality disorders. In F. E. Bloom & D. J. Kupfer (Eds.), *Psychopharmacology: The fourth generation of progress.* New York: Raven Press.

Coccaro, E. F., Siever, L. J., Klar, H. M., et al. (1989). Serotonergic studies in patients with affective and personality disorders: Correlates with suicidal and impulsive aggressive behavior. *Archives of General Psychiatry, 46,* 587–599; [Correction] 47, 124 (1990).

Cornelius, J. R., Brenner, R. P., et al. (1986). EEG abnormalities in borderline personality disorder: Specific or nonspecific? *Biological Psychiatry, 21,* 977–980.

Cornelius, J. R., Soloff, P. H., Perel, J. M., & Ulrich, R. F. (1991). A preliminary trial of fluoxetine in refractory borderline patients. *Journal of Clinical Psychopharmacology, 11,* 116–120.

Cowdry, R. W., & Gardner, D. L. (1988). Pharmacotherapy of borderline personality disorder: Alprazolam, carbamazepine, trifluoperazine, and tranylcypromine. *Archives of General Psychiatry, 45,* 111–119.

Davidson, J. R., Potts, N. S., Richichi, E. A., et al. (1993). Treatment of social phobia with clonazepam and placebo. *Journal of Clinical Psychopharmacology, 13,* 423–428.

De la Fuente, J. M., & Lotstra, F. (1994). A trial of carbamazepine in borderline personality disorder. *European Neuropsychopharmacology, 4,* 479–486.

Deltito, J. A., & Stam, M. (1989). Psychopharmacological treatment of avoidant personality disorder. *Comprehensive Psychiatry, 30,* 498–504.

Drake, M. E., Hietter, S. A., & Pakalnis, A. (1992). EEG and evoked potentials in episodic-dyscontrol syndrome. *Neuropsychobiology, 26,* 125–128.

Foster, H. G., Hillbrand, M., & Chi, C. C. (1989). Efficacy of carbamazepine in assaultive patients with frontal lobe dysfunction. *Progress in Neuropsychopharmacology and Biological Psychiatry, 13,* 865–874.

Giakas, W. J., Seibyl, J. P., & Mazure, C. M. (1990). Valproate in the treatment of temper outbursts. *Journal of Clinical Psychiatry, 51,* 525.

Gitlin, M. J. (1993). Pharmacotherapy of personality disorders: Conceptual framework and clinical strategies. *Journal of Clinical Psychopharmacology, 13,* 343–353.

Goldberg, S. C., Schulz, S. C., Schulz, P. M., Resnick, R. J., Hamer, R. M., & Friedel, R. O. (1986). Borderline and schizotypal personality disorder treatment with low-dose thiothixene versus placebo. *Archives of General Psychiatry, 43,* 680–686.

Goldman, M. J., & Grinspoon, L. (1990). Ritualistic use of fluoxetine by a former substance abuser. *American Journal of Psychiatry, 147,* 1377.

Hollander, E., Allen, A., Lopez, R. P., Bienstock, C. A., Grossman, R., Siever, L. J., Merkatz, L., & Stein, D. J. (2001). A preliminary double-blind, placebo-controlled trial of divalproax sodium in borderline personality disorder. *Journal of Clinical Psychiatry, 62,* 199–203.

Hyler, S. E., Skodol, A. E., Kellman, H. D., et al. (1990). Validity of Personality Diagnostic Questionnaire: Comparison between two structured interviews. *American Journal of Psychiatry, 147,* 1043–1048.

Hymowitz, P., Frances, A., Jacobsberg, L. B., et al. (1986). Neuroleptic treatment of schizotypal personality disorder. *Comprehensive Psychiatry, 27,* 267–271.

Javitt, D. C. (1999). Treatment of negative and cognitive symptoms. *Current Psychiatry Reports, 1,* 25–30.

Jensen, H. V., & Andersen, J. (1989). An open, noncomparative study of amoxapine in borderline disorders. *Acta Psychiatrica Scandinavica, 79,* 89–93.

Kaplan, H. I., & Sadock, B. J. (Eds.). (1995). *Comprehensive textbook of psychiatry* (Vol. 6). Baltimore: Williams & Wilkins.

Karson, C. N., Casanova, M. F., Kleinman, J. E., & Griffin, W. E. (1993). Choline acetyltransferase in schizophrenia. *American Journal of Psychiatry, 150,* 454–459.

Kavoussi, R. J., & Coccaro, E. F. (1993). The amphetamine challenge test correlates with affective lability in healthy volunteers. *Psychiatry Research, 48,* 219– 228.

Keck, P. E., Jr., McElroy, S. L., & Friedman, L. M. (1992). Valproate and carbamazepine in the treatment of panic and posttraumatic stress disorders, withdrawal states, and behavioral dyscontrol syndromes. *Journal of Clinical Psychopharmacology, 12*(1, Suppl.), 36–41.

Kirrane, R. M., & Siever, L. J. (2000). New perspectives on schizotypal personality disorder. *Current Psychiatry Reports, 2,* 62–66.

Koenigsberg, H. W., Anwunah, I., New, A., Mitropoulou, V., Schopick, F., & Siever, L. J. (1999). Relationship between depression and borderline personality disorder. *Depression and Anxiety, 10,* 158–167.

Koenigsberg, H. W., Goodman, M., Reynolds, D., Mitropoulou, V., Trestman, R., Kirrane, R., New, A. S., Anwunah, I., & Siever, L. J. (2001). Risperidone in the treatment of schizotypal personality disorder. *Biological Psychiatry* (abstracts), 56th Annual Meeting Society of Biological Psychiatry, New Orleans.

Lane, H. Y., Liu, C. C., & Chang, W. H. (1999). Risperidone for exclusively negative symptoms. *American Journal of Psychiatry, 156,* 335.

Links, P., Steiner, M., Boiago, I., & Irwin, D. (1990). Lithium therapy for borderline patients: Preliminary findings. *Journal of Personality Disorders, 4,* 173–181.

Markovitz, P. J., Calabrese, J. U., Schulz, S. C., et al. (1991). Fluoxetine in the treatment of borderline and schizotypal personality disorders. *American Journal of Psychiatry, 148,* 1064–1067.

Mattes, J. A. (1990). Comparative effectiveness of carbamazeipine and propranolol for rage outbursts. *Journal of Neuropsychiatry and Clinical Neuroscience, 2,* 159–164.

Montgomery, S. A., Montgomery, D. B., Green, M., et al. (1992). Pharmacotherapy in the prevention of suicidal behavior. *Journal of Clinical Psychopharmacology, 12*(2, Suppl.), 27S–31S.

Norden, M. J. (1989). Fluoxetine in borderline personality disorder. *Progress in Neuropsychopharmacology and Biological Psychiatry, 13,* 885–893.

Parsons, B., Quitkin, F. M., McGrath, P. J., et al. (1989). Phenelzine, imipramine, and placebo in borderline patients meeting criteria for atypical depression. *Psychopharmacology Bulletin, 25,* 524–534.

Pinto, O. C., & Akiskal, H. S. (1998). Lamotrigine as a promising approach to borderline personality: An open case series without concurrent *DSM-IV* major mood disorder. *Journal of Affective Disorders, 51,* 333–343.

Reich, J., Noyes, R., & Yates, W. (1989). Alprazolam treatment of avoidant personality traits in social phobic patients. *Journal of Clinical Psychiatry, 50,* 91–95.

Roy, A., De Jon, J., & Linnoila, M. (1989). Extroversion in pathological gamblers correlates with indices of noradrenergic function. *Archives of General Psychiatry, 46,* 679–681.

Salzman, C., Wolfson, A. N., Schatzberg, A., Looper, J., Henke, R., Albanese, M., Schwartz, J., & Miyawaki, E. (1995). Effects of fluoxetine on anger in symptomatic volunteers with borderline personality disorder. *Journal of Clinical Psychopharmacology, 15,* 23–29.

Schneier, F. R., Spitzer, R. L., & Gibbon, M. (1991). The relationship of social phobia subtypes and avoidant personality disorder. *Comprehensive Psychiatry,* 32, 496–502.

Schulz, S. C., Camlin, K. L., Berry, S. A., & Jesberger, J. A. (1999). Olanzepine safety and efficacy in patients with borderline personality disorder and comorbid dysthymia. *Biological Psychiatry, 46,* 1429–1435.

Schulz, S. C., Cornelius, J., Schulz, P. M., & Soloff, P. H. (1988). The amphetamine challenge test in patients with borderline personality disorder. *American Journal of Psychiatry, 145,* 809–814.

Serban, G., & Siegel, S. (1984). Response of borderline and schizotypal patients to small doses of thiothixene and haloperidol. *American Journal of Psychiatry, 141,* 1455–1458.

Sheard, M. J., Marini, J. L., Brideges, C. I., & Wagner, E. (1976). The effect of lithium on impulsive aggressive behavior in man. *American Journal of Psychiatry, 133,* 1409–1413.

Siever, L. J. (1991). The biology of the boundaries of schizophrenia. In C. A. Tamminga & S. C. Schulz (Eds.), *Schizophrenia: Advances in neuropsychiatry and neuropsychopharmacology: Vol. 1. Schizophrenia research.* New York: Raven Press.

Siever, L. J., et al. (1995). Brain structure/function and the dopamine system in schizotypal personality disorder. *Schizotypal Personality, 12,* 272–286.

Siever, L. J., Buchsbaum, M. S., New, A. S., Spiegel-Cohen, J., Wei, T., Hazlett, E. A., Sevin, E., Nunn, M., & Mitropoulou, V. (1999). d,l-fenfluramine response in impulsive personality disorder assessed with [18F]fluorodeoxyglucose positron emission tomography. *Neuropsychopharmacology, 20,* 413–423.

Siever, L. J., Amin, F., Coccaro, E. F., et al. (1991). Plasma HVA in schizotypal personality disorders. *American Journal of Psychiatry, 148,* 1246–1248.

Siever, L. J., Kalus, O. F., & Keefe, R. S. (1993). The boundaries of schizophrenia. *Psychiatric Clinics of North America, 16,* 217–244.

Silverman, J. M., & Pinkham, L. (1991). Affective and impulsive personality disorder traits in the relatives of patients with borderline personality disorder. *American Journal of Psychiatry, 148,* 1378–1385.

Silverman, J. M., Siever, L. J., Horvath, T. B., et al. (1993). Schizophrenia related and affective personality disorder traits in relatives of probands with schizophrenia and personality disorders. *American Journal of Psychiatry, 150,* 435–442.

Soloff, P. H., Corneluis, J. R., George, A., et al. (1993). Efficacy of phenelzine and haloperidol in borderline personality disorder. *Archives of General Psychiatry, 50,* 377–385.

Soloff, P. H., George, A., et al. (1986). Paradoxical effects of amitriptyline in borderline patients. *American Journal of Psychiatry, 143,* 1603–1605.

Soloff, P. H., George, A., Nathan, R. S., et al. (1989). Amitriptyline versus haloperidol in borderlines: Final outcomes and predictors of response. *Journal of Clinical Psychopharmacology, 9,* 238–246.

Stein, D. J., Berk, M., Els, C., Emsley, R. A., Gittelson, L., Wilson, D., Oakes, R., & Hunter, B. (1999). A double-blind placebo controlled trial of paroxetine in the management of social phobia (social anxiety disorder) in South Africa. *South African Medical Journal, 89,* 402–406.

Stein, D. J., & Hollander, E. (1993). Anxiety disorders and personality disorders. *Journal of Personality Disorders, 7,* 87–104.

Stein, D. J., Hollander, E., Cohen, L., & Frenkel, M. (1993). Neuropsychiatric impairment in impulsive personality disorders. *Psychiatry Research, 48,* 257–266.

Stein, D. J., Simeon, D., Frenkel, M., Islam, M., & Hollander, E. (1995). An open trial of valproate in borderline personality disorder. *Journal of Clinical Psychiatry, 56,* 506–510.

Stein, M. B., Chartier, M. J., Hazen, A. L., Kroft, C. D., Chale, R. A., Cote, D., & Walker, J. R. (1996). Paroxetien in the treatment of generalized social phobia: Open-label treatment and double-blind placebo-controlled discontinuation. *Journal of Clinical Psychopharmacology, 16,* 218–222.

Steinberg, B. J., Trestman, R., Mitropolous, V., et al. (1997). *Depressive response to physostigmine challenge in borderline personality disorder patients. Neuropsychopharmacology, 17,* 264–273.

Steinberg, B. J., Trestman, R. L., & Siever, L. J. (1994). The cholinergic and noradrenergic neurotransmitter systems affective instability in borderline personality disorder. In K. R. Silk (Ed.), *Biological and neurobehavioral studies in borderline personality disorder* (pp. 41–62). Washington, DC: American Psychiatric Association.

Tancer, M. E. (1993). Neurobiology of social phobia. *Journal of Clinical Psychiatry, 54*(12, Suppl.), 26–30.

Tandon, R., & Greden, J. F. (1989). Cholinergic hyperactivity and negative schizophrenic symptoms: A model of cholinergic/dopaminergic interactions in schizophrenia. *Archives of General Psychiatry, 46,* 745–753.

Torgersen, S. (1992). *The genetic transmission of borderline personality features displays multidimensionality* [New Abstracts]. Presented at the American College of Neuropsychopharmacology Annual Meeting, San Juan, Puerto Rico.

Trestman, R. L., deVegvar, M., & Siever, L. J. (1995). Treatment of personality disorders. In C. B. Nemeroff & A. F. Schatzberg (Eds.), *The APA textbook of psychopharmacology.* Washington, DC: American Psychiatric Press.

Uhde, T. W. (1994). A review of biological studies in social phobia. *Journal of Clinical Psychiatry, 55*(6, Suppl.), 17–27.

Versiani, M., Nardi, A. E., Mundim, F. D., et al. (1992). Pharmacotherapy of social phobia: A controlled study with moclobemide and phenelzine. *British Journal of Psychiatry, 161,* 353–360.

26

Efficacy, Effectiveness, and the Clinical Utility of Psychotherapy Research

Peter E. Nathan
Jack M. Gorman

The chapter begins with brief descriptions of the efficacy and effectiveness research models. An effort to put them in the context of psychotherapy research, including research on common factors more generally, follows. The successes and failures of psychotherapy research are then briefly reviewed from a historical perspective; recent research on efficacy and effectiveness is emphasized. The chapter then addresses whether the Dodo Bird metaphor continues to be valid or whether, instead, meaningful differences in efficacy and effectiveness among psychotherapies have been demonstrated. Throughout, the chapter examines the several factors leading clinicians largely to ignore the voluminous body of research on psychotherapy outcomes.

More than six decades ago, psychologist Saul Rosenzweig referred to the difficulty the mental health professionals of his time had distinguishing among the psychotherapies of the time in effectiveness. Rosenzweig (1936) reasoned that, if all psychotherapies affect patients equivalently, then, paraphrasing Lewis Carroll's Dodo Bird in *Alice in Wonderland* (1865/1962), "All have won and all must have prizes." Even though roughly 65 years separate the year of the Dodo Bird metaphor's birth from today—not to mention a world war, the Holocaust, Hiroshima and Nagasaki, a walk on the moon, Watergate, and Kenneth Starr—psychotherapy researchers still refer to Lewis Carroll's foot race when they want to make the point that most psychotherapies are pretty much interchangeable in effectiveness. This chapter takes another look at the validity of the Dodo Bird metaphor, especially in light of the psychotherapy research of the last decade that has distinguished two approaches to psychotherapy research, the *efficacy* model and the *effectiveness* model. The principal aim of the chapter is to determine whether these efforts to elucidate the two models has moved us closer to resolution of the Dodo Bird problem.

The chapter has an additional focus, however, one that necessitates recognition of a problem of similar longevity and importance. Closely related to the question of whether psychotherapy works and, if it does, which psychotherapies work best are questions around the lamentably low value psychotherapists and other mental health professionals more generally continue to attach to psychotherapy research. Despite the outpouring of research on psychotherapy over the past half century, by and large, the clinical activities of most psychotherapists remain largely untouched by findings from empirical research (Barlow, 1981; Kopta, Lueger, Saunders, & Howard, 1999; Nathan, 2000). This review of efficacy and effectiveness research, then, has an additional purpose; it is an effort to understand the determinants of the apparent decision by most clinicians largely to ignore the voluminous body of research on psychotherapy outcomes.

Although the methodology for randomized clinical trials involving psychoactive medications has been well worked-out and, because these studies are necessary for FDA approval, has a definite impact on routine clinical practice, efficacy trials in psychopharmacology are also prone to the complaints that they lack ecological validity. Clinicians insist that drugs approved by the FDA following rigorously conducted Phase III trials somehow stop working once they are released to the market. At the same time, they may continue to use medications that have failed to separate from placebo for a particular indication, insisting that in "real-life" situations they work. Once source of criticism of efficacy trials in psychopharmacology is the extensive exclusion criteria generally employed, so that patients with suicidal thoughts, comorbid medical and psychiatric illness, and mild disorders are typically not included in clinical trials but must be treated in clinical practice. Hence, though we have chosen to focus on the efficacy versus effectiveness dilemma in this chapter as it applies to psychotherapy research, many of the same concerns adhere to psychopharmacological research as well.

DISTINCTIONS BETWEEN EFFICACY AND EFFECTIVENESS STUDIES

Efficacy research is concerned above all with *replication*. As a consequence, efficacy studies require a number of research design specifications of much less importance to effectiveness research. Primary among them is the need to construct an *appropriate control condition* with which the experimental treatment can be compared, so that its impact can be assessed as clearly as possible. As a corollary, the emphasis on internal validity in efficacy research requires *random assignment of subjects* to either active or control conditions, to try to ensure the absence of systematic, subject-based bias. Efficacy studies also carefully specify the *type of treatment* provided, so that it can be replicated as closely as possible in subsequent studies. This consideration has led to the widespread and controversial use of *treatment manuals*, which are designed to ensure that the therapists conducting the intervention adhere to the dictates of the manual and thereby maintain therapeutic consistency. Finally, priority is given in efficacy studies to *well-defined groups of patients*, whose psychopathology is specified by means of objective measures of psychopathology.

Effectiveness research, by contrast, is concerned with *feasible, beneficial effects in real-world settings*. Persons needing treatment, regardless of diagnosis, comorbid psychopathology, or duration of illness, are the usual participants in effectiveness studies. Their therapists are rarely specifically trained in the research protocol or the treatments provided. Clinical considerations rather than the demands of the research design generally dictate the choice of the treatment method, as well as its frequency, duration, and means of outcome assessment. Although assignment of patients to treatments in effectiveness studies may be randomized, disguising the treatment to which the patient has been assigned is rarely feasible. Outcome assessments are often broadly defined, for example, in terms of changes in degree of disability, quality of life, or changes in personality, rather than targeted evaluations of symptoms.

Barlow (1996) characterized the outcomes of efficacy studies as "the results of a systematic evaluation of the intervention in a controlled clinical research context. Considerations relevant to the internal validity of these conclusions are usually highlighted" (p. 1051). By contrast, effectiveness research has to do with "the applicability and feasibility of the intervention in the local setting where the treatment is delivered" and is designed to "determine the generalizability of an intervention with established efficacy" (p. 1055).

In a nutshell, efficacy studies emphasize *internal validity* and *replicability*; effectiveness studies strive for *external validity* and *generalizability*.

COMMON FACTORS

Although this chapter, like this book, focuses on outcomes of psychotherapy that stem from differences in specific types or schools of psychotherapy, it is indisputable that variables common to all psychological treatments also carry a substantial amount of the treatment outcome variance. Hence, common factors may be responsible, at least in part, for the Dodo Bird phenomenon.

Lambert and Bergin (1994) viewed common factors as arising from three sources: the *therapist*, the *client or patient*, and the *therapeutic process*. They further divided all three into subfactors: support factors, such as therapeutic alliance, catharsis, and therapist warmth; learning factors, including corrective emotional experiences, insight, and feedback; and action factors, like cognitive mastery, modeling, and behavioral regulation. Many of these variables positively relate to outcome independently of the specific therapeutic techniques employed.

Emphasizing therapist variables in affirming the importance of common factors in psychotherapy outcomes, Beutler, Machado, and Neufeldt (1994) described them as extending across a very broad domain, from therapists' objective demographic characteristics and sociocultural backgrounds to more subjective factors like therapists' values, attitudes, and beliefs. They may also include factors quite specific to therapy (e.g., the therapist's role in the therapeutic relationship and his or her expectations for its success), as well as those well removed from it (e.g., therapists' cultural attitudes and emotional well-being). Therapist variables reflecting therapy-specific states, including the therapist's professional identity (Berman & Norton, 1985) and his or her therapeutic style and choice of interventions (Robinson, Berman, & Neimeyer, 1990), seem to exert an especially strong impact on therapy outcomes. Other therapist-specific factors like age and gender, by contrast, appear to affect outcomes to a lesser extent (Zlotnick, Elkin, & Shea, 1998).

With occasional exceptions, patient variables have not borne a robust relationship to therapeutic outcomes (Luborsky & Diguer, 1995). Although reviews by Strupp (1973) and Orlinsky and Howard (1986) concluded that process variables—the strength of the therapeutic bond, the skillfulness of therapeutic interventions, and the duration of the therapeutic relationship—impact on outcomes, process research has proven both difficult to carry out and not productive of consistent findings.

Having finished this brief excursion into the literature on the influence of common factors on therapeutic outcomes, let us return to our central theme, the impact of differences in psychotherapies on differences in psychotherapy outcomes. Our perspective will be historical and longitudinal, in an attempt to highlight and put into context crucial developments in a half century of psychotherapy outcome research.

PSYCHOTHERAPY OUTCOME RESEARCH: 1950s–1980s

While Hans Eysenck's 1952 evaluation of the effects of psychotherapy was not the first to assess psychotherapy outcomes, his recourse to data and willingness to reach unpopular conclusions distinguished his review from other early psychotherapy evaluations. Eysenck's controversial 1952 bottom line was that the psychotherapies in widest use at mid-century were largely ineffective. In response to critics of his conclusions, however, Eysenck acknowledged that the inadequate methodology of the research from which he had drawn his conclusions had forced him to qualify the most provocative of them.

Initiating this review of 40 years of psychotherapy outcome research with Eysenck's early evaluations emphasizes both the primitive state of psychotherapy research at mid-century and its discouraging findings on therapeutic effectiveness. The methodological shortcomings of this research ensured that the methodological subtleties on which current distinctions between efficacy and effective research are based were quite unavailable to the researchers of the time, including Eysenck. At the same time, the broader problem the efficacy/effectiveness distinction epitomizes—the perceived real-world irrelevance of much of the research on psychotherapy outcomes—was as much on the minds of the psychotherapists of Eysenck's time as it is today.

Two additional illustrations buttress this point: In his well-known reference to the "two disciplines of scientific psychology" in a 1957 presidential address to the American Psychological Association, Cronbach distinguished between correlational and experimental methodologies, concluding that only the latter detect causal agency. (It is only a modest stretch to substitute the current *efficacy* and *effectiveness* for Cronbach's *experimental* and *correlational*.) A few years later, Cohen (1965) made essentially the same point, when he lamented the proliferation of significant but meaningless results in psychotherapy research.

Notwithstanding these concerns, Bergin (1966) described six ways psychotherapy researchers had influenced psychotherapeutic practice, in an effort to counter the widespread view—held then and still held by many—that psychotherapy research impacts little on the clinical practice of psychotherapy.

In the early 1970s, a series of comprehensive reviews of the psychotherapy research literature focused on two additional themes: hard-won advances in the methodology of psychotherapy research and encouraging findings on the efficacy of new therapies, especially the behavior therapies and cognitive behavior therapies. Surprisingly, though, the reviews made little mention of the low frequency with which clinicians utilized psychotherapy research findings, even though the problem had been recognized and discussed a good deal earlier. It was less surprising that the distinction between efficacy and effectiveness research was not raised in these reviews; that distinction emerged only a good deal later, in the 1990s, when the continued maturation of psychotherapy research methods made it meaningful.

In their review of research on psychotherapeutic processes during the late 1960s, Gendlin and Rychlak (1970) repeated two observations, by now 20 years past, by Eysenck: They commented on both the inadequacy of psychotherapy research methods and the early promise of the behavior therapies. In a related review, Krasner (1971) observed that, while behavior therapy had developed from the experimental psychology laboratory, it had evolved even then into clinically effective procedures for behavior change. Nothing is said in this review, however, about behavior therapy in real-world clinical settings. A year later, the rhetoric remained the same: Howard and Orlinsky (1972), on reviewing a series of promising psychotherapeutic process studies, recorded no practitioner concerns about its value for them. Similarly, in their review of behavioral treatments 3 years later, Bergin and Suinn (1975) chronicled advances in both psychotherapy research methodology and the effectiveness of the behavioral and cognitive behavioral treatments but said nothing about the significance of these findings for psychotherapy in real-world clinical settings. In like fashion, Gomes-Schwartz, Hadley, and Strupp (1978) made no mention of the problems of transfer from laboratory to consulting room in their comprehensive review of outcomes of individual psychotherapy and behavior therapy 3 years later.

Perhaps it was optimism engendered by marked advances in research methods and the power of cognitive behavior therapy during this decade that led all of these reviewers to assume that the problem of transfer from the laboratory to the consulting room would be solved more easily than it has been. Or perhaps they simply failed to consider the issue or to think it important.

In the 1980s, however, researchers finally began to take up the issue of the clinical utility of psychotherapy research. One of the first was Barlow (1981), writing in a special issue of the *Journal of Consulting and Clinical Psychology*. Barlow's comments were provocative:

> At present, clinical research has little or no influence on clinical practice. This state of affairs should be particularly distressing to a discipline whose goal over the last 30 years has been to produce professionals who would integrate the methods of science with clinical practice to produce new knowledge. (p. 147)

Shapiro and Shapiro (1982, 1983) drew essentially the same conclusion following a meta-analysis of 143 contemporary psychotherapy outcome studies. Even though the statistical conclusions and internal validity of the studies included in the analysis were "generally satisfactory," these researchers concluded that their construct and external validity were "severely limited by unrepresentativeness of clinical practice" (1983, p. 42). The same year, Rosenthal (1983) lamented differences between the statistical and social importance of the effects of psychotherapy and suggested a statistical means of heightening the real-world usefulness of psychotherapy research findings. At exceptional variance to this consensus, Goldfried, Greenberg, and Marmar (1990) rather grandly concluded that "the development of methods for demonstrating clinical (in addition to statistical) significance (during the decade of the 1980s) has been one of the major advances in outcome research" (p. 661).

In summary, during the four decades from the 1950s through the 1980s, attributions of responsibility for the reluctance of clinicians to use research on psychotherapy outcomes in their practices appeared to shift from inadequate research methods and less than robust treatment outcomes to perceptions of a critical lack of correspondence between therapies and patients chosen for empirical study and those typically involved in real-world clinical practice. In turn, this issue also came to be seen, during the decade of the 1990s, as the major problem with the efficacy model.

PSYCHOTHERAPY OUTCOME RESEARCH: 1990s

A number of articles on psychotherapy published during the early 1990s tentatively moved toward and a number of others published in the mid-1990s developed and elaborated on the distinction between efficacy and effectiveness research. Thus, in a thoughtful 1991 review of contemporary psychotherapy outcome research, Persons emphasized the field's growing concerns with the questionable external validity of traditional efficacy research, concluding that designs of earlier psychotherapy outcome studies were clearly incompatible with the models of psychotherapy those studies were designed to evaluate. Persons assigned principal blame to the prevailing (efficacy) model's expectation that assignment of patients to standardized treatments would be done on the basis of diagnosis rather than a theory-driven psychological assessment of each individual. Her solution to this long-standing problem: "the case formulation approach to psychotherapy research," which requires development of an "assessment-plus-treatment protocol" based directly on the psychotherapeutic model itself.

The same year, Jacobson and Truax (1991) proposed to solve another common outcome research problem impacting on clinical utility: statistically significant pre- and posttherapy behavior change scores that possessed little apparent clinical significance. Recalling Jacobson's earlier characterization of clinically significant change as movement of someone out of the range of the dysfunctional population or into the range of the functional population, in a paper with Follette and Revenstorf (1984), Jacobson and Truax proposed three ways to operationalize the definition. An example:

> The level of functioning subsequent to therapy should fall within the range of the functional or normal population, where range is defined as within two standard deviations of the mean of that population. (p. 13)

In 1995, Ogles, Lambert, and Sawyer reanalyzed outcome data from the NIMH Treatment of Depression Collaborative Research Program (Elkin, 1994; Elkin et al., 1985, 1989), using Jacobson and Truax's 1991 criteria for assessing clinical significance. Although the initial analysis of the study's findings by Elkin and her colleagues in 1989 had revealed significant improvements in symptoms of depression following both psychological and pharmacological treatments, few statistically significant differences between treatment groups were revealed. Ogles and his colleagues (1995) accurately hypothesized that reanalysis according to the Jacobson and Truax criteria would be revealing of clinically significant differences between conditions, thereby revealing the therapeutic benefits of psychosocial treatments for depression.

In 1994, a subsample of 180,000 subscribers to *Consumer Reports* were asked a series of questions about their experiences with mental health professionals, physicians, medications, and self-help groups, in the largest survey to date of mental health treatment outcomes. The survey's principal findings, reported in the November 1995 issue of the magazine, included the following:

- Almost half of the respondents whose emotional state was "very poor" or "fairly poor" reported significant improvement following therapy.
- The longer psychotherapy lasted, the more it helped.
- Psychotherapy alone worked as well as combined psychotherapy and pharmacotherapy

In a 1995 *American Psychologist* article describing the study, Martin Seligman, a consultant to it, detailed the study's findings, listed its "methodological virtues and drawbacks," and identified eight characteristics of efficacy studies that differentiate them from effectiveness studies. Seligman (1995) concluded that the *Consumer Reports* survey "complements the [more traditional] efficacy method, [so that] the best features of these two methods can be combined into a more ideal method that will best provide empirical validation of psychotherapy" (p. 965).

A year later, the *American Psychologist* published a series of commentaries on Seligman's 1995 article that dealt largely with related issues, the real-world utility of psychotherapy research and the significance of the distinction between efficacy and effectiveness research. Goldfried and Wolfe (1996) proposed "a new outcome research paradigm that involves an active collaboration between researcher and practicing clinician" (p. 1007) that "individualizes the intervention on the basis of an initial assessment and case formulation" (p. 1013). Hollon (1996) concluded that, while efficacy studies "leave much to be desired," effectiveness designs are not a panacea, in large part because they cannot substitute "for the randomized controlled clinical trial when it comes to drawing causal inferences about whether psychotherapy (or any other treatment) actually works" (pp. 1029–1030). Jacobson and Christensen (1996) found the *Consumer Reports* study to be so seriously flawed that they could draw few conclusions from it. Like Hollon (1996), they also believed that "the randomized clinical trial is as good a method for answering questions of effectiveness as it is for answering questions of efficacy," despite its limitations (p. 1031). However, Howard et al. (1996) suggested moving away from treatment-focused research altogether, in favor of "patient-focused research," which attempts to monitor an individual's progress over the course of treatment and to provide feedback of this information to the practitioner, supervisor, or case manager.

In rejoinder, Seligman (1996) acknowledged the validity of many of the criticisms of the *Consumer Reports* study. Nonetheless, he insisted that the study had significant value:

> Both the experimental method (efficacy) and the observational method (effectiveness) answer complementary questions . . . [although] efficacy studies . . . cannot test long-term psychotherapy because long-term manuals cannot be written and patients cannot be randomized into two-year-long placebo controls, so the "empirical validation" of long-term therapy will likely come from effectiveness studies. (p. 1072)

Publication of practice guidelines by the American Psychiatric Association (e.g., 1993, 1994a, 1994b, 1995, 1996, 1997) and the Division of Clinical Psychology of the American Psychological Association (Chambless et al., 1996, 1998; Division 12 Task Force, 1995) generated strong negative reactions from those who questioned the clinical utility of the psychotherapy outcome research on which the guidelines were based (Nathan, 1998). Exemplifying these reactions were those of Sol Garfield (1996), a well-known psychotherapy researcher, who took strong exception to the initial list of "empirically validated treatments" published in 1995 by the Division 12 Task Force. A number of his concerns reflect the efficacy-effectiveness distinction, including the distortion to the psychotherapy process he believed manuals typically used in efficacy studies cause, as well as the incomparability of psychotherapy patients in efficacy studies and those in real-world psychotherapy settings. A number of others writing on the same issue (e.g., Fensterheim & Raw, 1996; Goldfried & Wolfe, 1998) expressed similar concerns.

In a review of the efficacy/effectiveness controversy in their 1999 *Annual Review* chapter reviewing contemporary psychotherapy research, Kopta, Lueger, Saunders, and Howard emphasized the continuing gap between clinical research and clinical practice. They suggested that part of the problem might lie in the field's preference for randomized clinical trials (RCTs), proposing instead "that this approach should be replaced by naturalistic designs, which can provide results more applicable to real clinical practice, therefore strengthening external validity" (p. 449). Thus, like Seligman (1996) and Howard et al. (1996), these authors endorsed effectiveness studies as the best means of understanding psychotherapy's impact in real-world clinical settings.

CONTEMPORARY EFFORTS TO INTEGRATE EFFICACY AND EFFECTIVENESS STUDIES

Four recent, innovative approaches to solving both the clinical utility problem and the effectiveness/efficacy controversy, three experimental, one statistical, have recently been proposed. All presume that neither efficacy studies alone nor effectiveness studies alone will be able to provide clinicians the help they require.

In introducing the first of these efforts, Norquist, Lebowitz, and Hyman (1999) distinguished between outcome research based on the "regulatory" or efficacy model, named for the detailed steps drug manufacturers must take to prove the safety and efficacy of their new products to the Federal Food and Drug Administration (FDA), and research that adheres to the "public health" or effectiveness model (research designed to evaluate the effectiveness of clinical interventions as they are likely to be delivered in the community). Norquist and his colleagues then described how the National Institute of Mental Health (NIMH), in consultation with basic scientists, advocates, and other federal agencies, will endeavor to bridge the gap between the two outcome research models.

A new research paradigm is envisioned. It will "combine the designs of traditional clinical and services research studies," thereby requiring compromises between the strict randomized designs of traditional clinical research and the more flexible observational designs of services research. Merging these designs will require the NIMH "to bring together methodologists with expertise across these fields to delineate what we currently know and what we don't [because it is] quite likely that new methods and statistical analytic approaches will need to be developed to address studies in the mental health area" (p. 6). To achieve the ambitious goals of the new paradigm, new methods and new statistical approaches will be required. New methods of grant review and a new research infrastructure to facilitate grant submission, review, and funding are also planned.

With similar goals in mind, Klein and Smith (1999) also proposed the establishment of "dedicated, multi-site efficacy/effectiveness clinics" to address the problems posed by the conflicting demands of internal and external validity in efficacy and effectiveness studies. These clinics would also be structured to examine such understudied treatment issues as compliance, comorbidity, refractory illness, and withdrawal syndromes, as well as adjunctive and maintenance treatments. The clinics would also facilitate the careful, reliable execution of empirical studies on process and outcome and would help gather outcome norms for well-defined populations on such variables as diagnosis, economic status, history, and comorbidity.

The proximate goal of the clinics that Smith and Klein (1999) envision would be to generate, across cooperating clinics, "a large volume of well-delineated patients [who] could be treated and studied who may have high comorbidity with medical, psychiatric, and substance abuse conditions" (p. 5). The distal goals would be both to develop benchmarks for expected treatment outcomes for these distinct groups of patients by means of normative sampling, and to generate hypotheses they would themselves ultimately be in a position to test.

Klein and Smith's proposal for efficacy/effectiveness clinics is long on enthusiasm, problem identification, and aspirations for change and a good deal shorter on concrete design, methodology, and details of statistical analyses. Although understandable at this early stage in the development of the concept, the relative lack of substance leaves the reader who appreciates some of the problems attendant on integrating efficacy and effectiveness studies uncertain whether the integration these authors propose can actually be brought about.

Most recently, Rounsaville, Carroll, and Onken (2001b) outlined a Stage Model of Behavioral Therapies Research. Originally proposed by Onken, Blaine, and Battjes (1997), the model details three sequential steps leading from an initial innovative clinical procedure through efficacy and then effectiveness testing.

> Stage I consists of pilot/feasibility testing, manual writing, training program development, and adherence/competence measure development for new and untested treatments. . . . Stage II initially consists of randomized clinical trials (RCTs) to evaluate efficacy of manualized and pilot-tested treatments which have shown promise or efficacy in earlier studies. Stage II research can also address mechanisms of action or effective components of treatment for those approaches with evidence of efficacy derived from RCTs. Stage III consists of studies to evaluate transportability of treatments for which efficacy has been demonstrated in at least two RCTs. Key Stage III research issues revolve around generalizability; implementation issues; cost effectiveness issues; and consumer/marketing issues. (pp. 133–134)

Commenting on the "stage model," Kazdin (2001) acknowledged the "critically important goal" of developing treatments that can be applied effectively in clinical work. At the same time, he emphasized the additional importance of addressing—and answering—such crucial scientific questions about new treatments as "why and how they work," questions that in his view the stage model as described by Rounsaville and his colleagues (2001) does not address.

In their response to Kazdin's (2001) commentary, Rounsaville, Carroll, and Onken (2001a) restated the critique in terms of three major omissions: "(a) lack of emphasis on theory-driven components to stage model research, (b) a failure to address the need for research on 'what are the mechanisms through which therapy operates and under what conditions is therapy likely to be effective and why,' and (c) an exclusive reliance on randomized clinical trials as the basis for evidence of efficacy/effectiveness of a treatment under study" (p. 152). They pointed to a number of their prior publications that demonstrated that they shared these concerns and would want them included in this effort, concluding that "implicit in Kazdin's characterization and reaction to the stage model is a cut-and-dried, assembly line view of the process," whereas they see it as "a tree, which has a directional, upward course, but a course that branches to catch the most light and to bear more than one fruit" (p. 154).

The NIMH effort to integrate efficacy and effectiveness research (NAMHC Workgroup, 1999; Niederehe, Street, & Lebowitz, 1999; Norquist, Lebowitz, & Hyman, 1999) assumes that the efficacy and effectiveness models, separately and jointly, lack the capacity to optimize internal and external validity. The Klein and Smith model of multisite efficacy/effectiveness clinics appears to draw the same conclusion, even though their proposal for solving the problem differs sharply from the NIMH proposal. The Rounsaville stage model seems to assume that the strengths of the two models, in succession, can be exploited to yield proven treatments. Unfortunately, at this point, like the other two proposals, the stage model optimistically projects ready solutions to problems in design, methodology, and statistical analysis that have yet to be solved by any psychotherapy researcher.

While statistical analyses of the psychotherapy outcome literature by Shadish and his colleagues (Shadish et al., 1996, 1997, in press) took a very different starting point from the three proposals for restructuring the venue of psychotherapy research just reviewed, the meta-analyses addressed a closely related set of issues and may have arrived at conclusions comparable to those to which the authors of the three earlier proposals might ultimately come. Using sophisticated random effects regression analyses to undertake secondary analyses of earlier meta-analyses, Shadish and his associates asked whether psychotherapy outcome studies ranging from less to more "clinically representative" differed in effectiveness according to a substantial array of outcome variables. They asked whether there are outcome differences in psychotherapy completed for efficacy research purposes and psychotherapy completed for effectiveness research purposes, whether substantive differences in results reflect substantive differences in research methods.

The meta-analyses failed to reveal any differences in therapeutic outcome as a function of where on the efficacy/effectiveness ("clinically representative") continuum a study fell. While these findings do not convert the real methodological differences between the efficacy/effectiveness research models to semantic ones, they do suggest that, in terms of one very important factor, clinical usefulness, the distinction may be more apparent than real. This research also confirmed prior findings indicating that therapy is more effective in larger doses, when outcome measures are highly tailored to treatment and, less consistently, when behaviorally oriented therapies are employed. These latter results buttress the view that the innovative data-analytic procedures used by Shadish's research team are sensitive to crucial variables affecting outcome.

WHERE HAVE WE BEEN, WHERE ARE WE GOING?

Where Have We Been?

From time to time, psychotherapy researchers in the 1950s and 1960s expressed concern that the statistical significance of their findings was rarely accompanied by clinical significance. Very little, though, was written during those years about the exceedingly modest impact psychotherapy research appeared to have on the practice of psychotherapy. This situation may well have been due in large part to the primitive state, by current standards, of the psychotherapy research methodologies of the time. The inadequate data from psychotherapy research during these years were wholly insufficient as bases for understanding or implementing treatment.

The 1970s witnessed marked advances in psychotherapy research methods and the parallel emergence of a variety of promising behavioral and cognitive behavioral treatments. Nonetheless, not much was written about how these advances might augment clinical practice, suggesting that the issue had not yet assumed importance in the eyes of psychotherapy researchers. Perhaps that omission reflected understandable caution in the face of the slow maturation of the research methodologies.

By the 1980s, however, researchers had recognized and begun to dwell in earnest on widespread concerns about how rarely psychotherapy research seemed to inform clinical practice. Enhancements in research methodology clearly played a role in the emergence of these concerns: They enabled researchers for the first time reliably to assess the comparative efficacy of different therapies. For this reason, the utility of psychotherapy research for clinical practice increasingly came to be scrutinized. Solutions that would facilitate the transfer of research findings from laboratory to consulting room tended to focus on efforts to make the prevailing psychotherapy research model—the efficacy model—more relevant to clinical practice. A few prescient commentators suggested integrating the distinct and different contributions of what we differentiate today as efficacy and effectiveness research. Others refocused the issue altogether by suggesting that emphasizing psychotherapeutic techniques as prime determinants of outcome might have a less substantial ultimate payoff for practitioners than emphasizing factors common to all therapies.

These general concerns about the usefulness of psychotherapy research coalesced early in the decade of the 1990s around the nature and significance of distinctions between psychotherapy outcome studies that examine efficacy and generalizability and those that examine effectiveness and feasibility. In this recent extended debate, some researchers determined that modest improvements in efficacy research ought to be sufficient to fix the problem, even though partial efforts of this kind thus far have not been successful. Others concluded that effectiveness studies alone represented the best hope for a solution, despite the randomization and control problems that solution engenders. Still others recommended a simultaneous tweaking of both models, to achieve an optimal mix of internal and external validity even though, conceptually and experimentally, that solution would be difficult to effect. Most recently, as we have noted, very ambitious proposals have been made to radically restructure institutions, including the NIMH, in order to facilitate an integration of efficacy and effectiveness research.

That, in brief, is where psychotherapy outcome research has been.

Where Are We Going?

Recent decades have witnessed clear, documented gains in psychotherapy effectiveness (Chambless & Ollendick, 2001; Roth & Fonagy, 1996). Marked advances in outcome research methodologies and conceptualizations, including most recently emphasis on the heuristically important distinction between the effectiveness and efficacy research models, have also taken place during this time. Moreover, there is now widespread recognition that behavioral and cognitive behavioral treatments—most often the object of efficacy studies—are treatments of choice for common anxiety and mood disorders. Nonetheless, the impact of research findings on psychotherapy outcomes still appears to be isolated from clinical practice, and many clinicians continue to choose to utilize methods and procedures that lack empirical support.

This situation has prevented psychotherapy researchers and psychotherapists from benefiting from the routine and easy transformation of research findings from the laboratory to the consulting room that seems to characterize psychopharmacology. Partly for this reason, consensus between psychotherapy researchers and clinicians is difficult to achieve even on issues that would seem obvious opportunities for agreement, like agreeing that treatments with strong empirical support are more likely to be effective than those without it.

However, there is clearly light at the end of the tunnel. One source is the recognition of the clinical utility of many of the cognitive behavioral treatments that have been the focus of the most intense empirical study. Another may be our intense preoccupation over the past several years with how to solve the efficacy/effectiveness paradox. While a number of solutions to the paradox posed by internal and external validity have been proposed, none has yet been proven ideal. Our view is that, within a shorter rather than a longer time, a solution will be found and the Dodo Bird metaphor will finally lose its currency. Exclusive endorsement of either research model alone will not do the job; efforts along those lines have not yielded much encouragement to date. Likewise, tinkering with both models simultaneously to achieve some optimal balance of the two does not seem to be the answer; experience does not suggest it will be. The most likely solution seems to be to take findings from the best efficacy studies and use them to design the most robust effectiveness studies. Then, in bootstrap fashion, alternating between the two approaches, meaningful and clinically relevant findings might well emerge. This back-and-forth variant of the Onken/Rounsaville/Carroll model makes the most sense to us, in large part because a reading of the literature suggests that when consensus has been reached on a pharmacological or psychological treatment that works, that is the means by which it has been achieved.

But resolving the efficacy/effectiveness paradox seems to be only part of a much more important unresolved issue. When and how will psychotherapy researchers and clinicians feel comfortable enough with each other to be able to benefit from the kind of mutual interaction that has proven fruitful elsewhere? That's the big question, and to it there is no ready answer, only, just now, some hope and some apprehension.

References

American Psychiatric Association. (1993). Practice guidelines for the treatment of major depressive disorder in adults. *American Psychiatric Association, 150*(4, Suppl.), 1–26.

American Psychiatric Association. (1994a). *Diagnostic and statistical manual of mental disorders* (4th ed.). Washington, DC: Author.

American Psychiatric Association. (1994b). Practice guideline for the treatment of patients with bipolar disorder. *American Journal of Psychiatry, 151*(12, Suppl.), 1–36.

American Psychiatric Association. (1995). Practice guideline for the treatment of patients with substance use disorders: Alcohol, cocaine, opioids. *American Journal of Psychiatry, 152*(11, Suppl.), 1–59.

American Psychiatric Association. (1996). Practice guideline for the treatment of patients with nicotine dependence. *American Journal of Psychiatry, 153*(10, Suppl.), 1–31.

American Psychiatric Association. (1997). Practice guideline for the treatment of patients with schizophrenia. *American Journal of Psychiatry, 154*(4, Suppl.), 1–63.

Barlow, D. H. (1981). On the relation of clinical research to clinical practice: Current issues. *Journal of Consulting and Clinical Psychology, 49,* 147–155.

Barlow, D. H. (1996). Health care policy, psychotherapy research, and the future of psychotherapy. *American Psychologist, 51,* 1050–1058.

Bergin, A. E. (1966). Some implications of psychotherapy research for therapeutic practice. *Journal of Abnormal Psychology, 71,* 235–246.

Bergin, A. E., & Suinn, R. M. (1975). Individual psychotherapy and behavior therapy. In M. R. Rosenzweig & L. W. Porter (Eds.), *Annual review of psychology* (Vol. 26, pp. 509–556). Palo Alto, CA: Annual Reviews.

Berman, J. S., & Norton, N. C. (1985). Does professional training make a therapist more effective? *Psychological Bulletin, 98,* 401–407.

Beutler, L. E., Machado, P. P. P., & Neufeldt, S. A. (1994). Therapist variables. In A. E. Bergin & S. L. Garfield (Eds.), *Handbook of psychotherapy and behavior change* (4th ed., pp. 229–269). New York: Wiley.

Carroll, L. (1962). *Alice's adventures in wonderland.* Harmondsworth, Middlesex, UK: Penguin Books. (Original work published 1865)

Chambless, D. L., Baker, M. J., et al. (1998). Update on empirically validated therapies, 2. *Clinical Psychologist, 51,* 3–16.

Chambless, D. L., & Ollendick, T. H. (2001). Empirically supported psychological interventions: Controversies and evidence. In S. T. Fiske, D. L. Schacter, & C. Zahn-Waxler (Eds.), *Annual review of psychology* (Vol. 52, pp. 685–716). Palo Alto, CA: Annual Review.

Chambless, D. L., Sanderson, W. C., et al. (1996). An update on empirically validated therapies. *Clinical Psychologist, 49,* 5–18.

Cohen, J. (1965). Some statistical issues in psychological research. In B. Wolman (Ed.), *Handbook of clinical psychology.* New York: McGraw-Hill.

Cronbach, L. J. (1957). Two disciplines of scientific psychology. *American Psychologist, 12,* 671–684.

Division 12 Task Force. (1995). Training in and dissemination of empirically-validated psychological treatments: Report and recommendations. *Clinical Psychologist, 48,* 3–23.

Elkin, I. (1994). The NIMH Treatment of Depression Collaborative Research Program: Where we began and where we are. In A. E. Bergin & S. L. Garfield (Eds.), *Handbook of psychotherapy and behavior change* (pp. 114–139). New York: Wiley.

Elkin, I., Parloff, M. B., Hadley, S. W., & Autry, J. H. (1985). NIMH Treatment of Depression Collaborative Treatment Program: Background and research plan. *Archives of General Psychiatry, 42,* 305–316.

Elkin, I., Shea, M. T., Watkins, J. T., Imber, S. D., Sotsky, S. M., Collins, J. F., Glass, D. R., Pilkonis, P. A., Leber, W. R., Docherty, J. P., Fiester, S. J., & Parloff, M. B. (1989). National Institute of Mental Health Treatment of Depression Collaborative Research Program: General effectiveness of treatments. *Archives of General Psychiatry, 46,* 971–982.

Eysenck, H. J. (1952). The effects of psychotherapy: An evaluation. *Journal of Consulting Psychology, 16,* 319–324.

Eysenck, H. J. (1960). *Behavior therapy and the neuroses.* Oxford: Pergamon Press.

Fensterheim, H., & Raw, S. D. (1996). Empirically validated treatments, psychotherapy integration, and the politics of psychotherapy. *Journal of Psychotherapy Integration, 6,* 207–215.

Garfield, S. L. (1996). Some problems associated with "validated" forms of psychotherapy. *Clinical Psychology: Science and Practice, 3,* 218–229.

Gendlin, E. T., & Rychlak, J. F. (1970). Psychotherapeutic processes. In P. H. Mussen & M. R. Rosenzweig (Eds.), *Annual review of psychology* (Vol. 21, pp. 148–190). Palo Alto, CA: Annual Reviews.

Goldfried, M. R., Greenberg, L., & Marmar, C. (1990). Individual psychotherapy: Process and outcome. In M. R. Rosenzweig & L. W. Porter (Eds.), *Annual* review of psychology (Vol. 41, pp. 659–688). Palo Alto, CA: Annual Reviews.

Goldfried, M. R., & Wolfe, B. E. (1996). Psychotherapy practice and research: Repairing a strained alliance. *American Psychologist, 51,* 1007–1016.

Goldfried, M. R., & Wolfe, B. E. (1998). Toward a more clinically valid approach to therapy research. *Journal of Consulting and Clinical Psychology, 66,* 143–150.

Gomes-Schwartz, B., Hadley, S. W., & Strupp, H. H. (1978). Individual psychotherapy and behavior therapy. In M. R. Rosenzweig & L. W. Porter (Eds.), *Annual review of psychology* (Vol. 29, pp. 435–472). Palo Alto, CA: Annual Reviews.

Hollon, S. D. (1996). The efficacy and effectiveness of psychotherapy relative to medications. *American Psychologist, 51,* 1025–1030.

Howard, K. I., Moras, K., Brill, P. L., Martinovich, Z., & Lutz, W. (1996). Evaluation of psychotherapy: Efficacy, effectiveness, and patient progress. *American Psychologist, 51,* 1059–1064.

Howard, K. I., & Orlinsky, D. E. (1972). Psychotherapeutic processes. In P. H. Mussen & M. R. Rosenzweig (Eds.), *Annual review of psychology* (Vol. 23, pp. 615–668). Palo Alto, CA: Annual Reviews.

Jacobson, N. S., & Christensen, A. (1996). Studying the effectiveness of psychotherapy: How well can clinical trials do the job? *American Psychologist, 51,* 1031–1039.

Jacobson, N. S., Follette, W. C., & Revenstorf, D. (1984). Psychotherapy outcome research: Methods for reporting variability and evaluating clinical significance. *Behavior Therapy, 15,* 336–352.

Jacobson, N. S., & Truax, P. (1991). Clinical significance: A statistical approach to defining meaningful change in psychotherapy research. *Journal of Consulting and Clinical Psychology, 59,* 12–19.

Kazdin, A. E. (2001). Progression of therapy research and clinical application of treatment require better understanding of the change process. *Clinical Psychology: Science and Practice, 8,* 143–151.

Klein, D. F., & Smith, L. B. (1999). Organizational requirements for effective clinical effectiveness studies. *Prevention and Treatment, 2,* Article 0002a.

Kopta, S. M., Lueger, R. J., Saunders, S. M., & Howard, K. I. (1999). Individual psychotherapy outcome and process research: Challenges leading to greater turmoil or a positive transition? In J. T. Spence, J. M. Darley, & D. J. Foss (Eds.), *Annual review of psychology* (Vol. 50, pp. 441–470). Palo Alto, CA: Annual Reviews.

Krasner, L. (1971). Behavior therapy. In P. H. Mussen & M. R. Rosenzweig (Eds.), *Annual review of psychology* (Vol. 22, pp. 483–532). Palo Alto, CA: Annual Reviews.

Lambert, M. J., & Bergin, A. E. (1994). The effectiveness of psychotherapy. In S. L. Garfield & A. E. Bergin (Eds.), *Handbook of psychotherapy and behavior change* (4th ed., pp. 143–189). New York: Wiley.

Luborsky, L., & Diguer, L. (1995, June). *The psychotherapist as a neglected variable: The therapist's treatment effectiveness.* Paper presented at the meeting of the Society for Psychotherapy Research, Vancouver, Canada.

Nathan, P. E. (1998). Practice guidelines: Not yet ideal. *American Psychologist, 53,* 290–299.

Nathan, P. E., Stuart, S. P., & Dolan, S. L. (2000). Research on psychotherapy efficacy and effectiveness: Between Scylla and Charybdis? *Psychological Bulletin, 126,* 964-981.

National Advisory Mental Health Council (NAMHC) Workgroup. (1999). *Bridging science and service.* Washington, DC: National Institute of Mental Health.

Niederehe, G., Street, L. L., & Lebowitz, B. D. (1999). NIMH support for psychotherapy research: Opportunities and questions. *Prevention and Treatment,* 2, Article 0003a.

Norquist, G., Lebowitz, B., & Hyman, S. (1999). Expanding the frontier of treatment research. *Prevention and Treatment, 2,* Article 0001a.

Ogles, B. M., Lambert, M. J., & Sawyer, J. D. (1995). Clinical significance of the National Institute of Mental Health Treatment of Depression Collaborative Research Program data. *Journal of Consulting and Clinical Psychology, 63,* 321–326.

Onken, L. S., Blaine, J. D., & Battjes, R. (1997). Behavior therapy research: A conceptualization of a process. In S. W. Henngler & R. Amentos (Eds.), *Innovative approaches from a difficult to treat populations* (pp. 477–485). Washington, DC: American Psychiatric Press.

Orlinsky, D. E., & Howard, K. I. (1986). Process and outcome in psychotherapy. In S. L. Garfield & A. E. Bergin (Eds.), *Handbook of psychotherapy and behavior change* (3rd ed.). New York: Wiley.

Persons, J. B. (1991). Psychotherapy outcome studies do not accurately represent current models of psychotherapy: A proposed remedy. *American Psychologist, 46,* 99–106.

Robinson, L. A., Berman, J. S., & Neimeyer, R. A. (1990). Psychotherapy for the treatment of depression: A comprehensive review of controlled outcome research. *Psychological Bulletin, 108,* 30–49.

Rosenthal, R. (1983). Assessing the statistical and social importance of the effects of psychotherapy. *Journal of Consulting and Clinical Psychology, 51,* 4–13.

Rosenzweig, S. (1936). Some implicit common factors in diverse methods in psychotherapy. *American Journal of Orthopsychiatry, 6,* 412–415.

Roth, A. D., & Fonagy, P. (1996). *What works for whom? A critical review of psychotherapy research.* New York: Guilford Press.

Rounsaville, B. J., Carroll, K. M., & Onken, L. S. (2001a). Methodological diversity and theory in the stage model: Reply to Kazdin. *Clinical Psychology: Science and Practice, 8,* 152–154.

Rounsaville, B. J., Carroll, K. M., & Onken, L. S. (2001b). A stage model of behavioral therapies research: Getting started and moving on from stage 1. *Clinical Psychology: Research and Practice, 8,* 133–142.

Seligman, M. E. P. (1995). The effectiveness of psychotherapy: The *Consumer Reports* study. *American Psychologist, 50,* 965–974.

Seligman, M. E. P. (1996). Science as an ally of practice. *American Psychologist, 51,* 1072–1079.

Shadish, W. R., Matt, G. E., Navarro, A. M., & Phillips, G. (in press). The effects of psychological therapies in clinically representative conditions: A meta-analysis. *Psychological Bulletin.*

Shadish, W. R., Matt, G. E., Navarro, A. M., Siegle, G., Crist-Christoph, P., et al. (1997). Evidence that therapy works in clinically representative conditions. *Journal of Consulting and Clinical Psychology, 65,* 355–365.

Shadish, W. R., & Ragsdale, K. (1996). Random versus nonrandom assignment in controlled experiments: Do you get the same answer? *Journal of Consulting and Clinical Psychology, 64,* 1290–1305.

Shapiro, D. A., & Shapiro, D. (1982). Meta-analysis of comparative therapy outcome studies: A replication and refinement. *Psychological Bulletin, 92,* 581–604.

Shapiro, D. A., & Shapiro, D. (1983). Comparative therapy outcome research: Methodological implications of meta-analysis. *Journal of Consulting and Clinical Psychology, 51,* 42–53.

Strupp, H. H. (1973). *Psychotherapy: Clinical, research, and theoretical issues.* New York: Jason Aronson.

Zlotnick, C., Elkin, I., & Shea, M. T. (1998). Does the gender of a patient or the gender of a therapist affect the treatment of patients with major depression. *Journal of Consulting and Clinical Psychology,* 655–659.

Author Index

Subject Index